Exam 220-221: A+ Core Hardware Service Technician Examination

Objective/Subobjective Topic   *Content*

DOMAIN 1.0 INSTALLATION, CONFIGURATION, AND UPGRADING

1.1 Identify basic terms, concepts, and functions of system modules, including how each module should work during normal operation and during the boot process. Examples of concepts and modules are	Chapter 1, "Basic Terms and Concepts"

- System board
- Power supply
- Processor/CPU
- Memory
- Storage devices
- Monitor
- Modem
- Firmware
- BIOS
- CMOS
- LCD (portables)
- Ports
- PDA (personal digital assistant)

1.2 Identify basic procedures for adding and removing field replaceable modules for both desktop and portable systems. Examples of modules:	Chapter 2, "Adding and Removing FRU Modules"

- System board
- Storage device
- Power supply
- Processor/CPU
- Memory
- Network Interface Card (NIC)
- Portable System Components:
  - AC adapters
  - DC controller
  - PC Card
- Input devices
- Hard drive
- Keyboard
- Video board
- Mouse

- Digital Camera
- LCD panel
- Pointing devices

1.3 Identify available IRQs, DMAs, and I/O addresses and procedures for device installation and configuration. Content might include the following:	Chapter 3, "System Resources"

- Standard IRQ settings
- Modems
- Floppy drive controllers
- Hexadecimal/Addresses
- USB port
- Infrared ports
- Hard drive controllers

1.4 Identify common peripheral ports, associated cabling, and their connectors. Content might include the following:	Chapter 4, "Peripherals and Ports"

- Cable types
- Cable orientation
- Serial versus parallel
- Pin connections

Examples of types of connectors:

- DB-9
- RJ-11
- BNC
- USB
- DB-25
- RJ-45
- PS2/MINI-DIN
- IEEE 1394

1.5 Identify proper procedures for installing and configuring IDE/EIDE devices. Content might include the following:	Chapter 5, "Installing Disk Devices"

- Master/Slave
- Devices per channel
- Primary/Secondary

1.6 Identify proper procedures for installing and configuring SCSI devices. Content might include the following:	Chapter 5, "Installing Disk Devices"

- Address/termination conflicts
- Cabling
- Types (for example, regular, wide, ultra-wide)
- Internal versus external
- Expansion slots, EISA, ISA, PCI
- Jumper block settings (binary equivalents)

1.7 Identify proper procedures for installing and configuring peripheral devices. Content might include the following:
 • Monitor/video card
 • USB peripherals and hubs
 • IEEE 1394
 • Portables:
   • Docking stations
   • PC Cards
   • Port replicators
   • Infrared devices
 • Modem
 • IEEE 1284
 • External Storage
	Chapter 6, "Installing and Configuring Peripheral Devices"

1.8 Identify hardware methods of upgrading system performance, procedures for replacing basic subsystem components, unique components and when to use them. Content might include the following:
 • Memory
 • Hard drives
 • Portable Systems:
   • Battery
   • Hard Drive
   • Type I, II, III cards
   • Memory
 • CPU
 • Upgrading BIOS
 • When to upgrade BIOS
	Chapter 7, "System Upgrading and Optimizing"

DOMAIN 2.0 DIAGNOSING AND TROUBLESHOOTING

2.1 Identify common symptoms and problems associated with each module and how to troubleshoot and isolate the problems. Content might include the following: • Processor/memory symptoms • Mouse • Floppy drive • Parallel ports • Hard drives • CD-ROM • DVD • Sound card/audio • Monitor/video • Motherboards • Modems • BIOS • USB • NIC • CMOS • Power supply • Slot covers • POST audible/visual error codes • Troubleshooting tools; that is, multimeter • Large LBA, LBA • Cables • Keyboard • Peripherals	Chapter 8, "Symptoms and Troubleshooting"

2.2 Identify basic troubleshooting procedures and how to elicit problem symptoms from customers. Content might include the following:
 • Troubleshooting/isolation/problem determination procedures
 • Determining whether hardware or software problem
 • Gathering information from user regarding, for example,
   • Customer environment
   • Situation when the problem occurred
   • Symptoms/error codes
	Chapter 9, "Basic Troubleshooting Techniques"

DOMAIN 3.0 PREVENTIVE MAINTENANCE

3.1 Identify the purpose of various types of preventive maintenance products and procedures and when to use them. Content might include the following: • Liquid cleaning compounds • Types of materials to clean contacts and connections • Non-static vacuums (chassis, power supplies, fans)	Chapter 10, "Preventive Maintenance"

3.2 Identify issues, procedures, and devices for protection within the computing environment, including people, hardware, and the surrounding workspace. Content might include the following:
 • UPS (uninterruptible power supply) and suppressors
 • Determining the signs of power issues
 • Proper methods of component storage for future use
 • Potential hazards and proper safety procedures relating to lasers:
   • High-voltage equipment
   • CRT
   • Power supply
	Chapter 11, "System Protection"

A+

Fourth Edition

Exams 220-221
220-222

Charles Brooks

Training Guide

A+ Training Guide, Fourth Edition

Copyright © 2003 by Que Certification

All rights reserved. No part of this book shall be reproduced, stored in a retrieval system, or transmitted by any means, electronic, mechanical, photocopying, recording, or otherwise, without written permission from the publisher. No patent liability is assumed with respect to the use of the information contained herein. Although every precaution has been taken in the preparation of this book, the publisher and author assume no responsibility for errors or omissions. Nor is any liability assumed for damages resulting from the use of the information contained herein.

International Standard Book Number: 0-7897-2844-3

Library of Congress Catalog Card Number: 2002109422

Printed in the United States of America

First Printing: November 2002
Reprinted with corrections: May 2003

05   04   03   5   4   3

Trademarks

All terms mentioned in this book that are known to be trademarks or service marks have been appropriately capitalized. Que Certification cannot attest to the accuracy of this information. Use of a term in this book should not be regarded as affecting the validity of any trademark or service mark.

Warning and Disclaimer

Every effort has been made to make this book as complete and as accurate as possible, but no warranty or fitness is implied. The information provided is on an "as is" basis. The author and the publisher shall have neither liability nor responsibility to any person or entity with respect to any loss or damages arising from the information contained in this book or from the use of the CD or programs accompanying it.

ASSOCIATE PUBLISHER
Paul Boger

EXECUTIVE EDITOR
Jeff Riley

DEVELOPMENT EDITOR
Susan Brown Zahn

MANAGING EDITOR
Thomas F. Hayes

PROJECT EDITOR
Carol Bowers

COPY EDITORS
Rhonda Tinch-Mize
Kitty Jarret

INDEXER
John Sleeva

PROOFREADER
Cindy Long

TEAM COORDINATOR
Rosemary Lewis

MULTIMEDIA DEVELOPER
Michael Hunter

INTERIOR DESIGNER
Louisa Adair

COVER DESIGNER
Charis Ann Santillie

Que Certification • 201 West 103rd Street • Indianapolis, Indiana 46290

A Note from Series Editor Ed Tittel

Congratulations on your purchase of the *A+ Training Guide*, the finest exam preparation book in the marketplace!

As Series Editor of the highly regarded Training Guide series, I can assure you that you won't be disappointed. You've taken your first step toward passing the 220-221 and 220-222 exams, and we value this opportunity to help you on your way!

As a "Favorite Study Guide Author" finalist in a 2002 poll of CertCities readers, I know the importance of delivering good books. You'll be impressed with Que Certification's stringent review process, which ensures the books are high-quality, relevant, and technically accurate. Rest assured that at least a dozen industry experts—including the panel of certification experts at CramSession—have reviewed this material, helping us deliver an excellent solution to your exam preparation needs.

Favorite Study Guide Author

We've also added a preview edition of PrepLogic's powerful, full-featured test engine, which is trusted by certification students throughout the world.

As a 20-year-plus veteran of the computing industry and the original creator and editor of the Exam Cram series, I've brought my IT experience to bear on these books. During my tenure at Novell from 1989 to 1994, I worked with and around its excellent education and certification department. At Novell, I witnessed the growth and development of the first really big, successful IT certification program—one that was to shape the industry forever afterward. This experience helped push my writing and teaching activities heavily in the certification direction. Since then, I've worked on more than 70 certification related-ed books, and I write about certification topics for numerous Web sites and for *Certification* magazine.

In 1997 when Exam Cram was introduced, it quickly became the best-selling computer book series since "*...For Dummies*," and the best-selling certification book series ever. By maintaining an intense focus on the subject matter, tracking errata and updates quickly, and following the certification market closely, Exam Cram was able to establish the dominant position in cert prep books.

You will not be disappointed in your decision to purchase this book. If you are, please contact me at etittel@jump.net. All suggestions, ideas, input, or constructive criticism are welcome!

Ed Tittel

Contents at a Glance

PART III FINAL REVIEW

PART IV APPENDICES

Table of Contents

7 System Upgrading and Optimizing   221

13 Random Access Memory   405

14 Motherboards   427

PART II: Operating System Technologies

PART III: Final Review

Fast Facts: Core Hardware Service Technician Exam   957

Fast Facts: Operating System Technologies Exam   977

Study and Exam Prep Tips   997

PART IV: Appendixes

About the Author

Charles J. Brooks is currently the president of Marcraft International Corporation, located in Kennewick, Washington, and is in charge of research and development. He is the author of several books, including *Speech Synthesis, Pneumatic Instrumentation, The Complete Introductory Computer Course, Radio-Controlled Car Project Manual,* and *IBM PC Peripheral Troubleshooting and Repair.* A former electronics instructor and technical writer with the National Education Corporation, Charles has taught and written on post-secondary EET curriculum, including introductory electronics, transistor theory, linear integrated circuits, basic digital theory, industrial electronics, microprocessors, and computer peripherals.

About the Technical Reviewers

These reviewers contributed their considerable hands-on expertise to the entire development process for *A+ Training Guide, Fourth Edition.* As the book was being written, these dedicated professionals reviewed all the material for technical content, organization, and flow. Their feedback was critical to ensuring that *A+ Training Guide, Fourth Edition* fits our readers' need for the highest-quality technical information.

Brian Alley has been in the PC industry since 1985. He has worked as a contract consultant primarily at law enforcement agencies installing networks and custom software. Joining Boston University's Corporate Education Center in 1992 as a contract instructor, Mr. Alley developed the first PC Service and Support course. This involved writing training materials, labs, and course outlines for PC Service and Support.

Additionally, Mr. Alley taught several Novell NetWare courses, Data Communications, Network, and applications programs. In 1995, Mr. Alley joined BUCEC as a full-time staff instructor, becoming the lead instructor for PC Service and Support and the A+ Certification programs. In his role as lead instructor, Mr. Alley regularly reviews new training materials, writes new labs, and qualifies new instructors. He has been contracted by a major computer training material publisher to serve as technical editor for three books currently in print and is working on soon-to-be-published new materials for Network +. Mr. Alley, as an MCT and MCSE, is currently certified to teach more than 20 Microsoft courses, including Windows 95, Windows 98, Windows NT, Windows 2000, and network-related topics. He has served as a subject matter expert for the 1995 A+ exam rewrite, and served as a

Beta tester for A+, Network +, Windows 98, Windows 2000, and several other products. He has served on the A+ Advisory Committee and the Internet + Advisory Committee. He is currently A+, iNet+, Server+, and Network+ certified in addition to being an MCT, MCP, and MCSE.

Jerald A. Dively has been involved in computers and computer networks for five years. He was the Workgroup manager for the Department of the Air Force for six years. While there, he was responsible for utilization and training for 90 workgroup managers. He has an A.S. degree in Network Administration and Business Administration. He was a systems administrator at a major Air Force installation in Texas, where he was responsible for a network consisting of 1,100 clients. He has written a CCNA Test Preparation book for a major publishing company and has reviewed many computer books. He now works as a network administrator and systems integrator in Florida. He has received his MSCE, CCNA, CNA, CNST, A+, Networking +, CST and other certifications.

Dedication

Once again, I want to thank my wife, Robbie, for her support throughout another book campaign. Without her support and help, I'm sure there would be no books by Charles Brooks.

Acknowledgments

I want to thank many individuals for their efforts in preparing this book.

My staff at Marcraft has worked diligently to make certain that this is a quality product. I want to thank Cathy Boulay and Mike Hall for their artistic efforts, which are demonstrated throughout the book.

I also owe a big thanks to Paul Havens, Wanda Dawson, Evan Samaritano, Grigoriy Ter-oganov, Yu Wen Ho, and Caleb Sarka of my Technical Services and Development staffs for many things, including turning my hands-on procedure ideas into working lab explorations, for their review and proofreading skills, and for their test-bank compilation work. Thanks also to Tony Tonda for all his work preparing user-support materials for the project.

I want to thank Brian Alley of Boston University for his invaluable insight on this project and his friendship.

Also, I want to give a big thanks to Jerry Dively, my other technical reviewer, for his diligent efforts to point me in the right directions. Input and suggestions from both of you have been very helpful in refining this book into the great educational and certification tool that it is.

As always, everyone I have worked with at Que Publishing has made this a pleasant experience. Jeff Riley, Susan Brown Zahn, and Carol Bowers, thanks again for another great life experience. Let's do another one sometime.

Finally, I want to thank all the people who purchased the first or second editions of the book and cared enough to share their feedback with me. You may see one of your suggestions in this version. Good luck with the exam, but I hope you don't need it after using this book and CD.

We Want to Hear from You!

As the reader of this book, *you* are our most important critic and commentator. We value your opinion and want to know what we're doing right, what we could do better, what areas you'd like to see us publish in, and any other words of wisdom you're willing to pass our way.

As an executive editor for Que Certification, I welcome your comments. You can email or write me directly to let me know what you did or didn't like about this book—as well as what we can do to make our books better.

Please note that I cannot help you with technical problems related to the *topic* of this book. We do have a User Services group, however, where I will forward specific technical questions related to the book.

When you write, please be sure to include this book's title and author as well as your name, email address, and phone number. I will carefully review your comments and share them with the author and editors who worked on the book.

Email: feedback@quepublishing.com

Mail: Jeff Riley
            Executive Editor
            Que Certification
            201 West 103rd Street
            Indianapolis, IN 46290 USA

For more information about this book or another Que title, visit our Web site at www.quepublishing.com. Type the ISBN (excluding hyphens) or the title of a book in the Search field to find the page you're looking for.

How to Use This Book

Que Certification has made an effort in its Training Guide series to make the information as accessible as possible for the purposes of learning the certification material. Here, you have an opportunity to view the many instructional features that have been incorporated into the books to achieve that goal.

CHAPTER OPENER

Each chapter begins with a set of features designed to allow you to maximize study time for that material.

List of Objectives: Each chapter begins with a list of the objectives as stated by the exam's vendor.

Objective Explanations: Immediately following each objective is an explanation of it, providing context that defines it more meaningfully in relation to the exam. Because vendors can sometimes be vague in their objectives list, the objective explanations are designed to clarify any vagueness by relying on the authors' test-taking experience.

OBJECTIVES

This chapter helps you to prepare for the Core Hardware module of the A+ Certification examination by covering the following objectives within the "Domain 1.0: Installation, Configuration, and Upgrading" section.

1.1 Identify basic terms, concepts, and functions of system modules, including how each module should work during normal operation and during the boot process.

Examples of concepts and modules are

- System board
- Power supply
- Processor /CPU
- Modem
- Memory
- Storage devices
- Monitor
- Firmware
- BIOS
- CMOS
- LCD (portable systems)
- Ports
- PDA (Personal Digital Assistant)

▶ All the objectives under Domain 1.0 of the A+ Core Hardware exam expect the potential candidate to show basic knowledge of typical personal computer hardware components. This objective basically asks you to identify typical PC components, know what they are called, know what they look like, and know a little bit about what they do. Almost nothing in the A+ exam asks you to know how these components work.

CHAPTER 1

Basic Terms and Concepts

Chapter Outline: Learning always gets a boost when you can see both the forest and the trees. To give you a visual image of how the topics in a chapter fit together, you will find a chapter outline at the beginning of each chapter. You will also be able to use this for easy reference when looking for a particular topic.

STUDY STRATEGIES

To prepare for the Installation, Configuration, and Upgrading objective of the Core Hardware exam,

▶ Read the objectives at the beginning of this chapter.

▶ Study the information in this chapter.

▶ Review the objectives listed earlier in this chapter.

▶ Perform any step-by-step procedures in the text.

▶ Answer the review questions at the end chapter and check your results.

▶ Use the PrepLogic test engine on the C that accompanies this book for additio review and exam questions concerning material.

▶ Review the exam tips scattered throug chapter and make certain that you are able with each point.

Study Strategies: Each topic presents its own learning challenge. To support you through this, Que Certification has included strategies for how to best approach studying in order to retain the material in the chapter, particularly as it is addressed on the exam.

INSTRUCTIONAL FEATURES WITHIN THE CHAPTER

These books include a large amount and different kinds of information. The many different elements are designed to help you identify information by its purpose and importance to the exam and also to provide you with varied ways to learn the material. You will be able to determine how much attention to devote to certain elements, depending on what your goals are. By becoming familiar with the different presentations of information, you will know what information will be important to you as a test-taker and which information will be important to you as a practitioner.

EXAM TIP

Know the parts of a typical system board and make sure that you can identify these components (and variations of them) from a pictorial or photographic representation. CompTIA likes to use hot-spot questions for these component identification questions, so you must be familiar with their relative sizes and typical placements on different types of system boards.

Exam Tip: Exam Tips appear in the margins to provide specific exam-related advice. Such tips may address what material is covered (or not covered) on the exam, how it is covered, mnemonic devices, or particular quirks of that exam.

Note: Notes appear in the margins and contain various kinds of useful information, such as tips on the technology or administrative practices, historical background on terms and technologies, or side commentary on industry issues.

Warning: In using sophisticated information technology, there is always potential for mistakes or even catastrophes that can occur through improper application of the technology. Warnings appear in the margins to alert you to such potential problems.

---

42   Part I   CORE HARDWARE SERVICE TECHNICIAN

NOTE

Data Vanishes Over long periods of time (such as 10 years or so), data will disappear from a magnetic disk.

Floppy Disk Drives

The PC uses floppy disk drives to store data on small, removable, flexible magnetic disks, like the one depicted in Figure 1.13. The typical floppy disk is a flexible, 3.5-inch diameter Mylar disk that has been coated with a ferromagnetic material. It is encased in a protective, hard plastic envelope that contains a low-friction liner that removes dust and contaminants from the disk as it turns within the envelope. These disks are relatively inexpensive and are easy to transport and store. In addition, they can easily be removed and replaced if they become full.

FIGURE 1.13
Floppy disks.

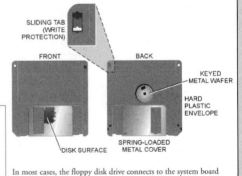

EXAM TIP

Be aware that the power supply's form factor and wattage ratings must be taken into account when ordering a replacement power supply for a system.

WARNING

Don't switch the P8/P9 connectors! Although they look alike, the voltage levels of each plug are different. Reversing them can cause severe damage.

In most cases, the floppy disk drive connects to the system board using a 34-pin ribbon cable. The cable has a color stripe along one edge of the cable to indicate the presence of Pin #1. This pin must be oriented correctly at both ends of the cable. In PC systems, the cable can provide for one or two floppy drives that will automatically be recognized as logical drives A: and B: by the system. The drive connected to the very end of the cable will be designated as drive A:.

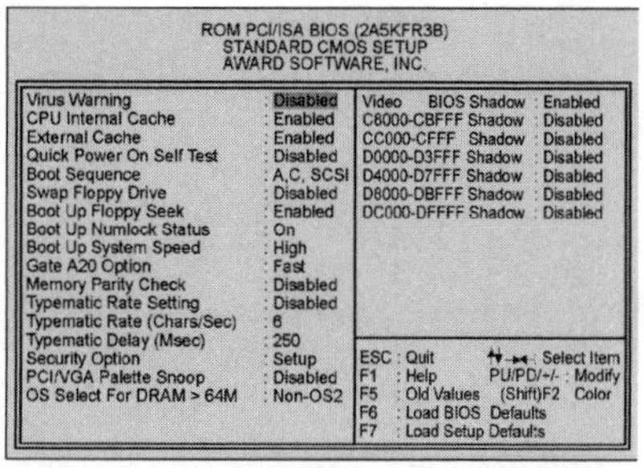

Chapter 1 BASIC TERMS AND CONCEPTS   65

FIGURE 1.31
A BIOS Features Setup screen.

```
          ROM PCI/ISA BIOS (2A5KFR3B)
              STANDARD CMOS SETUP
              AWARD SOFTWARE, INC.

Virus Warning                : Disabled   Video    BIOS Shadow  : Enabled
CPU Internal Cache           : Enabled    C8000-CBFFF Shadow   : Disabled
External Cache               : Enabled    CC000-CFFF  Shadow   : Disabled
Quick Power On Self Test     : Disabled   D0000-D3FFF Shadow   : Disabled
Boot Sequence                : A,C, SCSI  D4000-D7FFF Shadow   : Disabled
Swap Floppy Drive            : Disabled   D8000-DBFFF Shadow   : Disabled
Boot Up Floppy Seek          : Enabled    DC000-DFFFF Shadow   : Disabled
Boot Up Numlock Status       : On
Boot Up System Speed         : High
Gate A20 Option              : Fast
Memory Parity Check          : Disabled
Typematic Rate Setting       : Disabled
Typematic Rate (Chars/Sec)   : 6
Typematic Delay (Msec)       : 250
Security Option              : Setup     ESC : Quit          ↑↓←→ : Select Item
PCI/VGA Palette Snoop        : Disabled   F1  : Help      PU/PD/+/- : Modify
OS Select For DRAM > 64M     : Non-OS2    F5  : Old Values  (Shift)F2  Color
                                         F6  : Load BIOS  Defaults
                                         F7  : Load Setup Defaults
```

On Pentium-based system boards, the hardware configurations that enable various memory and I/O functions are established through the BIOS port-enabling settings. These settings usually include enabling the disk drives, keyboard, and video options, as well as the onboard serial and parallel ports. The user can also turn certain sections of the system's RAM on or off for shadowing purposes, as well as establish parity or non-parity memory operations through this screen.

CHALLENGE #3

Your system will not boot up to the hard drive, so you place a bootable floppy disk in the A: drive and try to restart the system. You watch the startup sequence closely and discover that the system does not appear to check the floppy disk drive for a disk. What should you do to get the system to look for the floppy disk?

NOTE   **Hands-On Activity** For hands-on experience with this concept, refer to Lab Procedure #2, "Boot Sequence," located on the CD that accompanies this book.

PERSONAL DIGITAL ASSISTANTS

Palmtop computers are a class of very small computers designed to fit in most users' hands. The palmtop market was diminished for

Figure: To improve readability, the figures have been placed in the margins wherever possible so they do not interrupt the main flow of text.

Challenge: Challenges provide you with a problem-solving scenario in which you must analyze a situation and suggest a solution. Answers appear at the end of the chapter.

EXTENSIVE REVIEW AND SELF-TEST OPTIONS

At the end of each chapter, along with some summary elements, you will find a section called "Apply Your Knowledge" that gives you several different methods with which to test your understanding of the material and review what you have learned.

CHAPTER SUMMARY

This chapter has presented a mini-course covering the basic organization and operation of the typical personal computer system. In particular, it has covered the fundamental hardware structures and components associated with PC-compatible personal computer systems. These discussions will underpin the more involved information related to these devices that will be presented in subsequent chapters.

At this point, review the objectives listed at the beginning of the chapter to be certain that you understand each point and can perform each task listed there. Afterward, answer the review questions that follow to verify your knowledge of the information.

KEY TERMS

- 5-pin DIN
- 6-pin mini-DIN
- Adapter cards
- Application-Specific Integrated Circuits (ASICs)
- AT-bus
- AT-Style
- ATX-Style
- Basic Input/Output System (BIOS)

Chapter Summary: Before the Apply Your Knowledge section, you will find a chapter summary that wraps up the chapter and reviews what you should have learned.

Key Terms: A list of key terms appears at the end of each chapter. These are terms you should know and be able to define.

Review Questions: These open-ended, short-answer questions allow you to quickly assess your comprehension of what you just read in the chapter. Instead of asking you to choose from a list of options, these questions require you to state the correct answers in your own words. Although you will not experience these kinds of questions on the exam, these questions will indeed test your level of comprehension of key concepts.

APPLY YOUR KNOWLEDGE

Review Questions

1. What is the main difference between AT and ATX power supplies?

   A. ATX power supplies require 240V AC input.

   B. The ATX power supply is controlled by a software switch on the system board.

   C. ATX power supplies deliver more power to the system.

   D. AT power supplies blow air onto the system board rather than out through the back of the unit.

2. Which type of storage is volatile?

   A. RAM

   B. CD-ROM

   C. Disk

   D. ROM

3. Which term does not describe the dot information produced by a color monitor?

   A. PEL

   B. Pixel

   C. Triad

   D. Picture element

4. Which system component executes software instructions and carries out arithmetic operations for the system?

   A. The microprocessor

   B. The CMOS RAM

   C. The BIOS

5. Which video standard is superior to the others listed?

   A. VGA

   B. SVGA

   C. XGA

   D. S3TV

6. PC-compatibles use a _____ connector for the VGA video function.

   A. 9-pin, female D-shell

   B. 15-pin, male D-shell

   C. 15-pin, female D-shell

   D. 25-pin, male D-shell

7. Disk drive tracks are composed of _____.

   A. sectors

   B. clusters

   C. FRUs

   D. magnetic spots

8. During startup, the memory of a computer is tested by _____.

   A. the CPU

   B. the CMOS setup program

   C. the POST

   D. the Interrupt Controller

9. Which of the following interfaces employs a 50-pin cable?

   A. An internal SCSI interface

   B. An EIDE interface

Chapter 1 BASIC TERMS AND CONCEPTS   73

APPLY YOUR KNOWLEDGE

C. Glass faceplate

D. Phosphor shield

27. If you were buying a new monitor, which of following has the best dot pitch?

    A. .24

    B. CYMK

    C. RBG

    D. .29

28. When two devices can send signals to each other at the same time over the same wire, this is called _____ communication.

    A. simplex

    B. half-duplex

    C. full-duplex

    D. multi-quadraplex

29. Which of the following describe differences between an ISA expansion slot and a PCI expansion slot? (Select all that apply.)

    A. PCI slots are shorter.

    B. PCI slots are 64-bits.

    C. PCI slots are primarily used for video graphics adapters.

    D. PCI slots are longer.

30. What type of electrical power is required by the LCD panel of a notebook computer?

    A. 100Hz AC

    B. Low voltage DC

    C. Low voltage AC

    D. 100Hz DC

Answers and Explanations

1. **B.** The ATX power supply is controlled by an electronic switch from the system board. Other differences between the ATX and AT power supplies include the monitor power passthrough is gone from the ATX design. ATX power supplies provide +3.3V through a new, keyed system board connector, and its fan blows into the system unit rather than out. For more information, see the section "Power Supplies."

2. **A.** RAM is a volatile type of memory—its contents disappear when power is removed from the memory. For more information, see the section "System Boards."

3. **C.** A color monitor employs a combination of three color phosphors—red, blue, and green—arranged in an adjacent group of dots or bars called pixels or PELS. A picture element, also referred to as a pixel, is created in a liquid crystal display's screen at each spot where a row and a column of electrodes intersect. For more information, see the section "Color Monitors."

4. **A.** The microprocessor is the major component of any system board. It can be thought of as the "brains" of the computer system because it reads, interprets, and executes software instructions, and also carries out arithmetic and logical operations for the system. For more information, see the section "Microprocessors."

5. **B.** Standard VGA resolution is defined as 720x400 pixels using 16 colors in text mode, and 640x480 pixels using 16 onscreen colors in graphics mode. However, improved resolution VGA systems, referred to as Super VGAs (SVGA), are now commonly available in formats of 1,024x768 with 256 colors, 1,024x768 with

Answers and Explanations: The correct answer and an explanation of it is supplied for each review question.

APPLY YOUR KNOWLEDGE

Suggested Readings and Resources

1. Free Online Dictionary of Computing
   http://foldoc.doc.ic.ac.uk/foldoc/index.html

2. PC Hardware Guide
   http://ctdp.tripod.com/hardware/pc/begin/index.html

3. VESA Bus
   http://webopedia.internet.com/TERM/V/VESA.html

4. PCI Bus
   http://webopedia.internet.com/TERM/P/PCI.html

5. Modem
   http://webopedia.internet.com/TERM/m/modem.html

7. Hard Disk Drive
   http://webopedia.internet.com/TERM/h/hard_disk_drive.html

8. Floppy Disk Drives
   www.pcguide.com/ref/fdd/

9. Storage/Tape Backup
   www.pctechguide.com/15tape.htm

10. Keyboard
    http://webopedia.internet.com/TERM/k/keyboard.html

11. CRT/Monitor
    www.pctechguide.com/06crtmon.htm

12. BIOS
    http://webopedia.internet.com/TERM/B/BIOS.html

Suggested Readings and Resources: Suggested Readings and Resources supply references for additional material such as books, articles, or online resources.

APPLY YOUR KNOWLEDGE

28. **C.** When a modem is used to send signals in only one direction, it is operating in simplex mode. Modems capable of both transmitting and receiving data are divided into two groups, based on their mode of operation. In half-duplex mode, modems exchange data, but only in one direction at a time. Multiplexing or full-duplex modems send and receive signal frequencies that will allow both modems to send and receive data simultaneously. For more information, see the section "Modems."

29. **A, B.** See Figure 1.6, which illustrates expansion slot connectors. For more information, see the section "Expansion Slots."

30. **B.** LCD panels operate with low voltage DC power. For more information, see the section "LCD Operation."

CHALLENGE SOLUTIONS

1. The system should include a CD-ROM drive and add-on speakers for listening to music stored on CDs. Likewise, you should install a modem to provide the system with the capability to connect to the Internet through a dial-up connection. In order to use the high-resolution graphics associated with the computer games, you should install a high-resolution video card and monitor. A printer should also be added to the system to provide the desired hard copy printouts from the Internet. For more information, see the section "Inside the System Unit."

Of course the system should provide the typical standard components—system board, hard and floppy drives, keyboard, and mouse. You should consider installing a large hard drive and plenty of RAM to fully exploit the multimedia capabilities of the games and other programs. A fast microprocessor is another consideration to be taken in this area.

2. Because the system reaches the single beep, you can tell that the basic hardware in her system is working okay. Between the time the system is turned on and the single beep is presented, the system is performing POST tests and initializing basic system hardware components—after the beep, the system searches for a boot record and tries to load an operating system—the problem must be related to one of these activities. For more information, see the section "Basic Input/Output Systems."

3. You must restart the computer and access its CMOS Setup utility screens. In one of its screens (probably the CMOS Setup utility screen), you should see the Boot Sequence option or an option to boot to the floppy drive. Activate this option in the CMOS and restart the system with the boot disk in the floppy drive. For more information, see the section "Advanced CMOS Utilities."

Challenge Solutions: A solution is presented for each challenge as well as an explanation for the solution.

Introduction

A+ Training Guide, Fourth Edition, is designed for those with the goal of certification as an A+ certified technician. It covers both the Core Hardware Service Technician (220-201) and Operating System Technologies (220-202) exams.

These exams measure essential competencies for a microcomputer hardware service technician with six months of on-the-job experience. You must demonstrate knowledge that would enable you to properly install, configure, upgrade, troubleshoot, and repair microcomputer hardware. This includes basic knowledge of desktop and portable systems, basic networking concepts, and printers. You also must demonstrate knowledge of safety and common preventive maintenance procedures.

This book is your one-stop shop. Everything you need to know to pass the exams is in here. You do not have to take a class in addition to buying this book to pass the exam. Depending on your personal study habits or learning style, however, you might benefit from buying this book and taking a class.

This book also can help advanced users and administrators who are not studying for the exam but are looking for a single-volume technical reference.

HOW THIS BOOK HELPS YOU

This book provides a self-guided tour of all the areas covered by the Core Hardware Service Technician and Operating System Technologies exams and identifies the specific skills you need to achieve your A+ certification. You also will find the features that make Que's training guides so successful: clear organization, helpful hints, tips, real-world examples, and step-by-step exercises. Specifically, this book is set up to help you in the following ways:

◆ **Organization**—This book is organized according to individual exam objectives. This book covers every objective that you need to know for the Core Hardware Service Technician and Operating System Technologies exams. The objectives are covered in the same order as they are listed by the certifying organization, CompTIA, to make it as easy as possible for you to learn the information. We also have attempted to make the information accessible in the following ways:

  • This introduction includes the full list of exam topics and objectives.

  • Each chapter begins with a list of the objectives to be covered.

  • Each chapter also begins with an outline that provides an overview of the material and the page numbers of where you can find particular topics.

  • Information on where the objectives are covered is also conveniently condensed on the tear card at the front of this book.

◆ **Instructional features**—This book has been designed to provide you with multiple ways to learn and reinforce the exam material. Following are some of the helpful methods:

- Objective explanations—As mentioned previously, each chapter begins with a list of the objectives covered in the chapter. In addition, immediately following each objective is an explanation in a context that defines it more meaningfully.

- Study strategies—The beginning of each chapter also includes strategies for studying and retaining the material in the chapter, particularly as it is addressed on the exam.

- Test tips—Exam tips appear in the margin to provide specific exam-related advice. Such tips might address what material is covered (or not covered) on the exam, how it is covered, mnemonic devices, and particular quirks of that exam.

- Review breaks and summaries—Crucial information is summarized at various points in the book in lists or tables. Each chapter ends with a summary as well.

- Key terms—A list of key terms appears at the end of each chapter. The key terms are also italicized the first time they appear in the text of the chapter.

- Notes—These appear in the margin and contain various kinds of useful information such as tips on technology or administrative practices, historical background on terms and technologies, or side commentary on industry issues.

- Warnings—When using sophisticated technology improperly, the potential for mistakes or even catastrophes to occur is ever-present. Warnings appear in the margin to alert you to such potential problems.

- Step by Steps—These are hands-on, tutorial instructions that lead you through a particular task or function relevant to the exam objectives.

- Lab exercises—Forty-four exercises or lab procedures are included on the CD that accompanies this book, providing you with more opportunities for hands-on learning and reinforcement of the concepts.

- Challenges—This instructional element requires you to analyze a situation and come up with a solution to a technical problem. It is included here in anticipation of the application questions that will begin to appear in the A+ exams. Answers appear in the "Apply Your Knowledge" section.

◆ **Extensive practice test options**—This book provides numerous opportunities for you to assess your knowledge and to practice for the exam. The practice options include the following:

- Review Questions—These questions appear in the "Apply Your Knowledge" section. They reflect the kinds of multiple-choice questions that appear on the A+ exams. Use them to practice for the exam and to help you determine what you know and what you need to review or study further. Answers and explanations for them are provided.

- Practice exam—A practice exam is included in the "Final Review" section for each exam (as discussed later).

- PrepLogic—The PrepLogic software included on the CD that accompanies this book provides even more practice questions. You also can purchase more questions; these questions are already on the CD and merely need to be "unlocked" so that you can access them.

◆ **Final Review**—This part of the book provides the following three valuable tools that can help you prepare for the exam:

- Fast Facts—This condensed version of the information contained in the book will prove extremely useful for last-minute review.

- Study and Exam Prep Tips—Read this section early on to help you develop study strategies. It also provides valuable exam-day tips and information.

- Practice Exam—A full practice test for each of the exams is included. Questions are written in the styles used on the actual exams. Use it to assess your readiness for the real thing.

The book includes several valuable appendixes as well, including a glossary (Appendix A), an overview of the A+ certification program (Appendix B), a description of what is on the CD-ROM (Appendix C), and an explanation of the PrepLogic test engine (Appendix D).

These and all the other book features mentioned previously will enable you to thoroughly prepare for the exam.

To register for the A+ exam, contact Marcraft at 800-441-6006. Special discounts are available for Que customers.

For more information about the exam or the certification process, contact Marcraft International or the CompTIA organization:

Marcraft International
Attn: A+ Certification
Exam Dept.
100 N. Morain St.
Kennewick, WA 99336
Tel: 800-441-6006
Fax: 509-374-1951
info@mic-inc.com
www.mic-inc.com

CompTIA Headquarters
450 E. 22nd St., Suite 230
Lombard, IL 60148-6158
Tel: 630-268-1818
Fax: 630-268-1834
info@comptia.org
www.comptia.org

A+ CORE HARDWARE SERVICE TECHNICIAN EXAMINATION BLUEPRINT

For A+ certification, you must pass both this examination and the A+ Operating System Technologies examination. As noted previously, the examination measures essential competencies for a microcomputer hardware service technician with six months of on-the-job experience.

The skills and knowledge measured by the examination are derived from an industry-wide job-task analysis and validated through a worldwide survey of 5,000 A+ certified professionals. The results of the worldwide survey were used in weighting the domains and ensuring that the weighting is representative of the relative importance of that content to the job requirements of a service technician with six months of on-the-job experience. The results of the job-task analysis and survey can be found in the following report:

CompTIA A+ Job Task Analysis (JTA) (November 2000)

This examination blueprint includes weighting, test objectives, and example content. Example topics and concepts are included to clarify the test objectives; do not construe these as a comprehensive list of the content of this examination.

The following table lists the domains measured by this examination and the approximate extent to which they are represented.

TABLE IN.1   DOMAIN REPRESENTATION

Domain	% of Examination (Approximately)
1.0 Installation, Configuration, and Upgrading	30%
2.0 Diagnosing and Troubleshooting	30%
3.0 Preventive Maintenance	5%
4.0 Motherboard/Processors/Memory	15%
5.0 Printers	10%
6.0 Basic Networking	10%
Total	100%

In terms of the exam itself, the examinee selects, from four response options, the one option that best completes the statement or answers the question. The exam directions read as follows:

> Read the statement or question and, from the response options, select only one letter that represents the most correct or best answer.

Distracters or wrong answers are response options that examinees with incomplete knowledge or skill would likely choose, but are generally plausible responses fitting into the content area.

The sections that follow outline the objectives for the exam and provide representative (but not necessarily complete) content areas that reflect each objective.

Domain 1.0 Installation, Configuration, and Upgrading

This domain requires the knowledge and skills required to identify, install, configure, and upgrade microcomputer modules and peripherals, following established basic procedures for system assembly and disassembly of field-replaceable modules. Elements include the ability to identify and configure IRQs, DMAs, I/O addresses, and set switches and jumpers.

Objectives and Representative Content

1.1   Identify basic terms, concepts, and functions of system modules, including how each module should work during normal operation and during the boot process.

Examples of concepts and modules are

- ◆ System board
- ◆ Power supply
- ◆ Processor/CPU
- ◆ Memory
- ◆ Storage devices
- ◆ Monitor
- ◆ Modem
- ◆ Firmware
- ◆ BIOS
- ◆ CMOS
- ◆ LCD (portables)
- ◆ Ports
- ◆ PDA (personal digital assistant)

1.2   Identify basic procedures for adding and removing field replaceable modules for both desktop and portable systems.

Examples of modules:

- ◆ System board
- ◆ Storage device

◆ Power supply

◆ Processor/CPU

◆ Memory

◆ Input devices

◆ Hard drive

◆ Keyboard

◆ Video board

◆ Mouse

◆ Network Interface Card

◆ Portable System Components:

  • AC adapters

  • Digital Camera

  • DC controller

  • LCD panel

  • PC Card

  • Pointing devices

1.3   Identify available IRQs, DMAs, and I/O addresses and procedures for device installation and configuration.

Content might include the following:

◆ Standard IRQ settings

◆ Modems

◆ Floppy drive controllers

◆ Hard drive controllers

◆ USB port

◆ Infrared ports

◆ Hexadecimal/Addresses

1.4   Identify common peripheral ports, associated cabling, and their connectors.

Content might include the following:

◆ Cable types

◆ Cable orientation

◆ Serial versus parallel

◆ Pin connections

Examples of types of connectors:

◆ DB-9

◆ DB-25

◆ RJ-11

◆ RJ-45

◆ BNC

◆ PS2/MINI-DIN

◆ USB

◆ IEEE 1394

1.5   Identify proper procedures for installing and configuring IDE/EIDE devices.

Content might include the following:

◆ Master/Slave

◆ Devices per channel

◆ Primary/Secondary

1.6   Identify proper procedures for installing and configuring SCSI devices.

Content might include the following:

◆ Address/termination conflicts

◆ Cabling

◆ Types (for example, regular, wide, ultra-wide)

◆ Internal versus external

◆ Expansion slots, EISA, ISA, PCI

◆ Jumper block settings (binary equivalents)

1.7   Identify proper procedures for installing and configuring peripheral devices.

Content might include the following:

◆ Monitor/video card

◆ Modem

◆ USB peripherals and hubs

◆ IEEE 1284

◆ IEEE 1394

◆ External Storage

◆ Portables:

  • Docking stations

  • PC Cards

  • Port replicators

  • Infrared devices

1.8   Identify hardware methods of upgrading system performance, procedures for replacing basic subsystem components, unique components, and when to use them.

Content might include the following:

◆ Memory

◆ Hard drives

◆ CPU

◆ Upgrading BIOS

◆ When to upgrade BIOS

◆ Portable Systems:

  • Battery

  • Hard Drive

  • Type I, II, III cards

  • Memory

Domain 2.0 Diagnosing and Troubleshooting

This domain requires the ability to apply knowledge relating to diagnosing and troubleshooting common module problems and system malfunctions. This includes knowledge of the symptoms relating to common problems.

Objectives and Representative Content

2.1   Identify common symptoms and problems associated with each module and how to troubleshoot and isolate the problems.

Content might include the following:

◆ Processor/memory symptoms

◆ Mouse

◆ Floppy drive

◆ Parallel ports

◆ Hard drives

◆ CD-ROM

◆ DVD

◆ Sound card/audio

◆ Monitor/video

◆ Motherboards

◆ Modems

◆ BIOS

◆ USB

◆ NIC

◆ CMOS

◆ Power supply

◆ Slot covers

◆ POST audible/visual error codes

◆ Troubleshooting tools, for example, multimeter

◆ Large LBA, LBA

◆ Cables

◆ Keyboard

◆ Peripherals

2.2   Identify basic troubleshooting procedures and how to elicit problem symptoms from customers.

Content might include the following:

◆ Troubleshooting/isolation/problem determination procedures

◆ Determining whether hardware or software problem

◆ Gathering information from user regarding, for example,

 • Customer environment

 • Symptoms/error codes

 • Situation when the problem occurred

Domain 3.0 Preventive Maintenance

This domain requires the knowledge of safety and preventive maintenance. With regard to safety, it includes the potential hazards to personnel and equipment when working with lasers, high-voltage equipment, ESD, and items that require special disposal procedures that comply with environmental guidelines. With regard to preventive maintenance, this includes knowledge of preventive maintenance products, procedures, environmental hazards, and precautions when working on microcomputer systems.

Objectives and Representative Content

3.1   Identify the purpose of various types of preventive maintenance products and procedures and when to use them.

Content might include the following:

◆ Liquid cleaning compounds

◆ Types of materials to clean contacts and connections

◆ Non-static vacuums (chassis, power supplies, fans)

3.2   Identify issues, procedures, and devices for protection within the computing environment, including people, hardware, and the surrounding workspace.

Content might include the following:

◆ UPS (uninterruptible power supply) and suppressors

◆ Determining the signs of power issues

◆ Proper methods of component storage for future use

◆ Potential hazards and proper safety procedures relating to lasers:

- High-voltage equipment
- Power supply
- CRT

◆ Special disposal procedures that comply with environmental guidelines:

- Batteries
- CRTs
- Toner kits/cartridges
- Chemical solvents and cans
- MSDS (Material Safety Data Sheet)

◆ ESD (electrostatic discharge) precautions and procedures:

- What ESD can do and how it might be apparent or hidden
- Common ESD protection devices
- Situations that could present a danger or hazard

Domain 4.0 Motherboard/Processors/ Memory

This domain requires knowledge of specific terminology, facts, ways, and means of dealing with classifications, categories, and principles of motherboards, processors, and memory in microcomputer systems.

Objectives and Representative Content

4.1   Distinguish between the popular CPU chips in terms of their basic characteristics.

Content might include the following:

◆ Popular CPU chips (Intel, AMD, Cyrix)

◆ Characteristics:

- Physical size
- Voltage
- Speeds
- Onboard cache or not
- Sockets
- SEC (Single Edge Contact)

4.2   Identify the categories of RAM (Random Access Memory) terminology, their locations and physical characteristics.

Content might include the following:

◆ Terminology:

- EDO RAM (Extended Data Output RAM)
- DRAM (Dynamic Random Access Memory)
- SRAM (Static RAM)
- RIMM (Rambus Inline Memory Module 184-pin)
- VRAM (Video RAM)
- SDRAM (Synchronous Dynamic RAM)
- WRAM (Windows Accelerator Card RAM)

◆ Locations and physical characteristics:

- Memory bank

- Memory chips (8-bit, 16-bit, and 32-bit)

- SIMMs (Single In-line Memory Module)

- DIMMs (Dual In-line Memory Module)

- Parity chips versus non-parity chips

4.3   Identify the most popular type of mother-boards, their components, and their architecture (bus structures and power supplies).

Content might include the following:

◆ Types of motherboards:

- AT (full and baby)

- ATX

◆ Components:

- Communication ports

- SIMM and DIMM

- Processor sockets

- External cache memory (Level 2)

◆ Bus architecture:

- ISA

- PCI

- AGP

- USB (Universal Serial Bus)

- VESA local bus (VL-Bus)

◆ Basic compatibility guidelines:

- IDE (ATA, ATAPI, ULTRA-DMA, EIDE)

- SCSI (Wide, Fast, Ultra, LVD (Low Voltage Differential))

4.4   Identify the purpose of CMOS (Complementary Metal-Oxide Semiconductor), what it contains, and how to change its basic parameters.

Examples of basic CMOS settings:

◆ Printer parallel port (uni/bidirectional, disable/enable, ECP, EPP)

◆ COM/serial port (memory address, interrupt request, disable)

◆ Floppy drive (enable/disable drive or boot, speed, density)

◆ Hard drive (size and drive type)

◆ Memory (parity, non-parity)

◆ Boot sequence

◆ Date/time

◆ Passwords

◆ Plug and Play BIOS

Domain 5.0 Printers

This domain requires knowledge of basic types of printers, basic concepts, printer components, how they work, how they print onto a page, paper path, care and service techniques, and common problems.

Objectives and Representative Content

5.1   Identify basic concepts, printer operations, and printer components.

Content might include the following:

◆ Types of printers:

- Laser

- Inkjet

- Dot matrix

◆ Types of printer connections and configurations:

- Parallel
- Network
- USB
- Infrared
- Serial

5.2   Identify care and service techniques and common problems with primary printer types.

Content might include the following:

◆ Feed and output

◆ Errors (printed or displayed)

◆ Paper jam

◆ Print quality

◆ Safety precautions

◆ Preventive maintenance

Domain 6.0 Basic Networking

This domain requires knowledge of basic network concepts and terminology, ability to determine whether a computer is networked, knowledge of procedures for swapping and configuring network interface cards, and knowledge of the ramifications of repairs when a computer is networked. The scope of this topic is specific to hardware issues on the desktop and connecting it to a network.

Objectives and Representative Content

6.1   Identify basic networking concepts, including how a network works and the ramifications of repairs on the network.

Content might include the following:

◆ Installing and configuring network cards

◆ Network access

◆ Full-duplex, half-duplex

◆ Cabling (twisted pair, coaxial, fiber optic, RS-232)

◆ Ways to network a PC

◆ Physical network topographies

◆ Increasing bandwidth

◆ Loss of data

◆ Network slowdown

◆ Infrared

◆ Hardware protocols

A+ Operating System Technologies Examination Blueprint

In addition to passing the Core Hardware exam, you must pass the Operating System Technologies exam to receive your certification. You must demonstrate basic knowledge of Windows 9x and 2000 for installing, configuring, upgrading, troubleshooting, and repairing microcomputer systems.

As with the Core Hardware exam, the skills and knowledge measured by this examination are derived from an industry-wide job-task analysis and validated through a worldwide survey of 5,000 A+ certified professionals. The results of the worldwide survey were used in weighting the domains and ensuring that the weighting is representative of the relative importance of that content to the job requirements of a service technician with six months of on-the-job experience. The results of the job-task analysis and survey can be found in the following report:

> CompTIA A+ Job Task Analysis (JTA) (November 2000)

This examination blueprint includes weighting, test objectives, and example content. Example topics and concepts are included to clarify the test objectives; they should not be construed as a comprehensive listing of the content of this examination.

The following table lists the domains measured by this examination and the approximate extent to which they are represented.

TABLE IN.2   DOMAIN REPRESENTATION

Domain	% of Examination (Approximately)
1.0 OS Fundamentals	30%
2.0 Installation, Configuration, and Upgrading	15%
3.0 Diagnosing and Troubleshooting	40%
4.0 Networks	15%
Total	100%

Domain 1.0 Operating System Fundamentals

This domain requires knowledge underlying DOS (Command prompt functions) in Windows 9x and Windows 2000 operating systems in terms of functions and structure, for managing files and directories, and running programs. It also includes navigating through the operating system from command-line prompts and Windows procedures for accessing and retrieving information.

Objectives and Representative Content

1.1   Identify the operating system's functions, structure, and major system files to navigate the operating system and how to get needed technical information.

Content might include the following:

◆ Major Operating System Functions:
  - Create folders
  - Checking OS version

◆ Major Operating System Components:
  - Explorer
  - My Computer
  - Control Panel

◆ Contrasts Between Windows 9x and Windows 2000

◆ Major system files: (what they are, where they are located, how they are used, and what they contain):
  - System, configuration, and user interface files
  - IO.SYS
  - BOOT.INI
  - WIN.COM
  - MSDOS.SYS
  - AUTOEXEC.BAT
  - CONFIG.SYS
  - COMMAND LINE PROMPT

◆ Memory management:
  - Conventional
  - Extended/upper memory

- High memory
- Virtual memory
- HIMEM.SYS
- EMM386.EXE

◆ Windows 9*x*:

- IO.SYS
- WIN.INI
- USER.DAT
- SYSEDIT
- SYSTEM.INI
- SETVER.EXE
- SMARTDRV.EXE
- MSCONFIG (98)
- COMMAND.COM
- DOSSTART.BAT
- REGEDIT.EXE
- SYSTEM.DAT
- RUN COMMAND
- DriveSpace

◆ Windows 2000:

- Computer Management
- BOOT.INI
- REGEDT32
- REGEDIT
- RUN CMD
- NTLDR
- NTDETECT.COM
- NTBOOTDD.SYS

◆ Command Prompt Procedures (Command syntax):

- DIR
- ATTRIB
- VER
- MEM
- SCANDISK
- DEFRAG
- EDIT
- XCOPY
- COPY
- FORMAT
- FDISK
- MSCDEX
- SETVER
- SCANREG

1.2   Identify basic concepts and procedures for creating, viewing, and managing files, directories, and disks. This includes procedures for changing file attributes and the ramifications of those changes (for example, security issues).

Content might include the following:

◆ File attributes—Read Only, Hidden, System, and Archive attributes

◆ File naming conventions (most common extensions)

◆ Windows 2000 COMPRESS, ENCRYPT

◆ IDE/SCSI

◆ Internal/External

◆ Backup/Restore

◆ Partitioning/Formatting/File System:

- FAT
- FAT16
- FAT32
- NTFS4
- NTFS5
- HPFS

◆ Windows-based utilities:

- ScanDisk
- Device Manager
- System Manager
- Computer Manager
- MSCONFIG.EXE
- REGEDIT.EXE (view information/back up registry)
- REGEDT32.EXE
- ATTRIB.EXE
- EXTRACT.EXE
- DEFRAG.EXE
- EDIT.COM
- FDISK.EXE
- SYSEDIT.EXE
- SCANREG
- WSCRIPT.EXE
- HWINFO.EXE
- ASD.EXE (Automatic Skip Driver)
- Cvt1.EXE (driver converter FAT16 to FAT32)

Domain 2.0 Installation, Configuration, and Upgrading

This domain requires knowledge of installing, configuring, and upgrading Windows 9*x* and Windows 2000. This includes knowledge of system boot sequences and minimum hardware requirements.

Objectives and Representative Content

2.1   Identify the procedures for installing Windows 9*x* and Windows 2000 for bringing the software to a basic operational level.

Content might include the following:

◆ Start Up

◆ Partition

◆ Format drive

◆ Loading drivers

◆ Run appropriate setup utility

2.2   Identify steps to perform an operating system upgrade.

Content might include the following:

◆ Upgrading Windows 95 to Windows 98

◆ Upgrading Windows NT Workstation 4.0 to Windows 2000

◆ Replacing Windows 9*x* with Windows 2000

◆ Dual boot Windows 9*x*/Windows NT 4.0/2000

2.3   Identify the basic system boot sequences and boot methods, including the steps to create an emergency boot disk with utilities installed for Windows 9*x*, Windows NT, and Windows 2000.

Content might include the following:

- ◆ Startup disk
- ◆ Safe mode
- ◆ MS-DOS mode
- ◆ NTLDR (NT Loader), BOOT.INI
- ◆ Files required to boot
- ◆ Creating Emergency Repair Disk (ERD)

2.4   Identify procedures for loading/adding and configuring application device drivers, and the necessary software for certain devices.

Content might include the following:

- ◆ Windows 9x Plug and Play and Windows 2000
- ◆ Identify the procedures for installing and launching typical Windows and non-Windows applications. (Note: there is no content related to Windows 3.1.)
- ◆ Procedures for setting up and configuring Windows printing subsystem:
  - • Setting default printer
  - • Installing/Spool setting
  - • Network printing (with help of LAN admin)

Domain 3.0 Diagnosing and Troubleshooting

This domain requires the ability to apply knowledge to diagnose and troubleshoot common problems relating to Windows 9x and Windows 2000. This includes understanding normal operation and symptoms relating to common problems.

Objectives and Representative Content

3.1   Recognize and interpret the meaning of common error codes and startup messages from the boot sequence, and identify steps to correct the problems.

Content might include the following:

- ◆ Safe mode
- ◆ No operating system found
- ◆ Error in CONFIG.SYS line XX
- ◆ Bad or missing COMMAND.COM
- ◆ HIMEM.SYS not loaded
- ◆ Missing or corrupt HIMEM.SYS
- ◆ SCSI
- ◆ Swap file
- ◆ NT boot issues
- ◆ Dr. Watson
- ◆ Failure to start GUI
- ◆ Windows Protection Error
- ◆ Event Viewer—Event log is full
- ◆ A device referenced in SYSTEM.INI, WIN.INI, Registry is not found

3.2   Recognize common problems and determine how to resolve them.

Content might include the following:

- ◆ Eliciting problem symptoms from customers
- ◆ Having customer reproduce error as part of the diagnostic process
- ◆ Identifying recent changes to the computer environment from the user

◆ Troubleshooting Windows-specific printing problems:

- Print spool is stalled

- Incorrect/incompatible driver for print

- Incorrect parameter

◆ Other common problems:

- General Protection Faults

- Illegal operation

- Invalid working directory

- System lock up

- Option (sound card, modem, input device) will not function

- Application will not start or load

- Cannot log on to network (option—NIC not functioning)

- TSR (Terminate Stay Resident) programs and virus

- Applications don't install

- Network connection

◆ Viruses and virus types:

- What they are

- Sources (floppy, emails, and so on)

- How to determine presence

Domain 4.0 Networks

This domain requires knowledge of network capabilities of Windows and how to connect to networks on the client side, including what the Internet is about, its capabilities, basic concepts relating to Internet access, and generic procedures for system setup. The scope of this topic is only what is needed on the desktop side to connect to a network.

Objectives and Representative Content

4.1   Identify the networking capabilities of Windows including procedures for connecting to the network.

Content might include the following:

◆ Protocols

◆ IPCONFIG.EXE

◆ WINIPCFG.EXE

◆ Sharing disk drives

◆ Sharing print and file services

◆ Network type and network card

◆ Installing and configuring browsers

◆ Configure OS for network connection

4.2   Identify concepts and capabilities relating to the Internet and basic procedures for setting up a system for Internet access.

Content might include the following:

◆ ISP

◆ TCP/IP

◆ IPX/SPX

◆ NetBEUI

◆ Email

◆ PING.EXE

◆ HTML

◆ HTTP://

◆ FTP

◆ Domain names (Web sites)

◆ Dial-up networking

◆ TRACERT.EXE

◆ NSLOOKUP.EXE

HARDWARE AND SOFTWARE YOU WILL NEED

As a self-paced study guide, this book was designed with the expectation that you will use your computer as you follow along through the exercises. You also will want to use the PrepLogic software and complete the labs on the CD that accompanies this book. Your computer should meet the following criteria:

◆ 32-bit operating system (Windows 9*x*/2000 or NT 4.0)

◆ 10MB hard drive space

◆ 16MB RAM

◆ IE 4.01 or later

◆ 640x480 video resolution with 256 colors or more

◆ CD-ROM drive

ADVICE ON TAKING THE EXAM

More extensive tips are found in the "Final Review" section titled "Study and Exam Prep Tips," but keep this advice in mind as you study:

◆ Read all the material. Make sure that your exam preparation is thorough. Do not just drop into the book and read around. Read through all the material. This book has included additional information not reflected in the objectives in an effort to give you the best possible preparation for the examination—and for the on-the-job experiences to come.

◆ Do the Step by Steps. This will provide you with another way of understanding the material as well as more information on how well you comprehend it.

◆ Use the questions to assess your knowledge. Do not just read the chapter content; use the questions to find out what you know and what you do not. Study some more, review, and then assess your knowledge again.

◆ Review the exam objectives. Develop your own questions and examples for each topic listed. If you can develop and answer several questions for each topic, you should not find it difficult to pass the exam.

Remember, the primary object is not to pass the exam—it is to understand the material. After you understand the material, passing the exam should be simple. Knowledge is a pyramid; to build upward, you need a solid foundation. This book and the CompTIA A+ certification program are designed to ensure that you have that solid foundation.

Good luck!

QUE

The staff of Que is committed to bringing you the very best in computer reference material. Each Que book is the result of months of work by authors and staff who research and refine the information contained within its covers.

As part of this commitment to you, the Que reader, Que invites your input. Please let us know if you enjoy this book, if you have trouble with the information or examples presented, or if you have a suggestion for the next edition.

Please note, however, that Que staff cannot serve as a technical resource during your preparation for the A+ certification exams or for questions about software- or hardware-related problems. Please refer instead to the documentation that accompanies the products or to the applications' Help systems.

If you have a question or comment about any Que book, there are several ways to contact Que Publishing. We will respond to as many readers as we can. Your name, address, and phone number will never become part of a mailing list or be used for any purpose other than to help us continue to bring you the best books possible. You can write to us at the following address:

Que Publishing, Attn: Jeff Riley, Executive Editor
201 W. 103rd Street, Indianapolis, IN 46290

If you prefer, you can fax Que Publishing at 317-581-4663.

You also can send email to Que at the following Internet address:

feedback@quepublishing.com

Thank you for selecting *A+ Training Guide, Fourth Edition*.

More About PrepLogic—For a complete description of the Que PrepLogic test engine, see Appendix D, "Using the *PrepLogic Practice Tests, Preview Edition* Software."

The objectives detailed in this section cover the A+ Core Hardware Service Technician exam and the A+ Operating Systems Technologies exam blueprints. This document was produced after the final technical and psychometric review of the item pool following the beta-testing period. This document reflects the topics and technologies that appear as part of the A+ Core Hardware exam.

The objectives listed here represent CompTIA's current outline. These certification exams went live on January 31, 2001.

Exam-Taking Advice—Although this book is designed to prepare you to take and pass the Core Hardware Service Technician and Operating System Technologies exams, there are no guarantees. Read this book, work through the questions and exercises, and when you feel confident, take the practice exam and additional exams using the PrepLogic test engine. This should tell you whether you are ready for the real thing.

When taking the actual certification exam, make sure that you answer all the questions before your time limit expires. Do not spend too much time on any one question. If you are unsure, answer it as best as you can; then mark it for review after you have finished the rest of the questions.

CORE HARDWARE SERVICE TECHNICIAN

This chapter helps you to prepare for the Core Hardware module of the A+ Certification examination by covering the following objectives within the "Domain 1.0: Installation, Configuration, and Upgrading" section.

1.1 Identify basic terms, concepts, and functions of system modules, including how each module should work during normal operation and during the boot process.

Examples of concepts and modules are

- **System board**
- **Power supply**
- **Processor /CPU**
- **Modem**
- **Memory**
- **Storage devices**
- **Monitor**
- **Firmware**
- **BIOS**
- **CMOS**
- **LCD (portable systems)**
- **Ports**
- **PDA (Personal Digital Assistant)**

▶ All the objectives under Domain 1.0 of the A+ Core Hardware exam expect the potential candidate to show basic knowledge of typical personal computer hardware components. This objective basically asks you to identify typical PC components, know what they are called, know what they look like, and know a little bit about what they do. Almost nothing in the A+ exam asks you to know how these components work.

CHAPTER 1

Basic Terms and Concepts

To prepare for the Installation, Configuration, and Upgrading objective of the Core Hardware exam,

▶ Read the objectives at the beginning of this chapter.

▶ Study the information in this chapter.

▶ Review the objectives listed earlier in this chapter.

▶ Perform any step-by-step procedures in the text.

▶ Answer the review questions at the end of the chapter and check your results.

▶ Use the PrepLogic test engine on the CD-ROM that accompanies this book for additional review and exam questions concerning this material.

▶ Review the exam tips scattered throughout the chapter and make certain that you are comfortable with each point.

INTRODUCTION

This chapter examines the fundamental organization and operations of a personal computer system. It lays the foundation for more in-depth topic discussions presented in later chapters.

The initial sections of the chapter cover the basic hardware components that make up the personal computer. It starts by describing the components typically found inside the system unit.

Next, the material moves into a discussion of how the basic computer system communicates and interacts with the world around it (that is, input, output, and I/O devices).

The final section of the chapter introduces the fundamental software components that work together to control the operation of the system's hardware. This discussion includes the system's BIOS and operating system software.

After completing this chapter, you should be able to identify the major components of a typical personal computer system and describe the function of each component. In addition, you should be able to describe the different levels of system software associated with a personal computer.

PC STANDARDS

The popularity of the original IBM PC-XT and PC-AT systems created a set of standards for hardware and software compatibility. The AT architecture became so popular that it was named the *Industry Standard Architecture* (*ISA*). Many of the decisions made in designing the PC-AT still influence the PC-compatible computer today. The AT architecture established industry standards for its

◆ Expansion bus

◆ System addressing

◆ Peripheral addressing

◆ System resource allocations

The majority of all current personal computers are based in some part on the original PC-AT design (but incorporate newer microprocessors, expansion buses, and memory management structures). For this reason, every computer technician should possess a thorough understanding of the architecture developed in these systems.

THE PC SYSTEM

As a technician, you should know and be able to identify the components found in a typical *personal computer* (*PC*) system. As shown in Figure 1.1, the PC is modular by design. It is called a system because it includes all the components required to have a functional computer.

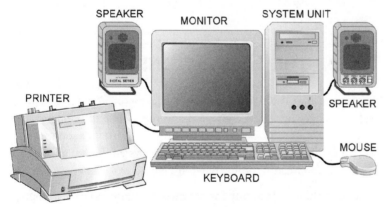

FIGURE 1.1
A typical personal computer system.

◆ *System unit*—The main computer cabinet housing containing the primary components of the system. This includes the main logic board (system board or motherboard), disk drive(s), switching power supply, and the interconnecting wires and cables.

◆ *Keyboard*—The most familiar computer input device, used to introduce characters and commands into the system. This is accomplished by incorporating a standard typewriter key layout with the addition of other specialized control and function keys.

◆ *Mouse*—A popular input device used with graphical user interfaces to point to, select, or activate images on the video monitor. By rolling the mouse along a surface, the user can cause a cursor on the display to move in a corresponding manner.

◆ *Video monitor*—A visual output device capable of displaying characters and graphics on a screen. Also, a name for a CRT computer display.

◆ *Character printer*—A hard copy output device that applies data to paper. Any printer that prints one character at a time. Normally, a dot-matrix, ink-jet, or a laser printer.

◆ *Speakers*—Audio output devices used to deliver voice, music, and coded messages.

INSIDE THE SYSTEM UNIT

The system unit is the main portion of the microcomputer system and is the basis of any PC system arrangement. The components inside the system unit can be divided into four distinct subunits: a switching power supply, the disk drives, the system board, and the options adapter cards, as illustrated in Figure 1.2.

Inside a desktop system unit, as depicted in Figure 1.3, the arrangement of its major components can be seen.

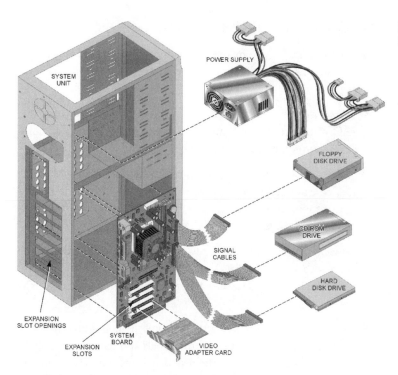

FIGURE 1.2
Internal system unit components.

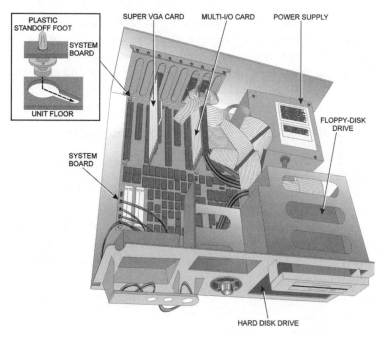

FIGURE 1.3
Inside a desktop unit.

EXAM TIP

Know the names of all the components of a typical PC system and be able to identify them by sight.

The major components of interest in a PC system are

◆ *System board*—The main component of a personal computer. It contains the major structures that make up a computer system.

◆ *Power supply*—The component in the system that converts the AC voltage from the commercial power outlet to the DC voltages required by the computer circuitry.

◆ *Disk drives*—The system's mass storage devices that hold data for an extended time, even when the power is removed from the system. Disk drives include floppy drives, hard drives, and CD-ROM drives.

◆ *Adapter cards*—Interface cards used to enhance the basic system with additional functions. Examples of common adapter cards include video display adapters, modems, and Local Area Network cards.

◆ *Signal cables*—Connecting cables, typically configured in a flat ribbon format, that pass control signals and data between system components such as the disk drives and the system board.

Two common form factors for desktop and tower computers currently exist. These form factors provide specifications for system board and adapter card sizes, mounting hole patterns for system boards and power supplies, microprocessor placement, and airflow. The ATX specification includes provisions for a software switch that enables users to turn off the system's power supply through software.

◆ *AT-Style*—The older form factor standard derived from PC-XT and PC-AT specifications.

◆ *ATX-Style*—A newer form factor standard that has been introduced to overcome problems found in the AT-Style designs.

For the most part, the component specifications for the AT and ATX form factors are incompatible. However, adapter cards from one system will fit in the other, and the basic I/O connection hardware is the same.

System Boards

The system board is the center of the PC-compatible microcomputer system. It contains the circuitry that determines the computing power and speed of the entire system. In particular, it contains the microprocessor and control devices that form the brains of the system. System boards are also referred to as motherboards and as planar boards. A typical system board layout is depicted in Figure 1.4.

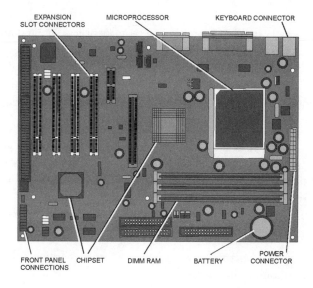

FIGURE 1.4
Parts of a typical system board.

The major components of interest on a PC system board are

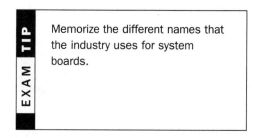

Memorize the different names that the industry uses for system boards.

♦ *Microprocessor/CPU*—The brains of the system. This component performs mathematical and logical computations at incredible speeds.

♦ *Primary Memory*—The system's primary memory elements.

♦ *RAM—Random Access Memory (RAM)* is quick enough to operate directly with the microprocessor and can be read from and written to as often as desired. RAM is a volatile type of memory—its contents disappear when power is removed from the memory.

EXAM TIP

Be aware of which memory types are volatile and what this means.

EXAM TIP

Know the parts of a typical system board and make sure that you can identify these components (and variations of them) from a pictorial or photographic representation. CompTIA likes to use hot-spot questions for these component identification questions, so you must be familiar with their relative sizes and typical placements on different types of system boards.

◆ *ROM—Read-Only Memory (ROM)* contains the computer's permanent startup programs. ROM is nonvolatile—its contents remain with or without power being applied.

◆ *Cache memory*—An area of special high-speed RAM reserved for improving system performance by holding information that the microprocessor is likely to use. Blocks of often used data are copied into the cache area to permit faster access times.

ROM devices store information in a permanent fashion, and are used to hold programs and data that do not change. RAM devices retain only the information stored in them as long as electrical power is applied to the IC. Any interruption of power will cause the contents of the memory to vanish. This is referred to as *volatile memory*. ROM, on the other hand, is *nonvolatile*.

◆ *Expansion slot connectors*—Connectors mounted on the system board into which the edge connectors of adapter cards can be plugged to achieve system expansion. The connector interfaces the adapter to the system's I/O channel and system buses. Therefore, the number of slots available determines the expansion potential of the system.

◆ *Chipset*—Microprocessor support ICs that coordinate the operation of the system.

Microprocessors

The microprocessor is the major component of any system board. It can be thought of as the *brains* of the computer system because it reads, interprets, and executes software instructions, and it also carries out arithmetic and logical operations for the system.

The original PC and PC-XT computers were based on the 8/16-bit 8088 microprocessor from Intel. The IBM PC-AT system employed a 16-bit 80286 microprocessor. Since then, Intel has introduced several different microprocessors for the PC market. These include devices such as the 80386DX and SX, the 80486DX and SX, the Pentium (80586), the Pentium Pro (80686), and Pentium II.

Intel used the SX notation to define reduced function versions of exiting microprocessors. (That is, the 80486SX was a version of the 80486DX that had some functionality removed.) SX devices were normally created to produce price variations that kept the Intel product competitive with those of other manufacturers.

Other IC manufacturers produce work-alike versions of the Intel processors that are referred to as clones. In response to clone microprocessor manufactures using their 80x86 nomenclature, Intel dropped the 80x86 numbering system after the 80486 and adopted the Pentium name so that they could copyright it.

All these microprocessors are backward compatible with the 8088; that is, programs written specifically for the 8088 can be executed by any of the other processors.

These microprocessors have employed a number of different package styles depending on their vintage and manufacturer. Notches and dots are placed on the various IC packages to provide important keys when replacing a microprocessor. These notches and dots specify the location of the IC's number 1 pin. This pin must be lined up with the pin-1 notch of the socket. The writing on the IC package is also significant. It contains the number that identifies the type of device in the package and normally includes a speed rating for the device.

| EXAM TIP | Know how to locate pin-1 of a microprocessor and be aware that this is one of the most important aspects of replacing or updating a microprocessor. |

| NOTE | **Reference Shelf** For more information, refer to the Electronic Reference Shelf, "How Microprocessors Work," located on the CD that accompanies this book. |

Configuration Settings

Each time the system is turned on or reset, the BIOS program checks the system's configuration settings to determine what types of optional devices have been included in the system. PCs feature a battery-powered RAM area that holds some of the system's advanced configuration information. This configuration storage area became known as *CMOS RAM*.

Many system-board designs include a rechargeable, Ni-CAD battery on their system boards to maintain the CMOS information when the system was turned off. However, in some newer systems, there are no rechargeable Ni-CAD batteries for the CMOS storage. Instead, the CMOS storage area and *Real Time Clock* (*RTC*) functions have been integrated with a 10-year, non-replaceable lithium cell in an independent RTC IC.

Because these configuration settings are the system's primary method of getting information about what options are installed, they must be set to accurately reflect the actual options being used with the system. If not, an error will occur. You should always suspect configuration problems when a machine fails to operate immediately after a new component has been installed.

The CMOS configuration values can be accessed for change by pressing the Delete key (or some key combination) during the boot-up procedure. Newer PCs possess the capability to automatically reconfigure themselves for new options that are installed. This feature is referred to as *Plug and Play* (*PnP*) capability.

Chipsets

Microprocessor manufacturers and third-party IC makers produce microprocessor-support chipsets that provide auxiliary services for each type of microprocessor. IC technology can produce millions of transistor circuits on a single small piece of silicon. Some VLSI devices contain complete computer modules.

NOTE

Reference Shelf   For more information, refer to the Electronic Reference Shelf, "The Chips," located on the CD that accompanies this book.

These devices are commonly referred to as *Application-Specific Integrated Circuits* (*ASICs*). By connecting a few ASIC devices together on a printed circuit board, computers that once inhabited an entire room have shrunk to fit on the top of an ordinary work desk, and now, into the palm of the hand. In some highly integrated Pentium system boards, the only ICs that remain are the microprocessor, a ROM BIOS chip, a three-IC chipset, and the system's memory modules.

Connectors and Jumpers

System boards and *Input/Output* (*I/O*) cards might use micro switches for configuration purposes. These micro switches are normally integrated into a DIP package, as illustrated in Figure 1.5. They might use a rocker or slide-switch mechanism to create the short or open condition. The switches are typically numbered sequentially and marked for On/Off positioning. Because the switches are so small, they can simply be marked with an On or Off or with a 1 or 0.

Figure 1.5 illustrates the operation of typical configuration jumpers and switches. A metal clip in the cap of the jumper creates an electrical short between the pins it is installed across. When the cap is removed, the electrical connection is broken and an electrically open condition is created.

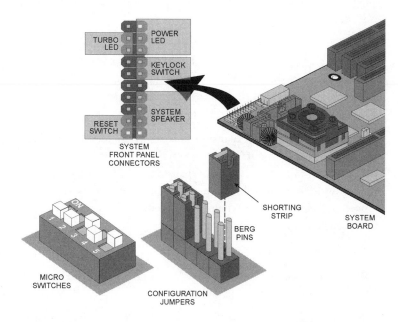

FIGURE 1.5
Jumpers and configuration switches.

PC-compatible system boards include switches and jumper blocks called *BERG connectors* (after the connector company that developed them) to select operating options such as processor and bus speeds. You might be required to alter these settings if you change a component or install a new module in the system.

The system board is connected to the front panel's indicators and controls through BERG connectors. Over time, these connection points have become fairly standard between cases. The normal connections are the power LED, hard drive activity indicator, system reset switch, and speaker system. Older AT style system boards also included turbo LED, turbo switch, and keylock switch connections to handle special high-speed operating modes and physical hardware—security locking devices.

NOTE

Reference Shelf For more information, refer to the Electronic Reference Shelf, "Buses and Support Devices," located on the CD that accompanies this book.

EXAM TIP

You should be able to recognize different expansion slot types from graphics of system board layouts. The most efficient way to do this is to memorize the size relationships between the different types and be aware of how they are most commonly arranged on the system board.

Expansion Slots

Most PCs use standardized *expansion slot* connectors that enable various types of peripheral devices to be attached to the system. Optional input/output devices, or their interface adapter boards, are plugged in to these slots to connect the devices to the system's address, data, and control buses.

The system board communicates with various I/O and memory systems through adapter boards that plug in to its expansion slots. These connectors are normally located along the left-rear portion of the system board so that the external devices they serve can access them through openings at the rear of the case.

Several different types of expansion slots are in use today. A particular system board can contain only one type of slot, or it can have a combination of different types of expansion slots. Be aware that adapter cards are compatible with particular types of slots, so it is important to know which type of slot is being used. The major expansion slot types are

- ◆ 8-bit PC-bus slots

- ◆ 16-bit AT-bus or Industry Standard Architecture (ISA) bus slots

- ◆ 32-bit Extended ISA (EISA) and Micro Channel Architecture (MCA) bus slots

- ◆ 32-bit *Video Electronics Standards Association (VESA)* and 32/64-bit *Peripheral Component Interconnect (PCI)* local bus slots

These expansion slots are depicted in Figure 1.6.

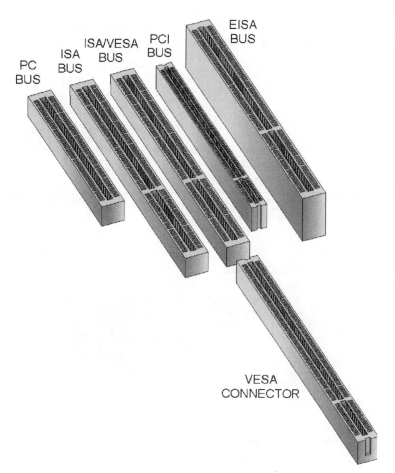

FIGURE 1.6
Expansion slot connectors.

POWER SUPPLIES

The system's *power supply unit* provides electrical power for every component inside the system unit. In older AT-style systems, it also passed the commercial alternating current (AC) through the On/Off switch to the display monitor.

The power supply delivers power to the system board and its expansion slots through the system board power connectors. The ATX system board connector is a 20-pin keyed connector. Figure 1.7 shows the wiring configuration diagram of an ATX system board power connector. Notice that it is keyed so that it cannot be installed incorrectly.

EXAM TIP

Be aware that ATX power supplies can be shut off through software from the system itself.

This connection contains a signal line that the system board can use to turn off the power supply. This is a power saving feature referred to as a *soft switch*.

FIGURE 1.7
The ATX system board power connector.

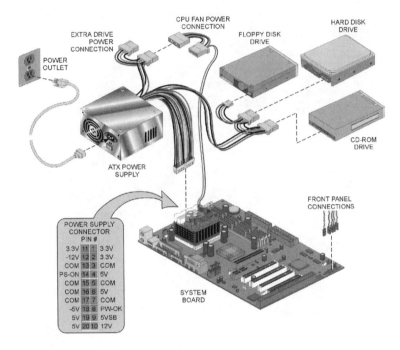

In AT-compatible power supplies, two six-wire bundles, typically marked P8 and P9, deliver power to the system board. The physical construction of these power connectors is identical. They are designed to plug in to the system board's P1 and P2 power plugs, respectively, as depicted in Figure 1.8. Although they look alike, the voltage levels of each plug are different. Reversing them can cause severe damage.

A good rule of thumb to remember when attaching these two connectors to the system board is that the black wires from each bundle should be side by side, as illustrated in the figure.

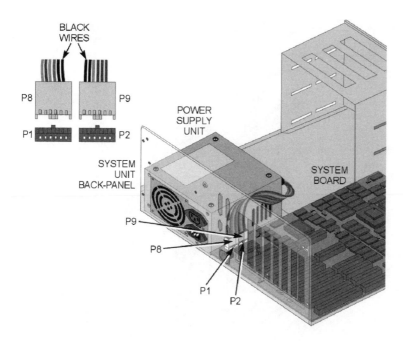

FIGURE 1.8
A P1/P2 to P8/P9 connection.

ADAPTER CARDS

The openness of the IBM PC XT and AT architectures, coupled with their overwhelming popularity, led manufacturers to develop a wide assortment of expansion devices for them. Most of these devices communicate with the basic system through adapter cards that plug in to the expansion slots of the system board, as illustrated in Figure 1.9. They typically contain the interfacing and controller circuitry for the peripheral. However, in some cases the entire peripheral can be included on the adapter card. Typical adapter cards used with PCs include

◆ Video adapter cards

◆ Modems

◆ Local Area Network cards

◆ Sound cards

FIGURE 1.9
Plugging in a typical adapter card.

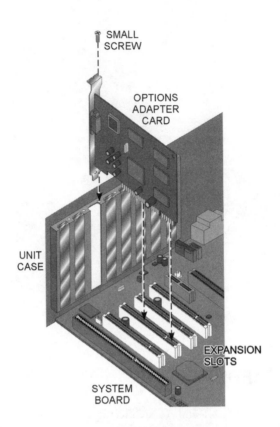

Video Adapter Cards

The video adapter card provides the interface between the system board and the display monitor. The most common type of video adapter card currently in use is the *Video Graphic Array (VGA) card*, like the one depicted in Figure 1.10. The system uses it to control video output operations.

Unlike most other computer components, the VGA video standard uses analog signals and circuitry rather than digital signals. The main component of most video adapter cards is a Video Controller IC. It is a microprocessor-like chip that oversees the operation of the entire adapter. It can access video RAM and video ROM memory units on the card. The video RAM chips hold the information that is to be displayed onscreen. Their size determines the card's video and color capacities. As the figure illustrates, the video output connector is a three-row, DB-15 female connector used with analog VGA displays.

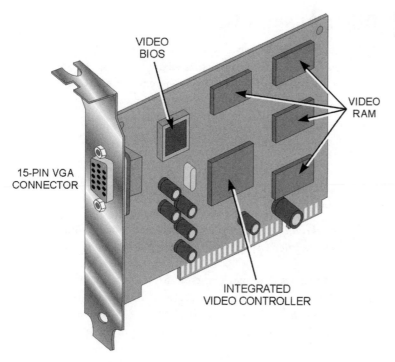

FIGURE 1.10
A typical VGA card.

Standard VGA resolution is defined as 720x400 pixels using 16 colors in text mode, and 640x480 pixels using 16 onscreen colors in graphics mode. However, improved resolution VGA systems, referred to as Super VGAs, are now commonly available in formats of 1,024x768 with 256 colors, 1,024x768 with 16 colors, and 800x600 with 256 colors. The SVGA definition continues to expand—with video controller capabilities ranging up to 1,280x1,024 (with reduced color capabilities) currently available in the market.

Standard VGA monitors employ a 31.5KHz horizontal scanning rate, whereas Super VGA monitors use frequencies between 35 and 48KHz for their horizontal sync, depending on the vertical refresh rate of the adapter card. Standard VGA monitors repaint the screen (vertical refresh) at a frequency of 60 or 70Hz, whereas Super VGA vertical scanning occurs at frequencies of 56, 60, and 72Hz.

EXAM TIP

Be aware of the resolution associated with a Standard VGA display.

Other Adapter Cards

Although the video display adapter card is typically the only adapter card required in the Pentium system, many other input/output functions can be added to the system through adapter cards. Some of the most popular I/O cards in modern Pentium systems include

◆ *Modem cards*—Used to carry out data communications through telephone lines

◆ *Local Area Network cards*—Used to connect the local system to a group of other computers so that they can share data and resources

◆ *Sound cards*—Used to provide high-quality audio output to the computer system

Figure 1.11 shows examples of these cards and their connections. Although they represent the most common options added to computer systems, there are many other I/O devices that can be plugged in to expansion slots to enhance the operation of the system.

FIGURE 1.11
Typical I/O cards.

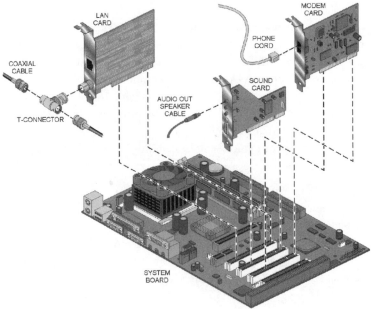

STORAGE DEVICES

Most secondary memory systems for computers have involved storing binary information in the form of magnetic charges on moving magnetic surfaces. However, optical storage methods such as CD-ROM and DVD have recently moved to rival magnetic storage for popularity.

Magnetic storage has remained popular because of three factors:

◆ It has a low cost-per-bit of storage.

◆ It is intrinsically nonvolatile in nature.

◆ It has successfully evolved upward in capacity.

The major magnetic storage media are floppy disks, hard disks, and tape.

The organizational structure of a typical magnetic disk is illustrated in Figure 1.12. A typical IBM floppy disk will have 40 or 80 tracks per surface. The tracks are divided into 8, 9, or 18 sectors each. In a PC-compatible system, each sector holds 512 bytes of data.

EXAM TIP

Be able to describe the organization of PC-compatible disks (that is, sectors, tracks) and recognize examples of them associated with different disk types.

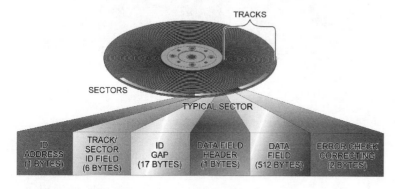

FIGURE 1.12
The organizational structure of a magnetic disk.

Disk Drives

The typical desktop PC system normally comes from the manufacturer with a *floppy disk drive* (*FDD*), a *hard disk drive* (*HDD*), and a *CD-ROM drive* installed.

NOTE

Data Vanishes   Over long periods of time (such as 10 years or so), data will disappear from a magnetic disk.

Floppy Disk Drives

The PC uses floppy disk drives to store data on small, removable, flexible magnetic disks, like the one depicted in Figure 1.13. The typical floppy disk is a flexible, 3.5-inch diameter Mylar disk that has been coated with a ferromagnetic material. It is encased in a protective, hard plastic envelope that contains a low-friction liner that removes dust and contaminants from the disk as it turns within the envelope. These disks are relatively inexpensive and are easy to transport and store. In addition, they can easily be removed and replaced if they become full.

FIGURE 1.13
Floppy disks.

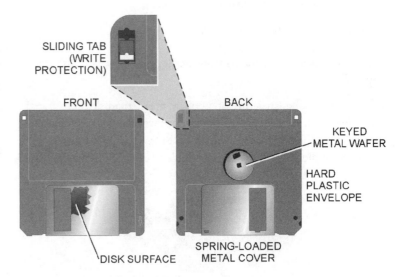

SLIDING TAB
(WRITE
PROTECTION)

FRONT   BACK

KEYED
METAL WAFER

HARD
PLASTIC
ENVELOPE

DISK SURFACE

SPRING-LOADED
METAL COVER

EXAM TIP

Be aware of the physical characteristics that determine which floppy drive will be designated as drive A:.

In most cases, the floppy disk drive connects to the system board using a 34-pin ribbon cable. The cable has a color stripe along one edge of the cable to indicate the presence of Pin #1. This pin must be oriented correctly at both ends of the cable. In PC systems, the cable can provide for one or two floppy drives that will automatically be recognized as logical drives A: and B: by the system. The drive connected to the very end of the cable will be designated as drive A:.

Hard Drives

The system's data storage potential is extended considerably through high-speed, high-capacity hard disk drive units like the one shown in Figure 1.14. Hard disk drives are the mainstays of mass data storage in PC-compatible systems. These units store much more information than floppy disks do. Modern hard drives typically have storage capacities ranging up to several gigabytes. Hard drives also differ from floppy-disk units in that they use rigid disks that are permanently sealed in a non-removable, vacuum-tight portion of the drive unit.

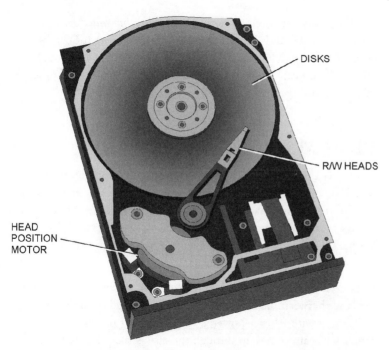

FIGURE 1.14
Inside a hard disk drive.

The disks have historically been aluminum platters coated with a nickel-cobalt or ferromagnetic material. Newer disk drives use ceramic platters. Two or more platters are usually mounted on a common spindle, with spacers between them, to allow data to be recorded on both sides of each disk. The drive's read/write mechanism is sealed inside a dust-free compartment along with the disks.

NOTE

Reference Shelf   For more information, refer to the Electronic Reference Shelf, "How Magnetic Disks Work," located on the CD that accompanies this book.

The rigid structure of the hard disk enables its tracks to be placed closer together than with floppy disks. This, in turn, makes its storage capacity very high. Typical hard disks can have between 315 and 2,048 tracks on each side of each platter. The term *cylinder* is used to refer to the collection of all the tracks possessing the same number on different sides of the disks (that is, track0/side0, track0/side1, track0/side2, and so on). Each track on the hard drive is divided into between 17 and 65 equal-size sectors, depending on the diameter of the disk. Sectors generally contain 512 bytes. The high speed at which the hard disk revolves also provides very rapid data transfer rates.

Most hard disk drives in modern PCs employ *Integrated Drive Electronics* (*IDE*) and *Small Computer System Interface* (*SCSI*) interfaces to connect them to the system. The IDE interface employs a 40-pin ribbon cable, whereas the SCSI interface uses several different cable sizes and types.

CD-ROM

Soon after the *compact disc* (*CD*) became popular for storing audio signals on optical material, the benefits of storing computer information in this manner became apparent. The term disc is used instead of disk to differentiate between magnetic disks and optical discs. With a CD, data is written digitally on a light-sensitive material by a powerful, highly focused laser beam.

EXAM TIP

Be aware of the amount of data that can be stored on a typical CD-ROM disc.

Data is encoded by the length and spacing of the blisters (pits), and the lands between them. The recorded data is read from the disc by scanning it with a lower-power, continuous laser beam. The scanning laser beam comes up through the disc, strikes the aluminized data surface, and is reflected back. Because there is no physical contact between the reading mechanism and the disc, the disc never wears out. Figure 1.15 illustrates this concept.

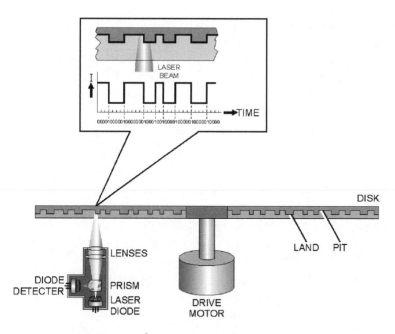

FIGURE 1.15
Encoding data on a CD-ROM.

The information on a compact disc is stored in one continuous spiral track—unlike magnetic disks where the data is stored in multiple, concentric tracks. The CD storage format still divides the data into separate sectors. However, the sectors of a CD-ROM disc are physically the same size. The disc spins counterclockwise and slows down as the laser diode emitter/detector unit approaches the outside of the disc. The average storage capacity of a CD-ROM disc is about 680MB.

CD-ROM Interfaces

The five choices of interface architectures commonly used with | CD-ROM drives are as follows:

◆ SCSI interfaces

◆ IDE/EIDE interfaces

◆ USB interfaces

◆ IEEE-1394 interfaces

◆ Proprietary interfaces

Because both the SCSI and IDE interfaces are system-level interfaces, most of their controller circuitry is actually located on the drives. In pre-Pentium systems, the SCSI and IDE drives employed host adapter cards that plugged in to the system board's expansion slots. In the Pentium environment, the IDE host adapter function has been integrated into the system board. The IDE interface connectors are located on the system board.

SCSI systems continue to use host adapter cards as their interface connectors. The host adapter provides a BERG pin connector for the system's internal SCSI ribbon cable. There are many versions of the SCSI standard, however, and several types of SCSI connecting cables. An internal SCSI CD-ROM drive must be capable of connecting to the type of SCSI cable being used. In a PC, this is most often a 50-pin ribbon cable. The SCSI interface is also widely used to connect external CD-ROM drives to systems. In external situations, a Centronics connector is normally employed with the SCSI cable.

EXAM TIP	Remember that most external CD-ROM drives employ a SCSI interface.

Digital Versatile Discs

Newer compact disc technologies have produced a high capacity disc, called a *digital versatile disc*, digital video disc, or *DVD* for short. These discs have capacities that range between 4.7 GB and 17 GB of data. Transfer rates associated with DVD drives range between 600Kbps and 1.3Mbps.

NOTE	**Reference Shelf** For more information about MPEG, video data compression, and multimedia, refer to the "How Multimedia Works" section of the Electronic Reference Shelf on the CD that accompanies this book.

Like CDs, DVDs are available in DVD-ROM (write-once) and DVD-RAM (rewritable) formats. There are also DVD-Audio and DVD-Video specifications that can store up to 75 songs or an entire full-length movie. The DVD-Video standard employs the MPEG-2 compression standard to compress and decompress video data on the disc.

The drives used for DVDs are backward compatible with old CD-ROM discs, and newer DVD drives can be used to read CD-R and CD-RW discs. Currently, there are two standards in the rewritable DVD field—the DVD-RAM standard being presented by the DVD consortium and the DVD-RW standard developed by a group of manufacturers that include Philips, Sony, and Hewlett Packard. The DVD-RAM format supports 2.6GB of storage per disc; the DVD-RW standard supports 3.0GB per disc.

Physically, the DVD drive looks and operates in the same manner as the traditional CD-ROM drive described earlier in this chapter. Newer manufacturing methods for the discs permit the minimum length of the pits and lands to be smaller. Therefore, they can be squeezed closer together on the disc. DVD drives also employ higher resolution lasers to decrease the track pitch (distance between adjacent tracks). Together, these two factors create the high data densities offered by DVD.

Tape Drives

Tape drive units are another popular type of information storage system. These systems can store large amounts of data on small tape cartridges. Tape drives are generally used to store large amounts of information that will not need to be accessed often, or quickly. Such applications include making backup copies of programs and data. This type of data security is a necessity with records such as business transactions, payroll, artwork, and so on.

PERIPHERALS AND PORTS

Peripherals are devices and systems that are added to the basic system to extend its capabilities. These devices and systems can be divided into three general categories: input, output, and memory systems. Peripheral devices are attached to the system through I/O port connections. Ports offer standard hardware connection and logical interface schemes that permit I/O device manufacturers to develop their products to predefined standards. PCs offer a wide variety of different port types to accommodate as many diverse device types as possible.

The standard peripherals used with PCs are keyboards, CRT monitors, and mice. Figure 1.16 depicts a sample system with these devices. Most PCs use detachable keyboards that are connected to the system by a coiled cable. This cable can plug into a 5-pin DIN or 6-pin mini-DIN (PS/2) connector located on the rear of the system board.

The connector is normally keyed so that it cannot be misaligned. The most widely used display device for current PCs is the *Video Graphics Array (VGA)* color monitor. The monitor's signal cable connects to a 15-pin, 3-row, female D-shell connector at the back of the system unit. A mouse can be connected to a PC by attaching it to a 9-pin D-shell or 6-pin mini-DIN connector at the rear of the system.

FIGURE 1.16
Typical PC peripherals.

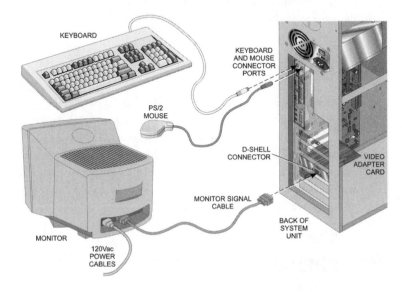

Some peripheral devices interact with the basic system architecture through adapter cards that plug in to the system board's expansion slots. The peripheral devices connect to the adapter cards through expansion slot openings in the back of the system unit. The physical port connector on the back of the computer might be located directly on the adapter card where the port circuitry is, or it might be connected to the port circuitry through an internal signal cable. As long as there are open expansion slots or other standard I/O connectors in a PC, it is possible to add compatible devices to the system.

Over time, many different types of connector have been used to implement different physical I/O port connections. Most I/O port connectors have become standardized. Typical I/O port connectors used with the PCs are shown in Figure 1.17.

EXAM TIP

Memorize the appearance, type, and pin configuration of the standard PC port connectors (that is, parallel ports use 25-pin, female D-shell connectors).

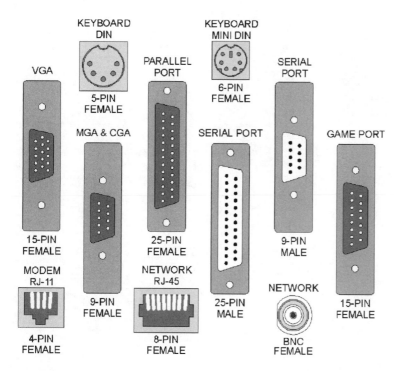

FIGURE 1.17
Typical I/O port connectors.

Keyboards

The keyboard type most widely used with desktop and tower units is a detachable, low profile 101/102-key model. Inside, a keyboard is basically an X-Y matrix arrangement of switch elements, as shown in Figure 1.18. To produce data from a key depression, the keyboard detects and identifies the depressed key and then encodes the closure into a digital character that the computer can use.

With the IBM PS/2 line, a smaller (0.25 inches), *6-pin mini-DIN* connector was adopted. This connector type has been adopted in the ATX specification for both the mouse and keyboard. Older AT-class systems use a larger, *5-pin DIN* connector. Other PC-compatibles use a modular, 6-pin AMP connector to interface the keyboard to the system. You should note that plugging hot-swappable devices such as the keyboard in to the system while it is turned on can cause a system crash or even damage parts of the system.

NOTE **Reference Shelf** For more information, refer to the Electronic Reference Shelf, "How Keyboards Work," located on the CD that accompanies this book.

FIGURE 1.18

101-key keyboard logic.

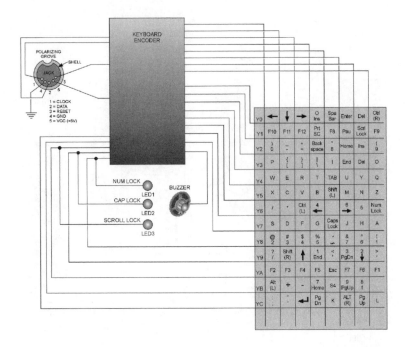

Monitors

The most widely used output device for personal computers is the *Cathode-Ray Tube* (*CRT*) *video display monitor*. The most widely used display device for current PCs is the VGA color monitor. The monitor's signal cable connects to a 15-pin D-shell connector at the back of the system unit. After the monitor, the next most often added output device is the character printer. These peripherals are used to produce hard copy output on paper. They convert text and graphical data from the computer into print on a page.

Video Displays

As an output device, the CRT monitor can be used to display alphanumeric characters and graphic images. A CRT is an evacuated glass tube with an electron gun in its neck, and a fluorescent coated surface opposite the electron gun. A typical CRT is depicted in Figure 1.19. When activated, the electron gun emits a stream of electrons that strike the fluorescent coating on the inside of the screen, causing an illuminated dot to be produced.

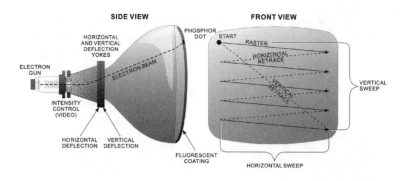

FIGURE 1.19
A Cathode ray tube.

The sweeping electron beam begins at the upper-left corner of the screen, and moves across its face to the upper-right corner, leaving a line across the screen. This is called a *raster line*. Upon reaching the right side of the screen, the trace is blanked out and the electron beam is repositioned to the left side of the screen—one line below the first trace—in an operation called the *horizontal retrace*. At this point, the horizontal sweep begins producing the second display line on the screen. The scanning continues until the horizontal sweep reaches the bottom of the screen. At that point, the electron beam is blanked again and returned to the upper-left corner of the screen in a move referred to as the *vertical retrace*, completing one field.

As the beam moves across the screen, it leaves an illuminated trace, which requires a given amount of time to dissipate. The amount of time depends on the characteristics of the fluorescent coating and is referred to as *persistence*. Video information is introduced to the picture by varying the voltage applied to the electron gun as it scans the screen. The human eye perceives only the picture due to the blanking of the retrace lines and the frequency at which the entire process is performed. Typically, a horizontal sweep requires about 63 microseconds to complete, whereas a complete field requires approximately 1/60 of a second.

Color Monitors

The monitor we have been discussing so far is referred to as a monochrome monitor because it is capable of displaying only shades of a single phosphor color. A color monitor, on the other hand, employs a combination of three color phosphors—red, green, and blue (RGB)—arranged in adjacent trios of dots or bars called picture elements, *pixels,* or *PELs*. By using a different electron gun for each element of the trio, the individual elements can be made to glow at different levels to produce almost any color desired.

The electron guns scan the front of a screen in unison—in the same fashion described earlier for a monochrome CRT. Color CRTs add a metal grid in front of the phosphor coating called a *shadow mask*. It ensures that an electron gun assigned to one color doesn't strike a dot of another color. The basic construction of a color CRT is shown in Figure 1.20.

FIGURE 1.20
Construction of a color CRT.

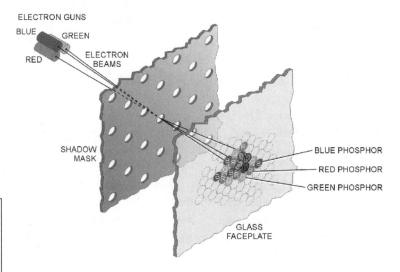

EXAM TIP

Be able to explain the purpose of a shadow mask in a monitor.

EXAM TIP

Be able to explain the definition of dot pitch.

NOTE

Reference Shelf   For more information, refer to the Electronic Reference Shelf, "How Video Displays Work," located on the CD that accompanies this book.

Screen Resolution

The quality of the image produced on the screen is a function of two factors: the speed at which the image is retraced on the screen and the number of pixels on the screen. The more pixels on a given screen size, the higher the image quality. This quantity is called *resolution*, and is often expressed in an X-by-Y format. Using this format, the quality of the image is still determined by how big the viewing area is. (That is, an 800x600 resolution on a 14-inch monitor will produce much better quality than the same number of pixels spread across a 27-inch monitor.)

Resolution can be expressed as a function of how close pixels can be grouped together on the screen. This form of resolution is expressed in terms of *dot pitch*. A monitor with a .28 dot pitch has pixels that are located .28mm apart. In monochrome monitors, dot pitch is measured from center to center of each pixel. In a color monitor, the pitch is measured from the center of one dot trio to the center of the next trio.

Other Peripherals

Mice, joysticks, trackballs, and touch pads belong to a category of input devices called *pointing devices*. They are all small, handheld input devices that enable the user to interact with the system by moving a cursor or some other screen image around the display screen and to choose options from an onscreen menu instead of typing commands from a keyboard. Because pointing devices make it easier to interact with the computer than other types of input devices, they are, therefore, friendlier to the user.

Newer printers might employ a standard parallel connection, a standard serial port connection, or both, as well as newer Universal Serial Bus or direct network connections. Common PC peripheral connections are depicted in Figure 1.21.

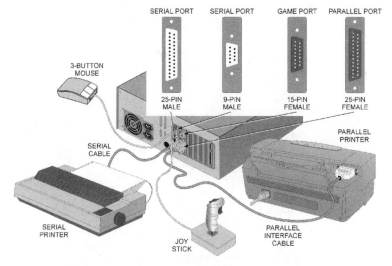

FIGURE 1.21
Typical peripheral connectors.

PORTABLE DISPLAY TYPES

Notebook and laptop computers use non-CRT displays, such as *Liquid Crystal Display* (*LCD*) and gas-plasma panels. These display systems are well suited to the portability needs of portable computers. They are much lighter and more compact than CRT monitors and require much less electrical energy to operate. Both types of display units can be operated from batteries.

EXAM TIP

Know that notebook display panels are powered by low-voltage DC power sources such as a battery or converter.

Liquid Crystal Displays

The most common flat-panel displays used with portable PCs are *Liquid Crystal Displays*. They are relatively thin, flat, and lightweight, and require very little power to operate. In addition to reduced weight and improved portability, these displays offer better reliability and longer life than CRT units.

LCD Operation

When a pixel is off, the molecules of the liquid crystal twist from one edge of the material to the other, as depicted in Figure 1.22. The spiral effect created by the twist polarizes light and prevents it from passing through the display. When an electric field is created between a row and column electrode, the molecules move, lining up perpendicular to the front of the display. This permits light to pass through the display, producing a single dot onscreen.

FIGURE 1.22
LCD operation.

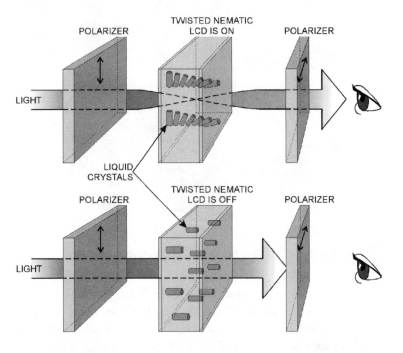

Depending on the orientation of the polarizers, the energized pixels can be made to look like a dark spot on a light screen or a light dot on a dark screen. In most notebook computers, the display is lit from behind the panel. This is referred to as *back lighting*. The level of back lighting is controlled through a small adjustable wheel built in to the LCD panel's housing.

Because no current passes through the display to light the pixels, the power consumption of LCD displays is very low. The screen is scanned by sequentially activating the panel's row and column electrodes. The pixels appear to be continuously lit because the scanning rate is very high. The electrodes can be controlled (turned on and off) using very low DC voltage levels. LCDs constructed in this manner are referred to as *dual-scan*, or *passive-matrix* displays. Advanced passive-matrix technologies are referred to as *Color Super-Twist Nematic* (*CSTN*) and *Double-Layer Super-Twist Nematic* (*DSTN*) displays.

An improved type of LCD is similar in design to the passive-matrix designs except that it places a transistor at each of the matrix row-column junctions to improve switching times. This technology produces an LCD display type referred to as an *active-matrix* display. The active matrix is produced by using *Thin Film Transistor* (*TFT*) arrays to create between one and four transistors for each pixel on a flexible, transparent film. TFT displays tend to be brighter and sharper than dual-scan displays. However, they also tend to require more power to operate and are therefore more expensive.

Color LCD displays are created by adding a three-color filter to the panel. Each pixel in the display corresponds to a red, blue, or green dot on the filter. Activating a pixel behind a blue dot on the filter will produce a blue dot onscreen. Like color CRT displays, the dot color on the screen of the color LCD panel is established by controlling the relative intensities of a three-dot (RGB) pixel cluster.

The construction of LCD displays prevents them from providing multiple-resolution options like an adapter-driven CRT display can. The resolution of the LCD display is dictated by the construction of the LCD panel.

EXAM TIP	Know what type of electrical power is used by an LCD panel.

MODEMS

If a peripheral is located at some distance from the computer (greater than 100 feet), they cannot be connected together by simply getting a longer cable. As the connecting cable gets longer, its natural resistance and distributive capacitance tend to distort digital signals until they are no longer digital.

In order to overcome this signal deterioration, a device called a *modem* (short for modulator/demodulator) is used to convert the parallel, digital signals of the computer in to serial, analog signals that are better suited for transmission over wire. A modem allows a computer to communicate with other computers through the telephone lines, as depicted in Figure 1.23.

FIGURE 1.23

Half-duplex and full-duplex communications.

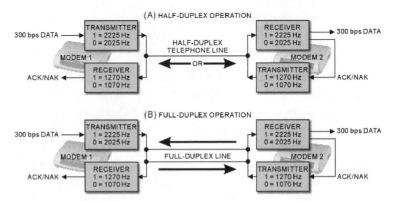

In its simplest form, a modem consists of two major blocks: a modulator and a demodulator. The *modulator* is a transmitter that converts the parallel/digital computer data into a serial/analog format for transmission. The *demodulator* is the receiver that accepts the serial/analog transmission format and converts it in to a parallel/digital format usable by the computer or peripheral.

When a modem is used to send signals in only one direction, it is operating in *simplex mode*. Modems capable of both transmitting and receiving data are divided into two groups, based on their mode of operation. In *half-duplex mode*, modems exchange data, but only in one direction at a time, as illustrated in Figure 1.24. Multiplexing the send and receive signal frequencies will allow both modems to send and receive data simultaneously. This mode of operation is known as *full-duplex mode*.

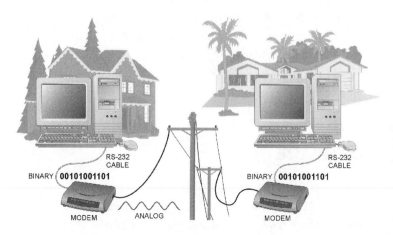

FIGURE 1.24
Modem communications.

EXAM TIP

Be able to state the difference between simplex, half-duplex, and full-duplex transmissions; and as you move through the text, be able to identify which communications systems use each type.

A modem can be either an internal or an external device, as illustrated in Figure 1.25. An internal modem is installed in one of the computer's expansion slots, and has its own interfacing circuitry. The external modem is usually a box that resides outside the system unit and is connected to one of the computer's serial ports by an *RS-232 serial cable*. These units depend on the interfacing circuitry of the computer's serial ports. Most PC-compatible computers contain two serial-port connections. Of course, both types of modems connect to an outside telephone line through a standard *RJ-11* connector. External modems also require a separate power source.

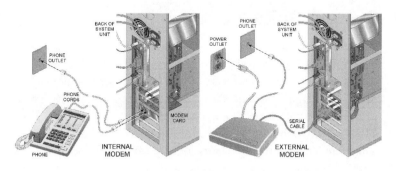

FIGURE 1.25
Internal and external modems.

CHALLENGE #1

Your employer wants to build a computer for his home and has asked you to give him a list of parts to shop for. He wants the system to be able to

- play his favorite music from CDs
- provide access to the Internet

NOTE

Reference Shelf   For more information, refer to the Electronic Reference Shelf, "How Modems Work," located on the CD that accompanies this book.

- play high-resolution video games
- create paper copies of Internet documents

List the components you would suggest that he purchase to build the computer system he wants.

Software

The term *software* refers to the logical instructions and data that can be stored in electronic form and used to control the operation of the computer. Three general classes of software can be discussed:

- ◆ system software
- ◆ applications software
- ◆ games and learning software

The bulk of the software discussed in this book deals with the system software category because this type of software requires more technical skills to manipulate and, therefore, most often involves the service person.

System Software

The system software category consists of special programs used by the system itself to control the computer's operation. Two classic examples of this type of software are the system's *Basic Input/Output System* (*BIOS*) program and the *Disk Operating System* (*DOS*). These programs control the operation of the other classes of software. The BIOS is located in a ROM IC device on the system board. Therefore, it is commonly referred to as *ROM BIOS*. The DOS software is normally located on a magnetic disk.

Basic Input/Output Systems

When a PC is turned on, the entire system is reset to a predetermined starting condition. From this state, it begins carrying out software instructions from its BIOS program. This small program is permanently stored in the ROM memory IC located on the system board.

The information stored in this chip represents all the inherent intelligence that the system has until it can load more information from another source, such as a disk drive or remote server computer. Taken together, the BIOS software (programming) and hardware (the ROM chip) are referred to as *firmware*. Some I/O devices, such as video and network adapter cards, have additional firmware that act as extensions to the system's BIOS.

A system's BIOS program is one of the keys to its compatibility. For example, to be IBM PC-compatible, the computer's BIOS must perform the same basic functions that the IBM PC's BIOS does. However, because the IBM BIOS software is copyrighted, the compatible's software must accomplish the same results that the original did, but it must do it in a different way.

The operation of starting the system and transferring control of it from the BIOS to the operating system is referred to as *booting* the system. If the computer is started from the **off** condition, the process is referred to as a *cold boot*. If the system is restarted from the **on** condition, the process is called a *reset*, or a *warm boot*.

During the execution of the BIOS firmware routines, three major sets of operations are performed.

1. First, the BIOS performs a series of diagnostic tests (called *POST* or *Power On Self Tests*) on the system to verify that it is operating correctly. The main functions provided by the POST are illustrated in Figure 1.26.

2. Next, the BIOS places starting values in the system's various programmable devices. These intelligent devices regulate the operation of different portions of the computer's hardware. This process is called *initialization*. The end of the POST/initialization process is typically marked by an audible signal such as a single beep. The system initialization process is described in Figure 1.27.

> **EXAM TIP**
>
> Be aware that when a PC is reset, its first action is to access the beginning of the ROM BIOS.

FIGURE 1.26
The steps of a bootup: Phase One—POST.

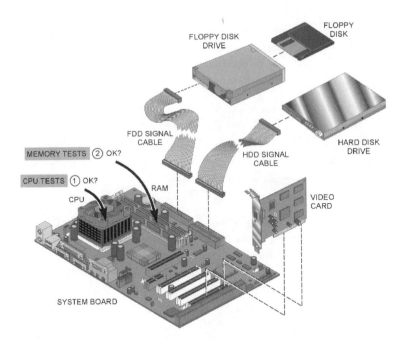

FIGURE 1.27
The steps of a bootup: Phase Two—
Initialization.

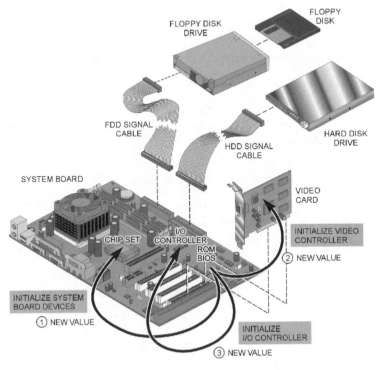

3. Finally, the BIOS performs the bootstrap loader sequence where it searches the system for a special program that it can use to load other programs into RAM. This program is called the *Master Boot Record* (*MBR*). The boot record contains information that enables the system to load a much more powerful control program, called the *disk operating system (DOS)*, into RAM memory. This operation is referred to as *bootup* and is depicted in Figure 1.28.

> **EXAM TIP**
>
> Remember that the single beep in the startup sequence marks the successful completion of the system's POST.

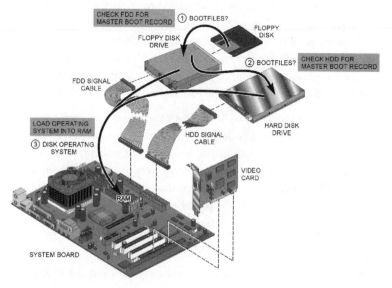

FIGURE 1.28
The steps of a bootup: Phase Three—Bootup

The boot process might take several seconds to perform depending on the configuration of the system. If a warm boot is performed or if the POST has been disabled, the amount of time required for the system to get into operation is decreased. After the operating system has been loaded into the computer's memory, the BIOS gives it control over the system. From this point, the operating system will oversee the operation of the system.

CHALLENGE #2

A friend is having trouble starting up her computer, and she has asked you to help. When you turn the system on, the video display comes on, and you can hear the disk drive spinning. Several different screens display, and then you hear a single beep from the computer. From your knowledge of system bootups, what can you tell your friend about her system?

OPERATING SYSTEMS

Operating systems are programs designed to control the operation of a computer system. Every portion of the system must be controlled and coordinated so that the millions of operations that occur every second are carried out correctly and on time. In addition, it is the job of the operating system to make the complexity of the personal computer as invisible as possible to the user.

A disk operating system, or DOS, is a collection of programs used to control overall computer operation in a disk-based system. These programs work in the background to enable the user of the computer to interact with it (that is, input characters from the keyboard, define a file structure for storing records, or output data to a monitor or printer). DOS is also responsible for finding and organizing your data and applications on the disk.

DOS can be divided into four distinct sections:

◆ *Boot files*—Take over control of the system from the ROM BIOS during startup.

◆ *Kernel files*—The basic set of files that make up the basic core of the operating system.

◆ *File management files*—Enable the system to manage information within itself.

◆ *Utility files*—Permit the user to manage system resources, troubleshoot the system, and configure the system.

CMOS SETUP UTILITIES

During the boot-up process, PCs check a battery-powered storage area on the system board, called the *CMOS RAM*, to determine what types of options were installed in the system. Users have access to this configuration information through their setup utility.

When the computer is set up for the first time, or when new options are added to the system, it might be necessary to run the computer's CMOS configuration setup utility. The values input through the setup utility are stored in the system's CMOS configuration registers where they are examined each time the system is booted up.

While performing its normal POST and boot-up functions, the BIOS displays an active RAM memory count as it is being tested. Immediately following the RAM test count, the BIOS program places a prompt on the display to tell the user that the *CMOS Setup* utility can be accessed by pressing a special key or key combination.

The keys, or key combinations, used to access the setup menus vary from one BIOS manufacturer to another. If the proper keys are not pressed within a predetermined amount of time, the BIOS program will continue with the boot-up process. If the keys are pressed during this time, however, the boot-up routine will be put on hold and the program will display a CMOS Setup Selection screen, similar to the one depicted in Figure 1.29.

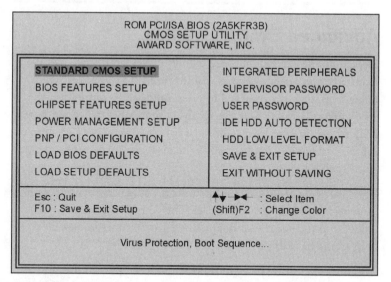

FIGURE 1.29
A CMOS Setup Selection screen.

Every system board model has a specific BIOS designed for it. Therefore, functions are specific to the design of system boards using that chipset. A typical Configuration Setup screen is shown in Figure 1.30. The user can enter specific configuration values in to the CMOS registers through this screen. The cursor on the screen can be moved from item to item using the keyboard's cursor control keys.

FIGURE 1.30
A CMOS Configuration Setup screen.

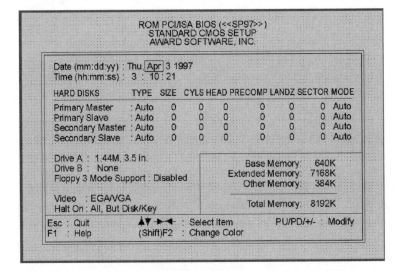

Advanced CMOS Utilities

Depending on the system board chipset maker, advanced CMOS Configuration screens, such as Chipset and BIOS Features Setup screens, are typically provided to extend the user's control over the configuration of the system. A relatively simple BIOS Features screen is illustrated in Figure 1.31. In this example, several boot-up options can be enabled in CMOS, such as the boot drive sequence and password enabling.

The CMOS boot-up sequence permits the system to boot up without checking all the drives in order. This setting might need to be adjusted to include the A: floppy drive if it becomes impossible to boot to the hard drive.

The *password* setting prevents users without the password from accessing the system. If the system has an unknown password, it will be necessary to clear the CMOS. Most system boards have a jumper that can be shorted to reset the CMOS to its default settings. If this option is used, you must reenter the original configuration information.

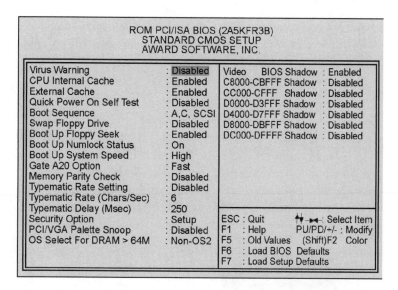

FIGURE 1.31
A BIOS Features Setup screen.

On Pentium-based system boards, the hardware configurations that enable various memory and I/O functions are established through the BIOS port-enabling settings. These settings usually include enabling the disk drives, keyboard, and video options, as well as the onboard serial and parallel ports. The user can also turn certain sections of the system's RAM on or off for shadowing purposes, as well as establish parity or non-parity memory operations through this screen.

CHALLENGE #3

Your system will not boot up to the hard drive, so you place a bootable floppy disk in the A: drive and try to restart the system. You watch the startup sequence closely and discover that the system does not appear to check the floppy disk drive for a disk. What should you do to get the system to look for the floppy disk?

> **NOTE**
>
> **Hands-On Activity**   For hands-on experience with this concept, refer to Lab Procedure #2, "Boot Sequence," located on the CD that accompanies this book.

PERSONAL DIGITAL ASSISTANTS

Palmtop computers are a class of very small computers designed to fit in most users' hands. The palmtop market was diminished for some time because of the difficulty of running Windows on such small displays. Human ergonomics also come into play when dealing with smaller notebooks. The smaller display screens become difficult to see, and keyboards become more difficult to use as the size of the keys decrease.

However, the market was revived by the introduction of palm tops as p*ersonal digital assistants* (*PDAs*). Figure 1.32 depicts a typical PDA. These handheld devices use a special stylus, referred to as a pen, to input data and selections instead of a keyboard or mouse. Basically the PDA is an electronic time management system that can also include computer applications such as word processors, spreadsheets, and databases.

FIGURE 1.32
A personal digital assistant.

The PDA's display is a touch-screen, LCD display that works in conjunction with a graphical user interface running on top of a specialized operating system. Some PDAs employ a highly modified, embedded (on a chip) version of the Microsoft Windows operating system, called Windows CE, as their operating system. These systems are particularly well suited for exchanging and synchronizing information with larger Windows-based systems.

Two items have made PDAs popular—their size and their capability of communicating with the user's desktop computer system. Early PDAs exchanged information with the full-sized computer through serial port connections. Newer models communicate with the user's desktop computer through USB ports, infrared communications links, or docking stations.

CHAPTER SUMMARY

This chapter has presented a mini-course covering the basic organization and operation of the typical personal computer system. In particular, it has covered the fundamental hardware structures and components associated with PC-compatible personal computer systems. These discussions will underpin the more involved information related to these devices that will be presented in subsequent chapters.

At this point, review the objectives listed at the beginning of the chapter to be certain that you understand each point and can perform each task listed there. Afterward, answer the review questions that follow to verify your knowledge of the information.

KEY TERMS

- 5-pin DIN
- 6-pin mini-DIN
- Adapter cards
- Application-Specific Integrated Circuits (ASICs)
- AT-bus
- AT-Style
- ATX-Style
- Basic Input/Output System (BIOS)
- BERG connectors
- Boot files
- Cache memory
- Cathode-Ray Tube (CRT)
- CD-ROM drive
- Character printer
- Chipset

CHAPTER SUMMARY

- CMOS RAM
- CMOS Setup
- Cold boot
- Compact Disc (CD)
- Digital Versatile Disc (DVD)
- Disk drives
- Disk Operating System (DOS)
- Dot pitch
- Expansion slots
- Extended ISA (EISA)
- File management files
- Firmware
- Floppy Disk Drive (FDD)
- Full-duplex mode
- Half-duplex mode
- Hard Disk Drive (HDD)
- Industry Standard Architecture (ISA)
- Initialization
- Input/Output (I/O)
- Integrated Drive Electronics (IDE)
- Kernel files
- Keyboard
- Liquid Crystal Display (LCD)
- Local Area Network cards

- Master Boot Record (MBR)
- Microprocessor/CPU
- Modem
- Mouse
- Nonvolatile
- Palmtop
- Password
- PELS
- Peripheral Component Interconnect (PCI)
- Peripherals
- Personal computer (PC)
- Personal Digital Assistants (PDAs)
- Pixels
- Plug and Play (PnP)
- Pointing devices
- Power On Self Tests (POST)
- Power supply
- Power-supply unit
- Primary Memory
- Read-Only Memory (ROM)
- Real Time Clock (RTC)
- Reset
- Resolution
- RJ-11

CHAPTER SUMMARY

- ROM BIOS
- RS-232 serial cable
- Shadow mask
- Signal cables
- Simplex mode
- Small Computer System Interface (SCSI)
- Soft switch
- Software
- Sound cards
- Speakers

- System board
- System unit
- Tape drive
- Utility files
- Video display monitor
- Video Electronics Standards Association (VESA)
- Video Graphic Array (VGA) card
- Video monitor
- Volatile memory
- Warm boot

APPLY YOUR KNOWLEDGE

Review Questions

1. What is the main difference between AT and ATX power supplies?

    A. ATX power supplies require 240V AC input.

    B. The ATX power supply is controlled by a software switch on the system board.

    C. ATX power supplies deliver more power to the system.

    D. AT power supplies blow air onto the system board rather than out through the back of the unit.

2. Which type of storage is volatile?

    A. RAM

    B. CD-ROM

    C. Disk

    D. ROM

3. Which term does not describe the dot information produced by a color monitor?

    A. PEL

    B. Pixel

    C. Triad

    D. Picture element

4. Which system component executes software instructions and carries out arithmetic operations for the system?

    A. The microprocessor

    B. The CMOS RAM

    C. The BIOS

    D. The U and V pipes

5. Which video standard is superior to the others listed?

    A. VGA

    B. SVGA

    C. XGA

    D. S3TV

6. PC-compatibles use a _____ connector for the VGA video function.

    A. 9-pin, female D-shell

    B. 15-pin, male D-shell

    C. 15-pin, female D-shell

    D. 25-pin, male D-shell

7. Disk drive tracks are composed of _____.

    A. sectors

    B. clusters

    C. FRUs

    D. magnetic spots

8. During startup, the memory of a computer is tested by _____.

    A. the CPU

    B. the CMOS setup program

    C. the POST

    D. the Interrupt Controller

9. Which of the following interfaces employs a 50-pin cable?

    A. An internal SCSI interface

    B. An EIDE interface

APPLY YOUR KNOWLEDGE

C. A VESA bus

D. An LPT port

10. An optical CD-ROM disk typically contains _____ of information.

    A. 420MB

    B. 600MB

    C. 680MB

    D. the Interrupt Controller

11. A good example of firmware is _____.

    A. CONFIG.SYS

    B. Windows 95

    C. DOS

    D. ROM BIOS

12. Which type of interface would you normally expect to encounter when installing an external CD-ROM drive?

    A. ISA

    B. IDE

    C. SCSI

    D. USB

13. Nonvolatile data can be stored in _____.

    A. Register

    B. Cache

    C. ROM

    D. RAM

14. Which of the following constitutes a valid boot-up sequence?

    A. POST, initialization, bootup

    B. Initialization, bootup, POST

    C. Bootup, POST, initialization

    D. Initialization, POST, bootup

15. The resolution for a video adapter operating in native VGA mode is ____.

    A. 350x468

    B. 640x480

    C. 800x600

    D. 1024x768

16. Replacing the power supply in an AT system requires that you also _____.

    A. reset the CMOS

    B. reinstall Windows

    C. match the P8 and P9 PS connectors to the P1 and P2 motherboard connectors, respectively

    D. replace the AC power cord

17. For computer boot-up purposes, the first set of instructions is stored in the _____.

    A. CMOS

    B. ROM BIOS

    C. CPU

    D. RAM

APPLY YOUR KNOWLEDGE

18. What is the rule for AT power connections? (Select the appropriate answer.)

    A. Red to orange

    B. Red to red

    C. Red to black

    D. Black to black

19. The LCD display on a portable computer is powered by _____.

    A. low voltage AC

    B. high voltage AC

    C. low voltage DC

    D. high voltage DC

20. Which are legitimate names for system boards? (Select two answers.)

    A. Circuit boards

    B. Daughterboards

    C. Motherboards

    D. Planar boards

21. Which type of system board uses a 5-pin DIN connector for the keyboard?

    A. NTX

    B. ATX

    C. PC-AT

    D. PS/2

22. Which pin is used to align a microprocessor for insertion?

    A. Pin 0

    B. Pin 1

C. Pin 10

D. Pin 8

23. What type of system bus expansion slot connector has two separate slots?

    A. PC-Bus

    B. ISA

    C. VESA

    D. PCI

24. A computer has two floppy disk drives. Which of them is the A: drive?

    A. The floppy drive that is first attached to the cable

    B. The floppy drive that is attached to the nearest connector

    C. The floppy drive that is attached to the connector at the end of the cable

    D. The floppy drive that is designated via its jumpers

25. Which of the following should be avoided when the computer is in operation?

    A. Removing CD-ROM disks

    B. Exchanging mice trackballs

    C. Pushing the ON/OFF switch

    D. Swapping keyboards

26. What is used to prevent the spreading of the electron beam on a color monitor?

    A. Shadow mask

    B. Color shield

APPLY YOUR KNOWLEDGE

C. Glass faceplate

D. Phosphor shield

27. If you were buying a new monitor, which of following has the best dot pitch?

A. .24

B. CYMK

C. RBG

D. .29

28. When two devices can send signals to each other at the same time over the same wire, this is called _____ communication.

A. simplex

B. half-duplex

C. full-duplex

D. multi-quadraplex

29. Which of the following describe differences between an ISA expansion slot and a PCI expansion slot? (Select all that apply.)

A. PCI slots are shorter.

B. PCI slots are 64-bits.

C. PCI slots are primarily used for video graphics adapters.

D. PCI slots are longer.

30. What type of electrical power is required by the LCD panel of a notebook computer?

A. 100Hz AC

B. Low voltage DC

C. Low voltage AC

D. 100Hz DC

Answers and Explanations

1. **B.** The ATX power supply is controlled by an electronic switch from the system board. Other differences between the ATX and AT power supplies include the monitor power passthrough is gone from the ATX design. ATX power supplies provide +3.3V through a new, keyed system board connector, and its fan blows into the system unit rather than out. For more information, see the section "Power Supplies."

2. **A.** RAM is a volatile type of memory—its contents disappear when power is removed from the memory. For more information, see the section "System Boards."

3. **C.** A color monitor employs a combination of three color phosphors—red, blue, and green—arranged in an adjacent group of dots or bars called pixels or PELS. A picture element, also referred to as a pixel, is created in a liquid crystal display's screen at each spot where a row and a column of electrodes intersect. For more information, see the section "Color Monitors."

4. **A.** The microprocessor is the major component of any system board. It can be thought of as the "brains" of the computer system because it reads, interprets, and executes software instructions, and also carries out arithmetic and logical operations for the system. For more information, see the section "Microprocessors."

5. **B.** Standard VGA resolution is defined as 720x400 pixels using 16 colors in text mode, and 640x480 pixels using 16 onscreen colors in graphics mode. However, improved resolution VGA systems, referred to as Super VGAs (SVGA), are now commonly available in formats of 1,024x768 with 256 colors, 1,024x768 with

APPLY YOUR KNOWLEDGE

16 colors, and 800x600 with 256 colors. The SVGA definition continues to expand, with video controller capabilities ranging up to 1,280x1,024 (with reduced color capabilities) currently available in the market. For more information, see the section "Video Adapter Cards."

6. **C.** The VGA/SVGA adapter on the back of the computer has a 15-pin, 3-row female D-shell connector. For more information, see the section "Peripherals and Ports."

7. **A.** Typical hard disks can have as many as 10,000 tracks on each side of each platter. Each track on the hard drive is divided into between 17 and 65 equal-size sectors, depending on the diameter of the disk. Sectors generally contain 512 bytes. For more information, see the section "Storage Devices."

8. **C.** The BIOS performs a series of diagnostic tests (called POST, or Power On Self Tests) on the system to verify that it is operating correctly. While performing its normal tests and boot-up functions, the BIOS displays an active RAM memory count as it is being tested. For more information, see the section "Basic Input/Output Systems."

9. **A.** An internal SCSI device must be capable of connecting to the type of SCSI cable being used. In a PC, this is most often a 50-pin ribbon cable. For more information, see the section "CD-ROM Interfaces."

10. **C.** The average storage capacity of a CD-ROM disc is about 680MB. For more information, see the section "CD-ROM."

11. **D.** The BIOS software (programming) and hardware (the ROM chip) are referred to as firmware. Some I/O devices, such as video and network adapter cards, have additional firmware that act

as extensions to the system's BIOS. For more information, see the section "Basic Input/Output Systems."

12. **C.** Most external CD-ROM drives employ SCSI interface connectors. For more information, see the section "CD-ROM Interfaces."

13. **C.** Read-Only Memory (ROM) contains the computer's permanent startup programs. ROM is nonvolatile—its contents remain with or without power being applied. For more information, see the section "System Boards."

14. **A.** When a PC is turned on, the entire system is reset to a predetermined starting condition. From this state, it begins carrying out software instructions from its BIOS program. This small program is permanently stored in the ROM memory IC located on the system board. First, the BIOS performs a series of diagnostic tests (called POST, or Power On Self Tests) on the system to verify that it is operating correctly. Next, the BIOS places starting values in the system's various programmable devices. These intelligent devices regulate the operation of different portions of the computer's hardware. This process is called initialization. Finally, the BIOS performs the bootstrap sequence where it searches the system for a special program that it can use to load other programs into RAM and start the operating system. For more information, see the section "Basic Input/Output Systems."

15. **B.** The default VGA resolution is defined as 640x480 pixels using 16 onscreen colors in graphics mode. For more information, see the section "Video Adapter Cards."

16. **C.** In AT-compatible power supplies, two six-wire bundles, typically marked P8 and P9, deliver

APPLY YOUR KNOWLEDGE

power to the system board. The physical construction of these power connectors is identical. They are designed to plug in to the system board's P1 and P2 power plugs, respectively. For more information, see the section "Power Supplies."

17. **B.** When a PC is turned on, it begins carrying out software instructions from its BIOS program. This small program is permanently stored in the ROM BIOS memory IC located on the system board. The information stored in this chip represents all the inherent intelligence that the system has until it can load more information from another source, such as a disk drive or remote server computer. For more information, see the section "Basic Input/Output Systems."

18. **D.** A good rule of thumb to remember when attaching these two connectors to the system board is that the black wires in each bundle should be next to each other in the middle. For more information, see the section "Power Supplies."

19. **C.** Liquid Crystal Displays are relatively thin, flat, and lightweight, and require very little power to operate. Notebook display panels are powered by low-voltage DC power sources such as a battery or converter. For more information, see the section "LCD Operation."

20. **C, D.** System boards are also referred to as motherboards and as planar boards. For more information, see the section "System Boards."

21. **C.** Older AT-class systems use a 5-pin DIN connector for the keyboard. For more information, see the section "Keyboards."

22. **B.** There are notches and dots on the various ICs that provide important keys when replacing a microprocessor. These notches and dots specify the location of the number 1 pin. This pin must be lined up with the pin-1 notch of the socket. For more information, see the section "Microprocessors."

23. **C.** A VESA expansion slot connector consists of an ISA slot and an additional VESA connector. For more information, see the section "Expansion Slots."

24. **C.** In PC systems, the cable can provide for one or two floppy drives that will automatically be recognized as logical drives A: and B: by the system. The drive connected to the very end of the cable will be designated as drive A:. For more information, see the section "Floppy Disk Drives."

25. **D.** Plugging hot-swappable devices such as the keyboard in to the system while it is turned on can cause a system crash or even damage parts of the system. For more information, see the section "Keyboards."

26. **A.** Color CRTs add a metal grid in front of the phosphor coating called a shadow mask. It ensures that an electron gun assigned to one color doesn't strike a dot of another color. For more information, see the section "Color Monitors."

27. **A.** Resolution can be expressed as a function of how close pixels can be grouped together on the screen. The closer the pixels to one another, the sharper the image. This form of resolution is expressed in terms of dot pitch. A monitor with a .28 dot pitch has pixels that are located .28mm apart. For more information, see the section "Screen Resolution."

APPLY YOUR KNOWLEDGE

28. **C.** When a modem is used to send signals in only one direction, it is operating in simplex mode. Modems capable of both transmitting and receiving data are divided into two groups, based on their mode of operation. In half-duplex mode, modems exchange data, but only in one direction at a time. Multiplexing or full-duplex modems send and receive signal frequencies that will allow both modems to send and receive data simultaneously. For more information, see the section "Modems."

29. **A, B.** See Figure 1.6, which illustrates expansion slot connectors. For more information, see the section "Expansion Slots."

30. **B.** LCD panels operate with low voltage DC power. For more information, see the section "LCD Operation."

CHALLENGE SOLUTIONS

1. The system should include a CD-ROM drive and add-on speakers for listening to music stored on CDs. Likewise, you should install a modem to provide the system with the capability to connect to the Internet through a dial-up connection. In order to use the high-resolution graphics associated with the computer games, you should install a high-resolution video card and monitor. A printer should also be added to the system to provide the desired hard copy printouts from the Internet. For more information, see the section "Inside the System Unit."

Of course the system should provide the typical standard components—system board, hard and floppy drives, keyboard, and mouse. You should consider installing a large hard drive and plenty of RAM to fully exploit the multimedia capabilities of the games and other programs. A fast microprocessor is another consideration to be taken in this area.

2. Because the system reaches the single beep, you can tell that the basic hardware in her system is working okay. Between the time the system is turned on and the single beep is presented, the system is performing POST tests and initializing basic system hardware components—after the beep, the system searches for a boot record and tries to load an operating system—the problem must be related to one of these activities. For more information, see the section "Basic Input/Output Systems."

3. You must restart the computer and access its CMOS Setup utility screens. In one of its screens (probably the CMOS Setup utility screen), you should see the Boot Sequence option or an option to boot to the floppy drive. Activate this option in the CMOS and restart the system with the boot disk in the floppy drive. For more information, see the section "Advanced CMOS Utilities."

APPLY YOUR KNOWLEDGE

Suggested Readings and Resources

1. Free Online Dictionary of Computing
   http://foldoc.doc.ic.ac.uk/foldoc/index.
   html

2. PC Hardware Guide
   http://ctdp.tripod.com/hardware/pc/begin/
   index.html

3. VESA Bus
   http://webopedia.internet.com/TERM/V/
   VESA.html

4. PCI Bus
   http://webopedia.internet.com/TERM/P/
   PCI.html

5. Modem
   http://webopedia.internet.com/TERM/m/
   modem.html

6. Sound Cards
   www.pctechguide.com/11sound.htm

7. Hard Disk Drive
   http://webopedia.internet.com/TERM/h/
   hard_disk_drive.html

8. Floppy Disk Drives
   www.pcguide.com/ref/fdd/

9. Storage/Tape Backup
   www.pctechguide.com/15tape.htm

10. Keyboard
    http://webopedia.internet.com/TERM/k/
    keyboard.html

11. CRT/Monitor
    www.pctechguide.com/06crtmon.htm

12. BIOS
    http://webopedia.internet.com/TERM/B/
    BIOS.html

13. Electronic Industries Alliance
    www.eia.org

14. PC Guide Index
    http://www.pcguide.com/topic.html

This chapter helps you to prepare for the Core Hardware module of the A+ Certification examination by covering the following objectives within the "Domain 1.0: Installation, Configuration, and Upgrading" section.

1.2 Identify basic procedures for adding and removing field replaceable modules for both desktop and portable systems.

Examples of modules:

- **System board**
- **Storage device**
- **Power supply**
- **Processor/CPU**
- **Memory**
- **Hard drive**
- **Keyboard**
- **Video board**
- **Mouse**
- **Network Interface Card (NIC)**

Portable system components:

- **AC adapters**
- **Digital cameras**
- **DC controllers**
- **LCD panel**
- **PC card**
- **Pointing devices**

CHAPTER 2

Adding and Removing FRU Modules

▶ Core objective 1.2 of the A+ exam states that the test taker should be able to identify basic procedures for adding and removing field replaceable modules. As the objective points out, every technician should be aware of typical personal computer components that can be exchanged in the field. They should be able to install, connect, and configure these components to upgrade or repair an existing system. The following sections of this chapter present standard procedures for installing and removing typical field replaceable units.

STUDY STRATEGIES

To prepare for the Installation, Configuration, and Upgrading objective of the Core Hardware exam,

▶ Read the objectives at the beginning of this chapter.

▶ Study the information in this chapter.

▶ Review the objectives listed earlier in this chapter.

▶ Perform any step-by-step procedures in the text.

▶ Answer the review questions at the end of the chapter and check your results.

▶ Use the PrepLogic test engine on the CD-ROM that accompanies this book for additional review and exam questions concerning this material.

▶ Review the exam tips scattered throughout the chapter and make certain that you are comfortable with each point.

INTRODUCTION

This chapter focuses on techniques and procedures for removing, installing, and configuring typical field replaceable hardware units (FRUs) associated with personal computer systems. These units include internal components such as system boards, power supplies, and disk drives as well as external devices such as keyboards, video displays, and mice.

The second section of the chapter covers FRUs located on the system board component. These devices include microprocessors, RAM and ROM devices, and batteries.

The final section of the chapter deals with replacing components primarily associated with portable computer systems. These devices include portable power sources, LCD panels, and PCMCIA cards.

After completing the chapter, you should be able to install, connect, and configure common computer hardware components to form a working system. In addition, you should be able to identify the components of portable systems and describe how they differ from typical desktop components. You should also be able to identify their unique problems.

REMOVING SYSTEM BOARDS

System boards are generally removed for one of two possible reasons. Either the system board has failed and needs to be replaced, or the user wants to install a new system board with better features. In either case, it will be necessary to remove the current system board and replace it. The removal procedure can be defined in five steps:

1. Remove all external I/O systems.

2. Remove the system unit's outer cover.

3. Remove the option adapter cards.

4. Remove the cables from the system board.

5. Remove the system board.

Removing External I/O Systems

Unplug all power cords from the commercial power outlet. Remove all peripherals from the system unit. Disconnect the mouse, keyboard, and monitor signal cable from the rear of the unit. Finally, disconnect the monitor power cable from the outlet (or the system unit in an AT-class computer). Figure 2.1 illustrates the system unit's back panel connections.

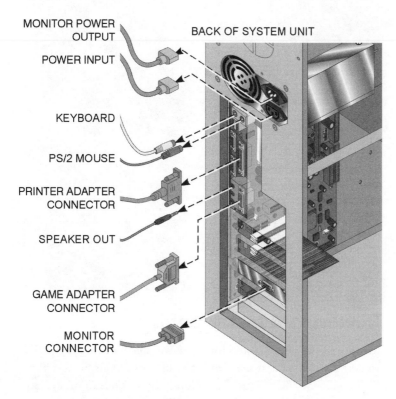

FIGURE 2.1
A system unit's back panel connections.

Removing the System Unit's Cover

Unplug the AC power cord from the system unit. Determine which type of case you are working with. If the case is a desktop model, does the cover slide off the chassis in a forward direction, bringing the front panel with it, or does it raise off the chassis from the rear? If the back lip of the outer cover folds over the edge of the back panel, the lid raises up from the back after the retaining screws are removed. If the retaining screws go through the back panel without passing through the lip, the outer cover will slide forward after the retaining screws have been removed.

Remove the screws that hold the cover to the chassis. Store the screws properly. Next, remove the system unit's outer cover, as illustrated in Figure 2.2, and set it aside. Slide the case forward. Tilt the case upward from the front and remove it from the unit. Or, lift the back edge of the outer cover to approximately 45 degrees, and then slide it toward the rear of the chassis.

FIGURE 2.2
Removing the case.

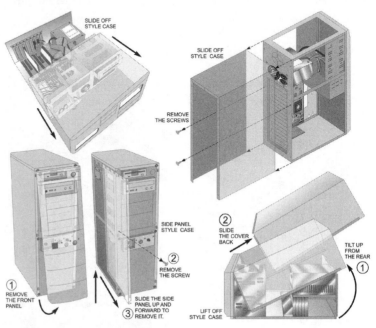

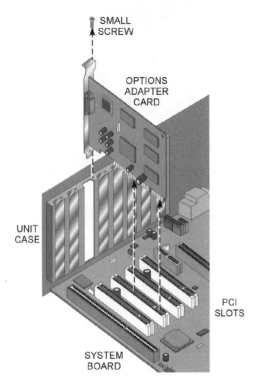

FIGURE 2.3
Removing adapter cards.

Removing Adapter Cards

Remove any cables or connectors from the adapter card noting where they originate. If the card is free of connections, remove the retaining screws that secure the options adapter cards to the system unit's back panel. Finally, remove the adapter cards from the expansion slots. It is a good practice to place adapter cards back into the same slots they were removed from, if possible. Store the screws properly. Refer to Figure 2.3 to perform this procedure.

Installing Adapter Cards

The process used to install adapter cards is normally the reverse of the removal process:

1. Check the adapter card's installation information for any manual configuration settings that might need to be made.

2. Remove the expansion slot cover from the system unit's back panel. Align the adapter card with the appropriate expansion slot and firmly push it into the slot.

3. Secure the card to the back panel of the system unit with a single screw.

4. Attach any external connections to the card (that is, attach the phone line to the modem card or attach the network cable to the LAN adapter).

5. Install any device drivers required (PnP devices should be detected by the operating system and automatically configured for operation. Additional or updated drivers can be loaded from the operating system (that is, enhancing the operation of a VGA card by loading an SVGA driver for the video display).

Removing the Cables from the System Board

Begin by disconnecting the floppy drive signal cable (smaller signal cable) and the hard drive signal cable (larger signal cable) from the card. Also disconnect any I/O port connections from the card before removing it from the expansion slot.

The system board provides an operator interface through a set of front panel indicator lights and switches. These indicators and switches connect to the system board by BERG connectors, as depicted in Figure 2.4.

The front panel connectors must be removed in order to exchange the system board. Make sure to mark them for identification purposes before removing them. This will ensure that they are reinstalled correctly.

Disconnect the power supply connections from the system board.

FIGURE 2.4
Front panel connections.

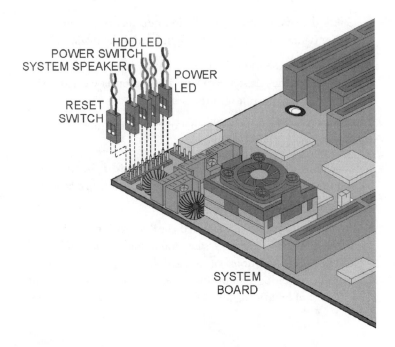

Removing the System Board

Verify the positions of all jumper settings on the old system board. Record these settings and verify their meanings before removing the board from the system. This might require the use of the board's user manual, if available. Remove the grounding screws that secure the system board to the chassis. Store the screws properly.

In a desktop unit that employs *plastic standoffs*, slide the system board toward the left (as you face the front of the unit) to free its plastic feet from the slots in the floor of the system unit. Tilt the left edge of the board up, and then lift it straight up and out of the system unit, as illustrated in Figure 2.5. If the system unit uses threaded, brass standoffs, simply remove all the retaining screws and lift the board out of the case.

In a tower unit that has plastic standoffs, slide the system board toward the bottom of the system unit to free its plastic feet from the slots in the side panel. Tilt the bottom edge of the board away from the unit and pull it straight out of the chassis, as shown in Figure 2.6.

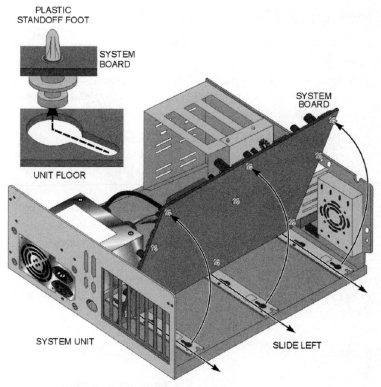

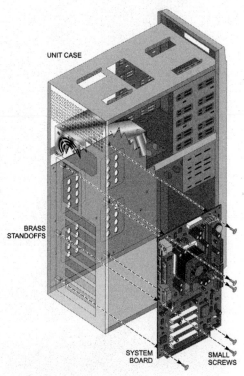

FIGURE 2.5
Removing the system board from a desktop case.

FIGURE 2.6
Removing the system board from a tower case.

SYSTEM BOARD DEVICES

The few serviceable devices on the system board include the following:

- ◆ The microprocessor
- ◆ The system RAM modules
- ◆ Specialized support ICs

As with the system board itself, there are really only two possible reasons for replacing any of these devices: to replace a failed unit or to upgrade the unit. In either case, technicians must be able to exchange the device and return the system to proper operation.

Installing Microprocessors

PC manufacturers mount microprocessors in *sockets* so that they can be replaced easily. This enables a failed microprocessor to simply be exchanged with a working unit. More often, though, the microprocessor is replaced with an improved version to upgrade the speed or performance of the system.

The notches and dots on the various ICs are important keys when replacing a microprocessor. They specify the location of the IC's number 1 pin. This pin must be lined up with the pin-1 notch of the socket for proper insertion. In older systems, the microprocessors had to be forcibly removed from the socket using an IC extractor tool. As the typical microprocessor's pin count increased, special *Zero Insertion Force (ZIF) sockets* were designed that permit the microprocessor to be placed in the socket without force and then be clamped in place. An arm-activated clamping mechanism in the socket shifts to the side, locking the pins in place. A ZIF socket and microprocessor arrangement is depicted in Figure 2.7.

FIGURE 2.7
A microprocessor and ZIF socket.

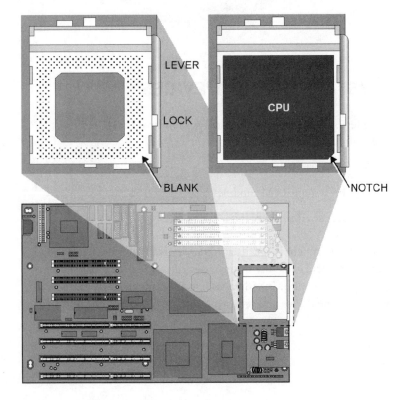

To release the microprocessor from the socket, the lever arm beside the socket must be pressed down and away from the socket. When it comes free from the socket, the arm raises up to release the pressure on the microprocessor's pins.

A notch and dot in one corner of the CPU marks the position of the processor's number 1 pin. The dot and notch should be located at the free end of the socket's locking lever for proper installation. Both the CPU and the socket have one corner that does not have a pin (or pin hole) in it. This feature prevents the CPU from being inserted into the socket incorrectly.

Modern processors generate a considerable amount of heat. To prevent this heat from reaching a destructive level for the device, all Pentium processors require CPU cooling fans and heat sinks. These units are available in glue-on and snap-on models. A special heat conducting grease is typically used with snap-on heat sinks to provide good thermal transfer between the microprocessor and the heat sink. Power for the fans is normally obtained from one of the system's options power connectors or from a special jumper block on the system board. These items must be installed before operating the microprocessor.

Pentium microprocessors come in a number of speed ratings and many use a dual-processor voltage arrangement. In addition, the processor might be a Pentium clone manufactured by someone other than Intel. The microprocessor's internal core voltage supply is controlled through a *voltage regulator module* (*VRM*) located on the system board. Older Pentium system boards employed jumpers to establish the proper +3V and CPU core voltage settings for the particular type of microprocessor being installed. These boards also use jumpers to establish the external/internal clock ratio for the microprocessor, as well as its external front-side bus frequency. Newer systems auto-detect the type of microprocessor installed through the PnP BIOS and configure these settings for their optimum values.

Installing Memory Modules

Modern system boards typically provide rows of *single in-line memory module* (*SIMM*) sockets and a single, *dual in-line memory module* (*DIMM*) socket. These sockets accept small, piggyback memory modules that can contain various combinations of DRAM devices.

Both SIMMs and DIMMs use edge connectors that snap into a retainer on the system board. The SIMMs used on Pentium boards are typically 72-pin SIMMs, whereas the DIMM socket accepts 168-pin DIMM units.

The SIMM modules can only be inserted in one direction because of a plastic safety tab at one end of the SIMM slot. The notched end of the SIMM module must be inserted into this end. To install a SIMM module, insert the module into the slot at a 45-degree angle, making sure that all the contacts are aligned with the slot. Rock the module into a vertical position so that it snaps into place and the plastic guides go through the SIMM's mounting holes. The metal clip should lock into place. To release the SIMM module, gently push the metal clips outward and rotate the module out of the slot. The DIMM module simply slides vertically into the socket and is locked in place by a tab at each end. These processes are illustrated in Figure 2.8.

FIGURE 2.8
Installing SIMM and DIMM modules.

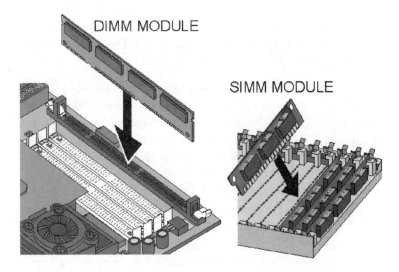

EXAM TIP

Know that SIMMs and DIMMs are keyed and that it is almost physically impossible to plug them in wrong.

Physically installing the RAM devices is all that is normally required. The system's PnP operation automatically detects the type of RAM installed and establishes proper settings for it during the boot process. Steps can be taken to optimize key RAM parameters through the CMOS setup utility. However, these parameters should only be changed by technicians who are aware of the implications of the changes they are making.

Installing Support ICs

In many system board designs, the ROM BIOS is installed in a *dual in-line package* (*DIP*) socket, as illustrated in Figure 2.9. This permits the BIOS to be upgraded by replacing the IC device in the socket. Many Pentium-class system boards have advanced BIOS devices that can be *flashed* (rewritten electrically) and still hold the information stored in them when the power is removed. In these cases, the BIOS device is likely to be a surface-mount device that is permanently soldered to the system board. However, other Pentium-class system boards have shifted the BIOS into *Plastic Leadless Chip Carrier* (*PLCC*) sockets.

FIGURE 2.9
Socket mounted ICs.

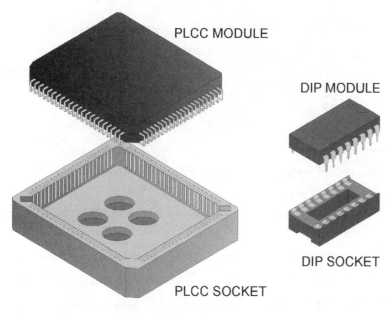

PLCC MODULE

DIP MODULE

DIP SOCKET

PLCC SOCKET

CHALLENGE #1

An employee in a remote office has called you for information about how to replace a system board in one of their desktop computers. He saw smoke coming from the microprocessor on the current system board and wants to replace it. Write a description of the process for replacing his system board that you can fax to his office. (The phone cord will not reach the location of the failed computer.)

POWER SUPPLIES

The function of the power supply is to deliver various levels of electrical power to the system's components. In order to exchange the power supply, its connections to the power source and other devices must be removed. Figure 2.10 illustrates the typical power-supply connections in a PC. The only other step involved in exchanging the power supply is to remove the screws that bind it to the system unit case.

FIGURE 2.10
Power-supply connections.

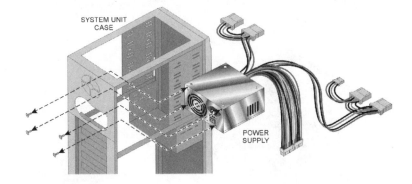

Use the following procedure to remove a power-supply unit from a system.

1. **Disconnect the exterior power connections from the system unit.**

   A. Unplug the power cord from the commercial receptacle.

   B. In an AT-class system, disconnect the monitor's power cord from the power supply.

2. **Disconnect the interior power connections.**

   A. Disconnect the power-supply connections from the system board.

   B. Disconnect the power-supply connector from the floppy disk drive.

   C. Disconnect the power-supply connector from the hard disk drive.

D. Disconnect the power-supply connector from the CD-ROM drive.

E. Disconnect the power-supply connector to the front-panel switch (if used in your case style).

3. **Remove the power-supply unit from the system.**

A. Remove the four retaining screws that secure the power-supply unit to the rear of the system unit. (Note that in some AT-style cases, an additional pair of screws is used along the front edge of the power supply to secure it to the metal bracket it is mounted on.)

B. Store the screws properly.

C. Remove the power supply from the system unit by lifting it out of the unit.

Installing Power Supplies

When ordering a replacement power supply, you must remember to take into account its form factor and its wattage rating requirements. The wattage rating is a measurement of the total power the supply can deliver to the system. More heavily equipped systems (that is, more disk drives and peripherals) require power supplies with higher wattage ratings.

When reinstalling an AT-style power supply, recall that although the P8 and P9 connectors that deliver power to the system board are alike, their voltage levels are different. Reversing them can cause severe damage.

The power connector labeled P8 should be plugged in to the circuit-board power connector labeled P1, whereas connector P9 is plugged in to the P2 connector next to it. As mentioned in Chapter 1, "Basic Terms and Concepts," a good rule of thumb to remember when attaching these two connectors to the system board is that the black wires in each bundle should be next to each other in the middle.

> **EXAM TIP**
>
> Be aware that the power supply's form factor and wattage ratings must be taken into account when ordering a replacement power supply for a system.

> **WARNING**
>
> **Don't switch the P8/P9 connectors!** Although they look alike, the voltage levels of each plug are different. Reversing them can cause severe damage.

EXAM TIP

Memorize the color code arrangement that shows a properly connected AT power supply/system board connector.

CHALLENGE #2

You are called to a large bank that is a customer of your computer repair company. It is using AT-style computers running Windows 3.1 operating systems. The computer shows no signs of life when the On/Off button is pressed, so you decide to replace the power supply. Neither the original power supply nor the new power supply has any markings on its connectors. There are also no markings for the power supply connection on the system board. What should you do to make certain that the power supply works properly in this system?

INPUT DEVICES

With the exception of the keyboard, the steps for installing input devices are similar to those of installing other I/O devices. The keyboard is different in that its installation procedure normally consists of simply plugging it in to the system board's keyboard connector.

Some input devices, such as the mouse, are so widely used that they plug in to one of the system's standard I/O ports. In the case of the mouse, it is almost standard procedure to plug it in to either the PS/2 mouse port or the 9-pin serial port on the back of the unit.

Other input devices might require that a proprietary adapter card be installed in one of the system's expansion slots to host them. These cards might have jumpers that must be set to configure them for the system. Plug and Play devices do not require physical configuration steps. The system will search for, detect, and configure PnP equipment during the boot process.

Some specialized input devices come with software drivers offered by the device's manufacturer that must be configured to work with the host system. These drivers must be installed before the device can function within the operating system.

Keyboards

Most ATX style, detachable keyboards use a round, (quarter-inch) *6-pin mini-DIN* connector (also referred to as a *PS/2 connector*).

Older AT-class systems employed a larger, half-inch, *5-pin DIN* connector to plug in to the PC's system board. Both of these connections are most often made through a round opening in the rear of the system unit's case. Figure 2.11 shows the various connection schemes used with detachable keyboards.

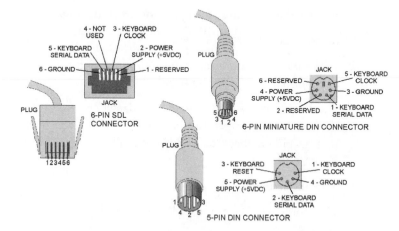

FIGURE 2.11
Connection schemes for PC keyboards.

Although many newer peripheral devices can safely be unplugged and reattached to the system while power is applied, this is not so with the standard keyboard. Plugging the keyboard in to the system while power is applied can cause the system board to fail due to the power surge and *electrostatic discharge* (*ESD*) that might occur between it and the system board.

> **EXAM TIP**
>
> Be aware that plugging non-hot swappable devices like the keyboard into the system while it is turned on can damage parts of the system.

Mice

In an ATX system, the mouse usually plugs in to a 6-pin PS/2 mini-DIN connector on the back of the system unit. This connector is identical to the keyboard connector and can easily be confused with it. In AT-class systems, the mouse is plugged in to a 9-pin serial port. This brings up a major point to consider when choosing a new mouse for an upgrade of an existing system or a replacement for a defective mouse—the type of connector that's required to attach it to the system.

> **EXAM TIP**
>
> Be aware that the mouse connector type is an important consideration in selecting a mouse for use.

In an ATX/Windows system, the steps for installing a mouse are simple—plug the mouse cable in to the mouse connector at the back of the unit. Then, turn the system on and let the operating system detect and automatically configure the mouse.

The only additional steps that might be required to get the mouse operational are to ensure that the port's hardware is properly selected and enabled, and that the mouse's driver software is installed.

However, installing a serial mouse in an AT (or ATX) class machine requires a little more effort.

1. **Configure the serial port for operation with the mouse.**

   A. Remove the system unit cover.

   B. Locate the serial port adapter function in the system (that is, on an AT or ATX system board).

   C. If a ribbon cable is used between the adapter and the D-shell connector, ensure that pin number 1 of the cable lines up with pin number 1 of the adapter, as illustrated by Figure 2.12.

   D. Start the system.

   E. When prompted, enter the CMOS setup utility.

   F. Check for any port enabling settings in the Extended CMOS screens.

   G. Turn the system off.

2. **Physically attach the mouse to the system**.

   A. Plug the mouse connector into the DB9M connector.

3. **Configure the mouse software.**

   A. Check the IRQ, COM port, and base-address settings for the serial port the mouse is attached to.

   B. Check the Control Panel to verify that the mouse driver is loaded and correct.

When the ATX specification adopted the same connector for both the keyboard and mouse, it introduced an opportunity to plug these devices in to the wrong connector. Later ATX models and peripherals have adopted an informal color coding system to differentiate between the mouse and keyboard connections—the keyboard connector and port are color coded purple, whereas the mouse connection is green.

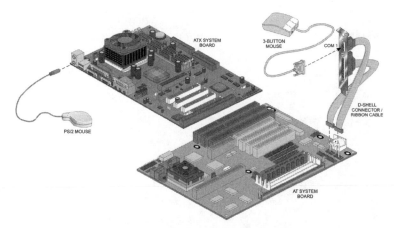

FIGURE 2.12
Attaching the mouse.

INSTALLING SOUND CARDS

Installing a *sound card* is similar to installing any other adapter card. Refer to the card's user guide to determine what hardware configuration settings might need to be made before inserting the card into the system. It might also be beneficial to run a diagnostic software package to check the system's available resources before configuring the card.

After the hardware configuration has been completed, simply install the card in one of the system's vacant expansion slots and secure it to the back panel of the system unit. Plug the microphone and speakers in to the proper *RCA mini jacks* on the card's back plate. With the card installed, the system loads its software drivers according to the directions in the user guide. Figure 2.13 depicts the connectors located on the back of a typical sound card.

EXAM TIP

Be aware that it is quite possible to confuse the mouse and keyboard connections on an ATX system.

FIGURE 2.13
Sound card connections.

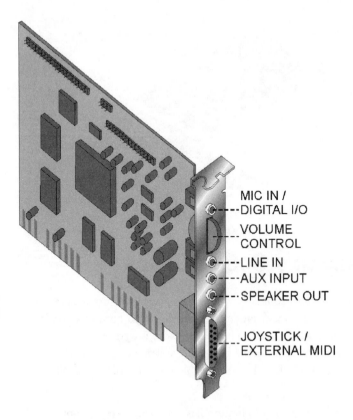

MIC IN /
DIGITAL I/O

VOLUME
CONTROL

LINE IN

AUX INPUT

SPEAKER OUT

JOYSTICK /
EXTERNAL MIDI

Most sound cards support microphones through stereo RCA jacks. A very similar speaker jack is also normally present on the back of the card. Depending on the card, the jack might be designed for mono or stereo output. An onboard volume control wheel might also protrude through the card's back plate.

INSTALLING SCANNERS AND DIGITAL CAMERAS

Two devices are designed to input graphical data into the computer. These devices are *scanners* and *digital cameras*. Scanners convert pictures, line art, photographs, and text into electronic signals that can be processed by software packages such as desktop publishers and graphic design programs. These programs, in turn, can display the image on the video display or can print it out on a graphics printer. Likewise, digital cameras produce digital snapshots that can be moved directly into the computer to be printed out or manipulated by graphics packages.

Although some older scanners employed proprietary adapter cards, most of these devices typically connect to one of the system's standard I/O ports. Scanners are typically connected to their host computers in a permanent fashion and employ the system's EPP or ECP-enabled parallel port, or its SCSI bus extension. On the other hand, digital cameras tend to be more mobile and are mostly plugged in to the computer simply to download pictures. Therefore, most digital cameras feature the capability of being connected to parallel ports, serial ports, and USB ports. Some cameras can also communicate through Firewire ports. USB and Firewire ports feature hot-swap capabilities that permit the camera to be plugged in to the system and removed while power is still applied.

Installing Storage Devices

For installation purposes, storage devices fall into one of two categories: internal and external. Internal devices are typically mounted in the system unit's drive bays. External devices normally connect to options adapter cards installed in the system board's expansion slots. Whereas internal devices typically derive their power from the system unit's power supply, external storage devices tend to employ separate, external power supply units.

Most internal storage devices conform to traditional disk drive form factors. Therefore, the hardware installation procedures for most storage devices are the same. To install a storage device in a disk drive bay,

1. Disconnect the system's power cord from the back of the unit.

2. Slide the device into one of the system unit's open drive bays.

3. Install two screws on each side to secure the unit to the disk drive cage.

4. If the unit is a 3-1/2 inch drive and it is being installed into a 5-1/4 inch drive bay, you will need to fit the drive with a universal mounting kit. These kits attach to the drive and extend its form factor so that it fits correctly in the 5-1/4 inch half-height space.

5. Connect the device's signal cable to the proper interface header on the system board (or on a host adapter card).

6. Connect the signal cable to the storage device. Use caution when connecting the disk drives to the adapter.

7. Make certain that the Pin 1 indicator stripe along one edge of the cable aligns with the Pin 1 position of the connectors on both the storage device and its controller.

8. Connect one of the power supply's optional power connectors to the storage device.

FDD Installation

The FDD installation procedure is simply sliding the FDD in to one of the system unit's open drive bays, installing two screws on each side to secure the drive to the system unit and connecting the signal and power cables to the drive. Figure 2.14 illustrates the steps required to install the floppy drive.

The PC-compatible FDD unit uses a 34-pin signal cable. The FDD signal cable is designed to accommodate two FDD units. If the drive is the only floppy in the system or intended to operate as the A: drive, connect it to the connector at the end of the cable. If it is being installed as a B: drive, attach it to the connector toward the center of the cable. A small twist of wires between the A: and B: connectors differentiates between the drives.

Reinstall the system unit's power cord and boot up the computer. As the system boots, move into the CMOS Setup utility and configure the CMOS for the type of FDD being installed.

> **EXAM TIP**
>
> Know what makes a floppy drive an A: or B: drive in a PC system.

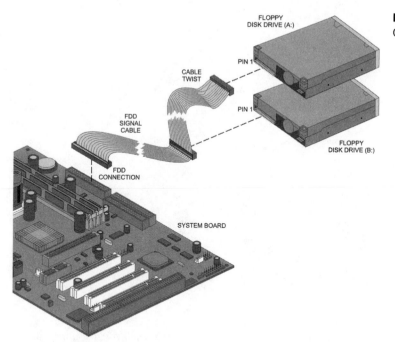

FIGURE 2.14
Connecting a drive's signal cable.

HDD Installation

The HDD hardware installation process is similar to that of other storage devices, as illustrated in Figure 2.15. However, the configuration and preparation of a typical hard disk drive is more involved than that of a floppy drive. You should confirm the IDE drive's Master/Slave/Single, or the SCSI drive's ID configuration setting before installing the unit in the drive bay. If a replacement hard drive is being installed for repair or upgrading purposes, the data on the original drive should be backed up to some other media before replacing it (if possible).

After completing the hardware installation process, the drive will need to be configured and formatted. Unlike floppy drives, which basically come in four accepted formats, hard disk drives are created in a wide variety of storage capacities. When the disk is created, its surface is electronically blank. With system-level drive types, the manufacturer performs the *low-level formatting* process. To prepare the hard disk for use by the system, three levels of preparation must take place. The order of these steps is as follows:

FIGURE 2.15
Installing a hard drive unit.

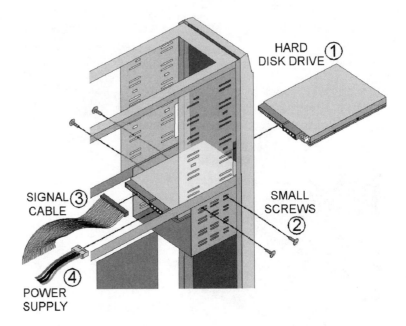

1. Set up the CMOS configuration for the drive (or allow the system to auto-detect it through the PnP boot-up process).

2. Partition the drive.

3. Perform a high-level format on the drive.

Logical and Physical Drives

Before a high-level format can be performed, a hard drive must be *partitioned*. The oldest versions of MS-DOS (2.*x*, 3.*x*) imposed a limit on the size of a drive at 32MB. As HDD technology advanced, the capacities of the physical drives eventually passed this limit. Fortunately, operating systems can partition, or divide, large physical drives into multiple *logical drives*. Each logical drive is assigned a different drive letter (that is, C, D, E, and so on up to Z) that the system will use to identify it.

Figure 2.16 illustrates the concept of creating multiple logical drives on a single hard drive. This is normally done for purposes of organization and increased access speeds. However, drives may also be partitioned to permit multiple operating systems to exist on the same physical drive.

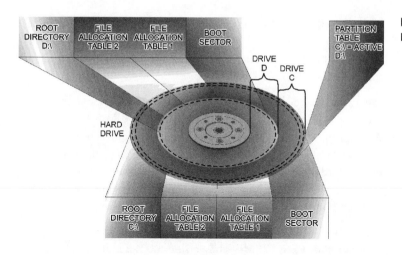

FIGURE 2.16
Partitions on a hard disk.

Basically, Microsoft Windows FAT-based operating systems provide for two types of partitions on an HDD unit. The first partition, or the *primary partition*, must exist as C: drive. The system files must be located in this partition, and the partition must be set to Active for the system to boot up from the drive. The *active partition* is the logical drive that the system will boot to.

After the primary partition has been established and properly configured, an additional partition, referred to as an *extended partition*, is also permitted. However, the extended partition can be further subdivided into 23 logical drives (all the letters in the alphabet minus a, b, and c). The extended partition cannot be deleted if logical drives have been defined within it.

The partitioning program for MS-DOS and Windows 9*x* is named *FDISK*. This program creates the disk's boot sector and a pair of blank *file allocation tables* (*FATs*). It also establishes partition parameters for the system's use in a special table called the *partition table*.

The partition table is created in the boot sector at the very beginning of the disk. It holds information about the location and starting point of each logical drive on the disk, along with the information about which partition has been marked as active and a *Master Boot Record* (*MBR*).

It is located at the beginning of the disk because this is the point where the system looks for boot-up information. When the system checks the boot sector of the physical disk during the boot process,

EXAM TIP

Know how many logical drives can be established under a FAT-based operating system.

it also checks to see which partition on the disk has been marked as active. It then jumps to that location, reads the information in that partition's boot record, and boots to the operating system it finds in that logical drive.

On a partitioned drive, there can only be one logical drive that is active at a time. When the system checks the MBR of the physical disk during the boot process, it also checks to see which partition on the disk has been marked as active and then boots to the partition boot record located in that logical drive. This arrangement enables a single physical disk to hold different operating systems that the system can boot to.

The FDISK utility in MS-DOS version 4.0 raised the maximum size of a logical drive to 128MB, and version 5.0 raised it to 528MB. The FDISK utility in Windows 9x provided upgraded support for very large hard drives. The original version of Windows 95 set a size limit for logical drives at 2GB. The FDISK version in the upgraded OSR2 version of Windows 95 extended the maximum partition size to 8GB.

CHALLENGE #3

You must install a new 12GB IDE drive in a customer's Windows 95 computer. He wants to use all of the drive's capabilities for storage. What should you do to ensure that he can use all the disk space he has purchased?

In Windows NT 4.0 and Windows 2000, the partitioning process should be performed through the Disk Administrator and Disk Management utilities, respectively. These utilities perform the same basic functions as the FDISK utility; however, they can also provide many additional functions associated with enterprise computing systems. When activated, they will show you the basic layout of the system's disks, including

◆ The size of each disk

◆ The size and file system type used in each logical drive

◆ The size and location of any unformatted (free) space on the drive

The *Disk Administrator* and *Disk Management* utilities can be used to create both traditional primary and extended partitions using FAT or NTFS organizational structures.

When newer operating system versions provided for partitions larger than 528MB, another limiting factor for the size of disk partitions was encountered—the BIOS. The standard AT-compatible BIOS had a hard drive capacity limit of 504MB. To overcome this, newer BIOS versions include an Enhanced mode that employs *logical block addressing (LBA)* techniques to permit the larger partition sizes available through the Windows operating systems to be used. This technique—known as *Enhanced Cylinder, Heads, Sectors (ECHS)*—effectively increases the number of R/W heads the system can recognize from 16 to 256. The parameters of 1,024 cylinders, 63 sectors/track, and 512 bytes/sector remains unchanged.

The partitioning procedure is performed by the operating system and creates logical structures on the disk that tell the system what files are on the disk and where they can be found. In MS-DOS and Windows 9*x* systems, the high-level format process updates the FAT tables and creates the root directory structure on the disk. In the case of Windows NT and Windows 2000 systems, the format operation might produce new FATs and root directories, or it might produce more flexible *Master File Table (MFT)* structures.

> **EXAM TIP**
>
> Be aware of the partition size limits associated with older OS versions and know how to overcome these limits when working with larger drives.

Installing CD-ROM Devices

Before installing an internal CD-ROM drive, confirm its Master/Slave/Single, or SCSI ID configuration setting. Afterward, install the CD-ROM unit in one of the drive bays, connect the power and signal cables, and load the CD-ROM driver software. In a Windows system, the operating system should automatically detect the CD-ROM drive and install the correct drivers for it as a part of the process.

If the interface type is different from that of the HDD, it will be necessary to install a controller card in one of the system's expansion slot. Finally, refer to the owner's manual regarding any necessary jumper or switch settings.

To connect the drive to the system, hook up the CD-ROM drive to the HDD signal cable, observing proper orientation. Connect the audio cable to the drive and to the sound card's CD Input connection (if a sound card is installed).

Configuring CD-ROM Devices

The CD-ROM drive must be properly configured for the system it is being installed in. In an IDE system, the Master/Slave setting must be confirmed. In a SCSI system, the ID setting must be correct. In a SCSI system, the only requirement is that a valid ID setting is configured. In an IDE system, however, some thought might be required as to how to configure the drive.

In Windows 9*x*, an advanced CD-ROM device driver called *CDFS* (*CD-ROM File System*) was implemented to provide protected-mode operation of the drive. Windows 9*x* retains the *MSCDEX files* for real-mode operation. If Windows 9*x* detects that the CDFS has taken over control of the CD-ROM on its initial bootup, it will REM any MSCDEX lines in the AUTOEXEC.BAT file.

You can enhance the performance of a Windows 9*x* system by establishing a supplemental *CD-ROM cache*. This cache enables the system to store pages of information cached from the CD in RAM memory, and as we already know, RAM access is always faster than accessing any other computer structure. The supplemental cache is established through the Control Panel's System icon as follows:

1. Under the System icon, click the Performance tab and select the File System button.

2. Set the Supplemental Cache Size slider to the desired cache size.

3. Set the Optimize Access Pattern setting to the Quad-speed or higher option. This will establish a 1,238KB supplemental cache (provided the system's RAM size is larger than 12MB).

4. Click the OK button and restart the system to create the cache.

> **EXAM TIP**
>
> Remember what type of device the MSCDEX file is used with and where it should be located.

> **EXAM TIP**
>
> Remember that the operation of the Windows 9x operating system is enhanced by establishing a supplemental cache for the CD-ROM.

> **NOTE**
>
> **Hands-On Activity**   For hands-on experience with this concept, refer to Lab Procedure #1, "Orientation," located on the CD that accompanies this book.

PORTABLE SYSTEM COMPONENTS

Portable computers typically contain all the devices that users need to perform work away from the office. However, there are additional items that users have become accustomed to using with their computers. For this reason, portables offer a wide range of I/O and expansion options to accommodate external FRU devices. The most common external devices used with portables include

◆ External power sources and supplies

◆ External I/O devices

◆ External disk drives

Portable Power Sources

Notebooks use detachable, rechargeable batteries and external power supplies, as illustrated in Figure 2.17. (Battery sizes vary from manufacturer to manufacturer.) They also employ power-saving circuits and ICs designed to lengthen the battery's useful time. The battery unit contains a recharging circuit that enables the battery to recharge while it is being used with the external power supply. Like other hardware aspects of notebook computers, there are no standards for their power-supply units.

Like other computer power-supply types, portable power supplies, also referred to as *AC adapters*, convert commercial AC voltage into a single DC voltage that the computer can use to power its components and recharge its batteries. Similar *DC-to-DC controllers* are available that permit notebook computers to draw power from a DC source, such as cigarette lighter sockets in automobiles. However, from manufacturer to manufacturer, these AC and DC power converters often employ different connector types and possess different DC voltage and current-delivery capabilities. Therefore, a power supply from one notebook computer will not necessarily work with another portable model.

When obtaining a replacement or accessory adapter or controller, the best choice is to get the suggested model from the notebook manufacturer. However, if you must get these devices from a third party, match the output voltage level of the original. Also make certain that the replacement unit is capable of delivering at least as much current as the original supply.

FIGURE 2.17
Laptop/notebook power supplies.

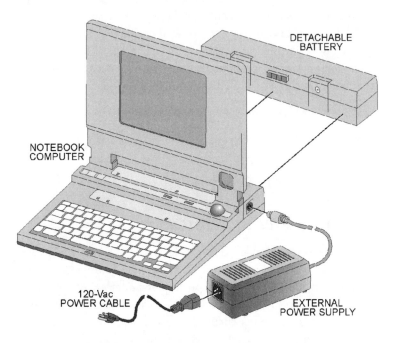

Because the premise of portable computers is mobility, it can be assumed that it should be able to run without being plugged in to an AC outlet. The question for most portables is how long will it run without being plugged in. This is the point where portable designs lead the industry. They continuously push forward in three design areas:

◆ Better battery design

◆ Better power-consumption devices

◆ Better power management

EXAM TIP

Be aware that the external power supply used with portable systems basically converts AC voltage into a DC voltage that the system can use to power its internal components and recharge its batteries.

External Portable I/O

Personal computer users are creatures of habit as much as anyone else. Therefore, as they moved toward portable computers, they wanted the types of features they had come to expect from their larger desktops and towers. These features typically include an alphanumeric keyboard, a video display, and a pointing device.

Most portables offer standard connectors to enable full-size keyboards and VGA monitors to be plugged in, as shown in Figure 2.18. The VGA connector is usually the standard 15-pin D-shell type; the external keyboard connector is generally the 6-pin mini-DIN (PS/2) type. When an external keyboard is plugged in, the built-in keyboard is disabled. The portable's software might enable both, or either display to remain active while the external monitor is connected.

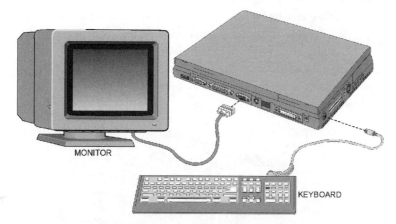

MONITOR

KEYBOARD

FIGURE 2.18
Attaching standard I/O devices.

The I/O ports included in most notebook computers consist of a single parallel port, a single serial port, an external VGA monitor connector, an external keyboard connector, and a docking-port expansion bus. Some models can be found with a second serial-port connector, but they are not common.

Figure 2.19 shows the port connections associated with most portable systems. This example places the connectors on the back of the unit, just as they would be in a typical desktop. Other units might place some of these connectors along the sides of the unit instead. High-end portables might include an array of other connectors, such as external microphone and speaker jacks. Some connectors might be hidden behind hinged doors for protection. These doors normally snap closed.

FIGURE 2.19

Notebook back-panel connections.

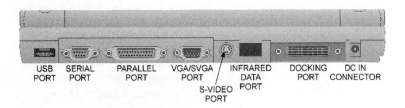

Liquid Crystal Displays

The LCD panel, illustrated in Figure 2.20, is constructed by placing thermotropic liquid crystal material between two sheets of glass. A set of electrodes is attached to each sheet of glass. Horizontal (row) electrodes are attached to one glass plate; vertical (column) electrodes are fitted to the other plate. These electrodes are transparent and let light pass through. A *picture element*, or *pixel* is created in the liquid crystal material at each spot where a row and a column electrode intersect. A special plate called a polarizer is added to the front and back of the display.

FIGURE 2.20

LCD construction.

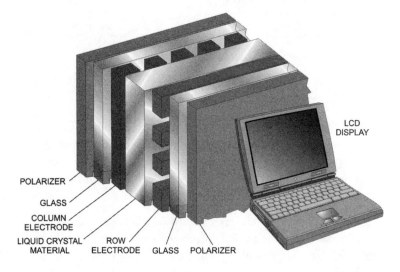

The complete LCD panel is mounted in a frame that also contains the control circuitry for the panel's electrode matrix. In a notebook computer, the frame is mounted between the two halves of its flip-up display housing, as illustrated in Figure 2.21. The display physically attaches to the body of the notebook by a pair of built in hinges. The display is free to rotate around a pair of rods in the main body. Electrically, a single cable is generally used to connect the entire panel assembly to the system board using a plug and socket arrangement.

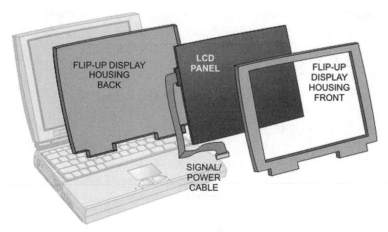

FIGURE 2.21
LCD display panel connections.

When an LCD panel fails, the most common repair is to replace the entire display panel/housing assembly. To replace the LCD panel, you must use an identical panel to ensure that it fits the plastic display housing. The upper half of the notebook body must be removed to provide access for plugging the display's signal cable in to the system board.

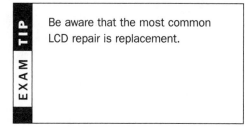

Be aware that the most common LCD repair is replacement.

PC Cards

In 1989, the *Personal Computer Memory Card International Association* (*PCMCIA*) developed the PCMCIA bus standard that was primarily intended to accommodate the needs of the space-conscious notebook and sub-notebook computer markets. A small form-factor expansion-card format, referred to as the PC Card standard, was also adopted for use. This format was derived from earlier proprietary laptop/notebook memory-card designs. Over time, the entire standard has come to be referred to as the *PC Card* standard. This is somewhat easier to say than PCMCIA.

The interface is designed so that cards can be inserted in to the unit while it is turned on (hot insertion).

The PC Card standard defines a methodology for software programmers to write standard drivers for PC Card devices. The standard is referred to as *socket services* and provides for a software head to identify the type of card being used, its capabilities, and its requirements. Although the card's software driver can be executed directly on the

EXAM TIP

Be aware that the PC Card enablers must be loaded in the operating system before the system can interact with a PC Card in one of its slots.

card (instead of moving it into RAM for execution), the system's *PC Card enablers* must be loaded before the card can be activated.

With the PC Card enablers loaded, a PC card can be installed in the system by shoving the card in to one of the system's PCMCIA slots, as illustrated in Figure 2.22. If the computer is running, the card services will detect that the card has been installed and the operating system will perform a PnP configuration process for it. If the device is present when the system is started up, it will be configured as part of the normal PnP boot process. Likewise, if the card is removed from the slot, the PC Card services will also detect this event and deactivate the device in the operating system.

FIGURE 2.22
Inserting a PC card.

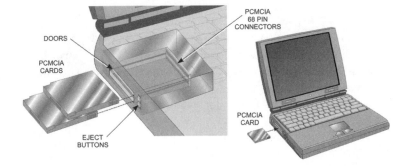

CHAPTER SUMMARY

KEY TERMS

- 5-pin DIN
- 6-pin mini-DIN
- AC adapters
- Active partition
- CDFS (CD-ROM File System)
- CD-ROM cache
- Color Super-Twist Nematic (CSTN)
- DC-to-DC controllers

This chapter has presented techniques and procedures used to install hardware components and bring them to an operational level. The initial sections of the system dealt with installing particular I/O devices. This information was followed by a discussion of FRU devices located on the system board. The system board is one of the only remaining components that can be upgraded without being totally replaced. The final section of the chapter focused expressly on I/O devices and systems associated with portable computer systems.

At this point, review the objectives listed at the beginning of the chapter to be certain that you understand each point and can perform each task listed there. Afterward, answer the review questions that follow to verify your knowledge of the information.

CHAPTER SUMMARY

- Digital cameras
- Disk administrator
- Disk management
- Double-Layer Super-Twist Nematic (DSTN)
- Dual In-Line Memory Module (DIMM)
- Dual In-line Pin (DIP)
- Electrostatic discharge (ESD)
- Enhanced Cylinder, Heads, Sectors (ECHS)
- Extended partition
- FDISK
- File Allocation Tables (FATs)
- Flashed
- Logical Block Addressing (LBA)
- Logical drives
- Low-level formatting
- Master Boot Record (MBR)
- Master File Table (MFT)
- MSCDEX files

- Partition table
- PC Card
- PC Card enablers
- Personal Computer Memory Card International Association (PCMCIA)
- Picture element
- Pixel
- Plastic Leadless Chip Carrier (PLCC)
- Plastic standoffs
- Portable computers
- Primary partition
- PS/2 connector
- RCA mini jacks
- Scanners
- Single In-Line Memory Module (SIMM)
- Sockets
- Sound card
- Voltage Regulator Module (VRM)
- Zero Insertion Force (ZIF)

APPLY YOUR KNOWLEDGE

Review Questions

1. What describes the typical configuration setting options associated with an IDE drive?

   A. Primary, Secondary, and Alternate

   B. Master, Slave, and Single

   C. Master, Secondary, and Alternate Primary

   D. Primary Master, Secondary Master, and Alternate Master

2. When can you safely disconnect a keyboard from a computer?

   A. When the computer is turned off

   B. Anytime while the computer is running

   C. While the computer is booting

   D. While the operating system is in safe mode

3. When selecting a mouse for a particular computer system, what is the most important consideration?

   A. The type of drivers that come with the mouse

   B. The length of the mouse cord

   C. The type of connector the mouse is equipped with

   D. The number of buttons the mouse has

4. Which standard ATX ports are often confused with each other?

   A. The serial and the VGA/SVGA ports

   B. The docking and the parallel ports

   C. The NIC card and MODEM connector ports

   D. The mouse and keyboard connections

5. What physical feature determines which floppy drive will be the A: drive in a two-floppy system?

   A. Connecting the color strip to pin 1

   B. Connecting the color strip to pin 34

   C. Connecting the FDD to the middle connector of the cable

   D. Connecting the FDD to the end connector of the cable

6. What is the highest drive letter that can be assigned to a logical drive in a FAT-based system?

   A. S

   B. W

   C. Z

   D. H

7. What type of hardware device is the MSCDEX file used with and where should it be located in the system?

   A. SVGA card. The video driver file is located in the `C:\Windows\System` directory.

   B. CD-ROM. The execution line should be in the Autoexec.bat file.

   C. HDD. The file is located in the boot sector and is an extension of the BIOS.

   D. FDD. The file is located in the `C:\Windows\System` directory.

8. What functions are performed by the external power supply of a portable computer system?

   A. Convert commercial AC voltage into DC voltage for system usage and battery charging.

   B. Convert commercial DC voltage into AC voltage for system usage and battery charging.

C. Store commercial power to recharge the battery.

D. Increase the voltage of commercial power for the computer.

9. Which of the following best describes the key to properly connecting an AT power supply to a baby AT-style system board?

A. P9 should be plugged in to P1, while P8 should be plugged in to P2.

B. P8 should be plugged in to P1, while P9 should be plugged in to P2.

C. It does not matter which power supply connector is plugged in to which circuit-board connector.

D. The connectors are configured so that the power supply will only plug in to the circuit board one way.

10. Which peripheral connection can be confused in an ATX system?

A. Modem, network

B. Mouse, keyboard

C. Printer, RCA

D. Video, gameport

11. The type of connectors usually associated with Audio-in and Audio-out ports are _____.

A. 25-pin, D-shells

B. RCA plugs and jacks

C. RJ-11 jacks and plugs

D. 15-pin, D-shells

12. When installing RAM memory modules, which of these potential problems is the most unlikely?

A. Installing two sticks of RAM with different memory sizes

B. Installing one stick of RAM with tin contacts and a second stick with gold contacts

C. Installing two sticks of RAM with different bus speeds

D. Installing a DIMM in a SIMM slot

13. What factors must be taken into account when ordering a new power supply?

A. Voltage and form factor

B. Total BTUs and amperage

C. Form factor and wattage

D. Noise and total BTUs

14. How many additional logical drives can be created in computer using a FAT-based operating system?

A. 1

B. 8

C. 23

D. 26

15. What is the partition size limit for Windows 95?

A. 32MB

B. 528MB

C. 2GB

D. 8GB

APPLY YOUR KNOWLEDGE

16. What is the most common repair for a failed LCD monitor?

    A. Demagnetize the LCD screen

    B. Replace the signal cable

    C. Replace the LCD panel

    D. Replace the computer

17. What system board feature is used to manage the installation and replacement of the microprocessor?

    A. ROM BIOS

    B. HSF

    C. ZIF

    D. Operating system

Answers and Explanations

1. **B.** You should confirm that the IDE drive is configured as a Master, Slave, or Single before installing the unit in the drive bay. For more information, see the section "HDD Installation."

2. **A.** Many newer peripheral devices can safely be unplugged and reattached to the system while power is applied; this is not so with the standard keyboard. Plugging the keyboard in to the system while power is applied can cause the operating system or even the system board to fail due to the power surge and Electrostatic Discharge (ESD). For more information, see the section "Keyboards."

3. **C.** Be aware that the mouse connector type is an important consideration in selecting a mouse for use. For more information, see the section "Mice."

4. **D.** When the ATX specification adopted the same connector for both the keyboard and mouse, it introduced an opportunity to plug these devices into the wrong connector. Later ATX models and peripherals have adopted an informal color-coding system (that is, purple for keyboards and green for mice). For more information, see the section "Mice."

5. **D.** If the drive is the only floppy in the system or intended to operate as the A: drive, connect it to the connector at the end of the cable. If it is being installed as a B: drive, attach it to the connector toward the center of the cable. For more information, see the section "FDD Installation."

6. **C.** The extended partition can be subdivided into 23 logical drives (all the letters in the alphabet minus a, b, and c). For more information, see the section "Logical and Physical Drives."

7. **B.** Windows 9x retains the MSCDEX files for real-mode operation of CDROM drives. If Windows 9x detects that the CDFS has taken over control of the CD-ROM on its initial bootup, it will REM any MSCDEX lines in the AUTOEXEC.BAT file. For more information, see the section "Configuring CD-ROM Devices."

8. **A.** Portable power supplies, also referred to as AC adapters, convert commercial AC voltage into a single DC voltage that the computer can use to power its components and use to recharge its batteries. For more information, see the section "Portable Power Sources."

9. **B.** The power connector labeled P8 should be plugged in to the circuit-board power connector labeled P1, while connector P9 is plugged in to the P2 connector next to it. A good rule of thumb to remember when attaching these two

connectors to the system board is that the two black wires in each bundle should be next to each other in the middle. For more information, see the section "Installing Power Supplies."

10. **B.** In an ATX system, the mouse usually plugs in to a 6-pin PS/2 mini-DIN connector on the back of the system unit. This connector is identical to the keyboard connector and can easily be confused with it. For more information, see the section "Mice."

11. **B.** The microphone and speakers are plugged in to the appropriate RCA jacks on the back of the sound card. For more information, see the section "Installing Sound Cards."

12. **D.** SIMM and DIMM slots are keyed, and it is almost physically impossible to plug them in wrong. For more information, see the section "Installing Memory Modules."

13. **C.** When ordering a replacement power supply, you must remember to take into account its form factor and its wattage rating requirements. The wattage rating is a measurement of the total power the supply can deliver to the system. More heavily equipped systems (that is, more disk drives and peripherals) require power supplies with higher wattage ratings. For more information, see the section "Installing Power Supplies."

14. **C.** The partition can be subdivided into 23 additional logical drives (all the letters of the alphabet minus a, b, and c). For more information, see the section "Logical and Physical Drives."

15. **C.** The oldest versions of MS-DOS (2.*x*, 3.*x*) imposed a limit on the size of a drive at 32MB. As HDD technology advanced, the capacities of the physical drives eventually passed this limit. The FDISK utility in MS-DOS version 4.0 raised the maximum size of a logical drive to 128MB and version 5.0 raised it to 528MB. The FDISK utility in Windows 9*x* provided upgraded support for very large hard drives. The original version of Windows 95 set a size limit for logical drives at 2GB. The FDISK version in the upgraded OSR2 version of Windows 95 extended the maximum partition size to 8GB. For more information, see the section "Logical and Physical Drives."

16. **C.** When an LCD panel fails, the most common repair is to replace the entire display panel/housing assembly. For more information, see the section "Liquid Crystal Displays."

17. **C.** Zero Insertion Force (ZIF) sockets were designed that permit the microprocessor to be placed in the socket without force and then be clamped in place. An arm-activated clamping mechanism in the socket shifts to the side, locking the pins in place. For more information, see the section "Installing Microprocessors."

Challenge Solutions

1. Although the microprocessor is an FRU device, it would not be a good idea to replace it in a unit where the original smoked. You could quickly ruin a perfectly good (and expensive) microprocessor by doing so.

   1. Remove all the external I/O systems attached to the computer.

   2. Remove the system unit's outer cover.

   3. Remove all the option adapter cards installed in the system.

APPLY YOUR KNOWLEDGE

4. Remove the power supply and front panel cables from the system board.

5. Remove the system board—remove the grounding screws that secure the system board to the chassis. Store the screws properly. In a desktop unit, slide the system board toward the left (as you face the front of the unit) to free its plastic feet from the slots in the floor of the system unit. Tilt the left edge of the board up, and then lift it straight up and out of the system unit.

6. Install the new system board and perform steps 5 through 1 in reverse order.

   For more information, see the section "Removing System Boards."

2. Make certain that the replacement power supply is an AT-style unit with an adequate power rating. Also be sure that you have the black wires from each bundle beside each other at the system board connection. For more information, see the section "Installing Power Supplies."

3. Subdivide the hard disk into multiple partitions. That way, each partition can be less than 2GB, which is Windows 95's maximum partition size. At a minimum, you would have six partitions, but you could have many more if need be (that is, 6x2GB = 12GB). For more information, see the section "Logical and Physical Drives."

Suggested Readings and Resources

1. System Components
   http://www.pcguide.com/ref/case/index.htm

2. Motherboard
   http://webopedia.internet.com/term/m/
   motherboard.html

3. FDD Installation
   http://www.pcguide.com/proc/physinst/
   fdd.htm

4. CD-ROM Installation
   http://www.pcguide.com/proc/physinst/
   cd-c.html

5. MSCDEX
   www.computerhope.com/mscdex.htm

6. MSCDEX Download
   www.driverzone.com/drivers/mscdex/

7. Logical Block Addressing
   http://whatis.techtarget.com/
   definition/0,,sid9_gci214074,00.html

8. Introduction to Major Flat Panel Display Technologies
   http://www.atip.or.jp/fpd/src/tutorial/
   fpd.html

This chapter helps you to prepare for the Core Hardware module of the A+ Certification examination by covering the following objectives within the "Domain 1.0: Installation, Configuration, and Upgrading" section.

1.3 Identify available IRQs, DMAs, I/O addresses, and procedures for device installation and configuration.

Content might include the following:

- **Standard IRQ settings**
- **Modems**
- **Floppy drive controllers**
- **Hard drive controllers**
- **USB ports**
- **Infrared ports**
- **Hexadecimal Addresses**

CHAPTER 3

System Resources

▶ An IBM-compatible PC system is a very flexible tool because it can be configured to perform so many tasks. By selecting appropriate hardware and software options, the same basic system can be customized to be an inventory-management business machine, a multimedia-development system, or a simple game machine.

▶ The computer technician must be able to determine what system resources are required for the device, what resources are available in the system, and how they can be allocated to successfully install hardware components in a PC. The following sections describe various standard I/O methods and peripheral connection schemes used to attach options to a PC system.

To prepare for the Installation, Configuration, and Upgrading objective of the Core Hardware exam,

▶ Read the objectives at the beginning of this chapter.

▶ Study the information in this chapter.

▶ Review the objectives listed earlier in this chapter.

▶ Perform any step-by-step procedures in the text.

▶ Answer the review questions at the end of the chapter and check your results.

▶ Use the PrepLogic test engine on the CD-ROM that accompanies this book for additional review and exam questions concerning this material.

▶ Review the exam tips scattered throughout the chapter and make certain that you are comfortable with each point.

INTRODUCTION

The most frequent operation that occurs in a personal computer involves the movement of information from one location to another. The initial section of the chapter deals with common methods of controlling the movement of data through the system.

Moving data through the system involves allocating system resources (that is, Interrupt Request channels, I/O addresses, and Direct Memory Address channels) to the system's different hardware devices. For this reason, the chapter also presents typical resource assignments associated with PC-compatible systems.

Because the computer industry references resource assignments in terms of hexadecimal addresses and values, the final section of the chapter presents a quick description of hexadecimal counting and addressing.

After completing the chapter, you should be able to describe standard PC resource assignments associated with common I/O connection points (ports) and devices. These assignments include IRQ channels, I/O and memory address ranges, and DMA channels.

EXTENDED I/O

In addition to the millions of possible memory locations in a PC, typically thousands of addresses are set aside for input and output devices in a system. In order for any device to operate with the system's microprocessor, it must have an address (or group of addresses) where the system can find it.

When discussing the standard I/O ports for PCs, it is common to differentiate between traditional standard ports that include

- ◆ Keyboard port
- ◆ Centronic parallel ports
- ◆ RS-232C serial ports
- ◆ Game ports

And newer standard ports that include

- ◆ PS/2 mouse and keyboard ports
- ◆ USB ports
- ◆ IEEE-1394 Firewire ports
- ◆ Infrared ports
- ◆ Improved parallel ports

Moving Data

The most frequent operation performed in a computer is the movement of information from one location to another. This information is moved in the form of words. Basically, there are two modes in which the words can be transferred. These modes are parallel mode—where an entire word is transferred from location A to location B by a set of parallel conductors at one instant—and serial mode—where the bits of the word are transmitted along a single conductor, one bit at a time.

Serial transfers require more time to accomplish than parallel transfers because a clock cycle must be used for each bit transferred. A parallel transfer requires only one clock pulse. Examples of both parallel and serial transfers are depicted in Figure 3.1.

> **NOTE**
>
> **Interface circuits** Interface circuits are necessary because the characteristics of most peripherals differ greatly from those of the basic computer. Most interface circuits in the PC-compatible world have been integrated into application-specific ICs.

FIGURE 3.1

Parallel and serial data transfers.

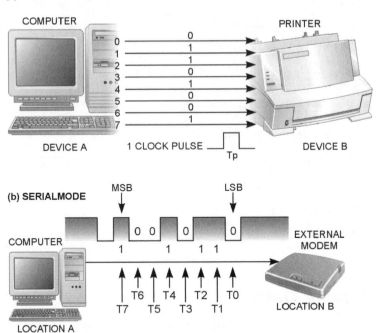

(a) PARALLEL MODE

(b) SERIALMODE

Initiating I/O Transfers

During normal program execution, the microprocessor constantly reads from or writes to memory locations. The program can also call on the microprocessor to read from or write to one of the system's I/O devices. Regardless of how the peripheral is connected to the system (serial or parallel), one of four methods can be used to initiate data transfer between the system and the peripheral. These four methods are listed as follows:

◆ *Polling*—The microprocessor examines the status of the peripheral under program control.

◆ *Programmed I/O*—The microprocessor alerts the designated peripheral by applying its address to the system's address bus.

◆ *Interrupt-driven I/O*—The peripheral alerts the microprocessor that it's ready to transfer data.

◆ *Direct Memory Access (DMA)*—The intelligent peripheral assumes control of the system's buses to conduct direct transfers with primary memory.

Polling and Programmed I/O

Both polling and programmed I/O represent software approaches to data transfer; interrupt-driven and DMA transfers, on the other hand, are basically hardware approaches. Using the polling method, the software periodically checks with the system's I/O devices to determine whether any device is ready to conduct a data transfer. The programmed I/O method calls for the microprocessor to alert the desired peripheral of an I/O operation by issuing its address to the address bus. The peripheral can delay the transfer by asserting its busy line.

> **NOTE**
>
> **Reference Shelf** For more information, refer to the Electronic Reference Shelf, "Initiating I/O Transfers," located on the CD that accompanies this book.

Interrupts

In the course of normal operations, the various I/O devices attached to a PC, such as the keyboard and disk drives, require servicing from the system's microprocessor. Because these service requests can happen at any time and tend to require immediate attention, I/O devices generally have the capability to interrupt the microprocessor while it is executing a program. The I/O device accomplishes this by issuing a *Maskable Interrupt (IRQ)* input signal to the microprocessor. Each device in a PC-compatible system that is capable of interrupting the microprocessor must be assigned its own, unique IRQ number. The system uses this number to identify which device is in need of service.

> **EXAM TIP**
>
> You should know that a device that requires service from the microprocessor must have access to its own IRQ channel.

Two varieties of interrupts are used in microcomputers:

- ◆ *Maskable Interrupts (IRQs)*—Interrupts that the system microprocessor can ignore under certain conditions.

- ◆ *Non-Maskable Interrupts (NMI)*—Very serious interrupts to which the system microprocessor must always respond. NMI conditions normally result in the system being shut down.

The device that requires service contacts the system's interrupt controller, which in turn contacts the system microprocessor and supplies it with information about where to service the device that issued the request. The processor stops what it is doing, stores the information that it is working with, jumps to the program servicing that interrupt, runs the service routine, and then returns to its original operation. A programmable interrupt controller, and its relationship to the system's microprocessor, is illustrated in Figure 3.2.

FIGURE 3.2

A programmable interrupt controller operation.

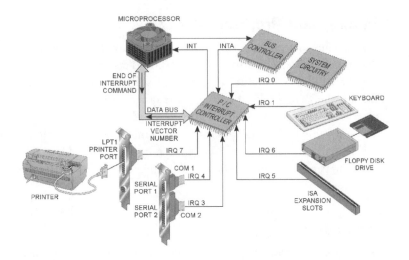

Of the 16 interrupt channels (IRQ0 through IRQ15) available, three are generally used inside the system board's chipset. Therefore, they do not have external IRQ pins. The other 13 IRQ inputs are available to the system for user-definable interrupt functions. Each IRQ input is assigned a priority level. IRQ0 is the highest, and IRQ7 is the lowest. IRQ-IRQ15 fit between IRQ1 and IRQ3 in the priority scheme. The internally connected channels are

> Channel 0 (IRQ0)—Timer/Counter interrupt is OK
>
> Channel 1 (IRQ1)—Keyboard buffer full
>
> Channel 2 (IRQ2)—Cascaded to INTC2
>
> Channel 8 (IRQ8)—Real-Time Clock interrupt
>
> Channel 9 (IRQ9)—Cascade between INTC1 and INTC2
>
> Channel 13 (IRQ13)—Math Coprocessor interrupt

Table 3.1 shows the designations for the various interrupt levels in the system.

TABLE 3.1

SYSTEM INTERRUPT LEVELS

Interrupt	Description	Interrupt	Description
NMI	I/O CHANNEL CHECK OR PARITY CHECK ERROR		
	INTC1		*INTC2*
IRQ0	TIMER/COUNTER ALARM	IRQ8	REAL-TIME CLOCK
IRQ1	KEYBOARD BUFFER FULL	IRQ9	CASCADE TO INTC1

Interrupt	Description	Interrupt	Description
IRQ2	CASCADE FROM INTC2	IRQ10	SPARE
IRQ3	SERIAL PORT 2 (COM 2 OR 4)	IRQ11	SPARE
IRQ4	SERIAL PORT 1 (COM 1 OR 3)	IRQ12	SPARE PS/2 MOUSE
IRQ5	PARALLEL PORT 2	IRQ13	COPROCESSOR
IRQ6	FDD CONTROLLER	IRQ14	PRIMARY IDE CTRL
IRQ7	PARALLEL PORT 1 (LPT1)	IRQ15	SECONDARY IDE CTRL

CHALLENGE #1

One of your co-workers is adding a wide carriage dot matrix printer to his workstation so that he can print multipart forms. He already has a color ink-jet printer attached to the computer using IRQ7. He has no idea of which resources to assign to the new printer. What will you tell him when he asks for help?

There are two serious system board-based conditions that will cause a *Non-Maskable Interrupt (NMI)* signal to be sent to the microprocessor. The first condition occurs when an active *IO Channel Check (IOCHCK) signal* is received from an adapter card located in one of the board's expansion slots. The other event that will cause an NMI signal to be generated is the occurrence of a *Parity Check (PCK)* error in the system's DRAM memory. Because these errors indicate that information from I/O devices or memory cannot be trusted, the NMI signal will cause the system to shut down without storing any of the potentially bad data.

Direct Memory Access

Direct Memory Access operations are very similar to interrupt-driven I/O operations, except that the controller does not ask the system microprocessor to stop what it is doing to manage the I/O operation. Instead, the DMA controller asks the microprocessor to get out of the way so that it can control the system and handle the I/O transfer. The DMA controller is a specialized microprocessor that can conduct the transfer much faster than the standard microprocessor can. Table 3.2 describes the system's DMA channel designations.

EXAM TIP

Memorize the system resources available in an ISA-compatible system and what their typical assignments are. There will be several questions about standard IRQ assignments on the exam.

EXAM TIP

Know what types of problems can cause an NMI to occur.

NOTE

Reference Shelf For more information, refer to the Electronic Reference Shelf, "How Interrupts Work," located on the CD that accompanies this book.

TABLE 3.2

SYSTEM'S DMA CHANNEL DESIGNATIONS

Channel	Function	Controller	Page Register Address
CH0	SPARE	1	0087
CH1	SDLC (NETWORK)	1	0083
CH2	FDD CONTROLLER	1	0082
CH3	SPARE	1	0081
CH4	CASCADE TO CNTR 1	2	
CH5	SPARE	2	008B
CH6	SPARE	2	0089
CH7	SPARE	2	008A

EXAM TIP

Know how many DMA channels are available in a typical AT-compatible PC.

EXAM TIP

Memorize the typical DMA channel assignments in a PC.

NOTE

Reference Shelf For more information, refer to the Electronic Reference Shelf, "How DMA Works," located on the CD that accompanies this book.

The system's FDD controller uses DMA channel 2 by default. Newer parallel port modes, such as ECP mode, can be assigned to any of the other open DMA channels. DMA channel 4 is used internally to cascade the two, four-channel DMA controllers together.

Onboard I/O

When dealing with a PC-compatible, there are two forms of I/O to contend with. These include the system board's onboard I/O as well as peripheral devices that interact with the system through its expansion slots.

Most of the I/O functions associated with PC-compatible systems have become so standardized that IC manufacturers produce them in single-chip ASIC formats. Figure 3.3 illustrates an ASIC for standard, AT-compatible system board functions.

Certain I/O connections have become standards associated with PC-compatibles. These include the system's parallel printer ports, RS-232 serial ports, and the game port. Figure 3.4 depicts an M/IO ASIC for standard peripheral control.

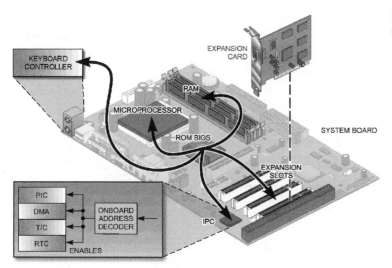

FIGURE 3.3
Onboard I/O.

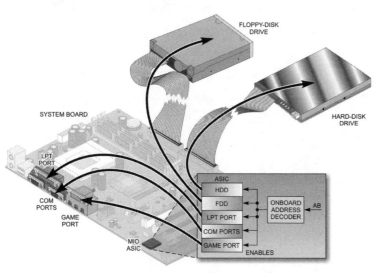

FIGURE 3.4
System I/O methods.

In both cases, the I/O controllers integrated into the ASIC are responsible for matching signal levels and protocols between the computer system and the I/O device. The system communicates with its onboard intelligent devices using I/O addresses. The onboard address decoder converts addresses from the address bus into enabling bits for the system's intelligent devices. These addresses are included in the overall I/O addressing map of the system.

In a PC-compatible system, standard I/O adapters employ the various *I/O port addresses* listed in Table 3.3. Notice that these addresses

> **EXAM TIP**
>
> Memorize the I/O port addresses for the first and second IDE controller.

are redundant with those stated for the system's interrupt vectors given in Table 3.4. PC-compatible computers handle addresses differently depending on whether they are identified in software as memory or I/O addresses.

TABLE 3.3

I/O PORT ADDRESSES

Hex Address	Device	Usage
000–01F	DMA Controller	System
020–03F	Interrupt Controller	System
040–05F	Timer/Counter	System
060–06F	Keyboard Controller	System
070–07F	Real-Time Clock, NMI Mask	System
080–09F	DMA Page Register	System
0A0–0BF	Interrupt Controller	System
0F0	Clear Math Coprocessor Busy	System
0F1	Reset Math Coprocessor	System
0F8–0FF	Math Coprocessor	System
170-177	Second IDE Controller	I/O
1F0–1F7	First IDE Controller	I/O
200–207	Game Port	I/O
278–27F	Parallel Printer Port #2	I/O
2F8–2FF	Serial Port #2	I/O
378–37F	Parallel Printer Port #1	I/O
3B0–3BF	MGA/first Printer Port	I/O
3D0–3DF	CGA	I/O
3F0–3F7	FDD Controller	I/O
3F8–3FF	Serial Port #1	I/O
FF80-FF9F	USB Controller	I/O

TABLE 3.4

SYSTEM MEMORY MAP

Address	Function
0–3FF	Interrupt Vectors
400–47F	ROM-BIOS RAM
480–5FF	BASIC and Special System Function RAM
600–9FFFF	Program Memory
0A0000–0BFFFF	VGA/EGA Display Memory
0B0000–0B0FFF	Monochrome Display Adapter Memory
0B8000–0BFFFF	Color Graphics Adapter Memory
0C0000–0C7FFF	VGA/SVGA BIOS
0C8000-0CBFFF	EIDE/SCSI ROM (also older HDD Types)
0D0000–0D7FFF	BIOS Extension Area ROM
0D0000–0DFFFF	LAN Adapter ROM
0E0000–0E7FFF	BIOS Extension Area ROM
0E8000–0EFFFF	BIOS Extension Area ROM
0F0000–0EFFFF	BIOS Extension Area ROM
0F4000–0EFFFF	BIOS Extension Area ROM
0F8000–0EFFFF	BIOS Extension Area ROM
0FC000–0FDFFF	ROM BIOS
0FE000–0FFFFF	ROM BIOS

CHALLENGE #2

A friend has called you because he is working on a system that has several legacy devices installed and he does not remember what resources are assigned to typical devices in a PC-compatible system. He needs for you to fax him a list of these devices. Because you have become a very successful computer technician, you are on a cruise and do not have access to your resource materials. What information can you send him from your memory?

Modems

As mentioned in Chapter 1, "Basic Terms and Concepts," modems come in two common types—internal and external. Both types of modems depend on a serial communication device called a *Universal Asynchronous Receiver-Transmitter* (*UART*) to carry out the serial-to-parallel and parallel-to-serial data conversions. In the case of an internal modem, the UART is normally located on the adapter card. With an external modem, the UART is usually provided by one of the PC's *serial communications* (*COM*) *ports*. The modem connects to the serial port through a standard RS-232 25-pin D-shell connector.

In the case of the internal modem, the UART in the modem normally replaces one of the two COM port UARTs provided by a typical PC system. If the COM port UART is not disabled, the system might have trouble differentiating between the two ports and a conflict can develop. Therefore, it is common practice to disable an onboard UART when an internal modem is installed. The COM ports can be enabled or disabled through the system's CMOS Setup—Peripherals screen.

In AT-style PCs, the first UART is normally used with the system's serial mouse. From the tables in this chapter, you can see that it resides at addresses 3F8 through 3FFh, uses IRQ4, and is assigned the designation of *COM1*. Therefore, the modem (or its host COM port) should be configured for addresses 278 through 27Fh, IRQ3, and *COM2*.

In ATX systems, the mouse has been provided with a special PS/2 mouse port, along with its own resources—including IRQ12. Therefore, a modem would be free to use COM1 or COM2 in these systems.

<table>
<tr><td>**EXAM TIP**</td><td>Be aware that you might need to disable the second onboard COM port to install an internal modem.</td></tr>
</table>

Floppy Drive Controllers

Most Pentium system boards contain the Floppy Disk drive Controller (FDC) circuitry and its physical interface connection. In older units, this circuitry and connector were typically located on an MI/O adapter card. The Pentium system board provides a standard 34-pin, two-row Berg connector as the FDD physical interface (typically labeled FD1). PC-compatible systems use a 34-pin flat ribbon cable as the FDD signal cable. This cable connects the system board's FDD interface with one or two floppy disk drives.

The FDC portion of the system board's chipset provides a programmable, logical interface for up to two FDD units. It resides in the I/O address range between locations 370 and 37Fh. The FDC receives and decodes instructions from the system to the floppy disk drive at these addresses. It also decodes these commands and generates the proper signals to carry out the command. Finally, it converts the data from the parallel format of the system to the encoded serial format used by the disk drive. The typical FDC divides the floppy disk into 80 tracks per side, with 9 or 18 512-byte sectors per side. This provides the system with 737,280 (720KB) or 1,474,560 (1.44MB) total bytes of storage on each diskette.

In a PC system, the FDC operates in conjunction with the system's DMA controller and is assigned to the DRQ-2 and DACK-2 lines. In operation, the FDC presents an active DRQ-2 signal to the DMA controller for every byte of data to be transferred. After the last byte has been transferred, the FDC interrupt is generated. The floppy disk drive controller is assigned the IRQ-6 channel in PC-compatible systems. The FDC generates an interrupt signal each time it receives a Read, Write, or Format command from the system.

> **EXAM TIP**
>
> Know which resources are used by the floppy disk drive system.

Hard Drive Controllers

Typical Pentium-based system boards include one or two enhanced IDE controllers to handle the hard disk drive hosting function. Each controller can handle up to two IDE drives. This provides the PC with the capability of controlling up to four IDE devices. The first drive at each connector is called the *master* and the second is called the *slave*. The first, or Primary IDE, controller is assigned IRQ14, whereas the Secondary controller uses IRQ15 to interrupt the system. The system board supplies two 40-pin BERG connectors that are typically labeled IDE1 and IDE2. Each connector corresponds to an IDE controller.

Generally, the master drive doesn't have anything to do with the operation of the slave drive. Whether a drive operates as master or slave is typically determined by the settings of configuration jumpers on each drive. If the drive is the only unit attached to the host connector, it can be configured as a single drive. The address decoding logic on the host adapter will then oversee the selection of either drive. The first IDE drive controller responds to I/O addresses between 1F0h and 1F7h, whereas the second answers to addresses between 170h and 177h.

Older hard drives required that the CMOS Setup parameters of the computer match the parameters of the drive that was connected to the system, specifying such things as the number of R/W heads and number of cylinders being used. In those units, the drive needed to match one of the configurations in the computer's drive-parameter tables. This table was a function of the system's BIOS. However, the last entry in the table was typically reserved for user entered parameters that could be used for drives not listed in the table.

Most of the newer IDE drives include a feature called *translation mode*. These drives add a microprocessor to the controller's electronics that determines what configuration the computer expects, and then adjusts itself to mimic that drive layout, within the limitations of the drive's geometry. Because of the sector translation and matching work the IDE controller performs, the host system is isolated from the actual layout of the heads and cylinders on the drive. It only sees its logical configuration presented by the controller, which matches the CMOS setting. This makes the IDE interface a system-level interface.

A growing number of system boards include SCSI interface support in their BIOS. However, very few include a physical onboard interface connection. This interface is typically found on a SCSI host adapter card that plugs in to one of the system's expansion slots.

USB Ports

Most ATX system boards include dual *Universal Serial Bus* (*USB*) connectors as a standard part of their I/O port offering. The onboard USB controller resides between the I/O addresses of FF80 and FF9Fh. The USB controller is also assigned an IRQ channel (such as IRQ10) by the PnP process.

The operation of the port connections is controlled by settings in the system board's CMOS Setup Utility. In most cases, it will be necessary to access the CMOS Setup Utility's PCI Configuration

EXAM TIP

Memorize the address ranges of the first and second IDE controllers in a PC system.

screen to enable the USB function and assign the ports IRQ channels to use. If no USB device is being used with the system, the IRQ
allocation should be set to <u>NA</u> to free up the IRQ line for use by
other devices.

Infrared Port

Infrared Data Association (*IrDA*) *ports* are very popular with notebook computers. These ports provide short-distance wireless connections for different IrDA-compliant devices, such as printers and personal digital assistants. Because the IrDA port communicates by
sending and receiving a serial stream of light pulses, it is normally
configured to work with the UART of the system's second serial
port. This arrangement must be established in the Peripherals page
of the CMOS Setup utility, as illustrated in Figure 3.5. In this manner, the infrared port is assigned the same system resources normally
reserved for the COM2/COM4 serial ports (that is, IRQ3, 2F8-
2FFh, or 2E8-2Efh).

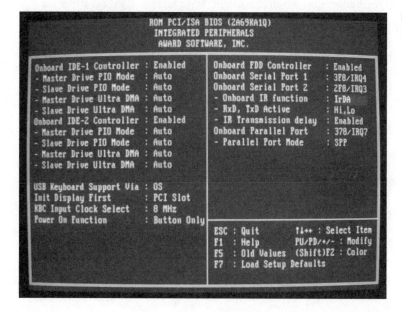

FIGURE 3.5
Enabling the infrared port.

To enable the IrDA port, the mode for the COM2 UART must be set to automatic and one of the infrared protocol settings (*HPSIR* or *ASKIR*) must be selected. In addition, the transmission duplex mode must be selected (normally half duplex). The operation of the infrared port and the second serial port are mutually exclusive. When the infrared option is enabled in CMOS, the second serial port will be disabled.

HEXADECIMAL ADDRESSES

Addresses in PC systems are always referred to by their hexadecimal value because digital computers are built on components that only work with two logic levels—either On/Off, High/Low, or 1/0. This corresponds directly to the Base-2 or *binary* numbering system. In the binary system, each piece of information represents a binary digit, or *bit*.

The power of the digital computer lies in how it groups bits of information into words. The basic word length in PCs is the 8-bit word called a *byte*. Some computers can handle data as 16, 32, and 64-bit words. With the byte as the basic data unit, it is easier for humans to speak of computer numbers in the Base-16 or *hexadecimal* (*hex*) numbering system. In this system, groups of 4 bits can be represented directly by a single hex character (that is, 1001 base2 = 09 base16). For human representation, the values in the numbering system run from 0 to 9 and then from A through F, as illustrated in Table 3.5.

| TABLE 3.5 |

DECIMAL, BINARY, AND HEXADECIMAL NUMBERS

Decimal (10)	Binary (2)	Hex (16)
0	0000	0
1	0001	1
2	0010	2
3	0011	3
4	0100	4
5	0101	5

Decimal (10)	Binary (2)	Hex (16)
6	0110	6
7	0111	7
8	1000	8
9	1001	9
10	1010	A
11	1011	B
12	1100	C
13	1101	D
14	1110	E
15	11111	F
16	0000	10

Although this might seem a little inconvenient for those of you not familiar with binary and hexadecimal systems, it is much easier to convey the number 3F8h to someone than it is 001111111000. The real difficulty of reconciling a hexadecimal value comes when you try to convert binary or hexadecimal values to the decimal (base 10) number system you are familiar with.

NOTE

Hands-On Activity For hands-on experience with this concept, refer to Lab Procedure #6, "PC Check," located on the CD that accompanies this book.

NOTE

Reference Shelf For more information, refer to the Electronic Reference Shelf, "Bits, Bytes, and Computer Words," located on the CD that accompanies this book.

CHAPTER SUMMARY

KEY TERMS

- ASKIR
- Binary
- Bit
- Byte
- COM1
- COM2
- Direct Memory Access (DMA)
- Hexadecimal (hex)
- HPSIR
- I/O port addresses
- Infrared (IrDA) ports
- Interrupt request (IRQ)
- Interrupt-driven I/O
- IO Channel Check (IOCHCK) signal
- Maskable Interrupts (IRQs)
- Non-Maskable Interrupts (NMI)
- Parity Check (PCK)
- Polling
- Programmed I/O
- Serial communications (COM) ports
- Translation mode
- Universal Asynchronous Receiver-Transmitter (UART)
- Universal Serial Bus (USB)

This chapter has described standard methods used to coordinate the movement of data throughout the personal computer. It has also presented standard system resource allocations for various types of I/O devices. Technicians must be aware of these typical assignments in order to isolate resource conflicts that may develop and to install non-Plug and Play hardware devices in systems. The chapter concluded with a short explanation of binary numbers and working with hexadecimal addressing.

At this point, review the objectives listed at the beginning of the chapter to be certain that you understand each point and can perform each task listed there. Afterward, answer the review questions that follow to verify your knowledge of the information.

APPLY YOUR KNOWLEDGE

Review Questions

1. On which I/O address would you find the second IDE controller in a PC-compatible system?

   A. 070

   B. 170

   C. 278

   D. 378

2. Which IRQ channel would you expect to be servicing an external modem in a PC system that was using a serial mouse in COM1 for input?

   A. IRQ 2

   B. IRQ 3

   C. IRQ 4

   D. IRQ 10

3. If you wanted to add a color ink-jet printer to a system with a secondary printer port that already had a laser printer attached to LPT1, how could you configure it?

   A. Connect the color printer to LPT2.

   B. Connect the color printer to COM1.

   C. Connect the color printer to COM2 so that the mouse can remain on COM1.

   D. Install a printer switch box so that both printers can use LPT1.

4. How many DMA channels are there in an AT-compatible system?

   A. 2

   B. 4

   C. 8

   D. 16

5. Which standard system device uses IRQ6?

   A. The keyboard

   B. Floppy disk drives

   C. The system board's DRAM Refresh circuitry

   D. The parallel printer port

6. What action normally accompanies installing an internal modem?

   A. Rebooting the system

   B. Pushing the reset button on the modem

   C. Disabling the second parallel port

   D. Disabling the second onboard COM port

7. What type of problem will create an NMI type of interrupt in the system? (Select all that apply.)

   A. A Parity Check (PCK) error in the system's DRAM memory

   B. IRQ conflict between devices

   C. When an active IO Channel Check (IOCHCK) signal is received from an adapter card located in one of the board's expansion slots

   D. Over-voltage of the system board

8. Which of the following describes the bit pattern that would appear on the address bus to activate the first serial port? (You may use a scientific calculator.)

   A. 0111110000

   B. 1001111000

   C. 1011111000

   D. 1111111000

APPLY YOUR KNOWLEDGE

9. What does the computer system typically use to stop the processes of the microprocessor so that attention can be given to the demands of a particular device?

   A. ATX

   B. ATA

   C. IRQ

   D. NMI

10. Which interrupt request channels are available for use through the ISA bus?

    A. IRQ 0-15

    B. IRQ 0-7, 14-15

    C. IRQ 3-7, 9-12, 14-15

    D. IRQ 1-4, 9-11

11. The IRQ1 channel is used _____ and cannot be used for other devices.

    A. for the system's internal time-of-day clock

    B. by the system's keyboard receiver

    C. by the floppy disk drive

    D. by the printer for LPT1

12. The IRQ0 channel is _____.

    A. used by the system's timer/counter and cannot be used for other devices

    B. used by the keyboard and cannot be used for other devices

    C. used by the floppy disk drive and cannot be used for other devices

    D. open and can be used for any device requiring an IRQ channel

13. Which interrupt is cascaded with IRQ2?

    A. IRQ5

    B. IRQ7

    C. IRQ9

    D. IRQ10

14. Which device normally uses IRQ7?

    A. A laser printer

    B. A modem

    C. A floppy disk drive

    D. A hard disk drive

15. IRQ4 is normally assigned to the device connected to the _____.

    A. COM1 port

    B. LPT1 port

    C. COM2 port

    D. LPT2 port

16. A floppy disk drive uses which of the following IRQs?

    A. IRQ2

    B. IRQ5

    C. IRQ6

    D. IRQ9

17. Which IRQ is the default assignment for the printer attached to LPT1?

    A. IRQ3

    B. IRQ5

    C. IRQ7

    D. IRQ13

APPLY YOUR KNOWLEDGE

18. What is the IRQ for COM1?

    A. IRQ1

    B. IRQ2

    C. IRQ3

    D. IRQ4

19. Which of the following combinations are correct? (Select all that apply.)

    A. IRQ1 is the default for COM2 and COM4.

    B. IRQ2 is the default for COM1 and COM3.

    C. IRQ3 is the default for COM2 and COM4.

    D. IRQ4 is the default for COM1 and COM3.

20. What is the standard IRQ for COM2?

    A. IRQ3

    B. IRQ4

    C. IRQ2

    D. IRQ1

21. On which I/O address would you find the primary IDE controller in a PC-compatible system?

    A. 070

    B. 170

    C. 1F0

    D. 3F8

22. Which standard PC device uses a DMA channel?

    A. LPT1

    B. COM1

    C. INTC1

    D. FDD

23. What I/O address range is typically assigned to the video controller BIOS?

    A. C000-C7FF

    B. C700-CFFF

    C. D000-C7FF

    D. D800-D8FF

24. Which IRQ channel is reserved for the Real-Time Clock module in an ATX system?

    A. IRQ0

    B. IRQ1

    C. IRQ8

    D. IRQ9

Answers and Explanations

1. **B.** The first or Primary IDE controller is assigned IRQ14 while the Secondary controller uses IRQ15 to interrupt the system. The I/O port address for the second IDE controller is 170h-177h. For a detailed listing, consult Table 3.3: I/O Port Addresses. For more information, see the section "Onboard I/O."

2. **B.** The modem (or its host COM port) should be configured to for addresses 278 through 27Fh, IRQ3, and COM2. For more information, see the section "Modems."

3. **A.** If you have a secondary printer port, the new printer should be configured to LPT2. For more information, see the section "Interrupts."

4. **C.** There are two DMA controllers of four channels each. One of these channels (CH4) is a cascade channel and is not available for designation.

APPLY YOUR KNOWLEDGE

Therefore, although there are eight DMA channels total, only seven are actually available. For more information, see the section "Direct Memory Access."

5. **B.** IRQ6 is normally assigned to the floppy disk drives (FDDs). For more information, see the section "Interrupts."

6. **D.** In the case of the internal modem, the UART in the modem normally replaces one of the two COM port UARTs provided by a typical PC system. If the COM port UART is not disabled, the system might have trouble differentiating between the two ports and a conflict can develop. Therefore, it is common practice to disable an onboard UART when an internal modem is installed. The COM ports can be enabled or disabled through the system's CMOS Setup—Peripherals screen. For more information, see the section "Modems."

7. **A, C.** There are two system board-based conditions that will cause a Non-Maskable Interrupt (NMI) signal to be sent to the microprocessor. The first condition occurs when an active IO Channel Check (IOCHCK) signal is received from an adapter card located in one of the board's expansion slots. The other event that will cause an NMI signal to be generated is the occurrence of a Parity Check (PCK) error in the system's DRAM memory. For more information, see the section "Interrupts."

8. **D.** The first serial port is 3F8h. This translates to a binary bit code of 1111111000. For more information, see the section "Onboard I/O."

9. **C.** In the course of normal operations, the various I/O devices attached to a PC, such as the keyboard and disk drives, require servicing from the system's microprocessor. Because these service requests can happen at any time and tend to require immediate attention, I/O devices generally have the capability to interrupt the microprocessor while it is executing a program. The I/O device accomplishes this by issuing an interrupt request (IRQ) input signal to the microprocessor. For more information, see the section "Interrupts."

10. **C.** See Table 3.1: System Interrupt Levels. For more information, see the section "Interrupts."

11. **B.** See Table 3.1: System Interrupt Levels. For more information, see the section "Interrupts."

12. **A.** See Table 3.1: System Interrupt Levels. For more information, see the section "Interrupts."

13. **C.** See Table 3.1: System Interrupt Levels. For more information, see the section "Interrupts."

14. **A.** See Table 3.1: System Interrupt Levels. For more information, see the section "Interrupts."

15. **A.** See Table 3.1: System Interrupt Levels. For more information, see the section "Interrupts."

16. **C.** See Table 3.1: System Interrupt Levels. For more information, see the section "Interrupts."

17. **C.** See Table 3.1: System Interrupt Levels. For more information, see the section "Interrupts."

18. **D.** See Table 3.1: System Interrupt Levels. For more information, see the section "Interrupts."

19. **C, D.** See Table 3.1: System Interrupt Levels. For more information, see the section "Interrupts."

20. **A.** See Table 3.1: System Interrupt Levels. For more information, see the section "Interrupts."

APPLY YOUR KNOWLEDGE

21. **C.** The first or Primary IDE controller is assigned IRQ14, whereas the Secondary controller uses IRQ15 to interrupt the system. The I/O port address for the primary IDE controller is 1F0h-1F7h. For a detailed listing, consult Table 3.3: I/O Port Addresses. For more information, see the section "Onboard I/O."

22. **D.** See Table 3.2: System's DMA Channel Designations. For more information, see the section "Direct Memory Access."

23. **A.** See Table 3.4: System Memory Map. For more information, see the section "Onboard I/O."

24. **C.** See Table 3.1: System Interrupt Levels. For more information, see the section "Interrupts."

Challenge Solutions

1. He should assign the new printer IRQ5, which is the standard second LPT port (LPT2) in a PC-compatible system. The system will be able to communicate with the printer at hex addresses 278-27Fh. For more information, see the section "Interrupts."

2. You should be able to fax him the following list:

170-177	Second IDE Controller
1F0-1F7	First IDE Controller
2F8-2FF	Serial Port #2
378-37F	Parallel Port #1
3F8-3FF	Serial Port #1

   For more information, see the section "Onboard I/O."

Suggested Readings and Resources

1. I/O Transfer Methods
   http://www.ebiz.com.pk/pakistan/dma.doc

2. IRQ
   http://webopedia.internet.com/TERM/I/IRQ.html

3. System Resources
   www.pcguide.com/ref/mbsys/res/

4. DMA
   http://www.pcguide.com/ref/mbsys/res/dma/

5. Introduction to Hexidecimal
   http://www.intuitor.com/hex/bases.html

This chapter helps you to prepare for the Core Hardware module of the A+ Certification examination by covering the following objectives within the "Domain 1.0: Installation, Configuration, and Upgrading" section.

1.4 Identify common peripheral ports, associated cabling, and their connectors.

Content might include the following:

- **Cable types**

- **Cable orientation**

- **Serial versus parallel**

- **Pin connections**

Examples of types of connectors:

- **DB-9**

- **DB-25**

- **RJ-11**

- **RJ-45**

- **BNC**

- **PS2/MINI-DIN**

- **USB**

- **IEEE-1394**

▶ The PC-compatible architecture has always permitted a wide variety of peripheral devices to be added to the system. Most of these devices are designed to employ some type of PC-compatible I/O connection method. As this A+ objective indicates, the computer technician must be able to recognize the type of port the device requires, locate standard I/O port connections, and determine what type of cabling is required to successfully connect the port and the device and to successfully add peripheral devices to a PC-compatible system.

CHAPTER 4

Peripherals and Ports

STUDY STRATEGIES

To prepare for the Installation, Configuration, and Upgrading objective of the Core Hardware exam:

▶ Read the objectives at the beginning of this chapter.

▶ Study the information in this chapter.

▶ Review the objectives listed earlier in this chapter.

▶ Perform any step-by-step procedures in the text.

▶ Answer the review questions at the end of the chapter and check your results.

▶ Use the PrepLogic test engine on the CD-ROM that accompanies this book for additional review and exam questions concerning this material.

▶ Review the exam tips scattered throughout the chapter and make certain that you are comfortable with each point.

INTRODUCTION

This chapter examines the different connection methods that have been devised for use with different common PC-compatible peripheral devices and ports. These methods include older parallel and serial ports as well as newer high-speed USB, Firewire, and IrDA port specifications. In the process of discussing the different port standards, the chapter also covers cabling specifications associated with those ports.

After completing the chapter, you should be able to identify the types of ports used by common PC-compatible I/O devices and locate standard I/O port connections in both AT and ATX class computer systems. In addition, you should be able to determine what type of cabling might be required to connect peripheral devices to specific ports.

STANDARD I/O PORTS

Although many different methods have been developed to connect devices to the PC-compatible system, there are three ports that have been standard since the original PCs were introduced. These are

◆ The IBM versions of the Centronics parallel port

◆ The RS-232C serial port

◆ The IBM game port

Two connection types have become standards for connecting networked computers together. These are

◆ *RJ-45 (Registered Jack)* Ethernet connectors

◆ *BNC (British Naval Connector)* Coaxial connectors

AT Ports

In an AT-style system, most peripheral devices interact with the basic system through adapter cards that plug in to the system board's expansion slots. The peripheral devices connect to the adapter cards through expansion slot openings in back of the system unit. Figure 4.1 illustrates external port connections for a basic AT-style system configuration.

FIGURE 4.1
AT back panel connections.

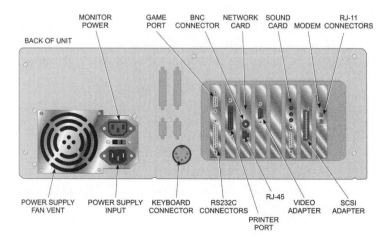

Beside the power connector is the power supply's fan vent. In a small opening near the power-supply openings is the circular, 5-pin DIN connector for connecting a keyboard to the system. Across the remainder of the back panel are eight expansion-slot openings.

Typical interface connections found in a PC system include two RS-232C connectors, a parallel printer port connector, and a game adapter connector. In this illustration, the two-row, 15-pin game-port connector is located on the sound card. On other systems, the locations of the various connectors may vary. The last connector on the back panel is the video adapter's monitor connector. This example features a VGA-compatible, three-row, 15-pin RGB color-output port connector. The three-row convention prevents the VGA connector from being confused with the two-row game port connector.

Other port connections likely to be found on the AT back panel include BNC and RJ-45 network connectors, RJ-11 telephone jacks for the modem, RCA jacks for the sound card's microphone and speakers, or a 50-pin Centronics connector on a SCSI host adapter card.

On early Pentium system boards, the basic I/O functions were integrated into the system board, but the standard I/O connectors were not included. These connections were made through ribbon cables that attached the physical port connector to the system board

EXAM TIP

Know what attribute prevents 15-pin VGA and game port connectors from being confused with each other.

that attached the physical port connector to the system board header. Figure 4.2 illustrates a sample arrangement for the standard I/O connectors (ports) of an AT-style system.

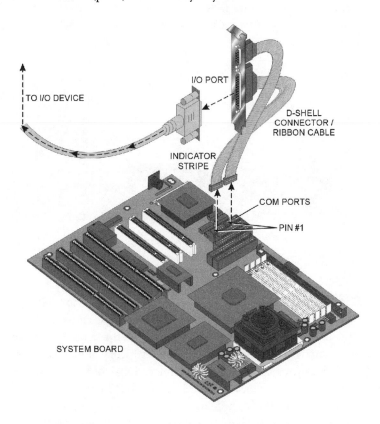

FIGURE 4.2
AT-style I/O port connections.

In AT systems, parallel I/O devices plug in to a DB-25F connector located on an expansion-slot cover or mounted directly in the back panel. The external connector is linked to a 26-pin BERG block on the system board through a ribbon cable and slot cover arrangement.

The same arrangement is true with the external RS-232C serial/asynchronous interface-port connections—COM1 and COM2. These ports support serial communications for I/O devices, such as mice and modems. A ribbon cable connects the system board's COM1 BERG connector to a DB-9M connector located on one of the unit's slot covers. In an AT system, this serial port is typically the system's first serial port and is normally the mouse connector. Another ribbon cable connects the system board's COM2 connection to a DB-25M connector on one of the expansion-slot covers. This connector serves as the second logical serial port.

EXAM TIP

You should receive several questions about the connections depicted in Figures 4.1 and 4.3. You should be able to identify each connector type shown and describe its characteristics and function.

ATX Ports

In an ATX system, the I/O port connections have been integrated into a vertical stack form factor located at the rear of the board. Figure 4.3 illustrates typical connectors found on the back of an ATX-style system.

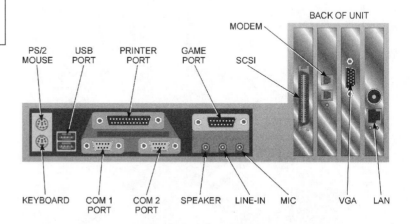

FIGURE 4.3
ATX back panel connections.

EXAM TIP

Be aware that the use of the 6-pin mini DIN in ATX systems can cause confusion between the keyboard and PS/2 mouse connection.

The ATX specification employs two 6-pin mini-DIN connectors (also referred to as PS/2 connectors) for the mouse and keyboard. Of course, the fact that both connections use the same type of connector can lead to problems if they are reversed. The standard also provides for two USB port connections, a DB-25F D-shell parallel printer port connector, two RS-232 serial COM ports implemented in a pair of DB-9M D-shell connectors, a DB-15F D-shell Game port, and an RCA audio port. Unlike the AT-style integrated I/O connections, these port connections require no system board connecting cables that can become defective.

The ATX system still makes provisions for a number of adapter cards to be used with the system. The physical port connectors on these cards conform to the I/O standards adopted by the PC community. Table 4.1 summarizes the types of connectors typically found on the back panel of both AT and ATX system units, along with their connector and pin count information.

TABLE 4.1

TYPICAL I/O PORTS

Port	AT	ATX
Keyboard	5-pin DIN	PS/2 6-pin mini-DIN
Mouse	xxxxxxx	PS/2 6-pin mini-DIN
COM1	DB-9M	DB-9M
COM2	DB-25M	DB-9M
LPT	DB-25F	DB-25F
VGA	DB-15F (3 row)	DB-15F (3 row)
Game	DB-15F (2 row)	DB-15F (2 row)
Modem	RJ-11	RJ-11
LAN	BNC/RJ-45	BNC/RJ-45
Sound	RCA mini-jacks	RCA mini-jacks
SCSI	Centronics 50-pin	Centronics 50-pin

EXAM TIP

Be able to identify a particular interface connection by the type and description of the connector it uses.

In an AT system, no connections are likely to be confused with each other except the COM1 and COM2 serial ports. In these systems, the keyboard uses a large round 5-pin DIN connector while the mouse uses the COM1 serial port. The connector type is an important consideration when purchasing a mouse—which type of connector will be needed for the system: 9-pin serial or 6-pin mini-DIN.

EXAM TIP

Be aware that the mouse connector type is an important consideration in selecting a mouse for use.

CHALLENGE #1

Your office is just getting networked, and you are in charge of getting the physical connections made to all the machines. In the CFO's office, you encounter a machine that has been running on a small accounting network for some time, but it doesn't have an RJ45 jack for the network cable. How can this be, and what should you do about it?

PARALLEL PORTS

Parallel ports have been a staple of the PC system since the original PCs were introduced. They have traditionally been the most widely used ports for connecting printers and other parallel devices to the computer. Figure 4.4 shows a typical parallel printer connection, using the IBM version of the Centronics standard. This interface enables the computer to pass information to the printer, 8 bits at a time, across the eight data lines. The other lines in the connection carry control signals (*handshaking* signals) back and forth between the computer and the printer.

FIGURE 4.4
Parallel printer connection.

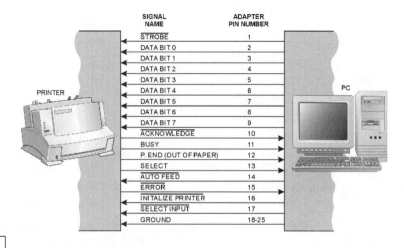

EXAM TIP

Know which types of connectors are used on each end of a standard parallel printer cable.

EXAM TIP

Know the recommended length of a standard parallel printer cable.

Printer Cabling

The original *Centronics interface* employed a 36-pin D-shell connector at the adapter and a 36-pin Centronics connector at the printer end. The IBM version of the interface, which became known as the *Standard Parallel Printer (SPP)* port specification, reduced the pin count to 25 at the computer end of the connection.

The cable length used for the parallel printer should be kept to less than 10 feet. If longer lengths are needed, the cable should have a low-capacitance value. The cable should also be shielded, to minimize *electromagnetic field interference (EFI)*. EFI is unwanted radio interference that can escape from improperly shielded cases and peripherals.

While the full implementation of the original SPP mode printer port could be used in a bi-directional manner, most PC manufacturers never implemented the two-way capabilities. Newer *Enhanced Parallel Port* (*EPP*) and *Extended Capabilities Port* (*ECP*) ports can be converted between unidirectional and bi-directional operation through the CMOS setup screen. If a bi-directional port is being used to support an I/O device, such as a local area network adapter or a high-capacity storage device, this feature would need to be checked at both a hardware and software level.

The parallel cable should also be checked to see that it complies with the *IEEE-1284* standard for use with bi-directional parallel ports. Using a traditional SPP cable could cause the device to operate erratically or fail completely.

LPT Handles

Microsoft operating systems keep track of the system's installed printer ports by assigning them the logical device names (handles) LPT1, LPT2, and LPT3. Whenever the system is booted up, the operating system searches the hardware for parallel ports installed at hex addresses 3BCh, 378h, and 278h consecutively.

If a printer port is found at 3BCh, the operating system assigns it the title of LPT1. If no printer port is found at 3BCh, but there is one at 378h, however, the operating system will assign LPT1 to the latter address. Likewise, a system that has printer ports at physical addresses 378h and 278h would have LPT1 assigned at 378h and LPT2 at location 278h.

The address of the printer port can normally be changed to respond as LPT1, LPT2, or LPT3, depending on the setting of address-selection jumpers. The printer port can also be disabled completely through these jumper settings.

The interrupt level of the printer port can be set at a number of different levels by changing its configuration jumpers or CMOS enabling setting. Normal interrupt request settings for printer ports in a PC-compatible system are IRQ5 or IRQ7. IRQ7 is normally assigned to the LPT1 printer port, whereas IRQ5 typically serves the LPT2 port, if installed.

EXAM TIP

As you study the I/O ports in this chapter, be aware of which ports provide bi-directional, half-duplex, and full-duplex operation.

EXAM TIP

Memorize the system resources that the PC typically assigns to parallel ports.

NOTE

Reference Shelf   For more information, refer to the Electronic Reference Shelf, "How a Parallel Printer Port Works," located on the CD that accompanies this book.

SERIAL PORTS

As the distance between the computer and a peripheral reaches a certain point (10 feet), it becomes less practical to send data as parallel words. An alternative method of sending data is to break the parallel words into their individual bits and transmit them, one at a time, in a serial bit stream over a single conductor.

Serial Transmission Modes

Two methods are used to provide the proper timing for serial transfers: The data bits can be sent synchronously (in conjunction with a synchronizing clock pulse) or asynchronously (without an accompanying clock pulse). The standard serial ports in a PC employ the asynchronous method. This method depends on the capability of two separate clocks, running at the same frequency, to remain synchronized for a short period of time. The transmitted material is sent character-by-character, with the beginning and end of each character framed by character start and stop bits. Between these marks, the bits of the character are sent at a constant rate, but the time interval between characters might be irregular, as illustrated in Figure 4.5.

FIGURE 4.5
Asynchronous transmission.

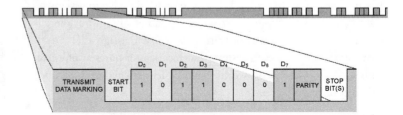

Although asynchronous transfer methods have been the standard for serial ports in the PC industry and synchronous ports were typically used in specialized applications, most of the newer ports and buses include a high-speed synchronous mode as a standard option.

UARTs

The original PC serial port adapters featured discrete 8250 UARTs with programmable baud rates from 50 to 9600 baud, a fully programmable interrupt system, and variable character lengths (5-, 6-, 7-, or 8-bit characters). In addition, the adapter added and removed start, stop, and parity bits; had false start-bit detection, line-break detection, and generation; and possessed built-in diagnostics capabilities.

Advanced high-performance UARTs include an onboard buffer that permits the UART to store, or transmit, a string of data without interrupting the system's microprocessor to handle them. These advanced UARTs enable serial ports to reach data transmission rates of up to 115Kbps. Although some features have changed between UART versions, they must still adhere to the basic 8250 UART structure to remain PC compatible.

Serial Cables

The original IBM version of the RS-232C standard calls for a 25-pin, male D-type connector, as depicted in Figure 4.6. It also designates certain pins for data transmission and receiving, along with a number of control lines. Normally, only nine of the pins are active for a given application. The other lines are used for secondary, or backup, lines and grounds.

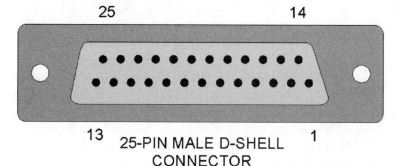

25   14

13   25-PIN MALE D-SHELL   1
CONNECTOR

FIGURE 4.6
RS-232C connector.

In addition to defining the type of connector to be used and the use of its individual pins, the RS-232 standard also establishes acceptable voltage levels for the signals on its pins. These levels are generally converted to and from standard digital logic level signals that can produce a maximum baud rate of 20,000 baud over distances of less than 50 feet, which is the recommended maximum length of an RS-232 cable. The RS-232C version extends this length to 100 feet.

EXAM TIP

Know the maximum recommended length of an RS-232 cable.

Even though the information in Figure 4.7 shows a designation for nearly every pin in the RS-232 connection (except 11, 18, and 25), many of the pins are not actually used in most serial cables. The figure illustrates the basic 25-pin to 25-pin variation of the RS-232 serial cable. In this example, the connection depicted is a straight through cabling scheme associated with PCs and PC XTs.

FIGURE 4.7
A 25-pin to 25-pin RS-232 cable.

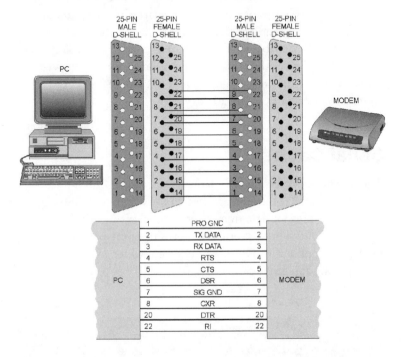

Since the advent of the PC AT, the system's first serial port has typically been implemented in a 9-pin, D-shell male connector on the computer. Figure 4.8 depicts a typical 9-pin to 25-pin connection scheme. Notice the crossover wiring technique employed for the TXD/RXD lines displayed in this example. This type of connection became popular with the 9-pin PC AT serial port.

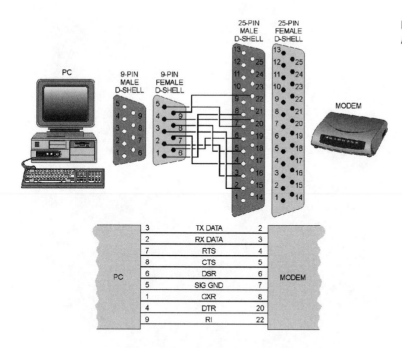

FIGURE 4.8
A 9-pin to 25-pin RS-232 cable.

PC		MODEM
3	TX DATA	2
2	RX DATA	3
7	RTS	4
8	CTS	5
6	DSR	6
5	SIG GND	7
1	CXR	8
4	DTR	20
9	RI	22

When the serial ports are located close enough together, a *null
modem* connection can be implemented. This type of connection—
also referred to as a *crossover cable*—permits two serial ports to communicate directly without using modems. A typical null modem
connection scheme is illustrated in Figure 4.9. Notice that, unlike
the unidirectional serial printer connection, the null modem connection scheme crosses pins 4 and 5 between the computer and modem
to facilitate two-way communications.

FIGURE 4.9
A null modem cable.

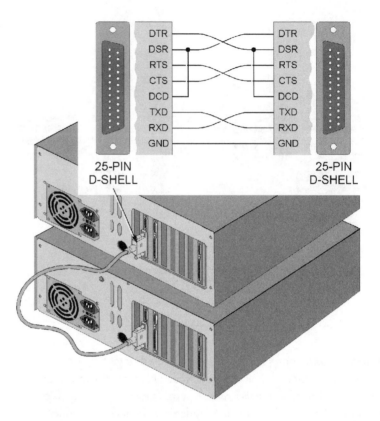

It should be apparent from the previous trio of figures that all serial cables are not created equal. Incorrect serial cabling can be a major problem when attaching third-party communication equipment to the computer. Read the modem's user manual carefully to make certain that the correct pins are being connected together.

Serial Port Names and Resources

As with parallel ports, DOS assigns COM port designations to the system's serial ports during bootup. COM port designations are normally COM1 and COM2 in most systems, but they can be extended to COM3 and COM4 in advanced systems.

Either RS-232 port can be designated as COM1, COM2, COM3, or COM4, as long as both ports are not assigned to the same COM port number. In most PCs, COM1 is assigned as port address hex 3F8h and uses IRQ channel 4. The COM2 port is typically assigned port address hex 2F8h and IRQ3. Likewise, COM3 uses IRQ4 and is assigned an I/O address of 3E8h; COM4 usually resides at 2E8 and uses IRQ3.

UNIVERSAL SERIAL BUS

A new serial interface scheme, called the *Universal Serial Bus* (*USB*), has been developed to provide a fast, flexible method of attaching up to 127 peripheral devices to the computer. The USB provides a connection format designed to replace the system's traditional serial- and parallel-port connections.

USB peripherals can be daisy chained, or networked together, using connection hubs that enable the bus to branch out through additional port connections. A practical USB desktop connection scheme is presented in Figure 4.10. In this example, some of the peripheral devices are simply devices, whereas others serve as both devices and connection hubs. The system provides a USB host connection that serves as the main USB connection.

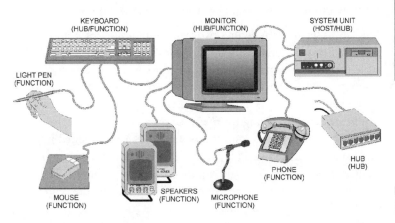

FIGURE 4.10
USB desktop connection scheme.

USB devices can be added to or removed from the system while it is powered up and fully operational. This is referred to as *hot-swapping* or *hot plugging* the device. The plug-and-play capabilities of the system will detect the presence (or absence) of the device and configure it for operation. In effect, the USB organizational structure is modified any time a device is added to or removed from the system.

EXAM TIP
Know the system addresses and other resources that a PC-compatible system uses for serial ports. It may be easy to remember that IBM set up these standards so that the odd-numbered COM ports use the even-numbered IRQ channel, and vice versa.

NOTE
Refeerence Shelf For more information, refer to the Electronic Reference Shelf, "How a Serial Port Works," located on the CD that accompanies this book.

EXAM TIP
Memorize the number of devices that can be attached to a USB port.

EXAM TIP
Be aware that USB devices can be plugged in and removed while power is applied and remember what this is called.

USB Cabling and Connectors

USB transfers are conducted over a four-wire cable, as illustrated in Figure 4.11. The signal travels over a pair of twisted wires (D+ and D–) in a 90-ohm cable. The differential signal and twisted-pair wiring provide minimum signal deterioration over distances and high noise immunity.

FIGURE 4.11
USB cable.

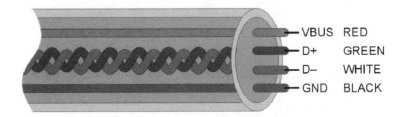

VBUS RED
D+   GREEN
D–   WHITE
GND   BLACK

> **EXAM TIP**
>
> Be aware that the USB bus supplies power to low-power devices, but devices requiring more power must include their own power sources.

The Vbus is the +5V (DC) power cord. The interface provides power to the peripheral attached to it. The root hub provides power directly from the host system to those devices directly connected to it. Hubs also supply power to the devices connected to them. Even though the interface supplies power to the USB devices, they are permitted to have their own power sources if necessary.

The USB specification defines two types of plugs: series-A and series-B. Series-A connectors are used for devices in which the USB cable connection is permanently attached to devices at one end. Examples of these devices include keyboards, mice, and hubs. Conversely, the series-B plugs and jacks are designed for devices that require detachable cabling (printers, scanners, and modems, for example). Both are four-contact plugs and sockets embedded in plastic connectors, as shown in Figure 4.12. The sockets can be implemented in vertical, right angle, and panel-mount variations. The icon used to represent a USB connector is depicted by the centers of the A and B "plug connectors."

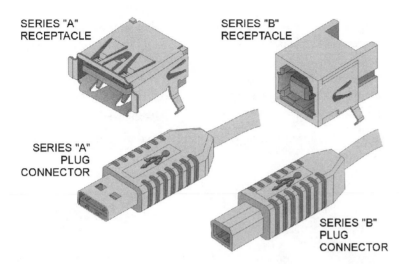

SERIES "A"
RECEPTACLE

SERIES "B"
RECEPTACLE

SERIES "A"
PLUG
CONNECTOR

SERIES "B"
PLUG
CONNECTOR

FIGURE 4.12
USB connectors.

The length limit for a USB cable serving a full speed device is 16 feet 5 inches (5 meters). Conversely, the length limit for cables used between low speed devices is 9 feet 10 inches (3 meters).

> **EXAM TIP**
>
> Know the length limits for full- and low-speed USB devices. It should help you to remember that the low-speed distance is actually shorter than the high-speed length.

FIREWIRE

While the USB specification was being refined for the computer industry, a similar serial interface bus was being developed for the consumer products market. Apple Computers and Texas Instruments worked together with the IEEE (Institute of Electrical and Electronic Engineers) to produce the *Firewire* (or *IEEE-1394*) specification. The new bus offers a very fast option for connecting consumer electronics devices, such as camcorders and DVDs, to the computer system.

The Firewire bus is similar to USB in that devices can be daisy chained to the computer using a single connector and host adapter. It requires a single IRQ channel, an I/O address range, and a single DMA channel to operate. Firewire is also capable of using a special high-speed Isochronous transfer mode described in Chapter 14, "Motherboards," to support data transfer rates up to 400Mbps. This actually makes the Firewire bus superior to the USB bus. Its high-speed capabilities make Firewire well suited for handling components, such as video and audio devices, which require real-time, high-speed data transfer rates.

> **EXAM TIP**
>
> Be aware that the Firewire bus is faster than the USB bus.

E X A M   T I P

Remember how many devices can
be attached to a single IEEE-1394
port.

A single IEEE-1394 connection can be used to connect up 63
devices to a single port. However, up to 1023 Firewire buses can be
interconnected. PCs most commonly use a PCI expansion card to
provide the Firewire interface. Although *audio/visual* (*A/V*) equipment typically employs 4-pin 1394 connectors, computers normally
use a 6-pin connector, with a 4-pin to 6-pin converter.

Figure 4.13 depicts the Firewire connector and plug most commonly
used with PCs.

FIGURE 4.13
Firewire plug and connector.

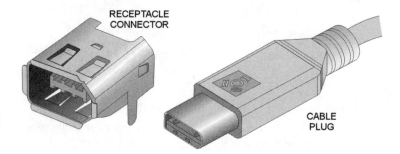

RECEPTACLE
CONNECTOR

CABLE
PLUG

The IEEE-1394 cable is composed of two twisted pair conductors
similar to those used in the local area networks. Like USB, it supports both PnP and hot swapping of components and provides
power to the peripheral devices through one pair of the twisted conductors in the interface cable.

Firewire is supported in both the Windows 9*x* and Windows
NT/2000 operating systems. Both operating systems support
advanced Firewire operations by including support for specifications
that define the way Firewire interfaces to a PC, the details for controlling specific audio-video devices over the IEEE-1394 bus, and
standard ways of encapsulating device commands over 1394 and is
essential for DVD players, printers, scanners, and other devices. In
addition, a new Home AV Interoperability (HAVi) standard is
directed at making Firewire devices plug-and-play capable in networks where no PC host is present.

A proposed version of the IEEE-1394 standard (titled P1394b) provides an additional electrical signaling method that permits data
transmission speeds of 800Mbps and greater. This proposal also
supports new transport media including glass and plastic optical
fiber, as well as *Category 5 copper cable*. Along with the new media
comes extended distances (for example, 100 meters over Cat-5
cable).

CHALLENGE #2

Your company is moving strongly into multimedia systems that include professional electronic music and video devices. Your boss has asked you which type of interface the company should standardize on. What should you tell the boss about this?

INFRARED PORTS

The *Infrared Data Association* (*IrDA*) has produced a wireless peripheral connection standard based on infrared light technology, similar to that used in consumer remote control devices. Many system board designs include an IrDA-compliant port standard to provide wireless communications with devices such as character printers, personal digital assistants, and notebook computers.

The same technology has been employed to carry out transfers between computer communications devices such as modems and local area network cards.

The IrDA standard specifies four protocols that are used with different types of devices:

◆ *IrLPT*—The protocol used with character printers to provide a wireless interface between the computer and the printer.

◆ *IrDA-SIR*—The standard infrared protocol used to provide a standard serial port interface with transfer rates ranging up to 115Kbps.

◆ *IrDA-FIR*—The fast infrared protocol used to provide a high-speed serial port interface with transfer rates ranging up to 4Mbps.

◆ *IrTran-P*—The protocol used to provide a digital image transfer standard for communications with digital image capture devices.

These protocols specify communication ranges up to 2 meters (6 feet), but most specifications usually state 1 meter as the maximum range. All IrDA transfers are carried out in half-duplex mode and must have a clear line of sight between the transmitter and receiver.

EXAM TIP

Remember that the IrLPT port is a new, high-speed printer interface that can be used to print from a wide array of computing devices.

EXAM TIP

Be aware of the stated range of an
IrDA-compliant infrared connection.

The receiver must be situated within 15 degrees of center with the
line of transmission.

The Windows operating system supports the use of infrared devices.
The properties of installed IrDA devices can be viewed through the
Device Manager. Likewise, connections to another IrDA computer
can be established through the Windows Network Dialup
Connections applet. By installing a *Point-to-Point Protocol* (*PPP*) or
an IrDA LAN protocol through this applet, you can conduct wireless communications with other computers without a modem or
network card.

CHALLENGE #3

Your assistant is setting up an IrDA printer in a remote location. He
has called you because he cannot get the system to see the
infrared printer connection. To check the printer, the assistant connected it to the host computer using a normal parallel interface
and it ran successfully. Which items should you suggest that your
assistant check to verify the operation of the infrared port?

CHAPTER SUMMARY

This chapter has dealt with common peripherals and ports associated with PC-compatible systems. The chapter presented two key A+ related figures—the standard AT and ATX back panel connection figures. These figures are very similar to those you will encounter on the actual A+ exam.

The AT-style back panel figure describes the older peripheral and port types associated with PC systems up to the first versions of Pentium class machines. The primary ports associated with these computers included parallel printer ports, serial communication ports, and game ports. Optional connections with this class of computers included various LAN and modem connections.

The ATX back panel figure shows those ports associated with newer Pentium class computers. Ports associated with these computers include the older serial and parallel ports in addition to newer USB, Firewire, and IrDA ports.

At this point, review the objectives listed at the beginning of the chapter to be certain that you understand each point and can perform each task listed there. Afterward, answer the review questions that follow to verify your knowledge of the information.

KEY TERMS

- Audio/visual (A/V)
- BNC (British Naval Connector)
- Category 5 copper cable
- Centronics interface
- Crossover cable
- Electromagnetic Field Interference (EFI)
- Enhanced Parallel Port (EPP)
- Extended Capabilities Port (ECP)
- Firewire
- Handshaking
- Hot plugging
- Hot-swapping
- IEEE-1284
- IEEE-1394
- Infrared Data Association (IrDA)
- IrDA-FIR
- IrDA-SIR
- IrLPT
- IrTran-P
- Null modem
- Parallel ports
- Point-to-Point Protocol (PPP)
- RJ-45 (Registered Jack)
- Standard Parallel Printer (SPP)
- Universal Serial Bus (USB)

APPLY YOUR KNOWLEDGE

Review Questions

1. Which new serial interface is faster?

   A. IrDA

   B. ECP

   C. IEEE-1394

   D. USB

2. How many devices can be attached to a single universal serial bus (USB) host?

   A. 63

   B. 127

   C. 255

   D. 511

3. What is the maximum recommended length of a standard parallel printer cable?

   A. 3 feet

   B. 10 feet

   C. 20 feet

   D. 30 feet

4. How long can an RS-232C serial cable be?

   A. 10 feet (3 meters)

   B. 25 feet (8.5 meters)

   C. 50 feet (15 meters)

   D. 150 feet (48 meters)

5. What is the maximum length of a full-speed USB segment?

   A. 3 meters

   B. 5 meters

   C. 10 meters

   D. 15 meters

6. How far can an IrDA-compliant device be placed away from the IrDA port and be expected to operate efficiently?

   A. 1 meter

   B. 5 meters

   C. 10 meters

   D. 20 meters

7. What wiring consideration must you take to create a null modem cable for use with two serial ports?

   A. Cable must be less than 3 meters long

   B. Must use a serial twisted pair (STP) cable

   C. Must use a parallel cable

   D. Cable must have crossed-over connections

8. What is the maximum data transmission speed specified by the standard infrared protocol?

   A. 64Kbps

   B. 115Kbps

   C. 128Kbps

   D. 4Mbps

APPLY YOUR KNOWLEDGE

9. IrLPT is described as an _____.

   A. infrared transmission protocol used as a standard serial port interface

   B. infrared transmission protocol that provides a high-speed serial port interface

   C. infrared transmission protocol that allows digital image transfer with image capture devices

   D. infrared transmission protocol used between a computer and a printer

10. What is the maximum length of a low-speed USB cable?

    A. 1 meter

    B. 3 meters

    C. 5 meters

    D. 10 meters

11. What type of port uses a DB-25F connector?

    A. VGA port

    B. Game port

    C. Printer port

    D. COM2 port

12. How is power supplied to a low-power USB device?

    A. Through a power cable

    B. From an external power supply

    C. Directly from the computer's power supply

    D. Through the USB cable

13. Which of these connectors can be easily confused in an ATX system? (Select all that apply.)

    A. Mouse

    B. Keyboard

    C. Monitor

    D. Joystick

14. Which IRQ channel and I/O address is typically used for standard serial ports?

    A. IRQ3, 3F8h

    B. IRQ6, 3F0h

    C. IRQ7, 378h

    D. IRQ15, 170h

15. Which IRQ channel and I/O address is typically used for standard parallel ports?

    A. IRQ3, 2F8h

    B. IRQ6, 3F0h

    C. IRQ7, 378h

    D. IRQ15, 170h

16. What IRQ is normally used for COM2?

    A. IRQ2

    B. IRQ3

    C. IRQ4

    D. IRQ5

17. What type of connectors are found on the ends of a standard parallel printer cable? (Select two.)

    A. DB-9F

    B. DB-25M

    C. DB-36M

    D. 36-pin Centronics

APPLY YOUR KNOWLEDGE

18. Which of these connectors is a VGA port?

    A. A

    B. B

    C. C

    D. D

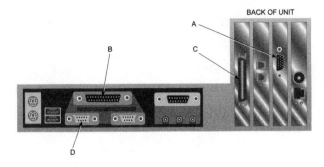

BACK OF UNIT

19. From the figure shown in question 18 that depicts an ATX back panel, which of these connectors is a SCSI port?

    A. A

    B. B

    C. C

    D. D

20. From the figure shown in question 18, which of these connectors is a printer port?

    A. A

    B. B

    C. C

    D. D

Answers and Explanations

1. **C.** Firewire (IEEE-1394) is capable of using the high-speed isochronous transfer mode described for USB to support data transfer rates up to 400Mbps. This actually makes the Firewire bus superior to the USB bus. For more information, see the section "Firewire."

2. **B.** The specification allows 127 devices (128 – 1) to be attached to the USB host. The host accounts for one of the 128 possible USB addresses. For more information, see the section "Universal Serial Bus."

3. **B.** The cable length used for the parallel printer should be kept to less than 10 feet. For more information, see the section "Printer Cabling."

4. **C.** The recommended maximum RS-232 cable length, as recognized by CompTIA, is 50 feet (15 meters). The maximum length for a standard RS-232C connection is actually 100 feet (33 meters). For more information, see the section "Serial Cables."

5. **B.** The limit of the full-speed USB connection is 5 meters without additional equipment. For more information, see the section "USB Cabling and Connectors."

6. **A.** Typically the transmission range of an IrDA device is specified as 0-2 meters, but the IrDA standard requires that the device have the ability to communicate within 1 meter. For more information, see the section "Infrared Ports."

APPLY YOUR KNOWLEDGE

7. **D.** The null modem connection scheme crosses pins 4 and 5 between the two units in order to facilitate two-way communications. This type of connection—also referred to as a crossover cable—permits two serial ports to communicate directly. For more information, see the section "Serial Cables."

8. **B.** The standard infrared protocol (IrDA-SIR) provides a standard serial port interface with transfer rates ranging up to 115Kbps. For more information, see the section "Infrared Ports."

9. **D.** IrLPT is a protocol that is used with character printers to provide a wireless interface between the computer and the printer. For more information, see the section "Infrared Ports."

10. **B.** The length limit for cables used between low-speed USB devices is 3 meters. For more information, see the section "USB Cabling and Connectors."

11. **C.** Parallel I/O devices (such as a printer) plug in to a DB-25F connector located on an expansion-slot cover or mounted directly in the back panel. For more information, see the section "AT Ports."

12. **D.** The USB bus supplies power to low-power devices, but devices requiring more power must include their own power sources. For more information, see the section "USB Cabling and Connectors."

13. **A, B.** The ATX specification employs two 6-pin mini-DIN connectors (also referred to as PS/2 connectors) for the mouse and keyboard. The fact that both connections use the same type of connector can lead to problems if they are reversed. For more information, see the section "ATX Ports."

14. **A.** In most PCs, COM1 is assigned as port address hex 3F8h and uses IRQ channel 4. The COM2 port is typically assigned port address hex 2F8h and IRQ3. Likewise, COM3 uses IRQ4 and is assigned an I/O address of 3E8h; COM4 usually resides at 2E8 and uses IRQ3. For more information, see the section "Serial Port Names and Resources."

15. **C.** IRQ7 is normally assigned to the LPT1 printer port, whereas IRQ5 typically serves the LPT2 port. LPT1 is assigned at 378h, and LPT2 at location 278h. For more information, see the section "LPT Handles."

16. **B.** The COM2 port is typically assigned port address hex 2F8h and IRQ3. For more information, see the section "Serial Port Names and Resources."

17. **B, D.** The original Centronics interface employed a 36-pin D-shell connector at the adapter and a 36-pin Centronics connector at the printer end. The IBM version of the interface, which became known as the Standard Parallel Printer (SPP) port specification, reduced the pin count to 25 (DB-25M) at the computer end of the cable. For more information, see the section "Printer Cabling."

18. **A.** See Figure 4.3: ATX Back Panel Connections. For more information, see the section "ATX Ports."

19. **C.** See Figure 4.3: ATX Back Panel Connections. For more information, see the section "ATX Ports."

20. **B.** See Figure 4.3: ATX Back Panel Connections. For more information, see the section "ATX Ports."

Challenge Solutions

1. The accounting network uses BNC cabling. You can either replace it with a RJ45 network so that you can hook it into your network, or add a RJ45 card to the CFO's computer to make it a gateway between the two networks. For more information, see the section "Standard I/O Ports."

2. You should tell your boss that the industry standard interface for professional music and multimedia work is the IEEE-1394 (or Firewire) specification. For more information, see the section "Firewire."

3. The properties of installed IrDA devices can be viewed through the Device Manager. Likewise, connections to another IrDA computer can be established through the Windows Network Dialup Connections applet. By installing a Point-to-Point Protocol (PPP) or an IrDA LAN protocol through this applet, you can conduct wireless communications with other computers without a modem or network card. For more information, see the section "Infrared Ports."

Suggested Readings and Resources

1. ATX
   http://www.webopedia.com/TERM/A/ATX.html

2. ATX Ports
   http://www.linux-1u.net/1U_Features/Color_IOShield.JPG

3. Extended Capability Port (ECP)
   www.fapo.com/ecpmode.htm

4. Enhanced Parallel Port (EPP)
   www.fapo.com/eppmode.htm

5. Serial Ports
   http://www.howstuffworks.com/serial-port.htm

6. Universal Serial Bus
   http://www.webopedia.com/TERM/U/USB.html

7. RJ-11 and RJ-45 Connectors
   www.starkelectronic.com/czp33a.htm

8. Connectors
   www.connectworld.net/c2.html

This chapter helps you to prepare for the Core Hardware module of the A+ Certification examination by covering the following objectives within the "Domain 1.0: Installation, Configuration, and Upgrading" section.

1.5 Identify proper procedures for installing and configuring IDE/EIDE devices.

Content might include the following:

- **Master/Slave**

- **Devices per channel**

- **Primary/Secondary**

1.6 Identify proper procedures for installing and configuring SCSI devices.

Content might include the following:

- **Address/Termination conflicts**

- **Cabling**

- **Types (for example, regular, wide, ultra-wide)**

- **Internal versus external**

- **External slots, EISA, ISA, PCI**

- **Jumper block settings (binary equivalents)**

CHAPTER 5

Installing Disk Devices

▶ Hard disk drives are the mainstay of mass data storage in PC-compatible systems. In contemporary PCs, IDE and SCSI drives are most commonly used. Therefore, computer technicians must be able to successfully install and configure both IDE and SCSI drives, as well as other devices that employ IDE and SCSI interfaces. This chapter covers the characteristics of these two interfaces, including standard variations and common connector types associated with each.

To prepare for the Installation, Configuration, and Upgrading objective of the Core Hardware exam,

▶ Read the objectives at the beginning of this chapter.

▶ Study the information in this chapter.

▶ Review the objectives listed earlier in this chapter.

▶ Perform any step-by-step procedures in the text.

▶ Answer the review questions at the end of the chapter and check your results.

▶ Use the PrepLogic test engine on the CD-ROM that accompanies this book for additional review and exam questions concerning this material.

▶ Review the exam tips scattered throughout the chapter and make certain that you are comfortable with each point.

INTRODUCTION

This chapter deals with the two types of disk drives commonly used with PC-compatible computers. These devices are based on the IDE and SCSI interface standards. The chapter provides important information about configuring both of these device types for use with PC systems.

The chapter begins with discussions of the IDE line of drives, which are more likely to be used in desktop PCs. This section includes information about successfully installing and configuring these devices for use.

The second half of the chapter deals with the different SCSI interface specifications and the devices that use it. Although SCSI interfaces are not as widely used in desktop PCs, they do find widespread acceptance in higher end PCs and server computers. This section provides key information about the different SCSI types, different types of cabling involved, and key information about how to configure SCSI devices for operation.

After completing the chapter, you should be able to describe proper procedures for installing and configuring IDE/EIDE and different types of SCSI disk drives and devices.

INTEGRATED DRIVE ELECTRONICS INTERFACE

The *Integrated Drive Electronics (IDE)* interface is a system-level interface. It is also referred to as the *AT Attachment (ATA)* interface. The IDE interface places most of the controller electronics on the drive unit. Therefore, data travels in parallel between the computer and the drive unit. The controller circuitry on the drive handles all the parallel-to-serial and serial-to-parallel conversions. This enables the interface to be independent of the host computer design. The host computer does not actually see the geometry of the disk, only the pattern that is presented to it by the IDE controller.

An IDE drive has low-level formatting information placed on itself by its manufacturer and is used by the controller for alignment and sector sizing of the drive. The IDE controller extracts the raw data (format and actual data information) coming from the R/W heads and converts it into signals that can be applied to the computer's buses.

The standard IDE interface uses a single 40-pin cable to connect the hard drives to the adapter card or system board. Some systems that employ system level interfaces, such as an IDE interface, employ an adapter card called a host adapter. These cards are referred to as host adapters rather than controller cards because they have no intelligent control devices on them. They simply offer physical extensions of the system buses to the I/O device. It should be apparent from Figure 5.1 that the IDE host adapter is quite simple because most of the interface signals originate directly from the system's extended bus lines. The relationship between the host adapter, the system buses, and the IDE interface are described in Figure 5.1.

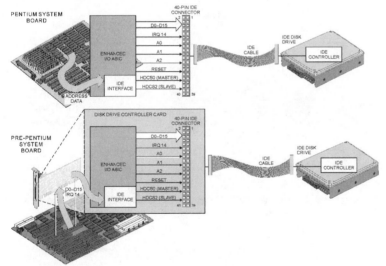

FIGURE 5.1
The host adapter, system buses, and IDE interface.

Configuring IDE Drives

The host adapter basically provides system bus level interfacing for the IDE devices. The interface includes buffering the system's address and data buses and providing the select signals that differentiate between a single drive system or the master and slave drives.

Most IDE drives come from the manufacturer configured for operation as a single drive, or as the master drive in a multidrive system. To install the drive as a second, or slave drive, it is usually necessary to install, remove, or move a jumper block, as illustrated in Figure 5.2. Some hosts disable the interface's Cable Select pin for slave drives. With these types of hosts, it is necessary to install a jumper for the *Cable Select* option on the drive. Consult the system's user manual to determine whether it supports this function.

Under Microsoft operating systems, the primary partitions of multiple IDE hard drives are assigned the first logical drive identifiers. If an IDE drive is partitioned into two logical drives, the system will identify them as the C: drive and the D: drive. If a second IDE drive is added as a slave drive with two additional logical drives, it will reassign the partitions on the first drive to be logical drives C: and E:, and the partitions on the slave drive will be D: and F:.

FIGURE 5.2
IDE master/slave settings.

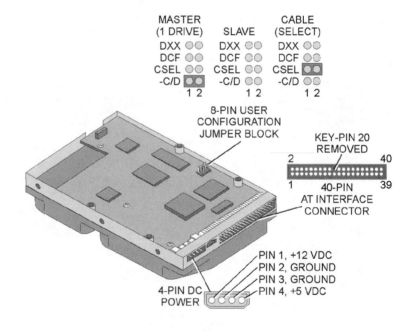

CHALLENGE #1

You are installing IDE drives in a new system. The buyers want to include a large HDD, a standard CD-ROM drive and a rewritable CD-ROM drive. Their company needs to have Windows 2000 and MS-DOS operating systems on the machine, so they want you to divide the hard drive into two equally sized drives. You connect the hard drive to the system board's IDE1 connector and the two CD-ROM drives to the cable connected to its IDE2 connector. How will their drive-specific MS-DOS programs need to be configured if DOS is placed on the drive's extended partition?

EXAM TIP

Remember the three configurations that can be set on an IDE drive.

Advanced EIDE Specifications

There are a variety of IDE-related specifications. The initial IDE standard was the IDE/ATA specification. The terms IDE and ATA are used to represent the same standard. This standard supported a maximum throughput of 8.3Mbps through the 40-pin IDE signal cable. Updated IDE specifications have been developed that enable more than two drives to exist on the interface.

The second IDE standard includes the ATA-2/EIDE/ATAPI specifications (the ATAPI standard is a derivative of the ATA-2 standard). This specification provides maximum throughput of 16.7Mbps through the 40-pin IDE signal cable. This new specification is called *Enhanced IDE* (*EIDE*), or the *ATA-2* interface, and permits up to four IDE devices to operate in a single system.

Under this specification, the host supplies two IDE interfaces that can each handle a master and a slave device in a daisy chained configuration. The first interface is the Primary IDE interface and is typically labeled IDE1. Likewise, the second IDE interface is the Secondary IDE interface and is usually marked as IDE2, as illustrated in Figure 5.3.

Actually, the update covers more than just increasing the number of drives that can be accommodated. It also provides for improved IDE drivers, known as the *AT Attachment Packet Interface* (*ATAPI*), for use with CD-ROM drives, as well as new DMA data transfer methods.

Continued development of the ATA standard has provided the ATA-3/Ultra ATA 33 specification that boosts throughput between the IDE device and the system to 33.3Mbps. This standard employs the 40-pin IDE signal cable and relies on the system to support the 33.3Mbps burst mode transfer operation through the *Ultra DMA* (*UDMA*) *protocol.*

FIGURE 5.3
IDE1 and IDE2 identification.

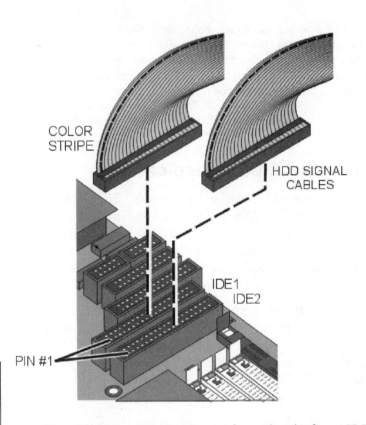

EXAM TIP
Remember how the Ultra ATA 66 interface cable can be identified.

EXAM TIP
Remember that IDE bus driver support is built in to the BIOS of system boards that have integrated IDE host adapters.

NOTE
Hands-On Activity   For hands-on experience with this concept, refer to Lab Procedure #4, "HDD Settings," located on the CD that accompanies this book.

In addition to the new Ultra DMA transfer modes, the fastest IDE enhancements, referred to as ATA-4/Ultra ATA 66 and Ultra ATA 100, extend the high data throughput capabilities of the bus by doubling the number of conductors in the IDE signal cable to 80. Although the number of wires has doubled, the IDE connector has remained compatible with the 40-pin IDE connection, but each pin has been provided with its own ground conductor in the cable. The *Ultra ATA 66* specification provides 66Mbps, whereas the *Ultra ATA 100* connection will provide 100Mbps.

When you are installing a newer EIDE drive in a system, if you use an older 40-wire IDE cable with a newer UDMA drive, the performance of the drive will be severely limited.

The IDE/EIDE interface has been the standard PC disk drive interface for some time. The IDE controller structure is an integrated portion of most PC system boards. This structure includes BIOS and chipset support for the IDE version the board will support, as well as the IDE host connector.

SMALL COMPUTER SYSTEM INTERFACE

The *Small Computer System Interface* (*SCSI*—often referred to as "scuzzy") standard, like the IDE concept, provides a true system-level interface for the drive. Nearly all the drive's controller electronics are located on the peripheral device. As with the IDE host adapter, the duties of the SCSI host adapter are reduced to mostly physical connection functions, along with some signal-compatibility handling. Under this arrangement, data arrives at the system interface in a form that is already usable by the host computer.

The original SCSI interface makes provisions for 8-bit parallel data transfers. This interface is still used to connect diverse types of peripherals to the system. As an example, a SCSI chain could be used to connect a controller to a hard drive, a CD-ROM drive, a high-speed tape drive, a scanner, and a printer. Additional SCSI devices are added to the system by daisy chaining them together. The input of the second device is attached to the SCSI output of the first device, and so forth.

EXAM TIP

Be aware of the different types of devices that might use a SCSI interface connection.

SCSI Cables and Connectors

The original SCSI standard has been implemented using a number of cable types. In PC-compatible systems, the SCSI interface uses a 50-pin signal cable arrangement. Internally, the cable is a 50-pin flat ribbon cable. However, a 50-pin shielded cable with Centronics-like connectors is used for external SCSI connections. The 50-pin SCSI connections are referred to as A-cables.

Advanced SCSI specifications have created additional cabling specifications. A 50-conductor alternative cable, using 50-pin D-shell connectors has been added to the A-cable specification for SCSI-2 devices. A second cable type, referred to as B-cable, was added to the SCSI-2 specification to provide 16- and 32-bit parallel data transfers. However, this arrangement employed multiple connectors at each end of the cable and never received widespread acceptance in the market. A revised 68-pin P-cable format, using D-shell connectors, was introduced to support 16-bit transfers in the SCSI-3 specification. A 68-pin Q-cable version was also adopted in SCSI for

32-bit transfers. The P and Q cables must be used in parallel to conduct 32-bit transfers.

For some PS/2 models, IBM used a special 60-pin Centronics-like connector for their SCSI connections. The version of the SCSI interface used in the Apple Macintosh employs a variation of the standard that features a proprietary, miniature 25-pin D-shell connector. These cabling variations create a hardware incompatibility between different SCSI devices. Likewise, some SCSI devices just will not work with each other because of software incompatibilities.

In addition, SCSI devices can be classified as internal or as external devices. An internal SCSI device has no power supply of its own and, therefore, must be connected to one of the system's options power connectors. On the other hand, external SCSI devices come with built-in or plug-in power supplies that need to be connected to a commercial AC outlet. Therefore, when choosing a SCSI device, always inquire about compatibility between it and any other SCSI devices installed in the system.

Figure 5.4 depicts a 25-pin D-shell, a 50-pin Centronics, and a 68-pin Centronics-type SCSI connector used for external connections. Inside the computer, the SCSI specification uses 50-pin and 68-pin ribbon cables with BERG pin connectors.

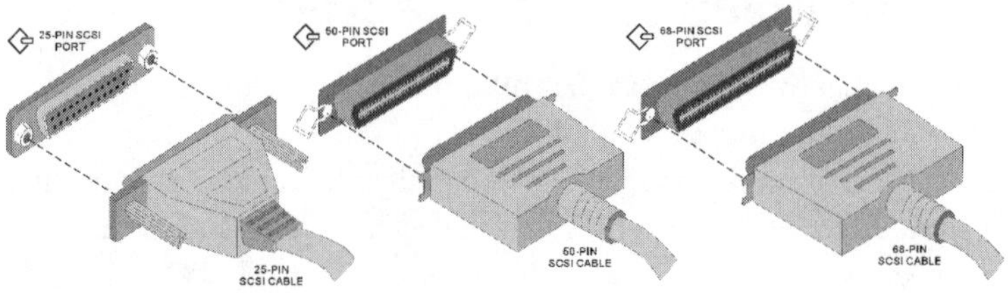

FIGURE 5.4
SCSI connectors.

SCSI Addressing

The SCSI specification permits up to eight SCSI devices to be connected together. The SCSI port can be daisy chained to permit up to six external peripherals to be connected to the system. To connect multiple SCSI devices to a SCSI host, all the devices, except the last one, must have two SCSI connectors: one for SCSI-In and one for SCSI-Out. It does not matter which connector is used for which function. If the device has only one SCSI connector, however, it must be connected to the end of the chain.

EXAM TIP

Remember how many devices can be daisy chained on a standard SCSI interface.

It is possible to use multiple SCSI host adapters within a single system to increase the number of devices that can be used. The system's first standard SCSI controller can handle up to seven (7) devices; an additional SCSI controller can boost the system to support up to 14 SCSI devices.

Each SCSI device in a chain must have a unique ID number assigned to it. Even though there are a total of eight possible *SCSI ID numbers* for each controller, only six are available for use with external devices. Most SCSI host adapter cards are set to SCSI-7 by default from their manufacturers. Historically, many manufacturers have classified the first internal hard drive as SCSI-0. In other cases, most notably IBM, the manufacturer routinely uses ID 2 for the first SCSI hard drive and ID 6 for the host adapter. In most newer systems, it typically doesn't matter which devices are set to which ID settings. However, if two SCSI devices in a system are set to the same ID number, one or both of them will appear invisible to the system. The priority levels assigned to SCSI devices are determined by their ID number, with the highest numbered device receiving the highest priority.

> **EXAM TIP**
> Be aware of how SCSI ID priorities are typically established and know which ID numbers are assumed automatically.

With older SCSI devices, address settings were established through jumpers on the host adapter card. Each device had a SCSI number selection switch or a set of configuration jumpers for establishing its ID number. Figure 5.5 illustrates a three-jumper configuration block that can be used to establish the SCSI ID number.

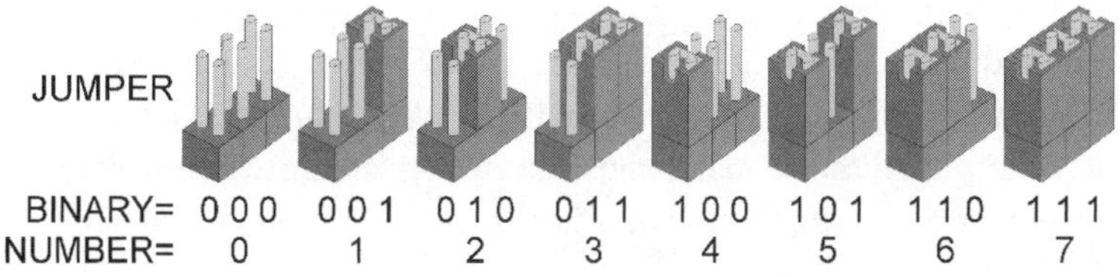

JUMPER

| BINARY= | 0 0 0 | 0 0 1 | 0 1 0 | 0 1 1 | 1 0 0 | 1 0 1 | 1 1 0 | 1 1 1 |
| NUMBER= | 0 | 1 | 2 | 3 | 4 | 5 | 6 | 7 |

FIGURE 5.5
Configuring a SCSI ID number.

In the figure, an open jumper pair can be counted as a binary 0, whereas a shorted pair represents a binary 1. With a three pair jumper block, it is possible to represent eight numbers (0 through 7). In PnP systems, the BIOS will configure the device addresses using information obtained directly from the SCSI host adapter during the boot-up process.

> **EXAM TIP**
> Know how to configure SCSI ID numbers using a 3-position, 2-pin jumper block.

CHALLENGE #2

You are installing a SCSI device on an AT-class machine and need to manually set the SCSI ID on the device. The device has a 3-position, 2-pin BERG jumper for configuration and you need to configure the device ID to 5. You have no documentation for the device, so you must guess at the setting. How would you arrange the three jumpers on the card? Explain your reasoning.

Before Plug-and-Play technology matured, SCSI hard drives were not configured as part of the system's CMOS setup function. However, newer BIOS versions are able to detect SCSI drives during the PnP process and can even be set to boot to a SCSI device. Older operating systems, such as DOS, Windows 3.*x*, and Windows 95 did not include support for SCSI devices. Therefore, SCSI drivers had to be loaded during the boot process before the system could communicate with the drive. However, Windows 9*x* and Windows 2000 do offer SCSI support. Because SCSI drives use a system level interface, they require no low-level formatting. Therefore, the second step involved in installing a SCSI drive is to partition it.

SCSI Termination

The SCSI daisy chain must be terminated with a resistor network pack at both ends. Single-connector SCSI devices are normally terminated internally. If not, a SCSI terminator cable (containing a built-in resistor pack) must be installed at the end of the chain. SCSI termination is a major cause of SCSI-related problems. Poor terminations cause a variety of different system problems including the following:

◆ Failed system startups

◆ Hard drive crashes

◆ Random system failures

The *terminating resistors* absorb electric energy at the ends of the daisy chain and prevent it from being reflected back into the cable where it can cause interference with other signals. The "ends of the chain" are the thought that you should concentrate on. If the host adapter is in the middle of the chain (say it supports one cable to an external connection and another to the internal hard drive and CD-ROM drive), it would not represent either end of the chain.

CHALLENGE #3

You are installing SCSI devices in a new system. Inside the case, there is a SCSI host adapter card, a hard disk drive, and a CD-ROM drive. The SCSI cabling runs from the host adapter to the hard drive and ends at the CD-ROM drive. External to the case, you must make connections for a SCSI flat bed scanner and a SCSI printer. The external cabling runs from the host adapter to the scanner and ends at the printer. Where should the terminator packs be installed?

SCSI Specifications

The maximum recommended length for a complete standard SCSI chain is 20 feet (6 meters). Unless the cables are heavily shielded, however, they become susceptible to data corruption caused by induced noise. Therefore, a maximum single SCSI segment of less than 3 feet (1 meter) is recommended. Don't forget the length of the internal cabling when dealing with SCSI cable distances. You can realistically count on about 3–5 feet of internal cable, so reduce the maximum total length of the chain to about 15 feet (4.5 meters).

An updated SCSI specification was developed by the ANSI committee to double the number of data lines in the standard interface. It also adds balanced, dual-line drivers that enable much faster data transfer speeds to be used. This implementation is referred to as *Wide SCSI-2*. The specification expands the SCSI specification into a 16/32-bit bus standard and increases the cable and connector specification to 68 pins.

An additional improvement increased the synchronous data transfer option for the interface from 5Mbps to 10Mbps. This implementation became known as *Fast SCSI-2*. Under this system, the system and the I/O device conduct non-data message, command, and status operations in 8-bit asynchronous mode. After agreeing on a larger,

EXAM TIP

Memorize the permissible lengths stated for SCSI cables and daisy chains.

or faster, file-transfer format, they conduct transfers using an agreed upon word size and transmission mode. The increased speed of the Fast SCSI specification reduced the maximum length of the SCSI chain to about 10 feet. Fast SCSI-2 connections use 50-pin connectors.

A third version brought together both improvements and became known as *Wide Fast SCSI-2*. This version of the standard doubles the bus size to 16 bits and employs the faster transfer methods to provide a maximum bus speed of 20Mbps supporting a chain of up to 15 additional devices.

A newer update, referred to as *Ultra SCSI*, makes provisions for a special high-speed serial transfer mode and special communications media, such as fiber-optic cabling. This update has been combined with both wide and fast revisions to produce:

◆ ULTRA SCSI

◆ ULTRA2 SCSI

◆ WIDE ULTRA SCSI

◆ WIDE ULTRA2 SCSI

◆ WIDE ULTRA3 SCSI

The addition of the Wide specification doubles the bus width and number of devices that can be serviced by the interface. Likewise, the Ultra designation indicates a speed increase because of improved technology. Combining the two technologies will yield a 4X increase in data throughput (that is, Wide Ultra SCSI = 40Mbps compared to Ultra SCSI = 20Mbps and Wide and Fast SCSI = 10).

The latest SCSI specification, referred to as *Ultra 320 SCSI*, boosts the maximum bus speed to 320Mbps, using a 16-bit bus and supporting up to 15 external devices. The Ultra 320 SCSI connection employs a special 80-pin *Single Contact Attachment* (*SCA*) *connector*.

The increased speed capabilities of the SCSI interfaces make them attractive for intensive applications such as large file servers for networks and multimedia video stations. However, the EIDE interface is generally more widely used because of its lower cost and nearly equal performance.

EXAM TIP

Know the number of devices that can be attached to IDE, EIDE, and standard SCSI interfaces.

Table 5.1 contrasts the specifications of the SCSI and IDE interfaces.

TABLE 5.1

SCSI/IDE SPECIFICATIONS

Interface	Bus Size	# Devices	Async. Speed	Sync. Speed
IDE (ATA-1)	16 bits	2	4MB/s	3.3/5.2/8.3MB/s
EIDE (ATA-2)	16 bits	4	4MB/s	11/16MB/s
SCSI (SCSI-1)	8 bits	7	2MB/s	5MB/s
Wide SCSI (SCSI-2)	8/16 bits	15	2MB/s	5MB/s
Fast SCSI (SCSI-2)	8/16 bits	7	2MB/s	5/10MB/s
Wide Fast SCSI (SCSI-2)	8/16 bits	15	2MB/s	10/20MB/s
Ultra SCSI	8 bits	7	2MB/s	10/20MB/s
Ultra WIDE SCSI (SCSI-3)	16 bits	15	2MB/s	10/20/40MB/s
Ultra2 SCSI	8 bits	7	2MB/s	10/20/40MB/s
Wide Ultra2 SCSI	16 bits	15	2MB/s	10/20/40/80MB/s
Wide Ultra3 SCSI	16 bits	15	2MB/s	10/20/40/160MB/s
Ultra320 SCSI	16 bits	15	2MB/s	10/20/40/320MB/s

CHAPTER SUMMARY

Modern PCs typically employ IDE disk drives for their mass storage needs. A second type of system level devices has also been adapted to PC-compatible systems—these are devices that employ versions of the SCSI interface.

This chapter covered the installation and configuration of these two types of devices in some detail. It began with discussions of the IDE and EIDE interface standards commonly associated with PC-compatible systems, The remainder of the chapter turned to installing and configuring the more complex (and less widely used) array of SCSI interface standards.

At this point, review the objectives listed at the beginning of the chapter to be certain that you understand each point and can perform each task listed there. Afterward, answer the review questions that follow to verify your knowledge of the information.

KEY TERMS

- AT Attachment (ATA)
- AT Attachment Packet Interface (ATAPI)
- ATA-2
- Cable select
- Enhanced IDE (EIDE)
- Fast SCSI
- Integrated drive electronics
- SCSI ID numbers
- Single Contact Attachment (SCA) connector
- Small Computer System Interface (SCSI)
- Terminating resistors
- Ultra ATA 100
- Ultra ATA 66
- Ultra DMA (UDMA) protocol
- Ultra SCSI
- Wide Fast SCSI-2
- Wide SCSI-2

APPLY YOUR KNOWLEDGE

Review Questions

1. Which of these configurations can be set on an IDE drive? (Select all that apply.)

   A. Master

   B. Primary

   C. Single

   D. Slave

2. How many devices can be daisy chained on a single standard SCSI controller?

   A. 2

   B. 7

   C. 8

   D. 15

3. On an ATX system board that integrates the EIDE interface connection into the board, how many devices can be attached to each interface connection?

   A. 1

   B. 2

   C. 3

   D. 4

4. What is the maximum permissible length for a standard SCSI daisy chain, including the internal cable?

   A. 10 feet

   B. 15 feet

   C. 20 feet

   D. 25 feet

5. What is the permissible length for a standard SCSI cable segment?

   A. 3 feet

   B. 6 feet

   C. 9 feet

   D. 12 feet

6. What distinctive feature enables you to quickly identify an Ultra ATA 66 interface cable?

   A. Connectors are blue.

   B. Cable is blue.

   C. Cable has 40 wires.

   D. Cable has 80 wires.

7. How are SCSI devices identified and differentiated from each other?

   A. By the order in which they are connected on the cable.

   B. Jumpers determine master/slave/single status.

   C. By the ID number that is assigned to the device.

   D. By the drive letter that is assigned to the device.

8. How is IDE support provided for system boards that have integrated IDE controllers?

   A. Through the BIOS firmware

   B. Through an installed driver

   C. By the operating system

   D. Through an installed application

9. If you are working on an older Pentium system board that supports a single IDE connector, how could you install a large HDD, a CD-ROM drive, and an IDE tape drive?

    A. Install a SCSI adapter card.

    B. Install an IDE adapter card.

    C. This type of motherboard can only use 1 IDE device.

    D. This type of motherboard can only use 2 IDE devices.

10. Which of these standard SCSI devices has the highest priority?

    A. SCSI-0

    B. SCSI-1

    C. SCSI-6

    D. SCSI-7

11. How many SCSI devices can be attached to a Wide SCSI host adapter?

    A. 7

    B. 8

    C. 15

    D. 16

12. Which SCSI ID is typically used for the system's internal hard disk drive?

    A. SCSI-0

    B. SCSI-1

    C. SCSI-7

    D. SCSI-8

13. What is the maximum length for an external standard SCSI daisy chain?

    A. 3 feet

    B. 10 feet

    C. 15 feet

    D. 20 feet

14. What is the maximum permissible length for a Fast SCSI daisy chain?

    A. 10 feet

    B. 15 feet

    C. 20 feet

    D. 25 feet

15. Which SCSI ID is typically used for the system's SCSI adapter?

    A. SCSI-0

    B. SCSI-6

    C. SCSI-7

    D. SCSI-8

16. If a 2-pin jumper block on an adapter card is used to represent a binary digit, what is the highest number that can be represented by a 3-jumper block combination?

    A. 3

    B. 7

    C. 8

    D. 16

APPLY YOUR KNOWLEDGE

17. After installing a scanner to the end of a SCSI daisy chain, you discover that both the scanner and your SCSI CD-ROM drive have stopped working. What is likely to be the problem?

    A. The ribbon cable is bad.

    B. The scanner is using an incompatible protocol.

    C. Both devices are set to slave.

    D. Both devices are using the same ID number.

18. When installing SCSI devices in a system, which device or devices should be terminated?

    A. All SCSI devices.

    B. The first and last SCSI device.

    C. Only the last SCSI device.

    D. SCSI devices do not require termination.

19. An internal SCSI ribbon cable is outfitted with a _____ connector.

    A. 25-pin

    B. 40-pin

    C. 50-pin

    D. 68-pin

20. Which of the following is not a valid SCSI connector?

    A. 25-pin DB

    B. 34-pin Centronics

    C. 50-pin Centronics

    D. 68-pin Centronics

21. You have been given an ISA SCSI host adapter to install. It has a single 3-pin jumper. How many different ID numbers are possible to assign on this card?

    A. 3

    B. 7

    C. 8

    D. 16

22. Which part of the system is responsible for assigning drive letters for IDE drives?

    A. BIOS

    B. User

    C. IDE controller

    D. Operating system

Answers and Explanations

1. **A, C, D.** Most IDE drives come from the manu-facturer configured for operation as a single drive, or as the master drive in a multidrive system. To install the drive as a second, or slave drive, it is usually necessary to install, remove, or move a jumper block. For more information, see the section "Configuring IDE Drives."

2. **B.** A system's first SCSI controller can handle up to seven (7) devices; an additional SCSI con-troller can boost the system to support up to 14 SCSI devices. For more information, see the section "SCSI Addressing."

APPLY YOUR KNOWLEDGE

3. **B.** The EIDE controller supplies two IDE interfaces that can each handle a master and a slave device in a daisy chained configuration. For more information, see the section "Configuring IDE Drives."

4. **C.** Maximum recommended length for a complete standard SCSI chain is 20 feet (6 meters). For more information, see the section "SCSI Specifications."

5. **A.** A maximum single SCSI segment of less than 3 feet (1 meter) is recommended. For more information, see the section "SCSI Specifications."

6. **D.** Ultra DMA (UDMA)—ATA-4/Ultra ATA 66 and Ultra ATA 100—extend the high data throughput capabilities of the ATA-3 bus by doubling the number of conductors in the IDE signal cable to 80. Although the number of wires has doubled, the IDE connector has remained compatible with the 40-pin IDE connection, but each pin has been provided with its own ground conductor in the cable. For more information, see the section "Advanced EIDE Specifications."

7. **C.** The priority levels assigned to SCSI devices are determined by their ID number, with the highest numbered device receiving the highest priority. Each SCSI device in a chain must have a unique ID number assigned to it. For more information, see the section "SCSI Addressing."

8. **A.** The IDE controller structure is an integrated portion of most PC system boards. This structure includes BIOS and chipset support for the IDE version the board will support, as well as the IDE host connector. For more information, see the section "Advanced EIDE Specifications."

9. **B.** Some older systems that employ system level interfaces, such as an IDE interface, employ an adapter card. These cards are referred to as host adapters rather than controller cards because they have no intelligent control devices on them. They simply offer physical extensions of the system buses (usually ISA slots) to the I/O device. For more information, see the section "Integrated Drive Electronics Interface."

10. **D.** The priority levels assigned to SCSI devices are determined by their ID number, with the highest numbered device receiving the highest priority. For more information, see the section "SCSI Addressing."

11. **C.** A Wide SCSI (SCSI-2) controller can control up to 15 additional devices. See Table 5.1: SCSI/IDE Specifications. For more information, see the section "SCSI Specifications."

12. **A.** Historically, manufacturers have classified the first internal hard drive as SCSI-0. For more information, see the section "SCSI Addressing."

13. **C.** Maximum recommended length for a complete standard SCSI chain is 20 feet (6 meters). You can realistically count on about 3–5 feet of internal cable, so reduce the maximum total length of the chain to about 15 feet (4.5 meters). For more information, see the section "SCSI Termination."

14. **A.** The Fast SCSI (Fast SCSI-2) specification allows transfers of up to 10Mbps, and reduces the maximum length of the SCSI chain to about 10 feet. Fast SCSI allows up to seven devices to be connected using a 50-pin connector. For more information, see the section "SCSI Specifications."

15. **C.** Traditionally, SCSI host adapter cards are set to SCSI-7 by default from their manufacturers. For more information, see the section "SCSI Addressing."

16. **B.** An open jumper pair can be counted as a binary 0, whereas a shorted pair represents a binary 1. With a three pair jumper block, it is possible to represent eight numbers (0 through 7). For more information, see the section "SCSI Addressing."

17. **D.** Each SCSI device in a chain must have a unique ID number assigned to it. Even though there are a total of eight possible SCSI ID numbers for each controller, only six are available for use with external devices. If two SCSI devices are set to the same ID number, one or both will appear invisible to the system. For more information, see the section "SCSI Addressing."

18. **B.** The SCSI daisy chain must be terminated with a resistor at both ends. For more information, see the section "SCSI Termination."

19. **C.** The SCSI interface uses a 50-pin signal cable arrangement. Internally, the cable is a 50-pin flat ribbon cable. For more information, see the section "SCSI Cables and Connectors."

20. **B.** The version of the SCSI interface used in the Apple Macintosh employs a variation of the standard that features a proprietary, miniature 25-pin D-shell connector. A 50-pin shielded cable with Centronics-like connectors is used for external SCSI connections. A revised 68-pin P-cable format, using Centronics connectors, was introduced to support 16-bit transfers in the SCSI-3 specification. For more information, see the section "SCSI Cables and Connectors."

21. **C.** With a three pair jumper block, it is possible to represent eight numbers—0 through 7. For more information, see the section "SCSI Addressing."

22. **D.** Under Microsoft operating systems, the primary partitions of multiple IDE hard drives are assigned the first logical drive identifiers. If an IDE drive is partitioned into two logical drives, the system will identify them as the C: drive and the D: drive. If a second IDE drive is added as a slave drive with two additional logical drives, it will reassign the partitions on the first drive to be logical drives C: and E:, and the partitions on the slave drive will be D: and F:. For more information, see the section "Configuring IDE Drives."

Challenge Solutions

1. The extended partition of the hard drive should show up as the E: drive. The primary partition will naturally be C:, whereas the master drive on IDE2 will be designated as drive D:. This will leave the F: designation for the slave drive on IDE2. For more information, see the section "Configuring IDE Drives."

2. The most logical arrangement of the jumpers to configure the device for ID 5 would be On/Off/On. This will digitally represent the binary number 5 (101) if the Jumper On condition is used to represent the value 1. For more information, see the section "SCSI Addressing."

3. The terminator packs should be installed on the printer and the CD-ROM drive. The host adapter does not represent either end of the chain; it is in the middle of the chain. For more information, see the section "SCSI Termination."

APPLY YOUR KNOWLEDGE

Suggested Readings and Resources

1. HDD Installation
   http://www.pcguide.com/proc/physinst/
   hdd.htm

2. ATA/IDE
   http://webopedia.internet.com/TERM/A/
   ATA.html

3. SCSI Trade Association
   www.scsita.org

4. SCSI Connectors
   www.paralan.com/sediff.html

5. SCSI Termination
   http://www.scsita.org/aboutscsi/
   SCSI_Termination_Tutorial.html

6. Tom's Storage Guide
   http://www6.tomshardware.com/storage/
   index.html

This chapter helps you to prepare for the Core Hardware module of the A+ Certification examination by covering the following objectives within the "Domain 1.0: Installation, Configuration, and Upgrading" section.

1.7 Identify proper procedures for installing and configuring peripheral devices.

Content might include the following:

- **Monitor/Video card**
- **Modem**
- **USB peripherals and hubs**
- **IEEE-1284**
- **IEEE-1394**
- **External storage**

Portable system components:

- **Docking stations**
- **PC Cards**
- **Port replicators**
- **Infrared devices**

▶ In addition to installing hard drives and peripheral devices that connect to standard I/O ports, technicians must be able to successfully install and configure peripheral devices (or systems) that connect to the system in other ways—such as through the system's expansion slots. This chapter deals with installing the system's video output components, internal and external modems, and alternative data storage systems.

CHAPTER 6

Installing and Configuring Peripheral Devices

OUTLINE

To prepare for the Installation, Configuration, and Upgrading objective of the Core Hardware exam,

▶ Read the objectives at the beginning of this chapter.

▶ Study the information in this chapter.

▶ Review the objectives listed earlier in this chapter.

▶ Perform any step-by-step procedures in the text.

▶ Answer the review questions at the end of the chapter and check your results.

▶ Use the PrepLogic test engine on the CD-ROM that accompanies this book for additional Review and Exam Questions concerning this material.

▶ Review the exam tips scattered throughout the chapter and make certain that you are comfortable with each point.

INTRODUCTION

This chapter covers installation and configuration processes associated with different peripheral devices commonly used with PC-compatible systems. These devices include video display systems, modems, and external storage systems.

The final section of the chapter deals with different types of peripheral devices typically associated with portable computer systems. These peripherals include external drive units, docking stations, and port replicators, along with PC Cards and services and infrared devices.

After completing the chapter, you should be able to successfully install and configure common peripheral devices, including video monitors, modems, and external storage devices.

VIDEO/MONITOR SYSTEMS

The *video display* is one of the easiest systems to add to the PC. The components associated with the video display are depicted in Figure 6.1. The video adapter card typically plugs in to one of the system's expansion slots. Most newer video adapter cards are designed for use with AGP slots. Some new video cards use an AGP video chip but are designed to fit in a PCI slot. Older video cards were designed to work with PCI or ISA slots. The monitor's signal cable plugs in to the 3-row, 15-pin female D-shell connector on the back of the video adapter card. The monitor's power cord should be plugged in to a commercial wall outlet. On AT-class systems, an outlet on the power supply could be used to turn the monitor on and off along with the system unit.

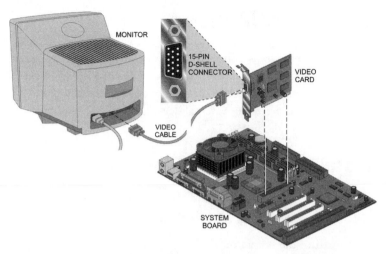

FIGURE 6.1
Installing video system components.

The Windows operating systems will recognize a new video card through the PnP process when the system is turned on. The PnP's New PCI or AGP device recognition utility will ask you to select the driver for the new video card. At this point, you can select the Windows Auto-detect option or you can manually install a driver from the adapter's utility disk. The default values for VGA/PCI-compatible adapters include a standard 640x480 pixel screen resolution at 16-colors, with a refresh rate of 60Hz.

The adapter's color, resolution, and refresh settings can be manually optimized through the Display icon in the Windows Control Panel. Some users prefer higher color values (that is, 32-bit instead of 16-, or 24-bit operation), whereas others prefer higher screen resolutions (1024x768 or higher). Generally, the fastest refresh rate possible is desirable. Some high-end video cards include an auto-optimize function that automatically adjusts the refresh rate for the selected resolution and monitor type.

In a command prompt mode—such as before Windows has been installed, or when working in one of the Windows 9x or Windows 2000 Safe Mode options—the video display should come up in standard VGA mode (640x480) with no further effort. If the Windows operating system is being used, the video adapter's driver must be loaded before the operating system can be run.

INSTALLING MODEMS

In most cases, the steps associated with installing a modem are identical to those involved with other peripheral devices. However, the steps for installing a modem will vary somewhat depending on whether it is an internal or external device.

Installing an Internal Modem

Use the following steps to install an internal modem.

1. **Prepare the system for installation.**

   A. Turn the system **off**.

   B. Remove the cover from the system unit.

   C. Locate a compatible empty expansion slot.

   D. Remove the expansion slot cover from the rear of the system unit.

2. **Configure the modem's IRQ and COM settings.**

   A. Refer to the modem user's manual regarding any IRQ and COM jumper or switch settings.

   B. Record the card's default IRQ and COM settings.

   C. Set the modem's configuration jumpers to operate the modem as COM2.

3. **Install the modem card in the system.**

   A. Install the modem card in the expansion slot.

   B. Reinstall the screw to secure the modem card to the back panel of the system unit.

   C. Connect the phone line to the appropriate connector on the modem, as shown in Figure 6.2.

   D. Connect the other end of the phone line to the commercial phone jack.

4. **Disable any competing COM ports (such as COM2 on the system board).**

   A. Disable COM2 in the CMOS Configuration utility.

5. **Finish the hardware installation.**

   A. Replace the system unit cover.

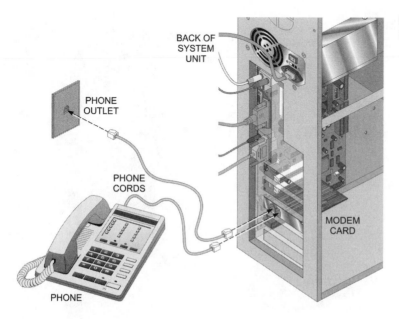

FIGURE 6.2
Installing an internal modem.

Installing an External Modem

Use the following steps to install an external modem.

1. **Make the modem connections.**

   A. Connect the serial cable to the 25-pin serial port at the rear of the system.

   B. Connect the opposite end of the cable to the RS-232 connector of the external modem unit.

   C. Connect the phone line to the appropriate connector on the modem.

   D. Connect the other end of the phone line to the phone system jack.

E. Optionally, connect the phone to the appropriate connector on the modem.

F. Verify that the power switch or power supply is turned off.

G. Connect the power supply to the external modem unit.

H. Verify this connection arrangement in Figure 6.3.

FIGURE 6.3
Installing an external modem.

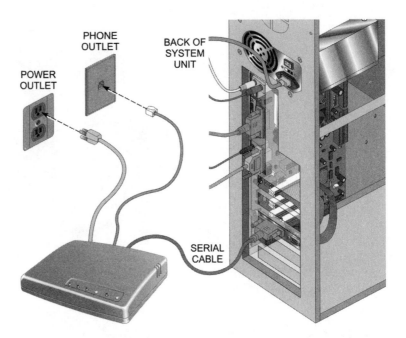

2. **Enable the system's internal support circuitry.**

   A. Remove the cover from system unit.

   B. Enable COM2 on the system board (through the CMOS Setup utility).

   C. Replace the system unit cover.

CHALLENGE #1

A customer has an internal ISA modem that they want you to install in a typical AT-style Pentium computer system. The system uses a serial mouse and has a sound card along with a printer attached to the first parallel port. The modem has jumpers that

can be used to configure the card for IRQ 3, 4, 5, or 7. What two
actions do you need to take to configure the modem for operation
in this system?

Modem Configuration

Examine the communications software being used to drive the
modem to determine which elements need to be configured using
the following steps.

1. **Install and configure the communications software
   package.**

   A. Locate the modem's communication software.

   B. Locate the software documentation.

   C. Locate the installation instructions inside the manual.

   D. Follow the instructions in the manual and on the screen to
      install the software.

   E. Configure the software to match the system's hardware
      settings.

2. **Set up Windows COM ports and character frame
   information.**

   A. Establish the baud rate, character frame, and flow control
      information in the Windows Control Panel.

   B. Set up the IRQ, COM port, and base address settings in
      the Control Panel for the COM port the modem is using.

Establishing Protocols

To maintain an orderly flow of information between the computer
and the modem, and between the modem and another modem, a
protocol, or set of rules governing the transfer of information, must
be in place. All the participants in the "conversation" must use the

same protocols to communicate. Two distinct classes of protocols are in widespread use with modems today. These include

◆ Hardware-oriented protocols—Protocols that are tied to the use of particular interface pins to control data flow. The most basic hardware protocol standard is the RS-232C serial-interface standard.

◆ Control-code–oriented protocols—Protocols in which control codes are sent across the data lines to control data flow, as opposed to using hardware control lines. Most data-flow control is performed using the control-code class of protocols. In this class of protocols, three types are in widespread use: X-ON/X-OFF, ACK/NAK, and ETX/ACK.

EXAM TIP

Know the fundamental difference between parity error checking and error-checking and correcting protocols.

Several *error-checking and correcting* (*ECC*) file transfer protocols have been developed for modem communications packages. These protocols are capable of not only detecting bit-level errors, but can also recalculate and repair the defective bit in the bit stream. The parity-checking scheme employed with common memory systems is simply a single-bit error checking operation. If an incorrect bit is detected in the memory read back, a Parity Check error is created and an NMI signal is passed to the microprocessor. Some of the more common modem protocols include Xmodem, Ymodem, Zmodem, and Kermit.

Advanced communication protocols use data compression techniques to reduce the volume of data that must be transmitted. Each protocol involves a mathematical algorithm that reads the data and converts it into encoded words. The modem at the receiving end must use the same algorithm to decode the words and restore them to their original form.

Character Framing

Within a particular protocol, a number of parameters must be agreed upon before an efficient exchange of information can occur. Chief among these parameters are character type and character framing. Basically, *character type* refers to the character set, or alphabet, understood by the devices. Depending on the systems, the character set might be an 8-bit ASCII line code, a 7-bit *ASCII code* (with an error-checking bit), or an *EBCDIC code*.

Character framing refers to the total number of the bits used to transmit a character. This includes the length of the coded character, as well as the number and type of overhead bits required for transmitting it. A common character-framing scheme calls for a start bit, seven data bits, an odd-parity bit, and a stop bit, as depicted in Figure 6.4. An additional bit is often added to the frame for error-checking purposes.

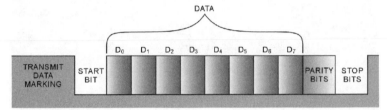

FIGURE 6.4
Asynchronous character format.

Although this is a typical character-framing technique, it is not universal throughout the industry. The problem here is one of device comprehension. The local unit might be using a 10-bit character frame consisting of a start bit, seven data bits, an odd-parity bit, and a stop bit. If the remote system is using something besides 7-bit, odd-parity ASCII, with one stop bit, however, the response from it would be unintelligible as anything written in English. The composition of the character frame must be the same at both the sending and receiving ends of the transmission.

CONFIGURING ADVANCED PORTS

Most new I/O ports and bus types (that is, USB, IEEE-1394, PCMCIA, and IrDA) feature hot insertion and removal capabilities for their devices, as well as PnP operation. The devices that connect to these ports and buses are designed to be plugged in and removed as needed. Installing these devices is practically a hands-off operation.

Installing a USB or Firewire device normally involves the following steps:

1. Enable the USB resources in the CMOS Setup screen, as illustrated in Figure 6. 5. In some cases, this involves enabling the port and reserving an IRQ resource for the device.

2. Plug the device in to an open USB connector.

3. Wait for the operating system to recognize the device and configure it through the PnP process.

FIGURE 6.5
Enabling the USB resources.

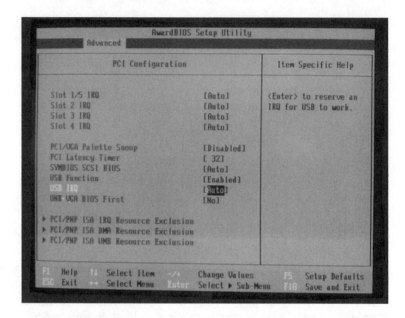

In the case of the Microsoft Windows 2000 operating system, it will detect the presence of the USB or Firewire device and start its Found New Hardware Wizard program, depicted in Figure 6.6, to guide you through the installation process. Simply follow the instructions provided by the wizard to set up the new device—there is no need to shut down or turn off the computer.

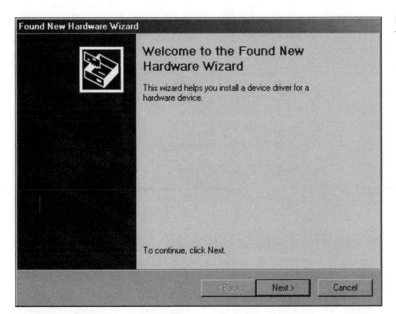

FIGURE 6.6
The Windows Found New Hardware Wizard.

IEEE-1284 Devices

Generally speaking, one of the least difficult I/O devices to add to a microcomputer system is a device that uses the system's parallel printer port. This is largely because, from the beginning of the PC era, a parallel printer has been one of the most standard pieces of equipment to add to the system.

This standardization has led to fairly direct installation procedures for most devices. Obtain an IEEE-1284 compliant cable and plug it in to the appropriate LPT port on the back of the computer. Connect the Centronic-compatible end of the cable to the device, plug the power cord in to the device, load a device driver to configure the software for the correct printer, and print.

Regardless of the type of device being installed, the steps for adding an IEEE-2184 device to a system are basically the same. Connect the device to the correct I/O port at the computer system. Make sure that the port is enabled. Set up the appropriate device drivers. Figure 6.7 summarizes these steps.

FIGURE 6.7
Printer steps.

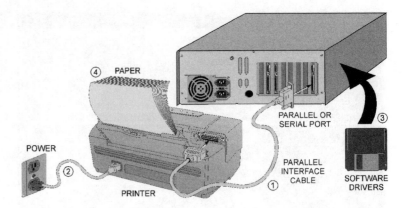

PERIPHERAL STORAGE DEVICES

External storage devices normally connect to options adapter cards installed in the system board's expansion slots. They also tend to employ separate, external power-supply units.

Several newer storage technologies, such as removable hard drive media, have been designed to take advantage of the enhanced parallel port specifications of modern systems. These devices can be connected directly into the system's parallel port, or can be connected to the system through another device that is connected to the port. The device's installation software is used to configure it for use in the system.

Installing External Storage Devices

The general procedure for installing external storage devices is

1. **Configure the device for operation.**

   A. Refer to the device's user manual regarding any configuration jumper or switch settings.

   B. Record the card's default configuration settings.

   C. Set the device's configuration jumpers to operate at the default setting.

2. **Install the device's adapter card (if necessary).**

   A. Turn the system off.

   B. Remove the cover from the system unit.

   C. Locate a compatible empty expansion slot.

   D. Remove the expansion slot cover from the rear of the system unit.

   E. Install the adapter card in the expansion slot.

   F. Reinstall the screw to secure the card to the back panel of the system unit.

3. **Make the device's external connections.**

   A. Connect the device's signal cable to the appropriate connector at the rear of the system.

   B. Connect the opposite end of the cable to the device.

   C. Verify that the power switch or power supply is turned off.

   D. Connect the power supply to the external storage unit.

4. **Configure the device's software.**

   A. Turn the system on.

   B. Check the CMOS Setup to ensure that the port setting is correct.

   C. Run the device's installation routine.

External Drive Units

The first laptops and notebooks incorporated the traditional single floppy-drive and single hard-drive arrangement that was typical in most desktop units. As CD-ROM drives and discs became the norm for new operating systems and software packages, a dilemma was created. There is simply not enough room in most notebook computers for three, normal-size drives. Even using reduced-size drives, the size limitations of most portables require that one of the three major drives be external.

Typically, the first item to be dropped from a new notebook design is the internal floppy drive. So much of the latest software is distributed on CD-ROM that those drives now have preference in newer designs. Because large volumes of software are still available on floppy disks (and so many users have cherished data stored on floppy disks), an external FDD is a common add-on option for new notebooks.

The external floppy comes as a complete unit with an external housing and a signal cable. As with other external devices, it requires an independent power source, such as an AC adapter pack. The external floppy drive's signal cable generally connects to a special FDD connector.

External CD-ROM Devices

Prior to the CD-ROM drive becoming an accepted part of the notebook PC, some manufacturers produced external CD-ROM drives for use with these machines. They are still available as add-ons for all types of PCs. External CD-ROM drives typically connect to a SCSI host adapter or to an enhanced parallel port. The latter connection requires a fully functional, bi-directional parallel port and a special software device driver.

Figure 6.8 illustrates the installation of an external SCSI CD-ROM drive. Because the drive is external, connecting it to the system usually involves connecting a couple of cables together. Connect the CD-ROM's power supply to the external drive unit. Before making this connection, verify that the power switch, or power supply, is turned off. Connect the signal cable to the computer. Finally, connect the opposite end of the cable to the external CD-ROM unit. Complete the installation by installing the CD-ROM driver software on the system's hard disk drive.

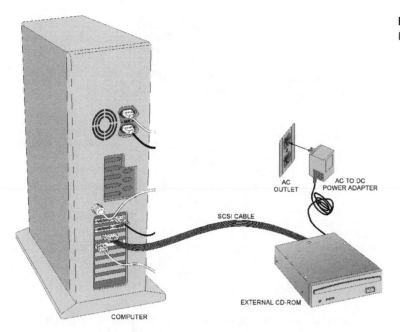

FIGURE 6.8
Installing an external CD-ROM drive.

PORTABLE PERIPHERALS

The basic portable should contain all the devices the user needs to perform work away from the office. Users have become accustomed to using additional items with their computers, however. For this reason, portable computers typically offer a full range of I/O port types. In addition, the portable computer manufacturers have produced an extensive array of products that can be added to a basic portable system to enhance its performance.

Docking Stations

A *docking station*, or docking port, is a specialized structure that permits the notebook unit to be inserted into it. When the notebook is inside, the docking port extends its expansion bus so that it can be used with a collection of desktop devices, such as an AC power source, a full-sized keyboard and CRT monitor, as well as modems, mice, and standard PC port connectors. Figure 6.9 depicts a typical docking station.

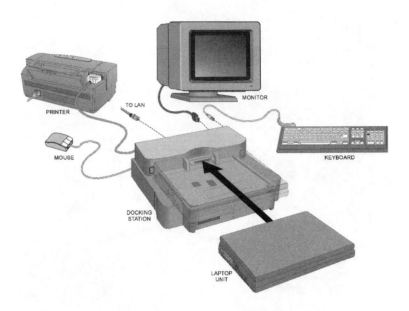

The notebook and the docking station communicate with each other through a special *docking-port connector* in the rear of the notebook. When the notebook is inserted into the docking station, its extension bus plugs in to the expansion connector in the notebook. Most docking stations provide standard full-size expansion slots so that non-notebook peripheral devices, such as network adapters and sound cards, can be used with the system. Docking stations might also provide additional PCMCIA slots for the notebook computer. When the notebook is in the docking station, its normal I/O devices (keyboard, display, and pointing device) are normally disabled and the docking station's peripherals take over.

Docking stations are proprietary to the portable computer they were designed to work with. The docking-port connection in the docking station must correctly align with the connector in the notebook. The notebook unit must also fit correctly within the docking-station opening. Because there are no standards for these systems, the chances of two different manufacturers locating the connectors or designing the same case outline are very remote.

Port Replicators

Many notebook computer manufacturers offer devices similar to docking stations that are called *port replicators*. These devices plug in to the notebook computer and contain common PC ports, such as serial and parallel ports. The purpose of theses devices is to permit users to attach portable computers to standard, non-portable devices such as printers and monitors.

Notebook manufacturers typically offer port replicators as additional proprietary options for their computers. Although these systems are similar to docking stations, they do not provide the additional expansion slots for adding options adapter cards and disk drives found in docking stations.

Installing PC Cards

Although portable computers do not include standard desktop expansion slots for adding peripheral devices to the system, they do typically include a couple of PC Card slots. Most notebooks provide two PCMCIA slots that can accept a wide variety of I/O device types. PC Cards are relatively easy to install in a PnP system that has the PCMCIA card services function running. Simply slide the card into an open PC Card slot and turn the machine on. The PnP function should detect the card in the slot and configure it with the proper drivers for the type of device it is.

The operating system must support the PCMCIA slots at two levels—at the socket level (universal support for all PCMCIA devices) and at the card level (specific drivers to handle the function of the particular card installed). Because PCMCIA cards are hot swappable, the operating system's socket service must update the system when a new card is installed or an existing card is removed. If not, the system would lose track of its actual resources. The card service portion delivers the correct device driver for the installed PC Card (that is, when a PC Card modem is removed and replaced with a LAN card, the operating system must automatically update its capability of controlling and using the new card).

In many cases, the PC Card must furnish a standard I/O connector for connection to the full sized world. Often, these connections are made through nonstandard connectors at the PC Card end but terminate in standard connectors at the I/O device end. For example, a PC Card LAN card, such as the one depicted in Figure 6.10, is not physically thick enough to accommodate a standard RJ-45 plug used with Ethernet networks. To overcome this, a thin connector is attached to the card and a standard connector is used at the other end of the cable. Depending on their specific function, some PC Cards require an external power supply to acquire enough power to operate efficiently.

FIGURE 6.10
PC Card connections.

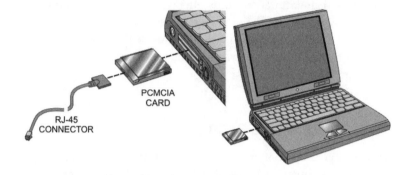

Installing PC Card Support

There are three possibilities for the card services utility to deliver the proper drivers to the card:

◆ The operating system, such as Windows 9*x* or Windows 2000, immediately recognizes the card and installs the driver without restarting.

◆ The operating system recognizes the card and has its driver, but needs to reboot the operating system for the driver to be loaded.

◆ The operating system does not recognize the card installed and requires an external driver to be loaded. Under Windows 9*x*, a PC Card Wizard is started to guide the user through the driver installation process. Windows 2000 does not supply a PC Card Installation wizard.

To install the PC Card (PCMCIA) Wizard on your Windows 9*x* system, you must navigate the Start, Settings, Control Panel path and access the Add/Remove Programs applet. Click the Windows Setup tab, select a category, and then click the Details tab. If you don't see the component listed in the Add/Remove Programs dialog box, it might be one that is only present on the Windows 9*x* distribution CD. In this case, you can download the component from an online service, such as The Microsoft Network, or from the Microsoft Download Service at the main Microsoft Web site.

At different times, you might want to stop a PC Card driver from being loaded. To turn off support for a PC Card, access the Device Manager tab and expand the PC Card slot node. Then, double-click the PC Card controller and in the Device usage area, check the Disable in This Hardware Profile check box option.

The proper procedure for removing a PC Card from the computer begins with clicking the PC Card status indicator on the taskbar. Then, select the command to stop the operation of the PC Card you want to remove. When the operating system prompts you, physically remove the PC Card from the system.

CHALLENGE #2

You are traveling away from your office, and you want to get as much work done on the airplane as possible. You notice that the notebook takes several minutes during the PnP configuration portion of the boot process. Your notebook has a PCMCIA modem and network card, and you want to disable these devices while you are traveling so that their drivers do not need to be loaded. How can you do this without permanently removing them? (You want to use them when you get back to the office.)

Infrared Devices

Installing an IrDA device in an infrared-enabled system is a fairly simple process. When an IrDA device is installed in the system, a Wireless Link icon appears in the Windows Control Panel as depicted in Figure 6.11. (Remember, infrared port operations must first be enabled through the CMOS Setup utility.) When another IrDA device comes within range of the host port, the *Infrared* icon will appear on the Windows desktop and in the taskbar. In the case of an IrDA printer, a printer icon will appear in the Printer folder.

EXAM TIP

Be aware that IrDA operations must be enabled in CMOS before any infrared activities can occur.

FIGURE 6.11
The Windows Wireless Link icon.

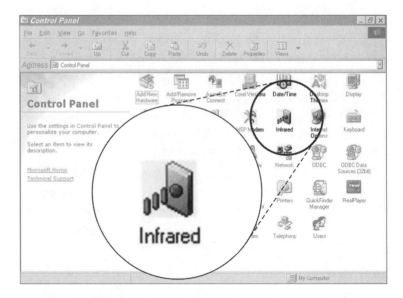

To turn on the infrared communication function, right-click the Infrared icon on the taskbar. Make sure that the *Enable Infrared* communication check box is checked. To turn off infrared communications, make sure that this item is not checked. When infrared communication has been turned off, the Search for Devices Within Range and Enable Plug and Play functions are also turned off. To engage support for infrared Plug-and-Play devices, right-click the Infrared icon on the taskbar.

Make sure that the Enable Plug and Play option is checked. Conversely, to turn off support for Plug-and-Play device installation, make sure that this item is not checked. It will only be available if the infrared and searching functions are enabled. If the taskbar icon is not visible, click the Related Topics option.

To install software for an infrared device, simply right-click the Infrared icon on the taskbar. Make sure that the Enable Plug and Play check box is checked and verify that the new device is within range. If you are not sure whether the device you are installing is Plug-and-Play capable, check its user's guide. If it is not a Plug-and-Play device, install its drivers by accessing the Add New Hardware icon in the Control Panel.

EXAM TIP

Be aware of how to know that an IrDA capable device is within range of a host system.

Infrared Monitor

Windows provides an *Infrared Monitor* utility that can be used to track the computer's activity. When this utility is running, it will alert you when infrared devices are within range of your computer by placing the Infrared icon on the taskbar. The Infrared Monitor not only notifies you when the computer is communicating with an infrared device, but it also indicates how well it is communicating. Other functions that can be performed through the Infrared Monitor include controlling how the system reports the status of the infrared activity it detects and what types of infrared activity it can conduct.

CHAPTER SUMMARY

This chapter has presented procedures for installing and configuring common PC-compatible peripheral devices, including video monitors, modems, and external storage devices. It also covered peripheral devices such as external drive units, docking stations and port replicators, and infrared devices. The chapter concluded with a discussion of installing PC Cards and services normally included with portable computer systems.

At this point, review the objectives listed at the beginning of the chapter to be certain that you understand each point and can perform each task listed there. Afterward, answer the review questions that follow to verify your knowledge of the information.

KEY TERMS

- ASCII code
- Docking station
- Docking-port connector
- EBCDIC code
- Enable infrared
- Error-checking and correcting (ECC)
- Infrared Monitor
- Port replicators
- Protocol
- Video display

APPLY YOUR KNOWLEDGE

Review Questions

1. What type of error checking is associated with parity operations?

   A. Single bit

   B. XOR

   C. 8-bit

   D. ECC

2. What is the standard resolution of a VGA card?

   A. 640x480 pixels

   B. 800x600 pixels

   C. 1024x768 pixels

   D. 1280x1024 pixels

3. How does the Windows operating system alert the user that an infrared device is within range to communicate with the host computer?

   A. An Infrared device icon appears in My Computer.

   B. An Infrared device icon appears in the taskbar.

   C. An Infrared device icon appears in the Control Panel.

   D. An Infrared device window pops up.

4. How do you install an IrDA device that is not PnP capable?

   A. Use the Add New Hardware wizard in the Control Panel.

   B. Use the Infrared icon in the Control Panel.

   C. Right-click the desktop and select Enable Wireless Link in the pop-up menu.

   D. Right-click the Infrared icon in the taskbar and select Enable Wireless Link from the pop-up menu.

5. What type of device would you expect to find in an AGP slot?

   A. AMR card

   B. SCSI card

   C. Video card

   D. Network card

6. Which interface type is normally associated with an external CD-ROM drive?

   A. EIDE

   B. SCSI

   C. USB

   D. Firewire

7. If you install an ISA modem that only has jumper settings for COM1 and COM2, what action do you need to take to make sure that it receives the proper resources in a PnP system?

   A. Set the modem to COM2 in CMOS.

   B. Set the COM port in CMOS to "auto."

   C. Enable the COM port in CMOS.

   D. Disable the competing COM port in CMOS.

8. What type of I/O device uses a 3-row, 15-pin female connector?

   A. Joystick

   B. Monitor

   C. Printer

   D. Modem

APPLY YOUR KNOWLEDGE

9. What type of error checking can repair the defective bit in the bit stream?

   A. Single bit

   B. XOR

   C. 8-bit

   D. ECC

10. What is the default color depth and refresh rate of a VGA adapter?

    A. 8-bit, 30Hz

    B. 16-bit, 60Hz

    C. 24-bit, 80Hz

    D. 32-bit, 90Hz

11. What is the first step to installing a USB device?

    A. Install the USB driver in the Add New Hardware Wizard.

    B. Enable the USB driver in Device Manager.

    C. Enable USB resources in CMOS.

    D. Right-click on the USB device icon in the taskbar and select Enable.

12. What internal device is usually not found in modern PC notebooks?

    A. Floppy drive

    B. CD-ROM drive

    C. USB port

    D. IrDA port

13. What device enables a notebook computer to be used with a desktop monitor, keyboard, and mouse?

    A. Portable station

    B. Desktop port

    C. Docking station

    D. Notebook port

14. What should you do first if you want to remove a PCMCIA card from a notebook computer?

    A. Uninstall the PC Card driver.

    B. Select the command to stop the operation of the PC Card you want to remove.

    C. Click on the PC Card icon in the taskbar.

    D. Pull the card from the computer.

15. What is the function of an Infrared Monitor?

    A. A standard video monitor that is attached to the computer via an IrDA port

    B. Identifies the type of device that is communicating via the IrDA port

    C. Alerts you when an infrared device is within range

    D. Controls the functions of the device that is communicating via the IrDA port

16. Where are IrDA operations enabled?

    A. Windows Control Panel

    B. Infrared Monitor

    C. CMOS Setup

    D. On the system board

Answers and Explanations

1. **A.** The parity-checking scheme employed with common memory systems is simply a single-bit error-checking operation. If an incorrect bit is detected in the memory read back, a Parity Check error is created and an NMI signal is passed to the microprocessor. For more information, see the section "Establishing Protocols."

2. **A.** Under the VGA video specification, the standard resolution setting is 640x480 pixels. For more information, see the section "Video/Monitor Systems."

3. **B.** When an IrDA device comes within range of the host port, the icon will appear on the Windows desktop and in the taskbar. In the case of an IrDA printer, a printer icon will appear in the Printer folder. For more information, see the section "Infrared Devices."

4. **A.** To install software for an infrared device, simply right-click the Infrared icon on the taskbar. Make sure that the Enable Plug and Play check box is checked and verify that the new device is within range. If you are not sure whether the device you are installing is Plug-and-Play capable, check its user's guide. If it is not a Plug-and-Play device, install its drivers by accessing the Add New Hardware icon in the Control Panel. For more information, see the section "Infrared Devices."

5. **C.** The video adapter card typically plugs in to one of the system's expansion slots. Most newer video adapter cards are designed for use with AGP slots. For more information, see the section "Video/Monitor Systems."

6. **B.** Most external drives use a SCSI interface connection. For more information, see the section "External CD-ROM Devices."

7. **D.** When installing a non-PnP modem, set the modem's configuration jumpers to operate the modem as COM2, and then disable the COM2 port in the CMOS utility. For more information, see the section "Installing an Internal Modem."

8. **B.** The monitor's signal cable plugs into the 3-row, 15-pin female D-shell connector on the back of the video adapter card. For more information, see the section "Video/Monitor Systems."

9. **D.** Error-Checking and Correcting (ECC) is capable of not only detecting bit-level errors, but can also recalculate and repair the defective bit in the bit stream. For more information, see the section "Establishing Protocols."

10. **B.** The default values for VGA/PCI-compatible adapters include a standard 640x480 pixel screen resolution at 16-colors, with a refresh rate of 60Hz. For more information, see the section "Video/Monitor Systems."

11. **C.** Installing a USB device normally involves enabling the USB resources in the CMOS setup screen. For more information, see the section "Configuring Advanced Ports."

12. **A.** Typically, the first item to be dropped from a new notebook design is the internal floppy drive. So much of the latest software is distributed on CD-ROM that those drives now have preference in newer designs. Because large volumes of software are still available on floppy disks (and so many users have cherished data stored on floppy disks), an external FDD is a common add-on option for new notebooks. For more information, see the section "External Drive Units."

13. **C.** A docking station, or docking port, is a specialized structure that permits the notebook unit to be inserted into it. When the notebook is inside, the docking port extends its expansion bus so that it can be used with a collection of desktop devices, such as an AC power source, a full-sized keyboard and CRT monitor, as well as modems, mice, and standard PC port connectors. For more information, see the section "Docking Stations."

14. **C.** The proper procedure for removing a PC Card from the computer begins with clicking the PC Card status indicator on the taskbar. Then, select on the command to stop the operation of the PC Card you want to remove. When the operating system prompts you, physically remove the PC Card from the system. For more information, see the section "Installing PC Card Support."

15. **C.** Windows provides an Infrared Monitor utility that can be used to track the computer's activity. When this utility is running, it will alert you when infrared devices are within range of your computer by placing the Infrared icon on the taskbar. The Infrared Monitor not only notifies you when the computer is communicating with an infrared device, it also indicates how well it is communicating. Other functions that can be performed through the Infrared Monitor include controlling how the system reports the status of the infrared activity it detects and what types of infrared activity it can conduct. For more information, see the section "Infrared Monitor."

16. **C.** The IrDA infrared functions must be enabled through the CMOS Setup utility before infrared operations can take place. For more information, see the section "Infrared Devices."

Challenge Solutions

1. The modem should be configured to use IRQ3 and COM2. The system board's internal COM2 channel should be disabled through the CMOS configuration utility to permit the UART on the internal modem to use this channel. The printer should be using IRQ7 by default while the sound card is most likely using IRQ5. For more information, see the section "Installing Modems."

2. The unused PC Card adapters could be temporarily disabled by making sure that the Enable Infrared Communication check box is checked. To turn off infrared communications, make sure that this item is not checked. When infrared communication has been turned off, the Search for Devices Within Range and Enable Plug and Play functions are also turned off. To engage support for infrared Plug and Play devices, right-click the Infrared icon on the taskbar.

   Make sure that the Enable Plug and Play option is checked. Conversely, to turn off support for Plug-and-Play device installation, make sure that this item is not checked. It will only be available if the infrared and searching functions are enabled. If the taskbar icon is not visible, click the Related Topics option. For more information, see the section "Installing PC Card Support."

APPLY YOUR KNOWLEDGE

Suggested Readings and Resources

1. Modem Installation
   http://www.waterwheel.com/Guides/how_to/
   modem/modems.htm

2. Introduction to the IEEE 1284-1994 Standard
   http://www.fapo.com/1284int.htm

3. Portable Computer Components
   http://www.pctechguide.com/25mob2.htm

4. Notebook Computer
   http://webopedia.internet.com/TERM/n/
   notebook_computer.html

5. Docking Station
   http://webopedia.internet.com/TERM/d/
   docking_station.html

6. Liquid Crystal Display
   http://webopedia.internet.com/TERM/L/
   LCD.html

This chapter helps you to prepare for the Core
Hardware module of the A+ Certification examination
by covering the following objectives within the
"Domain 1.0: Installation, Configuration, and
Upgrading" section.

**1.8 Identify hardware methods of upgrading
system performance, procedures for replacing
basic subsystem components, unique components, and when to use them.**

Content might include the following:

- **Memory**

- **Hard drives**

- **CPU**

- **Upgrading BIOS**

- **When to upgrade BIOS**

- **Portables:**

  - **Battery**

  - **Hard drive**

  - **Types I, II, III cards**

  - **Memory**

CHAPTER 7

System Upgrading and Optimizing

▶ The modular design of the PC-compatible system enables portions of the system to be upgraded as new or better components become available or as the system's application changes. As this A+ objective points out, computer technicians must be capable of upgrading the system's BIOS as part of a system upgrade. Technicians should also be able to optimize PC hardware to obtain the best performance possible for a given system configuration. The following sections cover upgradeable components found in common PC systems, including information about when and how to upgrade them.

STUDY STRATEGIES

To prepare for the Installation, Configuration, and Upgrading objective of the Core Hardware exam,

▶ Read the objectives at the beginning of this chapter.

▶ Study the information in this chapter.

▶ Review the objectives listed earlier in this chapter.

▶ Perform any step-by-step procedures in the text.

▶ Answer the review questions at the end of the chapter and check your results.

▶ Use the PrepLogic test engine on the CD-ROM that accompanies this book for additional review and exam questions concerning this material.

▶ Review the exam tips scattered throughout the chapter and make certain that you are comfortable with each point.

INTRODUCTION

Computer components are under continuous improvement. Therefore, the capabilities of existing computer systems quickly fall behind the leading edge of available PC technologies. This chapter examines typical options and procedures for upgrading and improving the operation of existing computer systems. Devices in a PC-compatible that are typically considered upgradeable components include microprocessors, RAM memory modules, the ROM BIOS, and hard disk drive units.

Because of their unique designs, portable systems tend to be much more difficult to upgrade than desktop computers. The final sections of the chapter focus on hardware components that can typically be used to upgrade portable computer systems. These devices include batteries, hard drives, PC cards, and RAM memory modules.

After completing the chapter, you should be able to evaluate an existing personal computer system and determine its suitability for upgrading. After determining to upgrade a given system, you should also be able to select proper microprocessor, RAM, BIOS, and HDD components to improve the operation of the system.

SYSTEM BOARD UPGRADING

In many situations, the best option for upgrading a PC system is to upgrade the entire system board. This is usually done to bring faster microprocessors and memory units together with newer chipsets and faster front side buses and I/O connections. However, in many cases, the components of the existing system board can be upgraded to provide additional performance at a lower cost than replacing the entire board.

There are typically five serviceable components on the system board. These include the following:

◆ The microprocessor

◆ The RAM modules

◆ The CMOS Backup battery

◆ The ROM BIOS IC

◆ The cache memory

Of the five items listed, three—the microprocessor, the RAM modules, and the ROM BIOS—can be exchanged to increase the performance of the system. These devices are often mounted in sockets to make replacing or upgrading them a relatively easy task.

Great care should be taken when exchanging these parts to avoid damage to the ICs from *electrostatic discharge* (*ESD*). In addition, care should be taken during the extraction and replacement of the ICs to avoid misalignment and bent pins. Make sure to correctly align the IC's pin #1 with the socket's pin #1 position.

Upgrading Microprocessors

Microprocessor manufacturers have devised upgrade versions for virtually every type of microprocessor in the market. It is also common for clone microprocessors to be pin-for-pin compatible with older Intel socket designs. This strategy allows the end user to realize a speed increase by upgrading, along with an increase in processing power.

Upgrading the processor is a fairly easy operation after gaining access to the system board. Simply remove the microprocessor from its socket and replace it with the upgrade. In older Pentium systems, such as Socket 7 system boards, you must configure the *Core Voltage*, *Bus Speed*, and *Bus Frequency Ratio* configuration jumpers to the correct settings for the processor being installed. These settings can be found in the system board's installation manual.

Four key items must be observed when changing the microprocessor:

◆ Make sure that the replacement microprocessor is hardware compatible (pin configuration, socket, or slot) with the original; otherwise, the system board will not support the new microprocessor type.

◆ Make certain to properly orient the new processor in the socket or slot so that its pin #1 (usually identified by a notch in one corner of the socket) matches the socket's/slot's pin #1.

◆ The system board must be configured correctly for the new processor type (manually or automatically).

◆ Verify that the existing BIOS can be upgraded to support the new microprocessor specifications.

Newer systems have the capability to auto-detect the proper configuration settings for the new microprocessor. These microprocessors exchange information with the system's PnP BIOS during the configuration portion of the boot procedure to obtain the optimum settings. Table 7.1 shows the upgrade paths available to the major microprocessor types used in PCs.

TABLE 7.1

MICROPROCESSOR UPGRADE PATHS

Number	*Pins*	*Voltages*	*Microprocessors*
Socket 7	321 SPGA	VRM (2.5v-3.6v)	Pentium (75MHZ-200MHz)
Socket 8	387 SPGA	VRM (2.2v-3.5v)	Pentium Pro
Slot 1	242 SECC/SEPP	VRM (1.5v-2.5v)	Celeron, Pentium II, Pentium III
Slot 2	330 SECC-2	VRM (1.5v-2.5v)	Xeon
Super Socket 7	321 SPGA	VRM (2.0v-3.5v)	AMD K6-2, K6-2+, K6-III, K6-III+, Pentium MMX, Pentium Pro
Socket 370	370 SPGA	VRM (1.1v-2.5v)	Cyrix III, Celeron, Pentium III
Slot A	242 Slot A	VRM (1.2v-2.2v)	AMD Athlon
Socket A	462 SPGA	VRM (12v-2.2v)	AMD Athlon, Duron
Socket 423	423 FC-PGA	VRM (1.7v)	Pentium IV (1.3 GHz-2.0GHz)

Number	*Pins*	*Voltages*	*Microprocessors*
Socket 478	478 FC-PGA	VRM (1.5v/1.7v)	Pentium IV (1.4GHz-2.2GHz)
Socket 603	603 INT-PGA	VRM (1.5v/1.7v)	Pentium IV Xeon (1.4GHz-2.2GHz)
Socket 418	418 INT-PGA	VRM (1.7v)	Itanium/Intel (733 MHz-800MHz)

If you install a new microprocessor in a system that does not have an *auto-detect function* for the microprocessor, you must make sure that

♦ The BIOS version will support the new processor.

♦ The Core Voltage, Bus Frequency, and Bus Ratio settings are properly configured for the new processor.

If these items are not set correctly, you might

♦ Burn up the new microprocessor

♦ Not get the system to start at all

♦ Encounter random errors during normal operations

♦ Fail to start the operating system

♦ Show an incorrect processor type or incorrect processor speed during the POST routines

EXAM TIP

Know why a computer would show an incorrect processor type or speed after a processor upgrade has been conducted.

NOTE

Hands-On Activity For hands-on experience with this concept, refer to Lab Procedure #9, "Configuring a Cisco Catalyst 1900 10BaseT Hub," located on the CD that accompanies this book.

NOTE

Hands-On Activity For hands-on experience with this concept, refer to Lab Procedure #9, "CPU Upgrading/Overclocking," located on the CD that accompanies this book.

Upgrading the BIOS

The system board's physical upgrade should also be accompanied by a logical upgrade. When the microprocessor is upgraded, the BIOS should also be upgraded to support it. In newer system boards, this can be accomplished by *flashing* (electrically altering) the information in the BIOS with the latest compatibility firmware. In these systems, new BIOS information is downloaded into the BIOS IC where it is permanently held until it is rewritten (even if power is removed form the IC). The flash download operation can be conducted from a floppy disk, from the hard drive, or from a manufacturer's Web site. In each case, the system is rebooted and the flash download's executable file is run to transfer the new information into the BIOS IC.

EXAM TIP

Know how to upgrade both flash and non-flash BIOS types.

EXAM TIP

Know what precautions to take before upgrading the system's BIOS.

If the system BIOS doesn't possess the flash option and does not support the new microprocessor, it will be necessary to obtain an updated BIOS IC that is compatible with the new processor (and with the system board's chip set). The old IC must be removed from the board and replaced by the new IC. If not, the entire system board will need to be upgraded. An upgraded BIOS can normally be obtained from the system board manufacturer.

Before flashing the BIOS, it is a good idea to make a backup copy of your BIOS settings on a floppy disk. This will enable you to recover to your old settings in the event that the new BIOS information will not work with your system. Make certain to record your CMOS Configuration information before flashing or changing out the BIOS device. This will permit you to reinstall those settings for the updated BIOS.

Upgrading Memory

Having more RAM on board enables the system to access more data from extended or expanded memory without needing to access the disk drive. This speeds up system operation considerably. Normally, upgrading memory amounts to installing new memory modules in vacant SIMM or DIMM slots. If the slots are already populated, it will be necessary to remove the existing memory modules to install faster or higher-capacity modules.

When upgrading memory in a newer PC, you must be aware of the following concerns:

◆ The types of memory that can be installed on the existing system board

◆ The makeup of the new modules (number and type of ICs on the modules)

◆ The speed rating of the memory module

You should consult the system board's user guide to determine what speed the memory devices must be rated for. You should be aware that RAM and other memory devices are rated in access time rather than clock speed. Therefore, a 70-nanosecond (ns) RAM device is faster than an 80-nanosecond device. You should also consult the manual to verify the types and arrangements of memory modules that can be used with the existing board. Finally, the guide should be checked for any memory configuration settings that must be made to accept the new memory capacity.

You should never mix memory types when upgrading a system board. If the new memory modules are not technically compatible with the existing memory, the old memory should be removed. Remember that just because the memory modules are physically compatible does not mean that they will work together in a system. Mismatched memory speeds and memory styles (registered/unregistered, buffered/un-buffered, ECC, and so on) can cause significant problems in the operation of the system. These problems can range from preventing bootup to creating simple soft memory errors.

If the system board has *cache memory* installed in sockets, some additional performance can be gained by optimizing the cache. Upgrading the cache on these boards normally requires that additional cache ICs be installed in vacant sockets. If the sockets are full but the system's cache size is less than its maximum, it will be necessary to remove the existing cache chips and replace them with faster, higher-capacity devices.

EXAM TIP	Be aware of the different concerns associated with upgrading RAM in a PC.
EXAM TIP	Be aware of the consequences of mixing memory types in a PC.

Making Upgrade Decisions

Before upgrading the system board's FRU units, check the cost of the proposed component upgrade against the cost of upgrading the system board itself. In many cases, the RAM from the original board can be used on a newer, faster model that should include a more advanced microprocessor. Before finalizing the choice to install a new system board, however, make sure that the current adapters, software, and peripherals will function properly with the updated board. If not, the cost of upgrading might be unexpectedly higher than just replacing an FRU component.

CHALLENGE #1

A customer has brought in his Socket-370 based computer and has told you that he wants to upgrade the system to get another year of good operation out of it. The system currently has a Celeron 600MHz processor, 64MB of DRAM, and a 2GB hard drive installed. What items can you suggest for upgrading this machine without replacing the system board? What additional system upgrades might be required to support these changes?

HDD UPGRADING

One of the key components in keeping the system up-to-date is the hard disk drive. Many newer programs place high demands on the hard drive to feed information, such as large graphics files or digitized voice and video, to the system for processing. Invariably, the system will begin to produce error messages saying that the hard drive is full. The first line of action is to use software disk utilities to optimize the organization of the drive. The second step is to remove unnecessary programs and files from the hard drive. Programs and information that is rarely, or never, used should be moved to an archival media, such as removable disks or tape.

In any event, there will come a time when it becomes necessary to determine whether the existing hard drive needs to be replaced, or another drive needs to be added to optimize the performance of the system. One guideline suggests that the drive should be replaced if the percentage of unused disk space drops below 20%.

Another reason to consider upgrading the HDD involves its capability to deliver information to the system efficiently. If the system is constantly waiting for information from the hard drive, replacing it with a faster drive should be considered as an option. Not all system slowdowns are connected to the HDD, but many are. Remember that the HDD is the mechanical part of the memory system and that everything else is electronic.

As with the storage space issue, HDD speed can be optimized through software configurations, such as a disk cache. After it has been optimized in this manner, however, any further speed increases must be accomplished by upgrading the hardware.

When considering an HDD upgrade, determine what the actual system's needs are for the hard drive. Multimedia-intensive applications can place heavy performance demands on the hard disk drive to operate correctly. Moving large image, audio, and video files into RAM on demand requires high performance from the drive. Critical HDD specifications associated with disk-drive performance include the following:

◆ *Access time*—The average time, expressed in milliseconds, required to position the drive's R/W heads over a specified track/cylinder and reach a specified sector on the track.

◆ *Track seek time*—The amount of time required for the drive's R/W heads to move between cylinders and settle over a particular track following the seek command being issued by the system.

◆ *Data transfer rate*—The speed, expressed in megabytes per second (Mbps), at which data is transferred between the system and the drive.

In contemporary systems, the choice of hard drives for high-performance applications alternates back and forth between IDE/EIDE drives and SCSI drives. The EIDE drives are competitive and relatively easy to install; the high-end SCSI specifications offer additional performance, but require additional setup effort and an additional host adapter card.

Before upgrading the HDD unit, make certain that the existing drive is providing all the performance that it can. Check for *SMARTDRV* or *VCACHE* arrangements at the software configuration level and optimize them if possible. Also, determine how much performance increase can be gained through other upgrading efforts (check the "System-Board Upgrading" section earlier in this chapter) before changing out the hard drive.

If the drive is being upgraded substantially, such as from a 500MB IDE drive to a 10GB EIDE drive, check the capabilities of the system's ROM BIOS. When the system's BIOS doesn't support large LBA or ECHS enhancements, the drive capacity of even the largest hard drive will be limited to 504MB. All newer BIOS support large LBA and ECHS enhanced drives.

EXAM TIP
Be aware that the BIOS might be a size-limiting factor in disk drive partition sizes.

EXAM TIP

Be aware of the effects of using newer EIDE devices with older IDE signal cables.

Finally, determine how much longer the unit in question is likely to be used before being replaced. If the decision to upgrade the HDD stands, ultimately, the best advice is to get the biggest, fastest hard drive possible. Don't forget to consider that a different I/O bus architecture might add to the performance increase.

When upgrading the hard drive, make sure that the correct cabling is being used to connect the drive to the system. You should know that installing a new ATA-66 or ATA-100 drive in a system using the old IDE cable will cause the drive's operation to be diminished to the level of the old drive. Without the new cables, communications with the drives will be limited to the lesser standard determined by the 40-conductor signal cable.

When upgrading SCSI drives, take care to ensure that the new drive is correctly configured and terminated for its position in the system. Verify that the SCSI host adapter will support the new drive type. For example, a standard SCSI-I host adapter will not support a Fast-Wide SCSI drive. The physical cable and the communication speed differences between the two specifications will not match.

CHALLENGE #2

Your EIDE hard drive is continually producing "Out of Hard Drive Space" error messages. These messages continue to be a problem even after you have optimized the drive through the Defrag utility and removed as much old information as possible. You are thinking of upgrading to a new high-speed, high-capacity 20GB ATA-100 drive. What system considerations do you need to resolve before buying this drive?

PORTABLE SYSTEM UPGRADING

As more and more desktop users began to use laptop and notebook computers, they demanded that additional peripheral systems be included. With the limited space inside portable units, it became clear that a new method for installing options had to be developed.

Batteries

The desktop world doesn't really pay much attention to *power-conservation* issues. Conversely, portable computer designers must deal with the fact that they are really tied to a battery. Older portable designs included the battery as an external, detachable device. These units normally contained rows of *Nickel Cadmium (Ni-Cad) batteries* wired together to provide the specified voltage and current capabilities for the portable. The housing was constructed to both hold the Ni-Cads and to attach to the portable case.

Typical Ni-Cad batteries offer operating times approaching two hours in some models. As with other devices that rely on Ni-Cads, computer battery packs constructed with this type of battery suffer from the charge/discharge cycle "memory effect" problem associated with Ni-Cads. A full recharge for some Ni-Cad packs could take up to 24 hours to complete. For these reasons, Ni-Cad battery packs have all but disappeared from the portable computer market.

Newer portable designs have switched to *nickel metal-hydride (NiMH)*, *lithium-ion (Li-ion)*, or *lithium-ion polymer batteries*. These batteries are often housed in a plastic case that can be installed inside the portable's case, as illustrated in Figure 7.1. Other designs use plastic cases that attach to the outside of the portable case. These batteries typically provide up to two or three hours of operation. It is best to run the battery until the system produces a "Battery Low" warning message, indicator, or chime.

It should take about two to three hours to fully recharge the typical Ni-MH battery pack and about four to five hours for a Li-ion pack. The battery packs should always be fully recharged before using. When the AC adapter is used, a trickle charge is applied to the battery pack to keep it in a fully charged condition. The AC adapter should be used whenever possible to conserve the battery.

FIGURE 7.1
Removing battery packs.

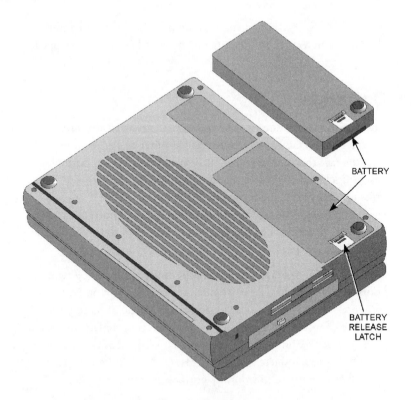

BATTERY

BATTERY
RELEASE
LATCH

Upgrading/Replacing Portable Drives

Smaller 2.5 inch form-factor hard drives, low-profile 3.5 inch floppy drives, and combination FDD/CD-ROM drives have been developed to address the portable computer market's need for compact devices. Older portables included one FDD and one HDD as standard equipment. Newer models tend to include a CD-ROM drive and an HDD as standard internal units. Figure 7.2 shows the placement of drives in a high-end notebook unit that includes one of each drive type.

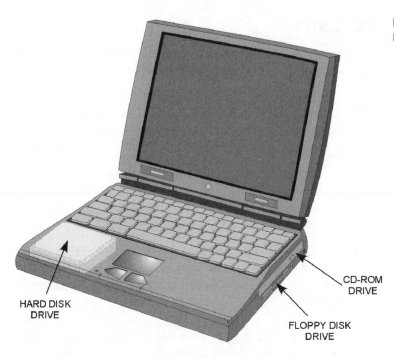

FIGURE 7.2
Portable disk drives.

HARD DISK
DRIVE

CD-ROM
DRIVE

FLOPPY DISK
DRIVE

Newer portable models include swappable drive bays that enable the combination of internal drives in the unit to be changed as dictated by the work being performed. In some units, a disk drive that is not needed for a particular task can be removed and replaced by an extra battery.

Three basic considerations should be observed when replacing disk drives in a portable computer:

◆ Their physical size and layout

◆ Their power consumption

◆ Whether the BIOS supports the new drive

Replacing an internal disk drive in a portable computer normally involves taking the computer case apart to gain access to the drive. Some older portables did feature hot-swappable internal drives, but these units have largely disappeared from the portable market.

PC Cards

Three types of PCMCIA cards currently exist. All three PC Card types adhere to the same credit card size form factor of 2.12x3.37 inches. However, they are created in three different thicknesses:

◆ Type I—The PCMCIA *Type I cards*, introduced in 1990, are 3.3mm thick and work as memory-expansion units.

◆ Type II—In 1991, *PCMCIA Type II cards* were introduced. They are 5mm thick and support virtually any traditional expansion function (typically a modem or LAN card), except removable hard drive units. Type II slots are backward compatible, so Type I cards will work in them.

◆ Type III—Currently, *PCMCIA Type III cards* are being produced. These cards are 10.5mm thick and are intended primarily for use with removable hard drives. Both Type I and Type II cards can be used in a Type III slot.

All three PC Card types employ a 68-pin, slide-in pin and socket arrangement. They can all be used with 8-bit or 16-bit data bus machines and operate on +5V or +3.3V supplies. The design of the cards enables them to be installed in the computer while it is turned on and running. Figure 7.3 shows the three types of PCMCIA cards.

EXAM TIP

Memorize the physical sizes of the three card standards. Also, know what applications each type of card is capable of.

FIGURE 7.3
PCMCIA cards.

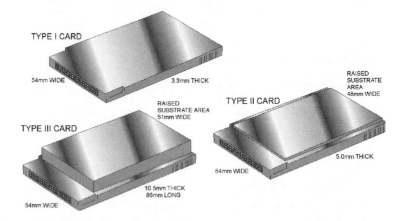

Most portable designs only include two Type II–sized PC-Card slots. These slots can physically accommodate two Type I or Type II cards, or a single Type III card. Type III cards only use one of the two *68-pin JEIDA connectors* but take up the entire opening. The PCMCIA interface is designed so that cards can be inserted into the unit while it is turned on (hot-swappable).

Even PC Card hard drives (with disks the size of a quarter) can be found in the notebook market. Other common PC Card adapters include fax/modems, SCSI adapters, network adapters, and IDE host adapters. The PCMCIA standard actually provides for up to 255 adapters—each capable of working with up to 16 cards. If a system implemented the standard to its extreme, it could, theoretically, work with more than 4,000 PC Cards installed.

EXAM TIP

Be aware that a single Type III PCMCIA card will normally take up both physical slots on a notebook computer.

Portable Memory

In portable computers, very few memory and memory-expansion hardware standards exist. Some designs use standard SIMM or DIMM modules for RAM, whereas others use special *Small Outline DIMM* (*SODIMM*) modules, or proprietary memory modules. Still other designs rely on PCMCIA memory-card modules for additional RAM.

The key to upgrading or replacing RAM in a portable PC can be found in its user's manual. Only those memory modules recommended by the portable manufacturer should be installed, and only in the configurations suggested. The voltage level support for the memory devices in portable computers is very critical. Using RAM devices that electrically overload this supply will cause memory errors to occur.

If the type of RAM device being installed is not one of the recommended types, the notebook might not be able to recognize the new memory. If the new RAM is being added to expand the existing banks of memory, the system might not recognize this additional RAM. The problem will show up in the form of a short memory count during the POST routines.

EXAM TIP

Know why notebook computers show short memory counts during the boot-up process.

However, if only the new RAM type is installed, the system could present a number of different symptoms, including

◆ Not working at all

◆ Giving beep coded error messages

◆ Producing soft memory errors

◆ Producing short memory counts in the POST

◆ Locking up while booting the operating system

As with disk drives, changing memory in a portable PC involves disassembling the computer case. Figure 7.4 shows the replacement of a SODIMM module in a particular notebook computer. The location and process of accessing the memory in the unit varies from manufacturer to manufacturer and model to model.

FIGURE 7.4
Replacing a SODIMM module.

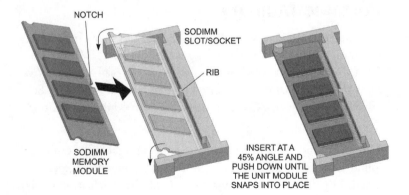

NOTCH

SODIMM SLOT/SOCKET

RIB

SODIMM MEMORY MODULE

INSERT AT A 45% ANGLE AND PUSH DOWN UNTIL THE UNIT MODULE SNAPS INTO PLACE

CHAPTER SUMMARY

KEY TERMS

• 68-pin JEIDA connectors

• Access time

• Auto-detect function

• Bus Frequency Ratio

• Bus Speed

• Cache memory

This chapter was dedicated to devices and techniques that can be used to upgrade existing systems and extend their usefulness. The initial sections of the chapter dealt with components that are typically used to upgrade desktop PC systems. The final sections of the chapter shifted the focus to components that can typically be used for upgrading of portable computers.

At this point, review the objectives listed at the beginning of the chapter to be certain that you understand each point and can perform each task listed there. Afterward, answer the review questions that follow to verify your knowledge of the information.

CHAPTER SUMMARY

- Core Voltage
- Data transfer rate
- Electrostatic discharge (ESD)
- Flashing
- Lithium-ion (Li-ion)
- Lithium-ion polymer batteries
- Nickel Cadmium (Ni-Cad) batteries
- Nickel metal-hydride (NiMH)
- PCMCIA Type II cards

- PCMCIA Type III cards
- Small Outline DIMM (SODIMM)
- SMARTDRV
- Track seek time
- Type I PCMCIA cards
- Type II PCMCIA cards
- Type III PCMCIA cards
- VCACHE

APPLY YOUR KNOWLEDGE

Review Questions

1. A flash BIOS is used for _____.

   A. resetting the default BIOS settings

   B. upgrading the BIOS without additional hardware

   C. inputting temporary BIOS settings for troubleshooting purposes

   D. making newer motherboards backward compatible

2. Under what conditions would you normally expect to upgrade the system's BIOS?

   A. Power comes on but the screen stays blank

   B. When you upgrade the microprocessor

   C. You forget the CMOS password

   D. Battery goes dead

3. You have three PCMCIA cards; a flash memory card, a modem, and a PC Card hard drive. Which of these cards can fit in the slots of a notebook computer that includes two standard Type II slots?

   A. Flash memory, hard drive

   B. Modem, hard drive

   C. Flash memory, modem

   D. Only the modem

4. If your BIOS does not have the capability to be altered electronically (flashed), how can you upgrade the system's microprocessor to a newer, faster version?

   A. Use an ultraviolet light to erase the ROM BIOS IC.

   B. Download an appropriate patch to the operating system from the manufacturer's Web site.

   C. Set the core voltage, bus frequency, and bus ratio manually using the jumpers.

   D. Replace the ROM BIOS IC with an upgraded version from the manufacturer.

5. The key to inserting a microprocessor is to _____.

   A. align pin #1 in the chip with pin #1 in the socket

   B. make sure to orient the writing on the top of the chip with that of the previous processor

   C. reattach the fan unit properly

   D. look for the arrow on the chip, and align it with the arrow on the pc board

6. Which type of PC Card would normally be used for a PCMCIA modem?

   A. Type I

   B. Type II

   C. Type III

   D. None of the above

APPLY YOUR KNOWLEDGE

7. A Type III PCMCIA card is _____ thick.

   A. 10.5mm

   B. 8mm

   C. 5mm

   D. 3.3mm

8. How many Type II PC Cards can normally be installed in a typical portable computer?

   A. 1

   B. 2

   C. 3

   D. 4

9. What effect does the BIOS have in upgrading the system's hard disk drives?

   A. Has no effect

   B. Allows the creation of partitions greater than 2 GB

   C. Needs LBA or ECHS support to allow drives larger than 528 MB

   D. Normally limits the size of partitions to 2GB

10. What is the most important step to be taken before upgrading the BIOS in a system?

    A. Make a backup copy of your BIOS data on a floppy disk and record all the CMOS configuration settings.

    B. Get the latest version of the BIOS from the manufacturer.

    C. Remove the BIOS IC from the motherboard.

    D. Install all updates to your operating system.

11. Why would a notebook computer only show 64MB of RAM after you have just upgraded the system to 256MB of RAM?

    A. Improper memory allocation by the operating system

    B. CMOS needs to be configured

    C. BIOS needs upgrading

    D. Incorrect memory type

12. What would cause the system to show the presence of a 600MHz Pentium III processor after you have just completed an upgrade to a 933MHz Pentium III processor? (Select all that apply.)

    A. Incompatible RAM type

    B. Motherboard BIOS version will not support the new processor

    C. Microprocessor is not aligned with pin #1

    D. Incorrect Core Voltage, Bus Frequency, or Bus Ratio settings

13. When upgrading the BIOS, what is the most important consideration?

    A. Erasing the existing ROM BIOS

    B. Writing the new ROM BIOS

    C. Getting the same version

    D. Getting the latest version

APPLY YOUR KNOWLEDGE

14. How can you upgrade an older computer system that uses a non-removable, non-flash ROM BIOS?

    A. Install a larger hard drive.

    B. Install more RAM.

    C. Replace the CPU.

    D. Replace the system board.

15. _____ mismatches can cause problems that range from preventing bootup to creating operating system or application failures.

    A. BIOS

    B. RAM

    C. Microprocessor

    D. Disk drive

16. You replace an ATA-33 drive with a new ATA-100 drive. What is the maximum data throughput when connecting an ATA-100 hard disk drive with the current 40-wire IDE cable?

    A. 10Mbps

    B. 33Mbps

    C. 66Mbps

    D. Will not work together

17. A Type II PCMCIA card is _____ thick.

    A. 10.5mm

    B. 8mm

    C. 5mm

    D. 3.3mm

Answers and Explanations

1. **B.** In newer system boards, the BIOS can be upgraded without changing the ROM IC by flashing (electrically altering) the information in the BIOS with the latest compatibility firmware. In these systems, new BIOS information is downloaded into the BIOS IC where it is permanently held until it is rewritten (even if power is removed from the IC). For more information, see the section "Upgrading the BIOS."

2. **B.** If you install a new microprocessor in a system that does not have an auto-detect function for the microprocessor, you must make sure that the BIOS version will support the new processor. A BIOS upgrade is necessary when the existing BIOS cannot support the new microprocessor. For more information, see the section "Upgrading Microprocessors."

3. **C.** Because of the physical size of the Type III card requires the space associated with two Type II cards, you cannot install the Type III card (that is, removable hard disk drive) with the other cards. For example, two Type II slots can physically accommodate one Type III card, two Type I cards, two Type II cards, or a combination of one Type I and one Type II card. Therefore, either a PC Card hard drive or both a flash memory card and a modem can be installed in the slots. For more information, see the section "PC Cards."

4. **D.** If the system BIOS doesn't possess the flash option and does not support the new microprocessor, it will be necessary to obtain an updated BIOS IC that is compatible with the new processor (and with the system board's chipset). The old IC will need to be removed from the

board and replaced by the new IC. This upgraded BIOS can normally be obtained from the system board manufacturer. For more information, see the section "Upgrading the BIOS."

5. **A.** The key factor to be considered when changing the microprocessor is to make certain to properly orient the new processor in the socket or slot so that its pin #1 (usually identified by a notch in one corner) matches the socket's/slot's pin #1. For more information, see the section "System Board Upgrading."

6. **B.** In 1991, PCMCIA Type II cards were introduced. They are 5mm thick and support virtually any traditional expansion function (typically a modem), except removable hard drive units. Type II slots are backward compatible, so Type I cards will work in them. For more information, see the section "PC Cards."

7. **A.** PCMCIA Type III cards are 10.5mm thick and are intended primarily for use with removable hard drives. For more information, see the section "PC Cards."

8. **B.** Most portable designs only include two Type II-sized PC Card slots. These slots can physically accommodate two Type I or Type II cards, or a single Type III card. Type III cards only use one of the two 68-pin JEIDA connectors but take up the entire opening. For more information, see the section "PC Cards."

9. **C.** If the drive is being upgraded substantially, such as from a 500MB IDE drive to a 10GB EIDE drive, check the capabilities of the system's ROM BIOS. When the system's BIOS doesn't support LBA or ECHS enhancements, the drive capacity of even the largest hard drive will be limited to 528MB. Almost all newer BIOS support

LBA and ECHS enhanced drives. For more information, see the section "HDD Upgrading."

10. **A.** Before flashing the BIOS, it is a good idea to make a backup copy of your BIOS settings on a floppy disk. This will enable you to recover to your old settings in the event that the new BIOS information will not work with your system. Make certain to record your CMOS Configuration information before flashing or changing out the BIOS device. This will permit you to reinstall those settings for the updated BIOS. For more information, see the section "Upgrading the BIOS."

11. **D.** If the type of RAM device being installed is not one of the recommended types, the PC might not be able to recognize the new memory. If the new RAM is being added to expand the existing banks of memory, the system might not recognize this additional RAM. The problem will show up in the form of a short memory count during the POST routines. For more information, see the section "Portable Memory."

12. **B, D.** If you install a new microprocessor in a system and the auto-detect function for the microprocessor does not work, you must make sure that 1) the BIOS version will support the new processor, and 2) the Core Voltage, Bus Frequency, and Bus Ratio settings are properly configured for the new processor. For more information, see the section "Upgrading Microprocessors."

13. **D.** When the system is upgraded, the BIOS should also be upgraded to support it. In newer system boards, this can be accomplished by flashing (electrically altering) the information in the BIOS with the latest compatibility firmware. The most recent full non-beta version of the BIOS

APPLY YOUR KNOWLEDGE

should be used for this upgrade. For more information, see the section "Upgrading the BIOS."

14. **D.** If you need to update the BIOS IC and it cannot be flashed or swapped, you will need to upgrade the entire system board. For more information, see the section "Upgrading the BIOS."

15. **B.** You should never mix memory types when upgrading a system board. If the new memory modules are not technically compatible with the existing memory, the old memory should be removed. Remember that just because the memory modules are physically compatible does not mean that they will work together in a system. Mismatched memory speeds and memory styles (registered/unregistered, buffered/un-buffered, ECC, and so on) can cause significant problems in the operation of the system. These problems can range from preventing bootup to creating simple soft memory errors. For more information, see the section "Upgrading Memory."

16. **B.** When upgrading the hard drive, make sure that the correct cabling is being used to connect the drive to the system. You should know that installing a new ATA-66 or ATA-100 drive in a system using the old IDE cable will cause the drive's operation to be diminished to the level of the old drive. Without the new cables, communications with the drives will be limited to the lesser standard determined by the 40-conductor signal cable. For more information, see the section "HDD Upgrading."

17. **C.** PCMCIA Type II cards are 5mm thick and support virtually any traditional expansion function, except removable hard drive units. For more information, see the section "PC Cards."

Challenge Solutions

1. The Celeron processor can be upgraded directly to a Pentium III, and the installed RAM can be expanded considerably. The hard drive capacity and speed can be increased as well. As a precaution, you should check the BIOS version to make certain that it will support these changes. For more information, see the section "System Board Upgrading."

2. If the drive is being upgraded substantially, such as from a 500MB IDE drive to a 10GB EIDE drive, check the capabilities of the system's ROM BIOS. When the system's BIOS doesn't support large LBA or ECHS enhancements, the drive capacity of even the largest hard drive will be limited to 528MB. All newer BIOS support large LBA and ECHS enhanced drives. For more information, see the section "HDD Upgrading."

APPLY YOUR KNOWLEDGE

Suggested Readings and Resources

1. Processor Physical Characteristics
   http://www.pcguide.com/ref/cpu/char/
   index.htm

2. The BIOS Survival Guide
   http://burks.brighton.ac.uk/burks/pcinfo/
   hardware/bios_sg/bios_sg.htm

3. BIOS Recovery Guide
   http://www.sysopt.com/articles/
   recoverbios/index.html

4. American Megatrends BIOS
   www.ami.com

5. Phoenix BIOS
   www.phoenix.com

6. Tom's RAM Guide
   http://www.tomshardware.com/mainboard/
   98q4/981024/index.html

7. HDD Installation and Upgrading
   http://pcsupport.about.com/cs/
   hdinstallupgrade/

8. Optimization
   http://www.pcmech.com/sysopt.htm

9. Nuts and Bolts of Notebook Computers
   http://www.tomshardware.com/mobile/01q1/
   010126/index.html

This chapter helps you to prepare for the Core Hardware module of the A+ Certification examination by covering the following objectives within the "Domain 2.0: Diagnosing and Troubleshooting" section.

2.1 Identify common symptoms and problems associated with each module and how to troubleshoot and isolate the problems.

Content might include the following:

- **Processor/Memory symptoms**
- **Mouse**
- **Floppy drive**
- **Parallel ports**
- **Hard drives**
- **CD-ROM**
- **DVD**
- **Sound Card/Audio**
- **Monitor/Video**
- **Motherboards**
- **Modems**
- **BIOS**
- **USB**
- **NIC**
- **CMOS**
- **Power supply**
- **Slot covers**
- **POST audible/visual error codes**
- **Troubleshooting tools (for example, multimeter)**
- **Large LBA, LBA**

CHAPTER

8

Symptoms and Troubleshooting

- **Cables**

- **Keyboard**

- **Peripherals**

▶ One of the primary responsibilities of every PC technician is to diagnose and troubleshoot computer problems. As this A+ objective points out, the technician should be able to identify common symptoms associated with computer components and to use those symptoms to effectively troubleshoot and repair the problem.

To prepare for the Diagnosing and Troubleshooting objective of the Core Hardware exam,

▶ Read the objectives at the beginning of this chapter.

▶ Study the information in this chapter.

▶ Review the objectives listed earlier in this chapter.

▶ Perform any step-by-step procedures in the text.

▶ Answer the review questions at the end of the chapter and check your results.

▶ Use the PrepLogic test engine on the CD-ROM that accompanies this book for additional review and exam questions concerning this material.

▶ Review the exam tips scattered throughout the chapter and make certain that you are comfortable with each point.

INTRODUCTION

When a computer system fails, there are generally two possible causes—hardware or software. This chapter is dedicated to symptoms and techniques associated with diagnosing and repairing failures associated with different hardware components.

The chapter is broken into individual sections dedicated to each type of hardware component. It begins with failures and symptoms associated with the power-supply unit and moves through system boards, input devices, video displays, disk drive systems, I/O ports, modems, and sound cards. Numerous symptoms and problem sources are presented for each of these components. Technicians need to be aware of the different symptoms produced by these devices so that they can move through the diagnostic and repair processes in the most efficient manner possible.

After completing the chapter, you should be able to identify common symptoms and problems associated with each hardware module and know how to isolate, troubleshoot, and repair the problems.

ISOLATING POWER-SUPPLY PROBLEMS

Typical symptoms associated with power-supply failures include

◆ No indicator lights visible, with no disk drive action, and no display on the screen. Nothing works, and the system is dead.

◆ The On/Off *indicator lights* are visible, but there is no disk drive action and no display on the monitor screen. The system fan might or might not run.

◆ The system produces a *continuous beep tone*.

Checking Dead Systems

Special consideration must be taken when a system is inoperable. In a totally inoperable system, there are no symptoms to give clues where to begin the isolation process. In addition, it is impossible to use troubleshooting software or other system aids to help isolate the problem.

When the system exhibits no signs of life—including the absence of lights—the best place to start looking for the problem is at the power supply. The operation of this unit affects virtually every part of the system. Also, the absence of any lights working usually indicates that no power is being supplied to the system by the power supply.

1. Begin by checking the external connections of the power supply. This is the first step in checking any electrical equipment that shows no signs of life.

2. Confirm that the power supply cord is plugged in to a functioning outlet.

3. Check the position of the On/Off switch.

4. Examine the power cord for good connection at the rear of the unit.

5. Check the setting of the 110/220 switch setting on the outside of the power supply. The normal setting for equipment used in the United States is 110.

6. Check the power at the commercial receptacle using a voltmeter, or by plugging in a lamp (or other 110-volt device) into the outlet.

Other Power-Supply Problems

The presence of the lights and the fan operation indicate that power is reaching the system and that at least some portion of the power supply is functional. This type of symptom results from the following two likely possibilities:

◆ A portion of the power supply has failed or is being overloaded. One or more of the basic voltages supplied by the power supply is missing while the others are still present.

◆ A key component on the system board has failed, preventing it from processing even though the system has power. A defective capacitor across the power input of the system board can completely prevent it from operating.

EXAM TIP

Remember the first step of checking out electrical equipment that appears dead.

WARNING

Turn It Off First!   Before changing any board or connection, always turn the system off first. In an ATX-style system, you should also disconnect the power cable from the power supply. This is necessary because even with the power switch off, some levels of voltages are still applied to the system board in these units.

TROUBLESHOOTING THE SYSTEM BOARD

As with any troubleshooting procedure, begin by observing the symptoms produced by bootup and operation. Observe the steps that lead to the failure and determine under what conditions the system failed. Were any unusual operations in progress? Note any error messages or beep codes. Refer to the *User Manuals* for the system board and peripheral units to check for configuration problems. Examine the *CMOS setup entries* for configuration problems. In Pentium systems, also check the advanced CMOS setup parameters to make certain that all the appropriate system board–enabling settings have been made.

The microprocessor, RAM modules, ROM BIOS, CMOS battery, and possibly cache ICs are typically replaceable units on the system board. If enough of the system is running to perform tests on these units, you can replace them. Problems with key system board components produce symptoms similar to those described for a bad power supply. Both the microprocessor and the ROM BIOS can be sources of such problems. You should check both by substitution when dead system symptoms are encountered, but the power supply is good.

In addition to containing the circuitry that directs all the system's operations, the system board contains a number of other circuits on which the rest of the system's components depend. These include the system's DRAM memory (which all software programs use) and the system's data, address, and signal buses (that is, expansion slots).

System Board Symptoms

Typical symptoms associated with system board hardware failures include

◆ The On/Off indicator lights are visible and the display is visible on the monitor screen, but there is no disk drive action and no bootup occurs.

◆ The On/Off indicator lights are visible and the hard drive spins up, but the system appears dead and there is no bootup.

◆ The system locks up during normal operation.

◆ The system produces a beep code with one, two, three, five, seven, or nine beeps.

◆ The system produces a beep code of one long and three short beeps.

◆ The system will not hold the correct date and time.

◆ An "8042 Gate A20 Error" message displays—Error getting into Protected mode.

◆ An "Invalid Switch Memory Failure" message displays.

◆ A "DMA Error" message displays—DMA Controller failed page register test.

◆ A "CMOS Battery Low" message displays, indicating failure of CMOS battery or CMOS checksum test.

◆ A "CMOS System Option Not Set" message displays, indicating failure of CMOS battery or CMOS checksum test.

◆ A "CMOS Checksum Failure" message displays, indicating CMOS battery low or CMOS checksum test failure.

◆ A 201 error code displays, indicating a RAM failure.

◆ A parity check error message displays, indicating a RAM error.

Typical symptoms associated with system board CMOS Setup failures include

◆ A "CMOS Inoperational" message displays—Failure of CMOS shutdown register.

◆ A "Display Switch Setting Not Proper" message displays—Failure to verify display type.

◆ A "CMOS Display Mismatch" message displays—Failure of display type verification.

◆ A "CMOS Memory Size Mismatch" message displays—System Configuration and Setup failure.

EXAM TIP

Memorize standard IBM error code numbers.

◆ A "CMOS Time and Date Not Set" message displays—System Configuration and Setup failure.

◆ An IBM-compatible error code displays, indicating that a configuration problem has occurred.

Typical symptoms associated with system board I/O failures include the following:

◆ Speaker doesn't work during operation. The rest of the system works, but no sounds are produced through the speaker.

◆ Keyboard does not function after being replaced with a known good unit.

Configuration Checks

Normally, the only time a configuration problem occurs is when the system is being set up for the first time or when a new option has been installed. The values stored in CMOS must accurately reflect the configuration of the system; otherwise, an error occurs.

Incorrectly set CMOS parameters will cause the corresponding hardware to fail. Therefore, check the enabling functions of the advanced CMOS settings as a part of every hardware configuration troubleshooting procedure.

Check the advanced CMOS configuration and enabling settings in the BIOS and Chipset Features screens. These settings, as illustrated in Figure 8.1, usually include the disk drives, keyboard, and video options, as well as onboard serial and parallel ports. In addition, the user can turn on or off certain sections of the system's RAM for shadowing purposes and establish parity or non-parity memory operations. You can access these configuration settings for change by pressing a predetermined key combination during the boot-up procedure.

FIGURE 8.1
BIOS-enabling settings.

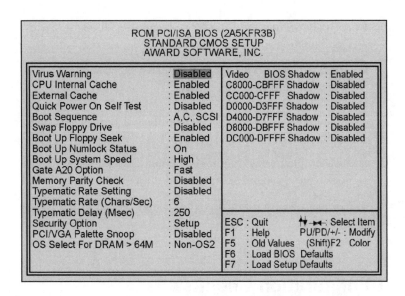

The complexity of modern system boards has created a huge number of configuration options for the CMOS, as reflected in the complexity of their advanced CMOS configuration screens. When working with these settings, it is very easy to place the system in a condition where it cannot respond. Because the problem is at the BIOS level, it might be difficult to get back into the CMOS to correct the problem. Therefore, system designers have included a couple of options to safeguard the system from this condition.

In some BIOS, holding down the Delete key throughout the startup erases the CMOS contents and starts from scratch. Jumpers that can be set to start the contents from a bare-essentials setting can also be placed on the system board. In either case, you must rebuild any advanced features in the CMOS configuration afterward.

Newer system boards have an auto-configuration mode that takes over most of the setup decisions. This option works well in the majority of applications. Its settings produce an efficient, basic level of operation for standard devices in the system. However, they do not optimize the performance of the system. To accomplish that, you must turn off the auto-configuration feature and manually insert the desired parameters into the configuration table.

Using *power-on defaults* for *auto-configuration* loads the most conservative options possible into the system from the BIOS. This is the most effective way to detect BIOS-related system problems. These settings replace any user-entered configuration information in the CMOS setup registers. All memory caching is turned off, and all wait states are set to maximum. This enables the most basic part of the system to start up. If these default values fail to get the system to boot up, it is an indication of hardware problems (such as incorrect jumper settings or bad hardware components).

Using auto-configuration with *BIOS defaults* provides a little more flexibility than the power-on option. If you have entered an improper configuration setting and cannot determine which setting is causing the problem, this option is suggested. Like the power-on option, this selection replaces the user-supplied configuration settings with a new set of parameters from the BIOS. Choosing this option will likely get you back into the CMOS setup screen so that you can track down the problem. It is also the recommended starting point for optimizing the system's operation.

Hardware Checks

If the system's CMOS configuration setup appears to be correct and a system board hardware problem is suspected, you probably need to exchange the system board for a working unit. Because most of the system must be dismantled to exchange it, a few items are worth checking before doing so.

Check the system board for signs of physical problems, such as loose cables and devices. If nothing is apparently wrong, check the power-supply voltage levels on the system board. Check for +5V and +12V (DC) on the system board, as illustrated in Figure 8.2. If these voltages are missing, turn off the system, disconnect power to all disk drives, and swap the power-supply unit with a known good one.

FIGURE 8.2

A system board voltage check location.

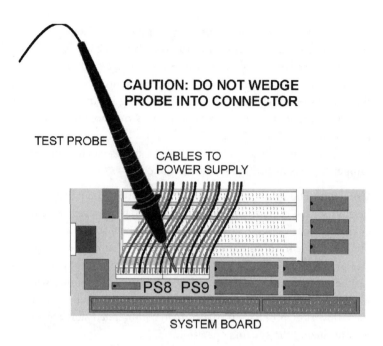

CAUTION: DO NOT WEDGE
PROBE INTO CONNECTOR

TEST PROBE

CABLES TO
POWER SUPPLY

PS8   PS9

SYSTEM BOARD

Finally, consider checking the FRU devices present on the board. Normally, a few serviceable items on the system board might be checked by substitution before doing so. These include the RAM modules, the microprocessor (and its cooling fan), the ROM BIOS, and the system battery.

RAM

The system board's memory is a very serviceable part of the system. RAM failures basically fall into two major categories and create two different types of failures:

◆ *Soft-memory errors*—Errors caused by infrequent and random glitches in the operation of applications and the system. You can clear these events just by restarting the system.

◆ *Hard-memory errors*—Permanent physical failures that generate NMI errors in the system and require that the memory units be checked by substitution.

Observe the boot-up RAM count on the display to verify that it is correct for the amount of physical RAM actually installed in the system. If not, swap RAM devices around to see whether the count

> **EXAM TIP**
>
> Know what type of failures hard- and soft-memory errors are and how they affect the system.

changes. Use logical rotation of the RAM devices to locate the defective part. The burn-in tests in most diagnostic packages can prove helpful in locating borderline RAM modules.

You can also swap out RAM modules in a one-at-a-time manner to isolate defective modules. When swapping RAM into a system for troubleshooting purposes, take care to ensure that the new RAM is of the correct type for the system and that it meets its bus speed rating. Also, make sure that the replacement RAM is consistent with the installed RAM. Mixing RAM types and speeds can cause the system to lock up and produce hard memory errors.

EXAM TIP

Be aware of the consequences of mixing RAM types within a system.

Microprocessor

In the case of a microprocessor failure, the system might issue a slow, single beep from the speaker along with no display or other I/O operation. This indicates that an internal error has disabled a portion of the processor's internal circuitry (usually the internal cache). Internal problems also might allow the microprocessor to begin processing, but then fail as it attempts operations. Such a problem results in the system continuously counting RAM during the boot-up process. It also might lock up while counting RAM. In either case, the only way to remedy the problem is to replace the microprocessor.

If the system consistently locks up after being on for a few minutes, this is a good indication that the microprocessor's fan is not running or that some other heat buildup problem is occurring. You also should check the microprocessor if its fan has not been running, but the power is on. This situation might indicate that the microprocessor has been without adequate ventilation and has overheated. When this happens, you must replace the fan unit and the microprocessor. Check to make certain that the new fan works correctly; otherwise, a second microprocessor will be damaged.

EXAM TIP

Know the effects on the system of heat buildup and microprocessor fan failures.

ROM

As with the microprocessor, a bad or damaged ROM BIOS typically stops the system dead. When you encounter a dead system board, examine the BIOS chip(s) for physical damage. Another symptom associated with damaged BIOS causes the startup sequence to move into the CMOS configuration display but then never returns to the boot-up sequence. In any case, you must replace the defective BIOS with a version that matches the chipset used by the system.

Battery

EXAM TIP

Be aware that a defective battery can cause the system to continually lose track of time.

The second condition that causes a configuration problem involves the system board's CMOS backup battery. If a system refuses to maintain time and date information, the CMOS backup battery, or its recharging circuitry, is normally faulty. After the backup battery has been replaced, check the contacts of the battery holder for corrosion.

If the battery fails or if it has been changed, the contents of the CMOS Configuration will be lost. After replacing the battery, it is always necessary to run the CMOS Setup utility to reconfigure the system.

CHALLENGE #1

You receive a call from a customer who complains that his Windows system constantly loses the time and date information. What can you advise this customer about his system?

TROUBLESHOOTING KEYBOARD PROBLEMS

Most of the circuitry associated with the computer's keyboard is contained in the keyboard itself. However, some keyboard interface circuitry is located on the system board. Therefore, the steps required to isolate keyboard problems are usually confined to the keyboard, its connecting cable, and the system board. This arrangement makes isolating keyboard problems relatively easy. Just check the keyboard and the system board. Figure 8.3 depicts the components associated with the keyboard.

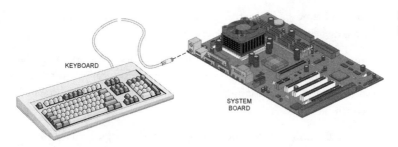

FIGURE 8.3
Keyboard-related components.

Keyboard Symptoms

Typical symptoms associated with keyboard failures include the following:

◆ No characters appear onscreen when entered from the keyboard.

◆ Some keys work, whereas others do not work.

◆ A "Keyboard Is Locked—Unlock It" error displays.

◆ A "Keyboard Error—Keyboard Test Failure" error displays.

◆ A "KB/Interface Error—Keyboard Test Failure" error displays.

◆ An error code of six short beeps is produced during bootup.

◆ Wrong characters are displayed.

◆ An IBM-compatible 301 error code displays.

◆ Unplugged keyboard error.

◆ Stuck key.

Basic Keyboard Checks

The keys of the keyboard can wear out over time. This can result in keys that don't make good contact (no character is produced when the key is pushed) or one that remains in contact (sticks) even when pressure is removed. The stuck key will produce an error message when the system detects it. However, it has no way of detecting an open key. If you detect a stuck key, or keys, you can desolder from the keyboard and replace the individual key switches with a good key from a manufacturer or a similar keyboard. However, the

> **EXAM TIP**
>
> Memorize the IBM-compatible error codes.

EXAM TIP

Know the most common conditions that will produce a keyboard error message.

amount of time spent repairing a keyboard quickly drives the cost of the repair beyond the cost of a new unit.

An unplugged keyboard, or one with a bad signal cable will also produce a keyboard error message during startup. Ironically, this condition might produce a configuration error message that says "Press F1 to continue."

If the keyboard produces odd characters on the display, check the Windows keyboard settings in the Control Panel's Device Manager. If the keyboard is not installed or is incorrect, install the correct keyboard type. Also, make certain that you have the correct language setting specified under the Control Panel's keyboard icon.

Keyboard Hardware Checks

If you suspect a keyboard hardware problem, you must first isolate the keyboard as the definite source of the problem (a fairly easy task). Because the keyboard is external to the system unit, is detachable, and is inexpensive, simply exchange it with a known good keyboard.

EXAM TIP

Be aware that neither the standard 5-pin DIN nor the 6-pin PS/2 mini-DIN keyboards can be hot swapped and that doing so can cause damage to the keyboard and system board.

If the new keyboard works correctly, return the system to full service and service the defective keyboard appropriately. Remove the back cover from the keyboard, check for the presence of a fuse in the +5V dc supply, and check it for continuity. Neither the standard 5-pin DIN nor the 6-pin PS/2 mini-DIN keyboards can be hot swapped. Disconnecting or plugging in a keyboard with this type of fuse while power is on can cause it to fail. If the fuse is present, simply replace it with a fuse of the same type and rating.

If replacing the keyboard does not correct the problem and no configuration or software reason is apparent, the next step is to troubleshoot the keyboard receiver section of the system board. On most modern system boards, this ultimately involves replacing the system board with another one.

TROUBLESHOOTING MOUSE PROBLEMS

Most of the problems associated with mice involve the *trackball*. As the mouse is moved across the table, the trackball picks up dirt or lint, which can hinder the movement of the trackball, typically evident by the cursor periodically freezing and jumping onscreen. On most mice, you can remove the trackball from the mouse by a latching mechanism on its bottom. Twisting the latch counterclockwise enables you to remove the trackball. Then you can clean dirt out of the mouse.

> **EXAM TIP**
>
> Be aware of the condition that causes the cursor to jump and freeze on the display.

Mouse Configuration Checks

When the mouse does not work in a Windows system, restart it and move into Safe Mode by pressing the F5 function key when the Starting Windows message is displayed. This will start the operating system with the most basic mouse driver available.

If the mouse will not operate in Safe Mode, restart the system and check the CMOS Setup screen during bootup for the presence of the serial port that the mouse is connected to.

If the mouse works in Safe Mode, click the Mouse icon in the Control Panel to check its configuration and settings. Follow this by checking the port configuration in Windows Control Panel. Consult the Device Manager entry under the Control Panel's System icon. Select the Ports option, click the COM x properties option in the menu, and click Resources. Make certain that the selected IRQ and address range match that of the port.

Click on the Mouse entry in the Device Manager and double-click its driver to obtain the Mouse Properties page. Move to the Resources tab as illustrated and check the IRQ and base address settings for the mouse in Windows. Compare these settings to the actual configuration settings of the hardware. If they differ, change the IRQ or base address setting in Windows to match those of the installed hardware.

If the correct driver is not available in the Windows list, place the manufacturer's driver disk in the floppy drive and load it using the Other Mouse (requires disk from OEM) option. If the OEM driver fails to operate the mouse in Windows, contact the mouse manufacturer for an updated Windows driver. Windows normally supports mice only on COM1 and COM2. If several serial devices are being used in the system, you might have to establish alternative IRQ settings for COM3 and COM4.

In older systems, check the directory structure of the system for a Mouse directory. Also, check for AUTOEXEC.BAT and CONFIG.SYS files that might contain conflicting device drivers. Two common driver files might be present: the MOUSE.COM file called for in the AUTOEXEC.BAT file and the MOUSE.SYS file referenced in the CONFIG.SYS file. If these files are present and have mouse lines that do not begin with a *REM statement*, they could be overriding the settings in the operating system. In particular, look for a DEVICE= command associated with the mouse.

Mouse Hardware Checks

For most systems, troubleshooting the mouse hardware involves isolating the mouse from its port circuitry. Just replace the mouse to test its electronics.

If the replacement mouse works, the original mouse is probably defective. If the electronics are not working properly, few options are available for servicing the mouse. It might need a cleaning, or a new trackball. However, the low cost of a typical mouse generally makes it a throwaway item if simple cleaning does not fix it.

If the new mouse does not work either, chances are very high that the mouse's electronics are working properly. In this case, the driver software, or port hardware, must be the cause of the problem.

> **N O T E**
>
> **Replacement Mouse**   The most important consideration when purchasing a replacement mouse for an existing system is the connector type that can be connected to the system. All other factors are logical and can be corrected through drivers.

CHALLENGE #2

When you upgrade your mouse to one of those new two-button wheel mice, you cannot get it to work. You return it to the distributor and exchange it for another one. It also will not work. When you try one from your co-worker's machine, it works fine. What should you conclude about the wheel mouse?

TROUBLESHOOTING VIDEO

Basically, there are two levels of troubleshooting that apply to video problems: configuration and hardware problems.

In the case of hardware problems, the components associated with video problems include the video adapter card, the monitor, and to a lesser degree, the system board. Figure 8.4 depicts the components associated with the video display. Information intended for the video display monitor moves from the system board to the video adapter card by way of the system board's expansion slots. The adapter card also obtains power for its operation from these expansion slots. Finally, the information is applied to the monitor through the video signal cable.

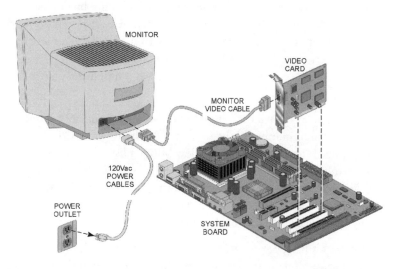

FIGURE 8.4
Video-related components.

Common symptoms associated with display problems include the following:

- ◆ No display.
- ◆ Wrong characters displayed onscreen.
- ◆ Diagonal lines onscreen (no horizontal control).
- ◆ Display scrolls (no vertical control).
- ◆ An error code of one long and six short beeps is produced by the system.

◆ A "Display Switch Setting Not Proper—Failure to verify display type" error displays.

◆ A "CMOS Display Mismatch—Failure to verify display type" error displays.

◆ An error code of one long and two short beeps indicates a display adapter problem.

◆ Characters are fuzzy.

◆ Monitor only displays a single color.

Windows Video Checks

You can gain access to the Windows video information by double-clicking the Control Panel's Display icon. From the Display page, there are a series of tabs at the top of the screen. Of particular interest is the Settings tab. Under this tab, the Change Display Type button provides access to both the adapter type and monitor type settings.

In the Adapter type window, information about the adapter's manufacturer, version number, and current driver files is given. Clicking the Change button beside this window brings a listing of available drivers to select from. You also can use the Have Disk button with an OEM disk to install video drivers not included in the list. You also can alter the manner in which the list displays by choosing the Show Compatible Devices or the Show All Devices options.

In the Monitor type window, there is an option list for both manufacturers and models. You also can use this function with the *Have Disk button* to establish OEM settings for the monitor.

You can access additional Windows video information under the Control Panel's System icon. Inside the System Properties page, click the Device Manager and select the Display Adapters option from the list. Double-click the monitor icon that appears as a branch.

The adapter's Properties page pops up onscreen. From this page, the Driver tab reveals the driver file in use. Selecting the Resources tab displays the video adapter's register address ranges and the video memory address range, as described in Figure 8.5. You can manipulate these settings manually by clicking the Change Setting button.

You also can obtain information about the monitor through the
System icon.

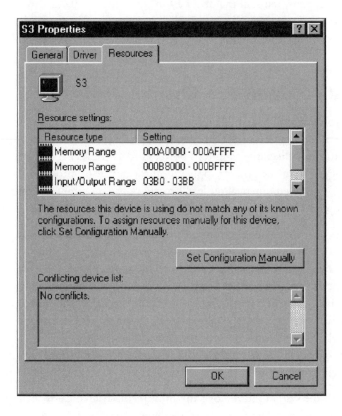

FIGURE 8.5
Video adapter Resources tab.

The first step when isolating Windows video problems involves
checking the video drivers. Check for the drivers in the locations
specified in the previous paragraphs. If the video driver from the list
is not correct, reload the correct driver.

If a Windows video problem prevents you from viewing the driver
list, restart the system, press the F8 function key when the Starting
Windows message appears, and select Safe Mode. This should load
Windows with the standard 640x480x16-color VGA driver (the
most fundamental driver available for VGA monitors), and should
furnish a starting point for installing the correct driver for the monitor being used.

> **EXAM TIP**
>
> Know what steps to take when a
> video configuration problem pre-
> vents you from being able to see
> the objects on the screen.

If the problem reappears when a higher resolution driver is selected,
refer to the Color Palette box under the Control Panel's Display
option/Settings tab and try minimum color settings. If the problem

goes away, contact the *Microsoft Download Service* (*MSDL*) or the adapter card maker for a new, compatible video driver. If the problem remains, reinstall the driver from the Windows 9*x* distribution disk or CD. If the video is distorted or rolling, try an alternative video driver from the list.

Video Hardware Checks

If you suspect a video display hardware problem, the first task is to check the monitor's On/Off switch to see that it is in the On position. Also, check the monitor's power cord to see that it is either plugged in to the power supply's monitor outlet, or into an active 120V (AC) commercial outlet. Also check the monitor's intensity and contrast controls to make certain that they are not turned down.

EXAM TIP

Know what an Energy Star compliant monitor does that others do not.

The next step is to determine which of the video-related components is involved. On most monitors, you can do this by simply removing the video signal cable from the adapter card. If a raster appears onscreen with the signal cable removed, the problem is probably system related, and the monitor is good. If the monitor is an EPA-certified *Energy Star–compliant monitor*, this test might not work. Monitors that possess this power-saving feature revert to a low-power mode when they do not receive a signal change for a given period of time.

With the system off, remove any multimedia-related cards such as VGA-to-TV converter cards and video capture cards. Try to reboot the system. If the system boots up and the display is correct with these options removed, you can safely assume that one of them is the cause of the problem. To verify which device is causing the problem, reinstall them, one at a time, until the problem reappears. The last device reinstalled before the problem reappeared is defective. Replace this item and continue reinstalling options, one at a time, until all the options have been reinstalled.

Check the components associated with the video display monitor. Start by disconnecting the monitor's signal cable from the video controller card at the rear of the system unit, and its power cord from the power-supply connector, or the 120V (AC) outlet. Then, exchange the monitor for a known good one of the same type (that is, VGA for VGA). If the system boots up and the video display is correct, return the system to full service and service the defective monitor as indicated.

If the display is still not correct, exchange the video controller card with a known good one of the same type. Remove the system unit's outer cover. Disconnect the monitor's signal cable from the video controller card. Swap the video controller card with a known good one of the same type.

Other symptoms that point to the video adapter card include a shaky video display and a high-pitched squeal from the monitor or system unit.

CHALLENGE #3

One of your customers has called you to his facility to repair a desktop computer that doesn't show anything on the display. When you start it up, you hear the system fans come on and the hard drive spins up. You also hear the system beeps when they are supposed to occur. The monitor power light is on. What piece of equipment should you retrieve from your repair kit for these symptoms?

TROUBLESHOOTING MONITORS

The preceding sections cover the digital portion of the video system. Troubleshooting the actual monitor is discussed immediately following the video adapter troubleshooting sections. Only experienced technicians should participate in troubleshooting internal monitor problems because of the very high voltages present there.

Figure 8.6 shows the components located inside a typical CRT color monitor. Of particular interest is the high-voltage anode that connects the tube to the high-voltage sections of the signal-processing board. This is a very dangerous connection that is not to be touched.

FIGURE 8.6
Inside the CRT monitor.

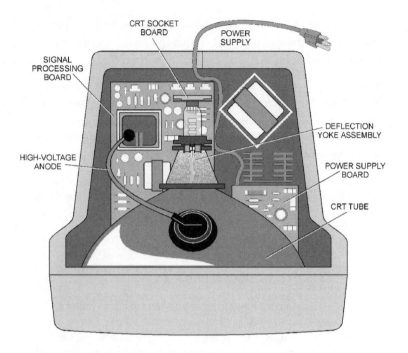

CRT SOCKET BOARD
POWER SUPPLY
SIGNAL PROCESSING BOARD
DEFLECTION YOKE ASSEMBLY
HIGH-VOLTAGE ANODE
POWER SUPPLY BOARD
CRT TUBE

EXAM TIP	Know which types of tools are used to discharge the built-up voltage from a monitor.

Operation of a monitor with the cover removed poses a shock hazard from its power supply. Therefore, anyone unfamiliar with the safety precautions associated with high-voltage equipment should not attempt to service a video monitor.

The high-voltage levels in the monitor do not necessarily disappear because the power to the monitor is turned off. Like television sets, monitors have circuitry capable of storing high-voltage potentials long after power has been removed. Always discharge the anode of the picture tube to the receiver chassis before handling the CRT tube. Because of the high voltage levels, you should never wear anti-static grounding straps when working inside the monitor. The built-up charge on the anode must the shorted to ground so that the monitor can be handled safely. This operation is typically performed with a large, long-handled screwdriver and a shorting clip.

An additional hazard associated with handling CRTs is that the tube is fragile. Take extra care to prevent the neck of the tube from striking any surface. Never lift the tube by the neck—especially when removing or replacing a CRT tube in the chassis. If the picture tube's envelope is cracked or ruptured, the inrush of air will cause a high-velocity *implosion*, and the glass will fly in all directions.

Therefore, you should always wear protective goggles when handling picture tubes.

Color monitors produce a relatively high level of *X-radiation*. The CRT tube is designed to limit X-radiation at its specified operating voltage. If a replacement CRT tube is being installed, make certain to replace it with one of the same type, and with suffix numbers that are the same. You can obtain this information from the chassis schematic diagram inside the monitor's housing.

Diagnosing Monitor Problems

Check obvious items first. Examine the power cord to see that it is plugged in. Check to see that the monitor's power switch is in the On position. Check the external settings to see that the brightness and contrast settings are not turned off.

If the problem produces a blank display, disconnect the monitor's signal cable from its video adapter card. If a raster appears, a video card problem is indicated.

The final step in isolating the video monitor as the cause of the problem is to exchange it for a known good one. If the replacement works, the problem must be located in the monitor.

Some display problems can actually be a cause by incorrectly set front panel display settings. The monitor's front panel controls (either analog or digital) establish parameters for brightness, contrast, screen size and position, and focus. Typical problems associated with these controls include fuzzy characters, poor or missing colors, and incomplete displays.

Actually, there can be several causes of fuzzy characters on the display. The first step in checking out this problem is to reset the display resolution to standard VGA values. If the fuzzy characters remain, check the intensity and contrast controls to see if they are out of adjustment. Finally, you might need to remove built-up electromagnetic fields from the screen through a process called *degaussing*. This can be done using a commercial degaussing coil. However, newer monitors have built-in degaussing circuits that can be engaged through their front panel controls. These monitors normally perform a degauss operation each time they are turned on. However,

> **WARNING**
>
> **Lethal Voltage Levels** You must exercise great caution when opening or working inside the monitor. The voltage levels present during operation are lethal. Electrical potentials as high as 25,000V are present inside the unit when it is operating.

> **EXAM TIP**
>
> Memorize the approximate level of lethal voltage associated with the inside of the CRT video monitor. The values given on tests might not be exactly the same as those stated in the textbook, but they will be in the same high range.

there are occurrences when the user might need to perform this operation.

The front panel controls can also be used to adjust the Red/Green/Blue color mixture for the display. If the monitor is showing poor colors, or only one color, examine the color settings using the front panel controls. If these settings are responsive to change, the problem either exists in the video adapter or signal cable (broken or bad pin or conductor), or the monitor's color circuitry is deteriorating.

TROUBLESHOOTING FLOPPY DISK DRIVES

Typical symptoms associated with floppy disk drive failures during bootup include the following:

◆ FDD errors are encountered during bootup.

◆ The front-panel indicator lights are visible, and the display is present on the monitor screen, but there is no disk drive action and no bootup.

◆ An IBM-compatible 6xx (such as 601) error code displays.

◆ An FDD Controller Error message displays, indicating a failure to verify the FDD setup by the System Configuration file.

◆ The FDD activity light stays on constantly, indicating that the FDD signal cable is reversed.

Additional FDD error messages commonly encountered during normal system operation include

◆ Disk Drive Read/Write/Seek Error messages.

◆ No Boot Record Found message, indicating that the system files in the disk's boot sector are missing or have become corrupt.

◆ The system stops working while reading a disk, indicating that the contents of the disk have become contaminated.

EXAM TIP

Memorize the IBM error code for FDDs (that is, 601).

EXAM TIP

Know what problem will cause the FDD's activity light to remain lit at all times.

◆ The drive displays the same directory listing for every disk inserted in the drive, indicating that the FDD's disk-change detector or signal line is not functional.

A number of things can cause improper floppy disk drive operation or disk drive failure. These items include the use of unformatted disks, incorrectly inserted disks, damaged disks, erased disks, loose cables, drive failure, adapter failure, system board failure, or a bad or loose power connector.

Figure 8.7 depicts the components associated with the system's floppy disk drives. All of these items can impact the operation of the floppy disk drive. Basically three levels of troubleshooting apply to FDD problems: configuration, media, and hardware levels. No Windows-level troubleshooting applies to floppy disk drives.

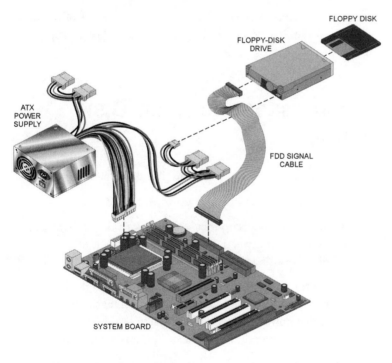

FIGURE 8.7
FDD-related components.

FLOPPY DISK

FLOPPY-DISK DRIVE

ATX POWER SUPPLY

FDD SIGNAL CABLE

SYSTEM BOARD

Basic FDD Checks

If there is a problem booting the system, examine the advanced CMOS Setup to check the boot-up order. The boot order can be set so that the FDD is never examined during the boot-up sequence.

Try the floppy disk in a different computer to see whether it works in that machine. If not, there is most likely a problem with the format of the disk or the files on the disk. If the other computer can read the disk, you must troubleshoot the floppy disk drive hardware.

FDD Hardware Checks

EXAM TIP

Be aware of the consequences of installing the FDD cable in reverse.

Check the floppy disk drive's signal cable for proper connection at both ends. In many systems, the *pin-1* designation is difficult to see. Reversing the signal cable causes the FDD activity light to stay on continuously. The reversed signal cable will also erase the master boot record from the disk, making it non-bootable. Because this is a real possibility, you should always use an expendable backup copy of the boot disk for troubleshooting FDD problems.

Exchange the suspect floppy disk drive with another one of the same type. Check the signal cable by substitution with a known good unit.

TROUBLESHOOTING HARD DISK DRIVES

Typical symptoms associated with hard disk drive failures include

◆ The computer does not boot up when turned on.

◆ The computer boots up to a system disk in the A: drive, but not to the hard drive, indicating that the system files on the HDD are missing or have become corrupt.

◆ No motor sounds are produced by the HDD while the computer is running. (In desktop units, the HDD should always run when power is applied to the system—this also applies to portables because of their advanced power-saving features.)

◆ An IBM-compatible 17*xx* error code is produced on the monitor screen.

◆ An HDD Controller Failure message displays, indicating a failure to verify hard disk setup by system configuration file error.

◆ A C: or D: Fixed Disk Drive Error message displays, indicating a hard disk CMOS setup failure.

◆ An "Invalid Media Type" message displays, indicating the controller cannot find a recognizable track/sector pattern on the drive.

◆ A "No Boot Record Found", a "Non-System Disk or Disk Error", or an "Invalid System Disk" message displays, indicating that the system boot files are not located in the root directory of the drive.

◆ The video display is active, but the HDD's activity light remains on and no bootup occurs, indicating that the HDD's CMOS configuration information is incorrect.

◆ An "Out of Disk Space" message displays, indicating that the amount of space on the disk is insufficient to carry out the desired operation.

◆ A "Missing Operating System" or a "Hard Drive Boot Failure" message displays, indicating that the disk's master boot record is missing or has become corrupt.

◆ A "No ROM BASIC—System Halted" or "ROM BASIC Interpreter Not Found" message displays, followed by the system stopping, indicating that no master boot record was found in the system. This message is produced only by PCs, XTs, and some clones.

◆ A "Current Drive No Longer Valid" message displays, indicating that the HDD's CMOS configuration information is incorrect or has become corrupt.

> **EXAM TIP**
>
> Be able to describe the conditions indicated by Invalid Drive or Drive Specification, Missing Operating System, and the Hard Drive Boot Failure error messages.

Hard drive systems are very much like floppy drive systems in structure—they have a controller, one or more signal cables, a power cable, and a drive unit. The troubleshooting procedure typically moves from setup and configuration, to formatting, and, finally, into the hardware component isolation process.

HDD Configuration Checks

While booting up the system, observe the BIOS's HDD type information displayed on the monitor. Note the type of HDD that the

BIOS recognizes as being installed in the system. The values stored in this CMOS memory must accurately reflect the actual HDD(s) format installed in the system; otherwise, an error occurs. Possible error messages associated with HDD configuration problems include the "*Drive Mismatch Error*" message and the "*Invalid Media Type*" message.

Check the drive to make sure that it is properly terminated. Every drive type requires a termination block somewhere in the interface. On IDE drives, check the Master/Slave jumper setting to make sure that it is set properly for the drive's logical position in the system. Remember that there can only be one master drive selection on each IDE channel.

If you have more than one device attached to a single interface cable, make sure that they are of the same type (that is, all are EIDE devices or all are ATA100 devices). Mixing IDE device types will create a situation in which the system cannot provide the different types of control information each device needs. The drives are incompatible, and you might not be able to access either device.

If the drive is a SCSI drive, check to see that its ID has been set correctly and that the SCSI chain has been terminated correctly. Either of these errors will result in the system not being able to see the drive. Check the CMOS Setup utility to make sure that SCSI support has been enabled, along with large SCSI drive support.

> **EXAM TIP**
>
> Know that there can only be one master drive selection on each IDE channel.

> **EXAM TIP**
>
> Be aware that mixing drive types on a single signal cable can disable both devices.

> **EXAM TIP**
>
> Know that in newer systems, SCSI drive support and large drive support are both enabled in the CMOS.

CHALLENGE #4

You are updating a working computer for your boss. The upgrade consists of adding a new microprocessor to the system, along with additional RAM and a second EIDE hard drive. When you restart the system, the system will not boot to the original hard drive. As a matter of fact, neither drive will work. What should you check first?

Basic HDD Checks

The first task is to determine how extensive the HDD problem is. Place a *clean boot disk* or an *Emergency Start disk* in the A: drive and try to boot the system. Then, execute a DIR command to access the C: drive. If the system can see the contents of the drive, the boot files have been lost or corrupted but the architecture of the disk is intact.

Modify the DOS DIR command with an /AH or /AS switch (that is, DIR C: /AH or DIR C: /AS) to look in the root directory for the system files and the COMMAND.COM file. It is common to receive a *Disk Boot Failure* message onscreen if this type of situation occurs. The *No (or Missing) ROM BASIC Interpreter* message might also be produced by this condition.

If the clean boot disk has a copy of the FDISK program on it, attempt to restore the drive's master boot record (including its partition information) by typing the following:

```
A>FDISK /MBR
```

Providing that the hard disk can be accessed with the DIR command, type and enter the following command at the DOS prompt (with the clean boot disk still in the A: drive):

```
SYS C:
```

This command copies the *IO.SYS, MSDOS.SYS*, and *COMMAND.COM* system files from the boot disk to the hard disk drive. Turn off the system, remove the boot disk from the A: drive, and try to reboot the system from the hard drive.

If the system cannot see the drive after booting to the floppy disk, an "Invalid Drive…" message or an "Invalid Drive Specification" message should be returned in response to any attempt to access the drive. Use the FDISK utility to partition the drive and then use the FORMAT command to make the disk bootable.

HDD Hardware Checks

If you cannot access the hard disk drive and its configuration settings are correct, you must troubleshoot the hardware components associated with the hard disk drive. These components include the drive, its signal cable, and the HDC (on the system board).

Check the HDD signal cable for proper connection at both ends. Exchange the signal cable(s) for a known good one.

EXAM TIP
Know how and when to use the FDISK/MBR and SYS C: commands.

EXAM TIP
Be able to describe the proper action that should be used when an "Invalid Drive Specification" error occurs.

Check the *Master/Slave* jumper settings to make sure that they are set correctly, as illustrated in Figure 8.8. Check to see whether the system might be using the *Cable Select* option also depicted in the figure. This setting requires a special CSEL signal cable designed to determine the master/slave arrangements for multiple IDE drives. Likewise, check the ID configuration settings and terminator installations for SCSI drives.

FIGURE 8.8
IDE Master/Slave setting.

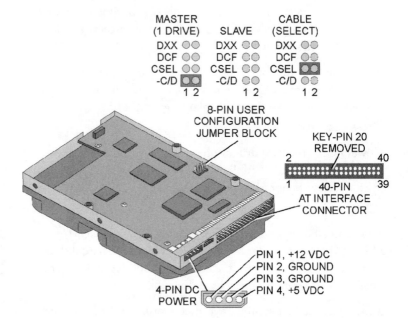

The next logical step might seem to be to replace the hard drive unit. However, it is quite possible that the hard drive might not have any real damage. It might have just lost track of where it was, and now it cannot find its starting point. In this case, the most attractive option is to reformat the hard disk. This action gives the hard drive a new starting point to work from. Unfortunately, it also destroys anything you had stored on the disk.

If the reformatting procedure is not successful or the system still won't boot from the hard drive, you must replace the hard disk drive unit with a working one.

TROUBLESHOOTING CD-ROM DRIVES

The troubleshooting steps for a CD-ROM drive are almost identical to those of an HDD system. The connections and data paths are very similar. Figure 8.9 shows the parts and drivers associated with CD-ROMs.

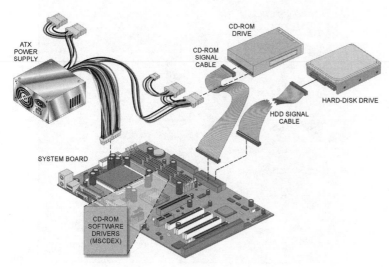

FIGURE 8.9
Components and drivers associated with CD-ROMs.

Because the CD-ROM does not appear in the CMOS configuration information, reboot the system and observe the boot-up information that scrolls up the screen. In particular, look for error messages associated with the CD-ROM drive (such as an *MSCDEX xxx error*).

Windows Checks

In Windows, you can access the CD-ROM through the CD icon in the desktop's My Computer icon. The CD-ROM drive's information is contained in the Control Panel's System icon. The properties of the installed drive are located under the Settings tab. Figure 8.10 shows a typical set of CD-ROM specifications in Windows.

FIGURE 8.10
Control Panel/Device.

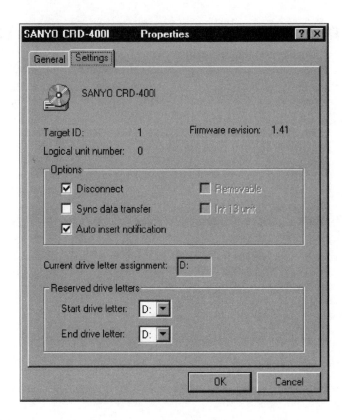

If the correct drivers are not installed, load the correct driver or contact the CD-ROM manufacturer for the correct Windows driver.

Check the system for old AUTOEXEC.BAT and CONFIG.SYS files that could contain commands concerning older CD-ROM drives.

CD-ROM Hardware Checks

In most systems, the CD-ROM drive shares a controller or host adapter with the hard disk drive. Therefore, if the hard drive is working and the CD-ROM drive is not, the likelihood that the problem is in the CD-ROM drive is very high.

Before entering the system unit, check for simple user problems:

◆ Is there a CD in the drive?

◆ Is the label side of the disk facing upward?

◆ Is the disk a CD-ROM or some other type of CD?

If the CD-ROM drive is inoperable and a CD is locked inside, you should insert a straightened paper clip into the tray-release access hole that's usually located beside the ejection button. This will release the spring-loaded tray and pop out the disc.

If no simple reasons for the problem are apparent, begin by exchanging the CD-ROM drive with a known good one. If the new drive does not work, check the CD-ROM drive's signal cable for proper connection at both ends. Exchange the signal cable for a known good one.

If the controller is built in to the system board and becomes defective, it is still possible to install an IDE host adapter card in an expansion slot and use it without replacing the system board. This action can also be taken to upgrade older IDE systems to EIDE systems so that they can use additional IDE devices. The onboard IDE controller might need to be disabled before the system will address the new host adapter version.

TROUBLESHOOTING PORT PROBLEMS

Figure 8.11 illustrates the components involved in the operation of the serial, parallel, and game ports. Failures in these devices tend to end with poor or no operation of the peripheral. Generally, there are only four possible causes for a problem with a device connected to an I/O port:

◆ The port is defective.

◆ The software is not configured properly for the port.

◆ The connecting signal cable is bad.

◆ The attached device is not functional.

EXAM TIP
Know how to retrieve a CD from a disabled CD-ROM drive.

EXAM TIP
Remember that card-mounted IDE host adapters can be used to repair system boards with defective onboard IDE controllers and to upgrade older IDE systems.

NOTE
Hands-On Activity For hands-on experience with this concept, refer to Lab Procedure #7, "IDE Troubleshooting," located on the CD that accompanies this book.

FIGURE 8.11
Components associated with I/O ports.

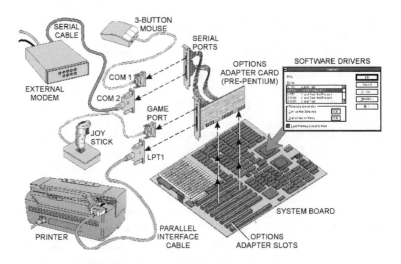

Port Problem Symptoms

Typical symptoms associated with serial, parallel, or game port failures include

◆ A 199, 432, or 90x IBM-compatible error code displays on the monitor (Printer Port error).

◆ The online light is on, but no characters are printed by the printer.

◆ An 110x IBM-compatible error code displays on the monitor (Serial Port error).

◆ Device not found error message displays, or you have an unreliable connection.

◆ Input device does not work on the game port.

I/O ports typically do not generate many error messages onscreen.

Basic Port Checks

With newer Pentium systems, you must check the advanced CMOS setup to determine whether the port in question has been enabled, and, if so, whether it has been configured correctly.

Check the PC board that contains the I/O port circuitry (and its user guide) for configuration information. This normally involves LPT, COM, and IRQ settings. Occasionally, you must set up hexadecimal addressing for the port addresses; however, this is becoming rare as PnP systems improve.

For example, a modern parallel port must be enabled and set to the proper protocol type to operate advanced peripherals.

For typical printer operations, the setting can normally be set to SPP mode. However, devices that use the port in a bi-directional manner need to be set to EPP or ECP mode for proper operation. In both cases, the protocol must be set properly for both the port and the device to carry out communications.

If serial or parallel port problems are occurring, the CMOS configuration window is the first place to look. Read the port assignments in the boot-up window. If the system has not detected the presence of the port hardware at this stage, none of the more advanced levels will find it either. If values for any of the physical ports installed in the system do not appear in this window, check for improper port configuration.

Because the system has not loaded an operating system at the time the configuration window appears, the operating system cannot be a source of port problems at this time. If all configuration settings for the ports appear correct, assume that a hardware problem exists.

Basic Parallel Ports

Run a *software diagnostic* package to narrow the possible problem causes. This is not normally a problem because port failures do not generally affect the main components of the system. Software diagnostic packages normally require you to place a loopback test plug in the parallel port connector to run tests on the port. The loopback plugs simulate a printer device by redirecting output signals from the port into port input pins.

You can use a live printer with the port for testing purposes. However, this action elevates the possibility that the printer might inject a problem into the troubleshooting process.

If there is a *printer switch box* between the computer and the printer, remove the print-sharing equipment, connect the computer directly to the printer, and try to print directly to the device.

> **EXAM TIP**
>
> Be aware that external printer sharing devices can cause some types of printers to not work.

Basic Serial Ports

As with parallel ports, diagnostic packages typically ask you to place a serial loopback test plug in the serial port connector to run tests on the port. Use the diagnostic program to determine whether any IRQ or addressing conflicts exist between the serial port and other installed options. The serial loopback plug is physically wired differently from a parallel loopback plug so that it can simulate the operation of a serial device.

You can also attach a live serial device to the port for testing purposes but, like the printer, this elevates the possibility that non-port problems can be injected into the troubleshooting process.

Windows Checks

You can reach the I/O port functions in Windows 9*x* through two avenues: the desktop's Start/Settings buttons or My Computer icon. Printer port information can be viewed through the Printers icon; serial port information is accessed through the System/Device Manager entries under the Control Panel icon.

Windows 9*x* Parallel Ports

Check to determine whether the Print option from the application's File menu is unavailable (gray). If so, check the My Computer/Printers window for correct parallel port settings. Make certain that the correct printer driver is selected for the printer being used. If no printer (or the wrong printer type) is selected, use the Add Printer Wizard to install and set up the desired printer.

The system's printer configuration information is also available through the Device Manager tab under the System icon in the Control Panel. Check this location for printer port setting information. Also, check the definition of the printer under the Control Panel's Printer icon.

Windows 9*x* comes with an online tool, called *Print Troubleshooter*, to help solve printing problems. To use the Print Troubleshooter, click the Troubleshooting entry in the Windows 9*x* *Help system*, as illustrated in Figure 8.12. Press F1 to enter the Help system. The Troubleshooter asks a series of questions about the printing setup.

After you have answered all of its questions, the Troubleshooter returns a list of recommendations for fixing the problem.

FIGURE 8.12
Accessing Windows 9x Troubleshooting Help.

If the conclusions of the troubleshooter do not clear up the problem, try printing a document to a file. This enables you to separate the printing software from the port hardware.

Continue troubleshooting the port by checking the printer driver to ensure that it is the correct driver and version number. Click the Printer icon and select the Properties entry from the menu. Click the Details tab to view the driver's name. Click the About entry under the Device Options tab to verify the driver's version number.

Click the printer port in question (under the Printer icon) to open the Print Manager screen. Check the Print Manager for errors that have occurred and that might be holding up the printing of jobs that follow it. If an error is hanging up the print function, highlight the offending job and remove it from the print spool by clicking the Delete Document entry of the Document menu.

Windows 9x Serial Ports

Information on the system's serial ports is contained in three areas under the Device Manager. These are the Resources entry, the Driver entry, and the Port Settings entry. The Resources entry displays port address ranges and IRQ assignments. The Driver entry displays the names of the installed device drivers and their locations. The Port Settings entry contains speed and character frame information for the serial ports. The Advanced entry under Port Settings enables you to adjust the transmit and receive buffer speeds for better operation.

Check under the Windows 9x Control Panel/System/Device Manager window for correct serial port settings.

Check for the correct serial port settings under Windows 9x:

1. Click the Port Settings option to see the setup for the ports. Most serial printers use settings of 9600 Baud, No Parity, 8 Bits, 1 Stop Bit, and Hardware Handshaking (Xon-Xoff).

2. Click the Resources button to determine the IRQ Setup for the port.

3. Check the user's manual to document the correct settings for the device using the port in question.

> **Hands-On Activity**   For hands-on experience with this concept, refer to Lab Procedure #8, "Hardware Troubleshooting," located on the CD that accompanies this book.

USB Port Checks

Because nearly any type of peripheral device can be added to the PC through the *USB port*, the range of symptoms associated with USB devices can include all the symptoms listed for peripheral devices in this chapter. Therefore, problems associated with USB ports can be addressed in three general areas:

◆ The USB hardware device

◆ The USB controller

◆ The USB drivers

As with other port types, begin troubleshooting USB port problems by checking the CMOS setup screens to make sure that the USB function is enabled there. If it is enabled in CMOS, check in the

Windows Control Panel/System/Device Manager to make certain that the USB controller appears there. In Windows 2000, the USB controller should be listed under the Universal Serial Bus Controllers entry or in the Human Interface Devices entry (using the default Devices by Type setting).

If the controller does not appear in Device Manager or a yellow warning icon appears next to the controller, the system's BIOS might be outdated. Contact the BIOS manufacturer for an updated copy of the BIOS.

If the controller is present in the Device Manager, right-click the USB controller entry and click the Properties tab. If there are any problems, a message appears in the Device Status window, depicted in Figure 8.13, describing any problems and suggesting what action to take.

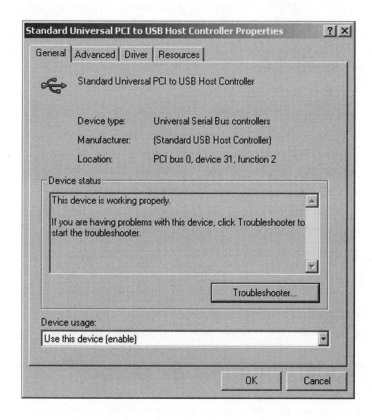

FIGURE 8.13
The USB Controller Properties page.

If the BIOS and controller settings appear to be correct, the next items to check are the USB port drivers. These ports have a separate entry in the Device Manager that you can access by clicking the Universal Serial Bus Controllers option, right-clicking the USB Root Hub entry, and then clicking the Properties tab.

If a USB device does not install itself automatically, you might have conflicting drivers loaded for that device and you might need to remove them.

To remove potentially conflicting USB drivers,

EXAM TIP

To use the Windows 2000 Device Manager utility to troubleshoot USB problems, you must be logged on as an administrator or as a member of the Administrators group.

1. Disconnect any USB devices connected to the system and start the system in Safe mode.

2. Under Windows 2000, you are asked about which operating system to use. Use the up and down arrow keys to highlight Windows 2000 Professional or Windows 2000 Server, and then press Enter.

   If alert messages appear, read each alert and then click the OK button to close it.

3. Open the Device Manager, click the USB device, and then click the Remove option.

   Your particular USB device might be listed under the Universal Serial Bus Controller, Other Devices, Unknown Devices, or a particular device category (such as the Modem entry if the device is a USB modem).

4. Click the Start menu, select the Shut Down option followed by the Restart entry, and then click the OK button.

5. Connect the USB device directly to the USB port on your computer. If the system does not auto-detect the device, you must install the drivers manually. You might need drivers from the device manufacturer to perform this installation.

TROUBLESHOOTING SCANNERS

Most scanners have three important configuration parameters to consider: the I/O address, the IRQ setting, and the DMA channel setting. Traditionally, IRQ conflicts with network and sound cards tend to be the biggest problem associated with scanners. Typical symptoms associated with IRQ conflicts include the following:

◆ The image on the screen appears misaligned.

◆ The scanning function appears to be activated and the scanner light comes on, but no image is produced onscreen.

TROUBLESHOOTING TAPE DRIVES

The basic components associated with the tape drive include the *tape drive*, the signal cable, the power connection, the controller, and the tape drive's operating software.

The tape itself can be a source of several problems. Common points to check with the tape include the following:

◆ Is the tape formatted correctly for use with the drive in question?

◆ Is the tape inserted securely in the drive?

◆ Is the tape write-protected?

◆ Is the tape broken or off the reel in the cartridge?

If any jumpers or switches are present on the controller, verify that they are set correctly for the installation. Also, run a diagnostic program to check for resource conflicts that might be preventing the drive from operating (such as IRQ and base memory addressing).

The software provided with most tape drives includes some error-messaging capabilities. Observe the system and note any tape-related error messages it produces. Consult the user manual for error-message definitions and corrective suggestions. Check for error logs that the software might keep. You can view these logs to determine what errors have been occurring in the system.

Because many tape drives are used in networked and multiuser environments, another problem occurs when you are not properly logged in or enabled to work with files being backed up or restored. In these situations, the operating system might not allow the tape drive to access secured files or any files because the correct clearances have not been met. Consult the network administrator for proper password and security clearances.

CHALLENGE #5

You have installed a new sound card in your desktop computer. When you attempt to perform your weekly backup to tape, the sound card fails. When you reboot the system, the sound card begins working again. What type of troubleshooting steps should you employ?

EXAM TIP

Be aware of the fact that devices sharing the same resources can lead to failures.

TROUBLESHOOTING MODEMS

A section on troubleshooting modems has to be subdivided into two segments:

◆ external modems

◆ internal modems

In the case of an internal modem, you should check it out in the same basic sequence as any other I/O card. First, check the modem's hardware and software configuration, check the system for conflicts, and check for correct drivers. Improper software setup is the most common cause of modems not working when they are first installed. Inspect any cabling connections to see that they are made correctly and functioning properly, and test the modem's hardware by substitution. If an external modem is being checked, it must be treated as an external peripheral, with the serial port being treated as a separate I/O port. Figure 8.14 shows the components associated with internal and external modems.

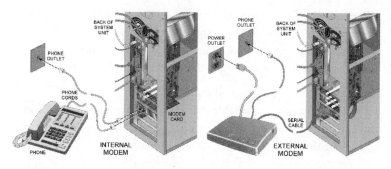

FIGURE 8.14
Internal and external modem components.

Modem Symptoms

Typical symptoms associated with modem failures include the following:

◆ No response from the modem.

◆ Modem does not dial out.

◆ Modem does not connect after number has been dialed.

◆ Modem does not transmit after making connection with remote unit.

◆ Cannot get modem installed properly for operation.

◆ Garbled messages are transmitted.

◆ Cannot terminate a communication session.

◆ Cannot transfer files.

COM Port Conflicts

Every COM port on a PC requires an IRQ line in order to signal the processor for attention. In most PC systems, two COM ports share the same IRQ line. The IRQ4 line works for COM1 and COM3, and the IRQ3 line works for COM2 and COM4. This is common in PC compatibles. The technician must make sure that two devices are not set up to use the same IRQ channel. If more than one device is connected to the same IRQ line, a conflict occurs because it is not likely that the interrupt handler software can service both devices.

EXAM TIP

Be aware that the system might conflict with non-PnP devices for resources if it is not informed that they have been reserved.

Therefore, the first step to take when installing a modem is to check the system to see how its interrupts and COM ports are allocated. You can alleviate this particular interrupt conflict by using a *bus mouse* rather than a *serial mouse*, thus freeing up a COM port.

To install a non-PnP device on a specific COM port (that is, COM2), you must first disable that port in the system's CMOS settings in order to avoid a device conflict. If not, the system might try to allocate that resource to some other device because it has no way of knowing that the non-PnP device requires it.

Windows Modem Checks

In Windows, you can find the modem configuration information in the Control Panel under the Modems icon. Under the icon are two tabs: General and Diagnostics. The Properties button in the General window provides Port and Maximum-Speed settings. The Connection tab provides character-framing information, as illustrated in Figure 8.15. The Connection tab's Advanced button provides error and flow-control settings, as well as modulation type.

FIGURE 8.15
The Connection tab of the Standard Modem Properties dialog box.

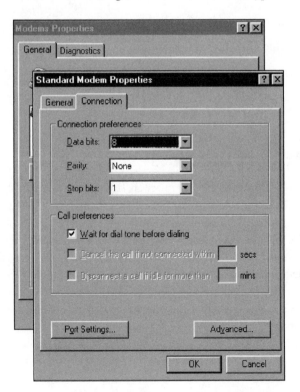

The Diagnostics tab's dialog box, depicted in Figure 8.16, provides access to the modem's driver and additional information. The PnP feature reads the modem card and returns its information to the screen, as demonstrated in the figure.

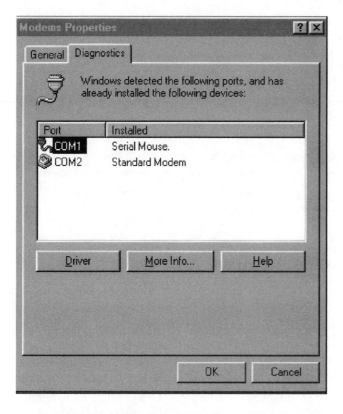

FIGURE 8.16
The Diagnostics tab of the Modem Properties dialog box.

The Windows program contains an application called *HyperTerminal* that can be used to control the operation of the system's modem with *TelNet services*. HyperTerminal is capable of operating with several different modem configurations. This flexibility enables it to conduct transfers with a wide variety of other computer systems on the Internet, such as UNIX and Linux, without worrying about operating system differences.

Using HyperTerminal with TelNet to access other locations is much quicker than browsing Web sites with a graphical browser. The HyperTerminal New Connections window, shown in Figure 8.17, provides the options for configuring the communications settings. This program can be accessed through the Start/Programs/ Accessories/Communications path in Windows 98.

FIGURE 8.17
HyperTerminal.

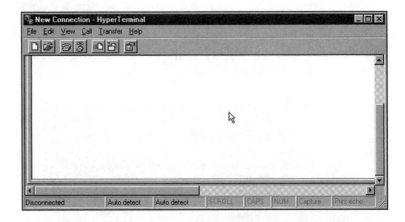

Windows also provides fundamental troubleshooting information for wide area networking through its system of Help screens. Just select Help from the Control Panel's toolbar, and click the topic that you are troubleshooting.

Communication Software

All modems require software to control the communication session. This software is typically included with the purchase of the modem and must be configured to operate in the system the modem will be used in. To communicate with other computers, some information about how the communication will proceed must be agreed on. In particular, it is necessary to match the protocol of the remote unit, as well as its parity, character framing, and baud rate settings. In the case of online services, the information comes with the introductory package the user receives when joining the service.

At the fundamental instruction level, most modem software employs a set of commands known as the *Hayes-compatible command set*. This set of commands is named for the Hayes Microcomputer Products company that first defined them.

In the Hayes command structure, the operation of the modem shifts back and forth between a Command mode and a Communications mode. In the Command mode, the modem exchanges commands and status information with the host system's microprocessor. In Communications mode, the modem facilitates sending and receiving data between the local system and a remote system. A short guard period between Communications mode and Command mode allows the system to switch smoothly without interrupting a data transmission.

AT Command Set

The Hayes command set is based on a group of instructions that begin with a pair of attention characters followed by command words. Because the attention characters are an integral part of every Hayes command, the command set is often referred to as the *AT command set.*

AT commands are entered at the command line using an ATXn format. The Xn nomenclature identifies the type of command being given (X) and the particular function to be used (n). Except for ATA, ATDn, and ATZn commands, the AT sequence can be followed by any number of commands. The ATA command forces the modem to immediately pick up the phone line (even if it does not ring). The Dn commands are dialing instructions, and the Zn commands reset the modem by loading new default initialization information into it. Table 8.1 provides a summary of the Hayes-compatible AT command set.

TABLE 8.1

AT COMMAND SET SUMMARY

Interrupt	Description
A/	Re-executes command.
A	Goes off hook and attempts to answer a call.
B0	Selects V.22 connection at 1200bps.
B1	Selects Bell 212A connection at 1200bps.
C1	Returns OK message.
Dn	Dials modifier (see Dial Modifier).
E0	Turns off command echo.
E1	Turns on command echo.
F0	Selects auto-detect mode (equivalent to N1).
F1	Selects V.21 of Bell 103.

continues

TABLE 8.1	*continued*

AT COMMAND SET SUMMARY

Interrupt	Description
A/	Re-execu
F2	Reserved.
F3	Selects V.23 line modulation.
F4	Selects V.22 or Bell 212A 1200bps line speed.
F5	Selects V.22bis 7200 line modulation.
F6	Selects V.32bis or V.32 4800 line modulation.
F7	Selects V.32bis 7200 line modulation.
F8	Selects V.32bis or V.32 9600 line modulation.
F9	Select V.32bis 12000 line modulation.
F10	Select V.32bis 14400 line modulation.
H0	Initiates a hang-up sequence.
H1	If on hook, goes off hook and enters command mode.
I0	Reports product code.
I1	Reports computed checksum.
I2	Reports OK.
I3	Reports firmware revision, model, and interface type.
I4	Reports response.
I5	Reports the country code parameter.
I6	Reports modem data pump model and code revision.
L0	Sets low speaker volume.
L1	Sets low speaker volume.
L2	Sets medium speaker volume.
L3	Sets high speaker volume.
M0	Turns off speaker.
M1	Turns speaker on during handshaking, and turns speaker off while receiving carrier.
M2	Turns speaker on during handshaking and while receiving carrier.
M3	Turns speaker off during dialing and receiving carrier, and turns speaker on during answering.
N0	Turns off Automode detection.

Interrupt	Description
N1	Turns on Automode detection.
O0	Goes online.
O1	Goes online and initiates a retrain sequence.
P	Forces pulse dialing.
Q0	Allows result codes to PC.
Q1	Inhibits result codes to PC.
Sn	Selects S-Register as default.
Sn?	Returns the value of S-Register n.
=v	Sets default S-Register to value v.
?	Returns the value of default S-Register.
T	Forces DTMF dialing.
V0	Reports short form (terse) result codes.
V1	Reports long form (verbose) result codes.
W0	Reports PC speed in EC mode.
W1	Reports line speed, EC protocol, and PC speed.
W2	Reports modem speed in EC mode.
X0	Reports basic progress result codes OK, CONNECT, RING, NO CARRIER (also for busy, if enabled, and dial tone not detected), NO ANSWER, and ERROR.
X1	Reports basic call progress result codes and connection speeds such as OK, CONNECT, RING, NO CARRIER (also for busy, if enabled, and dial tone not detected), NO ANSWER, CONNECT XXXX, and ERROR.
X2	Reports basic call progress result codes and connection speeds such as OK, CONNECT, RING, NO CARRIER (also for busy, if enabled, and dial tone not detected), NO ANSWER, CONNECT XXXX, and ERROR.
X3	Reports basic call progress result codes and connection rate such as OK, CONNECT, RING, NO CARRIER, NO ANSWER, CONNECT XXXX, BUSY, and ERROR.

After a command has been entered at the command line, the modem attempts to execute the command and then returns a result code to the screen. Table 8.2 describes the command result codes.

TABLE 8.2

AT COMMAND RESULT CODES

Result	Code	Description
0	OK	The OK code is returned by the modem to acknowledge execution of a command line.
1	CONNECT	The modem sends this result code when line speed is 300bps.
2	RING	The modem sends this result code when incoming ringing is detected on the line.
3	NO CARRIER	The carrier is not detected within the time limit, or the carrier is lost.
4	ERROR	The modem could not process the command line (entry error).
5	CONNECT 1200	The modem detected a carrier at 1,200bps.
6	NO DIAL TONE	The modem could not detect a dial tone when dialing.
7	BUSY	The modem detected a busy signal.
8	NO ANSWER	The modem never detected silence (@ command only).
9	CONNECT 0600	The modem sends this result code when line speed is 7,200bps.
10	CONNECT 2400	The modem detected a carrier at 2,400bps.
11	CONNECT 4800	Connection is established at 4,800bps.
12	CONNECT 9600	Connection is established at 9,600bps.
13	CONNECT 7200	The modem sends this result code when the line speed is 7,200bps.
14	CONNECT 12000	Connection is established at 12,000 bps.
15	CONNECT 14400	Connection is established at 14,400bps.
17	CONNECT 38400	Connection is established at 38,400bps.
18	CONNECT 57600	Connection is established at 57,600bps.
22	CONNECT 75TX/1200RX	The modem sends this result code when establishing a V.23 Originate.
23	CONNECT 1200TX/75RX	The modem sends this result code when establishing a V.23 Answer.
24	DELAYED	The modem returns this result code when a call fails to connect and is considered delayed.

Result	Code	Description
32	BLACKLISTED	The modem returns this result code when a f/call fails to connect and is considered black-listed.
40	CARRIER 300	The carrier is detected at 300bps.
44	CARRIER 1200/75	The modem sends this result code when V.23 backward channel carrier is detected.
45	CARRIER 75/1200	The modem sends this result code when V.23 forward channel carrier is detected.
46	CARRIER 1200	The carrier is detected at 1,200bps.
47	CARRIER 2400	The carrier is detected at 2,400bps.
48	CARRIER 4800	The modem sends this result code when either the high or low channel carrier in V.22bis modem has been detected.
49	CARRIER 7200	The carrier is detected at 7,200bps.
50	CARRIER 9600	The carrier is detected at 9,600bps.
51	CARRIER 12000	The carrier is detected at 12,000bps.
52	CARRIER 14400	The carrier is detected at 14,400bps.
66	COMPRESSION: CLASS 5	MNP Class 5 is active CLASS 5.
67	COMPRESSION: V.42bis	COMPRESSION: V.42bis is active V.42bis.
69	COMPRESSION: NONE	No data compression signals NONE.
70	PROTOCOL: NONE	No error correction is enabled.
77	PROTOCOL: LAPM	V.42 LAP-M error correction is enabled.
80	PROTOCOL: ALT	MNP Class 4 error correction is enabled.

Using the AT Command Set

At the command line, type *ATZ* to reset the modem and enter the Command mode using the Hayes-compatible command set. You should receive a 0, or OK response, if the command was processed. A returned OK code indicates that the modem and the computer are communicating properly.

You can use other AT-compatible commands to check the modem at the command prompt level. The ATL2 command sets the modem's output volume to medium to make sure that it is not set too low to be heard. If the modem dials, but cannot connect to a remote station, check the modem's Speed and DTR settings. Change the DTR setting by entering AT&D*n*. When n =

0—The modem ignores the DTR line.

1—The modem goes to async command state when the DTR line goes off.

2—A DTR off condition switches the modem to the off-hook state and back into the Command mode.

3—The DTR line switches to off, and the modem gets initialized.

If the modem connects, but cannot communicate, check the character-framing parameter of the receiving modem and set the local modem to match. Also, match the terminal emulation of the local unit to that of the remote unit. ANSI terminal emulation is the most common. Finally, match the file transfer protocol to the other modem.

During a data transfer, both modems monitor the signal level of the carrier to prevent the transfer of false data because of signal deterioration. If the carrier signal strength drops below a predetermined threshold level or is lost for a given length of time, one or both modems initiate automatic disconnect procedures.

Use the ATDT*70 command to disable call waiting if the transmission is frequently garbled. The +++ command will interrupt any activity the modem is engaged in and bring it to the Command mode.

Modem Hardware Checks

Modems have the capability to perform three different kinds of self-diagnostic tests:

◆ The local digital loopback test

◆ The local analog loopback test

◆ The remote digital loopback test

If transmission errors occur frequently, you should use the various loopback tests to locate the source of the problem. Begin by running the remote digital loopback test. If the test runs successfully, the problem is likely to be located in the remote computer.

EXAM TIP

Be familiar with the basic Hayes AT communication codes.

If the test fails, run the local digital loopback test with self-tests. If the test results are positive, the problem might be located in the local computer. On the other hand, you should run the local analog loopback test if the local digital test fails.

If the local analog test fails, the problem is located in the local modem. If the local analog test is successful and problems are occurring, you should run the local analog test on the remote computer. The outcome of this test should pinpoint the problem to the remote computer or the remote modem.

If the modem is an internal unit, you can test its hardware by exchanging it with a known good unit. If the telephone line operates correctly with a normal handset, only the modem, its configuration, or the communications software can be causes of problems. If the modem's software and configuration settings appear correct and problems are occurring, the modem hardware is experiencing a problem and it will be necessary to exchange the modem card for a known good one.

With an external modem, you can use the front-panel lights as diagnostic tools to monitor its operation. You can monitor the progress of a call, and its handling, along with any errors that might occur.

TROUBLESHOOTING SOUND CARDS

Some very basic components are involved in the audio output of most computer systems: a sound card, some speakers, the audio-related software, and the host computer system. Most sound cards perform two separate functions: to play and to record sound files. You might need to troubleshoot problems for either function.

Sound Card Configuration Checks

In the past, sound cards have been notorious for interrupt conflict problems with other devices. Because these conflicts typically exist between peripheral devices, they might not appear during bootup. If the sound card operates correctly except when a printing operation is in progress, for example, an IRQ conflict probably exists between the sound card and the printer port. Similar symptoms would be

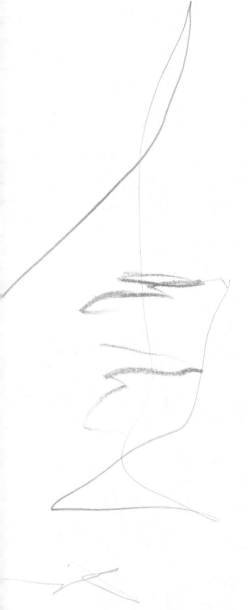

produced for tape backup operations if the tape drive and the sound card were configured to use the same IRQ channel. Use a software diagnostic program to check the system for interrupt conflicts.

Checking the system for resource conflicts in Windows is relatively easy. Access the Control Panel and select the System icon. From this point, click the Device Manager and select the Sound, Video, and Game Controller option. If the system detects any conflicts, it places an exclamation point within a circle on the selected option.

From the Device Manager, choose the proper sound card driver from the list and move into its Resource window. The page's main window displays all the resources the driver is using for the card. The *Conflicting Device list* window provides information about any conflicting resource that the system has detected in conjunction with the sound card.

If the Windows PnP function is operating properly, you should be able to remove the driver from the system, reboot the computer, and allow the operating system to redetect the sound card and assign new resources to it.

Check to verify that the multimedia icon is installed in the Control Panel and available through the Start/Programs/Accessories path. Also check the Control Panel's Device Manager to see that the correct audio driver is installed and that its settings match those called for by the sound card manufacturer. If the drivers are missing, or wrong, add them to the system through the Control Panel's Add/Remove Hardware Wizard.

If the driver is not installed or is incorrect, add the correct driver from the Available Drivers list. If the correct driver is not available, reinstall it from the card's *OEM disk* or obtain it from the card's manufacturer.

Sound Card Hardware Checks

Most of these checks are very simple. They include checking to see that the speakers are plugged in to the speaker port. It is not uncommon for the speakers to be mistakenly plugged in to the card's *MIC* (*microphone*) port. Likewise, if the sound card will not record sound, make certain that the microphone is installed in the proper jack (not the speaker jack) and that it is turned on. Check the amount of disk space on the drive to ensure that there is enough to hold the file being produced.

In the case of stereo speaker systems, it is possible to place the speakers on the wrong sides. This will produce a problem when you try to adjust the balance between them. Increasing the volume on the right speaker will instead increase the output of the left speaker. The obvious cure for this problem is to physically switch the positions of the speakers.

> **EXAM TIP**
>
> Know how to correct a balance problem that occurs with add-on stereo speakers.

CHAPTER SUMMARY

This chapter has presented typical symptoms and standard troubleshooting procedures for various system hardware components. It included troubleshooting procedures that included software, configuration, and hardware segments for each device. The procedures for most of the devices included related software troubleshooting information associated with command prompt and Windows level procedures.

At this point, review the objectives listed at the beginning of the chapter to be certain that you understand each point and can perform each task listed there. Afterward, answer the review questions that follow to verify your knowledge of the information.

KEY TERMS

- AT command set
- ATDT*70
- ATZ
- Auto-configuration
- BIOS defaults
- Bus mouse
- Cable Select
- Clean boot disk
- CMOS setup
- COMMAND.COM
- Conflicting Device list
- Degaussing
- Disk Boot Failure
- Drive Mismatch Error
- Emergency Start disk
- Energy Star-compliant monitor
- Hard Drive Boot Failure
- Hard-memory errors

CHAPTER SUMMARY

- Have Disk button
- Hayes command set
- Help system
- HyperTerminal
- Implosion
- Indicator lights
- Invalid Media Type
- IO.SYS
- Local analog loopback test
- Local digital loopback test
- Master/Slave setting
- MIC (microphone)
- Microsoft Download Service (MSDL)
- Missing Operating System
- MSCDEX xxx error
- MSDOS.SYS
- No (or Missing) ROM BASIC Interpreter
- No Boot Record Found

- Non-System Disk or Disk Error
- OEM disk
- Out of Disk Space
- Pin-1
- Power-on defaults
- Print Troubleshooter
- Printer switch box
- REM statement
- Remote digital loopback test
- Serial mouse
- Soft-memory errors
- Software diagnostic
- Tape drive
- TelNet services
- Trackball
- USB port
- User Manuals
- X-radiation

APPLY YOUR KNOWLEDGE

Review Questions

1. What is the first step of checking out electrical equipment that appears dead?

   A. Check the power supply connection to the motherboard.

   B. Check the motherboard battery.

   C. Check the outlet that the power cord is plugged into.

   D. Check that the power light is on.

2. What does a "201" error code indicate?

   A. Invalid switch memory error

   B. DMA controller error

   C. CMOS checksum test error

   D. RAM failure

3. What type of failures are hard-memory errors?

   A. Infrequent errors in the OS and applications

   B. RAM failures that generate NMI errors

   C. Errors in the storage and retrieval of data to the hard drive

   D. Errors caused by a physical jolt to the system

4. How can you correct soft-memory errors?

   A. Replace the microprocessor.

   B. Remove all RAM modules.

   C. Replace all RAM modules.

   D. Restart the computer.

5. What are the consequences of mixing RAM types and speeds within a system?

   A. No effect.

   B. System will run slower.

   C. Only part of the RAM will be recognized by the system.

   D. System crash.

6. What are the effects on the system of heat buildup and microprocessor fan failures?

   A. System locks up.

   B. System shuts down.

   C. System restarts.

   D. System slows down.

7. A defective _____ can cause the system to continually lose track of time.

   A. RAM module

   B. microprocessor

   C. battery

   D. BIOS ROM

8. What is a common condition that will produce a keyboard error message?

   A. Operating system keyboard settings are incorrect.

   B. Key is stuck down.

   C. Key is stuck open.

   D. Keyboard is plugged in wrong.

APPLY YOUR KNOWLEDGE

9. Which of the following connectors are used for devices that can be hot-swapped?

   A. 5-pin DIN

   B. 6-pin PS/2 mini-DIN

   C. RS-232C serial port

   D. USB port

10. What type of tool is used to discharge the built-up voltage from a CRT?

    A. Wrist strap

    B. Grounding wire

    C. Tweezers

    D. Heavy-duty screwdriver

11. What are the consequences of installing the FDD cable in reverse?

    A. FDD light stays on and erases the boot record on the disk.

    B. FDD doesn't spin.

    C. FDD light flashes and the drive will read the disk but cannot write to it.

    D. FDD will still work normally.

12. What action can be taken when you encounter an "Invalid Drive or Drive Specification" error message?

    A. Reinstall the operating system.

    B. Reformat the drive.

    C. Repartition the drive.

    D. Repartition and reformat the drive.

13. What condition is indicated by the "Missing Operating System" error message?

    A. Drive is not formatted.

    B. MBR is missing or corrupt.

    C. Operating system files are missing or corrupt.

    D. HDD cable is not attached.

14. What condition is indicated by the "Hard Drive Boot Failure" error message?

    A. Drive is not formatted.

    B. MBR is missing or corrupt.

    C. Operating system files are missing or corrupt.

    D. HDD cable is not attached.

15. How many master drive selections are there for each IDE channel?

    A. 1

    B. 2

    C. 3

    D. 4

16. What can happen when you mix different IDE drive types on a single signal cable?

    A. You will disable the master device.

    B. You will disable the slave device.

    C. You will disable both devices.

    D. The system will work normally.

17. In newer systems, where are the SCSI drive support and large drive support enabled?

    A. In the Device Manager

    B. In the CMOS Setup utility

    C. In the CONFIG.SYS file

    D. In the Registry

18. What command is used to restore a drive's master boot record and partition information?

    A. a. `SYS C:`

    B. `MBR /RENEW`

    C. `FDISK /MBR`

    D. `FORMAT C:`

19. How can a CD be retrieved from a disabled CD-ROM drive?

    A. Use a thin knife to gently pry the door open.

    B. Press the open/close button.

    C. Eject the disk using the operating system.

    D. Insert a straightened paper clip into the tray-release access hole in the front panel.

20. What can be done to repair system boards with defective onboard IDE controllers and to upgrade older IDE systems?

    A. Replace the system board.

    B. Replace the ROM BIOS.

    C. Install an IDE host adapter.

    D. Replace the IDE controller.

21. What must you do first if you want to troubleshoot a USB problem on a Windows 2000 system?

    A. Open Device Manager.

    B. Log on as a member of the Administrators group.

    C. Select the USB driver and click the properties button.

    D. Restart the system.

22. What AT command is used to reset a modem?

    A. `ATZ`

    B. `ATM`

    C. `ATW`

    D. `ATT`

23. How can a balance problem that occurs with add-on stereo speakers be corrected?

    A. Replace the speakers.

    B. Replace the sound card.

    C. Adjust the sound balance in the operating system.

    D. Swap the speaker positions.

24. How can you correct hard-memory errors?

    A. Replace the microprocessor.

    B. Remove all RAM modules.

    C. Replace all RAM modules.

    D. Restart the computer.

APPLY YOUR KNOWLEDGE

25. What command is used to restore the DOS files to the hard disk drive?

    A. SYS C:

    B. MBR /RENEW

    C. FDISK /MBR

    D. FORMAT C:

26. What does a "601" error code indicate?

    A. Invalid switch memory error

    B. FDD error

    C. CMOS checksum test error

    D. RAM failure

27. What action should be taken to clear up "fuzzy" characters on a CRT Display?

    A. Replace video card.

    B. Degauss CRT.

    C. Reinstall video driver.

    D. Reinstall operating system.

28. When you move the cursor across the screen, it randomly jumps and freezes. What should you do to correct this?

    A. Replace the mouse.

    B. Unplug the mouse and then plug it back in.

    C. Reinstall the mouse driver.

    D. Clean the dirt from inside the mouse.

29. What condition is indicated by the "Invalid Media Type" error message?

    A. Drive is not formatted.

    B. MBR is missing or corrupt.

    C. Operating system files are missing or corrupt.

    D. HDD cable is not attached.

30. When the system boots up, you can hear the fans start and the keyboard and drive lights flicker, but no display appears. What should you do first to troubleshoot this problem?

    A. Replace video card with a known good one of the same type.

    B. Unplug the monitor from the video card and then plug it back in.

    C. Exchange the monitor with a known good one of the same type.

    D. Replace the power supply with a known good one of the same type.

31. Booting to Windows results in a distorted image that prevents you from manipulating the operating system. What can you do to correct this problem?

    A. Reboot the system to the command line.

    B. Boot to Safe Mode and reinstall/configure the driver.

    C. Replace the video card.

    D. Replace the monitor.

32. An Energy Star Compliant monitor _____.

    A. uses more energy than non-ESC monitors

    B. shuts off automatically

    C. adjusts for room lighting automatically

    D. switches to low-power mode when no signal change occurs for a given period of time

33. What should you do if you intend to install a non-PnP device on a specific COM port?

    A. Disable the port using the motherboard jumper.

    B. Disable the port in Device Manager.

    C. Disable the port in CMOS.

    D. Manually allocate resources in Device Manger.

Answers and Explanations

1. **C.** Begin by checking the external connections of the power supply. This is the first step in checking any electrical equipment that shows no signs of life. For example, confirm that the power-supply cord is plugged in to a functioning outlet and check the position of the On/Off switch. For more information, see the section "Checking Dead Systems."

2. **D.** A 201 error code display indicates a RAM failure. For more information, see the section "System Board Symptoms."

3. **B.** Soft-memory errors are errors caused by infrequent and random glitches in the operation of applications and the system. You can clear these events just by restarting the system. Hard-memory errors are permanent physical failures that generate NMI errors in the system and require that the memory units be checked by substitution. For more information, see the section "RAM."

4. **D.** You can clear soft-memory errors just by restarting the system. For more information, see the section "RAM."

5. **D.** Make sure that the replacement RAM is consistent with the installed RAM. Mixing RAM types and speeds can cause the system to lock up and produce hard memory errors. For more information, see the section "RAM."

6. **A.** If the system consistently locks up after being on for a few minutes, this is a good indication that the microprocessor's fan is not running or that some other heat buildup problem is occurring. For more information, see the section "Microprocessor."

7. **C.** A defective motherboard battery can cause the system to continually lose track of time. For more information, see the section "Battery."

8. **B.** A stuck keyboard key will produce an error message when the system detects it. For more information, see the section "Basic Keyboard Checks."

9. **D.** Only the USB port has hot-swap capabilities. The standard 5-pin DIN and 6-pin PS/2 mini-DIN keyboards cannot be hot-swapped. Neither can the standard RS-232C serial port. Doing so can cause damage to the keyboard, the port, and the system board. For more information, see the section "Keyboard Hardware Checks."

10. **D.** The built-up charge on the monitor's anode must the shorted to ground so that the monitor can be handled safely. This operation is typically performed with a large, long-handled screwdriver and a shorting clip. For more information, see the section "Troubleshooting Monitors."

11. **A.** When the FDD signal cable is reversed, the FDD activity light stays on constantly and the boot record on the disk will be erased. For more information, see the section "FDD Hardware Checks."

APPLY YOUR KNOWLEDGE

12. **D.** If the system cannot see the drive after booting to the disk, an "Invalid Drive…" message or an "Invalid Drive Specification" message might be displayed in response to any attempt to access the drive. Use the FDISK utility to partition the drive and then use the FORMAT command to make the disk bootable. For more information, see the section "Basic HDD Checks."

13. **B.** A "Missing Operating System" message indicates that the disk's master boot record is missing or has become corrupt. For more information, see the section "Troubleshooting Hard Disk Drives."

14. **B.** A "Hard Drive Boot Failure" message indicates that the disk's master boot record is missing or has become corrupt. For more information, see the section "Troubleshooting Hard Disk Drives."

15. **A.** There can only be one master drive selection on each IDE channel. For more information, see the section "HDD Configuration Checks."

16. **C.** Mixing IDE device types will create a situation in which the system cannot provide the different types of control information each device needs. The drives are incompatible, and you might not be able to access either device. For more information, see the section "HDD Configuration Checks."

17. **B.** Check the CMOS Setup utility to make sure that SCSI support has been enabled, along with large SCSI drive support. For more information, see the section "HDD Configuration Checks."

18. **C.** If the clean boot disk has a copy of the FDISK program on it, you might attempt to restore the drive's master boot record (including its partition information) by typing the command FDISK /MBR. For more information, see the section "Basic HDD Checks."

19. **D.** If the CD-ROM drive is inoperable and a CD is locked inside, you should insert a straightened paper clip into the tray-release access hole that's usually located beside the ejection button. This will release the spring-loaded tray and pop out the disc. For more information, see the section "CD-ROM Hardware Checks."

20. **C.** If the IDE controller is built in to the system board and becomes defective, it is still possible to install an IDE host adapter card in an expansion slot and use it without replacing the system board. This action can also be taken to upgrade older IDE systems so that they can use additional IDE devices. The onboard IDE controller might need to be disabled before the system will address the new host adapter version. For more information, see the section "CD-ROM Hardware Checks."

21. **B.** To use the Windows 2000 Device Manager utility to troubleshoot USB problems, you must be logged on as an administrator or as a member of the Administrators group. For more information, see the section "USB Port Checks."

22. **A.** AT commands are entered at the command line using an ATX*n* format. The *Xn* nomenclature identifies the type of command being given (*x*) and the particular function to be used (*n*). The ATZ*n* commands reset the modem by loading new default initialization information. At the command line, just type **ATZ** to reset the modem. You should receive a **0**, or OK response if the command was processed. For more information, see the section "Using the AT Command Set."

23. **D.** In the case of stereo speaker systems, it is possible to place the speakers on the wrong sides. This will produce a problem when you try to adjust the balance between them. Increasing the volume on the right speaker will instead increase the output of the left speaker. The obvious cure for this problem is to physically switch the positions of the speakers. For more information, see the section "Sound Card Hardware Checks."

24. **C.** Hard-memory errors are permanent physical failures that generate NMI errors in the system and require that the memory units be checked by substitution. For more information, see the section "RAM."

25. **A.** Typing **SYS C:** at the DOS prompt will copy the IO.SYS, MSDOS.SYS, and COMMAND.COM system files from the boot disk to the hard disk drive. For more information, see the section "Basic HDD Checks."

26. **B.** A 601 error code display indicates a FDD failure. For more information, see the section "Troubleshooting Floppy Disk Drives."

27. **B.** Actually, there can be several causes of fuzzy characters on the display. The first step in checking out this problem is to reset the display resolution to standard VGA values. If the fuzzy characters remain, check the intensity and contrast controls to see if they are out of adjustment. Finally, you might need to remove built-up electromagnetic fields from the screen through a process called degaussing. This can be done using a commercial degaussing coil. However, newer monitors have built-in degaussing circuits that can be engaged through their front panel controls. These monitors normally perform a degauss operation each time they are turned on. However, there are occurrences when the user might need to perform this operation. For more information, see the section "Diagnosing Monitor Problems."

28. **D.** Most of the problems associated with mice involve the trackball. As the mouse is moved across the table, the trackball picks up dirt or lint, which can hinder the movement of the trackball, typically evident by the cursor periodically freezing and jumping onscreen. On most mice, you can remove the trackball from the mouse by a latching mechanism on its bottom. Twisting the latch counter-clockwise enables you to remove the trackball. Then you can clean dirt out of the mouse. For more information, see the section "Troubleshooting Mouse Problems."

29. **A.** An "Invalid Media Type" message indicates that the controller cannot find a recognizable track/sector pattern on the drive. For more information, see the section "Troubleshooting Hard Disk Drives."

30. **B.** If the video problem produces a blank display, disconnect the monitor's signal cable from its video adapter card. If a raster appears, a video card problem is indicated. For more information, see the section "Isolating Power-Supply Problems."

31. **B.** If the Windows video problem prevents you from seeing the desktop, restart the system, press the F8 function key when the Starting Windows message appears, and select Safe Mode. This should load Windows with the standard 640x480 16-color VGA driver (the most fundamental driver available for VGA monitors), and should furnish a starting point for installing the correct driver for the monitor being used. For more information, see the section "Windows Video Checks."

32. **D.** If the monitor is an EPA-certified, Energy Star–compliant, power-saving monitor, it can revert to a low-power mode when they do not receive a signal change for a given period of time. For more information, see the section "Video Hardware Checks."

33. **C.** To install a non-PnP device on a specific COM port (that is, COM2), you must first disable that port in the system's CMOS settings in order to avoid a device conflict. If not, the system might try to allocate that resource to some other device, since it has no way of knowing that the non-PnP device requires it. For more information, see the section "COM Port Conflicts."

Challenge Solutions

1. You should tell the customer that you think his system board battery is defective or that its charging circuitry is bad. If a system refuses to maintain time and date information, check the backup battery and the contacts of the battery holder for corrosion. Tell the customer to remove the system board battery if possible and clean its contacts with a contact cleaner or by gently using a pencil eraser. If cleaning the battery terminals does not cause the clock to keep proper time, replace the battery with a new one and allow it to completely charge. For more information, see the section "Battery."

2. If you install a new mouse in a working system and it does not work when you restart the system, chances are very high that the driver software or a port configuration setting must be the cause of the failure. For more information, see the section "Mouse Hardware Checks."

3. Because the system's light comes on and the hard drive spins, you can at least initially conclude that the system has power and that the power supply is working (although you might want to revisit these assumptions in some rare cases). The sound of the single beep indicates that the system has made it through the POST test and that most of the basic hardware (including the video controller) is working. However, the POST tests cannot check the monitor's internal operation (only its video adapter). Therefore, you should bring a replacement monitor to swap out the existing one. The presence of the light on the monitor only indicates that it is plugged in and turned on—not that it is working. If swapping the monitor does not clear up the problem, check the video driver to make sure that it is correct and replace the video adapter card last. For more information, see the section "Video Hardware Checks."

4. Check the drive to make sure that the Master/Slave jumper setting is set properly for the drive's logical position in the system. There can only be one master drive selection on each IDE channel. If you have more than one device attached to a single interface cable, make sure that all the devices are of the same type (that is, all are EIDE devices or all are ATA100 devices). Mixing IDE device types can create a situation in which the system cannot provide the different types of control information each device needs. The drives are incompatible, and you might not be able to access either device. For more information, see the section "HDD Configuration Checks."

APPLY YOUR KNOWLEDGE

5. You must be aware that when different devices share the same resources, this can lead to intermittent failures. Verify that they are set correctly for the installation. Run a diagnostic program or examine the Device Manager in Windows operating systems to check for resource conflicts that might be preventing the sound card from operating (such as IRQ and base memory addressing). For more information, see the section "Troubleshooting Tape Drives."

Suggested Readings and Resources

1. Troubleshooting
   http://www.pcmech.com/troubleshoot.htm

2. Technical Library
   http://www.pctusa.com/techlib.htm

3. General Troubleshooting Techniques
   www.pcguide.com/ts/gen/index.htm

4. Hardware Installation and Troubleshooting
   http://citabria.westmont.edu/tech/
   hardware.html

5. Troubleshooting the Motherboard and System Devices
   www.pcguide.com/ts/x/comp/mbsys/index.htm

6. Troubleshooting Keyboards
   http://www.pcguide.com/ts/x/comp/
   kb_Failure.htm

7. Problems with a Mouse
   www.colosys.net/computeraid/t6.htm

8. Troubleshooting Video Cards
   http://www.pcguide.com/ts/x/comp/video/
   index.htm

9. TV and Monitor Information
   http://ftp.unina.it/pub/electronics/
   repairfaq/REPAIR/F_crtfaq.html

10. Troubleshooting Floppy Drives
    http://support.microsoft.com/
    default.aspx?scid=kb;EN-US;q131690

11. Troubleshooting HDDs
    http://www.compguystechweb.com/
    troubleshooting/hardware/hd_q_and_a.html

12. Troubleshooting CD-ROM Drives
    http://www.techadvice.com/tech/C/CDROM_TS.
    htm

13. Troubleshooting Ports
    http://www.pcguide.com/ts/x/comp/io.htm

14. Troubleshooting Scanners
    http://www.waterwheel.com/Guides/
    Trouble_Shooting/scanner/scanners.htm

15. Troubleshooting Tape Drives
    http://stsdas.stsci.edu/documents/SUG/
    UG_54.html

16. Troubleshooting Modems
    http://www.modemsite.com/56k/trouble.asp

17. Troubleshooting Sound Cards
    http://netlab.gmu.edu/classwise/sound_card
    .html

This chapter helps you to prepare for the Core Hardware module of the A+ Certification examination by covering the following objectives within the "Domain 2.0: Diagnosing and Troubleshooting" section.

2.2 Identify basic troubleshooting procedures and how to elicit problem symptoms from customers. Content might include the following:

- **Troubleshooting/isolation/problem determination procedures**

- **Determine whether hardware or software problem**

- **Gather information from user regarding, for example,**

  - **Customer environment**

  - **Symptoms/Error codes**

  - **Situation when the problem occurred**

▶ One of the most important aspects of troubleshooting anything is the gathering of information about the problem at hand and the symptoms it is showing. One of the best sources for this type of information is the computer user. As this A+ objective states, the computer technician should be able to effectively acquire information from the customer (user) concerning the nature of a problem and then be able to practice basic troubleshooting methods to isolate and repair the problem.

CHAPTER 9

Basic Troubleshooting Techniques

STUDY STRATEGIES

To prepare for the Diagnosing and Troubleshooting objective of the Core Hardware exam,

▶ Read the objectives at the beginning of this chapter.

▶ Study the information in this chapter.

▶ Review the objectives listed earlier in this chapter.

▶ Perform any step-by-step procedures in the text.

▶ Answer the review questions at the end of the chapter and check your results.

▶ Use the PrepLogic test engine on the CD-ROM that accompanies this book for additional review and exam questions concerning this material.

▶ Review the exam tips scattered throughout the chapter and make certain that you are comfortable with each point.

INTRODUCTION

This chapter examines the basic tools and investigative techniques used to troubleshoot computer systems. It deals with the initial steps involved in computer problem solving. These steps include recognizing typical error and beep code messages, assessing the capabilities of the user or operator, differentiating between hardware and software problems, and identifying configuration problems.

The only hardware diagnostic tool that CompTIA references is the digital multimeter. The use of this test instrument is covered on a limited basis in the midsection of the chapter.

The final section of the chapter explains the concept of troubleshooting hardware devices using a FRU component swap process to isolate and repair hardware related problems.

After completing the chapter, you should be able to identify basic hardware troubleshooting procedures and describe good practices for eliciting problem symptoms from customers. In addition, you should be able to describe the basic use of a digital multimeter and know what readings you should expect when testing certain components.

DIAGNOSTIC AND REPAIR TOOLS

Anyone who wants to work on any type of equipment must have the proper tools for the task. The following sections discuss the tools and equipment associated with the testing and repair of digital systems.

The well-prepared technician's tool kit should contain a wide range of both flat-blade and Phillips-head screwdriver sizes. At a minimum, it should have a small jeweler's and a medium-size flat-blade screwdriver, along with a medium-size Phillips screwdriver. In addition, you might want to include a small set of miniature nut drivers, a set of Torx drivers, and a special nonconductive screwdriver-like device called an alignment tool.

You also need a couple of pairs of needle-nose pliers. These pliers are available in a number of sizes. You need at least one pair with a sturdy, blunt nose and one with a longer, more tapered nose. You also might want to get a pair that has a cutting edge built in to its jaws. You can perform this same function with a different type of pliers called diagonals, or crosscuts. Many technicians carry a pair of surgical forceps in addition to their other pliers.

Another type of tools associated with computer hardware repair are IC pullers, or IC extractors. These tools come in various styles and are used to remove ICs from sockets. Socket-mounted ICs are not as common on modern PC boards as they were in the past. Potential failures associated with the mechanical connections between sockets and chips, coupled with the industry's reliance on surface-mount soldering techniques, have led to far fewer socket-mounted chips. However, on some occasions, such as upgrading a ROM BIOS chip, the IC puller comes in handy.

In addition to these hardware tools, the technician should have a collection of software tools at his disposal. Typical software tools used by computer technicians include:

◆ Emergency boot/start disks to get broken systems started

◆ Antivirus utilities

◆ Hardware diagnostic utility packages

Using a Multimeter

A number of test instruments can help you to isolate computer hardware problems. One of the most basic pieces of electronic troubleshooting equipment is the *multimeter*. These test instruments are available in both analog and digital read-out form and can be used to directly measure electrical values of voltage (V), current, in milliamperes (mA) or amperes (A), and resistance, in ohms. Therefore, these devices are referred to as *VOMs (volt-ohm-millimeters)* for analog types, or *DMMs (digital multimeters)* for digital types.

Figure 9.1 depicts a digital multimeter. With a little finesse, you can use this device to check diodes, transistors, capacitors, motor windings, relays, and coils. This particular DMM contains facilities built in to the meter to test transistors and diodes. These facilities are in addition to its standard functions of current, voltage, and resistance measurement. However, in computer repair work, only the voltage and resistance functions are used extensively.

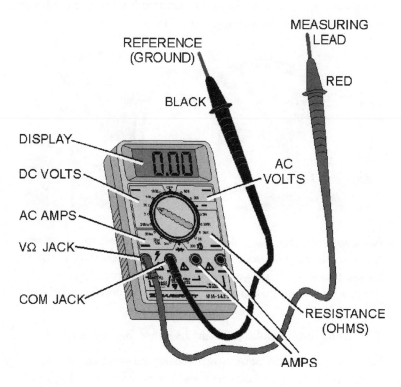

REFERENCE
(GROUND)

MEASURING
LEAD

FIGURE 9.1
A digital multimeter.

BLACK

RED

DISPLAY

DC VOLTS

AC AMPS

VΩ JACK

COM JACK

AC
VOLTS

RESISTANCE
(OHMS)

AMPS

The first step in using the multimeter to perform tests is to select the proper function. For the most part, you never need to use the current functions of the multimeter when working with computer systems. However, the voltage and resistance functions can be very valuable tools.

In computer troubleshooting, fully 99% of the tests made are DC voltage readings. These measurements most often involve checking the DC side of the power-supply unit. You can make these readings between ground and one of the expansion-slot pins, or at the system board power-supply connector. It is also common to check the voltage level across a system board capacitor to verify that the system is receiving power. The voltage across most of the capacitors on the system board is 5V (DC). The DC voltages that can normally be expected in a PC-compatible system are +12V, +5V, -5V, and -12V. The actual values for these readings might vary by 5% in either direction.

WARNING

Setting the Meter It is normal practice to first set the meter to its highest voltage range to make certain that the voltage level being measured does not damage the meter.

The *DC voltage function* is used to take measurements in live DC circuits. It should be connected in parallel with the device being checked. This could mean connecting the *reference lead* (black lead) to a ground point and the *measuring lead* (red lead) to a test point to take a measurement, as illustrated in Figure 9.2.

FIGURE 9.2
DC voltage check.

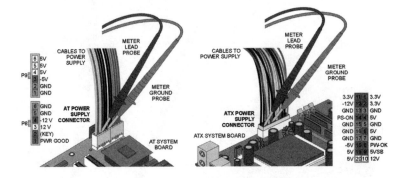

As an approximate value is detected, you can decrease the range setting to achieve a more accurate reading. Most meters allow for overvoltage protection. However, it is still a good safety practice to decrease the range of the meter after you have achieved an initial value.

The second most popular test is the resistance, or *continuity test*.

Failure to turn off the power when making resistance checks can cause serious damage to the meter and can pose a potential risk to the technician. Resistance checks require that you electrically isolate the component being tested from the system. For most circuit components, this means desoldering at least one end from the board.

The resistance check is very useful in isolating some types of problems in the system. One of the main uses of the resistance function is to test fuses. You must disconnect at least one end of the fuse from the system. You should set the meter on the 1k-ohm resistance setting. If the fuse is good, the meter should read near 0 ohms. If it is bad, the meter reads infinite. The resistance function also is useful in checking for cables and connectors. By removing the cable from the system and connecting a meter lead to each end, you can check the cable's continuity conductor by conductor to verify its integrity.

You also use the resistance function to test the system's speaker. To check the speaker, simply disconnect the speaker from the system and connect a meter lead to each end. If the speaker is good, the

> **WARNING**
>
> **Power Off** Unlike the voltage check, resistance checks are always made with power removed from the system.

meter should read near 8 ohms (although some smaller speakers might be 4 ohms). If the speaker is defective, the resistance reading should be 0 for shorts or infinite for opens.

Only a couple of situations involve using the AC voltage function for checking microcomputer systems. The primary use of this function is to check the commercial power being applied to the power-supply unit. As with any measurement, it is important to select the correct measurement range. However, the lethal voltage levels associated with the supply power call for additional caution when making such measurements. The second application for the AC voltage function is to measure ripple voltage from the DC output side of the power-supply unit. This particular operation is very rarely performed in field-service situations.

> **EXAM TIP**
>
> Know what readings to expect from a multimeter when testing fuses, speakers, and typical power-supply voltages in a PC.

CHALLENGE #1

One of your network administrator friends has called you about a problem she is having with her computer at home. She is not getting sound from her speaker and has checked all her software. She has asked you to explain to her how to check her speaker hardware. What should you tell her?

> **NOTE**
>
> **Hands-On Activity**   For hands-on experience with this concept, refer to Lab Procedure #5, "Digital Multimeter," located on the CD that accompanies this book.

INFORMATION GATHERING

The most important thing to do when checking a malfunctioning device is to be observant. Begin by talking to the person who reported the problem. You can obtain many clues from this person. Careful listening also is a good way to eliminate the user as a possible cause of the problems. Part of the technician's job is to determine whether the user could be the source of the problem—either trying to do things with the system that it cannot do, or not understanding how some part of it is supposed to work.

Gather information from the user regarding the environment the system is being used in, any symptoms or error codes produced by the system, and the situations that existed when the failure occurred.

> **NOTE**
>
> **Reference Shelf**   For more information, refer to the Electronic Reference Shelf, "Customer Satisfaction," located on the CD that accompanies this book.

> **EXAM TIP**
>
> Be well aware that the user is one of the most common sources of PC problems. In most situations, your first troubleshooting step should be to talk to the user.

Ask the user to demonstrate the procedures that led to the malfunction in a step-by-step manner. This communication can help you narrow down a problem to a particular section of the computer. Gain an understanding of the process she is trying to complete. Finally, remove the operator from the situation and observe the symptoms of a malfunction to verify the problem for yourself. Attempt to limit the problem to the hardware involved, the software package being used, and then to the operator.

CHALLENGE #2

You have been called to a business to repair a printing problem. When you arrive, you are told that the user is having trouble printing spreadsheets from his Microsoft Excel program. You are not an Excel or spreadsheet guru, so how do you go about servicing this problem?

Symptoms/Error Codes

Most PCs have reasonably good built-in self-tests that are run each time the computer is powered up. These tests can prove very beneficial in detecting hardware-oriented problems within the system. Whenever a self-test failure or setup mismatch is encountered, the BIOS might indicate the error through a blank screen, a *visual error message* on the video display, or an audio response (*beep codes*) produced by the system's speaker.

Some PCs issue numerically coded error messages on the display. Conversely, other PCs display a written description of the error. Tables 9.1 and 9.2 define the error messages and beep codes produced by a particular BIOS version from American Megatrends. The exact error messages and codes will vary between different BIOS manufacturers and from version to version.

TABLE 9.1

BEEP CODE MESSAGES

Number of Beeps	Problem Indicated
1	DRAM refresh failure
2	RAM failure (base 640kB)
3	System timer failure
5	Microprocessor failure
6	Keyboard controller failure
7	Virtual Mode Exception failure
9	ROM BIOS checksum failure
1 long, 2 short	Video controller failure
1 long, 3 short	Conventional and Extended test failure
1 long, 8 short	Display test failure

TABLE 9.2

VISUAL DISPLAY ERROR MESSAGES

System Halted Errors

CMOS INOPERATIONAL—Failure of CMOS shutdown register test

8042 GATE A20 ERROR—Error getting into protected mode

INVALID SWITCH MEMORY FAILURE—Real/Protected mode changeover error.

DMA ERROR—DMA controller failed page register test

DMA #1 ERROR—DMA device #1 failure

DMA #2 ERROR—DMA device #2 failure

Non-Fatal Errors—with Setup Option

CMOS BATTERY LOW—Failure of CMOS battery or CMOS checksum test

CMOS SYSTEM OPTION NOT SET—Failure of CMOS battery or CMOS checksum test

CMOS CHECKSUM FAILURE—CMOS battery low or CMOS checksum test failure

CMOS DISPLAY MISMATCH—Failure of display type verification

continues

TABLE 9.2	*continued*

VISUAL DISPLAY ERROR MESSAGES

Non-Fatal Errors—with Setup Option

CMOS MEMORY SIZE MISMATCH—System Configuration and Setup failure

CMOS TIMER AND DATE NOT SET—System Configuration and Setup failure in timer circuitry

Non-Fatal Errors—Without Setup Option

CH-X TIMER ERROR—Channel X (2, 1, or 0) TIMER failure

KEYBOARD ERROR—Keyboard test failure

KB/INTERFACE ERROR—Keyboard test failure

DISPLAY SWITCH SETTING NOT PROPER—Failure to verify display type

KEYBOARD IS LOCKED—Unlock it

FDD CONTROLLER ERROR—Failure to verify floppy disk setup by System Configuration file

HDD CONTROLLER FAILURE—Failure to verify hard disk setup by System Configuration file

C:DRIVE ERROR—Hard disk setup failure

D:DRIVE ERROR—Hard disk setup failure

INITIAL TROUBLESHOOTING STEPS

First, always try the system to see what symptoms you produce. Second, you must isolate the problem to either software- or hardware-related problems. Finally, you should isolate the problem to a section of the hardware or software.

Check any system jumper settings related to the symptom to determine that they are set correctly for the actual configuration of the system. Also check the BIOS' advanced CMOS configuration screens for any incorrect enabling settings.

Observe the Boot-up Procedure

Carefully observing the steps of a boot-up procedure can reveal a great deal about the nature of problems in a system. Faulty areas can be included or excluded from possible causes of errors during the boot-up process.

The observable actions of a working system's cold-boot procedure are listed as follows, in their order of occurrence:

1. When power is applied, the power supply fan activates.

2. The keyboard lights flash as the rest of the system components are being reset.

3. A BIOS message displays on the monitor.

4. A memory test flickers on the monitor.

5. The floppy disk drive access light comes on briefly (if enabled in the CMOS boot sequence.)

6. The hard disk drive access light comes on briefly.

7. The system beeps, indicating that it has completed its Power On Self Tests and initialization process. After this point, the operation of the machine has shifted to looking for and loading an operating system.

8. The floppy disk drive access light comes on briefly before switching to the hard drive. At this point in the process, the BIOS is looking for additional instructions (boot information)—first from the floppy drive and then from the hard drive (assuming that the CMOS setup is configured for this sequence).

9. When the system finds the boot files, the drive light will come on, indicating that the system is loading the operating system and configuration files.

10. For Windows machines, the "Starting Windows message" appears on the screen.

11. Windows loads its GUI components and takes over control of the system.

> **EXAM TIP**
> Memorize the order of the series of observable events that occur during the normal FAT bootup.

Determining Hardware/Software/Configuration Problems

One of the first steps in troubleshooting a computer problem (or any other programmable system problem) is to determine whether the problem is because of a hardware failure or faulty software. In most PCs, you can use a significant event that occurs during the startup process as a key to separating hardware problems from software problems: the single beep that most PCs produce between the end of the POST and the beginning of the startup process (step 7 in the preceding list).

Errors that occur, or are displayed, before this beep indicate that a hardware problem of some type exists. Up to this point in the operation of the system, only the BIOS and the basic system hardware have been active. The operating system side of the system does not come into play until after the beep occurs.

If the system produces an error message (such as "The System Has Detected Unstable RAM at Location x") or a beep code before the single beep occurs, the system has found a problem with the hardware. In this case, a bad RAM memory device is indicated.

Typically, if the startup process reaches the point in which the system's CMOS configuration information is displayed onscreen, you can safely assume that no hardware configuration conflicts exist in the system's basic components. After this point in the boot-up process, the system begins loading drivers for optional devices and additional memory. If the error occurs after the CMOS screen displays and before the boot-up tone, you must clean-boot the system and single-step through the remainder of the boot-up sequence.

You can still group errors that occur before the beep into two distinct categories:

◆ Configuration errors

◆ Hardware failures

A special category of problems tends to occur whenever a new hardware option is added to the system or when the system is used for the very first time. These problems are called configuration problems, or setup problems, and result from mismatches between the system's programmed configuration, held in CMOS memory, and the actual equipment installed in the system.

This mismatch also can exist between the system's CMOS configuration settings and the option's hardware jumper or switch settings. You can trace the majority of all problems that occur in computer systems back to configuration settings.

It is usually necessary to run the system's CMOS setup utility in the following three situations:

1. The first situation occurs when the system is first constructed.

2. The second occurrence happens if it becomes necessary to replace the CMOS backup battery on the system board.

3. Whenever a new or different option is added to the system (such as a hard drive, floppy drive, or video display), it might be necessary to run the Setup utility.

In most systems, the BIOS and operating system use Plug-and-Play techniques to detect new hardware that has been installed in the system. These components work together with the device to allocate system resources for the device. In some situations, the PnP logic will not be able to resolve all the system's resource needs and a configuration error will occur. In these cases, the user must manually resolve the configuration problem.

When you are installing new hardware or software options, be aware of the possibility of configuration errors occurring. If you encounter configuration (or setup) errors, refer to the installation instructions found in the new component's user manual. Table 9.3 lists typical configuration error codes and messages produced when various types of configuration mismatches occur.

TABLE 9.3

COMMON CONFIGURATION ERROR CODES

Configuration Error Message	Meaning
CMOS System Option Not Set	Failure of CMOS battery or CMOS Checksum test
CMOS Display Mismatch	Failure of display type verification
CMOS Memory Size Mismatch	System configuration and setup failure
Press F1 to Continue	Invalid configuration information
CMOS Time and Date Not Set	Failure of CMOS battery

> **EXAM TIP**
>
> Know the situation that causes a Press F1 to Continue error message to display.

If you cannot confirm a configuration problem, the problem most likely is a defective component. The most widely used repair method involves substituting known good components for suspected bad components. Other alternatives for isolating and correcting a hardware failure that appears before the bootup depend on how much of the system is operable.

After the single beep, the system begins looking for and loading the operating system. Errors that occur between the beep and the presentation of the operating system's user interface (command prompt or GUI) generally have three possible sources:

◆ Hardware failure (physical problem with the boot drive)

◆ Corrupted or missing boot files

◆ Corrupted or missing operating system files

Normally, symptoms can be divided into three sections: configuration problems, boot-up problems, and operational problems.

The system's configuration settings are normally checked first. It is important to observe the system's symptoms to determine in which part of the system's operation the fault occurs. The error messages depicted in Table 9.3 are errors that occur and are reported before the single beep tone is produced at the end of the POST routines.

After the single beep tone has been produced in the startup sequence, the system shifts over to the process of booting up to the operating system. Typical error messages associated with boot-up problems include the following:

◆ General Failure Error Reading Drive x

◆ Bad or Missing Command Interpreter

◆ Non-System Disk or Disk Error

◆ Bad File Allocation Table

Both configuration problems and boot-up problems can be caused by a hardware or operational failure. If the configuration settings are correct, but these symptoms are present, a hardware problem is indicated as the cause of the problem. Conversely, boot-up problems are typically associated with the operating system.

CHALLENGE #3

A remote customer calls and complains that she is receiving a Bad or Missing Command Interpreter error message and the system stops operating. She thinks she should replace her hard drive and wants you to order it for her. What should you tell her?

FIELD-REPLACEABLE UNIT TROUBLESHOOTING

Field-Replaceable Units (FRUs) are the portions of the system that you can conveniently replace in the field. Figure 9.3 depicts typical microcomputer FRUs. FRU troubleshooting involves isolating a problem within one section of the system. A section consists of one device such as a keyboard, video display, video adapter card, I/O adapter card, system board, disk drive, printer, and so on. These are typically components that can simply be exchanged for a replacement on site and require no actual repair work.

> **EXAM TIP**
>
> Know which devices in a typical PC system are FRU devices.

FIGURE 9.3
The typical FRUs of a microcomputer system.

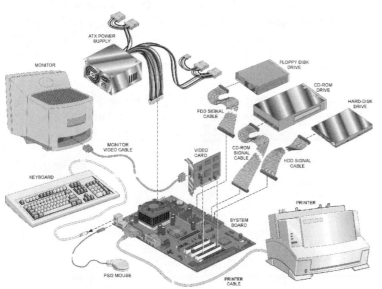

After a hardware error has been indicated, start troubleshooting the problem by exchanging components (cards, drives, and so on) with known good ones. Because *Metal Oxide Semiconductor (MOS)* devices might be on the board, you should ground yourself before performing this test. You can do so by touching an exposed portion of the unit's chassis, such as the top of the power supply.

If a diagnostic tool indicates that multiple components have failed, use the one-at-a-time exchange method, starting with the first component indicated, to isolate the original source of the problem. Test the system between each component exchange and work backward through the exchanged components after the system has started to function again.

CHAPTER SUMMARY

KEY TERMS

- Bad or Missing Command Interpreter
- Beep codes
- Configuration errors
- Continuity test
- DC voltage function
- DMMs (digital multimeters)
- Field-Replaceable Units (FRUs)
- Hardware failures
- Measuring lead
- Metal Oxide Semiconductor (MOS)
- Multimeter
- Non-System Disk or Disk Error
- Reference lead
- Visual error message

This chapter has covered fundamental troubleshooting tools and techniques. The first half of the chapter presented the basic tools and investigative techniques used to troubleshoot computer systems. It dealt with the early steps of computer problem solving, including differentiating between hardware and software problems and identifying configuration problems. The chapter also described areas of the computer system where a digital multimeter is typically used to test computer components.

At this point, review the objectives listed at the beginning of the chapter to be certain that you understand each point and can perform each task listed there. Afterward, answer the review questions that follow to verify your knowledge of the information.

APPLY YOUR KNOWLEDGE

Review Questions

1. What type of problem produces a "Press F1 to Continue" error message to be displayed?

   A. Floppy disk drive is defective.

   B. Operating system is missing from the hard drive.

   C. System needs to be reconfigured.

   D. Video display is defective.

2. What event marks the transition from basic hardware problems to boot-up problems?

   A. Operating system boot-up screen appears.

   B. Single beep sound.

   C. Power light comes on.

   D. Operating system bootup is completed.

3. What multimeter reading would you expect to receive from measuring a good 2-amp fuse?

   A. 0 ohms

   B. 2 ohms

   C. 15 ohms

   D. 30 ohms

4. Which multimeter reading should you expect from measuring a good speaker?

   A. Infinity

   B. 0 ohms

   C. 4 ohms

   D. 8 ohms

5. What meter reading would you expect from an open speaker?

   A. 0 ohms

   B. 4 ohms

   C. 8 ohms

   D. Infinite (or a blank display)

6. What type of computer component can you usually replace in the field?

   A. ERU

   B. FSU

   C. FRU

   D. FRC

7. What is the most important factor to consider when assessing the situation at a new troubleshooting call?

   A. The power supply

   B. The operating system

   C. The user

   D. The system configuration

8. What questions should you ask the user when you are first examining a defective unit? (Select all that apply.)

   A. How much experience do you have with this type of computer?

   B. What were you doing when the problem occurred?

   C. Was there an error message? What did it say?

   D. Is the unit new? Did it ever work?

APPLY YOUR KNOWLEDGE

9. Which of the following items would not be considered as an FRU that can be replaced in the field?

   A. Chassis

   B. Hard disk drive

   C. CPU

   D. Video card

10. What is the most commonly used repair technique?

    A. Replace all possible FRUs.

    B. Test each component on a test rig.

    C. Use a multimeter to test the signals from each component.

    D. Substitute known good parts for suspected bad components.

11. What is the most common type of malfunction observed after the installation of a new hardware or software component?

    A. Hardware problems

    B. Operating system problems

    C. Configuration problems

    D. Corrupted or missing files

12. After the system successfully POSTs, you see an error message "Bad or Missing Command Interpreter." What type of problem is this?

    A. Hardware problem

    B. Configuration problem

    C. Boot-up problem

    D. Operating system problem

13. During the boot-up procedure what action occurs before the memory test counts up?

    A. BIOS message appears on the screen.

    B. Floppy disk drive light comes on briefly.

    C. Hard disk drive light comes on briefly.

    D. POST is completed and the system beeps.

14. What are the voltages that should be expected when testing a PC?

    A. -1.2Vdc, +1.2Vdc, -0.5Vdc, +0.5Vdc

    B. -1.2Vac, +1.2Vac, -0.5Vac, +0.5Vac

    C. -3.3Vdc, +3.3Vdc, -1.5Vdc, +1.5Vdc

    D. -12Vdc, +12Vdc, -5Vdc, +5Vdc

15. Which of the following is not a software tool commonly used by a repair technician?

    A. Emergency boot disk

    B. Software diagnostics utility

    C. Hardware diagnostic utility

    D. Antivirus utility

Answers and Explanations

1. **C.** The system has encountered invalid configuration information during the boot-up process. Either the configuration has been set up incorrectly, or the hardware was unable to confirm the configuration settings. For more information, see the section "Determining Hardware/Software/Configuration Problems."

APPLY YOUR KNOWLEDGE

2. **B.** One of the first steps in troubleshooting a computer problem (or any other programmable system problem) is to determine whether the problem is because of a hardware failure or faulty software. In most PCs, you can use a significant event that occurs during the boot-up process as a key to separating hardware problems from software problems: the single beep that most PCs produce between the end of the POST and the beginning of the boot-up process. For more information, see the section "Observe the Boot-up Procedure."

3. **A.** One of the main uses of the resistance function is to test fuses. You must disconnect at least one end of the fuse from the system. You should set the meter on the 1k-ohm resistance setting. If the fuse is good, the meter should read near 0 ohms. If it is bad, the meter reads infinite. For more information, see the section "Using a Multimeter."

4. **D.** Disconnect the speaker from the system and connect a meter lead to each end. If the speaker is good, the meter should read near 8 ohms (although some smaller speakers might be 4 ohms). For more information, see the section "Using a Multimeter."

5. **D.** If the speaker is defective, the resistance reading should be 0 for shorts or infinite for opens. For more information, see the section "Using a Multimeter."

6. **C.** Field-Replaceable Units (FRUs) are the portions of the system that you can conveniently replace in the field. These are typically components that can simply be exchanged for a replacement on site and require no actual repair work.

For more information, see the section "Field-Replaceable Unit Troubleshooting."

7. **C.** The most important thing to do when checking a malfunctioning device is to be observant. Begin by talking to the person who reported the problem. You can obtain many clues from this person. Careful listening also is a good way to eliminate the user as a possible cause of the problems. Part of the technician's job is to determine whether the user could be the source of the problem—either trying to do things with the system that it cannot do, or not understanding how some part of it is supposed to work. For more information, see the section "Information Gathering."

8. **B, C, D.** When first examining a defective unit, gather information from the user regarding the environment the system is being used in, any symptoms or error codes produced by the system, and the situations that existed when the failure occurred. For more information, see the section "Information Gathering."

9. **A.** FRU troubleshooting involves isolating a problem within one section of the system. A section consists of one device such as a keyboard, video display, video adapter card, I/O adapter card, system board, disk drive, printer, and so on. For more information, see the section "Field-Replaceable Unit Troubleshooting."

10. **D.** The most widely used repair method involves substituting known good components for suspected bad components. For more information, see the section "Determining Hardware/Software/Configuration Problems."

11. **C.** When you are installing new hardware or software options, be aware of the possibility of a configuration error. If you encounter configuration (or setup) errors, refer to the installation instructions found in the new component's user manual. For more information, see the section "Determining Hardware/Software/Configuration Problems."

12. **C.** After the single beep tone has been produced in the startup sequence, the system shifts over to the process of booting up to the operating system. The "Bad or Missing Command Interpreter" error message is associated with boot-up problems. For more information, see the section "Determining Hardware/Software/Configuration Problems."

13. **A.** The observable actions of a working system's cold-boot procedure are listed as follows, in their order of occurrence: 1) When power is applied, the power supply fan activates; 2) The keyboard lights flash as the rest of the system components are being reset; 3) A BIOS message displays on the monitor; 4) A memory test flickers on the monitor; 5) The floppy disk drive access light comes on briefly (if enabled in the CMOS boot sequence); 6) The hard disk drive access light comes on briefly; 7)The system beeps, indicating that it has completed its Power On Self Tests and initialization process. After this point, the operation of the machine has shifted to looking for and loading an operating system. For more information, see the section "Observe the Boot-up Procedure."

14. **D.** The DC voltages that can normally be expected in a PC-compatible system are +12V, +5V, -5V, and -12V. The actual values for these readings might vary by 5% in either direction. For more information, see the section "Using a Multimeter."

15. **B.** Typical software tools used by computer technicians include emergency boot/start disks to get broken systems started, antivirus utilities, and hardware diagnostic software packages. For more information, see the section "Diagnostic and Repair Tools."

Challenge Solutions

1. Your friend needs to check the speaker using a simple ohmmeter check. She must remove the speaker from the system, gain access to the speaker itself, and measure across its two leads (caution her that all electrical power and signal sources must be removed from the speaker). The resistance reading on the meter should be about 8 ohms (although 4 ohms is a common value as well). If the reading is infinite (blank display), the speaker wire has opened (broken). If it is zero, the coil of wires has shorted (meaning that the signal cannot go through the coil to be applied to the physical speaker). For more information, see the section "Using a Multimeter."

2. Begin by having the user (who is supposed to be familiar with Excel) demonstrate the problem to you in a step-by-step manner. Have him describe his understanding of the process he is trying to complete.

APPLY YOUR KNOWLEDGE

Then, remove the operator from the situation and begin the troubleshooting process to limit the problem to the hardware involved, the software package being used, and then to the operator. For more information, see the section "Information Gathering."

3. You should tell your customer that the error she is reporting could be caused by a bad hard drive, but that it is more likely a missing or corrupted boot-up file that can be restored without replacing the hard drive. At the very least, more extensive troubleshooting should be conducted before buying a new drive. For more information, see the section "Determining Hardware/Software/Configuration Problems."

Suggested Readings and Resources

1. Using a Multimeter
   http://www.doctronics.co.uk/meter.htm

2. Beep Codes
   http://www.pctusa.com/beep.html

3. Error Codes
   www.sysopt.com/biosbmc.html

4. POST Card
   www.sysopt.com/post.html

5. Diagnostic Software
   www.windsortech.com/

6. DOS Boot Process
   http://www.pcguide.com/ref/hdd/file/structBoot-c.html

7. Motherboard Configuration Problems
   http://www.pcguide.com/proc/config/mb-c.html

8. Field-Replaceable Unit
   http://search390.techtarget.com/sDefinition/0,,sid10_gci761637,00.html

This chapter helps you to prepare for the Core Hardware module of the A+ Certification examination by covering the following objectives within the "Domain 3.0: Preventive Maintenance" section.

3.1 Identify the purpose of various types of preventive maintenance products and procedures and when to use them.

Content might include the following:

- **Liquid cleaning compounds**

- **Types of materials to clean contacts and connections**

- **Non-static vacuums (chassis, power supplies, and fans)**

▶ It has long been known that one of the best ways to fix problems with complex systems is to prevent problems before they happen. This is the concept behind preventive maintenance procedures. Breakdowns never occur at convenient times. By planning for a few minutes of nonproductive activities, hours of repair and recovery work can be avoided.

CHAPTER 10

Preventive Maintenance

STUDY STRATEGIES

To prepare for the Preventive Maintenance objective of the Core Hardware exam,

▶ Read the objectives at the beginning of this chapter.

▶ Study the information in this chapter.

▶ Review the objectives listed earlier in this chapter.

▶ Perform any step-by-step procedures in the text.

▶ Answer the review questions at the end of the chapter and check your results.

▶ Use the PrepLogic test engine on the CD-ROM that accompanies this book for additional review and exam questions concerning this material.

▶ Review the exam tips scattered throughout the chapter and make certain that you are comfortable with each point.

INTRODUCTION

Like all digital systems, a personal computer requires a certain level of ongoing care in order to deliver maximum performance over its full life cycle. This care is delivered in the form of preventive maintenance procedures designed to minimize the occurrence of problems and failures.

After completing the chapter, you should be able to select proper cleaning tools and products for use with different computer components. You should also be able to perform typical preventive maintenance procedures to keep the system healthy and performing at its optimum level.

CLEANING

Cleaning is a major part of keeping a computer system healthy. Therefore, the technician's tool kit should also contain a collection of cleaning supplies. Along with hand tools, it will need a lint-free, soft cloth (chamois) for cleaning the plastic outer surfaces of the system.

Outer-surface cleaning can be accomplished with a simple soap-and-water solution, followed by a clear, water rinse. Care should be taken to make sure that none of the liquid splashes or drips into the inner parts of the system. A damp cloth is easily the best general-purpose cleaning tool for use with computer equipment.

The cleaning should be followed by the application of an *antistatic spray* or *antistatic solution* to prevent the buildup of static charges on the components of the system. A solution composed of 10 parts water and one part common household fabric softener makes an effective and economical antistatic solution. To remove dust from the inside of cabinets, a small paintbrush is handy.

Another common problem is *corrosion*, or *oxidation buildup*, at electrical contact points. These buildups occur on electrical connectors and can reduce the flow of electricity through the connection. Some simple steps can be used to keep corrosion from becoming a problem. The easiest step in preventing corrosion is observing the correct handling procedures for printed circuit boards and cables. Never

> **EXAM TIP**
> Know the common methods of cleaning various computer components.

> **EXAM TIP**
> Know what types of materials/techniques can be used to clean different areas of the computer system.

EXAM TIP

Remember the different items that can be used to clean oxidation off the edge connectors of an I/O adapter card.

EXAM TIP

Be aware of the cause of chip-creep in sockets.

touch the electrical contact points with your skin because the moisture on your body can start corrosive action.

Even with proper handling, corrosion might occur over time. This oxidation can be removed in a number of ways. The oxide buildup can be gently rubbed off with an emery cloth, a common pencil eraser, or special solvent wipe. It can also be dissolved with an electrical-contact cleaner spray.

Socket-mounted devices should be reseated (removed and reinstalled to establish a new electrical connection) as a part of an anti-corrosion effort. This also overcomes the *chip-creep* effect that thermal cycling has on socket-mounted devices. Remember that these devices should be handled according to the metal oxide semiconductor handling guidelines to make certain that no electrostatic discharge damage occurs.

If you use the emery cloth, or rubber eraser, to gently clean your contacts, always rub toward the outer edge of the board or connector to prevent damage to the contacts. Rubbing the edge might lift the foil from the PC board. Printed–circuit-board connectors are typically very thin. Therefore, only rub hard enough to remove the oxide layer and take time to clean up any dust or rubber contamination generated by the cleaning effort.

Cleaning other internal components, such as disk drive read/write heads, can be performed using lint-free foam swabs and isopropyl alcohol or methanol. It's most important that the cleaning solution be one that dries without leaving a residue.

PREVENTIVE MAINTENANCE PROCEDURES

The environment around a computer system, and the manner in which the computer is used, determines greatly how many problems it will have. Occasionally dedicating a few moments of care to the computer can extend its *Mean Time Between Failures* (*MTBF*) period considerably. This activity, involving maintenance not normally associated with a breakdown, is called *Preventive Maintenance* (*PM*).

Computer equipment is susceptible to failures caused by dust buildup, rough handling, and extremes in temperature.

EXAM TIP

Know what environmental conditions, or activities, are most likely to lead to equipment failures.

Dust

Over time, *dust* builds up on everything it can gain access to. Many computer components generate static electrical charges that attract dust particles. In the case of electronic equipment, dust forms an insulating blanket that traps heat next to active devices and can cause them to overheat. Excessive heat can cause premature aging and failure. The best dust protection is a dust-tight enclosure. However, computer components tend to have less than dust-tight seals. In addition, power-supply and microprocessor fans pull air from outside through the system unit.

Another access point for dust is uncovered expansion-slot openings. Missing expansion-slot covers adversely affect the system in two ways. First, the missing cover permits dust to accumulate in the system, forming the insulating blanket described above which causes component overheating. Second, the heat problem is complicated further by the fact that the missing slot cover interrupts the designed airflow patterns inside the case, causing components to overheat because of missing or inadequate airflow.

EXAM TIP

Be aware of the effect that missing expansion-slot covers have on the operation of the system unit.

Smoke is a more dangerous cousin of dust. Like dust particles, smoke collects on all exposed surfaces. The residue of smoke particles is sticky and will cling to the surface. In addition to contributing to the heat buildup problem, smoke residue is particularly destructive to moving parts such as floppy disks, fan motors, and so forth.

Dust buildup inside system components can be taken care of with a soft brush. A static-free vacuum can also be used to remove dust from inside cases and keyboards. Be sure to use a static-free vacuum because normal vacuums are by their nature static generators. The static-free vacuum has special grounding to remove the static buildup it generates. Dust covers are also helpful in holding down dust problems. These covers are simply placed over the equipment when not in use and removed when the device is needed.

EXAM TIP

Know that computer vacuums have special grounding to dissipate static buildup that can damage computer devices.

Rough Handling

Rough handling is either a matter of neglect or a lack of knowledge about how equipment should be handled. Therefore, overcoming rough-handling problems requires that technicians be aware of proper handling techniques for sensitive devices, such as hard disk drives and monitors, and that they adjust their component-handling practices to compensate.

Heat Buildup

As mentioned earlier, excessive heat can cause premature aging and failure of electronic components. Identifying and controlling *heat buildup* problems can require some effort and planning. Microcomputers are designed to run at normal room temperatures. If the ambient temperature rises above about 85°F, heat buildup can become a problem. High humidity can also lead to heat-related problems and failures.

To combat heat problems, make sure that the area around the system is uncluttered so that free airflow around the system can be maintained. Make sure that the power supply's fan is operational. If not, replace the power-supply unit. Likewise, be sure that the microprocessor fan is plugged in and operational. It is very easy for a high-speed microprocessor to fry if its fan fails. A good rule of thumb is to install a fan on any large IC device running above 33MHz.

You should check the computer's ventilation frequently to make sure that papers and other desk clutter are not cutting off airflow to the unit. Check for other sources of heat buildup around the computer and its peripherals. These sources include

◆ Direct sunlight from an outside window

◆ Locations of portable heaters in the winter

◆ Papers/books piled up around the equipment

EXAM TIP

Be aware of the effects that high humidity conditions have on computer equipment.

EXAM TIP

Be aware that direct sunlight is a source of heat buildup in computer equipment.

If heat buildup still exists, check the outer cover to make sure that it is secured firmly to the machine and that all the expansion-slot covers are in place. These items can disrupt the designed airflow characteristics of the case. Finally, add an additional case fan to draw more air through the system unit.

CHALLENGE #1

When you arrive at a customer office to repair one of their key computers, you trace the problem down to a defective microprocessor. The system has apparently been upgraded several times over its lifetime—there are several open expansion slots and loose cables inside the system unit. There is also a layer of dust on all the internal components. What should you tell the manager when she asks you about what you have found?

Protecting Monitors

The PM associated with monitors consists of periodic cleaning, dusting, and good, commonsense practices around the monitor. Aerosol sprays, solvents, and commercial cleaners should be avoided because they can damage the screen and cabinet. The simple cleaning solution described earlier is fine for cleaning the monitor. Make sure that the monitor's power cord is disconnected from any power source before washing. The monitor's screen should be dried with a soft cloth after rinsing.

Very dangerous voltage levels (in excess of 25,000 volts; more than enough to kill or badly injure someone) exist inside the monitor's housing. Therefore, you should only remove the monitor's outer cabinet if you are fully qualified to work on CRT-based equipment. Figure 10.1 shows the areas of the monitor that should be avoided if you must work inside its housing.

FIGURE 10.1
Caution areas inside the monitor.

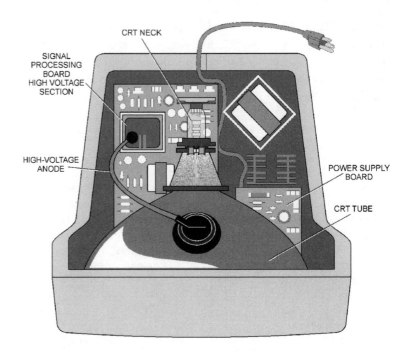

Protecting Hard Disk Drives

If a hard disk drive is to be transported or shipped, make sure to pack it properly. The forces exerted on the drive during shipment might be great enough to cause the R/W heads to slap against the disk surfaces, causing damage to both. Pack the drive unit in an oversized box, with antistatic foam all around the drive. You can also pack the drive in a box-within-a-box configuration—once again using foam as a cushion. Figure 10.2 illustrates this concept.

FIGURE 10.2
Proper packing of a hard drive for shipment.

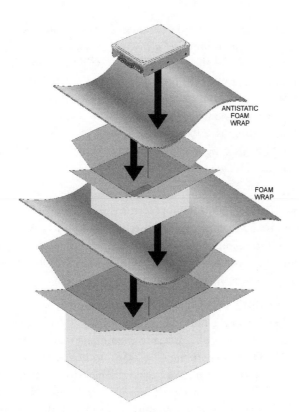

ANTISTATIC
FOAM
WRAP

FOAM
WRAP

At no time should the hard drive's housing, which protects the platters, be removed in open air. The drive's disks and R/W heads are
sealed in the airtight housing under a vacuum. The contaminants
floating in normal air will virtually ruin the drive. If the drive malfunctions, the electronic circuitry and connections can be tested; but
when it comes to repairs within the disk chamber, factory service or
a professional service facility with a proper clean room is a must!

To recover quickly from hardware failures, operator mistakes, and acts of nature, some form of *software backup* is essential with a hard disk system. Copies of the system backup should be stored in a convenient, but secure place. In the case of secure system backups, such as client/server networks, the backup copies should be stored where the network administrators can have access to them, but not the general public (that is, a locked file cabinet). Left unsecured, these copies could be used by someone without authority to gain access to the system or to its data.

Even *Emergency Repair Disks* associated with Windows 9x, Windows NT, and Windows 2000 should be stored in a secure location. These disks can also be used by people other than administrators to gain access to information in client/server networks. Many companies maintain a copy of their backup away from the main site. This is done for protection in case of disasters such as fire.

A number of hard disk drive software utilities are designed to optimize and maintain the operation of the hard disk drive. They should be used as part of a regular preventive maintenance program. The primary HDD utilities are the *CHKDSK, ScanDisk, Defrag, Backup*, and *antivirus* utilities that have been available with different versions of DOS and Windows since early MS-DOS versions. These utilities should be used on a regular scheduled basis to keep the system running to the best of its potential.

EXAM TIP

Be aware of the precautions that should be employed with storing system backups.

Protecting Floppy Disk Drives

Unlike hard disk drives, floppy drives are at least partially open to the atmosphere, and they can be handled on a regular basis. This opens the floppy disk drive to a number of maintenance concerns not found in hard disk drives. Also, removable disks are subject to extremes in temperature, exposure to magnetic and electromagnetic fields, bending, and airborne particles that can lead to information loss.

Never bring disks near magnetic-field producing devices, such as CRT monitors, television sets, or power supplies. They should also never be placed on, or near, appliances such as refrigerators, freezers, vacuum cleaners, and other equipment containing motors. Any of these can alter the information stored on the disk.

Additional measures to protect removable disks include storing them in a cool, dry, clean environment, out of direct sunlight. Excessive temperature will cause the disk and its jacket to warp. Take care when inserting the disk into the drive so as not to damage its jacket or the drive's internal mechanisms.

Protecting Input Devices

Input peripherals generally require very little in the way of preventive maintenance. An occasional dusting and cleaning should be all that's really required.

The keyboard's electronic circuitry is open to the atmosphere and should be vacuumed, as described in Figure 10.3, when you are cleaning around your computer area. Dust buildup on the keyboard circuitry can cause its ICs to fail because of overheating. The keyboard is the most vulnerable peripheral to damage caused by dust. To remove dirt and dust particles from inside the keyboard, disassemble the keyboard and carefully brush particles away from the board with a soft brush. A lint-free swab can be used to clean between the keys.

EXAM TIP

Remember that dust can settle into the keyboard through the cracks between the keys.

FIGURE 10.3
Cleaning the keyboard.

SMALL HAND-HELD VACUUM

When using a trackball mouse, keep its workspace clear, dry, and free from dust. The trackball should be removed and cleaned periodically. Use a lint-free swab to clean the X and Y trackball rollers inside the mouse, as described in Figure 10.4. Removing buildup from the trackball rollers with a sharp instrument—such as an Xacto

EXAM TIP

Know how to properly clean a track-ball mouse.

knife—can place cuts and divots in the roller and permanently damage the mouse.

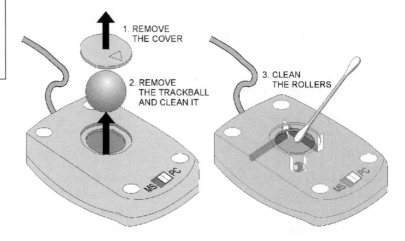

FIGURE 10.4
Cleaning the rollers in a trackball mouse.

CHAPTER SUMMARY

KEY TERMS

- Antistatic solution
- Antistatic spray
- Antivirus
- Backup
- Chip-creep
- CHKDSK
- Corrosion
- Defrag
- Dust
- Emergency Repair Disks
- Heat buildup
- Mean Time Between Failures (MTBF)

The focus of this chapter has been to present the key facets of a successful preventive maintenance program for personal computer systems. The initial section of the chapter dealt with typical computer cleaning chores. The rest of the chapter featured various preventive maintenance procedures associated with the system's different components.

At this point, review the objectives listed at the beginning of the chapter to be certain that you understand each point and can perform each task listed there. Afterward, answer the review questions that follow to verify your knowledge of the information.

CHAPTER SUMMARY

- Oxidation buildup
- Preventive Maintenance (PM)
- Rough handling

- ScanDisk
- Smoke
- Software backup

Review Questions

1. What effect does leaving off expansion-slot covers after performing an upgrade on the system have on its operation? (Select two answers.)

   A. Diminishes the ground potential of the system

   B. Permits dust to accumulate

   C. Interrupts airflow patterns inside the case

   D. Has no discernable effect on the system

2. Which peripheral item is most subject to problems created by environmental dust?

   A. Printer

   B. Floppy disk drive

   C. Mouse

   D. Keyboard

3. What precautions should be taken when storing backup copies of the systems disk drives?

   A. All personnel should have access to the backups.

   B. Only the network administrator should have access to the backup.

   C. All backups should be cleaned regularly.

   D. All backups should be tested regularly.

4. What are some of the most common sources of heat buildup that can be found around a PC installation? (Select all that apply.)

   A. Direct sunlight

   B. Excess body heat

   C. Location of heaters

   D. Papers piled on equipment

5. At what point does heat buildup become a problem for most PCs?

   A. Room temperatures above 85°F

   B. Room temperatures above 90°F

   C. Room temperatures above 95°F

   D. Room temperatures above 100°F

6. What is the effect of the thermal cycling of socket-mounted devices?

   A. Warping

   B. Oxidation

   C. Chip-creep

   D. Induction

7. What is the best type of cleaning tool for use on the exterior of computer components?

   A. Vacuum cleaner

   B. Damp cloth

   C. Brush

   D. Antistatic spray

8. What type of cleaning solution should be used on the exterior of computer components?

   A. Bleach and water

   B. Window cleaner

   C. Soap and water

   D. None

APPLY YOUR KNOWLEDGE

9. What should be done after cleaning the exterior of computer components?

   A. Use a small paintbrush to remove dust from their interiors.

   B. Rub them with a dry towel.

   C. Wipe them with a damp cloth.

   D. Apply a fabric softener and water solution to their exteriors.

10. How can you remove dust from the inside of the case?

   A. Use a small paintbrush.

   B. Rub gently with a dry towel.

   C. Wipe gently with a damp cloth.

   D. Apply a fabric softener and water solution.

11. What should you do if you suspect corrosion may cause a problem with a system component?

   A. Brush its contacts with a small paintbrush.

   B. Rub its contacts with a pencil eraser.

   C. Wipe its contacts gently with a damp cloth.

   D. Apply a fabric softener and water solution to the contacts.

12. _____ is/are unlikely to lead to equipment failure.

   A. Rough handling

   B. Dust buildup

   C. Temperature extremes

   D. Periodic system upgrades

13. What is the main reason to use a static-free vacuum?

   A. It is small and portable and allows you to get in between the keyboard keys and other small spaces.

   B. It is grounded.

   C. It generates less ESD.

   D. It has a spinning brush to pick up all the lint.

14. Which of the following can lead to problems with excess heat buildup?

   A. Open HVAC ducts

   B. Closed computer racks

   C. Closed window shades

   D. High humidity

15. Where should backup copies of the systems disk drives be located?

   A. System administrator's desk

   B. Offsite storage facility

   C. Computer room shelf

   D. Company president's file cabinet

16. How should you clean a trackball mouse?

   A. Use Xacto knife to clean buildup from the rollers.

   B. Use dry Q-tip swab to clean buildup from the rollers.

   C. Use damp cloth to clean buildup from the rollers.

   D. Use pencil eraser to clean buildup from the rollers.

APPLY YOUR KNOWLEDGE

Answers and Explanations

1. **B, C.** Missing expansion-slot covers adversely affect the system in two ways. First, the missing cover permits dust to accumulate in the system, forming an insulating blanket that traps heat next to active devices and causes them to overheat. Second, the heat problem is complicated further by the fact that the missing slot cover interrupts the designed airflow patterns inside the case, causing components to overheat because of missing or inadequate airflow. For more information, see the section "Dust."

2. **D.** Dust buildup on the keyboard circuitry can cause its ICs to fail because of overheating. For more information, see the section "Protecting Input Devices."

3. **B.** Copies of the system backup should be stored in a convenient, but secure place. In the case of secure system backups, such as client/server networks, the back-up copies should be stored where the network administrators can have access to them, but not the general public (that is, a locked file cabinet). Left unsecured, these copies could be used by someone without authority to gain access to the system or to its data. Many companies maintain a copy of their backup away from the main site. This is done for protection in case of disasters such as fire. For more information, see the section "Protecting Hard Disk Drives."

4. **A, C, D.** Sources of heat buildup around the computer and its peripherals include direct sunlight from an outside window, locations of portable heaters in the winter, and papers/books piled up around the equipment. For more information, see the section "Heat Buildup."

5. **A.** Microcomputers are designed to run at normal room temperatures. If the ambient temperature rises above about 85°F, heat buildup can become a problem. High humidity can also lead to heat-related problems. For more information, see the section "Heat Buildup."

6. **C.** Socket-mounted devices should be reseated (removed and reinstalled to establish a new electrical connection) as a part of an anti-corrosion effort. This also overcomes the chip-creep effect that thermal cycling has on socket-mounted devices. For more information, see the section "Cleaning."

7. **B.** A damp cloth is easily the best general-purpose cleaning tool for use with computer equipment. For more information, see the section "Cleaning."

8. **C.** Outer-surface cleaning can be accomplished with a simple soap-and-water solution, followed by a clear water rinse. Care should be taken to make sure that none of the liquid splashes or drips into the inner parts of the system. For more information, see the section "Cleaning."

9. **D.** The cleaning should be followed by the application of an antistatic spray or antistatic solution to prevent the buildup of static charges on the components of the system. A solution composed of 10 parts water and one part common household fabric softener makes an effective and economical antistatic solution. For more information, see the section "Cleaning."

10. **A.** To remove dust from the inside of cabinets, a small paintbrush is handy. For more information, see the section "Cleaning."

APPLY YOUR KNOWLEDGE

11. **B.** The oxide buildup that results from corrosion can be gently rubbed off with an emery cloth, a common pencil eraser, or a special solvent wipe. It can also be dissolved with an electrical-contact cleaner spray. For more information, see the section "Cleaning."

12. **D.** Computer equipment is susceptible to failures caused by dust buildup, rough handling, and extremes in temperature. For more information, see the section "Preventive Maintenance Procedures."

13. **C.** Be sure to use a static-free vacuum because normal vacuums are by their nature static generators. The static-free vacuum has special grounding to remove the static buildup it generates. For more information, see the section "Dust."

14. **D.** High humidity can also lead to heat-related problems. For more information, see the section "Heat Buildup."

15. **B.** Many companies maintain a copy of their backup away from the main site. This is done for protection in case of disasters such as fire. For more information, see the section "Protecting Hard Disk Drives."

16. **B.** When using a trackball mouse, keep its workspace clear, dry, and free from dust. The trackball should be removed and cleaned periodically. Use a lint-free swab to clean the X and Y trackball rollers inside the mouse. Removing buildup from the trackball rollers with a sharp instrument—such as an Xacto knife—can place cuts and divots in the roller and permanently damage the mouse. For more information, see the section "Protecting Input Devices."

Challenge Solution

1. You should tell her that the microprocessor has failed and you believe that it is related to heat buildup in the computer. Explain the importance of making sure that all of the back panel slot covers are in place and the need for periodic cleaning—both of which you have taken care of for now. Also describe other environmental issues the manager can be aware of that can cause such failures to occur. For more information, see the section "Heat Buildup."

Suggested Readings and Resources

1. PC Preventive Maintenance
   http://a1computers.net/pm.htm

2. PC Maintenance
   http://pcsupport.about.com/cs/maintenance/

3. Heat Buildup
   http://arar.essortment.com/
   computersmainte_rxwv.htm

4. Keep Your Computer Cool
   http://peripherals.about.com/library/
   weekly/aa052802a.htm

5. Preventive Maintenance
   http://www.pccomputernotes.com/
   newsletter/feb01/

This chapter helps you to prepare for the Core Hardware module of the A+ Certification examination by covering the following objectives within the "Domain 3.0: Preventive Maintenance" section.

3.2 Identify issues, procedures, and devices for protection within the computing environment, including people, hardware, and the surrounding workspace.

Content might include the following:

- **UPSs (uninterruptible power supplies) and suppressers**

- **Determining the signs of power issues**

- **Proper methods of storage of components for future use**

Potential hazards and proper safety procedures relating to lasers:

- **High-voltage equipment**

- **Power supply**

- **CRT**

Special disposal procedures that comply with environmental guidelines:

- **Batteries**

- **CRTs**

- **Toner kits/cartridges**

- **Chemical solvents and cans**

- **MSDS (Material Safety Data Sheet)**

ESD (electrostatic discharge) precautions and procedures:

- **What ESD can do; how it might be apparent or hidden**

- **Common ESD protection devices**

CHAPTER 11

System Protection

OBJECTIVES

▶ Computer technicians should be aware of potential environmental hazards and know how to prevent them from becoming a problem. Safety is an issue in every profession. Technicians should be aware of the potential hazards associated with certain areas of the computer and with certain types of peripheral equipment.

▶ Concerns for the world environment are at their highest. Many of the materials used in the construction of computer-related equipment can be harmful. Also, many of the products used to service computer equipment can also have an adverse effect on the environment. Therefore, the technician should be aware of requirements associated with the disposal of this equipment and these materials.

▶ PC repair personnel should be aware of the causes and damaging effects of ESD so that they can prevent its occurrence. A good place to start checking for environmental hazards is from the incoming power source. The following sections deal with power-line issues and solutions.

OUTLINE

To prepare for the Preventive Maintenance objective of the Core Hardware exam,

▶ Read the objectives at the beginning of this chapter.

▶ Study the information in this chapter.

▶ Review the objectives listed earlier in this chapter.

▶ Perform any step-by-step procedures in the text.

▶ Answer the review questions at the end of the chapter and check your results.

▶ Use the PrepLogic test engine on the CD-ROM that accompanies this book for additional review and exam questions concerning this material.

▶ Review the exam tips scattered throughout the chapter and make certain that you are comfortable with each point.

INTRODUCTION

This chapter deals with environmental hazards conditions that can damage computer equipment or injure the user or technician. These conditions include—power supply variations, electrostatic discharge conditions, and potentially hazardous areas of the system.

The chapter also describes procedures for properly disposing of computer equipment when it fails or reaches the end of its useful life cycle.

After completing the chapter, you should be able to describe different types of typical power-supply variations and describe equipment that can be employed to minimize or remove these variations from the system.

Likewise, you should be able to identify sources of ESD and specify precautions that can be taken to prevent static discharge. Finally, you should be able to identify potentially hazardous areas of the computer and its peripherals.

POWER-LINE PROTECTION

Digital systems tend to be sensitive to power variations and losses. Even a very short loss of electrical power can shut a digital computer down, resulting in a loss of any current information that has not been saved to a mass storage device.

Typical power supply variations fall into two categories:

◆ *Transients*—Over-voltage conditions that can be classified as spikes (measured in nanoseconds) or as surges (measured in milliseconds).

◆ *Sags*—Under-voltage conditions that include voltage sags and brownouts. A voltage sag typically lasts only a few milliseconds, whereas a brownout can last for a protracted period of time.

The effects of power-supply variations are often hard to identify as power issues. Brownouts and power failures are easy to spot because of their duration. However, faster acting disturbances can cause symptoms not easily traced to the power source. Spikes can be quite damaging to electronic equipment, damaging devices such as hard drives and modems. Other occurrences will just cause data loss. Sags can cause the system to suddenly reboot because it thinks the power has been turned off. These disturbances are relatively easy to detect because they typically cause any lights in the room to flicker.

In general, if several components go bad in a short period of time, or if components go bad more often than usual at a given location, these are good indicators of power-related issues. Likewise, machines that crash randomly and often could be experiencing power issues. If "dirty" power problems are suspected, a voltage-monitoring device should be placed in the power circuit and left for an extended period of time. These devices observe the incoming power over time and will produce a problem indicator if significant variations occur.

> **EXAM TIP**
> Be aware of how under-voltage and over-voltage situations are categorized (that is, time lengths).

Surge Suppressers

Inexpensive *power line filters*, called *surge suppressers*, are good for cleaning up dirty commercial power. These units passively filter the incoming power signal to smooth out variations. There are two factors to consider when choosing a surge suppresser:

◆ Clamping speed

◆ Clamping voltage

Surge suppressers will protect the system from damage up to a specified point. However, large variations, such as surges created when power is restored after an outage, can still cause considerable data loss and damage. In the case of startup surges, making sure that the system is turned off, or even disconnected from the power source, until after the power is restored is one option.

> **EXAM TIP**
> Know what type of devices will protect systems from minor power sags and power surges.

Uninterruptible Power Supplies

In the case of a complete shutdown, or a significant sag, the best protection from losing programs and data is an *uninterruptible power supply* (*UPS*).

> **EXAM TIP**
> Know what type of device prevents power interruptions that can corrupt data.

Uninterruptible power supplies are battery-based systems that monitor the incoming power and kick in when unacceptable variations occur in the power source. The term UPS is frequently used to describe two different types of power backup systems.

The first is a *standby power system*, and the second is a truly uninterruptible power system. The standby system monitors the power input line and waits for a significant variation to occur. The batteries in this unit are held out of the power loop and draw only enough current from the AC source to stay recharged. When an interruption occurs, the UPS senses it and switches the output of the batteries into an inverter circuit that converts the DC output of the batteries into an AC current and voltage that resembles the commercial power supply. This power signal is typically applied to the computer within 10 milliseconds.

The uninterruptible systems do not keep the batteries offline. Instead, the batteries and converters are always actively attached to the output of UPS. When an interruption in the supply occurs, no switching of the output is required. The battery/inverter section simply continues under its own power. Figure 11.1 shows how a UPS connects into a system.

FIGURE 11.1

Connecting the UPS in the system.

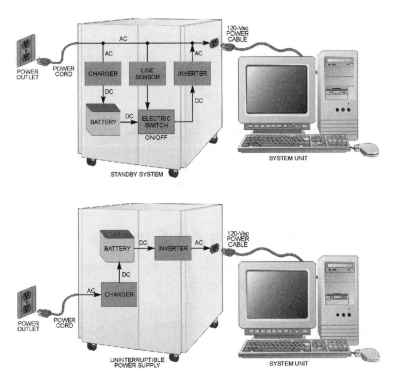

Standby systems don't generally provide a high level of protection from sags and spikes. They do, however, include additional circuitry to minimize such variations. Conversely, an uninterruptible system is an extremely good power-conditioning system. Because it always sits between the commercial power and the computer, it can supply a constant power supply to the system.

When dealing with either type of UPS system, the most important rating to be aware of is its *volt-ampere (VA) rating*. The VA rating indicates the capability of the UPS system to deliver both voltage (V) and current (A) to the computer, simultaneously. This rating differs from the device's wattage rating, and the two should not be used interchangeably. The wattage power rating is a factor of multiplying the voltage and current use, at any particular time, to arrive at a power consumption value. The VA rating is used in AC systems because peak voltage and current elements do not occur at the same instant. This condition is referred to as being out-of-phase with each other, and makes it slightly more difficult to calculate power requirements. In general, always make sure that the UPS system has a higher wattage capability than the computer requires, and likewise, that the VA rating of the UPS is higher than that required by the computer.

The other significant specification for UPS systems is the length of time they can supply power. Because the UPS is a battery-powered device, it uses an ampere-hour rating. This is the same time notation system used for automobile batteries and other battery-powered systems. The rating is obtained by multiplying a given current drain from the battery, for a given amount of time. (That is, a battery capable of sustaining 1.5 amps of output current for one hour would be rated at 1.5 amp-hours.)

The primary mission of the UPS is to keep the system running when a power failure occurs (usually, long enough to conduct an orderly shut down of the system). Because it's a battery-based system, it cannot keep the system running infinitely. For this reason, you should not connect non-essential, power-hungry peripheral devices such as a laser printer to the UPS supply. If the power goes out, it is highly unlikely that you will really have to print something before shutting the system down. If the UPS is being used to keep a critical system in operation during a power outage, the high current drain of the laser printer would severely reduce the length of time that the UPS could keep the system running.

EXAM TIP

Remember that non-essential peripheral devices should not be connected to UPS supplies.

PROTECTION DURING STORAGE

The best storage option for most computer equipment is the original manufacturer's box. These boxes are designed specifically to store and transport the device safely. They include form-fitting protective foam to protect the device from shock hazards. The device is normally wrapped in a protective antistatic bag or wrapper to defeat the effects of ESD.

Printed circuit boards are normally shipped on a thin piece of antistatic foam. The board is typically placed solder-side down on the foam. Both the foam and the board are placed in an antistatic bag and then into a storage box.

Hard disk drives are usually placed directly into a static bag and then placed in a thick foam box. The foam box is then inserted into a storage carton. Floppy drives typically receive less padding than HDD units do.

Monitors, printers, scanners, and other peripheral equipment should be stored in their original boxes, using their original packing foam and protective storage bag. The contours of the packing foam for these devices are not generally compatible from model to model or device to device. This is also the best packaging for transporting these devices. If the original boxes and packing materials are not available, make sure to use sturdy cartons and cushion the equipment well on all sides before shipping.

EXAM TIP

Know that the best device for transporting computer equipment is the original manufacturer's packaging, including the antistatic foam and bags used to pack it.

AVOIDING HIGH-VOLTAGE HAZARDS

In most IBM compatibles, there are only two potentially dangerous areas—inside the CRT display and inside the power-supply unit. Both of these areas contain electrical voltage levels that are lethal. However, both of these areas reside in self-contained units, and you normally won't be required to open either unit.

As a matter of fact, you should never enter the interior of a CRT cabinet unless you have been trained specifically to work with this type of equipment. The tube itself is dangerous if accidentally cracked. In addition, extremely high-voltage levels (in excess of 25,000 volts) might be present inside the CRT housing, even up to a year after electrical power has been removed from the unit.

EXAM TIP

Be aware of the voltage levels that are present inside a CRT cabinet.

In repair situations, the high voltage charge associated with video displays must be discharged. This is accomplished by creating a path from the tube's high-voltage anode to the chassis. With the monitor unplugged from the commercial power outlet, clip one end of an insulated jumper wire to the chassis ground of the frame. Clip the other end to a long, flat-blade screwdriver that has a well-insulated handle. While touching only the insulated handle of the screwdriver, slide the blade of the screwdriver under the rubber cup of the anode and make contact with its metal connection. This should bleed off the high-voltage charge to ground. Continue the contact for several seconds to ensure that the voltage has been fully discharged.

Never open the power-supply unit either. Some portions of the circuitry inside the power supply carry extremely high-voltage levels and have very high current capabilities.

Generally, no open *shock hazards* are present inside the system unit. However, you should not reach inside the computer while power is applied to the unit. Jewelry and other metallic objects do pose an electrical threat, even with the relatively low voltage present in the system unit.

Never have liquids around energized electrical equipment. It's a good idea to keep food and drinks away from all computer equipment at all times. When cleaning around the computer with liquids, make certain to unplug all power connections to the system, and its peripherals, beforehand. When cleaning external computer cabinets with liquid cleaners, take care to prevent any of the solution from dripping or spilling into the equipment.

Do not defeat the safety feature of *three-prong power plugs* by using two-prong adapters. The equipment ground of a power cord should never be defeated or removed. This plug connects the computer chassis to an earth ground through the power system. This provides a reference point for all the system's devices to operate from and supplies protection for personnel from electrical shock. In defeating the ground plug, a very important level of protection is removed from the equipment.

You should remove all power cords associated with the computer and its peripherals from the power outlet during thunder or lightning storms.

> **EXAM TIP**
>
> Be aware that a long, flat-blade screwdriver is the proper tool to use for discharging the high-voltage anode of a CRT tube.

> **EXAM TIP**
>
> Know the best way to protect computer equipment in an electrical storm.

Periodically examine the power cords of the computer and peripherals for cracked or damaged insulation. Replace worn or damaged power cords promptly. Never allow anything to rest on a power cord. Run power cords and connecting cables safely out of the way so that they don't become trip, or catch, hazards.

Don't apply liquid or aerosol cleaners directly to computer equipment. Spray cleaners on a cloth and then apply the cloth to the equipment. Freon-propelled sprays should not be used on computer equipment because they can produce destructive electrostatic charges.

Avoiding Laser and Burn Hazards

Laser printers contain many hazardous areas. The laser light can be very damaging to the human eye. In addition, there are multiple high-voltage areas in the typical laser printer and a high-temperature area to contend with as well.

It is sometimes necessary to bypass safety interlocks to isolate problems. When doing so, proper precautions must be observed, such as avoiding the laser light, being aware of the high temperatures in the fuser area, and taking proper precautions with the high-voltage areas of the unit. The laser light is a hazard to eyesight, the fuser area is a burn hazard, and the power supplies are shock hazards.

Another potential *burn hazard* is the printhead mechanism of a dot-matrix printer. During normal operation, it can become hot enough to be a burn hazard if touched.

Because computers do have the potential to produce these types of injuries, it is good practice to have a well-stocked first-aid kit in the work area. In addition, a Class-C fire extinguisher should be on hand. Class-C extinguishers are the type specified for use around electrical equipment. You can probably imagine the consequences of applying a water-based fire extinguisher to a fire with live electrical equipment around. The class, or classes, that the fire extinguisher is rated for are typically marked on its side.

EXAM TIP
Know the areas of the computer system that are dangerous for personnel, as well as how to prevent injury from these areas.

EXAM TIP
Remember the type of fire extinguisher that must be used with electrical systems, such as a PC.

DISPOSAL PROCEDURES

Most computer components contain some level of hazardous substances. Printed circuit boards consist of plastics, precious metals, fiberglass, arsenic, silicon, gallium, and lead. CRTs contain glass, metal, plastics, lead, barium, and rare earth metals. Batteries from portable systems can contain lead, cadmium, lithium, alkaline manganese, and mercury.

Although all these materials can be classified as hazardous materials, so far there are no widespread regulations when it comes to placing them in the landfill. Conversely, local regulations concerning acceptable disposal methods for computer-related components should always be checked before disposing of any electronic equipment.

Laser printer toner cartridges can be refilled and recycled. However, this should only be done for draft-mode operations, where very good resolution is not required. Ink cartridges from inkjet printers can also be refilled and reused. Like laser cartridges, they can be very messy to refill and often do not function as well as new cartridges do. In many cases, the manufacturer of the product will have a policy of accepting spent cartridges.

For both batteries and cartridges, the desired method of disposal is recycling. It should not be too difficult to find a drop site that will handle recycling these products. On the other hand, even nonhazardous, *Subtitle D dumpsites* can handle the hardware components if need be. Subtitle-D dumpsites are nonhazardous, solid waste dumpsites that have been designed to meet EPA standards set for this classification. These sites are designed to hold hazardous materials safely.

All hazardous materials are required to have *Material Safety Data Sheets* (*MSDS*) that accompany them when they change hands. They are also required to be on hand in areas where hazardous materials are stored and commonly used. The MSDS contains information about

◆ What the material is

◆ Its hazardous ingredients

◆ Its physical properties

◆ Fire and explosion data

> **EXAM TIP**
> Remember that toner cartridges from a laser printer should be recycled.

> **EXAM TIP**
> Remember that the proper disposal method for batteries is to recycle them.

◆ Reactivity data

◆ Spill or leak procedures

◆ Health hazard information

◆ Any special protection information

◆ Any special precaution information

These information sheets must be provided by the hazardous material supplier. Likewise, if you supply this material to a third party, you must also supply the MSDS for the material. These sheets inform workers and management about hazards associated with the product and how to handle it safely. It also provides instructions about what to do if an accident occurs involving the material.

ELECTROSTATIC DISCHARGE

EXAM TIP

Remember what the acronym ESD stands for.

EXAM TIP

Know that high voltage ratings do not make a particular contact point more dangerous than one with a lower voltage but a higher current potential.

The first step in avoiding *ESD* (*electrostatic discharge*) is being able to identify when and why it occurs. Electrostatic discharges are the most severe form of *electromagnetic interference* (*EMI*). The human body can build up static charges that range up to 25,000 volts. These buildups can discharge very rapidly into an electrically grounded body or device. Placing a 25,000-volt surge through any electronic device is potentially damaging to it.

At this point, you might be wondering if the 25,000 volts associated with video monitors is deadly, while the 10,000 to 25,000 volts associated with ESD is not harmful to humans. The reason for this is the difference in current-delivering capabilities created by the voltage. In electronics classes, we reiterate that "It isn't the voltage that will kill you, it's the current" (amperage). The capability of the voltage associated with a video monitor to push current through your body is significant (several amps), whereas the same capabilities associated with static are very low (micro-amps—thousandths of an amp). Therefore, it is possible for a lower voltage device with a higher current rating (such as a 110 Vac power supply) to be much more dangerous than a higher voltage source that has a lower current producing capability (such as static).

The most common causes of ESD are

◆ Moving people

◆ Improper grounding

◆ Unshielded cables

◆ Poor connections

◆ Moving machines

◆ Low humidity (hot and dry conditions)

When people move, their clothes rub together and can produce large amounts of electrostatic charge on their bodies. Walking across carpeting can create charges in excess of 1,000 volts. Motors in electrical devices, such as vacuum cleaners and refrigerators, also generate high levels of ESD. Some repair shops do not permit compressed air to be used for blowing dust out of keyboard and other computer equipment because it has erroneously been linked to creating ESD.

ESD is most likely to occur during periods of *low humidity*. If the relative humidity is below 50%, static charges can accumulate easily. ESD generally does not occur when the humidity is above 50%. Normal air conditioning works by removing moisture from the atmosphere. Therefore, its presence can increase the potential for ESD by lowering the humidity even farther. Anytime the static charge reaches around 10,000 volts, it is likely to discharge to grounded metal parts. In many high ESD situations, it can be useful to install a humidifier to raise the level of humidity in the work area.

> **EXAM TIP**
>
> Be aware that compressed air can be used to blow dust out of components and that it does not create ESD.

> **EXAM TIP**
>
> Memorize the conditions and actions that make ESD more likely to occur.

CHALLENGE #1

You have been asked to consult on the design of your company's new repair facility outside of Phoenix, Arizona. In particular, management wants to know how to equip the work areas of their new facility. You have not been to the site, but you know that it is in a hot desert environment. Also, the building will be air conditioned. How should you advise them about precautions that should be taken with the work area?

MOS Handling Techniques

MOS devices are sensitive to voltage spikes and static electricity discharges. The level of static electricity present on your body is high enough to destroy the inputs of a *CMOS device* if you touch its pins with your fingers.

Professional service technicians employ a number of precautionary steps when they are working on systems that might contain MOS devices. These technicians normally use a *grounding strap*, like the one depicted in Figure 11.2. These antistatic devices can be placed around the wrists or ankle to ground the technician to the system being worked on. These straps release any static present on the technician's body and pass it harmlessly to ground potential.

FIGURE 11.2
Typical antistatic devices.

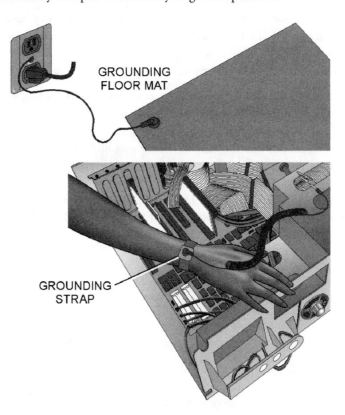

GROUNDING
FLOOR MAT

GROUNDING
STRAP

Antistatic wrist or ankle straps should never be worn while working on higher voltage components, such as monitors and power-supply units. Some technicians wrap a copper wire around their wrist or ankle and connect it to the ground side of an outlet. This is not a safe practice because the resistive feature of a true wrist strap is missing. As an alternative, most technician's work areas include antistatic mats made out of rubber or other antistatic materials that they stand on while working on the equipment. This is particularly helpful in carpeted work areas because carpeting can be a major source of ESD buildup. Some antistatic mats have ground connections that should be connected to the safety ground of an AC power outlet.

To avoid damaging static-sensitive devices, the following procedures will help to minimize the chances of destructive static discharges:

◆ Before touching any components inside the system, touch an exposed part of the chassis or the power-supply housing with your finger. Grounding yourself in this manner will ensure that any static charge present on your body is removed. This technique should be used before handling a circuit board or component. Of course, you should be aware that this technique only works safely when the power cord is attached to a grounded power outlet. The ground plug on a standard power cable is the best tool for overcoming ESD problems.

◆ Do not remove ICs from their protective tubes (or foam packages) until you are ready to use them. If you remove a circuit board, or component, containing static-sensitive devices from the system, place it on a conductive surface, such as a sheet of aluminum foil. It is a good practice to reseat any socket-mounted devices when handling a printed circuit board. Before removing the IC from its protective container, touch the container to the power supply of the unit in which it is to be inserted.

◆ Be aware that normal operating vibrations and temperature cycling can degrade the electrical connections between ICs and sockets over time. This gradual deterioration of electrical contact between chips and sockets is referred to as *chip-creep*.

◆ Use antistatic sprays or solutions on floors, carpets, desks, and computer equipment. An antistatic spray or solution, applied with a soft cloth, is an effective deterrent to static.

EXAM TIP

Know when not to wear an antistatic wrist strap.

EXAM TIP

Be aware of the effects that temperature cycling can have on socket-mounted devices.

◆ Install static-free carpeting in the work area. You can also install an antistatic floor mat as well. Install a conductive table-top to carry away static from the work area. Use antistatic mats on the work surface.

◆ Use a room humidifier to keep the humidity level above 50% in the work area.

Understanding Grounds

The term *ground* is often a source of confusion for the novice because it actually encompasses a collection of terms. Generically, ground is simply any point from which electrical measurements are referenced. However, the original definition of ground actually referred to the ground. This ground is called *earth ground*.

The movement of the electrical current along a conductor requires a path for the current to return to its source. In early telegraph systems and even modern power-transmission systems, the earth provides a return path, and hypothetically, produces an electrical reference point of absolute zero. Figure 11.3 depicts this type of ground.

FIGURE 11.3
Power transmission system.

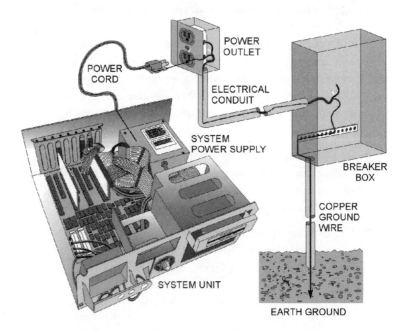

Grounding is an important aspect of limiting EMI in computer systems. Left unchecked, EMI can distort images on the video display, interfere with commercial communication equipment (such as radios and televisions), and corrupt data on floppy disks. In addition, EMI can cause signal deterioration and loss caused by improper cable routing. If a signal cable is bundled with a power cord, radiation from the power cord can be induced into the signal cable, affecting the signals that pass through it. Good grounding routes the induced EMI signals away from logic circuitry and toward ground potential, preventing it from disrupting normal operations. Unlike ESD, which is destructive, the effects of EMI can be corrected without damage.

Because the computer system is connected to an actual earth ground, it should always be turned off and disconnected from the wall outlet during *electrical storms*. This includes the computer and all of its peripherals. The electrical pathway through the computer equipment can be very inviting to lightning on its way to earth ground. The extremely high electrical potential of a lightning strike is more than any computer can withstand.

EXAM TIP

Remember that ESD is destructive and EMI is not.

CHAPTER SUMMARY

This chapter focused on environmental hazards that affect the operation of computer equipment. The initial sections of the chapter dealt with problems caused by fluctuations in the computer's incoming power line. Different types of universal power supplies were discussed, along with other power-line conditioning devices.

The next section of the chapter discussed proper storage methods for typical computer components.

Potentially hazardous areas of the computer and its peripherals were presented in the third major section of the chapter. Although not an intrinsically unsafe environment, some areas of a computer system can be harmful if approached unawares.

Cleaning materials and disposal of old and defective equipment were addressed in the next section of the chapter. MSDS records were also introduced.

KEY TERMS

- Brownouts
- Burn hazard
- Chip-creep
- CMOS device
- Earth ground
- Electrical storms
- Electromagnetic interference (EMI)
- Electrostatic discharge (ESD)
- Ground
- Grounding strap

CHAPTER SUMMARY

- Low humidity
- Material Safety Data Sheets (MSDS)
- Power-line filters
- Sags
- Shock hazards
- Spikes
- Standby power system
- Subtitle D dumpsites
- Surge suppressers
- Surges
- Three-prong power plugs
- Transients
- Uninterruptible power supply (UPS)
- Voltage sags
- Volt-ampere (VA) rating

The final section of the chapter described the danger and causes of electrostatic discharges and provided information about how to eliminate them.

At this point, review the objectives listed at the beginning of the chapter to be certain that you understand the information associated with each one and that you can perform each item listed there. Afterward, answer the review questions that follow to verify your knowledge of the information.

APPLY YOUR KNOWLEDGE

Review Questions

1. A _____ is an under-voltage condition that lasts for an extended period of time.

   A. sag

   B. brownout

   C. surge

   D. spike

2. A _____ is an under-voltage condition that lasts for a very short period of time.

   A. surge

   B. spike

   C. sag

   D. brownout

3. You should not wear a wrist grounding strap when _____.

   A. replacing an adapter card

   B. repairing a motherboard

   C. repairing a CRT

   D. adding or replacing RAM

4. The local weather report indicates that an electrical storm with severe winds is likely to occur in your area overnight. What reasonable precautions should you take to protect your computers?

   A. Monitor the computers until the storm passes.

   B. Plug the computers in to a surge protector.

   C. Turn off the computers.

   D. Unplug the computers.

5. _____ is the gradual deterioration of the electrical connection between the pins of an IC and its socket.

   A. Rust

   B. Degradation

   C. Chip-creep

   D. Tarnish

6. In terms of maintenance issues, how are the effects of ESD and EMI different?

   A. ESD is not destructive, whereas EMI can be very destructive.

   B. EMI is not destructive, whereas ESD can be very destructive.

   C. EMI improves system efficiency, whereas ESD can be very destructive.

   D. ESD improves system efficiency, whereas EMI can be very destructive.

7. Which voltage level is more dangerous, 110 Vac at 5 amps, or 25,000 Vac at 5 microamperes?

   A. Neither is particularly dangerous.

   B. 5 amps is much more dangerous than 5 microamperes.

   C. Both are extremely dangerous.

   D. 25,000 volts is much more dangerous than 110 volts.

APPLY YOUR KNOWLEDGE

8. A _____ is used to protect computer equipment from power-line variations or power outages.

   A. preliminary ESD

   B. surge protector

   C. USPS

   D. UPS

9. A _____ is used to protect computer equipment from very small over-voltage occurrences.

   A. USPS

   B. UPS

   C. surge suppresser

   D. preliminary ESD

10. Which device should not be connected to a UPS system?

    A. Mail server

    B. Laser printer

    C. Web server

    D. Workstation

11. What is the recommended method for handling empty toner cartridges?

    A. Recycle it.

    B. Throw it in the trash.

    C. Burn it in a certified incinerator.

    D. Turn it in to a licensed computer retailer.

12. What type of equipment should be used to minimize the chances of ESD during normal computer maintenance work?

    A. Surge protector

    B. Terrycloth towel

C. Wrist strap

D. Screwdriver

13. Damaging electrostatic discharge is most likely to occur when _____.

    A. working around rubber mats

    B. using test instruments on a system

    C. the humidity is low

    D. you accidentally get too close to the power-supply unit while it is operating

14. What is the recommended method for handling a dead battery?

    A. Recycle it.

    B. Throw it in the trash.

    C. Burn it in a certified incinerator.

    D. Recharge it.

15. What type of fire extinguisher should be used around computers?

    A. Class A

    B. Class B

    C. Class C

    D. Class D

16. What is the best tool for releasing the charge on a CRT anode?

    A. Your finger

    B. Terrycloth towel

    C. Wrist strap

    D. Screwdriver

APPLY YOUR KNOWLEDGE

17. What is the voltage level commonly found in a CRT?

    A. 25 volts

    B. 250 volts

    C. 25,000 volts

    D. 250,000 volts

18. What is the best device for transporting computer equipment?

    A. An antistatic bag

    B. A server rack

    C. A sturdy carton filled with Styrofoam peanuts

    D. The original packaging

19. If the light in the room dims for a few seconds each time the laser printer prints out, what type of line variation might you be dealing with?

    A. Sag

    B. Spike

    C. Surge

    D. Brownout

Answers and Explanations

1. **B.** A brownout is an under-voltage condition that lasts for a sustained period of time. For more information, see the section "Power-Line Protection."

2. **C.** A voltage sag is an under-voltage condition that lasts for a few milliseconds. For more information, see the section "Power-Line Protection."

3. **C.** A wrist strap is a conductor designed to carry electrical charges away from your body. In high-voltage environments such as those found inside a power-supply unit or a monitor, however, this safety device becomes a potential path for electrocution. For more information, see the section "MOS Handling Techniques."

4. **D.** For complete protection from potential lightning strikes, you should completely disconnect the computers from the commercial power source (unplug them from the outlets) so that there is no path for the lightning to follow. For more information, see the section "Avoiding High-Voltage Hazards."

5. **C.** Chip-creep, the degradation of the contact between an IC and its socket, occurs because of the effects of temperature cycling on the IC pins and the socket contacts. For more information, see the section "MOS Handling Techniques."

6. **B.** Electrostatic discharge (ESD) can send severe over-voltages into electrical equipment that have the potential to cause permanent damage to sensitive electronic components. Electromagnetic interference (EMI) is when strong electromagnetic fields can distort signals within the system, causing a partial or complete system crash. Unlike ESD, which is destructive, the effects of EMI can be corrected without damage. For more information, see the section "Understanding Grounds."

7. **B.** "It isn't the voltage that will kill you, it's the current" (amperage). The capability of the voltage associated with a video monitor to push current through your body is significant (several amps), whereas the same capabilities associated with static are very low (micro-amps—thousandths of an

APPLY YOUR KNOWLEDGE

amp). Therefore, it is possible for a lower voltage device with a higher current rating (such as a 110 Vac power supply) to be much more dangerous than a higher voltage source that has a lower current capability (such as static). For more information, see the section "Electrostatic Discharge."

8. **D.** The uninterruptible power supply (UPS) is the best protection against losing data or damaged components when power interruptions or variations occur. For more information, see the section "Uninterruptible Power Supplies."

9. **C.** A surge suppresser can protect an electrical device from small power variations only up to a point, but cannot handle sustained power-line problems. If the ratings of the suppresser are exceeded, the device it is guarding could be damaged. For more information, see the section "Surge Suppressers."

10. **B.** The laser printer should not be attached to the UPS. It is not required in an emergency situation, and it consumes a considerable amount of power. For more information, see the section "Uninterruptible Power Supplies."

11. **A.** Laser printer toner cartridges can be refilled and recycled. For more information, see the section "Disposal Procedures."

12. **C.** Professional service technicians employ a number of precautionary steps when they are working on systems that might contain MOS devices. These technicians normally use a grounding strap. These antistatic devices can be placed around the wrists or ankle to ground the technician to the system being worked on. These straps release any static present on the technician's body and pass it harmlessly to ground potential.

For more information, see the section "MOS Handling Techniques."

13. **C.** ESD is most likely to occur during periods of low humidity. If the relative humidity is below 50%, static charges can accumulate easily. ESD generally does not occur when the humidity is above 50%. In many high ESD situations, it can be useful to install a humidifier to raise the level of humidity in the work area. For more information, see the section "Electrostatic Discharge."

14. **A.** For both batteries and cartridges, the desired method of disposal is recycling. For more information, see the section "Disposal Procedures."

15. **C.** A Class-C (CO_2) fire extinguisher should always be on hand. Class-C extinguishers are the type specified for use around electrical equipment. For more information, see the section "Avoiding Laser and Burn Hazards."

16. **D.** In repair situations, the high voltage charge associated with video displays must be discharged. This is accomplished by creating a path from the tube's high-voltage anode to the chassis. With the monitor unplugged from the commercial power outlet, clip one end of an insulated jumper wire to the chassis ground of the frame. Clip the other end to a long, flat-blade screwdriver that has a well-insulated handle. While touching only the insulated handle of the screwdriver, slide the blade of the screwdriver under the rubber cup of the anode and make contact with its metal connection. This should bleed off the high voltage charge to ground. Continue the contact for several seconds to ensure that the voltage has been fully discharged. For more information, see the section "Avoiding High-Voltage Hazards."

APPLY YOUR KNOWLEDGE

17. **C.** Extremely high-voltage levels (in excess of 25,000 volts) might be present inside the CRT housing, even up to a year after electrical power has been removed from the unit. For more information, see the section "Avoiding High-Voltage Hazards."

18. **D.** The best storage option for most computer equipment is the original manufacturer's box. For more information, see the section "Protection During Storage."

19. **D.** A voltage sag typically lasts only a few milliseconds, whereas a brownout can last for a pro-tracted period of time. For more information, see the section "Power-Line Protection."

Challenge Solution

1. The facility should be equipped with a humidifier system to overcome the effects of the hot dry climate and the air conditioning. It should also have antistatic floor mats, antistatic desk mats, and antistatic wrist straps for the technicians. For more information, see the section "Electrostatic Discharge."

Suggested Readings and Resources

1. How Surge Suppression Works
   http://www.zerosurge.com/HTML/works2.html

2. UPS FAQ
   http://www.jetcafe.org/~npc/doc/ups-faq.html

3. UC Berkeley
   http://radsafe.berkeley.edu/nirsafman1101.pdf

4. Laser Hazards
   http://www.osha-slc.gov/SLTC/laserhazards/

5. ESD
   http://www.netlabs.net/hp/echase/

6. Handling MOS Devices
   http://www.claremicronix.com/pdfs/tone_signaling/AN-MOS-R1.pdf

7. Grounds
   http://www.amasci.com/emotor/ground.html

This chapter helps you to prepare for the Core Hardware module of the A+ Certification examination by covering the following objectives within the "Domain 4.0: Motherboard/Processors/Memory" section.

4.1 Distinguish between the popular CPU chips in terms of their basic characteristics.

Content might include the following:

- **Popular CPU chips (Intel, AMD, Cyrix)**
- **Characteristics:**
  - **Physical size**
  - **Voltage**
  - **Speeds**
  - **Onboard cache or not**
  - **Sockets**
  - **SEC (Single Edge Contact)**

▶ Computer technicians are often asked to upgrade existing systems with new devices, such as the microprocessor. Therefore, every technician should be aware of the characteristics of possible CPU upgrades and be able to determine whether a particular upgrade is physically possible and worthwhile.

▶ The successful technician must be aware of the capabilities of the different microprocessors available for use in a system. They must know what impact placing a particular microprocessor in an existing system can have on its operation. They must also be able to identify the type of processor being used and the system setting necessary to maximize its operation.

CHAPTER 12

Microprocessors

STUDY STRATEGIES

To prepare for the motherboard, processors, and memory objective of the Core Hardware exam:

▶ Read the objectives at the beginning of this chapter.

▶ Study the information in this chapter.

▶ Review the objectives listed earlier in this chapter.

▶ Perform any step-by-step procedures in the text.

▶ Answer the review questions at the end of the chapter and check your results.

▶ Use the PrepLogic test engine on the CD-ROM that accompanies this book for additional review and exam questions concerning this material.

▶ Review the exam tips scattered throughout the chapter and make certain that you are comfortable with each point.

INTRODUCTION

The system board is the main component of any personal computer system. This chapter examines the system board's main component—the microprocessor. These devices establish the basic capabilities of the entire computer system, so the technician must be aware of how to install, upgrade, and maintain them so that they provide optimum performance for the system.

The chapter describes the different Pentium class microprocessors in terms of their capabilities, speeds, and physical appearance.

The discussion goes on to describe typical socket specifications that have been developed for installing different microprocessors on system boards.

Finally, the chapter deals with configuring system boards to work with different microprocessor types.

After completing this chapter, you should be able to describe the basic characteristics and attributes associated with popular microprocessors. You should also be able to perform microprocessor installations and configurations, as well as to identify possible options for conducting microprocessor upgrades.

THE PENTIUM PROCESSOR

When IBM was designing the first PC, it chose the Intel 8088 microprocessor and its supporting chipset as the standard CPU for its design. This was a natural decision because one of IBM's major competitors (Apple) was using the *Motorola microprocessors* for its designs. The choice to use the Intel microprocessor still impacts the design of PC-compatible systems. As a matter of fact, the microprocessors used in the vast majority of all PC-compatible microcomputers include the Intel 8088/86, 80286, 80386, 80486, and Pentium (80586 and 80686) devices.

The original *Pentium processor* was a 32/64-bit design housed in a Ceramic Pin Grid Array package. Its registers and floating-point sections were identical to those of its predecessor, the 80486. It had a 64-bit data bus that enabled it to handle Quad Word data transfers.

> **NOTE** **Reference Shelf**   For more information, refer to the Electronic Reference Shelf, "How MACs Work," located on the CD that accompanies this book.

> **NOTE** **Reference Shelf**   For more information, refer to the Electronic Reference Shelf, "The 8088 Microprocessor," located on the CD that accompanies this book.

It also contained two separate 8KB caches, compared to only one in the 80486. One cache was used for instructions or code, whereas the other was used for data.

This original Pentium architecture has appeared in three generations. The first generation, code named the P5, came in a 273-pin PGA package and operated at 60 or 66MHz speeds. It used a single +5V (DC) operating voltage, which caused it to consume large amounts of power and generate large amounts of heat. It generated so much heat during normal operation that an additional CPU cooling fan was required.

The second generation of Pentiums, referred to as P54Cs, came in a 296-pin *Staggered Pin Grid Array* (*SPGA*) package and operated at 75, 90, 100, 120, 133, 150, and 166MHz in different versions. For these devices, Intel reduced the power-supply voltage level to +3.3V (DC) to consume less power and provide faster operating speeds. Reducing the power-supply level in effect moves the processor's high- and low-logic levels closer together, requiring less time to switch back and forth between them. The SPGA packaging made the second generation of Pentium devices incompatible with the first-generation system boards.

The second-generation devices also employed internal clock multipliers to increase performance. In this scenario, the system's buses run at the same speed as the clock signal introduced to the microprocessor. However, the internal clock multiplier causes the microprocessor to operate internally at some multiple of the external clock speed. (That is, a Pentium operating from a 50MHz external clock and using a 2x internal multiplier is actually running internally at 100MHz.)

The third generation of Pentium designs, designated as P55C, uses the 296-pin SPGA arrangement. This package adheres to the 321-pin Socket-7 specification designed by Intel. The P55C has been produced in versions that operate at 166, 180, 200, and 233MHz. This generation of Pentium devices operated at voltages below the +3.3 level established in the second generation of devices. The P55C is known as the *Pentium MMX* (*Multimedia Extension*) processor.

Figure 12.1 shows the pin arrangements for PGA and SPGA devices. Notice the uniformity of the PGA rows and columns versus the stagger in the rows and columns of the SPGA device.

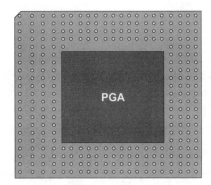

FIGURE 12.1
PGA and SPGA arrangements.

ADVANCED PENTIUM ARCHITECTURES

Intel has continued to advance its Pentium line of microprocessors by introducing additional specifications including the Pentium MMX, Pentium Pro, Pentium II, Pentium III, and Pentium 4 processors. At the same time, Intel's competitors have developed clone designs that equal or surpass the capabilities of the Intel versions.

Pentium MMX

In the *Pentium MMX* processor, the multimedia and communications processing capabilities of the original Pentium device were extended by the addition of 57 multimedia-specific instructions to the instruction set. Intel also increased the onboard *L1 cache* size to 32KB. The cache has been divided into two separate 16KB caches: the instruction cache and the data cache. The typical *L2 cache* used with the MMX was 256KB or 512KB, and it employed a 66MHz system bus.

The Pentium MMX processor was available in 166, 200, and 233MHz versions, and it uses a 321-pin, SPGA *Socket-7 format*. It required two separate operating voltages. One source was used to drive the Pentium processor core; the other was used to power the processor's I/O pins.

Pentium Pro

Intel departed from simply increasing the speed of its Pentium processor line by introducing the *Pentium Pro* processor. Although compatible with all the software previously written for the Intel processor line, the Pentium Pro was optimized to run 32-bit software.

However, the Pentium Pro did not remain pin-compatible with the previous Pentium processors. Instead, Intel adopted a 2.46x2.66 inches, 387-pin PGA configuration to house a Pentium Pro processor core and an onboard 256KB (or 512KB) L2 cache, and it employs a 60 or 66MHz system bus. The L2 cache complements the 16KB L1 cache in the Pentium core. Figure 12.2 illustrates this arrangement. Notice that although they are on the same PGA device, the two components are not integrated into the same IC. The unit is covered with a gold-plated, copper/tungsten *heat spreader*.

FIGURE 12.2
The Pentium Pro microprocessor.

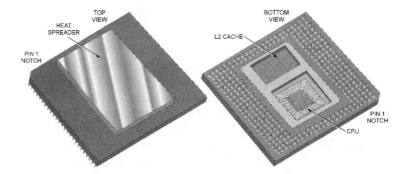

The L2 onboard cache stores the most frequently used data not found in the processor's internal L1 cache, as close to the processor core as it can be without being integrated directly into the IC. A high-bandwidth cache bus connects the processor and cache unit together. The bus (0.5 inches in length) allows the processor and external cache to communicate at a rate of 1.2Gbps.

The Pentium Pro was designed in a manner so that it could be used in typical, single-microprocessor applications or in multiprocessor environments, such as high-speed, high-volume file servers and workstations. Several dual-processor system boards have been designed for twin Pentium Pro processors. These boards are created with two Pentium Pro sockets so that they can operate with either a single or dual processors. When dual processors are installed, logic circuitry in the Pentium Pro's core manages the requests for access to the system's memory and 64-bit buses.

Pentium II

Intel radically changed the form factor of the Pentium processors by housing the *Pentium II* processor in a new, *Single-Edge Contact* (*SEC*) cartridge, depicted in Figure 12.3. This cartridge uses a special retention mechanism built in to the system board to hold the device in place.

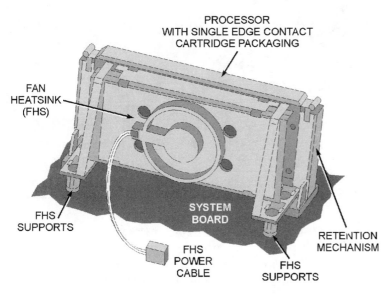

PROCESSOR
WITH SINGLE EDGE CONTACT
CARTRIDGE PACKAGING

FAN
HEATSINK
(FHS)

FHS
SUPPORTS

SYSTEM
BOARD

FHS
POWER
CABLE

FHS
SUPPORTS

RETENTION
MECHANISM

FIGURE 12.3
The Pentium II cartridge.

The proprietary 242-contact socket design is referred to as the *Slot 1 specification* and was designed to enable the microprocessor to operate at bus speeds in excess of 300MHz.

The cartridge also requires a special *Fan Heat Sink* (*FHS*) *module* and fan. Like the SEC cartridge, the FHS module requires special support mechanisms to hold it in place. The fan draws power from a special power connector on the system board or from one of the system's options power connectors.

Inside the cartridge, there is a substrate material on which the processor and related components are mounted. The components consist of the Pentium II processor core, a tag RAM, and an L2 burst SRAM. *Tag RAM* is used to track the attributes (read, modified, and so on) of data stored in the cache memory.

The Pentium II includes all the multimedia enhancements from the MMX processor, as well as retaining the power of the Pentium Pro's dynamic execution and 512KB L2 cache features, and it employs a 66 or 100MHz system bus. The L1 cache is increased to 32KB, whereas the L2 cache operates with a half-speed bus.

Figure 12.4 depicts the contents of the Pentium II cartridge.

EXAM TIP

Know which microprocessor employs half-speed cache.

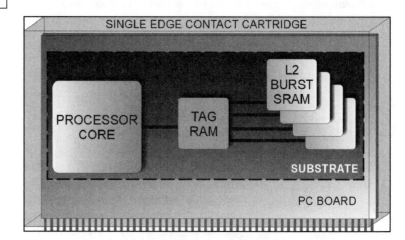

FIGURE 12.4
Inside the Pentium II cartridge.

EXAM TIP

Remember which components Intel included in the SEC cartridge.

A second cartridge type, called the *single-edged processor package* (*SEPP*), has been developed for use with the Slot 1 design. In this design, the boxed processor is not completely covered by the plastic housing as it is in the SECC design. Instead, the SEPP circuit board is accessible from the backside.

Pentium III

Intel followed the Pentium II processor with a new *Slot 1* compatible design it called the *Pentium III*. The original Pentium III processor (code-named Katmai) was designed around the Pentium II core, but increased the L2 cache size to 512KB. It also increased the speed of the processor to 600MHz, including a 100MHz *front side bus* speed.

Intel followed the Pentium III design with a less expensive version that it named the *Pentium Celeron*. Unlike the original Pentium III, the Celeron version featured a 66MHz bus speed and only 128KB of L2 cache. Initially, the Celeron Mendocino was packaged in the SECC cartridge.

Later versions of the Pentium III and Celeron processors were developed for the Intel *Socket 370 specification*. This design returned to a 370-pin, ZIF socket/SPGA package arrangement.

The first pin grid array versions of the Pentium III and Celeron processors conformed to a standard called the *Plastic Pin Grid Array* (*PPGA*) 370 specification. Intel repackaged its processors into a PGA package to fit this specification. The PPGA design was introduced to produce inexpensive, moderate performance Pentium systems. The design topped out at 533MHz with a 66MHz bus speed.

Intel upgraded the Socket 370 specification by introducing a variation called the *Flip Chip Pin Grid Array* (*FC-PGA*) 370 design. Intel made small modifications to the wiring of the socket to accommodate the Pentium III processor design. In addition, they employed a new 0.18 micron IC manufacturing technology to produce faster processor speeds (up to 1.12GHz) and front-side bus speeds (100MHz and 133MHz). However, the new design only provides 256KB of L2 cache.

Pentium III and Celeron processors designed with the 0.18 micron technology are referred to as the *Coppermine* and *Coppermine 128* processors, respectively. (The L2 cache in the Coppermine 128 is only 128KB.) Future Coppermine versions should employ 0.13 micron IC technology to achieve 1.4GHz operating speeds.

Intel has also introduced an edge-connector based *Slot 2 specification* that extends the Slot 1, boxed-processor scheme to a 330-contact design. For the Slot 2 design, Intel has produced three special versions of the Pentium III that they have named the *Pentium Xeon*. Each version features a different level of L2 cache (512KB, 1MB, 2MB). The Xeon designs were produced to fill different, high-end server needs.

> **EXAM TIP**
>
> Be able to state the difference between Pentium II and Pentium III processors.

Pentium 4

Late in 2000, Intel released its newest Pentium version called the Williamette 423, or *Pentium 4* microprocessor. It employs a modified Socket 370 PGA design that uses 423 pins and boasts operating speeds above 1.3GHz. The system bus has been increased from 64 to 128 bits and operates at 400MHz. Advanced plans for the Pentium 4 call for an improved 478-pin/533MHz bus version (Williamette 479).

In reality, the Pentium 4 is not a continuation of the Pentium design. It is actually a new design (IA-32 NetBurst architecture) based on .18 micron construction technology. In addition to the new front side bus size, the Pentium 4 features new WPNI (Williamette Processor New Instructions) instructions in its instruction set. The L1 cache size has been reduced from 16KB in the Pentium III to 8KB for the Pentium 4. The L2 cache is 256KB and can handle transfers on every clock cycle.

The operating voltage level for the Pentium 4 core is 1.7 volts. To dissipate the 55 watts of power (heat) that the microprocessor generates at 1.5GHz, the case incorporates a metal cap. In addition, firm contact between the microprocessor's case and the heat sink feature built in to the Pentium 4 system board must be maintained.

Pentium Clones

As mentioned earlier in this chapter, Intel abandoned the *80x86* nomenclature in favor of names that could be copyrighted in an effort to distance itself from the clone microprocessor manufacturers. When this occurred, the other manufacturers largely followed the 80x86 path, but eventually moved toward alternative numbering schemes as well.

AMD Processors

Advanced Micro Devices (*AMD*) offers several clone microprocessors: the 5x86 (X5), the 5x86 (K5), the K6, the K6PLUS-3D, and K7 microprocessors. The X5 offers operational and pin compatibility with the DX4. Its performance is equal to the Pentium and MMX processors. The K5 processor is compatible with the Pentium, and the K6 is compatible with the MMX. Both the K5 and K6 models are Socket-7 compatible, enabling them to be used in conventional Pentium and Pentium MMX system board designs (with some small modifications). The K6 employs an extended 64KB L1 cache that doubles the internal cache size of the Pentium II.

The K6PLUS-3D was operationally and performance compatible with the Pentium Pro, and the K7 is operationally and performance compatible with the Pentium II. However, neither of these units have a pin-out compatibility with another processor.

AMD continues to produce clone versions of Pentium processors. In some cases, the functions and performance of the AMD devices go beyond the Intel design they are cloning. Two notable AMD Pentium clone processors are the Athlon and the Duron.

The *Athlon* is a Pentium III clone processor. It is available in a Slot 1 cartridge clone, called the *Slot-A specification*. Figure 12.5 depicts the cartridge version of the Athlon processor along with a Slot A connector.

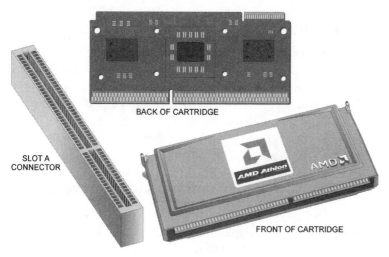

BACK OF CARTRIDGE

SLOT A
CONNECTOR

FRONT OF CARTRIDGE

FIGURE 12.5
The Slot-A Athlon processor.

The Athlon is also available in a proprietary SPGA *Socket-A* design that mimics the Intel Socket 370 specification. The Socket-A specification employs a 462-pin ZIF socket and is only supported by two available chipsets.

Three versions of the Athlon processor have been introduced so far. The first version was the K7 version that ran between 500MHz and 700MHz, provided a 128KB L1 cache and a 512KB L2 cache, employed a 100MHz system bus, and used Slot-A.

Subsequent Athlon versions have included the *K75* and *Thunderbird* versions. Both versions are constructed using the 0.18 micron manufacturing technology. The K75 processors ran between 750MHz and 1GHz. Like the K7 version, it provided a 128KB L1 cache and a 512KB L2 cache and employed a 100MHz system bus. The Thunderbird version runs between 750MHz and 1.2GHz, provides a 128KB L1 cache and a 256KB L2 cache, employs a 133MHz system bus, and features a Socket-A connection.

The *Duron* processor is a Celeron clone processor that conforms to the AMD Socket-A specification. The Duron features processor speeds between 600MHz and 800MHZ. It includes a 128KB L1 cache and a 64KB L2 cache and employs a 100MHz system bus. Like the newer Celerons, the Duron is constructed using 0.18 micron IC manufacturing technology.

Cyrix Processors

Like AMD, the Cyrix company has continued to develop clones of the various Pentium products. These clones include the Socket 370 compatible Celeron clone processor called the *Cyrix III* (originally called the Joshua Processor). The *Cyrix III* can be used in system boards designed for Celeron processors. However, the system's BIOS will need to be upgraded to work with the Cyrix clock multipliers. The latest version of the processor (the Samuel version) runs at 533MHz but supports a very fast 133MHz front side bus. It also possesses a large (128KB) L1 cache but has no support for an L2 cache.

Table 12.1 shows the relationship between the various numbering systems. In addition to the 80x86 numbering system, Intel used a Px identification up to the Pentium II. The Pentium II is identified as the Klamath processor. Subsequent improved versions have been dubbed Deschutes, Covington, Mendocino, Katmai, Willamette, Flagstaff (P7), Merced, and Tahoe.

TABLE 12.1			

CLONE PROCESSORS

Intel	Cyrix	AMD	NextGen
Pentium (P5/P54C)	M1 (6X86)	-K5(5X86)	NX586/686
Pentium MMX (P55C)	M2 (6X86MX)	-K6	
Pentium Pro (P6)	MXi	-K6PLUS-3D	
Pentium II	M3	-K7	
Pentium III	N/A	K75/Thunderbird	
Pentium Celeron	Cyrix III	Duron	

SOCKET SPECIFICATIONS

In addition to the clone processors, Intel has developed a line of upgrade microprocessors for its original units. These are referred to as *OverDrive* processors. The OverDrive unit might just be the same type of microprocessor running at a higher clock speed, or it might be an advanced architecture microprocessor designed to operate from the same socket/pin configuration as the original. To accommodate this option, Intel created specifications for eight socket designs, designated Socket-1 through Socket-8.

The specifications for Socket-1 through Socket-3 were developed for 80486SX, 80486DX, and 80486 OverDrive versions that use different pin numbers and power-supply requirements. Likewise, Socket-4 through Socket-6 deal with various Pentium and OverDrive units that use different speeds and power-supply requirements. The *Socket-7* design works with the fastest Pentium units and includes provision for a *voltage-regulator module* (*VRM*) to permit various power settings to be implemented through the socket.

The Socket-7 specification corresponds to the second generation of Pentium devices that employ SPGA packaging. It is compatible with the Socket-5, straight-row PGA specification that the first-generation Pentium processors employed. The Socket-8 specification is specific to the Pentium Pro processor.

The Socket 7 specification has been upgraded to include a new standard called Super Socket 7. This standard extends the use of the Socket 7 physical connector by adding a support signal required for implementing AGP slots and the 100MHz *front side bus (FSB)* specification. Microprocessors designed to use the Super Socket 7 specification include AMD's K6-2, K6-2+, and K6-III, along with Intel's Pentium MMX and Pentium Pro.

Although the Intel Slot 1 design was originally developed for the Pentium II, it also serves its Celeron and Pentium III processor designs. Like Socket 7, the Slot 1 specification provides for variable processor core voltages (2.8 to 3.3) that permit faster operation and reduced power consumption. In addition, some suppliers have created daughter boards containing the Pentium Pro processor that can be plugged into the Slot 1 connector. This combination Socket 8/Slot 1 device is referred to as a *slotket processor*.

The Slot 2 specification from Intel expands the Slot 1 SECC technology to a 330-contact (*SECC-2*) cartridge used with the Intel *Xeon processor*.

AMD produced a reversed version of the Slot 1 specification for its Athlon processor by turning the contacts of the Slot 1 design around. They titled the new design Slot A. Although serving the same ends as the Slot 1 design, the Slot A and Slot 1 microprocessor cartridges are not compatible.

In a departure from its proprietary Slot connector development, Intel introduced a new ZIF socket standard, called Socket 370, for use with its Celeron processor. There are actually two versions of the Socket 370 specification. The first is the PPGA 370 variation intended for use with *Plastic Pin Grid Array (PPGA)* version of the Celeron CPUs. The other is the *Flip Chip Pin Grid Array (FC-PGA)* version.

The term flip chip is used to describe a group of microprocessors that have provisions for attaching a heat sink directly to the microprocessor die. The processors in this category include the Cyrix III, Celeron, and Pentium III. Although the PPGA and FC-PGA processors will both plug in to the 370 socket, it does not mean that they will work in system boards designed for the other specification.

Likewise, AMD produced a 462-pin ZIF socket specification for the PGA versions of its Athalon and Duron processors. No other processors have been designed for this specification, and only two chipsets have been produced to support it.

Table 12.2 summarizes the attributes of the various industry socket and slot specifications.

TABLE 12.2

INDUSTRY SOCKET/SLOT SPECIFICATIONS

Number	Pins	Voltages	Microprocessors
Socket 1	169 PGA	5	80486 SX/DXx, DX4 Overdrive
Socket 2	238 PGA	5	80486 SX/DXx, Pentium Overdrive
Socket 3	237 PGA	5/3.3	80486 SX/DXx, Pent Overdrive
Socket 4	237 PGA	5	Pentium 60/66, 60/66 Overdrive
Socket 5	320 SPGA	3.3	Pentium 75-133, Pent Overdrive
Socket 6	235 PGA	3.3	Never Implemented
Socket 7	321 SPGA	VRM (2.5v-3.6v)	Pentium 75-200, Pent Overdrive
Socket 8	387 SPGA	VRM (2.2v-3.5v)	Pentium Pro
Slot 1	242 SECC/SEPP	VRM (1.5v-2.5v)	Celeron, Pentium II, Pentium III
Slot 2	330 SECC-2	VRM (1.5v-2.5v)	Xeon
Super Socket 7	321 SPGA	VRM (2.0v-3.5v)	AMD K6-2, K6-2+, K6-III, K6-III+, Pentium MMX
Socket 370	370 SPGA	VRM (1.1v-2.5v)	Cyrix III, Celeron, Pentium III
Slot A	242 Slot A	VRM (1.2v-2.2v)	AMD Athlon
Socket A	462 SPGA	VRM (12v-2.2v)	AMD Athlon, Duron
Socket 423	423 SPGA	1.75	Pentium 4
Socket 428	428 SPGA	VRM (1.5-1.75)	Pentium 4

> **EXAM TIP**
>
> Know which processors can be used with Slot 1 and Socket 370 connections. Also know which processors can be used in Slot A.

CHALLENGE #1

Your company does not want to replace all of its computers at this time. As a matter of fact, what it really wants to do is spend a little money to upgrade all its computers as much as it can now and wait as long as possible to replace them. As the Technical Service manager, they have asked you for a plan to upgrade the systems. You know that nearly all the systems in the company are Pentium II 350MHz machines. What is the most current, fastest upgrade you can recommend to your board of directors?

CLOCK SPEEDS

In the Pentium processor, two speed settings can be established for the microprocessor—one speed for its internal core operations and a second speed for its external bus transfers. These two operational speeds are tied together through an internal clock multiplier system. The Socket-7 specification enabled system boards to be configured for different types of microprocessors using different operating speeds. In older systems, the operating speed of the microprocessor was configured through external settings.

Prior to Pentium II, all Pentium processors used 50, 60, or 66MHz external clock frequencies to generate their internal operating frequencies. The value of the internal multiplier was controlled by external hardware jumper settings on the system board.

Pentium II processors moved to a 100MHz external clock and front side bus. The Pentium III and all slot processors up to 1GHz continued to use the 100MHz clock and FSB. However, beginning with the Pentium III Coppermine, the external clock speed was increased to 133MHz. At the same time, the Celeron processors retained the 66MHz clock and bus speeds up to the 800MHz Celeron versions.

The Pentium 4 processors use external clocks that run up to 400MHz. They have also used four different special memory buses with different memory types. In Pentium 4 systems, it is possible to set clock speeds for the memory and front side buses independently. The different bus versions work with different types of RDRAM and run at speeds of 400MHz, 600MHz, and 800MHz.

POWER-SUPPLY LEVELS

Beginning with the Pentium MMX, Intel adopted dual-voltage supply levels for the overall IC and for its core. Common Intel voltage supplies are +5/+5 for older units and +3.3/+3.3, +3.3/+2.8, +3.3/+1.8 for newer units. Clone processors can use compatible voltages (especially if they are pin compatible) or completely different voltage levels.

Common voltages for clone microprocessors include +5, +3.3, +2.5, and +2.2. The additional voltage levels are typically generated through special regulator circuits on the system board. In each case, the system board's user guide should be consulted any time the microprocessor is being replaced or upgraded.

HEAT SINKS AND FANS

The Pentium processor requires the presence of a heat-sinking device and a microprocessor fan unit for cooling purposes. As Figure 12.6 illustrates, these devices come in many forms including simple *passive heat sinks* and fan-cooled, *active heat sinks*.

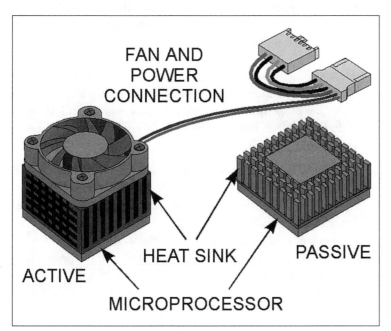

FIGURE 12.6
Microprocessor cooling systems.

Passive heat sinks are finned metal slabs that can be clipped or glued with a heat-transmitting adhesive onto the top of the microprocessor. The fins increase the surface area of the heat sink, enabling it to dissipate heat more rapidly. Active heat sinks add a fan unit to move air across the heat sink. The fan moves the heat away from the heat sink and the microprocessor more rapidly.

ATX-style systems employ power supplies that use a reverse-flow fan that brings in cool air from the back of the unit and blows it directly on the microprocessor. For this to work properly, the system board must adhere to the *ATX form factor* guidelines and place the microprocessor in the correct position on the system board. In theory, this design eliminates the need for special microprocessor cooling fans.

Configuring Microprocessors

Most Pentium system boards are designed so that they can support a number of different microprocessor types and operating speeds. In older Pentium systems, the microprocessor's configuration settings were established largely through jumpers on the system board. These settings typically included such items as

◆ *Microprocessor Type*—This setting manually tells the system what type of processor is installed. If this setting is incorrect, the system will assume that the installed processor is the one specified by the setting and try to interact with it on that basis. Depending on which microprocessor is indicated, the system POST might identify the processor incorrectly and still run— but not properly. In other cases, the processor might lock up during the POST or not run at all. In either case, the processor could be damaged.

◆ *Core-to-bus Speed Ratio*—Again, depending on the exact mismatch, the system might over clock the processor and run— but erratically. If the over clocking is less than 20%, the system might run without problems. However, the processor's life expectancy will be decreased. If the deviation is greater than 20%, the system might not come up at all and the processor might be damaged.

◆ *Bus Frequency Setting*—Configuring this setting incorrectly will cause the processor to run faster or slower. This is a common method employed by users to increase the operating speed of their older systems. If the variation is less than 20%, the system will probably work with a shortened processor life. Greater levels of over clocking the bus might cause the system to have random lock ups.

◆ *Core Voltage Level*—This setting establishes the voltage level that the microprocessor core will operate at. The setting is linked to the processor's speed and power dissipation. Normally, the microprocessor will not operate at all if the voltage level is more than 20% too low. Conversely, if you operate a processor at a voltage level that is higher than its specified value, this can cause physical damage to it.

In newer Pentium systems, the PnP process interrogates the processor during startup and configures it appropriately. This prevents the user from subjecting the processor to potentially destructive conditions, such as over clocking. In addition, these systems can monitor the health of the processor during operation and take steps to compensate for problems such as overheating.

In these systems, the BIOS version must support the parameters of the microprocessor. If a microprocessor upgrade is performed and the BIOS code does not fully support the new processor, all the error types listed for manual configuration can occur. For example, if an 850MHz Pentium III processor were installed in a system whose BIOS only supported processor speeds up to 600MHz, the BIOS will only report a processor speed of 600MHz during the POST portion of the startup. The system will actually be limited to running at 600MHz. For this reason, the capabilities of the system BIOS should always be examined when performing microprocessor upgrades.

Table 12.3 summarizes the characteristics of the various microprocessors associated with the A+ exam.

| EXAM TIP | Be aware of how older systems determine what type of microprocessor is installed and what its capabilities are. |

| EXAM TIP | Know why a processor would show an incorrect speed rating. |

TABLE 12.3

MICROPROCESSOR CHARACTERISTICS

Microprocessor	Diameter Size (mm)	VRM (volts)	Speeds (MHz)	Cache on Die (KB)	Cache on Cartridge	Cache on Board (KB)	Sockets or Slot Types
Pentium	23.1x23.1	2.5–3.6	75–299	L1—8+8	-	L2—256/512	Socket 7
Pentium MMX AMD - K6-2:K6-3	25.4x25.4	2.0–3.5	166–550	L1—16+16 32+32	- -	L2—255/1000	Socket Super 7
Pentium II/III Celeron (.25 micron)	25.4x25.4 18x62x140 Box	1.5–2.6	233–1000	L1—16+16	L2—256/512 128KB	- -	Slot 1
Xeon II/III (330) (.25 micron)	27.4x27.4 18x87x125 Box	1.5–2.6	500/550 700/900	L1—16+16	L2—512KB 1MB 2MB	- -	Slot 2
Pentium III Celeron (.25 micron)	25.4x25.4 Slug 27.4x27.4 Opening	1.1–2.5	300–566	L1—16+16 L2—128/256	- -	- -	Socket 370 PPGA
Pentium III (Copermine) Celeron (.18 micron)	9.3x11.3	1.1–2.5	566–1000	L1—16+16 L2—128/256	- -	- -	Socket 370 FC-PGA
Pentium III (Tualatin) Celeron (.13 micron)	31x31	1.1–2.5	800–1500	L1—16+16 L2—128/256/512	- -	- -	FC-PGA2
Pentium IV (.18 micron)	31x31	1.75	1300–2000	L1—12+8 L2—256	- -	- -	Socket 423 FC-PGA
Pentium IV (.18 micron) (.13 micron)	31x31 33x33	1.75 1.50	1400–2000 1800–2200	L1—12+8 L2—512	- -	- -	FC-PGA2
Pentium Xeon (.18 micron)	31x31	1.4–1.8 1.7	1400–2000	L1—12+8 L2—256	- -	- -	Socket 603 FC-BGA
Pentium Xeon (.13 micron)	35x35	1.4–1.8 1.475	1800–2200	L1—12+8 L2—512	- -	- -	Socket 603 FC-BGA2
Itanium(.18 micron) (266MHz)*	71.6x127.7	1.7	733/800	L1—16+16 L2—512	L3—2MB 4MB	- -	PAC-418
Athlon Duron	9.1x13.1	1.75	800–1400	L1—64+64	L2—256KB	-	Slot A 242 CPGA
Athlon Duron	11.1x11.6	1.75	733–1800	L1—64+64	L2—256	- -	Socket A 462 ORGA

*266MHz system bus and 133MHz address bus

CHALLENGE #2

Your company's board of directors approves your recommendation for upgrading their existing systems as outlined in challenge 1. When you upgrade the first system, you find that it is only running at 450MHz. What should you do to get the system up to the speed you recommended to the board?

CHAPTER SUMMARY

This chapter was dedicated to the different types of microprocessors commonly used in Pentium-class PC-compatible personal computers.

The chapter began by identifying the various microprocessor versions commonly found in Pentium-class PCs. It also described the basic characteristics associated with each processor type.

The chapter ended with a section dedicated to configuring microprocessors to work properly in different system boards.

At this point, review the objectives listed at the beginning of the chapter to be certain that you understand each point and can perform each task listed there. Afterward, answer the review questions that follow to verify your knowledge of the information.

KEY TERMS

- 80x86
- Active heat sinks
- Advanced Micro Devices (AMD)
- Athlon
- ATX form factor
- Bus Frequency Setting
- Coppermine
- Coppermine 128
- Core Voltage Level
- Core-to-bus Speed Ratio
- Cyrix III
- Duron
- Fan Heat Sink (FHS) module
- Flip Chip Pin Grid Array (FC-PGA)
- Front side bus (FSB)
- Heat spreader
- K75
- L1 cache

CHAPTER SUMMARY

- L2 cache
- Microprocessor Type
- Motorola microprocessors
- Passive heat sinks
- Pentium 4
- Pentium Celeron
- Pentium II
- Pentium III
- Pentium MMX (Multimedia Extension)
- Pentium Pro
- Pentium processor
- Plastic Pin Grid Array (PPGA)
- SECC-2
- Single-Edge Contact (SEC)

- Single-edged processor package (SEPP)
- Slot 1 specification
- Slot 2 specification
- Slot-A specification
- Socket 370 specification
- Socket-7
- Socket-7 format
- Socket-A
- Staggered Pin Grid Array (SPGA)
- Tag RAM
- Thunderbird
- Voltage-regulator module (VRM)
- Xeon processor

APPLY YOUR KNOWLEDGE

Review Questions

1. Explain how an older Socket-7 system knows what type of processor is installed in the system.

   A. CMOS setup utility

   B. Interrogation of the microprocessor

   C. Orientation of the microprocessor

   D. Jumpers on the motherboard

2. Which processors can be used in a Slot-A system board? (Select all that apply.)

   A. Athlon K7/550

   B. Duron/600

   C. Celeron/266

   D. Pentium II/233

3. Which processors can be used in a Socket 370 system?

   A. Pentium MMX, Celeron

   B. Celeron, Pentium III

   C. Pentium III, Pentium 4

   D. Celeron, Duron

4. If you upgrade a 600MHz processor to a 1.00GHz version and the system still shows a 600 MHz processor during the POST, what type of problem is indicated?

   A. Insufficient RAM

   B. Incompatible operating system

   C. Incompatible motherboard BIOS

   D. Defective microprocessor

5. Which microprocessor has cache memory that operates at half the core bus speed of the other microprocessor sections?

   A. Pentium Pro

   B. Pentium II

   C. Pentium III

   D. Celeron

6. Which type of system board sockets can accept a Pentium III microprocessor? (Select all that apply.)

   A. Slot 1

   B. Super Socket 7

   C. Socket 370

   D. Socket A

7. Which of the following is not a component of a Pentium II SEC cartridge?

   A. Processor core

   B. Tag RAM

   C. 262-contact socket interface

   D. L2 burst SRAM

8. What is the major difference between Pentium II and Pentium III microprocessors?

   A. L2 cache enlarged to 512KB

   B. Improved microprocessor die

   C. Improved to 128-bit system bus

   D. Lower voltage requirements

APPLY YOUR KNOWLEDGE

9. Which microprocessor works with a 66MHz front side bus?

    A. P75

    B. Pentium MMX

    C. PIII/450

    D. Duron/600

10. Which microprocessor can use a Slot 1 connection?

    A. Athlon K7/550

    B. Duron/600

    C. Celeron/266

    D. Pentium III/533

11. What is the appropriate socket for the Pentium Pro microprocessor?

    A. Socket 7

    B. Super Socket 7

    C. Socket 8

    D. Socket 370

12. What is the appropriate socket for the Pentium MMX microprocessor?

    A. Socket 7

    B. Super Socket 7

    C. Socket 8

    D. Socket 370

13. What is the appropriate socket for the original Celeron microprocessor?

    A. Slot 1

    B. Super Socket 7

    C. Socket 370

    D. Slot A

14. What is the appropriate socket for the Pentium II microprocessor?

    A. Slot 1

    B. Super Socket 7

    C. Socket 370

    D. Slot A

15. What is the appropriate socket for the Pentium 4 microprocessor?

    A. Socket A

    B. Super Socket 7

    C. Socket 370

    D. Socket 423

16. What is the appropriate socket for the Duron microprocessor?

    A. Socket A

    B. Super Socket 7

    C. Socket 370

    D. Socket 423

Answers and Explanations

1. **D.** The Socket 7 specification enabled system boards to be configured for different types of microprocessors using different operating speeds. In older systems, the operating speed of the microprocessor was configured through external settings (that is, jumpers on the motherboard). For more information, see the section "Clock Speeds."

2. **A, B.** The Athlon K7 version ran between 500MHz and 700MHz, provided a 128KB L1 cache and a 512KB L2 cache, employed a 100MHz system bus, and used Slot-A. The Duron processor is a Celeron clone processor that conforms to the AMD Socket-A specification. For more information, see the section "AMD Processors."

3. **B.** Later versions of the Pentium III and Celeron processors were developed for the Intel Socket 370 specification. For more information, see the section "Pentium III."

4. **C.** If an 850MHz Pentium III processor were installed in a system whose BIOS only supported processor speeds up to 600MHz, the BIOS will only report a processor speed of 600MHz during the POST portion of the startup. The system will actually be limited to running at 600MHz. For more information, see the section "Configuring Microprocessors."

5. **B.** The Pentium II L1 cache is increased to 32KB, whereas the L2 cache operates with a half-speed bus. For more information, see the section "Pentium II."

6. **A, C.** Intel followed the Pentium II processor with a new Slot 1 compatible design it called the Pentium III. Later versions of the Pentium III and Celeron processors were developed for the Intel Socket 370 specification. For more information, see the section "Pentium III."

7. **C.** The Pentium II's proprietary 242-contact socket design is referred to as the Slot 1 specification. For more information, see the section "Pentium II."

8. **A.** The original Pentium III processor (code named Katmai) was designed around the Pentium II core, but increased the L2 cache size

to 512KB. For more information, see the section "Pentium III."

9. **B.** In the Pentium MMX processor, the multimedia and communications processing capabilities of the original Pentium device were extended by the addition of 57 multimedia-specific instructions to the instruction set. Intel also increased the onboard L1 cache size to 32KB. The cache has been divided into two separate 16KB caches: the instruction cache and the data cache. The typical L2 cache used with the MMX was 256KB or 512KB, and employed a 66MHz system bus. For more information, see the section "Pentium MMX."

10. **C.** Initially, the Celeron was packaged in the Slot 1 (SECC) cartridge. For more information, see the section "Pentium III."

11. **C.** The Pentium Pro used Socket 8. See Table 12.2: Industry Socket/Slot Specifications. For more information, see the section "Pentium Pro."

12. **B.** The Pentium MMX uses Super Socket 7. See Table 12.2: Industry Socket/Slot Specifications. For more information, see the section "Pentium MMX."

13. **A.** The original Celeron used Slot 1. For more information, see the section "Pentium III."

14. **A.** The Pentium II used Slot 1. See Table 12.2: Industry Socket/Slot Specifications. For more information, see the section "Pentium II."

15. **D.** The Pentium 4 uses Socket 423 or Socket 478. See Table 12.2: Industry Socket/Slot Specifications. For more information, see the section "Pentium 4."

16. **A.** The Duron uses Socket A. See Table 12.2: Industry Socket/Slot Specifications. For more information, see the section "AMD Processors."

APPLY YOUR KNOWLEDGE

Challenge Solutions

1. You can potentially upgrade your Pentium II/Slot 1 machines to Pentium III class microprocessors that will run at up to 1GHz. For more information, see the section "Socket Specifications."

2. The old BIOS only supported processor speeds up to 450MHz. You now have processors capable of running 1GHz. You must upgrade the system BIOS to support higher operating speeds for the processor. With many Slot 1 system boards, you will not have any problems upgrading to 1GHz, provided you get the newest BIOS version. However, this is not true for every system board. You should have checked the chipset and BIOS information before purchasing the new microprocessors. There is a chance that you will only be able to upgrade to 600MHz. For more information, see the section "Configuring Microprocessors."

Suggested Readings and Resources

1. Great Microprocessors of the Past and Present
   www.cs.uregina.ca/~bayko/cpu.html

2. x86 Processor Information
   www.sandpile.org

3. Intel
   http://developer.intel.com/sites/developer/contents.htm

4. Pentium MMX
   www.sandpile.org/impl/p55.htm

5. Pentium Pro
   http://x86.ddj.com/intel.doc/686manuals.htm

6. Pentium II
   http://x86.ddj.com/intel.doc/p2manuals.htm

7. Pentium III
   http://www.geek.com/procspec/intel/pentium3consumer.htm

8. Pentium 4
   http://www.tomshardware.com/cpu/00q4/001120/

9. AMD
   http://www.amd.com/us-en/Processors/ProductInformation/0,,30_118,00.html

10. Cyrix
    http://www.via.com.tw/en/viac3/cyrix_MII.jsp

11. Microprocessor Sockets
    http://www.pcguide.com/ref/cpu/char/socket.htm

12. Clock Speed
    http://whatis.techtarget.com/definition/0,,sid9_gci211799,00.html

13. Heat Sink/Fan
    http://www.tomshardware.com/cpu/01q3/010917/

This chapter helps you to prepare for the Core Hardware module of the A+ Certification examination by covering the following objectives within the "Domain 4.0: Motherboard/Processors/Memory" section.

4.2 Identify the categories of RAM (random access memory) terminology, their locations, and physical characteristics.

Content might include the following:

- **Terminology:**

  - **EDO RAM (extended data output random access memory)**

  - **DRAM (dynamic random access memory)**

  - **SRAM (static random access memory)**

  - **RIMM (Rambus inline memory module 184 pins)**

  - **VRAM (video random access memory)**

  - **SDRAM (synchronous dynamic random access memory)**

  - **WRAM (Windows Accelerator Card random access memory)**

- **Locations and physical characteristics:**

  - **Memory bank**

  - **Memory chips (8-bit, 16-bit, and 32-bit)**

  - **SIMMs (single in-line memory module)**

  - **DIMMs (dual in-line memory module)**

  - **Parity chips versus non-parity chips**

▶ The system's microprocessor relies on the system board's memory units to correctly store and reproduce the data and programs that it needs for its operations. The operation of the system's memory units is so critical that if a single bit gets lost or becomes corrupt, a major interrupt error is created that in most cases results in a shutdown of the system.

CHAPTER 13

Random Access Memory

OBJECTIVES

▶ Because the operation of the system's RAM structures is so critical, every technician should be aware of the characteristics of different RAM devices and be able to determine whether a particular device is suited to a given application and whether it physically fits the system in question.

OUTLINE

To prepare for the motherboard, processors, and memory objective of the Core Hardware exam:

▶ Read the objectives at the beginning of this chapter.

▶ Study the information in this chapter.

▶ Review the objectives listed earlier in this chapter.

▶ Perform any step-by-step procedures in the text.

▶ Answer the review questions at the end of the chapter and check your results.

▶ Use the PrepLogic test engine on the CD-ROM that accompanies this book for additional review and exam questions concerning this material.

▶ Review the exam tips scattered throughout the chapter and make certain that you are comfortable with each point.

INTRODUCTION

This chapter provides an extended discussion of system RAM memory structures. It begins with descriptions of the various types of RAM memory devices commonly used in PC-compatible systems.

The second half of the chapter deals with memory organization and structures that are commonly employed with personal computers. Topics discussed here include SIMMs, DIMMs, memory banks, and error checking and correcting schemes.

Completing this chapter should enable you to differentiate between the different categories of RAM and identify their normal system board locations and physical characteristics. You should also be able to select appropriate RAM types for a given computer configuration.

MEMORY SYSTEMS

There are normally three types of semiconductor memory found on a system board. These include

◆ the system's ROM BIOS ICs

◆ the system's RAM memory

◆ the second-level cache memory

All the listed memory types are based on two types of semiconductor RAM technologies—*static RAM* (*SRAM*) and *dynamic RAM* (*DRAM*). Although they both perform the same basic storage functions, their methods of doing so are completely different. SRAM stores bits in a manner in which they will remain valid as long as power to the chip is not interrupted. On the other hand, DRAM requires periodic *refreshing* to maintain data, even if electrical power is applied to the chip.

Whether the RAM is made up of static or dynamic RAM devices, all RAM systems have the disadvantage of being *volatile*. This means that any data stored in RAM will be lost if power to the computer is disrupted for any reason. On the other hand, both types of RAM have the advantage of being fast, with the capability to be written to and read from with equal ease. ROM, on the other hand is classified as *nonvolatile* memory.

EXAM TIP

You should be aware that all forms of RAM are volatile and know what that means in terms of storing data.

Advanced DRAM

Both types of RAM are brought together to create an improved DRAM, referred to as *enhanced DRAM* (*EDRAM*). By integrating an SRAM component into a DRAM device, a performance improvement of 40% can be gained. An independent write path allows the system to input new data without affecting the operation of the rest of the chip. These devices are used primarily in L2 cache memories.

Another modified DRAM type, referred to as *synchronous DRAM* (*SDRAM*), employs special internal registers and clock signals to organize data requests from memory. Unlike asynchronous memory modules, SDRAM devices operate in synchronous with the system clock. Once an initial Read or Write access has been performed on the memory device, additional accesses can be conducted in a high speed burst mode that operates at one access per clock cycle.

Special internal configurations also speed up the operation of the SDRAM memory. The SDRAM device employs internal interleaving techniques that permit one side of the memory to be accessed while the other half is completing an operation. Because there are two versions of SDRAM (2-clock and 4-clock), you must make certain that the SDRAM type you are using is supported by the system board's chipset.

Advanced SDRAM

Advanced versions of SDRAM include

◆ *SDR-SDRAM*—Single Data Rate SDRAM. This version of SDRAM transfers data on one edge of the system clock signal.

◆ *SGRAM*—Synchronous Graphics RAM. This type of SDRAM is designed to handle high-performance graphics operations. It features dual-bank operations that permit two memory pages to be open at the same time.

◆ *ESDRAM*—Enhanced SDRAM. This advanced form of SDRAM employs small cache buffers to provide high data access rates. This type of SDRAM is used in L2 cache applications.

◆ *VCM-SDRAM*—Virtual Channel Memory SDRAM. This memory design has onboard cache buffers to improve multiple access times and to provide I/O transfers on each clock cycle. VCM-SDRAM requires a special chipset to support it.

◆ *DDR-SDRAM*—Double Data Rate SDRAM. This is a form of SDR-SDRAM that can transfer data on both the leading and falling edges of each clock cycle. This capability doubles the data transfer rate of traditional SDR-DRAM. It is available in a number of standard formats, including SODIMMs for portables.

◆ *EDDR-SDRAM*—Enhanced DDR SDRAM. An advanced form of DDR-SRAM that employs onboard cache registers to deliver improved performance.

<table>
<tr><td>EXAM TIP</td><td>Know the difference between EDO and Fast Page-Mode DRAM.</td></tr>
</table>

Extended data out (*EDO*) memory increases the speed at which RAM operations are conducted by cutting out the 10-nanosecond wait time normally required between issuing memory addresses. This is accomplished by not disabling the data bus pins between bus cycles. EDO is an advanced type of *fast page-mode DRAM* also referred to as *hyper page-mode DRAM*. The advantage of EDO DRAM is encountered when multiple sequential memory accesses are performed. By not turning off the data pin, each successive access after the first access is accomplished in two clock cycles rather than three.

<table>
<tr><td>EXAM TIP</td><td>Remember what type of application VRAM and WRAM are used in.</td></tr>
</table>

Special memory devices have also been designed to optimize video memory related activities. Among these devices are *video RAM* (*VRAM*) and *Windows RAM* (*WRAM*). In typical DRAM devices, access to the data stored inside is shared between the system microprocessor and the video controller. The microprocessor accesses the RAM to update the data in it and to keep it refreshed. The video controller moves data out of the memory to become screen information. Normally, both devices must access the data through the same data bus. VRAM employs a special dual-port access system to speed up video operations. WRAM, a special version of VRAM, is optimized to transfer blocks of data at a time. This allows it to operate at speeds of up to 150% of typical VRAM and costs up to 20% less.

A company named Rambus has designed a proprietary DRAM memory technology that promises very high data delivery speeds. The technology has been given a variety of different names that include *Rambus DRAM (RDRAM)*, *Direct Rambus DRAM (DRDRAM)*, and *Rambus inline memory module (RIMM)*. The RIMM reference applies to a special 184-pin memory module that is designed to hold the Rambus devices. However, their high-speed transfer modes generate considerably more heat than normal DIMMs. Therefore, RIMM modules include an aluminum heat shield, referred to as a *heat spreader*, to protect the chips from over-heating.

The Rambus technology employs a special, internal 16-bit data channel that operates in conjunction with a 400MHz clock. The 16-bit channel permits the device to operate at much higher speeds than more conventional 64-bit buses. Although Intel had expressed some interest in exploring the technology for its future system board designs, the fact that it is a proprietary standard might hinder its acceptance in the market.

As Figure 13.1 shows, RIMMs look similar to DIMMs, but they have a different pin count. RIMMs transfer data in 16-bit chunks. The faster access and transfer speed generates more heat.

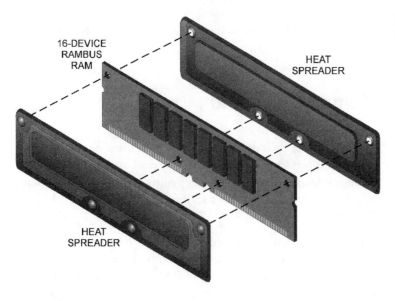

FIGURE 13.1
RIMMs.

SRAM

Like Dynamic RAM, SRAM is available in a number of different types. Many of the memory organization techniques described for DRAM are also implemented in SRAM.

◆ *Asynchronous SRAM*—Is standard SRAM and delivers data from the memory to the microprocessor and returns it to the cache in one clock cycle.

◆ *Synchronous SRAM*—Uses special clock signals and buffer storage to deliver data to the CPU in one clock cycle after the first cycle. The first address is stored and used to retrieve the data while the next address is on its way to the cache.

◆ *Pipeline SRAM*—Uses three clock cycles to fetch the first data and then accesses addresses within the selected page on each clock cycle.

◆ *Burst-mode SRAM*—Loads a number of consecutive data locations from the cache, over several clock cycles, based on a single address from the microprocessor.

In digital electronics terms, a buffer is a holding area for data shared by devices that operate at different speeds or have different priorities. These devices permit a memory module to operate without the delays that other devices impose. Some types of SDRAM memory modules contain buffer registers directly on the module. The buffer registers hold and retransmit the data signals through the memory chips.

Memory Overhead

DRAM devices, commonly used for the system's RAM, require periodic *refreshing* of their data to prevent it from disappearing. Some refreshing is performed by the system's normal memory reading and writing cycles. However, additional circuitry must be used to ensure that every bit in all the memory registers is refreshed within the allotted timeframe.

Another design factor associated with RAM is *data error detection*. A single, incorrect bit can shut down the entire system instantly. With bits constantly moving in and out of RAM, it is crucial that all the bits be transferred correctly. The most popular form of error detection in PC compatibles is *parity checking*. In this methodology, an extra bit is added to each word in RAM and checked each time it is used. Parity checking is a simple self test used to detect RAM readback errors. Like refreshing, parity checking requires additional circuitry and memory overhead to operate.

> **EXAM TIP**
>
> Be aware of what DRAM refreshing is and why it is performed.

> **EXAM TIP**
>
> Know that parity is a method of checking stored data for errors by adding an additional bit to each word when it is stored in memory.

When a parity error occurs, a Non-Maskable Interrupt (NMI) signal is generated in the system, causing the BIOS to execute its NMI handler routine. This routine will normally place a parity error message onscreen, along with an option to shut down the system or to continue. In other cases, the system will show a short memory count during the POST and lock up without an error message. Another possibility is that the system will count the memory, lock up, and reboot itself. If the memory error occurs higher in the physical memory device, this situation can occur after the operating system and applications have been loaded and started running.

ECC SDRAM is a type of SDRAM that includes a fault detection/correction circuit that can detect and fix memory errors without shutting down the system. Occasionally, the information in a single memory bit can change states, which in turn causes a memory error to occur when the data is read from memory. Using a parity memory scheme, the system can detect that a bit has flipped when the memory is read, but it can only display a "Parity Error" message and freeze up. Although this prevents the bad data from being used or written away in the system, it also erases all current data from RAM. An *ECC memory module* has the capability to detect and correct a single-bit error, or to detect errors in two bits. The latter condition causes a parity error shutdown to occur as described earlier.

> **EXAM TIP**
> Be aware of the types of problems that can create an NMI error and what the consequences of these errors are.

> **EXAM TIP**
> Know the difference between parity and ECC error detection systems.

CHALLENGE #1

You are called on to check out a failing computer in the production department. When you arrive, you find that the system is continually locking up and rebooting when the operating system loads. What type of problem is the system likely to be having, and what should you do about it?

Cache Memory

One method of increasing the memory-access speed of a computer is called *caching*. This memory management method assumes that most memory accesses are made within a limited block of addresses. Therefore, if the contents of these addresses are relocated into a special section of high-speed SRAM, the microprocessor could access these locations without requiring any wait states.

The original Intel Pentium had a built-in first-level cache that could be used for both instructions and data. The internal cache was divided into four 2KB blocks containing 128 sets of 16-byte lines each. Control of the internal cache is handled directly by the microprocessor. The microprocessor's internal first-level cache is also known as an *L1 cache*. Many of the older Pentium system boards extended the caching capability of the microprocessor by adding an external, second-level 256KB/512KB memory cache. Like the L1 cache, the second-level cache can also be referred to as an *L2 cache*.

Beginning with the Pentium Pro, Intel began placing the 256KB/512KB L2 cache in the same package with the Pentium processor core (however, it was not integrated directly into the actual IC design). In these cases, there is no additional cache memory on the system board.

The primary objective of the cache memory's control system is to maximize the ratio of hits to total accesses (*hit rate*) so that the majority of memory accesses are performed without wait states. One way to do this is to make the cache memory area as large as possible (thus raising the possibility of the desired information being in the cache). However, the relative cost, energy consumption, and physical size of SRAM devices work against this technique. Practical sizes for cache memories run between 16KB–512KB. However, the newest microprocessors (that is, *Xeon* and *Itanium*) used for server computers have created a third level—L3 cache. These microprocessors can support up to 4MB of cache in the cartridge. Figure 13.2 illustrates different placement schemes that have been used for providing cache memory.

EXAM TIP

Know where L1 cache memory is located.

EXAM TIP

Be aware that larger caches are not necessarily better than smaller caches—they need to be just right.

FIGURE 13.2
Cache locations.

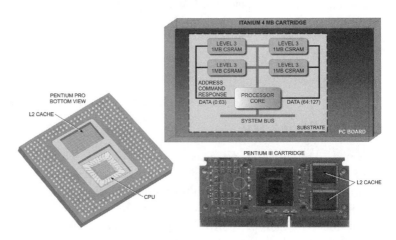

SIMMs, DIMMs, AND BANKS

In the second generation AT-compatible PCs, manufacturers began using snap-in memory modules that mounted vertically on the system board in sockets. The earliest versions of these snap-in modules were *single in-line memory modules* (*SIMMs*). To better accommodate Pentium microprocessors, system boards shifted over to larger *dual in-line memory modules* (*DIMMs*). Both types of memory modules employ special snap-in sockets that support the module firmly. They are also keyed so that they cannot be plugged in backward. SIMM modules were traditionally available in 30-pin and 72-pin versions; DIMMs are larger 168-pin boards.

SIMM and DIMM sockets are quite distinctive in that they are normally arranged side by side. However, they can be located anywhere on the system board. SIMMs typically come in 30-pin/8-bit or 72-pin/32-bit data-storage configurations. The 8-bit modules must be arranged in banks to match the data bus size of the system's microprocessor. To work effectively with a 32-bit microprocessor, a bank of four 8-bit SIMMs would need to be used. Conversely, a single 32-bit SIMM could do the same job.

DIMMs, on the other hand, typically come in 32-bit and 64-bit bus widths to service more powerful microprocessors. These devices must be organized properly to accommodate the size of the system's data bus. In both cases, the modules can be accessed in smaller 8- and 16-bit segments. SIMMs and DIMMs also come in 9-, 36-, and 72-bit versions that include parity-checking bits for each byte of storage (that is, a 36-bit SIMM provides 32 data bits and 4 parity bits—one for each byte of data).

PCs are typically sold with less than their full RAM capacity. This enables users to purchase a less expensive computer to fit their individual needs and yet retain the option to install more RAM if future applications call for it. SIMM and DIMM sizes are typically specified in an a-by-b format. For example, a 2x32 SIMM specification indicates that it is a dual, non-parity, 32-bit (4-byte) device. Using this scheme, the capacity is derived by multiplying the two numbers, and then dividing by 8 (or 9 for parity chips).

Some newer system boards feature a three-DIMM slot arrangement, referred to as a *split-bank arrangement*. When you are working with this board, you must refer to its user manual to determine what

EXAM TIP

Know how many pins are used in SIMMs and DIMMs.

EXAM TIP

Be aware of how many actual data bits are stored in memory devices that include parity.

EXAM TIP

Remember that it takes two 32-bit SIMM modules to make a bank for a 64-bit processor such as the Pentium.

EXAM TIP

Be aware of situations that will cause the system to "see" less than the actual amount of installed RAM.

types of memory can be used. The reason for this is that split-bank arrangements use a different specification for DIMM slot 1 than they do for DIMM slots 2 and 3. The odd slot will normally be organized into one bank while the other two slots combine to form the second bank. If you are not careful when populating these slots, you might create a situation in which the system's memory controller cannot access all the installed RAM.

CHALLENGE #2

You have been assigned to upgrade the memory in a number of your office's computers. When you open them, you discover that they have a three-slot DIMM arrangement. Also, you cannot locate a system board user manual for these computers. You install a 128MB DIMM in each slot. When you start the computer, you see from the POST that the system only recognizes 256MB of RAM. What happened to the other 128MB of RAM, and how can you get the system to recognize it?

A special form factor DIMM, called the *Small Outline DIMM (SO DIMM)* has been developed for use in notebook computers. The basic difference between SO DIMMs and regular DIMMs is that the SO DIMM is significantly smaller than the standard DIMM, so it takes up less space in notebook computers. Figure 13.3 depicts a 72-pin, a 144-pin, and a 200-pin SO DIMM. The 72-pin SO DIMM has a 32-bit data bus, whereas the 144-pin version is 64 bits wide.

CHALLENGE #3

Your friend has brought you his notebook computer and wants you to upgrade the memory in it. He has also brought several different 184-pin 512MB RIMM modules with him that he had in his office. What can you tell your friend about his upgrade?

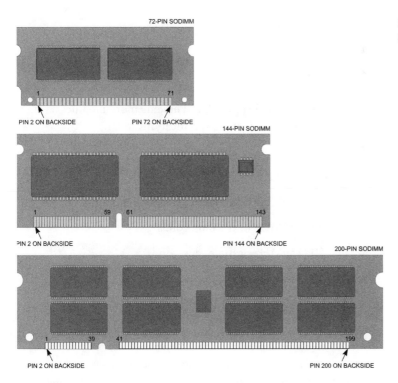

FIGURE 13.3
SO DIMM packages.

RAM Speeds

Another important factor to consider when dealing with RAM is its speed. Manufacturers mark RAM devices with speed information. DRAM modules are marked with a numbering system that indicates the number of clock cycles required for the initial Read operation, followed by information about the number of reads and cycles required to move a burst of data. As an example, a Fast Page Mode DRAM marked as 6-3-3-3 requires 6 cycles for the initial read and 3 cycles for each of three successive reads. This will move an entire 4-byte block of data. EDO and FPM can operate with bus speeds up to 66MHz.

SDRAM devices are marked a little differently. Because they are designed to run synchronously with the system clock and use no wait states, a marking of 3:3:3 at 100MHz on an SDRAM module specifies that

◆ The CAS signal setup time is 3 bus cycles.

◆ The RAS to CAS changeover time is 3 cycles.

◆ The RAS signal setup time is 3 clock cycles.

The bus speed is specified in MHz. These memory modules have been produced in the following specifications so far:

◆ PC66 (66MHz or 15 nanoseconds)

◆ PC83 (83MHz or 12 nanoseconds)

◆ PC100 (100MHz or 10 nanoseconds)

◆ PC133 (133MHz or 8 nanoseconds)

◆ PC150 (150MHz or 4.5 nanoseconds)

◆ PC166 (166MHz or 4 nanoseconds)

Continued advancements in memory module design have made the MHz and CAS time ratings obsolete. Onboard buffering and advanced access strategies have made these measurements inconsequential. Instead, memory performance is being measured by total *data throughput* (also referred to as *bandwidth*) and is being measured in terms of Gigabytes per second (Gbps). As an example, some of the new standard specifications include

◆ PC1600 (1.6Gbps/200MHz/2:2:2)

◆ PC2100 (2.1Gbps/266MHz/2:3:3)

◆ PC2400 (2.6Gbps/300MHz/3:3:3)

◆ PC2700 (2.6Gbps/333MHz/3:3:3)

◆ PC3200 (3.2Gbps/400MHz/3:3:3)

When dealing with RAMBUS memory devices, you should be aware that they use special, proprietary, high-speed buses to interact with the microprocessor. Because the memory bus is proprietary to the RAMBUS design, other memory types cannot be substituted for them. These devices have existed in four different speed ratings. The original RAMBUS devices were rated for 400MHz operation. As the following list indicates, newer RAMBUS devices can be used with even faster memory buses:

◆ PC-600 (600MHz RAMBUS/RDRAM/RIMM)

◆ PC-700 (700MHz RAMBUS/RDRAM/RIMM)

◆ PC-800 (800MHz RAMBUS/RDRAM/RIMM)

The system BIOS on these boards have a built-in autodetect function that can be used to automatically detect the type of memory devices that are installed and configure the memory bus specifically for it. Mixing memory device types can cause assorted memory errors including complete system failures, random lockups, and soft errors. If the autodetect setting is not selected in the BIOS, it is possible to set the system up to under clock or over clock the memory bus.

The system board's documentation will provide information about the types of devices it can use and their speed ratings. It is important to install RAM compatible with the bus speed that the system is running. Normally, installing RAM rated faster than the bus speed will not cause problems. However, installing slower RAM or mixing RAM speed ratings within a system might cause it not to start or to periodically lock up.

NOTE

RAMBUS Memory Devices The RAMBUS bank architecture is typically based on a two-slot arrangement. Both slots must be filled with matching memory modules for the memory system to work. For this reason, RAMBUS devices are typically sold as matching pairs.

EXAM TIP

Be aware of the consequences of mixing RAM with different speed ratings within a system.

CHAPTER SUMMARY

This chapter has examined the different types of memory devices used in the system board's different memory structures. It began with discussion of different DRAM and SRAM architectures before moving into the different types of memory overhead found in a typical PC's memory systems (that is, refreshing and parity checking).

At this point, review the objectives listed at the beginning of the chapter to be certain that you understand each point and can perform each task listed there. Afterward, answer the review questions that follow to verify your knowledge of the information.

KEY TERMS

- Asynchronous SRAM
- Bandwidth
- Burst-mode SRAM
- Caching
- Data error detection
- Data throughput
- Direct Rambus DRAM (DRDRAM)
- Dual in-line memory modules (DIMMs)
- Dynamic RAM (DRAM)

CHAPTER SUMMARY

- ECC memory module
- ECC SDRAM
- Enhanced DRAM (EDRAM)
- Extended data out (EDO)
- Fast page-mode DRAM
- Heat spreader
- Hit rate
- Hyper page-mode DRAM
- Itanium
- L1 cache
- L2 cache
- Non-volatile
- Parity checking
- Pipeline SRAM

- Rambus DRAM (RDRAM)
- Rambus inline memory module (RIMM)
- Refreshing
- Single in-line memory modules (SIMMs)
- Small Outline DIMM (SO DIMM)
- Static RAM (SRAM)
- Synchronous DRAM (SDRAM)
- Synchronous SRAM
- Video RAM (VRAM)
- Volatile
- Windows RAM (WRAM)
- Xeon

APPLY YOUR KNOWLEDGE

Review Questions

1. What are the effects of mixing RAM modules with different speed ratings?

   A. System will run at the speed of the slowest RAM stick.

   B. System will run normally.

   C. System will run at the speed of the memory bus.

   D. System might not run or will crash periodically.

2. What is WRAM typically used for?

   A. CMOS

   B. RAM

   C. Cache

   D. Video

3. Which type of RAM is faster, EDORAM or Fast Page-Mode DRAM?

   A. EDORAM is faster.

   B. Fast Page-Mode DRAM is faster.

   C. They are both the same.

   D. There is no such thing as Fast Page-Mode DRAM.

4. What type of error will a memory parity error create?

   A. Fatal exception error

   B. NMI error

   C. Corrupt Windows operation system file

   D. GPF error

5. How big is the data bus in a non-parity 72-pin RAM module?

   A. 8-bit

   B. 16-bit

   C. 32-bit

   D. 64-bit

6. Cache memory is used to _____.

   A. increase the speed of data access

   B. increase the size of memory available to programs

   C. store data in non-volatile memory

   D. augment the memory used for the operating system kernel

7. What method is used to correct single bit errors in RAM?

   A. Refreshing

   B. Parity

   C. ECC

   D. Latency

8. How many total bits need to be stored in RAM to provide parity for a 64-bit data bus?

   A. None

   B. 64

   C. 72

   D. 128

APPLY YOUR KNOWLEDGE

9. If the RAM count presented during the POST does not equal the amount of RAM actually installed in the system, what type of problem is the system having? (Select all that apply.)

    A. Using wrong RAM speed

    B. Using mixed RAM types

    C. Using split-bank RAM arrangement

    D. Bad voltage regulation from the power supply

10. Which types of memory are considered volatile?

    A. RAM

    B. Magnetic memory

    C. ROM BIOS

    D. CD-ROM disks

11. Where is the L1 cache located in a PC system?

    A. On the RAM

    B. On the motherboard

    C. On the microprocessor PCB

    D. On the microprocessor die

12. How many 32-bit SIMMs would be required to operate a Pentium MMX system board?

    A. 1

    B. 2

    C. 3

    D. 44

13. Which of the following are types of RAM?

    A. RDRAM

    B. ECC SDRAM

    C. CAS DRAM

    D. SO DIMM

14. What is the process of recharging a DRAM's memory bits called?

    A. Strobe

    B. Latency

    C. Refresh

    D. Survey

15. Which of the following describes volatile memory?

    A. Data disappears if the power goes off.

    B. Data will not disappear if the power goes off.

    C. Data is rewritable.

    D. The component is a potential fire hazard.

16. What is the term used to describe the method of checking memory for errors by adding an additional status bit to each byte?

    A. ECC

    B. CAS

    C. Parity

    D. Refreshing

17. How many pins/contacts are in a DIMM?

    A. 30

    B. 72

    C. 144

    D. 168

APPLY YOUR KNOWLEDGE

Answers and Explanations

1. **D.** Installing slower RAM or mixing RAM speed ratings within a system might cause it not to start or to periodically lock up. For more information, see the section "RAM Speeds."

2. **D.** Special memory devices have also been designed to optimize video memory related activities. Among these devices are video RAM (VRAM) and Windows RAM (WRAM). For more information, see the section "Advanced SDRAM."

3. **C.** Extended data out (EDO) memory increases the speed at which RAM operations are conducted by cutting out the 10-nanosecond wait time normally required between issuing memory addresses. This is accomplished by not disabling the data bus pins between bus cycles. EDO is an advanced type of fast page-mode DRAM also referred to as hyper page-mode DRAM. The advantage of EDO DRAM is encountered when multiple sequential memory accesses are performed. By not turning off the data pin, each successive access after the first access is accomplished in two clock cycles rather than three. For more information, see the section "Advanced SDRAM."

4. **B.** When a parity error occurs, a Non-Maskable Interrupt (NMI) signal is co-generated in the system, causing the BIOS to execute its NMI handler routine. This routine will normally place a parity error message onscreen, along with an option to shut down the system or to continue. In other cases, the system will show a short memory count during the POST and lock up without an error message. Another possibility is that the system will count the memory, lock up, and

reboot itself. If the memory error occurs higher in the physical memory device, this situation can occur after the operating system and applications have been loaded and started running. For more information, see the section "Memory Overhead."

5. **C.** SIMMs typically comes in 30-pin/8-bit or 72-pin/32-bit data-storage configurations. For more information, see the section "SIMMs, DIMMs, and Banks."

6. **A.** One method of increasing the memory-access speed of a computer is called caching. For more information, see the section "Cache Memory."

7. **C.** Using a Parity memory scheme, the system can detect that a bit has flipped when the memory is read, but it can only display a "Parity Error" message and freeze up. Although this prevents the bad data from being used or written away in the system, it also erases all current data from RAM. An ECC memory module has the capability to detect and correct a single-bit error or to detect errors in two bits. For more information, see the section "Memory Overhead."

8. **C.** SIMMs and DIMMs also come in 9-, 36-, and 72-bit versions that include parity-checking bits for each byte of storage (that is, a 36-bit SIMM provides 32 data bits and 4 parity bits—one for each byte of data). For more information, see the section "SIMMs, DIMMs, and Banks."

9. **C.** The system may have an incorrect RAM module installed in a split bank system board arrangement. Using wrong RAM speed or mixed RAM types can cause the system to lock up but should not produce a short RAM count. The system could also have a bad RAM module installed. For more information, see the section "SIMMs, DIMMs, and Banks."

10. **A.** Whether the RAM is made up of static or dynamic RAM devices, all RAM systems have the disadvantage of being volatile. This means that any data stored in RAM will be lost if power to the computer is disrupted for any reason. On the other hand, both types of RAM have the advantage of being fast, with the capability to be written to and read from with equal ease. ROM, on the other hand is classified as non-volatile memory. For more information, see the section "Memory Systems."

11. **D.** The microprocessor's internal first-level cache is also known as an L1 cache. For more information, see the section "Cache Memory."

12. **B.** It takes two 32-bit SIMM modules to make a bank for a 64-bit processor such as the Pentium. For more information, see the section "SIMMs, DIMMs, and Banks."

13. **C.** RDRAM, ECC SDRAM, and SO DIMMs are all types of memory modules. There are no such devices as CAS DRAMs. For more information, see the section "SIMMs, DIMMs, and Banks."

14. **C.** DRAM requires periodic refreshing to maintain data, even if electrical power is applied to the chip. For more information, see the section "Memory Overhead."

15. **A.** Whether the RAM is made up of static or dynamic RAM devices, all RAM systems have the disadvantage of being volatile. This means that any data stored in RAM will be lost if power to the computer is disrupted for any reason. ROM, on the other hand, is classified as non-volatile memory. For more information, see the section "Memory Systems."

16. **C.** The most popular form of error detection in PC compatibles is parity checking. In this methodology, an extra bit is added to each word in RAM and checked each time it is used. Parity checking is a simple self test used to detect RAM read-back errors. Like refreshing, parity checking requires additional circuitry and memory overhead to operate. For more information, see the section "Memory Overhead."

17. **D.** SIMM modules were traditionally available in 30-pin and 72-pin versions; DIMMs use larger 168-pin boards. For more information, see the section "SIMMs, DIMMs, and Banks."

Challenge Solutions

1. Even though there is no mention on the screen of a parity error, the symptoms seem to indicate that you have a bad memory location in a RAM device. You must isolate the bad device and replace it with one that will work properly. For more information, see the section "Memory Overhead."

2. The three-bank split bank slot arrangement has separated the memory into a 128MB section for the first slot and only 128MB for the second bank of two slots. These devices are not compatible with the organization of the board's slot configuration. You need to obtain the system board's user manual to determine what types and sizes of memory devices can be used. (If this occurs when you are using the specified types of memory devices, you might have a bad DIMM device in one of the slots.) For more information, see the section "SIMMs, DIMMs, and Banks."

APPLY YOUR KNOWLEDGE

3. You will probably need to tell your friend that you need the user manual for his notebook and that you doubt that the large RIMM modules he has supplied will work in the notebook computer. Notebook computers typically employ small outline DIMM devices (SO DIMMs) that use different pin configurations (that is, 72/144-pin versions) and operate from different voltage levels than normal DIMM devices do. For more information, see the section "SIMMs, DIMMs, and Banks."

Suggested Readings and Resources

1. Kingston's Ultimate Memory Guide
   www.kingston.com/tools/umg/default.asp

2. Ars Technica RAM Guide
   http://www.arstechnica.com/paedia/r/ram_
   guide/ram_guide.part1-1.html

3. System Memory Guide
   http://www.pcguide.com/ref/ram/index.htm

4. RAM Guide
   http://www.makeitsimple.com/articles/
   ramguide/

5. Cache Memory
   http://searchsystemsmanagement.techtar-
   get.com/sDefinition/0,,sid20_gci211730,00.
   html

6. Memory Management
   http://www.memorymanagement.org/articles/
   begin.html

This chapter helps you to prepare for the Core Hardware module of the A+ Certification examination by covering the following objectives within the "Domain 4.0: Motherboard/Processors/Memory" section.

4.3 Identify the most popular types of motherboards, their components, and their architecture (bus structures and power supplies).

Content might include the following:

- **Types of motherboards:**
  - **AT (full and baby)**
  - **ATX**
- **Components:**
  - **Communication ports**
  - **SIMM and DIMM**
  - **Processor sockets**
  - **External cache memory (Level 2)**
- **Bus architecture:**
  - **ISA**
  - **PCI**
  - **AGP**
  - **USB (Universal Serial Bus)**
  - **VESA local bus (VL-BUS)**
- **Basic compatibility guidelines:**
  - **IDE (ATA, ATAPI, ULTRA-DMA, EIDE)**
  - **SCSI (Wide, Fast, Ultra, LVD (Low Voltage Differential))**

▶ The system board is the main component in a PC-compatible microcomputer system. As this A+ objective indicates, technicians must be aware of the characteristics of different types of system boards in the marketplace. This will enable them to make intelligent choices about repairing, upgrading, or exchanging system boards.

CHAPTER 14

Motherboards

▶ The system board contains the components that form the basis of the computer system. Even though the system board's physical structure has changed over time, its logical structure has remained relatively constant. Since the original PC, the system board has contained the microprocessor, its support devices, the system's primary memory units, and the expansion-slot connectors.

STUDY STRATEGIES

To prepare for the motherboard, processors, and memory objective of the Core Hardware exam,

▶ Read the objectives at the beginning of this chapter.

▶ Study the information in this chapter.

▶ Review the objectives listed earlier in this chapter.

▶ Perform any step-by-step procedures in the text.

▶ Answer the review questions at the end of the chapter and check your results.

▶ Use the PrepLogic test engine on the CD-ROM that accompanies this book for additional review and exam questions concerning this material.

▶ Review the exam tips scattered throughout the chapter and make certain that you are comfortable with each point.

INTRODUCTION

The system board is the main component of any personal computer system. This chapter examines differences in the two main types of system boards commonly used in modern PC-compatible computers. These system boards typically adhere to either the ATX or baby AT form factor.

The ATX form factor is a newer design specification developed after the introduction of the Pentium microprocessor. It was introduced primarily to deal with the operation of the new processor and to overcome design limitations that became apparent as the older AT form factor specification aged.

The older AT (or Baby AT form factor) presents a larger system board with more IC devices on it and a greater number of I/O connections made directly on the board.

After completing this chapter, you should be able to describe the major architectural and operational differences between the standard system board types.

SYSTEM BOARD FORM FACTORS

The term *form factor* is used to refer to the physical size and shape of a device. However, with system boards, it also refers to their case style and power-supply compatibility, as well as to their I/O connection placement schemes. These factors must be considered when assembling a new system from components and in repair and upgrade situations in which the system board must be replaced.

The original IBM PC form factor established the industry standard for the PC, PC-XT, and PC-AT clone system boards. Although IBM produced a large AT format board, the industry soon returned to the PC-XT/Baby AT form factor. Several variations of the AT-class system board have been produced over time. Currently, there are really only two system board form factors that technicians must deal with. These are the older AT system boards and newer ATX system boards. While the AT-class of system boards has been around for a long time, the ATX class currently dominates the new computer market.

ATX System Boards

The newest system board designation is the *ATX form factor* developed by Intel for Pentium-based systems. This specification is an evolution of the older *Baby AT form factor* that moves the standard I/O functions to the system board.

The ATX specification basically rotates the baby AT form factor by 90 degrees, relocates the power-supply connection, and moves the microprocessor and memory modules away from the expansion slots.

Figure 14.1 depicts a Pentium-based, ATX system board that directly supports the FDD, HDD, serial, and parallel ports. The board is 12 inches (305mm) wide and 9.6 inches (244mm) long. A revised, *mini-ATX specification* allows for 11.2x8.2 inch system boards. The mounting-hole patterns for the ATX and mini-ATX system boards require a case that can accommodate the new boards. Although ATX shares most of its mounting-hole pattern with the baby-AT specification, it does not match exactly.

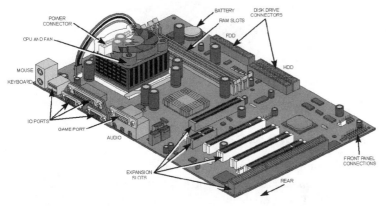

| EXAM TIP | Be able to identify the major components of an ATX system board from a graphical representation. |

FIGURE 14.1
An ATX Pentium system board.

The power-supply orientation enables a single fan to be used to cool the system. This feature results in reduced cost, reduced system noise, and improved reliability. The relocated microprocessor and memory modules enable full-length adapter cards to be used in the expansion slots while providing easy upgrading of the microprocessor, RAM, and I/O devices.

The fully implemented ATX format also has specifications for the power-supply and I/O connector placements. In particular, the ATX

EXAM TIP

Know which type of system board can use a software power-off switch.

specification for the power-supply connection calls for a single, 20-pin power cord between the system board and the power-supply unit rather than the typical P8/P9 cabling. As illustrated in Figure 14.2, the new cable adds a +3.3V (DC) supply to the traditional +/- 12V (DC) and +/- 5 V (DC) supplies. A software activated power switch can also be implemented through the ATX power-connector specification. The PS-ON and 5VSB (5V Standby) signals can be controlled by the operating system to perform automatic system shutdowns.

FIGURE 14.2
An ATX power-supply connector.

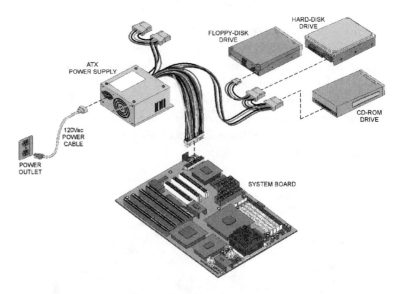

AT System Boards

The forerunner of the ATX system board was a derivative of the *Industry Standard Architecture* (*ISA*) system board developed for the IBM PC-AT. The original PC-AT system board measured 30.5x33 centimeters.

As the PC-AT design became the de facto industry standard, printed–circuit-board manufacturers began to combine portions of the AT design into larger IC devices to reduce the size of their system boards. These chipset-based system boards were quickly reduced to match that of the original PC and PC-XT system boards (22x33 centimeters). This particular system board size, depicted in Figure 14.3, is referred to as a *Baby AT system board*. The structures associated with this type of system board are referred to as AT-style architecture.

EXAM TIP

Be able to identify slot types and I/O ports from AT-style system board drawings.

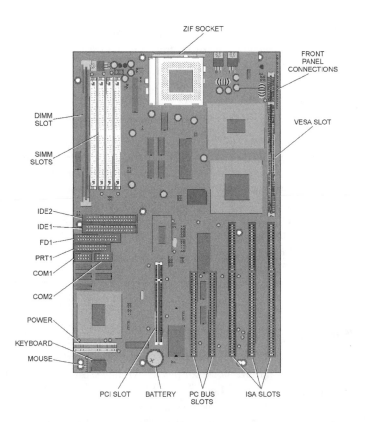

ZIF SOCKET

FRONT
PANEL
CONNECTIONS

DIMM
SLOT

VESA SLOT

SIMM
SLOTS

IDE2

IDE1

FD1

PRT1

COM1

COM2

POWER

KEYBOARD

MOUSE

PCI SLOT   BATTERY   PC BUS   ISA SLOTS
                      SLOTS

FIGURE 14.3
An AT-style system board.

System Board Compatibility

Obviously, the first consideration when installing or replacing a system board is whether it will physically fit (*form factor*) and work with the other system components (*compatibility*). In both of these situations, the following basic issues must be dealt with—the system board's form factor, its case style, and its power-supply connection type.

Standard PC, PC-XT, and Baby AT boards share the same mounting-hole patterns and can be exchanged freely with each other. However, the original PC-AT and ATX system boards have different mounting-hole pattern specifications. In addition to the mounting-hole alignment issue, the case openings for expansion slots and port connections must be compatible with those of the system board.

Various types of keyboard connectors have been used in different types of systems. The most common connectors used with PC keyboards are 6-pin PS/2 mini DINs, 5-pin DINs, and RJ-11 jacks.

EXAM TIP

Remember which system board types use a 5-pin DIN connector.

PC-XT- and AT-compatible systems have historically used the 5-pin DIN connector, whereas the 6-pin mini DIN is used with ATX systems.

CHALLENGE #1

You have been called in as a computer consultant for the world's third largest banking organization. It wants to upgrade its existing computer systems to Pentium class systems. When you arrive, you discover that old Windows 3.11 operating systems are still running on 80386 computers. These systems use baby AT system boards, 2/3 size Multi I/O cards, 9-pin serial mice, and 500MB IDE hard drives. What should you advise the customer to do in order to upgrade the machines with the least cost and the most advantage?

Power-Supply Considerations

Power-supply size, orientation, and connectors present another compatibility consideration. For example, an AT power supply cannot be installed in an ATX case. Because the AT bolt pattern is different from the ATX bolt pattern, it cannot be properly secured and grounded in the ATX case. Also, the single power connector from the ATX power supply will not connect to an AT system board's dual (P8/P9) power connector. Finally, true ATX fans are designed to blow air into the case from the rear—AT power supplies pull it through the case from the front.

PENTIUM CHIPSETS

IC manufacturers develop different chipsets to support different processors types. Most of the desktop Pentium designs feature a three-chip chipset that supports a combination PCI/ISA bus architecture. Figure 14.4 depicts a generic chipset arrangement for this type of system board.

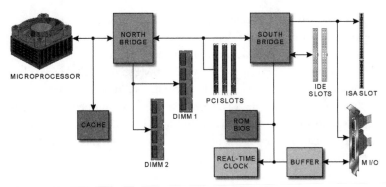

FIGURE 14.4
A typical Pentium chipset.

The major components of a typical Pentium chipset consist of

◆ A Memory Controller (called the North Bridge)

◆ A PCI-to-ISA Host Bridge (referred to as the South Bridge)

◆ An Enhanced I/O Controller

The Memory Controller provides the interface between the system's microprocessor, its various memory sections, and the PCI bus. In turn, the Host Bridge provides the interface between the PCI bus, the IDE bus, and the ISA bus. The Enhanced I/O chip interfaces the standard PC peripherals (LPT, COM, and FDD interfaces) to the ISA bus. This typical chipset arrangement can vary for a couple of reasons: The first is to include a specialized function, such as an AGP bus or USB interface. The second is to accommodate changes in bus specifications.

System Bus Speeds

Microprocessor and chipset manufacturers are continually developing products to speed up the operation of the system. One method of doing this is to speed up the movement of data across the system's data buses. When you examine the arrangement described in Figure 14.4, you should notice that the buses operating directly with the microprocessor and *North Bridge* are running at one speed, whereas the PCI bus is running at a different speed, and the ISA/MIO devices are running at still another speed. The chipset devices are responsible for coordinating the movement of signals and data between these different buses.

N O T E

Pentium Bus Speeds   Using an example of a current Pentium system board, the processor can run at 1.1GHz internally, whereas the front side bus runs at 133MHz, the PCI bus runs at 66MHz, the IDE bus runs at 100MHz (using UDMA100), and the ISA bus runs at 8MHz.

E X A M   T I P

Know which processors can be used with which system board bus speeds.

The buses between the microprocessor and the North Bridge are referred to as the *front side bus*, whereas the PCI and ISA buses are referred to as the *backside buses*. Historically, Pentium processors have operated at many speeds between 50MHz and 2.2GHz. At the same time, the front side buses have been operating at 66MHz, 100MHz, and 133MHz. Likewise, the PCI bus has operated at standard speeds of 33MHz, 44MHz, and 66MHz. Although the PCI bus speed has improved, the operating speed of the ISA bus has remained constant at 8MHz.

Expansion Bus Architectures

Expansion slots basically come in three formats: 8-bit, 16-bit, and 32-bit data buses. The PC-bus slot is the most famous example of an 8-bit expansion slot; the ISA slot is the consummate 16-bit expansion bus. The 32-bit expansion buses include the MCA bus, the EISA bus, the VESA bus, and the PCI bus. The AGP slot is a special version of the PCI bus connector. Figure 14.5 shows the size comparison between expansion-slot formats.

FIGURE 14.5
Expansion-slot size comparison.

8-Bit Slots

The 8-bit expansion slots in the original PC, PC-XT, and their compatibles became the de facto industry connection standard for 8-bit systems. It was dubbed the *PC-bus standard*. It featured an 8-bit, bidirectional data bus and 20 address lines for the I/O channel. It also provided six interrupt channels, control signals for memory and I/O read or write operations, clock and timing signals, and three channels of DMA control lines. In addition, the bus offered memory-refresh timing signals, and an I/O channel-check line for peripheral problems, as well as power and ground lines for the adapters that plug in to the bus.

16-Bit Slots

The overwhelming popularity of the IBM-PC AT established it as the 16-bit standard to which all other PC-compatible equipment is compared. Originally, this bus was called the *AT bus*. However, its widespread acceptance earned it the *Industry Standard Architecture (ISA)* title it now carries. As a matter of fact, the ISA slot is the most common expansion slot used with microcomputers. Even on system boards that have 32-bit and 64-bit expansion slots, it is not uncommon to find at least one ISA slot.

These expansion slots actually exist in two parts: the slightly altered, 62-pin I/O connector, similar to the standard PC-bus connector, and a 36-pin auxiliary connector. The new bus provided twice as many interrupt and DMA channels as the PC-bus specification, which made it possible to connect more peripheral devices to ISA systems. To maintain compatibility with older adapter cards, the transfer speed for the ISA bus was limited to the same speed as that of the older PC bus. Although the ISA bus ran at microprocessor-compatible speeds up to 10 or 12MHz Turbo speeds, incompatibility with slower adapter cards caused manufacturers to settle for running them at 8 or 8.33MHz in newer designs.

EXAM TIP

Remember that the ISA bus features a 16-bit data bus and runs at 8 or 8.33MHz.

32-Bit Architectures

As 32-bit microprocessors gained popularity, the shortcomings and restrictions of the 16-bit ISA bus became noticeable. Obviously, the

ISA bus could not support the full, 32-bit capabilities of micro-processors such as the 80386DX, the 80486DX, and the 64-bit Pentium. In addition, the physical organization of the signal lines in the ISA bus produced unacceptable levels of *Radio Frequency Interference (RFI)* as the bus speed increased. These factors caused designers to search for a new bus system to take advantage of the 32-bit bus and the faster operation of the processors.

Two legitimate 32-bit bus standards were developed to meet these challenges. They were the *Extended Industry Standard Architecture* (*EISA*) bus, which, as its name implies, was an extension of the existing ISA standard bus, and an IBM-sponsored, proprietary bus standard called *Micro Channel Architecture* (*MCA*). Although both 32-bit designs were revolutionary and competed for the market, both have passed from the scene. In both cases, market demand did not support these designs and they were eventually replaced by other more acceptable standards.

Local Bus Designs

In order to speed up the operation of their systems, system board manufacturers began to add proprietary bus designs to their board to increase the speed and bandwidth for transfers between the micro-processor and a few selected peripherals. This was accomplished by creating special local buses between the devices that would enable the peripherals to operate at speeds close to that of the micro-processor.

Because of industry moves away from anything related to ISA cards, the PCI bus has become the dominant force in system board designs. Each generation of PCI designs has provided fewer and fewer ISA buses. Current designs include three or four PCI slots, an AGP slot, and can include a single ISA connector for compatibility purposes (or none at all).

> **EXAM TIP**
>
> Remember which expansion-slot types are most prevalent on modern system boards.

PCI Local Bus

The *Peripheral Component Interconnect* (*PCI*) local bus design incorporates three elements: a low-cost, high-performance local bus; the automatic configuration of installed expansion cards (PnP); and the capability to expand with the introduction of new microprocessors and peripherals. The data-transfer performance of the PCI local bus is 132Mbps using a 32-bit bus and 264Mbps using a 64-bit bus. This is accomplished even though the bus has a maximum clock frequency of 33MHz.

The PCI peripheral device has 256 bytes of onboard memory to hold information as to what type of device it is. The peripheral device can be classified as a controller for a mass-storage device, a network interface, a display, or other hardware. The configuration space also contains control, status, and latency timer values. The latency timer register on the device determines the length of time that the device can control the bus for bus mastering operations.

The main component in the PCI-based system is the PCI bus controller, called the host bridge. This device monitors the microprocessor's address bus to determine whether addresses are intended for devices on the system board, in a PCI slot, or in one of the system board's other expansion slots.

The PCI bus specification uses multiplexed address and data lines to conserve the pins of the basic 124-pin PCI connector. Within this connector are signals for control, interrupt, cache support, error reporting, and arbitration.

The original PCI bus employed 32-bit address and data buses. Its specification also defined a 64-bit multiplexed address and data bus variation for use with 64-bit processors, such as the Pentium. Its clock line was originally defined for a maximum frequency of 33MHz and a 132Mbps transfer rate. However it can be used with microprocessors operating at higher clock frequencies (that is, 66MHz under the PCI 2.1 specification).

The PCI 2.2 version increase implemented a new slot structure to provide a true 64-bit data bus, as illustrated in Figure 14.6. The new PCI specification runs at 66MHz to provide a 264Mbps data throughput. The slot also features a reduced 3.3 Vdc power supply voltage to decrease signal interference levels for the 66MHz operations. The back portion of the slot remains pin and signal compatible with the older 32-bit PCI slots. Adapters placed in the 32-bit section can operate with the 5Vdc or 3.3V supply levels.

> **EXAM TIP**
>
> Know which expansion-slot specification employs a 124-pin connection.

FIGURE 14.6
32-bit and 64-bit PCI slots.

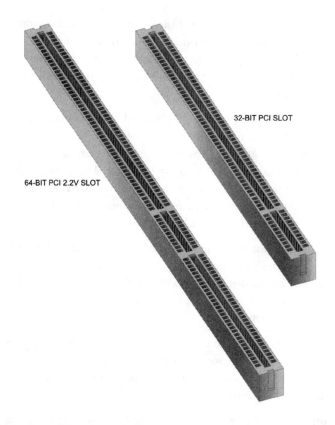

32-BIT PCI SLOT

64-BIT PCI 2.2V SLOT

PCI Configuration

The PCI standard is part of the PnP hardware standard. As such, the system's BIOS and system software must support the PCI standard. Although the PCI function is self-configuring, many of its settings can be viewed and altered through the CMOS Setup utility.

During a portion of the bootup known as the detection phase, the PnP-compatible BIOS checks the system for devices installed in the expansion slots to see what types they are, how they are configured, and which slots they are in. For PnP-compatible I/O cards, this information is held in a ROM device on the adapter card.

The BIOS reads the information from all the cards and then assigns each adapter a handle (logical name) in the *PnP registry*. It then stores the configuration information for the various adapters in the registry as well.

Next, the BIOS compares the adapter information to the system's basic configuration in search of resource conflicts. After evaluating the requirements of the cards and the system's available resources, the PnP routine assigns system resources to the cards as required.

Because the PnP process has no method for reconfiguring *legacy devices* during the resource assignment phase, it begins by assigning resources, such as IRQ assignments, to these devices before servicing the system's PnP devices.

Likewise, when the BIOS detects the presence of a new device during the detection phase, it will disable the resource settings of its existing cards, check to determine what resources are required and available, and then reallocate the system's resources as necessary.

Systems might in theory contain an unlimited number of PCI slots. Only four slots are normally included on most system boards because of signal loading considerations. The PCI bus includes four internal Interrupt lines (INTa through INTd or INT1 through INT4) that enable each PCI slot to activate up to four different interrupts. PCI interrupts should not be confused with the system's IRQ channels, although they can be associated with them if required by a particular device. In these cases, IRQ9 and IRQ10 are normally used.

> **EXAM TIP**
>
> Know which system resources the PnP system must assign first and why.

> **EXAM TIP**
>
> Know the process the PnP system employs to allocate resources to a new device in an existing system.

VESA Local Bus

The *VESA local bus* was developed by the Video Electronics Standards Association. This local bus specification, also referred to as the *VL-bus*, was originally developed to provide a local bus connection to a video adapter. Its functionality has since been defined for use with other adapter types, however, such as drive controllers and network interfaces.

The VL-bus defined a local bus that was originally designed for use with 80386 or 80486 microprocessors. It can operate at up to 66MHz if the VL-bus device is built directly on the system board. If the VL-bus devices are installed into an expansion slot, however, the maximum frequency allowed is 50MHz.

AGP Slots

EXAM TIP

Know what type of device is plugged in to an AGP slot.

Newer Pentium systems include an advanced *Accelerated Graphics Port* (*AGP*) interface for video graphics. The AGP interface is a variation of the PCI bus design that has been modified to handle the intense data throughput associated with three-dimensional graphics.

The AGP specification was introduced by Intel to provide a 32-bit video channel that runs at 66MHz in basic 1X video mode. The standard also supports two high-speed modes that include a 2X (5.33Mbps) and a 4X (1.07Gbps) mode.

The AGP standard provides for a direct channel between the AGP graphic controller and the system's main memory, instead of using the expansion buses for video data. This removes the video data traffic from the PCI buses. The speed provided by this direct link permits video data to be stored in system RAM instead of in special video memory.

The system board typically features a single slot that is supported by a Pentium/AGP-compliant chipset. System boards designed for portable systems and single-board systems might incorporate the AGP function directly into the board without using a slot connector.

EXAM TIP

You must be able to identify standard expansions slot types from different ATX and AT system board outline drawings.

Table 14.1 compares the capabilities of the various bus types commonly found in personal computers. It is quite apparent that the data-transfer rates possible with each new version increase dramatically. This is significant because the expansion bus is a speed-limiting factor for many of the system's operations. Every peripheral access made through the expansion slots requires the entire computer to slow down to the operating speed of the bus.

TABLE 14.1

EXPANSION BUS SPECIFICATIONS

Bus Type	Transfer Rate	Data Bits	Address Bits	Dma Channels	Int Channels
PC	1Mbps	8	20	4	6
ISA	16Mbps	16	24	8	11
VESA	150/275Mbps	32/64	32	None	1
PCI 2	132/264Mbps	32/64	32	None	3

Bus Type	Transfer Rate	Data Bits	Address Bits	Dma Channels	Int Channels
PCI 2.1	264/528Mbps	32/64	32	None	3
PCI 2.2	264Mbps	64	32	None	3
AGP	266/533/1,070Mbps	32	32	None	3

Expansion-Slot Considerations

The types of adapter cards used in the system are another concern when replacing a system board. Make sure that the new board has enough of the correct types of expansion slots to handle all the adapter cards that must be reinstalled. There is some upward compatibility between PC-bus, ISA, EISA, and VESA cards.

Also, some PC-bus cards can be installed in ISA, EISA, and VESA slots—although most cannot because of a small skirt on the bottom of the card that conflicts with the ISA extension portion of the slot. Both the EISA and VESA slots can accommodate ISA cards. Be aware that these relationships are not backward compatible. MCA and PCI are not compatible with any of the other bus types.

> **EXAM TIP**
>
> Be aware of which slot types are capable of accepting adapter cards designed for other slot types.

I/O CONNECTIONS

Pre-Pentium computers typically employed a Multi-I/O (MI/O) adapter card to provide standardized AT-compatible I/O (FDD, HDD, 1 parallel, 2 serial, 1 game port) connections. However, the Pentium chipsets have integrated these I/O functions into the system board by including their interfaces and controllers in the chipset.

Pentium AT Ports

Figure 14.7 illustrates a sample arrangement for the AT-style Pentium system board's standard I/O connectors (ports).

> **EXAM TIP**
>
> Be able to identify standard I/O connections from an AT-style system board drawing using their relative sizes and groupings.

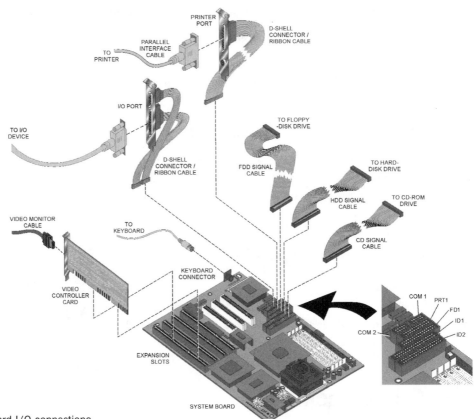

FIGURE 14.7
AT-class Pentium system board I/O connections.

Parallel I/O devices plug in to a DB-25F connector located on an expansion-slot cover. This port is connected to the system board at the 26-pin BERG pin block PRT1.

The RS-232C serial/asynchronous interface-port connections—COM1 and COM2—support serial communications for serial I/O devices, such as mice and modems. A ribbon cable connects the system board's COM1 connector to a DB-9M connector located on one of the unit's slot covers. This serial port is typically the system's first serial port and is normally the mouse connector.

Another ribbon cable connects the system board's COM2 connection to a DB-25F connector on one of the expansion-slot covers. This connector serves as the second logical serial port. Figure 14.8 illustrates the proper connection of the parallel- and serial-port ribbon cables to the AT-style system board.

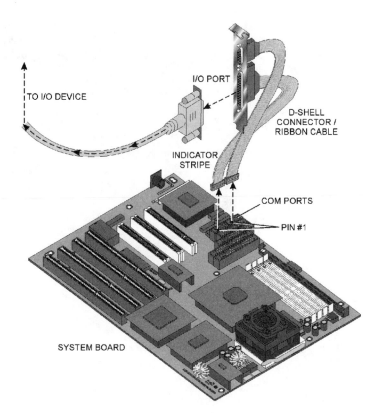

FIGURE 14.8
AT-Style parallel- and serial-port connections.

Pentium ATX Ports

On ATX-compliant system boards, the MIO port connections have been moved to a vertical stack form factor located at the rear of the board. Figure 14.9 depicts the standard arrangement of the I/O port connections in an ATX system.

> **EXAM TIP**
>
> You must be able to identify standard I/O connections types from different ATX and AT system board drawings by their relative sizes and locations.

FIGURE 14.9
ATX I/O connections.

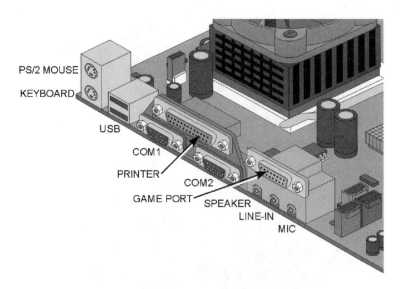

UNIVERSAL SERIAL BUS

The USB system is composed of a *USB host* and *USB devices*. The devices category consists of hubs and nodes. In any system, there is one USB host. This unit contains the interface that provides the USB host controller. The controller is actually a combination of USB hardware, firmware, and software. As mentioned earlier, up to 127 USB peripheral devices could plug in to each other, extending the bus to service up to 127 devices.

Many newer AT and ATX system boards feature built-in USB host ports. In the AT-style boards, the port is furnished as part of a BERG pin connection. The ports are converted to standard connectors through an additional back panel cable set that mounts in an open back panel slot.

ATX boards feature a pair of USB port connectors as part of their ATX port connection block. You can also find PCI card mounted USB ports that can be added to the system to permit even more USB devices to be attached to the system. These host ports function as the system's root hub.

The operation of the USB ports is controlled by settings in the CMOS Setup utility. In most cases, you will need to access the PCI Configuration Screen in the system's CMOS Setup Utility, enable the USB function, and assign the ports IRQ channels to use. If no USB device is being used, the IRQ allocation should be set to "NA" in order to free up the IRQ line for use by other devices.

USB Data Transfers

The USB specification provides for the following four types of transfers to be conducted:

◆ *Control transfers*—Are used by the system to configure devices at startup or time of connection. Other software can use control transfers to perform other device-specific operations.

◆ *Bulk data transfers*—Are used to service devices that can handle large batches of data (scanners and printers, for example). Bulk transfers are typically made up of large bursts of sequential data. The system arranges for bulk transfers to be conducted when the bus has plenty of capacity to carry out the transfer.

◆ *Interrupt transfers*—Are small, spontaneous transfers from a device used to announce events, provide input coordinate information, or transfer characters.

◆ *Isochronous transfers*—Involve large streams of data. This format is used to move continuous, real-time data streams such as voice or video. Data delivery rates are predetermined and correspond to the sampling rate of the device.

USB devices are rated as Full speed and Low speed devices based on their communication capabilities. Full speed USB devices operate at up to 480Mbps, whereas Low speed devices run at 12Mbps.

> **EXAM TIP**
>
> Be aware of the USB high-speed, data-streaming mode.

ONBOARD DISK DRIVE CONNECTIONS

Along with the I/O port connections, Pentium system boards moved the hard and floppy disk drive controller functions and interface connections to the system board, as illustrated in Figure 14.10. As is the case with most Pentium-based system boards, this example provides the system's IDE host adapter and floppy disk drive controller interface connections.

FIGURE 14.10
Pentium board disk drive connections.

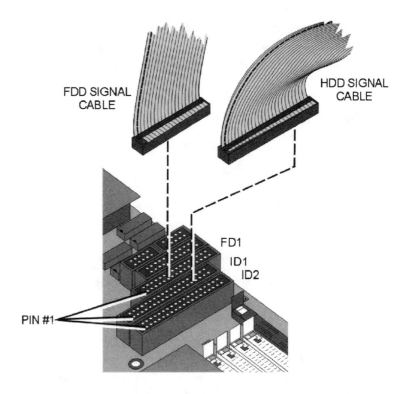

The FDC portion of the chipset can control two floppy disk drives whose signal cable connects to the system board at the 34-pin BERG block (labeled FD1 in Figure 14.10). As with any disk drive connections, caution must be taken when connecting the floppy disk drive signal cable to the system board; pin 1 of the connector must line up with the signal cable's indicator stripe.

IDE Connections

The IDE host adapter portion of the chipset is normally capable of controlling up to four IDE hard disks, CD-ROM drives, or other IDE devices. These adapters furnish two complete IDE channels—IDE1 and IDE2. Each EIDE channel can handle one master and one slave device. The hard drives and CD-ROM drives are connected to the system board's IDE connectors by 40-conductor ribbon cables at connectors ID1 or ID2.

EXAM TIP

Know how many devices can be attached to an IDE interface.

Recall that the primary partition of the drive attached to the ID1 connector will be designated as logical C: drive. If a second drive is attached to ID1 as a slave, its primary partition will be designated as logical D: drive. If there is an additional partition on the first drive, it will be designated as the E: drive. The hierarchy of assigning logical drive designations in the IDE interface calls for primary partitions to be assigned sequentially from ID1 master, ID1 slave, ID2 master, to ID2 slave. This is followed by assigning drive letters to the extended partitions for each drive in the same order.

The hard drives are connected in much the same manner as the floppy drives. The first hard drive is connected to the end of the cable farthest away from the ID1 or ID2 connector. Observe the same cable orientation that was used for connecting the floppy disk drives when connecting the cable to the FD1 connector for the hard drives. Figure 14.11 provides an example of the alignment of the FDD and HDD cables on the system board.

EXAM TIP

Know how partition and drive letters are assigned in an IDE system.

EXAM TIP

You must be able to identify IDE system board connections from different ATX and AT system board drawings by their relative sizes and locations.

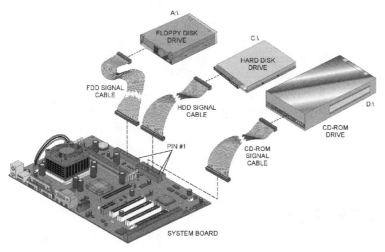

FIGURE 14.11
HDD and FDD system board connections.

You should remember that two similar cables are used with IDE devices. The newer ATA-4/Ultra ATA 66 and Ultra ATA 100 IDE enhancements provide higher data throughput by doubling the number of conductors in the signal cable to 80. The IDE connector has remained compatible with the original 40-pin IDE connection, but each pin has been provided with its own ground conductor in the cable. Both Ultra ATA versions support 33.3Mbps data rates

E X A M   **TIP**

Remember how the Ultra ATA 66 interface cable can be identified and what the effects of using the older signal cable have on these faster interfaces.

when used with a standard 40-pin/40-conductor IDE signal cable. Therefore, Ultra ATA 66 and 100 devices can still be used with systems that don't support the new IDE standards.

After the IDE hardware has been installed, its operating mode must be configured correctly through the system's CMOS Setup utility. Most newer systems possess an autodetect feature in the BIOS that communicates with the hard drives and automatically configures them for use. The physical geometry of the drive might be different than the logical arrangement that the controller displays to the CMOS. The IDE controller handles the translation between the drive parameters the system believes to exist and the actual layout of the drive. The CMOS Setup utility can be used to manually configure IDE channel selections. Both IDE channels can be Enabled, Disabled, or placed in Auto-detect mode through the CMOS. In addition, each channel's parameters can be manually configured through this utility.

Older BIOS versions provide for a manual PIO configuration setting. The ATA standards provide for different *Programmed I/O* (*PIO*) modes that offer higher performance capabilities. Most EIDE devices are now capable of operating in modes 3 or 4. However, the IDE port must be attached to the PCI bus to use these modes. Some system boards only place the IDE1 connection on this 64-bit bus, whereas the IDE2 connection is a function of the ISA bus. In these cases, devices installed on the IDE2 connector will only be capable of mode 2 operations. Newer BIOS versions do not offer manual PIO configuration capabilities.

SCSI Connections

E X A M   **TIP**

Be aware of the expansion-slot types that SCSI host adapter cards are commonly available for.

There is no industry-accepted equivalent for onboard *SCSI adapters* in desktop computers. On the other hand, the server computer portion of the industry has embraced onboard SCSI interfaces to support *RAID* backup operations. However, most desktop system boards require that a SCSI host adapter card be installed to support these types of devices. SCSI host adapters are typically available for use with ISA, EISA, and PCI bus interfaces.

The built-in SCSI connector on the system board will normally be made through a 50-pin BERG header. Like the IDE drives, support for the onboard SCSI controller must be established through the CMOS Setup utility. The system BIOS provides support for the built-in SCSI controller through its CMOS Setup utility, whereas add-on adapter cards feature a BIOS extension on the card.

CHALLENGE #2

Your colleague has faxed you a drawing of an old, stripped system board he is planning to repopulate for use as a Linux mail server. He is not sure about which components he must obtain to make it work again. From the drawing, shown in Figure 14.12, what can you tell him about what he will need to get the board up and running again?

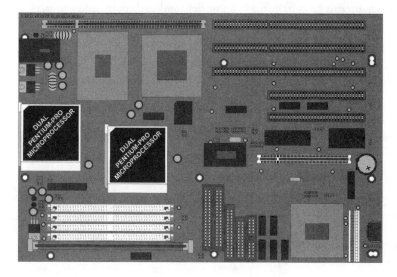

FIGURE 14.12

CHAPTER SUMMARY

KEY TERMS

- Accelerated Graphics Port (AGP)
- AT bus
- ATX form factor
- Baby AT form factor
- Baby AT system board
- Backside buses
- Bulk data transfers
- Compatibility
- Control transfers
- Expansion slots
- Extended Industry Standard Architecture (EISA)
- Form factor
- Front side bus
- Full speed
- Industry Standard Architecture (ISA)
- Interrupt transfers
- Isochronous transfers
- Legacy devices
- Low speed
- Micro Channel Architecture (MCA)
- Mini-ATX specification

This chapter has examined the major components and structures that make up typical PC-compatible system boards.

The chapter presented two key A+ related figures—the standard AT and ATX system board layout figures. These figures are very similar to those you will encounter on the actual A+ exam, although the figures on the actual exam are not drawn in a three-dimensional relief—they are flat line drawings.

In particular, you should be able to identify common structures and devices on these drawings by recognizing their relative sizes and placements on the designated system board type. These structures and devices include memory components, expansion slot types, batteries, processor sockets, and I/O connections.

At this point, review the objectives listed at the beginning of the chapter to be certain that you understand each point and can perform each task listed there. Afterward, answer the review questions that follow to verify your knowledge of the information.

CHAPTER SUMMARY

- North Bridge
- PC-bus standard
- Peripheral Component Interconnect (PCI)
- PnP registry
- Programmed I/O (PIO)

- RAID
- SCSI adapters
- USB devices
- USB host
- VESA local bus
- VL-bus

APPLY YOUR KNOWLEDGE

Review Questions

1. If you connect four, two-partition IDE drives to a system board, what will the drive designation be for the primary partition on the master drive of the secondary IDE controller?

   A. C:

   B. D:

   C. E:

   D. F:

2. At what speed does the ISA slot run?

   A. 8MHz

   B. 33MHz

   C. 66MHz

   D. 133MHz

3. From Figure 14.13, depicting an ATX mother-board, identify the ISA expansion slot.

   A. A

   B. B

   C. C

   D. D

4. From Figure 14.13, depicting an ATX mother-board, identify the AGP expansion slot.

   A. A

   B. B

   C. I

   D. N

5. From Figure 14.13, depicting an ATX mother-board shown in question 3, identify the IDE connectors.

   A. C

   B. J

   C. K

   D. M

6. From Figure 14.13, depicting an ATX mother-board shown in question 3, identify the battery.

   A. G

   B. H

   C. L

   D. O

7. From Figure 14.13, depicting an ATX mother-board, identify the DIMM slots.

   A. B

   B. I

   C. H

   D. N

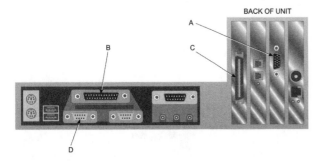

APPLY YOUR KNOWLEDGE

8. From Figure 14.14, depicting an AT motherboard, identify the VESA expansion slot.

   A. L

   B. M

   C. O

   D. R

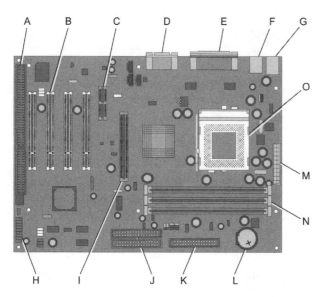

9. From Figure 14.14, depicting an AT motherboard, identify the COMM port connections.

   A. A

   B. C

   C. G

   D. L

10. From Figure 14.14, depicting an AT motherboard, identify the SIMM slots.

    A. A

    B. B

    C. M

    D. O

11. From Figure 14.14, depicting an AT motherboard, identify the FDD connector.

    A. C

    B. E

    C. F

    D. G

12. From Figure 14.14, depicting an AT motherboard, identify the keyboard connector.

    A. I

    B. J

    C. K

    D. Q

13. From Figure 14.14, depicting an AT motherboard, identify the front panel connector.

    A. I

    B. J

    C. K

    D. Q

APPLY YOUR KNOWLEDGE

14. Locate the power-supply connector from Figure 14.14, depicting an AT motherboard.

    A. I

    B. J

    C. P

    D. R

15. Locate the serial port connector in the diagram of an ATX backpanel shown in Figure 14.15.

    A. A

    B. B

    C. C

    D. D

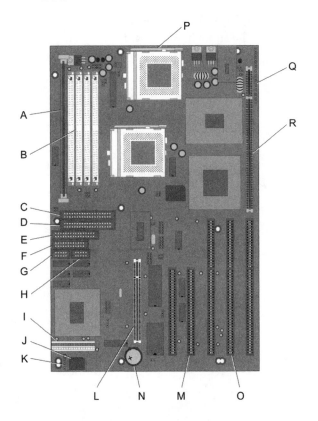

16. From Figure 14.15, depicting an ATX backpanel, locate the printer port.

    A. A

    B. B

    C. C

    D. D

17. What type of system board can use a software controlled power-off switch?

    A. XT

    B. AT

    C. ATX

    D. NTX

18. Which of the following is not part of the typical ATX motherboard?

    A. Game port

    B. Parallel printer port

    C. 5-pin DIN

    D. 6-pin DIN

19. What size is the data bus in an ISA slot?

    A. 8-bit

    B. 16-bit

    C. 32-bit

    D. 64-bit

20. Which of the following has an 8-bit data bus?

    A. ISA

    B. PCI

    C. AGP

    D. PC-bus

APPLY YOUR KNOWLEDGE

21. Which of the following have a 32-bit data bus? (Select all that apply.)

    A. ISA

    B. PCI

    C. AGP

    D. PC-bus

22. What type of expansion bus is the most common found on new motherboards?

    A. ISA

    B. PCI

    C. VESA

    D. PC-bus

23. What type of expansion bus uses an 124-pin slot?

    A. ISA

    B. PCI

    C. AGP

    D. PC-bus

24. What type of expansion card is plugged into an AGP slot?

    A. Graphics

    B. Modem

    C. Network

    D. Sound

25. Which of the following expansion slots can be used for an ISA card? (Select all that apply.)

    A. PC-bus

    B. EISA

    C. VESA

    D. PCI

26. What is the maximum data throughput for a low speed USB device?

    A. 1.5Mbps

    B. 12Mbps

    C. 60Mbps

    D. 480Mbps

27. What is the maximum data throughput when connecting an Ultra ATA 66 hard disk drive with a 40-pin IDE cable?

    A. 10Mbps

    B. 33Mbps

    C. 66Mbps

    D. Will not work together

28. Which IRQ resources are assigned in the PnP configuration process?

    A. Motherboard devices

    B. ISA devices

    C. PCI devices

    D. Legacy devices

29. What types of expansion slots might be used for a SCSI host adapter card? (Select all that apply.)

    A. AGP

    B. PCI

    C. ISA

    D. AMR

APPLY YOUR KNOWLEDGE

30. What type of device is connected to a 5-pin DIN connector?

    A. Mouse

    B. Printer

    C. Keyboard

    D. Joystick

Answers and Explanations

1. **C.** The hierarchy of assigning logical drive designations in the IDE interface calls for primary partitions to be assigned sequentially from ID1 master, ID1 slave, ID2 master, to ID2 slave. This is followed by assigning drive letters to the extended partitions for each drive in the same order. For more information, see the section "IDE Connections."

2. **A.** While the ISA bus originally ran at microprocessor-compatible speeds up to 10 or 12MHz Turbo speeds, incompatibility with slower adapter cards caused manufacturers to settle for running them at 8 or 8.33MHz in newer designs. For more information, see the section "16-Bit Slots."

3. **A.** Refer to Figures 14.1 and 14.4. For more information, see the section "ATX System Boards."

4. **C.** Refer to Figures 14.1 and 14.4. For more information, see the section "ATX System Boards."

5. **B.** Refer to Figure 14.1: An ATX Pentium system board. Along with the I/O port connections, Pentium system boards moved the hard and floppy disk drive controller functions and interface connections to the system board, as illustrated in Figure 14.9. For more information, see the section "ATX System Boards."

6. **C.** Refer to Figure 14.1: An ATX Pentium system board. For more information, see the section "ATX System Boards."

7. **D.** Refer to Figure 14.1: An ATX Pentium system board. For more information, see the section "ATX System Boards."

8. **D.** Refer to Figure 14.3: An AT-style system board. For more information, see the section "AT System Boards."

9. **C.** Refer to Figure 14.3: An AT-style system board. For more information, see the section "AT System Boards."

10. **B.** Refer to Figure 14.3: An AT-style system board. For more information, see the section "AT System Boards."

11. **B.** Refer to Figure 14.3: An AT-style system board. For more information, see the section "AT System Boards."

12. **B.** Refer to Figure 14.3: An AT-style system board. For more information, see the section "AT System Boards."

13. **D.** Refer to Figure 14.3: An AT-style system board. For more information, see the section "AT System Boards."

14. **A.** Refer to Figure 14.3: An AT-style system board. For more information, see the section "AT System Boards."

15. **D.** Refer to Figure 14.9: ATX I/O connections. For more information, see the section "Pentium ATX Ports."

APPLY YOUR KNOWLEDGE

16. **B.** Refer to Figure 14.9: ATX I/O connections. For more information, see the section "Pentium ATX Ports."

17. **C.** A software-activated power switch can also be implemented through the ATX power-connector specification. The PS-ON and 5VSB (5V Standby) signals can be controlled by the operating system to perform automatic system shutdowns. For more information, see the section "ATX System Boards."

18. **C.** PC-XT- and AT-compatible systems have historically used the 5-pin DIN connector, whereas the 6-pin mini DIN is used with ATX systems. For more information, see the section "System Board Compatibility."

19. **B.** The ISA bus features a 16-bit data bus and runs at 8 or 8.33MHz. For more information, see the section "Expansion Bus Architectures."

20. **D.** The PC-bus slot is the most famous example of an 8-bit expansion slot. For more information, see the section "Expansion Bus Architectures."

21. **B, C.** The 32-bit expansion buses include the MCA bus, the EISA bus, the VESA bus, and the PCI bus. The AGP graphics bus is a 32-bit bus. For more information, see the section "Expansion Bus Architectures."

22. **B.** Because of industry moves away from anything related to ISA cards, the PCI bus has become the dominant force in system board designs. Each generation of PCI designs has provided fewer and fewer ISA buses. Current designs include three or four PCI slots, an AGP slot, and might include a single ISA connector for compatibility purposes (or none at all). For more information, see the section "Local Bus Designs."

23. **B.** The PCI bus specification uses multiplexed address and data lines to conserve the pins of the basic 124-pin PCI connector. For more information, see the section "PCI Local Bus."

24. **A.** The AGP interface is a variation of the PCI bus design that has been modified to handle the intense data throughput associated with three-dimensional graphics. For more information, see the section "AGP Slots."

25. **B, C.** Both the EISA and VESA slots can accommodate ISA cards. For more information, see the section "Expansion-Slot Considerations."

26. **B.** Full speed USB devices operate at up to 480Mbps while low speed devices run at 12Mbps. For more information, see the section "USB Data Transfers."

27. **B.** All Ultra ATA versions support 33.3Mbps data rates when used with a standard 40-pin/40-conductor IDE signal cable. For more information, see the section "IDE Connections."

28. **D.** Because the PnP process has no method for reconfiguring legacy devices during the resource assignment phase, it begins by assigning resources, such as IRQ assignments, to these devices before servicing the system's PnP devices. For more information, see the section "PCI Configuration."

29. **B, C.** SCSI host adapters are typically available for use with ISA, EISA, and PCI bus interfaces. For more information, see the section "SCSI Connections."

30. **C.** Various types of keyboard connectors have been used in different types of systems. The most common connectors used with PC keyboards are 6-pin PS/2 mini DINs, 5-pin DINs, and

APPLY YOUR KNOWLEDGE

RJ-11 jacks. PC-XT- and AT-compatible systems have historically used the 5-pin DIN connector, whereas the 6-pin mini DIN is used with ATX systems. For more information, see the section "System Board Compatibility."

Challenge Solutions

1. You must advise the customer to completely upgrade their systems. The cases and power supplies are AT-style devices, and new system boards will not physically fit into these cases. Also, the newer ATX system will support 9-pin serial mice, but it is really set up for PS/2 mini-DIN mice. Finally, even the keyboards are physically incompatible (5-pin DIN) with the ATX system boards that you would need to install to upgrade the systems. For more information, see the section "System Board Form Factors."

2. The system board is an AT-style board which will require an AT-style case, keyboard, and power supply. It will also need an old ISA or PCI card for video. (There are no AGP slots on this example.) The system's memory slots will need to be filled with SIMM devices; the slots are too small for DIMMs. For more information, see the section "System Board Form Factors."

Suggested Readings and Resources

1. Tom's Motherboard Guide
   http://www.tomshardware.com/mainboard/index.html

2. ATX Motherboard Specification
   www.intel.com/design/motherbd/atx.htm

3. VIA Chipsets
   http://www.viatech.com/en/Products/prodindex.jsp

4. Intel Chipsets
   http://developer.intel.com/design/chipsets/linecard.htm

5. USB Specification
   www.usb.org/developers/docs.html

6. ISA Bus
   http://www.oreilly.com/reference/dictionary/terms/I/Industry_Standard_Architecture.htm

7. PCI Bus
   www.intel.com/design/chipsets/applnots/273011.htm

8. VESA Bus
   www.vesa.org

9. AGP Specification
   http://www.tomshardware.com/graphic/97q3/970805/index.html

This chapter helps you to prepare for the Core Hardware module of the A+ Certification examination by covering the following objectives within the "Domain 4.0: Motherboard/Processors/Memory" section.

4.4 Identify the purpose of CMOS (Complementary Metal-Oxide Semiconductor), what it contains, and how to change its basic parameters.

Example Basic CMOS Settings:

- **Printer parallel port—uni-, bi-directional, disable/enable, ECP, EPP**

- **COM/serial port—memory address, interrupt request, disable**

- **Floppy drive—enable/disable drive or boot, speed, density**

- **Hard drive—size and drive type**

- **Memory—parity, non-parity**

- **Boot sequence**

- **Date/Time**

- **Passwords**

- **Plug-and-Play BIOS**

▶ The configuration of every PC-compatible system is controlled by settings established in its CMOS Setup utility. Therefore, every technician should be aware of the contents of typical CMOS utilities and be able to properly manipulate the parameters they contain to achieve a fully functional unit and to optimize its performance.

CHAPTER 15

CMOS RAM

STUDY STRATEGIES

To prepare for the motherboard, processors, and memory objective of the Core Hardware exam,

▶ Read the objectives at the beginning of this chapter.

▶ Study the information in this chapter.

▶ Review the objectives listed earlier in this chapter.

▶ Perform any step-by-step procedures in the text.

▶ Answer the review questions at the end of the chapter and check your results.

▶ Use the PrepLogic test engine on the CD-ROM that accompanies this book for additional review and exam questions concerning this material.

▶ Review the exam tips scattered throughout the chapter and make certain that you are comfortable with each point.

INTRODUCTION

All modern PC-compatible systems rely on a structure called the CMOS RAM to store configuration information for the system's hardware and its peripherals. Some of the parameters stored in the CMOS are generated automatically, while other parameters can be established by the user.

As a technician, you should be aware of items in the CMOS RAM that can be configured or enabled to make the basic system work with its peripherals. This chapter deals with these items in a generic way, using a sample of a real CMOS utility to demonstrate common configurable items.

After completing this chapter, you should be able to describe the purpose of CMOS RAM, discuss what types of information a typical CMOS utility contains, and explain how to change its basic parameters.

CMOS SETUP UTILITIES

The CMOS Setup utility can be accessed during the POST process by pressing a designated key. The CMOS Setup utility's Main Menu screen, similar to the one depicted in Figure 15.1, appears whenever the CMOS Setup utility is engaged. This menu enables the user to select different configuration functions and exit choices. The most used entries include the Standard CMOS Setup, BIOS Features Setup, and Chipset Features Setup options. Selecting these or any of the other Main Menu options will lead you into the corresponding sub-menu.

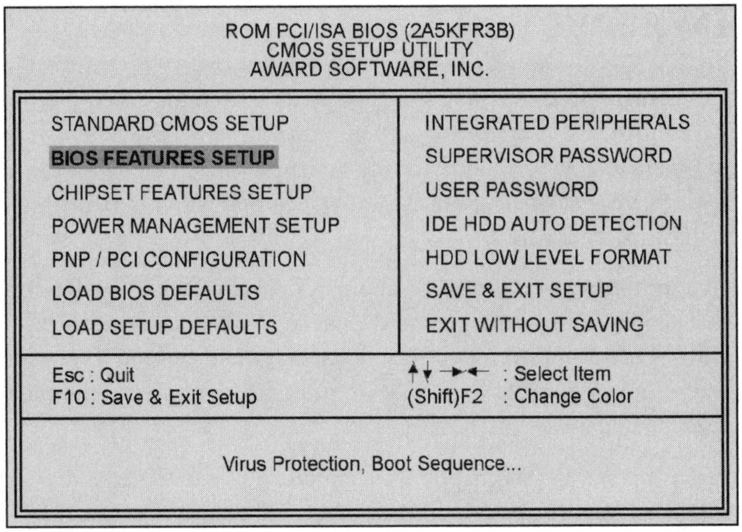

FIGURE 15.1

CMOS main menu screen.

```
             ROM PCI/ISA BIOS (2A5KFR3B)
                 CMOS SETUP UTILITY
                 AWARD SOFTWARE, INC.

  ┌─────────────────────────────┬──────────────────────────────┐
  │ STANDARD CMOS SETUP         │ INTEGRATED PERIPHERALS        │
  │ BIOS FEATURES SETUP         │ SUPERVISOR PASSWORD           │
  │ CHIPSET FEATURES SETUP      │ USER PASSWORD                 │
  │ POWER MANAGEMENT SETUP      │ IDE HDD AUTO DETECTION        │
  │ PNP / PCI CONFIGURATION     │ HDD LOW LEVEL FORMAT          │
  │ LOAD BIOS DEFAULTS          │ SAVE & EXIT SETUP             │
  │ LOAD SETUP DEFAULTS         │ EXIT WITHOUT SAVING           │
  ├─────────────────────────────┴──────────────────────────────┤
  │ Esc : Quit                        ↑↓ →←   : Select Item      │
  │ F10 : Save & Exit Setup          (Shift)F2  : Change Color   │
  ├─────────────────────────────────────────────────────────────┤
  │              Virus Protection, Boot Sequence...             │
  └─────────────────────────────────────────────────────────────┘
```

> **WARNING**
>
> **Set Values with Caution**   The settings in these menus permit the system to be configured and optimized for specific functions and devices. The default values are generally recommended for normal operation. Because incorrect Setup values can cause the system to fail, you should only change Setup values that really need to be changed. If changes are made that disable the system, pressing the Insert key on reset will override the settings and start the system with default values.

Other menu items typically include Power Management, PnP/PCI Configuration, Integrated Peripherals Control, and Password Maintenance Services. The CMOS Setup utility of a particular BIOS might contain these same options, options that perform the same functions under a different name, or it might not contain some of these options at all.

Standard CMOS Setup Functions

The standard CMOS Setup screens from various BIOS manufacturers all provide the same basic information. They can be used to set the system clock/calendar, establish disk drive parameters and video display type, and specify which types of errors will halt the system during the POST.

Time and Date

PC chipsets include a *Real-Time Clock* (*RTC*) function that keeps track of time and date information for the system. During the startup process, the operating system acquires the time and date information from the CMOS RTC module. This information is updated in the system once every second. The CMOS uses military time settings (that is, 13:00:00 = 1 p.m.). The PgUp and PgDn keys are used to change the setting after it has been selected using the arrow keys. Most BIOS versions support daylight savings time by adding an hour when daylight saving time begins and subtracting it when standard time returns.

Older system boards included a rechargeable, Ni-CAD battery to maintain the system's configuration information when it was turned off. In newer systems, there are no rechargeable Ni-CAD batteries for the CMOS storage. Instead, the CMOS storage area and RTC functions have been integrated with a 10-year non-replaceable lithium cell in an independent RTC IC module. Figure 15.2 shows different types of batteries found on different types of system boards. The first is a barrel style battery used on older system boards. The second is a disc battery used on newer system boards that do not integrate the battery and RTC modules into a single unit.

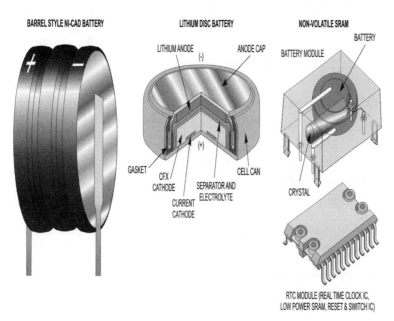

BARREL STYLE NI-CAD BATTERY

LITHIUM DISC BATTERY

LITHIUM ANODE (-)   ANODE CAP

GASKET   CFX CATHODE   SEPARATOR AND ELECTROLYTE   CELL CAN

(+)

CURRENT CATHODE

NON-VOLATILE SRAM

BATTERY

BATTERY MODULE

CRYSTAL

RTC MODULE (REAL TIME CLOCK IC, LOW POWER SRAM, RESET & SWITCH IC)

FIGURE 15.2
CMOS battery backup devices.

The final component is a non-volatile random access memory (*NVRAM* or *NOVRAM*) device that combines the battery and the RTC module into a single package. In the case of the barrel and disc batteries, it might be necessary to clean the battery terminals to remove oxide buildups if CMOS problems are encountered. The NOVRAM device can be removed and replaced. On some boards, this device is mounted in sockets for easy replacement. On other system boards, the RTC module can be soldered to the board.

If the power source or the backup battery becomes defective, the system's capability to keep proper time and date information will be impaired. On AT-style system boards, the backup battery was completely responsible for maintaining the information in the RTC. However, with ATX systems, there is a 5Vdc level present on the system board even when the system is turned off. On these boards, the power supply and the battery in the RTC module work together to keep the time and date information correct.

If the time is incorrect on a PC system, the easiest way to reset it is through the operating system. However, if the system continually fails to keep good time, you should start by checking that corrosion has not built up on the battery contacts. Clean the contacts with a pencil eraser and retry the battery. If that doesn't work, try replacing the battery. Next you should try replacing the RTC module. If this does not correct the time-keeping problem, the electronic circuitry that recharges the battery might be defective, and in this case you will need a new motherboard.

Disk Drives

Current BIOS versions typically support 360KB, 720KB, 1.2MB, 1.44MB, and 2.88MB floppy drive formats. The other area in this screen that might require some effort to set up is the HDD Parameters section. All BIOS versions come with a list of hard drive types that they can support directly. However, they also provide a position for user-definable drive settings. Historically, this has been referred to as the "Type 47" entry, but this entry can be located at any number in the list.

Newer BIOS versions possess *Auto Detect options* that automatically detect the type of hard drives installed in the system and load their parameters into the CMOS. Systems with Enhanced IDE capabilities support up to four IDE drives. In older BIOS versions, the CMOS did not typically display information about CD-ROM drives or SCSI devices. However, newer versions show both types of devices when running in Auto Detect mode.

When the Auto Detect option is chosen, the BIOS attempts to detect IDE devices in the system during the POST process. It will also attempt to determine the specifications and the optimum operating modes for those devices. The drive specifications can also be selected from a built-in list of drive parameters, or they can be entered directly using the User option at the end of the list.

EXAM TIP

Be aware of where to go to reset the system clock and what to check if the clock fails to keep proper time.

EXAM TIP

Know that you might be able to restore the CMOS configuration and clock functions by cleaning battery terminals on some system boards.

Four translation modes can be selected for each drive type: Auto, Normal, Large, and LBA. In *Auto mode*, the BIOS will attempt to determine the best operating mode for the drive. In *Normal mode*, the BIOS will support a maximum Cyl/Hds/Sec setting of 1024/16/63. For larger drives (above 1,024 cylinders or 528MB), the *Large* and *LBA modes* are used. The Large option can be used with large drives that do not support logical block addressing (LBA) techniques. For those drives that do, the LBA mode should be selected. In this mode, the IDE controller converts the sector/head/cylinder address into a physical block address that improves data throughput. Care must be taken when changing the translation mode setting in CMOS because all data on the drive can be lost in the process.

EXAM TIP

Know that the LBA mode for SCSI and IDE disk drives must be enabled in the CMOS to support hard drive sizes larger than 528MB.

EXAM TIP

Be aware that changing the translation mode setting for an existing drive might result in the loss of all data on the drive.

The BIOS Features Setup Screen

The BIOS Features Setup screen, depicted in Figure 15.3, provides access to options that extend the standard ISA BIOS functions. Many BIOS include a built-in Virus Warning utility that produces a warning message whenever a program tries to write to the boot sector of an HDD partition table. If a warning message is displayed under normal circumstances, a full-feature antivirus utility should be run on the system.

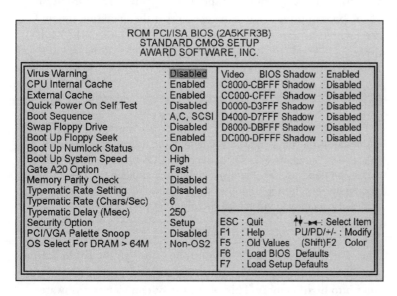

FIGURE 15.3
The BIOS Features Setup screen.

EXAM TIP

You should know that BIOS Virus Detection functions should be disabled when performing an operating system upgrade.

This function should be enabled for normal operations. However, it should be turned off when conducting an upgrade to the operating system. The built-in virus warning utility will check the drive's boot sector for changes. The changes that the new operating system will attempt to make to the boot sector will be interpreted as a virus, and the utility will act to prevent the upgrade from occurring.

Other boot-up options include Drive Seek Sequence, Numlock Status, and System Speed settings. The Feature Setup screen is used to configure different boot-up options. These options include establishing the system's boot-up sequence. The sequence can be set so that the system checks the floppy drive for a boot sector first or so that it checks the hard drive without checking the floppy drive.

The Drive A: option in the Drive Seek Sequence setting should be enabled if the system cannot boot to the hard disk drive and you have a clean boot or emergency repair floppy. Conversely, if you disable the A: seek function (by not selecting it as part of the boot seek sequence), you would not be able to use the A: drive to troubleshoot hard drive problems. The system would never access the floppy drive to see if it had a bootable disk in it. However, you can always enter the CMOS Setup utility and include it as part of the troubleshooting process.

EXAM TIP

Know the possible disk seek configuration possibilities and be aware of how they might affect the system in different circumstances.

This same logic comes into play for the CD-ROM drive on newer systems. In these systems, you should enable the CD-ROM as one of the boot options in the sequence so that the operating system CD can be used to start the system when it will not boot to the hard drive.

CHALLENGE #1

A friend gives you a copy of a simple game he has developed on a CD-ROM. The game is a self-booting MS-DOS based program, so it must be used to start the system. When you place the disc in the computer and turn it on, the system boots directly to the hard drive. How can you get the game to run on your system?

The system's *Shadow* feature is controlled through the BIOS Features screen. Shadowing can be used to copy various system firmware routines into high memory. This allows the system to read firmware from a 16-bit or 32-bit data bus rather than the normal 8-bit PC-compatible X-bus. In older systems, this feature was used to speed up firmware read operations. However, it also reduced the high memory space available for loading device drivers. Shadowing should only be enabled for individual sections of memory as needed.

Chipset Features Setup Functions

The Chipset Features screen contains advanced setting information that system designers and service personnel use to optimize the chipset. This information includes such items as wait-state timing for asynchronous SRAM read and writes, as well as EDO and Page-Mode RAM reads. Figure 15.4 shows a typical Chipset Features Setup screen.

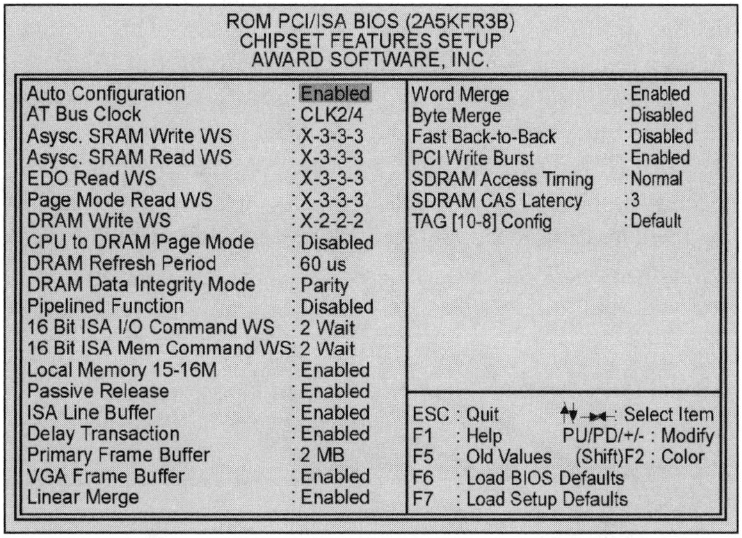

FIGURE 15.4
Chipset Features Setup screen.

```
                ROM PCI/ISA BIOS (2A5KFR3B)
                    CHIPSET FEATURES SETUP
                     AWARD SOFTWARE, INC.

 Auto Configuration      : Enabled    Word Merge          : Enabled
 AT Bus Clock            : CLK2/4     Byte Merge          : Disabled
 Asysc. SRAM Write WS    : X-3-3-3    Fast Back-to-Back   : Disabled
 Asysc. SRAM Read WS     : X-3-3-3    PCI Write Burst     : Enabled
 EDO Read WS             : X-3-3-3    SDRAM Access Timing : Normal
 Page Mode Read WS       : X-3-3-3    SDRAM CAS Latency   : 3
 DRAM Write WS           : X-2-2-2    TAG [10-8] Config   : Default
 CPU to DRAM Page Mode   : Disabled
 DRAM Refresh Period     : 60 us
 DRAM Data Integrity Mode: Parity
 Pipelined Function      : Disabled
 16 Bit ISA I/O Command WS : 2 Wait
 16 Bit ISA Mem Command WS: 2 Wait
 Local Memory 15-16M     : Enabled
 Passive Release         : Enabled
 ISA Line Buffer         : Enabled   ESC : Quit       ↑↓→←: Select Item
 Delay Transaction       : Enabled   F1  : Help       PU/PD/+/- : Modify
 Primary Frame Buffer    : 2 MB      F5  : Old Values   (Shift)F2 : Color
 VGA Frame Buffer        : Enabled   F6  : Load BIOS Defaults
 Linear Merge            : Enabled   F7  : Load Setup Defaults
```

The DRAM Refresh period and Data Integrity functions are also established here. This particular chipset features both *parity-error checking* and *error checking and correcting* (*ECC*) error-handling modes.

PnP/PCI Configuration Functions

In most newer PCs, the BIOS, peripheral devices and operating system employ *Plug and Play (PnP) technology* that enables the system to automatically determine what hardware devices are actually installed in the system and then to allocate system resources to those devices as required to configure and manage them. This removes some of the responsibility for system configuration from the user or the technician. All three of the system components listed must be PnP-compliant before automatic configuration can be carried out.

EXAM TIP

Know which portion of the BIOS is responsible for implementing the PnP process.

Basically, the PnP device communicates with the BIOS during the initialization phase of the startup to tell the system what type of device it is, where it is located in the system, and what its resource needs are. This information is actually stored on the device in the form of firmware. The BIOS stores the PnP information it collects from the devices in a special section of the CMOS RAM, known as the *Extended System Configuration Data (ESCD)* area. This information is stored in the same manner as standard BIOS settings are stored. The BIOS and operating system both access the ESCD area each time the system is restarted to see if any information has changed. This enables the BIOS and operating system to work together in sorting out the needs of the installed devices and assigning them needed system resources. Figure 15.5 illustrates the basic PnP process.

FIGURE 15.5
Plug-and-Play operations.

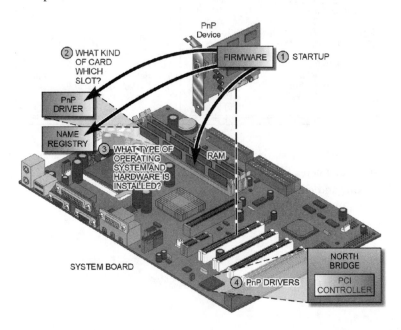

If no changes have occurred in the contents of the ESCD since the last startup occurred, the BIOS will detect this and skip that portion of the boot process. When a PnP operating system checks the ESCD to see if any hardware changes have occurred, it will react according-ly and record any changes it finds in the hardware portion of its Registry. On some occasions, the system's PnP logic might not be able to resolve all of its resource needs and a configuration error will occur. In these cases, the technician or the user will have to manual-ly resolve the configuration problem. The BIOS and operating sys-tem typically provide interfaces to the hardware configuration infor-mation so that users can manually override the system's Plug-and-Play resource assignments. The BIOS holds information about the system's resource allocations and supplies it to the operating system as required. This information can be displayed through the CMOS PnP/PCI Configuration Functions screen, as depicted in Figure 15.6. The operating system must be PnP-compatible to achieve the full benefits of the PnP BIOS. In most newer PCs, the standard operating system is Windows 9x or Windows 2000, which are both PnP compliant.

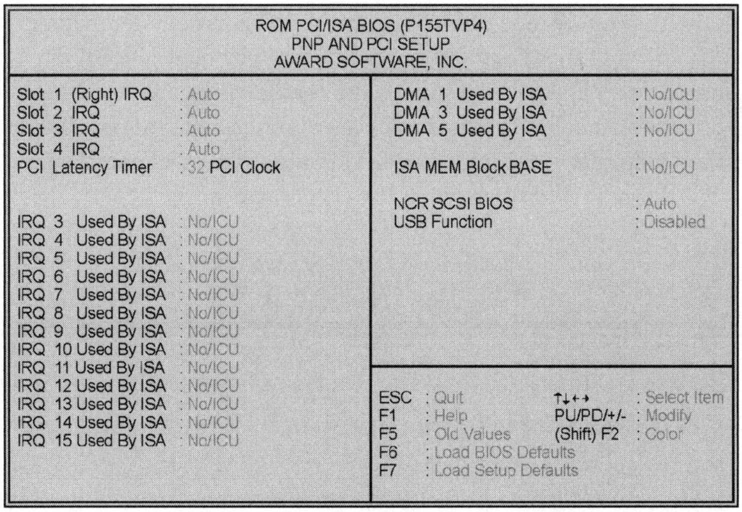

FIGURE 15.6
PnP/PCI Configuration Functions screen.

This CMOS utility can automatically configure all PnP devices if the Auto mode is enabled. Under this condition, the system's IRQ and DMA assignment fields disappear as the BIOS assigns them to the installed devices. When the configuration process is performed man-ually, each resource can be assigned as either a legacy device or a PnP/PCI device. The legacy device is one that is compatible with the original ISA slot and requires specific resource settings. The PnP/PCI device must be compliant with the PnP specification.

CHALLENGE #2

Your local area network connection to the Internet crashes often and tends to be down for some time. For these occasions, you want to establish a dial-up connection to the Internet from your office computer. Your boss does not want to buy a new PnP modem for your use. However, you have an old internal ISA modem in your desk drawer and want to install it in your system to perform this function through your office phone connection. What do you have to do to make this modem work in your plug-and-play system?

Integrated Peripherals Setup Functions

Most Pentium-based systems integrate the standard AT-compatible I/O functions into the system board. In these systems, the BIOS Integrated Peripherals screen provides configuration and enabling settings for the system board's IDE drive connections, floppy disk drive controller, onboard UARTs, and onboard parallel port. Figure 15.7 shows a typical Integrated Peripherals screen.

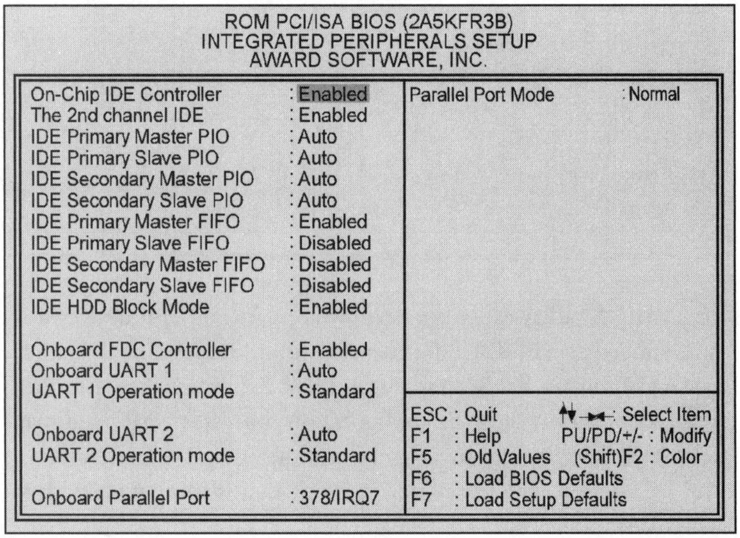

FIGURE 15.7
Integrated Peripherals screen.

```
ROM PCI/ISA BIOS (2A5KFR3B)
INTEGRATED PERIPHERALS SETUP
AWARD SOFTWARE, INC.

On-Chip IDE Controller      : Enabled    Parallel Port Mode        : Normal
The 2nd channel IDE         : Enabled
IDE Primary Master PIO      : Auto
IDE Primary Slave PIO       : Auto
IDE Secondary Master PIO    : Auto
IDE Secondary Slave PIO     : Auto
IDE Primary Master FIFO     : Enabled
IDE Primary Slave FIFO      : Disabled
IDE Secondary Master FIFO   : Disabled
IDE Secondary Slave FIFO    : Disabled
IDE HDD Block Mode          : Enabled

Onboard FDC Controller      : Enabled
Onboard UART 1              : Auto
UART 1 Operation mode       : Standard
                                         ESC : Quit       ↑↓←→: Select Item
Onboard UART 2              : Auto       F1  : Help        PU/PD/+/- : Modify
UART 2 Operation mode       : Standard   F5  : Old Values  (Shift)F2 : Color
                                         F6  : Load BIOS Defaults
Onboard Parallel Port       : 378/IRQ7   F7  : Load Setup Defaults
```

IDE Functions

The Integrated Peripherals screen is used to enable the onboard IDE controller. Each IDE device can also be enabled for Programmed Input/Output (PIO) modes. The PIO field enables the user to select any of four PIO modes (0–4) for each device. The PIO mode determines how fast data will be transferred between the drive and the system. The performance level of the device typically increases with each higher mode value.

The IDE HDD Block Mode selection should be set to Enabled for most new hard drives. This setting, also referred to as Large Block Transfer, Multiple Command, and Multiple-Sector Read/Write mode, supports LBA disk-drive operations so that partitions larger than 528MB can be used on the drive.

Implementing Ports

The other onboard I/O functions supported through the CMOS utility include enabling the FDD controller, selecting the logical COM port addressing and operating modes for the system's two built-in UARTs, and selecting logical addressing and operating modes for the parallel port.

The UARTs can be configured to support half-duplex or full-duplex transmission modes through an infrared port, provided the system board is equipped with one. This enables wireless communications with serial peripheral devices over short distances.

The parallel printer port can be configured for normal PC-AT compatible *standard parallel port* (*SPP*) operation, for extended bi-directional operation (*extended parallel port*, or *EPP*), for fast, buffered bi-directional operation (*extended capabilities port*, or *ECP*), or for combined ECP+EPP operation. The normal CMOS setting should be selected unless both the port hardware and driver software support EPP or ECP operation.

> **EXAM TIP**
>
> Remember that ECP and EPP modes for the parallel port must be enabled through the CMOS Setup utility.

Enhanced Parallel Port Operations

When EPP mode is selected in the port's configuration register, the standard and bi-directional modes are enabled. The functions of the port's pins are redefined under the EPP specification. When the EPP mode is enabled, the port can operate either as a standard, bi-directional SPP parallel port, or as a bi-directional EPP port. The software controlling the port will specify which type of operation is required.

The ECP mode provides a number of advantages over the SPP and EPP modes. In particular, it offers higher performance than either of the other modes. As with the EPP mode, the pins of the interface are redefined when ECP mode is selected in the system's CMOS. The ECP port is compatible with the standard LPT port and is used in the same manner when no ECP operations are called for. However, it also supports high-throughput DMA operations for both forward and reverse direction transfers.

Because both of the advanced parallel port modes operate in a bi-directional half duplex manner, they do require an IEEE-1284 compliant cable. Standard parallel cables designed for older SPP operations might not support these qualities.

> **EXAM TIP**
>
> Remember that the ECP specification employs DMA operations to provide the highest data throughput for a parallel port.

> **EXAM TIP**
>
> Be aware that a standard parallel printer cable should not be used with the bi-directional EPP or ECP devices.

> **NOTE**
>
> **Reference Shelf**   For more information, refer to the Electronic Reference Shelf, "The Parallel Port," located on the CD that accompanies this book.

CHALLENGE #3

A customer brings in a computer that has a laser printer and a scanner connected to the parallel port. The scanner is connected directly to the computer's parallel port, and the printer is connected to the scanner. The customer cannot get the scanner to work, but the printer operates correctly. What two actions should you perform to determine why the scanner does not work correctly?

Power-Management Functions

The *Power Management* fields enable the user to select from three power-saving modes: *Doze, Standby*, and *Suspend*. These are Green PC-compatible power-saving modes that cause the system to step down from maximum power usage. The Doze setting causes the microprocessor clock to slow down after a defined period of inactivity. The Standby mode causes the hard drive and video to shut down after a period of inactivity. Finally, everything in the system except the microprocessor shuts down in Suspend mode. Certain system events, such as IRQ and DRQ activities, cause the system to wake up from these modes and resume normal operation.

Passwords

The *Password Setting* options, depicted in Figure 15.8, enable the user to enter and modify passwords settings in the CMOS. Password protection can be established for the system so that a valid password must be entered each time the system boots up or when the Setup utility is entered. It can also be set up so that it is only required to access the Setup utility.

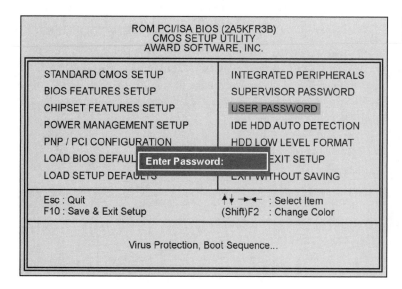

FIGURE 15.8
Password setting options.

Because the CMOS password controls access to all parts of the system, even before the bootup process occurs, there is some danger that the user will forget his password. When this occurs, it will be impossible to gain access to the system without completely resetting the contents of the CMOS RAM. On some system boards, this can be accomplished by shorting a special pair of jumpers on the board. With other systems, you will need to remove or short across the backup battery to reset the CMOS information. In ATX systems, it will also be necessary to unplug the power from the commercial outlet to reduce the voltage to the CMOS registers. When the contents of the CMOS are reset, you must manually restore any nondefault CMOS settings being used by the system.

EXAM TIP

Be aware of the affects of forgetting a CMOS password and know what steps must be taken to restore the system in this event.

NOTE

Hands-On Activity   For hands-on experience with this concept, refer to Lab Procedure #3, "CMOS Passwords and Resources," located on the CD that accompanies this book.

CHAPTER SUMMARY

KEY TERMS

- Auto mode

- Auto-Detect options

- Doze

- Error checking and correcting (ECC)

- Extended capabilities port (ECP)

- Extended parallel port (EPP)

- Extended System Configuration Data (ESCD)

- Large mode

- LBA mode

- NVRAM

- Parity-error checking

- Password Setting

- Plug and Play (PnP) technology

- Power Management

- Real-Time Clock (RTC)

- Shadow

- Standard parallel port (SPP)

- Standby

- Suspend

This chapter has explored CMOS Setup utilities in detail. It accomplished this by describing key elements from the CMOS screens of a particular computer system. Although the organization of the CMOS utility varies from model to model and chipset to chipset, the sample CMOS utility presented in this chapter was used to cover the major points of interest from a technician's perspective.

At this point, review the objectives listed at the beginning of the chapter to be certain that you understand each point and can perform each task listed there. Afterward, answer the review questions that follow to verify your knowledge of the information.

APPLY YOUR KNOWLEDGE

Review Questions

1. What should you do first if the system clock fails to keep proper time after being reset by the operating system?

   A. Reload the operating system.

   B. Replace the battery.

   C. Clean the battery contacts.

   D. Replace the motherboard.

2. What must be enabled in the CMOS to support hard drive sizes larger than 528MB, and to allow the IDE controller to convert the sector/head/cylinder addresses into a physical block address that improves data throughput?

   A. Auto

   B. LBA

   C. Normal

   D. Large

3. What might happen when you change the translation mode setting for an existing IDE drive?

   A. Loss of all data on the drive

   B. Access limited to the first 528MB of the drive

   C. Slower drive access times

   D. Deletion of the MBR

4. Which functions should be disabled when performing an operating system upgrade?

   A. EPP and ECP

   B. PnP resource allocation

   C. BIOS Virus detection functions

   D. RAM memory checks

5. When your computer boots up, you want it to search for a boot sector on a floppy, a CD-ROM drive, and then the hard disk drive. What boot sequence should you set in CMOS?

   A. A, C, SCSI

   B. A, C, CD-ROM

   C. CD-ROM, A, C

   D. A, CD-ROM, C

6. During which portion of the startup process does the BIOS communicate with the system's PnP devices?

   A. During the POST

   B. During the initialization phase

   C. During the OS bootstrap operation

   D. During the CMOS configuration process

7. Which utility must be used to enable the ECP and EPP modes for the parallel port?

   A. DMA

   B. CMOS

   C. FDISK

   D. BIOS

8. Which specification employs DMA operations to provide the highest data throughput for a parallel port?

   A. PPP

   B. SPP

   C. EPP

   D. ECP

APPLY YOUR KNOWLEDGE

9. What type of devices can be used with a half-duplex/bi-directional parallel printer cable? (Select all that apply.)

    A. USB devices

    B. SPP devices

    C. EPP devices

    D. ECP devices

10. What are the effects of forgetting a CMOS password?

    A. Cannot start the computer

    B. Cannot boot to the operating system

    C. Cannot log in to the computer

    D. Cannot shut down the computer

11. What action must be taken to restore the system if the CMOS password is forgotten in an ATX system?

    A. Change the Password Enable setting in CMOS.

    B. Remove the battery.

    C. Short the CMOS-enabling jumper and remove the battery.

    D. Unplug the computer from the wall and remove the battery.

12. Where is the PnP information stored in the BIOS?

    A. The RTC module

    B. The ESCD area

    C. The PnP Registry

    D. The Device Manager

13. The system's time and date information can be found in the _____.

    A. RAM

    B. ROM

    C. CMOS

    D. ROM BIOS

14. The system's time and date information is stored in the _____.

    A. System RAM

    B. ROM BIOS

    C. Real-Time Clock Registers

    D. CMOS Setup

15. What is the major difference between EPP and ECP operation of the parallel port?

    A. DMA mode

    B. Bi-directional

    C. 16-bit

    D. Serial

16. What type of communication is possible with an IEEE-1284 parallel cable?

    A. Bi-directional, half-duplex

    B. Bi-directional, full-duplex

    C. Simplex

    D. Selectable half or full-duplex

APPLY YOUR KNOWLEDGE

17. Which parallel port type has the highest throughput?

    A. ECP

    B. EPP

    C. XPP

    D. SPP

18. If you place a bootable floppy in drive A: and the system boots to drive C:, what action should you take to correct this?

    A. Reconfigure the drive seek sequence in the operating system control panel.

    B. Reconfigure the drive seek sequence in the CMOS setup utility.

    C. Disconnect the IDE cable to the drive to force the system to boot off of the floppy drive.

    D. Reconfigure the floppy jumpers to make it a bootable drive.

Answers and Explanations

1. **C.** If the time is incorrect on a PC system, the easiest way to reset it is through the operating system. However, if the system continually fails to keep good time, you should start by checking that corrosion has not built up on the battery contacts. Clean the contacts with a pencil eraser and retry the battery. If that doesn't work, try replacing the battery. Next you can try replacing the RTC module. If this does not correct the time keeping problem, the electronic circuitry that recharges the battery might be defective, and in this case you will need a new motherboard. For more information, see the section "Time and Date."

2. **B.** Four translation modes can be selected for each drive type: Auto, Normal, Large, and LBA. For larger drives (above 1,024 cylinders or 528MB), the Large and LBA modes are used. The Large option can be used with large drives that do not support logical block addressing (LBA) techniques. For those drives that do, the LBA mode should be selected. In this mode, the IDE controller converts the sector/head/cylinder address into a physical block address that improves data throughput. For more information, see the section "Disk Drives."

3. **A.** Care must be taken when changing the disk drive translation mode setting in CMOS because all data on the drive can be lost in the process. For more information, see the section "Disk Drives."

4. **C.** BIOS antivirus functions should be turned off when conducting an upgrade to the operating system. The built-in virus warning utility will check the drive's boot sector for changes. The changes that the new operating system will attempt to make to the boot sector will be interpreted as a virus, and the utility will act to prevent the upgrade from occurring. For more information, see the section "The BIOS Features Setup Screen."

5. **D.** The Feature Setup screen is used to configure different boot-up options. These options include establishing the system's boot-up sequence. The sequence can be set so that the system checks the floppy drive (A:) for a boot sector first or so that it checks the hard drive (C:) without checking the floppy drive. Other boot options include CD-ROM drives or a SCSI drive. For more information, see the section "The BIOS Features Setup Screen."

6. **B.** The PnP device communicates with the BIOS during the initialization phase of the startup to tell the system what type of device it is, where it is located in the system, and what its resource needs are. For more information, see the section "PnP/PCI Configuration Functions."

7. **B.** One of the onboard I/O functions supported through the CMOS utility includes selecting the operating modes for the parallel port. The parallel printer port can be configured for normal PC-AT compatible standard parallel port (SPP) operation, for extended bi-directional operation (extended parallel port, or EPP), for fast, buffered bi-directional operation (extended capabilities port, or ECP), or for combined ECP+EPP operation. The normal setting should be selected unless both the port hardware and driver software support EPP or ECP operation. For more information, see the section "Implementing Ports."

8. **D.** The ECP mode provides a number of advantages over the SPP and EPP modes. The ECP mode offers higher performance than either of the other modes. As with the EPP mode, the pins of the interface are redefined when ECP mode is selected in the system's CMOS. The ECP port is compatible with the standard LPT port and is used in the same manner when no ECP operations are called for. However, it also supports high-throughput DMA operations for both forward and reverse direction transfers. For more information, see the section "Enhanced Parallel Port Operations."

9. **C, D.** Because both of the advanced parallel port modes (that is, EPP and ECP) operate in a bi-directional half-duplex manner, they require an IEEE-1284 compliant cable. Standard parallel cables designed for older SPP operations might not support these qualities. For more information, see the section "Implementing Ports."

10. **B.** Because the CMOS password controls access to all parts of the system, even before the boot-up process occurs, there is some danger that the user will forget his password. When this occurs, it will be impossible to gain access to the system without completely resetting the contents of the CMOS RAM. For more information, see the section "Passwords."

11. **D.** On some system boards, resetting the contents of the CMOS can be accomplished by shorting a special pair of jumpers on the board. With other systems, you will need to remove or short across the backup battery to reset the CMOS information. In ATX systems, it will also be necessary to unplug the power from the commercial outlet to reduce the voltage to the CMOS registers. When the contents of the CMOS are reset, you must manually restore any non-default CMOS settings being used by the system. For more information, see the section "Passwords."

12. **B.** The BIOS stores the PnP information it collects from the devices in a special section of the CMOS RAM, known as the Extended System Configuration Data (ESCD) area. This information is stored in the same manner as standard BIOS settings are stored. The BIOS and operating system both access the ESCD area each time the system is restarted to see if any information has changed. This enables the BIOS and operating system to work together in sorting out the needs of the installed devices and assigning them needed system resources. For more information, see the section "PnP/PCI Configuration Functions."

APPLY YOUR KNOWLEDGE

13. **C.** The standard CMOS Setup screens from various BIOS manufacturers all provide the same basic information. For example, they can be used to set the date and time via the system clock/calendar. For more information, see the section "Time and Date."

14. **C.** During the startup process, the operating system acquires the time and date information from the CMOS RTC module. This information is updated in the system once every second. For more information, see the section "Time and Date."

15. **A.** The ECP mode supports high-throughput DMA operations for both forward and reverse direction transfers. For more information, see the section "Enhanced Parallel Port Operations."

16. **A.** Because both of the advanced parallel port modes operate in a bi-directional half-duplex manner, they do require an IEEE-1284 compliant cable. Standard parallel cables designed for older SPP operations might not support these qualities. For more information, see the section "Enhanced Parallel Port Operations."

17. **A.** The ECP mode offers higher performance than either the SPP or EPP modes. For more information, see the section "Enhanced Parallel Port Operations."

18. **B.** The Drive A: option in the Drive Seek Sequence setting should be enabled if the system cannot boot to the hard disk drive and you have a clean boot or emergency repair floppy. If you disable the A: seek function in the CMOS setup utility (by not selecting it as part of the book seek sequence), you would not be able to use the A: drive to troubleshoot hard drive problems. The

system would never access the floppy drive to see if it had a bootable disk in it. However, you can always enter the CMOS Setup utility and include it as part of the troubleshooting process. For more information, see the section "The BIOS Features Setup Screen."

Challenge Solutions

1. You must go into the CMOS Setup utility and make sure that the CD-ROM drive is one of the options selected in the Drive Seek Sequence. For more information, see the section "The BIOS Features Setup Screen."

2. There are actually several things that you should do to make this modem work in your system. The item we are most interested in, at this point, is the configuration information required by the CMOS. Older BIOS versions required that you manually disable the COM2 setting and reserve an IRQ setting for the modem in the PnP/PCI Configuration window. In a system with a PnP-compliant Windows 9x or Windows 2000 operating system, the operating system will detect the presence of some ISA devices and reserve a set of resources for it. However, you are still required to supply an acceptable software driver program for the device. For more information, see the section "PnP/PCI Configuration Functions."

3. If you consider the nature of the two devices, you will realize that the scanner is basically an input device, so its data must move back to the parallel port; whereas the printer is an output device, so information normally travels from the port to the printer. (The scanner is actually a bi-directional

APPLY YOUR KNOWLEDGE

device.) Check the parallel cables to make sure that they are IEEE-1284–compliant. The port must be configured for bi-directional support in the CMOS. Check the CMOS settings to make sure that EPP or ECP modes are selected. For more information, see the section "Enhanced Parallel Port Operations."

Suggested Readings and Resources

1. BIOS Companion
   www.sysopt.com/compex.html#TheBIOS

2. Award BIOS
   www.award.com/

3. Wim's BIOS
   http://www.wimsbios.com/

4. CMOS Help
   http://www.computerhope.com/help/cmos.htm

5. BIOS Setup Glossary
   http://www.abios.com/awdcmos1.html

6. CMOS Guide
   http://pcsupport.about.com/cs/cmos/

7. Intel Flash Memory
   http://developer.intel.com/design/flash/

8. EPP
   www.fapo.com/eppmode.htm

9. ECP
   www.fapo.com/ecpmode.htm

This chapter helps you to prepare for the Core Hardware module of the A+ Certification examination by covering the following objectives within the "Domain 5.0: Printers" section.

5.1 Identify basic concepts, printer operations, and printer components.

Content might include the following:

- **Paper-feeder mechanisms**
- **Types of printers:**
  - **Laser**
  - **Ink-jet**
  - **Dot-matrix**
- **Types of printer connections and configurations:**
  - **Parallel**
  - **Network**
  - **USB**
  - **Infrared**
  - **Serial**

▶ Printers are the second most common output peripheral used with PCs. As this A+ objective indicates, computer technicians must understand how the different types of printers operate, what their typical components are, and what printer components can be serviced in the field.

▶ Printers used with personal computers are available in many types and use various connection schemes. The computer technician must be able to connect a brand-x printer to a brand-y computer and configure them for operation. The connection method between the printer and the computer will affect many of the troubleshooting steps necessary to isolate printing problems. Likewise, connecting a printer to a network will affect how the technician approaches the configuration and troubleshooting.

CHAPTER 16

Basic Printer Concepts

STUDY STRATEGIES

To prepare for the Printers objective of the Core Hardware exam,

▶ Read the objectives at the beginning of this chapter.

▶ Study the information in this chapter.

▶ Review the objectives listed earlier in this chapter.

▶ Perform any step-by-step procedures in the text.

▶ Answer the review questions at the end of the chapter and check your results.

▶ Use the PrepLogic test engine on the CD-ROM that accompanies this book for additional review and exam questions concerning this material.

▶ Review the exam tips scattered throughout the chapter and make certain that you are comfortable with each point.

INTRODUCTION

The second most common type of output device used with personal computers is the character printer. These devices are employed to produce hard copy output of documents and graphics.

This chapter introduces the three types of character printers commonly used with personal computers. These include dot matrix, ink-jet, and laser printers. The chapter describes the basic structures and operation of all three types of printers.

The chapter also examines the different types of connection ports and interfaces used with these printers.

After completing the chapter, you should be able to identify important features associated with each type of printer. You should also be able to describe the basic operation of all three printer types.

PRINTER TYPES

Impact printers place characters on the page by causing a hammer device to strike an inked ribbon. The ribbon, in turn, strikes the printing surface (paper).

Several non-impact methods of printing are used in computer printers. Older, non-impact printers relied on special heat-sensitive or chemically reactive paper to form characters on the page. Newer methods of non-impact printing use ink droplets, squirted from a jet-nozzle device (ink-jet printers), or a combination of laser/xerographic print technologies (laser printers) to place characters on a page. Currently, the most popular non-impact printers use ink-jet or laser technologies to deliver ink to the page.

Basically, there are two methods of creating characters on a page. One method places a character on the page that is fully shaped, and fully filled in. This type of character is called a *fully formed character*. The other method involves placing dots on the page in strategic patterns to fool the eye into seeing a character. This type of character is referred to as a *dot-matrix character*.

FONTS

The term *font* refers to variations in the size and style of characters. With true fully formed characters, there is typically only one font available without changing the physical printing element. With all other printing methods, however, it is possible to include a wide variety of font types and sizes.

There are three common methods of generating character fonts: *bitmapped* (or *raster-scanned fonts*), *vector-based*, and *TrueType outline fonts*.

Bitmapped fonts store dot patterns for all the possible size and style variations of the characters in the set. Font styles refer to the characteristics of the font, such as normal, bold, and italic styles. Font size refers to the physical measurement of the character. Type is measured in increments of 1/72 of an inch. Each increment is referred to as a point. Common text sizes are 10-point and 12-point type.

Vector-based fonts store the outlines of the character styles and sizes as sets of mathematical formulas. Each character is composed of a set of reference points and connecting lines between them. These types of fonts can be scaled up and down to achieve various sizes.

The vector-based approach requires much less storage space to store a character set and all of its variations than would be necessary for an equivalent bitmapped character set. In addition, vector-based fonts can be scaled and rotated; bitmapped fonts typically cannot be scaled and rotated. Conversely, bitmapped characters can be printed out directly and quickly, but vector-based characters must be generated when called for.

TrueType fonts are a newer type of outline fonts commonly used with Microsoft Windows. These fonts are stored as a set of points and outlines used to generate a set of bitmaps. Special algorithms adjust the bitmaps so that they look best at the specified resolution. After the bitmaps have been created, Windows stores them in a RAM cache that it creates. In this manner, the font is only generated once when it is first selected. Afterward, the fonts are just called out of memory, thus speeding up the process of delivering them to the printer. Each TrueType character set requires an FOT and a TTF file to create all of its sizes and resolutions.

EXAM TIP
Be aware of the benefits and drawbacks of bitmapped characters.

EXAM TIP
Know which font types are generated by establishing starting points and then calculating mathematical formulas.

PRINTER MECHANICS

By the very nature of their operation, printers tend to be extremely mechanical peripherals. During the printing operation, the print mechanism must be properly positioned over each character cell in sequence. In most printers used with PCs, the character positioning action involves holding the paper stationary and stepping the printhead carriage across the page. The *printhead carriage* rides on rods that extend across the front of the page.

In addition to positioning the print mechanism for printing, all printer types must feed paper through the print area. The type of *paper handling mechanism* in a printer is somewhat dependent on the type of forms that will be used with the printer and its speed. There are two common methods of moving paper through the printer:

◆ *Friction-feed*—Uses friction to hold the paper against the printer's platen. The paper advances through the printer as the platen turns.

◆ *Pin-feed*—Pulls the paper through the printer by a set of pins that fit into the holes along the edge of the form, as shown in Figure 16.1. The pins can be an integral part of the platen or mounted on a separate, motor-driven tractor.

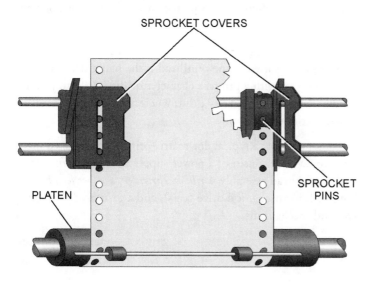

FIGURE 16.1
A tractor/pin-feed mechanism.

EXAM TIP

Know the major purpose of a tractor-feed mechanism and where it is
most commonly used.

Friction feed is normally associated with single-sheet printers. Platen pin-feed and pin tractors are usually employed with continuous and multilayer forms. These mechanisms can control paper slippage and misalignment created by the extra weight imposed by *continuous forms*. Platen pin-feed units can handle only one width of paper; tractors can be adjusted to handle various paper widths. Tractor feeds are used with very heavy forms, such as *multiple-part, continuous forms*, and are most commonly found on dot-matrix printers. Most ink-jet and laser printers use single-sheet feeder systems.

DOT-MATRIX PRINTERS

Dot-matrix characters are not fully formed characters. Instead, dot-matrix characters are printed in the form of dot patterns that represent the characters. The reader's eye fills in the gaps between the dots.

The printhead in a dot-matrix printer is a vertical column of *print wires* controlled by electromagnets. Dots are created on the paper by energizing selected electromagnets, which extend the desired print wires from the *printhead*. In the printhead, the permanent magnet keeps the wires pulled in until electromagnets are energized, causing them to move forward. The print wires impact an *ink ribbon*, which impacts the paper. Remember that the entire character is not printed in a single instant of time—it is printed in steps.

EXAM TIP

Remember the number of print
wires in typical dot-matrix printheads.

A typical printhead can contain 9, 18, or 24 print wires. The number of print wires used in the printhead is the major determining factor associated with a printer's character quality. A 9-pin printhead generally delivers draft quality print, whereas 24-pin printheads approach letter quality print.

The components of a typical dot-matrix printer are depicted in Figure 16.2. They consist of a power-supply board, a *main control board*, a printhead assembly, a *ribbon cartridge*, a *paper feed motor* (along with its mechanical drive gears), and a *printhead positioning motor* and mechanisms.

EXAM TIP

Remember what a main board in a
printer is called.

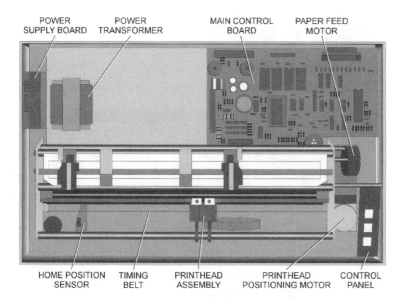

POWER SUPPLY BOARD   POWER TRANSFORMER   MAIN CONTROL BOARD   PAPER FEED MOTOR

HOME POSITION SENSOR   TIMING BELT   PRINTHEAD ASSEMBLY   PRINTHEAD POSITIONING MOTOR   CONTROL PANEL

FIGURE 16.2
Parts of a dot-matrix printer.

The control board contains the logic circuitry required to convert the signals received from the computer's printer port into character patterns. It also generates the control signals to properly position the printhead on the page, fire the correct combination of printhead wires to create the character, and advance the paper as needed. The onboard controller, character generators, and RAM and ROM are found on this control board.

The printer's interface can contain circuitry to handle serial data, parallel data, or a combination of the different interface types—Centronics parallel, RS-232 serial, SCSI, USB or IrDA. At the printer end of a Centronics parallel port, a 36-pin connector, like the one depicted in Figure 16.3, is used. Of course, the computer end of the cable should have a connector that is compatible with the interface being used (that is, a DB-25M connector to plug in to the system's DB-25F LPT port).

EXAM TIP

Be aware of the different types of interface connections commonly used with printers.

EXAM TIP

Remember the types of connectors used at both the computer and the printer ends of a parallel printer cable.

FIGURE 16.3
A parallel connection at the printer.

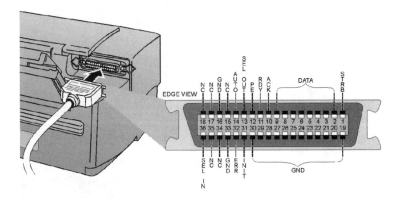

Printhead Mechanisms

The printhead unit is mounted in the printhead carriage assembly. This assembly rides on a bar that passes along the front of the platen. The printhead-positioning motor is responsible for moving the printhead mechanism across the page and stopping it in just the right places to print. The printhead rides back and forth across the printer on a pair of carriage rods. A timing belt runs between the printhead assembly and the printhead-positioning motor and converts the rotation of the motor into linear stepped movement of the printhead assembly across the page.

The paper-feed motor and gear train move the paper through the printer. This can be accomplished by driving the platen assembly. The platen can be used in two different ways to move the paper through the printer. After the paper has been wrapped half way around the platen, a set of rollers is used to pin the paper to the platen as it turns. This is friction-feed paper handling. The platen can have small pins that can drag the paper through the printer as the platen turns. In either case, the paper-feed motor drives the platen to move the paper.

The feed motor's gear train can also be used to drive the extended gear train of a tractor assembly, when it is installed. The gears of the feed motor mesh with those of the tractor, causing it to pull, or push, the paper through the printer.

INK-JET PRINTERS

Ink-jet printers produce characters by squirting a precisely controlled stream of ink drops onto the paper. The drops must be controlled very precisely in terms of their aerodynamics, size, and shape, or the drop placement on the page becomes inexact, and the print quality falters.

The drops are formed by one of two methods:

◆ *Thermal shock*—Heats the ink in a capillary tube, just behind the nozzle. This increases the pressure of the ink in the tube and causes it to explode through the opening.

◆ *Mechanical vibration*—Uses vibrations from a piezoelectric crystal to force ink through a nozzle.

The ink-jet nozzle is designed to provide the proper shape and trajectory for the ink drops so that they can be directed precisely toward the page. The nozzles are also designed so that the surface tension of the ink keeps it from running out of the nozzle uncontrollably.

> **EXAM TIP**
>
> Be able to identify the printer type that produces print by squirting ink at the page. Also, remember the techniques used to form the ink drops.

Ink-Jet Printer Components

Aside from the printing mechanism, the components of a typical ink-jet printer are very similar to those of a dot-matrix printer. Figure 16.4 illustrates these components.

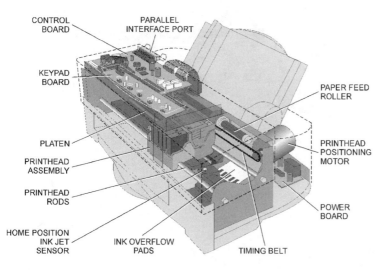

FIGURE 16.4
Ink-jet printer components.

The *ink cartridge* snaps into the printhead assembly, which rides in front of the platen on a rail or rod. The printhead assembly is positioned through a timing belt that runs between it and the positioning motor. A flexible cable carries ink-jet–firing information between the control board and the printhead. This cable folds out of the way as the printhead assembly moves across the printer.

The paper-feed motor turns a gear train that ultimately drives the platen. The paper is friction fed through the printer—between the platen and the pressure rollers. Almost all ink-jet printers used with microcomputer systems are single-sheet, friction-feed systems.

LASER PRINTERS

EXAM TIP
Know the formal name of the laser printer reproduction process.

The laser printer modulates a highly focused laser beam to produce CRT-like raster-scan images on a rotating drum, as depicted in Figure 16.5. This process was developed by Xerox and is referred to as *electrophotographic* reproduction.

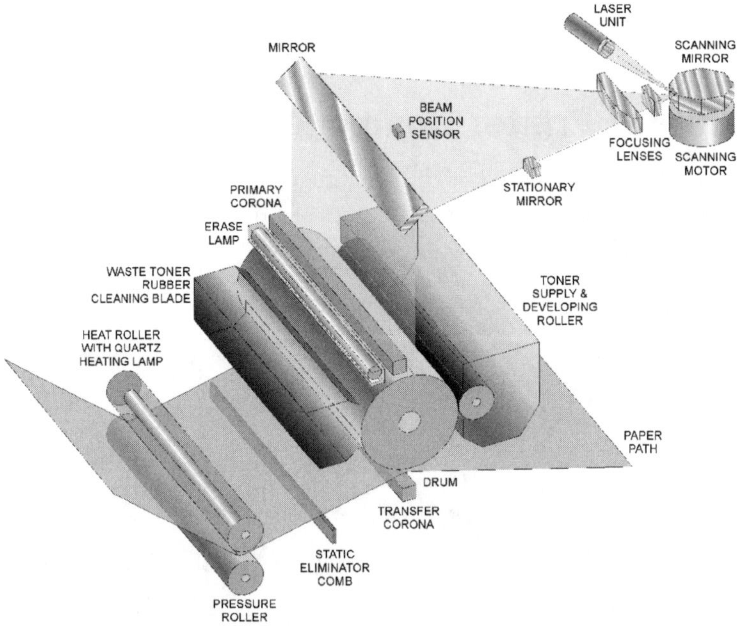

FIGURE 16.5
A typical laser printer.

The drum is coated with a *photosensitive plastic*, which is given a negative electrical charge over its surface. The modulated laser beam creates spots on the rotating drum. The spots written by the laser take on a positive electrical charge. A negatively charged toner material is attracted to the positively charged, written areas of the drum. The paper is fed past the rotating drum, and the toner is transferred to the paper. A pair of compression rollers and a high-temperature lamp work together to fuse the toner to the paper. Thus, the image, written on the drum by the laser, is transferred to the paper.

The laser beam scans the drum so rapidly that it is not practical to do the scanning mechanically. Instead, the beam is bounced off a rotating, polygonal (many-sided) mirror. The faces of the mirror cause the reflected beam to scan across the face of the drum as the mirror revolves. Using the highest dot densities available, these printers produce characters that rival typeset text.

Laser Printing Operations

From manufacturer to manufacturer, and model to model, the exact arrangement and combinations of components can vary in laser printers. However, the order of operations is always the same. The six stages of operation in a laser printer include

1. Cleaning
2. Conditioning
3. Writing
4. Developing
5. Transferring
6. Fusing

When character data is received from the host computer, it is converted into a serial bit stream, which is applied to the scanning laser. The *photosensitive drum* rotates as the pulse encoded laser beam is scanned across it. The laser creates a copy of the image on the photosensitive drum in the form of a relatively positive-charged drawing. This operation is referred to as *registration*.

EXAM TIP

Memorize the operational stages of a typical laser printer.

Before the laser writes on the drum, a set of *erase lamps* shine on the drum to remove any residual traces of the preceding image. This leaves the complete drum with a neutral electrical charge. A high voltage, applied to the *primary corona wire*, creates a highly charged negative field that conditions the drum to be written on by applying a uniform negative charge (-600V) to it.

As the laser writes on the drum, the drum turns through the toner powder, which is attracted to the charged image on the drum. *Toner* is a very fine powder, bonded to iron particles that are attracted to the charges written on the drum. The developer roller in the toner cartridge turns as the drum turns and expels a measured amount of toner past a restricting blade. A regulating AC voltage assists the toner in leaving the cartridge, but also pulls back some excess toner from the drum. Excess toner is recycled within the toner cartridge so that it can be used again.

Great care should be taken when installing a new drum unit in a laser printer. Exposing the drum to light for more than a few minutes can damage it. The drum should never be touched; this, too, can ruin its surface. Keep the unit away from dust and dirt, as well as away from humidity and high-temperature areas.

The *transfer corona wire* (*transfer roller*) is responsible for transferring the toner from the drum to the paper. The toner is transferred to the paper because of the highly positive charge the transfer corona wire applies to the paper. The positive charge attracts the negative toner particles away from the drum and onto the page. A special static-eliminator comb acts to prevent the positively charged paper from sticking to the negatively charged drum.

After the image has been transferred to the paper, a pair of *compression rollers*, in the *fusing unit* (fuser), act to press the toner particles into the paper while they melt them to it. The top roller, known as the *fusing roller*, is heated by a quartz lamp. This roller melts the toner to the paper as it exits the unit; the lower roller, known as the *compression roller*, applies pressure to the paper. A cleaning pad removes excess particles and applies a silicon lubricant to the roller to prevent toner from sticking to the Teflon-coated fusing roller.

A *thermal sensor* in the fusing unit monitors the temperature of the unit. This information is applied to the control circuitry so that it can control the fuser temperature between 140°C and 230°C. If the temperature of the fuser is not controlled correctly, it can cause

EXAM TIP

Know that you should never expose the drum of a laser printer to sunlight or any other strong light source.

EXAM TIP

Know the functions of the two corona wires in a laser printer.

severe damage to the printer and might also present a potential fire hazard.

A *thermal fuse* protects the fuser assembly from overheating and damaging the printer. The thermal fuse should normally snap back after the temperature condition is cleared. If the switch is open under cool conditions, it will need to be replaced.

A typical laser printer has sensors to determine what paper trays are installed, what size paper is in them, and whether the tray is empty. It also uses sensors to track the movement of the paper through each stage of the printer. This enables the controller to know where the page is at all times, and sequence the activities of the solenoids and clutches properly.

> **EXAM TIP**
>
> Remember the purpose of the thermal fuse in laser printers.

Electrophotographic Cartridges

In Hewlett-Packard printers, the main portion of the printing system is contained in the *electrophotographic cartridge*. This cartridge contains the toner supply, the corona wire, the drum assembly, and the developing roller. Figure 16.6 depicts the H-P configuration.

> **EXAM TIP**
>
> Memorize the parts of a typical laser printer cartridge. Also, be aware of what the H-P cartridge is called.

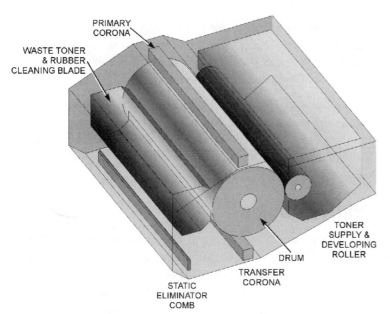

PRIMARY CORONA

WASTE TONER & RUBBER CLEANING BLADE

STATIC ELIMINATOR COMB

TRANSFER CORONA

DRUM

TONER SUPPLY & DEVELOPING ROLLER

FIGURE 16.6
The H-P cartridge configuration.

In other makes of laser printers, the basic components are often combined so that the printer consists of a developer unit, a toner cartridge, a drum unit, a fuser unit, and a cleaning pad. Making the developer unit and toner cartridge separate units means that changing the toner does not involve changing some of the other wear-prone components. Although it is less expensive to change toner, attention must be paid to how much the other units are wearing.

PAPER SPECIFICATIONS

EXAM TIP

Know how paper weight is specified and how many sheets are involved.

One of the biggest problems associated with any printer occurs when the wrong paper type, or paper type setting, is used. The most fundamental specification for paper is *paper weight*. Paper is specified in terms of its weight per 500 sheets at 22x17 inches (that is, 500 sheets of 22x17 inches, 21-pound bond paper will weigh 21 pounds).

PRINTER INSTALLATION

Generally speaking, one of the least difficult I/O devices to add to a microcomputer system is a parallel printer because, from the beginning of the PC era, a parallel printer has been one of the most standard pieces of equipment to add to the system.

Serial printers are slightly more difficult to set up because the communication definition must be configured between the computer and the printer. The serial port will need to be configured for speed, parity type, character frame, and protocol.

Printer Cables

One note of caution concerning parallel printer cables: The IEEE has established specifications for bi-directional parallel-printer cables (IEEE 1284). These cables affect the operation of EPP and ECP parallel devices. Using an older, noncompliant unidirectional cable with a bi-directional parallel device will prevent the device from communicating properly with the system and can prevent it from operating.

Some failures will produce error messages, such as "Printer Not Ready"; others will simply leave the data in the computer's print spooler. The symptom normally associated with this condition is that the parallel device just refuses to operate. If an ECP or EPP device successfully runs a self-test, but will not communicate with the host system, check the Advanced BIOS Setup screens to make certain that bi-directional printing has been enabled for the parallel port. If so, check the printer cable by substituting a known, IEEE 1284-compliant cable for it.

> **EXAM TIP**
>
> Be aware of the problems that can be created by using a noncompliant parallel cable with an IEEE-1284 bi-directional parallel device.

CHALLENGE #1

You are called out to a customer's site to check his laser printer. The printer sits on the desk next to the host computer and is attached to the 25-pin D-shell connector on the back of the system. When you start the printer, it shows no startup errors and will print a page from a self-test. So, you check the system's CMOS settings to verify that the printer port is enabled and that it is set for ECP operation. Still you cannot get the system to print a page from the printer. What should you check next?

Not all serial cables are created equal. In the PC world, RS-232 serial cables can take on several configurations. First of all, they might use either 9-pin or 25-pin D-shell connectors at either end of the cable. The cable for a particular serial connection will need to have the correct type of connector at each end. A typical printer serial cable will have a female 9-pin D-shell connector (DB-9F) that will connect to the PC's serial (COM) port, and a male 25-pin D-shell connector (DB-25M) that plugs in to the printer. Likewise, the connection scheme inside the cable can vary from printer to printer. Normally, the Transmit Data line (TXD–pin 2) from the computer is connected to the Receive Data line (RXD–pin 3) of the printer. Also, the Data Set Ready (DSR–pin 6) is typically connected to the printer's Data Terminal Ready (DTR–pin 20) pin. These connections are used as one method to control the flow of information between the system and the printer. If the printer's character buffer becomes full, it will signal the computer to hold up sending characters by deactivating this line.

> **EXAM TIP**
>
> Remember the types of connectors used at both the computer and the printer end of an RS-232 serial printer cable.

The recommended signal cable lengths associated with parallel and serial printers are

◆ Standard Parallel Printers—0–10 feet (3 meters), although some equipment manufacturers specify 6-feet (1.8 meters) maximums for their cables. You should believe these recommendations when you see them.

◆ RS-232 Serial Printers—10–50 feet (15.25 meters). However, some references use 100 feet as the acceptable length of an RS-232C serial cable. Serial connections are tricky enough without problems generated by the cable being too long. Make the cable as short as possible.

EXAM TIP

Know the recommended maximum length of a standard parallel printer cable and an RS-232 cable.

CHALLENGE #2

Your warehouse manager has come to you asking for a 20-foot printer cable so that he can move his wide carriage dot-matrix printer out of his office and into the warehouse where the noise level caused by the dot-matrix printer will not be a problem. He must use the dot-matrix printer because he has to print multipart invoice forms. What can you suggest to the warehouse manager that would solve his problem?

Infrared Printers

Many portable computer designs include an IrDA-compliant port to provide wireless communications with devices such as character printers. Figure 16.7 illustrates an IrDA-connected printer. The IrDA specification calls for communication ranges up to 2 meters (6 feet), but most implementations state 1 meter as the recommended maximum range. All IrDA transfers are carried out in half-duplex mode and must have a clear line of sight between the transmitter and receiver. The receiver must be situated within 15 degrees of center with the line of transmission.

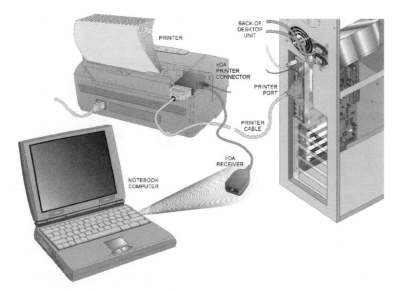

FIGURE 16.7
An IrDA printer connection.

The figure shows the infrared receiver mounted on a cable that connects to a standard port. This permits the receiver to be positioned in the best possible manner to maximize the IrDA line-of-sight and distance requirements.

> **EXAM TIP**
>
> Know the recommended and maximum distances specified for IrDA printer connections.

Networked Printers

If a printer is installed in a computer system that is part of a network, any other computer on the network can send work to the printer. Historically, the local computer is attached to the printer through one of the normal printing interfaces (that is, parallel serial or USB) and is also connected to the other remote computers through its network connection. In addition to the signal cable, the local computer's operating system must be configured to permit the remote stations on the network to print through it to its printer. This relationship is known as *print sharing*.

Newer printers, referred to as *Network-Ready printers*, come with built-in network interfacing that enables them to be connected directly into the Local Area Network. Most network printers contain an integrated network controller and Ethernet LAN adapter that enable it to work on the LAN without a supporting host computer.

Other printers can be connected directly to the Local Area Network through a device called a *Print Server port*. This device resembles a network hub in appearance and can be used to connect up to three printers directly into the network.

Whereas some older network printers used coaxial cable connections, newer network printers feature RJ-45 jacks for connection to twisted-pair Ethernet networks. It is relatively easy to determine whether a printer is networked by the presence of a coaxial or a twisted-pair network cable connected directly to the printer. The presence of the RJ-45 jacks on the back of the printer also indicate that the printer is network capable—even if it is not being used in that manner.

EXAM TIP

Know how to identify the presence of a network-ready printer.

NOTE

Reference Shelf For more information, refer to the Electronic Reference Shelf, "How Printers Work," located on the CD that accompanies this book.

CHALLENGE #3

Your office manager has come to you complaining about the noise level in the accounting office caused by the dot-matrix printers they have to use. The wide carriage dot-matrix printers are required because everyone in the department must print multipart invoices. After they have been printed, the invoices are separated from each other and taken to the warehouse for processing. The warehouse is well beyond the 10 feet range of the parallel printers you are using now. What option can you present to the office manager to lower the noise level in the accounting office?

CHAPTER SUMMARY

KEY TERMS

- Bitmapped fonts
- Cleaning
- Compression rollers
- Conditioning
- Continuous forms
- Developing
- Dot-matrix character
- Electrophotographic

The focus of this chapter has been on different types of character printers commonly used with PC-compatible computers. The opening section of the chapter presented an introduction to the different types of printers and provided a fundamental course in general printer structure and organization.

Following the general discussions of dot-matrix, ink-jet, and laser printer operations, the chapter focused on common types of printer connections and configurations.

At this point, review the objectives listed at the beginning of the chapter to be certain that you understand each point and can perform each task listed there. Afterward, answer the review questions that follow to verify your knowledge of the information.

CHAPTER SUMMARY

- Electrophotographic cartridge
- Erase lamps
- Font
- Friction-feed
- Fully formed character
- Fusing
- Fusing roller
- Fusing unit
- Ink cartridge
- Ink ribbon
- Ink-jet printers
- Main control board
- Mechanical vibration
- Multiple-part, continuous forms
- Network-ready printers
- Paper feed motor
- Paper handling mechanism
- Paper weight
- Photosensitive drum
- Photosensitive plastic
- Pin-feed

- Primary corona wire
- Print server port
- Print sharing
- Print wires
- Printhead
- Printhead carriage
- Printhead positioning motor
- Raster-scanned fonts
- Registration
- Ribbon cartridge
- Thermal fuse
- Thermal sensor
- Thermal shock
- Toner
- Transfer corona wire
- Transfer roller
- Transferring
- TrueType outline fonts
- Vector-based fonts
- Writing

APPLY YOUR KNOWLEDGE

Review Questions

1. Which of the following are true concerning bitmapped characters? (Select all that apply.)

   A. They store dot patterns for all the possible size and style variations of the characters in the set.

   B. Bitmapped fonts typically cannot be scaled and rotated.

   C. Bitmapped characters can be printed out directly and quickly.

   D. Each character is composed of a set of reference points and formulas.

2. Which font types are generated by establishing starting points and then calculating mathematical formulas?

   A. Bitmapped fonts

   B. Raster-scanned fonts

   C. Vector-based fonts

   D. TrueType outline fonts

3. What is the major purpose of a tractor-feed mechanism and where it is most commonly used?

   A. Used on dot-matrix printers that print continuous forms

   B. Used on ink-jet printers that print continuous forms

   C. Used on laser printers that print continuous forms

   D. Used on color printers that print continuous forms

4. How many print wires are in a typical dot-matrix printhead?

   A. 6, 10, or 12

   B. 6, 12, or 14

   C. 9, 12, or 18

   D. 9, 18, or 24

5. What is the main circuit board in a printer called?

   A. Printhead board

   B. Main control board

   C. Control panel

   D. Sensor board

6. Which of the following is not a type of interface connection commonly used with printers?

   A. IrDA

   B. SCSI

   C. IDE

   D. USB

7. What printer type produces print by squirting ink at the page?

   A. Thermal

   B. Ink-jet

   C. Laser

   D. Dot-matrix

APPLY YOUR KNOWLEDGE

8. What techniques are used to form the ink drops in an ink-jet printer? (Select two answers.)

   A. electromagnetic acceleration

   B. Mechanical vibration

   C. Air pressure

   D. Thermal shock

9. What are the operational stages of a typical laser printer?

   A. Cleaning, Conditioning, Writing, Transferring, Developing, Fusing

   B. Conditioning, Writing, Transferring, Developing, Fusing, Cleaning

   C. Cleaning, Conditioning, Writing, Developing, Transferring, Fusing

   D. Conditioning, Writing, Developing, Transferring, Fusing, Cleaning

10. You should never expose the drum of a laser printer to _____.

    A. cold

    B. a strong light source

    C. air

    D. toner

11. What are the functions of the two corona wires in a laser printer? (Select two answers.)

    A. Cleans the drum

    B. Fuses the toner to the paper

    C. Transfers toner from the drum to the paper

    D. Conditions the drum to be written on

12. What is the purpose of the thermal fuse in laser printers?

    A. Protects the paper from burning

    B. Protects the fuser assembly from overheating

    C. Fuses the toner image to the paper

    D. Heats the fusing unit

13. What is the H-P laser printer cartridge called?

    A. Cartridge assembly

    B. HP cartridge

    C. Electrophotographic cartridge

    D. Cartridge unit

14. You purchase a 24 pound standard weight of 24-pound bond paper. How many sheets are involved, and what size are they?

    A. 500 sheets, 8.5x11 inches

    B. 500 sheets, 17x22 inches

    C. 1000 sheets, 8.5x11 inches

    D. 1000 sheets, 17x22 inches

15. What problems can be created by using a non-compliant parallel cable with an IEEE-1284 bi-directional parallel device?

    A. Printer doesn't work.

    B. Printer output is jumbled.

    C. All characters print on the same line.

    D. Characters print, but not graphics.

APPLY YOUR KNOWLEDGE

16. What type of connectors are used at the computer and the printer ends of an RS-232 serial printer cable, respectively?

    A. 36-pin Centronics and DB-25F

    B. DB-25M and 36-pin Centronics

    C. DB-25F and DB-25M

    D. DB-9F and DB-25M

17. What is the recommended maximum length of an RS-232 cable?

    A. 10 feet (3 meters)

    B. 30 feet (9 meters)

    C. 50 feet (15 meters)

    D. 100 feet (30 meters)

18. What is the recommended maximum length of a standard parallel printer cable?

    A. 3 feet (1 meter)

    B. 10 feet (3 meters)

    C. 30 feet (9 meters)

    D. 50 feet (15 meters)

19. What are the recommended and maximum distances specified for IrDA printer connections?

    A. 1 meter, 2 meters

    B. 2 meters, 4 meters

    C. 3 meters, 6 meters

    D. 4 meters, 8 meters

20. How do you identify the presence of a network-ready printer? (Select two answers.)

    A. RJ-11 jacks on the back of the printer

    B. RJ-45 jacks on the back of the printer

    C. RS-232 port on the back of the printer

    D. Network cable connected to the printer

21. What types of connectors are used at the computer and the printer ends, respectively, of a parallel printer cable?

    A. 36-pin Centronics and DB-25F

    B. DB-25M and 36-pin Centronics

    C. DB-25M and DB-9F

    D. DB-9M and DB-25M

22. How does a dot-matrix printer place characters on a page?

    A. Precisely controlled drops of ink are squirted onto the paper.

    B. Magnetically charged ink particles are attracted to an ionized form on the paper.

    C. Magnetically controlled pins place dots on the paper.

    D. Fully formed metal characters force ink from a ribbon onto the paper.

23. What are the components found in a typical electrophotographic cartridge? (Select all that apply.)

    A. Developing roller

    B. Drum assembly

    C. Compression roller

    D. Corona wire

24. What is the function of the fuser unit in a laser printer?

    A. Squirts the ink onto the paper

    B. Cleans the excess toner off of the drum assembly

    C. Transfers toner to the paper

    D. Melts the toner onto the paper

25. How many pins are in a letter quality dot-matrix printer?

    A. 9

    B. 18

    C. 24

    D. 36

Answers and Explanations

1. **A, B, C.** Bitmapped fonts store dot patterns for all the possible size and style variations of the characters in the set. Bitmapped fonts typically cannot be scaled and rotated. Bitmapped characters can be printed out directly and quickly. For more information, see the section "Fonts."

2. **C.** Vector-based fonts store the outlines of the character styles and sizes as sets of mathematical formulas. Each character is composed of a set of reference points and connecting lines between them. These types of fonts can be scaled and rotated. For more information, see the section "Fonts."

3. **A.** Pin tractors are usually employed with continuous and multilayer forms. These mechanisms can control paper slippage and misalignment created by the extra weight imposed by continuous forms. Tractors can be adjusted to handle various paper widths. Tractor feeds are used with very heavy forms, such as multiple-part, continuous forms, and are most commonly found on dot-matrix printers. For more information, see the section "Printer Mechanics."

4. **D.** A typical printhead can contain 9, 18, or 24 print wires. The number of print wires used in the printhead is the major determining factor associated with a printer's character quality. For more information, see the section "Dot-Matrix Printers."

5. **B.** The main circuit board of a printer is referred to as the "main control board." For more information, see the section "Dot-Matrix Printers."

6. **C.** The printer's interface can contain circuitry to handle serial data, parallel data, or a combination of the different interface types—Centronics parallel, RS-232 serial, SCSI, USB, or IrDA. For more information, see the section "Dot-Matrix Printers."

7. **B.** Ink-jet printers produce characters by squirting a precisely controlled stream of ink drops onto the paper. For more information, see the section "Ink-Jet Printers."

8. **B, D.** The drops are formed by one of two methods: thermal shock or mechanical vibration. Thermal shock heats the ink in a capillary tube, just behind the nozzle. This increases the pressure of the ink in the tube and causes it to explode through the opening. Mechanical vibration uses the vibrations from a piezoelectric crystal to force ink through a nozzle. For more information, see the section "Ink-Jet Printers."

APPLY YOUR KNOWLEDGE

9. **C.** The six stages of operation in a laser printer include: cleaning, conditioning, writing, developing, transferring, and fusing. For more information, see the section "Laser Printing Operations."

10. **B.** Exposing a laser printer's drum to light, for more than a few minutes, can damage it. The drum should never be touched; this too, can ruin its surface. Keep the unit away from dust and dirt, as well as away from humidity and high-temperature areas. For more information, see the section "Laser Printing Operations."

11. **C, D.** A high voltage, applied to the primary corona wire, creates a highly charged negative field that conditions the drum to be written on by applying a uniform negative charge (-1000V) to it. The transfer corona wire is responsible for transferring the toner from the drum to the paper. For more information, see the section "Laser Printing Operations."

12. **B.** A thermal fuser protects the fuser assembly from overheating and damaging the printer. For more information, see the section "Laser Printing Operations."

13. **C.** In Hewlett-Packard laser printers, the main portion of the printing system is contained in the electrophotographic cartridge. For more information, see the section "Electrophotographic Cartridges."

14. **B.** Paper is specified in terms of its weight per 500 sheets at 22x17 inches (that is, 500 sheets of 22x17 inch, 21-pound bond paper will weigh 21 pounds). For more information, see the section "Paper Specifications."

15. **A.** The IEEE has established specifications for bi-directional parallel-printer cables (IEEE 1284). These cables affect the operation of EPP and ECP parallel devices. Using an older, noncompliant unidirectional cable with a bi-directional parallel device will prevent the device from communicating properly with the system and can prevent it from operating. Some failures will produce error messages, such as "Printer Not Ready"; others will simply leave the data in the computer's print spooler. The symptom normally associated with this condition is that the parallel device just refuses to operate. For more information, see the section "Printer Cables."

16. **D.** A typical serial printer cable will have either a female 9-pin D-shell connector (DB-9) or a female 25-pin D-shell connector that will connect to the PC's serial (COM) port and a male 25-pin D-shell (DB-25M) that plugs into the printer. For more information, see the section "Dot-Matrix Printers."

17. **C.** RS-232 serial printers have a recommended cable maximum cable length of 50 feet (¯15 meters). For more information, see the section "Printer Cables."

18. **B.** Standard parallel printers have a recommended cable maximum cable length of 10 feet (3 meters). For more information, see the section "Printer Cables."

19. **A.** The IrDA specification calls for communication ranges up to 2 meters, but most implementations state 1 meter as the recommended range. For more information, see the section "Infrared Printers."

APPLY YOUR KNOWLEDGE

20. **B, D.** It is relatively easy to determine whether a printer is networked by the presence of a coaxial or a twisted-pair network cable connected directly to the printer. The presence of the RJ-45 jacks on the back of the printer also indicate that the printer is network capable even if it is not being used in that manner. For more information, see the section "Networked Printers."

21. **B.** At the printer end of a parallel printer cable is a Centronics 36-pin connector. The computer end of the cable should have a DB-25M connector to plug into the system's DB-25F LPT port. For more information, see the section "Dot-Matrix Printers."

22. **C.** Dot-matrix characters are printed in the form of dot patterns that represent the characters. The printhead in a dot-matrix printer is a vertical column of print wires controlled by electromagnets. Dots are created on the paper by energizing selected electromagnets, which extend the desired print wires from the printhead. For more information, see the section "Dot-Matrix Printers."

23. **A, B, D.** The electrophotographic cartridge contains the toner supply, the corona wire, the drum assembly, and the developing roller. For more information, see the section "Electrophotographic Cartridges."

24. **D.** After the image has been transferred to the paper, a pair of compression rollers in the fusing unit act to press the toner particles into the paper while they melt them to it. The top compression roller, known as the fusing roller, is heated by a quartz lamp. This roller melts the toner to the paper as it exits the unit; the lower roller, known as the compression roller, applies pressure to the paper. A cleaning pad removes excess particles and applies a silicon lubricant to the roller to prevent toner from sticking to the Teflon-coated fusing roller. For more information, see the section "Laser Printing Operations."

25. **C.** A 9-pin printhead generally delivers draft quality print while 24-pin printheads approach letter quality print. For more information, see the section "Dot-Matrix Printers."

Challenge Solutions

1. You have checked the host computer and the printer. The only item left unchecked in the printing sub-system is the signal cable. For more information, see the section "Printer Cables."

2. You could install a serial printer in the warehouse. The range provided by the serial interface would enable you to move the printer to the warehouse without moving the computer out of the office. For more information, see the section "Printer Cables."

3. In this situation, you could place the dot-matrix printer in the warehouse and connect it to the network. The accounting staff would then have to print across the network to the warehouse. For more information, see the section "Networked Printers."

APPLY YOUR KNOWLEDGE

Suggested Readings and Resources

1. Printers, definitions
   `http://webopedia.internet.com/Hardware/`
   `Output_Devices/Printers/`

2. Dot-matrix Printer
   `http://webopedia.internet.com/TERM/d/`
   `dot_matrix_printer.html`

3. Ink-jet Printer
   `http://webopedia.internet.com/TERM/i/`
   `ink_jet_printer.html`

4. Ink-jet Printers Guide
   `www.pctechguide.com/13inkjets.htm`

5. Laser Printer Guide
   `www.pctechguide.com/12lasers.htm`

6. Printer Cables
   `http://www.cablesnmor.com/printer.html`

7. Infrared Printer Adaptor
   `http://www.actisys.com/actir100.html`

8. Spooling
   `http://webopedia.internet.com/TERM/s/`
   `spooling.html`

This chapter helps you to prepare for the Core Hardware module of the A+ Certification examination by covering the following objectives within the "Domain 5.0: Printers" section.

5.2 Identify care and service techniques and common problems with primary printer types.

Content might include the following:

- **Feed and output**
- **Errors (printed or displayed)**
- **Paper jam**
- **Print quality**
- **Safety precautions**
- **Preventive maintenance**

▶ Printers are connected to personal computers, and they break down. Therefore, computer technicians should be familiar with common printer problems and be able to demonstrate acceptable service techniques. The following sections deal with typical problems encountered with dot-matrix, ink-jet, and laser printers. They also include troubleshooting methods associated with each type of printer.

CHAPTER 17

Servicing Printers

STUDY STRATEGIES

To prepare for the Printers objective of the Core Hardware exam,

▶ Read the objectives at the beginning of this chapter.

▶ Study the information in this chapter.

▶ Review the objectives listed earlier in this chapter.

▶ Perform any step-by-step procedures in the text.

▶ Answer the review questions at the end of the chapter and check your results.

▶ Use the PrepLogic test engine on the CD-ROM that accompanies this book for additional review and exam questions concerning this material.

▶ Review the exam tips scattered throughout the chapter and make certain that you are comfortable with each point.

INTRODUCTION

Printers tend to be very mechanical devices, and like all other computer equipment, will eventually fail to operate. When this happens, it must be diagnosed and repaired like other equipment. This chapter presents techniques and tools used to troubleshoot and repair printer problems. It also provides common preventative maintenance procedures for use with the different types of printers.

After completing the chapter, you should be able to identify common symptoms produced by errors by different areas of the various printer types and apply the proper tools and techniques required to correct the indicated problem.

TROUBLESHOOTING DOT-MATRIX PRINTERS

The classical first step in determining the cause of any printer problem is to determine which part of the printer-related system is at fault—the host computer, the signal cable, or the printer.

Nearly every printer is equipped with a built-in *self-test*. The easiest way to determine whether the printer is at fault is to run its self-test routine. If the self-test runs and prints clean pages, most of the printer has been eliminated as a possible source of problems. The problem could be in the computer, the cabling, or the interface portion of the printer. If the printer fails the self-test, however, it will be necessary to troubleshoot the printer's problem.

Like other peripheral devices, printers can be configured to operate in different modes. In the case of dot-matrix printers, the configuration settings are normally entered into the printer through the buttons of its control panel. Typical dot-matrix configuration settings include printer mode, perforation skip (for continuous forms), automatic line feed at the bottom of the page, paper-handling type,

> **EXAM TIP**
>
> Know what it means if the printer produces a satisfactory self-test printout but will not print from the computer.

ASCII character codes (7 bit or 8 bit), and basic character sets. Other quantities that can be configured on a dot-matrix printer can include print font, character pitch, and form length.

Dot-Matrix Printer Power-Supply Problems

If the printer will not function and displays no lights, no sounds, and no actions, the power supply is generally involved. Check the online light. If the printer is offline, no print action will occur. A missing or improperly installed ribbon cartridge will also prevent the unit from printing. Plug a lamp or other device in the outlet to verify that it is operative. Check to see that the power cord is plugged securely in to the printer and the socket. Make sure that the power switch is turned on.

Check the power supply's fuse to make sure that it is good. If the fuse is blown, replace it with a fuse of the same type and rating. Fuses do not usually blow unless another component fails. The other possible cause of excessive current occurs when a motor (or its gear train) binds and cannot move. Check the drive mechanisms and motors for signs of binding. If none of the printer sections work when everything is connected and power is applied, you should exchange the power-supply board for a new unit.

Ribbon Cartridges

The single item in a dot-matrix printer that requires the most attention is the *ribbon cartridge*. It is considered a consumable part of the printer and must be changed often. The ink ribbon is stored in a controlled wad inside the cartridge, and moves across the face of the platen, as depicted in Figure 17.1. A take-up wheel draws new ribbon out of the wad as it is used.

> **EXAM TIP**
>
> Remember that the ribbon cartridge is the item in a dot-matrix printer that requires the most attention.

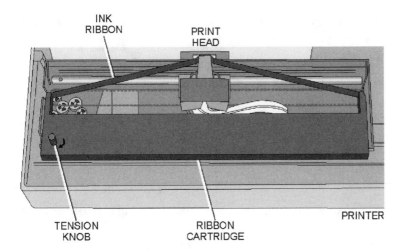

INK
RIBBON

PRINT
HEAD

TENSION
KNOB

RIBBON
CARTRIDGE

PRINTER

FIGURE 17.1
The printer ribbon cartridge.

As the ribbon wears out, the printing will become faint and uneven.
When the print becomes noticeably faint, the cartridge should be
replaced. Most dot-matrix printers use a snap-in ribbon cartridge. To
replace a typical ribbon cartridge, move the printhead carriage
assembly to the center of the printer. Remove the old cartridge by
freeing it from its clips, or holders, and then lifting it out of the
printer. Tighten the ribbon tension by advancing the tension knob
on the cartridge in a counterclockwise direction until the ribbon is
taut. Snap the cartridge in to place, making certain that the ribbon
slides between the printhead and the ribbon mask. Slide the printhead assembly back and forth on the rod to check for proper ribbon
movement.

EXAM TIP

Be aware of what the most likely
cause of uneven or faded print is in
a dot-matrix printer and know how
to correct it.

Printhead Not Printing

If the printhead is moving, but not printing, begin by checking the
printer's head gap lever to make sure that the printhead is not too
far back from the paper. If the printhead does not operate, components involved include—the printhead, the flexible signal cable
between the control board and the printhead, the control board, and
possibly the power-supply board.

If none of the printhead's print wires are being energized, the first
step should be to exchange the control board for a known good one
of the same type. If the new control board does not correct the

problem, replace the printhead. A power-supply problem could also cause the printhead to not print.

A related problem occurs when one or more of the print wires do not fire. If this is the case, check the printhead for physical damage. Also check the flexible signal cable for a broken conductor. If the control board is delivering any of the other print-wire signals, the problem is most likely associated with the printhead mechanism. Replace the printhead as a first step. If the problem continues after replacing the printhead, however, exchange the control board for a new one.

If the tops of characters are missing, the printhead is misaligned with the platen. It might need to be reseated in the printhead carriage, or the carriage assembly might need to be adjusted to the proper height and angle.

If the output of the printer gets lighter as it moves from left to right across the page, it might become necessary to adjust the spacing between the platen and the printhead carriage rod to obtain proper printing.

To exchange a dot-matrix printhead assembly, make sure that it is cool enough to be handled. These units can get hot enough to cause a serious burn.

Printhead Not Moving

If the printhead is printing, but not moving across the page, a single block of print will be generated on the page. When this type of problem occurs, the related components include the printhead positioning motor, the timing belt, the home position and timing sensors, the control board, and possibly the power-supply board.

With the power off, manually move the printhead to the center of the printer. Turn the printer on to see whether the printhead seeks the home position at the far-left side of the printer. If it moves to the left side of the printer and does not shut off, or does not return to the center of the printer, the home position sensor is malfunctioning and should be replaced.

If the printhead moves on startup, but will not move during normal printing, the control board should be replaced. In the event that the

---

EXAM TIP

Know what causes tops of characters to be missing from dot-matrix characters and how to correct the problem.

EXAM TIP

Know the most likely cause of print that fades from one side of the page to the other.

EXAM TIP

Remember that the printheads of dot-matrix printers generate a great deal of heat and can be a burn hazard when working on these units.

printhead assembly will not move at any time, the printhead positioning motor should be replaced. If the print is skewed from left to right as it moves down the page, the printer's bi-directional mode settings might be faulty, or the home position/end-of-line sensors might be defective.

Paper Not Advancing

When the paper does not advance, the output will normally be one line of dark blocks across the page. Examine the printer's paper-feed selector lever to make sure that it is set properly for the type of paper feed selected (that is, friction feed, pin feed, or tractor feed). If the paper feed is set correctly, the printer is online, and the paper will not move, it will be necessary to troubleshoot the paper-handling motor and gear train. Check the motor and gear train by setting the printer to the offline mode and holding down the *Form Feed (FF)* button.

EXAM TIP
Know the type of output that will be generated by a dot-matrix printer when the paper advance does not work.

If the feed motor and gear train work from this point, the problem must exist on the control board, with the interface cable, the printer's configuration, or in the computer system. If the motor or the gear train do not respond, unplug the paper-feed motor cable and check the resistance of the motor windings. If the windings are open, replace the paper-feed motor.

CHALLENGE #1

You get a call from your warehouse manager complaining about the serial printer you installed in his warehouse in the previous chapter. It seems that soon after you installed the new dot-matrix printer, the text on the multipart forms became uneven from side to side and print on an uphill slant. When you check out the printer, you determine that the paper is slipping from the weight of the multipart continuous forms. What can you do to fix this printing problem on the new printer?

TROUBLESHOOTING INK-JET PRINTERS

As with the dot-matrix printer, the first step in determining the cause of an ink-jet printer problem is to determine which part of the printer system is at fault—the host computer, the signal cable, or the printer.

Ink-Jet Printer Configuration Checks

Ink-jet printers are equipped with built-in self-tests. The easiest way to determine whether the printer is at fault is to run its self-tests.

A color ink-jet printer uses four ink colors to produce color images: Cyan, Magenta, Yellow, and Black (referred to as *CMYK color*). To create other colors, the printer prints a predetermined percentage of the basic colors in close proximity to each other. You can also configure the basic appearance of color and grayscale images produced by the ink-jet printer.

Ink Cartridges

The single item in an ink-jet printer that requires the most attention is the ink cartridge (or cartridges).

The density of the printout from an ink-jet printer can be adjusted through its printing software. However, when the print becomes noticeably faint or the resolution becomes unacceptable, the cartridge will need to be replaced. Most ink-jet printers use a self-contained, snap-in ink cartridge, like the one shown in Figure 17.2. Some models have combined ink cartridges that replace all three colors and the black ink at the same time. Other models use individual cartridges for each color.

EXAM TIP

Be aware that print density can be adjusted through software in an ink-jet printer.

EXAM TIP

Know what the symptoms are of an ink-jet printer cartridge going dry.

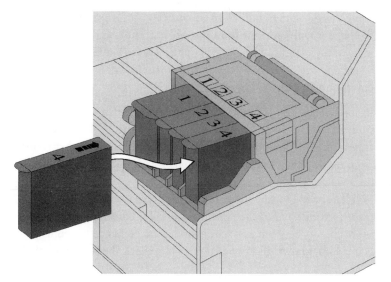

FIGURE 17.2
Self-contained, snap-in ink cartridge.

You can pop an ink cartridge out of the printhead assembly and thereby inspect the ink jets. If any, or all, of the jets are clogged, it is normally possible to clear them by gently wiping the face of the cartridge with a swab. A gentle squeeze of the ink reservoir can also help to unblock a clogged jet. The surface tension of the ink keeps it from running out of the nozzle when it is not energized. Using solvents to clear blockages in the jets can dilute the ink, reduce its surface tension characteristics, and allow it to flow uncontrollably through the jet.

To replace a typical ink cartridge, move the printhead carriage assembly to the center of the printer. Remove the old cartridge by freeing it from its clips or holders and lifting it out of the printer. After replacing the ink cartridge, you should cycle the printer on so that it will go through its normal warm up procedures. During these procedures, the printer performs a thorough cleaning of the ink-jet nozzles and gets the ink flowing correctly from the nozzles.

EXAM TIP

Be aware of the consequences of using a solvent to unclog an ink-jet nozzle.

Printhead Not Printing

If the printhead is moving, but not printing, begin by checking the ink supply in the print cartridge. The reservoir does not have to be completely empty to fail. Next, attempt to print from the self-test. If the printer will not print from the self-test, the components involved include the printhead, the flexible signal cable (between the control board and the printhead), the main control board, and possibly the power-supply board.

If none of the ink jets are firing, you should exchange the ink cartridges for new ones. If a single ink jet is not firing, the output will appear as white lines on the page—replace the cartridge that is not working. If one of the jets is activated all the time, black or colored lines will be produced on the page. To isolate the cause of these problems, perform the following actions one at a time—replace the print cartridge, check the flexible cabling for continuity and for short-circuits between adjacent conductors, exchange the control board for a known good one, and finally, check the power supply.

Printhead Not Moving

If the printhead is printing, but not moving across the page, a single block of print will normally be generated on the page. When this type of problem occurs, the related components include the printhead-positioning motor, the timing belt, the home position sensor, the control board, and possibly the power supply. Figure 17.3 depicts these components.

FIGURE 17.3
Printhead-positioning components.

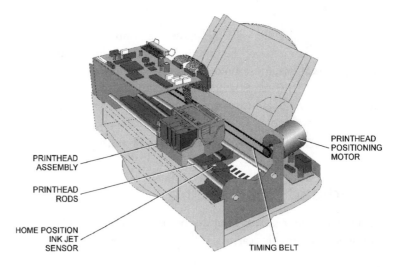

With the power off, manually move the printhead to the center of the printer. Turn the printer on to see whether the printhead seeks the home position at the far end of the printer. If the printhead moves to the end of the printer and does not shut off, or does not return to the center of the printer, the home position sensor is malfunctioning and should be replaced. If the printhead moves on startup, but will not move during normal printing, the control board should be replaced. In the event that the printhead assembly will not move at any time, check to see whether the printer is in *Maintenance Mode*. In this mode, the printer typically keeps the printhead assembly in the home position. If no mode configuration problems are present, the printhead-positioning motor should be replaced.

> EXAM TIP
>
> Be aware of the Maintenance Mode setting in ink-jet printers and that this setting can adversely affect troubleshooting procedures.

Paper Not Advancing

When the paper does not advance in an ink-jet printer, the output will normally be a thick, dark line across the page. Check the control panel to see that the printer is online. If the printer is online and the paper will not move, you must troubleshoot the paper-handling motor and gear train. Check the motor and gear train by setting the printer to the offline mode and holding down the Form Feed button.

If the printer's paper thickness selector is set improperly or the rollers in its paper-feed system become worn, the paper can slip as it moves through the printer and cause disfigured graphics to be produced. Check the printer's paper thickness settings. If they are correct and the print output is disfigured, you will need to replace the paper-feed rollers.

> EXAM TIP
>
> Know what types of problems can cause disfigured print in an ink-jet printer.

TROUBLESHOOTING LASER PRINTERS

Many of the problems encountered in laser printers are similar to those found in other printer types. For example, notice that most of the symptoms listed in the following section relate to the printer not printing, or not printing correctly, and not moving paper through the printer.

EXAM TIP

Memorize places where paper jams are likely to occur in a laser printer.

EXAM TIP

Remember that paper jams in a laser printer can be caused by incorrect paper settings.

WARNING

Laser Printer Dangers Unlike other printer types, the laser printer tends to have several high-voltage and high-temperature hazards inside it. To get the laser printer into a position in which you can observe its operation, it will be necessary to defeat some interlock sensors. This action will place you in potential contact with the high-voltage, high-temperature areas mentioned previously. Take great care when working inside the laser printer.

EXAM TIP

Be aware that laser printers can be a source of electrocution, eye damage (from the laser), and burns (from the fuser assembly).

Because of the extreme complexity of the laser printer's paper handling system, *paper jams* are a common problem. This problem tends to increase in frequency as the printer's components wear from use. Basically, paper jams occur in all three main sections of the printer. These sections are

- The pickup area
- The registration area
- The fusing area

If the rubber separation pad in the pickup area is worn excessively, more than one sheet of paper can be drawn into the printer, causing it to jam.

If additional, optional paper-handling features—such as *duplexers* (for double-sided copying) and *collators* (for sorting)—can contribute to the possibility of jams as they wear. Paper problems can also cause jams to occur. Using paper that is too heavy or too thick can result in jams, as can overloading paper trays. Similarly, using the wrong type of paper can defeat the separation pad and allow multiple pages to be drawn into the printer at one time. In this case, the multiple sheets might move through the printer together or they might result in a jam. Using coated paper stock can be hazardous because the coating might melt or catch fire.

Printer Is Dead or Partially Disabled

If the printer does not start up, check all the normal, power supply-related components (that is, power cord, power outlet, internal fuses, and so on). If the printer's fans and lights are working, other components that are associated with a defective power supply include the main motor and gear train, the high-voltage corona wires, the drum assembly, and the fusing rollers.

If the high-voltage portion of the power supply that serves the corona wires and drum sections is defective, the image delivered to the page will be affected. If the high-voltage section of the power supply fails, the transfers of toner to the drum, and then to the paper, cannot occur. In addition, the Contrast control will not be operational either.

In cases of partial failure, the image produced will have a washed-out appearance. Replace the high-voltage section of the power supply and/or the drum unit. If a separate corona wire is used, let the printer cool sufficiently and replace the wire. Never reach into the high-voltage, high-temperature corona area while power is applied to the printer. Also, avoid placing conductive instruments in this area.

If the DC portion of the power supply fails, the laser beam will not be produced, creating a "Missing Beam" error message. The components involved in this error are the laser/scanning module, the control board, and the DC portion of the power supply.

If the printer remains in a constant state of startup, this is equivalent to the computer not passing the POST portion of the boot-up process. If the printer starts up to an offline condition, there is likely a problem between the printer and the host computer's interface. Disconnect the interface cable to see whether the printer starts up to a ready state. If so, the problem is in the host computer, its interface, its configuration, or its signal cable.

Check to determine whether the printer is connected to the system through a print-sharing device. If so, connect the printer directly to the system and test it. It is not good practice to use laser printers with these types of devices. A better arrangement is to install, or just use, an LPT2 port to attach an additional printer to the system. Beyond two printers, it would be better to network the printers to the system.

EXAM TIP
Know what conditions will cause the Contrast control on a laser printer to not work.

EXAM TIP
Be aware that laser printers are not good candidates for use with print-sharing devices.

Print on Page Is Missing or Bad

Many of the problems encountered in laser printers are associated with missing, or defective print on the page. Normal print delivery problems fall into eight categories. These include

- Black pages
- White (blank) pages
- Faint print
- Smudged print
- Random specks on the page
- White lines along the page

◆ Faulty print at regular intervals on the page

◆ Print missing from some portion of the page

A black page indicates that toner has been attracted to the entire page. This condition could be caused by a failure of the primary corona, the laser-scanning module, or the main control board. If the laser is in a continuous on condition, the entire drum will attract toner. Likewise, if the primary corona is defective, the uniform negative charge will not be developed on the drum to repel toner. Replace the primary corona and/or drum assembly. If the problem continues, replace the laser-scanning module and the main control board.

On the other end of the spectrum, a white (or blank) page indicates that no information is being written on the drum. This condition basically involves the laser-scanning module, the control board, and the power supply. Another *white-page fault* occurs when the corona wire becomes broken, contaminated, or corroded, so that the attracting charge between the drum and paper is severely reduced.

Specks and stains on the page might be caused by a worn cleaning pad or by a defective corona wire. If the cleaning pad is worn, it will not remove excess toner from the page during the fusing process. If the corona wire's grid does not regulate the charge level on the drum, dark spots will appear in the print. To correct these situations, replace the corona assembly by exchanging the toner cartridge or drum unit. Also, replace the cleaning pad in the fusing unit. If the page still contains specks after changing the cartridge, run several pages through the printer to clear excess toner that might have collected in the printer.

White lines, which run along the length of the page, are normally a sign of poorly distributed toner. Try removing the toner cartridge and gently shaking it to redistribute the toner in the cartridge. Another cause of white lines is a damaged or weakened corona wire. Check and clean the corona wires, if accessible, or replace the module containing the corona wires.

Faint print in a laser printer can be caused by a number of different things. If the contrast control is set too low, or the toner level in the cartridge is low, empty, or poorly distributed, the print quality can appear washed out. Correcting these symptoms is fairly easy; adjust

---

EXAM TIP

Know what types of problems produce blank pages from a laser printer.

the contrast control, remove the toner cartridge, inspect it, shake it gently (if it is a sealed unit), and retry it.

If the print does not improve, replace the toner cartridge. Other causes of faint print include a weakened corona wire or a weakened high-voltage power supply that drives it. Replace the unit that contains the corona wire. Replace the high-voltage power supply. Make sure that latent voltages have been drained off the high-voltage power supply before working with it.

Faults in the print output that occur at regular intervals along the page are normally caused by mechanical problems. When roller and transport mechanisms begin to wear in the printer, bad registration and bad print appear in cyclic form. This can be attributed to the dimensions of cyclic components such as the drum, developing roller in the toner cartridge, or fusing rollers. When you have cyclic problems, examine the various mechanical components for wear or defects.

Missing print is normally attributed to a bad or misaligned laser-scanning module. If this module is not correctly installed, it cannot deliver lines of print to the correct areas of the page. Likewise, if the scanning mirror has a defect or is dirty, portions of the print will not be scanned on the drum. Another cause of missing print involves the toner cartridge, and low, or poorly distributed toner. If the toner does not come out of the cartridge uniformly, areas of missing print can be created. A damaged or worn drum can also be a cause of repeated missing print. If areas of the drum will not hold the charge properly, toner will not transfer to it, or to the page, correctly.

Smudged print is normally a sign of a failure in the fusing section. If the fusing roller's temperature or pressure is not sufficient to bond the toner to the page, the print will smudge when touched. When the heating element or lamp in the fusing area does not receive adequate AC power from the power supply, the toner will not affix to the page as it should. This condition will result in smudged output. Examine the fuser unit, the power supply, and the fusing roller's heating unit.

> **EXAM TIP**
>
> Know what type of problem is created when the fuser fails in a laser printer.

CHALLENGE #2

One of your customers calls you complaining that the pages coming out of his laser printer have spots where the print does not show up. He has changed the toner cartridge, but nothing improved. Now he wants your advice on what to do next. What should you tell him?

Paper Will Not Feed or Is Jammed

If the paper will not feed at all, the place to begin checking is the paper tray area. The paper trays have a complex set of sensors and pickup mechanisms that must all be functioning properly to begin the paper handling. Because of the complexity of the paper-pickup operation, jams are most likely to occur in this area.

Check the paper tray to make sure that there is paper in it, and that it has the correct size of paper in it. Each tray in a laser printer has a set of tabs that contact sensor switches to tell the control circuitry that the tray is installed and what size paper is in it. A mechanical arm and photo detector are used to sense the presence of paper in the tray. If these switches are set incorrectly, the printer could print a page that was sized incorrectly for the actual paper size.

If the paper feeds into the printer, but jams after the process has begun, troubleshoot the particular section of the printer where the jam is occurring—pickup, registration, fusing area, and output devices (collators and duplexers). This information is generally presented to the user through the laser printer's display panel. Figure 17.4 describes the paper path through a typical laser printer.

EXAM TIP

Be aware of the consequences of incorrectly setting the paper tray switches in a laser printer.

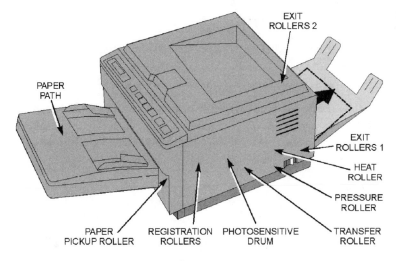

FIGURE 17.4
The paper path.

Another cause for laser printer jams is the presence of some obstruction in the paper path. Check for pieces of paper that have torn loose and lodged in the printer's paper path. In most laser printers, mechanical components are part of a replaceable module (that is, the drum unit, the developing unit, or the fusing unit). If the motor and all the exposed gears are working, replace these units one at a time.

Many times, a paper jam error indication will remain even after the paper has been removed from the laser printer. This is typically caused by a safety interlock error. Simply opening the printer's main access door should clear the error.

EXAM TIP

Be aware that you might need to open the printer's access door to clear a paper jam after the jammed paper has been removed.

PREVENTIVE MAINTENANCE AND SAFETY ISSUES

Because printers tend to be much more mechanical than other types of computer peripherals, they require more effort to maintain. Printers generate pollutants, such as paper dust and ink droplets, in everyday operation. These pollutants can build up on mechanical parts and cause them to wear. As the parts wear, the performance of the printer diminishes. Therefore, printers require periodic cleaning and adjustments to maintain good performance.

Dot-Matrix Printers

Clean the printer's roller surfaces. Use a damp, soft cloth to clean the surface of the platen. Rotate the platen through several revolutions. Do not use detergents or solvents on the rollers.

Use a non-fibrous swab, dipped in alcohol, to clean the face of the dot-matrix printhead. This should loosen up paper fibers and ink that can cause the print wires to stick. Apply a small amount of oil to the face of the printhead.

Ink-Jet Printers

Most ink-jet printers require cleaning and adjustments similar to those described for dot-matrix printers.

Laser Printers

Use a vacuum cleaner to remove dust buildup and excess toner from the interior of the laser printer. Care should be taken to remove all excess toner from the unit. Vacuum or replace the printer's *ozone filter* as a normal step in its PM schedule. Because water can mix with the toner particles in the printer, using wet sponges or towels to clean up toner inside the laser printer can create a bigger mess than the original one you were cleaning up. Remove the toner cartridge before vacuuming. Clean the laser printer's rollers using a damp cloth or denatured alcohol.

In most laser printers, the toner cartridges are designed so that they can be refilled. At this time, the third-party refill cartridges are not typically as good as those from the manufacturer. However, they tend to be much cheaper than original equipment cartridges. If the output from the printer does not have to be very high quality, refilled toner cartridges might be an interesting topic to examine. To date, no regulations govern the disposal of laser-printer cartridges.

WARNING

Cleaning the Printer   Cleaning the printer and its mechanisms periodically adds to its productivity by removing contaminants that cause wear. Vacuum the inside of the unit after applying antistatic solution to the vacuum's hose tip. Wipe the outside with a damp cloth, also using antistatic solution. Brush any contaminant buildup from the printer's mechanical components using a soft-bristled brush. Never lubricate the platen assembly of the printer.

EXAM TIP

Remember acceptable methods for cleaning laser printers.

CHAPTER SUMMARY

This chapter has presented troubleshooting procedures for each type of printer. Each procedure was divided into logical areas associated with typical printer symptoms and repairs.

The final section of the chapter featured preventative maintenance procedures that apply to the different printer types.

At this point, review the objectives listed at the beginning of the chapter to be certain that you understand each point and can perform each task listed there. Afterward, answer the review questions that follow to verify your knowledge of the information.

KEY TERMS

- Black page
- CMYK color
- Collators
- Duplexers
- Faint print
- Fusing area
- Maintenance Mode
- Missing print
- Ozone filter
- Paper jams
- Pickup area
- Registration area
- Ribbon cartridge
- Self-test
- Smudged print
- White-page fault

APPLY YOUR KNOWLEDGE

Review Questions

1. What does it mean if the printer produces a satisfactory self-test printout but will not print from the computer?

   A. The printer is the problem.

   B. The printer is not the problem.

   C. The cabling is the problem.

   D. The computer is the problem.

2. What item in a dot-matrix printer requires the most attention?

   A. Printhead

   B. Ribbon cartridge

   C. Tension knob

   D. Control panel

3. What is the most likely cause of uneven or faded print in a dot-matrix printer?

   A. Misaligned printhead

   B. Misaligned platen

   C. Worn out ribbon

   D. Worn out printhead

4. How do you correct the problem of uneven or faded print in a dot-matrix printer?

   A. Adjust the ink ribbon.

   B. Replace the ink ribbon cartridge.

   C. Replace the printhead.

   D. Adjust the platen.

5. What causes the tops of characters to be missing from a dot-matrix printer?

   A. Printhead is misaligned.

   B. Printhead is too far back from the paper.

   C. Ribbon is worn out.

   D. Printhead is worn out.

6. How do you correct the problem in which the tops of characters are missing from a dot-matrix printer? (Select two answers.)

   A. Reseat the printhead in the printhead cartridge.

   B. Reseat the platen.

   C. Carriage assembly might need to be adjusted to the proper height and angle.

   D. Replace the ribbon.

7. What is the most likely cause of print that fades from one side of the page to the other?

   A. Ribbon needs replacing.

   B. Printhead needs adjusting.

   C. Platen needs to be reseated.

   D. Printhead needs replacing.

8. The _____ of dot-matrix printers generate a great deal of heat and can be a burn hazard when working on these units.

   A. ribbons

   B. platens

   C. printheads

   D. paper trays

APPLY YOUR KNOWLEDGE

9. What type of output will be generated by a dot-matrix printer when the paper advance does not work?

    A. One or more dark lines are running down the page.

    B. One dark line crosses the page.

    C. Whole page is black.

    D. Whole page is white.

10. Where is print density adjusted in an ink-jet printer?

    A. Software

    B. Control panel

    C. Platen knob

    D. System tray

11. What are the symptoms of an ink-jet printer cartridge going dry? (Select two answers.)

    A. Black streaks run down the page.

    B. Resolution becomes unacceptable.

    C. One dark line crosses the page.

    D. Print becomes noticeably faint.

12. What are the consequences of using a solvent to unclog an ink-jet nozzle? (Select all that apply.)

    A. Dilutes the ink

    B. Reduces its surface tension characteristics

    C. Unblocks a clogged jet

    D. Allows ink to flow uncontrollably

13. Which ink-jet printer setting can adversely affect troubleshooting procedures?

    A. Tray selector

    B. Page feed

    C. Self-test

    D. Maintenance Mode

14. What types of problems can cause smudged or disfigured print in an ink-jet printer? (Select all that apply.)

    A. Platen is misaligned.

    B. Paper thickness selector is improperly set.

    C. Paper feed rollers are worn.

    D. The ribbon is worn out.

15. Where are paper jams likely to occur in a laser printer? (Select all that apply.)

    A. Fusing area

    B. Registration area

    C. Control area

    D. Pickup area

16. Paper jams in a laser printer can be caused by _____. (Select all that apply.)

    A. using paper that is too thick

    B. incorrect paper settings

    C. using coated paper

    D. using colored paper

APPLY YOUR KNOWLEDGE

17. Which type of printer can be a source of electrocution, eye damage, and burns?

    A. Laser

    B. Dot-matrix

    C. Ink-jet

    D. Daisy-wheel

18. What type of problem will produce blank pages from a laser printer? (Select all that apply.)

    A. Contrast is set too low.

    B. Failure in the fusing section.

    C. Bad or misaligned laser-scanning module.

    D. Corona wire is broken, contaminated, or corroded.

19. What are the consequences of incorrectly setting the paper tray switches in a laser printer? (Select two answers.)

    A. Pages are smudged.

    B. Paper will not feed.

    C. Page is sized incorrectly for the actual paper size.

    D. Pages are all white.

20. After a jammed paper has been removed, what may need to be done to clear the paper jam?

    A. Set the printer to the Online mode.

    B. Disconnect the interface cable.

    C. Open the printer's access door.

    D. Use the Form Feed button.

21. What is an acceptable method for cleaning laser printers?

    A. Wet sponges

    B. Vacuum cleaner

    C. Towels

    D. Detergent

22. Which type of printer is not a good candidate for use with print-sharing devices?

    A. Laser

    B. Dot-matrix

    C. Ink-jet

    D. Daisy-wheel

23. What type of problem will produce smudged pages from a laser printer?

    A. Contrast is set too low.

    B. Failure in the fusing section.

    C. Bad or misaligned laser-scanning module.

    D. Corona wire is broken, contaminated, or corroded.

Answers and Explanations

1. **B.** The easiest way to determine whether the printer is at fault is to run its self-test routine. If the self-test runs and prints clean pages, most of the printer has been eliminated as a possible source of problems. The problem could be in the computer, the cabling, or the interface portion of the printer. If the printer fails the self-test, however, it will be necessary to troubleshoot the printer's problem. For more information, see the section "Troubleshooting Dot-Matrix Printers."

APPLY YOUR KNOWLEDGE

2. **B.** The single item in a dot-matrix printer that requires the most attention is the ribbon cartridge. It is considered a consumable part of the printer and must be changed often. For more information, see the section "Ribbon Cartridges."

3. **C.** As the ribbon wears out, the printing will become faint and uneven. For more information, see the section "Ribbon Cartridges."

4. **B.** When the print becomes noticeably faint, the cartridge should be replaced. Most dot-matrix printers use a snap-in ribbon cartridge. To replace a typical ribbon cartridge, move the printhead carriage assembly to the center of the printer. Remove the old cartridge by freeing it from its clips, or holders, and then lifting it out of the printer. Tighten the ribbon tension by advancing the tension knob on the cartridge in a counter-clockwise direction until the ribbon is taut. Snap the cartridge into place, making certain that the ribbon slides between the printhead and the ribbon mask. Slide the printhead assembly back and forth on the rod to check for proper ribbon movement. For more information, see the section "Ribbon Cartridges."

5. **A.** When the tops of characters are missing, the printhead is misaligned with the platen. For more information, see the section "Printhead Not Printing."

6. **A, C.** The printhead might need to be reseated in the printhead carriage, or the carriage assembly might need to be adjusted to the proper height and angle. For more information, see the section "Printhead Not Printing."

7. **B.** If the output of the printer gets lighter as it moves from left to right across the page, it might become necessary to adjust the printhead mechanism to obtain proper printing. For more information, see the section "Printhead Not Printing."

8. **C.** To exchange the printhead assembly, make sure that it is cool enough to be handled. These units can get hot enough to cause a serious burn. For more information, see the section "Printhead Not Printing."

9. **B.** When the paper does not advance, the output will normally be one line of dark blocks across the page. For more information, see the section "Paper Not Advancing."

10. **A.** The density of the printout from an ink-jet printer can be adjusted through its printing software. However, when the print becomes noticeably faint or the resolution becomes unacceptable, the cartridge will need to be replaced. For more information, see the section "Ink Cartridges."

11. **B, D.** When the print becomes noticeably faint or the resolution becomes unacceptable, the cartridge will need to be replaced. For more information, see the section "Ink Cartridges."

12. **A, B, D.** The surface tension of the ink keeps it from running out of the nozzle when it is not energized. Using solvents to clear blockages in the jets can dilute the ink, reduce its surface tension characteristics, and allow it to flow uncontrollably through the jet. For more information, see the section "Ink Cartridges."

13. **D.** In the event that the printhead assembly will not move at any time, check to see whether the printer is in Maintenance Mode. In Maintenance Mode, the printer typically keeps the printhead assembly locked in the home position. For more information, see the section "Printhead Not Moving."

APPLY YOUR KNOWLEDGE

14. **B, C.** If the printer's paper thickness selector is set improperly or the rollers in its paper feed system become worn, the paper can slip as it moves through the printer and cause disfigured graphics to be produced. For more information, see the section "Paper Not Advancing."

15. **A, B, D.** Because of the extreme complexity of the laser printer's paper handling system, paper jams are a common problem. This problem tends to increase in frequency as the printer's components wear from use. Basically, paper jams occur in all three main sections of the printer. These sections are the pickup area, the registration area, and the fusing area. For more information, see the section "Troubleshooting Laser Printers."

16. **A, B, C.** Using paper that is too heavy or too thick can result in jams, as can overloading paper trays. Similarly, using the wrong type of paper can defeat the separation pad and allow multiple pages to be drawn into the printer at one time. In this case, the multiple sheets might move through the printer together, or they might result in a jam. Using coated paper stock can be hazardous because the coating might melt or catch fire. For more information, see the section "Troubleshooting Laser Printers."

17. **A.** Laser printers can be a source of electrocution, eye damage (from the laser), and burns (from the fuser assembly). The laser printer tends to have several high-voltage and high-temperature hazards inside it. To get the laser printer into a position in which you can observe its operation, it will be necessary to defeat some interlock sensors. This action will place you in potential contact with the high-voltage, high-temperature areas in the printer. Take great care when working inside the laser printer. For more information, see the section "Troubleshooting Laser Printers."

18. **C, D.** A white (or blank) page indicates that no information is being written on the drum. This condition basically involves the laser-scanning module, the control board, and the power supply. Another white-page fault occurs when the corona wire becomes broken, contaminated, or corroded so that the attracting charge between the drum and paper is severely reduced. For more information, see the section "Print on Page Is Missing or Bad."

19. **B, C.** The paper trays have a complex set of sensors and pickup mechanisms that must all be functioning properly. Each tray in a laser printer has a set of tabs that contact sensor switches to tell the control circuitry that the tray is installed and what size paper is in it. A mechanical arm and photo detector are used to sense the presence of paper in the tray. For more information, see the section "Paper Will Not Feed or Is Jammed."

20. **C.** A paper jam error indication might remain even after the paper has been removed from the laser printer. This is typically caused by a safety interlock error. Simply opening the printer's main access door should clear the error. For more information, see the section "Paper Will Not Feed or Is Jammed."

21. **B.** Use a vacuum cleaner to remove dust buildup and excess toner from the interior of the laser printer. Clean the laser printer's rollers using a damp cloth or denatured alcohol. For more information, see the section "Laser Printers."

22. **A.** When troubleshooting a remote printer, check to see whether the printer is connected to the system through a print-sharing device. If so, connect the printer directly to the system, and try it. It is not good practice to use laser printers with these

types of devices. A better arrangement is to install, or just use, an LPT2 port to attach an additional printer to the system. Beyond two printers, it would be better to use network-capable printers. For more information, see the section "Printer Is Dead or Partially Disabled."

23. **B.** Smudged print in a laser printer is normally a sign of a failure in the fusing section. If the fusing roller's temperature, or pressure, is not sufficient to bond the toner to the page, the print will smudge when touched. Examine the fuser unit, the power supply, and the fusing roller's heating unit. For more information, see the section "Print on Page Is Missing or Bad."

Challenge Solutions

1. You should contact the printer manufacturer to obtain a tractor feed mechanism for the printer. The tractor feed will move the heavy forms through the printer in a straight line. The tractor must be obtained from the original printer manufacturer because they are proprietary to the printer they are mounted on. For more information, see the section "Paper Not Advancing."

2. Missing print is normally attributed to a bad or misaligned laser-scanning module. If this module is not correctly installed, it cannot deliver lines of print to the correct areas of the page. Likewise, if the scanning mirror has a defect or is dirty, portions of the print will not be scanned on the drum. Another cause of missing print involves the toner cartridge and low or poorly distributed toner. If the toner does not come out of the cartridge uniformly, areas of missing print can be created. A damaged or worn drum can also be a cause of repeated missing print. If areas of the drum will not hold the charge properly, toner will not transfer to it or to the page correctly.

Because he has already changed the toner cartridge, you should tell him to wait for a qualified printer technician. The problems he is having indicate that he is past the point of things that users can be expected to repair. For more information, see the section "Print on Page Is Missing or Bad."

APPLY YOUR KNOWLEDGE

Suggested Readings and Resources

1. Driver
   `http://webopedia.internet.com/TERM/d/`
   `driver.html`

2. Handshaking
   `http://webopedia.internet.com/TERM/h/`
   `handshaking.htm/`

3. Troubleshooting Peripheral I/O Ports
   `www.pcguide.com/ts/x/comp/io.htm`

4. Printer and Photocopier Troubleshooting and Repair
   `http://www.repairfaq.org/REPAIR/`
   `F_printfaq.html`

5. Troubleshooting Laser Printers
   `http://imprints.ucsd.edu/lps/`
   `troubleshoot.html`

6. Laser Printer Troubleshooting Tip-Sheet
   `http://www.tufftest.com/pctbx-content-`
   `7.htm`

7. Apple Printers
   `http://www.apple.com/support/`

8. Brother Printers
   `http://www.brother.com/usa/printer/`
   `printer_cntr.html`

9. Canon Printers
   `http://consumer.usa.canon.com/`
   `techsupport/index.html`

10. Epson Printers
    `http://support.epson.com/troubleshooting.`
    `html`

11. HP Printers
    `http://www.hp.com/cposupport/nonjsnav/`
    `prhome.html`

12. IBM Printers
    `http://www-1.ibm.com/support/`

13. Lexmark Printers
    `http://www.lexmark.com/support/index.html`

14. NEC Printers
    `http://printers.nectech.com/printers/index`
    `.htm`

15. Xerox Printers
    `http://www.xerox.com/`

This chapter helps you to prepare for the Core Hardware module of the A+ Certification examination by covering the following objectives within the "Domain 6.0: Basic Networking" section.

6.1 Identify basic networking concepts, including how a network works and the ramification of repairs on the network.

Content might include the following:

- **Installing and configuring network cards**

- **Network access**

- **Full-duplex, half-duplex**

- **Cabling: Twisted pair, Coaxial, Fiber-Optic, RS-232**

- **Ways to network a PC**

- **Physical Network Topologies**

- **Increasing bandwidth**

- **Loss of data**

- **Network slowdown**

- **Infrared**

- **Hardware protocols**

▶ Within a very short time span, the use of *local area networks (LANs)* has grown immensely. Because LANs have become such an integral part of commercial computer systems, the PC technician must understand how they function.

▶ LANs are communication systems designed to connect computers together in a relatively close proximity. These connections enable users attached to the network to share resources such as printers and modems. LAN connections also enable users to communicate with each other and share data among their computers. In concept, a minimum of three stations must be connected to have a true LAN.

CHAPTER 18

Basic Networking Concepts

▶ When discussing LANs, there are two basic topics to consider—the LAN's topology (hardware connection method) and its protocol (communication control method).

OUTLINE

STUDY STRATEGIES

To prepare for the Basic Networking objective of the Core Hardware exam,

▶ Read the objectives at the beginning of this chapter.

▶ Study the information in this chapter.

▶ Review the objectives listed earlier in this chapter.

▶ Perform any step-by-step procedures in the text.

▶ Answer the review questions at the end of the chapter and check your results.

▶ Use the PrepLogic test engine on the CD-ROM that accompanies this book for additional review and exam questions concerning this material.

▶ Review the exam tips scattered throughout the chapter and make certain that you are comfortable with each point.

INTRODUCTION

Local area networks have become a very common part of the computer system, particularly in the workplace. This chapter deals with local area networking from the local desktop computer level. The involvement of the computer repair technician in network-related problems is normally limited because these systems typically fall under the authority of a network administrator in most enterprise (business) settings.

The chapter presents a short course on basic networking terminology and concepts. It begins by describing typical computer connection schemes or topologies. This section also features a presentation about the different transmission media (that is, copper and fiber cables, infrared and Rf wireless links) commonly used with computer networks.

The second major topic of the chapter centers on the two contemporary network access protocols in use—Ethernet and Token Ring. This topic extends to cover Fiber optic, infrared, and wireless LAN specifications.

The chapter then moves into Installing LAN adapter (NIC) cards. This is the highest level networking operation actually performed by A+ level technicians.

The final sections of the chapter focus on LAN repair functions. This information is presented for A+ level operations and will acquaint the A+ technician with the concept of working with a network administrator to diagnose and repair network-related problems.

After completing the chapter, you should be able to identify different LAN topologies and describe their basic characteristics. You should also be able to install and configure a typical LAN adapter and bring the local computer on line with the network.

LAN TOPOLOGIES

Network topologies are physical connection/configuration strategies. Let's first address CompTIA's definition of a network. CompTIA defines a network as a minimum of two computers connected together so that they can share resources. However, if only two units are connected, point-to-point communications software and a simple null modem could be employed. The null modem could be constructed using the RS-232 serial cable method described in Chapter 4, "Peripherals and Ports," or it could be made up of a copper networking cable, using RJ-45 connectors. In this case, the cable would be known as a *crossover cable* instead of a null modem.

With this in mind, we can say that LAN topologies fall into four types of configurations:

◆ Bus

◆ Ring

◆ Star

◆ Mesh

Figure 18.1 illustrates all four topologies.

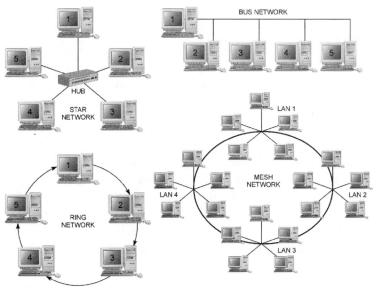

EXAM TIP
Be aware that under CompTIA's definition, a LAN can exist with only two computers.

EXAM TIP
Know that two computers can be connected together and communicate without the benefit of a network.

FIGURE 18.1
Star, bus, ring, and mesh configurations.

EXAM TIP
Be able to recognize network topologies from this type of drawing.

In the *bus* topology, the stations, or nodes, of the network connect to a central communication link. Each node has a unique address along the bus that differentiates it from the other users on the network. Information can be placed on the bus by any node. The information must contain network address information about the node, or nodes that the information is intended for. Other nodes along the bus will ignore the information.

In a *ring* network configuration, the communication bus is formed into a closed loop. Each node inspects the information on the LAN as it passes by. A repeater, built in to each ring LAN card, regenerates every message not directed to it and sends the message to the next appointed node. The originating node eventually receives the message back and removes it from the ring.

Ring topologies tend to offer very high data transfer rates but require additional management overhead. The additional management is required for dependability. If a node in a ring network fails, the entire network could fail. To overcome this, ring designers have developed rings with Primary and Secondary data paths. If a break occurs in a primary link, the network controller can reroute the data onto the secondary link to avoid the break.

In a *star* topology, the logical layout of the network resembles the branches of a tree. All the nodes are connected in branches that eventually lead back to a central unit. Nodes communicate with each other through the central unit. The central station coordinates the network's activity by polling the nodes, one by one, to determine whether they have any information to transfer. If so, the central station gives that node a predetermined slice of time to transmit. If the message is longer than the time allotted, the transmissions are chopped into small packets of information that are transmitted over several polling cycles.

The *mesh* design offers the most basic network connection scheme. In this design, each node has a direct physical connection to all the other nodes in the network. Although the overhead for connecting a mesh network topology together in a LAN environment is prohibitive, this topology is employed in two very large network environments—the public telephone system and the Internet.

LOGICAL TOPOLOGIES

It should be easy to visualize the connections of the physical topologies just described if the nodes simply connected to each other. However, this is typically not the case in newer LAN arrangements because most LAN installations employ connection devices, such as hubs and routers, that alter the appearance of the actual connection scheme. Therefore, the logical topology will not match the appearance of the physical topology. The particulars of the connection scheme are hidden inside the connecting device. It is not uncommon for a logical ring or mesh topology to be implemented in a physical star topology.

NETWORK CONTROL STRATEGIES

When you begin to connect computers to other computers and devices so that they can share resources and data, the issue of how and who will control the network comes up very quickly. Control of a network can be implemented in two ways:

◆ As a *peer-to-peer network* in which each computer is attached to the network in a ring or bus fashion and is equal to the other units on the network

◆ As a *client/server network* in which dependent workstations, referred to as clients, operate in conjunction with a dedicated master computer (server)

Figure 18.2 illustrates a typical peer-to-peer network arrangement. In this arrangement, the users connected to the network can decide to share access to different network resources, such as hard drives and printers.

EXAM TIP

Be aware that resource sharing in a peer-to-peer network is determined at the local node.

FIGURE 18.2
A peer-to-peer network.

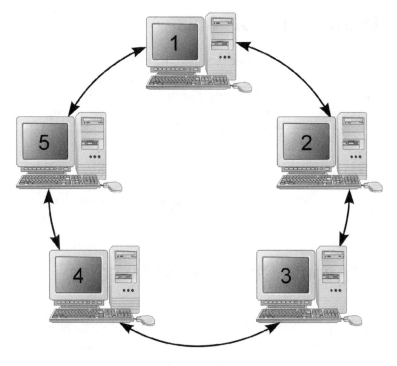

EXAM TIP

Be aware that the nodes in peer-to-peer networks can serve as both clients and servers for different functions.

In a peer-to-peer network, control of the local unit is fairly autonomous. The nodes in this type of network configuration usually contain local hard drives and printers that the local computer has control of. These resources can be shared at the discretion of the individual user. A common definition of a peer-to-peer network is one in which all the nodes can act as both clients and servers of the other nodes under different conditions.

Figure 18.3 depicts a typical client/server LAN configuration. In this type of LAN, control tends to be very centralized. The server typically holds the programs and data for its client computers. It also provides security and network policy enforcement.

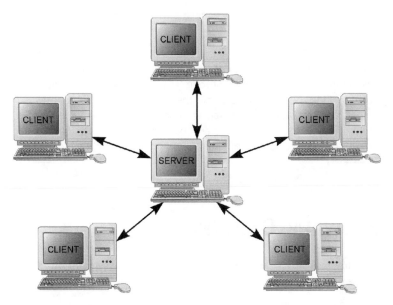

FIGURE 18.3
A client/server network.

The major advantages of the client/server networking arrangement include

◆ Centralized administration

◆ Data and resource security

EXAM TIP	Be aware of the characteristic differences between peer-to-peer and client/server networks.

CHALLENGE #1

You are setting up a new production room for creating textbooks and multimedia presentations. You will employ writers, artists, document layout and paste up professionals, multimedia animators, and multimedia presentation designers. Your board of directors has asked you for input about how to set up the system. They are anticipating tying everyone into the company's existing client/server network, but someone has suggested looking into peer-to-peer networks. What will you recommend to them and why?

CHALLENGE #2

Your board of directors has asked you to give them a report on implementing a peer-to-peer network for the entire company. This would include the development room from challenge 1 and would also include the accounting office, the technical services department, and the warehouse/shipping department. They have been told that peer-to-peer networks are relatively inexpensive and very flexible. What would you tell them about implementing this idea?

NETWORK CABLING

Basically four media are used to transmit data between computers. These media include

◆ Copper cabling

◆ Fiber optic cabling

◆ Infrared light

◆ Wireless radio frequency (RF) signals

Under the heading of copper cabling, there are basically two categories to consider: twisted-pair and coaxial cabling. *Twisted-pair* cabling consists of two or more pairs of wires twisted together to provide noise reduction. The twist in the wires cause induced noise signals to tend to cancel each other out. In this type of cabling, the number of twists in each foot of wire indicates its relative noise immunity level.

When discussing twisted pair cabling with data networks, there are two basic types to consider: *unshielded twisted pair (UTP)* and *shielded twisted pair (STP)*. UTP networking cable contains four pairs of individually insulated wires as illustrated in Figure 18.4. STP cable is similar with the exception that it contains an additional foil shield that surrounds the four pair wire bundle. The shield provides extended protection from induced electrical noise and cross talk by supplying a grounded path to carry the induced electrical signals away from the conductors in the cable.

FIGURE 18.4
UTP and STP cabling.

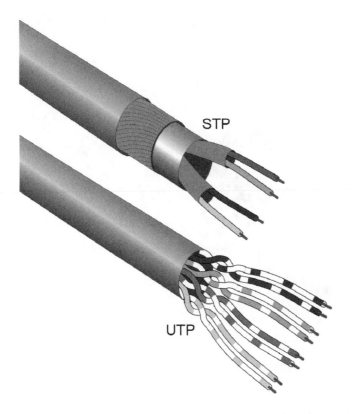

Coaxial Cable

Coaxial cable is familiar to most people as the conductor that carries cable TV into their homes. Coax has a single copper conductor in its center and a protective braided copper shield around it, as illustrated in Figure 18.5.

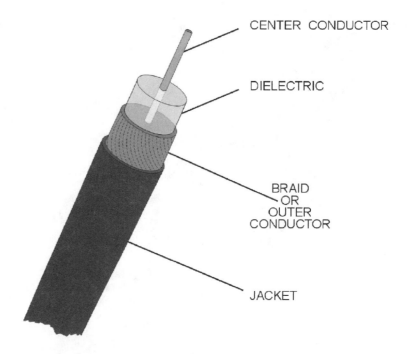

FIGURE 18.5
Coaxial cable.

UTP Cable

UTP cable specifications have been established jointly by two groups—the Electronic Industry Association and the Telecommunications Industry Association (TIA). They have categorized different grades of cable along with connector, distance, and installation specifications to produce the EIA/TIA UTP wiring category (CAT) ratings for the industry (that is, Cat3 and *Cat5 cabling*). Table 18.1 lists the industry's various Cat cable ratings that apply to UTP data communications cabling. Cat5 cabling is currently the most widely used specification for data communication wiring.

TABLE 18.1

UTP CABLE CATEGORY RATINGS

Category	Maximum Bandwidth	Wiring Types	Applications
3	16MHz	100Ω UTP Rated Category 3	10Mbps Ethernet 4Mbps Token Ring
4	20MHz	100Ω UTP Rated Category 4	10Mbps Ethernet 16Mbps Token Ring
5	100MHz	100Ω UTP Rated Category 5	100Mbps TPDDI 155Mbps ATM

Category	Maximum Bandwidth	Wiring Types	Applications
5E	160MHz	100Ω UTP Rated Category 5E	1.2Gbps 1000BASE-T High-Speed ATM
6 Proposed	200-250MHz	100Ω UTP Rated Category 6	1.2Gbps 1000BASE-T High-Speed ATM and beyond
7 Proposed	600-862MHz	100Ω UTP Rated Category 7	1.2Gbps 1000BASE-T High-Speed ATM and beyond

The connector and color-coded connection scheme specified for 4-pair, Cat 5 UTP network cabling is illustrated in Figure 18.6. UTP cabling is terminated in an 8-pin *RJ-45 plug*. The color code for attaching the connector to the cable is also provided in the figure.

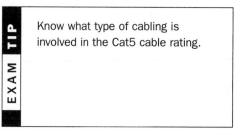

EXAM TIP

Know what type of cabling is involved in the Cat5 cable rating.

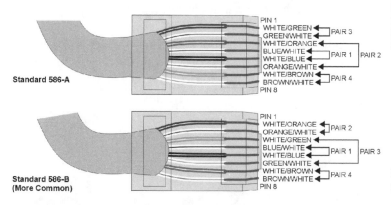

FIGURE 18.6
UTP Cable Connections.

Fiber-Optic Cable

Fiber-optic cable is plastic or glass cable designed to carry voice or digital data in the form of light pulses. The signals are introduced into the cable by a laser diode and bounce along its interior until reaching the end of the cable. At the end, a light detecting circuit receives the light signals and converts them back into usable information. This type of cabling offers potential signaling rates in excess of 200,000Mbps. However, use with current access protocols still limits fiber-optic LAN speeds to 100Mbps.

Because light moving through a fiber-optic cable does not attenuate (lose energy) as quickly as electrical signals moving along a copper conductor, segment lengths between transmitters and receivers can be much longer with fiber-optic cabling. In some fiber-optic applications, the maximum cable length can range up to 2 kilometers.

Fiber-optic cable also provides a much more secure data transmission medium than copper cable because it cannot be tapped without physically breaking the conductor. Basically, light introduced into the cable at one end does not leave the cable except through the other end. In addition, it electrically isolates the transmitter and receiver so that no signal level matching normally needs to be performed between the two ends.

As a matter of fact, getting the light out of the cable without significant attenuation is the key to making fiber-optic connections. The end of the cable must be perfectly aligned with the receiver and be free from scratches, film, or dust that would distort or filter the light.

In Figure 18.7, the connector on the left is a *Straight Tip (ST) connector*, and the one on the right is an *SC connector*. The SC connector is the dominant connector for fiber-optic Ethernet networks. In both cases, the connectors are designed so that they correctly align the end of the cable with the receiver.

EXAM TIP

Know what type of networks employ ST and SC connectors.

FIGURE 18.7
Fiber-optic cable connectors.

NETWORK ACCESS PROTOCOLS

In a network, some method must be used to determine which node has use of the network's communications paths, and for how long it can have it. The network's hardware protocol handles these functions, and is necessary to prevent more than one user from accessing the bus at any given time.

If two sets of data are placed on the network at the same time, a data collision occurs and data is lost. Basically, there are two de-facto networking protocols in use: Ethernet and Token Ring.

Ethernet

The standard specification for Ethernet has been published by the International Electrical and Electronic Association (IEEE) as the *IEEE-802.3 Ethernet protocol*. Its methodology for control is referred to as *carrier sense multiple access with collision detection (CSMA/CD)*. Using this protocol, a node that wants to transfer data over the network first listens to the LAN to determine whether it is in use. If the LAN is not in use, the node begins transmitting its data. If the network is busy, the node waits for the LAN to clear for a predetermined time, and then takes control of the LAN.

If two nodes are waiting to use the LAN, they will periodically attempt to access the LAN at the same time. When this happens, a data collision occurs, and the data from both nodes is rendered useless. The receiver portion of the Ethernet controller monitors the transmission to detect collisions.

When it senses the data bits overlapping, it halts the transmission, as does the other node. The transmitting controller generates an abort pattern code that is transmitted to all the nodes on the LAN, telling them that a collision has occurred. This alerts any nodes that might be waiting to access the LAN that there is a problem.

The receiving node dumps any data that it might have received before the collision occurred. Other nodes waiting to send data generate a random timing number and go into a holding pattern. The timing number is a waiting time that the node sits out before it tries to transmit. Because the number is randomly generated, the odds against two of the nodes trying to transmit again at the same time are very low.

The Ethernet strategy provides for up to 1,024 users to share the LAN. From the description of its collision-recovery technique, however, it should be clear that with more users on an Ethernet LAN, more collisions are likely to occur, and the average time to complete an actual data transfer will be longer.

Ethernet Specifications

Ethernet is classified as a bus topology. The original Ethernet scheme was classified as a 10Mbps transmission protocol. The maximum length specified for Ethernet is 1.55 miles (2.5km), with a maximum segment length between nodes of 500 meters. This type of LAN is referred to as a 10BASE-5 LAN by the IEEE organization.

The XXBaseYY IEEE nomenclature designates that the maximum data rate across the LAN is 10Mbps, that it is a baseband LAN (verses broadband), and that its maximum segment length is 500 meters. One exception to this method is the 10BASE-2 implementation. The maximum segment length for this specification is 185 meters (almost 200).

Newer Ethernet implementations produce LAN speeds of up to 100Mbps using UTP copper cabling. For these networks, the IEEE adopted *10BASET, 100BASET,* and *100BASETX* designations, indicating that they are operating on twisted-pair cabling and depend on its specifications for the maximum segment length.

The 100BASE designation is referred to as *Fast Ethernet.* The TX version of the Fast Ethernet specification employs two pairs of twisted cable to conduct high-speed, full-duplex transmissions. The cables used with the TX version can be Cat 5 UTP or STP. There is also a *100BASEFX Fast Ethernet* designation that indicates the network is using fiber-optic cabling. This specification is described later in this chapter.

Network cards capable of supporting both transmission rates are classified as 10/100 Ethernet cards. The recommended maximum length of a 10/100BASET segment is 100 meters. One problem with using 10/100BASE cards in a system is that the presence of a single 10BASET card in the network can slow down the entire network.

EXAM TIP

Be aware that the 10BASEXX system roughly uses the XX value to represent the distance (in meters) that a network segment can be. (The notable exception is the 185 meter BASE-2 value—it's almost 200 meters.)

EXAM TIP

Know which types of cabling are used to support the different IEEE standards.

EXAM TIP

Memorize the maximum cable lengths associated with different networking standards.

Ethernet Connections

Ethernet connections can be made through 50-ohm, coaxial cable (10BASE-5), thinnet coaxial cable (10BASE-2), or UTP cabling (10BASE-T).

The original UTP LAN specification had a transmission rate that was stated as 1Mbps. Using UTP cable, a LAN containing up to 64 nodes can be constructed with the maximum distance between nodes set at 250 meters. Figure 18.8 depicts typical coaxial and UTP connections.

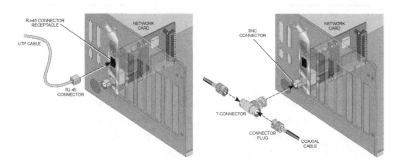

FIGURE 18.8
Typical UTP and coax connections.

Coaxial cables are attached to equipment through *BNC (British Naval Connectors)* connectors. In a 10BASE-2 LAN, the node's LAN adapter card is usually connected directly to the LAN cabling, using a T-connector (for peer-to-peer networks), or by a BNC connector (in a client/server LAN).

UTP LAN connections are made through modular *RJ-45 registered jacks* and plugs. RJ-45 connectors are very similar in appearance to the RJ-11 connectors used with telephones and modems. However, the RJ-45 connectors are considerably larger than the RJ-11 connectors. Some Ethernet adapters include 15-pin sockets that allow special systems, such as fiber-optic cabling, to be interfaced to them. Other cards provide specialized ST connectors for fiber-optic connections.

Table 18.2 summarizes the different Ethernet specifications.

> **EXAM TIP**
>
> Know the types of connectors and physical cable types used with each network type.

> **EXAM TIP**
>
> Know what type of cable 10BASE-T and 100BASE-T use.

| TABLE 18.2 |

ETHERNET SPECIFICATIONS

Classification	Conductor	Maximum Segment Length	Nodes	Maximum Length	Transfer Rate
10BASE-2	RG-58	185m	30/1024	250m	10Mbps
10BASE-5	RG-8	500m	100/1024	2.5km	10Mbps
10BASE-T	UTP/STP	100m/200m	2/1024	2.5km	10Mbps
100BASE-T	UTP	100m	2/1024	2.5km	100Mbps
100BASE-FX	FO	412m	1024	5km	100Mbps

Token Ring

Token Ring is a *token-passing protocol* operating on a ring topology. The token is a small frame that all nodes can recognize instantly. This access protocol standard specification is referred to as the *IEEE-802.5 Token Ring Protocol.*

In a token-passing system, contention for use of the LAN between different nodes is handled by passing an electronic enabling code, called a token, from node to node. Only the node possessing the token can have control of the LAN. Figure 18.9 depicts the Token Ring concept.

FIGURE 18.9
The Token Ring concept.

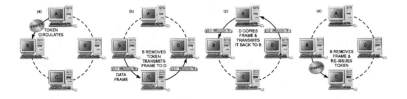

The token is passed from node to node along the LAN. Each node is allowed to hold the token a prescribed amount of time. After sending its message, or after its time runs out, the node must transfer the token to the next node. If the next node has no message, it just passes the token along to the next designated node. Nodes do not have to be in numeric sequence; their sequences are programmed in the network management software. All nodes listen to the LAN during the token-passing time.

The Token Ring cabling is a two-pair, shielded twisted-pair cable. The main cable is called the trunk cable, and the individual drops are referred to as the interface cable. The cables are grouped together in hardware units called concentrators. Internally, the concentrator's ports are connected into a ring configuration. In this manner, the concentrator can be placed in a convenient area, and have nodes positioned where they are needed. Some Token Ring adapters provide nine-pin connectors for *shielded twisted-pair (STP)* cables as well.

The data-transfer rate stated for Token Ring systems is between 4- and 16Mbps. Token-passing is less efficient than other protocols when the network load is light. It evenly divides the network's usage among nodes, however, when traffic is heavy. It can also be extremely vulnerable to node crashes when that node has the token. LAN adapter cards are typically designed to monitor the LAN for such occurrences so that they can be corrected without shutting down the entire network.

The IEEE specifications for both Ethernet (802.3) and Token Ring (802.5) make provisions for a high-speed, full-duplex mode (two-way simultaneous communication). This mode is normally encountered in large networks that have multiple servers. Its primary use is to perform backup functions between the large system servers where a lot of data must be moved through the network. In full-duplex mode, the standard Ethernet transfer rate of 10Mbps is boosted to 20Mbps; the Token Ring rate is raised to 32Mbps. This mode is rarely encountered on desktop client units. These units tend to operate in half-duplex (two-way communication, but in only one direction at a time) mode.

> **EXAM TIP**
>
> Be aware that Ethernet and Token Ring networks have full-duplex capabilities.

Fiber-Optic LANs

As indicated earlier in this chapter, fiber-optic cabling offers the prospect of very high performance links for LAN implementation. It can handle much higher data-transfer rates than copper conductors and can use longer distances between stations before signal deterioration becomes a problem. In addition, fiber-optic cable offers a high degree of security for data communications: Because it does not radiate EMI signal information that can be detected outside the conductor, it does not tap easily, and it shows a decided signal loss when it is tapped into.

Fiber Ethernet Standards

The IEEE organization has created several fiber optic variations of the Ethernet protocol. They classify these variations under the IEEE-803 standard. These standards are referenced as the 10/100BASE-F specification. Variations of this standard include

- *10BASE-FP*—This specification is used for passive star networks running at 10Mbps. It employs a special hub that uses mirrors to channel the light signals to the desired node.

- *10BASE-FL*—This specification is used between devices on the network. It operates in full-duplex mode and runs at 10Mbps. Cable lengths under this specification can range up to 2 kilometers.

- *100BASE-FX*—This protocol is identical to the 10BASE-FL specification with the exception that it runs at 100Mbps. This particular version of the specification is referred to as Fast Ethernet because it can easily run at the 100Mbps rate.

The FDDI Ring Standard

A Token Ring-like network standard has been developed around fiber-optic cabling: the *Fiber Distributed Data Interface (FDDI)* specification. The FDDI network was design to work almost exactly like a Token Ring network—with the exception that it works on two counter-rotating rings of fiber-optic cable.

FDDI employs token passing access control and provides data transfer rates of 100Mbps. Using the second ring, FDDI can easily handle multiple frames of data moving across the network at any given time. Of course, the dual ring implementation provides additional network dependability because it can shift over to a single ring operation if the network controller senses that a break has occurred in one of the rings.

Infrared LANs

The *IrDA infrared transmission* specification makes provisions for multiple IrDA devices to be attached to a computer so that it can have multiple, simultaneous links to multiple IrDA devices. Figure 18.10 shows how IrDA links can be used to share computers and devices through a normal Ethernet hub. In these scenarios, the *IrDA link* provides the high-speed transmission media between the Ethernet devices.

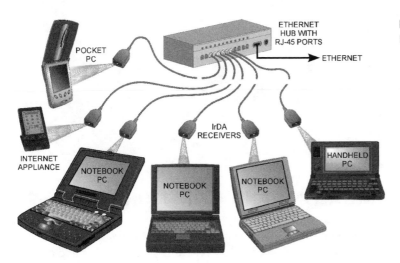

FIGURE 18.10
IrDA networking.

Wireless LANs

Recently, a variety of *wireless local area networking (WLAN* or *LAWN)* specification has been introduced into the market. These networks connect computer nodes together using high-frequency radio waves. The IEEE organization has presented a specification titled *IEEE-802.11* to describe its wireless networking standard.

A typical wireless LAN, depicted in Figure 18.11, consists of a wireless LAN adapter card with an RF antenna. The WLAN adapter cards in the various systems of the LAN communicate with each other and a host system through an Access Point device. Current wireless LANs operate in the range of 1Mbps transfer rates. Wireless LAN adapters are typically available in the form of PCI and PCM-CIA cards.

FIGURE 18.11
A wireless LAN.

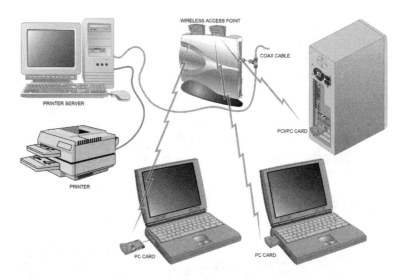

INSTALLING AND CONFIGURING LANs

A portion of the A+ Core Hardware objective 6.1 states that the test taker should be able to: Identify procedures for swapping and configuring network interface cards. Because PC technicians are typically responsible for maintaining the portion of the network that attaches to the computer, they must be able to install, configure, and service the network adapter card and cable.

LAN Adapter Cards

In a LAN, each computer on the network requires a *network adapter card* (also referred to as a network interface card or *NIC*), and every unit is connected to the network by some type of cabling. These cables are typically either twisted-pair wires, thick or thin coaxial cable, or fiber-optic cable.

LAN adapter cards must have connectors that are compatible with the type of LAN cabling being used. Many Ethernet LAN cards come with both an RJ-45 and a BNC connector, so the cards can be used in any type of Ethernet configuration.

Each adapter must have an adapter driver program loaded in its host computer to handle communications between the system and the

> **WARNING**
>
> **Use the User Guide** Although some cards might have jumper instructions printed directly on themselves, the card's user manual is normally required to configure it for operation. Great care should be taken with the user manual because its loss might render the card useless. At the very least, the manufacturer would have to be contacted to get a replacement.

adapter. These are the Ethernet and Token Ring drivers loaded to control specific types of LAN adapter cards.

In addition to the adapter drivers, the network computer must have a network protocol driver loaded. This program can be referred to as the transport protocol, or just as the protocol. It operates between the adapter and the initial layer of network software to package and un-package data for the LAN. In many cases, the computer can have several different protocol drivers loaded so that the unit can communicate with computers that use other types of *protocols*.

Typical protocol drivers include the *Internetworking Packet Exchange/Sequential Packet Exchange (IPX/SPX)* model produced by Novell, and the standard *Transmission Control Protocol/Internet Protocol (TCP/IP)* developed by the U.S. military for its ARPA network.

Installing LANs

Installing a LAN card in a PC follows the basic steps of installing most peripheral cards. Place the adapter card in a vacant expansion slot and secure it to the system unit's back plate. Then, connect the LAN card to the network as directed by the manufacturer's installation guide and load the proper software drivers for the installed adapter. Figure 18.12 illustrates connecting the computer to the LAN, using UTP or coaxial cable. If UTP cabling is being used, the line drop to the computer would come from a concentrator like the one depicted.

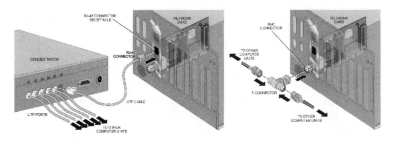

FIGURE 18.12
Connecting the computer to the LAN.

The following three important pieces of information are required to configure the LAN adapter card for use:

◆ The interrupt request (IRQ) setting the adapter will use to communicate with the system

◆ The I/O port address the adapter will use to exchange information with the system

◆ The base memory address the adapter will use as a starting point in memory for DMA transfers

Some adapters might require that a DMA channel be defined for proper operation.

EXAM TIP

Know the system resources normally required by network adapter cards.

NETWORK REPAIR

A portion of the A+ Core Hardware objective 6.1 states that the test taker should be able to—identify the ramifications of repairs on the network. Normally, you should begin troubleshooting a general network problem by determining what has changed since it was running last. If the installation is new, it will need to be inspected as a setup problem. Check to see if any new hardware or software has been added. Has any of the cabling been changed? Have any new protocols been added? Has a network adapter been replaced or moved? If any of these events has occurred, begin by checking them specifically.

Troubleshooting LANs

EXAM TIP

Be aware that in a network environment, no unit really functions alone. Unlike working on a standalone unit, the steps performed on a network computer might affect the operation of other units on the network.

Be aware that in a network environment, no unit really functions alone. Unlike working on a standalone unit, the steps performed on a network computer might affect the operation of other units on the network.

Disconnecting a unit from a network that uses coaxial cable, for example, creates an un-terminated condition in the network. A bad cable or connector can also cause this condition to exist. As a matter of fact, the majority of all network failures involve bad cabling, connectors, and connections.

◆ Data moving through the network can be lost.

◆ A general slowdown of data movement across the network can occur because of reduced bandwidth.

◆ Nodes might not be able to "see" or connect to each other.

If a unit must be removed from the network, it is good practice to place a terminator in the empty connector where the unit was attached. This should allow the other units to function without the problems associated with an open connection. Care must be taken to ensure that the proper value of terminating resistor is used. Substituting a terminator from an obsolete ARCnet network into an Ethernet system might create as many problems as the open connection would have. However, they might be harder to track down. Systems that use concentrators have fewer connection problems when a unit needs to be removed for servicing.

Even if the unit does not need to be removed from the network, diagnostic efforts and tests run across the network can use a lot of the network's bandwidth. This reduced bandwidth causes the operation of all the units on the network to slow down just because of the added usage of the network.

Because performing work on the network can affect so many users, it is good practice to involve the network administrator in any such work being performed. This person can run interference for any work that must be performed that could disable the network or cause users to lose data.

LAN Configuration Checks

As with any peripheral device, its configuration must be correct for the software that is driving the peripheral and for the adapter card it is communicating through. An improperly configured network adapter card can prevent the system from gaining access to the network.

Many newer network cards possess Plug-and-Play capabilities. With other non-PnP network cards, such as most ISA NIC cards, it is necessary to configure the card manually through hardware jumpers, or through logical configuration settings in the *BIOS Extension* EPROM.

EXAM TIP

Be aware of the affects that a missing terminator or bad cable/connector can have on an Ethernet network.

EXAM TIP

Be aware of the effects that running applications across the network can have on its performance.

EXAM TIP

Be aware that many ISA NIC cards are not PnP configurable, so they must be configured manually.

Security Access Problems

One of the major concerns in most network environments is *data security*. Because all the data around the network is potentially available to anyone else attached to the Net, all LAN administration software employs different levels of security. *Passwords* are typically used at all software levels to lock people out of hardware systems, as well as out of programs and data files.

Logon passwords and scripts are designed to keep unauthorized personnel from accessing the system or its contents. Additional passwords can be used to provide access to some parts of the system, and not others. (That is, lower-level accounting personnel may be allowed access to accounts receivable and payable sections of the business management software package, but not allowed into the payroll section.) A series of passwords can be used to deny access to this area.

In other LAN management packages network administrators can control access and privilege levels to programs and data through the operating system's security system. These settings can be established to completely deny access to certain information or to allow limited access rights to it. An example of limited rights would be the ability to read data from a file, but not be able to manipulate it (write, delete, print, or move it) in any way.

The reason for discussing security at this point is because established security settings can prevent the technician from using any, or all, of the system's resources. In addition, having limited access to programs can give them the appearance of being defective. Because of this, the service technician must work with the network administrator when checking a networked machine. The administrator can provide the access, and the security relief, needed to repair the system. The administrator can also keep you away from data that might not be any of your business.

LAN Hardware Checks

Check the activity light on the back plate of the LAN card (if available) to determine whether the network is recognizing the network adapter card. If the lights are active, the connection is alive. If not, check the adapter in another node. Check the cabling to make sure that it is the correct type and that the connector is properly attached. A *LAN cable tester* is an excellent device to have in this situation.

In a network, no node is an island, and every unit has an impact on the operation of the network when it is on line. Changes made in one part of a network can cause problems, and data loss, in other parts of the network. You should be aware that changing hardware and software configuration settings for the adapter might have adverse effects when the system is returned to the network. In addition, changing hard drives in a network node can have a negative impact on the network when the unit is brought back online.

EXAM TIP

Be aware of what activity from the light on the NIC's back plate means.

CHALLENGE #3

You have been called to a customer site to repair a networking problem. The user cannot see any other computers on her network. You check the drivers for the NIC, and you check the protocols that are installed in the operating system and they appear to be okay. You also check the NIC and see that the light on its back panel is not glowing. What items should you check next?

CHAPTER SUMMARY

This chapter has presented basic networking in three parts: "Basic Networking Concepts," "Installing and Configuring LANs," and "Network Repair."

The "Basic Networking Concepts" section presented basic networking terminology and concepts. Major topics of this section included network topologies, types of networks, and connection schemes.

The second portion of the chapter dealt with installing and configuring basic network hardware.

The final section of the chapter concerned network troubleshooting and the possible complications of performing repair work on an operational network.

At this point, review the objectives listed at the beginning of the chapter to be certain that you understand each point and can perform each task listed there. Afterward, answer the review questions that follow to verify your knowledge of the information.

KEY TERMS

- 100BASE-FX
- 100BASEFX Fast Ethernet
- 100BASET
- 100BASETX
- 10BASE-FL
- 10BASE-FP
- 10BASET
- BIOS Extension
- Carrier sense multiple access with collision detection (CSMA/CD)

CHAPTER SUMMARY

- Cat5 cabling
- Client/server network
- Data security
- Fiber Distributed Data Interface (FDDI)
- Fiber-optic cable
- IEEE-802.11
- IEEE-802.3 Ethernet protocol
- IEEE-802.5 Token Ring Protocol
- Internetworking Packet Exchange/Sequential Packet Exchange (IPX/SPX)
- IrDA infrared transmission
- IrDA link
- LAN cable tester
- Local area networks (LANs)
- Network adapter card (NIC)

- Passwords
- Peer-to-peer network
- Protocols
- RJ-45 plug
- RJ-45 registered jacks
- SC connector
- Shielded twisted pair (STP)
- Straight Tip (ST) connector
- Token Ring
- Token-passing protocol
- Transmission Control Protocol/Internet Protocol (TCP/IP)
- Unshielded twisted pair (UTP)
- UTP cable
- Wireless local area networking (WLAN or LAWN)

APPLY YOUR KNOWLEDGE

Review Questions

1. From the network topologies shown in Figure 18.13, identify the bus topology.

   A. A

   B. B

   C. C

   D. D

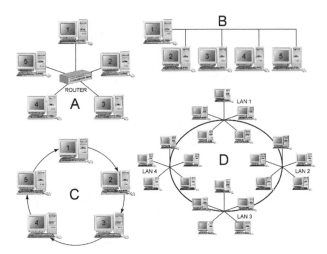

FIGURE 18.13

2. From the network topologies shown in Figure 18.13, identify the ring topology.

   A. A

   B. B

   C. C

   D. D

3. From the network topologies shown in Figure 18.13, identify the star topology.

   A. A

   B. B

   C. C

   D. D

4. From the network topologies shown in Figure 18.13, identify the mesh topology.

   A. A

   B. B

   C. C

   D. D

5. Under CompTIA's definition, a LAN can exist with as few as _____ computers.

   A. two

   B. three

   C. four

   D. five

6. Nodes in _____ networks can serve as both clients and servers for different functions.

   A. client/server

   B. peer-to-peer

   C. token ring

   D. non-differentiated

APPLY YOUR KNOWLEDGE

7. What are the major advantages of client/server over peer-to-peer networks? (Select all that apply.)

   A. Less cable to maintain

   B. Centralized administration

   C. Data and resource security

   D. Low cost

8. What type of cabling is involved in the CAT5 cable rating?

   A. Thin coaxial

   B. UTP

   C. STP

   D. Thick coaxial

9. What type of networks employ SC connectors?

   A. Token ring fiber-optic

   B. Peer-to-peer UTP

   C. Client-server UTP

   D. Ethernet fiber-optic

10. _____ networks have full-duplex capabilities. (Select two answers.)

    A. Ethernet

    B. Token Ring

    C. Fiber-optic

    D. ARCnet

11. What type of Ethernet network uses RG-58 cable?

    A. 10BASE-2

    B. 10BASE-5

    C. 10BASE-T

    D. 100BASE-FX

12. What type of cable do 10BASE-T and 100BASE-T use?

    A. UTP

    B. STP

    C. Fiber-optic

    D. RG-58

13. Which type of cabling is used to support the 100BASE-FX IEEE standard?

    A. Fiber-optic

    B. UTP

    C. STP

    D. Thick coaxial

14. What is the maximum segment length associated with the 10BASE-5 LAN networking standard?

    A. 100m

    B. 185m

    C. 200km

    D. 500m

15. What is the maximum segment length associated with the 10BASE-2 networking standard?

    A. 100m

    B. 185m

    C. 200km

    D. 500m

APPLY YOUR KNOWLEDGE

16. What system resources are normally required by network adapter cards? (Select all that apply.)

    A. Interrupt request (IRQ) setting

    B. I/O port address

    C. DMA address

    D. Base memory address

17. Which of the following actions is likely to crash the local area network?

    A. Shutting down a workstation on a 10BASE-5 LAN

    B. Shutting down a workstation on a 10BASE-T LAN

    C. Disconnecting a workstation on a 10BASE-5 LAN

    D. Disconnecting a workstation on a 10BASE-T LAN

18. What effects will a missing terminator or bad cable/connector have on an Ethernet network? (Select all that apply.)

    A. Network nodes might stop functioning.

    B. Lost data.

    C. Network slowdown.

    D. Network nodes are not visible to each other.

19. What effects will running applications across the network have on its performance?

    A. The unit running the application will not have access to other parts of the network.

    B. The units on the network might slow down.

    C. The units on the network will communicate faster.

    D. The units on the network might crash.

20. Older ISA NICs might require _____ .

    A. an RS-232 cable

    B. manual configuration

    C. PnP configuration

    D. a power cord

21. What does the activity from the light on the network adapter's back plate mean?

    A. The connection is alive.

    B. Data is being uploaded.

    C. Data is being downloaded.

    D. Data is being encrypted.

22. An RJ-45 connector is most commonly used with _____.

    A. disk drive units

    B. fiber-optic cabling

    C. coaxial cabling

    D. unshielded twisted-pair cabling

23. Which connector is not used with network cables?

    A. BNC

    B. RJ-45

    C. SCSI

    D. ST

24. What is the maximum cable length for a 10BASE-T network?

    A. 250m

    B. 500m

    C. 2500m

    D. 5000m

Answers and Explanations

1. **B.** In the bus topology, the stations, or nodes, of the network connect to a central communication link. Each node has a unique address along the bus that differentiates it from the other users on the network. Information can be placed on the bus by any node. The information must contain network address information about the node or nodes that the information is intended for. Other nodes along the bus will ignore the information. For more information, see the section "LAN Topologies."

2. **C.** In a ring network configuration, the communication bus is formed into a closed loop. Each node inspects the information on the LAN as it passes by. A repeater, built in to each ring LAN card, regenerates every message not directed to it and sends it to the next appointed node. The originating node eventually receives the message back and removes it from the ring. For more information, see the section "LAN Topologies."

3. **A.** In a star topology, the logical layout of the network resembles the branches of a tree. All the nodes are connected in branches that eventually lead back to a central unit. Nodes communicate with each other through the central unit. The central station coordinates the network's activity by polling the nodes, one by one, to determine whether they have any information to transfer. If so, the central station gives that node a predetermined slice of time to transmit. If the message is longer than the time allotted, the transmissions are chopped into small packets of information that are transmitted over several polling cycles. For more information, see the section "LAN Topologies."

4. **D.** The mesh design offers the most basic network connection scheme. In this design, each node has a direct physical connection to all the other nodes in the network. Although the overhead for connecting a mesh network topology together in a LAN environment is prohibitive, this topology is employed in two very large network environments—the public telephone system and the Internet. For more information, see the section "LAN Topologies."

5. **A.** Under CompTIA's definition, a LAN can exist with as few as two (2) computers. For more information, see the section "LAN Topologies."

6. **B.** The nodes in a peer-to-peer network configuration usually contain local hard drives and printers that the local computer has control of. These resources can be shared at the discretion of the individual user. A common definition of a peer-to-peer network is one in which all the nodes can act as both clients and servers of the other nodes under different conditions. For more information, see the section "Network Control Strategies."

7. **B, C.** The major advantages of the client/server networking arrangement include centralized administration and data and resource security. For more information, see the section "Network Control Strategies."

8. **B.** EIA/TIA have categorized different grades of cable along with connector, distance, and installation specifications to produce the EIA/TIA UTP wiring category (CAT) ratings for the industry (that is, CAT3 and CAT5 cabling). CAT5 cabling is currently the most widely used specification for data communication wiring. For more information, see the section "UTP Cable."

9. **D.** The SC connector is the dominant connector for fiber optic Ethernet networks. For more information, see the section "Fiber-Optic Cable."

10. **A, B.** The IEEE specifications for both Ethernet (802.3) and Token Ring (802.5) make provisions for a high-speed, full-duplex mode (two-way simultaneous communication). This mode is normally encountered in large networks that have multiple servers. Its primary use is to perform backup functions between the large system servers in which a lot of data must be moved through the network. In full-duplex mode, the standard Ethernet transfer rate of 10Mbps is boosted to 20Mbps; the Token Ring rate is raised to 32Mbps. This mode is rarely encountered on desktop client units. These units tend to operate in half-duplex (two-way communication, but in only one direction at a time) mode. For more information, see the section "Token Ring."

11. **A.** The 10BASE-2 Ethernet specification uses the RG-58 coaxial cable and has a maximum segment length of 185 meters. For more information, see the section "Ethernet Connections."

12. **A.** Newer Ethernet implementations produce LAN speeds of up to 100Mbps using unshielded twisted-pair (UTP) copper cabling. For these networks, the IEEE adopted 10BASE-T, 100BASE-T, and 100BASE-TX designations, indicating that they are operating on twisted-pair cabling and depend on its specifications for the maximum segment length. For more information, see the section "Ethernet Connections."

13. **A.** The 100BASE-FX Fast Ethernet designation indicates that the network is using fiber-optic cabling. For more information, see the section "Fiber Ethernet Standards."

14. **D.** The 10BASE-5 LAN has a maximum segment length of 500m. For more information, see the section "Ethernet Specifications."

15. **B.** The 10BASE-2 LAN has a maximum segment length of 185m. For more information, see the section "Ethernet Specifications."

16. **A, B, D.** Three important pieces of information are required to configure the LAN adapter card for use: The interrupt request (IRQ) setting the adapter will use to communicate with the system, the I/O port address the adapter will use to exchange information with the system, and the base memory address that the adapter will use as a starting point in memory for DMA transfers. For more information, see the section "Installing LANs."

17. **C.** Disconnecting a unit from a network that uses coaxial cable creates an un-terminated condition in the network that might cause it to crash. For more information, see the section "Troubleshooting LANs."

18. **B, C, D.** A bad cable or connector can cause an un-terminated condition in the network. This condition can cause several different types of problems: Data moving through the network can be lost, a general slowdown of data movement across the network can occur because of reduced bandwidth, and nodes might not be able to "see," or connect to, each other. For more information, see the section "Troubleshooting LANs."

19. **B.** Performing diagnostic efforts and running tests across the network can use a lot of the network's bandwidth. This reduced bandwidth causes the operation of all the units on the network to slow down because of just the added usage of the network. For more information, see the section "Troubleshooting LANs."

20. **B.** With non-PnP network cards, such as most ISA NIC cards, it is necessary to configure the card manually through hardware jumpers, or through logical configuration settings in the BIOS Extension EPROM. For more information, see the section "LAN Configuration Checks."

21. **A.** The activity light on the back plate of the LAN card (if available) is used to determine whether the network is recognizing the network adapter card. If the lights are active, the connection is alive. For more information, see the section "LAN Hardware Checks."

22. **D.** Unshielded Twisted Pair (UTP) cabling is terminated with an 8-pin RJ-45 plug. For more information, see the section "UTP Cable."

23. **C.** A SCSI cable is used to connect SCSI devices to the computer. For more information, see the section "Network Cabling."

24. **C.** The 10BASE-T Ethernet specification uses the CAT5 UTP cable and has a maximum cable length of 2500 meters (2.5km). For more information, see the section "Ethernet Connections."

Challenge Solutions

1. A peer-to-peer network is very well suited to this type of environment. The different workers in this scenario need to be able to exchange different types of information between their different work areas. The administrative overhead is minimal in a peer-to-peer network. Also, the information these workers generate can be very intense when it passes across the network. Graphics and multimedia files tend to be quite large and can tie up a network. By creating a peer-to-peer network for the development staff, the main company network will not be required to handle these files. For more information, see the section "Network Control Strategies."

2. In the case of the company's other network requirements, a client/server environment is much better suited for the accounting and warehouse/shipping functions. In most companies, the accounting and payroll information is normally considered confidential and protected. This normally includes inventory and shipping information. The advanced security functions associated with client/server systems are very important in these situations. For more information, see the section "Network Control Strategies."

3. You should check the drop cable to the computer to make sure that it is plugged in and that it is wired correctly (check its color code). Also check the device it is connecting to (that is, the hub or router). For more information, see the section "LAN Hardware Checks."

APPLY YOUR KNOWLEDGE

Suggested Readings and Resources

1. LAN Topologies
   http://www.cisco.com/univercd/cc/td/doc/
   cisintwk/ito_doc/introlan.htm#xtocid6

2. Logical Topologies
   http://www.networkmagazine.com/article/
   NMG20000727S0011

3. UTP Cable
   http://support.3com.com/infodeli/tools/
   hubs/suprstac/ss100/ssii100/appa.htm

4. Fiber-Optic Cable
   http://www.arcelect.com/fibercable.htm

5. Charles Spurgeon's Ethernet Page
   http://www.ethermanage.com/ethernet/
   ethernet.html

6. Token Ring
   http://www.rad.com/networks/1997/nettut/
   token_ring.html

7. Wireless LAN
   http://www.proxim.com/learn/library/
   whitepapers/wp2001-06-what.html

8. Network Hardware Drivers
   www.otex.org/manual/chap10.htm

9. Ethernet Card Configuration
   www.cse.bris.ac.uk/pcs/kb/3comcfg.htm

10. CISCO Troubleshooting Assistance
    http://www.cisco.com/warp/public/779/smbiz
    /service/troubleshooting/ts.htm

11. CISCO Tutorials and References
    http://www.cisco.com/warp/public/779/smbiz
    /service/knowledge/tutorials.htm

12. CISCO Cable and Port Pinouts
    http://www.cisco.com/warp/public/779/smbiz
    /service/knowledge/pinouts/

OPERATING SYSTEM TECHNOLOGIES

This chapter helps you to prepare for the Operating System Technologies module of the A+ Certification examination by covering the following objective within the "Domain 1.0: Operating System Fundamentals" section. Coverage of this objective is continued in Chapter 20, "Navigating Operating Systems."

1.1 Identify the operating system's functions, structure, and major system files to navigate the operating system and how to get to needed technical information.

Content might include the following:

- **Major operating system functions:**
  - **Create folders**
  - **Checking OS Version**
- **Major operating system components:**
  - **Explorer**
  - **My Computer**
  - **Control Panel**
- **Contrasts between Windows 9x and Windows 2000**
- **Major system files: what they are, where they are located, how they are used, and what they contain**
- **System, configuration, and user interface files:**
  - **IO.SYS**
  - **BOOT.INI**
  - **WIN.COM**
  - **MSDOS.SYS**
  - **AUTOEXEC.BAT**
  - **CONFIG.SYS**
  - **COMMAND LINE PROMPT**

CHAPTER 19

Operating System Fundamentals

- **Memory management:**
  - **Conventional**
  - **Extended/upper memory**
  - **High memory**
  - **Virtual memory**
  - **HIMEN.SYS**
  - **EMM386.exe**
- **Windows 9x:**
  - **IO.SYS**
  - **WIN.INI**
  - **USER.DAT**
  - **SYSEDIT**
  - **SYSTEM.INI**
  - **SETVER.EXE**
  - **SMARTDRV.EXE**
  - **MSCONFIG (98)**
  - **COMMAND.COM**
  - **DOSSTART.BAT**
  - **REGEDIT.EXE**
  - **SYSTEM.DAT**
  - **RUN COMMAND**
  - **DriveSpace**
- **Windows 2000:**
  - **Computer Management**
  - **BOOT.INI**
  - **REGEDT32**
  - **REDEDIT**
  - **RUN CMD**
- **NTLDR**
- **NTDETECT.COM**
- **NTBOOTDD.SYS**
- **Command prompt procedures (command syntax):**
  - **DIR**
  - **ATTRIB**
  - **VER**
  - **MEM**
  - **SCANDISK**
  - **DEFRAG**
  - **EDIT**
  - **XCOPY**
  - **COPY**
  - **FORMAT**
  - **FDISK**
  - **MSCDEX**
  - **SETVER**
  - **SCANREG**

▶ The computer technician must be familiar with the functions and structure of operating systems that he might encounter in the field. Currently, the major operating systems associated with personal computers are Windows 9x and Windows 2000. Both operating systems provide a DOS-like command-line interface that works separate from their GUIs. Although "DOS is dead" for consumers, the technician will often need to resort to the command-line interface to isolate and correct problems within the operating system.

▶ Although CompTIA has chosen to begin its Objective Map with a section concerning identifying the OS version and creating directories, followed by a section on major operating system components (Explorer, My Computer, and Control Panel), we feel that this information is better grouped with navigating the operating systems and accessing tools and technical information. Therefore, we have used this chapter to identify the different key operating system's functions, structure, and major system files. Navigating and manipulating different operating systems will be covered in detail in Chapter 20.

STUDY STRATEGIES

To prepare for the Operating System Fundamentals objective of the Operating Systems Technologies exam,

▶ Read the objectives at the beginning of this chapter.

▶ Study the information in this chapter.

▶ Review the objectives listed earlier in this chapter.

▶ Perform any step-by-step procedures in the text.

▶ Answer the review questions at the end of the chapter and check your results.

▶ Use the PrepLogic test engine on the CD-ROM that accompanies this book for additional review and exam questions concerning this material.

▶ Review the exam tips scattered throughout the chapter and make certain that you are comfortable with each point.

INTRODUCTION

All computer systems require an operating system to guide and control the operation of its hardware and to link specialized application software to the hardware. This chapter deals with basic operating system structures and operations. It uses the Microsoft MS-DOS operating system as an example because it represents one of the most fundamental operating systems available.

This chapter begins with a short description of the various types of operating systems used with microprocessor-based systems, such as single- and multiprocess, multiuser, and multitasking systems.

The second major section of the chapter deals with traditional memory organization and management strategies for Microsoft operating systems.

The third major portion of the chapter covers Windows 9x functions, structures, and major files. This is followed by a similar discussion of the Windows NT and Windows 2000 operating systems.

After completing the chapter, you should be able to describe the relationship between the system's BIOS, command-line operations, and graphical user interfaces.

You should also be able to describe the structures and major system files associated with the MS-DOS, Windows 9x, and Windows NT/2000 operating systems.

OPERATING SYSTEM BASICS

Literally thousands of different operating systems are in use with microcomputers. The complexity of each operating system typically depends on the complexity of the application the microcomputer is designed to fill. There are two basic types of operating systems used with personal computers:

- *single-process systems*—Systems that can work on only one task at one time

- *multiple-process systems*—Systems that can work on several tasks at one time

Multiple process operations can be organized in three different ways:

- *multiuser*—Systems that accommodate more than one user at once

- *multitasking*—Systems that work on more than one task at a time

- *multiprocessor*—Systems that divide the processing load into threads and distribute them between different processors

In multiuser and multitasking operations, the appearance of simultaneous operation is accomplished by switching between different tasks in a predetermined order. The multiuser system switches between different users at multiple locations, whereas multitasking systems switch between different applications at a single location. In a multiprocessor operating system, tasks are divided among multiple microprocessors. This type of operation is referred to as *parallel processing*.

MICROSOFT DISK OPERATING SYSTEMS

Most microcomputers use a bootstrapping process to load the operating system into RAM. Bootstrapping describes an arrangement in which the operating system is loaded into memory by a smaller program called the bootstrap loader. In personal computers, the bootstrap operation is one of the functions of the ROM BIOS. The operating system can be loaded from a ROM chip, a floppy disk, a hard disk drive, or from another computer. Loading the more-powerful operating system files from the disk increased the system's onboard intelligence considerably.

The bootstrap process is primarily used in disk drive–based systems to load an operating system that can control such a system. MS-DOS is a disk operating system for IBM PC-compatible computers. In its day, it was easily the most popular operating system in the world. It is also the basis from which Windows 9x derives its underlying organization.

Although the concept of *MS-DOS* has largely disappeared from the consumer computer market, its structure and command-line interface have not gone away for the technician. Many diagnostic and troubleshooting situations exist in which the technician must have a firm understanding of DOS structures and command-line operations. Therefore, we will begin with a description of the MS-DOS boot operation and structure and then use it to contrast the Windows 9*x* and Windows NT/2000 operating systems.

MS-DOS Structure

The main portions of the MS-DOS operating system are the *IO.SYS*, *MSDOS.SYS*, and *COMMAND.COM* files. IO.SYS and MSDOS.SYS are special hidden system files that do not show up in a normal directory listing.

The IO.SYS file moves the system's basic I/O functions into memory and then implements the MS-DOS default control programs, referred to as device drivers, for various hardware components. These include

- ◆ The boot disk drive

- ◆ The console display and keyboard

- ◆ The system's time-of-day clock

- ◆ The parallel and serial communications port

Conversely, the MSDOS.SYS file provides default support features for software applications. These features include

- ◆ Memory management

- ◆ Character input and output

- ◆ Real-time clock access

- ◆ File and record management

- ◆ Execution of other programs

There is a little known MS-DOS system requirement that the MSDOS.SYS file must maintain a size in excess of 1KB.

The operating system is responsible for providing the system's user interface. In MS-DOS, the COMMAND.COM command interpreter contains the operating system's most frequently used

EXAM TIP

Be aware of the minimum file size specification associated with the MSDOS.SYS file.

commands. It also provides the system's primary user interface in the form of the command prompt. The command prompt for most command-line based operating systems is some type of character on the screen (that is, c:\>). The command line is the space immediately following the command prompt on the screen. All commands are typed in this space. They are executed by pressing the Enter key on the keyboard.

When a command is entered at the command-line prompt, the COMMAND.COM program examines it to see whether it is an internal or an external DOS command. Internal commands are understood directly by COMMAND.COM; external commands are stored in a directory called \DOS. If it is one of the internal commands, the COMMAND.COM file can execute it immediately. If not, COMMAND.COM looks in the \DOS directory for the command program.

When MS-DOS runs an application, COMMAND.COM finds the program, loads it into memory, and then gives it control of the system. When the program is shut down, it passes control back to the command interpreter.

The remainder of the MS-DOS operating system is composed of utility programs to carry out DOS operations such as formatting disks (Format), printing files (Print), and copying files (XCOPY).

MS-DOS Configuration Files

In the MS-DOS system, there are two special configuration files, known as *CONFIG.SYS* and *AUTOEXEC.BAT* that can be included in the boot process. These programs are used to optimize the system for operations in particular functions, or with different options. These files can also be found in systems that have been upgraded to a Windows operating system. In these cases, they supply backward compatibility with older hardware and software products.

As the system moves through the boot procedure, the BIOS checks in the root directory of the boot disk for the presence of the CONFIG.SYS file. Afterward, it searches for the COMMAND.COM interpreter, and finally looks in the root directory for the AUTOEXEC.BAT file. Both the CONFIG.SYS and AUTOEXEC.BAT files play key roles in optimizing the system's memory and disk drive usage. Their involvement in the boot process can be summarized as follows:

1. The BIOS searches drives for master boot record.

2. The Primary Bootstrap Loader moves master boot record into memory.

3. The system executes Secondary Bootstrap Loader from master boot record.

4. The Secondary Bootstrap Loader moves IO.SYS and MSDOS.SYS into memory.

5. IO.SYS runs the MSDOS.SYS file to load memory and file management functions.

6. IO.SYS checks for CONFIG.SYS file in root directory.

7. If CONFIG.SYS is found, IO.SYS will use it to reconfigure the system in three read sequences (device, install, and shell).

8. IO.SYS loads COMMAND.COM.

9. COMMAND.COM checks for the AUTOEXEC.BAT file in the root directory.

10. If the AUTOEXEC.BAT file is found, COMMAND.COM will carry out the commands found in the file.

11. If no AUTOEXEC.BAT file is found, COMMAND.COM will display the time and date prompt on the display.

While the system is operating, the BIOS continues to perform several important functions. It contains routines on which the operating system calls to carry out basic services.

CONFIG.SYS

The CONFIG.SYS program is responsible for

◆ Setting up any memory managers being used

◆ Configuring the DOS program for use with options devices and application programs

◆ Loading device-driver software into memory and installing memory-resident programs.

> **EXAM TIP**
>
> Memorize the sequence in which files are loaded in a DOS startup.

EXAM TIP

Know which statements and commands are normally located in the CONFIG.SYS file.

These activities are illustrated in the sample CONFIG.SYS file:

```
1    Device=C:\DOS\HIMEM.SYS
     Device=C:\DOS\EMM386.EXE 1024 RAM
2    FILES=30          BUFFERS=15
     STACKS=9,256
3    DEVICE=C:\DOS\SMARTDRV.SYS 1024
     DOS=HIGH,UMB
     DEVICEHIGH=C:\MOUSE\MOUSE.SYS
     DEVICEHIGH=C:\DOS\RAMDRIVE.SYS 4096/a
```

Memory Managers

In the first section, the system's memory-manager programs are loaded. In this case, the *HIMEM.SYS* command loads the DOS *extended memory driver (XMS)*. This driver manages the use of extended memory installed in the system so that no two applications use the same memory locations at the same time. This memory manager should normally be listed in the CONFIG.SYS file before any other memory managers or devices drivers.

HIMEM.SYS also creates a 64KB area of memory just above the 1MB address space called the *high memory area (HMA)*. With this, the DOS=HIGH statement is used to shift portions of DOS from conventional memory into the HMA.

EXAM TIP

Know the purpose and function of the HIMEM.SYS file.

The *EMM386.EXE* program provides the system's microprocessor with access to the *upper memory area (UMA)* of RAM. Operating together with the HIMEM.SYS program, this program enables the system to conserve conventional memory by moving device drivers and memory-resident programs into the UMA.

Files, Buffers, and Stacks

In the second section of the CONFIG.SYS file are the commands that define DOS for operation with optional devices and applications. The FILES command causes the DOS program to establish the number of files that DOS can handle at any one time at 30. This just happens to be the minimum number required to load Windows for operation. The BUFFERS command sets aside 15 blocks of RAM memory space for storing data being transferred to and from disks. Similarly, the STACKS command establishes the number and length of some special RAM memory storage operations at nine memory stacks, with each being 256 bytes long.

Device Drivers

Device drivers are loaded in the third part of the file. Device drivers are programs that tell DOS how to control specific devices. `DEVICE-HIGH=C:\MOUSE\MOUSE.SYS` is a command that loads a third-party device driver supporting the particular mouse being used with the system.

The *SMARTDRV.SYS* driver establishes a disk cache in an area of extended memory as a storage space for information read from the hard disk drive. A cache is a special area of memory reserved to hold data and instructions recently accessed from another location. A disk cache holds information recently accessed from the hard disk drive. Information stored in RAM is much quicker to access than if it were on the hard drive.

When a program or DOS operation requests more data, the SMARTDRV program redirects the request to check in the cache memory area to see whether the requested data is there. If SMART-DRV finds the information in the cache, it will operate on it from there. If the requested information is not in the cache, the system will access the hard drive for it. Using this technique, the overall operating speed of the system is improved. When the system is shut down, SMARTDRV copies the most current information onto the hard drive.

The 1024 modifier establishes a memory cache size of 1MB (1024KB of memory) in extended memory. This is a typical cache size for SMARTDRV; however, 2MB (2048KB) is probably the most efficient size for the cache because the larger the cache size, the greater the chance that the requested information will be in the cache.

The *RAMDRIVE.SYS* driver simulates the organization of a hard disk drive in RAM memory. This type of drive is called a virtual disk. In this case, the `DEVICEHIGH=` command loads the RAMDRV into the upper memory area rather than the base memory area, where a simple `DEVICE=` command would run it.

MS-DOS comes with several other standard device driver programs. These include

- ◆ KEYBOARD.SYS
- ◆ DISPLAY.SYS

♦ ANSI.SYS

♦ DRIVER.SYS

♦ PRINTER.SYS

EXAM TIP

Know which driver assigns logical drive letters to the system's floppy drives.

From the list, you can see that these basic drivers are included to control the operation of the system's most basic input and output devices and ports. KEYBOARD.SYS is the default keyboard definition file. The DISPLAY.SYS driver supports code-page switching for the monitor type in use by the system. A code page is the set of 256 characters that DOS can handle at one time, when displaying, printing, and manipulating text. ANSI.SYS supports ANSI escape-code sequences used to modify the function of the system's display and keyboard. This file is also required to display colors on the monitor under DOS. *DRIVER.SYS* creates the logical drive assignments for the system's floppy drives (that is, A: and B:). Finally, the PRINTER.SYS driver supports code-page switching for parallel ports. All these drivers are normally found in the DOS directory.

AUTOEXEC.BAT

After completing the CONFIG.SYS operation, DOS searches for the presence of a file called the AUTOEXEC.BAT file. This file contains a batch of DOS commands that will automatically be carried out when DOS is loaded into the system.

Refer to the following sample AUTOEXEC.BAT file:

```
DATE
TIME
PROMPT=$P$G
SET TEMP=C:\TEMP
PATH=C:\;C:\DOS;C:\MOUSE
SMARTDRV.EXE 2048 1024
CD\
DIR
```

The first two commands cause the operating system to prompt you for the date and time (because DOS does not automatically do this when an AUTOEXEC.BAT file is present). The PROMPT=PG command causes the active drive and directory path to be displayed on the command line. The SET TEMP line sets up an area for holding data temporarily in a directory named TEMP.

The *PATH command* creates a specific set of paths that DOS will use to search for executable (EXE, COM, and BAT) files. In this example, DOS will search for these files first in the root directory (`C:\`), followed by the DOS directory (`C:\DOS`), and finally through the Mouse directory (`C:\MOUSE`). This statement effectively lets a MOUSE.COM or MOUSE.EXE driver program—normally located in the Mouse directory—to be executed from anywhere in the system. Upon receiving the `MOUSE` command, the operating system looks through all the directories in the path until it finds the specified filename.

The *syntax* (punctuation and organization) of the `PATH` command is very important. Each entry must be complete from the root directory and must be separated from the preceding entry by a semicolon. There should be no spaces in the `PATH` command.

> **EXAM TIP**
> Know which commands are normally located in a typical AUTOEXEC.BAT file.

Windows Initialization Files

The original Windows 3.*x* operating environment was introduced between MS-DOS and the Windows 9*x* operating systems. Windows 3.*x* was a separate graphical environment that worked on top of the DOS operating system. It was built on a number of *Initialization (.INI) files* that held the system's hardware and software configuration information. The major Windows 3.*x* initialization files included

- ◆ WIN.INI
- ◆ CONTROL.INI
- ◆ WINFILE.INI
- ◆ PROGMAN.INI
- ◆ SYSTEM.INI

Current versions of Windows 9*x* and Windows 2000 continue to include these files for compatibility reasons. The `\Windows` directory can also contain several other INI files. When a new Windows application is installed, it might very well install its own INI file at that time. These files can be modified to customize, or optimize, the program's execution.

> **EXAM TIP**
> Be aware of how Windows versions before Windows 95 organized and monitored the system's configuration information.

Parameters in INI files are typically modified through normal Windows menus or pop-up dialog boxes. Other parameters can only be changed by directly modifying the INI files. Changes to the files are automatically updated whenever Windows is exited.

Basic Memory Management

Decisions were made in the original IBM PC design, and thereby, the MS-DOS operating system that ran it, that still affect design of PCs and operating systems. Technicians who work on PC-compatible systems must understand how they allocate memory and how that memory can be manipulated to provide the best system performance.

DOS Memory Organization

The original PC-DOS version was constructed in two sections. The first 640KB of memory was reserved for use by the DOS operating system and its programs. The remaining section was reserved for use by the BIOS and the system's peripherals (that is, the video card, the hard drive controller card, and so on). This arrangement consumed the entire 1MB addressing range associated with the 8088 microprocessor used in the original PCs.

As more powerful microprocessors entered the market, MS-DOS retained the limitations imposed on it by the original version to remain compatible with older machines and software. Special add-on programs called memory managers were created to enable the system to access and use the additional memory capabilities available with more powerful microprocessors.

Basic Memory Organization

Basically, MS-DOS could recognize the following classifications of memory: *conventional memory*, *upper memory blocks*, *high memory area*, *expanded memory*, *extended memory*, and *virtual memory*. Because of compatibility issues, these decisions have carried over into the address allocations of all DOS-based PC compatibles, as described in Figure 19.1.

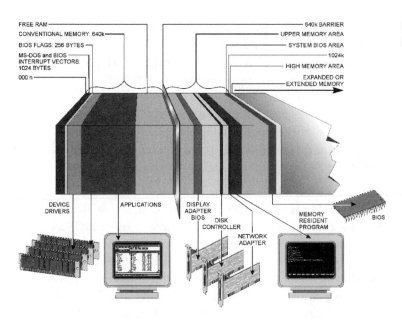

FREE RAM
CONVENTIONAL MEMORY: 640k
BIOS FLAGS: 256 BYTES
MS-DOS and BIOS INTERRUPT VECTORS: 1024 BYTES
000 h

640k BARRIER
UPPER MEMORY AREA
SYSTEM BIOS AREA
1024k
HIGH MEMORY AREA
EXPANDED OR EXTENDED MEMORY

DEVICE DRIVERS
APPLICATIONS
DISPLAY ADAPTER BIOS
DISK CONTROLLER
NETWORK ADAPTER
MEMORY RESIDENT PROGRAM
BIOS

FIGURE 19.1
PC memory allocations.

Conventional Memory

Conventional memory (locations 00000h through 9FFFFh) is the standard memory area for all PC-compatible systems. It traditionally holds the operating system, the interrupt vector tables, and relocated ROM BIOS tables. The remaining space in the conventional memory area is referred to as DOS Program Memory. (Programs written to operate under PC-DOS or MS-DOS use this area for program storage and execution.)

The Upper Memory Area

The *upper memory area (UMA)* occupies the 384KB portion of the PC's address space from A0000h to FFFFFh. This space is not normally considered as part of the computer's total address space because programs cannot store information in this area. Instead, the area is reserved to run segments of the system's hardware. Address spaces from A0000h through BFFFFh are dedicated addresses set aside for the system's video display memory. The system's ROM BIOS occupies the address space between locations FE000h and FFFFFh.

Between the video memory and system BIOS areas, addresses are reserved to hold BIOS extension programs for add-on hardware adapters. Typical BIOS extensions include those for hard drive adapters, advanced video adapters, and network adapters. After the BIOS extensions are in place, the typical UMA still has many unused memory areas that can have information mapped (copied) into them. This space is segmented into 64KB sections called *upper memory blocks (UMBs)*. The primary use for these blocks is to hold installable device drivers and other memory resident programs moved out of the conventional memory area. By moving these programs out of the conventional memory area, more space is made available there for use by application programs.

PCs also use this area to incorporate a memory-usage scheme called *Shadow RAM* to improve their overall performance. With this feature, the contents of the system BIOS and/or adapter BIOS are rewritten (shadowed) into faster extended memory RAM locations. The operating system then re-maps the ROM addresses to the corresponding RAM locations through unused portions of the UMA. Shadowing enables the system to operate faster when application software makes use of any of the BIOS' CALL routines.

Extended Memory

With the advent of the 80286 microprocessor and its protected operating mode, it became possible to access physical memory locations beyond the 1-megabyte limit of the 8088. Memory above this address is generally referred to as *extended memory*.

Modern operating systems can take full advantage of extended memory through the Protected Addressing modes of the more advanced microprocessors. This capability to manage higher memory enables the system to free up more of the base memory area for use by applications programs.

Virtual Memory

The term *virtual memory* is used to describe memory that isn't what it appears to be. Virtual memory is actually disk drive space that is manipulated to seem like RAM. Software creates virtual memory by swapping files between RAM and the disk drive. This memory management technique effectively creates more total memory for the system's applications to use. When the system runs out of available RAM, it shifts data to the virtual memory swap file on the disk drive. However, because a major transfer of information involves the hard disk drive, an overall reduction in speed is encountered with virtual memory operations.

EXAM TIP

Know what actions operating systems take when they run out of available RAM.

The following list describes the types of swap files supported by the various Microsoft operating systems:

◆ Temporary swap files—Windows 3.*x*

◆ Permanent swap files—Windows 3.*x*, NT, 2000

◆ Variable swap files—Windows 9*x*

Windows 9*x* swap files do not require contiguous drive space and can be established on compressed drives that use virtual device drivers. The size of the Windows 9*x* swap file, called *WIN386.SWP*, is variable and is dynamically assigned. Control of Windows 9*x* virtual memory operations is established through the Control Panel's System\Performance tab. The default and recommended setting in Windows 9*x* is Let Windows Manage My Virtual Memory Settings.

In Windows 2000, the virtual memory functions are located under the Control Panel's System icon. The Windows NT and Windows 2000 pagefiles (named *PAGEFILE.SYS*) are created when the operating system is installed. Its default size is typically set at 1.5 times the amount of RAM installed in the system. It is possible to optimize the system's performance by distributing the swap file space between multiple drives. It can also be helpful to relocate it away from slower or heavily used derives. The swap file should not be placed on mirrored or striped volumes. Also, don't create multiple swap files on logical disks that exist on same physical drive.

> **EXAM TIP**
>
> Memorize the filenames of the virtual memory swap files used in each operating system.

Flat Memory Models

Unlike MS-DOS, Windows 3.*x*, or Windows 9*x*, other operating systems, such as Windows NT, Windows 2000, UNIX, and Linux do not employ the address segmentation features of the Intel microprocessors to divide up the computer's memory allocations. Because segments can overlap, memory usage errors can occur when an application attempts to write data into a space being used by the operating system or by another application.

Using the *Flat Memory Model*, the memory manager sections map each application's memory space into contiguous pages of physical memory. Using this method, each application is mapped into a truly unique address space that cannot overlap any other address space. The lack of segment overlap reduces the chances of applications interfering with each other and helps to ensure data integrity by providing the operating system and other processes with their own memory spaces.

Figure 19.2 illustrates the Flat Memory Model concept. In this example, the 32-bit address produced by the microprocessor contains three parts dictated by the operating system. This arrangement guarantees that there is only one method of entering the page space—through this table. Therefore, there is no chance for poorly written software to stray into a page it has not been assigned.

FIGURE 19.2
Flat memory model.

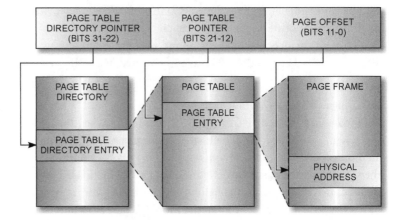

Optimizing Memory

The real objective in memory management in DOS and Windows 9x is to free up as much conventional memory as possible for use by DOS-based programs. The first step in this process is to use the DOS *MEM command* to determine how much memory is actually in the system and how it is organized. Figure 19.3 shows a typical memory map displayed by the MEM command.

```
C:\>

C:\>mem

Memory Type          Total  =  Used  +  Free

Conventional          640K      47K      593K
Upper                   0K       0K        0K
Reserved              384K     384K        0K
Extended (XMS)      7,168K   2,112K    5,056K

Total memory        8,192K   2,559K    5,633K

Total under 1 MB      640K      47K      593K

Largest executable program size        593K  (607,312 bytes)
Largest free upper memory block          0K       (0 bytes)
MS-DOS is resident in the high memory area.
```

FIGURE 19.3
The MEM display.

When the MEM command is executed without any modifying switches, the system's free and used memory space is displayed. Adding a Page (/p) switch to the line causes the output to stop at the end of each screen full of information. In versions of MS-DOS before release 6.0, the /p switch produced a program function that displayed the status of programs currently loaded into memory. Likewise, using a Debug (/d) switch with the MEM command will show the status of currently loaded programs and internal drivers. Another switch, called the Classify (/c) switch, displays the status of programs in conventional memory and the UMA. In addition, it provides each program's size in decimal and hex notation, along with a summary of memory usage and the largest memory blocks available. The MEM command can only be used with one switch at a time.

WINDOWS 9x FUNCTIONS, STRUCTURES, AND MAJOR FILES

The computer technician must be familiar with the functions and structure of different operating systems that might be encountered in the field. The major operating systems associated with personal computers are Windows 9x and Windows 2000. Both operating systems provide a DOS-based, command-line interface that works separately from their GUIs. The technician will often need to use this interface to isolate and correct problems within the operating system. This section focuses on Windows 9x.

Windows Evolution

Because of the huge installed base of Windows 3.x and Windows 95 products, every technician needs to be familiar with these operating systems for at least the immediate future. The 9x version of Windows (including ME) has been produced as five distinct products:

◆ Windows 95

◆ Windows 95 OSR2

◆ Windows 98

◆ Windows 98SE

◆ Windows Millennium Edition

Windows 95

In 1995, Microsoft released a radically different looking Windows environment called *Windows 95*. It offered improved multimedia support for video and sound file applications, Plug-and-Play hardware support, 32-bit advanced multitasking functions, improved email and fax capabilities through Microsoft Exchange, and the Microsoft Network for easy wide area network usage.

Windows 95 offered full built-in Plug-and-Play capability. When it was combined with a hardware system that implemented PnP BIOS, expansion slots, adapter support, and that was supported with PnP adapter drivers, fully automated configuration and reconfiguration could take place.

Even though Windows 95 was optimized for running 32-bit applications, it was still fully compatible with 16-bit Windows 3.x and MS-DOS applications. It could be installed over either of these operating system versions as a direct upgrade. The only real concern when installing Windows 95 over either of these operating systems was that the existing system had the hardware resources needed to run Windows 95.

Windows 95 OSR2

Windows 95 OSR2, also known as *Windows 95 (b)*, is an upgrade of the original Windows 95 package and includes patches and fixes for version 1, along with Microsoft Internet Explorer 3.0 and Personal Web Server. It also includes an enhanced file allocation table system, referred to as FAT32.

In addition to the FAT32 system, OSR2 offered improved power management (APM) functions, bus mastering support, MMX multimedia support, and enhanced PCMCIA functions over version 1 (which was referred to as OSR1, or Service Pack 1). Also new in OSR2 was HDD/CD-ROM DMA access support. This feature was located in the Control Panel/System/Device Manager/Disk Drives window.

Windows 98

Microsoft's *Windows 98* replaced the Windows 95 operating system. Although many of its features remained basically the same as those of Windows 95, Windows 98 did bring certain new items to the system. Most notably, it extended the desktop to the Internet, creating a Web-based desktop environment. This feature was designed to make Internet (or Intranet) access as seamless as possible for the user. It also enabled Windows 98 to perform unattended, self-upgrades directly from the Microsoft Web site when new items or repairs were released.

In 1999, Microsoft produced an improved version of Windows 98 that became known as *Windows 98SE (Second Edition)*. This edition was basically the original Windows 98 platform with all of the patches incorporated. However, it did transform a relatively unstable operating system into a very stable platform. Along with the patches, Windows 98SE offered additional device drivers and Internet Explorer repair tools. Its only notable new feature was built-in Internet connection sharing. This feature enables a Windows 98 machine to act as a proxy server for other nodes in a network. The proxy acts as the connection point to the Internet for all of the computers on the LAN.

Windows Millennium

Windows Millennium Edition (ME) is the latest variation of the Windows 9*x* line of consumer operating systems. However, although it operates in a manner similar to Windows 98, it incorporates more of the look and feel of the Windows 2000 commercial operating system discussed in the next chapter.

Windows ME minimizes the user's access to the command prompt functions. It also includes a number of new self-repairing capabilities that perform some of the technician's repair functions automatically. Many of the items we will discuss in this chapter, and in the operating system troubleshooting chapters (26 and 27), have been moved to new, Windows 2000-like locations in Windows ME.

Windows 9*x* Structure

The Windows 9*x* program is loaded when the startup routine locates and executes the file named *WIN.COM*. This file resides in the \Windows folder and is responsible for loading the Windows operating system. When fully installed, the Windows 9*x* structure is depicted in Figure 19.4.

FIGURE 19.4

The Windows 9x organizational structure.

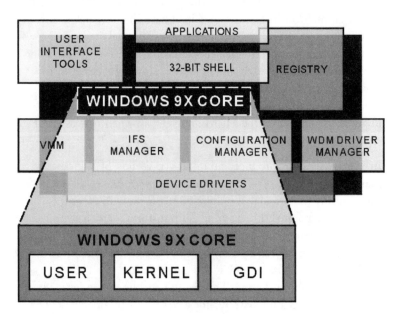

The Windows 9x Core consists of three components: the Kernel, the GDI, and the USER files. Their functions are basically the same for both Windows 95 and Windows 98 architectures. The Kernel is the foundation of the system. It includes basic memory and I/O management, task scheduling, error (exception) handling, and program execution functions. The USER files manage input from hardware devices and output to the user interface components (that is, to the icons and screen structures). The GDI components control what appears on the video display and from the printer.

The Kernel files (KERNEL32.DLL and KERNEL386.EXE) contain the Windows 9x core and load its device drivers. The GDI files provide the base of the graphical device interface; the USER files provide the user interface. The GDI files graphically represent and manage the system's hardware devices.

Any *WIN.INI*, *SYSTEM.INI*, and *WINFILE.INI* files that previously existed are included in the Windows directory to maintain compatibility functions with older software. These files are retained for use with older 16-bit applications and are not necessary for the operation of Windows 9x applications. These files must be checked if the Windows 9x system has conflicts with any 16-bit applications.

The Windows 9x shell program is normally the Windows 9x desktop.

Windows 9x possesses system boot-up files that replace the MS-DOS files described earlier in this chapter. The Windows 9x version of IO.SYS is a real-mode operating system that replaces the DOS version. It also takes over many of the functions associated with the CONFIG.SYS file. An MSDOS.SYS file is created to retain compatibility with older applications. However, the Windows 9x VMM32 and VxD files take over control of the system from the IO.SYS file during the startup process. Windows 9x supplies its own version of COMMAND.COM as well.

No CONFIG.SYS or AUTOEXEC.BAT files are created when Windows 9x is installed in a new system. These files are also not required by Windows 9x to start up or to run. Even so, both files will be retained from the previous operating system in upgraded systems to maintain compatibility with older applications. However, entries in the CONFIG.SYS file override the values in the Windows 9x IO.SYS file.

EXAM TIP

Be aware of the file that is used to load the Windows environment into memory.

The Windows 9*x* IO.SYS file also handles some of the AUTOEX-EC.BAT commands. In both cases, the system uses REM statements to deactivate those CONFIG.SYS and AUTOEXEC.BAT functions implemented in the IO.SYS file. Similarly, the functions of the SYSTEM.INI and WIN.INI files have been moved to the *Windows 9x Registry*.

Windows 9*x* provides a mechanism for automatically starting programs whenever the operating system starts by adding them to the system's Startup folder. You can accomplish this by accessing the Start Menu's Programs tab and then selecting the Add option. From here you can simply browse until the desired program is found and then double-click on it. Finish the addition by clicking the Next button and then double-clicking on the Startup folder. These programs can be bypassed for troubleshooting purposes by pressing the left-Shift key during startup.

> **EXAM TIP**
> Remember how to prevent the items in the Windows 9*x* Startup folder from running at startup.

Optimizing Windows 9*x* Performance

As mentioned earlier, establishing a supplemental cache for the CD-ROM drive can enhance the efficiency of a Windows 9*x* system. This cache enables data to be paged between the CD and the system (or hard disk). The supplemental cache is established through the Control Panel's System icon:

1. Under the System icon, click the Performance tab and select the File System button.

2. Set the Supplemental Cache Size slider to the desired cache size.

3. Set the Optimize Access Pattern for setting to the Quad-speed or higher option (unless you have an old single- or double-speed drive). This will establish a 1,238KB supplemental cache (provided the system's RAM size is larger than 12MB).

4. Click the OK button and restart the system to create the cache.

> **EXAM TIP**
> Know how to optimize the operation of a CD-ROM drive in Windows 9*x*.

In a pure 32-bit Windows 9*x* environment, very little memory management is needed. In these systems, new 32-bit virtual device drivers (VxDs) are automatically loaded into extended memory during the boot-up process. This eliminates the need for DEVICE= and

LOADHIGH commands for devices that have VxDs and Windows 9*x* application programs. However, when 16-bit device drivers or DOS applications are being used, Windows must create a real-mode DOS environment for them. For this reason, Windows 9*x* will execute a CONFIG.SYS and/or AUTOEXEC.BAT file that it encounters during bootup.

If no DOS-based drivers or applications are in the system, the CONFIG.SYS and AUTOEXEC.BAT files are not necessary. However, the Windows 9*x* version of the IO.SYS file will automatically load the Windows 9*x* version of the HIMEM.SYS file during bootup. This file must be present for Windows 9*x* to boot up. There are likely to be multiple versions of the HIMEM.SYS file in a Windows 9*x* system. (There could be three or more versions.)

If a Windows 9*x* system has a CONFIG.SYS, AUTOEXEC.BAT, or .INI file that has been held over from a previous operating system, you should be aware that any unneeded commands in these files have the potential to reduce system performance. In particular, the SMARTDRV function from older operating systems will inhibit dynamic VCACHE operation and slow the system down. The VCACHE driver establishes and controls a disk cache in an area of RAM as a storage space for information read from the hard disk drive, CD-ROM, and other drives and file operations.

> **EXAM TIP**
>
> Know what function the VCACHE utility performs in a Windows 9*x* system.

If the system runs slowly, check the CONFIG.SYS and AUTOEXEC.BAT files for SMARTDRV and any other disk cache software settings. Remove these commands from both files to improve performance. Also, remove any Share commands from the AUTOEXEC.BAT file.

The SYSTEM.INI, WIN.INI, PROTOCOL.INI, CONFIG.SYS and AUTOEXEC.BAT files can be modified through the System Editor (Sysedit) in Windows 9*x*. This utility can be accessed by typing the Sysedit command in the Start/Run dialog box.

> **EXAM TIP**
>
> Be aware of the effect that active commands in a CONFIG.SYS, AUTOEXEC.BAT, or INI file can have on the operation of an advanced Windows operating system.

Windows 98 Components

The Windows 98 structure is organized as depicted in Figure 19.5. The Windows Registry, Configuration Manager, Virtual Machine Manager, and Installable File System (IFS) Manager operate between the Windows 9*x* core and the device drivers that service the system's hardware. On the other side of the Windows 9*x* core, applications running on the system are accessed through the new 32-bit Shell and User Interface tools.

FIGURE 19.5
The Windows 98 organizational structure.

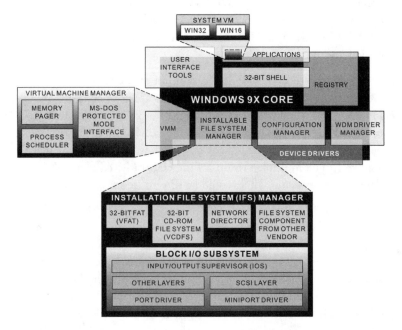

The 32-bit Windows 98 structure basically builds on the Windows 95 structure. However, Windows 98 did add enhanced video display support, power management functions, and additional hardware support. It also featured built-in Internet Explorer functions.

Windows 9x Registries

In Windows 9*x*, the system's configuration information is held in a large hierarchical database called the *Registry*. The Registry structure is primarily used to hold information about system hardware that has been identified by the enumeration or detection processes of the Plug-and-Play system. When a device is installed in the system, Windows 9*x* detects it, either directly or through the system's bus managers, and searches the registry and installed media sources for an appropriate driver. When the driver is found, it is recorded in the registry along with its selected settings.

The Registry also holds information that enables the system to serve and track multiple users. It does this by retaining user- and configuration-specific information that can be used to customize the system

EXAM TIP

Know what type of database Windows uses for its Registry.

to different users, or to different configuration situations. This includes the local hardware configuration, the network environment, file associations, and user configurations.

The contents of the Windows 9*x* Registry are located in two files located in the \Windows directory. These are the *USER.DAT* and *SYSTEM.DAT* files. The USER.DAT file contains user-specific information, whereas the SYSTEM.DAT file holds hardware- and computer-specific profiles and setting information.

Each time Windows 95 boots up successfully, these files are backed up with a .DA0 extension. The contents of the Windows 95 Registry can be viewed and altered through the Registry Editor (*REGEDIT.EXE*) utility, as depicted in Figure 19.6. If the system experiences a Registry corruption problem, the *USER.DA0* and *SYS-TEM.DA0* files can be renamed to DAT files and used to restore the Registry to its previous working configuration.

EXAM TIP

Know which two files make up the Windows 95 Registry and where they are located in the system.

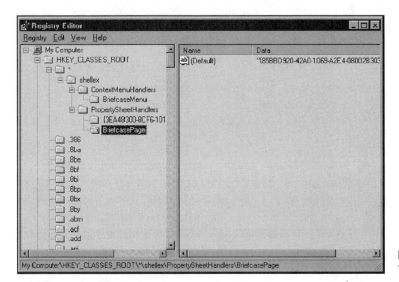

FIGURE 19.6
The Windows 9x Registry Editor.

The contents of the Registry are not backed up in the same way under Windows 98 that they were in Windows 95. The Windows 98 system makes up to five backup copies of the Registry structure each time it successfully starts Windows. The backed-up contents of the Windows 98 Registry are stored in the \Windows\Sysbckup

EXAM TIP

Know where the Windows 98 Registry files are stored and what they are called.

directory in the form of *cabinet (.CAB) files*—not as .DA0 files. These files contain the following Registry-related files:

◆ System.dat

◆ System.ini

◆ User.dat

◆ Win.ini

The Sysbckup folder is a hidden folder. To examine its contents, you must remove the hidden attribute from it. Inside the folder, the backup files are stored under an RB0*XX*.CAB format, where *XX* is a sequential backup number given to the file when it is created. Running the Scanreg /Restore command will also produce a listing of the available backup files to select from for troubleshooting purposes.

If you examine the My Computer heading using the RegEdit option, you will find six categories listed. The head keys all start with an HKEY_ notation. Most of the HKEY titles should appear very descriptive of their contents. Under My Computer, the categories are

◆ HKEY_CLASSES_ROOT—The Classes_Root key divides the system's files into two groups by file-extension type and by association. This key also holds data about icons associated with the file.

◆ HKEY_CURRENT_USER—The Current_User key holds the data about the user-specific configuration settings of the system, including color, keyboard, desktop, and start settings. The values in the Current_User key reflect those established by the user who is currently logged on to the system. If a different user logs on, the contents of the Users key is moved into the Current_User key.

◆ HKEY_USERS—The Users key contains the information about the various users who have been defined to log on to the system. The information from the Current_User key is copied into this section whenever a user logs off the system or when the system is shut down.

◆ HKEY_LOCAL_MACHINE—The Dyn_Data key and Current_Config keys work with the Local_Machine key.

◆ HKEY_DYN_DATA—The Dyn_Data key works with the branch of the Local_Machine key that holds PnP dynamic status information for various system devices including current status and problems.

◆ HKEY_CURRENT_CONFIG—The Current_Config key works with the Local_Machine branch containing current information about hardware devices.

EXAM TIP

Memorize the basic function of each Registry key.

CHALLENGE #1

One of your friends calls you to get some advice about his computer. He was reading an article about changing his Windows 98 system so that it would run games faster. The article mentioned making changes in the Registry, so he did—through the Registry Editor. Now his system will not run, and he does not know how to get it going again. What can you do to help him?

NOTE

Hands-On Activity For hands-on experience with this concept, refer to Lab Procedure #13, "Advanced Windows Me," located on the CD that accompanies this book.

Windows 9x System Policies

Because Windows 9x provides multiuser operations, operational policies are necessary to govern the rights and privileges of different users. Windows 9x System Policies establish guidelines to restrict user access to the options in the Control Panel and desktop. They also enable administrators to customize the desktop and configure network settings.

When a user logs on to the system, Windows 9x checks that user's configuration information. When found, the policy information associated with that user is moved into the Registry and replaces the existing settings. This information is held in the CONFIG.POL file. Policies can be established for individual users, for defined groups of users, for a specific computer, for a network environment, or for default settings.

The system policies that govern these functions are established and modified using an editor similar to the Registry Editor, called the *System Policy Editor (Poledit)*. The Policy Editor is another tool that can be used to access the information in the Registry. Unlike the

RegEdit utility, the Policy Editor can only access subsets of keys. The Registry Editor can access the entire Registry.

Normally, the use of the Poledit tool is restricted to the network administrator. Therefore, it is not normally installed on users' computers. The utility is located on the Windows 9x CD, under the Admin folder so that only the keeper of the CD can adjust the system's policies. The path to access the Policy Editor on the CD is ADMIN\APPTOOLS\POLEDIT. Once located, it can be executed by entering **Poledit** in the Start/Run dialog box.

WINDOWS NT/2000 STRUCTURES AND MAJOR FUNCTIONS

As previously mentioned, computer technicians must be familiar with the functions and structure of operating systems that they might encounter in the field. Windows 2000 is one of the major operating systems currently associated with personal computers. It is a successor of the Windows NT line of operating systems developed specifically for use in business computing applications.

Windows NT

While Microsoft developed and improved the Windows 3.x and Windows 9x products for desktop use by the general population, it also developed a more robust and complicated operating system for corporate client/server networking installations. This new windowed operating system was introduced as Windows New Technology, or Windows NT.

Windows NT was built around a new operating system kernel that focused on enhanced reliability, scalability, and security elements required for corporate applications, while retaining the strengths of the Windows operating system.

The Windows NT operating system actually exists as three distinct products:

◆ A workstation operating system

◆ A server operating system

◆ An extended server operating system to manage large
enterprise networks

Although all three Windows NT product types are referenced in this
chapter, the scope of the A+ examination deals with the Workstation
versions of the software. Therefore, the discussions in this chapter
will primarily be aimed at these portions of the Windows NT platform. When aspects of the Server side of the package must be mentioned, this will be pointed out.

Although there have been several versions of the Windows NT operating system, the A+ examination has limited its involvement to the
two most recent versions. These are Windows NT 4.0 and the
newest version of NT, called Windows 2000. In most parts of the
chapter, these two versions will be referenced as a single topic.

A *client/server network*, depicted in Figure 19.7, is one in which
standalone computers, called *clients*, are connected to and administered by a master computer called a *server*. Collectively, the members
of the group make up a body called a *domain*. The members of the
domain share a common directory database and are organized in levels. Every domain is identified by a unique name and is administered as a single unit having common rules and procedures.

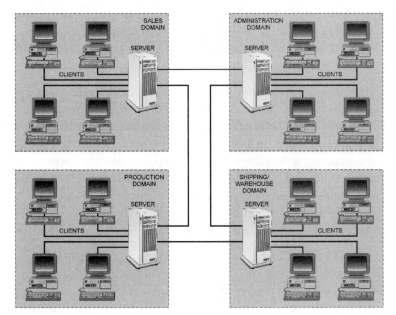

FIGURE 19.7
A client/server or domain-based network.

Windows NT Workstation

The Windows NT Workstation operating system can be employed as a client workstation in a client/server network, or it can be used as an operating system for a standalone computer that's not connected to anything. However, Windows NT was designed to work in a strong network environment. As such, many of the features that make Windows 9x packages easier to use are not located in Windows NT workstation.

Windows NT 4.0 Workstation supports advanced multitasking and multiprocessor operations. It can maintain different hardware profiles for multiple configurations within the same system. The Windows NT memory management system does a much better job of protecting applications from violating each other's space than the Windows 9x products do. Finally, Windows NT workstation provides a much higher level of file, folder, and resource security than the 9x versions do. Windows NT can control access to these resources through passwords and logins on the desktop or through a central security database located on a server in a client/server relationship.

Windows NT Server

The *Windows NT 4.0 Server* package provides the same features and functions found in the Windows NT Workstation. However, the Server package also provides the tools necessary to administer and control a network from its central location.

Recall that in a *peer-to-peer workgroup* setting, all the nodes can act as servers for some processes and clients for others. In a domain-based network, the network is controlled from a centralized server (domain controller). In a Windows NT network, this concept is embodied by the location where the Administration and Security databases are kept. In the workgroup, each machine maintains its own security and administration databases. In a domain environment, the server is responsible for keeping the centralized user account and security databases.

In the Windows NT Client/Server environment, two types of domain controllers exist—*Primary Domain Controllers (PDC)* and *Backup Domain Controllers (BDC),* as shown in Figure 19.8. The PDC contains the directory database for the network. This database contains information about user accounts, group accounts, and computer accounts. You might also find this database referred to as the *Security Accounts Manager (SAM)*. BDCs are servers within the network that are used to hold read-only backup copies of the directory database. A network can contain one or more BCDs. These servers are used to authenticate user logons. Authentication is the process of identifying an individual as who they claim to be. This process is normally based on usernames and passwords.

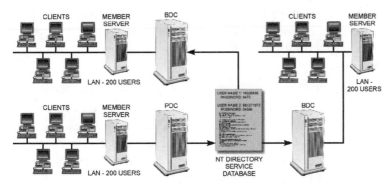

FIGURE 19.8
A PDC/BDC arrangement in a network.

Three types of workstation operating systems are supported in a Windows NT domain. These include Windows 9*x*, Windows NT Workstation, and Windows NT Server—set up for standalone use. However, servers are not normally used as workstations so that network operations are not slowed down or interrupted by local tasks.

Enterprise Networks

As mentioned earlier, Windows NT 4.0 is sold in two different versions—a Standard NT Server and an extended Enterprise Server version. *Enterprise networks* are those networks designed to facilitate business-to-business or business-to-customer operations. Because monetary transactions and customers' personal information travel across the network in these environments, enterprise networks feature facilities for additional, highly protective security functions.

Most enterprise networks are actually *intranets*. An intranet is a network built on the TCP/IP protocol that belongs to a single organization. It is, in essence, a private Internet. Like the Internet, intranets are designed to share information and are accessible only to the organization's members with authorization.

A *firewall* blocks unauthorized outside users from accessing the intranet site. A relatively new concept, called *extranet*, is being used to describe intranets that grant limited access to authorized outside users, such as corporate business partners.

Windows 2000

Windows 2000 is the successor of the Windows NT 4.0 operating system. As a matter of fact, it was originally titled Windows NT 5. This operating system brings together the stability and security of Windows NT 4.0 and the Plug-and-Play capabilities of Windows 9*x*.

Windows 2000 also includes built-in support for many new technologies including DVD drives, USB devices, Accelerated Graphics Ports, multifunction adapter cards, and a full line of PC cards. Finally, Windows 2000 provides a new, distributed directory service for managing resources across an enterprise, FAT 32 support, and the Internet Explorer 5 Web browser.

As with previous NT versions, Windows 2000 comes in two basic variations: the corporate workstation version, titled Windows 2000 Professional, and the network server version, called Windows 2000 Server. The server product is also available in two extended enterprise versions—*Windows 2000 Advanced Server* and *Windows 2000 Datacenter Server.*

The workstation side of Windows 2000 has been named *Windows 2000 Professional.* This operating system is designed to be the reliable, powerful desktop for the corporate computing world. It has been designed to be easier to set up and configure than previous Windows NT platforms. Windows 2000 Professional employs several wizards, such as the New Hardware Wizard and the Network Connection Wizard, to make installation and configuration processes easier for users.

Windows 2000 Professional extends and improves the Windows 9*x* user interface. It also brings Plug-and-Play to the NT workstation. The hardware supported by Windows 2000 Professional has been upgraded to include those items commonly found in newer systems.

The standard Windows 2000 Server package can manage up to 4GB of RAM and is capable of distributing work between two microprocessors at the same time. This type of operation is referred to as

Symmetrical Microprocessing (SMP). If Windows 2000 Server has been installed as an upgrade to an existing Windows NT 4.0 Server, it can support up to four different microprocessors simultaneously.

The Advanced Server edition can support up to eight symmetrical processors and up to 8GB of memory. These features enable it to function well in medium size networks running between 100 and 500 concurrent users. Similarly, the Windows 2000 Datacenter Server edition can handle up to 64GB of RAM and 32 processors. This will enable it to support up to 1000 simultaneous users with heavy processing demands.

Windows NT/2000 Structure

When fully installed, the Windows NT logical structure exists, as depicted in Figure 19.9. It is a modular operating system that permits advances in computing technology to be integrated into the system efficiently. The operating system exists in two basic layers, referred to as modes. These two layers are the Kernel Mode and the User Mode.

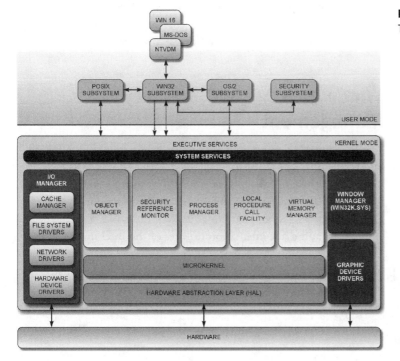

FIGURE 19.9
The Windows NT organizational structure.

Basically, the operating system runs in the *Kernel Mode*, whereas applications run in *User Mode*. The Kernel Mode is the operating mode in which the program has unlimited access to all memory, including those of system hardware, the User Mode applications, and other processes (such as I/O operations). The User Mode is a more restrictive operating mode in which no direct access of hardware is permitted.

APIs are routines, protocols, and tools built in to the operating system that provide application designers with consistent building blocks to design their applications with. For the user, these building blocks lead to consistent interfaces being designed for all applications. Likewise, the *Windows NT Hardware Abstraction Layer (HAL)* is a library of hardware drivers that operate between the actual hardware and the rest of the system. These software routines act to make the architecture of every device look the same to the operating system. The Microkernel works closely with the HAL to keep the system's microprocessor as busy as possible. It does this by scheduling threads for introduction to the microprocessor on a priority basis.

The Win32k Executive Services block provides all the basic operating system functions for the NT environment. It is made up of a number of managers that support activities such as basic operating system services, application environments, and APIs for the various types of applications that the Windows NT system can handle.

Windows NT/2000 Memory Management

The Windows NT memory management scheme employs a full 32-bit architecture with a flat memory model. In the Windows NT model, the *Virtual Memory Manager (VMM)* assigns unique memory spaces to every active 32-bit and 16-bit application. Unlike MS-DOS, Windows 3.*x*, and Windows 9*x*, Windows NT does not employ the address segmentation features of the Intel microprocessors. Because memory segments can overlap in the segmented model, memory usage errors can occur when an application attempts to write data into a memory space allocated to the operating system or another application.

The VMM maps each application's memory space into contiguous, 4KB pages of physical memory. Using this method, each application is mapped into a truly unique address space that cannot overlap any other address space. The lack of segment overlap reduces the chances of applications interfering with each other and helps to ensure data integrity by providing the operating system and other processes with their own memory spaces.

Windows NT Virtual Memory

When the VMM has exhausted the physical RAM locations available, it maps memory pages into virtual memory addresses. Windows NT establishes virtual memory by creating the PAGE-FILE.SYS file on the disk. The VMM shifts data between RAM memory and the disk in 4KB pages. This theoretically provides the operating system with a total memory space that equals the sum of the system's physical RAM and the capacity of the hard disk drive.

To take advantage of high RAM capacity, Windows NT automatically tunes itself to take advantage of all available RAM. The VMM dynamically balances RAM between paged memory and the virtual memory disk cache.

Windows NT Registries

Like Windows 9*x*, Windows NT and Windows 2000 use multipart databases, called the Registry, to hold system and user configuration information. However, the Windows NT and Windows 2000 Registries are not compatible with the Windows 9*x* Registries. This makes the Windows 9*x* and Windows NT/2000 operating systems basically incompatible with each other. The contents of the Windows NT Registry are physically stored in five files referred to as *hives*. Hives represent the major divisions of all the *Registry's keys*, subkeys, subtrees, and values.

> **EXAM TIP**
>
> Be aware that Windows 9*x* and Windows NT/2000 Registries are incompatible.

The hives of the Windows NT Registry are

- ◆ The SAM hive

- ◆ The Security hive

- ◆ The Software hive

◆ The System hive

◆ The Default hive

These files are stored in the \Winnt\System32\Config directory, along with a backup copy and log file for each hive. Configuration information about every user who has logged in to the system is maintained in a named subfolder of the \Winnt\Profiles directory. The actual user configuration file is named Ntuser.dat (that is, \Winnt\Profiles\Charles\Ntuser.dat). In Windows 2000, the Ntuser.dat file is stored in \Documents_and_Settings\username.

The major Windows NT hives and their files are as described in Table 19.1.

TABLE 19.1

MAJOR WINDOWS NT HIVES AND THEIR FILES

Subtree/Key	File	Log File
HKEY_LOCAL_MACHINE\SOFTWARE	SOFTWARE	SOFTWARE.LOG
HKEY_LOCAL_MACHINE\SECURITY	SECURITY	SECURITY.LOG
HKEY_LOCAL_MACHINE\SYSTEM	SYSTEM	SYSTEM.LOG
HKEY_LOCAL_MACHINE\SAM	SAM	SAM.LOG
HKEY_CURRENT_USER	USERxxx	USERxxx.LOG
	ADMINxxx	ADMINxxx.LOG
HKEY_USERS\DEFAULT	DEFAULT	DEFAULT.LOG

The HKEY_LOCAL_MACHINE subtree is the Registry's major branch. It contains five major keys. The SAM and SECURITY keys hold information such as user rights, user and group information for domain or workgroup organization, and password information. The HARDWARE key is a database built by device drivers and applications during bootup. The database is updated each time the system is rebooted. The SYSTEM key contains basic information about startup including the device drivers loaded and which services are in use. The *Last*

Known Good Configuration settings are stored here. Finally, the SOFT-WARE key holds information about locally loaded software, including file associations, OLE information, and configuration data.

The second most important subtree is HKEY_USERS. It contains a sub-key for each local user who accesses the system. These subkeys hold Desktop settings and user profiles. When a server logs in across a domain, the subkey is stored on the Domain Controller.

The Windows NT/2000 Control Panel Wizards are designed to cor-rectly make changes to the Registry in a manner that the operating system can understand. Editing the Registry directly opens the possi-bility of changing an entry in a manner that Windows NT cannot accept, and thereby, crashing the system. In either event, it is a good practice to back up the contents of the Registry before installing new hardware or software, or modifying the Registry directly. The *Rdisk.exe* utility, located in the \Winnt\System32 folder can be used to create a backup copy of the Windows NT Registry in the \Winnt\Repair folder.

Windows 2000 relies on the same Registry structure used in previ-ous Windows NT versions. For this reason, it is not compatible with Windows 9*x* Registries. As with Windows NT 4.0, the user settings portion of the Registry is stored in the *NTUSER.DAT* file located in the \Documents_and_Settings\username folder. The System portions of the Registry are stored in the SOFTWARE, SYSTEM, SECURI-TY and SAM hives. These files are stored in the \Winnt\System32\Config folder.

The contents of the Registry can be edited directly using the Windows NT/2000 RegEdit utility. Although there is a copy of the RegEdit tool in Windows 2000, it was designed to work with Windows 9*x* clients. The editor used to manage the Windows 2000 Registry is *Regedit32.exe*. This file is located in the \Winnt\System32 folder. However, in some instances, such as Registry searches, the RegEdit utility offers superior operation, even in Windows 2000. As with the Windows 9*x* versions, most changes to the Registry should be performed through the Wizards in the Windows NT/2000 Control Panels.

EXAM TIP

Know how to make a backup copy of the Registry in Windows NT 4.0.

EXAM TIP

Be aware of the utility used to directly edit Registry entries of the various operating systems.

NOTE

Hands-On Activity For hands-on experience with this concept, refer to Lab Procedure #26, "Windows 2000 Registry," located on the CD that accompanies this book.

CHALLENGE #2

You have been sent to a customer site to upgrade one of his old Windows NT 4.0 workstations to Windows 2000 Professional. Because the equipment is getting a little old, you want to protect the system in case you need to reinstall it. You are not too familiar with Windows NT, but you know that there is a utility for creating a backup of the system's Registry. What is this utility named and where can you access it?

Active Directory

The central feature of the Windows 2000 architecture is the *Active Directory (AD)* structure. Active Directory is a distributed database of user and resource information that describes the makeup of the network (that is, users and application settings).

The Active Directory arranges domains in a hierarchy and establishes trust relationships among all of the domains in a tree-like structure. A *tree* is a collection of objects that share the same DNS name. Active Directory can subdivide domains into organizational units (that is, sales, admin, and so on) that contain other units, or leaf objects, such as printers, users, and so on. Conversely, Windows 2000 can create an organizational structure containing more than one tree. This structure is referred to as a *forest*.

Trusts are relationships that enable users to move between domains and perform prescribed types of operations. Rights are the permission settings that control a user's (or groups of users') authority to access objects and perform operations (such as reading or writing a file). Administrative Rights provide authority to users down to the Organizational Unit level.

The primary tool for working with the Active Directory is the Active Directory Users and Computers applet, located in the Start/Settings/Control Panel path. The organizational units of a domain contain users, groups, and resources. This Active Directory management tool, depicted in Figure 19.10, is used to add users, groups, and Organizational Units (OUs) to the directory.

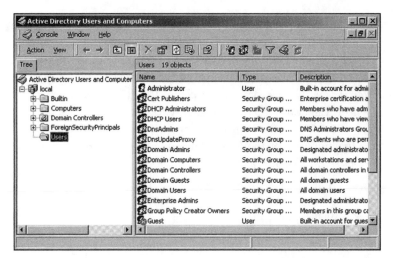

FIGURE 19.10
Active Directory Manager.

Although the Active Directory structure is designed primarily to help manage a network, it can also be a valuable desktop tool. The Active Directory Service running on a Windows 2000 Server enables Windows 2000 Professional installations to locate printers, disk drives, and other network devices across the network.

Administering Windows 2000

Windows NT and 2000 are both designed to be used in an administrated LAN environment. As such, they must provide network administrators with the tools necessary to control users and data within the network. To empower the network administrator, Windows 2000 furnishes five powerful administrative tools:

- ◆ System policies
- ◆ User profiles
- ◆ Groups
- ◆ Network shares
- ◆ NTFS rights

Each of these tools is designed to enable administrators to limit, or grant, users access to files, folders, services, and administrator-level services.

Computer Management Consoles

Windows 2000 concentrates many of the system's administration tools in a single location—under the Control Panel's *Administrative Tools icon*. The tools are combined in the *Windows 2000 Computer Management Console*, depicted in Figure 19.11. The Management Console can also be accessed by right-clicking the My Computer icon and selecting the Manage option from the pop-up menu. As the figure illustrates, the console includes three primary *Microsoft Management Consoles (MMCs):*

◆ System Tools

◆ Storage

◆ Services and Applications

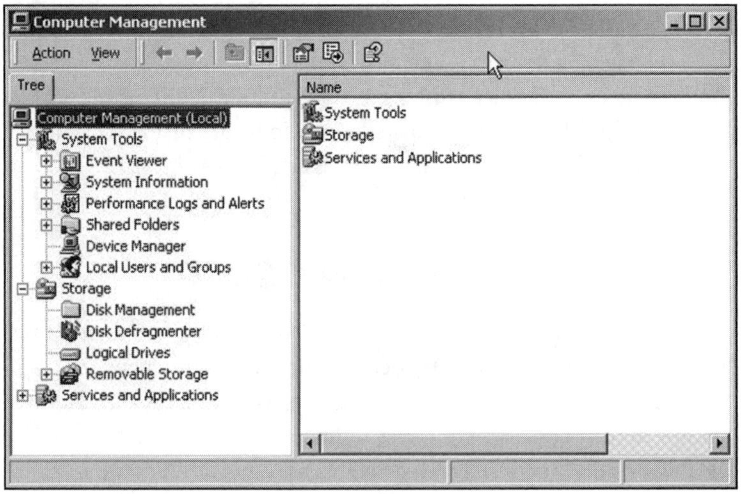

FIGURE 19.11

The Windows 2000 Computer Management console.

The *System Tools console* provides a collection of tools that can be used to view and manage system objects. They can also be used to track and configure all the system's hardware and software. It can also be used to configure network options and view system events.

Likewise, the *Storage console* provides a standard set of tools for maintaining the system's disk drives. These tools include the Disk

Management tool, the Disk Defragmenter utility, and a Logical Drives utility. The Disk Management tool enables the user to create and manage disk partitions and volumes. The Disk Defragmenter is used to optimize file operations on disks by rearranging their data into the most effective storage pattern for reading and writing. Finally, the Logical Drives tool shows a listing of all the logical drives in the system, including remote drives that have been mapped to the local system.

The Services and Applications console includes an advanced set of system management tools. These tools include the *Windows Management Instrumentation (WMI)* tools, a listing of all the system's available services, and access to the Windows 2000 Indexing functions. The WMI tools are used to establish administrative controls with another computer, provide logging services, view user security settings, and enable the Windows 2000 advanced scripting services.

Some of the Windows 2000 management consoles are not loaded when the operating system is installed. However, they are available for installation from the Windows 2000 CD. These consoles are referred to as *snap-ins*. In addition to the Control Panel path, all of the installed MMCs can be accessed through the `Start/Programs/Administrative Tools` path.

Windows 2000 Device Manager

Windows 2000 employs the Windows 9x–like Device Manager illustrated in Figure 19.12. The Device Manager replaces the Windows NT Diagnostic utility found in Windows NT 4.0. As with Windows 9x, the Windows 2000 Device Manager plays a major role in modifying hardware configurations and for troubleshooting hardware problems encountered in Windows 2000.

EXAM TIP Be aware of where the disk management tools are located in Windows 2000.

NOTE **Hands-On Activity** For hands-on experience with this concept, refer to Lab Procedure #16, "Windows 2000 Administrative Tools," and Lab Procedure #17, "Windows 2000 Computer Management," located on the CD that accompanies this book.

FIGURE 19.12

The Windows 2000 Device Manager.

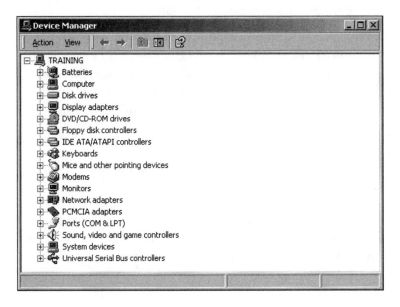

The Windows 2000 Device Manager utility can be accessed by clicking its button located under the Hardware tab of the Control Panel's System properties page. However, in Windows 2000, the Device Manager is usually accessed through the Computer Management Console. Operation of the Device Manager is very similar to its Windows 9*x* counterparts. It can be used to identify installed ports, update device drivers, and change I/O settings for hardware installed in the system.

Even though entries in the Registry can be altered through the Regedt32 and RegEdit utilities, the safest method of changing hardware settings is to change their values through the Device Manager.

EXAM TIP

Know that the safe method of changing Registry entries is to let the system do it through the Device Manager.

Windows NT/2000 Group Policies

In Windows 2000, policies are established through the *Group Policy Editor (GPE)*. Administrators use this editor to establish which applications different users or groups may have access to, as well as to control applications on the user's desktop.

With Group Policies, administrators can institute a large number of detailed settings for users throughout an enterprise—without establishing each setting manually. GPOs can be used to apply a large number of changes to machines and users through the Active Directory structure. These changes appear in the GPE under three headings:

◆ Software Installation settings

◆ Windows settings

◆ Administrative templates

Command Prompt Procedures

As mentioned at the beginning of the chapter, both operating systems provide a command-line interface that works separately from their GUIs. Although "DOS is dead" for consumers, the technician must often resort to the command-line interface to isolate and correct problems within the operating system.

The operating system is responsible for providing the system's user interface. The main user interface for MS-DOS is the *command line*. The command line is the space immediately following the *command prompt* on the screen. All command line operations are executed by typing their names in this space. They are executed by pressing the Enter key on the keyboard.

Windows 9*x*, Windows NT, and Windows 2000 provide a *Command Prompt window*. However, unlike Windows 9*x*, when this feature is engaged in Windows NT, no separate DOS version is being accessed. Windows NT simply provides a DOS-like interface that enables users to perform some command-line functions. There is no MS-DOS icon in the Windows NT system. To access the DOS emulator in Windows 9*x* or Windows NT 4.0, select the Run option from the Start menu and type the word COMMAND in the Run dialog box. To access this function in Windows 2000, enter CMD in the dialog box. This will produce the command-line prompt similar to the one displayed in Figure 19.13.

EXAM TIP

Know how to access the Command Prompt interface in Windows 9*x* and Windows 2000.

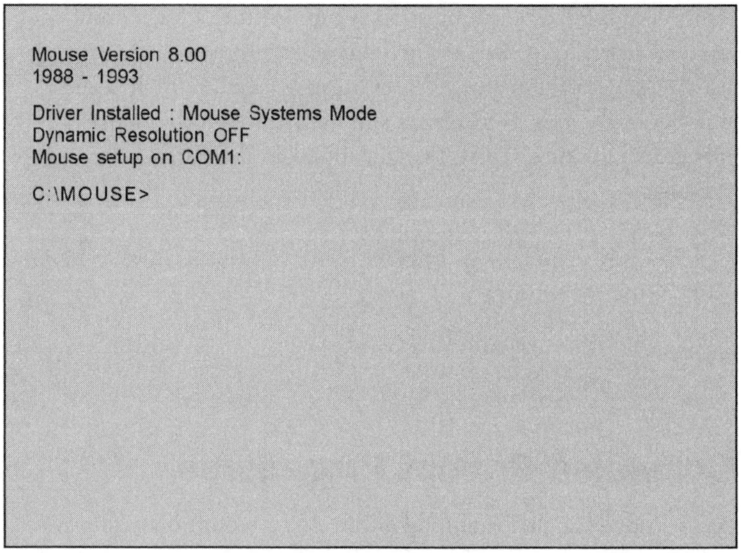

FIGURE 19.13

The Windows Command Prompt interface.

```
Mouse Version 8.00
1988 - 1993

Driver Installed : Mouse Systems Mode
Dynamic Resolution OFF
Mouse setup on COM1:

C:\MOUSE>
```

EXAM TIP

Know which file types can be executed directly from the command-line prompt.

From the command prompt, all command-line functions can be entered and executed. Application programs can also be started from this prompt. These files can be discerned by their filename extensions. Files with .COM, .EXE, or .BAT extensions can be started directly from the prompt. The .COM and .EXE file extensions are reserved by DOS and can only be generated by programs that can correctly configure them. BAT files are simply ASCII text files that have been generated by writing command prompt functions in a text editor and saving them as a file. Because BAT files contain commands mixed with COM and EXE files, they can be executed directly from the command line.

Programs with other types of extensions must be associated with one of these three file types to be operated. As an example, the executable component of a word processor could be a file called WORDPRO.EXE. Document files produced by word processors are normally given filename extensions of .DOC (for document) or .TXT (for text file).

The user can also enter commands on the command line to perform DOS functions. These commands can be grouped into drive-level commands, directory-level commands, and file-level commands. The format for using commands is as follows:

```
COMMAND (space) SOURCE location (space) DESTINATION loca-
tion
COMMAND (space) location
COMMAND
```

The first example illustrates how command prompt operations that involve a source and a final destination, such as moving a file from one place to another, are entered. The second example illustrates how single-location command prompt operations, such as formatting a disk in a particular disk drive, are specified. The final example applies to commands that occur in a default location, such as obtaining a listing of the files on the current disk drive. Many of these commands can be modified by placing one or more software switches at the end of the command. A switch is added to the command by adding a space, a fore-slash (/), and a single letter:

```
COMMAND (space) option /switch
```

Common command switches include /P for page, /W for wide format, and /S for system. Different switches are used to modify different DOS commands. To obtain a listing of the switch definitions available with each command, simply type the command at the prompt followed by /?.

Typical command-line functions (commands and utility programs) used by technicians in the Windows 9*x* and Windows NT/2000 environments include

- ◆ ATTRIB
- ◆ COPY
- ◆ DEFRAG
- ◆ DIR
- ◆ EDIT
- ◆ FDISK
- ◆ FORMAT
- ◆ MEM
- ◆ MSCDEX
- ◆ SETVER
- ◆ ScanDisk
- ◆ SCANREG
- ◆ VER
- ◆ XCOPY

Although CompTIA has included these commands and utilities at this point in their Objective Map, we feel that they are better covered in conjunction with other topics—such as diagnosing and troubleshooting. Therefore, we have simply listed them here in context with using command-line functions. Explanations for the functions these commands and utilities perform are described in detail in Chapter 28, "Networking with Windows."

NOTE   **Hands-On Activity**   For hands-on experience with this concept, refer to Lab Procedure #12, "Windows Me Command Prompt Navigating," located on the CD that accompanies this book.

CHALLENGE #3

A co-worker has just had her Windows 98 computer upgraded to Windows 2000 Professional. The computer is connected to the company network and serves as a client to the company's file server. She wants to access the command prompt to run an older MS-DOS application, but she cannot find the MS-DOS icon in the Control Panel, so she asked you how to get to the command line in Windows 2000. What can you tell her?

CHAPTER SUMMARY

KEY TERMS

- Active Directory (AD)
- Active Directory Users and Computers
- Administrative Rights
- Administrative Tools icon
- AUTOEXEC.BAT
- Backup Domain Controllers (BDC)
- Cabinet (.CAB) files
- Client/server network
- Clients
- Command line

This chapter has examined basic operating systems in depth. It concentrated in particular on the ROM BIOS and command prompt disk operating systems.

The initial section introduced the various types of operating systems used with microprocessor-based systems. Items covered in this section included, single- and multiprocess, multiuser, and multitasking systems.

A major portion of the chapter focused on the function, structure, and major system files of MS-DOS, Windows 9x, and Windows NT/2000. The MS-DOS information is included to provide a simplified example of common operating system functions and to introduce elements that still reside in computer systems to maintain compatibility with older systems.

At this point, review the objectives listed at the beginning of the chapter to be certain that you understand each point and can perform each task listed there. Afterward, answer the review questions that follow to verify your knowledge of the information.

CHAPTER SUMMARY

- Command prompt
- Command Prompt window
- COMMAND.COM
- CONFIG.SYS
- Conventional memory
- Domain
- DRIVER.SYS
- EMM386.EXE
- Enterprise networks
- Expanded memory
- Extended memory
- Extended memory driver (XMS)
- Firewall
- Flat Memory Model
- Forest
- GDI
- High memory area (HMA)
- HIMEM.SYS
- Hives
- Initialization (.INI) files
- Intranets
- IO.SYS
- Kernel
- Kernel Mode
- Last Known Good configuration

- Leaf objects
- MEM command
- Microsoft Management Consoles (MMCs)
- MS-DOS
- MSDOS.SYS
- Multiple-process systems
- Multiprocessor
- Multitasking
- Multiuser
- NTUSER.DAT
- PAGEFILE.SYS
- PATH command
- Peer-to-peer workgroup
- Permission settings
- Primary Domain Controllers (PDC)
- RAMDRIVE.SYS
- Rdisk.exe
- REGEDIT.EXE
- Regedit32.exe
- Registry
- Registry's keys
- Rights
- Scanreg /Restore

CHAPTER SUMMARY

- Security Accounts Manager (SAM)
- Server
- Shadow RAM
- Single-process systems
- SMARTDRV.SYS
- Snap-ins
- Storage console
- Syntax
- System Policy Editor (Poledit)
- System Tools console
- SYSTEM.DA0
- SYSTEM.DAT
- SYSTEM.INI
- Tree
- Trust relationships
- Upper memory area (UMA)
- Upper memory blocks (UMBs)
- USER files
- User Mode
- USER.DA0
- USER.DAT
- Virtual memory

- Virtual Memory Manager (VMM)
- WIN.COM
- WIN.INI
- WIN386.SWP
- Windows 2000 Advanced Server
- Windows 2000 Computer Management Console
- Windows 2000 Datacenter Server
- Windows 2000 Professional
- Windows 95
- Windows 95 (b)
- Windows 95 OSR2
- Windows 98
- Windows 98SE (Second Edition)
- Windows 9x Registry
- Windows Millennium Edition (ME)
- Windows NT 4.0 Server
- Windows NT 4.0 Workstation
- Windows NT Hardware Abstraction Layer (HAL)
- WINFILE.INI

APPLY YOUR KNOWLEDGE

Review Questions

1. What is the minimum file size specification associated with the MSDOS.SYS file?

   A. 16 bits

   B. 1 KB

   C. 2 KB

   D. 4 KB

2. How did the Windows versions before Windows 95 organize and monitor the system's configuration information?

   A. .LOG files

   B. .CFG files

   C. .DAT files

   D. .INI files

3. What is the purpose of the HIMEM.SYS file?

   A. Expanded memory management

   B. Extended memory management

   C. OS configuration management

   D. Creates the UMA

4. Which driver assigns logical drive letters to the system's floppy drives?

   A. DRIVER.SYS

   B. DISPLAY.SYS

   C. ANSI.SYS

   D. KEYBOARD.SYS

5. Which of these statements is normally located in the CONFIG.SYS file? (Select all that apply.)

   A. `PATH=C:\,C:\DOS,C:\MOUSE,C:\PROGRAMS`

   B. `DEVICE=C:\DOS\EMM386.EXE`

   C. `DOS=HIGH,UMB`

   D. `FILES=30`

6. Which of these commands are normally located in a typical AUTOEXEC.BAT file? (Select all that apply.)

   A. `PROMPT=$P$G`

   B. `SET TEMP=C:\TEMP`

   C. `DOS=HIGH,UMB`

   D. `SMARTDRV`

7. What actions does the operating system take when it runs out of available RAM?

   A. Writes data to memory addresses that are not used frequently

   B. Writes data to the hard disk drive

   C. Writes data to virtual memory

   D. Writes data to cache

8. What virtual memory swap file is used in Windows 9x?

   A. TEMP.SWP

   B. WIN.SWP

   C. WIN386.SWP

   D. PAGEFILE.SYS

APPLY YOUR KNOWLEDGE

9. What file is used to load up the Windows environment?

   A. START.EXE

   B. IO.SYS

   C. WIN.COM

   D. AUTOEXEC.BAT

10. What steps can be performed to optimize the operation of a system running a Windows 98 operating system? (Select all that apply.)

    A. Create a supplemental CD-ROM cache.

    B. REM out unneeded items (such as SMRT-DRV) in the CONFIG.SYS and AUTOEX-EC.BAT files.

    C. Run the defrag utility.

    D. Delete CONFIG.SYS and AUTOEXEC.BAT.

11. What function does the VCACHE utility perform in a Windows 9x system?

    A. Creates and manages the HMA

    B. Creates and manages a disk cache in RAM

    C. Creates and manages a RAM cache

    D. Creates and manages the UMB

12. How are the items in the Windows 9x Startup folder prevented from running at startup?

    A. Press left+Ctrl during startup.

    B. Press left+Alt during startup.

    C. Press left+Shift during startup.

    D. Press Tab during startup.

13. What effect can active commands in a CONFIG.SYS, an AUTOEXEC.BAT, or an INI file have on the operation of an advanced Windows operating system?

    A. Runs faster

    B. Runs better with older devices

    C. Runs more slowly

    D. Runs better with older programs

14. What files make up the Windows 9x Registry?

    A. USER.SYS, SYSTEM.SYS

    B. USER.LOG, SYSTEM.LOG

    C. USER.REG, SYSTEM.REG

    D. USER.DAT, SYSTEM.DAT

15. What is the basic function of the HKEY_CLASSES_ROOT Registry key?

    A. User-specific configuration

    B. Associates icons with files

    C. PnP status data

    D. Current information about devices

16. What is the basic function of the HKEY_CURRENT_USER Registry key?

    A. User-specific configuration

    B. User logon data

    C. PnP status data

    D. Current information about devices

APPLY YOUR KNOWLEDGE

17. What is the basic function of the HKEY_USERS Registry key?

    A. User-specific configuration

    B. User logon data

    C. PnP status data

    D. Current information about devices

18. What is the basic function of the HKEY_DYN_DATA Registry key?

    A. User-specific configuration

    B. User logon data

    C. PnP dynamic status data

    D. Current information about devices

19. What is the basic function of the HKEY_CURRENT_CONFIG Registry key?

    A. User-specific configuration

    B. User logon data

    C. PnP dynamic status data

    D. Current information about devices

20. Where are the Registry backup files located in Windows 98?

    A. c:\

    B. c:\Windows

    C. c:\Windows\Registry

    D. c:\Windows\Sysbckup

21. Where are the files that make up the Windows 9x Registry located in the system?

    A. c:\

    B. c:\Windows

    C. c:\Windows\Registry

    D. c:\Windows\Sysbckup

22. What utility is used to create a backup copy of the Registry in Windows NT 4.0?

    A. RDISK

    B. BACKUP

    C. SYSBACK

    D. REGBACK

23. What utility is used to directly edit Registry entries in Windows 9x?

    A. EDIT

    B. SYSEDIT

    C. REGEDIT

    D. REGEDT32

24. What is the safest method of changing Registry entries in Windows 2000?

    A. Use REGEDIT

    B. Use a file editor

    C. Use Device Manager

    D. Use REGEDT32

APPLY YOUR KNOWLEDGE

25. How is the DOS emulator accessed in Windows 2000?

    A. PROMPT

    B. CMD

    C. COMMAND

    D. DOS

26. Where are the disk drive tools located in Windows 2000?

    A. System Information

    B. System Tools

    C. Device Manager

    D. Computer Management

27. Which of these file types cannot be executed directly from the command-line prompt in Windows 2000?

    A. .SYS

    B. .COM

    C. .EXE

    D. .BAT

28. What virtual memory swap file is used in Windows 2000?

    A. TEMP.SWP

    B. WIN.SWP

    C. WIN386.SWP

    D. PAGEFILE.SYS

Answers and Explanations

1. **B**. There is a little known MS-DOS system requirement that the MS-DOS.SYS file must maintain a size in excess of 1KB. For more information, see the section "MS-DOS Structure."

2. **D**. Windows 3.*x* was built on a number of Initialization (.INI) files that held the system's hardware and software configuration information. For more information, see the section "Windows Initialization Files."

3. **B**. HIMEM.SYS loads the DOS extended memory driver (XMS). This driver manages the use of extended memory installed in the system so that no two applications use the same memory locations at the same time. This memory manager should normally be listed in the CONFIG.SYS file before any other memory managers or device drivers. HIMEM.SYS also creates a 64KB area of memory just above the 1MB address space called the high memory area (HMA). With this, the DOS=HIGH statement is used to shift portions of DOS from conventional memory into the HMA. For more information, see the section "Memory Managers."

4. **A**. DRIVER.SYS creates the logical drive assignments for the system's floppy drives (that is, A: and B:). For more information, see the section "Device Drivers."

APPLY YOUR KNOWLEDGE

5. **B, C, D**. A sample CONFIG.SYS file might consist of command lines such as

```
Device=C:\DOS\HIMEM.SYS
Device=C:\DOS\EMM386.EXE 1024 RAM
FILES=30
BUFFERS=15
STACKS=9,256
DEVICE=C:\DOS\SMARTDRV.SYS 1024
DOS=HIGH,UMB
DEVICEHIGH=C:\MOUSE\MOUSE.SYS
DEVICEHIGH=C:\DOS\RAMDRIVE.SYS 4096/a
```

For more information, see the section "CONFIG.SYS."

6. **A, B, D**. A sample AUTOEXEC.BAT file might consist of command lines such as

```
DATE
TIME
PROMPT=$P$G
SET TEMP=C:\TEMP
PATH=C:\;C:\DOS;C:\MOUSE
SMARTDRV.EXE 2048 1024
CD\
DIR
```

For more information, see the section "AUTOEXEC.BAT."

7. **C**. Virtual memory is disk drive space that is manipulated to seem like RAM. Software creates virtual memory by swapping files between RAM and the disk drive. This memory management technique effectively creates more total memory for the system's applications to use. When the system runs out of available RAM, it shifts data to the virtual memory swap file on the disk drive. However, because there is a major transfer of information that involves the hard disk drive, an overall reduction in speed is encountered with virtual memory operations. For more information, see the section "Virtual Memory."

8. **C**. The size of the Windows 9x swap file (WIN386.SWP) is variable and is dynamically assigned. For more information, see the section "Virtual Memory."

9. **C**. IO.SYS loads the WIN.COM file into RAM, which controls the loading and testing of the Windows 9x core components. For more information, see the section "Windows 9x Structure."

10. **A, B, C**. Establishing a supplemental cache for the CD-ROM drive can enhance the efficiency of a Windows 9x system. If a Windows 9x system has a CONFIG.SYS and AUTOEXEC.BAT file that has been held over from a previous operating system, you should be aware that any unneeded commands in these files have the potential to reduce system performance. In particular, the SMARTDRV function from older operating systems will inhibit dynamic VCACHE operation and slow the system down. Defragmenting the hard disk drive will improve optimization by improving the read/write times. For more information, see the section "Optimizing Windows 9x Performance."

11. **B**. The VCACHE driver establishes and controls a disk cache in an area of RAM as a storage space for information read from the hard disk drive, CD-ROM, and other drives and file operations. For more information, see the section "Optimizing Windows 9x Performance."

12. **C**. The programs in the Startup folder can be bypassed for troubleshooting purposes by pressing the left+Shift key during startup. For more information, see the section "Windows 9x Structure."

APPLY YOUR KNOWLEDGE

13. **C.** If the system runs slowly, check the CONFIG.SYS and AUTOEXEC.BAT files for SMART-DRV and any other disk cache software settings. Remove these commands from both files to improve performance. Also, remove any Share commands from the AUTOEXEC.BAT file. The SYSTEM.INI, WIN.INI, PROTOCOL.INI, CONFIG.SYS, and AUTOEXEC.BAT files can be modified through the System Editor (Sysedit) in Windows 9x. For more information, see the section "Optimizing Windows 9x Performance."

14. **D.** The contents of the Windows 9x Registry are located in two files: USER.DAT and SYSTEM.DAT. For more information, see the section "Windows 9x Registries."

15. **B.** The Classes_Root key divides the system's files into two groups by file-extension type and by association. This key also holds data about icons associated with the file. For more information, see the section "Windows 9x Registries."

16. **A.** The Current_User key holds the data about the user-specific configuration settings of the system, including color, keyboard, desktop, and start settings. The values in the Current_User key reflect those established by the user who is currently logged on to the system. If a different user logs on, the contents of the Users key are moved into the Current_User key. For more information, see the section "Windows 9x Registries."

17. **B.** The Users key contains the information about the various users who have been defined to log on to the system. The information from the Current_User key is copied into this section whenever a user logs off the system or when the system is shut down. For more information, see the section "Windows 9x Registries."

18. **C.** The Dyn_Data key works with the branch of the Local_Machine key that holds PnP dynamic status information for various system devices including current status and problems. For more information, see the section "Windows 9x Registries."

19. **D.** The Current_Config key works with the Local_Machine branch containing current information about hardware devices. For more information, see the section "Windows 9x Registries."

20. **D.** The Windows 98 system makes up to five backup copies of the Registry structure each time it successfully starts Windows. The backed up contents of the Registry are stored in the \Windows\Sysbckup directory in the form of cabinet (.CAB) files—not as .DA0 files. For more information, see the section "Windows 9x Registries."

21. **B.** The contents of the Windows 9x Registry are located in two files located in the \Windows directory. For more information, see the section "Windows 9x Registries."

22. **A.** The RDISK.EXE utility, located in the \Winnt\System32 folder, can be used to create a backup copy of the Windows NT Registry in the \Winnt\Repair folder. For more information, see the section "Windows 9x Registries."

23. **C.** Although there is a copy of the REGEDIT.EXE tool in Windows 2000, it was designed to work with Windows 9x clients. For more information, see the section "Windows 9x Registries."

APPLY YOUR KNOWLEDGE

24. **C**. Even though entries in the Registry can be altered through the REGEDT32 and REGEDIT utilities, the safest method of changing hardware settings is to change their values through the Device Manager. For more information, see the section "Windows 2000 Device Manager."

25. **B**. To access the DOS emulator in Windows 9*x*, select the Run option from the Start menu and type the word COMMAND in the Run dialog box. To access this function in Windows 2000, enter CMD in the dialog box. For more information, see the section "Command Prompt Procedures."

26. **D**. The Windows 2000 Computer Management Console can be accessed by right-clicking the My Computer icon and selecting the Manage option from the pop-up menu. The console includes the System Tools, Storage, and Services and Applications consoles. The Storage console provides a standard set of tools for maintaining the system's disk drives. These tools include the Disk Management tool, the Disk Defragmenter utility, and a Logical Drives utility. For more information, see the section "Computer Management Consoles."

27. **A**. From the command prompt, files with .COM, .EXE, or .BAT extensions can be started directly. For more information, see the section "Command Prompt Procedures."

28. **D**. Windows NT/2000 establishes virtual memory by creating the PAGEFILE.SYS file on the disk. For more information, see the section "Virtual Memory."

Challenge Solutions

1. He must get the system started with a boot disk so that he can have access to the system. Then, he must run the Scanreg /Restore command from the command prompt. This will produce a list of the available backup files to select from for troubleshooting purposes. The Sysbckup folder is a hidden folder, so you must remove the hidden attribute from it to examine its contents. Inside the folder, the Registry backup files are stored under an RB0*XX*.CAB format. Your friend should choose the newest version from the list and have the utility extract it onto the disk. Then he should be able to reboot the system and start it. For more information, see the section "Windows 9*x* Registries."

2. It is the Rdisk.exe utility, it is located in the \Winnt\System32 folder, and it can be used to create a backup copy of the Windows NT Registry in the \Winnt\Repair folder. For more information, see the section "Windows NT Registries."

3. Windows 2000 does not include an MS-DOS icon in the Control Panel as Windows 98 did. Instead, she must access the command prompt through the Windows 2000 Start/Run menu option. In the Run dialog box that pops up, she must type CMD and click on the OK button to access the command prompt. For more information, see the section "Command Prompt Procedures."

APPLY YOUR KNOWLEDGE

Suggested Readings and Resources

1. DOS Tutorial
   http://www.butterwick0.freeserve.co.uk/
   tutor/menu.html

2. DOS Structure
   http://www.patersontech.com/Dos/Byte/
   InsideDos.htm

3. DOS Tips
   http://www.pctusa.com/Dos/dos_3.html

4. CONFIG.SYS and AUTOEXEC.BAT
   http://www.butterwick0.freeserve.co.uk/
   tutor/part_5.html

5. .INI File
   http://www.webopedia.com/TERM/_/_INI_file.
   html

6. DOS Memory Management
   http://support.microsoft.com/
   default.aspx?scid=kb;EN-US;q95555

7. DOS/Windows Memory Management
   http://www.billssite.com/memory.htm

8. Virtual Memory
   http://www.howstuffworks.com/
   virtual-memory1.htm

9. Early Evolution of Windows
   http://www.engr.uconn.edu/lc_web/help/
   ntintro/evolution.html

10. Optimizing Windows 9x/Me Startup
    http://www.extremetech.com/
    article2/0,3973,10409,00.asp

11. Windows Registry
    http://webopedia.internet.com/TERM/R/
    Registry.html

12. Windows NT/2000
    http://www.winsupersite.com/showcase/
    ty_intro.asp

13. DLL
    http://webopedia.com/TERM/D/DLL.html

This chapter helps you to prepare for the Operating System Technologies module of the A+ Certification examination by covering the following objective within the "Domain 1.0: Operating System Fundamentals" section. Chapter 19 covered the different key operating system's functions, structure, and major system files. Navigating and manipulating different operating systems will be covered in detail in this chapter.

1.1 Identify the operating system's functions, structure, and major system files to navigate the operating system and know how to get to needed technical information.

Content might include the following:

- **Major Operating System functions:**
    - **Creating folders**
    - **Checking OS Version**
- **Major Operating System components:**
    - **Explorer**
    - **My Computer**
    - **Control Panel**

▶ The previous chapter addressed the first portion of the Operating System Technologies objective 1.1—identify the operating system's functions, structure, and major system files. In this chapter, we will take up the second half of the objective—identify how to navigate the operating system and how to get to needed technical information.

▶ Computer technicians must be familiar with the functions and structure of operating systems that they might encounter in the field. The major operating systems associated with personal computers are Windows 9*x* and Windows 2000. Both provide an MS-DOS–like command-line interface that works independently from their GUIs. As a technician, you will often need to use this interface to isolate and correct problems associated with the operating system.

CHAPTER 20

Navigating Operating Systems

STUDY STRATEGIES

To prepare for the Operating System Fundamentals objective of the Operating Systems Technologies exam,

▶ Read the objectives at the beginning of this chapter.

▶ Study the information in this chapter.

▶ Review the objectives listed earlier in this chapter.

▶ Perform any step-by-step procedures in the text.

▶ Answer the review questions at the end of the chapter and check your results.

▶ Use the PrepLogic test engine on the CD-ROM that accompanies this book for additional review and exam questions concerning this material.

▶ Review the exam tips scattered throughout the chapter and make certain that you are comfortable with each point.

INTRODUCTION

Most PCs are disk drive-based systems (that is, they rely on disk drives for their data storage functions). In the PC, the disk drive system is based on a tree-like disk/directory/sub-directory/file organizational structure.

This chapter describes this disk and directory architecture in some detail. Because technicians often have to work on PCs when they are not working properly, the chapter focuses on navigating through Microsoft operating systems from a command-line environment. This environment permits the technician to work in the system without the complications of the GUI structures associated with Windows.

The chapter also describes proper methods for navigating through the Windows 9x and Windows 2000 environments using the major user interfaces of Windows 9x and Windows 2000.

After completing the chapter, you should be able to navigate through the Windows 9x, Windows NT 4.0, and Windows 2000 operating system to get to needed programs and tools.

WORKING FROM THE COMMAND LINE

Disk storage is organized in a manner that can be compared to a filing cabinet. The logical disk drives can be thought of as drawers of the cabinet, while the hanging folders are associated with *directories* (directories are represented by *folders* in graphical interfaces such as Windows), and the items inside the folders are files.

Disk-based systems manage data blocks by giving them *filenames*. A *file* is simply a block of logically related data given a single name and treated as a single unit. Like the contents of the folders, files can be programs, documents, drawings or other illustrations, sound files, and so on.

To locate a particular file, you must know which drive, directory, and subdirectory it is located in. In Microsoft operating systems, the path to any file in the system can be written as a direction to the computer so it will know where the file is located. The format for specifying a path is as follows:

```
C:\directory name\subdirectory name\filename
```

Under the old *MS-DOS* operating systems, a basic filename of up to eight characters was permitted. The filename could also have an extension of up to three characters. The extension was separated from the main portion of the filename by a period and is normally used to identify what type of file it is.

Drives and Disks

The Microsoft operating systems reserve the letters A: and B: for the first and second floppy drives. Multiple hard disk drive units can be installed in the system unit, along with the floppy drives. Likewise, Microsoft operating systems recognize the first logical hard drive in the system as the C: drive. Disk management utilities can be used to partition a single, physical hard disk drive into two or more volumes that the system recognizes as logical drives C:, D:, and so on. Figure 20.1 illustrates how the various disk drives are seen by a typical, standalone system.

> **NOTE**
>
> **Filename Extensions** Filename extensions are not actually required for most files. However, they become helpful in sorting between files in a congested system. You should be aware that the operating system reserves some three-letter combinations, such as .COM and .SYS, for its own use.

FIGURE 20.1
The system's disk drives.

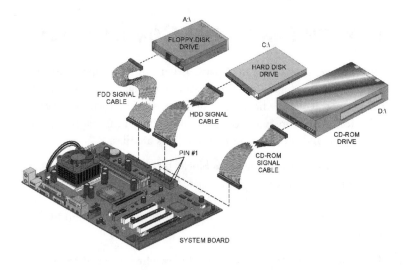

Drive-Level Command Operations

The following command-line commands pertain to drive-level operations. They must be typed at the command prompt, and they carry out the instruction along with any drive modifiers given.

◆ FORMAT:—Used to prepare a new disk for use with an operating system. Actual data locations are marked off on the disk for the tracks and sectors, and bad sectors are marked. In addition, the directory is established on the disk. New diskettes must be formatted before they can be used.

C:\>FORMAT A:—Creates the track, sector, and the file system structure on the specified disk (in this case, the A: floppy drive).

C:\>FORMAT A:/S—Causes three system files (boot files—IO.SYS, MSDOS.SYS, and COMMAND.COM) to be copied into the root directory of the disk after it has been formatted.

◆ SETVER:—Sets the OS version number that the system reports to an application. Programs designed for previous OS versions might not operate correctly under newer versions unless the version has been set correctly:

C:> SETVER C:—This entry will cause all the files on the C: drive to be listed in the operating system version table.

◆ VER:—If the current operating system version is not known, typing VER at the command prompt will display it onscreen. These commands are particularly useful in networking operations where multiple computers are connected together to share information. In these applications, several versions of operating system might exist on different machines attached to the network.

> **NOTE**
>
> **Drive Letters**   The figure shows a CD-ROM drive as drive D: because this is becoming the most common PC configuration. In the case of networked systems, logical drive letters can be extended to define up to Z drives. These drives are actually the hard drives located in remote computers. The operating system in the local machine treats them as additional logical drives (that is, F:, G:, and so on). Under Windows 2000, drives can be given names, and the 26 logical drive limit imposed by the alphabet is done away with.

Directories

In hard drive–based systems, it is common to organize related programs and data into areas called *directories*. This makes them easier to find and work with because modern hard drives can hold large amounts of information. Microsoft directories can hold up to 512 directory or filename entries.

> **EXAM TIP**
>
> Be aware that Microsoft directories can hold up to 512 directory or filename entries.

The following DOS commands are used for directory-based operations. The format for using them is identical to disk-related commands discussed earlier.

- `DIR:`—Gives a listing of the files on the disk that is in the drive indicated by the drive specifier.

  `C:\>DIR or DIR B:`—(If `DIR` is used without any drive specifier, the contents of the drive indicated by the prompt will be displayed.) The command can also be used with modifiers to alter the way in which the directory is displayed. The `C:\>DIR/W` command displays the entire directory at one time across the width of the display, whereas the `C:\>DIR/P` command displays the contents of the directory one page at a time.

- `MKDIR (MD):`—Creates a new directory in an indicated spot in the directory tree structure.

  `C:\>MD C:\DOS\`*XXX*—Creates a new subdirectory named *XXX* in the path that includes the ROOT directory (`C:\`) and the `DOS` directory.

- `CHDIR (CD):`—Changes the location of the active directory to a position specified with the command.

  `C:\>CD C:\DOS`—Changes the working directory from the `C:` root directory to the `C:\>DOS` directory.

- `RMDIR (RD):`—Erases the directory specified in the command. You cannot remove a directory until it is empty and you cannot remove the directory if it is currently active.

  `C:\>RD C:\DOS\forms`—Would remove the DOS subdirectory `forms`, provided it was empty.

- `PROMPT:`—Changes the appearance of the command prompt.

  `C:\>PROMPT $P$G`—Causes the form of the prompt to change from simply `C:` to `C:\` and causes the complete path from the main directory to the current directory to be displayed at the DOS prompt (that is, `C:\>DOS`).

- `TREE:`—Lists all the directory and subdirectory names on a specified disk.

  `C:\>TREE C:`—Displays a graphical representation of the organization of the C hard drive.

◆ DELTREE:—Removes a selected directory and all the files and subdirectories below it.

C:\>DELTREE C:\DOS\DRIVER\MOUSE—Deletes the subdirectory Mouse and any subdirectories it might have.

NOTE **Hands-On Activity** For hands-on experience with this concept, refer to Lab Procedure #12, "Windows Me Command Prompt Navigating," located on the CD that accompanies this book.

NAVIGATING WINDOWS 9x

When Windows 95 or 98 is started, it produces the basic desktop screen depicted in Figure 20.2. The desktop is the primary graphical user interface for Windows 9x. As with previous Windows products, it uses icons to quickly locate and run applications. In Windows 9x, however, the Start button provides the starting point for most functions.

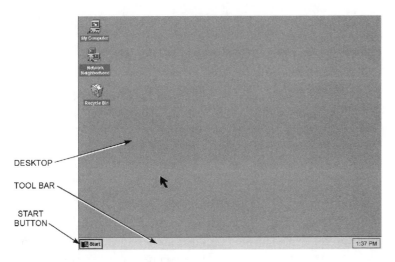

FIGURE 20.2
The Windows 9x desktop screen.

Windows is a *task-switching* environment. Under this type of environment, several applications can be running at the same time. In some cases, a particular application might be running on the desktop while others are running out of view. When you have multiple applications open in Windows, the window currently being accessed is called the active window and appears in the foreground (over the top of the other windows). The activity of the other open windows is suspended, as denoted by their gray color, and they run in the background.

Select key combinations can be used to navigate through the Windows environment using the keyboard. The most common keys include the Alt, Esc, Tab, and Enter keys. These keys are used to move between the different windows structures and make selections (that is, the Tab key is used to move forward through different options, whereas the Shift+Tab combination is used to move backward through available options).

Special key combinations enable the user to move between tasks easily. By pressing the Alt and Tab keys together, you can quickly select one of the open applications. Similarly, the Alt+Esc key combination enables the user to cycle through open application windows. Pressing the Ctrl+Esc keys will pop up the Start menu.

EXAM TIP

Memorize the desktop's shortcut key combinations.

Windows 95 Desktop

The Desktop interface provides an easy method for starting tasks and making resource connections. Desktop icons are referred to as shortcuts because the primary method of accessing applications is through the Start menu. Applying a traditional double-click to the icon starts the application or brings up its window.

In addition to the normal left-click and double-click functions, Windows 95 and Windows 98 both employ the right mouse button for some activities. This is referred to as *right-clicking*, or as *alternate-clicking* for right-handers, and is used to pop-up a menu of functions onscreen. The right-click menus in Windows 9*x* are context sensitive, so the information they contain applies to the item being clicked on.

Alternate-clicking on an icon produces a *pop-up menu*, similar to the left-hand menu in Figure 20.3. These menus enable the user to open, cut, or copy a folder (an icon that represents a directory), create a shortcut, delete or rename a folder, or examine properties of the folder.

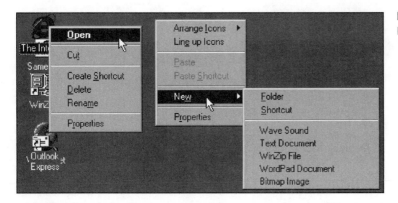

FIGURE 20.3
Right-click menus.

In the case of one of the system's hardware devices, the menu will permit you to perform such functions as sharing the device or checking its properties. These menus might contain additional items inserted by applications that they serve.

Right-clicking in an open area of the desktop produces a pop-up menu similar to the one displayed in the right half of the figure. This menu enables the user to arrange icons on the desktop, create new folders and shortcuts, and see the properties of the system's video display.

> **EXAM TIP**
> Memorize the common options found in the My Computer right-click menu.

Windows 98 Desktop

In its basic form, the Windows 98 Desktop is very similar to that of the Windows 95 Desktop. However, some additional features of the new desktop enable the user to quickly access a wide variety of resources. Additional items of interest on the Windows 98 desktop include an extended icon system, a QuickLaunch Toolbar, user-defined toolbars, and active desktop elements.

In a multiple user system, the \Windows\Profiles directory contains a folder for each user that logs on to the system. These folders contain the individual user's USER.DAT files, along with a number of their desktop-related folders. These folders include each user's

◆ Desktop folder

◆ Favorites folder

◆ History folder

NOTE

Cookie Info   Cookies are collections of information samples from different user's visits to a Web site.

- ◆ Internet Explorer Cookies folder
- ◆ Temporary Internet Files folder
- ◆ My Documents folder
- ◆ NetHood folder
- ◆ Recent folder
- ◆ Start Menu folder

Locating, Accessing, and Retrieving Information in Windows 9*x*

In its most basic form, the Windows 9*x* desktop features three standard icons: My Computer, Network Neighborhood, and the Recycle Bin.

The major user interfaces in Windows 9*x* include

- ◆ My Computer
- ◆ Pop-up dialog boxes
- ◆ The Start menu
- ◆ Windows Explorer
- ◆ Internet Explorer
- ◆ Network Neighborhood

My Computer

The *My Computer* icon is the major user interface for Windows 9*x*. It enables the user to see the local system's contents and manage its files. Double-clicking the My Computer icon produces the My Computer window, which displays all the system's disk drives as icons and represents the Control Panel and system printers as folders.

Double-clicking one of the drive icons produces a display of its contents onscreen. This information can also be displayed in several different formats using the View option. Selecting the Options entry in the View menu produces the Options window displayed in Figure 20.4. This window consists of three tabs (screens): Folders, View, and File Types.

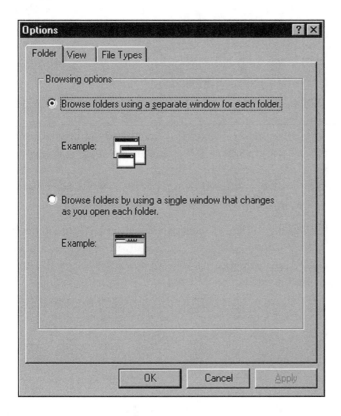

FIGURE 20.4
The View\Options window.

The General tab supplies information about how the desktop will display windows as the user browses through multiple windows. The View window is used to define how the folders and files in the selected window will be displayed onscreen. This screen also determines which types of files will be displayed. To see hidden and system files, select the View tab and click on the Show Hidden Files button. The File Types screen lists the types of files that the system can recognize. New file types can be registered in this window.

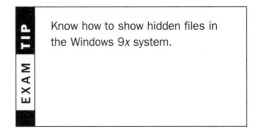

EXAM TIP

Know how to show hidden files in the Windows 9x system.

The Control Panel and Printers folders under My Computer contain information about the system and its printers. The Windows 9x Control Panel is the user interface employed to manage hardware devices attached to the system. The Windows 98 Control Panel is explored in greater detail in a later section of this chapter.

The Printers folder displays the computer's installed printer types. As with other icons in the My Computer window, the printers can be displayed as small icons, large icons, in a simple list, or in a list with details. Details include such items as printer type, number of documents to print, current status, and any comments generated by the print controller.

Windows 9x Pop-Up Menus

Most Windows 9x windows have menu bars that provide pop-up menus on the screen when they are accessed by clicking on their titles or by pressing the Alt key and their underlined character (that is, the Alt+F combination will pop up the File menu). Typical menu bar options include File, Edit, View, and Help. Options that apply to the current window are displayed as dark text. Options that are not applicable to the window will be grayed out.

The File option on the My Computer menu bar (as well as other user interface windows) can be used to perform many file and directory management procedures. When a disk drive icon is selected, clicking on the File option will produce a menu that includes provisions for creating a new folder, formatting the disk, sharing a drive with the network community, backing up the contents of the drive, or displaying its properties.

The File menu's Properties option displays general information about the drive, such as FAT type, capacity, free space, and used space. This option also provides a notice of how much time has elapsed since the last error-checking, backup, and defragmentation operations were performed on the selected drive.

The Windows 95 View menu option, depicted in Figure 20.5, is one of the most used features of the menu bar. It can be used to alter the manner in which the contents of the window are displayed. The drives and folders in the selected window can be displayed as large icons. However, they can be reduced to small icons, displayed as a list, or displayed with name, type, size, and free space details. Other options in the menu can be used to organize the icons within the window.

EXAM TIP

Know what is indicated when menu options are grayed.

EXAM TIP

Be aware of the different locations in Windows where new folders can be created and remember the primary method of creating a new folder.

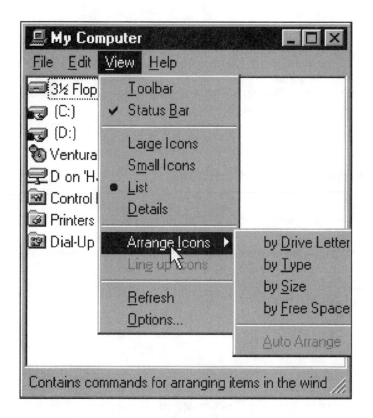

FIGURE 20.5
The View menu.

A check mark located next to the menu option indicates that the item is currently in use. The large dot next to the item indicates that it is the currently selected option.

In Windows 98, the My Computer options have been rearranged slightly from those of the Windows 95 My Computer window. In particular, the Options entry under the View menu has been replaced by Folder Options entry. The tabs in this window are titled General, View, and File Types. As with the Windows 95 version, the View/Folder Options/View window is used to define how folders and files will be displayed and to determine which types of files will be displayed.

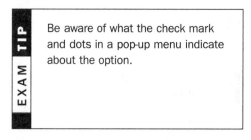

EXAM TIP

Be aware of what the check mark and dots in a pop-up menu indicate about the option.

EXAM TIP

Know how to navigate to various parts of Windows 9x through the My Computer icon.

CHALLENGE #1

You are working at a Help Desk position when you get a call from a user saying that her mouse has stopped working in the middle of her writing project and she doesn't know how to save her work without it. What should you tell her to do?

Network Neighborhood

The *Network Neighborhood* icon provides quick information about the world around the system when it's used in a networked environment. Small computer icons represent the various computers attached to the network. They enable the user to browse through the network. Double-clicking on any of the icons will produce a listing of the resources the selected computer offers—such as disk drives and printers.

The Recycle Bin

The *Recycle Bin* is a storage area for deleted files, and enables you to retrieve such files if they are deleted by mistake. When you delete a folder or file from the Windows system, it removes the first three letters of its name from the drive's FAT so that it is invisible to the system. However, the system records its presence in the Recycle Bin. The system is free to reuse the space on the drive because it does not know that anything is there. As long as it hasn't been overwritten with new data, or it hasn't been removed from the Recycle Bin, it can be restored from the information in the Recycle Bin. If it has been thrown out of the bin but has not been overwritten, it can be recovered using a third-party software utility for recovering deleted files.

The Recycle Bin icon should always be present on the desktop. It can only be removed through the Registry. If its icon is missing, there are two alternatives to restoring it: establish a shortcut to the Recycle Bin using a new icon, or just reinstall Windows 9x. This action will always place the Recycle Bin on the desktop.

In the case of removable media, such as floppy disks and removable hard drives, the Recycle Bin does not retain the files deleted from these media. When a file or folder is removed from one of these devices, the information is deleted directly from the system.

EXAM TIP

Know what happens to files moved into the Recycle Bin.

EXAM TIP

Know how to replace the Recycle Bin's icon in a Windows 9x system.

EXAM TIP

Be aware that information deleted from a removable media is not moved into the Recycle Bin. Therefore, no recovery is possible for this information.

CHALLENGE #2

A customer has called your Help Desk complaining that she has mistakenly removed a project that she have been working on for several months from her hard drive. She wants to know if your company can extract erased data from disk drives. With good questioning techniques, you determine that she is using a Pentium 4 machine with lots of RAM and a huge hard disk drive. In addition, she has a R/W CD-ROM drive and she is running Windows 2000 Professional. She does not have a tape drive for backup and because the system is very new, she has never performed a backup on it. What if anything, can you do to help this customer?

The Taskbar

Just to the right of the Start button is an area called the *Taskbar*. This area is used to display the applications currently open. Each time a program is started or a window is opened, a corresponding button appears on the Taskbar. To switch between applications, just click on the desired program button to make it the active window. The button will disappear from the Taskbar if the program is closed.

Right-clicking on the taskbar at the bottom of the screen produces a menu that can be used to control the appearance of the taskbar and open windows onscreen.

The Taskbar can be moved around the display by clicking and dragging it to the left, right, or top of the screen. It can be hidden just off screen by clicking its edge and then dragging it toward the edge of the display. If the Taskbar is hidden, pressing the Ctrl+Esc key combination will retrieve it and bring it to the screen. This will pop up the Start menu along with the Taskbar. Enter the Start/Settings/Taskbar and Start Menu option to change the Taskbar settings so that it will not be hidden. You can also locate an absent Taskbar by moving the mouse around the edges of the screen until the shape of the cursor changes.

Likewise, pressing the Tab key will cycle control between the Start menu, the Quick launch icons, the Taskbar, and the desktop icons. This key can also be helpful in navigating the system if the mouse fails.

> **EXAM TIP**
>
> Know how to move around the desktop, Start menu, and Taskbar using the keyboard.

The Start Menu

All operations begin from the Start button. When you click on the button, a pop-up menu of options appears, as illustrated in Figure 20.6. This Windows 95 menu normally contains the options Programs, Documents, Settings, Find, Help, Run, and Shut Down.

FIGURE 20.6
The Start button menu.

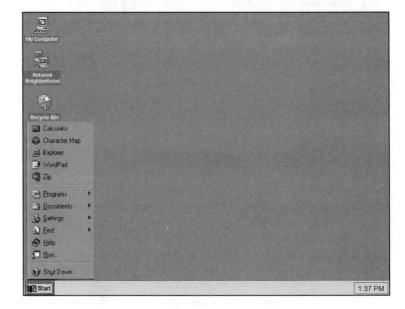

Placing the cursor over designated menu items will cause any submenus associated with that option to pop up onscreen. An arrow to the right of the option indicates that a submenu is available. To open the selected item, just left-click on it and its window will appear on the desktop.

The Programs submenu, depicted in Figure 20.7, has several options that include Accessories, Online Services, Start Up, Windows 9*x* Training, MS-DOS Prompt, and Windows Explorer.

The MS-DOS prompt is also accessed through the Programs option. The Start menu's Documents entry displays a list of documents previously opened.

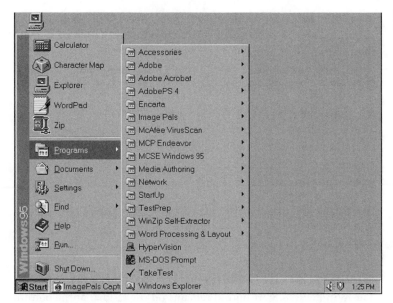

FIGURE 20.7
The Programs submenu.

The Settings option displays values for the system's configurable components. It combines previous Windows functions, such as copies of the Control Panel and Print Manager folders, as well as access to the Windows 9x taskbar.

The Find utility is used to locate folders, files, mail messages, and shared computers. The Find function can be accessed directly from the Start menu, or it can be reached by right-clicking on the My Computer icon. The selection from the Start menu allows files, folders, and computers to be searched for. The My Computer version searches only for files and folders. To locate a file, just type its name in the Named window, tell the system which drive or drive to look in, and click Find. Standard DOS wildcards can be included in the search name.

The Help file system provides extensive information about many Windows 9x functions and operations. It also supplies an exhaustive list of guided troubleshooting routines for typical system components and peripherals.

The Run option is used to start programs or open folders from a command-line dialog box. Executable files can be started by typing their filename in the dialog box and then clicking the OK button. The Browse button can be used to locate the desired file by looking through the system's file structure.

The Start button is also used to correctly shut down Windows 9x. The Shut Down entry in the Start menu is used to shut down the system, restart the computer, or log the user off. It must be used for exiting the system to avoid damaging files and to ensure that your work is properly saved.

In the Windows 9x Accessories folder in Start/Programs, you will find items such as Communications, Entertainment, Games, and System Tools.

Windows 98 Start Menu

The Windows 98 Start button remains on the taskbar at the bottom of the screen. Although most of the entries are carry-overs from Windows 95, the Log Off User and Favorites entries are new.

Windows 98 permits individuals in multiuser systems to log on to and operate in Windows 98 environments that have been specifically configured for their work needs. The Log Off User option is used to return the system to its natural setup. The Log Off entry might not appear in some installations, such as standalone machines that are not connected to a network environment.

The Favorites entry is included to enable users to store locations of often-used files. These files can be local to the machine, located on a local area network, or remotely located on the Internet. The Internet Explorer checks Web sites specified in the Favorites folder regularly for updated information.

The *Shut Down option* from the menu has been changed so that only three possible methods are listed for shutting down the session. They are Shut Down, Restart (warm boot), and Restart in MS-DOS mode. Windows 98 also includes a Standby option in the Shut Down menu. This option enables the user to put the system in a power conservation mode when it will not be active for some time. Standby keeps Windows ready to go when an event happens, but does not keep the system I/O devices awake.

Additional items can be added to the Start Menu so that they can be used directly from this menu. In doing so, the normal method of clicking Start, pointing to the Program option, and moving through sub-menus can be avoided. To move a frequently used item to the top of the Start Menu, simply drag its icon to the Start button on the Taskbar.

Windows 9x Control Panels

The Windows *Control Panel* is the primary user interface for managing the Windows system. It contains a collection of Windows-specific applications and utilities (referred to as *applets*) that control different components of the operating system.

The *Control Panel* in Windows 95 can be accessed from multiple locations within the system. One Control Panel folder is located under the My Computer icon; another copy can be found under the Start\Settings path. Both folders access the Control Panel window, depicted in Figure 20.8. This window contains icons for managing every device attached to the system. The Control Panel icon provides access to the configuration information for each of the system's installed devices specific to its type.

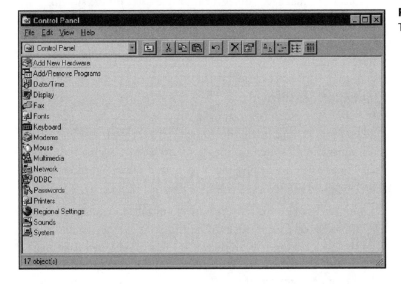

EXAM TIP

Know how to navigate to various parts of Windows 9*x* through the Start menus.

NOTE

Hands-On Activity For hands-on experience with this concept, refer to Lab Procedure #11, "Windows Me Navigating," located on the CD that accompanies this book.

FIGURE 20.8
The Windows 95 Control Panel.

Double-clicking on any of the device icons will produce a Properties dialog box for that device. Each box is different in that it contains information specific to the selected device. These dialog boxes might have a number of different folder tabs located along their tops. Each tab is labeled with the type of information it holds. Clicking on a tab displays additional information for that dialog page.

The most important uses of the Control Panel are as follows:

◆ Adding or removing new hardware or software components to the system

◆ Modifying system device settings

◆ Modifying desktop items

The Windows 98 Control Panel remains the user's primary interface for configuring system components. It has been enlarged to control a number of new functions. In addition to the Windows 95 configuration icons, Windows 98 adds Infrared Device Control options, an Internet Configuration tool, a Power Management utility, support for Scanners/Digital cameras, and additional modem and communication control functions in the form of a Telephony utility. The final addition to the Control Panel is the Users icon that provides tools to establish and manage profiles for multiple users on the system.

The Windows 98 Control Panel can be accessed through the My Computer icon on the Desktop or through the Settings entry in the Start menu.

Installation Wizards

The *Add New Hardware* icon brings the *Hardware Installation Wizard* into action. It will immediately ask the user whether Windows should search for the new hardware through a PnP-style detection process. Clicking the Next option causes Windows to conduct the hardware-detection operation.

If the device is not PnP, or if it must be installed manually because Windows 9x could not detect it, selecting the No option and clicking the Next button will produce a hardware components list. The Hardware Wizard will guide the manual installation process from this point and prompts the user for any necessary configuration information. If Windows 9x does not support the new device, you must click the Have Disk button and load drivers supplied by the device's manufacturer.

The *Add/Remove Programs icon* leads to the Install/Uninstall screen. This page can be used to install new programs from floppy disks or CDs by just clicking the Install button. Conversely, programs listed in the Programs window can be removed from the system by highlighting their title and clicking the Add/Remove button. The Add/Remove Programs applet is also used to bring auxiliary Windows components into the system. These components include Accessibility Options for physically, visually, or audibly challenged users.

The Windows Setup tab of the Add/Remove Programs applet is used to add or remove selected Windows 9x components, such as communications packages or additional system tools. The Startup Disk tab is used to create a clean startup disk for emergency start purposes after a crash. This disk can be used to boot the system to the command prompt (not the Windows desktop) so that you can begin troubleshooting failed startups. The Windows 98 start disk provides CD-ROM support that is not available with the Windows 95 start disk.

> **EXAM TIP**
>
> Know what action is required to install hardware devices not directly supported by Windows 9x.

> **NOTE**
>
> **Hands-On Activity** For hands-on experience with this concept, refer to Lab Procedure #18, "Windows Me Plug-and-Play," located on the CD that accompanies this book.

> **EXAM TIP**
>
> Remember the location of the Control Panel screen that is used to create a Windows Startup Disk.

CHALLENGE #3

A friend gave you a copy of several quaint old MS-DOS-based games on CD. When you put the CD in the drive, there is no Auto-run action for the CD. You want to install the game on your PC, but you're not sure how to go about it. Where should you look first to install the game under Windows 98?

The System Icon

One of the main Control Panel icons is the *System icon*. Clicking this icon produces the System Properties window. This window features tabs for general information, the device manager, hardware profiles, and system performance. The General tab supplies information about the system's operating system version, microprocessor type and RAM capacity, as well as its ownership and registration.

> **EXAM TIP**
>
> Memorize the types of information provided by the General tab of the System Properties page.

EXAM TIP

Be aware of the paths that can be used to access the Device Manager.

EXAM TIP

Memorize the pathway to the Device Manager's Properties screens.

Device Manager

The *Device Manager* utility provides a graphical representation of the devices configured in the system. This interface can be used to identify installed ports, update device drivers, and change I/O settings. It can also be used to manually isolate hardware and configuration conflicts. The problem device can be examined to see where the conflict is occurring. In Windows 9*x*, the Device Manager can be accessed through the Start/Settings/Control Panel/System path.

The Device Manager contains a set of buttons that permit its various functions to be accessed. These buttons include Properties, Refresh, Remove, and Print. Typical Device Manager Properties pages provide tabs that can be used to access General information, device settings, device drivers information, and device resources requirements and usage. Each device might have some or all these tabs available depending on the type of device it is and what its requirements are.

The information under the tabs can be used to change the properties associated with the selected device. This often becomes necessary when resource conflicts occur in a system that has legacy devices installed. The Device Manager can be used to identify possible causes of these IRQ, DMA, I/O, and memory-settings conflicts.

Hardware Profiles

The System icon's Hardware Profiles tab provides a window that can be used to establish different hardware configuration profiles to be implemented at startup. Most systems do not require any additional profiles. The System icon's Performance tab displays information about the system's installed RAM, system resource usage, virtual memory settings, and disk FAT type.

NAVIGATING WINDOWS NT/2000

Many of the Windows NT/2000 structures and navigation methods should appear very familiar after reading the Windows 9*x* material. With Windows NT version 4.0, Microsoft introduced a Windows 9*x*–like user interface to the Windows NT operating system. This included the Desktop with its icons, the pop-up Start menu, and the Tool Bar.

Windows NT/2000 Desktops

The Windows NT/2000 desktops include most of the same features found in their Windows 9x counterpart. The standard desktop icons in Windows NT 4.0 are the same as those in Windows 9x (that is, My Computer, Network Neighborhood, Inbox, and the Recycle Bin). If the operating system is installed on a standalone unit that does not have a network card installed, the Network Neighborhood icon will not be present on the desktop. The standard desktop icons for Windows 2000 include My Computer, My Documents, My Network Places, and the Recycle Bin). The functions of these icons are identical to those described for the Windows 9x versions.

Like Windows 9x, Windows NT and Windows 2000 operations typically begin from the Start menu that pops up when the Start button is clicked. The Windows NT Start menu contains Programs, Documents, Settings, Find, Help, Run, and Shut Down options. As with the desktop icons, the operations of the Windows NT Start Menu options are identical to the descriptions of their Windows 9x counterparts.

The My Documents concept has been expanded in Windows 2000 to include a My Pictures folder that acts as the default location to hold graphic files. The Windows 2000 dialog boxes include an image preview function that allows the user to locate graphic files efficiently. The dialog box View menu option enables the user to toggle between Large and Small icons, Details, and Thumbnail views.

The My Network Places folder replaces the Network Neighborhood folder employed in previous Windows NT and 9x versions. This utility enables the user to create shortcut icons to network shares on the desktop. A network share is an existing shared resource (that is, printer, drive, modem, or folder) located on a remote system. The new icon acts as an alias to link the system to the share point on the remote unit.

Locating, Accessing, and Retrieving Information in Windows NT/2000

The process of locating, accessing, and retrieving information in Windows NT and Windows 2000 is virtually the same as with the Windows 9x operating systems.

The major Windows NT/2000 user interfaces are

◆ My Computer

◆ Start menu

◆ Windows Explorer

◆ Internet Explorer (must be added on in Windows NT)

◆ Network Neighborhood (My Network Places in Windows 2000)

◆ Windows 2000 dialog boxes (windows)

These interfaces provide users with access to all the major areas of the system. The My Computer window enables users to access every hardware device in the system. The Start menu provides the user with access to the system regardless of what else is occurring in the system. In doing so, it provides access to the system's installed applications, a search engine for finding data in the system, and the operating system's Help file structure.

The Windows NT Windows Explorer graphically displays the entire computer system in a hierarchical tree structure. This enables the user to manipulate all the system's software and hardware. Similarly, the Network Neighborhood window extends the Windows Explorer structure to include network and domain structures. The Internet Explorer supplies the system with a tightly linked Web connection.

Windows 2000 offers extended common dialog boxes for File/Open, File/Print, and File/Save options. These dialog boxes provide easy organization and navigation of the system's hard drives, as well as providing navigation columns that grant quick access to frequently used folders, such as the My Documents and My Pictures folders.

Windows 2000 also includes powerful new search capabilities for searching the local hard drive and the Web. The new HTML-like Search function in Windows 2000 replaces the Start menu's Find option from previous Windows desktops. The Search feature provides three distinct search options—For Files and Folders, On the Internet, and For People.

NOTE

Hands-On Activity For hands-on experience with this concept, refer to Lab Procedure #15, "Windows 2000 Navigation," located on the CD that accompanies this book.

CHAPTER SUMMARY

This chapter has concentrated on disk and directory architectures used in Microsoft-based PCs. It has also presented information about how to navigate through command line, Windows 9x, and Windows 2000 environments.

The chapter also included a guide to command-line functions and usage, as well as methods of working in the major user interfaces of Windows 9x and Windows 2000.

At this point, review the objectives listed at the beginning of the chapter to be certain that you understand each point and can perform each task listed there. Afterward, answer the review questions that follow to verify your knowledge of the information.

KEY TERMS

- Add New Hardware icon
- Add/Remove Programs applet
- Add/Remove Programs icon
- Alternate clicking
- Control Panel
- Device Manager
- Directories
- File
- Filename Extensions
- Filenames
- Folders
- Hardware Installation Wizard
- Hardware Profiles
- MS-DOS
- My Computer
- My Network Places
- Network Neighborhood
- Pop-up menu
- Recycle Bin
- Right clicking
- Show Hidden Files button
- Shut Down option
- Start button
- System icon
- Taskbar
- Task-switching
- Windows 2000 dialog boxes
- Windows Explorer

APPLY YOUR KNOWLEDGE

Review Questions

1. What desktop's shortcut key combination enables the user to cycle through open application windows?

   A. Alt+Tab keys

   B. Ctrl+Esc keys

   C. Shift+Tab keys

   D. Alt+Esc keys

2. How can hidden and system files be shown in the Windows 9x system?

   A. Double-click on My Computer, click on File and select Properties from the menu, click the View tab and then click on Show Hidden Files button.

   B. Double-click on My Computer, click on Tools and select Folder Options from the menu, click the View tab and then click on Show Hidden Files and Folders button.

   C. Double-click on My Computer, click on View and select Options from the menu, click the View tab and then click on Show Hidden Files button.

   D. Double-click on My Computer, click on Edit and select Folder Options from the menu, click the View tab and then click on Show Hidden Files button.

3. What is indicated when menu options are grayed?

   A. Options applicable to the selected item

   B. Options not applicable to the selected item

   C. Options currently in use

   D. Options that are not installed

4. What is the primary location in Windows where new folders can be created?

   A. Select a parent directory, click the File menu, and then select New Folder.

   B. Select a parent directory, click the Edit menu, and then select New Folder.

   C. Select a parent directory, click the Edit menu, and select New and then Folder.

   D. Select a parent directory, click the File menu, and select New and then Folder.

5. What do the check marks in a pop-up menu indicate about the option?

   A. The option was previously deleted.

   B. The option is currently selected.

   C. The item needs to be installed.

   D. The item is currently in use.

6. What do the dots in a pop-up menu indicate about the option?

   A. The item is currently in use.

   B. The item needs to be installed.

   C. The option is currently selected.

   D. The option is not available.

7. What happens to files moved into the Recycle Bin?

   A. The filename is changed to make it invisible to the system.

   B. The file is deleted.

   C. The file is archived and held for later deletion.

   D. The file is overwritten.

APPLY YOUR KNOWLEDGE

8. What happens to information that was deleted from a removable media?

   A. Deleted from the file system.

   B. Moved into the Recycle Bin.

   C. Relocated to the System Backup directory.

   D. The file is archived and held for later deletion.

9. How can the Recycle Bin's icon be replaced in a Windows 9x system? (Select two answers.)

   A. Establish a new shortcut to the Recycle Bin.

   B. Copy and paste the icon.

   C. Reinstall Windows 9x.

   D. Create a new folder and rename it "Recycle Bin."

10. How can you move around the desktop, Start menu, and Taskbar by just using the keyboard?

    A. Esc

    B. Tab

    C. The Arrow keys

    D. Ctrl

11. What action is required to install hardware devices not directly supported by Windows 9x?

    A. The system must be rebooted.

    B. Install a driver for a similar device from the same manufacturer.

    C. The item cannot be installed.

    D. It must be installed manually.

12. How is a Startup Disk created in Windows 9x?

    A. Start/Programs/Accessories/System Tools and then select Backup

    B. Start/Settings/Control Panel/Add-Remove Programs and then click the Startup tab

    C. Start/Settings/Control Panel/System and then click the Startup tab

    D. Start/Programs/Accessories/System Tools and then click the System Information

13. What type of information is provided by the General tab of the System Properties page? (Select all that apply.)

    A. Microprocessor type and RAM capacity

    B. Operating system version

    C. Date of OS installation

    D. Registered owner

14. Which path can be used to access the Device Manager?

    A. Start/Settings/Control Panel and then double-click on Device Manager

    B. Start/Settings/Control Panel/System and then click on the Device Manager tab

    C. Start/Settings/Control Panel/System click on the Hardware tab, and then click on Device Manager

    D. Start/Programs/Accessories/System Tools and then select Device Manager

APPLY YOUR KNOWLEDGE

15. Which function in Device Manager will allow you to manage and configure a device driver?

    A. Properties

    B. Resources

    C. Settings

    D. Options

16. How do you navigate to the System Tools in Windows 9x?

    A. Start/Settings/Control Panel/System Tools

    B. Start/Settings/Control Panel/Administrative Tools/System Tools

    C. Start/Programs/Accessories/Administrative Tools/System Tools

    D. Start/Programs/Accessories/System Tools

17. What is the maximum number of directories or files that can be held by another directory?

    A. 32

    B. 64

    C. 256

    D. 512

Answers and Explanations

1. **D**. Special key combinations enable the user to move between tasks easily. The Alt+Esc key combination enables the user to cycle through open application windows. For more information, see the section "Navigating Windows 9x."

2. **C**. The View window is used to define how the folders and files in the selected window will be displayed onscreen. It also determines which types of files will be displayed. To see hidden and system files, double-click on My Computer, click on View and select Options from the menu, click the View tab and then click on Show Hidden Files button. For more information, see the section "My Computer."

3. **B**. Options that are not applicable to the selected item will be grayed out. For more information, see the section "Windows 9x Pop-Up Menus."

4. **D**. To create a new folder in Windows, select a parent directory and then click on the File menu, move the cursor to the New entry, slide across to the Folder option and click on it. A new unnamed folder icon will appear in the right window. For more information, see the section "Windows 9x Pop-Up Menus."

5. **D**. A check mark located next to the menu option indicates that the item is currently in use. For more information, see the section "Windows 9x Pop-Up Menus."

6. **C**. The large dot next to the item indicates that it is the currently selected option. For more information, see the section "Windows 9x Pop-Up Menus."

7. **A**. The Recycle Bin is a storage area for deleted files, and enables you to retrieve such files if they are deleted by mistake. When you delete a folder or file from the Windows system, it removes the first three letters of its name from the drive's FAT so that it is invisible to the system. However, the system records its presence in the Recycle Bin.

APPLY YOUR KNOWLEDGE

The system is free to reuse the space on the drive because it does not know that anything is there. As long as it hasn't been overwritten with new data or it hasn't been removed from the Recycle Bin, it can be restored from the information in the Recycle Bin. If it has been thrown out of the bin but has not been overwritten, it can be recovered using a third-party software utility for recovering deleted files. For more information, see the section "The Recycle Bin."

8. **A**. In the case of removable media, such as floppy disks and removable hard drives, the Recycle Bin does not retain the files deleted from these media. When a file or folder is removed from one of these devices, the file information is deleted directly from the file system. For more information, see the section "The Recycle Bin."

9. **A, C**. If the Recycle Bin icon is missing, there are two alternatives to restoring it: establish a shortcut to the Recycle Bin using a new icon, or just reinstall Windows 9x. For more information, see the section "The Recycle Bin."

10. **B**. Pressing the Tab key will cycle control between the Start menu, the Quick launch icons, the Taskbar, and the desktop icons. This key can also be helpful in navigating the system if the mouse fails. For more information, see the section "The Taskbar."

11. **D**. If the device is not PnP, or if it must be installed manually because Windows 9x could not detect it, selecting the No option and clicking Next will produce a hardware component list. The Hardware Wizard guides the manual installation process from this point and prompts the user for any necessary configuration information.

If Windows 9x does not support the device, you must click the Have Disk button and load drivers supplied by the device's manufacturer. For more information, see the section "Installation Wizards."

12. **B**. In the Control Panel, the Windows Startup tab of the Add/Remove Programs applet is used to create a clean startup disk for emergency start purposes after a crash. For more information, see the section "Installation Wizards."

13. **A, B, D**. The General tab supplies information about the system's operating system version, registered owner, microprocessor type and RAM capacity, as well as its ownership and registration. For more information, see the section "The System Icon."

14. **B**. In Windows 9x, the Device Manager can be accessed through the Start/Settings/Control Panel/System path, and then clicking on the Device Manager tab. For more information, see the section "Device Manager."

15. **A**. The Device Manager page contains a set of buttons that permit its various functions to be accessed. These buttons include Properties, Refresh, Remove, and Print. Typical Device Manager Properties pages provide tabs that can be used to access general information, device settings, device drivers information, and device resources requirements and usage. For more information, see the section "Device Manager."

16. **D**. In the Windows 9x Accessories folder in Start/Programs you will find items such as Communications, Entertainment, Games, and System Tools. For more information, see the section "The Start Menu."

APPLY YOUR KNOWLEDGE

17. **D.** Microsoft directories can hold up to 512 directory or filename entries. For more information, see the section "Directories."

Challenge Solutions

1. You should tell the caller to press the Alt and F keys at the same time to pop up the application's File menu. Next, she should press the S or A key to Save the work to disk. She might also need to press the Enter key to activate the command.

   After the work has been saved, she should press the Ctrl+Esc key combination to bring up the Start menu. From this point, she can use the up/down arrow keys to move to the Shut Down option. Pressing the Enter key will start the shut-down process. For more information, see the section "Windows 9x Pop-Up Menus."

2. You should simply have the customer check her Recycle Bin and restore the data herself. Because the drive is large and she has made no indication that she has cleaned out the Bin after the data was erased, there is no reason to think that the data is not in the Bin. For more information, see the section "The Recycle Bin."

3. Your best bet is to try the Add/Remove Software applet in the Control Panel. This utility is responsible for installing all software in the Windows environment. For more information, see the section "Installation Wizards."

Suggested Readings and Resources

1. DOS Command Line Navigation
   http://www.tnd.com/camosun/elex130/
   dostutor1.html

2. ScanDisk
   http://webopedia.internet.com/TERM/S/
   ScanDisk.html

3. Hard Drive Utilities
   www.codemicro.com/badsector.htm

4. Windows 95 Desktop
   www.bus.msu.edu/nrc/class/95/desktop.html

5. Windows 95 Explorer
   www.bus.msu.edu/nrc/class/95/explorer.html

6. Windows 95 FAQ
   http://www.pctusa.com/win95.html

7. Windows 98 FAQ
   http://www.pctusa.com/win98.html

8. Windows 98 Tutorial
   http://www.baycongroup.com/win98/
   win9800.htm

9. Windows NT Tutorial
   http://www.utexas.edu/business/
   accounting/nt/

This chapter helps you to prepare for the Operating System Technologies module of the A+ Certification examination by covering the following objective within the "Domain 1.0: Operating System Fundamentals" section. This chapter focuses on creating and managing files. Coverage of this objective is continued in Chapter 22, which focuses on disk management.

1.2 Identify basic concepts and procedures for creating, viewing, and managing files, directories, and disks. This includes procedures for changing file attributes and the ramifications of those changes (for example, security issues).

Content might include the following:

- **File attributes—Read-Only, Hidden, System, and Archive attributes**

- **File-naming conventions (most common extensions)**

- **Windows 2000 COMPRESS, ENCRYPT**

▶ Disk-based computers handle information in bundles called files. Therefore, computer technicians must be able to create and manipulate files in the major operating system versions. This chapter covers file handling and conventions in MS-DOS, Windows 9*x*, and Windows NT/2000.

CHAPTER 21

Creating and Managing Files

STUDY STRATEGIES

To prepare for the Operating System Fundamentals objective of the Operating Systems Technologies exam,

▶ Read the objectives at the beginning of this chapter.

▶ Study the information in this chapter.

▶ Review the objectives listed earlier in this chapter.

▶ Perform any step-by-step procedures in the text.

▶ Answer the review questions at the end of the chapter and check your results.

▶ Use the PrepLogic test engine on the CD-ROM that accompanies this book for additional review and exam questions concerning this material.

▶ Review the exam tips scattered throughout the chapter and make certain that you are comfortable with each point.

INTRODUCTION

This chapter deals with how computers handle and store programs and data. With disk-based systems, this involves creating and manipulating organizational structures called files and directories. All Microsoft operating systems basically use the same structures and organization. Only the specific steps used to manipulate the structure differ between the various operating system versions.

The first section of the chapter covers basic file creation and management principles using the MS-DOS operating system as an example. In particular, the material deals with file management commands and naming conventions implemented under the DOS operating system.

The next section of the chapter switches to procedures associated with handling files in Windows 9*x* systems. This section continues by examining files in the Windows NT and Windows 2000 operating systems. This information includes how file management and naming conventions differ in Windows NT and Windows 2000. It also describes methods of encrypting files for security and for compressing folders and files under Windows 2000.

The chapter concludes by examining the Windows Explorer user interface. This is the user interface designed to enable users to organize and manipulate files and directories through a tree-like graphical environment.

After completing the chapter, you should be able to create, view, and manage files, directories, and disks from a command line or through the Windows GUIs. You should also be able to implement procedures for changing file attributes in all these operating system types.

FILES AND FILENAMES

Disk-based systems store and handle related pieces of information in groups called *files*. The system recognizes and keeps track of the different files in the system by their *filenames*. Therefore, each time a new file is created, it is given a unique filename that the operating system can use to identify and store it. Actually, computers can have different files with the same names, but they must be located in different directories. The real naming rule is that each file in a given directory is required to have a different filename from any other file in the directory. If two files with the same name were present in the same directory, the computer has no mechanism to differentiate between them so it would become confused and fail to operate properly.

MS-DOS FILES

Files are created by application programs or through programming packages. When they are created, they are assigned a filename. In an MS-DOS environment, there are a few rules you must remember when creating new filenames. The MS-DOS filename consists of two parts—a name and an extension. The filename is a combination of alphanumeric characters and is between one and eight characters in length. The extension is an optional addition to the name that begins with a period, and is followed by between one and three characters.

You should remember the seven items below when assigning and using filenames:

◆ All files must have a filename.

◆ All filenames must be different from any other filename in the system, or on the disk presently in use.

◆ DOS filenames are up to eight characters long with an optional three-character extension (separated from the basic filename by a period).

◆ When using a filename in a command, you must also use its extension, if one exists.

◆ Some special characters are not allowed in filenames. These are: [,], :, ;, +, =, \, /, <, >, ?, and ,.

◆ When telling DOS where to carry out a command, you must tell it on which disk drive the operation is to be performed. The drive must be specified by its letter name followed by a colon (that is, A:, B:, C:, and so on).

◆ The complete and proper way to specify a file calls for the drive specifier, the filename, and the filename extension, in that order (that is, A:filename.ext).

The following DOS commands are used to carry out file-level operations. The format for using them is identical to the disk and directory-related commands discussed earlier. However, the command must include the filename and its extension at the end of the directory path. Depending on the operation, the complete path might be required, or a default to the currently active drive will be assumed.

◆ COPY—The file copy command copies a specified file from one place (disk or directory) to another.

C:\>COPY A:filename.ext B: is used if the file is to have the same name in its new location; the second filename specifier can be omitted.

C:\>COPY A:filename.ext B:filename.ext

◆ XCOPY—This command copies all the files in a directory, along with any subdirectories and their files. This command is particularly useful in copying files and directories between disks with different formats (that is, from a 1.2MB disk to a 1.44MB disk):

C:\>XCOPY A: B: /s

This command would copy all the files and directories from the disk in drive A: (except hidden and system files) to the disk in drive B:. The /s switch instructs the XCOPY command to copy directories and subdirectories.

◆ DEL or ERASE—These commands allow the user to remove unwanted files from the disk when typed in at the DOS prompt:

C:\>DEL filename.ext

C:\>ERASE B:filename.ext

A great deal of care should be taken when using these commands. If a file is erased accidentally, it might not be retrievable.

◆ REN—Enables the user to change the name or extension of a filename:

C:\>REN A:filename.ext newname.ext

C:\>COPY A:filename.ext B:newname.ext

EXAM TIP

Know which characters can legally be used in a DOS filename.

Using this command does not change the contents of the file, only its name. The original filename (but not the file) is deleted. If you want to retain the original file and filename, a copy command, using different filenames, can be used.

◆ TYPE—Shows the contents of a designated file on the monitor screen.

`C:\>TYPE AUTOEXEC.BAT` will display the contents of the AUTOEXEC.BAT file.

◆ FC—This file-compare command compares two files to see if they are the same. This operation is normally performed after a file copy has been performed to ensure that the file was duplicated and located correctly:

`C:\>FC A:filename.ext B:`

If the filename is to be changed during the copy operation, the command would have to be typed as

`C:\>FC A:filename.ext B:newname.ext`

◆ ATTRIB—Changes file attributes such as Read-only (+R or -R), Archive (+A or -A), System (+S or -S), and Hidden (+H or -H). The + and − signs are to add or subtract the attribute from the file.

`C:\>ATTRIB +R C:\DOS\memos.doc`

EXAM TIP

Memorize the different DOS file attributes and be able to use the various attribute switch settings.

This command sets the file MEMOS.DOC as a read-only file. Read-only attributes protect the file from accidentally being overwritten. Similarly, one of the main reasons for giving a file a Hidden attribute is to prevent it from accidentally being erased. The System attribute is reserved for use by the operating system and marks the file as a system file.

DOS SHORTCUTS

When using filenames in command-line operations, the filename appears at the end of the directory path in the source and destination locations. The * notation is called a *wild card* and allows operations to be performed with only partial source or destination information. Using the notation as *.* tells the software to perform the designated command on any file found on the disk using any filename and extension.

A question mark (?) can be used as a wild card to represent a single character in a filename or extension. Multiple question marks can be used to represent multiple characters in a filename or extension.

> **EXAM TIP**
>
> Memorize the MS-DOS wild card characters and be able to use their variations.

WINDOWS 9X FILES

The Windows 9x file system does away with the 8+3 character filename system implemented under DOS. In Windows 9x, long filenames of up to 255 characters can be used, so they can be more descriptive in nature. When these filenames are displayed in non-Windows 9x systems, they are truncated (shortened) to fit the 8.3 DOS character format and identified by a tilde character (~) followed by a single-digit number.

The tilde character is placed in the seventh character position of the filename to show that the filename is being displayed in a shortened manner, as an alias for the full-length filename. The number following the mark will have a value of 1 assigned to it unless another file has already been assigned the alias with a 1 value. Customers with older operating systems might overlook files because they are saved in this manner.

The tilde will be inserted into the seventh character space for up to nine iterations of similar filenames. After that, Windows will replace the sixth character for iterations up to 99. Windows 95 applies this same convention to the naming of directories as well. To change a long directory name from the command line requires that quotation marks be placed around the name. Consider the following examples:

- ◆ oldlongfile.txt = oldlon~1.txt
- ◆ oldlongtable.txt = oldlon~2.txt
- ◆ oldlonggraphic.txt = oldlo~63.txt

> **EXAM TIP**
>
> Know how Windows 9x handles similar long file names in an MS-DOS compatible format. Additional characters can be used in the Windows 95 long filenames. These characters include +, ,, :, =, [, and]. Blank spaces can also be used in long filenames.

Windows NT/2000 Files

EXAM TIP

Be aware of the maximum numbers of characters that can be used for Windows NT and Windows 2000 filenames.

EXAM TIP

Know which characters can legally be used in a Windows 2000 filename.

From Windows NT 4.0 forward, the NT operating system has been able to handle long filenames. Filenames in Windows NT can be up to 256 characters long. Windows NT uses a proprietary method for reducing long filenames to MS-DOS–compatible 8.3 filenames. Instead of simply truncating the filename, inserting a tilde, and then assigning a number to the end of the filename, Windows NT performs a mathematical operation on the long name to generate a truly unique MS-DOS compatible filename.

Filenames in Windows 2000 can be up to 215 characters long, including spaces. Windows 2000 uses a proprietary method for reducing long filenames to MS-DOS–compatible 8.3 filenames. Windows 2000 filenames cannot contain the following characters: /, \, :, *, ?, ", |.

Basically, the Windows NT 4.0 and Windows 2000 algorithms employed to produce DOS-compatible filenames remove any characters that are illegal under DOS, remove any extra periods from the filename, truncate the filename to six characters, insert a tilde, and add an ID number to the end of the name. However, when five or more names are generated that would result in duplicate short names, Windows NT changes its truncation method. Beginning with the sixth filename, the first two characters of the name are retained, the next four characters are generated through the mathematical algorithm, and, finally, a tilde with an ID number is attached to the end of the name. This method is used to create DOS-compliant short filenames for MS-DOS, Windows 3.*x*, and Windows 9*x*–compliant FAT systems, as well as the proprietary *Windows NT file system (NTFS)*.

CHALLENGE #1

A customer has an important business file on his Windows 2000 machine that has boot problems. He can gain access to the drive using a Start disk. However, when he views the disk from the command line, he cannot find the FutureBusinessPlansandMarketing.doc file. He has asked you to help him locate the file because he must give a presentation based on it in one hour. When you view the drive, there are literally several hundreds of files on the drive. What can you do for him?

File Encryption and Compression

The NTFS file system employed in Windows 2000 provides two new file types that technicians must deal with: *encrypted files* and *compressed files*. The Windows 2000 NTFS system provides an *Encrypted File System* (*EFS*) utility that is the basis of storing encrypted files on NTFS volumes. Once a file or folder has been encrypted, only the user who encrypted it can access it. The original user can work with the file or folder just as he would a regular file. However, other users cannot open or share the file. (But, they can delete it.)

For other users to be able to access the file or folder, it must first be decrypted. The encryption protection disappears when the file or folder is moved to a non-NTFS partition. Only files on NTFS volumes can be encrypted. Conversely, system and compressed files cannot be encrypted.

Files and folders can be encrypted from the command line using the *cipher command*. Information about this command and its many switches can be obtained by typing **cipher /?** at the command prompt. Files can also be encrypted through the Windows Explorer. Encryption is treated as a file attribute in Windows 2000. Therefore, to encrypt a file, you simply need to access its properties page by right-clicking on it and selecting the Properties option from the pop-up menu. Move to the Advanced Attributes screen under the General tab and click the Encrypt contents to secure data check box, as illustrated in Figure 21.1. Decrypting a file is a simple matter of clearing the check box.

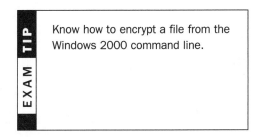

EXAM TIP

Know how to encrypt a file from the Windows 2000 command line.

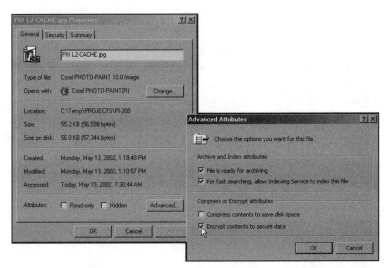

FIGURE 21.1
Encrypting a file.

The Windows Explorer can also be used to compress files and folders on NTFS volumes. As with the encryption function, Windows 2000 treats NTFS compression as a file attribute. To compress a particular file or folder, right-click on it in the Windows Explorer and then select the Properties option followed by the Advanced button to access its advanced properties screen. Click in the Compress Contents to Save Disk Space check box to compress the file or folder.

Likewise, an entire drive can be compressed through the My Computer icon. From the File menu, select the Properties option and click in the Compress Contents to Save Disk Space check box.

As with the encryption function, Windows 2000 files and folders can only be compressed on NTFS volumes. If you move a file into a compressed folder, the file will be compressed automatically. These files cannot be encrypted while they are compressed. Compressed files can be marked so that they are displayed in a second color for easy identification. This is accomplished through the Folder Options setting in the Control Panel. From this page, select the View tab and click in the Display Compressed Files and Folder with Alternate Color check box. The only other indication that you will have concerning a compressed or encrypted file or folder is an attribute listing when the view setting is configured to display in Web style.

WINDOWS EXPLORER

The File Management functions in Windows 9x and NT/2000 is performed through the *Windows Explorer* interface. This manager is located under the Start/Programs path from the desktop. By clicking on the Windows Explorer entry, the system's directory structure will appear, as shown in Figure 21.2. You can access the Windows Explorer by right-clicking on the Start button, or on the My Computer icon, and then selecting the Explore option.

The Windows Explorer enables the user to copy, move, and erase files on any of the system's drives. Its screen is divided into two parts. The left side displays the system's directory tree, showing all the directories and subdirectories of its available drives.

EXAM TIP

Know how to identify a compressed file in Windows 2000.

NOTE

Hands-On Activity   For hands-on experience with this concept, refer to Lab Procedure #25, "Windows 2000 Disk Management," located on the CD that accompanies this book.

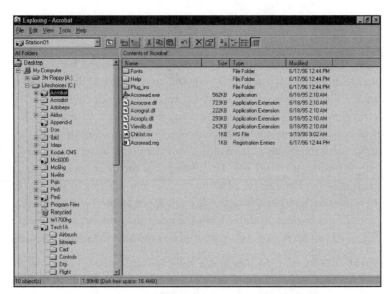

FIGURE 21.2

The Windows 9x Explorer screen.

In the Windows environment, directories and subdirectories are referred to and depicted as folders (and subfolders). Any drive or directory can be selected by clicking on its icon or folder. You can expand the contents of the folder by clicking on the *node* (+ sign) beside the folder. Conversely, the contents of the same folder can be contracted by clicking on the minus (-) sign node in the same box.

The Windows Explorer is not limited to just showing the directories, subdirectories, and files on local drives. It will also display drives and folders from throughout the network environment. The contents of the local drives are displayed at the top of the directory tree. If the system is connected to a network, the additional resources available through the network are displayed below those of the local system, as a continuation of its tree structure.

One noticeable difference exists between the Windows 9x and Windows 2000 main tree structures in Windows Explorer—the Printers folder has been removed from the main tree and placed as a sub-branch of the Control Panel folder.

The right side of the Windows Explorer screen displays the files of the selected directory. The status bar at the bottom of the screen provides information about the number and size of the files in the selected directory. The View menu on the Explorer menu bar can be used to set the display for large or small icons, as well as simple or

EXAM TIP

Know how to navigate to various parts of Windows 9x through the Windows Explorer.

detailed lists. The Explorer's View functions are the same as those described for the My Computer menu bar.

The Windows Explorer is also used to perform disk and file management functions, such as formatting and copying disks. Right-clicking on a folder icon will produce a menu that includes a Send To option. Moving the mouse to this entry will produce a submenu that can be used to send a selected folder or file to a floppy disk drive or to the desktop. Several files or folders can be selected for copying using the Shift key. The contents of the right-click menu change in the Explorer, depending on the item that is selected. Because the right-click function is context sensitive, the menu produced for a folder will differ from the one displayed for a document file. Each menu has options that apply to the selected item.

Right-clicking on a document file will produce a pop-up menu with options that enable the user to copy, cut, rename, open, or print the document from the Windows Explorer. This menu also provides options to create a shortcut for the document or to change its attributes.

By default, Windows Explorer does not show .SYS, .INI, or .DAT files. To view these types of hidden files in Windows Explorer, you must change their attributes. Changing file attributes from the Windows Explorer involves right-clicking on the desired file, selecting the Properties option from the pop-up list, moving to the General page, and clicking on the desired attribute boxes. To see hidden and system files in Windows Explorer, click the View menu option, select the Folder Options entry, click the View tab, and check the Show All Files box. If you experience difficulty with this operation from the Windows environment, you can always access the file from the command prompt and change its attributes with the ATTRIB command.

Selecting the Open option from the pop-up list will cause Windows to examine the document to determine what type of file it is. After this has been established, Windows will attempt to start the appropriate application and open the file.

EXAM TIP

Know how to rename a file in Windows 2000.

EXAM TIP

Be familiar with efficient methods of changing file attributes from the Windows Explorer.

EXAM TIP

Know which file types are normally not shown in Windows Explorer.

CHALLENGE #2

You are working through a customer's system that is set up so that it can dual boot into MS-DOS or Windows 98. You want to verify the sizes of the IO.SYS and MS.SYS files for each operating system. However, when you try to check them out through the Windows Explorer, you can't find them. Where did they go, and how do you find them?

The Windows File Menu

The Windows Explorer's File menu enables users to perform typical file management functions such as opening and closing selected files, saving files or changing their names or locations, and printing files. The File menu also includes an entry at the top titled New. Clicking on this option produces the New options submenu depicted in Figure 21.3. This menu is used to create new folders, shortcuts, and files.

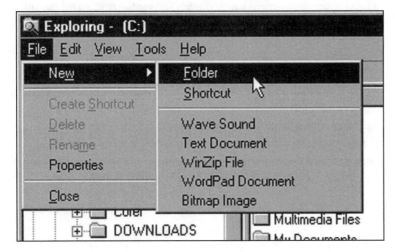

FIGURE 21.3
The New option.

To create a new folder in Windows Explorer, select a parent directory by highlighting it in the left window. Then click the File menu button, move the cursor to the New entry, slide across to the Folder option, and click on it. A new unnamed folder icon will appear in the right Explorer window.

EXAM TIP

Be able to create a new folder or file using Windows Explorer.

The same process is used to create new files. A file icon can be produced for any of the registered file types. Right-clicking on the new icon will produce the menu with options to rename the icon, create a shortcut for it, and establish its properties (including its attributes).

When a *shortcut* is created, Windows does not place a copy of the file or application in every location that references it. Instead, it creates an icon in each location and defines it with a link to the actual location of the program in the system. This reduces the amount of disk space required to reference the file from multiple locations. A small arrow in the lower-left corner of the icon identifies it as a Shortcut icon.

CHAPTER SUMMARY

KEY TERMS

- Cipher command
- Compressed files
- Encrypted File System (EFS)
- Encrypted files
- Filenames
- Files
- Node
- Shortcut
- Wild card
- Windows Explorer
- Windows NT file system (NTFS)

This chapter has dealt with file and directory manipulation in the three Major Microsoft operating systems/environments. The first part of the chapter covered basic file creation and management principles in a command-line environment.

The chapter then moved on to discuss file management and naming conventions under Windows NT and Windows 2000—including encrypting files and compressing folders and files in Windows 2000.

The chapter concluded with an investigation of using the Windows Explorer utility to manage files and directory structures in the Windows operating system.

At this point, review the objectives listed at the beginning of the chapter to be certain that you understand each point and can perform each task listed there. Afterward, answer the review questions that follow to verify your knowledge of the information.

APPLY YOUR KNOWLEDGE

Review Questions

1. Which of the following characters cannot be used in a DOS filename? (Select two answers.)

   A. ?

   B. &

   C. >

   D. #

2. Which DOS file attribute is reserved for use by the operating system?

   A. Read-only

   B. Archive

   C. System

   D. Hidden

3. Which DOS wild card characters tell the software to perform the designated command on any file found on the disk using any filename and extension?

   A. #.#

   B. *.*

   C. ?.?

   D. +.+

4. You have a file named "Arizona's best places to see.jpg" in the folder c:\pictures. You can see the file in Windows Explorer. But when you view this directory in the command prompt, why can't you see this file?

   A. Windows doesn't display long filenames at the command prompt.

   B. It is displayed as Arizon~1.jpg in the command prompt.

   C. The Windows command prompt deleted the file.

   D. When viewing the file system using the command prompt, it's not in the c:\pictures directory.

5. What is the maximum number of characters that can be used for Windows 2000 filenames?

   A. 64

   B. 215

   C. 255

   D. 256

6. What is the maximum number of characters that can be used for Windows 9x filenames?

   A. 64

   B. 215

   C. 255

   D. 256

7. Which of the following characters are not allowed to be used in a Windows 2000 filename? (Select two answers.)

   A. :

   B. *

   C. &

   D. #

8. What command is used to encrypt files and folders from the Windows 2000 command line?

   A. Protect

   B. Uuencode

   C. Encrypt

   D. Cipher

APPLY YOUR KNOWLEDGE

9. How do you identify a compressed file in Windows 2000? (Select two answers.)

   A. File or folder is listed in a second color.

   B. File or folder is listed in italic.

   C. File or folder shows compressed/archive attribute listing.

   D. File or folder is given a vice-clamp icon.

10. How do you navigate to various parts of Windows 9x through the Windows Explorer?

   A. Expand a folder contents listing by clicking on the minus sign (-) to expand it, and repeat until you locate the target file/folder.

   B. Expand a folder contents listing by clicking on the plus sign (+) to expand it, and repeat until you locate the target file/folder.

   C. Expand a folder contents listing by clicking on the star sign (*) to expand it, and repeat until you locate the target file/folder.

   D. Expand a folder contents listing by clicking on the backslash sign (\) to expand it, and repeat until you locate the target file/folder.

11. Which file types are normally not shown in Windows Explorer? (Select two answers.)

   A. .PCX

   B. .DAT

   C. .BMP

   D. .INI

12. Which method is used to change file attributes from the Windows Explorer?

A. Right-click on the file and select Properties.

B. Edit the appropriate Registry entry with Regedt32.

C. Highlight the file and choose the Select Options entry in the System Tools menu.

D. Highlight the file and choose the Select Options entry in the View menu.

13. How do you create a new folder using Windows Explorer?

   A. Select a parent directory, click the File menu, and then select New Folder.

   B. Select a parent directory, click the Edit menu, and then select New Folder.

   C. Select a parent directory, click the Edit menu, select New, and then Folder.

   D. Select a parent directory, click the File menu, select New, and then Folder.

14. How do you rename a file in Windows?

   A. Double-click on the file and enter the new name.

   B. Right-click the file and then select Rename from the pop-up menu.

   C. Click on the file and enter the new name.

   D. Click on the file and then select Rename from the pop-up menu.

15. Which DOS file attribute is used to define the user's ability to edit that file?

   A. Read-only

   B. Archive

   C. System

   D. Hidden

APPLY YOUR KNOWLEDGE

16. What is the maximum number of characters that can be used for Windows NT filenames?

    A. 64

    B. 215

    C. 255

    D. 256

17. Which DOS file attribute is used to define whether a file can be viewed in Windows Explorer?

    A. Read-only

    B. Archive

    C. System

    D. Hidden

Answers and Explanations

1. **A, C.** Some special characters are not allowed in filenames. These are [,], :, ;, +, =, \, /, <, >, ?, and ,. For more information, see the section "MS-DOS Files."

2. **C.** The System attribute (+s, -s) is reserved for use by the operating system and marks the file as a system file. For more information, see the section "MS-DOS Files."

3. **B.** Using the notation *.* tells the software to perform the designated command on any file found on the disk using any filename and extension. The * notation is called a wild card and allows operations to be performed with only partial source or destination information. For more information, see the section "DOS Shortcuts."

4. **B.** In Windows 9x, long filenames of up to 255 characters can be used, so they can be more descriptive in nature. When these filenames are displayed in DOS systems, they are truncated (shortened) to fit the 8.3 DOS character format and identified by a tilde character (~) followed by a single-digit number. The tilde character is placed in the seventh character position of the filename, to show that the filename is being displayed in a shortened manner, as an alias for the full-length filename. The number following the mark will have a value of 1 assigned to it unless another file has already been assigned the alias with a 1 value. For more information, see the section "Windows 9x Files."

5. **B.** Filenames in Windows 2000 can be up to 215 characters long, including spaces. For more information, see the section "Windows NT/2000 Files."

6. **C.** In Windows 9x, long filenames of up to 255 characters can be used so that they can be more descriptive in nature. For more information, see the section "Windows 9x Files."

7. **A, B.** Windows 2000 filenames cannot contain the following characters: /, \, :, *, ?, ", and |. For more information, see the section "Windows NT/2000 Files."

8. **D.** Files and folders can be encrypted from the command line using the cipher command. Information about the cipher command and its many switches can be obtained by typing **cipher /?** at the command prompt. For more information, see the section "File Encryption and Compression."

APPLY YOUR KNOWLEDGE

9. **A, C.** Compressed files can be marked so that they are displayed in a second color for easy identification through the Folder Options setting in the Control Panel. From this page, select the View tab and select the Display Compressed Files and Folder with Alternate Color check box. The only other indication that you will have concerning a compressed or encrypted file or folder is an attribute listing when the view setting is configured to display in Web style. For more information, see the section "File Encryption and Compression."

10. **B.** In the Windows environment, directories and subdirectories are referred to, and depicted as, folders (and subfolders). Any drive or directory can be selected by clicking on its icon or folder. You can expand the contents of the folder by clicking on the node (+ sign) beside the folder. Conversely, the contents of the same folder can be contracted by clicking on the minus (-) sign node in the same box. For more information, see the section "Windows Explorer."

11. **B, D.** By default, Windows Explorer does not show .SYS, .INI, or .DAT files. For more information, see the section "Windows Explorer."

12. **A.** Changing file attributes from the Windows Explorer involves right-clicking on the desired file, selecting the Properties option from the pop-up list, moving to the General page, and clicking on the desired attribute boxes. For more information, see the section "Windows Explorer."

13. **D.** To create a new folder in Windows Explorer, select a parent directory by highlighting it in the left window. Then click the File menu button, move the cursor to the New entry, slide across to the Folder option, and click on it. A new unnamed folder icon will appear in the right Explorer window. For more information, see the section "Windows Explorer."

14. **B.** A file icon can be produced for any of the registered file types. Right-clicking on the icon will produce a pop-up menu with options to rename the icon, create a shortcut for it, and establish its properties (including its attributes). For more information, see the section "Windows Explorer."

15. **A.** The read-only attribute protects the file from being improperly edited or accidentally being overwritten. For more information, see the section "MS-DOS Files."

16. **D.** Filenames in Windows NT can be up to 256 characters long. For more information, see the section "Windows NT/2000 Files."

17. **D.** The hidden attribute protects the file from being viewed in Windows Explorer. This is intended to prevent the accidental erasure of these files. For more information, see the section "MS-DOS Files."

Challenge Solutions

1. Because it is a Windows 2000 drive, the filenames are truncated when they are viewed from the command line. The customer should be looking for a file named *XXXXXX*1.DOC. For more information, see the section "Windows 9*x* Files."

2. Windows Explorer does not show .SYS, .INI, or .DAT files by default. To view these types of hidden files in Windows Explorer, click the View menu option, select the Folder Options entry, click the View tab, and check the Show All Files box. For more information, see the section "Windows Explorer."

APPLY YOUR KNOWLEDGE

Suggested Readings and Resources

1. DOS Filenames
   http://ou800doc.caldera.com/DOS_others/
   DOS_filenames.html

2. DOS Commands
   http://www.computerhope.com/msdos.htm

3. Wild Card Characters
   http://unixhelp.ed.ac.uk/tasks/defining.
   html

4. DOS Filename Truncation
   http://www.york.ac.uk/services/cserv/help/
   win95/w95h-14.htm

5. Managing Files in Windows 2000
   http://www.cs.ncl.ac.uk/modules/2001-
   02/csc131/Guide121.pdf

6. NTFS File Encryption
   http://www.brienposey.com/
   working_with_ntfs_encryption.htm

7. NTFS File Compression
   http://www.pcguide.com/ref/hdd/file/ntfs/
   otherCompr-c.html

8. Windows Explorer: Managing Your Files
   http://www.duke.edu/~dhewitt/tutorials/
   explorer/explor.html

This chapter helps you to prepare for the Operating System Technologies module of the A+ Certification examination by covering the following objective within the "Domain 1.0: Operating System Fundamentals" section. Coverage of file creation and management is included in Chapter 21.

1.2 Identify basic concepts and procedures for creating, viewing, and managing files, directories, and disks. This includes procedures for changing file attributes and the ramifications of those changes (for example, security issues).

Content might include the following:

- **IDE/SCSI**

- **Internal/External**

- **Backup/Restore**

- **Partitioning/Formatting/File system:**

  - **FAT**

  - **FAT16**

  - **FAT32**

  - **NTFS4**

  - **NTFS5**

  - **HPFS**

- **Windows-based utilities:**

  - **ScanDisk**

  - **Device Manager**

  - **System Manager**

  - **Computer Manager**

  - **MSCONFIG.EXE**

  - **REGEDT32.EXE**

  - **ATTRIB.EXE**

  - **EXTRACT.EXE**

CHAPTER *22*

Basic Disk Management

▶ The components in a computer system that require the most attention from a computer technician are its disk drives. These devices fill up and slow down the operation of the system. They also fail more often than less-mechanical parts of the system. Therefore, the technician must be able to perform typical disk-management procedures. Among other things, you should be familiar with the operation of the ScanDisk utility, the Windows Backup and Restore functions, the defragmentation utility, Windows disk management utilities, and file system partitioning/formatting functions.

▶ In addition to managing the system's disk drives, the technician must be able to locate and use the other system management utilities available to them. The Windows operating systems provide a wealth of troubleshooting tools that can be used to isolate and correct operating system problems. In this chapter, we will investigate the most widely used Windows utilities.

STUDY STRATEGIES

To prepare for the Operating System Fundamentals objective of the Operating Systems Technologies exam,

▶ Read the objectives at the beginning of this chapter.

▶ Study the information in this chapter.

▶ Review the objectives listed earlier in this chapter.

▶ Perform any step-by-step procedures in the text.

▶ Answer the review questions at the end of the chapter and check your results.

▶ Use the PrepLogic test engine on the CD-ROM that accompanies this book for additional review and exam questions concerning this material.

▶ Review the exam tips scattered throughout the chapter and make certain that you are comfortable with each point.

INTRODUCTION

This chapter explores basic disk organization and management issues in Microsoft-based systems. It also examines standard operating system utilities associated with Windows 9x, Windows NT, and Windows 2000.

The chapter begins by describing typical steps employed to prepare a disk drive for use by an operating system. This includes such practices as drive partitioning and high-level formatting the drive to prepare it for use.

The chapter then moves on to cover the organizational structure of disks—boot sectors, FAT tables, and root directories associated with MS-DOS and Windows 9x systems—as well as boot records and Master File Tables in Windows NT and 2000.

The next section of the chapter describes the advantages associated with the NTFS file management system native to Windows NT and Windows 2000. Information in this section also covers the use of basic and dynamic disks and volumes that can be established and manipulated in Windows 2000 systems.

The final sections of the chapter are dedicated to system management utilities used with PCs. These utilities include disk management—related programs such as CHKDSK, ScanDisk, defrag, and backup utilities.

The discussion also includes operating system utilities such as Troubleshooting Tools, System Tools, Configuration Troubleshooting Tools, Device Driver Tools and the System Resource Monitor and the Event Viewer.

After completing the chapter, you should be able to prepare the disk for use by the system. You should also be able to select the proper type of file system for use in a given computer situation. You should also be able to locate and use the various disk drive, system configuration, and troubleshooting tools available in Windows 9x and Windows NT/2000 systems.

MICROSOFT DISK STRUCTURES

The Microsoft MS-DOS, Windows 3.*x* and Windows 9*x* operating systems manage data on disk drives through a *File Allocation Table* (*FAT*) arrangement devised by Bill Gates for the original PC-DOS. Windows NT and Windows 2000 disk organization is based on a more dynamic *Master File Table* (*MFT*) structure. To prepare the disk for use by the system, three levels of preparation must take place. These are, in order

- the *low-level format* (below DOS)
- the *partition* (DOS—FDISK command)
- the *high-level format* (DOS—Format command)

In a PC, floppy disks basically come in four accepted formats: 360KB, 720KB, 1.2MB, 1.44MB, and 2.88MB. When they are formatted to one of these standards, the system performs the low- and high-level formats in the same operation. Floppy disks cannot be partitioned into logical disks; therefore, no partition operation needs to be performed.

The low-level format marks off the disk into cylinders and sectors and defines their placement on the disk. In older device-level drive types, the user was required to perform the low-level format using the DOS *Debug* program or through software diagnostic packages that came with a low-level formatter program. However, newer drive types come from the manufacturer with the low-level format already installed. These drives (that is, IDE and SCSI drives) should never have a low-level format operation performed on them.

Installing a new operating system on a hard drive has evolved into the five basic steps that follow:

1. Partition the drive for use with the operating system.

2. Format the drive with the basic operating system files.

3. Run the appropriate Setup utility to install the complete operating system.

4. Load all the drivers necessary for the operating system to function with the system's installed hardware devices.

5. Reboot the system to activate all the system components.

> **EXAM TIP**
>
> Memorize the proper order of operations for preparing a disk drive for use.

Drive Partitioning

Physical hard disk drives can be divided into multiple *logical drives*. This operation is referred to as *partitioning* the drive. With earlier versions of MS-DOS, partitioning became necessary because the capacity of hard drives exceeded the capability of the existing FAT structure to track all the possible sectors.

By creating a second logical drive on the hard disk, another complete file tracking structure is created on the drive. The operating system sees this new structure on the hard drive as a completely new logical disk. Therefore, it must have a new, unique drive letter assigned to it. Figure 22.1 illustrates the concept of creating multiple logical drives on a single hard drive. This is normally done for purposes of organization and increased access speeds. However, many users partition their drives so that they can hold multiple operating systems.

FIGURE 22.1
HDD partitions.

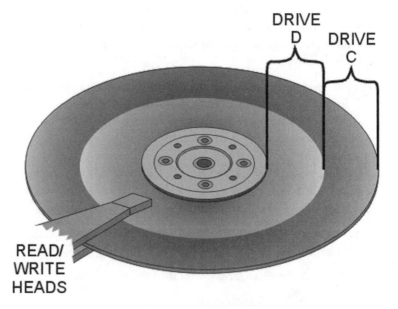

Basically, Microsoft's FAT-based file systems provide for two partitions on an HDD unit. The first, or *primary partition* must exist as drive C. After the primary partition has been established and properly configured, an additional partition, referred to as an *extended partition*, is also permitted. However, the extended partition can be subdivided into 23 logical drives. The extended partition cannot be deleted if logical drives have been defined within it. The *active partition* is the logical drive that the system will boot to. The system files must be located in this partition, and the partition must be set to "Active" for the system to boot up from the drive.

On a partitioned drive, a special table, called the *Partition table*, is created in the Master boot sector at the very beginning of the disk. This table holds information about the location and starting point of each logical drive on the disk, along with the information about which partition has been marked as active and a *Master Boot Record (MBR)*.

The Partition table is located at the beginning of the disk because this is the point where the system looks for boot information. When the system checks the MBR of the physical disk during the boot process, it also checks to see which partition on the disk has been marked as active. It then jumps to that location, reads the information in that partition boot record, and boots to the operating system in that logical drive.

The partitioning program for MS-DOS, Windows 9*x*, UNIX, and Linux is named FDISK. This program creates the disk's boot sector, two blank FAT tables, and establishes partition parameters (partition table) for the system's use.

EXAM TIP

Be aware of how the primary partition, extended partitions, and the active partition are related.

CHALLENGE #1

You have a customer who has a new computer with Windows 2000 Professional installed on it. However, she has several Linux based applications that she routinely uses and wants to move those applications onto the new computer. How can you help her do this?

High-Level Formatting

The high-level format procedure is used to load the operating system into the partition. On a FAT (MS-DOS, Windows 9*x*) disk, the high level format can be performed using the Format command from the command prompt or as a part of the operating system installation process. In a FAT-based system, this operation re-creates the two *file allocation tables (FATs)* along with a Root Directory on the disk. These elements tell the system what files are on the disk and where they can be found. Modifying the Format command with a /S after the drive letter designation causes the operating system files to be moved to the drive.

Figure 22.2 describes the organization of a FAT disk and illustrates the position of the boot sector, file allocation tables, and the root directory. The remainder of the disk is dedicated to data storage. The first area on each logical FAT-based disk, or partition, is the boot sector. Although all formatted partitions have this sector, they do not all have the optional master boot record located in the sector. Only those partitions created to be bootable have this record.

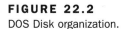

FIGURE 22.2
DOS Disk organization.

File Allocation Tables

The second logical section of a FAT-based disk is occupied by the file allocation tables. This area is a table of information about how the disk is organized. Basically, the system logs the usage of the disk's space in this table.

In older versions of DOS, the amount of space dedicated to tracking the sectors on the disk was 16 bits. Therefore, only 65,536 sectors could be accounted for. This parameter limited the size of a DOS partition to 32MB (33,554,432 bytes). To more effectively manage the disk space, newer operating system versions divide the disk into groups of logically related sectors called allocation units, or clusters. In a *FAT-based* system, the *cluster* is the smallest piece of manageable information.

EXAM TIP

Know what the smallest unit of storage in a disk-based system is.

The sectors on a FAT-based disk hold 512 bytes each. On the other hand, files can be of any length. Therefore, a single file can occupy several sectors on the disk. The file system breaks the file into sector-sized chunks and stores it in a cluster of sectors. In this manner, the FAT system uses the cluster to track files rather than sectors. Because the file allocation table only has to handle information for a cluster, rather than for each sector, the number of files that can be tracked in a given-length table is greatly increased.

In version b of Windows 95, also referred to as OSR2, Microsoft supplied an improved file management system that increased the entries in the FAT from 16 bits to 32-bit (called *FAT32*). This was done to make more efficient use of large hard drives (larger than 2GB). Under the previous FAT16 structure, large drives used large partitions, which, in turn, required large cluster sizes and wasted a lot of disk space. The FAT32 format in OSR2 supports hard drives of up to 2 Terabytes (TB) in size. FAT32 uses 4KB cluster sizes for partitions up to 8GB in size.

The Root Directory

The disk section following the FAT tables is the disk's *root directory*. This is a special directory present on every FAT-based disk. It is the main directory of every logical disk, and serves as the starting point for organizing information on the disk. Each directory and subdirectory (including the root directory) can hold up to 512 32-byte entries that describe each of the files in them.

Because each root directory entry is 32 bytes long, each disk sector can hold 16 entries. On a hard disk drive, normally 32 sectors are set aside for the root directory. Therefore, the root directory for such a disk can accommodate up to 512 entries.

Technically, every directory on a disk is a *subdirectory* of the root directory. All additional directories branch out from the root directory in a tree-like fashion. Therefore, a graphical representation of the disk drive's directory organization is called a *directory tree*. Figure 22.3 depicts the directory organization or a typical hard drive.

EXAM TIP
Know the size of sectors in an IBM/PC compatible disk.

EXAM TIP
Remember the number of entries that directories in a FAT-based system can hold.

EXAM TIP
Be aware of the maximum number of entries that can exist in the root directory of a FAT-based disk.

FIGURE 22.3
The DOS directory tree structure.

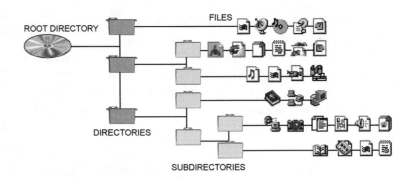

FAT32

Earlier versions of DOS and Windows supported what is now termed as FAT16 (or FAT 12). The *OSR2* version of Windows 95 introduced the FAT32 file allocation table. As described earlier, the size of the operating system's FAT determines the size of the clusters for a given-size disk partition. Of course, smaller cluster sizes are better because even a single byte stored in a cluster will remove the entire cluster from the available storage space on the drive. This can add up to a lot of wasted storage space on larger drives.

To use the FAT32 system, the hard drive must be formatted using the FDISK/FORMAT functions in OSR2. This makes FAT32 incompatible with older versions of Windows (even *Windows 95(a)* and Windows NT) and with disk utilities and troubleshooting packages designed for FAT12/16 systems.

To use the FAT32 FDISK function in OSR2, it is necessary to enable the Large Disk Support option. After completing the FDISK operation, manually reboot the system and perform a FORMAT operation using the OSR2 CD, or start disk.

To verify that a hard drive is formatted with FAT32, select the My Computer option from the desktop and right-click on the C: drive icon. This will produce the [C:] Properties window. The Type entry should read Local Disk [FAT 32].

OSR2 does not require that the FAT32 system be used. It will operate just as well, if not better, using the FAT16 format. Depending on the application of the system, the system might actually run slower with FAT32. Remember that FAT32 is designed to optimize storage space, not performance.

In Windows 9*x*, it is possible to convert partitions created on a FAT16 drive into a FAT32 file system using the *CVT.EXE* command-line utility. This operation can also be performed by accessing the *Drive Converter (FAT 32)* utility through the Start/Programs/Accessories/System Tools path. Selecting this option will run the *CVT1.EXE* file that starts the Drive Converter Wizard. The main drawback to doing this is that there is some possibility of data corruption and loss. Not surprisingly, there is no utility for converting FAT32 partitions to FAT16.

EXAM TIP

Know how to convert FAT16 partitions to FAT32 partitions.

Virtual File Allocation Table

Windows 9*x* streamlines the 32-bit file and disk-access operations by removing both the DOS and the BIOS from the access equation, allowing the operating system to always run in protected memory mode so that no mode switching need occur. Because the system does not normally have to exit and reenter protected mode, performance is increased considerably.

Microsoft refers to this portion of the system as the Protected Mode FAT File System. It is also called the Virtual File Allocation Table or *VFAT*. As its full name implies, the VFAT provides a Protected mode method of interacting with the file system on the disk drive. VFAT operates in 32-bit mode; however, the actual FAT structure of the disk remains as 12-bit or 16-bit allocations.

The VFAT system replaces the SMARTDRV disk-caching utility with a protected-mode driver named VCACHE. Under VCACHE, the size of the cache data pool is based on the amount of free memory in the system rather than a fixed amount. The program automatically allocates blocks of free memory to caching operations as needed. Under Windows 9*x*, the VCACHE driver controls the cache for the system's CD-ROM drive, as well as for hard disk and file operations.

EXAM TIP

Know that the VCACHE utility replaces the SMARTDRV utility for disk caching in Windows 9*x*.

Windows NT File System

In addition, Windows NT offers its own proprietary *Windows NT File System (NTFS)*. The NTFS structure is designed to provide better data security and to operate more efficiently with larger hard drives than FAT systems do.

The NTFS4 structure found in Windows NT 4.0 uses 64-bit entries to keep track of storage on the disk (as opposed to the 16- and 32-bit entries used in FAT and FAT32 systems). The core component of the NTFS system is the *Master File Table* (*MFT*). This table replaces the FAT in a MS-DOS compatible system and contains information about each file being stored on the disk.

The system files produced during the NTFS formatting process include

0/1. A pair of MFT files (the real one and a shorter backup version)

2. A Log file to maintain transaction steps for recovery purposes

3. A Volume file that includes the volume name, NTFS version, and other key volume information

4. An Attribute definition table file

5. A Root Filename file that serves as the drive's root folder

6. A Cluster Bitmap that represents the volume and indicates which clusters are in use

7. The partition boot sector file

8. A Bad Cluster file containing the locations of all bad sectors identified on the disk

9. A Quota Table for tracking allowable storage space on the disk for each user

10. An Upper Case Table for converting lowercase characters to Unicode uppercase characters

Figure 22.4 illustrates the organization of an NTFS disk volume. The first information in the NTFS volume is the 16-sector Partition Boot Sector. The sector starts at physical sector-0 and is made up of two segments—The BIOS Parameter Block and the Code section. The BIOS Parameter Block holds information about the structures of the volume and disk file system. The information in the Code section describes the method to be used to locate and load the start-up files for the specified operating system. This code loads the Windows NT bootstrap loader file NTLDR in Intel-based computers running Windows NT.

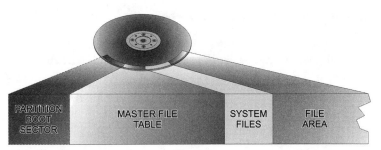

FIGURE 22.4
The organization of an NTFS disk volume.

The MFT contains information about each folder and file on the volume. The NTFS system relates to folders and files as a collection of attributes (that is, filename, security information, and data). The system allocates space in the MFT for each file or folder based on the cluster size being used by the disk.

For large files that cannot be identified by a single MFT record, multiple MFT records are employed. The first record contains a pointer to additional MFT records. The original MFT record contains the file or folder's standard information followed by index links to other MFT records that have index links to the actual data runs. In these cases, the data is stored outside the table and can theoretically range up to 16EB (exabytes—2^{60}).

Like FAT systems, NTFS systems use the cluster as the basic unit of disk storage. In Windows 4.0, NTFS clusters can range between 512 bytes and 64KB, depending on the size of the drive and how the disk was prepared. Clusters can range up to 64KB when established using the FORMAT command from the command prompt. However, cluster sizes are limited to a maximum of 4KB when using the Windows NT Disk Manager to handle the disk organization. The default cluster size is determined by the volume size and can be specified in the Disk Administrator utility.

The smaller cluster size of the NTFS format makes it more efficient than FAT formats for storing smaller files. It also supports larger drives (over 1GB) much more efficiently than FAT16 or FAT32 structures. The NTFS system is more complex than the FAT systems and, therefore, is not as efficient for smaller drives.

EXAM TIP

Be aware of the circumstances that make one file system more useful than the other.

Windows NT Disk Partitions

Windows NT can be used to partition a hard drive so that different operating systems can be used in each partition (and in extended partitions). The NTFS format lacks compatibility with other operating systems. Therefore, it will not allow other operating systems to access files on the NTFS drive. This can be a problem on partitioned drives that support multiple operating systems.

Windows NT employs very difficult terminology when referring to types of disk partitions. The disk partition where the BIOS looks for the master boot record is called the *System Partition*, whereas the partition containing the Windows NT operating system is called the *Boot Partition*. Either, or both, types of partitions can be formatted with the FAT or NTFS file systems. In practice, both partition types can be assigned to a single partition, or they can exist as separate partitions.

NTFS Advantages

The Windows 2000 operating system supports several file management system formats including FAT, FAT16, FAT32, *CDFS* (the *Compact Disk File System* is used on CD-ROM disks), and NTFS4, along with the new improved NTFS format referred to as *NTFS5*. This version enables administrators to establish user hard disk quotas limiting the amount of hard drive space users can have access to. The new NTFS system also offers enhanced system security. Windows 2000 NTFS provides an encrypted file system and secure network protocol and authentication standards.

Although Windows 2000 does support several different file systems (that is, FAT, FAT16, FAT32, CDFS, NTFS4, and NTFS5), in most situations, the NTFS system offers better performance and features than a FAT16 or FAT32 system. The exceptions to this occur when smaller drives are being used, other file systems are being used on the same drive, or the operating system crashes.

In most other situations, the NTFS system offers the following benefits over other file management systems:

◆ More efficient drive management because of its smaller cluster size capabilities.

◆ Support for very large drives is made possible by its 64-bit clustering arrangement.

> **EXAM TIP**
>
> Be aware of the different file system types supported by Windows 2000.

◆ Increased folder and file security capabilities.

◆ Recoverable file system capabilities.

◆ Built-in RAID support.

EXAM TIP

Memorize the advantages associated with using the NTFS file system.

Although the NTFS4 file management system in Windows NT 4.0 provided directory level access and use controls, it did not control user rights to individual files. However, in Windows 2000 administrators are given new tools that enable them to limit what the user can do to any given file or directory.

CHALLENGE #2

You have a physical disk in your computer that has two partitions—both of which are formatted with FAT 16. In one partition you are running Windows 95, and in the other you are running Windows NT4.0. Because Windows 95 is becoming very old and you do not want to keep it up, you upgrade the Windows 95 partition to Windows 2000 and use the NTFS5 file system. When you start up the system using the Windows 2000 partition, there is no problem. However, when you boot into the Windows NT4.0 partition, the new partition is not available. What should you do to correct this problem?

Basic and Dynamic Disks and Volumes

The Windows 2000 *Disk Management utility* is a graphical tool that handles two distinctive types of disks—*basic disks* and *dynamic disks*. A *basic disk* is a physical disk that contains partitions, drives, or volumes created with Windows NT 4.0 or earlier operating systems. Dynamic disks are physical disks created from basic disks using the Windows 2000 Disk Management utility. These disks can only hold dynamic volumes (not partitions, volumes, or logical drives). Dynamic disks are not created directly on new drives—they must be created from basic disks under Windows 2000.

The Disk Management utility enables Windows 2000 to create and handle *dynamic volumes*, created on *dynamic disks*. It contains a Dynamic Volume Management feature that permits the capacity of an existing volume to be extended without rebooting or reformatting. In addition, using dynamic disks, Windows 2000 escapes the four-volume limit inherent with other Microsoft operating systems. It also features a new user interface that enables administrators to configure drives and volumes located in remote computers.

There are five different types of dynamic volumes:

◆ *Simple volume*—Contains disk space from a single disk, and can be easily extended if necessary, as depicted in Figure 22.5.

FIGURE 22.5
Simple volumes.

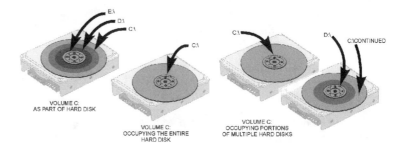

◆ *Spanned volume*—Contains disk space from two or more disks (up to a maximum of 32), as illustrated in Figure 22.6. The amount of disk space derived from each disk can vary.

FIGURE 22.6
Spanned volumes.

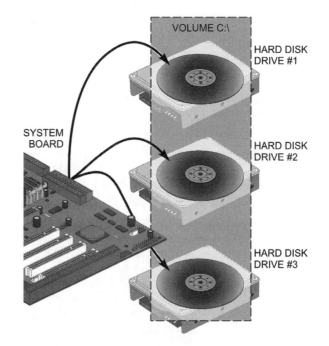

◆ *Mirrored volume*—Two volumes on different disks that are the same size and contain exactly the same data, as shown in Figure 22.7. In the event that one of the disks fails, the other will continue functioning, providing disk fault tolerance (RAID 1).

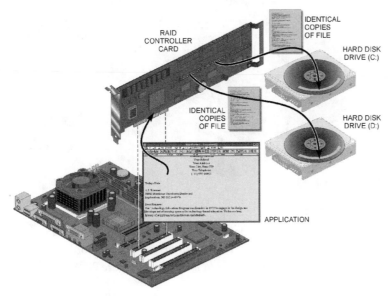

FIGURE 22.7
Mirrored volumes.

◆ *Striped volume*—Contains disk space from two or more disks (up to a maximum of 32), as illustrated in Figure 22.8. The amount of disk space derived from each disk must be the same.

FIGURE 22.8
Striped volumes.

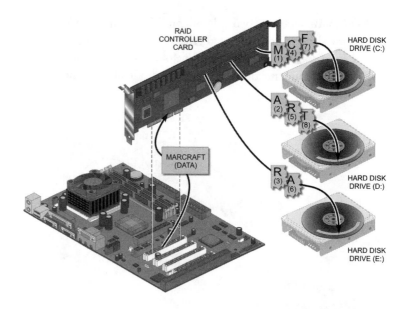

◆ *RAID 5 volume*—Also known as striped volumes with tolerance, provides disk fault tolerance. The data is divided into
64KB chunks and written to all drives in a fixed order. A five-
disk RAID 5 configuration is shown in Figure 22.9.

FIGURE 22.9
Five-Disk RAID 5 system.

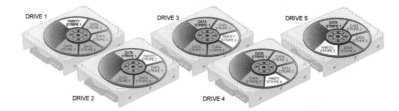

Only systems running Windows 2000 can access dynamic volumes.
Therefore, basic volumes should be established on drives that
Windows 9x or Windows NT 4.0 systems need to access. If a
dynamic volume is present on a drive, the file management systems
associated with the other operating systems will not be able to see or
access the dynamic drives or volumes.

To install Windows 2000 on a dynamic volume, it must be either a simple or a mirrored volume, and it must be a volume that has been upgraded from a basic volume. Installing Windows 2000 on the volume requires that it have a partition table, which dynamic volumes do not have unless they have been upgraded from a basic volume. Basic volumes are upgraded by converting a basic disk to a dynamic disk. Under Windows 2000, basic volumes are converted to dynamic volumes using the Disk Management tool (follow the path Start/Run, and enter **DISKMGMT.MSC** into the text box, and then click the OK button). Windows 2000 will not support dynamic volumes on portable computers. Mirrored and RAID-5 volumes are only supported on Windows 2000 Servers.

Dynamic volumes are managed through the Windows 2000 *Disk Management snap-in* tool, depicted in Figure 22.10. This snap-in is located in the Computer Management console. To access the *Disk Manager*, navigate the Start/Settings/Control Panel/Administrative Tools path. Double-click the Computer Management icon and click on the Disk Management entry.

> **EXAM TIP**
>
> Know what the requirements are for creating a dynamic volume in Windows 2000.

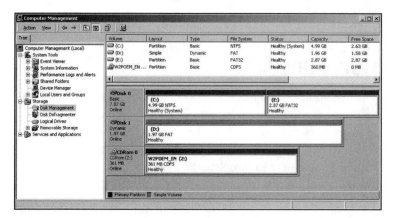

FIGURE 22.10
Windows 2000 Disk Management tool.

Because working with dynamic volumes is a major administrative task, you must be logged in as an administrator or as a member of Windows 2000's Administrators group in order to carry out the procedure. Also, system and boot volumes cannot be formatted as dynamic volumes.

> **NOTE**
>
> **Hands-On Activity**   For hands-on experience with this concept, refer to Lab Procedure #25, "Windows 2000 Disk Management," located on the CD that accompanies this book.

High Performance File System

IBM followed their successful PC-AT system with a line of personal computers called PS/2 (Personal System 2). The line was advertised around a proprietary 32-bit bus, called Micro Channel Architecture (MCA), and a new GUI-based operating system called OS/2 (Operating System 2). The PS/2 line has long since faded into the background of PC hardware, but the OS/2 software continues in some circles.

At the heart of the OS/2 operating system is the *High Performance File System* (*HPFS*). It provided a very robust file system for its time. The HPFS structure retained the FAT directory structure, but featured long filenames (up to 254 characters) and volume sizes up to 8GB. Under HPFS, the unit of management was changed to physical sectors rather than clusters.

Its other attributes include good performance when directories contain several files, built-in fault tolerance, fragmentation resistance, and good effectiveness when working with large partitions. The HPFS file system is only accessible under the OS/2 and Windows NT 3.51 operating systems.

> **NOTE**
>
> **High Performance File System**
> Although HPFS is listed in the Objectives for this section, it does not seem to actually appear as a question topic in the exam. However, it has been used as an incorrect answer in many of the questions.

HDD Utilities

The operation of hard drives can slow down with general use. Files stored on the drive can be erased and moved, causing parts of them to be scattered around the drive. This causes the drive to reposition the R/W heads more often during read and write operations, thereby requiring more time to complete the process.

Five important utilities can be used to optimize and maintain the operation of the hard disk drive. These are the CHKDSK, ScanDisk, defrag, backup, and antivirus utilities. With the exception of ScanDisk, which is a Windows utility, all these utilities have been available since early MS-DOS versions.

In Windows 9x, these functions are located in several areas of the system. The icons for backup, ScanDisk, and defrag are located in the Programs/Accessories/System Tools path. The executable file for ScanDisk can be found in `C:\Windows\Command`; the Defrag program is under `C:\Windows`. The Backup utility is located in `C:\Program_Files\Accessories` in Windows 9x and is located in

C:\WINNT\SYSTEM32 in Windows NT/2000. The built-in antivirus function is missing from Windows 9x. An add-on program from a second party should be used. The MSAV and MWAV programs from DOS and Windows 3.x, respectively, can be found in the C:\DOS directory if Windows 9x was installed as an upgrade.

The simplest way to access the HDD tools in Windows 9x is to open My Computer and right-click on the icon for the hard disk drive you want to use. Next, select the Properties option from the context-sensitive pop-up menu. Then, simply click on the Tools tab to gain access to the three most useful Windows HDD utilities: ScanDisk, Backup, and Defrag.

> **EXAM TIP**
>
> Remember where the main HDD utility programs are located in the Windows 9x environments.

CHKDSK

The DOS CHKDSK (*Check Disk*) command is a command line utility that has remained in use with Windows 3.x, 9x, NT, and 2000 and is used to recover lost allocation units from the hard drive. These lost units occur when an application terminates unexpectedly and causes the file management system to lose track of where some parts of the file are stored. The total file becomes segmented into undefined pieces that can still be read by the utility but cannot be associated with a particular filename in the FAT. Files can also become cross-linked when the file management system loses track of some portion of the file. In these cases, part of a second file might be written into a sector that actually belonged to another file and they become linked to each other at that spot.

Over a period of time, lost units can pile up and occupy large amounts of disk space. To remove lost units from the drive, an /F modifier is added to the command so that the lost units will be converted into files that can be investigated, and removed if necessary. In some cases, the converted file is a usable data file that can be rebuilt for use with an application. The CHKDSK /F command is often used before running a drive defragmentation program.

ScanDisk

A similar program, called *ScanDisk*, is available in DOS 6.x and Windows 9x. ScanDisk searches the disk drive for disconnected file clusters and converts them into a form that can be checked and manipulated. This enables the user to determine whether there is

EXAM TIP

Be aware of what events will cause ScanDisk to run automatically.

any information in the *lost clusters* that can be restored. ScanDisk also detects, and deletes if necessary, *cross-linked files*. Cross-linked files occur when information from two or more files is mistakenly stored in the same sector of a disk.

In addition to locating and converting lost clusters on the disk drive, the ScanDisk utility can detect and delete cross-linked files from the drive. It can also make corrections to file and disk errors that it detects. ScanDisk can be run from the command line or as a Windows utility program. As with other disk utilities, only a Windows version of ScanDisk should be used on a Windows system. Using a DOS-based version of ScanDisk might cause data loss rather than optimization because the DOS version does not lock out the system when the file structure is being modified. By default, the command-line version of ScanDisk runs automatically during Startup whenever the operating system detects that the system was not shut down properly.

The Windows 9x version of ScanDisk actually provides two ScanDisk utilities: an MS-DOS-based version that remains on the Windows 9x startup disk and a Windows-compatible graphics-based version (ScanDskw) that can be run from the Windows 9x environment. The MS-DOS version (ScanDisk) was designed to run from the Startup disk's command line in emergency recovery operations.

The Windows version is located in the Start/Programs/Accessories/System Tools path. It can be run from the Start/Run dialog box by typing `ScanDisk`, or it can be initiated through the drive's Tools Properties dialog box. The Windows version can repair long filenames and is the recommended version for repairing disks.

EXAM TIP

Know the difference between the Standard and Thorough ScanDisk operations.

The standard ScanDisk operation examines the system's directory and file structure. However, a Thorough option can be selected to examine the physical disk surface as well as its files and directories. If potential defects exist on the surface, ScanDisk can be used to recover data stored in these areas.

Backup

Backup utilities enable the user to quickly create extended copies of files, groups of files, or an entire disk drive. This operation is normally performed to create backup copies of important information

NOTE

Hands-On Activity   For hands-on experience with this concept, refer to Lab Procedure #23, "Windows Me Disk Management," located on the CD that accompanies this book.

for use in the event that the drive crashes or the disk becomes corrupt. The `Backup` and `Restore` functions can be used to back up and retrieve one or more files to another disk.

Because a backup of related files is typically much larger than a single floppy disk, serious backup programs allow information to be backed up to a series of disks; they also provide file compression techniques to reduce the size of the files stored on the disk. Of course, it is impossible to read or use the compressed backup files in this format. To be usable, the files must be decompressed (expanded) and restored to the DOS file format.

The *Microsoft Backup and Restore disk management utility* can be found in both Windows 9*x* and Windows 2000. However, it is not automatically installed when Windows is set up. If the user decides to install this feature, the actual backup file (Backup.exe) is placed in the `C:\Program_Files\Accessories` directory. Windows also creates a shortcut icon for the backup utility in the `C:\Windows\Start Menu\Programs\Accessories\System Tools` directory.

> **EXAM TIP**
>
> Know where the `Backup` and `Restore` functions are located in the Windows environment.

Backup Types

Most backup utilities allow backups to be performed in a number of ways. Typically, backups fall into four categories:

- ◆ Full or Total
- ◆ Incremental
- ◆ Selective
- ◆ Differential (or modified only)

In a full, or total backup, the entire contents of the designated disk are backed up. This includes directory and subdirectory listings and their contents. This backup method requires the most time each day to backup, but also requires the least time to restore the system after a failure. Only the most recent backup copy is required to restore the system.

Three partial backup techniques are used to store data, but yet conserve space on the storage media: *Incremental backups, selective backups,* and *differential backups.*

In an incremental backup operation, the system backs up those files that have been created or changed since the last backup. Restoring the system from an incremental backup requires the use of the last full backup and each incremental backup taken since then. However, this method requires the least amount of time to back up the system but the most amount of time to restore it.

To conduct a selective backup, the operator moves through the tree structure of the disk marking, or tagging, directories and files to be backed up. After all the desired directories/files have been marked, they are backed up in a single operation.

Specifying a differential backup causes the backup utility to examine each file to determine whether it has changed since the last full backup was performed. If not, it is bypassed. If the file has been altered, however, it will be backed up. This option is a valuable time saving feature in a periodic backup strategy. To restore the system, you need a copy of the last full backup and the last differential backup.

HDD Defragmentation

In the normal use of the hard disk drive, files become fragmented on the drive. This file *fragmentation* creates conditions that cause the drive to operate more slowly. Fragmentation occurs when files are stored in non-continuous locations on the drive. This happens when files are stored, retrieved, modified, and rewritten because of differences in the sizes of the before and after files.

Because the fragmented files do not provide for efficient reading by the drive, it takes longer to complete multi-sector read operations. The defragmentation program realigns the positioning of related file clusters to speed up the operation of the drive.

The *Microsoft Defrag* utility has been available since the later versions of MS-DOS (with the exception of Windows NT). In Windows 9*x* and Windows 2000, the *Defragmenter utility* is located under the `Start/Programs/Accessories/System Tools` path. In Windows 2000, the Defragmenter can be accessed through the `Start/Settings/Control Panel/Administrative Tools/Computer Management` path.

EXAM TIP

Know which backup type requires the least amount of time to perform and the least amount of effort to restore the system.

EXAM TIP

Be aware that the defragmentation process will provide more efficient and faster operation of your system.

EXAM TIP

Know where to locate the Windows 2000 Defrag utility.

OPERATING SYSTEM UTILITIES

Successful troubleshooting of operating systems requires tools. In addition to the startup tools already described (clean boot disks and single-step, boot-up utilities), a number of other utilities are available through the Windows operating systems to isolate and correct operating system problems.

Many of these utilities can be added directly to the startup disk so that they will be readily available in emergency situations. Some of the utilities that should be added to the startup disk include the following:

- ◆ SCANDISK.EXE—Checks the disk for lost clusters and cross-linked files and can examine disks and their contents for errors.

- ◆ DEFRAG.EXE—Realigns the file structure on the disk to optimize its operation.

- ◆ MEM.EXE—Used to view system memory organization.

- ◆ SYSEDIT.EXE/REGEDIT.EXE—These utilities can be used to edit Windows 9x system structures such as CONFIG.SYS, AUTOEXEC.BAT, and INI files, as well as the Windows 9x Registry structure.

- ◆ FDISK.EXE—Used to create, view, and manage partitions on a hard disk.

- ◆ ATTRIB.EXE—Can be employed to change the attribute of files (such as hidden, read-only, and system files) so that they can be seen and manipulated for troubleshooting purposes.

- ◆ FORMAT.COM—Used to establish the high-level format on disk drives.

- ◆ SYS.COM—Used to copy key system files to a disk so that it will be self-booting.

In the case of Windows 9x, the Create Startup Disk option under the Add/Remove Programs tab includes most of these utilities on the emergency start disk when it is created. Other utilities that can be very helpful in troubleshooting operating system problems include the Microsoft Diagnostic program and the Windows 9x Device Manager.

Windows 98 Troubleshooting Tools

Microsoft includes an extensive set of system troubleshooting tools in Windows 9*x*. It has also expanded the built-in Troubleshooting menu located in the Windows 9*x* Help functions. All of these items have been included to assist in the location and correction of Windows-related problems.

The System Tools

The following list identifies the Windows 98 troubleshooting tools:

- Microsoft System Information
- Windows Report Tool
- MS-DOS Report Tool
- Dr. Watson
- System File Checker
- Registry Checker
- System Configuration Utility
- Automatic Skip Driver Agent
- Version Conflict Manager
- Scheduling Tasks
- Maintenance Wizard
- Microsoft Backup
- Microsoft System Recovery
- Digital Signal Check
- Signature Verification Tool
- Windows Update

The *Microsoft System Information* tool (*MSINFO32.EXE*) is located at `Program Files\Common Files\Microsoft Shared\MSINFO`. You can use this utility to view system hardware resources, installed devices, and drivers. It can also be used to view reports generated by Web-based Windows and MS-DOS Report Tools. This enables remote service providers to inspect MSINFO information from local units across a LAN or WAN.

MSINFO is typically started by clicking the System Information option in the Start menu's /Programs/Accessories/System Tools path. If Windows 98 does not run, the program can be executed by typing MSINFO32 at the DOS command prompt. When the utility starts, the System Information screen depicted in Figure 22.11 appears.

> **Hands-On Activity**   For hands-on experience with this concept, refer to Lab Procedure #22, "Windows Me System Information," located on the CD that accompanies this book.

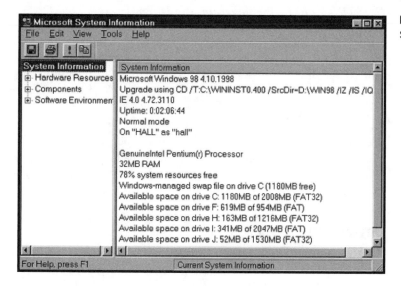

FIGURE 22.11
System Information screen.

The *Windows Report Tool* (*WINREP.EXE*) is located in the Windows directory and provides a copy of the MSINFO information in HTML format. The *MS-DOS Report Tool* (*DOSREP.EXE*), also located in the Windows directory, provides a snapshot of the system files and can upload it to an FTP site when Windows is not working.

The *System File Checker utility* (*SFC.EXE*) checks the system files for changed, deleted, or possibly corrupt files. If it finds such files, it attempts to extract the original version of the file from Windows files. This file can be found in the Windows\System folder. However, you can simply click the System File Checker entry in the System Information Tools menu to activate this utility.

Windows 98 also includes a pair of Registry checker utilities (*SCANREG.EXE* and *SCANREGW.EXE*) to scan, fix, back up, and restore Registry files. The SCANREG file is a DOS-based program, whereas SCANREGW is a Windows-based version. The command-line version is located in the Windows\Command directory, whereas the Windows version is just in the \Windows directory.

System Configuration Troubleshooting Tools

Windows 98 has a collection of configuration-related troubleshooting tools. These utilities include the *System Configuration Utility (MSCONFIG.EXE)*, the *Automatic Skip Driver Agent (ASD.EXE)*, and the *Version Conflict Manager (VCMUI.EXE)*.

The System Configuration Utility enables you to examine the system's configuration through a check-box system. By turning different configuration settings on and off, problem settings can be isolated and corrected by a process of elimination. You can access this utility through the System Information screen. From the Tools menu, select the System Configuration Utility. This tool is especially useful in controlling which programs will automatically be loaded at Startup. This is discussed in more detail in Chapter 26, "Troubleshooting OS Setup/Startup Problems."

Device Driver Tools

In cases in which the configuration problem is more severe, you can use the Automatic Skip Driver Agent. This utility senses and skips configuration steps that prevent Windows 98 from starting.

Finally, the Version Conflict Manager automatically installs Windows 98 drivers over other drivers that it finds—even if these drivers are newer. The System Configuration Manager is located in the Windows\System directory, whereas the other two utilities are found under the Windows directory.

To minimize the adverse affects of poorly written device drivers on the system, Microsoft works with hardware suppliers and signs (certifies) their drivers for Windows 98 compatibility by adding special digital codes to them. This *Driver Signing* tool is valuable to administrators who do not want users to introduce questionable devices and drivers into the system.

The *Signature Verification Tool (SIGVERIF.EXE)* is used to check files to determine whether Microsoft has signed them. It also determines whether the files have been modified since they were signed.

EXAM TIP

Be aware of the functions performed by the different system configuration utilities in Windows 98.

EXAM TIP

Be aware of driver signing and know why it is implemented.

Finally, the Windows Update utility (IEXPLORE.EXE) is a Windows 98 extension located on the Microsoft Web site (www.microsoft.com/windowsupdate). It enables you to update the system's files and drivers with new or improved versions over the Web.

System Monitor

Two other valuable utilities in Windows 9*x* are the *System Monitor* and the *System Resource Meter* programs. The System Monitor can be used to track the performance of key system resources for both evaluation and troubleshooting purposes. If system performance is suspect but there is no clear indication of what might be slowing it down, the System Monitor can be used to determine which resource is operating at capacity, thereby limiting the performance of the system.

Typical resources that the System Monitor is capable of tracking include those associated with processor usage and memory management. Results can be displayed in real time using Statistical mode, Line Chart mode, or Bar Chart mode. Figure 22.12 illustrates the monitor operating in Line Chart mode. The System Monitor can be set up to run on top of other applications so that it can be used to see what effect they are having on the system.

NOTE

Hands-On Activity For hands-on experience with this concept, refer to Lab Procedure #42, "Windows 2000 Software Version Update Management," located on the CD that accompanies this book.

EXAM TIP

Be aware of which Windows 9*x* utility can be used to monitor certain resource activities.

FIGURE 22.12
Using the System Monitor.

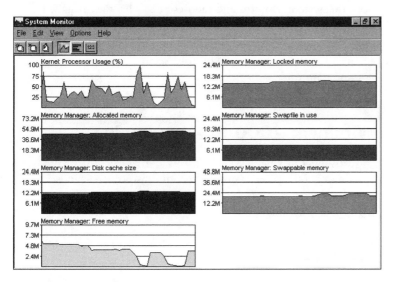

The Resource Meter, depicted in Figure 22.13, is a simple bar chart display that shows the percent usage of the system resources, user resources, and GDI resources. When activated, the meter normally resides as an icon on the extreme right side of the Task Bar, at the bottom of the desktop. Double-clicking the icon brings the bar chart display to the desktop. As with the System Monitor, the Resource Meter can be used to evaluate hardware and software performance.

FIGURE 22.13
Using the Resource Meter.

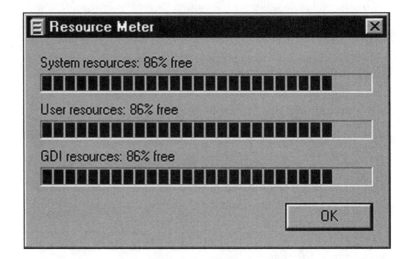

Both the System Monitor and the Resource Meter are installed through the Setup tab under the Control Panel's Add/Remove Programs applet. From the Setup tab, highlight the System Tools entry and click on the Details button. Select the utilities and click the Apply button.

Windows 2000 System Tools

As mentioned in Chapter 19, "Operating System Fundamentals," Windows 2000 clusters a number of administrative, diagnostic, and troubleshooting tools under the Control Panel's Microsoft Management Console.

Event Viewer

In Windows 2000, significant events (such as system events, application events, and security events) are routinely monitored and stored.

These events can be viewed through the *Event Viewer* utility depicted in Figure 22.14. As described earlier, this tool is located under the Control Panel/Administrative Tools/Computer Management path.

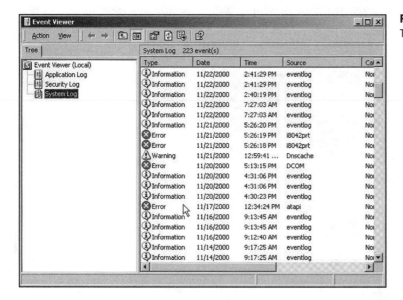

FIGURE 22.14
The Windows 2000 Event Viewer.

System events include items such as successful and failed Windows component startups, as well as successful loading of device drivers. Likewise, application events include information about how the system's applications are performing. Not all Windows applications generate events that the Event Viewer will log. Finally, security events are produced by user actions such as logons and logoffs, file and folder accesses, and creation of new Active Directory accounts.

The Event Viewer produces three categories of system and application events:

◆ *Information events*—Events that indicate an application, service, or driver has loaded successfully. These events require no intervention.

◆ *Warning events*—Events that have no immediate impact, but that could have future significance. These events should be investigated.

◆ *Error events*—Events that indicate an application, service, or driver has failed to load successfully. These events require immediate intervention.

NOTE — **Hands-On Activity**   For hands-on experience with this concept, refer to Lab Procedure #16, "Windows 2000 Administrative Tools," located on the CD that accompanies this book.

System Information

The *Windows 2000 System Information utility* provides five subfolders of information about the system, as illustrated in the right pane of Figure 22.15. These folders include a system summary, a list of hardware resources being used, a list of I/O components in the system, a description of the system's current software environment, and a description of the Windows Internet Explorer.

FIGURE 22.15

The System Information tool.

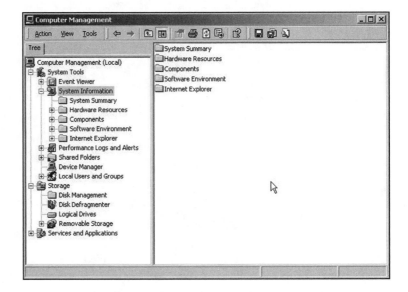

As with the Windows 98 System Information tool, the Windows 2000 version can be used to enable remote service providers to inspect the system's information across a LAN environment. To save system information to a file, right-click the System Information entry and select the Save As option from the resulting menu. Saving this information enables you to document events and conditions when errors occur. You can use the results of different system information files to compare situations and perhaps determine what changes might have occurred to cause the problem.

Using Device Manager

The Device Manager utility is basically an easy-to-use interface for the Windows 9x and Windows 2000 Registries. It can be accessed through the Control Panel's System icon. You can use the Device Manager to identify installed ports, update device drivers, and change I/O settings. It can also be used to manually isolate hardware and configuration conflicts. Through the Device Manager, the problem device can be examined to determine where the conflict is occurring.

In the Device Manager display, the presence of plus (+) and (-) signs in the nodes of the devices indicates expandable and collapsible information branches at those nodes.

The Device Manger will display an *exclamation point* (!) inside a yellow circle whenever a device is experiencing a direct hardware conflict with another device. The nature of the problem is described in the device's Properties dialog box. Similarly, when a *red X* appears at the device's icon, the device has been disabled because of a user-selection conflict.

This situation can occur when a user wants to disable a selected device without removing it. For example, a user who travels and uses a notebook computer might want to temporarily disable device drivers for options that aren't used in travel. This arrangement can be established through the Device Manager's Disable in This Hardware Profile option. Selecting this setting will prevent the driver from loading up until it is reactivated and is located in the Properties window for the particular device.

When a device conflict is suspected, simply click the offending device in the listing, right-click on the item, select Properties from the pop-up menu, and then click the Resources tab to examine the Conflicting Device's List, depicted in Figure 22.16. You can also access the Properties window by double-clicking on the device driver name.

EXAM TIP

Memorize symbols used by the Windows Device Manager.

EXAM TIP

Be aware of how to temporarily disable device drivers that are not needed in certain situations, yet retain them in the system for future use.

EXAM TIP

Know how to find conflicts using the Windows Device Manager.

FIGURE 22.16
The Device Manager Resources page.

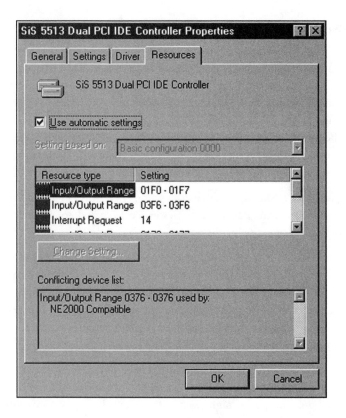

Normal causes for conflict include devices sharing IRQ settings, I/O address settings, DMA channels, or base memory settings. The most common conflicts are those dealing with the IRQ channels. Nonessential peripherals, such as sound and network adapters, are most likely to produce this type of conflict.

When a device conflict is reported through the Resource tab's Conflicting Devices list, record the current settings for each device, refer to the documentation for each device to determine what other settings might be used, and change the settings for the most flexible device. If either device continues to exhibit problems, reset the configurations to their original positions and change the settings for the other device.

> **NOTE**
>
> **Hands-On Activity**   For hands-on experience with this concept, refer to Lab Procedure #18, "Windows Me Plug-and-Play," located on the CD that accompanies this book.

System Editors

The Windows operating systems contain three important editors: the *System Editor* (*SysEdit*), the *Registry Editor* (*RegEdit and*

RegEdt32), and the *Policy Editor* (*PolEdit*). Windows 2000 also includes a very powerful *Group Policy Editor* (*GPE*).

Later versions of DOS contained a small text editor program (*EDIT.COM*) that enabled users to easily modify text files. This utility is started by typing the **EDIT** command along with the filename at the command prompt. In Windows, this editor is the System Editor (SYSEDIT.EXE). To start the SysEdit function, select the Run option from the Start menu and type **SYSEDIT** in the Run dialog box.

Windows 9*x* contains three editors: SysEdit, RegEdit, and PolEdit. The Windows 9*x* SysEdit function is used to modify text files, such as any INI files in the system, as well as the CONFIG.SYS and AUTOEXEC.BAT files.

Windows 2000 includes two Registry editors: RegEdit and RegEdt32. Both utilities enable you to add, edit, and remove Registry entries and to perform other basic functions. However, specific functions can be performed only in one editor or the other.

RegEdt32 is the Registry editor that has historically been used with Windows NT. It presents each subtree as an individual entity, in a separate window. RegEdit is the Registry editor that was introduced with Windows 95, and also was included with Windows NT 4.0. The subtrees are presented as being part of the same entity in a single window.

The Find capabilities of RegEdt32 are accessed from the View menu, and are very limited. You can search only for keys, not assigned values or their corresponding data. This is the equivalent of being able to search for folders in the file system, but not for files. Also, you can initiate a search in only one subtree at a time. The Find capabilities of RegEdit are accessed through the Edit menu, and are very strong. You have the option to search for keys and assigned values, and you can search all subtrees at once. RegEdit also enables you to save frequently accessed Registry locations as favorites to enable quicker access.

Using Dr. Watson

The main tool for isolating and correcting *General Protection Faults* (*GPFs*) is the *Dr. Watson* utility provided in all Windows versions. It

EXAM TIP

Be aware of which Windows utilities can be used to make changes to the Registry in Windows 2000.

WARNING

Edit Registry Warning Editing the Registry with RegEdit or RegEdt32 should be done only when you have no other alternative. These editors bypass all the safeguards provided by the standard utilities and permit you to enter values that are invalid or that conflict with other settings. Incorrect editing of the Registry can cause Windows 2000 to stop functioning correctly, prompting a significant amount of troubleshooting or a reinstallation of the operating system.

is used to trace problems that appear under certain conditions, such as starting or using a certain application. When Dr. Watson is started, it runs in the background with only an icon appearing on the taskbar to signify that it is present. For problems such as a GPF that cannot be directly attributed to the Windows operating system, an application program might be the source of the problem and the Dr. Watson utility should be set up to run in the background as the system operates.

EXAM TIP

Know which Windows utility can be used to monitor the operation of application packages and log errors so that they can be reported to software developers for repairing their programs.

As the system operates, the Dr. Watson utility monitors the code moving through the system and logs its key events in the DRWATSON.LOG file. When a system error occurs, the Dr. Watson log contains a listing of the events that were going on up to the time of the failure. This log provides programmers with a detailed listing of the events that led up to the failure. The information is automatically stored in the log file that can be provided to software developers, or to Microsoft, so that they can debug their software and produce patches for it. In many cases, the program will describe the nature of the error and possibly suggest a fix.

The Dr. Watson utility is not located in any of the Windows 98 menus. To use it, you must execute the program from the Start menu's Run option by typing the name **drwatson** in the dialog box, and clicking OK to start the log file. This will cause the Dr. Watson icon to appear on the taskbar. Dr. Watson also can be started through the Tools menu in the System Information screen. This option is located in the `Programs\Accessories\System Tools` path.

EXAM TIP

Be aware of where the Dr. Watson utility is located and what it is used for.

Windows Help Files

Windows 9x, NT 4.0, and 2000 come with built-in troubleshooting Help file systems. This feature includes troubleshooting assistance for a number of different Windows problems. The *Windows 9x* and *Windows 2000 Troubleshooters* are much more expansive than the Windows NT Troubleshooters. In all three systems, the Troubleshooter utilities can be accessed from the Start menu, or from the Help menu entry on the taskbar.

The *Windows Troubleshooters* are a special type of help that is available in Windows 9x and 2000. These utilities enable you to pinpoint problems and identify solutions to those problems. Troubleshooters ask a series of questions and then provide you with detailed troubleshooting information based on your responses to those questions.

The *Windows 98* and *Windows 2000 Help functions* include both the local help, such as that supplied by Windows 95, as well as online help through a built-in Web browser. The online help enables the system to access Microsoft's significant online help resources. You can access the troubleshooters in many ways, including through context-sensitive Help, through the Help option on the Start menu, and through the Device Manager.

CHAPTER SUMMARY

This chapter was dedicated to basic disk drive management issues. It began with an explanation of how disks are organized and then moved into an extended discussion of standard disk-management utilities.

The presentation quickly moved to the organizational structure of disks in MS-DOS, Windows 9*x*, and Windows NT/2000 systems. It then went on to discuss the advantages of the NTFS file management system features in Windows NT and Windows 2000.

The chapter concluded with extended discussions of disk management, standard operating system utilities, and troubleshooting tools in Windows operating systems.

At this point, review the objectives listed at the beginning of the chapter to be certain that you understand each point and can perform each task listed there. Afterward, answer the review questions that follow to verify your knowledge of the information.

KEY TERMS

- Active
- Active partition
- Automatic Skip Driver Agent (ASD.EXE)
- Backup
- Basic disks
- Boot Partition
- Cluster
- Compact Disk File System (CDFS)
- Cross-linked files
- CVT.EXE
- CVT1.EXE
- Debug
- Defragmenter utility
- Differential backups
- Directory tree
- Disk Management snap in

CHAPTER SUMMARY

- Disk Management utility
- Disk Manager
- DOS CHKDSK (Check Disk)
- Dr. Watson
- Drive Converter (FAT 32)
- Driver Signing
- Dynamic disks
- Dynamic volumes
- EDIT.COM
- Event Viewer
- Exclamation point (!)
- Extended partition
- FAT32
- FAT-based
- File allocation table (FAT)
- Fragmentation
- General Protection Faults (GPFs)
- Group Policy Editor (GPE)
- High Performance File System (HPFS)
- High-level format
- Incremental backups
- Logical drives
- Lost clusters
- Low-level format
- Master Boot Record

- Master File Table (MFT)
- Microsoft Backup and Restore disk management utility
- Microsoft Defrag
- Microsoft System Information
- Mirrored volume
- MS-DOS Report Tool (DOS-REP.EXE)
- MSINFO32.EXE
- NTFS4
- NTFS5
- OSR2
- Partition
- Partition Table
- Policy Editor (PolEdit)
- Primary partition
- RAID 5 volume
- Registry Editor (RegEdit and RegEdt32)
- Restore
- Root directory
- ScanDisk
- SCANREG.EXE
- SCANREGW.EXE
- Selective backups
- Signature Verification Tool (SIGVERIF.EXE)

CHAPTER SUMMARY

- Simple volume
- SMARTDRV
- Spanned volume
- Striped volume
- Subdirectory
- System Configuration Utility (MSCONFIG.EXE)
- System Editor (SysEdit)
- System File Checker utility (SFC.EXE)
- System Monitor
- System Partition
- System Resource Meter
- VCACHE

- Version Conflict Manager (VCMUI.EXE)
- VFAT
- Windows 2000 Help functions
- Windows 2000 System Information utility
- Windows 2000 Troubleshooters
- Windows 95(a)
- Windows 98 Help functions
- Windows NT File System (NTFS)
- Windows Report Tool (WIN-REP.EXE)
- Windows Troubleshooters
- Windows Update utility (IEX-PLORE.EXE)

APPLY YOUR KNOWLEDGE

Review Questions

1. What is the proper order of operations for preparing a disk drive for use?

   A. Format, Partition, Run Setup, Reboot, Load drivers

   B. Partition, Format, Run Setup, Load drivers, Reboot

   C. Format, Partition, Run Setup, Load drivers, Reboot

   D. Partition, Format, Run Setup, Reboot, Load drivers

2. What are the primary characteristics of an active partition?

   A. The first partition on the drive

   B. Can be divided into 23 logical drives

   C. Cannot be deleted if logical drives have been defined within it

   D. The logical drive that the system will boot to

3. What is the smallest unit of storage on a disk that can be manipulated by the operating system?

   A. Pixel

   B. Bit

   C. Cluster

   D. Byte

4. What is the size of a sector in an IBM/PC compatible disk?

   A. 512 bytes

   B. 8 bytes

   C. 16 bytes

   D. 1024 bytes

5. How many items can be placed in a directory in a FAT-based system?

   A. 128

   B. 256

   C. 512

   D. 1024

6. What is the maximum number of items that can exist in the root directory of a FAT-based disk?

   A. 255

   B. 256

   C. 512

   D. 1024

7. Which command-line utility can be used to convert FAT16 partitions to FAT32 partitions?

   A. CONVERT.EXE

   B. CVT.EXE

   C. 1CVT.EXE

   D. CNVRT.EXE

8. What utility replaces the SMARTDRV utility for disk caching in Windows 9x?

   A. VCACHE

   B. RAMDISK

   C. CACHEDISK

   D. RAMCACHE

APPLY YOUR KNOWLEDGE

9. Which file system is the most efficient for the storage of small files?

   A. FAT

   B. VFAT

   C. FAT32

   D. NTFS

10. What is required to create a dynamic volume in Windows 2000?

    A. Convert a FAT32 volume using the Disk Management tool.

    B. Convert a primary volume using the Disk Management tool.

    C. Convert a basic volume using the Disk Management tool.

    D. Convert an extended volume using the Disk Management tool.

11. Where can you locate the three main HDD utility programs in the Windows 9x environments?

    A. Start/Programs/Accessories/System Tools

    B. Start/Programs/Accessories/Computer Management

    C. Right-click on a disk drive's icon, select Properties, and then click the Tools tab.

    D. Right-click on a disk drive's icon and select Tools.

12. What event will cause ScanDisk to run automatically?

    A. During a cold boot

    B. At the beginning of a new week

C. The operating system detects that the system was not shut down properly.

   D. Whenever the OS is updated

13. What is the difference between the Standard and Thorough ScanDisk operations?

    A. Standard only examines file tables.

    B. Standard does not examine the physical disk surface.

    C. Standard only examines system files.

    D. Standard does not examine the cluster map.

14. Where are the `Backup` and `Restore` functions located in Windows 2000?

    A. Start/Programs/Accessories/System Tools and then select Backup

    B. Start/Settings/Control Panel/System and then click the Backup tab

    C. Start/Settings/Control Panel and then double-click the Backup tool

    D. Start/Programs/Accessories and then select Backup

15. Which backup methodology requires the least amount of time to perform and the most amount of effort to restore the system?

    A. Full

    B. Differential

    C. Incremental

    D. Selective

APPLY YOUR KNOWLEDGE

16. The _____ process will provide more efficient and faster operation of your system.

    A. ScanDisk

    B. Defragmentation

    C. CHKDSK

    D. Backup

17. Which method will **not** access the Windows 2000 Defragmentation utility?

    A. Start/Programs/Accessories/System Tools and then select Disk Defragmenter

    B. Start/Settings/Control Panel/Administrative Tools and then double-click Computer Management

    C. Start/Programs/Accessories and then select Disk Defragmenter

    D. Open My Computer, right-click on the drive icon and select Properties from the contextual menu, click the Tools tab, and then click the Defragment Now button

18. Which Windows 9x utility can be used to monitor the operation of application packages and log any errors?

    A. ScanDisk

    B. Report Tool

    C. Conflict Manager

    D. Dr. Watson

19. Where is the Dr. Watson utility?

    A. Start/Programs/Accessories/System Tools and then select Dr. Watson

    B. Start/Settings/Control Panel/Administrative Tools and then double-click Dr. Watson

    C. Start/Programs/Accessories/System Tools, select System Information, and then click on the Tools menu and select Dr. Watson

    D. Start/Programs/Accessories and then select Dr. Watson

20. Where would you locate information about conflicts found in Device Manager?

    A. Open Device Manager, double-click on the device driver's name, and then click the Resources tab

    B. Start/Programs/Accessories/System Tools, select System Information, and then click the Resources tab

    C. Start/Settings/Control Panel, double-click on System, and then click the Resources tab

    D. Open Device manager and then click the Resources tab

21. What does the exclamation point (!) inside a yellow circle mean when used by the Windows Device Manager?

    A. The device has been disabled because of a user-selection conflict.

    B. It indicates expandable and collapsible information branches.

    C. The device is experiencing a direct hardware conflict with another device.

    D. The device is not installed properly.

APPLY YOUR KNOWLEDGE

22. In Windows 9*x*, how are device drivers temporarily disabled when they are not needed in certain situations, yet retained in the system for future use?

    A. By opening Device Manger and selecting Disable in the device's Properties window

    B. By opening Device Manager, right-clicking on the device, and selecting Disable from the pop-up menu

    C. By opening System Information, clicking on Hardware Resources, and then right-clicking on the device and selecting Disable

    D. Start/Settings/Control Panel, open System, click on Hardware Resources, and then right-click on the device and select Disable

23. Which of the following are advantages associated with using the NTFS file system? (Select all that apply.)

    A. Data security

    B. Larger drives

    C. Handles small drives efficiently

    D. 64-bit entries to keep track of items

24. In Windows 9*x*, which utility is used to control programs that run at startup?

    A. STARTREG

    B. MSCONFIG

    C. REGEDIT

    D. REGEDT32

25. Which Windows utility can be used to make changes to the Registry in Windows 2000?

    A. REGEDIT32

    B. SYSEDIT

    C. REGEDIT

    D. POLEDIT

26. What file system format is used to store files on a CD-ROM?

    A. FAT

    B. NTFS

    C. HPFS

    D. CDFS

27. What are the primary characteristics of an extended partition?

    A. The first partition on the drive

    B. Can be divided into 23 logical drives

    C. Cannot be deleted if logical drives have been defined within it

    D. The logical drive that the system will boot to

28. If the backup utility is installed in Windows 2000, it is located in which directory or subdirectory?

    A. `C:\WINNT\SYSTEM32`

    B. `C:\PROGRAM FILES\ACCESSORIES\SYSTEM TOOLS`

    C. `C:\WINNT\SYSTEM`

    D. `C:\PROGRAM FILES`

APPLY YOUR KNOWLEDGE

29. What command can be used to repair segmented files in Windows 9x?

    A. DISKSCAN /F

    B. CHECKDSK /F

    C. SCANDISK /F

    D. CHKDSK /F

30. Which utility is used to ensure that only Microsoft-approved drivers are installed on the system?

    A. MSINFO32.EXE

    B. SCANREGW.EXE

    C. SIGVERIF.EXE

    D. SCF.EXE

31. Which utility is used to view real-time system performance in Windows 9x?

    A. System Information

    B. System Monitor

    C. Computer Management

    D. Task Manager

Answers and Explanations

1. **B.** Installing a new operating system on a hard drive has evolved into the five basic steps that follow:

    Partition the drive for use with the operating system.

    Format the drive with the basic operating system files.

    Run the appropriate Setup utility to install the complete operating system.

    Load all the drivers necessary for the operating system to function with the system's installed hardware devices.

    Reboot the system to activate all the system components.

    For more information, see the section "Microsoft Disk Structures."

2. **D.** The active partition is the logical drive that the system will boot to. The system files must be located in this partition, and the partition must be set to Active for the system to boot up from the drive. For more information, see the section "Drive Partitioning."

3. **C.** To more effectively manage the space on the disk, newer operating system versions divide the disk into groups of logically related sectors, called allocation units, or clusters. In a FAT-based system, the cluster is the smallest piece of manageable information. For more information, see the section "File Allocation Tables."

4. **A.** The sectors on a FAT-based disk hold 512 bytes each, and files can be of any length. For more information, see the section "File Allocation Tables."

5. **C.** Each directory and subdirectory (including the root directory) can hold up to 512 32-byte entries that describe each of the files in them. For more information, see the section "The Root Directory."

APPLY YOUR KNOWLEDGE

6. **C.** Because each root directory entry is 32 bytes long, each disk sector can hold 16 entries. On a hard disk drive, normally 32 sectors are set aside for the root directory. Therefore, the root directory for such a disk can accommodate up to 512 entries. For more information, see the section "The Root Directory."

7. **B.** It is possible to convert partitions created on a FAT16 drive into a FAT32 file system using the CVT.EXE command-line utility. This operation can also be performed by accessing the Drive Converter (FAT 32) utility through the Start/Programs/Accessories/System Tools path. Selecting this option will run the CVT1.EXE file that starts the Drive Converter Wizard. For more information, see the section "FAT32."

8. **A.** The VFAT system replaces the SMARTDRV disk-caching utility with a protected-mode driver named VCACHE. For more information, see the section "Virtual File Allocation Table."

9. **D.** The smaller cluster size of the NTFS file system makes it more efficient than FAT formats for storing smaller files. For more information, see the section "Windows NT File System."

10. **C.** To create a dynamic volume, it must be either a simple or a mirrored volume and it must be a volume that can be upgraded from a basic volume. Installing Windows 2000 on the volume requires that it have a partition table, which dynamic volumes normally do not have unless they have been upgraded from a basic volume. Basic volumes are converted to dynamic volumes using the Disk Management tool (follow the path Start/Run, enter DISKMGMT.MSC into the text box, and then click the OK button). For more information, see the section "Basic and Dynamic Disks and Volumes."

11. **A, C.** The icons for backup, ScanDisk, and Defrag are located in the Programs/Accessories/System Tools Path. The simplest way to access the HDD tools in Windows 9*x* is to open My Computer, right-click on the icon for the hard disk drive you want to use, and then select Properties from the contextual pop-up menu. Now just click on the Tools tab, and you have access to the three most useful HDD utilities: ScanDisk, Backup, and Defrag. For more information, see the section "HDD Utilities."

12. **C.** By default, the command-line version of ScanDisk runs automatically during Startup whenever the operating system detects that the system was not shut down properly. For more information, see the section "ScanDisk."

13. **B.** The standard ScanDisk operation examines the system's directory and file structure. However, a Thorough option can be selected to examine the physical disk surface as well as its files and directories. If potential defects exist on the surface, ScanDisk can be used to recover data stored in these areas. For more information, see the section "ScanDisk."

14. **A.** The Backup utility is located in the C:\Windows\Start Menu\Programs\Accessories\System Tools directory. For more information, see the section "Backup."

15. **C.** In an incremental backup operation, the system backs up those files that have been created or changed since the last backup. Restoring the system from an incremental backup requires the use of the last full backup and each incremental backup taken since then. Therefore, this method requires the least amount of time to back up the system, but the most amount of time to restore it. For more information, see the section "Backup Types."

APPLY YOUR KNOWLEDGE

16. **B.** Because the fragmented files do not provide for efficient reading by the drive, it takes longer to complete multi-sector read operations. The defragmentation program realigns the positioning of related file clusters to speed up the operation of drive access operations. For more information, see the section "HDD Defragmentation."

17. **C.** In Windows 9*x* and Windows 2000, the Defragmenter utility is located under the Start/Programs/Accessories/System Tools path. In Windows 2000, the Defragmenter can also be accessed through the Start/Settings/Control Panel/Administrative Tools/Computer Management path. For more information, see the section "HDD Defragmentation."

18. **D.** The Dr. Watson utility provided in all Windows versions is used to trace problems that appear under certain conditions, such as starting or using a certain application. When Dr. Watson is started, it runs in the background with only an icon appearing on the taskbar to signify that it is present. As the system operates, the Dr. Watson utility monitors the code moving through the system and logs its key events in the DRWATSON.LOG file. For more information, see the section "Using Dr. Watson."

19. **C.** Dr. Watson also can be started through the Tools menu in the System Information screen. This option is located in the Programs\Accessories\System Tools path. For more information, see the section "Using Dr. Watson."

20. **A.** When a device conflict is suspected, simply click the offending device in the listing, right-click on the item and select Properties from the pop-up menu, and then click the Resources tab to examine the Conflicting Device's List. You can also access the Properties window by double-clicking on the device driver name. For more information, see the section "Using Device Manager."

21. **C.** The Device Manger will display an exclamation point (!) inside a yellow circle whenever a device is experiencing a direct hardware conflict with another device. The nature of the problem is described in the device's Properties dialog box. For more information, see the section "Using Device Manager."

22. **A.** This arrangement can be established through the Device Manager's Disable in This Hardware Profile option. This setting will keep the driver from loading up until it is reactivated, and is located in the Properties window for that particular device. For more information, see the section "Using Device Manager."

23. **A, B, D.** The NT File System (NTFS) structure is designed to provide better data security and to operate more efficiently with larger hard drives than FAT systems do. The NTFS4 structure found in Windows NT 4.0 uses 64-bit entries to keep track of storage on the disk (as opposed to the 16- and 32-bit entries used in FAT and FAT32 systems). The smaller cluster size of the NTFS format makes it more efficient than FAT formats for storing smaller files. It also supports larger drives (over 1GB) much more efficiently than FAT16 or FAT32 structures. For more information, see the section "NTFS Advantages."

APPLY YOUR KNOWLEDGE

24. **B**. The System Configuration Utility (MSCON-FIG.EXE) enables you to examine the system's configuration through a check-box system. By turning different configuration settings on and off, problem settings can be isolated and corrected by a process of elimination. You can access this utility through the System Information screen. From the Tools menu, select the System Configuration Utility. This tool is especially useful in controlling which programs will load at startup. For more information, see the section "System Configuration Troubleshooting Tools."

25. **C**. Windows 2000 includes two Registry editors: RegEdit and RegEdt32. Both utilities enable you to add, edit, and remove Registry entries and to perform other basic functions. However, specific functions can be performed only in one editor or the other. RegEdt32 is the Registry editor used with Windows NT/2000. RegEdit is the Registry editor introduced with Windows 95. For more information, see the section "System Editors."

26. **D**. The file system used on CD-ROM disk is called the CDFS (Compact Disk File System). For more information, see the section "NTFS Advantages."

27. **B, C**. After the primary partition has been established and properly configured, an additional partition, referred to as an extended partition, is also permitted. However, the extended partition can be subdivided into 23 logical drives. The extended partition cannot be deleted if logical drives have been defined within it. For more information, see the section "Drive Partitioning."

28. **A**. The Backup utility is located in C:\WINNT\SYSTEM32 in Windows NT/2000. For more information, see the section "HDD Utilities."

29. **D**. The DOS CHKDSK (Check Disk) command is a command-line utility that has remained in use with Windows 3.*x*, 9*x*, NT, and 2000, and is used to recover lost allocation units from the hard drive. These lost units occur when an application terminates unexpectedly and causes the file management system to lose track of where some parts of the file are stored. The total file becomes segmented into undefined pieces that can still be read by the utility but cannot be associated with a particular filename in the FAT. Over a period of time, lost units can pile up and occupy large amounts of disk space. To remove lost units from the drive, an /F modifier is added to the command so that the lost units will be converted into files that can be investigated, and removed if necessary. In some cases, the converted file is a usable data file that can be rebuilt for use with an application. The CHKDSK /F command is often used before running a drive defragmentation program. For more information, see the section "CHKDSK."

30. **C**. To minimize the adverse affects of poorly written device drivers on the system, Microsoft works with hardware suppliers and signs (certifies) their drivers for Windows 98 compatibility by adding special digital codes to them. This Driver Signing tool is valuable to administrators who do not want users to introduce questionable devices and drivers into the system. The Signature Verification Tool (SIGVERIF.EXE) is used to check files to determine whether Microsoft has signed them. It also determines whether the files have been modified since they were signed. For more information, see the section "Device Driver Tools."

APPLY YOUR KNOWLEDGE

31. **B.** The System Monitor can be used to track the performance of key system resources for both evaluation and troubleshooting purposes. If system performance is suspect but there is no clear indication of what might be slowing it down, the System Monitor can be used to determine which resource is operating at capacity, thereby limiting the performance of the system. For more information, see the section "System Resource Monitor."

Challenge Solutions

1. You must create two partitions on the disk and format one with a Windows 2000 file management system (that is, FAT32 or NTFS) and the other with a Linux file management system. Although we make this sound simple, this is not always the case. However, some steps can be observed to make the process simpler. If the disk does not already have two partitions available, you must normally repartition the drive to create them. Afterward, you can install each operating system in one of the partitions. You might be aware that third-party utilities exist that can be used to repartition a disk without losing existing data, but this function is not directly available in Windows 2000. For more information, see the section "Drive Partitioning."

2. Although the NTFS file system can be used with NTFS, FAT16, FAT32 and CDFS, the FAT16 file management system has no tools for working with the other file management formats. Therefore, it is not even aware of the NTFS partition. You should change the second partition to use NTFS so that it will be able to access the first partition. For more information, see the section "NTFS Advantages."

APPLY YOUR KNOWLEDGE

Suggested Readings and Resources

1. Major Disk Structures
   http://www.pcguide.com/ref/hdd/file/struct.htm

2. Drive Partitioning
   http://www.newlogic.co.uk/kbase/fdisk/page1.htm

3. File Allocation Tables
   http://www.oreilly.com/reference/dictionary/terms/F/File_Allocation_Table.htm

4. NTFS File System
   http://www.digit-life.com/articles/ntfs/

5. RAID.edu
   www.acnc.com/raid.html

6. HPFS File System
   http://www.seds.org/~spider/spider/OS2/HPFS/hpfs.html

7. CHKDSK, ScanDisk, and Defrag
   http://www.shiningstar.net/geek/html/pc_maint.html

8. Troubleshooting
   http://www.codemicro.com/windows.htm

9. Drivers HQ
   www.drivershq.com/mainhome.html

10. Conflict Resolution
    www.pcguide.com/ref/mbsys/res/confl.htm

11. Windows NT Event Viewer
    http://www.eicon.com/support/helpweb/dcnten/evntview.htm

12. Device Manager
    http://support.microsoft.com/default.aspx?scid=kb;EN-US;q133240

13. Using Dr. Watson
    http://www.winguides.com/registry/category.php/60/

This chapter helps you to prepare for the Operating System Technologies module of the A+ Certification examination by covering the following objectives within the "Domain 2.0: Installation, Configuration, and Upgrading" section.

2.1 Identify the procedures for installing Windows 9*x* and Windows 2000 for bringing the software to a basic operational level.

Content might include the following:

- **Start up**

- **Partition**

- **Format drive**

- **Load drivers**

- **Run appropriate setup utility**

2.2 Identify steps to perform an operating system upgrade.

Content might include the following:

- **Upgrading Windows 95 to Windows 98**

- **Upgrading from Windows NT Workstation 4.0 to Windows 2000**

- **Replacing Windows 9*x* with Windows 2000**

- **Dual booting Windows 9*x*/Windows NT 4.0/2000**

▶ Operating systems must be installed on new computers to make them work. In addition, operating system versions change at a rapid pace, and most computers will have their operating system upgraded at least once in their lifetime. Therefore, technicians must be able to install operating systems on new machines and repair operating system problems. They must also be able to upgrade operating systems to new versions (that is, Windows 9*x* and Windows NT 4.0 systems to Windows 2000 systems). This chapter deals with installing and upgrading Windows 9*x* and Windows 2000 operating systems and getting them to a functional level.

CHAPTER 23

Installing and Upgrading Operating Systems

To prepare for the Installation, Configuration, and Upgrading objective of the Operating Systems Technologies exam,

▶ Read the objectives at the beginning of this chapter.

▶ Study the information in this chapter.

▶ Review the objectives listed earlier in this chapter.

▶ Perform any step-by-step procedures in the text.

▶ Answer the review questions at the end of the chapter and check your results.

▶ Use the PrepLogic test engine on the CD-ROM that accompanies this book for additional review and exam questions concerning this material.

▶ Review the exam tips scattered throughout the chapter and make certain that you are comfortable with each point.

INTRODUCTION

This chapter deals with installing, configuring, and upgrading operating systems. It begins by providing system requirements and procedures for installing Windows 9x and Windows 2000 operating systems. Part of accomplishing this task involves establishing compliance with the minimum system resource requirements associated with the different Windows packages.

The second half of the chapter covers the steps involved in performing operating system upgrades from previous versions to the various Windows 9x or Windows 2000 operating systems. This includes knowing which operating systems can be upgraded directly to the new version and which ones must be upgraded in a two-step process.

After completing the chapter, you should be able to execute procedures for installing Windows 9x and Windows 2000 and bring them to a basic operational level (Desktop display). You should also be able to perform operating upgrades between major operating systems.

DISK PREPARATION

Installing the operating system on a new hard drive has evolved into the four basic steps outlined in this A+ objective:

1. Partition the drive for use with the operating system.

2. Format the drive with the basic operating system files.

3. Run the appropriate setup utility to install the complete operating system.

4. Load all the drivers necessary to enable the operating system to work with the system's installed hardware devices.

INSTALLING WINDOWS 95

EXAM TIP

Remember that Windows 95 requires that a FAT16 partition exist on the drive where it is being installed.

EXAM TIP

Memorize the minimum, recommended, and preferred CPU specifications for running Windows 95.

EXAM TIP

Memorize the minimum and recommended amounts of memory specified to start Windows 95.

The Windows 95 operating system must be installed over an existing operating system. In particular, its installation program must find a recognizable FAT16 partition on the drive. This prevents it from being installed over some other type of operating system, such as Windows NT or Novell NetWare OS.

The Windows 95 system must be at least an 80386DX or higher machine, operating with at least 4MB of RAM (8MB is recommended). Although the 80386DX is the listed minimum microprocessor for running Windows 95, the recommended processor is the 80486DX; the Pentium processors are actually the preferred microprocessor for running Windows 95. Likewise, 4MB might be the minimum RAM option, with 8MB being the recommended option, but 16MB, 32MB, or 64MB are preferred for running Windows 95.

The system should also possess a mouse and a VGA or better monitor. The system's hard drive should have at least 20MB of free space available to successfully install Windows 95.

In addition, the Windows 95 setup routine provides for different types of installations to be established, including Typical, Portable, Compact, and Custom. All these options install different combinations of the possible Windows 9x system. Therefore, they all have different system requirements for proper installation.

To perform a *Typical installation* in a DOS system requires a minimum of 40MB of free drive space. Conversely, conducting a *Compact installation* on the same system would only require 30MB. When the installation is being conducted from a Windows 3.1 or Windows for Workgroup environment, the free space requirements drop to 30MB Typical/20MB Compact for Windows 3.1 and 20MB Typical/10MB Compact for Windows for Workgroups. The total required free space can range up to 85MB when a Custom install is conducted using all the Windows 95 options.

To run the Windows 95 Setup program from DOS,

1. Boot the computer.

2. Insert the Windows 95 Start Disk (Disk 1) in the A: drive, or place the Windows 95 CD in the CD-ROM drive.

3. Move to the drive that contains the Windows 95 Installation files.

4. At the DOS prompt, type **Setup** and press the Enter key.

5. Follow the directions from the screen and enter the information requested by the program for the type of installation being performed.

INSTALLING WINDOWS 98

Unlike Windows 95, Windows 98 does not need to be installed over an existing operating system. Only the Upgrade version of Windows 98 requires an existing operating system such as MS-DOS, Windows 3.1x, or Windows 95. The distribution CD for the full version of Windows 98 can be used to boot the system and provide options to partition and format the drive.

To install Windows 98, the system hardware must be at least an 80486DX/66 or higher machine, operating with at least 16MB of RAM. The system should also possess a modem, a mouse, and a 16-color VGA or better monitor. The system's hard drive should have between 120- and 355MB of free space available to successfully install Windows 98. The actual amount of disk space used depends on the type of installation being performed (Typical, Custom, Portable, Compact, New, Upgrade, and so on.). Typical installations use between 170- and 225MB of disk space.

The installation is carried out in the five-step procedure as follows:

1. Preparing to Run Windows 98 Setup—During this part of the procedure, Setup performs the following steps to prepare the Windows 98 Setup Wizard to guide the user through the installation process.

2. Collecting Information About Your Computer—After the Setup files have been extracted to the hard drive, the Setup Wizard begins operation by presenting the Microsoft Licensing Agreement and asking the user to enter the Product Key number. The product key can be found on the software's Certificate of Authenticity, or on the CD's liner. On stand-alone machines, this number must be entered correctly to

EXAM TIP

Memorize the hardware requirements for installing Windows 98.

continue the installation. Conversely, there will not be any Product Key request when Windows 98 is being installed across a network.

After the registration information has been gathered, Setup begins to collect information about the system.

After gathering this information, the Setup routine stops to prompt the installer to create an *Emergency Startup Disk* and then begins installing Windows 98 files to the selected drive.

3. Copying Windows 98 Files to Your Computer—This portion of the operation begins when the Start Copying Files dialog box appears on the screen. The complete operation of this phase is automated so that no external input is required. However, any interruption of the Setup operation during this period might prevent the system from starting up again. In this event, it will be necessary to re-run the Setup routine from the beginning.

4. Restarting Your Computer—After Setup has copied the Windows 98 files into their proper locations, it will present a prompt to restart the system. Doing so enables the newly installed Windows 98 functions to become active. The restart will be conducted automatically if no entry is detected within 15 seconds.

5. Setting Up Hardware and Finalizing Settings—After the system has been restarted, Setup finalizes the installation of the operating system.

INSTALLING WINDOWS NT/2000

The installation process for Windows NT versions, including Windows 2000, can be a little more difficult than that of the Windows 9x versions. In particular, the lack of extensive hardware and software compatibilities requires some advanced planning before installing or upgrading to Windows NT.

The first issue to deal with is the hardware compatibility issue. Windows NT makes no claim to maintaining compatibility with a wide variety of hardware devices. If the current hardware does not appear in the *Microsoft Hardware Compatibility List* (*HCL*), you are on your own for technical support.

The second factor to sort out is which file management system should be used. Windows NT can be configured to use either a typical FAT-based file system, or its own proprietary NTFS file system.

INSTALLING WINDOWS 2000 PROFESSIONAL

The minimum hardware requirements for installing Windows 2000 Professional on a PC-compatible system are

◆ Microprocessor—133MHz Pentium (P5 equivalent or better)

◆ RAM—64MB (4GB maximum)

◆ HDD Space—650MB or more free on a 2GB drive

◆ VGA Monitor

For installation from a CD-ROM, a 12*x* drive is required. If the CD-ROM drive is not bootable, a high-density 3.5-inch floppy drive is also required.

Before installing Windows 2000 Professional from the CD, it is recommended that the file checkupgradeonly be run. This file is located on the installation CD under \i386\winnt32 and checks the system for possible hardware compatibility problems. The program generates a text file report named upgrade.txt that can be found under the \Windows folder. It contains Windows 2000 compatibility information about the system, along with a list of potential complications.

If your system has hardware devices that are not on the Windows 2000 Hardware Compatibility List, you should contact the manufacturer of the device to determine whether they have new, updated Windows 2000 drivers for their device. Many peripheral makers have become very proactive in supplying updated drivers for their devices—often, posting their latest drivers and product compatibility information on their Internet Web sites, where they can be downloaded by customers. The second alternative is to try the device with

| EXAM TIP | Memorize the minimum system requirements for installing Windows 2000 Professional. |

EXAM TIP

Know what to do if you encounter hardware devices not listed on the Windows 2000 HCL.

EXAM TIP

Know which files are used to start a Windows 2000 install from 16-bit and 32-bit operating systems.

Windows NT or Windows 9x drivers to see if it will work. The final option is to get a device that is listed on the Windows 2000 HCL.

To conduct a new Windows 2000 Professional installation, you will need the Windows 2000 Professional distribution CD. If the installation is being performed on a system that cannot boot to the CD-ROM drive, you will also need Windows 2000 Professional Setup disks.

The first step in the Setup process is to choose whether the installation is a *Clean Install* or an *Upgrade.* If a new installation is being performed, the Setup program will install the Windows 2000 files in the \WINNT folder.

For a CD-ROM install, boot the system to the existing operating system and then insert the Windows 2000 Professional distribution CD in the CD-ROM drive. If the system detects the CD in the drive, simply click the Install Windows 2000 option. If not, start Setup through the Run command prompt dialog box. In Windows 9x and NT 4.0, click the Start button and then select the Run option from the menu. At the prompt, enter the location of the Windows 2000 start file (*Winnt.exe* or *Winnt32.exe*) on the distribution CD (that is, `d:\i386\Winnt32.exe`). In the case of 16-bit operating systems, such as MS-DOS or Windows 3.x, the Winnt.exe option should be used. Winnt32.exe is used with 32-bit operating systems.

To install Windows 2000 Professional across a network, it will be necessary to establish a shared connection between the local unit and the system containing the Windows 2000 Professional Setup files.

You will also need a Windows 2000 Professional–compatible NIC. At the command prompt, enter the path to the remote Winnt32.exe file (or Winnt.exe file).

CHALLENGE #1

You have been tasked with changing one of your office computers that had been running Windows 95 over to Windows 2000 Professional. The company has purchased a new, high-capacity hard drive for the machine. As you move through the pre-installation preparation, you notice that the machine contains a modem and a LAN card that you cannot find on the Microsoft HCL for Windows 2000 Pro. What should you do to get the system running and back in service?

OPERATING SYSTEM UPGRADING

As mentioned earlier, it is not uncommon for a computer to have its operating system upgraded, possibly several times, during its life span. The following sections of this chapter cover upgrading from DOS or Windows 9x environments to the Windows 9x or Windows 2000 operating systems.

Upgrading to Windows 98

When Windows 98 is installed on a current Windows 95 machine using the existing settings, the Setup program acquires information about the system's hardware, applications, and utilities from the existing Registry entries. The existing information is simply migrated into the new Windows 98 structure. In this manner, a lot of time is saved because the system does not have to run a full hardware detection routine or configure the system's hardware. The Setup routine also skips the option of selecting a Setup type (that is, Custom, Typical, etc.).

During phase 1 of the Windows 98 upgrade, the system checks for the presence of antivirus software in the system. The Setup routine might fail if the CMOS Antivirus function is enabled. If this occurs, the SETUPLOG.TXT file should be checked for information about the antivirus test. In some cases, the Setup program might ask that the antivirus software be disabled so that it can have access to the Master Boot Record. Setup will also modify the AUTOEXEC.BAT file, causing it to run a file called SUWARN.BAT. This file reboots the system in case of a failure and presents an explanation of why the Setup failed.

In phase 2 of the upgrade, the real-mode ScanDisk operation is carried out, and Setup runs the SCANREGW.EXE file to check the existing Registry for corruption during this phase. The Setup routine also provides a prompt that permits the current DOS or Windows System Files to be saved in case an uninstall operation is required for Windows 98 at some future time.

The Setup routine copies the Windows 98 files to the computer during phase 3. This segment of the process begins with the appearance of the Start Copying Files dialog box on the screen. The complete operation of this phase is automated and requires no external intervention. However, any interruption of the Setup operation during this period might prevent the system from starting up again. In this event, it will be necessary to repeat the entire Setup routine form the beginning.

In phase 4, the Restart operation includes a step in which the Setup routine modifies the WIN.INI, SYSTEM.INI, and Registry files to include the appropriate Windows 98 entries. Likewise, an existing AUTOEXEC.BAT or CONFIG.SYS file will be examined for device drivers and Terminate and Stay Resident programs that might be incompatible with the upgraded installation. The results of this check are logged in a hidden file at C:\Windows\Inf_folder\Setupc.inf. The Setup routine disables the questionable entries in these files by using REM statements.

You should be aware that active antivirus software might prevent Windows 98 from being installed to a system. These utilities see the changes to the new operating system's core files as a virus activity and will work to prevent them from occurring. Any antivirus programs should be disabled prior to running Windows 98 Setup. The program can be re-enabled after the setup process has been completed.

In cases where it is desirable to install Windows 98 into some directory other than the C:\Windows directory, click on the Other Directory button in the Select Directory dialog box, depicted in Figure 23.1, and select the Next option. This will produce the Change Directory dialog box. Type the new directory name in the dialog box and click on the Next button. The new directory will be created automatically, if it does not already exist.

EXAM TIP

Be aware that antivirus utilities can prevent operating system upgrades from occurring.

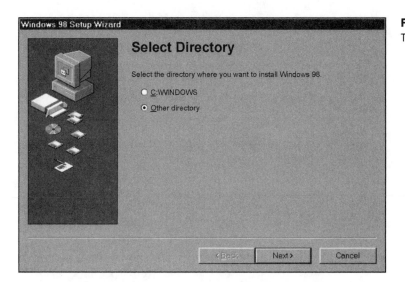

FIGURE 23.1
The Select Directory dialog box.

If Windows 98 is installed in a new directory, it will be necessary to reinstall any Windows-based applications in the system. This will be required in order for the applications to function properly. The applications' support DLLs will not be able to automatically access the Windows 98 structure in the new directory. Likewise, existing .GRP and .INI files will not work unless Windows 98 has been installed in the Windows directory.

Upgrading to Windows 2000

Systems can be upgraded directly to Windows 2000 Professional from Windows 9x operating systems, as well as Windows NT 3.51 and 4.0 workstations. This includes older NTFS, FAT16, and FAT32 installations. When you install Windows 2000, it can recognize all three of these file system types. If the computer is running a different Microsoft operating system, that OS version must be upgraded to one of these versions before it can be upgraded to Windows 2000. Otherwise, a clean install must be performed from a full version of the operating system. Table 23.1 lists the acceptable Windows 2000 upgrade routes.

TABLE 23.1

Windows 2000 Upgrade Routes

Current Operating System	Upgrade Path
Windows 95 and Windows 98	Windows 2000 Professional only
Windows NT 3.51 and 4.0 Workstation	Windows 2000 Professional only
Windows NT 3.51 and 4.0 Server	Any Windows 2000 Product
Windows NT 3.1 and 3.5	Must be upgraded to NT 3.51 or 4.0 first, and then to Windows 2000
Windows 3.x	Must be upgraded to Windows 95 or 98 first, then to Windows 2000 Professional

EXAM TIP

Memorize the acceptable paths for upgrading from older Windows operating systems to Windows 2000.

The easiest upgrade path to Windows 2000 is from the Windows NT 4.0 operating system. Upgrading from Windows 9x is potentially more difficult.

As with previous Windows NT products, Windows 2000 does not attempt to remain compatible with older hardware and software. Therefore, some applications might not be compatible with Windows 2000 and might run poorly or fail completely after an upgrade.

CHALLENGE #2

One of your customers has an office network made up of a Windows 4.0 Server with three Windows NT 3.5 workstations, two Windows 98 workstations, one Windows NT 4.0 workstation, and one Windows 3.51 workstation. He wants to test out Windows 2000 Professional on one of his computers to see how it works and to begin getting his users accustomed to Windows 2000. He wants to do this with as little hassle as possible. What would you suggest he do to accomplish these goals?

Upgrading to Windows 2000 is suggested for users who have an existing Windows operating system that is compatible with Windows 2000 and who want to maintain their existing data and preference settings.

1. To upgrade a system to Windows 2000 from a previous operating system using a CD-ROM install, boot the system to the existing operating system and then insert the Windows 2000 Professional distribution CD in the CD-ROM drive.

2. If the system detects the CD in the drive, simply click the Install Windows 2000 option. If not, start Setup through the Run command. In Windows 9x and NT 4.0, click Start and select the Run option from the menu. In Windows 3.x and NT 3.51, click File and then select the Run option from that menu.

3. At the prompt, enter the location on the Windows 2000 start file (Winnt.exe or Winnt32.exe) on the distribution CD (that is, d:\i386\Winnt32.exe). In the case of Windows 3.x, the Winnt.exe option should be used.

4. Specify whether the installation will be a Clean Install or an Upgrade.

5. Follow the instructions the Installation Wizard places on the screen, entering any information required.

> **EXAM TIP**
>
> Be aware that in a current Windows 2000 system, you should be able to reinstall Windows 2000 by simply starting the system with the Windows 2000 distribution CD in the drive so that it can be Auto-detected.

To upgrade Windows 2000 Professional from a previous operating system across a network, it will be necessary to establish a shared connection between the local unit and the system containing the Windows 2000 Professional Setup files.

1. Boot the local unit to the existing operating system and establish a connection with the remote unit.

2. At the command prompt, enter the path to the remote Winnt32.exe file. (Use the Winnt.exe file if a 16-bit older operating system is being used on the local unit.) The Winnt command is used with 16-bit operating systems such as DOS or Windows 3x. The Winnt32 version is used with 32-bit operating systems including Windows 95, 98, NT3.5, and NT4.0.

3. Choose the Upgrade Your Computer to Windows 2000 option.

4. Follow the instructions the Setup Wizard places on the screen, entering any information required.

CHALLENGE #3

You place the Windows 2000 Professional distribution CD in the drive of a Windows 98 machine, and nothing happens. You want to upgrade the system to Windows 2000, but there is no Auto-detection or self-starting feature for the CD-ROM. What do you need to do to install the Windows 2000 OS?

DUAL BOOTING

In a *dual-boot system*, a startup menu is established that can be used to boot the system into different operating systems on the disk. Depending on which OS option the user selects from the menu, the system will retrieve the correct set of files and then use them to boot the system.

Dual Booting with Windows 9*x*

Establishing a dual-boot configuration makes it possible to install Windows 9*x* and some other operating system on an existing system and then be able to select which operating system to boot the system with. To accomplish this, Windows 9*x* swaps versions of the boot files back and forth between their standard names and a designated set of backup names.

The first step in establishing a Windows 9*x* dual-boot system is to install the Windows 9*x* operating system into a new directory. The Windows 9*x* Setup routine locates and stores existing MS-DOS files under .DOS extensions when it is installed as an upgrade over a previous operating system. In particular, the AUTOEXEC.BAT, COMMAND.COM, CONFIG.SYS, IO.SYS, and MSDOS.SYS files are stored with this extension.

To dual boot with an MS-DOS version, the system must have a copy of MS-DOS 5.0 or higher already running on it. If the Windows 9*x* installation is a new setup, the dual-boot option can be configured during the installation process. When prompted by the Setup utility to use the C:\Windows directory or specify another directory for the Windows files, choose a new directory for the Windows 9x installation. The Windows 9x Setup program will automatically adjust the existing DOS, CONFIG.SYS, and AUTOEXEC.BAT files for the new operating system.

The original DOS versions of the IO.SYS, MSDOS.SYS, COMMAND.COM, CONFIG.SYS, and AUTOEXEC.BAT files are stored in the root directory using a .DOS extension. If the system is started with the other operating system, the Windows 9x versions of AUTOEXEC.BAT, COMMAND.COM, CONFIG.SYS, IO.SYS, and MSDOS.SYS are stored under .W40 extensions, and the renamed DOS versions of the files are returned to their normal extensions.

Dual Booting with Windows NT/2000

Windows NT can be set up to dual boot with DOS or Windows 9x operating systems. This option provides a method for the system to boot up into a Windows NT environment or into a DOS/Windows 9x environment. In such cases, a Startup menu appears on the display that asks which operating system should be used. Establishing either of these dual-boot conditions with Windows NT/2000 requires that the MS-DOS or Windows 9x operating systems must be installed first. Make certain to install Windows 2000 in a new folder so that it does not overwrite the original operating system.

Although it is possible for Windows 2000 to share a partition with Windows 9x or Windows NT4.0, this produces some potentially undesirable situations. Normally, you should install Windows 2000 and the other operating system in separate partitions.

The major drawback of dual booting with Windows NT or Windows 2000 is that the other operating systems are not capable of using applications installed in the other operating system's partition. Therefore, software to be used by both operating systems must be installed in the system twice—once for each operating system partition. Even when you permit Windows 2000 to share the same partition with a Windows 9x or Windows NT OS, you will need to reinstall the system's applications so that their install programs can modify the Windows 2000 Registry.

EXAM TIP

Be aware of which operating system versions are aware of other partition types in a dual-boot situation.

As indicated in Chapter 22, "Basic Disk Management," care must also be taken when formatting partitions in a Windows NT dual-boot system. The native file management formats of Windows NT/2000 and the other operating systems are not compatible. If the disk is formatted with NTFS, the DOS or Windows 9x operating systems will not be able to read the files in the NTFS partition. These operating systems are not "*NTFS Aware.*" However, Windows NT and Windows 2000 can both operate with the FAT file systems used by DOS and Windows 3.x/9x. Therefore, it is recommended that logical drives in a dual-boot system be formatted with the FAT system.

CHAPTER SUMMARY

KEY TERMS

- Clean Install
- Compact installation
- Dual-boot system
- Emergency Startup Disk
- Microsoft Hardware Compatibility List (HCL)
- NTFS Aware
- Typical installation
- Upgrade
- Winnt.exe
- Winnt32.exe

This chapter has focused on installing, configuring, and upgrading operating systems. The initial section of the chapter presented system requirements and procedures for installing Windows 9x and Windows 2000 and bringing them up to a basic operating level.

The second half of the chapter covered the process of performing upgrades from previous operating system versions to the Windows 9x or Windows 2000 operating systems.

At this point, review the objectives listed at the beginning of the chapter to be certain that you understand each point and can perform each task listed there. Afterward, answer the review questions that follow to verify your knowledge of the information.

Review Questions

1. Windows 9*x* requires that a _____ partition exist on the drive where it is being installed.

   A. NTFS

   B. FAT16

   C. FAT32

   D. HPFS

2. What are the minimum, recommended, and preferred CPU specifications for running Windows 95?

   A. 8088, 80286, 80386DX

   B. 80286, 80386DX, 80486DX

   C. 80386DX, 80486DX, Pentium

   D. 80486DX, Pentium, Pentium II

3. What are the minimum, recommended, and preferred amounts of memory specified to start Windows 95?

   A. 2MB, 4MB, 8MB

   B. 4MB, 8MB, 16MB

   C. 8MB, 16MB, 32MB

   D. 16MB, 32MB, 64MB

4. What are the minimum hardware requirements for installing Windows 98 onto a standard desktop PC?

   A. 80386DX/33 CPU, 4MB RAM, 20MB HDD space

   B. 80486DX/66 CPU, 8MB RAM, 120MB HDD space

   C. 80486DX/66 CPU, 16MB RAM, 170MB HDD space

   D. Pentium CPU, 16MB RAM, 225MB HDD space

5. What should you do if you encounter hardware devices not listed on the Windows 2000 HCL?

   A. Download appropriate drivers from the device manufacturer's Web site.

   B. Use a driver from a similar model from the same manufacturer in the Add New Hardware Wizard's list of supported devices.

   C. Install the device without drivers.

   D. Devices not directly supported by the Windows 2000 HCL cannot be installed.

6. What utilities can prevent operating system upgrades from occurring?

   A. Multiple-OS loader

   B. Encryption

   C. Compression/archive

   D. Antivirus

7. What are the minimum hardware requirements needed to install Windows 2000 Professional?

   A. 80486DX/66 CPU, 32MB RAM, 650MB HDD space

   B. Pentium 75 CPU, 32MB RAM, 650MB HDD space

   C. Pentium 100 CPU, 64MB RAM, 650MB HDD space

   D. Pentium 133 CPU, 64MB RAM, 650MB HDD space

APPLY YOUR KNOWLEDGE

8. What type of file system should you put on a partition, if you intend to dual boot Windows 9*x* and Windows NT off of that partition?

   A. FAT

   B. FAT32

   C. NTFS

   D. HPFS

9. Which command is used to start a Windows 2000 installation from a 16-bit operating system?

   A. WIN2K

   B. WINNT

   C. WINNT16

   D. WINNT32

10. Which command is used to start a Windows 2000 installation from a 32-bit operating system?

    A. WIN2K

    B. WINNT

    C. WINNT16

    D. WINNT32

11. Your system currently has Windows 3.11 installed on it. What is the upgrade path to Windows 2000?

    A. Upgrade to Windows 95 and then upgrade to Windows 2000.

    B. Upgrade to Windows Me and then upgrade to Windows 2000.

    C. Upgrade to Windows NT and then upgrade to Windows 2000.

    D. Upgrade directly to Windows 2000.

12. Which of these methods can be used to upgrade a Windows 95 computer to Windows 2000? (Select all that apply.)

    A. Open the command prompt, navigate to the CD-ROM drive; then enter the command **SETUP**, and then click on Install Windows 2000.

    B. Open the command prompt, navigate to the CD-ROM drive, change to the I386 sub-directory; then enter the command **SETUP**, and then click on Install Windows 2000.

    C. Open the command prompt, navigate to the CD-ROM drive, change to the I386 sub-directory, and then enter the command **WINNT32**.

    D. Boot to the desktop, insert the Windows 2000 CD, and then click on Install Windows 2000.

Answers and Explanations

1. **B.** Windows 9*x* operating systems must be installed over an existing operating system. In particular, the Windows 9*x* installation program must find a recognizable MS-DOS FAT16 partition on the drive. For more information, see the section "Installing Windows 95."

2. **C.** The Windows 95 system must be at least an 80386DX or higher machine. The recommended processor is the 80486DX; the Pentium processors are the preferred microprocessor for running Windows 95. For more information, see the section "Installing Windows 95."

APPLY YOUR KNOWLEDGE

3. **B.** For a Windows 95 installation, 4MB is the minimum RAM option, 8MB is the recommended option, and 16MB, 32MB, or 64MB are preferred for running Windows 95. For more information, see the section "Installing Windows 95."

4. **C.** To install Windows 98, the system hardware must be at least an 80486DX/66 or higher machine, operating with at least 16MB of RAM. The system should also possess a modem, a mouse, and a 16-color VGA or better monitor. The system's hard drive should have between 120MB (for a portable computer) and 355MB of free space available to successfully install Windows 98. The actual amount of disk space used depends on the type of installation being performed (Typical, Custom, Portable, Compact, New, Upgrade, and so on). Typical installations use between 170- and 225MB of disk space. For more information, see the section "Installing Windows 98."

5. **A.** If your system has hardware devices that are not on the Windows 2000 Hardware Compatibility List, you should contact the manufacturer of the device to determine whether they have new, updated Windows 2000 drivers for their device. Many peripheral makers have become very proactive in supplying updated drivers for their devices—often, posting their latest drivers and product compatibility information on their Internet Web sites, where they can be downloaded by customers. The second alternative is to try the device with Windows NT or Windows 9x drivers to see if it will work. The final option is to get a device that is listed on the Windows 2000 HCL. For more information, see the section "Installing Windows NT/2000."

6. **D.** Active antivirus software might prevent Windows 98 from being installed to a system. These utilities see the changes to the new operating system's core files as a virus activity and will work to prevent them from occurring. Any antivirus programs should be disabled prior to running Windows 98 Setup. The program can be re-enabled after the setup process has been completed. For more information, see the section "Upgrading to Windows 98."

7. **D.** The minimum hardware requirements for installing Windows 2000 Professional on a PC-compatible system are: Pentium 133 (P5 equivalent or better); 64MB RAM; 650MB or more of free space on a 2GB drive; and a VGA-compatible Monitor. For installation from a CD-ROM, a 12x drive is required. If the CD-ROM drive is not bootable, a high-density 3.5-inch floppy drive is also required. For more information, see the section "Installing Windows 2000 Professional."

8. **A.** The native file management formats of Windows NT/2000 and the other operating systems are not compatible. If the disk is formatted with NTFS, the DOS or Windows 9x operating system will not be able to read the files in the NTFS partition. These operating systems are not "NTFS Aware." However, Windows NT and Windows 2000 can both operate with the FAT file systems used by DOS and Windows 3.x/9x. Therefore, it is recommended that logical drives in a dual-boot system be formatted with the FAT system. For more information, see the section "Dual Booting with Windows NT/2000."

---

9. **B.** The WINNT command is used with 16-bit operating systems such as DOS or Windows 3.*x*. The WINNT32 version is used with 32-bit operating systems including Windows 95, 98, NT3.5, and NT4.0. For more information, see the section "Installing Windows 2000 Professional."

10. **D.** The WINNT32 version is used with 32-bit operating systems including Windows 95, 98, NT3.5, and NT4.0. The WINNT command is used with 16-bit operating systems such as DOS or Windows 3.*x*. For more information, see the section "Installing Windows 2000 Professional."

11. **A.** Windows 3.*x* must be upgraded to Windows 95 or 98 first, and then to Windows 2000 Professional. For more information, see the section "Upgrading to Windows 2000."

12. **A, C, D.** To upgrade a system to Windows 2000 from a previous operating system using a CD-ROM installation, you can: 1) boot the system to the existing operating system, insert the Windows 2000 Professional distribution CD in the CD-ROM drive, and click on Install Windows; 2) Start Setup through the Run command (In Windows 9*x* and NT 4.0, click Start and select the Run option from the menu. In Windows 3.*x* and NT 3.51, click File and then select the Run option from that menu.). At the prompt, enter the location on the Windows 2000 start file (Winnt.exe or Winnt32.exe) on the distribution CD (that is, d:\i386\Winnt32.exe). In the case of Windows 3.*x*, the Winnt.exe option should be used. For more information, see the section "Upgrading to Windows 2000."

Challenge Solutions

1. The best solution is to purchase a modem and LAN card that are listed on the HCL. This is your best guarantee of compatibility. The second best option is to determine the device manufacturer, attempt to locate their Web site, and download Windows 2000-compatible drivers for the devices. Because the devices are not in the HCL, there is a very good chance that you will not be able to use them. For more information, see the section "Installing Windows NT/2000."

2. The best way for this company to test Windows 2000 Pro in its system is to upgrade the Windows NT 4.0 workstation. This is the most effective and easiest upgrade path to Windows 2000. The next best option would be upgrading the Windows NT 3.51 computer to Windows 2000 Pro. The other upgrade paths are more involved and might require more compatibility effort to successfully install the new operating system. For more information, see the section "Upgrading to Windows 2000."

3. You will need to manually start the Windows 2000 Setup routine. To accomplish this, you must boot the system to the existing operating system with the Windows 2000 Professional distribution CD in the CD-ROM drive. Then, start the Windows 2000 Setup Wizard from the command prompt. (Run dialog box in Windows.) At the command prompt, enter the location on the Windows 2000 Winnt32.exe start file on the distribution CD (that is, d:\i386\Winnt32.exe) and follow the instructions the Setup Wizard places on the screen. For more information, see the section "Upgrading to Windows 2000."

APPLY YOUR KNOWLEDGE

Suggested Readings and Resources

1. Installing Windows 95
   http://malektips.envprogramming.com/
   windows_95_installation_and_upgradingtoc.
   html

2. Installing Windows 98
   http://support.microsoft.com/
   default.aspx?scid=kb;EN-US;q188881

3. Installing Windows 2000 Pro
   http://www.winsupersite.com/showcase/
   win2k_pro_install.asp

4. Upgrading to Windows 98
   http://www.windows-
   help.net/windows98/start-01.shtml

5. Upgrading to Windows 2000
   http://www.microsoft.com/windows2000/
   professional/howtobuy/upgrading/default.
   asp

6. Configuration
   http://webopedia.internet.com/TERM/c/
   configuration.html

7. Dual Boot with Windows
   http://windows.about.com/cs/dualboot/

8. How to Dual Boot Windows 9*x*/Me and 2000
   Pro
   http://www.duxcw.com/digest/Howto/
   software/windows/dual/

This chapter helps you to prepare for the Operating System Technologies module of the A+ Certification examination by covering the following objective within the "Domain 2.0: Installation, Configuration, and Upgrading" section.

2.3 Identify the basic system boot sequences and boot methods, including the steps to create an emergency boot disk with utilities installed for Windows 9x, Windows NT, and Windows 2000.

Content might include the following:

- **Startup disk**

- **Safe mode**

- **MS-DOS mode**

- **NTLDR (NT Loader), BOOT.INI**

- **Files required to boot**

- **Creating an Emergency Repair Disk (ERD)**

▶ Booting up the disk operating system is one of the most critical times in the operation of the computer. A technician must know the general sequence of events that should occur during this process. By knowing this information, the technician can observe the process and watch for telltale symptoms of operation system startup problems. Therefore, this chapter deals with booting up operating systems including Windows 9x, Windows NT, and Windows 2000.

CHAPTER 24

Starting the System

To prepare for the Installation, Configuration, and Upgrading objective of the Operating Systems Technologies exam,

▶ Read the objectives at the beginning of this chapter.

▶ Study the information in this chapter.

▶ Review the objectives listed earlier in this chapter.

▶ Perform any step-by-step procedures in the text.

▶ Answer the review questions at the end of the chapter and check your results.

▶ Use the PrepLogic test engine on the CD-ROM that accompanies this book for additional review and exam questions concerning this material.

▶ Review the exam tips scattered throughout the chapter and make certain that you are comfortable with each point.

INTRODUCTION

One of the major activities in which operating systems fail is the startup process. This chapter describes basic boot-up sequences associated with the MS-DOS, Windows 9x, and Windows NT/2000 operating systems. Understanding this information becomes particularly important when the system fails to start up and you must troubleshoot it.

The chapter goes on to describe alternative methods that can be used to start the system and circumvent potential problems that might be preventing the system from starting.

The chapter concludes with explanations of how to create a Windows 9x Emergency start disk with utilities installed and a Windows 2000 Emergency Repair Disk.

After completing the chapter, you should be able to identify the major events that occur during the startup process and relate them to different groups of components in the system. You should also be able to use alternative methods to start the system to isolate potential problems that are preventing the system from starting. Finally, you should also know where and how to create a Windows 9x Emergency start disk with utilities installed and a Windows 2000 Emergency Repair Disk.

THE BOOT PROCESS

PC system boards use an IC chip to hold the system's BIOS firmware. This chip contains the programs that handle the startup of the system, the changeover to disk-based operations, video and printer output functions, and a Power On Self Test.

POST Tests and Initialization

The *Power On Self Test* (*POST*) test is actually a series of tests that are performed each time the system is turned on. The different tests check the operation of the microprocessor, the keyboard, the video display, the floppy and hard disk drive units, as well as both the RAM and ROM memory units.

When the system is first turned on or reset, the system applies a *Reset signal* to the microprocessor and other intelligent system board components, causing them to clear most of their internal registers. However, the microprocessor sets its Instruction Pointer register to the address at the beginning of the ROM BIOS program. This is not coincidental. When the system is started up, the microprocessor must begin taking instructions from this ROM location to initialize the system for operation.

Initial POST Checks

The initial BIOS startup steps are illustrated in Figure 24.1.

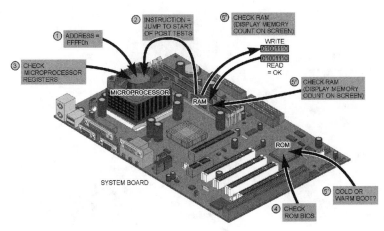

FIGURE 24.1
The Startup sequence.

The first instruction that the microprocessor executes causes it to jump to the POST routines where it verifies that the BIOS program is accurate and checks the system's installed RAM (including the system's CMOS RAM). During the memory tests, the POST displays a running memory count to show that it is testing and verifying the individual memory locations. Next, the POST verifies the operation of the microprocessor's registers and performs tests on the ROM-BIOS chip.

At this point, the program checks to determine whether the system is being started from an off condition or being reset from some other state. When the system is started from an off condition, a *cold boot* is being performed. Conversely, simultaneously pressing Ctrl+Alt+Del while the system is in operation will generate a reset signal in the system and cause it to perform a shortened boot-up routine. (Some of the POST memory tests will be skipped.) This operation is referred to as a *warm boot*. This action permits the system to be shut down and restarted without turning it off.

System Initialization

If the system passes the initial POST, the BIOS routine will initialize the system's intelligent devices. During this part of the program, startup values stored in the ROM chip are moved into the system's programmable devices (that is, Interrupt Controller, DMA Controller, chipset, and so on) to make them functional. The steps of the initialization process are described in Figure 24.2.

FIGURE 24.2
System initialization.

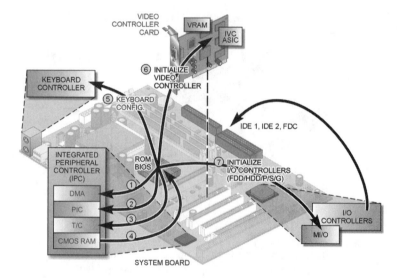

The BIOS routines read configuration information from the system's CMOS RAM to determine what type of display (VGA, SVGA, and so on) is being used with the system. After this parameter has been established, the routine tests the video adapter's RAM memory. If it passes these tests, the system displays a cursor symbol on the monitor.

Additional POST Checks

After the system's display adapter has been checked, the BIOS routines test all additional RAM on the system board and execute the system's built-in setup program to configure its day/time setting, its hard disk and floppy disk drive types, and the amount of memory actually available to the system. Following the final memory test, the keyboard and the I/O devices and adapters are tested. The steps of the additional POST process are described in Figure 24.3.

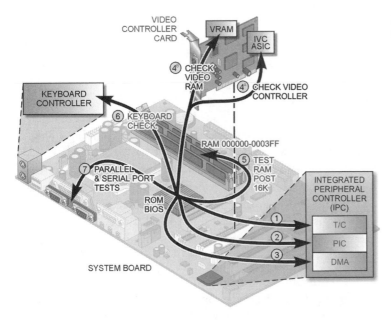

FIGURE 24.3
Completion of the POST test.

After the initialization and POST tests are completed, the BIOS checks in the Upper Memory Area for BIOS extension programs. System designers created this memory area so that new or nonstandard BIOS routines could be added to the basic BIOS structure. These extended firmware routines match software commands from the system to the hardware they support. Therefore, the software running on the system does not need to be directly compatible with these hardware devices.

Video cards contain video BIOS code extensions, as do different types of HDD controller cards. Network adapter cards are another type of device that commonly uses BIOS extensions. These extensions enable the computer to be connected to other computers in the local area and will cause the local computer to load up and operate from the operating system of a remote computer. The system can accommodate as many extensions as will mathematically fit within the allotted memory area.

At the completion of the POST and Initialization operations, the BIOS routines of most systems cause a single, short tone to be produced by the speaker circuitry. The single beep indicates that the POST portion of the bootup has been successfully completed. This is an important point in the overall troubleshooting scheme for hardware/software/configuration problems.

PLUG-AND-PLAY

In the case of *Plug-and-Play* systems, the BIOS must also communicate with the adapter cards located in the expansion slots to determine what their characteristics are. Even in a system using a PnP-compliant operating system, such as Windows 9*x* or Windows 2000, the BIOS must also be PnP compatible before the system can recognize and manipulate system resources. When the system is turned on, the PnP devices involved in the boot-up process become active in their default configuration. Other logical devices, not required for bootup, start up in an inactive mode until the operating system can configure them.

Before starting the boot-up sequence, the PnP BIOS checks the devices installed in the expansion slots to see what types they are, how they are configured, and which slots they are in. It then assigns each adapter a software handle (name) and stores their names and configuration information in a RAM table. Next, the BIOS compares the adapter information to the system's basic configuration, looking for resource conflicts. If no conflicts are detected, all the devices required for bootup are activated.

The operating system is left with the task of activating the remaining intelligent devices and resolving any resource conflicts that the BIOS detected but could not resolve. If the PnP function is not working for a particular device, or the operating system cannot resolve the remaining resource conflicts, it will be necessary for the user to perform manual configurations.

NOTE

Hardware Detection   The Windows 9*x* Plug-and-Play process can be examined by printing out its DETLOG.TXT file. The printout of this file is located under the C:\ root directory and provides a step-by-step listing of the operating system's hardware detection process. It demonstrates the order of resource allocation, as well as the process of detecting and assigning resources to the system's various hardware devices.

MS-DOS BOOTUP

The boot-up process begins when the BIOS starts looking through the system for a *Master Boot Record (MBR)*. This record can reside on drive A: or C:, or at any other location in the system. A simple single-operating system, single-disk boot-up process is described in Figure 24.4. As you can see, it is a multiple-access operation that uses two different bootstrap routines to locate and load two different boot records.

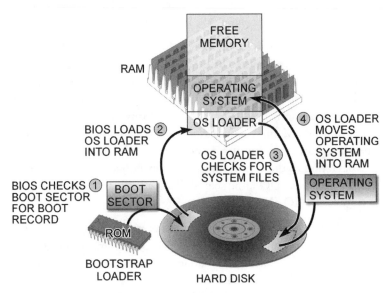

FIGURE 24.4
The Bootstrap operation.

The very first section on any logical disk is called the *boot sector*. This section contains information about how the disk is organized. It can also contain the small, optional master boot record that can access a larger, more powerful *Bootstrap Loader* program located in the root directory of the logical disk.

In most systems, the master boot record is found at sector 1, head 0, and track 0 of the first logical hard drive. Some texts might refer to the first sector as sector 0, keeping with the idea that the first one of anything in a digital system is 0. If the disk possesses a master boot record, it can boot up the hardware system to the operating system. The disk is then referred to as a bootable disk. If not, the disk is just a data disk that can be used for storing information.

Traditionally, BIOS programs will search for the master boot record in floppy disk drive A: first. In later models, the BIOS looked first in the floppy drive, or drives, and then in the hard disk drive. In newer systems, the order that the BIOS uses to search for the MBR is governed by information stored in the system's CMOS configuration RAM. The order can be set to check the floppy drive first and then the hard drive, to check the hard drive first, to check the hard drive only, or most recently, to check the CD-ROM drive.

If the BIOS does not locate the boot record in one of the indicated drives, it will most likely display a "Non-System Disk or Disk Error" or "ROM BASIC Interpreter Not Found" message on the screen.

EXAM TIP

Know what types of error messages are produced when no valid MBR is found in a system.

When an MBR is located, the bootstrap loader moves the boot record into system RAM to be executed. This record contains the Secondary Bootstrap Loader, also referred to as the *Operating System Loader*. This routine looks for an operating system boot record, typically located on the disk. When found, it loads the bigger boot record into RAM and begins executing it. This boot record brings special operating system files into memory so that they can control the operation of the system (that is, the operating system). In the case of Microsoft DOS, the special files loaded by the OS boot record are the IO.SYS and MSDOS.SYS files.

In the MS-DOS system, the IO.SYS file executes the contents of the MSDOS.SYS file and looks for the MS-DOS command processor and moves it into system RAM along with the operating system support files. The default command processor for MS-DOS is a system file called COMMAND.COM. This file processor provides the basic user interface called the command line and interprets the input entered at the command prompt.

EXAM TIP

Remember the files involved in the MS-DOS boot process and the order of their execution.

The following list summarizes the files required to boot an MS-DOS system, along with their execution order:

1. IO.SYS

2. MSDOS.SYS

3. CONFIG.SYS

4. COMMAND.COM

5. AUTOEXEC.BAT

Altering Boot-up Steps

MS-DOS made provisions to permit the basic boot process to be modified through two special configuration files—CONFIG.SYS and AUTOEXEC.BAT. Because these files added complexity to the startup process and often prevented systems from booting, later versions included special keystrokes that could be used to skip the execution of these files or to move through them one step at a time for troubleshooting purposes. When these options were used, the system would boot up with a complete set of default settings. No installable device drivers were installed, the current directory was set to C:\DOS, and the user often received a "Bad or missing command interpreter" message. When this message was received, the system would ask the user to manually enter the path to the COMMAND.COM file.

The special function keys available during the MS-DOS Startup are summarized as follows:

- ◆ *F5* (also *Left Shift key*)—Skips CONFIG.SYS and AUTOEXEC.BAT files

- ◆ *F8*—Proceeds through the CONFIG.SYS and AUTOEXEC.BAT files one step at a time waiting for Confirmation from the user.

> **EXAM TIP**
>
> Know which function keys can be used during the MS-DOS boot process to alter it.

WINDOWS 9X STARTUP

Windows 9x takes over the complete boot-up function as a normal part of its operation. This seamless bootup might be convenient but can offer some interesting problems when the system will not boot—there's no stable command-line level to fall back to for troubleshooting purposes. Basically, the Windows 9x boot sequence occurs in five phases:

- ◆ Phase 1: Bootstrap with the BIOS—During the bootstrap process, the BIOS is in control of the system and functions as described in the DOS boot section.

- ◆ Phase 2: Loading DOS drivers and TSR files—After the disk boot, IO.SYS checks the system's hardware profile to determine its actual configuration. This profile is a function of the

EXAM TIP

Be aware of which file loads the Windows 9*x* operating system into the system.

BIOS detection process during the initialization phase. IO.SYS begins loading default drivers that were previously taken care of by the CONFIG.SYS file.

◆ Phase 3: Real-mode initialization of static Virtual Device Drivers (VxDs)—The system checks the SYSTEM.DAT file for the first part of the Registry file and processes it. SYSTEM.DAT is a hidden file that contains all the system's hardware configuration information, including the PnP and application settings. It is always located under the \Windows folder. Afterward, IO.SYS loads the WIN.COM file to control the loading and testing of the Windows 9*x* core components.

◆ Phase 4: Protected-mode switchover—After loading all the static VxDs, the system shifts the microprocessor into protected-mode operation and begins loading the protected-mode components of the operating system.

◆ Phase 5: Loading Remaining Components—Following the initialization process, the final Windows 9*x* components are loaded into the system. During this period,

- The KERNEL32.DLL and KERNEL386.EXE files are executed.
- The GDI.EXE and GDI32.EXE files are executed.
- The USER.EXE and USER32.EXE files are executed.
- All fonts and other associated resources are loaded.
- The WIN.INI file values are checked.
- The Windows 9*x* shell and machine policies are loaded.
- The Windows desktop components are loaded.

EXAM TIP

Be aware of the two files that make up the different Windows 9*x* Registries and where they are located.

Windows 9*x* searches the `Hkey_Local_Machine` key and the user's home directory for user profile information. Windows 9*x* creates a folder for each user who logs on to the system. This profile is held in the \Windows\Profiles subdirectory. Each profile contains a USER.DAT file (the second half of the Registry) that holds the Registry information for that user. It also contains a number of other files that customize the desktop just for that user. As with the SYSTEM.DAT file, the USER.DAT file is backed up as USER.DA0 each time the Windows 95 system is rebooted. Under Windows 98, the USER.DAT backup is part of the rb000x.cab files.

In Chapter 19, "Operating System Fundamentals," we mentioned that the USER.DAT and SYSTEM.DAT files were located in the \Windows folder. The difference between that statement and the preceding one is that for single-user systems, these files are located in the \Windows folder. However, in multiple-user systems, Windows keeps profile information about all of its users in the \Windows\Profiles folder.

The Windows 9x startup sequence can be summarized as follows:

1. POST tests.

2. PnP configuration.

3. OS bootstrap looks for MBR.

4. System loads IO.SYS.

5. IO.SYS loads and executes CONFIG.SYS (if present).

6. IO.SYS loads MSDOS.SYS.

7. IO.SYS loads and executes COMMAND.COM.

8. COMMAND.COM looks for and executes AUTOEXEC.BAT (if present).

9. Windows 9x Core files are loaded (Starting Windows notice displayed).

10. Windows 9x checks the Startup folder.

Alternative Windows 9x Startup Modes

The Windows 9x *Startup menu* (not to be confused with the desktop's Start menu), depicted in Figure 24.5, can be accessed on a non-starting system by holding down the F8 function key when the "Starting Windows 9x" display is onscreen. The menu offers several startup options, including Normal, Logged, Safe, Step-by-Step Confirmation, and Command Prompt modes.

EXAM TIP

Memorize the files involved the Windows 9x startup process and the order of their execution.

EXAM TIP

Know which files are required to boot Windows 9x to the Starting Windows notice.

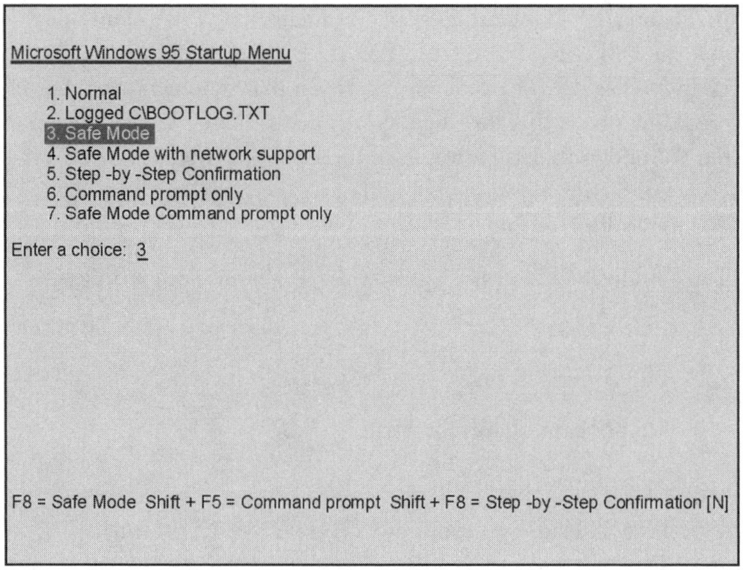

FIGURE 24.5
The Startup menu.

```
Microsoft Windows 95 Startup Menu

    1. Normal
    2. Logged C\BOOTLOG.TXT
    3. Safe Mode
    4. Safe Mode with network support
    5. Step -by -Step Confirmation
    6. Command prompt only
    7. Safe Mode Command prompt only

Enter a choice:  3




F8 = Safe Mode  Shift + F5 = Command prompt  Shift + F8 = Step -by -Step Confirmation [N]
```

> **EXAM TIP**
>
> Be aware that the BOOTLOG.TXT file is not created during startup. It has to be initiated with the Logged mode option.

If the Normal option is selected, the system just tries to restart as it normally would, loading all of its normal startup and Registry files. The Logged option also attempts to start the system in normal mode, but keeps an error log file that contains the steps performed and outcome. This text file (*BOOTLOG.TXT*) can be read with any text editor or printed out on a working system.

Safe Mode

If Windows 9*x* determines that a problem has occurred that prevented the system from starting, it will attempt to restart the system in *Safe mode*. This mode bypasses several startup files to provide access to the system's configuration files. This Startup mode can also be accessed by pressing the F5 function key when the "Starting Windows 9*x*" message is displayed onscreen.

> **EXAM TIP**
>
> Know which drivers are loaded into the system when it is started in Safe mode.

In Safe mode, the minimal device drivers (keyboard, mouse, and standard-mode VGA drivers) are active to start the system. However, the CD-ROM drive will not be active in Safe mode.

In *step-by-step confirmation mode*, the system displays each startup command line by line and waits for a confirmation from the keyboard before moving ahead. This enables an offending startup command to be isolated and avoided so that it can be replaced or removed. This option is obtained by pressing the *F8 function key* at the Startup menu.

Command Prompt Modes

Other startup options might also be available from the menu depending on the configuration of the system. Some options start the system and bring it to a DOS-like command prompt. Selecting the *Command Prompt Only mode* causes the system to boot up to the command line, using the startup files and the Registry.

If this option will not start the system, reboot the computer and select the Safe Mode Command Prompt Only option from the Startup menu. This option performs the same function as pressing the Shift and F5 keys simultaneously (Shift+F5) during the boot-up process. The system will start in Safe mode with minimal drivers (while not executing any of the startup files) and will produce the command-line prompt.

WIN Switches

When Windows 9*x* refuses to start up, a number of options are available for starting it from the command line. After gaining access to the system using a boot disk, you should attempt to start Windows by typing the **WIN** command at the command prompt. The *WIN command* can be modified by the inclusion of command switches that define the scope of the command. For example, starting Windows using a /D switch is often helpful in isolating possible areas of the operating system as problem sources (that is, WIN /D). These switches are covered in more detail in Chapter 26, "Troubleshooting OS Setup/Startup Problems."

You can use a question mark as a switch with the WIN command (that is, WIN /?) to show a listing of all the switches associated with the command. You can use these switches to start Windows with various portions of the operating system disabled. If the system runs with a particular section disabled, at least some portion of the problem can be linked to that area.

NOTE

Safe Mode with Network Support
Windows 98 does not officially support Safe mode with Network Support. However, the Safe mode version can be accessed by pressing the F6 function key during startup.

EXAM TIP

Memorize the function keys associated with the various Safe mode startup options.

EXAM TIP

Be aware that the WIN / switches are a viable method of starting Windows 9*x* systems for troubleshooting.

CHALLENGE #1

A client has called you up from her hotel room. She is traveling to a convention and her Windows 9x notebook computer hangs up after displaying the "Starting Windows" notice on the display. She does not know how to begin troubleshooting the problem, and there is no technical support around the hotel. She needs the notebook to be running tomorrow so that she can give a Power Point slide show presentation at the convention. What two things can you suggest for getting past the "Starting..." message so that she can try to repair her computer?

WINDOWS NT STARTUP

The sequence of events in the Windows NT/2000 boot and startup processes is similar to those presented for DOS and Windows 9x systems. The main differences are found in the terminology and filenames that Windows NT employs.

Like any other PC system, the Windows NT–based PC starts up by running the POST test, performing an initialization of its intelligent system devices, and performing a system boot process. It is in the boot process that the descriptions of the two operating systems diverge.

When the BIOS executes the Master Boot Record on the hard drive, the MBR examines the disk's partition table to locate the active partition. The boot process then moves to the boot sector of that partition (referred to as the *partition boot sector*) located in the first sector of the active partition. Here it finds the code to begin loading the secondary bootstrap loader from the root directory of the boot drive.

In the case of a Windows NT partition, the bootstrap loader is the NT Loader file named *NTLDR*. This file is the Windows NT equivalent of the DOS IO.SYS file and is responsible for loading the NT operating system into memory. Afterward, NTLDR passes control of the system to the Windows NT operating system.

Next, a temporary, miniature file system that can read both FAT and NTFS file structures is loaded to aid NTLDR in reading the rest of the system. Recall that Windows NT has the capability to work in either FAT or proprietary NTFS partitions. However, at this stage of the boot process, the operating system is still uncertain as to which system it will be using.

With the minifile system in place, the NTLDR can locate and read a special, hidden boot loader menu file named *BOOT.INI*. NTLDR uses this text file to generate the *Boot Loader Menu* that is displayed on the screen. If no selection is made after a given period of time, the default value is selected.

If Windows NT is the designated operating system to be used, the NTLDR program executes a hardware detection file called *NTDE-TECT.COM*. This file is responsible for collecting information about the system's installed hardware devices and passing it to the NTLDR program. This information is later used to upgrade the Windows NT Registry files.

If a different operating system is to be loaded, as directed by the Boot Loader Menu entry, the NTLDR program loads a file called *BOOTSECT.DOS* from the root directory of the system partition and passes control to it. From this point, the BOOTSECT file is responsible for loading the desired operating system.

Finally, the NTLDR program examines the partition for a pair of files named *NTOSKRNL.EXE* and *HAL.DLL*. NTOSKRNL.EXE is the Windows NT kernel file that contains the Windows NT core and loads its device drivers. HAL.DLL is the Hardware Abstraction Layer driver that holds the information specific to the CPU that the system is being used with.

Even though NTLDR reads the NTOSKRNL and HAL files at this time, it does not load or execute them. Instead, it uses a file named *NTDETECT.COM* to gather information about the hardware devices present and passes it to the NTLDR. (Note: This should not be confused with the PnP enumeration process that occurs later in the Windows 2000 boot process.) The information gathered by NTDETECT is stored to be used later for updating the Hardware Registry hive.

After the information has been passed back to NTLDR, it opens the System Hive portion of the Registry to find the Current Control Set. At this point, the system displays the Starting Windows NT logo on the display along with a sliding progress bar that shows the degree of progress being made in loading the drivers. After the

EXAM TIP

Memorize the names and functions of the files involved in the Windows NT/2000 boot process and know which order they are executed in.

NOTE

Using NTBOOTDD.SYS If the Windows NT system employs a SCSI disk drive, a driver file named NTBOOTDD.SYS will need to be present in the root directory of the system partition. This condition must also be noted in the BOOT.INI file by placing a mark in its SCSI(x) or Multi(x) locations. The NTLDR program can also load driver files that have been renamed as NTBOOTDD.SYS to enable Windows NT 4.0 and Windows 2000 to use drives greater than 8GB in size (even EIDE drives).

EXAM TIP

Be aware of what the NTBOOTDD.SYS file does in a Windows NT/2000 system.

EXAM TIP

Be aware that the old Last Known Good Hardware Configuration settings are not replaced until a user actually logs on to the system.

drivers have been loaded, the NTLDR program passes control to the NTOSKRNL file to complete the boot sequence.

When NTOSKRNL gains control of the system, it initializes the HAL.DLL file (along with the *BOOTVID.DLL* file in Windows 2000) and shifts the video display to graphics mode. It then initializes the drivers prepared by NTLDR and uses the NTDETECT information to create a temporary Hardware Hive in memory. Finally, NTOSKRNL executes a *Session Manager* file titled *SMSS.EXE* to carry out pre-start functions such as running a boot-time version of CHKDSK called *AUTOCHK*. It also establishes parameters concerning the Windows NT paging file (*PAGEFILE.SYS*) to hold RAM memory swap pages.

Alternative Windows NT Startup Modes

Unlike the Windows 9x products, Windows NT 4.0 provides very few options when it starts up. The user is normally offered two options. The NTLDR file causes the system to display a selection menu of which operating system to boot from, along with an option to start the system in VGA mode. The menu listing is based on what NTLDR finds in the Boot.ini file. If the VGA option is selected, the system will start up as normal—with the exception that it will only load the standard VGA driver to drive the display.

The second option presented is the Last Known Good Hardware Configuration mode option. Selecting this option will cause the system to start up using the configuration information that it recorded the last time a user successfully logged on to the system. The option appears on the screen for a few seconds after the operating system selection has been made. You must press the Spacebar while the option is displayed on the screen to select this startup mode. If no selection is made, the system continues on with a normal startup as previously outlined, using the existing hardware configuration information.

WINDOWS 2000 STARTUP

The Windows 2000 boot process is nearly identical to the Windows NT bootup. The major events in the Windows 2000 startup include

1. NTLDR looks into memory, and the OS loader V5.0 message appears on screen.

2. NTLDR switches processor to 32-bit flat memory mode.

3. NTLDR starts mini-file system (FAT or NTFS) to read disk files.

4. NTLDR reads Boot.ini file and displays the Advanced Boot Options menu on screen.

5. NTLDR runs Ntdetect.com to gather system hardware information. Ntdetect checks for key hardware items.

6. NTLDR loads Ntoskrnl and hal files into memory and passes the hardware information to it.

7. NTLDR reads the SYSTEM Registry key, places it in memory, and implements the hardware profile (configuration and control set) from the proper Registry.

8. NTLDR loads startup device drivers into memory.

9. NTLDR passes control to the Ntoskrnl file.

10. Ntoskrnl creates the Registry's HARDWARE key from the information gathered earlier by Ntdetect.

11. Ntoskrnl executes additional device drivers.

12. Ntoskrnl starts the SMSS.EXE session file.

13. The Win32 subsection runs the WINLOGON.EXE and LSASS.EXE programs, the Ctrl+Alt+Del window is presented on the display, and the logon screen is displayed.

14. The SCREG.EXE service controller program starts and loads all remaining services specified in the Registry, including the Windows 2000 shell and desktop.

> **EXAM TIP**
>
> Memorize the files involved in the Windows 2000 startup process and know the order of their execution.

The Windows NT/2000 logon enables the operating system to be configured differently for individual users. Normal logon involves entering a username and password. If no logon information is entered, default values will be loaded into the system.

Alternative Windows 2000 Startup Modes

The Windows 2000 operating system incorporates a number of Windows 9x–like startup options that can be engaged to get the system up and running in a given state to provide a starting point for troubleshooting operations. The Windows 2000 Advanced Options Menu, depicted in Figure 24.6, contains several options that can be of assistance when troubleshooting startup failures. To display this menu, press F8 at the beginning of the Windows 2000 startup process.

FIGURE 24.6

The Advanced Options menu.

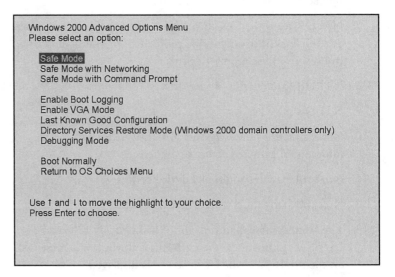

The Windows 2000 Startup Menu basically provides the same Safe Mode options as the Windows 9x operating systems—that is, Boot Normally, Safe Mode, Safe Mode with Networking, and Safe Mode with Command Prompt. The Windows 2000 Start menu also provides a number of Windows NT-like options:

◆ Enable Boot Logging—Creates a log file called
NTBTLOG.TXT in the root folder. This log is very similar to
the BOOTLOG.TXT file described earlier in that it contains
a listing of all the drivers and services that the system attempts
to load during startup and can be useful when trying to determine what service or driver is causing the system to fail.

◆ Enable VGA Mode—When selected, this option boots the system normally, but uses only the standard VGA driver. If you
have configured the display incorrectly and are unable to see
the Desktop, booting in to VGA Mode will enable you to
reconfigure those settings.

◆ Last Known Good Configuration—Starts Windows 2000
using the settings that existed the last time a successful user
logon occurred. All system setting changes made since the last
successful startup are lost. This is a particularly useful option if
you have added or reconfigured a device driver that is causing
the system to fail.

◆ Debugging Mode—Starts Windows 2000 in a kernel debug
mode that will enable special debugger utilities to access the
kernel for troubleshooting and analysis.

SELF-BOOTING DISKS

Boot disks are referred to by different names depending on which
operating system you are discussing. In MS-DOS, it was simply
referred to as a clean boot disk. Under Windows 9*x*, it is called an
Emergency Start disk. Windows NT and Windows 2000 refer to
these as *Setup disks*. In all the operating system versions, this tool
provides a well-defined point to begin troubleshooting operating
system problems.

However, to make a simple MS-DOS boot disk, you must install the
files required to boot to an MS-DOS command prompt—IO.SYS,
MSDOS.SYS and COMMAND.COM. The CONFIG.SYS and
AUTOEXEC.BAT files are helpful in configuring a bootup, but are
not required in order to boot to a command prompt. To make the
boot disk truly useful, you should include at least a few utilities that

EXAM TIP

Know which types of files should be included on a typical boot disk.

can be used to provide initial troubleshooting functions after you have gained access to the system. These functions include partitioning, formatting, file editing, and diagnostic utilities.

Creating a Windows 95 Emergency Start Disk

In the event that the Windows program becomes nonfunctional, it will be necessary to use the Emergency Start disk to gain access to the system so that you can restore it to proper operation. The Windows 9x Start disk will only boot the system up to the command prompt. From this point, you will need to be familiar with command-line operations so that you can employ tools and utilities that will get the system up and running again.

During the Windows setup operation, the software provides an option for creating an Emergency Start disk. This option should be used for every Windows 9x installation. Setup copies the operating system files to the disk, along with utilities for troubleshooting start-up problems. The disk can then be used to boot up the system in safe mode and display a command-line prompt. The Emergency Start disk can also be used to replace lost or damaged system files on the hard disk.

EXAM TIP

Be aware of the two methods of creating Emergency Start disks in Windows 9x and know when these disks should be employed.

An Emergency Start disk can also be created through the Control Panel's Add/Remove Programs icon. This option is normally used to create a new startup disk after new hardware has been installed or when configuration information has been changed.

In addition to creating a startup floppy disk, Windows 95 transfers a number of diagnostic files to the disk, including the following:

- ATTRIB.EXE
- COMMAND.COM
- EDIT.COM
- FDISK.EXE
- FORMAT.COM
- IO.SYS
- MSDOS.SYS

- ◆ REGEDIT.EXE
- ◆ SCANDISK.EXE
- ◆ SCANDISK.INI
- ◆ SYS.COM

Because the Windows 95 system settings are basically contained in the two Registry files SYSTEM.DAT and USER.DAT, it is not uncommon to back them up on the Emergency Start disk. This operation is performed with the RegEdit utility's Export function. The Export function can be used to save a selected branch or the entire Registry as a REG text file.

In addition to the .DAT Registry files, you might want to include copies of any CONFIG.SYS, AUTOEXEC.BAT, WIN.INI, SYSTEM.INI, and CD-ROM driver files on the Emergency Start disk. These files can be quite useful for maintaining compatibility with installed hardware and software applications. The CD-ROM driver (that is, MSCDEX.EXE) should be included to provide CD-ROM support for access to the utilities on the Windows distribution CD.

The Registry backup file can be used to restore the Registry to the system after a crash. Once again, this involves using the RegEdit Import function to restore the Registry for use. The RegEdit Import function can be performed using the Windows-based version, or it can be conducted from the command line using the real-mode version located on the Emergency Start disk.

The REGEDIT /C command should not be used except for cases where the Registry is heavily corrupted. It must have a complete image of the Registry to be used in this manner. Also realize that Windows 9x backs up the Registry files each time it is started. There should be several iterations of the Registry files that could be renamed and copied over the existing Registry files to repair them.

The Windows 98 Emergency Start Disk

Like the Windows 95 Emergency Start disk, the Windows 98 version is basically a boot disk with key Windows 98 utilities included—to assist in restarting the system when Windows 98 doesn't boot. This disk can be created during the installation process or by

EXAM TIP — Know which files should be present on a Windows 9x Emergency Start disk.

EXAM TIP — Understand the nature of why the recommended files should be added to the Emergency Start disk.

EXAM TIP

Know where to make Emergency Start Disks in Windows 9x.

EXAM TIP

Know that real-mode drivers must be available to support CD-ROM drive operation in Safe mode.

EXAM TIP

Be aware of the function of the Extract command and of the file type used to store files on the Windows 9x distribution CD.

accessing the Startup disk tab in the Control Panel's Add/Remove Programs window.

In addition to the necessary system files required to start the system in a minimal, real-mode condition, the Windows 98 Startup disk provides a number of diagnostic programs and a trio of real-mode CD-ROM drivers (MSCDEX.EXE for IDE drives and BTDC-DROM.SYS and ASPICD.SYS for SCSI drives) to enable the CD-ROM drive to operate in Safe Mode.

CHALLENGE #2

You have started a customer's computer in Safe mode because it has repeatedly failed to start Windows 95. After reaching Safe mode, you put the Windows CD in the drive but cannot access it. What do you need to do to access the CD-ROM drive so that you can run repair utilities from it?

The Windows 98 Emergency Start disk includes real-mode SCSI CD-ROM support, provides a RAMDrive, and features a new *Extract command* (*EXT.EXE*) to work with *EXTRACT.EXE*. The Extract command is used to pull necessary files from the *cabinet* (.*CAB*) files on the Windows 98 distribution CD.

CHALLENGE #3

A customer has accidentally erased the SCANDISK.EXE file from her Windows 98 notebook computer. What is the least intrusive method that you can use to recover her file and get the ScanDisk function back in operation?

Windows NT/2000 Emergency Disks

In the Windows NT/2000 arena, there are two different types of troubleshooting-related disks that the technician should have on hand. These are

◆ Setup disks

◆ Emergency Repair disk

Setup disks are the equivalent of the Windows 9*x* Startup Disk. Windows NT 4.0 generates a three-disk set, whereas Windows 2000 creates a four-disk set. Unlike the Windows 9*x* Start disk, the Setup disks do not bring the system to a command prompt. Instead, they initiate the Windows Setup process.

Both Windows NT 4.0 and Windows 2000 provide for an *Emergency Repair Disk* (*ERD*) to be produced. The ERD is different from the Setup disks in that it is intended for use with an operational system when it crashes. It is not a bootable disk and must be used with the Setup disks or the Windows distribution CD.

Whereas the Setup disks are uniform for a given version of Windows NT, the ERD is specific to the machine it is created from. It contains a copy of the SAM in Windows NT and the Registry in Windows 2000. When dealing with the NT ERD, it is necessary to manually copy the Registry files to the disk.

Windows NT/2000 Setup Disks

The *Windows NT Setup disks* basically perform three functions. They load a miniature file system into the system, initialize its drives, and start the installation process. All Windows NT Setup disks are the same for all machines running that version of the operating system. To create Setup disks under Windows NT 4.0, you must install the Windows NT distribution CD in the system and type **WINNT /ox** at the command prompt.

Under Windows 2000, you must place the distribution CD in the drive and launch the MakeBootDisk utility to create the four disk images for its Windows 2000 Setup disks. You can also create Setup disks from the command prompt using the MAKEBT32.EXE file for Windows 2000. These disks can also be made from the Start/Run/Browse/CD-ROM path. From the CD, select the BOOT-DISK option, followed by the MAKEBT32.EXE command.

> **EXAM TIP**
>
> Be aware of the different ways that Setup disks are created in Windows NT 4.0 and Windows 2000.

Windows NT 4.0 ERD

During the installation process, Windows NT Setup asks whether you want to create an Emergency Repair Disk. You can also create an ERD later using the *Repair Disk program* (*RDISK.EXE*). To do so, select the Run option from the Start menu, enter the CMD command in the Run dialog box, and then type **RDISK** at the command prompt.

EXAM TIP

Know what the RDISK command is used for in a Windows NT 4.0 system.

EXAM TIP

Know where ERDs are created in Windows NT 4.0 and in Windows 2000.

When Windows NT is installed, the Setup routine stores Registry information in the \system32\config folder and creates a \repair folder to hold key files.

Windows 2000 ERD

The Windows 2000 Setup routine prompts you to create an ERD during the Installation process. The ERD can also be created using the Windows 2000 Backup utility located under the Programs/Accessories/System tools path. The Windows 2000 ERD disk contains configuration information specific to the computer that will be required during the emergency repair process.

CHALLENGE #4

One of your associates has called you because he is a Windows 2000 technician, but he has been assigned to repair a Windows NT 4.0 workstation. He needs an Emergency Repair Disk for the machine and cannot find it. Also, he is not familiar with Windows NT 4.0 and does not know where to create this disk. What can you tell him to help him out?

CHAPTER SUMMARY

KEY TERMS

- AUTOCHK
- Boot disks
- Boot Loader Menu
- BOOT.INI
- BOOTLOG.TXT
- BOOTSECT.DOS
- BOOTSECT.DOS
- Bootstrap Loader

This chapter presented the steps of the basic boot-up sequences for DOS and Windows systems in detail. It also described alternative startup methods that can be used to isolate potential sources of startup problems.

This section also included step-by-step procedures for creating Windows 9x Emergency start disks and Windows 2000 Emergency Repair Disks.

At this point, review the objectives listed at the beginning of the chapter to be certain that you understand each point and can perform each task listed there. Afterward, answer the review questions that follow to verify your knowledge of the information.

CHAPTER SUMMARY

- BOOTVID.DLL
- Cabinet (.CAB)
- Cold boot
- Command Prompt Only mode
- Emergency Repair Disk (ERD)
- Emergency Start disk
- Extract command (EXT.EXE)
- EXTRACT.EXE
- F5
- F8
- F8 function key
- HAL.DLL
- Left Shift key
- MakeBootDisk
- MAKEBT32.EXE
- Master Boot Record (MBR)
- NTBOOTDD.SYS
- NTDETECT.COM
- NTLDR
- NTOSKRNL.EXE

- PAGEFILE.SYS
- Plug and Play
- Power On Self Test (POST)
- Rdisk
- REGEDIT /C
- Repair Disk program (RDISK.EXE)
- Reset signal
- Safe Mode
- Session Manager
- Setup disks
- Shift+F5
- SMSS.EXE
- Startup menu
- Step-by-step confirmation mode
- Warm boot
- WIN command
- Windows NT Setup disks
- WINNT /ox

APPLY YOUR KNOWLEDGE

Review Questions

1. What type of error message is produced when no valid MBR is found in a system?

   A. Non-System Disk

   B. Invalid Media Type

   C. No Partition Found

   D. Disk Not Found

2. What is the order of execution for the files involved in the MS-DOS boot process?

   A. IO.SYS, MSDOS.SYS, COMMAND.COM, CONFIG.SYS, AUTOEXEC.BAT

   B. IO.SYS, MSDOS.SYS, CONFIG.SYS, AUTOEXEC.BAT, COMMAND.COM

   C. IO.SYS, MSDOS.SYS, CONFIG.SYS, COMMAND.COM, AUTOEXEC.BAT

   D. MSDOS.SYS, IO.SYS, CONFIG.SYS, COMMAND.COM, AUTOEXEC.BAT

3. Which function key can be used to alter the MS-DOS boot process?

   A. F1

   B. F4

   C. F5

   D. F11

4. Which file loads the Windows 9x operating system into the system?

   A. START.EXE

   B. IO.SYS

   C. WIN.COM

   D. AUTOEXEC.BAT

5. Which files make up the Windows 9x Registry? (Select two answers.)

   A. REG.DAT

   B. SYSTEM.DAT

   C. HIVE.DAT

   D. USER.DAT

6. What are the two methods for creating Emergency Start disks in Windows 9x? (Select two answers.)

   A. format a: /c.

   B. In the Add/Remove Programs Properties window, select the Startup Disk tab.

   C. Select the option during installation.

   D. Right-click on the desktop and select Create System Disk.

7. Which files are involved in the Windows 9x startup process, and what is the order of their execution?

   A. IO.SYS, CONFIG.SYS, MSDOS.SYS, COMMAND.COM, AUTOEXEC.BAT, WIN.COM, KERNEL32.DLL, KERNEL386.EXE, GDI.EXE, GDI32.EXE, USER.EXE, USER32.EXE, fonts, WIN.INI

   B. IO.SYS, MSDOS.SYS, CONFIG.SYS, COMMAND.COM, AUTOEXEC.BAT, WIN.COM, KERNEL32.DLL, GDI32.EXE, USER.EXE, USER32.EXE, fonts, WIN.INI

   C. MSDOS.SYS, IO.SYS, CONFIG.SYS, COMMAND.COM, AUTOEXEC.BAT, WIN.COM, KERNEL32.DLL, GDI32.EXE, USER.EXE, USER32.EXE, fonts, WIN.INI

   D. IO.SYS, MSDOS.SYS, CONFIG.SYS, COMMAND.COM, AUTOEXEC.BAT, WIN.COM, KERNEL32.DLL, KERNEL386.EXE, GDI.EXE, GDI32.EXE, fonts, WIN.INI

APPLY YOUR KNOWLEDGE

8. Which of these files is included on the Windows 9x startup disk?

   A. WIN.COM

   B. FDISK.EXE

   C. PAGEFILE.SYS

   D. NTLDR

9. Which files must be present on a DOS boot disk? (Select all that apply.)

   A. IO.SYS

   B. MSDOS.SYS

   C. COMMAND.COM

   D. CONFIG.SYS

10. What is the utility used to retrieve a file from a cabinet (.CAB) archive file located on the Windows 9x distribution CD?

    A. EXPAND

    B. RESTORE

    C. COPY

    D. EXT

11. When in Safe mode, the BOOTLOG.TXT file has to be initiated with the _____ option.

    A. Network Support

    B. Command Prompt

    C. logged mode

    D. step-by-step confirmation

12. Which items are loaded into the system when it is started in Safe mode?

    A. BOOT.INI, CONFIG.SYS

    B. NTDETECT, BOOT.INI, NTLDR

    C. Mouse, keyboard, VGA

    D. Network adapter, mouse, keyboard

13. Which of these function key commands is associated with booting to startup menu?

    A. F5

    B. Shift+F5

    C. F6

    D. F8

14. Which of these function key commands is associated with booting to standard Safe mode?

    A. F5

    B. Shift+F5

    C. F6

    D. F8

15. What are the names of the files involved in the Windows NT boot process, and which order they are executed in?

    A. BOOT.INI, NTLDR, NTOSKRNL.EXE, NTDETECT.COM

    B. NTLDR, BOOT.INI, NTOSKRNL.EXE, NTDETECT.COM

    C. BOOT.INI, NTLDR, NTDETECT.COM, NTOSKRNL.EXE

    D. NTLDR, BOOT.INI, NTDETECT.COM, NTOSKRNL.EXE, HAL.DLL

APPLY YOUR KNOWLEDGE

16. What is the swap file in Windows NT/2000 called?

    A. SWAP.SYS

    B. PAGEFILE.SYS

    C. WIN386.SWP

    D. WINSWAP.SWP

17. Which command is used to create Setup disks in Windows NT 4.0?

    A. MAKEBT

    B. WINNTCD /O

    C. WINNT /OX

    D. MAKEBT32

18. What is the RDISK command used for in a Windows NT 4.0 system?

    A. Create an ERD

    B. Restore a backup

    C. Restore a file system to a previous good condition

    D. Make a backup to a disk

19. What are two methods of creating an ERD in Windows 2000? (Select two answers.)

    A. During setup

    B. Use the Add/Remove Programs utility

    C. Use the Backup utility

    D. Use the Startup Disk utility

20. The old Last Known Good Hardware Configuration settings are not replaced until _____.

    A. a user logs off the system

    B. a user shuts down the operating system

    C. a user boots the operating system

    D. a user logs on to the system

21. What command can you use from the command line to show a listing of all the Windows 9x boot-up switches?

    A. WIN ?

    B. WIN /?

    C. WIN /HELP

    D. WIN /H

22. In a Windows NT/2000 system, the NTBOOTDD.SYS file is used to _____.

    A. boot the system

    B. enable SCSI disk drives

    C. detect bootup errors

    D. enable double-density booting

23. Which file is not required to boot the Windows NT 4.0 operating system?

    A. BOOT.INI

    B. NTLDR

    C. NTDECT.COM

    D. HAL.DLL

24. Which file must be present on the Windows 9*x* startup disk to provide CD-ROM support?

    A. MSCDDVR.EXE

    B. CDDRVR.SYS

    C. MSCDEX.EXE

    D. CDFS.SYS

25. What is the file type used to store files on the Windows 9*x* distribution CD?

    A. .ZIP

    B. .EXE

    C. .CAB

    D. .TAR

Answers and Explanations

1. **A**. If the BIOS does not locate the boot record in one of the indicated drives, it will most likely display a "Non-System Disk," "Disk Error," or "ROM BASIC Interpreter Not Found" message on the screen. For more information, see the section "MS-DOS Bootup."

2. **C**. The files required to boot an MS-DOS system, and their execution order, are: IO.SYS, MSDOS.SYS, CONFIG.SYS, COMMAND.COM, AUTOEXEC.BAT. For more information, see the section "MS-DOS Bootup."

3. **C**. The special function keys available during the MS-DOS Startup are F5 (also Left Shift key)— skips CONFIG.SYS and AUTOEXEC.BAT files—and F8 —proceeds through the CONFIG.SYS and AUTOEXEC.BAT files one step at

a time. For more information, see the section "Altering Boot-up Steps."

4. **C**. IO.SYS loads the WIN.COM file into RAM, which controls the loading and testing of the Windows 9*x* core components. For more information, see the section "Windows 9*x* Startup."

5. **B, D**. The system checks the SYSTEM.DAT file for the first part of the Registry file and processes it. SYSTEM.DAT is a hidden file that contains all the system's hardware configuration information, including the PnP and application settings. It is always located under the \Windows folder. Windows 9*x* searches the Hkey_Local_Machine key and the user's home directory for user profile information. Windows 9*x* creates a folder for each user who logs on to the system. This profile is held in the \Windows\Profiles subdirectory. Each profile contains a USER.DAT file (the second half of the Registry) that holds the Registry information for that user. It also contains a number of other files that customize the desktop just for that user. As with the SYSTEM.DAT file, the USER.DAT file is backed up as USER.DA0 each time the Windows 95 system is rebooted. Under Windows 98, the USER.DAT backup is part of the rb000x.cab files. For more information, see the section "Windows 9*x* Startup."

6. **B, C**. An Emergency Startup Disk is an essential tool for troubleshooting in Windows 9*x*. There are two methods for creating this disk. When you install the Windows 9*x* operating system, you will be asked if you want to create such a disk. For all other situations, you will need to use the Add/Remove Programs tool in the Control Panel. When you open the Add/Remove Programs utility, just click on the Startup Disk tab and run the wizard. The file on this disk that is used to boot

APPLY YOUR KNOWLEDGE

the system is WIN.COM. For more information, see the section "Creating a Windows 95 Emergency Start Disk."

7. **A**. The Windows 9x startup sequence can be summarized as follows:

1. POST tests.

2. PnP configuration.

3. OS bootstrap looks for member.

4. System loads IO.SYS.

5. IO.SYS loads and executes CONFIG.SYS (if present).

6. IO.SYS loads MSDOS.SYS.

7. IO.SYS loads and executes COMMAND.COM.

8. COMMAND.COM looks for and executes AUTOEXEC.BAT (if present).

9. IO.SYS loads WIN.COM (the Starting Windows notice is displayed).

10. The KERNEL32.DLL and KERNEL386.EXE files are executed.

11. The GDI.EXE and GDI32.EXE files are executed.

12. The USER.EXE and USER32.EXE files are executed.

13. All fonts and other associated resources are loaded.

14. The WIN.INI file values are checked.

15. The Windows 9x shell and machine policies are loaded.

16. The Windows desktop components are loaded.

17. Windows 9x checks the Startup folder.

For more information, see the section "Windows 9x Startup."

8. **B**. The Windows 9x Emergency Startup Disk contains several useful utilities including FDISK, FORMAT, SYS, EDIT ATTRIB, REGEDIT, and SCANDISK. For more information, see the section "Creating a Windows 95 Emergency Start Disk."

9. **A, B, C**. The files required to boot to an MS-DOS command prompt are IO.SYS, MSDOS.SYS, and COMMAND.COM. The CONFIG.SYS and AUTOEXEC.BAT files are helpful in configuring a bootup, but are not required in order to boot to a command prompt. For more information, see the section "MS-DOS Bootup."

10. **D**. The Windows 98 Emergency Start disk features a new Extract command (EXT.EXE) to work with EXTRACT.EXE. The Extract command is used to pull necessary files from the cabinet (.CAB) files on the Windows 98 distribution CD. For more information, see the section "The Windows 98 Emergency Start Disk."

11. **C**. If the Normal option is selected, the system tries to restart as it would normally, loading all of its normal startup and Registry files. The Logged option also attempts to start the system in normal mode, but keeps an error log file that contains the steps performed and outcome. This text file (BOOTLOG.TXT) can be read with any text editor or printed out on a working system. For more information, see the section "Alternate Windows 9x Startup Modes."

APPLY YOUR KNOWLEDGE

12. **C**. In Safe mode, the minimal device drivers (keyboard, mouse, and standard-mode VGA drivers) are active to start the system. However, the CD-ROM drive will not be active in Safe mode. For more information, see the section "Safe Mode."

13. **D**. The Startup Menu allows you to access all the standard Safe modes and others (including Normal, Logged, and standard Command Prompt Only modes), which can be accessed by pressing F8. For more information, see the section "Alternative Windows 9x Startup Modes."

14. **A**. Standard Safe Mode can be accessed by pressing F5 when the "Starting Windows 9x" message is displayed on the screen. For more information, see the section "Safe Mode."

15. **D**. The Windows NT/2000 boot sequence includes NTLDR, BOOT.INI, NTDETECT.COM, NTOSKRNL.EXE, and HAL.DLL. For more information, see the section "Windows NT Startup."

16. **B**. The Windows NT paging file (PAGEFILE.SYS) is used to hold RAM memory swap pages. For more information, see the section "Windows NT Startup."

17. **C**. To create Setup disks under Windows NT 4.0, you must install the Windows NT distribution CD in the system and type **WINNT /ox** at the command prompt. For more information, see the section "Windows NT/2000 Setup Disks."

18. **A**. You can create a Windows NT ERD using the Repair Disk program (RDISK.EXE). To do so, select the Run option from the Start menu, enter the **CMD** command in the Run dialog box, and then type **RDISK** at the command prompt. For more information, see the section "Windows NT 4.0 ERD."

19. **A, C**. The Windows 2000 Setup routine prompts you to create an ERD during the Installation process. The ERD can also be created using the Windows 2000 Backup utility located under the Programs/Accessories/System tools path. For more information, see the section "Windows 2000 ERD."

20. **D**. The old Last Known Good Hardware Configuration settings are not replaced until a user actually logs on to the system. For more information, see the section "Alternative Windows NT Startup Modes."

21. **B**. You can use a question mark as a switch with the WIN command (that is, WIN /?) to show a listing of all the switches associated with the command. You can use these switches to start Windows with various portions of the operating system disabled. For more information, see the section "WIN Switches."

22. **B**. If the Windows NT system employs a SCSI disk drive, a driver file named NTBOOTDD.SYS will need to be present in the root directory of the system partition. This condition must also be noted in the BOOT.INI file by placing a mark in its SCSI(x) or Multi(x) locations. The NTLDR program can also load driver files that have been renamed as NTBOOTDD.SYS to enable Windows NT 4.0 and Windows 2000 to use drives greater than 8GB in size (even EIDE drives). For more information, see the section "Windows NT Startup."

23. **C**. The Windows NT/2000 boot sequence includes the files NTLDR, BOOT.INI, NTDETECT.COM, NTOSKRNL.EXE, and HAL.DLL. For more information, see the section "Windows NT Startup."

24. **C.** You might want to include copies of any CD-ROM driver files on the Emergency Start disk. The CD-ROM driver (that is, MSCDEX.EXE) should be included to provide CD-ROM support for access to the utilities on the Windows distribution CD. For more information, see the section "Creating a Windows 95 Emergency Start Disk."

25. **C.** Files for the repair and update of the Windows 9x operating system can be extracted from the cabinet (.CAB) archive files on the Windows 98 distribution CD. For more information, see the section "The Windows 98 Emergency Start Disk."

Challenge Solutions

1. There are two possible ways to start Windows 9x if it hangs up before reaching the desktop display. The first is to press the F8 key to access the Startup menu so that Safe mode or another startup method can be selected. The second method is to start the system with a boot disk and use the WIN/D command to start Windows. Either of these options should permit you to begin troubleshooting the Windows environment. For more information, see the section "WIN Switches."

2. You must load the MSCDEX.EXE driver for the CD-ROM drive in to the system. This will enable the CD-ROM to operate under Safe mode. (Remember that in Safe mode, only the keyboard, video display, and mouse drivers are loaded into the system.) For more information, see the section "The Windows 98 Emergency Start Disk."

3. You must install the Windows 98 Emergency Startup disk and extract the SCANDISK.EXE file from the .cab file using (edb.cab) the Extract command. For more information, see the section "The Windows 98 Emergency Start Disk."

4. You should tell him to select the Run option from the desktop's Start menu, enter the CMD command in the Run dialog box, and then type **rdisk** at the command prompt. For more information, see the section "Windows NT 4.0 ERD."

APPLY YOUR KNOWLEDGE

Suggested Readings and Resources

1. POST
   http://www.yale.edu/pclt/BOOT/POST.HTM

2. Plug-and-Play
   http://www.pcmech.com/show/cards/143/

3. Plug-and-Play Guide
   www.pcguide.com/ref/mbsys/res/pnp.htm

4. DOS Bootup
   http://www.pccomputernotes.com/
   operating_systems/dosboot.htm

5. DOS System Files
   http://pclt.cis.yale.edu/pclt/BOOT/DOS.HTM

6. Windows 95 Startup
   http://support.microsoft.com/directory/
   article.asp?ID=KB;EN-
   US;Q174018&FR=1&LNG=ENG&SA=PER&

7. Windows 98 Startup
   http://www.geocities.com/~budallen/98start
   .html

8. Kernel32.dll
   http://webopedia.internet.com/TERM/k/
   kernel32_dll.html

9. Windows 9x Safe Mode
   http://service4.symantec.com/SUPPORT/
   tsgeninfo.nsf/docid/1999101916343139

10. Windows 95/98 Win.com Command-Line
    Switches
    http://support.microsoft.com/
    default.aspx?scid=kb;EN-US;q142544

11. Windows 2000 Startup
    http://www.microsoft.com/windows2000/
    techinfo/reskit/en/ProRK/prbd_std_nfkh.htm

12. Windows 9x Emergency Start Disk
    http://www.pcworld.com/howto/article/
    0,aid,44202,00.asp

13. Windows NT/2000 Emergency Repair Disk
    (ERD)
    http://is-it-
    true.org/nt/nt2000/atips/atips32.shtml

This chapter helps you to prepare for the Operating System Technologies module of the A+ Certification examination by covering the following objective within the "Domain 2.0: Installation, Configuration, and Upgrading" section.

2.4 Identify procedures for loading/adding and configuring application device drivers, and the necessary software for certain devices.

Content might include the following:

- **Windows 9x Plug-and-Play and Windows 2000**

- **Identify the procedures for installing and launching typical Windows and non-Windows applications. (Note: There is no content related to Windows 3.1.)**

- **Procedures for setup and configuration of the Windows printing subsystem:**

  - **Setting Default printer**

  - **Installing/Spool setting**

  - **Network printing (with help of LAN admin)**

▶ The flexibility of the PC system has always rested on the capability to add third-party items to the system as desired. The operating system handles these additions through software device drivers. Therefore, the technician must be able to install and configure device drivers for the operating system being used.

▶ Printers are the second most used output devices for the PC. As with other software and hardware components, users add and change these items often. Therefore, the technician must be able to add new printers to the system and make them functional. This includes setting up their parameters in the operating system.

CHAPTER 25

Working with Devices, Applications, and Printers

▶ As with operating system versions and printers, users add and update application software packages frequently. The technician must be able to install these packages, both Windows and DOS based, and be able to bring them to a fully functional level.

To prepare for the Installation, Configuration, and Upgrading objective of the Operating Systems Technologies exam,

▶ Read the objectives at the beginning of this chapter.

▶ Study the information in this chapter.

▶ Review the objectives listed earlier in this chapter.

▶ Perform any step-by-step procedures in the text.

▶ Answer the review questions at the end of the chapter and check your results.

▶ Use the PrepLogic test engine on the CD-ROM that accompanies this book for additional review and exam questions concerning this material.

▶ Review the exam tips scattered throughout the chapter and make certain that you are comfortable with each point.

INTRODUCTION

In the PC environment, peripherals that we add to the basic system require a unique software program called a driver to interface the physical device to the system and its operating system.

The chapter initially presents procedures for loading/adding device drivers for typical hardware devices in Windows 9x and Windows 2000 systems. The information in this sections deals with the Plug-and-Play capabilities of the Windows 9x and Windows 2000 operating systems. However, it also deals with their hardware installation wizards that are employed when the system cannot identify or configure devices.

Most applications written for Windows 9x or Windows NT/2000 contain built-in utilities that will normally install the application with minimal user intervention. The chapter discussion switches over to describe procedures for installing and running Windows and non-Windows applications in both Windows 9x and Windows 2000 systems.

The final section of the chapter describes procedures for installing printers in the Windows 9x and Windows 2000 environments. It also includes information about conducting network printing across a local area network with the help of the network administrator.

After completing the chapter, you should be able to load drivers for the three major operating systems. You should also be able to identify procedures for installing and launching typical Windows and non-Windows applications. In addition, you should be able to execute procedures for setting up and configuring the Windows printing subsystems.

LOADING AND ADDING DEVICE DRIVERS

One of the reasons for the success of the PC-compatible system is its open architecture and its versatility. This versatility is the result of an architecture that permits all types of devices to be added to it. In the PC world, this is accomplished through the use of software device drivers that interface diverse equipment to the basic system. Although the process for installing equipment and their drivers in a PC has become increasingly easy, the technician must still be able to install whatever drivers are necessary.

Windows 9x Device Drivers

The PnP-compliant design of Windows 9x makes installing most new hardware nearly automatic (as long as the new device is also PnP compatible). The PnP function will automatically detect new PnP-compliant hardware when it is started. If the device is not PnP compliant, or the system just can't detect it for some reason, it will be necessary to use the *Windows 9x Add New Hardware Wizard*.

The Hardware Wizard is a series of screens that will guide the installation process for the new device. The new card or device should already be installed in the system before running this procedure. The Add New Hardware icon can be found under the Control Panel option of the Settings menu. It can also be accessed through the Hardware tab of the System Properties window.

If the Wizard does not detect the hardware, the user can attempt to locate the device in the Wizard's list of supported devices. The only other option for installing hardware devices is to obtain an *OEM disk* or CD for the device that has Windows 9x drivers. If the driver disc does not have an *AutoStart function*, it will be necessary to click the Have Disk button and supply the file's location to complete the installation process.

Windows NT/2000 Device Drivers

As mentioned earlier, Windows NT does not support as many hardware devices as the Windows 9x platforms do. However, Windows NT still offers support for a fairly wide range of disk drive types, VGA video cards, network interface cards, tape drives, and printers. To determine what devices Windows NT or Windows 2000 supports, it is necessary to consult the *Hardware Compatibility List* for the version of Windows NT/2000 being used.

EXAM TIP

Know where the Add New Hardware applet is located in the Windows 9x and Windows 2000 environments.

EXAM TIP

Be aware of your options for installing drivers not directly supported by the Windows 9x operating system.

NOTE

Hands-On Activity For hands-on experience with this concept, refer to Lab Procedure #25, "Windows Me Video Drivers," located on the CD that accompanies this book.

NOTE

Hardware Compatibility List   The Hardware Compatibility List information for the version of Windows NT/2000 being used can be obtained from the Microsoft Web site (www.microsoft.com/st/hcl).

EXAM TIP

Know where to begin looking for Windows NT/2000 device drivers not supplied directly from Microsoft.

NOTE

Hands-On Activity   For hands-on experience with this concept, refer to Lab Procedure #41, "Windows Me Software Version Update Management," located on the CD that accompanies this book.

If drivers for the device being installed are not listed at this location, there is a good chance the device will not operate or will not operate well in the Windows NT environment. If this is the case, the only recourse is to contact the device's manufacturer for *Windows NT drivers*. It is a good idea to check the manufacturer's Web site for updated drivers that can simply be downloaded.

CHALLENGE #1

You are working in a music production facility that uses high-end MIDI devices (high end professional sound cards and devices) to generate and manipulate musical instruments and sounds. You want to upgrade your production computers, but you worry that these specialized sound cards will not be compatible with the Windows 2000 Professional operating system. The cards and devices are working under Windows 98 and they tend to be somewhat expensive compared to other computer devices. How can you determine whether this is a good thing to do?

Windows NT 4.0 does not possess Plug-and-Play capabilities, although it does feature some autodetection capabilities. It also has no Add New Hardware Wizard. Devices must be installed manually under Windows NT 4.0—either through the icons in the Control Panel or through installation routines provided by the equipment manufacturer.

Windows 2000 supports a wide array of newer hardware devices. These devices include DVD, USB, and IEEE 1394 devices. Microsoft works with hardware vendors to certify their drivers. These drivers are digitally signed so that they can be loaded automatically by the system.

Adding new devices to Windows 2000 is accomplished through the Add New Hardware icon located in the Control Panel. Figure 25.1 depicts the Windows 2000 Control Panel icons. As with Windows 9*x* systems, the Windows 2000 Control Panel is used to add or remove new hardware and software components to the system, modify device settings, and modify desktop items.

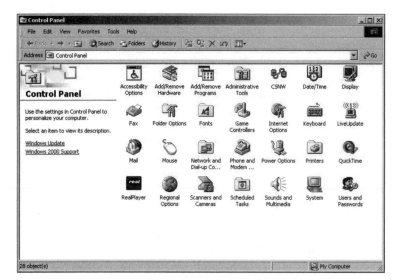

FIGURE 25.1
Windows 2000 Control Panel icons.

Double-clicking on a device icon in the Control Panel will produce a Properties dialog box for that device. The dialog box holds configuration information specific to that device. The tabs located along the tops of the dialog boxes can be used to review and change settings and drivers for the device.

> **NOTE**
>
> **Hands-On Activity**   For hands-on experience with this concept, refer to Lab Procedure #19, "Windows 2000 Plug-and-Play," located on the CD that accompanies this book.

WORKING WITH APPLICATIONS

Another factor that makes PC-compatible systems so widely accepted is the fact that so many software applications are available for them. Because these applications are, for the most part, not installed by the computer maker, technicians must be able to successfully install application software and configure it according to the customer's specifications.

Windows Applications

Like the Hardware Wizard, Windows offers the user assistance in installing new programs. The *Add/Remove Programs icon* under the Control Panel is used to install new programs automatically.

The main page of the Add/Remove window is the Install/Uninstall tab, which is used to add and remove the desired software package.

The upper half of the page contains the Install button that is clicked to start the software installation process.

EXAM TIP

Be aware of the best response to the possibility of deleting shared files in a Windows system.

Some Windows 9x applications might share support files (such as .DLLs) with other applications. In these instances, the Uninstall utility will produce a dialog box asking about deleting the shared files. The best response is to keep the file to avoid disabling the other application. If the files are to be deleted, a backup should be made before running the *Uninstall utility* so that the files can be replaced if needed.

Windows Setup

The Windows 9x Setup tab, depicted in Figure 25.2, is also located under the Control Panel's Add/Remove Programs icon. This utility permits different Windows 9x components to be added to or removed from the system. Windows Configuration settings can be changed through its dialog boxes. The window in the center of the Setup page provides a list of the standard Windows 9x groups, along with their total sizes.

FIGURE 25.2
The Windows 9x Setup page.

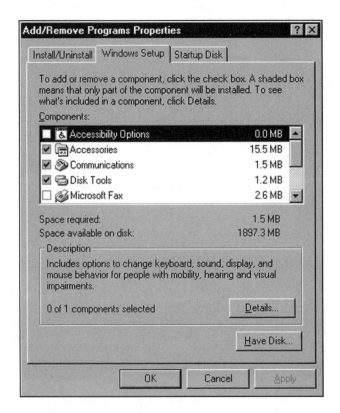

Most software manufacturers include a proprietary setup program for their Windows 9x applications. These programs normally run directly from the CD-ROM when they are inserted into the drive for the first time (unless the AutoPlay function is disabled).

For applications that don't feature the automatic installation function, or if the AutoPlay function is disabled, the software must be installed manually. This is accomplished through the Have Disk button. Clicking this button will produce a dialog box asking for the name and location of the application's installation file. Most software suppliers will provide a SETUP.EXE or INSTALL.EXE file to handle the actual installation and configuration process for their software.

One of the optional groups that you might typically leave out is the *Accessibility options*. This group contains programs that modify the operations of the Windows keyboard—audio and video output for use by those who have physical conditions that inhibit their use of the computer. If you require visual warning messages for hearing disabilities or special color controls for visual difficulties, install this component and select the options that you need access to. When the Accessibility options are installed, the icon appears in the Control Panel, and when they're removed, it disappears. This option uses 4.6MB of disk space when it is installed.

CHALLENGE #2

Your company has just hired a new person for the accounting department. The new person is hearing impaired and needs the computer to display visual warnings and messages to replace the audible signals normally provided by the computer. The computer in the accounting department is running Windows 98. What must you do to establish these settings for the new employee?

Launching Windows Applications

In the command-line environment, starting or launching an application is a simple matter of typing the name of its executable file at the command prompt of the directory that it was installed in. However, in the Windows environment, starting an application is as

EXAM TIP
Know where to set up an application that does not feature automated installation utilities.

NOTE
Hands-On Activity For hands-on experience with this concept, refer to Lab Procedure #35, "Windows Me Accessories," located on the CD that accompanies this book.

EXAM TIP
Know where to access options that can be selected to enable users with physical challenges to use the computer.

NOTE
Hands-On Activity For hands-on experience with this concept, refer to Lab Procedure #24, "Windows 2000 Accessories," located on the CD that accompanies this book.

simple as double-clicking on its icon, or selecting it from the pop-up Start/Programs menu.

Actually, there are several acceptable methods of launching an application in the Windows environment. These include

◆ From the Start menu, select the Programs option, click on the folder where the desired application is, and double-click its filename.

◆ From the Start menu, select the Run entry, and then enter the full path and filename for the desired executable file.

◆ Double-click the application's filename in Windows Explorer or in My Computer.

◆ In My Computer or Windows Explorer, select the desired application file and then click the File menu option from the Menu Bar. From the pop-up menu, select the Open option. (You can also right-click on the application and choose Open.)

◆ Create a shortcut icon on the desktop for the application so that it can be started directly from the desktop by simply double-clicking its icon.

EXAM TIP

Be aware of the various methods of launching an application in the Windows environment.

DOS and Windows 9*x*

DOS-based applications are installed in Windows 9*x* by simply running their executable file from the Run dialog box or from the Windows 9*x* Explorer. If the file has never been run under Windows 9*x*, the operating system creates a default entry in its *APPS.INF* file for that program. A copy of the new entry is also used to create a *Program Information File* (*PIF*) for the application. A PIF file is a file created to serve as a bridge between a DOS-based application and the Windows environment in older versions of Windows. These files contain information about how much memory the application requires and which system resources it needs.

Nearly every DOS-based program should run successfully in Windows 9*x*. Even DOS programs that require access to all the system's resources can run successfully in the Windows 9*x* MS-DOS mode. In this mode, basically all but a small portion of Windows exits from memory. When the application is terminated, Windows restarts and returns to the desktop screen.

MS-DOS mode is established for the application by configuring its properties in the Advanced dialog box under the My Computer/application name/Properties/Program tab. This tab only exists for MS-DOS specific files. To enter MS-DOS mode, select the Shut Down option in the Start menu, and then click the Restart in MS-DOS mode option.

When Windows is restarted in MS-DOS mode, a batch file named *DOSSTART.BAT* runs automatically. It is used to load real-mode DOS drivers for devices such as mice, sound cards, or joysticks. You will find it located in the \Windows directory, provided that you have installed software that requires real-mode DOS drivers. If not, the file might be absent from the directory. As time passes, there are fewer applications remaining that require a real-mode DOS environment. Therefore, most computers will never have their DOSSTART.BAT programs activated.

If a DOS application takes up the entire screen in Windows 9*x*, it will be necessary to press the Alt+Enter key combination to switch the application into a window. The Alt+Tab key combination switches the screen to another application. Some applications might grab the entire screen and cover the Toolbar and Start menu button when maximized. When this occurs, it will be necessary to resize the application's window through the Screen tab to access the Toolbar. You can press the Ctrl+Esc keys at any time to access the Windows 9*x* Start menu.

EXAM TIP	Be aware of the DOSSTART.BAT file's function.

EXAM TIP	Know the consequences of running DOS utilities from a Windows environment and how to solve problems associated with DOS applications running in the Windows environment.

CHALLENGE #3

Your boss has started up an old MS-DOS game program, and it has taken over his entire screen. He does not know how to regain control of his system to get out of the game and get back to the Windows 9*x* GUI that he is familiar with. He has called you for advice about getting back to his desktop. What should you tell him to do?

In some cases, MS-DOS and Windows 3.*x* applications will not run well under Windows 9*x* platforms. This is usually due to the application being written specifically to run under these older operating systems. In Windows 98, Microsoft included a *Make Compatible*

EXAM TIP

Know how to bring applications written specifically for older Microsoft operating systems into compatibility with Windows 9*x*.

utility that can be used to establish compatibility between the application and the operating system. This utility can be executed from the Start/Run path by typing `mkcompat.exe` in the Run dialog box.

Windows NT 4.0 Applications

The Windows NT environment employs an Add/Remove Programs Wizard to assist users in installing new applications. The Windows NT Add/Remove Programs icon is located in the main Control Panel. Double-clicking on this icon produces the Add/Remove Programs dialog box. Any application that employs a Setup.exe or Install.exe installation routine can be installed through this window. Clicking the Install button will cause the system to request the location of the installation program.

In addition to third-party applications, the Add/Remove Programs Wizard can be used to install or remove optional components of the Windows NT operating system. Clicking on the Windows NT Setup tab under the Properties box produces a list of Windows NT components that can be selected for inclusion or removal from the Windows NT system.

Windows 2000 Application Installer

EXAM TIP

Be aware that applications might install DLL files that can damage the operation of other applications that use the same DLL file.

Windows 2000 features a new, more versatile MSI applications installer called the *Windows 2000 Application Installer*. This program is designed to better handle DLL files in the Windows 2000 environment. In previous versions of Windows, applications would copy similar versions of shared DLL files, and other support files, into the \Windows folder. When a new application overwrites a particular DLL file that another application requires for proper operation, a problem is likely to occur with the original software package.

The Windows 2000 Application Installer enables applications to check the system before introducing new DLLs to the system. Software designers who want their products to carry the Windows 2000 logo must write code that does not place proprietary support files in the \Windows directory—including DLL files. Instead, the DLL files are located in the application's folder.

Windows Installer–compatible applications can repair themselves if they become corrupted. When the application is started, the operating system checks the properties of its key files. If a key file is missing or appears to be damaged, it will invoke the Installer and prompt the user to insert the application distribution CD. When the CD has been inserted, the Installer automatically reinstalls the file in question.

Windows 9*x* and Windows NT

Microsoft did not intend for the Windows NT and Windows 9*x* systems to be compatible with each other. There is no direct pathway between the two and no direct upgrade path from Windows 9*x* to Windows NT. Because both rely on Registry structures and because those structures are incompatible with each other, there is no way to bring them together. For this reason, Microsoft does not recommend or support a dual-booting operation of the two operating systems. However, the Windows 2000 design does provide a path for upgrading from Windows 9*x* platforms.

DOS and Windows NT

Like Windows 9*x*, Windows NT and Windows 2000 provide a Command Prompt window. However, unlike Windows 9*x*, when this feature is engaged in Windows NT or Windows 2000, no separate DOS version is being accessed. Windows NT simply provides a DOS-like interface that enables users to perform some MS-DOS functions. There is no MS-DOS icon in the Windows NT system. To access the DOS emulator, select the Run option from the Start menu and type the command CMD or COMMAND into the dialog box and press the OK button. COMMAND is an older Windows 9*x* version of the utility that is not fully compatible with Windows NT/2000.

> **EXAM TIP**
> Know how to access the command prompt environment in Windows NT and Windows 2000.

PRINTING IN WINDOWS

A portion of the A+ Operating System Technologies objective 2.4 states that the test taker should be able to identify the procedures for changing options, configuring, and using the Windows printing

EXAM TIP

Know where to access the Print Manager in both Windows 9x and Windows NT/2000.

subsystem. The Windows environment supplies the printing function for all its applications.

Printing from nearly any Windows package is as simple as choosing the Print option from the application's File menu. All printing activities in both Windows 9x and in Windows 2000 are controlled through the Windows Print Manager. In both Windows versions, the Print Manager can be found in the My Computer folder, or it can be accessed through the Start/Settings path. Another path to the Print Manager exists in the Control Panel.

Printing in Windows 9x

In Windows 9x, the *Print Manager* function and its support components have been integrated into a single print–processing architecture, referred to as the *print spooler*. This integration provides smooth printing in a background mode and quick return-to-application time. The key to this operation is in how the print spooler sends data to the printer—data is only moved to the printer when it is ready. Therefore, the system is never waiting for the printer to digest data that has been sent to it.

EXAM TIP

Be aware of the various methods of printing documents in Windows 9x.

To print an open file in Windows 9x, simply move to the application's File menu and click on the Print option. If the file is not open, it is still possible to print files in Windows 9x. Under the My Computer icon, right-clicking on a selected file will produce a Print option in a pop-up menu. Files can be printed using the same right-click menu method from the Windows Explorer screen. Documents can also be dragged and dropped on to a printer icon in the Printers folder, in the Network Neighborhood listing, or on the desktop. Obviously, this option can be performed with both local and remote networked printers.

The settings for any printer can be changed through the My Computer icon on the desktop or through the Printers option under the Start menu's Settings entry. The process is the same for both routes—simply double-click on the Printer folder, right-click on the desired printer, and select its Properties entry from the pop-up menu.

EXAM TIP

Know where and how to change the settings for a printer under the Windows 9x operating system.

To view documents waiting to be printed from the print spooler, double-click on the desired printer's icon in the Printer folder. This will display the existing print queue, as illustrated in Figure 25.3.

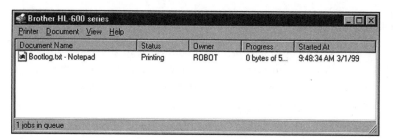

FIGURE 25.3
Windows 9x Print Queue display.

Unlike earlier Windows Print Managers, closing the Print window does not interrupt the *print queue* in Windows 9x. The fact that the *print spooler service* runs in its own 32-bit virtual environment means that printer hang-ups will not lock up the system. The print jobs in the queue will be completed unless they are deleted from the list.

> **EXAM TIP**
>
> Know the value that the Print Spooler provides for printing operations in Windows 9x.

CHALLENGE #4

You have sent a document to your local printer for printing when you notice that you have not included some key information that needed to be in the document. Nothing has come out of the printer, so you check the Windows 9x Printer queue in an attempt to delete the document before it prints. However, nothing is there. What can you do to get the document back?

Installing Printers in Windows 9x

Windows 9x automatically adopts any printers that have been established prior to its installation. If no printers are already installed, the Setup program will automatically run the *Add Printer Wizard* to permit a printer to be installed. Each printer in the system has its own print window and icon to work from. The Wizard can be accessed at any time through the Windows 9x My Computer icon or Start menu. From the Start menu, move to the Settings entry and click on the Printers option. Likewise, through the My Computer icon, or the Control Panel window, double-click on the Printers folder or icon.

To install a printer in Windows 9x, open the Printers folder and double-click the Add Printers icon. From this point, the Printer Wizard guides the installation process. Because Windows 9x has

EXAM TIP

Know the identifying feature of a print server.

EXAM TIP

Memorize the procedures that can be used for installing a network printer in Windows 9x.

EXAM TIP

Know how to install printer drivers in Windows 9x if the particular device is not listed in the standard Windows driver listings.

NOTE — **Hands-On Activity**   For hands-on experience with this concept, refer to Lab Procedure #20, "Windows Me Printers," located on the CD that accompanies this book.

built-in networking support, the printer can be a local unit (connected to the computer) or a remote unit located somewhere on the network. If the physical printer is connected to a remote computer, referred to as a *print server*, the remote unit must supply the printer drivers and settings to control the printer. Likewise, the print server must be set up to share the printer with the other users on the network.

To install the network printer, access the Network Neighborhood icon on the desktop, select the remote computer's network name and the remote unit's printer name, and right-click on the Install option. After the remote printer has been installed, the local computer can access it through the Network Neighborhood icon.

If the printer is not recognized as a model supported by the Windows 9x driver list, OEM drivers can be installed from a device manufacturer's installation disk, which contains the *OEMSETUP.INF* file. After locating the appropriate INF file, simply right-click on the file and select the Install option from the context-sensitive menu.

Printing in Windows 2000

The methods used to print a document in Windows 2000 are identical to those used under Windows 9x. Likewise, the Windows 2000 operating system employs a print spooler processing architecture similar to that found in Windows 9x. This structure provides smooth printing in a background mode and quick return-to-application time. The Windows 2000 print spooler is actually a series of 32-bit virtual device drivers and DLLs that process threads in the background and pass them to the printer when it is ready (that is, the application prints to the Windows printer driver, the driver controls the operation of the spooler, and the driver prints to the printer from the spooler).

In a network printing operation, the print spooler must run on both the local server and the remote client systems. The user can start and stop the local print spooler process through the Control Panel's Services icon. If the spooler service is stopped by the user, it must be restarted before printing can occur again—unless the printer driver has been configured to bypass the spooler. Also, the local user is not capable of controlling the print operation to a server. The server print function is managed independently.

The Windows 2000 Printers dialog box enables users to sort between different printers based on their attributes. Windows 2000 Professional possesses the capability of printing across the Internet using the new standards-based *Internet Printing Protocol (IPP)*. Using this protocol, Windows 2000 Professional can print to a URL, view the print queue status using an Internet browser, and install print drivers across the Internet.

Establishing Printers in Windows 2000

Like Windows 9*x*, Windows 2000 will automatically adopt any printers that have been established prior to its installation in the system. If no printers have been installed, the Setup routine will run its Add Printer Wizard to permit a printer to be installed. The Wizard can be accessed at any time through the My Computer icon or through the Start Menu. To install a printer from the Start menu, navigate the Start/ Settings/Printers path and open the Printers folder. Then, double-click the Add Printer icon. From this point, the Printer Wizard will guide the installation process.

To install local printers, choose the My Computer selection and click the Next button. Normally, the LPT1 options should be selected from the list of port options. Next, the Add Printer Wizard will produce a list of manufacturers and models to choose from. Simply select the correct manufacturer and the desired model from the list and inform the Wizard about the location of the \I386 directory to fetch the driver from. If the \I386 directory has been copied to the hard drive, it will be faster to access the driver there. If not, the Windows NT distribution CD will be required.

As with Windows 9*x*, if the printer is not recognized as a model supported by the Windows NT/2000 driver list, OEM drivers can be installed from a disk containing the OEMSETUP.INF file. Select the Have Disk option from the Add Printer Wizard screen.

NOTE   **Hands-On Activity**   For hands-on experience with this concept, refer to Lab Procedure #21, "Windows 2000 Printers," located on the CD that accompanies this book.

CHAPTER SUMMARY

KEY TERMS

- Accessibility options
- Add Printer Wizard
- Add/Remove Programs icon
- APPS.INF
- AutoStart function
- CMD
- DOSSTART.BAT
- Hardware Compatibility List
- Make Compatible utility
- Mkcompat.exe
- OEM disk
- OEMSETUP.INF
- Print Manager
- Print queue
- Print server
- Print spooler service
- Program Information File (PIF)
- Uninstall utility
- Windows 2000 Application Installer
- Windows 9x Add New Hardware Wizard
- Windows NT drivers

This chapter began with a discussion of procedures for loading/adding device drivers for Windows 9x and Windows 2000 systems. Although the Windows operating systems' PnP process can detect and automatically install a large number of different hardware devices, technicians must still know how to install devices that the system cannot identify or configure.

The next section of the chapter presented procedures for installing and running Windows and non-Windows applications in both Windows 9x and Windows 2000 systems.

The final section of the chapter identified procedures for installing printers in the Windows 9x and Windows 2000 environments. It also dealt with changing options, configuring, and using the Windows 9x and Windows 2000 printing subsystems.

At this point, review the objectives listed at the beginning of the chapter to be certain that you understand each point and can perform each task listed there. Afterward, answer the review questions that follow to verify your knowledge of the information.

Review Questions

1. How do you activate the Add New Hardware applet located in the Windows 9x and Windows 2000 environments? (Select all that apply.)

   A. Start/Programs/Accessories/System Tools and then select Add New Hardware

   B. Start/Settings/Control Panel and then open Add New Hardware

   C. Right-click on My Computer, select Properties from the contextual menu, click on the Hardware tab, and then click the Hardware Wizard button

   D. Start/Settings/Control Panel, click on the Hardware tab, and then click the Hardware Wizard button

2. What are your options for installing drivers not directly supported by the Windows 9x operating system? (Select all that apply.)

   A. Use a driver from a similar model from the same manufacturer in the Add New Hardware Wizard's list of supported devices.

   B. Attempt to locate the specific device in the Add New Hardware Wizard's list of supported devices.

   C. Obtain an OEM installation disk or CD for the device that has the Windows 9x drivers.

   D. Devices not directly supported by Windows cannot be installed.

3. Where are device drivers not supplied directly from Microsoft usually located?

   A. On the device manufacturer's Web site

   B. On the Windows OS installation CD

   C. At `http://www.microsoft.com/downloads/search.asp`

   D. At `http://www.windrivers.com/`

4. When uninstalling an application, what is the best response to the possibility of deleting shared files?

   A. Remove all files

   B. Remove the file

   C. Keep all files

   D. Keep the file

5. Where is the tool that allows you to set up an application that does not feature an automated installation utility?

   A. Right-click on the desktop, select Properties from the contextual menu, and then click on the Add-Remove Programs tab

   B. Right-click on My Computer, select Properties from the contextual menu, and then click on the Add-Remove Programs tab

   C. Start/Settings/Control Panel/System, and then click on the Add-Remove Programs tab

   D. Start/Settings/Control Panel, and then open Add-Remove Programs

APPLY YOUR KNOWLEDGE

6. If they are installed, where are options accessed that can enable users with physical challenges to use the computer?

A. Start/Settings/Control Panel/System and then click the Accessibility Options tab

B. Start/Settings/Control Panel and then open the Accessibility Options utility

C. Right-click on My Computer and then click the Accessibility Options tab

D. Right-click on the taskbar, select Properties from the contextual menu, and then click the Accessibility Options tab

7. What are the various methods of launching an application in the Windows environment? (Select all that apply.)

A. Start/Programs, select the application's entry, and then select the shortcut to the executable file

B. Start/Run, enter the full path and filename to the executable file, and then click the OK button

C. Browse to the application's folder in Windows Explorer, and then double-click the application's executable file

D. Browse to the application's folder in Windows Explorer, click on the executable file to highlight it, and then click the Edit menu and select the Open option

8. You are running a DOS program under Windows, and its display has taken up the full screen. What can you do if you want to switch to another application while this one is running?

A. Ctrl+Esc

B. Ctrl+Tab

C. Alt+Tab

D. Alt+Esc

9. What is the most common type of file that might be installed by an application, which will damage the operation of another application that might attempt to use the same file?

A. .DLL

B. .EXE

C. .COM

D. .CAB

10. What is an appropriate command that will access the command prompt environment in Windows NT and Windows 2000?

A. CMD

B. COMMAND

C. GO

D. RUN

11. Where is the Print Manager accessed in Windows 9x? (Select all that apply.)

A. Network Neighborhood

B. My Computer

C. Start/Settings/Control Panel

D. Start/Settings

APPLY YOUR KNOWLEDGE

12. What are the methods of printing documents in Windows 9x? (Select all that apply.)

    A. Right-click the file and choose Print from the contextual menu

    B. Highlight the file, click on the File menu, and select Print

    C. Open the file and select Print from the Edit menu

    D. Drag and drop the file onto the Printer icon

13. Where and how are the settings changed for a printer under the Windows 9x operating system? (Select all that apply.)

    A. Start/Settings/Printers, select the printer, click the File menu, and select Properties

    B. Start/Run/Printers, select the printer, click the Tools menu, and select Properties

    C. My Computer/Printers, right-click on the printer and select Properties from the contextual menu

    D. My Computer/Printers, select the printer, click the File menu, and select Settings

14. Which Windows 9x service loads files to memory for later printing?

    A. Print spooler

    B. Networking

    C. Protected storage

    D. Printer

15. What are the required features of a print server?

    A. Remote network computer, printer services shared over the network

    B. Remote network computer, printer drivers pre-installed, printer settings preconfigured, access controlled by the primary domain controller

    C. Remote network computer, printer drivers pre-installed, printer settings preconfigured, printer services shared over the network, TCP/IP installed

    D. Remote network computer, printer drivers pre-installed, printer settings preconfigured, printer services shared over the network

16. Which procedure can be used for installing a network printer in Windows 9x?

    A. Start/Run, navigate to the remote network printer, highlight it, and click the OK button

    B. Start/Settings/Control Panel/Printers, navigate to the remote network printer; then right-click on it and select Install from the pop-up menu

    C. Start/Settings/Printers, navigate to the remote network printer; then right-click on it and select Install from the pop-up menu

    D. Open Network Neighborhood, navigate to the remote network printer; then right-click on it and select Install from the pop-up menu

17. How are printer drivers installed in Windows 9x if the particular device is not listed in the standard Windows driver listings?

    A. Install a similar driver from this manufacturer that is listed.

    B. Locate the appropriate INF file and double-click the file.

    C. Locate the appropriate INF file and select Install after right-clicking the file.

    D. You cannot install unlisted devices drivers.

APPLY YOUR KNOWLEDGE

18. What is the function of the DOSSTART.BAT file?

    A. Makes DOS commands available under Windows.

    B. Loads real-mode DOS drivers.

    C. Loads virtual mode DOS drivers.

    D. This file serves no function in Windows.

19. You have an employee who is hearing impaired and needs visual warning messages. Where do you set these up?

    A. Start/Settings/Control Panel/System and then click the Accessibility Options tab

    B. Start/Settings/Control Panel/Add Remove Programs and select the Windows Setup option

    C. Right-click on My Computer and then click the Accessibility Options tab

    D. Right-click on the taskbar, select Properties from the contextual menu, and then click the Accessibility Options tab

20. What utility can be used to make older Microsoft applications compatible with the Windows 9x operating system?

    A. mscompat

    B. mkcompat

    C. doscompt

    D. Wincompt

Answers and Explanations

1. **B, C, D**. The Add New Hardware icon can be found under the Control Panel option of the Settings menu. It can also be accessed through the Hardware tab of the System Properties window. For more information, see the section "Windows 9x Device Drivers."

2. **B, C**. If the wizard does not detect the hardware, the user can attempt to locate the device in the wizard's list of supported devices. The only other option for installing hardware devices is to obtain an OEM disk or CD for the device that has Windows 9x drivers. For more information, see the section "Windows 9x Device Drivers."

3. **A**. Contact the device's manufacturer for appropriate Windows drivers. It is a good idea to regularly check the manufacturer's Web site for updated drivers that can simply be downloaded. For more information, see the section "Windows NT/2000 Device Drivers."

4. **C**. The best response is to keep all these files to avoid disabling another application. If the files are to be deleted, a backup should be made before running the Uninstall utility so that the files can be replaced if needed. For more information, see the section "Windows Applications."

5. **D**. The Control Panel's Add/Remove Programs tool permits different Windows 9x components to be added to or removed from the system. For more information, see the section "Windows Setup."

6. **B**. One of the optional groups that you might typically leave out during installation is the Accessibility Options utility. This group contains programs that modify the operations of the Windows keyboard—audio and video output for use by those who have physical conditions that inhibit their use of the computer. When the Accessibility option is installed, its icon appears in the Control Panel and when it is removed, the icon disappears. For more information, see the section "Windows Setup."

7. **A**, **B**, **C**. There are several acceptable methods of launching an application in the Windows environment. These include: From the Start menu, select the Applications entry, click the folder where the desired application is and double-click its filename; From the Start menu, select the Run entry, and then enter the full path and filename for the desired executable file; Double-click the application's filename in Windows Explorer or in My Computer; Click the File menu option from the Menu Bar in My Computer or Windows Explorer, and select the Open option; You can also right-click on the application and choose Open. For more information, see the section "Launching Windows Applications."

8. **C**. If a DOS application takes up the entire screen in Windows 9*x*, it will be necessary to press the Alt+Enter key combination to switch the application into a window. The Alt+Tab key combination switches the screen to another application. For more information, see the section "DOS and Windows 9*x*."

9. **A**. Windows 2000 features a new, more versatile MSI applications installer called the Windows 2000 Application Installer. This program is designed to better handle DLL files in the Windows 2000 environment. In previous versions of Windows, applications would copy similar versions of shared DLL files, and other support files, into the \Windows folder. When a new application overwrites a particular DLL file that another application requires for proper operation, a problem is likely to occur with the original software package. For more information, see the section "Windows 2000 Application Installer."

10. **A**. To access the DOS emulator, select the Run option from the Start menu and type the command **CMD** or **COMMAND** into the dialog box and press the OK button. COMMAND is an older Windows 9*x* version of the utility that is not fully compatible with Windows NT/2000. For more information, see the section "DOS and Windows NT."

11. **B**, **C**, **D**. The Print Manager can be found in My Computer, in the Control Panel, or it can be accessed through the Start/Settings path. For more information, see the section "Printing in Windows."

12. **A**, **B**, **D**. To print an open file in Windows 9*x*, simply move to the application's File menu and click on the Print option. If the file is not open, it is still possible to print files in Windows 9*x*. Under the My Computer icon, right-clicking on a selected file will produce a Print option in a pop-up menu. Files can be printed using the same right-click menu method from the Windows Explorer screen. Documents can also be dragged and dropped onto a printer icon in the Printers folder, in the Network Neighborhood listing, or on the desktop. Obviously, this option can be performed with both local and remote networked printers. For more information, see the section "Printing in Windows 9*x*."

APPLY YOUR KNOWLEDGE

13. **A, C**. The settings for any printer can be changed through the My Computer icon on the desktop or through the Printers option under the Start menu's Settings entry. The process is the same for both routes—simply double-click on the Printer folder, right-click on the desired printer, and select its Properties entry from the pop-up menu. For more information, see the section "Printing in Windows 9*x*."

14. **A**. Unlike earlier Windows Print Managers, closing the Print window does not interrupt the print queue in Windows 9*x*. The fact that the print spooler service runs in its own 32-bit virtual environment means that printer hang-ups will not lock up the system. The print jobs in the queue will be completed unless they are deleted from the list. For more information, see the section "Printing in Windows 9*x*."

15. **D**. Because Windows 9*x* has built-in networking support, the printer can be a local unit (connected to the computer) or a remote unit located somewhere on the network. If the physical printer is connected to a remote computer, referred to as a print server, the remote unit must supply the printer drivers and settings to control the printer. Likewise, the print server must be set up to share the printer with the other users on the network. For more information, see the section "Installing Printers in Windows 9*x*."

16. **D**. To install the network printer, access the Network Neighborhood icon on the desktop, navigate to the remote computer's network name, the remote unit's printer name, and then right-click on the Install option. After the remote printer has been installed, the local computer can access it through the Network Neighborhood icon. For more information, see the section "Installing Printers in Windows 9*x*."

17. **C**. If the printer is not recognized as a model supported by the Windows 9*x* driver list, OEM drivers can be installed from a device manufacturer's installation disk, which contains the OEMSETUP.INF file. After locating the appropriate INF file, just right-click on the file and select Install from the contextual menu. For more information, see the section "Installing Printers in Windows 9*x*."

18. **B**. When Windows is restarted in MS-DOS mode, a batch file named DOSSTART.BAT runs automatically. It is used to load real-mode DOS drivers for devices such as mice, sound cards, or joysticks. You will find it located in the \Windows directory, provided that you have installed software that requires real-mode DOS drivers. If not, the file might be absent from the directory. As time passes, there are fewer applications remaining that require a real-mode DOS environment. Therefore, most computers will never have their DOSSTART.BAT programs activated. For more information, see the section "DOS and Windows 9*x*."

19. **B**. If you require visual warning messages for hearing disabilities or special color controls for visual difficulties, install this component and select the options that you need access to. When the Accessibility option is installed, its icon appears in the Control Panel and when it is removed, the icon disappears. For more information, see the section "Windows Setup."

APPLY YOUR KNOWLEDGE

20. **B**. In some cases, MS-DOS and Windows 3.*x* applications will not run well under Windows 9*x* platforms. This is usually due to the application being written specifically to run under these older operating systems. In Windows 98, Microsoft included a Make Compatible utility that can be used to establish compatibility between the application and the operating system. This utility can be executed from the Start/Run path by typing `mkcompat.exe` in the Run dialog box. For more information, see the section "DOS and Windows 9*x*."

Challenge Solutions

1. Begin by checking for the MIDI devices and cards on the Windows 2000 HCL. This can be accomplished on the Windows 2000 distribution CD or at the Microsoft Web site. If the devices are not listed there, there is a good chance the devices will not operate or will not operate well with Windows 2000. Your only remaining recourse is to contact the device manufacturers for Windows 2000–compatible drivers. Begin by checking the manufacturer's Web sites for updated drivers that can simply be downloaded. Unless there is some other compelling reason to upgrade the operating system, the best choice would be to stick with a system that is working and producing money. For more information, see the section "Windows NT/2000 Device Drivers."

2. The Windows 9*x* Accessibility Options can be accessed through the Setup tab located under the Control Panel's Add/Remove Programs icon. This group contains programs that modify the operations of the Windows keyboard—audio and video output to provide visual warning messages for your employees with hearing disabilities. For more information, see the section "Windows Setup."

3. The game has taken over the system and is running in full screen mode. To get back to the desktop environment, he should press the Alt+Enter key combination to switch the application into a window. If the application has grabbed the entire screen and covered the Toolbar and Start menu button, it will be necessary to resize the application's window through the Screen tab to access the Toolbar. The Start menu can be accessed at any time by pressing the Ctrl+Esc keys. For more information, see the section "DOS and Windows 9*x*."

4. The fact that the document does not appear in the Printer queue indicates that it has already been processed and sent to the printer. In Windows 98, data is only moved to the printer from the print spooler when the printer is ready. Therefore, the system is never waiting for the printer to digest data that has been sent to it. At this point, there is no way to retrieve the document because the operating system cannot reach over into the printer to get it back through the printer interface. For more information, see the section "Printing in Windows 9*x*."

APPLY YOUR KNOWLEDGE

Suggested Readings and Resources

1. Win Drivers
   http://www.windrivers.com/

2. Driver Guide
   http://www.driverguide.com/

3. Drivers HQ
   http://www.drivershq.com/

4. Driver Zone
   http://www.driverzone.com/

5. Windows Applications
   http://www.teckies.com/tutor/win09.html

6. Installing a Network Printer
   http://support.pa.msu.edu/Help/FAQs/
   Windows/Faq-w00001.html

7. Printing in Windows 95
   http://www.winplanet.com/winplanet/
   tutorials/796/1/

8. Printing in Windows NT
   http://www.winplanet.com/winplanet/
   tutorials/811/1/

This chapter helps you to prepare for the Operating System Technologies module of the A+ Certification examination by covering the following objective within the "Domain 3.0: Diagnosing and Troubleshooting" section.

3.1 Recognize and interpret the meaning of common error codes and startup messages from the boot sequence, and identify steps to correct the problem.

Content might include the following:

- **Safe Mode**

- **No operating system found**

- **Error in CONFIG.SYS line XX**

- **Bad or missing COMMAND.COM**

- **HIMEM.SYS not loaded**

- **Missing or corrupt HIMEM.SYS**

- **SCSI**

- **Swap file**

- **NT boot issues**

- **Dr. Watson**

- **Failure to start GUI**

- **Windows Protection Error**

- **Event Viewer; Event log is full**

- **A device referenced in SYSTEM.INI, WIN.INI, or Registry is not found**

▶ Troubleshooting operating system problems involves the same steps as any other logical troubleshooting procedure. The steps are just adapted to fit the structure of the operating system. Analyze the symptoms displayed, isolate the error conditions, correct the problem, and test the repair.

CHAPTER 26

Troubleshooting OS Setup/Startup Problems

▶ Operating system problems can be divided into three basic categories:

- Setup problems (those that occur during installation or upgrading)

- Startup problems (those that occur when the system is booting up)

- Operational problems (those that occur during the normal course of operations)

▶ By isolating a particular software problem to one of these areas, the troubleshooting process becomes less complex.

▶ Setup problems typically involve failure to complete an OS install or upgrade operation. In some cases, this can leave the system stranded between an older OS version and a newer OS version, making the system unusable.

▶ Startup problems usually produce conditions that prevent the system hardware and software from coming up and running correctly. These problems fall into two major groups—Hardware configuration problems and operating system boot-up problems.

▶ Operational problems are problems that occur after the system has booted up and started running. These problems fall into three main categories:

- When performing normal application and file operations

- When printing

- When performing network functions

To prepare for the Diagnosing and Troubleshooting objective of the Operating Systems Technologies exam,

▶ Read the objectives at the beginning of this chapter.

▶ Study the information in this chapter.

▶ Review the objectives listed earlier in this chapter.

▶ Perform any step-by-step procedures in the text.

▶ Answer the review questions at the end of the chapter and check your results.

▶ Use the PrepLogic test engine on the CD-ROM that accompanies this book for additional review and exam questions concerning this material.

▶ Review the exam tips scattered throughout the chapter and make certain that you are comfortable with each point.

INTRODUCTION

This chapter is dedicated to diagnosing and troubleshooting operating system problems. One of the three major types of operating system problems is those that occur when new hardware, applications, or operating systems are added to the system. The first major portion of the chapter deals with troubleshooting setup problems.

The second major section of the chapter examines troubleshooting Windows 9x startup problems. The major topics discussed include Windows 9x boot problems, using Safe mode and other alternative startup modes, using Windows 9x log files, and using the Windows 98 Startup disk.

The final section of the chapter changes to discussions of Windows 2000 startup problems. Information in this section includes Windows 2000 boot problems, Windows 2000 startup tools, and the Windows 2000 Recovery Console.

After completing the chapter, you should be able to relate a given error condition to a portion of the system and suggest proper steps for diagnosing and repairing these problems in both Windows 9x and Windows 2000 systems. You should also be able to apply the correct troubleshooting tools to Windows 9x and Windows 2000 problems.

TROUBLESHOOTING SETUP PROBLEMS

Setup problems are those errors that occur during the process of installing the operating system on the hard disk drive. One of the most common OS setup problems involves situations in which the system's hard drive does not have enough free space to carry out the installation process. When this occurs, you must remove files from the disk until you have cleared enough room to perform the installation.

Setup problems also occur when the system's hardware will not support the operating system that is being installed. These errors can include the following:

◆ Microprocessor requirements

◆ Memory speed mismatches

◆ Insufficient memory problems

◆ Incompatible device drivers

The memory speed mismatch or mixed RAM-type problem might produce a Windows Protection Error message during the installation process. This error indicates that the operating system is having timing problems that originate from the RAM memory used in the system. Correcting this problem involves swapping the system's RAM for devices that meet the system's timing requirements.

It is not uncommon for mouse or video drivers to fail during the installation of an operating system. If the video driver fails, you must normally turn off the system and attempt to reinstall the operating system from scratch. Conversely, if the mouse driver fails during the install, it is possible to continue the process using the keyboard. This problem is normally self-correcting after the system reboots.

A similar problem occurs when the operating system is looking for a PS/2 mouse and the system is using a serial mouse. It will not detect the serial mouse, and you will need to complete the installation process using the keyboard. Afterward, you can check the CMOS Port Settings for the serial port the mouse is connected to and install the correct driver for the serial mouse if necessary.

The best way to avoid hardware-compatibility problems is to consult Microsoft's Web site to see whether the hardware you are using is compatible with the operating system version you are installing.

EXAM TIP
Be aware that RAM speed mismatches can cause OS installation failures.

Windows 9*x* Setup Problems

Windows 9*x* draws from the existing FAT structure when it is being installed. Therefore, an interruption, or a crash, during the installation process might leave the system with no workable operating system in place. If this occurs, you must boot the system from a bootable floppy disk and reinstall Windows 9*x* from that point.

If the system crashes during the hardware detection phase of a Windows 9x install, Microsoft recommends that you simply reboot the system until the installation process is successful. The Windows Setup Wizard will mark startup steps that have failed and bypass them the next time you attempt to install the operating system. The failed steps are recorded in the Setuplog text file.

The Windows 9x installation files are stored on the installation disk in a compressed Cabinet (CAB) file format. Therefore, they cannot just be copied over to the hard drive to repair files damaged in an aborted installation. The best recovery method for this situation is to boot the system to a floppy disk, run FDISK to repartition the drive, format the drive, and run the Windows 9x Setup utility (provided that your data was backed up beforehand).

If programs or hardware options fail to run properly after a system has been upgraded to a Windows 9x operating system, you should determine whether they require specific real-mode drivers to be retained in the CONFIG.SYS and AUTOEXEC.BAT files. Recall that during the Restart phase of the installation process, Windows 9x deactivates files that it perceives as incompatible, or unnecessary, by placing a Remark (REM) statement at the beginning of the line. This might cause different applications or hardware to fail if they require these specific entries for operation. Be aware that restoring the driver can cause other problems within Windows 9x. The best choice is always to contact the software or hardware manufacturer for a Windows 9x driver.

Windows NT/2000 Setup Problems

When an attempt to install Windows NT or Windows 2000 fails, a Stop screen error will normally result. Stop errors occur when Windows NT or Windows 2000 detects a condition from which it cannot recover. The system stops responding, and a screen of information with a blue or black background display, as illustrated in Figure 26.1, appears. Stop errors are also known as Blue Screen errors, or as the *Blue Screen of Death* (*BSOD*).

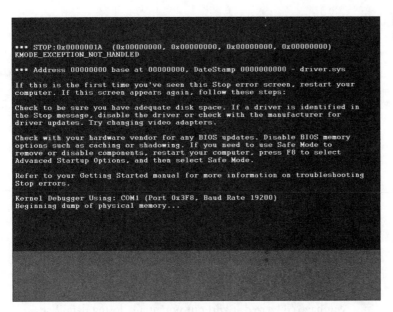

FIGURE 26.1
Stop error or Blue Screen error.

Some other problems can typically occur during the Windows 2000 installation process. These problems include items such as the following:

◆ Noncompliant hardware failures.

◆ Insufficient resources.

◆ File system type choices.

◆ WINNT32.EXE will not run from the command-line errors.

Ways to correct these particular installation-related problems include the following:

◆ Verify Hardware Compatibility—The hardware-compatibility requirements of Windows NT and Windows 2000 are more stringent than those of the Windows 9x platform. When either of these operating systems encounters hardware that is not compatible during the setup phase, they will fail.

   Make certain to check the Hardware Compatibility List to ensure that your hardware is compatible with Windows 2000. If the hardware is not listed, contact the hardware vendor to determine whether they support Windows 2000 before starting the installation.

EXAM TIP

Be aware that you should check the hardware manufacturer's Web sites for updated device drivers before installing Windows 2000.

◆ Verify Minimum System Resource Requirements—Also, make certain that your hardware meets the minimum hardware requirements, including the memory, free disk space, and video requirements. When the Windows NT or Windows 2000 Setup routines detect insufficient resources (that is, processor, memory, or disk space), it either informs you that an error has occurred and halts or it just hangs up and refuses to continue the install.

◆ Establish the File System Type—Decide which file system you are going to use. If you are going to dual boot to Windows 98 and have a drive that is larger than 2GB, you must choose FAT32. Choosing NTFS for a dual boot system renders the NTFS partition unavailable when you boot into Windows 98. FAT16 does not support drives larger than 2GB. You can upgrade from FAT16 to FAT32 or from FAT32 to NTFS. However, you can never revert to the older file system after you have converted it without potentially losing data. You should also be aware that Windows NT does not support FAT32 partitions. Therefore, Windows NT 4.0 or earlier cannot be used on a Windows 9x drive. Consider using the lowest common file system during installation and upgrade later.

◆ WINNT32 will not run from the command prompt—The WINNT32.EXE program is designed to run under a 32-bit operating system and will not run from the command line. It is used to initiate upgrades from Windows 9x or Windows NT to Windows 2000. From a 16-bit operating system, such as MS-DOS or Windows 95a, you must run the WINNT.EXE program from the command line to initiate the installation of Windows 2000.

Upgrade Problems

You will encounter many of the same problems performing an operating system upgrade that you do when performing a clean install. To review, these problems are normally related to the following:

◆ Insufficient hard drive or partition sizes

◆ Memory speed mismatches

◆ Insufficient memory problems

◆ Incompatible device drivers

While performing upgrade operations, you can also encounter problems created by version incompatibilities. New versions of operating systems are typically produced in two styles: *full versions* and *upgrade versions*. Normally, you cannot use a full version of the operating system to upgrade an existing operating system. Doing so will produce an *Incompatible Version* error message telling you that you cannot use this version to upgrade. You must either obtain an upgrade version of the operating system or partition the drive and perform a new installation (losing your existing data).

You must have the appropriate version of the upgrade for the existing operating system. (That is, Windows 98SE comes in two versions—one upgrades both Windows 95 and Windows 98, whereas the other version upgrades only Windows 98.)

In order to determine the current version of a Windows operating system running on a computer, right-click on the My Computer icon, select the properties option from the pop-up menu, and select the General tab of the System Properties page. Another way to get the version of Windows is to open Windows Explorer, click on the Help menu, and select About Windows.

> **EXAM TIP**
> Know how to display the current version of Windows information for a system.

TROUBLESHOOTING STARTUP PROBLEMS

Fortunately, only a few problems can occur during the startup process of a disk-based computer. These problems include the following:

◆ Hardware problems.

◆ Configuration problems.

◆ Bootup (or OS-startup) problems.

◆ Operating system desktop GUI won't load.

> **NOTE**
> **Boot-up Process Single Beep** A key troubleshooting point occurs at the single beep in the boot-up process of most computers. If the system produces an error message or a beep-coded error signal before the beep, the problem is hardware related. On the other hand, if the error message or beep code is produced after the single beep occurs, the problem is likely to be associated with starting up the operating system. At this point, the problem becomes an operating system startup problem.

When dealing with a disk operating system, the following four things can prove very useful to help you isolate the cause of startup problems:

◆ Error messages and beep codes

◆ Single-step startup procedures

◆ Clean boot disks (Emergency Start Disks)

◆ System log files

The following list identifies the preliminary steps involved in troubleshooting startup problems:

1. Try to reboot the system.

2. Check system log files if available to determine where the process was interrupted.

3. Perform a clean boot with minimal configuration settings to remove any nonessential elements from the process.

4. Perform a single-step bootup to isolate any driver problems that are preventing bootup from taking place.

If the system will not boot up correctly, you must try to boot the system to a minimum configuration in order to establish a point to begin troubleshooting the problem from. This startup method enables you to bypass any unnecessary configuration and normally involves using a clean boot disk or the Emergency Start disk to start the system.

If the system boots up from the minimal condition, the problem exists in the bypassed files. Restart the system and select a startup mode that single steps through the configuration and startup file sequence.

The single-step startup procedure enables you to isolate the problem command. If the system crashes while trying to execute a particular command, restart the boot-up process and skip the offending command. Repeat the process until the system reaches bootup. Track all offending commands so that you can correct them individually. Check the *syntax* (spelling, punctuation, and usage) of any offending lines.

When the system will boot to the clean boot disk, but will not boot up to the hard drive and has no configuration or startup file errors, a problem exists in the operating system's boot files. These errors typically return some type of *Bad or Missing Command Interpreter* message, or a *Disk Boot Failure* message. Basically, three conditions produce these types of error messages:

◆ The Master Boot Record or Command interpreter file cannot be found on the hard drive, and no bootable disk is present in the A: drive.

◆ The Master Boot Record or operating system's Command interpreter file is not located in the partition's root directory. This message is likely when installing a new hard drive or a new operating system version.

◆ The user has inadvertently erased the Master Boot Record or operating system Command interpreter file from the hard drive, possibly during the process of establishing a dual-boot disk or when setting up a multiple operating system environment.

The Missing Command Interpreter error can be repaired by restoring the boot record and operating system files to the hard disk. To do so, you normally copy or extract the files from the clean boot disk to the hard drive. In a FAT environment, if the boot disk contains a copy of the FDISK command, you can use the FDISK /MBR command to restore the hard drive's Master Boot Record, along with its partition information. The command SYS:*X* (where *X* is the drive designation) is used to restore the command interpreter.

> **EXAM TIP**
>
> Be aware of the FDISK /MBR command for repairing damaged master boot records, and SYS C: is used to restore missing command interpreters.

Windows 9*x* Startup Problems

Windows 9*x* includes several built-in troubleshooting tools including several Safe-Mode startup options, a trio of system log files, and an extensive interactive troubleshooting Help file system. Windows 9*x* also includes three important tools that can be used when a Windows 9*x* system is having startup problems: the Emergency Start (clean boot) disk, Safe modes, and the step-by-step startup sequence. With Windows 9*x*, the clean boot disk is referred to as an Emergency Start disk. To access the Safe modes and the single-step with confirmation startup process, press the Shift and F8 function

EXAM TIP

Memorize the shortcut keys used to skip startup sections and to single step through the boot-up process.

keys simultaneously when the Starting Windows 9*x* message appears onscreen.

The special function keys available during the Windows 9*x* startup are

- ◆ F5—Safe mode
- ◆ F6—Safe mode with Network Support
- ◆ F8—Step-by-Step Confirmation mode
- ◆ Shift+F5—Safe mode Command Prompt Only

Typical Windows 9x startup error messages include the following:

- ◆ HIMEM.SYS not loaded.
- ◆ Unable to initialize display adapter.
- ◆ Device referenced in WIN.INI could not be found.
- ◆ Bad or missing COMMAND.COM.
- ◆ Swap file corrupt.
- ◆ Damaged or missing core files.
- ◆ Device referenced in SYSTEM.INI could not be found.
- ◆ Correcting Windows 9*x* Startup Problems.

The generic process for isolating the cause of a Windows 9*x* startup problem is as follows:

1. Use the Emergency Start disk to gain access to the system and the hard drive.

2. If necessary, repair the system files and command interpreter files.

3. Attempt to boot up into Safe mode to see whether the problem is driver related.

4. Reboot the system into the step-by-step confirmation startup mode to isolate configuration and driver problems. Continue single stepping through the startup process until all offending steps have been identified and corrected.

5. Review the Windows 9*x* log files for problem steps.

Specific Problem Areas

Each of the specific problem areas suggested in the preceding error messages is discussed in this section.

HIMEM.SYS Problems

In the case of the HIMEM.SYS error, use the System Editor to check the syntax and correctness of the entry in the CONFIG.SYS file if present. With Windows 9x, the HIMEM.SYS statement must be present in the \Windows directory and must be the correct version for the operating system to run. Check the HIMEM.SYS file to make sure that it is the correct version and in the correct location. In the case of a Windows 9x upgrade, as many as three versions of HIMEM.SYS might be present in the system.

> **EXAM TIP**
>
> Know where to go and how to correct HIMEM.SYS errors in MS-DOS and Windows 9x environments.

Initializing the Display Adapter

The Unable to Initialize Display Adapter error message indicates that errors are occurring during the hardware-detection phase of the Windows 9x PnP boot-up routine. These errors normally occur either because the Windows 9x PnP function cannot detect the hardware component or because it cannot reconcile the adapter's needs to the available system resources. However, do not assume that just because Windows 9x is running PnP is in effect and working. The system's BIOS and the peripheral devices must also be PnP-compliant for the auto-detection function to work.

Windows 9x Boot Problems

Key Windows 9x files prevent the system from starting up if they become corrupted. These files include those associated with the Master Boot Record, the boot sector, the FATs, and the Windows Core files. Errors that occur between the single beep that marks the end of the POST and the appearance of the Starting Windows 9x message on the screen are associated with the boot sector. Problems that show up between the "Starting Windows..." message and the appearance of the Desktop involve the Windows core files.

When the IO.SYS file is corrupted in Windows 9x, the system hangs up before the "Starting Windows..." message appears and produces a *System Disk Invalid error* message onscreen.

If the MSDOS.SYS file is missing or corrupted, Windows will display a blue screen with an "Invalid VxD Dynamic Link" message and fail to start up. Other MSDOS.SYS-related problems relate to the Registry, the Extended Memory Manager (XMS), and the Installable File System Manager (IFSMGR). These problems produce errors that appear during startup and are caused by syntax errors in the [Paths] section of the file. Be aware that the MSDOS.SYS file in Windows 9x is used to provide startup options, load some drivers, and establish paths for certain system files. You should check these entries if Windows 9x does not start properly.

Likewise, the COMMAND.COM problem produces an error message onscreen and fails to start up Windows. You can repair the missing COMMAND.COM error by using the DOS COPY and SYS commands. These commands copy the COMMAND.COM and system files from the clean boot disk to the hard drive. As mentioned earlier, if the boot disk contains a copy of the FDISK command, you can use the FDISK/MBR command to restore the hard drive's Master Boot Record, along with its partition information.

As mentioned previously, the following conditions produce a Bad or Missing COMMAND.COM error message:

◆ The COMMAND.COM file cannot be found on the hard drive, and no bootable disk is present in the A: drive.

◆ The COMMAND.COM file is not located in the hard drive's root directory. This message is likely when installing a new hard drive or a new DOS version.

◆ The user inadvertently erases the COMMAND.COM file from the hard drive.

EXAM TIP

Know how to use the Attrib command to view hidden system files.

To correct these problems, start the system using the Emergency Start disk. At the command prompt, type **SYS C:** to copy the IO.SYS, MSDOS.SYS, and COMMAND.COM files onto the hard disk. You can use the DOS Attribute command to verify that the hidden system files have been successfully copied to the disk (that is, Attrib -r -s -h C:\IO.SYS and Attrib -r -s -h C:\MSDOS.SYS to make them visible and to remove their read-only and system status).

The COMMAND.COM file can also be restored from the command line or through the Windows Explorer. To restore the COMMAND.COM file from the command line, start the system from the startup disk and use the Copy command to transfer the file manually. The COMMAND.COM file can also be dragged from the startup disk to the root directory of the hard drive using the Windows 9*x* My Computer or Windows Explorer functions. As with the manual copy procedure, the COMMAND.COM file's read-only, system, and hidden attributes must be removed so that it can be manipulated within the system.

Missing Windows Core File Problems

To locate and correct the *"Missing Core File" problem* cited earlier, check for corrupted files on the disk drive. To accomplish this, start the system in Safe mode using the Command Prompt Only option. When the command prompt appears, move to the Windows Command directory and run the ScanDisk utility. If ScanDisk detects corrupted files, you must replace them. The ScanDisk utility can locate and fix several types of problems on the hard drive. These problems include corrupted FATs, long filenames, lost clusters and cross-linked files, tree structure problems, and bad sectors on the drive.

The ScanDisk version used with a Windows 9*x* system must be the one specifically designed for that operating system. (That is, a Windows 95 ScanDisk version should not be used on a Windows 98 system.) Using other versions might not work correctly and could result in data loss. When using ScanDisk to isolate startup problems, the Windows 9*x* version used should be the version located on the particular computer's Emergency Start disk, and it should be the version that runs from the command prompt.

You can use the Windows 9*x* Setup function to verify or repair damaged Windows operating system files. To accomplish this, run the Setup utility and select the Verify option when presented by the Setup procedure. You then can repair damaged system files without running a complete reinstall operation.

If corrupted Windows 9*x* files are found in the system, it is not possible to simply copy new ones onto the drive from the CD. Instead, you must run Setup using the distribution CD and the Validate/Restore option.

EXAM TIP

Know what causes bad or missing COMMAND.COM errors and how to correct them.

CHALLENGE #1

One of your assistants has deleted a print manager file from his Windows 98 workstation. How can you restore this file to the system from the Windows CD so that he can print out his normal documentation?

EXAM TIP

Know the effects of checking the Disable Virtual Memory setting in Windows 9x.

Swap File Problems

The Windows 9x swap file is controlled through the System icon in the Control Panel. From this point, enter the Performance page and click its Virtual Memory button. Typically, the Let Windows Manage Virtual Memory option should be selected. If the system locks up and does not start, the swap file might have become corrupted or the Virtual Memory setting might have been changed to Disabled. In either case, you must reinstall Windows 9x to correct the problem.

Initialization File Problems

EXAM TIP

Be aware of the steps required to repair a missing INI error type.

The device or driver files referenced in the *Missing INI Files* error messages should be checked to make certain that they have been properly identified and that their location and path are correct. If they are not, use the System Editor to make the necessary changes by installing the specified device driver in the designated INI file. If the path and syntax is correct for the indicated files, you should reload the INI file from the Emergency Startup disk.

Errors in the CONFIG.SYS and AUTOEXEC.BAT files will produce the "Error in CONFIG.SYS Line *XX*" or "Error in AUTOEXEC.BAT Line *XX*" messages. The line specified by the *XX* in the error message contains a syntax (spelling, punctuation, or usage) error that prevents it from running. Syntax errors can also produce an Unrecognized command in CONFIG.SYS message. These errors are caused by missing or corrupt files referenced in the CONFIG.SYS or AUTOEXEC.BAT files. To correct these errors, use one of the system's text editors—such as SYSEDIT, to correct the designated line in the file, reload the indicated file with a known good copy, and restart the computer.

EXAM TIP

Know how to correct problems that cause an error message about a particular line in a CONFIG.SYS or AUTOEXEC.BAT file.

Figure 26.2 provides a graphic illustration of the Windows 9x startup sequence. It lists the order of event occurrences in each major startup stage and provides typical types of problems that might be encountered in each stage.

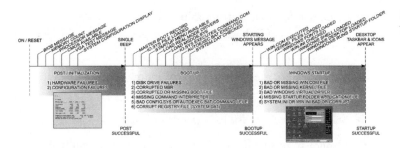

FIGURE 26.2
The Windows 9x startup sequence.

Using Safe Mode

If Windows determines that there is a problem that will prevent the system from starting, or if it senses that the Registry has become corrupt, it will automatically attempt to restart the system in Safe mode. As mentioned earlier, this mode bypasses several startup files to provide access to the system's configuration settings. In Safe mode, the minimal device drivers (keyboard, mouse, and standard-mode VGA drivers) are active to start the system. However, the CD-ROM drive will not be active in Safe mode.

As Figure 26.3 shows, Windows 9x has six Safe Mode Startup options—Normal, Logged, Safe Mode, Step-by-Step Confirmation, Command Prompt Only, and Safe Mode Command Prompt Only. Each option is customized for specific situations and disables selected portions of the system to prevent them from interfering with the startup process.

NOTE

Safe Mode with Network Support
Windows 98 does not officially support Safe mode with Network Support. However, you can access this mode by pressing the F6 function key during the startup process.

FIGURE 26.3
The Startup menu.

```
Microsoft Windows 95 Startup Menu

   1. Normal
   2. Logged C:\BOOTLOG.TXT
   3. Safe Mode
   4. Safe Mode with network support
   5. Step -by -Step Confirmation
   6. Command prompt only
   7. Safe Mode Command prompt only

Enter a choice: 3




F8 = Safe Mode  Shift + F5 = Command prompt  Shift + F8 = Step -by -Step Confirmation [N]
```

The standard Safe Mode startup, initiated by pressing the F5 key when the "Starting Windows…" message is present, is used when the system

◆ Will not start after the "Starting Windows…" message appears onscreen

◆ Stalls repeatedly or for long periods of time

◆ Cannot print to a local printer after a complete troubleshooting sequence

◆ Has video display problems

◆ Slows down noticeably, or does not work correctly

The Step-by-Step Confirmation option enables you to check each line of the startup procedure individually. In doing so, the Step-by-Step option enables you to verify which drivers are being loaded, temporarily disable any offending drivers, and check other startup errors that might be indicated through error messages.

The Step-by-Step Confirmation option is obtained by pressing the F8 function key at the Startup menu, and should be employed when the system

◆ Fails while loading the startup files

◆ Needs to load real-mode drivers

◆ Displays a Registry Failure error message

EXAM TIP

Memorize the function key used to access Step-by-Step Confirmation mode in Windows 9x.

The Safe Mode with Network Support option is used in networked environments when the system

◆ Stops responding when a remote network is accessed

◆ Cannot print to a remote printer

◆ Stalls during startup and cannot be started using a normal Safe Mode startup

---

CHALLENGE #2

You attempt to change the video driver on a customer's Windows 98 computer because you believe that he should be able to get more performance out of his video card. However, when you reboot the machine, you only have horizontal streaks across the screen. You know that you should restart the system in a mode that will permit you to access the display setup, but you are not sure which mode you should select. Which Windows 9*x* startup mode is the best choice to accomplish this without wasting a lot of extra time?

Command Prompt Modes

The *Safe Mode Command Prompt Only* option loads only COM-MAND.COM and the disk-compression utility files (DriveSpace or DoubleSpace), if present. This option should be chosen when the system fails to start in Safe mode. You can enter this mode directly during the startup process by pressing Shift+F5 when the "Starting Windows ..." message is onscreen.

The Safe Mode Command Prompt Only option can be used to

◆ Employ command-line switches, such as WIN /d:x

◆ Employ command-line tools, such as DOS editors

◆ Avoid loading HIMEM.SYS or IFSHLP.SYS

A Safe Mode Without Compression option appears only in systems using compressed drives. In operation, it is similar to the Command Prompt Only option—with the exception that no compression drivers are loaded. The following list provides reasons for selecting the Safe Mode without Compression option:

◆ The system stops responding when a compressed drive is accessed.

◆ A Corrupt *CVF* (*Compressed Volume File*) error displays during startup.

◆ When Safe Mode and Safe Mode Command Prompt Only options fail to start the system.

NOTE

Hands-On Activity   For hands-on experience with this concept, refer to Lab Procedure #27, "Windows Me Safe Mode," located on the CD that accompanies this book.

CHALLENGE #3

When you attempt to start a client's Windows 9x computer, the system reaches the "Starting Windows..." prompt and then locks up. You try to start the system in standard Safe mode, but it still locks up when the desktop GUI come to the screen. What items could be causing this problem, and how should you repair it?

Using WIN Switches

As mentioned in Chapter 24, "Starting the System," starting Windows 9x from the command prompt using a /D switch is often helpful in isolating different areas of the operating system as possible problem sources (that is, WIN /D). You can modify the /D switch to start Windows in a number of different configurations:

◆ Using a /D:F switch disables 32-bit disk access.

◆ The :M and :N variations start Windows in Safe mode, or Safe mode with networking mode.

◆ An :S modifier inhibits Windows from using address space between hexadecimal addresses F0000h and FFFFFh.

◆ The :V variation prevents Windows from controlling disk transfers. Instead, HDD interrupt requests are handled by the BIOS.

◆ The :X switch prevents Windows from using the area of memory between hexadecimal addresses A000h and FFFFh.

EXAM TIP

Be aware of different ways to start the Windows 9x system when it will not boot normally.

Other switches can be used with the WIN command. The WIN /B switch causes Windows to start in logged mode and to produce a BOOTLOG.TXT file during startup. This option enables you to determine whether specific device drivers are stalling the system. Logged mode can also be selected by pressing the F8 key while the Starting Windows 9x message is onscreen. After selecting the Logged option, restart the system using the Safe Mode Command Prompt Only option. Then, use a text editor to examine the contents of the BOOTLOG.TXT file and determine which driver has failed to load.

Windows 9x Log Files

Windows 9x maintains four log files—BOOTLOG.TXT, SETU-PLOG.TXT, DETLOG.TXT, and DETCRASH.LOG. These files maintain a log of different system operations and enable you to see what events occurred leading up to a failure. The TXT files can be read with Notepad, DOS Editor, or any other text editor.

BOOTLOG.TXT

The *BOOTLOG.TXT* file contains the sequence of events conducted during the startup of the system. The original BOOTLOG.TXT file is created during the Windows 9x setup process. You can update the file by pressing the F8 key during Startup or by starting Windows 9x with a WIN /B switch. It is not updated automatically each time the system is started.

> **EXAM TIP**
>
> Know which log file is not generated automatically during the Windows startup process.

SETUPLOG.TXT

The *SETUPLOG.TXT* file holds setup information that was established during the installation process. The log file exists in seven basic sections, and entries are added to the file as they occur in the setup process. Therefore, it can be read to determine what action was in process when a setup failure occurred. The file is stored on the system's root directory and is used in Safe Recovery situations.

DETLOG.TXT

This *Detect Crash log* file is created when the system crashes during the hardware detection portion of the startup procedure. It contains information about the detection module that was running when the crash occurred. It is a binary file and cannot be read directly. However, a text version of the file, named DETLOG.TXT, is available under the root directory of the drive.

The *DETLOG.TXT* file holds the text equivalent of the information in the DETCRASH.LOG file. This file can be read with a text editor to determine which hardware components have been detected by the system and what its parameters are. This printout is really a detailed explanation of the hardware-detection phase of the system's PnP operation.

> **NOTE**
>
> **Hands-On Activity** For hands-on experience with this concept, refer to Lab Procedure #28, "Windows Me Setup Log Files," located on the CD that accompanies this book.

Using the Windows 98 Startup Disk

If the system will not make it to the Startup menu, you must boot the system with the Startup disk and begin checking the operating system on the boot drive. After gaining access to the system, you can use the built-in troubleshooting aids on the Windows 9*x* startup disks to isolate the cause of the problem. When the system is booted with a Windows 98 Startup disk, a menu such as the following displays:

1. Start the computer with CD-ROM support.
2. Start the computer without CD-ROM support.
3. View the Help file.

Using Windows 98 System Tools on Startup Problems

In addition to the clean-boot, Safe mode, and log file functions previously described, the Windows 98 distribution CD contains a wealth of other troubleshooting tools that you can use to isolate and correct problems.

If a startup problem disappears when the system is started using any of the Windows 9*x* Safe modes, use the System Configuration utility (MSCONFIG.EXE) to isolate the conflicting items. Of course, you might need to enter this command from the command line.

Select the Diagnostic Startup option from the General tab to interactively load device drivers and software options. When the Startup menu appears, select the Step-by-Step option. Begin by starting the system with only the CONFIG.SYS and AUTOEXEC.BAT files disabled. If the system starts, move into those tabs and step through those files, one line at a time, using the Selective Startup option. The step-by-step process is used to systematically enable/disable items until all the problem items have been identified. If an entry is marked with a Microsoft Windows logo, it is used when the Selective Startup option is disabled.

If the problem does not go away, you can use the Advanced button on the General tab to inspect lower-level configuration settings, such as real-mode disk accesses and VGA standard video settings. You also can start the Device Manager from the MSCONFIG View option. This will permit the protected-mode device drivers to be inspected. The

MSINFO-Problem Devices section also should be examined to check for possible problem causing devices. Other items to check include missing or corrupted system files (using the System File Checker utility), corrupted Registry entries (using the Registry Checker), viruses (using a virus checker program), and hardware conflicts using the CMOS Configuration screens.

When a potential problem setting has been identified in the CONFIG.SYS, AUTOEXEC.BAT, or Registry, use the *Automatic Skip Driver* utility to automatically isolate and disable the suspect line. Select the *ASD* option from the System Information's Tools menu, select the operation that has failed by marking it in the Hardware Troubleshooting Agent dialog box, and then select the Details option. This action should cause the Enumerating a Device dialog box to provide recommendations for correcting any problems. This normally involves replacing the driver disabled by the ASD utility. This series of automated tests basically replaces the manual isolation method performed with the Step-by-Step Startup option.

The Windows 98 system might contain up to five backup copies of the Registry structure. If the system fails to start up after installing some new software or hardware component, run the Registry Checker utility using the /Restore option (ScanReg /Restore) to return the Registry to its previous condition. Simply type **ScanReg /Restore** at the command prompt to view a list of available backup copies. Generally, the most recent version should be selected for use.

Windows 2000 Startup Problems

If Windows 2000 fails to boot, the first troubleshooting step is to determine whether the computer is failing before or after the operating system takes control. If the startup process makes it to the beep that indicates the end of the POST, but you do not see the operating system Boot Selection menu, the problem is probably one of the following:

◆ System partition

◆ Master Boot Record

◆ Partition boot sector

EXAM TIP

Know what types of problems the MSCONFIG.EXE utility is used for.

EXAM TIP

Know which Windows 9x utility can be used to restore backup copies of the Registry to the system.

NOTE

Hands-On Activity For hands-on experience with this concept, refer to Lab Procedure #43, "Windows Me OS Faults," located on the CD that accompanies this book.

These types of problems are usually the result of hard disk media failures, or a virus, and must be repaired before the operating system will function. Typical symptoms associated with hard disk media failures include the following:

◆ Blue screen or Stop message appears.

◆ Bootup stops after the POST.

◆ The Boot Selection menu is never reached.

◆ An error message is produced.

Windows 2000 displays a number of error messages related to these problems, including the following:

◆ Missing Operating System

◆ Disk Read Error

◆ Invalid Partition Table

◆ Hard Disk Error (or Absent/Failed)

◆ Insert System Disk

◆ Error Loading Operating System

The *"Error Loading Operating System"* message indicates that the system partition was located but could not start the operating system. The system partition on that drive could be missing or misidentified. Use the FDISK utility to search for and set the system partition properly.

<table>
<tr><td>

EXAM TIP

</td><td>

Know which files must be present to boot Windows NT/2000 and how to correct problems associated with the Windows NT boot sequence.

</td></tr>
</table>

The BOOT.INI or NTLDR files also could be missing or have become corrupted. If you receive a message indicating that a *"Kernel File Is Missing"* or that the *"NTLDR Could Not Be Found,"* the partition boot sector is okay, but the NTLDR file is probably corrupt. Use the command prompt ATTRIB utility to change the attributes. Copy the file over from the Startup disk to the root folder. All the startup files, including NTLDR, BOOT.INI, NTDETECT, and NTOSKRNL, can be restored from the Emergency Repair Disk.

The Missing Operating System and Invalid Partition Table errors indicate a problem with the Master Boot Record. Use the FDISK /MBR command to replace the Master Boot Record. Although this works well on a standalone drive, it does not work with disks that contain partitions or logical drives that are part of striped or volume sets. You also should not perform this procedure on drives that use third-party translation, partitioning, or dual-boot programs.

Figure 26.4 graphic illustrates the Windows 2000 startup process. In addition to listing the order of events that occur in each distinct startup stage, it also describes various types of problems typically encountered during each stage.

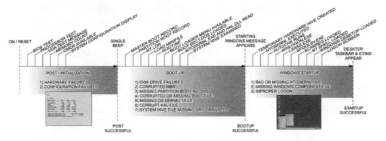

FIGURE 26.4
The Windows 2000 startup sequence.

Windows 2000 Startup Tools

Windows 2000 provides a wealth of tools for recovering from a startup problem, including the following:

◆ Windows 2000 Safe Mode options

◆ Windows 2000 Recovery Console

◆ Windows 2000 Emergency Repair Disk

Using Windows 2000 Start Modes

In addition to the Windows 9x–like Safe Mode startup options, Windows 2000 includes a pair of Windows NT–like Start options. As mentioned in Chapter 24, during startup the Windows 2000 NTLDR file causes the system to display a boot selection menu that includes options to start the system in VGA mode and in a Last Known Good Hardware Configuration mode.

If the VGA option is selected, the system will start as normal— except that it will only load the standard VGA display driver. This option was introduced with the Windows NT 4.0 version for the express purpose of managing video driver problems. Selecting the Last Known Good Hardware Configuration mode option will start the system using the configuration information that it recorded the last time a user successfully logged onto the system. This option is extremely valuable for sorting out Windows NT/2000 configuration problems.

CHALLENGE #4

While you are working on a customer's Windows 2000 system, you notice that the display resolution is running well below what you expect from his video card. When you attempt to change the video driver to get better display performance out of it, you only see horizontal streaks across the screen after you reboot the machine. Which Windows 2000 startup mode provides the best choice for quickly accessing the display setup so you can correct it?

NOTE

Hands-On Activity   For hands-on experience with this concept, refer to Lab Procedure #29, "Windows Me Safe Mode," located on the CD that accompanies this book.

Windows 2000 Recovery Console

The *Recovery Console* is a command-line interface that provides you with access to the hard disks and many command-line utilities when the operating system will not boot. The Recovery Console can access all volumes on the drive, regardless of the file system type. However, if you have not added the Recovery Console option prior to a failure, you will not be able to employ it and will need to use the Windows 2000 Setup disks instead. You can use the Recovery Console to perform tasks such as the following:

◆ Copy files from a floppy disk, CD, or another hard disk to the hard disk used for bootup, enabling you to replace or remove files that might be affecting the boot process. Because of the security features built in to Windows 2000, you are only granted limited access to certain files on the hard drive. You cannot copy files from the hard drive to a floppy or other storage device under these conditions.

◆ Control the startup state of services, enabling you to disable a service that could potentially be causing the operating system to crash.

◆ Add, remove, and format volumes on the hard disk.

◆ Repair the MBR or boot sector of a hard disk or volume.

◆ Restore the Registry.

You can use the Recovery Console to restore the Windows 2000 Registry. Every time you back up the system state data with Windows 2000 backup, a copy of the Registry is placed in the \Repair\RegBack folder. If you copy the entire contents of this folder or only particular files to \System32\Config (which is the folder where the working copy of the Registry is stored), you can restore the Registry to the same condition as last time you performed a System State data backup. It is recommended that you create a copy of the files located in \System32\Config prior to restoring the other files from backup. This will enable you to restore the Registry to its original condition if necessary. The Recovery Console can be started from the Repair option on the Windows 2000 Setup disk or distribution CD. After installing the Recovery Console, it can be accessed through the Advanced options menu at startup.

> **EXAM TIP**
>
> Know which Windows 2000 utility can be used to restore backup copies of the Registry to the system.

Performing Emergency Repairs in Windows NT/2000

The *Emergency Repair Disk* (*ERD*) provides another repair option in the event that Safe Mode and the Windows 2000 Recovery Console do not enable you to repair the system. If you have already created an ERD, you can start the system with the Windows 2000 Setup CD or the Setup floppy disks, and then use the ERD to restore core system files.

The Emergency Repair Process can perform the following functions:

◆ Repair the boot sector

◆ Repair the startup files

◆ Replace the system files

> **EXAM TIP**
>
> Be aware that the Windows 2000 Emergency Repair Process is designed to repair the operating system only, and cannot be of assistance in repairing application or data problems.

To perform an emergency repair,

1. Boot the system from the Window 2000 CD. If the system cannot boot from CD, you will need to boot with the Setup Boot Disk, which is the first of four Setup floppies that will be required. The setup floppies can be created with MAKE-BOOT.EXE, which is in the \BOOTDISK folder off the root of the Windows 2000 CD.

2. When the text-mode portion of Setup begins, follow the initial prompts. When you reach the Welcome to Setup screen depicted in Figure 26.5, press R to repair the Windows 2000 installation.

NOTE

Hands-On Activity For hands-on experience with this concept, refer to Lab Procedure #44, "Windows 2000 OS Faults," located on the CD that accompanies this book.

3. When prompted, choose the *Emergency Repair Process* by pressing R.

4. When prompted, press F for Fast repair.

5. Follow the instructions and insert the Emergency Repair Disk into the floppy drive when prompted.

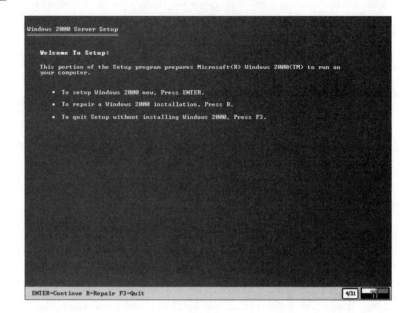

FIGURE 26.5
Repairing a Windows 2000 installation.

CHAPTER SUMMARY

KEY TERMS

- /Restore
- ASD
- Automatic Skip Driver
- Bad or Missing Command Interpreter
- Blue Screen of Death (BSOD)
- BOOTLOG.TXT
- CVF (Compressed Volume File)

This chapter has focused on diagnosing and troubleshooting operating system setup and startup problems. The first section of the chapter examined installation problems encountered in Windows 9x and Windows 2000 systems.

The final two sections dealt with startup problems. First, those associated with Windows 9x systems, and then those typically encountered when starting up Windows NT/2000 systems. These sections presented typical startup error messages and related them to probable causes for each type of system. Full discussions of Safe-mode startups and other alternative startup processes were presented along with the different log files available in the Windows operating systems.

CHAPTER SUMMARY

At this point, review the objectives listed at the beginning of the chapter to be certain that you understand each point and can perform each task listed there. Afterward, answer the review questions that follow to verify your knowledge of the information.

- Detect Crash log
- DETLOG.TXT
- Disk Boot Failure
- Emergency Repair Disk (ERD)
- Emergency Repair Process
- Error Loading Operating System message
- FDISK/MBR
- Full versions
- Incompatible Version error
- Kernel File Is Missing
- Missing Core File problem
- Missing INI Files error
- NTLDR Could Not Be Found
- Recovery Console
- Safe Mode Command Prompt Only
- ScanReg /Restore
- SETUPLOG.TXT
- Shift+F5
- Syntax
- System Disk Invalid error
- Upgrade versions

APPLY YOUR KNOWLEDGE

Review Questions

1. _____ speed mismatches can cause OS installation failures.

   A. Bus

   B. RAM

   C. Microprocessor

   D. Disk drive

2. What should be checked before installing Windows 2000?

   A. The hardware manufacturer's Web sites for updated device drivers

   B. The expiration date for the operating system

   C. The speed of the hard disk drive

   D. Your Internet connection

3. How can the current version of Windows be displayed? (Select all that apply.)

   A. Open Windows Explorer, click on the Help menu, and select About Windows.

   B. Open Windows Explorer, click on the File menu, and select Properties.

   C. Right-click on My Computer and select Properties from the contextual menu.

   D. Right-click on the desktop and select Properties from the contextual menu.

4. Which command is commonly used to repair the error "Missing Command Interpreter"?

   A. `copy a:\command.com c:\command.com`

   B. `fdisk /mbr`

   C. `format c: /c`

   D. `command.com c:xcopy`

5. What shortcut keys are used to skip normal start-up in the Windows 9x startup process? (Select all that apply.)

   A. F1

   B. F5

   C. F8

   D. F11

6. What shortcut keys are used to single-step through the boot-up process?

   A. F1

   B. F5

   C. F8

   D. F11

7. In a Windows 9x system, which file would you access to correct a HIMEM.SYS error reported during startup?

   A. COMMAND.COM

   B. AUTOEXEC.BAT

   C. CONFIG.SYS

   D. MSDOS.SYS

8. What command is used to view hidden system files?

   A. `attrib -r -s -h c:\*.sys`

   B. `attrib +r +s +h c:\*.sys`

   C. `fa -r -s -h c:\*.sys`

   D. `fa +r +s +h c:\*.sys`

9. You have just encountered a "Bad or Missing COMMAND.COM" error. How should it be corrected?

    A. Boot to an emergency startup disk. At the command prompt, type **SYS C:**.

    B. Boot to an emergency startup disk. At the command prompt, type **fdisk /mbr**.

    C. Boot to an emergency startup disk. At the command prompt, type **format c: /s**.

    D. Boot to an emergency startup disk. At the command prompt, type **copy a:\command.com c:\command.com**.

10. How do you correct a problem identified by an error message about a particular line in a CONFIG.SYS or AUTOEXEC.BAT file?

    A. Reinstall Windows.

    B. Delete the config.sys or autoexec.bat file.

    C. At the command prompt, type **sys c:**.

    D. Use **SYSEDIT** to correct the line in the file.

11. What are the effects of checking the Disable Virtual Memory setting in Windows 9*x*?

    A. Operating system runs slowly.

    B. Operating system fails to start.

    C. Applications will not start.

    D. Mouse stops working.

12. Which drivers are loaded into the system when it is started in Safe Mode?

    A. Standard mouse, keyboard, VGA drivers

    B. Standard mouse, keyboard, VGA, CD-ROM drivers

    C. Standard mouse, keyboard, VGA, network drivers

    D. Standard mouse, keyboard, VGA, CD-ROM, network drivers

13. Which function key is used to access Safe Mode in Windows 9*x*?

    A. F1

    B. F5

    C. F8

    D. F11

14. How can a Windows 9*x* system be started when it will not boot normally? (Select all that apply.)

    A. F5

    B. F8

    C. **WIN /D**

    D. **WIN /V**

15. Which log file is not generated automatically during the Windows startup process?

    A. BOOTLOG.TXT

    B. SETUPLOG.TXT

    C. DETLOG.TXT

    D. DETCRASH.LOG

16. What types of problems is the MSCONFIG.EXE utility used for?

    A. Desktop configuration

    B. Registry configuration

    C. Network configuration

    D. System configuration

APPLY YOUR KNOWLEDGE

17. Which Windows 9x utility can be used to restore backup copies of the Registry to the system?

    A. Regback

    B. Restore

    C. Backup

    D. Scanreg

18. Which of these files does not need to be present to boot Windows NT/2000?

    A. NTLDR

    B. BOOT.INI

    C. NTDETECT.COM

    D. I/O.SYS

19. Which of the following is not a function of the Emergency Repair Process in Windows 2000?

    A. Repair the disk drive's boot sector

    B. Repair the system's Startup files

    C. Repair corrupted data files

    D. Repair failed applications

20. In Windows 2000, which utility can be used to access hard drives and command-line utilities when the system will not boot?

    A. Recovery Console

    B. Computer Management Console

    C. Device Manager

    D. REGEDT32.EXE

21. In Windows 2000, which utility can be used to restore the Registry from a backup if you cannot boot to a GUI?

    A. Backup

    B. Regback

    C. Recovery console

    D. Scanreg

22. The Emergency Repair Process is designed to _____ and cannot be of assistance in repairing application or data problems.

    A. repair the file system

    B. repair the operating system

    C. repair the network configuration

    D. repair the desktop configuration

23. If you receive a HIMEM.SYS error in a Windows 9x system, where must you go to correct it?

    A. `C:\WINDOWS\SYSTEM32`

    B. `C:\WINDOWS\CONFIG.SYS`

    C. `C:\WINDOWS`

    D. `C:\WINDOWS\COMMAND`

Answers and Explanations

1. **B.** A memory speed mismatch or mixed RAM-type problem might produce a Windows Protection Error message during the installation process. This error indicates that the operating system is having timing problems that originate from the RAM memory used in the system. Correcting this problem involves swapping the system's RAM for devices that meet the system's timing requirements. For more information, see the section "Troubleshooting Setup Problems."

2. **A**. Contact the hardware vendor for all of your components to determine whether they support Windows 2000 before starting the installation. At the same time, you can download the latest updates to the device drivers. For more information, see the section "Windows NT/2000 Setup Problems."

3. **A**, **C**. The simplest method to determine the current version of a Windows operating system running on a computer is to right-click on the My Computer icon, select the properties option from the pop-up menu, and select the General tab of the System Properties page. For more information, see the section "Upgrade Problems."

4. **B**. The "Missing Command Interpreter" error can be repaired by restoring the boot record and operating system files to the hard disk. To do so, you normally copy or extract the files from the clean boot disk to the hard drive. In a FAT environment, if the boot disk contains a copy of the FDISK command, you can use the FDISK /MBR command to restore the hard drive's Master Boot Record, along with its partition information. For more information, see the section "Troubleshooting Startup Problems."

5. **B**, **C**. The special function keys available during the Windows 9x startup are

   F5—Safe mode

   F6—Safe mode with Network Support

   F8—Step-by-Step Confirmation mode

   Shift+F5—Safe mode Command Prompt Only

   For more information, see the section "Windows 9x Startup Problems."

6. **C**. The special function keys available during the Windows 9x startup includes F8—Step-by-Step Confirmation mode. For more information, see the section "Windows 9x Startup Problems."

7. **C**. In the case of the HIMEM.SYS error, use the System Editor to check the syntax and correctness of the entry in the CONFIG.SYS file if present. Look for the line DEVICE=C:\DOS\HIMEM.SYS. With Windows 9x, the HIMEM.SYS statement must be present and correct for the operating system to run. Also check the HIMEM.SYS file to make sure that it is the correct version and in the correct location. In the case of a Windows 9x upgrade, as many as three versions of HIMEM.SYS might be present in the system, though there will always be one copy in C:\WINDOWS. For more information, see the section "HIMEM.SYS Problems."

8. **A**. You can use the DOS Attribute command to view the hidden system files (that is, Attrib -r -s -h c:*.SYS) to make them visible and to remove their read-only and system status. For more information, see the section "Windows 9x Boot Problems."

9. **A**, **D**. The following conditions produce a Bad or Missing COMMAND.COM error message: The COMMAND.COM file cannot be found on the hard drive, and no bootable disk is present in the A: drive; The COMMAND.COM file is not located in the hard drive's root directory. This message is likely when installing a new hard drive or a new DOS version; The user inadvertently erases the COMMAND.COM file from the hard drive. To correct these problems, start the system using the emergency start disk. At the command prompt, type **SYS C:** to copy the IO.SYS, MSDOS.SYS, and COMMAND.COM files

APPLY YOUR KNOWLEDGE

onto the hard disk. You can also use the copy command to make a copy of COMMAND.COM on the hard drive. For more information, see the section "Windows 9x Boot Problems."

10. **D**. Errors in the CONFIG.SYS and AUTOEXEC.BAT files will produce the "Error in CONFIG.SYS Line *XX*" or "Error in AUTOEXEC.BAT Line *XX*" messages. The line specified by the *XX* in the error message contains a syntax (spelling, punctuation, or usage) error that prevents it from running. Syntax errors can also produce an "Unrecognized Command in CONFIG.SYS" message. These errors are caused by missing or corrupt files referenced in the CONFIG.SYS or AUTOECE.BAT files. To correct these errors, use one of the system's text editors, such as SYSEDIT, to correct the designated line in the file, reload the indicated file with a known good copy and restart the computer. For more information, see the section "Initialization File Problems."

11. **B**. If the system locks up and cannot be restarted, the Virtual Memory setting might have been changed to Disabled. For more information, see the section "Swap File Problems."

12. **A**. In Safe mode, the minimal device drivers (keyboard, mouse, and standard-mode VGA drivers) are active to start the system. However, the CD-ROM drive will not be active in Safe mode. For more information, see the section "Using Safe Mode."

13. **B**. Safe mode can be accessed at bootup by pressing the F5 key. For more information, see the section "Using Safe Mode."

14. **A, B, C**. Starting Windows 9x from the command prompt using a /D switch is often helpful in isolating different areas of the operating system as possible problem sources (that is, WIN /D). You can modify the /D switch to start Windows in a number of different configurations: Using a /D:F switch disables 32-bit disk access; The :M and :N variations start Windows in Safe mode, or Safe mode with networking mode; An :S modifier inhibits Windows from using address space between hexadecimal addresses F0000h and FFFFFh; The :V variation prevents Windows from controlling disk transfers. Instead, HDD interrupt requests are handled by the BIOS; The :X switch prevents Windows from using the area of memory between hexadecimal addresses A000h and FFFFh. Other switches can be used with the WIN command. The WIN /B switch causes Windows to start in logged mode and to produce a BOOTLOG.TXT file during startup. This option enables you to determine whether specific device drivers are stalling the system. Logged mode can also be selected by pressing the F8 key while the Starting Windows 9x message is onscreen. After selecting the Logged option, restart the system using the Safe Mode Command Prompt Only option. Then, use a text editor to examine the contents of the BOOTLOG.TXT file and determine which driver has failed to load. For more information, see the section "Command Prompt Modes."

15. **A**. The BOOTLOG.TXT file contains the sequence of events conducted during the startup of the system. The original BOOTLOG.TXT file is created during the Windows 9x setup process. You can update the file by pressing the F8 key

during Startup, or by starting Windows 9x with a WIN /b switch. It is not updated automatically each time the system is started. For more information, see the section "BOOTLOG.TXT."

16. **D**. If a startup problem disappears when the system is started using any of the Windows 9x Safe modes, use the System Configuration utility (MSCONFIG.EXE) to isolate the conflicting items. Of course, you might need to enter this command from the command line. For more information, see the section "Using Windows 98 System Tools on Startup Problems."

17. **D**. The system might contain up to five backup copies of the Registry structure. If the system fails to start up after installing some new software or hardware component, run the Registry Checker utility using the /restore option (that is, scanreg /restore) to return the Registry to its previous condition. Simply type **SCANREG /RESTORE** at the command prompt to view a list of available backup copies. Generally, the most recent version should be selected for use. For more information, see the section "Using Windows 98 System Tools on Startup Problems."

18. **D**. The Windows NT/2000 bootstrap finds NTLDR. NTLDR reads the BOOT.INI and displays operating system choices. NTLDR loads NTDETECT.COM, which builds a hardware list and returns to NTLDR. NTLDR loads NTOSKRNL.EXE. NTOSKRNL.EXE loads and initializes Windows NT/2000 using information from the Registry to load and initialize drivers and other system settings. For more information, see the section "Windows 2000 Startup Problems."

19. **C, D**. In Windows 2000, the Emergency Repair Process can be used to repair the boot sector, repair the startup files, and replace the system files. However, you should be aware that the Windows 2000 Emergency Repair Process is designed to repair the operating system only, and cannot be of assistance in repairing application or data problems. For more information, see the section "Performing Emergency Repairs in Windows NT/2000."

20. **A**. The Recovery Console is a command-line interface that provides you with access to the hard disks and many command-line utilities when the operating system will not boot. The Recovery Console can access all volumes on the drive, regardless of the file system type. However, if you have not added the Recovery Console option prior to a failure, you will not be able to employ it and will need to use the Windows 2000 Setup disks instead. For more information, see the section "Windows 2000 Recovery Console."

21. **C**. Every time you back up the system state data with Windows 2000 backup, a copy of the Registry is placed in the \Repair\RegBack folder. If you must use the command line provided by the recovery console to restore the registry, copy the entire contents of this folder or only particular files to \System32\Config (which is the folder where the working copy of the Registry is stored); you can restore the Registry to the same condition as last time you performed a System State data backup. It is recommended that you create a copy of the files located in \System32\Config prior to restoring the other files from backup. This will enable you to restore the Registry to its original condition if necessary. For more information, see the section "Windows 2000 Recovery Console."

APPLY YOUR KNOWLEDGE

22. **B**. The Emergency Repair Process can perform the following functions: repair the boot sector; repair the startup files; and replace the system files. The Windows 2000 Emergency Repair Process is designed to repair the operating system only, and cannot be of assistance in repairing application or data problems. For more information, see the section "Performing Emergency Repairs in Windows NT/2000."

23. **C**. With Windows 9*x*, the HIMEM.SYS statement must be present and correct for the operating system to run. Also check the HIMEM.SYS file to make sure that it is the correct version and in the correct location. In the case of a Windows 9*x* upgrade, as many as three versions of HIMEM.SYS might be present in the system, though there will always be one copy in C:\WINDOWS. For more information, see the section "HIMEM.SYS Problems."

Challenge Solutions

1. The *XXXXX* file can be restored from the Windows 98 distribution CD. However, it is stored there in Cabinet (.CAB) format. You will need to use the Extract (Ext.exe) command to retrieve the file from the CD. For more information, see the section "Missing Windows Core File Problems."

2. In this situation, using Windows 98, the most efficient mode that you can use to reset the video driver is standard Safe mode. Step-by-Step and Command Prompt Only modes involve additional steps and do not provide an opportunity to change the video driver. For more information, see the section "Using Safe Mode."

3. One of the Windows 98 files being loaded after the WIN.COM file is executed is corrupt or missing and should be identified and replaced. You should restart the system using the Step-by-Step Confirmation option that will enable you to check each line of the startup procedure individually. In doing so, you can verify which components and drivers are being loaded, temporarily disable any offending files or drivers, and check other startup errors that might be indicated through error messages. For more information, see the section "Command Prompt Modes."

4. In this situation, using Windows 2000 Professional, the most efficient mode that you can use to reset the video driver is VGA Mode. This mode was actually introduced in Windows NT 4.0 to provide efficient management of the video driver under the Windows NT platform. In Windows 2000, you can change the video driver through this mode with a single reboot operation (actually, you would not need to reboot at all to simply change the resolution of the existing driver). Using Safe Mode to change the video driver in Windows 2000 would require that you reboot the system twice to complete the operation. For more information, see the section "Using Safe Mode."

APPLY YOUR KNOWLEDGE

Suggested Readings and Resources

1. The Universal Troubleshooting Process
   `http://www.troubleshooters.com/tuni.htm`

2. Troubleshooting Windows Setup Problems
   `http://support.microsoft.com/`
   `default.aspx?scid=kb;EN-US;q310064`

3. Troubleshooting Windows 95 Startup
   Problems
   `http://support.microsoft.com/`
   `default.aspx?scid=kb;EN-US;q136337`

4. Troubleshooting Windows 98 Startup
   Problems
   `http://support.microsoft.com/`
   `default.aspx?scid=kb;EN-US;q188867`

5. Troubleshooting Windows 95 Using Safe
   Mode
   `http://support.microsoft.com/`
   `default.aspx?scid=kb;EN-US;q156126`

6. Starting Safe Mode Command Prompt
   `http://pshopelementssupport.adobe.com/`
   `adobeknowbase/root/public/`
   `pm1033.htm?DREID=8574`

7. Using WIN Switches
   `http://support.microsoft.com/`
   `default.aspx?scid=kb;EN-US;q142544`

8. BOOTLOG.TXT
   `http://www.tafe.sa.edu.au/institutes/`
   `torrens-valley/programs/eit/pcsupport/`
   `bootlog.htm`

9. Log Files
   `http://www.pe.net/~rlewis/Resources/`
   `logfiles.html`

10. Registry Troubleshooting
    `http://docs.rinet.ru:8083/Registratura/htm`
    `/toc.htm`

This chapter helps you to prepare for the Operating System Technologies module of the A+ Certification examination by covering the following objective within the "Domain 3.0: Diagnosing and Troubleshooting" section.

3.2 Recognize common problems and determine how to resolve them.

Content might include the following:

- **Eliciting problem symptoms from customers**

- **Having customer reproduce error as part of the diagnostic process**

- **Identifying recent changes to the computer environment from the user**

- **Troubleshooting Windows-specific printing problems:**

  - **Print spool is stalled**

  - **Incorrect/incompatible driver for print**

  - **Incorrect parameter**

- **Other common problems:**

  - **General protection faults**

  - **Illegal operation**

  - **Invalid working directory**

  - **System lockup**

  - **Option (Sound card, modem, input device) will not function**

  - **Application will not start or load**

  - **Cannot log on to network (option—NIC not functioning)**

  - **TSR (Terminate and Stay Resident) programs and virus**

  - **Applications don't install**

  - **Network connection**

CHAPTER *27*

Common OS Operational Problems

- **Viruses and virus types:**
  - **What they are**
  - **Sources (floppy, emails, and so on)**
  - **How to determine their presence**

▶ As with hardware problems, every technician should be able to effectively acquire information from the customer concerning the nature of a software problem and then involve the user in the troubleshooting process as required.

▶ The Windows operating environment and operating system provide the printing functions for all the applications in a Windows system. The successful technician must be able to recognize and correct printing problems related to the Windows environment. After the operating system has been started and become functional, another set of problems can exist that fall into the category called operational problems. As with startup problems, the technician must be able to identify and correct operational problems associated with the operating system.

▶ Viruses have become a major cause of problems in the personal computer environment. The technician must be aware of how typical viruses work, how they are contracted, and how to deal with them.

To prepare for the Diagnosing and Troubleshooting objective of the Operating Systems Technologies exam,

▶ Read the objectives at the beginning of this chapter.

▶ Study the information in this chapter.

▶ Review the objectives listed earlier in this chapter.

▶ Perform any step-by-step procedures in the text.

▶ Answer the review questions at the end of the chapter and check your results.

▶ Use the PrepLogic test engine on the CD-ROM that accompanies this book for additional review and exam questions concerning this material.

▶ Review the exam tips scattered throughout the chapter and make certain that you are comfortable with each point.

INTRODUCTION

This chapter deals with troubleshooting operating system problems that occur after the system has been successfully booted to a command prompt or desktop environment. Problems in this category are referred to as *operational problems*.

This chapter covers common operational problems that occur in Windows 9*x* and Windows 2000 systems. Typical operational problems include memory usage problems, application problems, printing problems, and networking problems.

The second portion of the chapter deals specifically with problems and troubleshooting procedures associated with printing in Windows.

The final section of the chapter discusses computer viruses. Typical symptoms and precautions for preventing virus infections are presented during the discussion.

After completing the chapter, you should be able to relate common Windows operational problems to the symptoms they produce and suggest remedies for these problems. You should also be able to identify Windows-specific printing problems and implement procedures for correcting them. Finally, you should be able to identify common symptoms produced by viruses and describe preventive measures that can be employed to avoid infections.

COMMON OS OPERATIONAL PROBLEMS

After the operating system has been started and becomes functional, particular types of problems come into play. Many of these problems are documented in this A+ objective. It indicates that the technician must be able to identify and correct operational problems associated with the operating system. To this end, this chapter deals specifically with OS operational symptoms and problems, including the following:

◆ Memory usage

◆ Application

◆ Printing

◆ Networking

Memory Usage Problems

Memory usage problems occur when the operating system, or one of its applications, attempts to access an unallocated memory location. When these memory conflicts occur, the data in the violated memory locations is corrupted and may crash the system. In older Windows versions, these types of problems were labeled *General Protection Faults* (*GPF*) and were generally the product of data protection errors induced by poorly written programs.

Although Windows 9*x* provides a much better multitasking environment than its predecessors, applications can still attempt to access unallocated memory locations or attempt to use another application's space. These actions create a software exception error in the system. When these memory conflicts occur, the system might either return an error message or simply stop processing. Because of the severity of the GPF problems in early Windows versions, Microsoft chose to use memory usage error messages in Windows 9*x* that say "*This Application Has Performed an Illegal Operation and Is About to Be Shut Down.*" When this happens, Windows might take care of the error and permit you to continue operating by simply pressing a specific key combination.

Some memory usage errors are nonfatal and provide an option to ignore the fault and continue working or to just close the application. These errors are generally caused by Windows applications and can sometimes be tracked to dynamic link library (DLL) files associated with a particular application. Although the application might continue to operate, it is generally not stable enough to continue working on an extended basis. It is recommended that the application be used only long enough to save any existing work.

Windows NT and Windows 2000 employ a flat memory management scheme that does not use the segmented memory mapping features associated with the Intel microprocessors. Therefore, these operating systems have very few memory usage problems.

Optional Devices Will Not Operate

The system's basic devices are configured as part of the system's PnP startup process in both Windows 9*x* and Windows NT/2000 systems. However, this doesn't mean that all the system's devices are in working order or that they will remain in working order while the system is on. Optional devices such as modems, sound cards, and advanced I/O devices might configure properly as part of the PnP process and then fail to operate after the system starts.

As an example, many video cards are capable of displaying very high-resolution screens at high refresh rates. However, some monitors do not have the same capabilities. When you configure the video card with settings that the monitor cannot display, symptoms can range from a simple blank screen to several ghost images being displayed onscreen. After the initial installation, the video drivers are always changed while Windows is operating.

To correct this problem under Windows 9*x*, start the system in Safe mode. This action causes Windows to load a basic VGA video driver, enabling you to then change the display properties of the video card. In a Windows 2000 system, you should select the VGA Mode option to gain access to the video configuration by loading a standard VGA driver.

Similarly, adding input devices, such as a new mouse or joystick, can create problems where the new device does not work under the Windows environment. In the Windows operating system, there are several tools to help identify and isolate hardware related problems. These tools include the Device Manager (located under the Control Panel's System icon), the Hardware Troubleshooter procedures (located under the Help entry of the Start menu), and the various hardware-related icons in the Control Panel.

CHALLENGE #1

You believe your video display can produce a much higher resolution display than it is currently providing, so you change the video driver in you Windows 2000 Professional system. When you apply the new setting, you cannot see anything on the display. What should you do to regain control of your display?

Applications Will Not Install

In both Windows 9x and Windows 2000, most applications will autorun when their distribution CD is placed in the drive. The Autorun feature presents a user interface on the display that will guide the user through the installation process. If the Autorun feature in Windows 2000 is disabled in the drive's Properties page, the automatic interface will not start and the installation will not be performed. In Windows 9x, the Autorun feature is a function of the Registry and is not generally available to the user.

You should check the distribution CD for the presence of the Autorun.inf file. If it is present and no Autorun action occurs, you should examine the CD-ROM drive's Properties page to ensure that the Autorun function is enabled.

Some applications do not include the Autorun function as part of their installation scheme and are typically installed through the Control Panel's Add/Remove Programs applet. If the application is not on the *Windows 2000 Application Compatibility Toolkit (ACT—* the software equivalent of the HCL listing), the application might not install on the system or operate properly. This tool can be downloaded from the Microsoft Upgrade Web page.

Logon Problems

Login problems are common types of problems that can occur during startup (even though it is not actually a startup problem) or when trying to access different applications and utilities. Basically, in network and inter-networked computer environments, users cannot log on to systems and applications unless they have the proper authorization to do so. These problems tend to be very common in secure environments such as local and wide area networks.

The most common logon problem is the forgotten or invalid username and password. Invalid usernames and passwords typically result from poor typing or from having the Caps Lock function turned on. Users can also be prevented from logging on because of network station or time restrictions imposed by administrators. You should check with the network administrator to see whether the user's rights to the system have been restricted.

Windows 9x Operating Problems

Aside from the application, printing, and networking problem categories listed earlier, if the Windows 9x operating system starts up properly, only a limited number of things can go wrong afterward. The disk drive can run out of space, files can become corrupt, or the system can lock up because of software exception errors. When these problems occur, the system can either return an error message or simply stop processing.

Drive Space and Memory Problems

The System Information utility in the `\Programs\Accessories\System_Tools` path can be used to view the disk drive's space parameters. You also can check the drive's used/available space information by performing a `CheckDisk` operation on it.

If the system produces an Out of Memory error in Windows 9x, it is very unlikely that the system is running out of RAM—unless you are running DOS-based applications. In Windows 9x, this error indicates that the system is running out of memory space altogether—RAM and virtual.

Run the Windows System Monitor utility described later in this chapter to observe system memory usage and determine the nature of the error. If you are running DOS-based applications, you can optimize the system's use of conventional memory by running the old DOS MEMMAKER utility from the \Tools\Oldmsdos directory on the Windows distribution CD.

You can view the system's swap file settings through the Control Panel's System/Performance/Virtual Memory option or through the System Tool's System Information utility. Any lost clusters taking up space on the drive can be identified and eliminated using the ScanDisk utility. A heavily used, heavily fragmented hard drive can affect the system's virtual memory and produce memory shortages as well. Run the Defrag utility to optimize the storage patterns on the drive.

EXAM TIP

Be aware of the part that the disk drive plays in Windows 9x memory management and how to optimize its use.

If the system is running a FAT16 drive, you can free up additional space by converting it to a FAT32 drive. Use the CVT1.EXE command of the *Drive Converter* (*GFAT 32*) utility, as described in Chapter 22, "Basic Disk Management." The smaller sector clustering arrangement available through FAT32 frees up wasted space on the drive. The drawbacks of performing this upgrade are that you have some risk of losing data if a failure occurs in the conversion process and that larger files will have slightly slower read/write times than they did under FAT16.

EXAM TIP

Memorize which command-line utility can be used to convert the disk drive file system from FAT to FAT32.

If these corrective actions do not clear the memory error, you will need to remove unnecessary files from the drive, or install a larger drive. If the system begins to run out of hard disk space, remember that up to five backup copies of the Registry might be on the drive. This is a function of using the SCANREGW utility to check out the Registry structure for corruption. Each backup can be up to 2MB in size and can be removed to free up additional disk drive space.

Stalled Applications

If the system locks up or an application stalls, it is often possible to regain access to the Close Program dialog box by pressing the Ctrl+Alt+Del key combination. When the Close Program dialog box appears, you can close the offending application and continue operating the system without rebooting.

EXAM TIP

Know how to clear a stalled application in the Windows environment.

As an example, in Windows *9x* the *Windows Explorer* shell (EXPLORER.EXE) might crash and leave the system without a Start button or *Taskbar*. To recover from this condition, use the Ctrl+Alt+Del combination to access the Close Programs dialog box and shut the system down in a proper manner. Pressing the Ctrl+Alt+Del combination again will immediately shut down the operating system and any unsaved data in other open applications.

The Alt+F4 key combination can also be used to close active windows. Pressing this key combination in an application stops the application and moves to the next active application in the task list. If the Alt+F4 combination is pressed when no applications are active, the Windows Shut Down menu will appear on the display. This will enable you to conduct an orderly Shut Down or Restart of the system.

EXAM TIP

Memorize the functions associated with the Alt+F4 key combination.

EXAM TIP

Know the function of the Dr. Watson utility and where its information is stored in the system.

If the application repeatedly locks the system up, you must reinstall the application and check its configuration settings. The Dr. Watson utility also proves very useful in detecting application faults. When activated, Dr. Watson intercepts the software actions, detects the failure, identifies the application, and provides a detailed description of the failure. The information is automatically transferred to the disk drive and stored in the \Windows\Drwatson*.WLG file. You can view and print the information stored in the file from a word processor.

CHALLENGE #2

You are using a number of different applications on a Windows 9x system, but when you open a spreadsheet program, it hangs up and the system will not do anything. What is the best method to safely restart the system and retain the information you have in the other open applications?

If a DOS-based program is running and the system locks up, you must restore Windows 9x. To accomplish this, attempt to restart the system from a cold boot. If the system starts in Windows 9x, check the Properties of the DOS application. This information can be obtained by locating the program through the My Computer or Windows Explorer interface, right-clicking on its filename, and selecting the Properties option from the pop-up menu.

From the Properties page, select the Programs tab and then click the Advanced button to view the file's settings, as depicted in Figure 27.1. If the application is not already set for MS-DOS–mode operation, click the box to select it. Also select the Prevent MS-DOS–based Programs from Detecting Windows option. Return to the failing application to see whether it will run correctly in this environment.

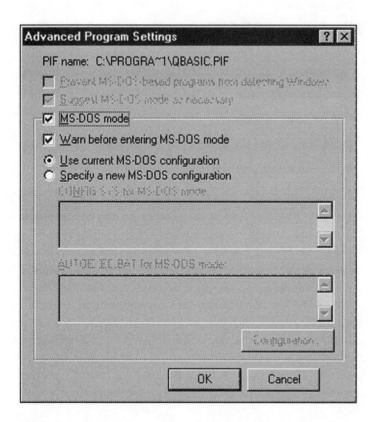

FIGURE 27.1
DOS Program properties.

Windows 98 occasionally produces an error message that says you are running out of resources. This message indicates that the operating system believes that it has exhausted all the system's real and virtual memory. Although the message tells you to correct the problem by shutting down applications, and it provides an endless series of application shutdown dialog windows, this process almost never works. Even shutting the applications down through the *Close Program dialog box* will not restore the system. Therefore, you should shut down the system and restart it. This action normally clears the problem.

Windows 2000 Operating Problems

You should be aware of some typical symptoms that can pop up during the normal operation of the Windows 2000 operating system, including the following:

◆ User cannot log on.

◆ You cannot recover an item that was deleted by another user.

◆ You cannot recover any items deleted.

◆ The video adapter supports higher resolution than the monitor does.

◆ You cannot find key files using Windows utilities.

When Windows 2000 is first installed, the only usable account is the Administrator account—the Guest account is disabled by default. Someone who has administrative privileges must create any additional user accounts. Each user account is given a password and username. If a user cannot log on, check his password. The password is case sensitive, so verify that the Caps Lock key is not an issue. If you forget the Administrator password and have not created any other accounts with Administrator privileges, you must reinstall Windows 2000.

EXAM TIP

Be aware that files deleted from remote and removable storage devices do not appear in the Recycle Bin.

You cannot recover an item that has been deleted by another user because the Recycle Bin is maintained on a user-by-user basis. If one user deletes something, only that user can recover it. You must log on as the user who deleted the items. Files and folders deleted from a floppy disk or network drive are permanently deleted and cannot be recovered. After the Recycle Bin fills to capacity, any newly deleted file or folder added causes older deleted items to be automatically deleted for the Recycle Bin.

Troubleshooting Application Problems

One of the other major operational problems that affect operating systems involves the application programs running in the system. Recall that in the Microsoft world, if the application is a BAT, EXE, or COM file, it should start when its name is properly entered on the command line. If such an application will not start in a command-line environment, you have a few basic possibilities to consider: It has been improperly identified; it is not located where it is supposed to be, or the application program is corrupted.

Check the spelling of the filename and reenter it at the command prompt. Also, verify that the path to the program has been presented correctly and thoroughly. If the path and filename are correct, the application might be corrupted. Reinstall the application and try to start it again.

Windows 9x Application Problems

As with other GUI-based environments, Windows 9x applications hide behind icons. The properties of each icon must correctly identify the filename and path of the application's executable file; otherwise, Windows will not be able to start it. Likewise, when a folder or file—accessed by the icon or by the shortcut from the Windows 9x Start menu—is moved, renamed, or removed, Windows will again not be able to find it when asked to start the application. Check the application's Properties to verify that the filename, path, and syntax are correct. Application Properties can be accessed by right-clicking on their desktop icon, as well as by right-clicking their entry in the Start menu, My Computer page, or Windows Explorer screen.

> **EXAM TIP**
>
> Be aware of the different methods of accessing an application's properties.

Most applications require Registry entries to run. If these entries are missing or corrupt, the application will not start. In addition, Windows 9x retains the DLL structure of its Windows 3.x predecessor under the \Windows\System directory. Corrupted or conflicting DLL files prevent applications from starting. To recover from these types of errors, you must reinstall the application.

Windows 2000 Application Problems

Windows 2000 might suffer the same types of application problems described for the Windows 9x versions:

◆ Incorrect application properties (filename, path, and syntax)

◆ Missing or corrupt Registry entries

◆ Conflicting DLL files

> **EXAM TIP**
>
> Know what items to look for when applications will not start.

Because Windows NT and Windows 2000 are typically used in client/server networks, some typical administrative problems associated with files, folders, and printers can pop up during their normal operations. These problems include such things as the following:

◆ Users cannot gain access to folders.

◆ Users send a print job to the printer, but cannot locate the documents.

◆ Users have Read permissions to a folder, but they can still make changes to files inside the folder.

◆ Users complain that they can see files in a folder but cannot access any of the files.

A user's inability to gain access to folders can come from many places. In the Windows NT/2000 environment, they might not have permissions that will enable them to access different files and folders. This is an administrative decision and can only be overcome by an administrator establishing permission levels that will permit access.

If the print job is visible in the spooler but does not print, this can be caused by the printer availability hours being set for times other than when you submitted the print job.

If users have Read permission for a folder, but can still make changes to files inside it, their file permissions must be set to Full Control, Write, or Modify. These permissions are applied directly to the file and override the folder permission of Read. You can correct this condition by changing the permissions on the individual files or at the folder level, allowing the permissions to propagate to files within the folder.

When users complain that they can see files in a folder but cannot access any of the files, they might have been assigned the List permission at the folder level. The List permission enables users to view the contents of the folder only, denying them all other permissions, including Read and Execute.

CHALLENGE #3

You have just installed a new Windows 2000 Professional operating system upgrade on a co-worker's machine. In the process of testing it, you discover that her word processor application will not start from the desktop icon. How should you go about troubleshooting this problem?

Locating Hidden Files

By default, Windows 2000 hides known filename extensions. If you cannot see filename extensions, open the Windows Explorer, click Tools, click Folder Options, click the View tab, and then locate and deselect the Hide File Extensions for Known Files option.

Likewise, Windows 2000, by default, does not display hidden or system files in Explorer. To see hidden or system files, open the Windows Explorer, click Tools, click Folder Options, click the View tab, and then locate and select the Show Hidden Files and Folders option.

> **EXAM TIP**
>
> Be aware that Windows 2000 does not show hidden and system files by default. Also, know how to display these file types from the Windows environment.

Windows 2000 Task Manager

In Windows NT and Windows 2000, the Close Program dialog window is referred to as the Task Manager. This utility can be used to determine which applications in the system are running or stopped, as well as which resources are being used. You can also determine general microprocessor and memory usage levels are.

When an application hangs up in these operating systems, you can access the Task Manager window depicted in Figure 27.2 and remove it from the list of tasks. The Windows 2000 Task Manager can be accessed by pressing Ctrl+Alt+Del or by pressing Ctrl+Shift+Esc. You can also access the Task Manager by right-clicking the system tray and selecting Task Manager from the pop-up contextual menu. The Ctrl+Shift+Esc key sequence moves directly into Task Manager while the Ctrl+Alt+Del selection opens the Windows Security menu screen, which offers Task Manager as an option.

> **EXAM TIP**
>
> Be able to access the Task Manager in Windows 2000, and be aware that it can be used to remove non-functioning applications from the system.

FIGURE 27.2
Task Manager.

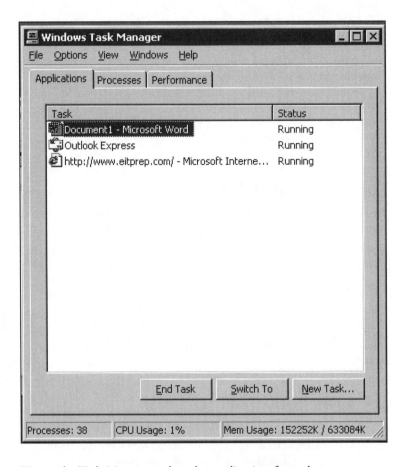

To use the Task Manager, select the application from the Applications tab and press the End Task button. If prompted, press the End Task button again to confirm the selection. The Performance tab provides a graphical summary of the system's CPU and memory usage. The Process tab provides information that can be helpful in tracking down problems associated with slow system operation.

CHALLENGE #4

You are using a commercial customer tracking database application on a Windows 2000 Professional system when the system hangs up and will not do anything. What is the best method to safely gain control of the system and remove the offending application?

WINDOWS-RELATED PRINTING PROBLEMS

A portion of the A+ Operating System Technologies objective 3.2 states that the test taker should be able to "recognize Windows-specific printing problems and identify the procedures for correcting them."

In a Windows-based system, the Windows environment controls the printing function through its drivers. Check the printer driver using the Control Panel's Print icon to make certain that the correct driver is installed. Substitute the standard VGA driver and try to print a document.

Determine whether the Print option from the application's File menu is unavailable (gray). If so, check the Windows Control Panel/Printers window for correct parallel port settings. Make certain that the correct printer driver is selected for the printer being used. If no printer type or the wrong printer type is selected, simply set the desired printer as the default printer.

Check to see whether there is a printer switch box between the computer and the printer. If so, remove the print sharing equipment and connect the computer directly to the printer.

Troubleshooting Windows Printing Problems

If a printer is not producing anything in a Windows 9x/NT/2000 environment even though print jobs have been sent to it, check the Print Spooler to see whether any particular type of error has occurred. To view documents waiting to be printed, double-click the desired printer's icon.

Return to the Printer folder, right-click the printer's icon, click Properties, and then select Details. From this point, select *Spool Settings* and select the Print Directly to the Printer option. If the print job goes through, there is a spooler problem. If not, the hardware and printer driver are suspect.

EXAM TIP

Remember how to test the operation of the Windows Print Spooler when the printer will not print.

To check spooler problems, examine the system for adequate hard disk space and memory. If the *Enhanced Metafile* (*EMF*) *Spooling* option is selected, disable it, clear the spooler, and try to print. To check the printer driver, right-click the printer icon, select the Properties option, and click the Details option. Reload or upgrade the driver if necessary.

If the printer operation stalls during the printing operation, some critical condition must have been reached to stop the printing process (that is, the system was running but stopped). Restart the system in Safe mode and try to print again. If the system still will not print, check the print driver, the video driver, and the amount of space on the hard disk drive. Delete backed up spool files (SPL and TMP) in the System/Spool/Printers directory.

CHALLENGE #5

When you arrive at the customer's machine, he tells you that he has been sending files to the local printer but nothing comes out. When you check the local print queue, you see the files sitting there and determine that they are not moving. What steps should you take to get the printer back into operation?

Troubleshooting Network Printing Problems

The complexity of printing across a network is much greater than local printing because of the need for additional network drivers and protocols. Many problems encountered when printing over the network involve components of the network operating system. Therefore, both the networking and printing functions must be checked.

When printing cannot be carried out across the network, verify that the local computer and the network printer are set up for remote printing. In Windows, this involves sharing the printer with the network users. The local computer that the printer is connected to, referred to as the print server, should appear in the Windows 9*x*

Network Neighborhood window of the remote computer. If the local computer cannot see files and printers at the print server station, file and print sharing might not be enabled there.

In Windows 9*x*, file and printer sharing can be accomplished at the print server in a number of ways. First, double-click the printer's icon in the My Computer window or the Windows Explorer screen. Select the Printer/Properties/Sharing option and then choose the desired configuration. The second method uses right-clicking on the printer's icon, followed by selecting Share in the Context menu, and choosing the desired configuration. The final method is similar except that you right-click the printer's icon, click Properties, Sharing, and then choose the configuration.

Run the printer's *self-test* to verify that its hardware is working correctly. If it will not print a test page, there is obviously a problem with the printer hardware. Next, troubleshoot the printer hardware. When the operation of the hardware is working, attempt to print across the network again.

Next, determine whether the print server can print directly to the printer. Open a document on the print server and attempt to print it. If the file will not print directly to the local printer, there is a problem in the local hardware. Troubleshoot the situation as a local, standalone printer problem.

If the local print server operation is working, verify the operation of the network by attempting to perform other network functions, such as transferring a file from the remote unit to the print server. In Windows 9*x*, open the Control Panel's Printer folder and select the Properties entry in the drop-down File menu. Check the information under the Details and Sharing tabs.

If other network functions are operational, verify the printer operation of the local computer. If possible, connect a printer directly to the local unit and set its print driver up to print to the local printer port. If the file prints to the local printer, a network/printer driver problem still exists. Reload the printer driver and check the network print path, as depicted in Figure 27.3. The correct format for the UNC network pathname is \\computer_name\shared_device_name.

> **EXAM TIP**
> Be aware that not having File and Print sharing enabled will cause computers to not "see" the other computers across the network.

> **EXAM TIP**
> Know how to create a UNC path from a local computer to a remote printer, or a directory located on a remote computer.

FIGURE 27.3
Checking the printer path.

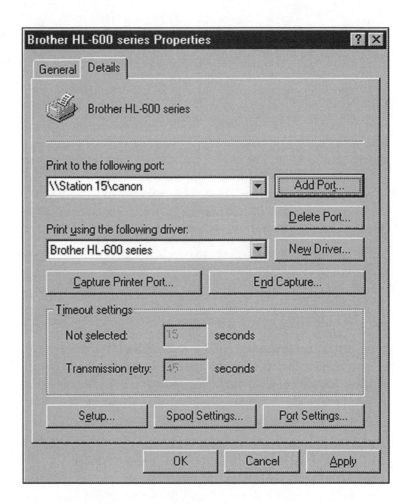

VIRUSES

Computer viruses are destructive programs designed to replicate and spread on their own. Viruses are created to sneak into personal computers. Sometimes these programs take control of a machine to leave a humorous message, and sometimes they destroy data. After they infiltrate one machine, they can spread into other computers through infected disks that friends and coworkers pass around or through local and wide area network connections.

Common Viruses

There are basically three types of viruses, based on how they infect a computer system:

◆ A boot-sector virus—This type of virus copies itself onto the boot sector of floppy and hard disks. The virus replaces the disk's original boot-sector code with its own code. This allows it to be loaded into memory before anything else is loaded. Once in memory, the virus can spread to other disks.

◆ A file infector—File infectors are viruses that add their virus code to executable files. After the file with the virus is executed, it spreads to other executable files. A similar type of virus, called a macro virus, hides in the macro programs of word processing document files. These files can be designed to load when the document is opened or when a certain key combination is entered. In addition, these types of viruses can be designed to stay resident in memory after the host program has been exited (similar to a TSR program), or they might just stop working when the infected file is terminated.

◆ A Trojan horse—This type of virus appears to be a legitimate program that might be found on any system. Trojan horse viruses are more likely to do damage by destroying files, and they can cause physical damage to disks.

A number of different viruses have been created from these three virus types. They have several different names, but they all inflict basically the same damage. After the virus file has become active in the computer, it basically resides in memory when the system is running. From this point, it might perform a number of different types of operations that can be as complex and damaging as the author designs them to be.

As an example, a strain of boot-sector virus, known as *CMOS virus*, infects the hard drive's Master Boot Record and becomes memory resident. When activated, the virus writes over the system's configuration information in the CMOS area. Part of what gets overwritten is the HDD and FDD information. Therefore, the system cannot boot up properly. The initial infection comes from booting from an infected floppy disk. The virus overwrites the CMOS once in every 60 bootups.

A similar boot-sector virus, referred to as the *FAT virus*, becomes memory resident in the area of system memory where the IO.SYS and MSDOS.SYS files are located. This allows it to spread to any non–write-protected disks inserted into the computer. In addition, the virus moves the system pointers for the disk's executable files to an unused cluster and rewrites the pointers in the FAT to point to the sector where the virus is located. The result is improper disk copies, inability to back up files, large numbers of lost clusters, and all executable files being cross-linked with each other.

In another example, a file infector virus strain, called the *FAT table* virus, infects EXE files but does not become memory resident. When the infected file is executed, the virus rewrites another EXE file.

EXAM TIP

Know how the different types of viruses attack the system.

Virus Symptoms

Because viruses tend to operate in the background, it is sometimes difficult to realize that the computer has been infected. Typical virus symptoms include the following:

◆ Hard disk controller failures.

◆ Disks continue to be full even when files have been deleted.

◆ System cannot read write-protected disks.

◆ The hard disk stops booting, and files are corrupted.

◆ The system will boot to floppy disk, but will not access the HDD.

◆ An Invalid Drive Specification message usually displays when attempting to access the C: drive.

◆ CMOS settings continually revert to default even though the system board battery is good.

◆ Files change size for no apparent reason.

◆ System operation slows down noticeably.

◆ Blank screen when booting (flashing cursor).

◆ Windows crashes.

◆ The hard drive is set to DOS compatibility, and 32-bit file access suddenly stops working.

◆ Network data transfers and print jobs slow down dramatically.

Common practices that increase the odds of a machine being infected by a virus include use of shareware software, software of unknown origin, or bulletin board software. One of the most effective ways to reduce these avenues of infection is to buy shrink-wrapped products from a reputable source.

Another means of virus protection involves installing a virus-scanning program that checks disks and files before using them in the computer. Several other companies offer third-party virus-protection software that can be configured to operate in various ways. If the computer is a standalone unit, it might be nonproductive to have the antivirus software run each time the system is booted up. It would be much more practical to have the program check floppy disks only because this is the only possible entryway into the computer.

A networked or online computer has more opportunity to contract a virus than a standalone unit because viruses can enter the unit over the network or through the modem. In these cases, setting the software to run at each bootup is more desirable. Most modern antivirus software includes utilities to check files downloaded to the computer through dial-up connections, such as from the Internet.

With Windows 95, Microsoft abandoned integrated antivirus protection. Therefore, you must use third-party antivirus programs with Windows 9x and Windows 2000.

> **EXAM TIP**
>
> Know how viruses are spread.

CHALLENGE #6

A customer calls you to his site complaining that the wide-carriage, dot-matrix printer in his accounting department is running very slowly and that they cannot get all their invoices printed for today's shipping purposes. When you check their print queue, you see that the print jobs for the invoices are stacked up in the queue but that they are being processed. The accounting manager tells you that they typically don't have any problems getting their invoices printed and that nothing out of the ordinary has been done to the computer to make it slow down. What items should you check to determine the cause of the slow down?

> **NOTE**
>
> **Hands-On Activity** For hands-on experience with this concept, refer to Lab Procedure #30, "Windows 2000 Virus Protection," located on the CD that accompanies this book.

CHAPTER SUMMARY

KEY TERMS

- Close Program dialog box
- CMOS virus
- Computer viruses
- CVT1.EXE
- Drive Converter (GFAT 32)
- Enhanced Metafile (EMF) Spooling
- FAT table
- FAT virus
- General Protection Faults (GPF)
- Login problems
- Self-test
- Spool Settings
- Taskbar
- This Application Has Performed an Illegal Operation and Is About to Be Shut Down
- Windows 2000 Application Compatibility Toolkit (ACT)
- Windows Explorer

This chapter contained material associated with typical operational problems associated with Microsoft operating systems. Once again, Windows 9x and Windows 2000 systems were discussed, and typical error messages and symptoms were related to probable causes for both types of systems. An extended discussion of Windows utilities was presented in this section as well.

The second section of the chapter was dedicated to printing problems associated with the different Windows operating systems. Specific types of printing problems were presented, along with procedures for correcting them.

The final topic the chapter dealt with was computer viruses. Different types of viruses were described, along with ways to protect computer systems against them.

At this point, review the objectives listed at the beginning of the chapter to be certain that you understand each point and can perform each task listed there. Afterward, answer the review questions that follow to verify your knowledge of the information.

APPLY YOUR KNOWLEDGE

Review Questions

1. What part does the disk drive play in Windows 9x memory management?

    A. The page file is located on the hard disk drive.

    B. Real memory storage is on the hard disk drive.

    C. The memory registers are located on the hard disk drive.

    D. The swap file is located on the hard disk drive.

2. How is disk drive performance optimized?

    A. ScanDisk

    B. Clean up to improve free disk space

    C. Defrag

    D. Convert the file system to FAT16

3. How is a stalled application cleared in the Windows 9x environment?

    A. Press Ctrl+Alt+Del, select Task Manager, highlight all non-responding applications, and click End Task

    B. Press Ctrl+Alt+Del and close all non-responding applications

    C. Start/Settings/Control Panel/Add-Remove Programs, select the offending program, and click Remove

    D. Start/Programs/Accessories/System Tools/System Manager and close all non-responding applications

4. What are the two possible functions associated with the Alt+F4 key combination?

    A. Stops an application or opens the Shut Down Windows menu

    B. Stops an application or restarts the computer

    C. Opens the Close Program window or opens the Shut Down Windows menu

    D. Switches the active window or opens the Shut Down Windows menu

5. What is the function of the Dr. Watson utility?

    A. Analyzes system failures

    B. Analyzes virus activity

    C. Detects and logs an application failure

    D. Detects and logs unauthorized user access

6. Where is the Dr. Watson utility information stored in the system?

    A. \Windows\Drwatson*.WLG

    B. \Drwatson*.WLG

    C. \Program Files\Drwatson*.WLG

    D. \Windows\System\Drwatson*.WLG

7. Which command-line utility can be used to convert the disk drive file system from FAT to FAT32?

    A. CNVRT1.EXE

    B. CONVERT.EXT

    C. CVT1.EXE

    D. CONVTER.EXE

APPLY YOUR KNOWLEDGE

8. What type of deleted files do not appear in the Recycle Bin? (Select two answers.)

   A. System files

   B. Files from remote devices

   C. Files from removable storage devices

   D. Hidden files

9. How are hidden and system files displayed from the Windows 2000 environment?

   A. Start/Settings/Control Panel/System/Folder Options/View tab; then locate and select the Show Hidden Files and Folders option

   B. Open Windows Explorer/Tools/Folder Options; then locate and select the Show Hidden Files and Folders option

   C. Start/Programs/Accessories/System Tools/Folder Options/View tab; then locate and select the Show Hidden Files and Folders option

   D. Open Windows Explorer/Tools/Folder Options/View tab; then locate and select the Show Hidden Files and Folders option

10. What methods can be used to access an MS-DOS application's Properties?

    A. Right-click on the filename and select Properties from the contextual menu.

    B. Click on the filename to highlight it and then select Properties from the View menu.

    C. Click on the filename to highlight it and then select Properties from the Edit menu.

    D. Click on the filename to highlight it and then select Properties from the Tools menu.

11. When applications will not start in Windows, what items should be looked for? (Select all that apply.)

    A. Conflicting DLL files

    B. Incorrect application properties

    C. Missing or corrupt registry entries

    D. Incompatibility with operating system

12. The _____ in Windows 2000 can be used to remove non-functioning applications from the system.

    A. Close Program tool

    B. Task Manager tool

    C. Close Application tool

    D. Computer Management tool

13. How is the operation of the Windows 9x Print Spooler tested when the printer will not print?

    A. Start/Settings/Printers, right-click on the printer icon, select Properties, and then click on the Print Test Page button

    B. Start/Settings/Printers, click on the printer icon to highlight it, click on the File menu, select Properties, and then click on the Print Test Page button

    C. Start/Settings/Printers, right-click on the printer icon, select Properties, click on the Details button, select Spool Settings, and then select the Print Directly to Printer option

    D. Start/Settings/Printers, right-click on the printer icon, select Properties, click on the Advanced tab, and then select the Print Directly to Printer option

14. How is a UNC path created from a local computer to a remote printer or a directory located on a remote computer?

    A. `//shared_resource_name`

    B. `//computer_name/shared_resource_name`

    C. `\\shared_resource_name`

    D. `\\Computer_name\shared_resource_name`

15. How does a Trojan horse virus attack a system?

    A. It replaces a disk's original boot-sector code.

    B. It adds code to a legitimate program.

    C. It appears to be a normal program.

    D. Attack occurs when a document is opened.

16. Which of the following represents the least likely method to spread computer viruses?

    A. Installing downloaded software

    B. Sending MS Word documents over email

    C. Installing shrink-wrapped commercial software

    D. Transferring a file via a floppy disk

17. What happens when the Ctrl+Alt+Del keys are pressed twice?

    A. Computer shuts down.

    B. Computer restarts.

    C. The Close Program window opens.

    D. The currently running application will shut down.

18. How can you kill an application in Windows 2000? (Select all that apply.)

    A. Right-click the system tray, select Task Manager from the contextual menu, click the Applications tab, highlight the application, and click End Task

    B. Press Ctrl+Alt+Esc, click on Task Manager, click the Applications tab, highlight the application, and click End Task

    C. Press Ctrl+Shift+Esc, click the Applications tab, highlight the application, and click End Task

    D. Press Ctrl+Alt+Del, click on Task Manager, click the Applications tab, highlight the application, and click End Task

19. How does a macro virus attack a system?

    A. It replaces a disk's original boot-sector code.

    B. It adds code to a legitimate program.

    C. It appears to be a normal program.

    D. Attack occurs when an infected document is opened.

20. What is a common reason for not seeing a remote printer in Windows 9x Network Neighborhood?

    A. Inadequate access rights

    B. File and printer sharing not enabled

    C. Improper printer name

    D. No driver loaded

APPLY YOUR KNOWLEDGE

Answers and Explanations

1. **D**. A heavily used, heavily fragmented hard drive can affect the system's virtual memory (in particular the swap file) and produce memory shortages as well. For more information, see the section "Drive Space and Memory Problems."

2. **C**. You should run the Defrag utility to optimize the storage patterns on the drive and thus improve read/write times and virtual memory performance. For more information, see the section "Drive Space and Memory Problems."

3. **B**. If the system locks up or an application stalls, it is often possible to regain access to the Close Program dialog box by pressing the Ctrl+Alt+Del key combination. After the Close Program dialog box appears, you can close the offending application and continue operating the system without rebooting. For more information, see the section "Stalled Applications."

4. **A**. The Alt+F4 key combination can be used to close active windows. Pressing this key combination in an application stops the application and moves to the next active application in the task list. If the Alt+F4 combination is pressed when no applications are active, the Shut Down Windows menu will appear on the display. This will enable you to conduct an orderly Shut Down or Restart of the system. For more information, see the section "Stalled Applications."

5. **C**. The Dr. Watson utility proves very useful in detecting application faults. When activated, Dr. Watson intercepts the software actions, detects the failure, identifies the application, and provides a detailed description of the failure. For more information, see the section "Stalled Applications."

6. **A**. The Dr Watson information is automatically transferred to the disk drive and stored in the \Windows\Drwatson*.WLG file. You can view and print the information stored in the file from a word processor. For more information, see the section "Stalled Applications."

7. **C**. You can free up additional space by converting a FAT16 drive to a FAT32 drive using the CVT1.EXE command-line utility. The smaller sector clustering arrangement available through FAT32 frees up wasted space on the drive. For more information, see the section "Drive Space and Memory Problems."

8. **B, C**. Files and folders deleted from a floppy disk or network drive are permanently deleted and cannot be recovered. For more information, see the section "Windows 2000 Operating Problems."

9. **D**. To see hidden or system files, open the Windows Explorer, click Tools, click Folder Options, click the View tab, and then locate and select the Show Hidden Files and Folders option. For more information, see the section "Locating Hidden Files."

10. **A**. The Properties of a DOS application can be obtained by locating the program through the My Computer or Windows Explorer interface, right-clicking on its filename, and selecting the Properties option from the pop-up menu. For more information, see the section "Windows 9x Application Problems."

11. **A, B, C**. Windows 2000 might suffer the same types of application problems described for the Windows 9x versions: incorrect application properties (filename, path, and syntax); missing or corrupt Registry entries; conflicting DLL files.

For more information, see the section "Windows 2000 Application Problems."

12. **B.** In Windows NT and Windows 2000, the Close Program dialog window is replaced by the Task Manager. This utility can be used to determine which applications in the system are running or stopped, as well as which resources are being used. You can also determine what general microprocessor and memory usage levels are. A non-functioning application can be removed using Task Manager in Windows 2000. For more information, see the section "Windows 2000 Task Manager."

13. **C.** To test the Printer spooler, access the Printer folder through the Start/Settings/Printers path, right-click the printer's icon, click Properties, and then select Details. From this point, select Spool Settings and select the Print Directly to the Printer option. If the print job goes through, there is a spooler problem. If not, the hardware and printer driver are suspect. For more information, see the section "Troubleshooting Windows Printing Problems."

14. **D.** The correct format for the UNC network path to a shared network device is `\\computer_name\shared_resource_name`. For more information, see the section "Troubleshooting Network Printing Problems."

15. **C.** A Trojan appears to be a legitimate program that might be found on any system. Trojan horse viruses are more likely to do damage by destroying files, and they can cause physical damage to disks. For more information, see the section "Common Viruses."

16. **C.** Common practices that increase the odds of a machine being infected by a virus include use of shareware software, software of unknown origin, or bulletin board software. One of the most effective ways to reduce these avenues of infection is to buy shrink-wrapped products from a reputable source. For more information, see the section "Virus Symptoms."

17. **A.** To recover from conditions in which you cannot control the operating system properly, use the Ctrl+Alt+Del combination to access the Close Programs dialog box and shut the system down in a proper manner. If you cannot use the mouse, pressing the Ctrl+Alt+Del combination again will immediately shut down the operating system and any unsaved data in other open applications. For more information, see the section "Stalled Applications."

18. **A, C, D.** There are several methods for accessing Task Manager in Windows 2000: press Ctrl+Alt+Del and then click on the Task Manager button; press Ctrl+Shift+Esc; right-click the system tray; select Task Manager from the pop-up contextual menu. For more information, see the section "Windows 2000 Task Manager."

19. **D.** A macro virus hides in the macro programs of word processing document files. These files can be designed to load when the document is opened or when a certain key combination is entered. In addition, these types of viruses can be designed to stay resident in memory after the host program has been exited (similar to a TSR program), or they might just stop working when the infected file is terminated. For more information, see the section "Common Viruses."

20. **B**. When printing cannot be carried out across the network, verify that the local computer and the network printer are set up for remote printing. In Windows, this involves sharing the printer with the network users. The local computer that the printer is connected to, referred to as the print server, should appear in the Windows 9*x* Network Neighborhood window of the remote computer. If the local computer cannot see files and printers at the print server station, file and print sharing might not be enabled there. For more information, see the section "Troubleshooting Network Printing Problems."

Challenge Solutions

1. To correct this problem under the Windows 2000 system, you should select the VGA Mode option to gain access to the video configuration by loading a standard VGA driver. This action causes Windows to start the system normally using the standard VGA video driver, enabling you to then change the display properties of the video card. For more information, see the section "Optional Devices Will Not Operate."

2. If the system locks up or an application stalls, it is often possible to regain access to the Close Program dialog box by pressing the Ctrl+Alt+Del key combination. After the Close Program dialog box appears, you can close the offending application and continue operating the system without rebooting.

   Pressing the Ctrl+Alt+Del key combination twice will restart the system, but the unsaved information in the other open applications would be lost. For more information, see the section "Stalled Applications."

3. In Windows, the properties of each icon must correctly identify the filename and path of the application's executable file. If not, Windows will not be able to start the application. If the folder or file containing the executable were moved, renamed, or removed in the upgrade, Windows would not be able to find it when asked to start the application. Check the application's Properties to verify that its filename, path, and syntax are correct. Application Properties can be accessed by right-clicking on the desktop icon, as well as by right-clicking the entry in the Start menu, My Computer page, or Windows Explorer screen.

   One of the applications core files, such as a dll, could have been erased, or become corrupted in the upgrade. In this case, you would need to reinstall the application. For more information, see the section "Windows 2000 Application Problems."

4. In Windows 2000, pressing the Ctrl+Shift+Esc key combination will directly access the Task Manager window so that you can remove nonfunctioning applications from the list of tasks. For more information, see the section "Windows 2000 Task Manager."

5. Begin by making sure that the printer is not in an offline condition and that the physical connection is correct. Next, change the settings in the Printer Properties page so that it prints directly to the port, instead of to the spooler. If the information begins moving to the printer, reinstall the printer driver. This should reset the spooler in the process. Other options for repairing the spooler include extracting the spooler files from the Windows distribution CD or simply reinstalling the operating system. For more information, see

APPLY YOUR KNOWLEDGE

the section "Troubleshooting Windows Printing Problems."

6. This is a classic symptom of a virus infection. The virus is using excessive amounts of memory, slowing down the computer's operation. The other possible cause of this symptom is a nearly full hard drive. The lack of space for the print spooler and other temporary files caused by either of these situations make it difficult for the system to process information for the printer. Check the hard drive's Temporary folders for TMP files that have accumulated on there. For more information, see the section "Virus Symptoms."

Suggested Readings and Resources

1. General Protection Faults
   http://support.microsoft.com/
   default.aspx?scid=kb;EN-US;q82710

2. Fatal Exception Error
   http://support.microsoft.com/
   default.aspx?scid=kb;en-us;Q150314

3. Converting from FAT to FAT32
   http://www.happytech.net/Articles/
   KenWincel/Fat32Info.htm

4. Ctrl+Alt+Del
   http://www.atlguide2000.com/eng/win2k/
   ctrldel.htm

5. Locating Hidden Files
   http://digital.ni.com/public.nsf/web-
   search/42c48f8709e53ce886256b6d006334d7?Op
   enDocument

6. Microsoft's Super Hidden Files
   http://netsecurity.about.com/library/
   weekly/aa020402a.htm

7. Windows 2000 Task Manager
   http://www.labmice.net/troubleshooting/
   taskmgr.htm

8. Windows-Related Printing Problems
   http://www.michigan.gov/sos/1,1607,7-127-
   1633_11976_12001-31042--CI,00.html

9. Troubleshooting Network Printing
   http://www.iup.edu/helpdesk/service/pc/
   network/netprint.shtm

10. Symantec Antivirus Center
    http://www.symantec.com/avcenter/

11. Boot-Sector Virus
    http://www.itsecurity.com/asktecs/jul2101.
    htm

12. Method to Detect a Boot-Sector Virus in Windows
    http://support.microsoft.com/
    default.aspx?scid=kb;EN-US;q82923

13. Trojan
    http://www.xtra.co.nz/help/
    0,,5739-544116,00.html

This chapter helps you to prepare for the Operating System Technologies module of the A+ Certification examination by covering the following objective within the "Domain 4.0: Networks" section.

4.1 Identify the networking capabilities of Windows including procedures for connecting to the network.

Content might include the following:

- **Protocols**

- **IPCONFIG.EXE**

- **WINIPCFG.EXE**

- **Sharing disk drives**

- **Sharing print and file services**

- **Network type and network card**

- **Installing and configuring browsers**

- **Configure OS for network connection**

▶ Local area networks have become a major part of the personal computer market. The prevalence of local area networks (LANs) in businesses requires that PC technicians know how to install and maintain LAN equipment and software.

CHAPTER 28

Networking with Windows

OUTLINE

STUDY STRATEGIES

To prepare for the Networks objective of the Operating Systems Technologies exam,

▶ Read the objectives at the beginning of this chapter.

▶ Study the information in this chapter.

▶ Review the objectives listed earlier in this chapter.

▶ Perform any step-by-step procedures in the text.

▶ Answer the review questions at the end of the chapter and check your results.

▶ Use the PrepLogic test engine on the CD-ROM that accompanies this book for additional review and exam questions concerning this material.

▶ Review the exam tips scattered throughout the chapter and make certain that you are comfortable with each point.

INTRODUCTION

The network operating system is responsible for providing the networking functions of computers connected to a local area network. This chapter begins with a section that describes basic local area network hardware and resource sharing.

The second section of the chapter describes networking as it applies to the Windows 9x environment. In particular, this section focuses on the Network Neighborhood applet and the Network Icon in the Control Panel where networking is managed in the Windows 9x systems. The section also deals with installing and configuring network components and managing network printing with Windows 9x.

The next section of the chapter focuses on networking with Windows 2000. As with the Windows 9x section, this section deals primarily with the My Network Places applet and Windows 2000 Network Control Panel. The section also covers network printing with Windows 2000.

The third major section of the chapter is dedicated to troubleshooting local area network problems. The first portion of this section covers Windows 9x networking problems, whereas the remainder of the troubleshooting information deals with Windows 2000 networking problems.

The final section of the chapter deals with networking with the Novell NetWare network operating system.

After completing the chapter, you should be able to identify the networking capabilities of Windows 9x and Windows 2000, including procedures configuring both systems for connecting to the local area network. You should also be able to use Windows network troubleshooting utilities to locate the source of networking problems.

NETWORK HARDWARE

Networking PCs begins with the network type and card. The type of network determines which transfer protocol you need to load, and the network card determines which adapter driver you can install.

The *Network Interface Card (NIC)* must be configured to communicate with the system software. With older legacy network cards, you accomplished this by setting hardware jumpers to a specified pattern on the card before it was installed in the computer. With newer ISA and PCI cards, this is accomplished through the plug-and-play process. The typical parameters that must be established for the NIC include the IRQ level (IRQ-5/10/11/15), Base I/O port address (300h/210h/220h), and the Base memory address (D0000h/C800h).

RESOURCE SHARING

The concept of sharing directories, files, and hardware resources is central to the design of any *network operating system (NOS)*. The overriding features that distinguish a NOS system from a DOS system are the sharing and security features of the NOS. These features are typically manifested in passwords, permission levels, and access rights for the system's users.

EXAM TIP

Know what the DOS SHARE command does.

In later versions of DOS, however, Microsoft added the SHARE.EXE command to provide file-sharing and -locking capabilities for files on a local hard disk drive. These capabilities enabled multiple users to access the same file at the same time in a networked or multitasking environment. With version 3.11, the Windows operating system added built-in, peer-to-peer networking capabilities to the operating environment and titled it *Windows for Workgroups (WfW)*.

In a network environment, only shared directories and resources can be accessed across the network. The sharing function is instituted at the remote computer. In Windows, the presence of a hand under the folder or device icon notifies other potential users that this resource or directory has been shared and can be accessed.

To access a shared remote resource, the local operating system must first connect to it. When the connection is established with a remote drive or folder, the local operating system creates a new logical drive on the local machine to handle the shared directory. Normally, the local file management system assigns the directory the next available drive letter in the local system.

The path to the shared resource contains a little more information than the path to a local directory. The remote path must include the remote computer's name and shared resource name (directory or printer). It also must be expressed using the *universal naming convention* (*UNC*) format. This format begins with a pair of back slashes followed by the computer name and the resource name. Each name in the path is separated by a single backslash. Therefore, the format of a shared path is `\\computer name\directory name`.

Valid computer names in Windows 9*x* can be up to 15 characters in length and cannot contain any blank spaces. In Windows 2000 using the TCP/IP protocol, computer names can range up to 63 characters in length and should be made up of the letters A through Z, numbers 0 through 9, and hyphens.

<table>
<tr><td>EXAM TIP</td><td>Know the specifications for setting up computer names in a given operating system.</td></tr>
</table>

NETWORKING WITH WINDOWS 9*x*

In Windows 9*x*, the peer-to-peer local area networking function is an integral part of the system. The heart of the Windows 9*x* networking system is contained in the desktop's Network Neighborhood icon and the Control Panel's Network icon.

Network Neighborhood

The Network Neighborhood display, depicted in Figure 28.1, is the primary network user interface for Windows 9*x*. It is used to browse and access shared resources on the LAN—in a method similar to that used with the Windows Explorer for a local hard drive. Most directory- and file-level activities, such as opening and saving files, can be performed through the Network Neighborhood screen.

FIGURE 28.1
Network Neighborhood.

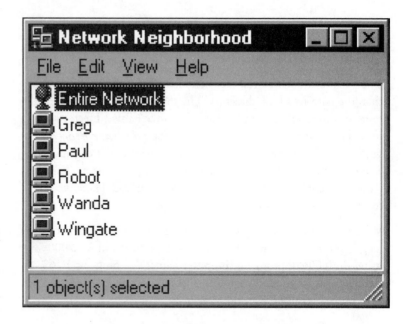

Microsoft networks group logically related computers together in workgroups for convenient browsing of resources. The local computer is a part of a workgroup. Double-clicking the Network Neighborhood icon displays the printers and folders available in the workgroup. If the desired computer does not display, double-click the Entire Network icon. This action displays any other workgroups in the system, along with any additional printers and folders that are available.

If the Network Neighborhood window is empty or if its icon is missing, networking connections have not been established. If this is the case, you must correctly configure networking on the local unit to connect to any other computers on the network. This is accomplished through the Control Panel's Network icon.

Mapping a Drive

It is possible for the local system to assign a logical drive letter to the remote unit, or folder. This is referred to as *mapping the drive* letter to the resource. This mapping enables non-Windows 9x applications running on the local computer to use the resource across the network.

A drive map is a very important tool in a network environment. It allows a single computer to act as though it possesses all the hard drives that reside in the network. The operating system coordinates the access to various systems so that drives located on other physical machines show up as logical drives on the local machine. This shows up in the Windows Explorer and My Computer screens, as illustrated in Figure 28.2.

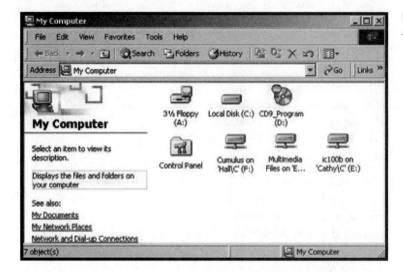

FIGURE 28.2
A mapped drive display.

The primary reason to map a drive in a network environment is because some applications cannot recognize volume names. They can see only drive letters. In Windows 9x, the number of recognizable drive letters is 26 (A-Z). Some network operating systems can recognize an extended number of drive letters (for example, A-Z and AA-ZZ). By using unique volume names to identify drives, however, the Windows 2000 system is capable of recognizing a vast number of network drives.

For a local system to access a remote resource, the resource must be shared, and the local user must have a valid network user ID and password. The user's assigned rights and permissions are tied to his or her password throughout the network—either through individual settings or through group settings.

To map (assign) a drive letter to a remote network computer, or folder, open the Windows Explorer. From the Tools menu, select the Map Network Drive option. This will display the Map Network Drive dialog box, as illustrated in Figure 28.3.

FIGURE 28.3
The Map Network Drive dialog box.

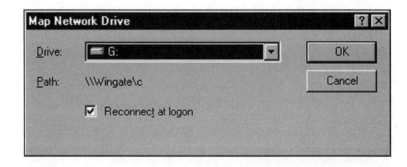

EXAM TIP

Be aware of how to apply the UNC format to shared resources.

EXAM TIP

Know what will cause a mapped drive to disappear from a system when it is shut down and restarted.

Windows attempts to assign the next available drive letter to the computer or folder indicated in the Path dialog box. Establishing the map to the resource is a simple matter of entering the required path and share name in the dialog box, using the UNC format (*host_name**drive_path**shared_resource_name*). The format always begins with double slashes \\.

The Reconnect at Logon option must be selected in the Map Network Drive page for the drive mapping to become a permanent part of the system. If the option is not selected when the user logs off, the mapped drive information disappears and needs to be remapped for any further use. If a red X appears on the icon of a properly mapped drive, this indicates that the drive is no longer available. Its host computer might be turned off, the drive might have been removed, or it might no longer be on the same path. If the drive was mapped to a particular folder and the folder name has been changed, the red X will also appear.

The Network Icon in Control Panel

The Control Panel's Network screen, shown in Figure 28.4, provides configuration and properties information about the system's networks. The system's installed network components are listed under the Network Configuration tab.

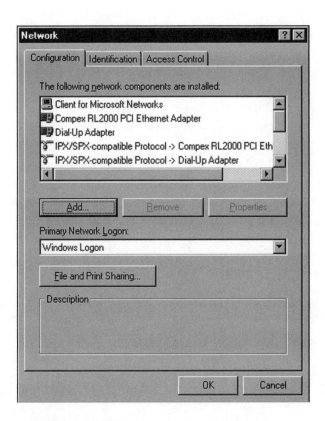

FIGURE 28.4
The Network Control Panel screen.

Double-clicking an installed adapter's driver, or clicking the Properties button when the driver is highlighted, produces its Configuration information page. The Add and Remove buttons on this page are used to install and remove network drivers from the system.

The Primary Network Logon window is used to establish which type of network Windows 9x will enter when it starts up. This proves particularly helpful on systems that might be working in multiple network environments (such as a computer that might need to access Microsoft network resources in some situations and Novell network resources at other times).

The File and Print Sharing button is used to select the first level of resource sharing for the local unit. Sharing can be individually enabled/disabled for file and printer accesses from remote computers.

Installing Network Components

After the network adapter card has been configured and installed, the next step in setting up the computer on the network is to load its drivers, protocols, and services. In most Windows 9*x* installations, the majority of these steps can be accomplished by simply rebooting the computer so that Windows can detect the network adapter.

The Windows 9*x* networking utilities should produce an adapter driver, a *Microsoft Client protocol*, and a *Novell NetWare Client protocol* in the Network Configuration window in a typical installation. A default set of file and print sharing services also are loaded. The only items that must be installed manually are the protocols for the particular type of network being used. Clicking the Add button in the Network Configuration page brings up the Select Network Component Type screen depicted in Figure 28.5.

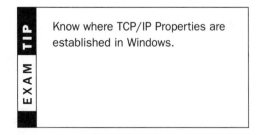

EXAM TIP

Know where TCP/IP Properties are established in Windows.

FIGURE 28.5
The Select Network Component Type screen.

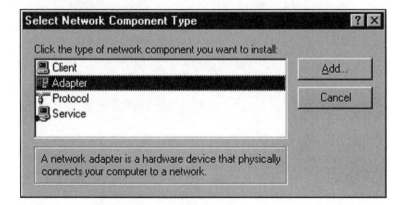

The types of networking components include four categories:

◆ *Client*—Software that enables the system to use files and printers shared on other computers

◆ *Adapter*—Drivers that control the physical hardware connected to the network

◆ *Protocol*—Rules that the computers use to govern the exchange of information across the network

◆ *Service*—Utilities that enable resources and provide support services, such as automated backup, remote registry, and network monitoring facilities

If a particular network type is not supported in the standard listings, the Components page features a Have Disk button that permits the system to upload Windows-compatible drivers and protocols.

Because the boot-up detection process loads the adapter driver, two types of clients to choose from, and a set of sharing parameters, most installation procedures require only that the appropriate protocols be loaded for the network type. In a Microsoft network application, these usually include the *NetBEUI* and *IPX/SPX* (also known as *NWLink*) protocols for the LAN. An additional *TCP/IP* protocol can be added for Internet support.

In a Windows network, the set of rules that govern the exchange of data between computers is the *NetBIOS Extended User Interface* (*NetBEUI*) protocol. This protocol works in most purely Windows networks so that no other protocol is called for. All the devices on the network must use the same protocol to be able to communicate with each other. If an additional protocol is required, choose the Add Protocol option in the Network Components dialog box to add another protocol. *Network adapters* can typically handle up to four different protocols.

Although NetBEUI is easy to implement, it is a non-routable protocol. Because NetBEUI uses broadcast techniques to find other nodes on the network, it has no inherent capabilities to access nodes outside of the immediate physical network segment. Therefore, it is not used in wide area networking applications. However, NetBEUI is required to support dial up *Remote Access Services* (*RAS*) through a modem. The RAS service uses the NetBEUI protocol to navigate through a network after you have dialed into it. Both the calling client and the receiving server in the LAN must be running NetBEUI. If either computer does not have this protocol active, the client will be able to connect with the LAN, but will not be able to navigate through it.

IPX/SPX is a Novell network protocol for LANs, and TCP/IP is the Internet protocol supported by Windows 9x and Windows NT/2000.

EXAM TIP

Remember the meaning of the term NetBEUI and know what type of network operating system it belongs to.

EXAM TIP

Be aware that NetBEUI is required to navigate a dial-up connection to a local area network.

NOTE

Hands-On Activity For hands-on experience with this concept, refer to Lab Procedure #34, "Windows Me Network Operations," located on the CD that accompanies this book.

NETWORK PRINTING WITH WINDOWS 9x

Until recently, network printing in Windows was normally a matter of creating and linking an icon on the local unit with a shared physical device attached to a remote computer. Newer printers have built-in network adapters and require no host computer to operate on the network.

The standard method of installing a printer in Windows 9x is to activate the Add Printer Wizard through the Printers folder. This folder provides a central location for adding and managing printer operations. The Add Printer Wizard asks a number of questions about how the printer will be used. Because you are installing a remote network printer, you must supply the complete path to the printer (or browse the network to find its location). The Printers folder can be accessed in the following manners:

◆ Start/Settings/Printers

◆ My Computer/Printers

◆ Control Panel/Printers

You can also use the Network Neighborhood icon to browse the network until you locate the desired computer. Then double-click it so that the designated printer displays. A hand under the icon indicates a shared printer. In addition, you can install a remote printer by clicking and dragging its icon into the local Printers window and then dropping it anywhere inside the window.

The next step in setting up the remote printer is to assign it a unique printer name. In a network environment, this name should have some relevance to what type of printer it is or what relationship it has to the local unit.

The final step in setting up the printer is to configure its icon properties as if it were a local printer. Right-click the printer icon and select Properties. Enter all the information required to bring the printer to operation.

NETWORKING WITH WINDOWS 2000

During the Windows 2000 Installation process, the network portion of the operating system must be configured to function as a workgroup node or as part of a domain.

A *workgroup* is a collection of networked computers assigned the same workgroup name. Any user can become a member of a workgroup by specifying the particular workgroup's name during the setup process. Conversely, a *domain* is a collection of networked computers established and controlled by a network administrator. Recall that domains are established for security and administration purposes.

My Network Places

In the Windows 2000 system, the Network Neighborhood folder has been replaced with a more powerful My Network Places folder. The new folder includes new *Recently Visited Places* and *Computers Near Me* views. The Add Network Place options enable you to more easily establish connections to other servers on the network. The user can establish shortcuts to virtually every server on the network.

Network and Dial-Up Connections

The Network icon under the Windows 2000 Control Panel has been changed to the Network and Dial-Up Connections folder. It provides access to the *Network and Dial-Up Connections applet*. This applet provides several key functions associated with local and wide area networking, such as installing new network adapter cards and changing their settings, changing network component settings, and installing TCP/IP.

The functions associated with the Windows 2000 Local Area Connections Properties include

- ◆ *Services*—Used to add, remove, or configure network services such as DNS, WINS, and DHCP functions.

- ◆ *Protocols*—Used to add, remove, or configure network protocols for specific types of network environments.

◆ *Adapters*—Used to add, remove, or configure NIC cards for operation with the system. This includes loading drivers and assigning system resources to the adapter.

To configure any of these functions for a given component, access the *Local Area Connection Properties* page, highlight the desired component, and click the Install button. Other functions affecting the Networking and Dial-Up connections in Windows 2000 include the following:

◆ *Network Identification*—Specifies the computer name and the workgroup or domain name to which it belongs. Under TCP/IP, computer names can be up to 63 characters but should be limited to 15 characters or fewer. They can use the numbers 0-9, letters A-Z (and a-z), as well as hyphens. Using other characters might prevent other nodes from finding your computer or the network. This option is located under the System icon in the Control Panel.

◆ *Bindings*—Sets a potential pathway between a given network service, a network protocol, and a given network adapter. The order of the bindings can affect the efficiency of the system's networking operations. To establish bindings, access the Network and Dial-Up Connections page and click the Advanced entry on its drop-down menu bar. Then select the Advanced Settings option from the menu.

EXAM TIP

Memorize which network items can be set through the Windows 2000 Networking and Dial-Up connection applet's Local Area Connections Properties.

NOTE

Hands-On Activity   For hands-on experience with this concept, refer to Lab Procedure #37, "Windows 2000 Networking," located on the CD that accompanies this book.

Network Printing with Windows 2000

Windows NT 4 and Windows 2000 provide installation wizards to guide the network printer installation. If the physical printer is connected to a remote computer, referred to as a print server, the remote unit must supply the printer drivers and settings to control the printer. The print server must also be configured to share the printer with the other users on the network.

To install the network printer, access the My Network Places icon on the desktop, navigate the network to locate and open the remote computer's network name, right-click on the remote unit's printer name, select the Connect option from the pop-up menu, and follow the directions provided by the Windows Add Printer Wizard. When the Wizard produces a dialog box asking whether to install the selected printer, click the OK button. This should produce the Add Printer Wizard driver selection dialog window, depicted in Figure 28.6. After the remote printer has been installed, the local computer can access it through the My Network Places icon.

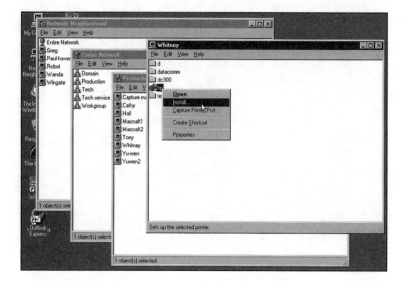

FIGURE 28.6

Installing a network printer in Windows 2000.

Sharing Printers in Windows 2000

To share a printer under Windows 2000, select the Printers option from the Start/Settings path. Right-click the printer to be shared and select the Sharing option. This action produces the Sharing tab depicted in Figure 28.7. From this page, click the Shared As option, enter a share name for the printer, and click the OK button. Unlike the Windows 9x systems, you must have administrative rights to make these changes in Windows 2000.

FIGURE 28.7
Sharing a printer in Windows 2000.

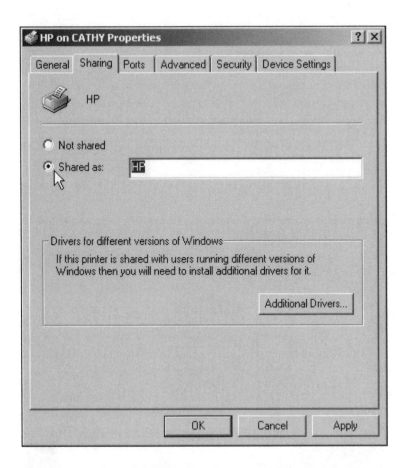

To connect to a printer on the network, select the Printers option from the Start/Settings path and double-click the Add Printer icon. When the Welcome to the Add Printer Wizard page displays, click the Next button to move forward. In the Local or Network Printer page, select the Network Printer option, click the Next button, and then enter the network printer name. Use the UNC format to specify the path to the printer being connected to. If the printer's name is not known, click the Type the Printer Name option or click the Next to Browse for a Printer option.

Connecting to a printer over the Internet (or the company intranet) is as simple as selecting the Connect to Printer on the Internet or on Your Intranet option and entering the URL address of the printer. The URL must be expressed in standard *HTTP addressing format* (that is, `http://servername/printer/`). The connection wizard will guide the connection process from this point.

Troubleshooting Local Area Networks

Generally, the order of isolating LAN problems is as follows:

1. Check the local networking software

2. Check the cabling and connectors

3. Check the NIC adapter

Most network adapter cards come from the manufacturer with a disk, or CD-ROM, of drivers and diagnostic utilities for that particular card. You can run these diagnostic utilities to verify that the LAN hardware is functioning properly. However, it might be easier to run the Windows PING utility from the command prompt and attempt to connect to the network. In a LAN environment, you will need to know the IP address, or the name of a remote computer in the network that you can direct the PING to. Both PING and TRACERT can be used to identify the IP address of a known network address.

Cabling is one of the biggest problems encountered in a network installation. Is it connected? Are all the connections good? Is the cable type correct? Has there been any termination, and if so, has it been done correctly? The most efficient way to test network cable is to use a *line tester* to check its functionality.

With *UTP cabling*, simply unplug the cable from the adapter card and plug it in to the tester. If coaxial cable is used, you must unplug both ends of the cable from the network, install a terminating resistor at one end of the cable, and plug the other end into the tester. The tester will perform the tests required to analyze the cable and connection.

Windows 9x Networking Problems

In Windows 9x, you should run the Add New Hardware Wizard and allow it to detect the network hardware. This should point out any hardware-related network problems. However, you might also want to click the Network icon in the Control Panel to review the NIC settings. Use the *Detected Config* option from the adapter's Resources tab if the NIC settings are not known.

If the network adapter is installed and the cabling is connected correctly, the operating system's network support must be checked. The

---

EXAM TIP

Know which network utility can be used to identify the address of a known remote location.

EXAM TIP

Be aware that cabling faults represent the number one reason for LAN failures.

EXAM TIP

Know what type of device is commonly used to make checks on LAN cables.

most obvious items to check are those found in the Properties pages of the Network Neighborhood window. Possible reasons for not being able to log on to the network include the following:

◆ Incorrect services settings (Configuration tab)

◆ Incorrect protocol settings (Configuration tab)

◆ Incorrect adapter settings (Configuration tab)

◆ Incorrect primary network logon settings (Configuration tab)

◆ Missing computer name (Identification tab)

◆ Missing workgroup name (Identification tab)

Begin the troubleshooting process by checking the system for resource conflicts that might involve the network adapter card. You can obtain this information by accessing the Control Panel's Device Manager. If a conflict exists, an exclamation point (!) should appear beside the network adapter card in the listing. If Windows thinks the card is working properly, the Device Manager displays a normal listing.

If a conflict is detected, move into the network adapter's Properties page and check the adapter's resources against those indicated by the card's diagnostic utility. The conflict must be resolved between the network adapter and whatever device is using its resources.

If the adapter resources are okay, the next step depends on the type of symptom being encountered:

◆ Can any units be seen on the network?

◆ Can other units be seen but not used?

EXAM TIP

Be aware of factors that will prevent users from browsing the network.

If the network cannot be seen in the Network Neighborhood or the network cannot be browsed from this utility, the network protocols and drivers should be checked. *Network adapters* and *protocols* are checked through the Control Panel's Network icon. Check the protocols listed in the Configuration tab's Installed Components window. Compare these to those listed on working units in the workgroup. Each machine must have all the clients and protocols other machines are using; otherwise, it will not be possible to browse the network. The local computer and the Entire Network icon should be present, but the other units will not be visible.

If you can browse the network but cannot access or use certain resources in remote locations, sharing is not turned on in the remote unit or the local unit does not have proper access rights to that resource. To use the remote resource across the network, the system's File and Print functions must be turned on and its Share function must be enabled. Turning on the File and Print functions places the local resources in the network's Browse listing.

> **EXAM TIP**
>
> Know which items and settings affect the abilities to use resources across the network.

CHALLENGE #1

You are working in a Windows 2000 Client/Server network, and you discover that you cannot use a shared drive on another computer. What should you do to troubleshoot access to the drive?

However, this does not enable the Share function. The Share function is established by supplying the system with a valid share name. In addition, the computer must be running Client for Microsoft Networks for File and Print to be available on a Microsoft network. If this client service is not installed, the File and Print functions will be unavailable for use (grayed out). The Client for Microsoft Networks services component must be installed in the Select Network Component Type screen.

> **EXAM TIP**
>
> Be aware of problems that cause computers or resources to not appear on the network.

Windows 2000 Networking Problems

Because Windows NT/2000 systems are typically involved in client/server networks, the types of problems encountered are somewhat different from those found in Windows 9x network environments. Some typical networking problems can occur during normal Windows 2000 operations, including such things as the following:

◆ The user cannot see any other computers on the local network.

◆ The user cannot see other computers on different networks.

◆ The clients cannot see the DHCP server, but do have an IP address.

◆ The clients cannot obtain an IP address from a DHCP server that is on the other side of a router.

EXAM TIP

Know what the presence of a light on the NIC card indicates.

As mentioned earlier, a major cause of connectivity problems is the physical layer. Check to see that the computer is physically connected to the network and that the status light is glowing (normally green). The presence of the light indicates that the NIC sees network traffic.

If a client cannot see any other computers on the network, improper IP addressing might be occurring. This is one of the most common problems associated with TCP/IP. Users must have a valid IP address and subnet to communicate with other computers. If the IP address is incorrect, invalid, or conflicting with another computer in the network, you will only be able to see your local computer, but you will not be able to see others on the network.

One reason for an incorrect IP address problem occurs when the local system in a TCP/IP network is looking for a *DHCP Server* that is not present. In some LANs, a special server called a DHCP Server is used to dynamically assign IP addresses to its clients in the network. In large networks, each segment of the network would require its own DHCP Server to assign IP addresses for that segment. If the DHCP Server were missing, or not functioning, none of the clients in that segment would be able to see the network.

Likewise, if a DHCP client computer were installed in a network segment that did not use DHCP, it would need to be reconfigured manually with a static IP address. The *DHCP settings* are administered through the TCP/IP Properties window. This window is located under the Start/Settings/Networking and Dial-up Connections option. From this point, open the desired Local Area or Dial-up Connection and click the Properties button. DHCP operations are covered in more detail later in this chapter.

EXAM TIP

Know the primary TCP/IP tools used to troubleshoot network problems.

Begin the troubleshooting process for this type of problem by checking the TCP/IP Properties under the Network icon. Next, check the current TCP/IP settings using the command line IPCONFIG/ALL (or the WINIPCFG) utility. They will display the current IP settings and offer a starting point for troubleshooting. Afterward, use the PING utility to send test packets to other local computers you have found. The results of this action indicate whether the network is working.

CHALLENGE #2

You have installed a new Windows 2000 Professional client in your network and manually assigned it a valid IP address. However, when you try to browse the network, nothing shows up. What network utilities should you use to get the new system into operation?

If users can see other local computers in a TCP/IP network, but cannot see remote systems on other networks, you might be having routing problems. Determine that the address for the *default gateway* (router) listed in the TCP/IP properties is valid. Use the NET VIEW command to see whether the remote computer is available. If the user is relying on the My Network Places feature to see other computers, a delay in updating the Browse list might cause remote systems to not be listed. The NET VIEW command directly communicates with the remote systems and displays available shares.

If the clients have an IP address of 169.254.*xxx.xxx*, it is because they cannot communicate with the DHCP server. Windows 2000 automatically assigns the computer an IP address in the 169.254 range if it cannot be assigned an address from a DHCP server.

Many routers do not pass the broadcast traffic generated by *DHCP clients*. If clients cannot obtain an IP address from a DHCP server that is located on the other side of a router, the network administrator must enable the forwarding of *DHCP packets*, or place a DHCP server on each side of a router.

CHALLENGE #3

You work in a large corporation that has just converted all of its Windows NT Workstation client computers in your network over to Windows 2000 Professional. The network uses a DHCP server to provide IP addresses for the clients. In the process of upgrading the system, you have also moved one of the workstations to a new location in the network. However, when you bring the network back up, all the clients come up perfectly except the unit that was relocated—it cannot connect to the network. What should you look for as you try to get the unit back in operation?

Networking with Novell NetWare

In a Novell NetWare system, check the root directory of the workstation for the *NETBIOS* and *IPX.COM* files. The NETBIOS file is an emulation of IBM's Network *Basic Input/Output System* (*NetBIOS*), and represents the basic interface between the operating system and the LAN hardware. This function is implemented through ROM ICs, located on the network card. The *Internetworking Packet Exchange* (*IPX*) file passes commands across the network to the file server.

The NETBIOS and IPX protocols must be bound together in order to navigate the Novell network from a computer using a Windows operating system. This is accomplished by enabling the NETBIOS bindings in the IPX protocol Properties in the Network Properties window.

The *Open Datalink Interface* (*ODI*) file is the Novell network shell that communicates between the adapter and the system's applications. Older versions of NetWare used a shell program called NETx. These files should be referenced in the AUTOEXEC.BAT or NET.BAT files.

EXAM TIP

Be aware of the elements that are required to navigate through a Novell network from a computer running a Microsoft operating system.

CHALLENGE #4

You are working on a Windows 2000 Professional client computer that has IPX loaded. You are working in a Novell LAN, however, you find that you cannot browse the network. What should you check to gain access to the LAN?

CHAPTER SUMMARY

This chapter has focused on the software side of networking, concentrating on the major operating systems. The initial section of this chapter dealt with the fundamentals of installing and configuring local area networking under Windows 9x and Windows NT/2000.

In the second major section of the chapter, procedures for establishing and administering networked printers in both Windows 9x and Windows 2000 were described in detail.

A major portion of the chapter was dedicated to providing step-by-step instructions for troubleshooting and repairing LAN problems. This material included descriptions of hardware troubleshooting symptoms and procedures, as well as Windows 9x and Windows 2000–specific network troubleshooting information.

The final section of the chapter discussed the particulars of working with Novel Netware networks.

At this point, review the objectives listed at the beginning of the chapter to be certain that you understand each point and can perform each task listed there. Afterward, answer the review questions that follo w to verify your knowledge of the information.

KEY TERMS

- Adapters
- Basic Input/Output System (NetBIOS)
- Bindings
- Computers Near Me
- Default gateway
- Detected Config
- DHCP clients
- DHCP packets
- DHCP Server
- DHCP settings
- Domain
- HTTP addressing format
- Internetworking Packet Exchange (IPX)
- IPCONFIG/ALL
- IPX.COM
- IPX/SPX
- Line tester
- Local Area Connection Properties
- Mapping the drive
- Microsoft Client protocol
- NET VIEW command
- NetBEUI
- NETBIOS

CHAPTER SUMMARY

- NetBIOS Extended User Interface (NetBEUI)
- Network adapters
- Network and Dial-Up Connections applet
- Network Identification
- Network operating system (NOS)
- Novell NetWare Client protocol
- NWLink
- Open Datalink Interface (ODI)
- PING
- Protocols

- Recently Visited Places
- Remote Access Services (RAS)
- Services
- SHARE.EXE
- TCP/IP
- Universal naming convention (UNC)
- UTP cabling
- Windows for Workgroups (WfW)
- WINIPCFG
- Workgroup

APPLY YOUR KNOWLEDGE

Review Questions

1. What does the DOS command SHARE.EXE do?

   A. Allows multiple users to share the same Internet connection

   B. Allows multiple users to access a network printer

   C. Allows multiple users to log in to a single workstation

   D. Allows file sharing over a network

2. What are the specifications for setting up computer names in Windows 2000?

   A. Up to 15 characters, A to Z, 0 to 9, hyphens, no spaces

   B. Up to 63 characters, A to Z, 0 to 9, hyphens, no spaces

   C. Up to 255 characters, A to Z, 0 to 9, hyphens, no spaces

   D. Up to 256 characters, A to Z, 0 to 9, hyphens, no spaces

3. How is the UNC format applied to shared resources?

   A. `//shared_resource_name`

   B. `//host_name/shared_resource_name`

   C. `\\shared_resource_name`

   D. `\\host_name\drive_path\ shared_resource_name`

4. Which of the following will cause a mapped drive to disappear from a system when it is shut down and restarted?

   A. The name of the mapped folder has been changed.

   B. The Reconnect at Logon option is not selected.

   C. The path to the mapped folder has changed.

   D. The host computer for the mapped folder is turned off.

5. Where can the TCP/IP protocol be manually installed in Windows 9x?

   A. In the Select Network Component Type screen through the Network Configuration page

   B. In the Network Component Type screen through the Dial-up Connections page

   C. In the Protocol Installation screen through the Local Area Connection page

   D. In the Protocol screen of the Network Configuration page

6. What is the meaning of the term NetBEUI?

   A. Network Basic Encrypted User Interconnection

   B. Network Broadcast Expanded User Interface

   C. NetBIOS Extended User Interface

   D. NetBIOS Broadcast Expanded User Interface

APPLY YOUR KNOWLEDGE

7. What type of network operating system does NetBEUI belongs to?

   A. Windows

   B. NetWare

   C. Internet

   D. Intranet

8. _____ is required to navigate a local area network when using a RAS dial-up connection.

   A. IPX

   B. NetBEUI

   C. TCP/IP

   D. PPP

9. What is the number one reason for LAN installation failures?

   A. Cabling faults

   B. NOS failures

   C. Excessive traffic

   D. Incorrect protocol

10. What type of device is commonly used to make checks on a LAN cable?

    A. Volt-meter

    B. Multi-meter

    C. Line (cable) tester

    D. OTDR

11. What problems can cause a network not to be seen in the Network Neighborhood?

    A. Insufficient access rights.

    B. Incorrect computer name.

C. Incompatible protocols loaded.

D. Sharing is not turned on.

12. What does the presence of a light on the NIC card indicate?

    A. NIC driver is functioning.

    B. Downloading data.

    C. Uploading data.

    D. NIC sees network traffic.

13. What is the primary TCP/IP tool used to troubleshoot network connectivity problems?

    A. IPCONFIG

    B. ARP

    C. NET VIEW

    D. PING

14. What element(s) are required to navigate through a Novell network from a computer running a Microsoft operating system?

    A. Installing the NetBEUI protocol

    B. Binding the NETBIOS and IPX protocols

    C. Binding the ODI and IPX protocols

    D. Installing the IPX protocol

15. Which network utilities can be used to identify the IP address of a known remote location?

    A. PING and TRACERT

    B. NetSTAT and NET VIEW

    C. ARP and NET VIEW

    D. IPCONFIG and WINIPCFG

APPLY YOUR KNOWLEDGE

16. Which network items can be set through the Windows 2000 Networking and Dial-Up connection applet's local area connections properties? (Select all that apply.)

    A. Allowing DHCP

    B. Adding the DNS service

    C. Configuring network protocols

    D. Configuring network adapter cards

17. Which of the following is a valid computer name for a Windows 9x workstation connected to a LAN?

    A. MY COMPUTER

    B. THERECANBEONLYONE

    C. H-1-T-H-3-R-3

    D. TERMINAL 4

Answers and Explanations

1. **D**. In later versions of DOS, Microsoft added the SHARE.EXE command to provide file-sharing and -locking capabilities for files on a local hard disk drive. These capabilities enabled multiple users to access the same file at the same time in a networked or multitasking environment. For more information, see the section "Resource Sharing."

2. **B**. Valid computer names in Windows 9x can be up to 15 characters in length and cannot contain any blank spaces. In Windows 2000 using the TCP/IP protocol, computer names can range up to 63 characters in length and should be made up of the letters A through Z, numbers 0 through 9, and hyphens. For more information, see the section "Resource Sharing."

3. **D**. Establishing the map to the resource is a simple matter of entering the required path and share name in the dialog box, using the UNC format (`\\host_name\drive_path\shared_resource_name`). For more information, see the section "Mapping a Drive."

4. **B**. The Reconnect at Logon option must be selected in the Map Network Drive page for the drive mapping to become a permanent part of the system. If the option is not selected when the user logs off, the mapped drive information disappears and needs to be remapped for any further use. If a red X appears on the icon of a properly mapped drive, this indicates that the drive is no longer available. Its host computer might be turned off, the drive might have been removed, or it might no longer be on the same path. If the drive was mapped to a particular folder and the folder name has been changed, the red X will also appear. For more information, see the section "Mapping a Drive."

5. **A**. The Windows 9x networking utilities should produce an adapter driver, a Microsoft Client protocol, and a Novell NetWare Client protocol in the Network Configuration window in a typical installation. A default set of file and print sharing services also is loaded. The only items that must be installed manually are the protocols for the particular type of network being used. Clicking the Add button in the Network Configuration/Properties screen brings up the Select Network Component Type screen. From here, you can select Protocol and click the Add button to begin installation of a network protocol. For more information, see the section "Installing Network Components."

APPLY YOUR KNOWLEDGE

6. **C**. In a Windows-only network, the default set of rules that govern the exchange of data between computers is the NetBIOS Extended User Interface (NetBEUI) protocol. For more information, see the section "Installing Network Components."

7. **A**. In a Windows-only network, the default set of rules that govern the exchange of data between computers is the NetBIOS Extended User Interface (NetBEUI) protocol. Because of its limitations, this protocol is not used in non-Windows environments. For more information, see the section "Installing Network Components."

8. **B**. The NetBEUI protocol is required to support dial-up Remote Access Services (RAS) through a modem. The RAS service uses NetBEUI to navigate through a network after you have dialed into it. Both the calling client and the receiving server in the LAN must be running NetBEUI. If either computer does not have this protocol active, the client will be able to connect with the LAN, but will not be able to navigate through it. For more information, see the section "Installing Network Components."

9. **A**. Cabling is one of the biggest problems encountered in a network installation. You should check to be make sure that it is connected, and then check for good connections, proper cable type, and correct termination. For more information, see the section "Troubleshooting Local Area Networks."

10. **C**. The most efficient way to test network cable is to use a line tester to check its functionality. With UTP cabling, simply unplug the cable from the adapter card and plug it into the tester. If coaxial cable is used, you must unplug both ends of the cable from the network, install a terminating resistor at one end of the cable, and plug the other end in to the tester. The tester will perform the tests required to analyze the cable and connection. For more information, see the section "Troubleshooting Local Area Networks."

11. **C**. If the network cannot be seen in the Network Neighborhood or the network cannot be browsed from this utility, the network protocols and drivers should be checked. Each machine must have all the clients and protocols other machines on the network are using; otherwise, it will not be possible to browse the network. For more information, see the section "Windows 9x Networking Problems."

12. **D**. In order to check to see that the computer is physically connected to the network, examine the status light and make certain it is glowing (normally green). The presence of the light indicates that the NIC sees network traffic. For more information, see the section "Windows 2000 Networking Problems."

13. **A**. You can check the current TCP/IP settings using the IPCONFIG tool from the command line (for example, C:> ipconfig /all) or the WINIPCFG utility. For more information, see the section "Windows 2000 Networking Problems."

APPLY YOUR KNOWLEDGE

14. **B**. The NETBIOS and IPX protocols must be bound together in order to navigate the Novell network from a computer using a Windows operating system. This is accomplished by enabling the NETBIOS bindings in the IPX protocol Properties in the Network Properties window. For more information, see the section "Networking with Novell NetWare."

15. **A**. Both PING and TRACERT can be used to identify the IP address of a known network address. For more information, see the section "Troubleshooting Local Area Networks."

16. **B**, **C**, **D**. Items that can be accessed through the Windows 2000 Local Area Connections Properties screen include configuring the network adapter; turning on and off clients, file and printer sharing and protocols; installing and uninstalling services (such as DNS); accessing the properties for the installed network services; and toggling the taskbar network connection icon. For more information, see the section "Network and Dial-Up Connections."

17. **C**. Valid computer names in Windows 9x can be up to 15 characters in length and cannot contain any blank spaces. In Windows 2000 using the TCP/IP protocol, computer names can range up to 63 characters in length and should be made up of the letters A through Z, numbers 0 through 9, and hyphens. For more information, see the section "Resource Sharing."

Challenge Solutions

1. If you can browse the network but cannot access or use certain resources—such as a shared drive—in remote locations, the sharing function is not enabled in the remote unit (or the local unit does not have proper access rights to that resource). The user at the remote unit, or the network administrator, must provide you with the proper sharing or permissions to access the remote resource. For more information, see the section "Windows 2000 Networking Problems."

2. Use the IPCONFIG/ALL utility for Windows 98/NT/2000 systems, or use the WINIPCFG utility for Windows 95 systems. They will both display the current IP settings and offer a starting point for troubleshooting. For more information, see the section "Windows 2000 Networking Problems."

3. Check to see if there is a router between the old and new segments that the computer is attached to. Many routers do not pass the broadcast traffic generated by DHCP clients. If clients cannot obtain an IP address from a DHCP server that is located on the other side of a router, the network administrator must enable the forwarding of DHCP packets or place a DHCP server on each side of a router. For more information, see the section "Windows 9x Networking Problems."

4. The NETBIOS and IPX protocols must be bound together in order to navigate the Novell network from a computer using a Windows operating system. This is accomplished by enabling the NETBIOS bindings in the IPX protocol Properties in the Network Properties window. For more information, see the section "Networking with Novell NetWare."

APPLY YOUR KNOWLEDGE

Suggested Readings and Resources

1. Network Hardware
   http://www.networknews.co.uk/Products/
   Hardware/Network%20Hardware

2. DOS SHARE Command
   www.otex.org/manual/chap13.htm

3. Sharing Resources
   http://www.onecomputerguy.com/networking/
   sharing.htm

4. Networking with Windows 9*x*
   http://www.atomic-
   matrix.com/win98/Overview%20of%20Windows%2
   098%20Network%20Configuration.htm

5. Network Neighborhood
   http://www.wown.com/j_helmig/browse.htm

6. Mapping a Drive
   http://www.admin.ias.edu/pc/documents/
   q1005.html

7. Network Printing with Windows 9*x*
   http://support.microsoft.com/
   default.aspx?scid=kb;en-us;q243075

8. Networking with Windows 2000
   http://www.onecomputerguy.com/networking.
   htm

9. My Network Places
   http://www.winsupersite.com/showcase/
   win2k_980918.asp

10. The Windows 2000 Network Control Panel
    http://www.xtra.co.nz/help/
    0,,6155-840041,00.html

11. Network Printing with Windows 2000
    http://winservices.web.cern.ch/
    winservices/docs/PrinterWizard/

12. Troubleshooting Local Area Networks
    http://www.annoyances.org/exec/show/
    category04

13. Understanding DHCP
    www.cisco.com/warp/public/779/smbiz/
    service/knowledge/tcpip/dhcp.htm

14. Novell NetWare Protocols
    http://www.cisco.com/univercd/cc/td/doc/
    cisintwk/ito_doc/netwarep.htm

This chapter helps you to prepare for the Operating System Technologies module of the A+ Certification examination by covering the following objective within the "Domain 4.0: Networks" section.

4.2 Identify concepts and capabilities relating to the Internet and basic procedures for setting up a system for Internet access.

Content might include the following:

- **ISP**
- **TCP/IP**
- **IPX/SPX**
- **NetBEUI**
- **Email**
- **PING.EXE**
- **HTML**
- **HTTP://**
- **FTP**
- **Domain names (Web sites)**
- **Dial-up networking**
- **TRACERT.EXE**
- **NSLOOKUP.EXE**

▶ The Internet is the most famous example of wide area networking. With so many people going online, the technician must understand how the Internet is organized. The tremendous popularity of the Internet, and its heavy concentration on PC platforms, requires that the PC technician understand how the Internet is organized and how the PC relates to it. The successful technician also must be able to establish and maintain Internet connections using the major operating systems and dial-up networking software.

CHAPTER 29

Internet Concepts

To prepare for the Networks objective of the Operating Systems Technologies exam,

▶ Read the objectives at the beginning of this chapter.

▶ Study the information in this chapter.

▶ Review the objectives listed earlier in this chapter.

▶ Perform any step-by-step procedures in the text.

▶ Answer the review questions at the end of the chapter and check your results.

▶ Use the PrepLogic test engine on the CD-ROM that accompanies this book for additional review and exam questions concerning this material.

▶ Review the exam tips scattered throughout the chapter and make certain that you are comfortable with each point.

INTRODUCTION

This chapter focuses on the wide area networking functions associated with the Windows 9x and Windows 2000 operating systems. The main focus of the chapter deals with different methods of accessing the Internet.

The chapter begins with a section dedicated to configuring and using Windows 9x and Windows 2000 dial-up networking utilities to access the Internet. Information in this section focuses on the TCP/IP protocol central to the workings of the Internet. It also covers the functions typically provided by Internet service providers.

The second major section of the chapter deals with using IP addresses on the Internet and how these addresses are related to Internet Domains. The information about IP addressing continues with discussions of the Domain Naming Service (DNS) that provides addressing oversight for the Internet and the Dynamic Host Configuration Protocol (DHCP) that is used to automatically assign these addresses to some users.

The next section of the chapter describes concepts associated with the World Wide Web. Information in this section includes discussions of the Web Browser utilities used to navigate the Web and view its contents. The section continues with information about the File Transfer Protocol and Email functions associated with the Web.

The chapter then moves into discussions about wide area networking with Windows 9x along with additional information about the Windows 2000 Internet access infrastructure.

A major portion of the chapter is dedicated to troubleshooting typical WAN/Internet problems. In addition to presenting common symptoms and repairs encountered in WAN environments, the section provides an extensive discussion of the network troubleshooting tools available with Windows 9x and Windows 2000.

After completing the chapter, you should be able to identify concepts and capabilities relating to the Internet and describe basic procedures for preparing a system to provide Internet access.

WIDE AREA NETWORKS

A *wide area network* (*WAN*) is very similar in concept to a widely distributed client/server LAN. In a wide area network, computers are typically separated by significant distances. WANs can be connected together by several different types of communication systems. The communication paths created by these systems are referred to as links. Most users connect to the network via standard telephone lines, using dial-up modems. *Dial-up connections* are generally the slowest way to connect to a network, but they are inexpensive to establish and use.

Other users, who require quicker data transfers, contract with the telephone company to use special, high-speed *Integrated Service Digital Network* (*ISDN*) lines, or newer *Digital Subscriber Lines* (*DSL*) connections. These types of links require a digital modem to conduct data transfers. Because the modem is digital, no analog conversion is required.

Users who require very high volumes will lease dedicated T1 and T3 lines from the telephone company. These applications generally serve businesses that put several of their computers or networks online. After the information is transmitted, it might be carried over many types of communications links—including fiber-optic cables, satellite up and down links, UHF, and microwave transmission systems—on its way to its destination.

The Internet

The most famous WAN is the Internet. The Internet is actually a network of networks working together. The main communication path for the Internet is a series of networks, established by the U.S. government, to link supercomputers together at key research sites.

TCP/IP

The language of the Internet is *Transport Control Protocol/Internet Protocol* (*TCP/IP*). No matter what type of computer platform or software is being used, the information must move across the

EXAM TIP

Know what TCP/IP is and what it does.

EXAM TIP

Know the advantages of using the TCP/IP protocol. Also, be aware that TCP/IP supports dial-up, Ethernet, and Token Ring networking.

EXAM TIP

Be able to describe the pathway that should be used to manually establish IP address and Subnet Mask settings.

EXAM TIP

Be aware of common services that ISPs provide their Internet customers.

Internet in this format. This protocol calls for data to be grouped together, in bundles, called *network packets*. The *TCP/IP packet* is designed primarily to permit message fragmentation and reassembly.

It is considered to be one of the most secure of the network protocols. Because no one actually owns the TCP/IP protocol, it was adopted as the transmission standard for the Internet. It was so widely accepted by the Internet community that virtually every network operating system supports it, including Apple, MS-DOS/Windows, UNIX, Linux, OS/2 and even networked printers. It can also be used on any topology (that is, dial-up, Ethernet, Token Ring, and so on). Therefore, all these computer types can exchange data across a network using the TCP/IP protocol.

In the Windows operating systems, the TCP/IP settings are established through the Start/Settings/Control Panel/Network/TCP-IP adapter/Properties path. From this location, you can click on the IP Address tab to establish the desired method of obtaining an IP address (that is, automatically from a DHCP Server, or manually, by specifying a static IP address). If you choose the option to Specify an IP address, you must enter the IP address and Subnet Mask settings.

Internet Service Providers

Connecting all the users and individual networks together are *Internet service providers* (*ISPs*). ISPs are companies that provide the technical gateway to the Internet. These companies own blocks of access addresses that they assign to their customers to give the customer an identity on the network.

Service that most ISPs deliver to their customers include

◆ Internet identity through IP Addresses

◆ Email services through POP3 and SMTP servers

◆ Internet News Service through USENET archive servers

◆ Internet routing through DNS servers

IP Addresses

The blocks of Internet access addresses that ISPs provide to their customers are called the *Internet Protocol addresses*, or *IP addresses*. The IP address makes each site a valid member of the Internet. This is how individual users are identified to receive file transfers, email, and file requests.

IP addresses exist in the numeric format of *xxx.yyy.zzz.aaa*. Each address consists of four 8-bit fields (octets) separated by dots (.). This format of specifying addresses is referred to as *dotted-decimal notation*. The decimal numbers are derived from the binary address that the hardware understands.

Each IP address consists of two parts: the *network address* and the *host address*. The network address identifies the entire network; whereas the host address identifies an intelligent member within the network (router, a server, or a workstation).

Three classes of standard IP addresses are supported for LANs: Class A, Class B, and Class C. These addresses occur in four-octet fields like the example.

◆ *Class A addresses* are reserved for large networks and use the last 24 bits (the last three octets or fields) of the address for the host address. The first octet always begins with a 0, followed by a 7-bit number. Therefore, valid Class A addresses range between 001.*x.x.x* and 126.*x.x.x*. This permits a Class A network to support 126 different networks with nearly 17 million hosts (nodes) per network.

◆ *Class B addresses* are assigned to medium-sized networks. The first two octets can range between 128.*x.x.x* and 191.254.0.0. The last two octets contain the host addresses. This enables Class B networks to include up to 16,384 different networks with approximately 65,534 hosts per network.

◆ *Class C addresses* are normally used with smaller LANs. In a Class C address, only the last octet is used for host addresses. The first three octets can range between 192.*x.x.x* and 223.254.254.0. Therefore, the Class C address can support approximately 2 million networks with 254 hosts each.

Sections of the network can be grouped together into subnets that share a range of IP addresses. These groups are referred to as *intranet*s. (Actually, a true intranet requires that the segment have a protective gateway to act as an entry and exit point for the segment.) In most cases, the gateway is a device called a *router*. A router is an intelligent device that receives data and directs it toward a designated IP address.

NOTE

Where's 127? The 127.*x.x.x* address range is a special block of addresses reserved for testing network systems. The U.S. government owns some of these addresses for testing the Internet backbone. The 127.0.0.1 address is reserved for testing the bus on the local system.

Some networks employ a firewall as a gateway to the outside. A *firewall* is a combination of hardware and software components that provide a protective barrier between networks with different security levels. The firewall is configured by an administrator so that it will only pass data to and from designated IP addresses and TCP/IP ports.

Subnets are created by masking off (hiding) the network address portion of the IP address on the units within the subnet. This, in effect, limits the mobility of the data to those nodes within the subnet because they can reconcile only addresses from within their masked range. There are three common reasons to create a subnet:

◆ To isolate one segment of the network from all the others— Suppose, for example, that a large organization has 1,000 computers; all of which are connected to the network. Without segmentation, data from all 1,000 units would run through every other network node. The effect of this would be that everyone else in the network would have access to all the data on the network and the operation of the network would be slowed considerably by the uncontrolled traffic.

◆ To efficiently use IP addresses—Because the IP addressing scheme is defined as a 32-bit code, there are only a certain number of possible addresses. Although 126 networks with 17 million customers might seem like a lot, in the scheme of a worldwide network system, that's not a lot of addresses to go around.

◆ To utilize a single IP address across physically divided locations—For example, subnetting a Class C address between remotely located areas of a campus would permit half of the 253 possible addresses to be allocated to one campus location, and the other half can be allocated to hosts at the second location. In this manner, both locations can operate using a single Class C address.

Internet Domains

The IP addresses of all the computers attached to the Internet are tracked using a listing called the *Domain Name System* (*DNS*)—a database organizational structure whereby higher-level Internet servers keep track of assigned domain names and their corresponding IP addresses for systems on levels under them. (That is, it is responsible for resolving *DNS names* to particular IP addresses.) This system evolved as a way to organize the members of the Internet into a hierarchical management structure.

The DNS structure consists of various levels of computer groups called *domains*. Each computer on the Internet is assigned a domain name, such as mic-inc.com. The mic-inc portion of the name is the user friendly domain name assigned to the Marcraft site. The .com notation at the end of the address is a top-level domain that defines the type of organization or country of origin associated with the address. In this case, the .com designation identifies the user as a commercial site.

The following list identifies the Internet's top-level domain codes:

.biz = Business names and trademarks

.com = Commercial businesses

.edu = Educational institutions

.gov = Government agencies

.info = Special products, events, interests, and services

.int = International organizations

.mil = Military establishments

.name = Personalized domain names

.net = Networking organizations

.org = Non-profit organizations

On the Internet, domain names are specified in terms of their *Fully Qualified Domain Names (FQDN)*. An FQDN is a human-readable address that describes the location of the site on the Internet. It contains the hostname, the domain name, and the top-level domain name. For example, the name www.oneworld.owt.com is an FQDN.

The letters www represent the *hostname*. The hostname specifies the name of the computer that provides services and handles requests for specific Internet addresses. In this case, the host is the World Wide Web. Other types of hosts include FTP and HTTP sites.

The .owt extension indicates that the organization is a domain listed under the top-level domain heading. Likewise, the .oneworld entry is a subdomain of the .owt domain. It is very likely one of multiple networks supported by the .owt domain.

The Internet software communicates with the service provider by embedding the TCP/IP information in a *Point-to-Point Protocol* (*PPP* shell for transmission through the modem in analog format.) The communications equipment, at the service provider's site, converts the signal back to the digital TCP/IP format. Older units running UNIX used a connection protocol called *Serial Line Internet Protocol* (*SLIP*) for dial-up services.

When you connect to a service provider, you are connecting to its computer system, which, in turn, is connected to the Internet through routers. The router intercepts network transmissions, determines which part of the Internet they are intended for, and then determines the best routing scheme for delivering the message to its intended address. The routing schedule is devised from the known, available links through the Internet and the amount of traffic detected on various segments. The router then transfers the message to a *network access point* (*NAP*).

NOTE

Hands-On Activity   For hands-on experience with this concept, refer to Lab Procedure #40, "Windows Me Internet Domain Names," located on the CD that accompanies this book.

Dynamic Host Configuration Protocol

In addition to its domain name tracking function, the DNS system resolves (links) individual domain names of computers to their current IP address listings. Some IP addresses are permanently assigned to a particular domain name so that whenever the domain name is issued on the Internet, it always accesses the same IP address. This is referred to as static IP addressing. However, most ISPs use a dynamic IP addressing scheme for allocating IP addresses.

If an ISP wants to service 10,000 customers within its service area, using static IP addressing, it needs to purchase and maintain 10,000 IP addresses. Because most Internet customers are not online all the time, however, their IP addresses are not always in use. Therefore, the ISP can purchase a reasonable number of IP addresses that it can hold in a bank and dynamically assign to its users as they log on to their service. When the user logs off, the IP address returns to the bank for other users.

The *Dynamic Host Configuration Protocol* (*DHCP*) is an Internet protocol that can be used to automatically assign IP addresses to devices on a network using TCP/IP. This simplifies network administration because software, rather than an administrator, assigns and keeps track of IP addresses. For this reason, many ISPs use the dynamic IP addressing function of DHCP to provide access to their dial-up users. The protocol automatically delivers IP addresses, subnet mask and default router configuration parameters, and other configuration information to the devices on the network.

The dynamic addressing portion of the protocol also means that computers can be added to a network without manually assigning them unique IP addresses. As a matter of fact, the devices can be issued a different IP address each time they connect to the network. In some networks, the device's IP address can even change while it is still connected. DHCP also supports a mix of static and dynamic IP addresses.

The most important configuration parameter carried by DHCP is the IP address. A computer must initially be assigned a specific IP address that is appropriate for the network it is attached to. It must also be an IP address not assigned to any other computer on that network. If a computer moves to a new network, it must be assigned a new IP address for that new network. DHCP can be used to manage these assignments automatically. The DHCP client support is built in to Windows 9x, Windows NT 4.0 Workstation, and Windows 2000 Professional. Windows NT 4 and Windows 2000 Server versions include both client and server support for DHCP.

> **EXAM TIP**
>
> Be aware that dynamic IP addressing is performed by DHCP.

CHALLENGE #1

You work as a service representative for an Internet service provider. One day, you receive a call from a customer wondering why her IP address changes periodically. She really doesn't have a problem with the operation of her computer, so what do you tell her?

Internet Transmissions

The TCP/IP protocol divides the transmission into packets of information suitable for retransmission across the Internet. Along the way, the information passes through different networks that are organized at different levels. Depending on the routing scheme, the packets might move through the Internet using different routes to get to the intended address. At the destination, however, the packets are reassembled into the original transmission. Figure 29.1 illustrates this concept.

As the message moves from the originating address to its destination, it might pass through LANs, mid-level networks, *routers*, *repeaters*, *hubs*, *bridges*, and *gateways*. A mid-level network is just another network that does not require an Internet connection to carry out communications.

FIGURE 29.1
Packets moving through the Internet.

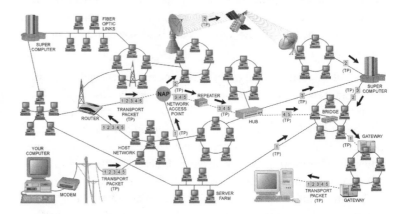

ISDN

ISDN service offers high-speed access to the public telephone system. However, ISDN service requires digital modems. Not only does the end user require a digital modem, but also the telephone company's switch gear equipment must be updated to handle digital switching. This fact has slowed implementation of ISDN services until recently.

Digital Subscriber Lines

The telephone companies have begun to offer a new high bandwidth connection service to home and business customers in the form of *Digital Subscriber Lines* (*DSL*). This technology provides high-speed communication links by using the existing telephone lines to generate bandwidths ranging up to 9Mb/s or more. However, distance limitations and line quality conditions can reduce the actual throughput that can be achieved with these connections.

The term xDSL is used to refer to all types of DSL collectively. There are two main categories of DSL—*Asynchronous DSL (ADSL)* and *Synchronous DSL (SDSL)*. Two other types of xDSL technologies that have some promise are *High-data-rate DSL (HDSL)* and *Symmetric DSL (SDSL)*. SDSL is referred to as symmetric because it supports the same data rates for upstream and downstream traffic. Conversely, ADSL (also known as rate-adaptive DSL) supports different data transfer rates when receiving data (referred to as the downstream rate) and transmitting data (known as the upstream rate).

xDSL is similar to the ISDN arrangements in that they both operate over existing copper *POTS (Plain Old Telephone System)* telephone lines. Also, they both require short geographical cable runs (less than 20,000 feet) to the nearest central telephone office. However, xDSL services offer much higher transfer speeds. In doing so, the xDSL technologies use a much greater range of frequencies on the telephone lines than the traditional voice services do. In addition, DSL technologies use the telephone lines as a constant connection so that users can have access to the Internet and email on a 24/7 basis. There is no need to connect with an ISP each time you want to go online.

The World Wide Web

The *World Wide Web (WWW)* is a menu system that ties together Internet resources from around the world. These resources are scattered across computer systems everywhere. Web servers inventory the Web's resources and store address pointers, referred to as links, to them.

Each Web site has a unique address called its *universal resource locator (URL)*. URLs have a format similar to a DOS command line. To access a Web site, the user must place the desired URL on the network. Each URL begins with http://. These letters stand for *Hypertext Transfer Protocol*, and identify the address as a Web site. The rest of the address is the name of the site being accessed (that is, http://www.mic-inc.com is the home page of Marcraft, located on a server at One World Telecommunications). Each Web site begins with a home page. The home page is the menu to the available contents of the site.

Web Browsers

As the Internet network has grown, service providers have continued to provide more user-friendly software for exploring the World Wide Web. These software packages are called *browsers*, and are based on hypertext links. These links are used to create hypermedia documents that can contain information from computer sites around the world. A hypermedia document can contain text, graphics, and animation, as well as audio and video sequences. Inside a hypermedia document, the links enable the user to move around the document in a nonlinear manner.

EXAM TIP

Be aware of the language used to build the WWW.

Browsers use hypertext links to interconnect the various computing sites in a way that resembles a spider's web—hence the name, Web. Browsers enable graphical pages to be displayed using a mixture of text, graphics, audio, and video files. Browsers translated the Hypertext Markup Language (HTML) files that were used to create the Web and that ultimately link the various types of files together. These files can be recognized in older systems by their abbreviated .HTM file extension.

EXAM TIP

Memorize the Internet-related abbreviations and acronyms.

File Transfer Protocol

A special application, called the *File Transfer Protocol* (*FTP*), is used to upload and download information to, and from, the Net. FTP is a client/server type of software application. The server version runs on the host computer, and the client version runs on the user's station.

EXAM TIP

Memorize the different file types associated with Internet operations and know what their functions are.

To access an FTP site, the user must move into an FTP application and enter the address of the site to be accessed. After the physical connection has been made, the user must log on to the FTP site by supplying an account number and password. When the host receives a valid password, a communication path opens between the host and the user site, and an FTP session begins.

Around the world, thousands of FTP host sites contain millions of pages of information that can be downloaded free of charge. However, most FTP sites are used for file transfers of things like driver updates and large file transfers that are too large for email operations.

FTP Authentication

FTP sites exist on the Internet in two basic formats—private and public. To access most private sites, you must connect to the site and input a username and password designated by the FTP host. Most *public FTP sites* employ *anonymous authentication* for access to the site. Anonymous authentication is an interaction that occurs between the local browser and the FTP host without involving the remote user. (That is, no username or passwords are required to gain access.)

Email

One of the most widely used functions of WANs is the *electronic mail (email)* feature. This feature enables Internet users to send and receive electronic messages to each other over the Internet. As with the regular postal service, email is sent to an address, from an address. With email, however, you can send the same message to several addresses at the same time, using a mailing list.

On the Internet, the message is distributed in packets, as with any other TCP/IP file. At the receiving end, the email message is reassembled and stored in the recipient's mailbox. When the recipient opens his email program, the email service delivers the message and notifies the user that it has arrived. The default email reader supported by the Windows 9*x* Outlook Express applet is the *POP3* standard. Likewise, it includes a standard *Simple Mail Transfer Protocol (SMTP)* email utility for outgoing email.

When setting up an email account, you must supply the following configuration information:

◆ Account name

◆ Password

◆ POP3 Server address

◆ SMTP Server address

EXAM TIP

Be aware that FTP sites employ anonymous authentication for access.

NOTE

Hands-On Activity For hands-on experience with this concept, refer to Lab Procedure #39, "Windows Me FTP/Telnet," located on the CD that accompanies this book.

WIDE AREA NETWORKING WITH WINDOWS 9x

EXAM TIP

Know what the Telephony Application Programming Interface (TAPI) is and what it does.

The primary way to connect to the Internet with Windows 9x is through a dial-up networking connection (using a modem). The dial-up communications system in Windows 9x offers many improvements over previous operating systems. Under Windows 9x, applications can cooperatively share the dial-up connections through its *Telephony Application Programming Interface* (*TAPI*). This interface provides a universal set of drivers for modems and COM ports to control and arbitrate telephony operations for data, faxes, and voice.

The Windows 9x Internet Connection

To establish dial-up Internet connection using the Windows 9x operating systems, follow these steps:

1. Configure the Windows 9x Dial-Up Networking feature.
2. Establish the Windows 9x modem configuration.
3. Set up the ISP dial-up connection information.
4. Establish the server address for the connection (if required by the ISP).
5. Set up the Internet Explorer (or other browser).
6. Connect to the Internet.

Configuring the Dial-Up Networking Feature

To set up *Dial-Up Networking* to connect to the Internet, turn on the computer, double-click the My Computer icon on the Desktop, and click the Dial-Up Networking icon. You can also reach this icon through the Start button. Choose the Programs option from the Start menu, point at the Accessories entry, and click the Dial-Up Networking entry.

If this option has never been set up before, a Welcome to Dial-Up Networking message comes up. Press the Next button to advance into the Make New Connection screen. At this point, enter the name of the Internet service provider in the Type window.

Establishing the Windows 9x Modem Configuration

Click the Configure button and set the maximum speed value to its fastest available setting to allow compression and smoother connection. Next, click the Connection tab to see the modem Connection Preferences information, as illustrated in Figure 29.2.

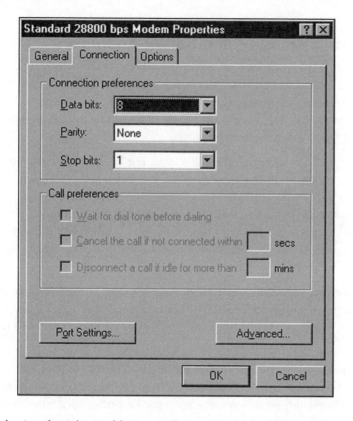

FIGURE 29.2
The Connection Preferences Window.

Selecting the Advanced button will permit you to add any extra settings desired for the installed modem. For example, an M0 setting should turn the volume on your modem off so that it is quiet when connecting to the Internet. Click the OK button to return to the Modem Preferences window.

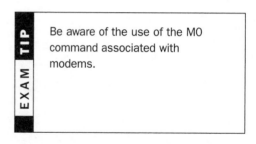

EXAM TIP

Be aware of the use of the M0 command associated with modems.

When in Rome When using the dial-up networking functions outside the United States, several configuration settings must be changed. Most international telephone systems do not feature the same dial tone/ring characteristics used in the United States. If your modem fails to detect a dial tone in a foreign country, you will need to disable the modem's dial tone detection feature. This is accomplished by accessing the Connections tab under the Control Panel/Modems path and then clearing the check box beside the Wait for Dial Tone Before Dialing option. You might also need to increase the cancel call waiting period if connections from your calling location take a relatively long time to make. This is accomplished by increasing the number of seconds in the Cancel the Call If Not Connected setting under the Connection tab.

Hands-On Activity For hands-on experience with this concept, refer to Lab Procedure #31, "Windows Me Dial-Up Access," located on the CD that accompanies this book.

Entering the ISP Dial-Up Connection Information

From the Modem Preferences window, click the OK button to move into the Make New Connection entry. Click the Next button to advance to the phone number entry page. Enter the dial-in phone number of your ISP—area code and local number. If a dialing prefix is required, such as 9, set this up as well. If the number is a long-distance number, Windows will detect this during dialing and automatically enter the appropriate long-distance prefix (that is, a 1 in the United States).

Establishing IP and Server Addresses

Most ISPs use *dynamic IP address assignments* for their customers. The DHCP service makes this possible by dynamically assigning IP addresses to the server's clients. This service is available in both Windows 9x and Windows NT/2000 and must be located on both the server and the client computers.

Some users require that their IP address not be changed. Therefore, they purchase an IP address from the ISP that is always assigned to them. Of course, this removes an assignable address from the ISP's bank of addresses, but the customer normally pays a great deal more for the constant address. In these situations, it might be necessary to enter the IP address information into the Internet connection's TCP/IP configuration.

Likewise, some ISPs might assign static server addresses that must be entered manually; others assign their server addresses dynamically and, therefore, do not require this information to be entered into the TCP/IP configuration.

When the ISP requires a server and/or IP address to be supplied, simply move into the Dial-Up Networking window and right-click the Internet Connection icon. Select the Properties option from the list and move into the Server Types page, depicted in Figure 29.3.

From this page, verify the Dial-Up Server type—usually PPP for Windows 9x, Windows NT, and Windows 2000—and click the TCP/IP Settings button. Set the TCP/IP settings as directed by the ISP's instructions. If specific values are entered into this page, the ISP connects the system to the Internet through a specific server address.

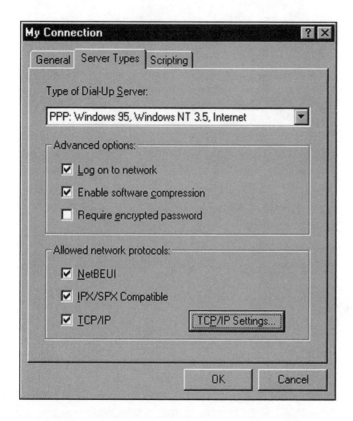

FIGURE 29.3
The Server Types page.

Click the Specify Name Server Address button and enter the Primary DNS and Secondary DNS addresses provided to you by the ISP. The screen should be similar to the one depicted in Figure 29.4.

FIGURE 29.4
TCP/IP Settings numbers.

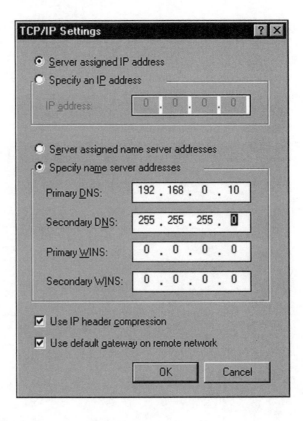

WINS

Although DNS is the naming service used by the Internet, it is not the only name-resolution service used with PCs. In the case of Windows LANs, the Microsoft preferred naming system is the *Windows Internet Naming Service* (*WINS*). This service can be used to translate IP addresses to NetBIOS names within a Windows LAN environment. The LAN must include a Windows name server running the WINS server software that maintains the IP address/NetBIOS name database for the LAN.

Each client in the WINS LAN must contain the WINS client software and be WINS enabled. In Windows 9x, you can establish the *WINS client* service through the Control Panel's Network icon. On the Network page, select the TCP/IP LAN adapter from the list and click the Properties button. Select the WINS Configuration tab to obtain the page shown in Figure 29.5, and enable the WINS resolution function. Then, enter the IP address of the *WINS server*.

> **EXAM TIP**
>
> Know what DNS and WINS are, what they do, and how they are different.

> **NOTE**
>
> **Hands-On Activity** For hands-on experience with this concept, refer to Lab Procedure #32, "Windows Me TCP/IP Setup," located on the CD that accompanies this book.

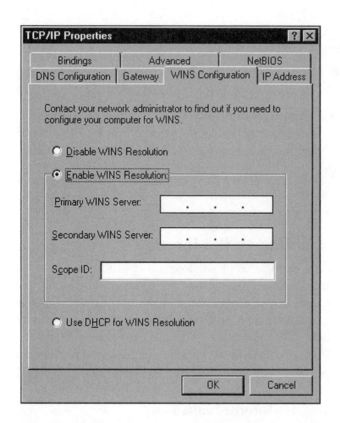

FIGURE 29.5
WINS enabling.

Setting Up the Internet Explorer Browser

Windows 9*x* includes a default browser called *Internet Explorer* (*IE*).
Unless a different browser is installed, Windows 9*x* places the IE
icon on the desktop and automatically refers to this browser for
Internet access. In order to browse the Internet using the IE, you
must configure it for use. You can do so in three different ways:

◆ From the IE View menu, select the Internet Options entry.

◆ Right-click the desktop Internet icon and click the Properties
tab.

◆ Click the Internet icon under the Start/Settings/Control Panel
path.

Selecting one of these options leads to an Internet Options page or
Internet Properties page. From either page, choose the Connection
tab and click the Connect button to bring up the Windows Internet
Connection Wizard and feature the Get Connected page. Pressing

the Next button provides three possible options for setting up the Internet connection and the browser:

◆ I want to choose an Internet service provider and set up an Internet account. (MSN is the default.)

◆ I want a new connection on this computer to my existing Internet account using my phone line or local area network (LAN).

◆ I already have an Internet connection set up on this computer, and I do not want to change it.

Connecting to the Internet

To access the Internet in Windows, double-click the icon of the new connection. Enter the username and password supplied by your ISP. Click the Connect option. You should hear the modem dialing at this point. A Connecting To window should appear on the screen, displaying the status of the modem. When it comes up, the Connected To window should minimize to the taskbar. The system is now connected to the Internet.

Setting Up Internet Email

Windows systems that run Microsoft Internet Explorer 4.0 or newer have a built-in email manager called *Outlook Express* that resides on the desktop taskbar. To set up an email account, open Outlook Express and click on the drop-down Tools menu. From the menu, choose the Account option, click the Add button, and select the Mail entry.

On successive screens, you will need to enter

◆ Your display name (the name that will be displayed to those receiving emails from you) email address

◆ Internet Mail Server information (POP3 and SMTP server names) for incoming and outgoing mail

◆ The ISP-supplied Mail Account name and password

At the end of the setup process, you simply click the Finish button to complete the email setup.

NOTE

Hands-On Activity   For hands-on experience with this concept, refer to Lab Procedure #38, "Internet Client Setup for IE 5.5," located on the CD that accompanies this book.

WIDE AREA NETWORKING WITH WINDOWS NT/2000

Older versions of Windows NT refer to all aspects of the dial-up networking function as *Remote Access Services* (*RAS*). With Windows NT 4.0, however, Microsoft changed the nomenclature to Dial-Up Networking on its client side elements. Microsoft did so to maintain compatibility with Windows 9*x* descriptions. The server side elements are still referred to as RAS. This same convention is used in the Windows 2000 product.

Windows NT Workstation provides all the software tools required to establish an Internet connection. These include a TCP/IP network protocol and the Windows NT Workstation Dial-Up Networking component. The Dial-Up Networking component is used to establish a link with the ISP over the public telephone system. This link also can be established over an ISDN line. Windows NT versions from 4.0 forward feature the built-in Microsoft Internet Explorer Web browser and a personal Web Server.

The Windows 2000 Internet Infrastructure

Windows 2000 replaces the Network Settings utility from the Windows NT 4.0 Control Panel with a New Network Connections folder, located in the My Computer applet. To create a dial-up connection in Windows 2000, click the Make New Connection icon in the My Computer Network Connections folder. This action opens the Windows 2000 Network Connection Wizard that guides the connection process. The Wizard requires information about the type of connection, modem type, and the phone number to be dialed. The connection types offered by the Wizard include private networks, virtual private networks, and other computers.

Establishing the Windows 2000 Modem Configuration

Under Windows 2000, the operating system should detect, or offer to detect, the modem through its Plug-and-Play facilities. It might also enable you to select the modem drivers manually from a list in the Control Panel.

After the modem has been detected, or selected, it appears in the Windows 2000 Modem list. The settings for the modem can be examined or reconfigured by selecting the modem from the list and clicking its Properties tab. In most cases, the device's default configuration settings should be used.

Establishing Dialing Rules

For Windows 2000 to connect to a network or dial-up connection, it must know what rules to follow in establishing the communication link. These rules are known as the Dialing Rules. In Windows 2000, the Dialing Rules are configured through the Start/Settings/Control Panel/Phone and Modem Options path. If the connection is new, a Location Information dialog window displays, enabling you to supply the area code and telephone system information.

To create a new location, click the New button and move through the General, Area Code Rules, and Calling Card tabs to add information as required. The default rules for dialing local, long-distance, and international calls are established under the General tab. These rules are based on the country or region identified on this page. Ways to reach an outside line (such as dialing 8 or 9 to get an outside line in a hotel or office building) are also established here. Similarly, the Area Code Rules information modifies the default information located under the General tab. As its name implies, the information under the Calling Cards tab pertains to numbers dialed using a specific calling card or long-distance company.

Establishing Dial-Up Internet Connections

The Windows 2000 *Internet Connection Wizard* provides an efficient way to establish Internet connectivity. You can use the Internet Connection Wizard to set up the Web browser, the Internet email account, and the newsgroup reader. To create the Internet connection to an existing account with an ISP, you need to know the following:

◆ The ISP's name

◆ The user name and password

◆ The ISP's dial-in access number

If the system is equipped with a cable modem or an Asymmetrical Digital Subscriber Line (ADSL), the ISP will need to furnish any additional connection instructions. The cable modem is a device that transmits and receives data through cable television connections. Conversely, ADSL is a special, high-speed ADSL modem technology that transmits data over existing telephone lines. The Internet Connection Wizard collects this information and then creates the Internet connection.

To connect to the Internet, select the Internet Connection Wizard option from the Start/Programs/Accessories/Communications path. If the connection is new, the Location Information dialog box displays, along with the Dialing Rules defined in the preceding section of this chapter. You also need to click the I Want to Sign Up for a New Internet Account option, click the Next button, and follow the Wizard's instructions.

Establishing Internet Connection Sharing

Windows 2000 makes it possible to share resources such as printers, folders, and Internet connections across a network. Sharing an Internet connection allows several computers to be connected to the Internet through a single dial-up connection. These connections can be made individually, or simultaneously, with each user maintaining the ability to employ the same services they did when their computer was connected directly to the Internet.

To establish *Internet connection sharing*, you must log on to the computer using an account that has administrator rights. Afterward, click Start/Settings and select the Network and Dial-Up Connections option. Right-click the connection to be shared and select the Properties option. The Internet Connection Sharing screen displays, as depicted in Figure 29.6.

FIGURE 29.6
The Internet Connection Sharing screen.

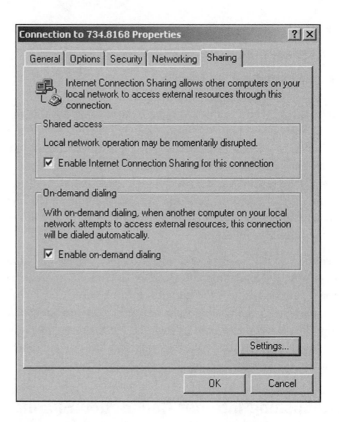

FIGURE 29.6
The Internet Connection Sharing screen.

Troubleshooting WAN Problems

The quickest items to check in a WAN application are the dial-up network software settings. Check the spelling of the Fully Qualified Domain Name to make sure that it is spelled exactly as it should be. If the spelling is wrong, no communications will take place. The major difference in checking WAN problems occurs in checking the Internet-specific software, such as the browser.

Most of the WAN troubleshooting steps from the local computer level involve the modem. The modem hardware should be examined. If the hardware is functional, the operating system's driver and resource configuration settings must be checked.

In Windows 9*x*, you can find the modem configuration information in the Control Panel under the Modems icon. This icon has two tabs: the General tab and the Diagnostics tab. The Properties button in the General window provides Port and Maximum Speed settings. The Connection tab provides character-framing information. The Connection tab's Advanced button provides Error and Flow Control settings, as well as Modulation Type.

The ISP establishes an Internet access account for each user. These accounts are based on the user's account name and password that are asked for each time the user logs on to the account. Forgetting or misspelling either item will result in the ISP rejecting access to the Internet. Most accounts are paid for on a monthly schedule. If the account isn't paid up, the ISP might cancel the account and deny access to the user. In either of these situations, if the user attempts to log on to the account, he will repeatedly be asked to enter his account name and password until a predetermined number of failed attempts has been reached.

> **EXAM TIP**
>
> Be aware of reasons that ISP accounts become invalid and what the consequences of this situation are.

CHALLENGE #2

Your friend has called you on the telephone because he cannot get on the Internet and he don't know enough about his computer or the Internet to fix his problem. When you ask him to describe what is happening, he tells you that he gets to the login screen that asks for his username and password, but each time he puts them in, the same screen reappears. He wants to know if you think he has a virus. What two things can you tell him to check? Is one of those items running an antivirus program?

The most common communication error is the Disconnected message. This message occurs for a number of reasons, including a noisy phone line or random transmission errors. You can normally overcome this type of error by just retrying the connection. Other typical error messages include the following:

◆ *No Dial Tone*—This error indicates a bad or improper phone-line connection, such as the phone line plugged in to the modem's line jack rather than the phone jack.

◆ *Port In Use*—This error indicates a busy signal or an improper configuration parameter.

◆ *Can't Find Modem*—This error indicates that the PnP process did not detect the modem or that it has not been correctly configured to communicate with the system.

If the system cannot find the modem, reboot it so that Windows can attempt to redetect the modem. If rebooting does not detect the modem, check any hardware configuration settings for the modem and compare them to the settings in the Control Panel's Device Manager. These values can be checked through the Control Panel's Modems/Properties page. However, the Device Manager must be used to make changes to these settings.

If the modem is present, move into the Device Manager and check the modem for resource conflicts. If there is a conflict with the modem, an exclamation point (!) should appear alongside the modem listing. If you detect a conflict, move into the Modems Properties page and check the modem's resources. Also, record the Connection Preferences from the Connection page and make certain that the character-framing configuration is correct. The conflict must be resolved between the modem and whatever device is using its resources.

If no conflict is indicated, move into the Diagnostics page and highlight the installed device. Click the More Info button. This action causes Windows to communicate with the modem hardware. If no problems are detected by this test, Windows 9*x* displays the modem's port information, along with a listing of the AT commands that it used to test the hardware, as illustrated in Figure 29.7. If an error is detected during the Windows testing, an error message displays onscreen. These messages are similar to those previously listed.

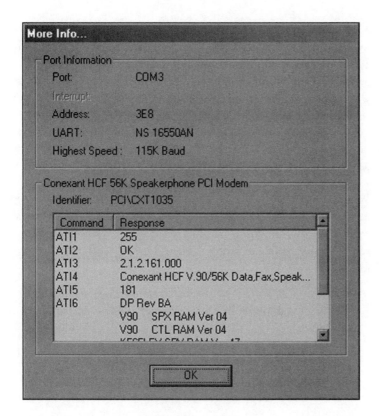

FIGURE 29.7
Modem Properties More Info response.

If the modem tests are okay, check the Username and Password settings. This can be accomplished through the My Computer/Dial-Up Networking path, or through the Start/Programs/Accessories/Communications/Dialup Networking path in Windows 98.

In the Dial-Up Networking window, right-click the desired connection icon and select the Properties option from the list. Check the phone number and modem type on the General page. Next move into the Server Types page and check Type of Dial-Up Server installed. For Windows Internet dial-up service, this is typically a "PPP, Internet, Windows NT, Windows 98" connection. Also, disable the NetBEUI and IPX/SPX settings from the page and make certain that the TCP/IP setting is enabled.

Most ISPs employ DHCP to assign IP, DNS, and Gateway addresses to clients for dial-up accounts. Therefore, in a dial-up situation, the Server Assigns IP Address option and the Server Assigns Name Server Address option are normally enabled. In the case of intranets with in-house clients, the network administrator determines how the values are assigned—statically or via DHCP.

Network Troubleshooting Tools

When TCP/IP is installed in Windows 9*x* or Windows 2000, a number of TCP/IP troubleshooting tools are automatically installed with it. All *TCP/IP utilities* are controlled by commands entered and run from the command prompt. These TCP/IP tools include the following:

◆ *Address Resolution Protocol (ARP) command*—This utility enables you to modify IP-to-Ethernet address-translation tables.

◆ *FTP*—This utility enables you to transfer files to and from FTP servers.

◆ *PING*—This utility enables you to verify connections to remote hosts.

◆ *NETSTAT*—This utility enables you to display the current TCP/IP network connections and protocol statistics. A similar command, called NBTSTAT, performs the same function using NetBIOS over the TCP/IP connection.

◆ *Trace Route (TRACERT)*—This utility enables you to display the route, and a hop count, taken to a given destination. The route taken to a particular address can be set manually using the ROUTE command.

◆ *IPCONFIG*—This command-line utility enables you to determine the current TCP/IP configuration (MAC address, IP address, and subnet mask) of the local computer. It also can be used to request a new TCP/IP address from a DHCP server. IPCONFIG is available in both Windows 98 and Windows 2000. Windows 95 did not support IPCONFIG.

EXAM TIP

Know which TCP/IP utility can be used to display the path of a transmission across a network.

The IPCONFIG utility can be started with two important option switches—/renew and /release. These switches are used to release and update IP settings received from a DHCP server. The /all switch is used to view the TCP/IP settings for all of the adapter cards that the local station is connected to.

◆ WINIPCFG—This is a GUI version of the IPCONFIG command available only in Windows 95. The various command-line switches available with the IPCONFIG command are implemented in graphical buttons. Like IPCONFIG, WINIPCFG can be used to release and renew IP addresses leased from a DHCP server.

◆ NSLOOKUP.EXE—This is a Windows 2000 TCP/IP utility that can be entered at the command prompt to query Internet (DNS) name servers interactively. It has two modes—interactive and non-interactive. In interactive mode, the user can query name servers for information about various hosts and domains. Non-interactive mode is used to print just the name and requested information for a host or domain. NSLOOKUP is only available when the TCP/IP protocol has been installed.

EXAM TIP

Know which TCP/IP utilities can be used to release and renew IP address information from a DHCP server.

EXAM TIP

Know which TCP/IP utilities show the host IP address.

CHALLENGE #3

You are setting up a network of old Windows 95 and 98 computers that have been donated to a school by a local company. Which utilities must you use to view the TCP/IP settings for all the adapter cards in the network?

EXAM TIP

Know where TCP/IP utilities are run from.

Although all of these utilities are useful in isolating different TCP/IP problems, the most widely used commands are PING and TRACERT.

The PING utility sends *Internet Control Message Packets (ICMP)* to a remote location and then waits for echoed response packets to be returned. The command waits for up to one second for each packet sent and then displays the number of transmitted and received packets. You can use the command to test both the name and IP address of the remote unit. A number of switches can be used to set parameters for the ping operation. Figure 29.8 depicts the information displayed by a typical ping operation.

EXAM TIP

Know which Windows tools to employ to check out network-related problems.

FIGURE 29.8
A Ping operation.

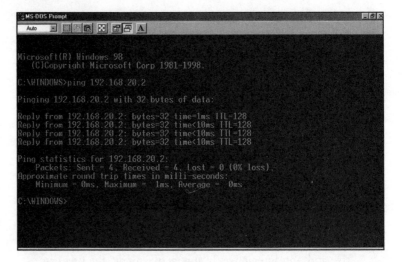

Most Internet servers do not respond to ICMP requests created by pinging. However, you can use the PING utility to access. By doing so, you can get a reply that will verify that TCP/IP, DNS, and gateway are working. The TRACERT utility traces the route taken by ICMP packets sent across the network, as described in Figure 29.9. Routers along the path return information to the inquiring system and the utility displays the hostname, IP address, and round-trip time for each hop in the path.

FIGURE 29.9
A TRACERT operation.

Because the TRACERT report shows how much time is spent at each router along the path, it can be used to help determine where network slow downs are occurring.

NOTE   **Hands-On Activity**   For hands-on experience with this concept, refer to Lab Procedure #33, "Windows Me TCP/IP Utilities," and Lab Procedure #36, "Windows 2000 TCP/IP," located on the CD that accompanies this book.

CHALLENGE #4

You are supposed to demonstrate the operation of the company's network to some executives and you want to display the path that your TCP/IP packets are traveling to get to a remote network location. Which utilities can you use to accomplish this?

CHAPTER SUMMARY

This chapter focused on wide area networking functions of the Windows 9x and Windows 2000 operating systems. The first section of the chapter included a discussion of Internet basics, including procedures for configuring and using a dial-up network configuration to access the Internet.

The chapter then moved forward with a section of information about IP addresses on the Internet and how these addresses are related to Internet Domains. This included discussions of the DNS and DHCP functions in Windows 9x and Windows 2000.

The next major section of the chapter focused on a section of the Internet known as the World Wide Web. It covered Web Browsers used to navigate the Web and view its contents and included information about the FTP and email functions of the Web.

The fourth major section of the chapter dealt with the wide area networking capabilities of both the Windows 9x and Windows 2000 operating systems.

The final section of the chapter provided instructions for troubleshooting Internet access problems. This section also included an extensive discussion of the network tools found in Windows and how they can be applied to troubleshooting WAN-related problems.

At this point, review the objectives listed at the beginning of the chapter to be certain that you understand each point and can perform each task listed there. Afterward, answer the review questions that follow to verify your knowledge of the information.

KEY TERMS

- Anonymous authentication
- Asynchronous DSL (ADSL)
- Bridges
- Browsers
- Class A addresses
- Class B addresses
- Class C addresses
- Dial-up connections
- Dial-Up Networking
- Digital Subscriber Lines (DSL)
- DNS names
- Domain Name System (DNS)
- Dotted-decimal notation
- Dynamic Host Configuration Protocol (DHCP)
- Dynamic IP address assignments
- Electronic mail (email)
- File Transfer Protocol (FTP)

CHAPTER SUMMARY

- Fully Qualified Domain Names (FQDN)
- Gateways
- High-data-rate DSL (HDSL)
- Host address
- Hostname
- Hubs
- Hypertext Markup Language (HTML)
- Hypertext Transfer Protocol
- Integrated Service Digital Network (ISDN)
- Internet connection sharing
- Internet Connection Wizard
- Internet Control Message Packets (ICMP)
- Internet Explorer (IE)
- Internet Protocol addresses
- Internet service providers (ISPs)
- IP addresses
- IPCONFIG
- NETSTAT
- Network Access Point (NAP)
- Network address
- Network packets
- NSLOOKUP.EXE
- Outlook Express
- PING

- Point-to-Point Protocol (PPP)
- POP3
- POTS (Plain Old Telephone System)
- Public FTP sites
- Remote Access Services (RAS)
- Repeaters
- Routers
- Serial Line Internet Protocol (SLIP)
- Simple Mail Transfer Protocol (SMTP)
- Synchronous DSL (SDSL)
- TCP/IP packet
- TCP/IP utilities
- Telephony Application Programming Interface (TAPI)
- Trace Route (TRACERT)
- Transport Control Protocol/Internet Protocol (TCP/IP)
- Universal Resource Locator (URL)
- Wide area network (WAN)
- Windows Internet Naming Service (WINS)
- WINIPCFG
- WINS client
- WINS server
- World Wide Web (WWW)

APPLY YOUR KNOWLEDGE

Review Questions

1. What is TCP/IP?

   A. Protocol used to send remote network commands

   B. Protocol used to send email

   C. Protocol used to allow remote interrupt masking

   D. Protocol used on the Internet

2. What does TCP/IP do? (Select all that apply.)

   A. Allows messages to be routed to a specific computer

   B. Bundles data into network packets

   C. Allows messages to be fragmented and reassembled

   D. Provides basic encryption to data packets

3. What are the advantages of using the TCP/IP protocol? (Select all that apply.)

   A. Can be used on any network typology

   B. Common to most operating systems

   C. Non-proprietary (no one owns it)

   D. Encrypted

4. What describes the pathway used to manually establish IP address and Subnet Mask settings?

   A. Start/Settings/Control Panel/Network/TCP-IP adapter/Properties

   B. Start/Settings/Network/TCP-IP adapter/Properties

   C. Start/Control Panel/TCP-IP adapter/Properties

   D. Start/Control Panel/Network/TCP-IP Properties

5. What protocol supports dialup, Ethernet, and Token Ring networking?

   A. TCP/IP

   B. UDP

   C. RAS

   D. IPX

6. What services do all ISPs provide their Internet customers? (Select all that apply.)

   A. Spam filtering

   B. Internet identity through IP addresses

   C. DNS routing

   D. Email services

7. Dynamic IP addressing is performed by
   _____.

   A. LMHOST

   B. IMAP

   C. DHCP

   D. DNS

8. On a Microsoft-based LAN, what is the preferred naming service?

   A. DNS

   B. LMHOST

   C. NetBIOS

   D. WINS

APPLY YOUR KNOWLEDGE

9. What modem string command will turn off the dialing sound?

   A. M0

   B. M1

   C. S0

   D. S1

10. What are the possible reasons that I could log in to my Internet account yesterday, but it won't work today? (Select all that apply.)

    A. Password has expired.

    B. Incorrect username or password.

    C. Failure to pay fee.

    D. Thunderstorm.

11. Which TCP/IP utility can be used to release and renew IP address information from a DHCP server?

    A. NETSTAT

    B. TRACERT

    C. PING

    D. IPCONFIG

12. Which TCP/IP utilities show the host IP address? (Select all that apply.)

    A. NETSTAT

    B. NSLOOKUP

    C. IPCONFIG

    D. WINIPCFG

13. Which Windows tools are employed to check out network-related problems?

    A. WINS utilities

    B. DHCP utilities

    C. DNS utilities

    D. TCP/IP utilities

14. Where are TCP/IP utilities run from?

    A. Command prompt

    B. Start/Run

    C. Start/Program Files/Accessories/System Tools

    D. Start/Settings/Control Panel/Network

15. Which TCP/IP utility displays the address of a known remote location?

    A. PING

    B. NETSTAT

    C. IPCONFIG

    D. NSLOOKUP

16. Which TCP/IP utility can be used to display the path of a transmission across a network?

    A. PING

    B. NETSTAT

    C. TRACERT

    D. NSLOOKUP

17. What type of protocol is commonly associated with the World Wide Web?

    A. FTP

    B. TCP/IP

    C. HTTP

    D. PPP

18. What language is used to create the pages that make up the Web?

    A. C++

    B. HTML

    C. Java

    D. Net

19. Anonymous authentication is used for which type Internet service?

    A. Web server

    B. Email server

    C. FTP server

    D. Secure server

20. Windows 9x uses which function to share dial-up connections?

    A. TCP/IP

    B. UDP

    C. RAS

    D. TAPI

Answers and Explanations

1. **D**. The language of the Internet is Transport Control Protocol/Internet Protocol (TCP/IP). No matter what type of computer platform or software is being used, the information must move across the Internet in this format. For more information, see the section "TCP/IP."

2. **B, C**. This protocol calls for data to be grouped together, in bundles, called network packets. The TCP/IP packet is designed primarily to permit message fragmentation and reassembly. For more information, see the section "TCP/IP."

3. **A, B, C**. It is considered to be one of the most secure of the network protocols. Because no one actually owns the TCP/IP protocol, it was adopted as the transmission standard for the Internet. It was so widely accepted by the Internet community that virtually every network operating system supports it, including Apple, MS-DOS/Windows, UNIX, Linux, OS/2 and even networked printers. It can also be used on any topology (that is, dial-up, Ethernet, Token Ring, and so on). Therefore, all these computer types can exchange data across a network using the TCP/IP protocol. For more information, see the section "TCP/IP."

4. **A**. In most Windows operating systems, the TCP/IP settings are established through the Start/Settings/Control Panel/Network/TCP-IP adapter/Properties path. From this location, you can click on the IP Address tab to establish the desired method of obtaining an IP address (that is, automatically from a DHCP Server, or manually, by specifying a static IP address). If you choose the option to Specify an IP address, you must enter the IP address and Subnet Mask settings. For more information, see the section "TCP/IP."

5. **A**. TCP/IP can be used on any topology (that is, dial-up, Ethernet, Token Ring, and so on). Therefore, all these computer types can exchange data across a network using the TCP/IP protocol. For more information, see the section "TCP/IP."

APPLY YOUR KNOWLEDGE

6. **B, C, D**. Service that most ISPs deliver to their customers include: Internet identity through IP Addresses, Email services through POP3 and SMTP servers, Internet News Service through USENET archive servers, and Internet routing through DNS servers. For more information, see the section "Internet Service Providers."

7. **C**. A Dynamic Host Configuration Protocol (DHCP) server will automatically assign a unique IP address to hosts on the network (usually by the ISP). For more information, see the section "Dynamic Host Configuration Protocol."

8. **D**. Although DNS is the naming service used by the Internet, it is not the only name-resolution service used with PCs. In the case of Windows LANs, the Microsoft preferred naming system is the Windows Internet Naming Service (WINS). For more information, see the section "WINS."

9. **A**. An M0 setting should turn the volume on your modem off so that it is quiet when connecting to the Internet. For more information, see the section "Establishing the Windows 9x Modem Configuration."

10. **B, C**. Internet accounts are based on the user's account name and password that are asked for each time the user logs on to the account. Forgetting or misspelling either item will result in the ISP rejecting access to the Internet. Most accounts are paid for on a monthly schedule. If the account isn't paid up, the ISP might cancel the account and deny access to the user. In either of these situations, if the user attempts to log on to the account, he will repeatedly be asked to enter his account name and password until a predetermined number of failed attempts has been reached. For more information, see the section "Troubleshooting WAN Problems."

11. **D**. The IPCONFIG utility can be started with two important option switches—/renew and /release. These switches are used to release and update IP settings received from a DHCP server. For more information, see the section "Network Troubleshooting Tools."

12. **C, D**. IPCONFIG and WINIPCFG will display the network information for the local host, including the host IP address. For more information, see the section "Network Troubleshooting Tools."

13. **D**. When TCP/IP is installed in Windows 9x or Windows 2000, a number of TCP/IP network troubleshooting tools are automatically installed with it. For more information, see the section "Network Troubleshooting Tools."

14. **A**. All TCP/IP utilities are controlled by commands entered and run from the command prompt. For more information, see the section "Network Troubleshooting Tools."

15. **A, D**. The PING utility will enable you to verify connections to remote hosts and display the IP address. In interactive mode, the user can employ NSLOOKUP to query name servers for information about various hosts and domains. Non-interactive mode is used to print just the name and requested information for a host or domain. NSLOOKUP is only available when the TCP/IP protocol has been installed. For more information, see the section "Network Troubleshooting Tools."

16. **C**. The TRACERT utility enables you to display the route, and a hop count, taken to a given destination. For more information, see the section "Network Troubleshooting Tools."

APPLY YOUR KNOWLEDGE

17. **C.** The World Wide Web (WWW) can be accessed by using the Hypertext Transfer Protocol (HTTP). For more information, see the section "The World Wide Web."

18. **B.** The Hypertext Markup Language (HTML) files are used to create the Web, and link the various types of files together. These files can usually be recognized by their abbreviated .HTM file extension. For more information, see the section "Web Browsers."

19. **C.** Most public FTP sites employ anonymous authentication for access to the site. Anonymous authentication is an interaction that occurs between the local browser and the FTP host without involving the remote user (that is, no username or passwords are required to gain access). For more information, see the section "FTP Authentication."

20. **D.** Under Windows 9*x*, applications can cooperatively share the dial-up connections through its Telephony Application Programming Interface (TAPI). This interface provides a universal set of drivers for modems and COM ports to control and arbitrate telephony operations for data, faxes, and voice. For more information, see the section "Wide Area Networking with Windows 9*x*."

Challenge Solutions

1. Many ISPs use the dynamic IP addressing function of DHCP to provide access to their dial-up users. The protocol automatically delivers IP addresses, subnet mask and default router configuration parameters, and other configuration information to the devices on the network. The dynamic addressing portion of the protocol also means that computers can be added to a network without manually assigning them unique IP addresses. As a matter of fact, the devices can be issued a different IP address each time they connect to the network. In some networks, the device's IP address can even change while it is still connected. For more information, see the section "Dynamic Host Configuration Protocol."

2. Forgetting or misspelling either his username or password will result in his ISP refusing him access to the Internet. Also, if the account isn't paid up, the ISP might have cancelled his account and deny him access. In either case, when he attempts to log on to his account, he will repeatedly be asked to enter his account name and password until a predetermined number of failed attempts has been reached. For more information, see the section "Troubleshooting WAN Problems."

3. The IPCONFIG utility enables you to determine the current TCP/IP configuration (MAC address, IP address, and subnet mask) of the local computer. It also might be used to request a new TCP/IP address from a DHCP server. IPCONFIG is available in both Windows 98 and Windows 2000. Windows 95 did not support IPCONFIG. In Windows 95, the WINIPCFG utility performed this function. It is a GUI version of the IPCONFIG command available only in Windows 95. The various command-line switches available with the IPCONFIG command are implemented in graphical buttons. For more information, see the section "Network Troubleshooting Tools."

4. TRACERT is the traditional TCP/IP tool used to show packet routes to a remote location. For more information, see the section "Network Troubleshooting Tools."

APPLY YOUR KNOWLEDGE

Suggested Readings and Resources

1. Wide Area Networks
   http://www.techfest.com/networking/wan.htm

2. TCP/IP
   http://www.cisco.com/univercd/cc/td/doc/
   cisintwk/ito_doc/ip.htm

3. Internet Service Providers
   http://www.phdsystems.com/tutorials/
   internet/isp/sld01.html

4. IP Addresses
   http://www.phdsystems.com/tutorials/
   internet/ipadress/sld01.html

5. Internet Domains
   http://www.phdsystems.com/tutorials/
   internet/domname/sld01.html

6. Understanding PPP and PPP Authentication
   www.cisco.com/warp/public/779/smbiz/
   service/knowledge/wan/ppp_auth.htm

7. Dynamic Host Configuration Protocol
   http://www.networkmagazine.com/article/
   NMG20000727S0025

8. ISDN
   http://www.cisco.com/univercd/cc/td/doc/
   cisintwk/ito_doc/isdn.htm

9. Digital Subscriber Lines
   http://www.networkmagazine.com/article/
   NMG20000725S0008

10. File Transfer Protocol
    http://www.pbs.org/uti/guide/ftp.html

11. Email
    http://www.pbs.org/uti/guide/email.html

12. The World Wide Web
    http://www.pbs.org/uti/guide/www.html

13. Web Browsers
    http://www.learnthenet.com/english/html/
    12browser.htm

14. Configuring the Dial-Up Networking Feature
    http://www.msu.edu/user/cic/dialup/
    pc-dial/win98/98dial.html

15. WINS
    http://www-tus.csx.cam.ac.uk/
    pc_support/Win98/wins/

16. ISP Logon Problems
    http://support.microsoft.com/search/
    preview.aspx?scid=kb;en-us;Q161986

17. Establishing Internet Connection Sharing
    http://www.annoyances.org/exec/show/
    ics_2000

18. Troubleshooting WAN Problems
    http://www.webcom.com/llarrow/trouble.html

19. Networking Troubleshooting Tools
    http://www.hildrum.com/TCPIPutil.html

PART

III

FINAL REVIEW

Fast Facts: Core Hardware Service Technician Exam

Fast Facts: Operating Systems Technologies Exam

Study and Exam Prep Tips

Practice Exam: Core Hardware Service Technician

Practice Exam: Operating Systems Technologies

The fast facts listed in this chapter and the following chapter are designed as a refresher of key points and topics required to succeed on the A+ certification exam. By using these summaries of key points, you can spend an hour prior to your exam refreshing your knowledge of key topics to ensure that you have a solid understanding of the objectives and information required to succeed in each major area of the exam.

CompTIA has established two modules for the A+ examination: the Core Hardware Service Technician module and the Operating System Technologies module. The information here is organized to follow the sequence of the Core Hardware Service Technician module test objectives, and each domain that follows includes the key points from each chapter in this book. If you have a thorough understanding of the key points here, chances are good that you will pass the exam.

Part I, "Core Hardware Service Technician," is dedicated to the six domains covered in the Core Hardware Service Technician module. Now that you have read those chapters, answered all the review and exam questions at the ends of the chapters, and explored the PrepLogic test engine on the CD-ROM that accompanies the book, you are ready to take the exam.

Albert Einstein supposedly said, "Everything should be as simple as possible, but not simpler." These fast facts are designed as a quick study aid that you can use in less than an hour just prior to taking the exam. This chapter cannot serve as a substitute for knowing the material supplied in all the chapters in the book. However, its key points should refresh your memory on critical topics. In addition to the information located here, remember to review the Glossary terms, which are intentionally not covered here.

Fast Facts

Core Hardware Service Technician Exam

CompTIA uses the following domains to arrange the objectives for the Core Hardware Service Technician module:

1.0 Installation, Configuration, and Upgrading

2.0 Diagnosing and Troubleshooting

3.0 Preventive Maintenance

4.0 Motherboard/Processors/Memory

5.0 Printers

6.0 Basic Networking

1.0 INSTALLATION, CONFIGURATION, AND UPGRADING

This domain requires knowledge and skills required to identify, install, configure, and upgrade microcomputer modules and peripherals. The main points follow:

◆ System boards are also referred to as *motherboards* and as *planar boards*.

◆ Notches and dots on the various ICs provide important keys for replacing a microprocessor. These notches and dots specify the location of the number 1 pin, which must be lined up with the pin-1 notch of the socket.

◆ The ATX system board power connector contains a signal line that the system board can use to turn off the power supply. This is a power-saving feature referred to as a soft switch.

◆ A good rule of thumb to remember when attaching the two AT-style power-supply connectors to the system board is that the black wires from each bundle should be side-by-side.

◆ Standard VGA resolution is defined as 720×400 pixels using 16 colors in text mode and 640×480 pixels using 16 onscreen colors in graphics mode.

◆ A typical IBM floppy disk has 40 or 80 tracks per surface. The tracks are divided into 8, 9, or 18 sectors each. In a PC-compatible system each sector holds 512 bytes of data.

◆ The drive connected to the very end of the cable is designated as drive A:.

◆ The average storage capacity of a CD-ROM is about 680MB.

◆ The SCSI interface is widely used to connect external CD-ROM drives to systems. A Centronics connector is normally used with an external SCSI cable.

◆ A color CRT has a metal grid called a *shadow mask* in front of the phosphor coating. The shadow mask ensures that an electron gun assigned to one color doesn't strike a dot of another color.

◆ Resolution can be expressed as a function of how close pixels can be grouped together onscreen. This form of resolution is expressed in terms of *dot pitch*. A monitor with a .28 dot pitch has pixels that are located .28mm apart. In monochromatic monitors, dot pitch is measured from center to center of each pixel. In a color monitor, the pitch is measured from the center of one dot trio to the center of the next trio.

◆ Notebook and laptop computers use non-CRT displays, such as LCDs and gas-plasma panels. Both types of display units can be operated from batteries.

◆ When a modem is used to send signals in only one direction, it is operating in simplex mode.

◆ In *half-duplex mode*, modems exchange data, but only in one direction at a time. Multiplexing the send and receive signal frequencies allows both modems to send and receive data simultaneously. This mode of operation is known as *full-duplex mode*.

◆ When a PC is turned on, the entire system is reset to a predetermined starting condition. From that state, it begins carrying out software instructions from its BIOS program.

◆ A SIMM module can be inserted in only one direction because of a plastic safety tab at one end of the SIMM slot.

◆ SIMMs and DIMMs are keyed, and it is almost physically impossible to plug them in incorrectly.

◆ When ordering a replacement power supply, you must remember to take into account the system's form factor and wattage rating requirements. The wattage rating is a measurement of the total power the supply can deliver to the system. Heavily equipped systems require power supplies with higher wattage ratings.

◆ A good rule of thumb to remember when attaching the two power connectors labeled P8 and P9 to the system board is that the black wires in each bundle should be next to each other, in the middle.

◆ Plugging a keyboard in to a system while power is on may cause the system board to fail due to the power surge and ESD that may occur between it and the system board.

◆ When choosing a new mouse for an upgrade of an existing system or a replacement for a defective mouse, you need to consider the type of connector that's required to attach it to the system.

◆ When the ATX specification adopted the same connector for both the keyboard and mouse, it introduced an opportunity to plug these devices into the wrong connectors.

◆ The FDD signal cable is designed to accommodate two FDD units. If the drive is the only floppy drive in the system or is intended to operate as the A: drive, you should connect it to the connector at the end of the cable. If it is being installed as a B: drive, you should attach it to the connector toward the center of the cable. A small twist of wires between the A: and B: connectors differentiates between the drives.

◆ After the primary partition has been established and properly configured, an additional partition, referred to as an *extended partition*, is also permitted. However, the extended partition may be further subdivided into 23 logical drives (all the letters in the alphabet minus a, b, and c).

◆ The FDISK utility in MS-DOS version 4.0 raised the maximum size of a logical drive to 128MB, and version 5.0 raised it to 528MB. The FDISK utility in Windows 9x provided upgraded support for very large hard drives. The original version of Windows 95 set a size limit for logical drives at 2GB. The FDISK version in the upgraded OSR2 version of Windows 95 extended the maximum partition size to 8GB.

◆ When newer operating system versions provide for partitions larger than 528MB, another limiting factor for the size of disk partitions is encountered: the BIOS. The standard AT-compatible BIOS had a hard drive capacity limit of 504MB. To overcome this, newer BIOS versions include an Enhanced mode, which employs LBA techniques to permit the larger partition sizes that are available through the Windows operating systems to be used.

◆ In Windows 9*x*, an advanced CD-ROM device driver called CDFS was implemented to provide protected-mode operation of the drive. Windows 9*x* retains the MSCDEX files for real-mode operation.

◆ Like other computer power-supply types, a portable power supply, also referred to as an *AC adapter*, converts commercial AC voltage into a single DC voltage that the computer can use to power its components and recharge its batteries. Similar DC-to-DC controllers are available that permit notebook computers to draw power from DC sources such as cigarette lighter sockets in automobiles.

◆ When an LCD panel fails, the most common repair is to replace the entire display panel/housing assembly. To replace the LCD panel, you must use a panel that is identical to the original, to ensure that it fits the plastic display housing.

◆ Because no current passes through the display to light the pixels, the power consumption of LCD displays is very low. The electrodes can be controlled (that is, turned on and off) by using very low DC voltage levels.

◆ Although the PC card's software driver can be executed directly on the card (instead of being moved into RAM for execution), the system's PC card enablers must be loaded before the card can be activated.

◆ Each device in a PC-compatible system that is capable of interrupting the microprocessor must be assigned its own unique IRQ number. The system uses the IRQ numbers to identify which device is in need of service.

◆ Two serious system board–based conditions cause an NMI signal to be sent to the microprocessor. One condition occurs when an active IOCHCK signal is received from an adapter card located in one of the board's expansion slots. The other condition that causes an NMI signal to be generated is the occurrence of a PCK error in the system's DRAM memory.

◆ The system's FDD controller uses DMA channel 2 by default.

◆ In the case of an internal modem, the UART in the modem normally replaces one of the two COM port UARTs provided by a typical PC system. If the COM port UART is not disabled, the system may have trouble differentiating between the two ports, and a conflict may develop. Therefore, it is common practice to disable an onboard UART when an internal modem is installed.

◆ In a PC system, the FDC operates in conjunction with the system's DMA controller and is assigned to the DRQ-2 and DACK-2 lines.

◆ The floppy disk drive controller is assigned to the IRQ-6 channel in PC-compatible systems.

◆ The first IDE drive controller responds to I/O addresses between 1F0h and 1F7h, and the second responds to addresses between 170h and 177h.

◆ The ATX specification employs two 6-pin mini-DIN connectors (also referred to as *PS/2 connectors*) for the mouse and keyboard. Of course, the fact that both connections use the same type of connector can lead to problems if they are reversed.

◆ The connector type is an important consideration when you purchase a mouse. You need to consider which type of connector will be needed for the system—9-pin serial or 6-pin mini-DIN.

◆ The cable length used for a parallel printer should be kept to less than 10 feet (3m).

◆ If a printer port is found at 3BCh, the operating system assigns it the title LPT1. If no printer port is found at 3BCh, but there is one at 378h, however, the operating system assigns LPT1 to the latter address. Likewise, a system that has printer ports at physical addresses 378h and 278h would have LPT1 assigned at 378h and have LPT2 at location 278h.

◆ You can set the interrupt level of the printer port to a number of different levels by changing its configuration jumpers or CMOS enabling setting. Normal interrupt request settings for printer ports in a PC-compatible system are IRQ5 and IRQ7. IRQ7 is normally assigned to the LPT1 printer port, and IRQ5 typically serves the LPT2 port, if installed.

◆ The RS-232 standard can produce a maximum baud rate of 20,000 baud over distances of less than 50 feet (15.25m), which is the recommended maximum length of an RS-232 cable. The RS-232C version extends the length to 100 feet (30.5m).

◆ Either RS-232 port may be designated as COM1, COM2, COM3, or COM4, as long as both ports are not assigned to the same COM port number. In most PCs, COM1 is assigned as port address hex 3F8h and uses IRQ channel 4. The COM2 port is typically assigned port address hex 2F8h and IRQ3. Likewise, COM3 uses IRQ4 and is assigned the I/O address 3E8h; COM4 usually resides at 2E8 and uses IRQ3.

◆ USB has been developed to provide a fast, flexible method of attaching up to 127 peripheral devices to a computer.

◆ USB devices can be added to or removed from a system while it is powered up and fully operational. This is referred to as *hot-swapping* or

hot-plugging the device. The PnP capabilities of the system detect the presence (or absence) of the device and configure it for operation.

◆ The root hub provides power directly from the host system to the devices that are directly connected to it. Hubs also supply power to the devices that are connected to them. Even though the interface supplies power to the USB devices, the USB devices are permitted to have their own power sources if necessary.

◆ The length limit for a USB cable serving a full-speed device is 16 feet, 5 inches (5m). Conversely, the length limit for cables used between low-speed devices is 9 feet, 10 inches (3m).

◆ FireWire is capable of using the high-speed isochronous transfer mode described for USB to support data transfer rates up to 400Mbps. This makes the Firewire bus superior to the USB bus.

◆ The IrDA standard specifies that IrLPT is used with character printers to provide a wireless interface between a computer and a printer.

◆ IrDA protocols specify communication ranges up to 6.6 feet (2m), but most specifications usually state 3.3 feet (1m) as the maximum range.

◆ In most cases, the IDE drive comes from the manufacturer configured for operation as a single drive, or as the master drive in a multidrive system. To install the drive as a second, or slave, drive, you usually need to install, remove, or move a jumper block. Some hosts disable the interface's Cable Select pin for slave drives. With these types of hosts, it is necessary to install a jumper for the Cable Select option on the drive.

◆ The EIDE, or the ATA-2 interface, permits up to four IDE devices to operate in a single computer system.

◆ In addition to the new DMA transfer modes, the fastest IDE enhancements—referred to as Ultra, ATA 4/Ultra ATA 66, and Ultra ATA 100—extend the high data throughput capabilities of the bus by doubling the number of conductors in the IDE signal cable to 80. Although the number of wires has doubled, the IDE connector has remained compatible with the 40-pin IDE connection, but each pin has been provided with its own ground conductor in the cable.

◆ The IDE controller structure is an integrated portion on most PC system boards. This structure includes BIOS and chipset support for the IDE version the board will support, as well as the IDE host connector.

◆ A SCSI chain could be used to connect a controller to a hard drive, a CD-ROM drive, a high-speed tape drive, a scanner, and a printer.

◆ A system's first standard controller can handle up to 7 devices; an additional SCSI controller can boost the system to support up to 14 SCSI devices.

◆ The priority levels assigned to SCSI devices are determined by their ID numbers, with the highest-numbered device receiving the highest priority.

◆ The maximum recommended length for a complete standard SCSI chain is 20 feet (6m). You can realistically count on about 3 to 5 feet (1m to 1.5m) of internal cable, so you should reduce the maximum total length of the chain to about 15 feet (4.5m).

◆ The latest SCSI specification, referred to as Ultra 320 SCSI, boosts the maximum bus speed to 320Mbps, uses a 16-bit bus, and supports up to 15 external devices.

◆ Several ECC file transfer protocols have been developed for modem communications packages. These protocols are capable of detecting bit-level errors and can also recalculate and repair a defective bit in the bit stream. The parity-checking scheme employed with common memory systems is simply a single-bit error-checking operation. If an incorrect bit is detected in the memory that is read back, a parity check error is created and an NMI signal is passed to the microprocessor. Some of the most common modem protocols include Xmodem, Ymodem, Zmodem, and Kermit.

◆ When an IrDA device is installed in a system, a Wireless Link icon appears in the Windows Control Panel. (Remember that infrared port operations must first be enabled through the CMOS Setup utility.) When another IrDA device comes within range of the host port, the icon appears on the Windows desktop and in the taskbar. In the case of an IrDA printer, a printer icon appears in the Printer folder.

◆ If you install a new microprocessor in a system that does not have an auto-detect function for the microprocessor, you must make sure that the BIOS version will support the new processor and that the Core Voltage, Bus Frequency, and Bus Ratio settings are properly configured for the new processor. If these items are not set correctly, you could burn up the new microprocessor, not get the system to start at all, encounter random errors during normal operations, fail to start the operating system, or get an incorrect processor type or an incorrect processor speed during the POST routines.

◆ When the microprocessor is upgraded, the BIOS should also be upgraded to support it. In newer system boards, this can be accomplished by flashing (that is, electrically altering) the information in the BIOS with the latest compatibility firmware.

◆ If the system BIOS doesn't possess the flash option and does not support the new micro-processor, you need to obtain an updated BIOS IC that is compatible with the new processor (and with the system board's chipset). The old IC must be removed from the board and replaced by the new IC. This upgraded BIOS can normally be obtained from the system board manufacturer.

◆ Before you flash the BIOS, it is a good idea to make a backup copy of your BIOS settings on a floppy disk. This enables you to recover to your old settings in the event that the new BIOS infor-mation does not work with your system.

◆ Mismatched memory speeds and memory styles (registered/unregistered, buffered/unbuffered, ECC, and so on) can cause significant problems in the operation of a system. These problems can range from preventing bootup to creating simple soft-memory errors.

◆ When the system's BIOS doesn't support LBA or ECHS enhancements, the drive capacity of even the largest hard drive is limited to 528MB. Almost all newer BIOS versions support LBA and ECHS enhanced drives.

◆ Installing a new ATA-66 or ATA-100 drive in a system by using the old IDE cable causes the drive's operation to be diminished to the level of the old drive. Without a new cable, communica-tion with the drives is limited to the lesser stan-dard determined by the 40-conductor signal cable.

◆ PCMCIA Type I cards, which were introduced in 1990, are 3.3mm thick and work as memory-expansion units.

◆ PCMCIA Type II cards are 5mm thick and sup-port virtually any traditional expansion function (typically a modem), except removable hard drive units. Type II slots are backward compatible, so Type I cards work in them.

◆ PCMCIA Type III cards are 10.5mm thick and are intended primarily for use with removable hard drives. Both Type I and Type II cards can be used in Type III slots.

◆ A PCMCIA Type III card uses only one of the two 68-pin JEIDA connectors, but it takes up the entire opening.

2.0 DIAGNOSING AND TROUBLESHOOTING

This domain requires the ability to apply knowledge related to diagnosing and troubleshooting common module problems and system malfunctions, including knowledge of the symptoms related to common prob-lems. The main points follow:

◆ The first step in checking any electrical equip-ment that shows no signs of life is to check the external connections of the power supply.

◆ A 201 error code indicates a RAM failure.

◆ RAM failures basically fall into two major cate-gories and create two different types of failures: soft-memory errors and hard-memory errors. *Soft-memory errors* are errors caused by infrequent and random glitches in the operation of applica-tions and the system. You can clear these events just by restarting the system. *Hard-memory errors* are permanent physical failures that generate NMI errors in the system and require that the memory units be checked by substitution.

◆ You need to make sure that the replacement RAM is consistent with the installed RAM. Mixing RAM types and speeds can cause a system to lock up and produce hard-memory errors.

◆ If only the new RAM type is installed, a system could present a number of different symptoms, including producing short memory counts in the POST.

◆ If a system consistently locks up after being on for a few minutes, this is a good indication that the microprocessor's fan is not running or that some other heat buildup problem is occurring.

◆ If a system refuses to maintain time and date information after the backup battery has been replaced, you should check the contacts of the holder for corrosion.

◆ A typical symptom associated with keyboard failures is an IBM-compatible 301 error code display.

◆ When a system detects a stuck key on a keyboard, it produces an error message.

◆ An unplugged keyboard or a keyboard with a bad signal cable produces a keyboard error message during startup.

◆ Disconnecting or plugging in a keyboard while power is on can cause the keyboard to fail.

◆ As the mouse is moved, the trackball picks up dirt or lint, which can hinder the movement of the trackball and cause the cursor to periodically freeze and jump onscreen.

◆ If a Windows video problem prevents you from seeing the driver, you should restart the system, press the F8 function key when the Starting Windows message appears, and select Safe Mode. This should load Windows with the standard 640×480 16-color VGA driver (the most fundamental driver available for VGA monitors), and it should furnish a starting point for installing the correct driver for the monitor being used. If the monitor is an EPA-certified Energy Star–compliant monitor, this test might not work. Monitors

that possess this power-saving feature revert to a low-power mode when they do not receive a signal change for a given period of time.

◆ Due to the high voltage levels, you should never wear antistatic grounding straps when working inside a monitor.

◆ The built-up charge on an anode must the shorted to ground so the monitor can be handled safely. This operation is typically performed with a large, long-handled screwdriver and a shorting clip.

◆ The voltage levels that are present in a computer during operation are lethal. Electrical potentials as high as 25,000 volts are present inside a unit when it is operating.

◆ You can remove built-up electromagnetic fields from the screen through a process called degaussing, which can be done by using a commercial degaussing coil. However, newer monitors have built-in degaussing circuits that can be engaged through the front panel controls.

◆ A typical symptom associated with floppy disk drive failures during bootup is the display of an IBM-compatible 6xx (such as 601) error code.

◆ A typical symptom associated with floppy disk drive failures during bootup is the FDD activity light staying on constantly, indicating that the FDD signal cable is reversed.

◆ Reversing the FDD signal cable causes the FDD activity light to stay on continuously. The reversed signal cable also erases the master boot record from the disk, making it nonbootable.

◆ A typical symptom associated with hard disk drive failures is the display of an "Invalid Media Type" message, which indicates that the controller cannot find a recognizable track/sector pattern on the drive.

◆ A typical symptom associated with hard disk drive failures is the display of "No Boot Record Found," "Non-System Disk or Disk Error," and "Invalid System Disk" messages, which indicate that the system boot files are not located in the root directory of the drive.

◆ A typical symptom associated with hard disk drive failures is the display of a "Missing Operating System" or "Hard Drive Boot Failure" message, which indicates that the disk's master boot record is missing or has become corrupt.

◆ A typical symptom associated with hard disk drive failures is the display of a "Current Drive No Longer Valid" message, which indicates that the hard disk drive's CMOS configuration information is incorrect or has become corrupt.

◆ On IDE drives, you should check the Master/Slave jumper setting to make sure it is set properly for the drive's logical position in the system.

◆ Mixing IDE device types creates a situation in which the system cannot provide the different types of control information each device needs. The drives are incompatible, and you may not be able to access either device.

◆ You should check the CMOS Setup utility to make sure that SCSI support has been enabled, along with large SCSI drive support.

◆ If a system can see the contents of a drive, the boot files have been lost or corrupted, but the architecture of the disk may be intact. You should attempt to restore the drive's master boot record (including its partition information) by typing A>FDISK /MBR.

◆ If a system cannot see a drive after booting to the floppy disk, an "Invalid Drive..." message or an "Invalid Drive Specification" message should be returned in response to any attempt to access the drive. You can use the FDISK utility to partition the drive and then use the FORMAT command to make the disk bootable.

◆ If the CD-ROM drive is inoperable and there is a CD-ROM locked inside it, you should insert a straightened paper clip into the tray-release access hole that's usually located beside the Ejection button. This releases the spring-loaded tray and pops out the CD-ROM.

◆ If a controller is built in to a system board and becomes defective, you may be able to install an IDE host adapter card in an expansion slot and use it without replacing the system board.

◆ If there is a printer switch box between the computer and the printer, you can remove the print-sharing equipment, connect the computer directly to the printer, and try to print directly to the device.

◆ To use the Windows 2000 Device Manager utility to troubleshoot USB problems, you must be logged on as an administrator or as a member of the Administrators group.

◆ To install a non-PnP device on a specific COM port (such as COM2), you must first disable that port in the system's CMOS settings in order to avoid a device conflict. If you do not, the system might try to allocate that resource to some other device because it has no way of knowing that the non-PNP device requires it.

◆ One of the main uses of the resistance function is to test fuses. If a fuse is good, the meter should read near 0 ohms. If the fuse is bad, the meter should read infinite.

◆ You can use the resistance function to test a system's speaker. To check a speaker, disconnect the speaker from the system and connect a meter lead to each end. If the speaker is good, the meter should read around 8 ohms (although some smaller speaker may be 4 ohms).

◆ The user is one of the most common sources of PC problems.

◆ If a system produces an error message (such as "The System Has Detected Unstable RAM at Location x") or a beep code before the single beep occurs, the system has found a problem with the hardware. Such a case indicates a bad RAM memory device.

◆ FRUs are the portions of a system that you can conveniently replace in the field. FRU troubleshooting involves isolating a problem within one section of the system. A section consists of one device such as a keyboard, video display, video adapter card, I/O adapter card, system board, disk drive, printer, and so on. These are typically components that can simply be exchanged for replacements onsite and require no actual repair work.

3.0 PREVENTIVE MAINTENANCE

This domain requires knowledge of safety and preventive maintenance. With regard to safety, this domain covers the potential hazards to personnel and equipment when working with high-voltage equipment and items that require special disposal procedures to comply with environmental guidelines. With regard to preventive maintenance, this domain covers knowledge of preventive maintenance products, procedures, environmental hazards, and precautions you should take when working on computer systems. The main points follow:

◆ Outer-surface cleaning can be accomplished with a simple soap-and-water solution, followed by a clear water rinse.

◆ A damp cloth is the best general-purpose cleaning tool for use with computer equipment.

◆ Socket-mounted devices should be reseated (that is, removed and reinstalled to establish a new electrical connection) as part of an anticorrosion effort. Doing this overcomes the chip-creep effect that thermal cycling has on socket-mounted devices.

◆ Computer equipment is susceptible to failures caused by dust buildup, rough handling, and extremes in temperature.

◆ Missing expansion slot covers adversely affect a system in two ways. First, a missing cover permits dust to accumulate in the system, forming an insulating blanket that causes components to overheat. Second, the heat problem is complicated further by the fact that the missing slot cover interrupts the designed airflow patterns inside the case, causing components to overheat due to lack of or inadequate airflow.

◆ You should use a static-free vacuum because normal vacuums are, by nature, static generators. A static-free vacuum has special grounding to remove the static buildup it generates.

◆ You should check for sources of heat buildup around a computer and its peripherals, including direct sunlight from an outside window.

◆ Copies of the system backup should be stored in a convenient but secure place. In the case of secure system backups, such as those for client/server networks, backup copies should be stored where the network administrators can access them but others cannot (for example, in a locked file cabinet). Left unsecured, these copies could be used by someone without authority to gain access the system or to its data.

◆ A keyboard's electronic circuitry is open to the atmosphere and should be vacuumed when you are cleaning around your computer area. Dust buildup on the keyboard circuitry can cause its ICs to fail due to overheating.

- A mouse's trackball should be removed and cleaned periodically. You should use a lint-free swab to clean the X and Y trackball rollers inside the mouse.

- Typical power supply variations fall into two categories: transients and sags. *Transients* are overvoltage conditions, and *sags* are an undervoltage conditions. Transients can be classified as spikes (measured in nanoseconds) or as surges (measured in milliseconds). Sags can include voltage sags (which typically last only a few milliseconds) and brownouts (which can last for a protracted period of time).

- Inexpensive power line filters called *surge suppressers* are good for cleaning up dirty commercial power.

- In the case of a complete shutdown or a significant sag, the best protection against losing programs and data is a UPS.

- A battery-based UPS cannot keep a system running infinitely. For this reason, you should not connect nonessential, power-hungry peripheral devices such as laser printers to a UPS supply.

- Monitors, printers, scanners, and other peripheral devices should be stored in their original boxes, using their original packing foam and protective storage bags.

- Extremely high voltage levels (in excess of 25,000 volts) may be present inside the CRT housing, even up to a year after electrical power has been removed from the unit.

- In repair situations, the high voltage charge associated with video displays must be discharged. This is accomplished by creating a path from the tube's high-voltage anode to the chassis. With the monitor unplugged from the commercial power outlet, you clip one end of an insulated jumper wire to the chassis ground of the frame, and you clip the other end to a long, flat-blade screwdriver that has a well-insulated handle.

- In laser printers, the laser light is a hazard to eyesight, the fuser assembly is a burn hazard, and the power supply is a shock hazard.

- A potential burn hazard is the printhead mechanism of a dot-matrix printer.

- A Class C fire extinguisher should be present in the work area. Class C extinguishers are the type specified for use around electrical equipment.

- Laser printer toner cartridges can be refilled and recycled.

- For both batteries and printer cartridges, the desired method of disposal is recycling.

- ESD is the most severe form of EMI. The human body can build up static charges that range up to 25,000 volts. These buildups can discharge very rapidly into an electrically grounded body or device. A 25,000-volt surge can be damaging to any electronic device.

- The ability of the voltage associated with a video monitor to push current through the human body is significant (several amps), but the same ability associated with static is very low (microamps; that is, thousandths of an amp). Therefore, it is possible for a lower-voltage device with a higher current rating (such as a 110-volt AC power supply) to be much more dangerous than a higher-voltage source that has a lower current-producing capability (such as static).

- Some repair shops do not permit compressed air to be used for blowing dust out of keyboards and other computer equipment because it has erroneously been linked to creating ESD.

◆ ESD is most likely to occur during periods of low humidity. If the relative humidity is below 50%, static charges can accumulate easily. ESD generally does not occur when the humidity is above 50%. Normal air-conditioning works by removing moisture from the atmosphere, creating low-humidity conditions. Therefore, humidifiers are often used to correct this condition.

◆ You should never wear antistatic wrist or ankle straps while working on high-voltage components, such as monitors and power supply units.

◆ Normal operating vibrations and temperature cycling can degrade the electrical connections between ICs and sockets over time. This gradual deterioration of electrical contact between chips and sockets is referred to as *chip-creep*.

◆ Good grounding routes the induced EMI signals away from logic circuitry and toward ground potential, preventing the signals from disrupting normal operations. Unlike ESD effects, which are destructive, EMI effects can be corrected without damage.

◆ Because a computer system is connected to an actual earth ground, it should always be turned off and disconnected (along with its peripherals) from the power outlet during electrical storms.

4.0 MOTHERBOARD/ PROCESSORS/MEMORY

This domain requires knowledge of specific terminology and facts, along with ways and means of dealing with classifications, categories, and principles of motherboards, processors, and memory in computer systems. The main points follow:

◆ A Pentium II processor includes all the multimedia enhancements from the MMX processor, and it retains the power of the Pentium Pro's dynamic execution and 512K L2 cache features and employs a 66MHz or 100MHz system bus. The L1 cache is increased to 32K, and the L2 cache operates with a half-speed bus.

◆ The original Pentium III processor (code-named Katmai) was designed around the Pentium II core, but increased the L2 cache size to 512K. It also increased the speed of the processor to 600MHz, including a 100MHz front-side bus speed.

◆ Although the Intel Slot 1 design was originally developed for the Pentium II processor, it is also used in Celeron and Pentium III processor designs.

◆ AMD produced a reversed version of the Slot 1 specification for its Athlon processor by turning around the contacts of the Slot 1 design. AMD titled the new design Slot A. Although these two slot designs serve the same ends, the Slot A and Slot 1 microprocessor cartridges are not compatible.

◆ In older Pentium systems, the microprocessor's configuration settings are established largely through jumpers on the system board.

◆ The BIOS version must support the parameters of the microprocessor. If a microprocessor upgrade is performed and the BIOS code does not fully support the new processor, all the error types listed for manual configuration can occur.

◆ Whether RAM is made up of static or dynamic RAM devices, all RAM systems have the disadvantage of being volatile. This means that any data stored in RAM is lost if power to the computer is disrupted for any reason.

◆ EDO is an advanced type of fast page-mode DRAM that is also referred to as *hyper page-mode DRAM*. The advantage of EDO DRAM is encountered when multiple sequential memory accesses are performed. Because the data pin is not turned off, each successive access after the first access is accomplished in two clock cycles rather than three.

◆ Special memory devices have been designed to optimize video memory–related activities. Among these devices are VRAM and WRAM.

◆ DRAM devices, which are commonly used for a system's RAM, require periodic refreshing of their data. Some refreshing is performed by the system's normal memory reading and writing cycles. However, additional circuitry must be used to ensure that every bit in all the memory registers is refreshed within the allotted timeframe.

◆ The most popular form of error detection in PC compatibles is parity checking. With this methodology, an extra bit is added to each word in RAM and checked each time it is used. Parity checking is a simple self-test that is used to detect RAM read-back errors.

◆ When a parity error occurs, an NMI signal is generated in the system, causing the BIOS to execute its NMI handler routine, which normally places a parity error message onscreen, along with an option to shut down the system or to continue.

◆ Another possibility when a parity error occurs is that the system counts the memory, locks up, and reboots itself. If the memory error occurs high in the physical memory device, this situation can occur after the operating system and applications have been loaded and started running.

◆ ECC SDRAM is a type of SDRAM that includes a fault-detection/correction circuit that can detect and fix memory errors without shutting down the system.

◆ By using a parity memory scheme, a system can detect that a bit has flipped when the memory is read, but it can only display a "Parity Error" message and freeze up. Although this prevents the bad data from being used or written away in the system, it also erases all current data from RAM. An ECC memory module has the ability to detect and correct a single-bit error or to detect errors in 2 bits.

◆ A microprocessor's internal first-level cache is also known as an *L1 cache*.

◆ The primary objective of the cache memory's control system is to maximize the ratio of hits to total accesses (that is, the *hit rate*) so that the majority of memory accesses are performed without wait states. One way to do this is to make the cache memory area as large as possible (thus raising the possibility of the desired information being in the cache). However, the relative cost, energy consumption, and physical size of SRAM devices work against this technique. Practical sizes for cache memories run between 16K and 512K.

◆ SIMM modules were traditionally available in 30-pin and 72-pin versions; DIMMs are larger 168-pin boards.

◆ SIMMs and DIMMs come in 9-, 36-, and 72-bit versions that include parity-checking bits for each byte of storage (for example, a 36-bit SIMM provides 32 data bits and 4 parity bits—1 for each byte of data).

◆ Split-bank arrangements use a different specification for DIMM slot 1 than they do for DIMM slots 2 and 3. The odd slot is normally organized into one bank, and the other two slots combine to form the second bank. If you are not careful when populating these slots, you can create a situation in which the system's memory controller cannot access all the installed RAM.

◆ It is important to install RAM that is compatible with the bus speed at which the system is running. Normally, installing RAM that is rated faster than the bus speed does not cause problems. However, installing slower RAM, or mixing RAM speed ratings within a system may cause it not to start or to periodically lock up.

◆ A software-activated power switch can be implemented through the ATX power-connector specification. The PS-ON and 5VSB signals can be controlled by the operating system to perform automatic system shutdowns.

◆ The most common connectors used with PC keyboards are 6-pin PS/2 mini-DINs, 5-pin DINs, and RJ-11 jacks. PC-XT- and AT-compatible systems have historically used 5-pin DIN connectors, and ATX systems use 6-pin mini-DINs.

◆ Although the ISA bus originally ran at microprocessor-compatible speeds up to 10MHz or 12MHz turbo speeds, incompatibility with slower adapter cards caused manufacturers to settle for running them at 8MHz or 8.33MHz in newer designs.

◆ Due to industry moves away from anything related to ISA cards, the PCI bus has become the dominant force in system board designs. Current designs include three or four PCI slots and an AGP slot; they may include a single ISA connector for compatibility purposes or no ISA connector.

◆ The PCI bus specification uses multiplexed addresses and data lines to conserve the pins of the basic 124-pin PCI connector. Within this connector are signals for control, interruption, cache support, error reporting, and arbitration.

◆ Because the PnP process has no method for reconfiguring legacy devices during the resource assignment phase, it begins by assigning

resources, such as IRQ assignments, to these devices before servicing the system's PnP devices.

◆ When the BIOS detects the presence of a new device during the detection phase, it disables the resource settings of its existing cards, checks to determine what resources are required and available, and then reallocates the system's resources as necessary.

◆ Newer Pentium systems include an advanced AGP interface for video graphics. The AGP interface is a variation of the PCI bus design that has been modified to handle the intense data throughput associated with three-dimensional graphics.

◆ There is some upward compatibility between PC-Bus, ISA, EISA, and VESA cards. Both the EISA and VESA slots can accommodate ISA cards.

◆ The USB specification provides *interrupt transfers*, which are small, spontaneous transfers from a device that are used to announce events, provide input coordinate information, or transfer characters.

◆ USB devices are rated as full-speed (480Mbps) and low-speed (12Mbps) devices based on their communication capabilities. The length limit for a cable serving a full-speed device is 16 feet, 5 inches (5m). The length limit for cables used between low-speed devices is 9 feet, 10 inches (3m).

◆ The IDE host adapter portion of a chipset is normally capable of controlling up to four IDE hard disks, CD-ROM drives, or other IDE devices.

◆ The hierarchy of assigning logical drive designations in the IDE interface calls for primary partitions to be assigned sequentially from ID1 master, to ID1 slave, to ID2 master, to ID2 slave. Next, the system assigns drive letters to the extended partitions for each drive in the same order.

◆ Two similar cables are used with IDE devices. The newer ATA 4/Ultra ATA 66 and Ultra ATA 100 IDE enhancements provide increased data throughput by doubling the number of conductors in the signal cable to 80.

◆ SCSI host adapters are typically available for use with ISA, EISA, and PCI bus interfaces.

◆ If the time is incorrect on a PC system, the easiest way to reset it is through the operating system. However, if the PC system continually fails to keep good time, you should ensure that corrosion has not built up on the battery contacts. You should clean the contacts with a pencil eraser and retry the battery. If that doesn't work, you can try replacing the battery. Next, you can try replacing the RTC module. If this does not correct the time-keeping problem, the electronic circuitry that recharges the battery may be defective; in this case, you need a new motherboard.

◆ For larger drives (above 1,024 cylinders or 528MB), the Large and LBA modes are used. The Large option can be used with large drives that do not support LBA techniques. For drives that do support LBA techniques, the LBA mode should be selected. In LBA mode, the IDE controller converts the sector/head/cylinder address into a physical block address that improves data throughput.

◆ Care must be taken when changing the translation mode setting in CMOS because all data on the drive can be lost in the process.

◆ The BIOS antivirus utility should be enabled for normal operations. However, it should be turned off when you conduct an upgrade of the operating system. The built-in virus warning utility checks the drive's boot sector for changes. The changes that the new operating system attempts to make to the boot sector are interpreted as a virus, and the utility tries to prevent the upgrade from occurring.

◆ You use the Feature Setup screen to configure different boot-up options, including establishing the system's boot-up sequence. The sequence can be set so that the system checks the floppy drive for a boot sector first or so that it checks the hard drive without checking the floppy drive.

◆ You should enable the CD-ROM drive as one of the boot options in the sequence, so that the operating system CD-ROM can be used to start the system when it will not boot to the hard drive.

◆ The BIOS stores the PnP information it collects from the devices in a special section of the CMOS RAM that is known as the *ESCD area*. This information is stored in the same manner in which standard BIOS settings are stored.

◆ The parallel printer port can be configured for normal PC-AT-compatible SPP operation; for extended bi-directional operation (that is, EPP operation); for fast, buffered bi-directional operation (that is, ECP operation); or for combined ECP+EPP operation. The normal CMOS setting should be selected unless both the port hardware and the driver software support EPP and/or ECP operation.

◆ The ECP mode provides a number of advantages over the SPP and EPP modes. In particular, it offers higher performance than either of the other modes.

◆ The ECP port is compatible with the standard LPT port and is used in the same manner as the LPT port when no ECP operations are called for. However, it also supports high-throughput DMA operations for both forward and reverse transfers.

◆ Because both of the advanced parallel port modes operate in a bi-directional half-duplex manner, they require an IEEE 1284–compliant cable. Standard parallel cables designed for older SPP operations may not support these qualities.

◆ There is some danger that a user will forget his or her password. When this occurs, it is impossible for the user to gain access to the system unless you completely reset the contents of the CMOS RAM. On some system boards, this can be accomplished by shorting a special pair of jumpers on the board. With other systems, you need to remove or short across the backup battery to reset the CMOS information.

◆ When you try to reset the contents of the CMOS RAM in ATX systems, it is necessary to unplug the power from the commercial outlet to reduce the voltage to the CMOS registers. When the contents of the CMOS are reset, you must manually restore any nondefault CMOS settings being used by the system.

5.0 Printers

This domain requires knowledge of basic types of printers, basic printer concepts, printer components, how printers work, how printers print onto a page, the paper path, printer care and service techniques, and common printer problems. The main points follow:

◆ Vector-based fonts store the outlines of the character styles and sizes as sets of mathematical formulas. Each character is composed of a set of reference points and connecting lines between the reference points. These types of fonts can be scaled up and down to achieve various sizes.

◆ Vector-based fonts require much less storage space to store a character set and all its variations than is necessary for an equivalent bitmapped character set. In addition, vector-based fonts can be scaled and rotated; bitmapped fonts typically cannot be scaled and rotated. Conversely, bitmapped characters can be printed out directly and quickly, but vector-based characters must be generated when called for.

◆ Tractor feeds are used with very heavy forms, such as multiple-part, continuous forms, and are most commonly found on dot-matrix printers.

◆ A typical printhead may contain 9, 18, or 24 print wires. The number of print wires used in the printhead is the major determining factor associated with a printer's character quality. A 9-pin printhead generally delivers draft-quality print, and 24-pin printheads approach letter-quality print.

◆ The components of a typical dot-matrix printer include a power-supply board, a main control board, a printhead assembly, a ribbon cartridge, a paper-feed motor (along with its mechanical drive gears), and a printhead positioning motor and mechanisms.

◆ A printer's interface may contain circuitry to handle serial data, parallel data, or a combination of the different interface types: Centronics parallel, RS-232 serial, SCSI, USB, or IrDA.

◆ Ink-jet printers produce characters by squirting a precisely controlled stream of ink drops onto paper. The drops must be controlled very precisely in terms of their aerodynamics, size, and shape, or the drop placement on the page becomes inexact, and the print quality falters.

◆ The six stages of operation in a laser printer are cleaning, conditioning, writing, developing, transferring, and fusing.

◆ A high voltage applied to the primary corona wire in a printer creates a highly charged negative field that conditions the drum to be written on, by applying a uniform negative charge (–600 volts) to it.

◆ Great care should be taken when installing a new drum unit in a laser printer. Exposing the drum to light for more than a few minutes may damage it. The drum should never be touched because touching it can ruin its surface. You should keep the unit away from dust, dirt, humidity, and high temperatures.

◆ The transfer corona wire (that is, transfer roller) is responsible for transferring toner from the drum to the paper.

◆ A thermal sensor in the fuser unit of a printer monitors the temperature of the unit. This information is applied to the control circuitry so that it can control the fuser temperature between 140°C and 230°C. If the temperature of the fuser is not controlled correctly, it may cause severe damage to the printer and may also present a potential fire hazard.

◆ In Hewlett-Packard printers, the main portion of the printing system is contained in the electrophotographic cartridge, which contains the toner supply, the corona wire, the drum assembly, and the developing roller.

◆ The most fundamental specification for paper is paper weight. Paper is specified in terms of its weight per 500 sheets of 22-inch×17-inch paper (for example, 500 sheets of 22-inch×17-inch 21-pound bond paper weighs 21 pounds).

◆ You should heed this caution concerning parallel printer cables: The IEEE has established specifications (IEEE 1284) for bi-directional parallel-printer cables. These cables affect the operation of EPP and ECP parallel devices. Using an older, noncompliant unidirectional cable with a bi-directional parallel device prevents the device from communicating properly with the system and may prevent it from operating.

◆ Not all serial cables are created equal. In the PC world, RS-232 serial cables can have several configurations. First, they may use either 9-pin or 25-pin D-shell connectors. The recommended signal cable lengths associated with parallel printers are 0 to 10 feet (0m to 3m), although some equipment manufacturers specify 6 feet (1.8m) maximums for their cables. You should believe these recommendations when you see them. The recommended signal cable lengths associated with RS-232 serial printers are 10 to 50 feet (3m to 15.25m). However, some references use 100 feet (30.5m) as the acceptable length of an RS-232C serial cable.

◆ The IrDA specification calls for communication ranges up to 6.5 feet (2m), but most implementations state 3 feet (1m) as the recommended range.

◆ Although some older network printers use coaxial cable connections, newer network printers feature RJ-45 jacks for connection to twisted-pair Ethernet networks. It is relatively easy to determine whether a printer is networked by the presence of a coaxial or a twisted-pair network cable connected directly to the printer. The presence of the RJ-45 jacks on the back of the printer also indicate that the printer is network capable, even if it is not being used in that manner.

◆ Nearly every printer is equipped with a built-in self-test. The easiest way to determine whether a printer is at fault when problems arise is to run its self-test routine. If the self-test runs and prints clean pages, most of the printer has been eliminated as a possible source of problems. The problem could be in the computer, the cable, or the interface portion of the printer. If the printer fails the self-test, however, it is necessary to troubleshoot the printer's problem.

◆ The item in a dot-matrix printer that requires the most attention is the ribbon cartridge.

◆ As a dot-matrix printer's ribbon wears out, the printing becomes faint and uneven. When the print becomes noticeably faint, the cartridge should be replaced.

◆ If the tops of characters are missing, the printer's printhead is misaligned with the platen. It might need to be reseated in the printhead carriage, or the carriage assembly might need to be adjusted to the proper height and angle.

◆ If the output of a printer gets lighter as it moves from left to right across the page, you might need to adjust the spacing between the platen and the printhead carriage rod to obtain proper printing.

◆ To exchange a dot-matrix printhead assembly, you should make sure that it is cool enough to be handled. Printheads can get hot enough to cause serious burns.

◆ When paper does not advance in a printer, the output is normally one line of dark blocks across the page.

◆ The item in an ink-jet printer that requires the most attention is the ink cartridge (or cartridges).

◆ The density of the printout from an ink-jet printer can be adjusted through the printer's printing software. When the print becomes noticeably faint or the resolution becomes unacceptable, the cartridge needs to be replaced.

◆ Using a solvent to clear blockages in the jets can dilute the ink, reduce its surface tension characteristics, and allow it to flow uncontrollably through the jet.

◆ If a printhead assembly will not move at any time, check to see whether the printer is in Maintenance mode. In this mode, the printer typically keeps the printhead assembly in the home position. If no mode configuration problems are present, the printhead-positioning motor should be replaced.

◆ If the printer's paper thickness selector is set improperly or the rollers in its paper-feed system become worn, paper can slip as it moves through the printer and cause disfigured graphics to be produced. You should check the printer's paper thickness settings. If they are correct and the print output is disfigured, you need to replace the paper-feed rollers.

◆ Paper jams occur in all three main sections of the printer: the pickup area, the registration area, and the fuser area.

◆ Using paper that is too heavy or too thick can result in jams, as can overloading paper trays. Similarly, using the wrong type of paper can defeat the separation pad and allow multiple pages to be drawn into the printer at one time.

◆ If the high-voltage section of a laser printer's power supply fails, the transfer of toner to the drum and then to the paper cannot occur. In addition, the Contrast control is not operational.

◆ If you are having printer problems, you should check to see whether the printer is connected to the system through a print-sharing device. If it is, you should connect the printer directly to the system and test it. It is not a good practice to use laser printers with print-sharing devices.

◆ A black page indicates that toner has been attracted to the entire page. This condition could be caused by a failure of the primary corona, the laser-scanning module, or the main control board.

◆ A white, or blank, page indicates that no information is being written on the drum. This condition involves the laser-scanning module, the control board, and the power supply. Another white-page fault occurs when the corona wire becomes broken, contaminated, or corroded, so that the attracting charge between the drum and paper is severely reduced.

◆ Specks and stains on a page may be caused by a worn cleaning pad or by a defective corona wire. If the cleaning pad is worn, the pad cannot remove excess toner from the page during the fusing process. If the corona wire's grid does not regulate the charge level on the drum, dark spots appear in the print.

◆ Faint print from a laser printer can be caused by a number of different situations. If the contrast control is set too low or the toner level in the cartridge is low, empty, or poorly distributed, the print quality can appear washed out.

◆ If toner does not come out of a laser printer toner cartridge uniformly, areas of missing print can be created. A damaged or worn drum can also be a cause of repeated missing print. If areas of the drum do not hold the charge properly, toner is not transferred to it or to the page correctly.

◆ Smudged print is normally a sign of a failure in the fusing section. If the fuser roller's temperature or pressure is not sufficient to bond the toner to the page, the print smudges when it is touched.

◆ If paper feeds into a printer but jams after the process has begun, you should troubleshoot the particular section of the printer where the jam is occurring—pickup, registration, fuser area, and output devices (that is, collators and duplexers).

◆ Many times, a paper jam error indication remains even after the paper has been removed from the laser printer. This is typically caused by a safety interlock error. Simply opening and closing the printer's main access door should clear the error.

◆ You can use a vacuum cleaner to remove dust buildup and excess toner from the interior of a laser printer. Care should be taken to remove all excess toner from the unit.

◆ You should vacuum or replace a printer's ozone filter as a normal step in its preventive maintenance schedule.

6.0 BASIC NETWORKING

This domain requires knowledge of basic networking concepts and terminology, ability to determine whether a computer is networked, knowledge of procedures for swapping and configuring NICs, and knowledge of the ramifications of repairs when a computer is networked. The main points follow:

◆ Be aware that under CompTIA's definition, a LAN can be composed of only two computers. If only two units are connected, point-to-point communications software and a simple null modem could be used.

◆ In a peer-to-peer network arrangement, the users connected to the network can decide to share access to different network resources, such as hard drives and printers.

◆ A common definition of a peer-to-peer network is one in which all the nodes can act as both clients and servers of the other nodes under different conditions.

◆ The major advantages of the client/server networking arrangement include centralized administration and data and resource security.

◆ The IEEE's XXBase-YY nomenclature provides three pieces of information about the LAN. For example, 10Base-5 designates that the LAN has a maximum data rate of 10Mbps, that it is a baseband LAN (verses broadband), and that its maximum segment length is 500m.

◆ The cables used in a TX network can be Category 5 UTP or STP. The 100Base-FX Fast Ethernet designation indicates that the network is using fiber-optic cable.

◆ The recommended maximum length of a 10/100Base-T segment is 330 feet (100m).

◆ UTP LAN connections are made through modular RJ-45 jacks and plugs.

◆ The three important pieces of information required to configure a LAN adapter card for use are the IRQ setting (which the adapter uses to communicate with the system), the I/O port address (which the adapter uses to exchange information with the system), and the base memory address (which the adapter uses as a starting point in memory for DMA transfers).

◆ In a network environment, no unit really functions alone. Unlike on a standalone unit, the steps performed on a network computer may affect the operation of other units on the network.

◆ A bad cable or connector can cause a condition in which the user cannot see any other computers on the network. As a matter of fact, the majority of all network failures involve bad cable, connectors, and connections.

◆ Even if a unit does not need to be removed from a network, diagnostic efforts and tests run across the network can use a lot of the network's bandwidth. This reduced bandwidth causes the operation of all the units on the network to slow down, due to the added usage of the network.

◆ Many newer network cards possess PnP capabilities. With non-PnP network cards, such as most ISA NICs, it is necessary to configure the cards manually through hardware jumpers or through logical configuration settings in the BIOS Extension EPROM.

◆ You should check the activity light on the back plate of a LAN card (if available) to determine whether the network is recognizing the network adapter card. If the lights are active, the connection is alive.

The fast facts listed in this chapter and the preceding chapter are designed as a refresher of key points and topics required to succeed on the A+ certification exam. By using these summaries of key points, you can spend an hour prior to your exam refreshing your knowledge of key topics to ensure that you have a solid understanding of the objectives and information required to succeed in each major area of the exam.

CompTIA has established two modules for the A+ examination: the Core Hardware Service Technician module and the Operating System Technologies module. The information here is organized to follow the sequence of the Operating System Technologies module test objectives, and each domain that follows includes the key points from each chapter in this book. If you have a thorough understanding of the key points here, chances are good that you will pass the exam.

Part II, "Operating System Technologies," is dedicated to the four domains covered in the A+ Operating System Technologies module. Now that you have read those chapters, answered all the review and exam questions at the ends of the chapters, and explored the PrepLogic test engine on the CD-ROM that accompanies the book, you are ready to take the exam.

This chapter is designed as a quick study aid that you can use in less than an hour just before taking the exam. Its key points should jog your memory in critical areas. In addition to the information located in this chapter, remember to review the Glossary terms, which are intentionally not covered here.

CompTIA uses the following domains to arrange the objectives for the Operating System Technologies module:

1.0 Operating System Fundamentals
2.0 Installation, Configuration, and Upgrading
3.0 Diagnosing and Troubleshooting
4.0 Networks

Fast Facts

OPERATING SYSTEM TECHNOLOGIES EXAM

1.0 OPERATING SYSTEM FUNDAMENTALS

This domain requires knowledge of DOS (command-prompt functions), Windows 9x, and Windows 2000 operating systems in terms of functions and structures for managing files and directories and running programs. This domain also requires knowledge of navigating through the operating system from the command-line prompts and Windows procedures for accessing and retrieving information. The main points are as follows:

◆ There is a little-known MS-DOS system requirement that the MSDOS.SYS file must maintain a size in excess of 1K.

◆ The HIMEM.SYS command loads the DOS extended memory driver (XMS), which manages the use of extended memory installed in the system so that no two applications use the same memory locations at the same time.

◆ DRIVER.SYS creates the logical drive assignments for the system's floppy drives (that is, A: and B:).

◆ Windows 3.x is a separate graphical environment that works on top of the DOS operating system. It is built on a number of initialization (.INI) files that hold the system's hardware and software configuration information.

◆ Software creates virtual memory by swapping files between RAM and the disk drive. This memory management technique effectively creates more total memory for the system's applications to use. When the system runs out of available RAM, it shifts data to the virtual memory swap file on the disk drive.

◆ The size of the Windows 9x swap file, called WIN386.SWP, is variable and is dynamically assigned.

◆ The Windows NT and Windows 2000 pagefile (named PAGEFILE.SYS) is created when the operating system is installed.

◆ Windows 9x is loaded when the startup routine locates and executes the file named WIN.COM.

◆ Windows 9x provides a mechanism for automatically starting programs whenever the operating system starts: You can add them to the system's Startup folder. You can then bypass these programs for troubleshooting purposes by pressing the Left-Shift key during startup.

◆ Establishing a supplemental cache for the CD-ROM drive can enhance the efficiency of a Windows 9x system.

◆ If a Windows 9x system has a CONFIG.SYS, AUTOEXEC.BAT, or .INI file that has been held over from a previous operating system, any unneeded commands in these files have the potential to reduce system performance. In particular, the SMARTDRV function from older operating systems inhibits dynamic VCACHE operation and slows the system.

◆ If a Windows 9x system runs slowly, check the CONFIG.SYS and AUTOEXEC.BAT files for SMARTDRV and any other disk cache software settings.

◆ The SYSTEM.INI, WIN.INI, PROTOCOL.INI, CONFIG.SYS, and AUTOEXEC.BAT files can be modified through the System Editor (Sysedit) in Windows 9x.

◆ In Windows 9x, the system's configuration information is held in a large hierarchical database called the Registry.

◆ The contents of the Windows 9x Registry are located in two files in the \Windows directory: USER.DAT and SYSTEM.DAT. The USER.DAT file contains user-specific information, and the SYSTEM.DAT file holds hardware- and computer-specific profiles and setting information.

◆ Each time Windows 95 boots up successfully, the USER.DAT and SYSTEM.DAT files are backed up and given the .DA0 extension.

◆ The backed-up contents of the Windows 98 Registry are stored in the \Windows\Sysbckup directory in the form of cabinet (.CAB) files, not as .DA0 files.

◆ The Sysbckup folder is a hidden folder. To examine its contents, you must remove the hidden attribute from it. Inside the folder, the backup files are stored in the format RB0XX.CAB, where XX is a sequential backup number that is given to the file when it is created.

◆ The Current_User key (HKEY_CURRENT_USER) holds data about the user-specific configuration settings of the system, including color, keyboard, desktop, and startup settings.

◆ Windows NT establishes virtual memory by creating the PAGEFILE.SYS file on disk. The VMM shifts data between RAM and the disk in 4K pages.

◆ The Windows NT and Windows 2000 Registries are not compatible with the Windows 9x Registries. This makes the Windows 9x and Windows NT/2000 operating systems basically incompatible with each other. The contents of the Windows NT Registry are physically stored in five files, referred to as *hives*. Hives represent the major divisions of all the Registry's keys, subkeys, subtrees, and values.

◆ The Rdisk.exe utility, which is located in the \Winnt\System32 folder, can be used to create a backup copy of the Windows NT Registry in the \Winnt\Repair folder.

◆ The contents of the Registry can be edited directly by using the Windows NT/2000 RegEdit utility. Although there is a copy of the RegEdit tool in

Windows 2000, it was designed to work with Windows 9x clients. The editor used to manage the Windows 2000 Registry is Regedit32.exe, and it is located in the \Winnt\System32 folder.

◆ The Storage Console provides a standard set of tools for maintaining the system's disk drives. These tools include the Disk Management tool, the Disk Defrag utility, and the Logical Drives utility.

◆ All the installed MMCs can be accessed either through the Control Panel or by selecting Start, Programs, Administrative Tools.

◆ In Windows 2000 the Device Manager is usually accessed through the Computer Management Console.

◆ Even though entries in the Registry can be altered through the RegEdt32 and RegEdit utilities, the safest method of changing hardware settings is to change their values through the Device Manager.

◆ To access the DOS emulator in Windows 9x or Windows NT 4.0, you select the Run option from the Start menu and type COMMAND in the Run dialog box.

◆ To access the DOS emulator in Windows 2000, you select the Run option from the Start menu and type CMD in the Run dialog box.

◆ Files with .COM, .EXE, or .BAT extensions can be started directly from the command prompt.

◆ In hard drive–based systems, it is common to organize related programs and data into areas called *directories*. This makes them easy to find and work with because modern hard drives can hold large amounts of information. The directories in the various version of Microsoft operating systems can hold up to 512 directory or filename entries.

◆ Special key combinations enable a user to move between tasks easily. By pressing the Alt+Tab, a user can quickly select one of the open applications. Similarly, the Alt+Esc key combination enables the user to cycle through open application windows. Pressing Ctrl+Esc causes the Start menu to open.

◆ Alternate-clicking an icon produces a pop-up menu that enables the user to open, cut, or copy a folder (an icon that represents a directory), create a shortcut, delete or rename a folder, or examine properties of the folder.

◆ You use the View window to define how the folders and files in the selected window should be displayed onscreen.

◆ To see hidden and system files, you can select the View tab and click the Show Hidden Files button.

◆ Options that apply to the current window are displayed as dark text. Options that are not applicable to the window are grayed out.

◆ When a disk drive icon is selected, clicking the File option produces a menu that includes provisions for creating a new folder, formatting a disk, sharing a drive with the network community, backing up the contents of the drive, and displaying a drive's properties.

◆ A check mark located next to the menu option indicates that the item is currently in use.

◆ When you delete a folder or file from the Windows system, Windows removes the first three letters of its name from the drive's FAT so that it is invisible to the system. However, the system records the presence of the deleted file or folder in the Recycle Bin. The system is free to reuse the space on the drive because it does not know that anything is there. As long as it hasn't been overwritten with new data or been removed from the Recycle Bin, the file or folder can be restored from the Recycle Bin.

◆ If the Recycle Bin icon is missing, there are two ways to restore it: Establish a shortcut to the Recycle Bin by using a new icon or reinstall Windows 9x, which always places the Recycle Bin on the desktop.

◆ The Recycle Bin does not retain the files deleted from removable media, such as floppy disks and removable hard drives. When a file or folder is removed from one of these devices, the information is deleted directly from the system.

◆ If the Taskbar is hidden, pressing the Ctrl+Esc key combination retrieves it and brings it to the screen. This pops up the Start menu, along with the Taskbar. You can enter the start, settings, Taskbar, and start menu options to change the Taskbar settings so that the Taskbar is not hidden.

◆ The Control Panel is the primary user interface for assigning ports for printers and mouse devices, as well as for specifying how various peripheral devices respond.

◆ The Windows 98 Control Panel is the user's primary interface for configuring system components.

◆ The Hardware Wizard guides the manual installation process from the hardware component list and prompts the user for any necessary configuration information. If Windows 9x does not support a device, you must click the Have Disk button and load the drivers supplied by the device's manufacturer.

◆ You use the Windows Setup tab of the Add/Remove Programs applet to add or remove selected Windows 9x components, such as communications packages or additional system tools.

You use the Windows Startup Disk tab to create a clean startup disk for emergency startup after a crash.

◆ The System Properties window features the tabs General Information, Device Manager, Hardware Profiles, and Performance. The General tab supplies information about the system's operating system version, registered owner, microprocessor type and RAM capacity, and ownership and registration.

◆ In Windows 9x you can access the Device Manager by selecting Start, Settings, Control Panel, and then clicking the System icon.

◆ The Device Manager contains a set of buttons that permit its various functions to be accessed. These buttons include Properties, Refresh, Remove, and Print.

◆ MS-DOS does not allow some special characters in filenames: [,], :, ;, +, =, \, /, <, >, ?, and ,.

◆ You use ATTRIB to change file attributes such as Read-only (+R or –R), Archive (+A or –A), System (+S or –S), and Hidden (+H or –H). The + and – signs add or subtract the attribute from the file.

◆ The * notation is called a *wildcard*, and it allows operations to be performed with only partial source or destination information. Using the notation *.* tells the software to perform the designated command on any file found on the disk, using any filename and extension.

◆ A question mark (?) can be used as a wildcard to represent a single character in a filename or extension.

◆ When long filenames are displayed in non-Windows 9x systems, they are truncated (shortened) to fit the 8.3 DOS character format and identified with a tilde character (~), followed by a single-digit number.

◆ The tilde character (~) is inserted into the seventh character space for up to nine iterations of similar filenames. After that, Windows replaces the sixth character, for iterations up to 99. Windows 95 applies this same convention to the naming of directories.

◆ From Windows NT 4.0 forward, the NT operating system has been able to handle long filenames. Filenames in Windows NT can be up to 256 characters long.

◆ Filenames in Windows 2000 can be up to 215 characters long, including spaces.

◆ Windows 2000 filenames cannot contain the following characters: /, \, :, *, ?, ", and |.

◆ You can obtain information about the cipher command and its many switches by typing cipher /? at the command prompt.

◆ To encrypt a file, you can access its properties page by right-clicking it and selecting the Properties option from the pop-up menu. Then, you Move to the Advanced Attributes screen under the General tab and click the Encrypt Contents to Secure Data check box.

◆ To compress a particular file or folder, right-click it in Windows Explorer and then select the Properties option followed by the Advanced button to access its advanced properties screen. Click the Compress Contents to Save Disk Space check box to compress the file or folder.

◆ You can mark compressed files so that they are displayed in a second color for easy identification. You do this through the Folder Options setting in the Control Panel. From this page, you select the View tab and click in the Display Compressed Files and Folder with Alternate Color check box. The only other indication you receive concerning a compressed or encrypted file or folder is an attribute listing when the view setting is configured to display in Web style.

◆ You can expand the contents of a folder by clicking the plus (+) sign node beside the folder. Conversely, you can contract the contents of a folder by clicking the minus (–) sign node.

◆ Right-clicking a document file in Windows Explorer or My Computer produces a pop-up menu with options that enable the user to copy, cut, rename, open, or print the document.

◆ By default, Windows Explorer does not show .SYS, .INI, or .DAT files.

◆ Changing file attributes from Windows Explorer involves right-clicking the desired file, selecting the Properties option from the pop-up list, moving to the General page, and clicking the desired attribute boxes.

◆ To create a new folder in Windows Explorer, you select a parent directory by highlighting it in the left window. Then, you click the File menu button, move the cursor to the New entry, and slide across to the Folder option and click it.

◆ Right-clicking a new icon produces a menu that has options to rename the icon, create a shortcut for the icon, and establish the icon's properties (including its attributes).

◆ A small arrow in the lower-left corner of an icon identifies the icon as a shortcut icon.

◆ Installing a new operating system on a hard drive takes five basic steps: Partition the drive for use with the operating system, format the drive with the basic operating system files, run the appropriate Setup utility to install the complete operating system, load all the drivers necessary for the operating system to function with the system's installed hardware devices, and reboot the system to activate all the system components.

◆ The first, or primary, partition exists as drive C:. After the primary partition has been established and properly configured, an additional partition, referred to as an *extended partition*, is also permitted. The extended partition may be subdivided into 23 logical drives.

◆ The high-level format procedure is used to load an operating system into a partition.

◆ In a FAT-based system, a *cluster* is the smallest piece of manageable information.

◆ The sectors on a FAT-based disk hold 512 bytes each.

◆ Each directory and subdirectory (including the root directory) can hold up to 512 32-byte entries that describe each of the files in them.

◆ On a hard disk drive, 32 sectors are normally set aside for the root directory. Therefore, the root directory for such a disk can accommodate up to 512 entries.

◆ In Windows 9*x* it is possible to convert partitions created on a FAT16 drive into a FAT32 file system by using the CVT.EXE command-line utility. This operation can also be performed by accessing the Drive Converter (FAT32) utility by selecting Start, Programs, Accessories, System Tools, Drive Converter. Selecting this option runs the CVT1.EXE file, which starts the Drive Converter Wizard. The main drawback to doing this is that there is some possibility of data corruption and loss. Not surprisingly, there is no utility for converting FAT32 partitions to FAT16.

◆ The VFAT system replaces the SMARTDRV disk-caching utility with a protected-mode driver named VCACHE.

◆ The smaller cluster size of the NTFS format makes it more efficient than FAT formats for storing smaller files. It also supports larger drives (over 1GB) much more efficiently than FAT16 or FAT32 structures. NTFS is more complex than the FAT systems and therefore is not as efficient for smaller drives.

◆ Windows 2000 supports several file management system formats, including FAT, FAT16, FAT32, CDFS (which is used on CD-ROMs), and NTFS4, along with the new and improved NTFS5.

◆ NTFS offers the following benefits over other file management systems: More efficient drive management due to its smaller cluster size capabilities; support for very large drives, made possible by its 64-bit clustering arrangement; increased folder and file security capabilities; recoverable file system capabilities; and built-in RAID support.

◆ To install Windows 2000 on a dynamic volume, the volume must be either simple or mirrored, and it must be a volume that has been upgraded from a basic volume.

◆ You can convert basic volumes to dynamic volumes by using the Disk Management tool. You do this by selecting Start, Run, entering DISKMGMT.MSC in the text box, and then clicking the OK button.

◆ In Windows 9x, the Disk Management functions are located in several areas of the system. You can find the icons for Backup, ScanDisk, and Disk Defrag by selecting Start, Programs, Accessories, System Tools, and then the appropriate program. The executable file for ScanDisk can be found in C:\Windows\Command. The Disk Defrag program is under C:\Windows. The Backup utility is located in C:\Program_Files\Accessories in Windows 9x and in C:\WINNT\SYSTEM32 in Windows NT/2000.

◆ Over time, lost units can pile up and occupy large amounts of disk space. To remove lost units from the drive, you can add the /F modifier to the CHKDSK command, to convert the lost units into files that can be investigated and removed if necessary. In some cases, the converted file is a usable data file that can be rebuilt for use with an application. You often use the CHKDSK /F command before running a drive defragmentation program.

◆ By default, the command-line version of ScanDisk runs automatically during startup whenever the operating system detects that the system was not shut down properly.

◆ The standard ScanDisk operation examines the system's directory and file structure. However, a thorough option can be selected to examine the physical disk surface, as well as its files and directories. If potential defects exist on the surface, ScanDisk can be used to recover data stored in these areas.

◆ If a user decides to install the Windows Backup feature, the actual Backup utility file (Backup.exe) is placed in the C:\Program Files\Accessories directory. Windows also creates a shortcut icon for the Backup utility in the C:\Windows\Start Menu\Programs\Accessories\System Tools directory.

◆ In a full, or total, backup, the entire contents of the designated disk are backed up, including directory and subdirectory listings and their contents. This backup method requires the most time each day for backing up, but it also requires the least time for restoring the system after a failure because only the most recent backup copy is required to restore the system.

◆ Restoring a system from an incremental backup requires the use of the last full backup and each incremental backup taken since that full backup was made. This method requires the least time for backing up the system but the most time for restoring the system.

◆ The differential backup option is a valuable time-saving feature in a periodic backup strategy. To restore a system, you need a copy of the last full backup and the last differential backup.

◆ The Disk Defrag program realigns the positioning of related file clusters to speed up the operation of the drive.

◆ In Windows 2000 you can access the Disk Defrag program by selecting Start, Settings, Control Panel, clicking the Administrative Tools icon, and then selecting Computer Management.

◆ To minimize the adverse effects of poorly written device drivers on a system, Microsoft works with hardware suppliers and signs (that is, certifies) their drivers for Windows 98 compatibility by adding special digital codes to them. This driver-signing tool is valuable to administrators who do not want users to introduce questionable devices and drivers into the system.

◆ The System Monitor can be used to track the performance of key system resources for both evaluation and troubleshooting purposes. If system performance is suspect but there is no clear indication of what might be slowing down the system, the System Monitor can be used to determine which resource is operating at capacity, thereby limiting the performance of the system.

◆ The Device Manager displays an exclamation point (!) inside a yellow circle whenever a device is experiencing a direct hardware conflict with another device. The nature of the problem is described in the device's Properties dialog box.

◆ When a red X appears at a device's icon, the device has been disabled because of a user-selection conflict. This situation can occur when a user wants to disable a selected device without removing it, and this arrangement can be established through the Device Manager's Disable in This Hardware Profile option. Selecting this setting keeps the driver from loading until it is reactivated and is located in the Properties window for the particular device.

◆ When you suspect a device conflict, you can click the name of the offending device in the Device Manager listing, right-click the item, select Properties from the pop-up menu, and then click the Resources tab to examine the conflicting device's list. You can also access the Properties window by double-clicking the device driver name.

◆ Windows 2000 includes two Registry editors: RegEdit and RegEdt32. Both of these utilities enable you to add, edit, and remove Registry entries and perform other basic functions. However, you can perform specific functions only in one editor or the other.

◆ RegEdt32 is the Registry editor that has historically been used with Windows NT.

◆ As a system operates, the Dr. Watson utility monitors the code moving through the system and logs its key events in the DRWATSON.LOG file. The Dr. Watson log contains a list of the events that were going on up to the time of a system error occurrence.

◆ Dr. Watson can also be started through the Tools menu in the System Information screen. You can find this option by selecting Start, Programs, Accessories, System Tools, Dr. Watson.

2.0 INSTALLATION, CONFIGURATION, AND UPGRADING

This domain requires knowledge of installing, configuring, and upgrading DOS, Windows 3.*x*, and Windows 95. This domain requires knowledge of system boot sequences. The main points are as follows:

◆ Windows 95 must be installed over an existing operating system. In particular, the Windows 95 installation program must find a recognizable FAT16 partition on the drive.

◆ A Windows 95 system must be at least an 80386DX or higher machine, operating with at least 4MB of RAM (8MB is recommended).

◆ Although 80386DX is the listed minimum microprocessor for running Windows 95, the recommended processor is an 80486DX; Pentium processors are actually the preferred microprocessors for running Windows 95. Likewise, 4MB may be the minimum RAM option, with 8MB being the recommended option, but 16MB, 32MB, and 64MB are preferred for running Windows 95.

◆ To install Windows 98, the system hardware must be at least an 80486DX/66 or higher machine, operating with at least 16MB of RAM. The system should also possess a modem, a mouse, and a 16-color VGA or better monitor. The system's hard drive should have between 120MB and 355MB of free space available to successfully install Windows 98.

◆ The minimum hardware requirements for installing Windows 2000 Professional on a PC-compatible system are a 133MHz Pentium P5 equivalent or better microprocessor, 64MB to 4GB maximum of RAM, 650MB or more free hard drive space on a 2GB drive, and VGA monitor.

◆ If your system has hardware devices that are not on the Windows 2000 Hardware Compatibility List, you should contact the manufacturer of the device to determine whether it has new, updated Windows 2000 drivers for the device.

◆ In the case of 16-bit operating systems, such as MS-DOS or Windows 3.*x*, the Winnt.exe option should be used. Winnt32.exe is used with 32-bit operating systems.

◆ Any antivirus programs should be disabled prior to running Windows 98 Setup. Antivirus programs can be reenabled after the setup process has been completed.

◆ The easiest upgrade path to Windows 2000 is from the Windows NT 4.0 operating system. Upgrading from Windows 9*x* is potentially more difficult.

◆ In a Windows 2000 system, you should be able to install Windows 2000 by simply starting the system with the Windows 2000 distribution CD-ROM in the drive so that it can be auto-detected.

◆ If a disk is formatted with NTFS, DOS and Windows 9*x* operating systems are not able to read the files in the NTFS partition. These operating systems are not NTFS aware. However, Windows NT and Windows 2000 can both operate with the FAT file systems used by DOS and Windows 3.*x*/9*x*.

◆ If the BIOS does not locate the boot record in one of the indicated drives, it is likely to display a "Non-System Disk or Disk Error" or "ROM BASIC Interpreter Not Found" message onscreen.

◆ The following files, in the following order, are required to boot an MS-DOS system: IO.SYS, MSDOS.SYS, CONFIG.SYS, COMMAND.COM, and AUTOEXEC.BAT.

◆ Pressing the F5 key, or the Left-Shift key, during MS-DOS startup skips over the CONFIG.SYS and AUTOEXEC.BAT files. Pressing the F8 key proceeds through the CONFIG.SYS and AUTOEXEC.BAT files one step at a time, waiting for confirmation from the user.

◆ IO.SYS loads the WIN.COM file to control the loading and testing of the Windows 9x core components.

◆ Windows 9x creates a folder for each user who logs on to the system. This profile is held in the \Windows\Profiles subdirectory. Each profile contains a USER.DAT file (the second half of the Registry) that holds the Registry information for that user. It also contains a number of other files that customize the desktop for that user. As with the SYSTEM.DAT file, the USER.DAT file is backed up as USER.DA0 each time the Windows 95 system is rebooted. Under Windows 98, the USER.DAT backup is part of the rb000x.cab files.

◆ When the Logged option is selected, the system attempts to start in normal mode, but it keeps an error log file (BOOTLOG.TXT) that contains the steps performed and the outcomes. You can read the BOOTLOG.TXT file with any text editor, or you can print it out on a working system.

◆ You can access Safe mode by pressing the F5 function key when the Starting Windows 9x message is displayed onscreen.

◆ In Safe mode, the minimal device drivers (keyboard, mouse, and standard-mode VGA drivers) are active to start the system. However, the CD-ROM drive is not active in Safe mode.

◆ In step-by-step confirmation mode, the system displays each startup command line-by-line and waits for a confirmation from the keyboard before moving ahead.

◆ You can obtain the step-by-step confirmation mode option by pressing the F8 function key at the startup menu.

◆ The Safe Mode Command Prompt Only option performs the same function as pressing Shift+F5 during the boot-up process.

◆ After gaining access to a system by using a boot disk, you should attempt to start Windows by typing the WIN command at the command prompt.

◆ If a Windows NT system employs a SCSI disk drive, a driver file named NTBOOTDD.SYS needs to be present in the root directory of the system partition. The NTLDR program can also load driver files that have been renamed NTBOOTDD.SYS to enable Windows NT 4.0 and Windows 2000 to use drives larger than 8GB (even EIDE drives).

◆ Selecting the Last Known Good Hardware Configuration mode option causes the system to start up by using the configuration information that it recorded the last time a user successfully logged on to the system.

◆ To make a boot disk truly useful, you should include at least a few utilities that can be used to provide initial troubleshooting functions after you have gained access to the system. These functions include partitioning, formatting, file editing, and diagnostic utilities.

◆ During the Windows setup operation, the software provides an option for creating an Emergency Start disk. You should use this option for every Windows 9x installation. An Emergency Start disk can also be created through the Control Panel's Add/Remove Programs icon.

◆ The Windows 98 version of the Emergency Start disk is basically a boot disk with key Windows 98 utilities included, to assist in restarting the system when Windows 98 doesn't boot. You can create this disk during the installation process or by accessing the Startup disk tab in the Control Panel's Add/Remove Programs window.

◆ In addition to the necessary system files required to start the system in a minimal, real-mode condition, the Windows 98 Startup disk provides a number of diagnostic programs and a trio of real-mode CD-ROM drivers (MSCDEX.EXE for IDE drives and BTDCDROM.SYS and ASPICD.SYS for SCSI drives), to enable the CD-ROM drive to operate in safe mode.

◆ You can use the Extract command to pull necessary files from the cabinet (.CAB) files on the Windows 98 distribution CD-ROM.

◆ To create setup disks in Windows NT 4.0, you must install the Windows NT distribution CD-ROM in the system and type WINNT /ox at the command prompt.

◆ In Windows 2000 you must place the distribution CD in the drive and launch the MakeBootDisk utility to create the four disk images for the Windows 2000 Setup disks. You can also create a setup disk from the command prompt by using the MAKEBT32.EXE file for Windows 2000. You can also make these disks by selecting Start, Run, clicking Browse, and then selecting the CD-ROM drive. Then select the BOOTDISK option, followed by the MAKEBT32.EXE command.

◆ You can create an ERD after the operating system installation by using the Repair Disk program (RDISK.EXE). To do so, select Start, Run, enter the CMD command in the Run dialog box, and then type RDISK at the command prompt.

◆ The Windows 2000 Setup routine prompts you to create an ERD during the installation process. You can also create an ERD by using the Windows 2000 Backup utility, which you can find by selecting Programs, Accessories, System Tools, Backup.

◆ You can find the Add New Hardware icon under the Control Panel option of the Settings menu. You can also access it through the Hardware tab of the System Properties window.

◆ If the Add New Hardware Wizard does not detect the hardware, the user can attempt to locate the device in the wizard's list of supported devices. The only other option for installing hardware devices is to obtain for the device an OEM disk or CD-ROM that contains Windows 9x drivers. If the driver disk/CD-ROM does not have an AutoStart function, you need to click the Have Disk button and supply the file's location to complete the installation process.

◆ To determine what devices Windows NT or Windows 2000 supports, you must consult the Hardware Compatibility List for the version of Windows NT/2000 being used.

◆ If drivers for the device being installed are not listed in the Hardware Compatibility List, there is a good chance the device will not operate, or will not operate well in the Windows NT environment. If this is the case, the only recourse is to contact the device's manufacturer for Windows NT drivers. It is a good idea to check the manufacturer's Web site for updated drivers that can be downloaded.

◆ Some Windows 9x applications may share support files (such as .DLL files) with other applications. In these instances, the Uninstall utility produces a dialog box that asks about deleting the shared files. The best response is to keep the file to avoid disabling the other applications. If the files are to be deleted, you should make a backup before running the Uninstall utility so that the files can be replaced if needed.

◆ For applications that don't feature the automatic installation function, or if the AutoPlay function is disabled, the software must be installed manually. You do this by clicking the Have Disk button. A dialog box then asks for the name and location of the application's installation file. Most software suppliers provide a SETUP.EXE file or an INSTALL.EXE file to handle the installation and configuration process for their software.

◆ One of the optional Windows components that you may not choose to install is the Accessibility options group. This group contains programs that modify the operations of the Windows keyboard and audio and video output for use by those who have physical conditions that inhibit their use of the computer.

◆ When Windows is restarted in MS-DOS mode, a batch file named DOSSTART.BAT runs automatically. This file is used to load real-mode DOS drivers for devices such as mouse devices, sound cards, or joysticks.

◆ If a DOS application takes up the entire screen in Windows 9x, you should press Alt+Enter to switch the application into a window. The Alt+Tab key combination switches the display to another application.

◆ Some applications grab an entire screen, covering the toolbar and Start menu, when maximized. When this occurs, you need to resize the application's window through the Screen tab to access the toolbar. You can press Ctrl+Esc at any time to access the Windows 9x Start menu.

◆ In Windows 98 Microsoft includes a Make Compatible utility that can be used to establish compatibility between the application and the operating system. You can execute this utility by selecting Start, Run and then typing mkcompat.exe in the Run dialog box.

◆ In versions of Windows before Windows 2000, applications copy similar versions of shared DLL files and other support files into the \Windows folder. When a new application overwrites a particular DLL file that another application requires for proper operation, a problem is likely to occur with the original software package.

◆ To access the DOS emulator, you can select Start, Run, type the command CMD or COMMAND in the dialog box, and then press the OK button.

◆ All printing activities in both Windows 9x and Windows 2000 are controlled through the Windows Print Manager, which you can find in the My Computer folder or access by selecting Start, Settings, Printers. You can also access the Print Manager via the Control Panel.

◆ To print an open file in Windows 9x, move to the application's File menu and select the Print option. If the file is not open, you can still print the file in Windows 9x. Under the My Computer icon, right-clicking a selected file produces a Print option in a pop-up menu. You can use this right-clicking method to print files from Windows Explorer. You can also print files by dragging and dropping them onto a printer icon in the Printers folder, in the Network Neighborhood, or on the desktop.

◆ You can change the settings for any printer through the My Computer icon on the desktop or by selecting Start, Settings, Printers. The process is the same for both routes: Simply double-click the Printer folder, right-click the desired printer, and select the printer's Properties entry from the pop-up menu.

◆ Because the print spooler service runs in its own 32-bit virtual environment, printer hangups do not lock up a system. The print jobs in the queue are completed unless they are deleted from the list.

◆ If a physical printer is connected to a remote computer, referred to as a *print server*, the remote unit must supply the printer drivers and settings to control the printer. Likewise, the print server must be set up to share the printer with the other users on the network.

◆ To install a network printer, click the Network Neighborhood icon on the desktop, select the remote computer's network name, select the remote unit's printer name, and right-click on the Install option. After the remote printer has been installed, the local computer can access it through the Network Neighborhood icon.

◆ If a printer is not recognized as a model supported by the Windows 9*x* driver list, you can install an OEM driver from a device manufacturer's installation disk that contains the OEMSETUP.INF file.

3.0 DIAGNOSING AND TROUBLESHOOTING

This domain requires the ability to apply knowledge to diagnose and troubleshoot common problems relating to Windows 9*x* and Windows 2000. The main points are as follows:

◆ A memory speed mismatch or mixed RAM problem might produce a "Windows Protection Error" message during the installation process. This error indicates that the operating system is having timing problems that originate from the RAM memory used in the system.

◆ You should check the Hardware Compatibility List to ensure that your hardware is compatible with Windows 2000. If any part of your hardware is not listed, contact the hardware vendor to determine whether it supports Windows 2000 before starting the installation.

◆ To determine the current version of a Windows operating system running on a computer, alternate-click the My Computer icon, select the Properties option from the pop-up menu, and select the General tab of the System Properties page.

◆ You can repair a system after a "Missing Command Interpreter" error by restoring the boot record and operating system files to the hard disk. To do so, you normally copy or extract the files from a clean boot disk to the hard drive. In a FAT environment, if the boot disk contains a copy of the FDISK command, you can use the FDISK /MBR command to restore the hard drive's master boot record, along with its partition information.

◆ The special function keys available during the Windows 9*x* startup are F5 (safe mode), F6 (safe mode with network support), F8 (step-by-step confirmation mode), and Shift+F5 (safe mode, command-prompt only).

◆ If a HIMEM.SYS error occurs, you can use the System Editor to check the syntax and correctness of the entry in the CONFIG.SYS file, if present. With Windows 9*x*, the HIMEM.SYS statement must be present in the Windows directory and must be correct in order for the operating system to run.

◆ The following conditions produce a bad or missing COMMAND.COM error message: The COMMAND.COM file cannot be found on the hard drive and no bootable disk is present in the A: drive; the COMMAND.COM file is not located in the hard drive's root directory (this message is likely when installing a new hard drive or a new DOS version); and the user inadvertently erases the COMMAND.COM file from the hard drive.

◆ You can use the DOS Attrib command to verify that the hidden system files have been successfully copied to the disk (that is, Attrib -r -s -h c:\IO.SYS and Attrib -r -s -h C:\MSDOS.SYS to make them visible and to remove their read-only and system status).

◆ To restore the COMMAND.COM file from the command line, you can start the system from the startup disk and use the Copy command to transfer the file manually.

◆ As with the manual copy procedure, the COMMAND.COM file's Read-only, System, and Hidden attributes must be removed in order for the file to be manipulated within the system.

◆ If the system locks up and does not start, the swap file may have become corrupted or the virtual memory setting may have been changed to Disabled. In either case, you must reinstall Windows 9x to correct the problem.

◆ You should check the device or driver files referenced in "Missing INI Files" error messages to make certain that they have been properly identified and that their location and path are correct. If they are not, you can use the System Editor to make the necessary changes by installing the specified device driver in the designated INI file.

◆ Errors in the CONFIG.SYS and AUTOEXEC.BAT files produce the "Error in CONFIG.SYS Line XX" and "Error in AUTOEXEC.BAT Line XX" messages. The line specified by the XX in the error message contains a syntax (spelling, punctuation, or usage) error that prevents it from running. Syntax errors can also produce an "Unrecognized command in CONFIG.SYS" message. These errors are caused by

missing or corrupt files referenced in the CONFIG.SYS or AUTOECE.BAT files. To correct these errors, use one of the system's text editors, such as SYSEDIT, to correct the designated line in the file, reload the indicated file with a known good copy, and restart the computer.

◆ You can enter step-by-step confirmation mode by pressing the F8 function key at the Startup menu.

◆ Starting Windows 9x from the command prompt by using WIN /D is often helpful for isolating different areas of the operating system as possible problem sources.

◆ The BOOTLOG.TXT file contains the sequence of events conducted during the startup of the system. The original BOOTLOG.TXT file is created during the Windows 9x setup process. You can update the file by pressing the F8 key during startup or by starting Windows 9x with a WIN /b command. The BOOTLOG.TXT file is not updated automatically each time the system is started.

◆ If a Windows 9x startup problem disappears when the system is started by using any of the Safe mode options, you should use the System Configuration utility (MSCONFIG.EXE) to isolate the conflicting items. You might need to enter this command from the command line. Select the Diagnostic Startup option from the System Configuration Utility's General tab to interactively load device drivers and software options. If the problem does not go away, you can use the Advanced button on the General tab to inspect lower-level configuration settings, such as real-mode disk access settings and VGA standard video settings.

◆ You can start the Device Manager from the MSCONFIG View option. This permits the protected-mode device drivers to be inspected. You should examine the MSINFO-Problem Devices section (which you access by selecting Start, Programs, Accessories, System Tools, System Information, Components, Problem Devices) to check for possible problem-causing devices. Other items to check include missing or corrupted system files (which you check by using the System File Checker utility), corrupted Registry entries (which you check by using the Registry Checker), viruses (which you check by using a virus-checking program), and hardware conflicts (which you check by using the CMOS configuration screens).

◆ A Windows 98 system may contain up to five backup copies of the Registry structure. If the system fails to start up after you install a new software or hardware component, you can run the Registry Checker utility by using the /Restore option (that is, ScanReg /Restore) to return the Registry to its previous condition. Simply type ScanReg /Restore at the command prompt to view a list of available backup copies. Generally, you should select the most recent version for use.

◆ If the system fails to start up after you install a new software or hardware component, the BOOT.INI and NTLDR files could be missing or have become corrupted. If you receive the message "Kernel File Is Missing" or the message "NTLDR Could Not Be Found," the partition boot sector is okay, but the NTLDR file is probably corrupt.

◆ All the startup files, including NTDETECT and NTOSKRNL, can be restored from an ERD.

◆ You can use the Recovery Console to restore the Windows 2000 Registry. Every time you back up the system state data with Windows 2000 Backup utility, a copy of the Registry is placed in the \Repair\RegBack folder.

◆ The Windows 2000 emergency repair process is designed to repair the operating system only; it is not helpful in repairing application or data problems.

◆ You can identify and eliminate any lost clusters that take up space on a drive by using the ScanDisk utility. A heavily used, heavily fragmented hard drive can affect the system's virtual memory and produce memory shortages. You can run the Disk Defrag utility to optimize the storage patterns on the drive.

◆ If a system is running a FAT16 drive, you can free up additional space by converting it to a FAT32 drive by using the CVT1.EXE command of the Drive Converter (FAT32) utility. The smaller sector clustering arrangement available through FAT32 frees up wasted space on the drive. The drawback of performing this upgrade is that you risk losing data if a failure occurs in the conversion process.

◆ If a system locks up, or if an application stalls, you can often regain access to the Close Program dialog box by pressing Ctrl+Alt+Del. When the Close Program dialog box appears, you can close the offending application and continue operating the system without rebooting.

◆ You can use Alt+F4 to close active windows. Pressing this key combination in an application stops the application and moves to the next active application in the task list. If you press Alt+F4 when no applications are active, the Windows Shut Down menu appears, enabling you to conduct an orderly shutdown or restart of the system.

◆ The Dr. Watson utility is useful for detecting application faults. When it is activated, Dr. Watson intercepts software actions, detects failures, identifies applications, and provides detailed descriptions of failures. The information is automatically transferred to the disk drive and stored in the \Windows\Drwatson*.WLG file. You can view and print the information stored in the file from a word processor.

◆ Within a multiuser system, you cannot recover an item that has been deleted by another user because the Recycle Bin is maintained on a user-by-user basis. If one user deletes something, only that user can recover it. You must log on as the user who deleted the items. Files and folders deleted from a floppy disk or network drive are permanently deleted and cannot be recovered.

◆ You can access application properties by right-clicking on the application's desktop icon or by right-clicking its entry in the Start menu, My Computer, or Windows Explorer.

◆ Windows 2000 may suffer the same types of application problems described for the Windows 9x versions: incorrect application properties (file-name, path, and syntax), missing or corrupt Registry entries, and conflicting DLL files.

◆ By default, Windows 2000 does not display hidden or system files in Explorer. To see hidden or system files, you need to open Windows Explorer, click Tools, click Folder Options, click the View tab, and select the Show Hidden Files and Folders option.

◆ You can access the Windows 2000 Task Manager by pressing Ctrl+Alt+Del or by pressing Ctrl+Shift+Esc. Ctrl+Shift+Esc moves you directly into Task Manager, and Ctrl+Alt+Del opens the Windows Security menu screen, which offers Task Manager as an option.

◆ To check print spooler problems, you can examine the system for adequate hard disk space and memory. If the EMF Spooling option is selected, you should disable it, clear the spooler, and try to print. To check the printer driver, right-click the Printer icon, select the Properties option, and click the Details option. Then, reload or upgrade the driver if necessary.

◆ When printing cannot be carried out across a network, you should verify that the local computer and the network printer are set up for remote printing. In Windows this involves sharing the printer with the network users. The local computer that the printer is connected to, referred to as the *print server*, should appear in the Windows 9x Network Neighborhood window of the remote computer.

◆ If a local computer cannot see files and printers at the print server station, file and print sharing may not be enabled there.

◆ The correct format for the UNC network path-name is `\\computer_name\shared device_name`.

◆ Common practices that increase the odds of a machine being infected by a virus include use of shareware software, software of unknown origin, and bulletin board software. One of the most effective ways to reduce these avenues of infection is to buy shrink-wrapped products from a reputable source.

4.0 NETWORKS

This domain requires knowledge of network capabilities of DOS and Windows, and how to connect to networks, including what the Internet is about, the Internet's capabilities, basic concepts relating to Internet access, and generic procedures for system setup. The main points are as follows:

◆ In later versions of DOS, Microsoft added the SHARE.EXE command to provide file-sharing and -locking capabilities for files on a local hard disk drive. These capabilities enabled multiple users to access the same file at the same time in a networked or multitasking environment.

◆ Valid computer names in Windows 9x can be up to 15 characters in length and cannot contain any blank spaces.

◆ In Windows 2000, using the TCP/IP protocol, computer names can range up to 63 characters in length and should be made up of the letters A through Z, numbers 0 through 9, and hyphens.

◆ Establishing the map to a resource is a simple matter of entering the required path and share name in the dialog box, using the UNC format (*host_name**drive_path**shared_resource_name*).

◆ The Reconnect at Logon option must be selected in the Map Network Drive page in order for the drive mapping to become a permanent part of the system. If the option is not selected when the user logs off, the mapped drive information disappears and needs to be remapped for any further use.

◆ The Control Panel's Network screen provides configuration and properties information about the system's networks. The system's installed network components are listed under the Network Configuration tab.

◆ Clicking the Add button in the Network Configuration page brings up the Select Network Component Type screen.

◆ In a Windows network, the set of rules that govern the exchange of data between computers is the NetBEUI protocol. NetBEUI works in most purely Windows networks, so no other protocol is needed.

◆ NetBEUI is required to support dial-up RAS through a modem. RAS uses the NetBEUI protocol to navigate through a network after you have dialed in to it. Both the calling client and the receiving server in the LAN must be running NetBEUI. If either computer does not have this protocol active, the client is able to connect with the LAN but is not able to navigate through it.

◆ It might be easier to run the Windows PING utility from the command prompt and attempt to connect to the network than to run the manufacturer's diagnostic utilities to verify that the LAN hardware is functioning properly. In a LAN environment, you need to know the IP address, or the name of a remote computer in the network, to which you direct the PING.

◆ Cable is one of the biggest problems encountered in a network installation. Is the cable correctly connected? Are all the connections good? Is the cable type correct? Has there been any cable termination, and if so, has it been done correctly?

◆ With UTP cable, you can unplug a cable from an adapter card and plug it into a tester. With coaxial cable, you must unplug both ends of the cable from the network, install a terminating resistor at one end of the cable, and plug the other end of the cable into the tester. The tester performs the tests required to analyze the cable and connection.

◆ If a network cannot be seen in the Network Neighborhood or a network cannot be browsed from this utility, you should check the network protocols and drivers. You check network adapters and protocols through the Control Panel's Network icon.

◆ If you can browse a network but cannot access or use certain resources in remote locations, either sharing is not turned on in the remote unit or the local unit does not have proper access rights to that resource. To use the remote resource across the network, the system's File and Print functions must be turned on, and its Share function must be enabled.

◆ Turning on the Windows File and Print Sharing functions places the local resources in the network's Browse listing.

◆ Many connectivity problems originate in the Physical layer. You should check to see that a computer is physically connected to the network and that the status light is glowing (normally green). The presence of the light indicates whether the NIC sees any network traffic.

◆ You begin the troubleshooting process for a connectivity problem by checking the TCP/IP properties under the Network icon. Next, you should check the current TCP/IP settings by using the command-line IPCONFIG /ALL (or the WINIPCFG) utility to display the current IP settings, which offers a starting point for troubleshooting. Then, you can use the PING utility to send test packets to other local computers you have found. The results of this action indicate whether the network is working.

◆ You can use the NET VIEW command to see whether a remote computer is available.

◆ Many routers do not pass the broadcast traffic generated by DHCP clients. If a client cannot obtain an IP address from a DHCP server that is located on the other side of a router, the network administrator must enable the forwarding of DHCP packets or place a DHCP server on each side of the router.

◆ The NetBIOS and IPX protocols must be bound together in order to navigate a Novell network from a computer that uses a Windows operating system. This is accomplished by enabling the NetBIOS bindings in the IPX protocol properties in the Network Properties window.

◆ The ODI file is the Novell network shell that communicates between the adapter and the system's applications. Older versions of NetWare use a shell program called NETx. These files should be referenced in the AUTOEXEC.BAT or NET.BAT files.

◆ Know the language of the TCP/IP. No matter what type of computer platform or software is being used, the information must move across the Internet in TCP/IP format. TCP/IP calls for data to be grouped together, in bundles called *network packets*. A TCP/IP packet is designed primarily to permit message fragmentation and reassembly.

◆ TCP/IP is considered one of the most secure of the network protocols. Because no one actually owns TCP/IP, it was adopted as the transmission standard for the Internet. It was so widely accepted by the Internet community that virtually every network operating system supports it, including Apple, MS-DOS/Windows, UNIX, Linux, OS/2, and even networked printers. It can also be used on any topology (for example, dial-up, Ethernet, Token Ring).

◆ In Windows you can set TCP/IP settings by selecting Start, Settings, Control Panel, clicking the Network icon, selecting TCP/IP Adapter, and clicking Properties.

◆ Services that most ISPs deliver to their customers include Internet identity through IP addresses, e-mail services through POP3 and SMTP servers, Internet news service through Usenet archive servers, and Internet routing through DNS servers.

◆ DHCP is an Internet protocol that can be used to automatically assign IP addresses to devices on a network that uses TCP/IP. DHCP simplifies network administration because software, rather than an administrator, assigns and keeps track of IP addresses.

◆ Browsers enable pages to be displayed graphically, using a mixture of text, graphics, audio, and video files. They translate the HTML files that are used to create the Web and that ultimately link the various types of files together.

◆ FTP is used to upload and download information to and from the Internet. FTP is a client/server type of software application.

◆ Most public FTP sites allow anonymous authentication for access to the site. Anonymous authentication is an interaction that occurs between the local browser and the FTP host, without involving the remote user (that is, no usernames or passwords are required to gain access).

◆ In Windows 9x applications can cooperatively share dial-up connections through TAPI. TAPI provides a universal set of drivers for modems and COM ports to control and arbitrate telephony operations for data, fax, and voice traffic.

◆ Selecting the Advanced button on the modem's Properties Connection tab permits you to add any extra settings desired for an installed modem. For example, an M0 setting should turn the volume on your modem off so that it is quiet when you connect to the Internet. You can click the OK button to return to the Modem Properties window.

◆ Although DNS is the naming service used by the Internet, it is not the only name-resolution service used with PCs. In the case of Windows LANs, the Microsoft preferred naming system is WINS. WINS can be used to translate IP addresses to NetBIOS names within a Windows LAN environment.

◆ An ISP establishes an Internet access account for each user. These accounts are based on the users' account names and passwords, which are requested each time the users log on to the accounts. Forgetting or misspelling either the username or password results in the ISP rejecting access to the Internet. Most accounts are paid for monthly. If an account isn't paid up, the ISP may cancel the account and deny access to the user. In either of these situations, if the user attempts to log on to the account, her or she is repeatedly asked to enter the username and password, until a predetermined number of failed attempts has been reached.

◆ All TCP/IP utilities are controlled by commands that are entered and run from the command prompt.

◆ The TRACERT utility enables you to display the route, and a hop count, taken to a given destination. The route taken to a particular address can be set manually by using the ROUTE command.

◆ The IPCONFIG utility can be used with two important option switches: /renew and /release. These switches update and release IP settings received from a DHCP server.

◆ NSLOOKUP.EXE is a Windows 2000 TCP/IP utility that can be entered at the command prompt to query Internet (DNS) name servers interactively. It has two modes: interactive and non-interactive. In interactive mode, the user can query name servers for information about various hosts and domains. Non-interactive mode is used to print just the name and requested information for a host or domain. Nslookup is available only when TCP/IP has been installed.

◆ Although a number of utilities are useful in isolating TCP/IP problems, the most widely used utilities are PING and TRACERT.

◆ The PING utility sends ICMP packets to a remote location and then waits for echoed response packets to be returned. You can use PING to test both the name and IP address of the remote unit.

◆ The TRACERT utility traces the route taken by
ICMP packets sent across a network. Routers
along the path return information to the inquiring system, and the utility displays the hostname,
IP address, and round-trip time for each hop in
the path.

These study and exam prep tips provide you with some general guidelines to help prepare for the A+ certification exams. The information is organized into two main sections. The first section addresses your pre-exam preparation activities and covers general study tips. Following this are some tips and hints for the actual test-taking situation. Before tackling those areas, however, you should think a little bit about how you learn.

LEARNING AS A PROCESS

To better understand the nature of preparation for the exams, it is important to understand learning as a process. You are probably aware of how you best learn new material. You might find that outlining works best for you, or you might need to see things, as a visual learner. Whatever your learning style, test preparation takes place over time. Obviously, you cannot start studying for these exams the night before you take them; it is very important to understand that learning is a developmental process. And as part of that process, you need to focus on what you know and what you have yet to learn.

Learning takes place when we match new information to old information. You have some previous experience with computers, and now you are preparing for these A+ certification exams. Using this book, software, and supplementary materials will not just add incrementally to what you know; as you study, you will actually change the organization of your knowledge, as you integrate this new information into your existing knowledge base. This will lead you to a more comprehensive understanding of the tasks and concepts outlined in the exam objectives and of computing in general. Again, this happens as a repetitive process rather than as a singular event. Keep this model of learning in

Study and Exam Prep Tips

mind as you prepare for the exams, and you will make good decisions concerning what to study and how much more studying you need to do.

STUDY TIPS

There are many ways to approach studying, just as there are many different types of material to study. The following tips, however, should work well for the type of material covered on the A+ certification exams.

Study Strategies

Although individuals vary in the ways they learn, some basic principles apply to everyone. You should adopt some study strategies that take advantage of these principles. One of these principles is that learning can be broken into various depths. Recognition (of terms, for example) exemplifies a surface level of learning in which you rely on a prompt of some sort to elicit recall. Comprehension or understanding (of the concepts behind the terms, for example) represents a deeper level of learning. The ability to analyze a concept and apply your understanding of it in a new way represents an even deeper level of learning.

Your learning strategy should enable you to know the material at a level or two deeper than mere recognition. This will help you do well on the exams. You will know the material so thoroughly that you can easily handle the recognition-level types of questions used in multiple-choice testing. You will also be able to apply your knowledge to solve new problems.

Macro and Micro Study Strategies

One strategy that can lead to deeper learning includes preparing an outline that covers all the objectives and subobjectives for the particular exam you are working on. You should delve a bit further into the material and include a level or two of detail beyond the stated objectives and subobjectives for the exam. Then you can expand the outline by coming up with a statement of definition or a summary for each point in the outline.

An outline provides two approaches to studying. First, you can study the outline by focusing on the organization of the material. You can work your way through the points and subpoints of your outline, with the goal of learning how they relate to one another. You should be certain, for example, that you understand how each of the main objective areas is similar to and different from the others. Then you should do the same thing with the subobjectives: Be sure you know which subobjectives pertain to each objective area and how they relate to one another.

Next, you can work through the outline, focusing on learning the details. You should memorize and understand terms and their definitions, facts, rules and strategies, advantages and disadvantages, and so on. In this pass through the outline, you should attempt to learn detail rather than the big picture (the organizational information that you worked on in the first pass through the outline).

Research has shown that attempting to assimilate both types of information at the same time seems to interfere with the overall learning process. To perform best on the exam, separate your studying into these two approaches.

Active Study Strategies

You should develop and exercise an active study strategy. You should write down and define objectives, subobjectives, terms, facts, and definitions. In human information-processing terms, writing forces you to engage in active encoding of the information. Just reading over the information exemplifies more passive processing.

Next, you should determine whether you can apply the information you have learned by attempting to create examples and scenarios on your own. You should think about how or where you could apply the concepts you are learning. Again, you should write down this information so that you can process the facts and concepts in a more active fashion.

Common-Sense Strategies

Finally, you should also follow common-sense practices when studying. You should study when you are alert, reduce or eliminate distractions, take breaks when you become fatigued, and so on.

Pretesting Yourself

Pretesting enables you to assess how well you are learning. One of the most important aspects of learning is what has been called meta-learning. *Meta-learning* has to do with realizing when you know something well or when you need to study some more. In other words, meta-learning involves recognizing how well or how poorly you have learned the material you are studying.

For most people, this can be difficult to assess objectively. Practice tests are useful because they objectively reveal what you have learned and what you have not learned. You should use this information to guide review and further study. Developmental learning takes place as you cycle through studying, assessing how well you have learned, reviewing, and assessing again until you feel you are ready to take the exam.

You might have noticed the practice exams included in this book. You should use them as part of the learning process. The PrepLogic software on the CD-ROM also provides a variety of ways to test yourself before you take the actual exams. By using the practice exams, you can take an entire timed practice test quite similar in nature to the actual Core Hardware Service Technician and Operating System Technologies exams. You can use the PrepLogic Adaptive Exam option to take the same test in an adaptive testing environment. This mode monitors your progress as you are taking the test, and it offers you more difficult questions as you succeed. By using the Study Mode option, you can set a time limit, focus only on a particular objective domain (such as Diagnosing and Troubleshooting or Basic Networking) and also receive instant feedback on your answers.

You should set a goal for your pretesting. A reasonable goal would be to score consistently in the 90% range.

See Appendix D, "Using the *PrepLogic Practice Tests, Preview Edition* Software," for a more detailed explanation of the test engine.

EXAM PREP TIPS

A+ certification exams start out as standardized, computerized, fixed-form exams that reflect the knowledge domains established by CompTIA. After being in use for some period of time, the questions in the test banks become stable, and CompTIA converts its tests to adaptive delivery mode.

Fixed-Form Exams

An original fixed-form computerized exam is based on a fixed set of exam questions. The individual questions are presented in random order during a test session. If you take the same exam more than once, you see the same number of questions, but you don't necessarily see exactly the same questions. This is because two or three final forms are typically assembled for such exams. These are usually labeled Forms A, B, and C.

As suggested previously, the final forms of a fixed-form exam are identical in terms of content coverage, number of questions, and allotted time, but the questions differ. You might notice, however, that some of the same questions appear on, or rather are shared among, different final forms. When questions are shared among multiple final forms of an exam, the percentage of sharing is generally small. Many final forms share no questions, but some older exams may have a 10% to 15% duplication of exam questions on the final exam forms.

Fixed-form exams also have a fixed time limit in which you must complete the exam. The PrepLogic test engine on the CD-ROM that accompanies this book provides fixed-form exams.

Finally, the score you achieve on a fixed-form exam is based on the number of questions you answer correctly. The exam's passing score is the same for all final forms of a given fixed-form exam.

Table 1 shows the formats for the exams.

TABLE 1 TIME AND NUMBER OF QUESTIONS, BY EXAM

Exam	Time Limit, in Minutes	Number of Questions
Core Hardware Service Technician	90	69
Operating System Technologies	90	70

This might seem like ample time for each question, but remember that many of the scenario questions are lengthy word problems that can ramble on for paragraphs and/or include several exhibits. Your 90 minutes of exam time can be consumed very quickly.

Keep in mind that to pass the Core Hardware Service Technician exam, a score of at least 683 on a scale of 100 to 900 is required. To pass the Operating System Technologies exam, a score of at least 614 on a scale of 100 to 900 on the same scale is required.

Adaptive Exams

When CompTIA converts its exams to an adaptive-delivery format, as discussed previously, the number of questions you are asked decreases. The adaptive test engine measures your performance as you move through the test and adjusts the difficulty level of the questions you receive. If you answer introductory questions correctly, you are shifted to more difficult questions, until you have earned enough points to pass the test. Therefore, you should see only between 20 and 25 questions in an adaptive exam, versus the 70 question in the fixed-form tests. The adaptive engine also ends the exam if it detects that you have been mathematically eliminated from passing the test. The main point to remember when preparing for the exam is that the fixed-form and adaptive tests use the same question pools.

Examinees at different levels of ability see quite different sets of questions in an adaptive exam. Examinees who demonstrate little expertise with the subject matter continue to be presented with relatively easy questions. Examinees who demonstrate a high level of expertise are presented with progressively more difficult questions. Individuals of both levels of expertise may answer the same number of questions correctly, but because the higher-expertise examinee can correctly answer more difficult questions, he or she receives a higher score and is more likely to pass the exam.

The typical design for the adaptive exam is as follows:

◆ The exam contains 20–25 questions.

◆ You are allowed 90 minutes of testing time (although this is likely to be reduced to 45–60 minutes in the near future).

◆ Question review is not allowed, providing no opportunity for you to change your answers.

The Adaptive-Exam Process

Your first adaptive exam will be unlike any other testing experience you have had. In fact, many examinees have difficulty accepting the adaptive testing process because they feel that they are not provided the opportunity to adequately demonstrate their full expertise.

You can take consolation in the fact that adaptive exams are painstakingly put together after months of data gathering and analysis and that adaptive exams are just as valid as fixed-form exams. The rigor introduced through the adaptive testing methodology means that there is nothing arbitrary about the exam items seen. It is also a more efficient means of testing, requiring less time to conduct and complete than the traditional fixed-form methodology.

As you can see in Figure 1, a number of statistical measures drive the adaptive examination process. The statistic that is most immediately relevant to you is the ability estimate. Accompanying this test statistic are the standard error of measurement, the item characteristic curve, and the test information curve.

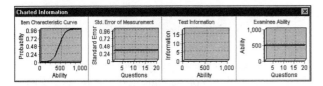

FIGURE 1
Microsoft's adaptive testing demonstration program.

The standard error, which is the key factor in determining when an adaptive exam terminates, reflects the degree of error in the exam ability estimate. The item characteristic curve reflects the probability of a correct response relative to examinee ability. Finally, the test information statistic provides a measure of the information contained in the set of questions the examinee has answered, again relative to the ability level of the individual examinee.

When you begin an adaptive exam, the standard error has already been assigned a target value below which you must drop in order for the exam to conclude. This target value reflects a particular level of statistical confidence in the process. The examinee ability is initially set to the mean possible exam score.

As the adaptive exam progresses, questions of varying difficulty are presented. Based on your pattern of responses to these questions, the ability estimate is recalculated. At the same time, the standard error estimate is refined from its first estimated value, toward the target value. When the standard error reaches the target value, the exam is terminated. Thus, the more consistently you answer questions of the same degree of difficulty, the more quickly the standard error estimate drops, and the fewer questions you end up seeing during the exam session. This situation is depicted in Figure 2.

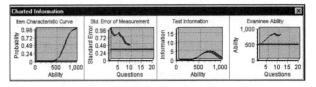

FIGURE 2
The changing statistics in an adaptive exam.

As you might suspect, one good piece of advice for taking an adaptive exam is to treat every exam question as if it were the most important. The adaptive scoring algorithm attempts to discover a pattern of responses that reflects a level of proficiency with the subject matter. Incorrect responses almost guarantee that additional questions must be answered (unless, of course, you get every question wrong). This is because the scoring algorithm must adjust to information that is not consistent with the emerging pattern.

Putting It All Together

Given all these different pieces of information, we now present a set of tips that will help you successfully tackle the A+ certification exams.

More Pre-Exam Prep Tips

Generic exam-preparation advice is always useful. Tips include the following:

◆ Become familiar with PCs and operating systems. Hands-on experience is one of the keys to success. Review the hands-on exercises on the CD that accompanies this book.

◆ Review the current exam-preparation guide at the CompTIA Web site.

◆ Memorize foundational technical detail, but remember that you need to be able to think your way through questions as well.

◆ Take any of the available practice tests. We recommend the ones included in this book and the ones you can create by using the PrepLogic software on the CD-ROM.

◆ Look at the CompTIA Web site for samples and demonstration items.

Tips for During the Exam Session

The following generic exam-taking advice that you have heard for years applies when taking an A+ certification exam:

◆ Take a deep breath and try to relax when you first sit down for your exam session. It is very important to control the pressure you might (naturally) feel when taking exams.

◆ You will be provided with scratch paper. Take a moment to write down any factual information and technical detail that you have committed to short-term memory.

◆ Carefully read all information and instruction screens. These displays have been put together to give you information that is relevant to the exam you are taking.

◆ Read the exam questions carefully. Reread each question to identify all relevant detail.

◆ Do not rush, but also do not linger on difficult questions. The questions vary in degree of difficulty. Don't let yourself be flustered by a particularly difficult or verbose question.

◆ If session time remains after you have completed all questions (and if you aren't too fatigued!), review your answers. Pay particular attention to questions that seem to have a lot of detail or that involve graphics.

◆ As for changing your answers, the general rule of thumb here is don't! If you read the question carefully and completely and you felt like you knew the right answer, you probably did. Do not second-guess yourself. If as you check your answers, one clearly stands out as being incorrectly marked, of course you should change it. If you are at all unsure, however, go with your first instinct.

If you have done your studying and follow the preceding suggestions, you should do well. Good luck!

This exam simulates the CompTIA A+ Core Hardware Service Technician exam. It is representative of what you should expect on the actual exam. The answers and the explanations for the answers follow the questions. It is strongly suggested that when you take this exam, you treat it just as you would the actual exam. Time yourself, read carefully, and answer all the questions as best you can. There are 69 questions, just as there are on the actual fixed-length exam. Set a 90-minute time limit for yourself. This is the amount of time you are given to take the real thing. The questions reflect the amount of coverage given to each domain in the exam:

Domain	Percentage of Exam	Number of Questions
1.0 Installation, Configuration, and Upgrading	30%	21
2.0 Diagnosing and Troubleshooting	30%	21
3.0 Preventive Maintenance	5%	3
4.0 Motherboard/Processors/Memory	15%	10
5.0 Printers	10%	7
6.0 Basic Networking	10%	7

You should take the exam and score it, and if you score less than 75%, you should try rereading the chapters on the domains with which you had trouble.

Practice Exam

Core Hardware Service Technician

EXAM QUESTIONS

1. The POST program can be found in _____.

    A. the BIOS chips

    B. the DOS disk

    C. the Windows program

    D. the CMOS RAM chip

2. An AT-compatible system has _____ DMA channels.

    A. 2

    B. 4

    C. 8

    D. 16

3. AGP stands for _____.

    A. Another Graphics Port

    B. Apple Graphics Port

    C. Advanced Graphics Port

    D. Accelerated Graphics Port

4. The purpose of the rechargeable battery on a system board is _____.

    A. to back up the contents of RAM memory, in case of a power fluctuation

    B. to keep the microprocessor's registers alive, in case of a power fluctuation

    C. to maintain the contents of CMOS RAM, in case of a power fluctuation

    D. to maintain the system's time-of-day chip, in the event of a power fluctuation

5. IRQ4 is normally assigned to _____.

    A. COM1

    B. COM2

    C. LPT1

    D. LPT2

6. IRQ7 is generally assigned to _____.

    A. COM1

    B. COM2

    C. LPT1

    D. LPT2

7. A USB device can be located a maximum distance of _____ from the host.

    A. 10 feet (3m)

    B. 16 feet (5m)

    C. 22 feet (7m)

    D. 30 feet (10m)

8. The recommended maximum length of an RS-232 serial connection is _____.

    A. 10 feet (3m)

    B. 25 feet (8.5m)

    C. 50 feet (15m)

    D. 100 feet (33m)

9. The recommended maximum length of a Centronics parallel connection is _____.

    A. 10 feet (3m)

    B. 25 feet (8.5m)

    C. 50 feet (15m)

    D. 100 feet (33m)

10. What type of connectors are used with IBM-compatible versions of the parallel printer port?

    A. 36-pin D-shell connectors

    B. 9-pin D-shell connectors

    C. 25-pin D-shell connectors

    D. 25-pin edge connectors

11. Serial ports transmit data _____.

    A. 1 bit at a time

    B. 1 byte at a time

    C. when a clock pulse is applied to them

    D. in one direction only

12. Standard parallel ports transmit data _____.

    A. 1 bit at a time

    B. 8 bits at a time

    C. when a clock pulse is applied to them

    D. in one direction only

13. A 25-pin female D-shell connector, located on the back of a PC, is used as _____.

    A. the COM1 serial port

    B. the COM2 serial port

    C. the LPT1 parallel port

    D. the game port

14. _____ transmissions are conducted at irregular intervals, using start and stop bits.

    A. Serial

    B. Parallel

    C. Synchronous

    D. Asynchronous

15. The COM2 and COM4 serial port settings are normally assigned to _____.

    A. IRQ1

    B. IRQ2

    C. IRQ3

    D. IRQ4

16. A .28 dot pitch monitor has _____.

    A. .28 inches between pixels onscreen

    B. .28mm between pixels onscreen

    C. .28 inches between characters onscreen

    D. .28mm between characters onscreen

17. An IEEE 1394 FireWire port can support a maximum of _____ devices.

    A. 8

    B. 23

    C. 58

    D. 63

18. How many pins does a Wide SCSI 2 connector have?

    A. 68

    B. 50

    C. 25

    D. 9

19. How many logical drives can be created by using Microsoft operating systems?

    A. 8

    B. 23

    C. 38

    D. 44

20. An IDE hard drive interface on a system board that does not contain an enhanced BIOS has a maximum disk partition size of _____.

    A. 528MB

    B. 1GB

    C. 2GB

    D. 32MB

21. A 15-pin D-shell connector would probably be used as a _____.

    A. SCSI port

    B. printer port

    C. serial port

    D. game port

22. What system component can cause problems to appear in all of a system's other components?

    A. The system board

    B. The expansion slots

    C. The power supply

    D. The hard disk drive

23. When using the ohmmeter function of a DMM to perform tests, you must always _____.

    A. connect the meter in series with the device being tested

    B. connect the meter in parallel with the device being tested

    C. remove the device being tested from the circuit board

    D. open the circuit that contains the device being tested

24. Which of the following command-line functions can be used to restore a corrupted boot record to a Windows 9*x* hard disk drive?

    A. `RESTORE /C:`

    B. `MAKEBOOT C:`

    C. `RECOVER /MB`

    D. `FDISK /MBR`

25. What is the major difference between AT and ATX power supplies?

    A. An ATX power supply requires 240-volt AC input.

    B. An ATX power supply is controlled by a software switch on the system board.

    C. An ATX power supply delivers more power to the system.

    D. An AT power supply blows air onto the system board rather than out through the back of the unit.

26. If the power supply's fan runs and the hard drive spins up, but the system appears dead, what is the most likely cause of the problem?

    A. The monitor is just turned off.

    B. An I/O card is defective and has the system buses disabled.

    C. The floppy disk drive is defective.

    D. The system board is bad.

27. Cyrix III CPUs can be used in which of the following slots or sockets?

    A. Socket A

    B. Slot 1

    C. Slot A

    D. Socket 370

28. What type of cable is used in a 100Base-TX system?

   A. Cat 4 STP

   B. Cat 5 UTP

   C. Cat 6 STP

   D. Cat 3 UTP

29. What item in a system's CMOS settings can prevent you from upgrading the operating system software?

   A. The hard disk drive Type setting

   B. The USB Enable setting

   C. The Virus Warning function

   D. The Auto-Detect hard drive setting

30. You have been asked by a customer to install an additional hard drive in an older AT-style computer that has only one IDE controller. The system already has a hard drive and a CD-ROM drive installed. How can you handle the request?

   A. Add a SCSI controller to the system.

   B. Install a new IDE cable with an additional connector on it.

   C. Connect the hard drive to the B: floppy disk drive connector.

   D. Install an IDE host adapter card in the system.

31. What action should logically be taken as a first step if a "Disk Boot Failure" error message is received during bootup?

   A. Replace the hard disk drive.

   B. Replace the disk drive controller.

   C. Boot the system from a boot floppy and type SYS C:.

   D. Replace the floppy disk drive.

32. What is the transmission range of an IrDA device?

   A. 1m

   B. 5m

   C. 10m

   D. 20m

33. If a functioning system fails to boot up after a new sound card is installed, what is the most likely cause of the problem?

   A. The sound card is bad.

   B. The system board does not have enough RAM to accommodate the new card.

   C. An interrupt-level conflict exists between the sound card and some other device in the system.

   D. The sound card has a DMA conflict with another system device.

34. An ATA interface can provide for how many drive connections?

   A. 7

   B. 4

   C. 15

   D. 2

35. What type of device would you expect to find in an AGP slot?

   A. Video display adapter

   B. Modem card

   C. Local area network card

   D. Sound card

36. The best way to transport a PC board is
    _____.

    A. in an antistatic bag

    B. in a shielded box

    C. in a Styrofoam container

    D. inside aluminum foil

37. You should not wear a wrist grounding strap
    when _____.

    A. repairing a CRT

    B. replacing an adapter card

    C. repairing a motherboard

    D. adding or replacing RAM

38. ESD can especially become a problem in condi-
    tions that are _____.

    A. hot and dry

    B. cool and dry

    C. hot and humid

    D. cool and humid

39. When disposing of a CRT, you should first
    _____.

    A. pack it in its original container

    B. discharge the HV anode

    C. check applicable local ordinances

    D. smash the CRT's glass envelope with a
       hammer

40. When replacing the fuser assembly in a laser
    printer, you should be careful because _____.

    A. it has sharp edges

    B. it may leak toner

    C. it may be hot

    D. it may be broken

41. When a system comes back on following a power
    outage, the primary concern is _____.

    A. to print the remaining jobs in the queue

    B. to recover any lost data

    C. to reestablish Internet connections

    D. to guard against power surges to the system

42. What can be done to protect a computer system
    and its data from the effects of a sudden shut-
    down or significant power sag?

    A. Use a battery backup for the system's CMOS
       settings.

    B. Use a UPS unit.

    C. Use a surge suppressor on the power supply.

    D. Use a backup generator.

43. Most ATX Pentium system boards use which
    combination of extension bus types?

    A. VESA, ISA, and PCI

    B. ISA, AGP, and MCA

    C. ISA, PCI, and VESA

    D. ISA, AGP, and PCI

44. Cache memory is used to _____.

    A. increase the speed of data accesses

    B. increase the amount of memory that is avail-
       able to programs

    C. store data in nonvolatile memory

    D. augment the memory that is used for the
       operating system kernel

45. The Pentium MMX CPU can fit into which of the following sockets?

    A. Socket 8

    B. Socket A

    C. Socket 370

    D. Super Socket 7

46. What types of microprocessors can be used in a Slot A system board?

    A. Athlon

    B. Duron

    C. XEON

    D. Pentium IV

47. In a Pentium II–based system board, the L2 cache is located _____.

    A. on an expansion card

    B. in the microprocessor cartridge

    C. on the system board

    D. on the microprocessor

48. An ATX-type system board supports _____.

    A. a soft power switch

    B. a total of 16 expansion slots

    C. universal expansion slots

    D. a RAM memory capacity of 256MB

49. A 72-pin memory module is known as a _____.

    A. SIMM

    B. DIMM

    C. DRAM

    D. PRAM

50. Where is WRAM used in a PC system?

    A. System RAM

    B. Video RAM

    C. Cache RAM

    D. Flash RAM

51. What is the most likely condition indicated by light printout of a dot-matrix printer?

    A. Printhead misalignment

    B. Worn platen

    C. Spent ribbon

    D. Incorrect printer setup

52. Which of the following items should be checked when a laser printer produces blank pages?

    A. Fuser assembly

    B. Toner cartridge

    C. Transfer corona

    D. Conditioning roller

53. Paper weight is specified in terms of _____.

    A. pounds

    B. pounds per 8.5-inch×11-inch sheets

    C. pounds per 17-inch×22-inch sheets

    D. pounds per 11-inch×17-inch sheets

54. The flow of operations in a laser printer can be summarized as _____.

    A. condition, clean, transfer, fuse, write, develop

    B. condition, transfer, fuse, clean, write, develop

    C. clean, condition, transfer, fuse, develop, write

    D. clean, condition, write, develop, transfer, fuse

55. Paper jams are most likely to occur in which laser printer area?

    A. Paper pickup area

    B. Transfer area

    C. Fusing area

    D. Registration area

56. A customer calls, saying he has a CD stuck in a nonfunctioning drive and wants to know how to get it out. What do you tell the customer?

    A. Remove the top of the drive housing from the drive unit.

    B. Push a paper clip into the hole near the activity light.

    C. Use a small knife to pry the drawer open just enough to get the disc out.

    D. Apply 110-volt AC directly to the power-supply connections on the back of the drive to eject the disc.

57. Which function can be performed by a Type III PCMCIA card, but not by Type I or Type II cards?

    A. Removable HDD functions

    B. Memory expansion functions

    C. Serial port functions

    D. Parallel port functions

58. Notebook computers do not have _____.

    A. RAM memory

    B. power connections

    C. floppy drives

    D. ISA expansion slots

59. What must occur in order for a PCMCIA card to work properly?

    A. The TCP/IP protocol must be active.

    B. A COM3 port must be added to the system.

    C. A special jumper must be set on the motherboard.

    D. A PC card–enabling driver must be loaded.

60. Which system can be classified as a bus topology?

    A. Ethernet

    B. FDDI

    C. Token Ring

    D. PS/2

61. An RJ-45 connector is most commonly used with _____.

    A. disk drive units

    B. fiber-optic cable

    C. coaxial cable

    D. unshielded twisted-pair cable

62. The maximum length of a 10Base-2 Ethernet network segment is _____.

    A. 15m

    B. 185m

    C. 520m

    D. 1,050m

63. If all the drives in an IDE system stop working when a new drive is installed, what is the most likely cause?

  A. The new drive has not been partitioned.

  B. The CMOS settings for the new drive have not been enabled in the BIOS.

  C. The old drive is not compatible with the new drive type.

  D. The master and slave settings of the two drives are conflicting.

64. In a peer-to-peer network _____.

  A. each node contains a security database of users

  B. all nodes can only be clients

  C. all nodes must act as servers

  D. all nodes can act as servers or clients under different circumstances

65. Your system will not boot to the hard drive, so you try to start it with a boot disk in the A: drive. However, the system still refuses to boot up. What should you do next?

  A. Change the Boot Sequence setting in the CMOS Setup utility to check the A: drive first.

  B. Replace the floppy drive and the signal cable, and then restart the system.

  C. Replace the hard drive and the signal cable, and then reinstall the operating system and applications.

  D. Replace the boot disk with a working disk.

66. When you start a Windows-based system in safe mode with standard VGA drivers, at what resolution does the monitor operate?

  A. 640×480

  B. 800×600

  C. 1024×768

  D. 800×400

67. Which I/O connections in an ATX system can be confusing?

  A. The COM1 and COM2 serial ports

  B. The mouse and keyboard ports

  C. The VGA video and game ports

  D. The modem and LAN ports

68. What items are found in an SEC cartridge?

  A. Toner, primary corona, and drum

  B. Microprocessor and L2 cache

  C. Fan and heat sink module

  D. A sealed disk drive unit

69. The accounting department manager complains that each time her backup tape drive runs, the system's sound card fails. What should you do about this problem?

  A. Tell the manager to run backups at night or during off-hours to avoid conflicts with other devices and systems.

  B. Install a new power supply with a higher wattage rating so that the drive does not spike the sound card when it runs.

  C. Install an external tape drive that has its own power supply.

  D. Check for conflicting IRQ and DMA settings.

ANSWERS TO EXAM QUESTIONS

1. **A.** The POST program is one of the three primary components of the ROM BIOS firmware. This program is located in the BIOS chip (or chips) on the system board.

2. **C.** The AT system uses the equivalent of two 8237 4-channel DMA controllers to complete the 8-channel AT-compatible DMA function. However, 1 of the channels in the primary DMA controller is used to funnel all the secondary channels through. Therefore, only 7 channels are actually available for use by the system.

3. **D.** The Accelerated Graphics Port (AGP) was created by Intel, based on the PCI slot, but it is designed especially for the throughput demands of three-dimensional graphics adapters.

4. **C.** The system board uses the rechargeable battery to maintain power to the system's CMOS RAM area. This area has been used to hold the system's configuration information since the early days of the 80286 AT systems. Because this area is actually RAM, even a short loss of power results in the loss of the configuration information.

5. **A.** In a PC-compatible system, IRQ4 is generally assigned to the COM1 serial port. The COM2 port is assigned IRQ3. For these two ports, it might be easy to remember that there is an even/odd reversal between the IRQ and COM values.

6. **C.** In a PC-compatible system, IRQ7 is generally assigned to the LPT1 parallel port. The LPT2 port is typically assigned IRQ5.

7. **B.** The limit of the USB 1.1 connection is 16 feet (5m) without additional equipment.

8. **C.** The recommended maximum RS-232 cable length, as recognized by CompTIA, is 50 feet (15m). The maximum length for a standard RS-232C connection is 100 feet (33m).

9. **A.** The stated maximum length of a Centronics parallel printer cable is 10 feet (3m). Some manufacturers call for a maximum of 6 feet (2m) in their documentation. These distances should be taken seriously.

10. **C.** At the back of the computer, the connector specified for the IBM printer port is a 25-pin female D-shell connector. The original Centronics specification called for a 36-pin D-shell connector, but that was not used in the PC. However, the 36-pin Centronics connector is still used at the printer end of the cable.

11. **A.** Serial ports pass data back and forth as a string of single bits. The UARTs in serial ports enable the ports to both transmit and receive data. In asynchronous mode, the timing of the data through a port is controlled by start and stop bits placed at the beginning and end of each character.

12. **B.** A parallel port passes a complete byte (8 bits) of data through the port at one time. The transmission of the data is synchronized by a control signal handshaking sequence that goes on between the port and the peripheral device. Currently, two types of bi-directional parallel printer ports are on the market.

13. **C.** A 25-pin female D-shell connector is almost always the LPT1 parallel port connector. In cases in which there are two such connectors, one should be LPT1 and the other should be LPT2. The game port uses a 15-pin female D-shell connector; serial ports use 9-pin and 25-pin male D-shells.

14. **D**. Asynchronous (that is, without timing) transmissions are conducted at irregular intervals. They use start and stop bits to define the data character sandwiched between them.

15. **C**. COM2 and COM4 (both even numbers) are assigned to IRQ3 (an odd number) in the PC-compatible environment.

16. **B**. The .28 dot pitch monitor has .28mm between the centers of each pixel on the face of a color monitor.

17. **D**. With an IEEE 1394 bus, you can connect up to 63 devices together. When IEEE 1394.1 bus bridges become available, it will become possible to connect more than 60,000 devices by using an IEEE 1394 bus.

18. **A**. Advanced SCSI connectors, such as those used with Wide SCSI 2, have 68 contacts/pins.

19. **B**.The drive can be partitioned into a primary partition and an extended partition. The extended partition can be subdivided into 23 logical drives (labeled D through Z).

20. **A**. Without large drive support from the BIOS, the IDE drive specification can handle only drives up to 528MB (which is very small by current standards).

21. **D**. There are two possibilities for the purpose of a 15-pin female D-shell connector on the back of the computer. The first is a 3-row version used with the VGA video standard; the second is a 2-row version used for game ports, to which joysticks and other game devices can be connected.

22. **C**. The power supply must deliver power to every portion of the basic system. Even the adapter cards receive power from the power supply through the system board's expansion slots. Therefore, a problem with the power supply could be manifested in any part of the system.

23. **D**. The ohmmeter function uses an internal battery to control the environment being checked. Therefore, it is very important that power in the circuit being tested be removed. In addition, at least one end of the component being tested must be disconnected from the system. This prevents any of the control current from the battery from being directed away through other circuits to which the device may be connected, which would cause the reading taken to be inaccurate.

24. **D**. From the boot disk containing a copy of the FDISK utility, you can run the FDISK program with the /MBR switch to replace the master boot record on a hard disk. This should be followed by using the SYS C: command to copy the system files over to the drive. Be aware that the IO.SYS, MS.SYS, and COMMAND.COM files are different for Windows 9*x* and MS-DOS, so using different operating system versions on an existing installation should not be done unless absolutely necessary.

25. **B**. The ATX power supply is controlled by an electronic switch from the system board. Other differences between the ATX and AT power supplies include the fact that the monitor's power pass through is gone from the ATX design, ATX power supplies provide +3.3V, AXT uses a new, keyed, system board connector, and the ATX fan blows into the system unit rather than out.

26. **D**. Under the conditions cited, the power supply is clearly receiving power (because the fan is running and the hard drive spins up) and is providing power to the disk drive unit. Otherwise, the system appears dead. The system board is the logical next choice because the problem does not appear to be confined to a particular part of the system (such as just the disk drive or monitor boot-up actions).

27. **D**. The Cyrix III processor was designed specifically to fit in a Socket 370 system.

28. **B**. 100Base-TX LAN systems are connected together by Cat 5 UTP cable.

29. **C**. The BIOS Anti Virus setting is designed to prevent boot-sector viruses from infecting the system and making the computer unusable. However, this same utility also prevents the upgrading software from writing to the boot sector of the hard drive. Therefore, it is necessary to disable this feature before upgrading.

30. **D**. A standard ATA/IDE interface can have only two devices attached to it (master and slave). To install more devices, you must install an ATA2/EIDE host adapter card in one of the system's PCI slots.

31. **C**. A "Disk Boot Failure" error message indicates that the system could not find the boot record it was looking for on the drive. This record could be missing or corrupted. If it is missing, the drive may not have been formatted. If it is corrupted, the boot record needs to be restored. Booting to a floppy disk enables you to attempt to access the hard drive. If the hard drive cannot be accessed, you should repartition and reformat the drive. If the drive can be seen but not booted, you should install the system files to it from the floppy disk by using the sys command.

32. **A**. Typically the transmission range of an IrDA device is specified as 0m to 2m, but the IrDA standard requires that the device have the ability to communicate from at least 1m.

33. **C**. If the system refuses to boot up after a new option has been installed, it is a good guess that it has detected a conflict between the new device and one of the other system devices and that it wants you to get the conflict straightened out before it will go back to work.

34. **D**. A standard ATA connection can support a maximum of one master device and one slave device.

35. **A**. Newer Pentium systems include an advanced AGP interface for video graphics. The AGP interface is a variation of the PCI bus design that has been modified to handle the intense data throughput associated with three-dimensional graphics. Most new video adapter cards are designed for use with AGP slots.

36. **A**. A printed circuit board is typically shipped in an antistatic bag, if it is not already installed in a system. It is also are typically shipped with an antistatic foam sheet along the solder side of the board. This scenario has been designed and refined by the PC board manufacturers for shipping products around the world safely. This is also the best method for transporting PC boards.

37. **A**. A wrist strap is a conductor designed to carry electrical charges away from your body. In high-voltage environments such as those found inside a power-supply unit or a monitor, however, this safety device becomes a potential path for electrocution.

38. **A**. ESD tends to form when conditions are hot and dry. These conditions provide the low humidity that ESD requires in order to form.

39. **C**. Although there are not any national requirements for disposing of computer equipment, there may be local requirements in your area. You need to check the dumpsite regulations before disposing of computer equipment of any kind.

40. **C**. The fuser assembly in a laser printer is a burn hazard. It is one of the three types of hazards present in laser printers: burn, vision damage, and electric shock.

41. **D**. When power is restored after an outage, every piece of equipment that has a power switch in the On position draws maximum power. This places a very high initial load on the power-supply system and results in short-term fluctuations—power surges and sags. These fluctuations can wreak havoc and cause damage with a digital system.

42. **B**. Surge suppressors can filter out minor variations in incoming power, but they have no active components to actually compensate for large variations such as major sags or total power outages.

43. **D**. Historically, the vast majority of all Pentium system boards have used a combination of ISA and PCI slots to service the system. With the advent of ATX-compliant system boards, the AGP slot for video graphics adapters became a common addition.

44. **A**. Cache memory of any type—and there are several applications for caching—is used to speed up a system's access to data. It is volatile memory, and it always operates in parallel with some other memory type (for instance, RAM or disk memory).

45. **D**. The Super Socket 7 PPGA socket is a derivation of the Socket 7 specification, with the addition of support for a 100MHz front-side bus specification.

46. **A**. AMD produced a reversed-version of the Slot 1 specification for its Athlon processor by turning around the contacts of the Slot 1 design. AMD called the new design Slot A. Although the Slot A design serves the same ends as the Slot 1 design, the Slot A and Slot 1 microprocessor cartridges are not compatible with one another.

47. **B**. In the Pentium Pro and Pentium II microprocessor designs, the L2 cache has been migrated from the system board to the same substrate on which the microprocessor is constructed. This provides extremely fast access of the cache by the processor core.

48. **A**. One of the features of the ATX specification is the addition of a software On/Off switch that is activated by a single key. This is not a new idea; it has been available in the Apple Macintosh design for some time.

49. **A**. The 72-pin memory module is the larger-sized SIMM. The smaller, original module is a 30-pin version. DIMMs, on the other hand, are physically larger, physically different, and have 168 pins.

50. **B**. Windows RAM or WRAM is designed specifically for use as video memory. It is a special version of VRAM that has been optimized to transfer blocks of video data at a time. This enables WRAM to operate at speeds of up to 150% the speeds of typical VRAM devices.

51. **C**. Light print produced by any type of printer typically indicates that the primary printing element is wearing out or running low. In the case of a dot-matrix printer, this is the ink ribbon.

52. **C**. A blank page indicates that no information is being written on the drum. This condition basically involves the laser-scanning module, the control board, and the power supply. Another blank-page fault occurs when the corona wire becomes broken, contaminated, or corroded, so that the attracting charge between the drum and paper is severely reduced.

53. **C**. The most fundamental specification for paper is paper weight. Paper is specified in terms of its weight per 500 sheets at 22 inches by 17 inches (for example, 500 sheets of 22-inch×17-inch, 21-pound bond paper weighs 21 pounds).

54. **D.** In a laser printer, the drum is cleaned to remove and excess toner, conditioned by applying a uniform charge to its surface, and written on with the new information to be printed. The image on the drum is developed by attracting toner to the electronic image, and then it is transferred to the paper. Finally, the toner image is fused to the paper.

55. **A.** Picking up something as thin as a piece of paper without wrinkling it is difficult for humans. It is also a difficult undertaking for a mechanical laser printer. The paper pickup area is the leading place for paper jams to occur in a laser printer.

56. **B.** Pushing a straightened paper clip into the small opening on the front panel of the drive mechanically releases the CD tray from the drive and lets it open. This is the only nondestructive way to remove a disc from a nonfunctioning CD-ROM drive.

57. **A.** The Type III PCMCIA specification was designed specifically to enable PC cards to handle removable disk drive systems. Of course, this specification remains compatible with the memory usage specification for Type I and the general I/O functions of Type II cards.

58. **D.** There is not enough room in a portable computer case for traditional expansion slots. This is one of the traditional drawbacks of portable computers and the basic reason that PC cards exist.

59. **D.** The PCMCIA specification allows for hot insertion of PC cards in the system. However, the system's PC card–enabling drivers must be loaded and running so that it can interrogate the card and configure it for use when it is added to the system.

60. **A.** Ethernet runs as a bus topology. ARCnet and Token Ring networks operate as ring topologies.

61. **D.** The RJ-45 registered jack is the connector specified for use with UTP cable. Coaxial cable uses BNC connectors, and fiber cable uses ST connectors.

62. **B.** The 10Base-2 specification is a misuse of the naming methodology because such a LAN cannot be 200m long (although 185m is close to 200m). The extra distance may compensate for the equipment links that must be used at the end of the network to connect to the user.

63. **D.** If the original drive was working but stopped when the new drive was installed, a device conflict is indicated. (Recall that installing a new device is one of the times when a configuration conflict is likely to occur.) In the case of IDE devices, the most common device conflicts occur due to master/slave settings. If these settings are wrong, the system cannot differentiate between the devices to communicate with them; therefore, no boot or drive recognition is possible with these devices.

64. **D.** In a peer-to-peer network, all nodes can act as servers or clients under different circumstances. They can access files and folders on other nodes if they are shared and can make their resources available to other members of the network by marking them as shared.

65. **A.** With newer CMOS configuration options, it is common to set up the system boot sequence to skip checking the A: floppy disk drive. This makes the boot-up process a couple seconds faster. However, when a boot-up problem occurs, the system has no reason to check the A: drive. Therefore, the technician must go into the CMOS settings to direct the system toward the A: drive during bootup.

66. **A.** Under the VGA video specification, the standard resolution setting is 640×480 pixels.

67. **B**. Because the ATX specification uses 6-pin PS/2 mini-DIN connectors for both the keyboard and mouse connections, it is very easy to confuse the two when installing the system's peripherals. This is a particularly interesting choice of connectors considering past connectivity choices (such as video and COM port connections) that have been confusing to users and technicians.

68. **B**. The SEC cartridge is the container that Intel designed to hold its Pentium II microprocessor and its L2 cache. The package was designed to plug in to the proprietary Intel Slot 1 design.

69. **D**. If two devices attempt to use the same system resources at the same time, they have conflicts. The resources they are sharing (such as IRQ and DMA channels) attempt to refer to different service routines that were never written for them or to incorrect memory locations. Therefore, at least one of the devices is doomed to fail due to improper service support.

This exam simulates the CompTIA A+ Operating System Technologies exam. It is representative of what you should expect on the actual exam. The answers and the explanations for the answers follow the questions. It is strongly suggested that when you take this exam, you treat it just as you would the actual exam. Time yourself, read carefully, and answer all the questions as best you can. There are 70 questions, just as there are on the actual exam. Set a 90-minute time limit for yourself. This is the amount of time you are given to take the real thing. The questions reflect the amount of coverage given to each domain in the exam:

Domain	Percentage of Exam	Number of Questions
1.0 Operating System Fundamentals	30%	22
2.0 Installation, Configuration, and Upgrading	15%	10
3.0 Diagnosing and Troubleshooting	40%	28
4.0 Networks	15%	10

You should take the exam and score it, and if you score lower than 75%, you should try rereading the chapters on the domains with which you had trouble.

Practice Exam

Operating System Technologies

EXAM QUESTIONS

1. Which statement is not normally a part of the
   CONFIG.SYS file?

   A. FILES=20

   B. BUFFERS=20

   C. STACKS=65,000

   D. PATH=C:\WINDOWS;C:\DOS

2. The purpose of a device driver is to _____.

   A. tell the operating system device how to interface with an external device

   B. provide more useful memory by moving
   device control data to extended memory

   C. improve performance of installed devices by
   optimizing access patterns

   D. modify application programs to work correctly with devices attached to the system

3. Which of the following commands is not proper
   for use in the AUTOEXEC.BAT file?

   A. Echo

   B. Pause

   C. Loadhigh

   D. Files

4. Memory-manager programs are loaded from
   _____.

   A. the AUTOEXEC.BAT file

   B. BIOS

   C. the CONFIG.SYS file

   D. CMOS

5. Which of the following file types cannot be run
   from the DOS prompt?

   A. .BAT

   B. .EXE

   C. .RUN

   D. .COM

6. _____ interprets input from the DOS
   prompt.

   A. IO.SYS

   B. MSDOS.SYS

   C. COMMAND.COM

   D. BIO.COM

7. In Windows 2000 which utility would you use to
   rewrite scattered parts of files into contiguous
   sectors on a hard disk?

   A. The Add/Remove Hardware applet

   B. The Disk Defrag utility

   C. The Disk Cleanup utility

   D. The Backup utility

8. The MYFILE.EXE file is located in the C:\Test
   directory. To execute the file from anywhere, you
   _____.

   A. add C:\Test to the Path statement.

   B. add the line C:\Test\MYFILE.EXE to the
   CONFIG.SYS file.

   C. add the line DEVICE=MYFILE.EXE to the
   AUTOEXEC.BAT file.

   D. add ;C:\TEST to the Path statement.

9. To configure the file `MYFILE.TXT` as read-only, you use the _____ DOS command.

   A. `ATTRIB +A MYFILE.TXT`

   B. `ATTRIB -A MYFILE.TXT`

   C. `ATTRIB +R MYFILE.TXT`

   D. `ATTRIB-R MYFILE.TXT`

10. What is the primary GUI for Windows 9x?

    A. The monitor

    B. The desktop GUI

    C. The command prompt

    D. The keyboard

11. You are installing new hardware in a Windows 2000 system that does not use PnP. From where can you install the drivers for the new devices?

    A. The Add/Remove Hardware Wizard

    B. The System Properties icon

    C. The Device Manager utility

    D. The Add New Programs Wizard

12. In Windows 9x a filename can be up to _____ characters long.

    A. 8

    B. 16

    C. 32

    D. 255

13. When Windows 95 boots up successfully, the Registry files are backed up and given the _____ extension.

    A. `.DAT`

    B. `.DOC`

    C. `.DA0`

    D. `.DMM`

14. The ScanDisk utility runs automatically in a Windows 9x or 2000 system _____.

    A. each time the system is shut down

    B. once a week

    C. according to the schedule established in the Computer Management Console

    D. whenever Windows is shut down incorrectly

15. In Windows 9x the command used to edit the Registry is _____.

    A. `SysEdit`

    B. `RegEdit`

    C. `AutoEdit`

    D. `WinEdit`

16. Where can a startup disk be created in the Windows 9x environment?

    A. In the Add/Remove Programs Wizard

    B. In the `\System Tools` directory

    C. In Windows Explorer

    D. In the Start menu's Run dialog box

17. If an application hangs up in Windows 2000, you should _____.

    A. press Alt+Tab, click Applications, and close applications that are not responding

    B. press Ctrl+Alt+Del, click Task Manager, click Applications, and close applications that are not responding

    C. press Ctrl+Esc, click Applications, and select the appropriate application to close

    D. turn off the power to the system unit and restart

18. A customer cannot find the file QUESTIONPOOL.DOC while searching in MS-DOS mode. The customer should _____.

    A. look for a abbreviated name for the file, such as QUESTI~1.DOC

    B. assume that the file has been deleted

    C. look for the file in Windows 95 instead

    D. look for an abbreviated name for the file, such as QUESTION.DOC

19. ScanDisk does all the following except _____.

    A. relocate data into sequential sectors

    B. check the FAT

    C. review the filenames

    D. locate cross-referenced sectors

20. Which Windows 2000 command starts a new instance of the Windows 2000 command-prompt interpreter?

    A. Run

    B. Execute

    C. Start

    D. CMD

21. Which command-line utility can be used to convert FAT16 partitions into FAT32 partitions?

    A. CONVERT

    B. CNVT1632

    C. CVT.EXE

    D. PARTCHNG

22. PAGEFILE.SYS is _____.

    A. the Windows 98 virtual memory swap file

    B. the Windows 98 expanded memory manager

    C. the Windows 2000 virtual memory swap file

    D. the Windows 2000 expanded memory manager

23. Which file is responsible for loading Windows 2000?

    A. BOOT.INI

    B. KERNEL32.EXE

    C. WIN.COM

    D. NTLDR

24. Windows 2000 is based on which new file system?

    A. NTFS3

    B. NTFS4

    C. NTFS5

    D. HPFS

25. How do upper memory and high memory differ?

    A. There is no difference.

    B. Upper memory is any memory above 1MB.

    C. High memory is the memory between 640K and 1MB.

    D. High memory is the first 64K area of memory above 1MB.

26. The Windows 9x System Monitor can be used to _____.

    A. view monochromatic graphics in color

    B. input TV signals directly

    C. reproduce U.S. currency

    D. detect major system bottlenecks

27. What is the purpose of HIMEM.SYS?

    A. It controls the shadow RAM operations.

    B. It loads programs into expanded memory.

    C. It loads the ROM BIOS into the high memory area.

    D. It loads programs into extended memory.

28. Memory from 0K to 640K is called _____ memory.

    A. enhanced

    B. conventional

    C. expanded

    D. extended

29. What are the minimum hardware requirements for installing Windows 2000 Professional?

    A. 133MHz Pentium processor with 64MB RAM installed

    B. 150MHz Pentium processor with 32MB RAM installed

    C. 166MHz Pentium processor with 24MB RAM installed

    D. 266MHz Pentium processor with 32MB RAM installed

30. To install Windows 9x on the system's D: drive, you _____.

    A. disconnect the C: drive from the system before installing Windows

    B. copy the Windows directory to the D: drive after Windows has been installed

    C. click the Other Directory option during the setup routine and change the install path

    D. Use the Move function in Windows Explorer to move the Windows directory to the D: drive after Windows has been installed

31. To install a network printer from Windows 9x, you _____.

    A. select File, Print from the application, and then click the Printer button and select the printer

    B. select Start, Settings, Printers, and then select the printer to install

    C. click the My Computer icon, click the Printers folder, and select the printer

    D. click the Network Neighborhood icon, computer name, printer name, and then right-click Install

32. Which startup mode is not a Window 9x mode?

    A. Normal mode

    B. Safe mode

    C. Standard mode

    D. MS-DOS mode

33. Identify the correct sequence of events that occur when Windows 2000 is started?

    A. NTLDR, NTDETECT.COM, BOOT.INI

    B. BOOT.INI, NTDETECT.COM, NTLDR

    C. NTDETECT.COM, NTLDR, BOOT.INI

    D. NTLDR, BOOT.INI, NTDETECT.COM

34. The purpose of safe mode in Windows is to _____.

    A. start Windows with minimal drivers loaded

    B. single-step through the Windows startup process

    C. skip all the Windows configuration steps

    D. start Windows with an MS-DOS command line

35. What partition must be on the hard disk drive to install Windows 95?

    A. CDFS

    B. NTFS

    C. FAT

    D. HPFS

36. The boot sequence for Windows 9x is _____.

    A. POST, Bootstrap Loader, IO.SYS, MSDOS.SYS, COMMAND.COM, CONFIG.SYS

    B. POST, Bootstrap Loader, IO.SYS, CONFIG.SYS, COMMAND.COM, MSDOS.SYS, AUTOEXEC.BAT

    C. POST, Bootstrap Loader, IO.SYS, CONFIG.SYS, MSDOS.SYS, COMMAND.COM, AUTOEXEC.BAT

    D. POST, Bootstrap Loader, IO.SYS, CONFIG.SYS, MSDOS.SYS, AUTOEXEC.BAT, COMMAND.COM

37. Which Windows 2000 administrative tool can you use to view several administrative tools, such as Event Viewer and Device Manager, in one window?

    A. Tool Viewer

    B. Services and Applications

    C. Computer Management Console

    D. Performance Meter

38. To single-step through the Windows 9x boot process, you press _____ while the Starting Windows message is onscreen.

    A. F3

    B. F4

    C. F5

    D. F8

39. To boot directly into safe mode, you press _____ while the Starting Windows 9x message is onscreen.

    A. F3

    B. F4

    C. F5

    D. F8

40. If PnP is not working in Windows, from where can you install a device driver?

    A. The Start menu

    B. The My Computer window

    C. The Add/Remove Programs Wizard

    D. The Add New Hardware Wizard

41. Which is not an acceptable way to install a device driver in Windows 9x?

    A. Let the PnP function install it.

    B. Use the Device Manager to install it.

    C. Use the Add New Hardware Wizard to install it.

    D. Use the Add/Remove Programs Wizard to install it.

42. You suspect that a program is causing errors in a Windows 2000 system, but the system is not reporting any errors. What tool would you use to view errors in the system?

    A. Event Viewer

    B. Local Security Policy

    C. Services

    D. Component Services

43. The main reason to encrypt a file is to _____.

    A. reduce its size

    B. protect it from unauthorized access

    C. prepare it for backup

    D. include it in the startup sequence

44. Which of the following is not true regarding the boot sector?

    A. It contains the MBR.

    B. It contains the disk's partition table.

    C. It resides on each disk partition.

    D. It contains information about the drive and disk.

45. You can enter boot logging mode by pressing ___ at Windows 2000 startup.

    A. F1

    B. Ctrl

    C. F8

    D. Esc+F4

46. Which of the following protocols was designed to be used with a Novell network?

    A. TCP/IP

    B. IrLAN

    C. IPX/SPX

    D. NetBEUI

47. VxDs for Windows 9x are designed for _____ operation.

    A. 8-bit

    B. 16-bit

    C. 32-bit

    D. 64-bit

48. What type of networking is included as the default in Windows 9x?

    A. None

    B. Peer-to-peer

    C. Client-based

    D. Workstation

49. A customer has asked you to install a 5GB hard drive in his Windows 95b machine. He wants to use the entire drive but does not want to change his operating system. What's the minimum number of partitions you must have in order to utilize the whole drive?

    A. 1

    B. 2

    C. 3

    D. 4

50. Which protocol enables a network server to assign an IP address to a network node?

    A. RAS

    B. DNS

    C. DHCP

    D. WINS

51. Which of the following presents the least likely cause of computer virus infections?

    A. Shareware programs

    B. Bulletin board software

    C. User-copied software

    D. Shrink-wrapped original software

52. To replace a missing or corrupt Windows 9x file from the Windows 9x CD-ROM, you use _____.

    A. SUBTRACT.EXE

    B. COMPACT.EXE

    C. EXTRACT.EXE

    D. LOCATE.EXE

53. A system is running in Windows 9x and then stops. Restarting the system is unsuccessful. What is the problem?

    A. The power supply is bad.

    B. The virtual memory function is enabled.

    C. The virtual memory function is disabled.

    D. The hard drive controller is defective.

54. If an application freezes in Windows 9x, you can press _____ to remove the offending task.

    A. Alt+Tab

    B. Ctrl+Alt+Del

    C. Esc

    D. Alt+Esc

55. What TCP/IP utility is commonly used to test a remote network node to see whether it is active?

    A. IPCONFIG

    B. ARP

    C. PING

    D. WinIPCFG

56. When comparing thorough ScanDisk operation with standard ScanDisk operation, _____.

    A. thorough operation checks the files and folders on the drive that you specify

    B. standard operation checks the disk surface on the drive that you specify

    C. thorough operation checks the disk surface, files, and folders on the drive that you specify

    D. standard operation checks the disk surface, files, and folders on the drive that you specify

57. To share a printer in Windows 9x, you _____.

    A. double-click its icon, select Printer, Properties, Sharing, and choose the configuration

    B. right-click its icon, select Sharing, and choose the configuration

    C. right-click its icon, select Properties, Sharing, and choose the configuration

    D. perform any of the first three choices, A–C

58. If a printer attached to a Windows computer is not producing any output, even though pages are being sent to the printer, what should you do?

    A. Check the printer driver.

    B. Check the print Spooler.

    C. Check the printer Pool.

    D. Check file and print sharing.

59. Device Manager can do all the following except _____.

    A. update drivers

    B. change peripheral I/O settings

    C. check for viruses

    D. identify installed ports

60. The Device Manager displays a red X symbol when _____.

    A. a device is disabled due to some type of user selection conflict

    B. a device is experiencing a direct hardware conflict with another device

C. the selected device is not present on the system

D. the selected device is not operating properly and requires repair

61. In Windows 9*x* where do you go to correct any conflicting IRQs?

A. Print Manager

B. Device Manager

C. File Manager

D. System Manager

62. Which of the following is the correct UNC network pathname format?

A. \\server_name\computer_name\user_name

B. \\computer_name\share_name

C. \\user_name\computer_name\share_name

D. \\computer_name\user_name\share_name

63. How can you see hidden files in Windows 2000?

A. Edit the appropriate Registry entry.

B. Right-click My Computer, select Properties, click the View tab, and change to the appropriate setting.

C. Run Explorer, click the Tools menu, select Folder Options, click the View tab, and change to the appropriate setting.

D. Right-click the desktop, click Properties, click the View tab, and change to the appropriate setting.

64. ISPs _____.

A. install modems

B. provide Internet addresses

C. install cable

D. create Internet browsers

65. A customer wants to use an installed modem for Internet operation. You should _____.

A. install another modem and get the ISP information

B. get the ISP information

C. install Dial-Up Networking and enter the ISP information

D. install Dial-Up Networking

66. In Windows 2000 Professional, where are TCP/IP utility programs run?

A. At the MS-DOS command prompt

B. At the TCP/IP Properties window

C. At the window that appears when you double-click the file TCPIP.COM

D. At the Run window, which is accessed via the Start menu

67. What condition causes other network users to not be able to see any files on your local machine?

A. You have not enabled the File and Print Sharing option on the local computer.

B. The remote computers have not enabled the File and Print Sharing option for your computer.

C. The local computer is password protected, and the users have not entered the correct password to gain access.

D. The remote computers do not have their directories shared.

68. What file type is not associated with the Internet?

    A. HTML

    B. FTP

    C. X.40

    D. POP3

69. What could cause a properly mapped drive to disappear when the system is rebooted?

    A. The installed network protocol has been corrupted.

    B. The network interface card is bad.

    C. The Reconnect at Logon option has not been selected.

    D. Mapped drives must always be reentered when the system is rebooted.

70. Which TCP/IP utility traces the connection path from your terminal to a remote Internet address?

    A. NBTSTAT

    B. NETVIEW

    C. TRACERT

    D. PING

ANSWERS TO EXAM QUESTIONS

1. **D**. The PATH command is associated and properly used in the AUTOEXEC.BAT file. The other answers are all valid CONFIG.SYS files.

2. **A**. The device driver is a piece of interfacing software that tells the operating system how to communicate with and manage an external device. Applications use the driver, through the operating system, to address devices, but the driver does not alter the application.

3. **D**. The Files statement is properly used in the CONFIG.SYS file. The other answers are legitimate AUTOEXEC.BAT statements.

4. **C**. The CONFIG.SYS file's statements are responsible for loading the system's memory managers. This normally involves the HIMEM.SYS and EMM386 lines.

5. **C**. There is no system extension .RUN. All the other file types can be executed directly from the DOS command line.

6. **C**. The COMMAND.COM command interpreter is responsible for accepting input from the DOS command line and interpreting it for the system.

7. **B**. The Defrag utility rearranges files and unused space on the hard disk into contiguous blocks so that the drive can operate more efficiently.

8. **D**. The Path statement in the AUTOEXEC.BAT file sets up the system with an automatic search order for executing files. To make a file, such as MYFILE.EXE, able to be executed from anywhere, the filename must be added to the Path statement (with a semicolon at the beginning).

9. **C**. The +R switch modifies the ATTRIB command to mark the specified file as read-only. The -R switch is used to remove such a specification from the file.

10. **B**. The desktop is the primary GUI for Windows 9x. Within the desktop, the My Computer icon is the primary navigation tool for the system, and Windows Explorer serves as the primary file-management tool. The Start menu is the secondary user interface for navigation.

11. **A**. The Add/Remove Hardware Wizard is used to install and configure hardware devices.

12. **D**. The file-management system in Windows 9x can accommodate filenames up to 255 characters in length. This allows for very descriptive filenames to be used to represent the contents of a file.

13. **C**. The Windows 95 startup procedure produces a backup copy of SYSTEM.DAT and USER.DAT each time the system successfully boots up. Before storing these copies, the system renames the old SYSTEM and USER files with the .DA0 extension and saves them.

14. **D**. ScanDisk is scheduled to run only when Windows 2000 does not shut down correctly. It runs in DOS mode before Windows boots up.

15. **B**. The utility for directly modifying the Windows 9x Registry is RegEdit. You can start this utility from the command line by executing the REGEDIT.EXE file.

16. **A**. An emergency startup disk for Windows 9x can be created in the setup process during installation. Alternatively, it can be created at any time via the Add/Remove Programs utility.

17. **B**. These are the steps for entering Task Manager: Press Ctrl+Alt+Del, click the Task Manager, click Applications, and close the applications that are not responding. You can use Task Manager to view applications, processes, and system performance, and to shut down anything that is not responding.

18. **A**. If the file was saved with a Windows 9x long filename, a directory listing does not display the name in its entirety. Instead, the name is truncated (shortened) and displayed with a tilde character (~) in the seventh position of the filename. A numeric character, beginning with 1, is inserted into the eighth character position, to show that it is the first iteration of the truncated filename (for example, QUESTI~1.DOC). If other filenames are

created with the same first six characters, they are labeled as the second, third, and so on iterations.

19. **A**. The ScanDisk utility does not relocate blocks of data into sequential sectors. This is the function of the Disk Defrag utility.

20. **D**. The CMD command is used to start the Windows 2000 command interpreter. It can be used to set the environment variables of the new interpreter.

21. **C**. In Windows 9x it is possible to convert partitions created on a FAT16 drive into a FAT32 file system by using the CVT.EXE command-line utility. This operation can also be performed by accessing the Drive Converter (FAT32) utility by selecting Start, Programs, Accessories, System Tools, Drive Converter.

22. **C**. PAGEFILE.SYS is a swap filename used in Windows NT or 2000. When a computer is running low on memory, Windows NT or 2000 can use hard drive space, PAGEFILE.SYS, to simulate RAM.

23. **D**. The NTLDR file, along with NTDETECT, loads the Windows NT/2000 operating system into memory.

24. **C**. The newest NTFS file system (NTFS5) is included in Windows 2000. It has some encryption and administrative enhancements over its predecessors.

25. **D**. Upper memory is the area of RAM in the PC memory map between 640K and 1MB. It has existed since the original PC design. High memory is the 64K area just above the 1MB mark that is created by the segmented offset addressing style of the Intel microprocessor. The high memory area comes into existence when the HIMEM.SYS driver is loaded in the CONFIG.SYS file.

26. **D**. The Windows 9x System Monitor is designed to monitor the operation of key system resources and graphically identify processing bottlenecks that occur.

27. **D**. HIMEM.SYS has two functions. It is the memory manager responsible for controlling any other memory managers in the system. It also provides access to the extended memory area and creates the high memory area.

28. **B**. Memory between 0K and 640K was originally referred to as *base memory* in the original PC. When additional memory became available in the PC-AT, however, in the form of expanded and then extended memory, this area of memory began to be called *conventional memory*.

29. **A**. These are the requirements set by Microsoft for installation of the Windows 2000 Professional operating system: 133MHz processor with 64 MB RAM installed.

30. **C**. Even if the Typical option is selected for the installation, the Windows 9x Setup utility enables the user to specify a new directory where the Windows 9x files are to be placed. This new directory can be located on a different drive.

31. **D**. You install a network printer in Windows 9x by accessing the Network Neighborhood through its desktop icon, selecting the remote computer's network name, and then selecting the remote printer's name. From this point, you right-click the Install option to install the printer in the local system.

32. **C**. There is no standard mode in the Windows 9x world. Normal mode is just the normal Windows 9x startup. Safe mode is a special troubleshooting mode that loads only the minimum number of device drivers required to get the basic parts of the system operational. MS-DOS mode is a command-prompt-only mode that simulates the DOS environment.

33. **A**. The correct sequence is NTLDR, NTDETECT.COM, BOOT.INI. BOOT.INI next passes control to OSLOADER.EXE.

34. **A**. Safe mode is a special troubleshooting mode that loads only the minimum number of device drivers required to get the basic parts of the system operational. This includes a reduced version of the Windows GUI environment. If the system will not function in this mode, a command-prompt-only mode is available that removes even these few drivers. Safe mode startup also provides a step-by-step boot-up mode that you can use to single-step through the boot-up process and identify steps that cause the system to crash.

35. **C**. The Windows 95 Setup routine must find a copy of a FAT16 partition running on the intended drive where it is supposed to install Windows 95.

36. **C**. When Windows 9x boots, the system initialization occurs and POST tests are performed. The Bootstrap Loader finds the MBR and loads the Windows version of the IO.SYS file. IO.SYS checks the CONFIG.SYS file for system configuration parameters. IO.SYS then loads the MSDOS.SYS file and checks its information. IO.SYS then looks for and executes the COMMAND.COM file, which in turn looks for and executes the AUTOEXEC.BAT file if it finds one. Be aware that in a pure Windows 9x installation, no CONFIG.SYS or AUTOEXEC.BAT file is present. The order of events in all the other possible answers is incorrect.

37. **C**. The Computer Management Console combines many of tools, including System Information, Performance Logs, Shared Folders, Local Users, Disk Management and Defragmenter, Logical Drives, and Services and Applications.

38. **D**. The Step-by-Step Startup option can be accessed by pressing the F8 key while the Starting Windows message is onscreen. This action brings up the Start menu, from which you can select any of the various Windows startup modes.

39. **C**. Pressing the F5 key while the system is starting up boots the system directly into safe mode. The system also defaults to safe mode if it detects a configuration problem that the PnP function cannot sort out.

40. **D**. The Control Panel's Add New Hardware Wizard must be used to manually install a device driver in the Windows system.

41. **D**. The Add/Remove Programs Wizard cannot be used to install a device driver. All the other methods can be used to install a device driver.

42. **A**. The Event Viewer administrative tool is used to view and manage the logs of system, program, and security events that occur in the computer.

43. **B**. You encrypt files to protect them from access by other users. You can encrypt files by using different cipher strengths. The files can be decrypted after they are sent to the user.

44. **B**. The boot sector does not contain information about the size and layout of the disk. That is the function of the partition table.

45. **C**. Pressing the F8 key during startup causes Windows 2000 to display the Bootup Options menu, which includes options such as Safe Mode.

46. **C**. IPX/SPX was designed for use with Novell NetWare networks.

47. **C**. VxDs are designed for 32-bit virtual-mode operations under Windows 9x.

48. **B**. By default, Windows 9x provides easy-to-use peer-to-peer networking software. It can be set up as a client or a workstation for Windows NT, Windows 2000, UNIX, or Novell NetWare networks, but this is not its default networking scheme.

49. **A**. Windows 95b allows the use of the FAT32 file system. FAT32 allows partitions of up to 2TB in size.

50. **C**. DHCP enables the host server to automatically assign IP addresses and subnet masks every time a client computer begins a network session.

51. **D**. The least likely (but not foolproof) source of virus infections is original manufacturer, shrink-wrapped software. Most reputable software manufacturers test their software and systems for viruses before placing them in the marketplace. All the other sources of software listed provide a much higher possibility for viruses to have been attached to the software.

52. **C**. In Windows 9x the installation files are stored on the distribution disks, or disc, in a compressed .CAB format. These files can be moved and expanded into the system by using the Windows EXTRACT.EXE command in MS-DOS mode.

53. **C**. If the Virtual Memory function is disabled in Windows 9x, the system stops running at some point, and you are unable to restart it.

54. **B**. Because Windows 9x employs preemptive multitasking, it is possible to exit to the Windows task list, remove the offending task, and continue processing. You access the Windows 9x task list by pressing the Ctrl+Alt+Del key combination.

55. **C**. The PING command is one of the key tools for troubleshooting TCP/IP. PING causes a data packet to be sent to a specified IP address and returned to your machine.

56. **C**. The thorough ScanDisk option only checks the system's files and folders for cross-linked files to repair, and it also examines the disk surface for physical defects.

57. **D**. All the answers provided for this question can be used to share a printer with the system.

58. **B**. If a printer is not producing anything in a Windows 9x/NT/2000 environment, even though print jobs have been sent to it, you should check the print spooler to see whether any particular type of error has occurred. To view documents waiting to be printed, double-click the desired printer's icon. Return to the Printer folder, right-click the printer's icon, click Properties, and then select Details. From this point, select Spool Settings and select the Print Directly to the Printer option. If the print job goes through, there is a spooler problem. If it does not, the hardware and printer driver are suspect.

59. **C**. There is no virus-checking function in the Device Manager. In Windows 9x there is no integrated virus detection or correction; this feature must be added from a third-party supplier.

60. **A**. An X associated with a device listed in the Device Manager indicates that the device has been disabled by a user selection conflict.

61. **B**. The Device Manger lists all the hardware installed in the system, along with the resources that the hardware has been allotted. By selecting the device from the list and clicking its driver, you can enter the device's Resources tab and change its IRQ settings.

62. **B**. The correct UNC path begins with two slashes and has both the computer name and the share name for the device.

63. **C**. In Windows 2000 the appearance of file extension is controlled through the View tab in Folder Options.

64. **B**. ISPs provide Internet addresses for their users. ISPs purchase blocks of IP addresses that they rent to their customers so that they can have access to the Internet and identities on the Web.

65. **C**. If a working modem is already installed in the system, only two things need to occur: Windows needs to have its Dial-Up Networking feature operational, and it needs to be loaded with the ISP's contact and configuration information.

66. **A**. All TCP/IP utilities are controlled by commands entered at the MS-DOS command prompt (for instance, C:>).

67. **A**. The File and Print Sharing option on the local computer must be enabled in order for other network locations to see these resources on your system. If the options were not enabled, others would not be able to see or access your resources.

68. **C**. There is no X.40 file format. HTML is the format used to create Internet documents and pages. FTP is used to transfer files across the Internet, and POP3 is an email protocol format.

69. **C**. The Reconnect at Logon box is often overlooked when someone is mapping a drive. When the user logs off, the drive map disappears and must be reentered at the next logon.

70. **C**. The command TRACERT *hostname*, where *hostname* is the IP address or DNS name of a host, traces the path of a network connection to that remote host.

APPENDIXES

Glossary

A

A: drive   The commonly understood term designating the first floppy disk drive in Microsoft's DOS microcomputer operating system.

Accelerated Graphics Port (AGP)   A newer 32-bit video interface specification based on the PCI bus design. Instead of using the PCI bus for video data, the AGP system provides a dedicated point-to-point path between the video graphics controller and system memory. The AGP bus was designed specifically to handle the high data-transfer demands associated with 3D graphic operations.

ACK (ACKnowledge)   A data communications code used by the receiver to tell the transmitter it is ready to accept data. During a data transfer, this signal is continually used to indicate successful receipt of the last data character or block and to request more.

Active Directory (AD)   The central feature of the Windows 2000 architecture. It is a distributed database of user and resource information that describes the makeup of the network (that is, users and application settings). It also is a way to implement a distributed authentication process. The Active Directory replaces the domain structure used in Windows NT 4.0. This feature helps to centralize system and user configurations, as well as data backups on the server in the Windows 2000 network.

active partition   The disk partition that possesses the system files required to boot the system. This is the logical drive that the system reads at bootup.

adapter   A device that permits one system to work with and connect to another. Many I/O device adapters interface with the microcomputer by plugging in to the expansion slots on the system board. These specialized circuit boards are often called adapter cards.

Add New Hardware Wizard   Windows 9x/2000 applet designed to guide the installation process for non-PnP hardware. When installing Plug-and-Play devices, the Add New Hardware Wizard should not be used. Instead, the Windows PnP function should be allowed to detect the new hardware. The new hardware must be installed in the computer before running the Wizard.

Add/Remove Programs Wizard   Windows 9x/2000 applet designed to guide the installation or removal of application programs. This utility also can be used to install or remove optional Windows components, such as Accessibility options, or to create a Windows Start disk.

add/remove windows components   Windows 9x/2000 utilities that can be used to change optional hardware (Add New Hardware) and software (Add/Remove Programs) components installed in the system. These utilities are located in the Windows Control Panel.

address   The unique location number of a particular memory storage area, such as a byte of primary memory, a sector of disk memory, or of a peripheral device itself.

address bus   A unidirectional pathway that carries address data generated by the microprocessor to the various memory and I/O elements of the computer. The size of this bus determines the amount of memory a particular computer can use and therefore is a direct indication of the computer's power.

American Standard Code for Information Interchange (ASCII)   The 7-bit binary data code used in all personal computers, many minicomputers, and also in communications services. Of the 128 possible character combinations, the first 32 are used for printing and transmission control. Because of the 8-bit byte used in digital computers, the extra bit can be used either for parity checking or for the extended ASCII set of characters, which includes foreign language characters and line-draw graphic symbols.

Application Specific Integrated Circuit (ASIC)   A very large scale device designed to replace a large block of standardized PC circuitry. After the parameters of the device achieve a pseudo standard usage status, IC manufacturers tend to combine all the circuitry for that function into a large IC custom designed to carry out that function. Examples include integrated VGA controllers, integrated MI/O controllers, and integrated peripheral controllers.

asynchronous transmission   A method of serial data transmission in which the receiving system is not synchronized, by a common clock signal, with the transmitting system.

AT Attachment (ATA)   Also known as IDE. A system-level interface specification that integrates the disk drive controller on the drive itself. The original ATA specification supports one or two hard drives through a 16-bit interface using Programmed I/O (PIO) modes.

The ATA-2 specification, also known as EIDE or Fast ATA, supports faster PIO and DMA transfer modes, as well as logical block addressing (LBA) strategies.

AT bus   Also referred to as ISA (Industry Standard Architecture) bus. The 16-bit data bus introduced in the AT class personal computer that became the industry standard for 16-bit systems.

ATTRIB   The DOS command used to change attributes assigned to files (for instance, system, read-only, and hidden status).

attribute   Properties of DOS files. Special file attributes include system, read-only, and hidden status. These conditions can be altered using the external DOS command ATTRIB.

ATX form factor   A newer system board form factor that improves on the previous Baby AT form factor standard by reorienting the system board by 90 degrees. This makes for a more efficient design, placing the IDE connectors nearer to the system unit's drive bays and positioning the microprocessor in line with the output of the power supply's cooling fan.

AUTOEXEC.BAT   An optional DOS program that the system's command interpreter uses to carry out customized startup commands at bootup.

B

backup   An operation normally performed to create backup copies of important information in case the drive crashes or the disk becomes corrupt. Backup utilities enable the user to quickly create extended copies of files, groups of files, or an entire disk drive.

backup domain controller (BDC)   Backup domain controllers are servers within the network that are used to hold read-only backup copies of the directory database. A network can contain one or more BCDs. These servers are used to authenticate user logons.

Backup Wizard   An automated software routine in Windows 2000 designed to lead users through a step-by-step process of configuring and scheduling a backup job.

BAT file (Batch file)   A filename extension used to identify a batch file in Microsoft DOS versions. A batch file, created by a word processor, contains a list of DOS commands that are executed as if each were typed and entered one at a time.

baud rate   The number of electrical-state changes per second on a data communications line. At lower speeds, the baud rate and the bits-per-second rate are identical. At higher speeds, the baud rate is some fraction of the bits-per-second rate.

binary   This means two. In conjunction with digital computers, all data is processed only after being converted into binary numbers consisting of the two digits, 0 and 1.

Basic Input Output System (BIOS)   See ROM BIOS.

bit (binary digit)   One digit of a binary number (0 or 1). Groups of bits are manipulated together by a computer into various storage units called nibbles, bytes, words, or characters.

bitmap   A term used in computer graphics to describe a memory area containing a video image. One bit in the map represents one pixel on a monochrome screen; whereas in color or grayscale monitors, several bits in the map can represent one pixel.

Blue Screen   A kernel-mode stop that indicates a failure of a core operating system function. Also known as the Blue Screen of Death because the system stops processing and produces a blue screen instead of risking catastrophic memory and file corruption.

boot   To start the computer. It refers to the word bootstrap because the straps help in pulling boots on, just as the bootable disk helps the computer to get its first instructions.

Boot menu   The Startup options screen menu displayed during the Windows 2000 boot-up process. This menu is produced when the F8 function key is depressed while the Starting Windows message is onscreen. This menu is generated by the BOOT.INI boot loader menu file. Options in this menu include the variety of operating systems installed on the computer. If no selection is made from this menu after a given time, the default value is selected.

boot partition   The disk partition that possesses the system files required to load the operating system into memory. Also referred to as the active partition.

boot sector   The first sector on a disk (or partition). On bootable disks or partitions, this sector holds the code (called the boot record) that causes the system to move the operating system files into memory and begin executing them.

bootable disk   A disk that starts the operating system. Normally refers to a floppy disk containing the computer operating system.

BOOT.INI   BOOT.INI is a special, hidden boot loader menu file used by the NTLDR during the boot-up process to generate the Boot Loader menu that is displayed onscreen. If no selection is made from this menu after a given time, the default value is selected.

BOOTSECT.DOS   A Windows NT file used to load operating systems other than Windows NT. If an entry from the boot loader menu indicates an operating system other than Windows NT is to be loaded, the NTLDR program loads the BOOTSECT.DOS file from the root directory of the system partition and passes control to it. From this point, the BOOTSECT file is responsible for loading the desired operating system.

Bootstrap Loader   A term used to refer to two different software routines involved in starting a system and loading the operating system. The Primary Bootstrap Loader is a firmware routine that locates the boot record required to load the operating system into memory. The OS loader takes over from the primary bootstrap loader and moves the operating system into memory (known as booting the OS).

bits per second (bps)   A term used to measure the speed of data being transferred in a communications system.

bus   A parallel collection of conductors that carry data or control signals from one unit to another.

bus master   Any class of intelligent devices that can take control of the system buses of a computer.

byte   The most common word size used by digital computers. It is an 8-bit pattern consisting of both a high- and a low-order nibble. Computers of any size are frequently described in terms of how many bytes of data can be manipulated in one operation or cycle.

C

C: drive   This is the commonly understood term designating the system or first hard disk drive in the DOS and OS/2 microcomputer operating systems.

cache   An area of high-speed memory reserved for improving system performance. Blocks of often used data are copied into the cache area to permit faster access times. A disk cache memory is an area of RAM used to hold data from a disk drive that the system may logically want to access, thereby speeding up access.

cache controller   A highly automated memory controller assigned the specific task of managing a sophisticated cache memory system.

carriage   The part in a printer or typewriter that handles the feeding of the paper forms.

cartridge   A removable data-storage module containing disks, magnetic tape, or memory chips and inserted into the slots of disk drives, printers, or computers.

cathode ray tube (CRT)   The vacuum tube used as the display screen for both TVs and computer terminals. Sometimes, the term is used to mean the terminal itself.

central processing unit (CPU)   The part of the computer that does the thinking. It consists of the control unit and the arithmetic logic unit. In personal computers, the CPU is contained on a single chip, whereas on a minicomputer, it occupies one or several printed circuit boards. On mainframes, a CPU is contained on many printed circuit boards. Its power comes from the fact that it can execute many millions of instructions in a fraction of a second.

Centronics interface   The 36-pin standard for interfacing parallel printers and other devices to a computer. The plug, socket, and signals are defined.

Certificate   A security service used to authenticate the origin of a public key to a user possessing a matching private key.

character printer   Any printer that prints one character at a time, such as a dot-matrix printer or a daisy wheel.

chip   The common name for an integrated circuit (IC). Preceded by the development of the transistor, ICs can contain from several dozen to several million electronic components (resistors, diodes, transistors, and so forth) on a square of silicon approximately 1/16- to 1/2-inch wide and around 1/30th of an inch in thickness. The IC can be packaged in many different styles depending on the specific use for which it is intended.

chipset   A group of specifically engineered ICs designed to perform a function interactively.

CHKDSK   A DOS disk-maintenance utility used to recover lost allocation units from a hard drive. These lost units occur when an application terminates unexpectedly. Over a period of time, lost units can pile up and occupy large amounts of disk space.

Clear To Send (CTS)   An RS-232 handshaking signal sent from the receiver to the transmitter indicating readiness to accept data.

client   Workstation that operates in conjunction with a master server computer that controls the operation of the network.

client/server network   Workstations or clients that operate in conjunction with a master server computer to control the network.

clock   An internal timing device. Several varieties of clocks are used in computer systems. Among them are the CPU clock, the real-time clock, a timesharing clock, and a communications clock.

cluster   Clusters are organizational units used with disk drives to represent one or more sectors of data. These structures constitute the smallest unit of storage space on the disk.

CMOS Setup   A software setup program used to provide the system with information about what options are installed. The configuration information is stored in special CMOS registers that are read each time the system boots up. Battery backup prevents the information from being lost when power to the system is removed.

Complementary Metal-Oxide Semiconductor (CMOS)   A MOS technology used to fabricate IC devices. It is traditionally slower than other IC technologies, but it possesses higher circuit-packing density than other technologies. CMOS ICs are sensitive to voltage spikes and static discharges and must be protected from static shock.

cold boot   Booting a computer by turning the power on.

color monitor   Also known as RGB monitors, these display types allow the user to run text and/or color-based applications such as graphics drawing and CAD programs. There are two basic RGB type monitors: digital (TTL) and analog. Analog RGB monitors allow the use of many more colors than digital RGB monitors.

color printer   Any printer capable of printing in color, using thermal-transfer, dot-matrix, electrophotographic, electrostatic, inkjet, or laser-printing techniques.

COM1   The label used in Microsoft DOS versions assigned to serial port #1.

COMMAND.COM   The DOS command interpreter that is loaded at the end of the boot-up process. It accepts commands issued through the keyboard or other input devices and carries them out according to the command's definition. These definitions can be altered by adding switches to the command.

command prompt   A screen symbol that indicates to the user that the system is ready for a command. It usually consists of the current drive letter, followed by a colon and a blinking cursor.

compatible   A reference to any piece of computer equipment that works like, or looks like, a more widely known standard or model. A PC-compatible, or clone, is a PC that, although physically differing somewhat from the IBM-PC, runs software developed for the IBM-PC and accepts its hardware options.

Computer Management Console   A Windows 2000 management console that enables the user to track and configure all the system's hardware and software. It also can be used to configure network options and view system events.

computer names   A name created for a computer by a network administrator. This name identifies the computer to other members of the network. It is generally recommended that computer names be 15 characters or less. If the computer has the TCP/IP networking protocol installed, however, its name can range up to 63 characters long but should contain only the numbers 0–9, the letters A–Z and a–z, and hyphens. It is possible to use other characters, but doing so might prevent other users from finding your computer on the network.

CONFIG.SYS   A Microsoft operating system configuration file that, upon startup, is used to customize the system's hardware environment. The required peripheral device drivers (with .SYS file extensions) are initialized.

configuration   A customized computer system or communications network composed of a particular number and type of interrelated components. The configuration varies from system to system, requiring that some means be established to inform the system software about what options are currently installed.

Configuration Manager   A component of the Windows PnP system that coordinates the configuration process for all devices in the system.

continuous forms   Paper sheets that are joined together along perforated edges and used in printers that move them through the printing area with motorized sprockets. Sprockets can fit into holes on both sides of the paper.

control bus   A pathway between the microprocessor and the various memory, programmable, and I/O elements of the system. Control bus signals are not necessarily related to each other and can be unidirectional or bidirectional.

control character   A special type of character that causes some event to occur on a printer, display, or communications path such as a line feed, a carriage return, or an escape.

control panels   The Windows components used to customize the operation and appearance of Windows functions. In Windows 9x and Windows NT/2000, the control panels can be accessed through the Start button/Settings route or under the My Computer icon on the desktop.

control protocols   Protocols that configure the communication interface to the networking protocols employed by the system. Each network transport supported under Windows 2000 has a corresponding control protocol.

cursor   The movable, display screen symbol that indicates to the user where the action is taking place. The text cursor is usually a blinking underline or rectangle, whereas the graphics cursor can change into any predetermined shape at different parts of the screen.

cursor keys   Special keyboard keys that can be used to move the cursor around the display screen. Enhanced keyboards have two clusters of cursor keys so that the numeric keypad portion of the keyboard can be used separately.

cyclic redundancy check (CRC)   The error-checking technique that ensures communications-channel integrity by utilizing division to determine a remainder. If the transmitter and receiver do not agree on what the remainder should be, an error is detected.

cylinder   The combination of all tracks, normally on multiple-platter disk drives, that reside at the same track number location on each surface.

D

data   Information assembled in small units of raw facts and figures.

data bus   A bidirectional pathway linking the microprocessor to memory and I/O devices—the size of which usually corresponds to the word size of the computer.

Data Communications Equipment (DCE) A communications device, usually a modem, that establishes, maintains, and terminates a data-transfer session. It also serves as a data converter when interfacing different transmission media.

data compression Most compression algorithms use complex mathematical formulas to remove redundant bits, such as successive 0s or 1s from the data stream. When the modified word is played back through the decompression circuitry, the formula reinserts the missing bits to return the data stream to its original state.

Data Encryption Standard (DES) A U.S. standard method of encrypting data into a secret code. Down-level clients employ the DES standard to encrypt user passwords.

Data Set Ready (DSR) An RS-232 handshaking signal sent from the modem to its own computer to indicate its ability to accept data.

Data Terminal Ready (DTR) An RS-232 handshaking signal that is sent to a modem by its own computer to indicate a readiness to accept data.

default The normal action taken, or setting used, by the hardware or software when the user does not otherwise specify.

defragmentation Disk maintenance operation performed to optimize the use of disk space by moving scattered file fragments into continuous chains to speed up data retrieval from the drive.

demodulator A device that removes the data from the carrier frequency and converts it to its originally unmodulated form.

DEVICE= CONFIG.SYS commands used to load specified device drivers into memory at bootup. For instance, the statement DEVICE=C:\MOUSE\MOUSE.SYS loads a mouse driver from the MOUSE directory. Used as DEVICEHIGH=, the command will load the specified device driver into the upper memory blocks, thereby freeing up conventional memory space.

device driver Special memory-resident program that tells the operating system how to communicate with a particular type of I/O device, such as a printer or a mouse.

Device Manager A Windows 95/98/2000 Control Panel utility that provides a graphical representation of devices in the system. It can be used to view resource allocations and set hardware configurations properties for these devices. This utility also can be used to identify and resolve resource conflicts between system devices. The Device Manager is located under the Control Panel's System icon.

diagnostics Software programs specifically designed to test the operational capability of the computer memory, disk drives, and other peripherals. The routines are available on disks or on ROM chips. Errors might be indicated by beep codes or visual reports. They can normally point to a board-level problem, but not down to a particular component, unless the routine has been written for a particular board being used in the system under test. A complete system failure would require a ROM-based diagnostic program as opposed to a disk-based routine.

dial-up networking Methods of accessing the public telephone system to carry on data-networking operations. These methods include modem, ISDN, and DSL accesses.

DIMMs Dual in-line memory modules. DIMMs are 168-pin plug-in memory modules similar to SIMMs.

direct I/O An I/O addressing method that uses no address allocations, but requires extra control lines.

Direct Memory Access (DMA) The capability of certain intelligent, high-speed I/O devices to perform data transfers themselves, with the help of a special IC device called a DMA controller.

directory   A hierarchical collection of disk files organized under one heading and simulating the concept of a drawer in a file cabinet. In the structure of a disk drive system, the directory is the organizational table that holds information about all files stored under its location. This information includes filename, size, time and date of when it was last changed, and its beginning location on the disk.

disk   A term usually applied to a removable, floppy disk memory-storage device.

disk arrays   A collection of multiple disk drives operating under the direction of a single controller for the purpose of providing fault tolerance and performance. Data files are written on the disks in ways that improve the performance and reliability of the disk drive subsystem, as well as to provide detection and corrective actions for damaged files. Redundant Array of Inexpensive Disks (RAID) 5 in Windows 2000.

disk drive   The peripheral storage device that reads and writes data to spinning magnetic or optical disks. The drive can either hold removable disks or contain permanent platters.

disk operating system (DOS)   Can be a generic term, but in most cases, it refers to the Microsoft family of computer operating systems (PC-DOS for IBM equipment or MS-DOS for compatibles).

docking station   Special platforms designed to work with portable computers to provide additional I/O capacity. The docking station is designed so that the portable computer is inserted into it for access to the docking station's expansion slots, additional storage devices, and other peripheral devices, such as full size keyboards and monitors. No standards exist for docking stations, so they must be purchased for specific types of portable computers.

domain   Collectively, a domain is a group of members that share a common directory database and are organized in levels. Every domain is identified by a unique name and is administered as a single unit having common rules and procedures.

domain name   A unique name that identifies a host computer site on the Internet.

Domain Name Service (DNS)   A database organizational structure whereby higher level Internet servers keep track of assigned domain names and their corresponding IP addresses for systems on levels under them. The IP addresses of all the computers attached to the Internet are tracked by this listing system. DNS evolved as a way to organize the members of the Internet into a hierarchical management structure that consists of various levels of computer groups called domains. Each computer on the Internet is assigned a domain name, which corresponds to an additional domain level.

dot-matrix printer   A type of printer that forms its images out of one or more columns of dot hammers. Higher resolutions require a greater number of dot hammers to be used.

dot pitch   A measurement of the resolution of a dot matrix. The width of an individual dot in millimeters describes a display's resolution, with the smaller number representing the higher resolution. The number of dots per linear inch describes a printer's resolution, with the higher number representing the higher resolution.

drive   (1) An electromechanical device that moves disks, discs, or tapes at high speeds so that data can be recorded on the media, or read back from it. (2) In the organizational structure of a DOS system, a drive can be thought of as the equivalent of a file drawer that holds folders and documents. (3) In electronic terms, it is a signal output of a device used to activate the input of another device.

dual booting A condition that can be established on a hard disk drive that holds two or more operating systems. A preboot option is created that enables the system to be booted from one of the designated operating systems (for instance, Windows 98 or Windows 2000 Professional).

Dynamic Host Configuration Protocol (DHCP) Software protocol that dynamically assigns IP addresses to a server's clients. This software is available in both Windows 9*x* and Windows NT/2000 and must be located on both the server and the client computers (installed on servers and activated on clients). This enables ISPs to provide dynamic IP address assignments for their customers.

dynamic link library (DLL) files Windows library files that contain small pieces of executable code that can be shared between Windows programs. These files are used to minimize redundant programming common to certain types of Windows applications.

Dynamic Random Access Memory (DRAM) A type of RAM that will lose its data, regardless of power considerations, unless it is refreshed at least once every two milliseconds.

E

edge connector The often double-sided row of etched lines on the edge of an adapter card that plugs in to one of the computer's expansion slots.

Electrically Erasable Programmable Read-Only Memory (EEPROM) A type of nonvolatile semiconductor memory device that allows erasure and reprogramming from within a computer using special circuitry. These devices allow specific memory cells to be manipulated, instead of requiring a complete reprogramming procedure (as in the case of EPROMs).

electromagnetic interference (EMI) A system-disrupting electronic radiation created by some other electronic device. The FCC sets allowable limits for EMI, in Part 5 of its Rules and Regulations. Part A systems are designed for office and plant environments, and Part B systems are designed for home use.

electron gun The device by which the fine beam of electrons is created that sweeps across the phosphor screen in a CRT.

Electronics Industries Association (EIA) An organization, founded in 1924, made up of electronic parts and systems manufacturers. It sets electrical and electronic interface standards such as the RS-232C.

electrostatic discharge (ESD) As it applies to computer systems, a rapid discharge of static electricity from a human to the computer, because of a difference of electrical potential between the two. Such discharges usually involve thousands of volts of energy and can damage the IC circuits used to construct computer and communications equipment.

Emergency Repair Disk (ERD) A disk created to repair the Windows NT/2000 system when its boot disk fails. ERD provides another option if Safe mode and the Recovery Console do not provide a successful solution to a system crash. If you have already created an ERD, you can start the system with the Windows NT/2000 Setup CD or the Setup floppy disks, and then use the ERD to restore core system files.

Enhanced Cylinder Head Sector (ECHS) format BIOS translation mode used to configure large hard drives (more than 504MB) for operation. This mode is an extended CHS mode and is identical to Large and LBA modes. However, reconfiguring drives to other configuration settings risks the prospects of losing data.

Enhanced IDE (EIDE)   An improved version of the Integrated Drive Electronics interface standard. The new standard supports data transfer rates up to four times that of the original IDE standard. It also makes provisions for supporting storage devices of up to 8.4GB in size, as opposed to the old standard's limit of 528MB. The new standard is sometimes referred to as Fast ATA or Fast IDE.

enterprise networks   Enterprise networks are those networks designed to facilitate business-to-business or business-to-customer operations. Because monetary transactions and customers' personal information travels across the network in these environments, enterprise networks feature facilities for additional highly protective security functions.

Erasable Programmable Read-Only Memory (EPROM)   A type of nonvolatile semiconductor memory device that can be programmed more than once. Selected cells are charged using a comparatively high voltage. EPROMs can be erased by exposure to a source of strong ultraviolet light—at which point they must be completely reprogrammed.

ergonomics   The study of people-to-machine relationships. A device is considered to be ergonomic when it blends smoothly with a person's body actions.

error checking   The act of testing the data transfer in a computer system or network for accuracy.

Esc key (Escape key)   This keyboard key is used to cancel an application operation or to exit some routine.

Ethernet   A popular network topology that uses Carrier Sense Multiple Access with Collision Detection (CSMA/CD) for collision detection and avoidance. Ethernet can be physically implemented as either a bus or a star network organization.

expanded memory (EMS)   A memory-management strategy for handling memory beyond the 1MB of conventional memory. Using this strategy, the additional memory is accessed in 16K pages through a window established in the upper memory area.

Expanded Memory Manager (EMM)   Any software driver that permits and manages the use of expanded memory in 80386 and higher machines.

Expanded Memory Specification (EMS)   A method of using memory above one megabyte on computers using DOS. Co-developed by Lotus, Intel, and Microsoft, each upgrade has allowed for more memory to be used. EMS is dictated by the specific application using it. In 286 machines, EMS is installed on an adapter card and managed by an EMS driver. See Expanded Memory Manager (EMM).

expansion slot   The receptacle mounted on the system board into which adapter cards are plugged to achieve system expansion. The receptacle interfaces with the I/O channel and system bus; therefore, the number of slots available determines the expansion potential of the system.

Extended Industry Standard Architecture (EISA)   A PC bus standard that extends the AT bus architecture to 32 bits and allows older PC and AT boards to plug in to its slot. It was announced in 1988 as an alternative to the IBM Micro Channel.

extended memory   The memory above 1MB in Intel 286 and higher computers, and used for RAM disks, disk-caching routines, and for locating the operating system files in recent versions of Microsoft DOS.

extended memory (XMS)   A memory-management strategy for handling memory beyond the 1MB of conventional memory. Using this strategy, Windows and Windows-based programs directly access memory above the 1MB marker. Extended memory requires that the HIMEM.SYS memory manager be loaded in the DOS CONFIG.SYS.

extended partition   Secondary partitions that can be created after the drive's primary partition has been established. It is the only other partition allowed on a disk after the primary partition is made using FDISK. However, an extended partition can be subdivided into up to 23 logical drives.

Extended System Configuration Data (ESCD)   A portion of CMOS memory that holds PnP configuration information.

F

FDISK command   The disk utility program that permits the partitioning of the hard disk into several independent disks.

field replaceable unit (FRU)   The components of the system that can be conveniently replaced in the field.

file   Any program, record, table, or document stored under its own filename.

file allocation table (FAT)   A special table located on a formatted DOS disk that tracks where each file is located on the disk.

file menu   A drop-down menu attached to Windows graphical interfaces whose options enable users to open, move, copy and delete selected folders, files, or applications.

file systems   File-management systems. The organizational structures that operating systems employ to organize and track files. Windows 2000 employs the NTFS5 file system to perform these functions. It is a hierarchical directory system that employs directories to organize files into a tree-like structure.

File Transfer Protocol (FTP)   An application layer protocol that copies files from one FTP host site to another.

filenames   Names assigned to files in a disk-based system. These systems store and handle related pieces of information in groups called files. The system recognizes and keeps track of the different files in the system through their names. Therefore, each file in the system is required to have a filename that differs from that of any other file in the directory.

FireWire   Also known as IEEE 1394, FireWire is a very fast I/O bus standard designed to support the high-bandwidth requirements of real-time audio/visual equipment. The IEEE-1394 standard employs streaming data-transfer techniques to support data transfer rates up to 400Mbps. A single FireWire connection can be used to connect up to 63 external devices.

firmware   A term used to describe the situation in which programs (software) are stored in ROM ICs (hardware) on a permanent basis.

floppy disk   Also called a diskette, a removable secondary storage medium for computers, composed of flexible magnetic material and contained in a square envelope or cartridge. A floppy disk can be recorded and erased hundreds of times.

flow control   A method of controlling the flow of data between computers. The receiving system signals the sending PC when it can and cannot receive data. Flow control can be implemented through hardware or software protocols. Using the software method, the receiving PC sends special code characters to the sending system to stop or start data flow. XON/XOFF is an example of a software flow-control protocol.

folders   Icons that represent directories. In Windows 9x/NT/2000, directories and subdirectories are referred to and depicted as folders.

Folder Options   Options that enable the users to change the appearance of their desktops and folder content, and to specify how their folders will open. Users can select whether they want a single window to open, as opposed to cascading windows, and they can designate whether folders will open with a single-click or double-click. This option also can be used to turn on the Active Desktop, change the application used to open certain types of files, or make files available when they are not online with the network. Changes made in Folder Options apply to the appearance of the contents of Windows Explorer (including My Computer, My Network Places, My Documents, and Control Panel) windows.

font   One set of alphanumeric characters possessing matching design characteristics such as typeface, orientation, spacing, pitch, point size, style, and stroke weight.

forests   A group of one or more Active Directory domain trees that trust each other. Unlike directory trees, forests do not share a contiguous namespace. This permits multiple namespaces to be supported within a single forest. In the forest, all domains share a common schema, configuration, and global catalog.

form feed   The moving of the next paper form into the proper printing position, accomplished either by pressing the Form Feed (FF) button on the printer or by sending the printer the ASCII form-feed character.

FORMAT command   A Microsoft DOS utility that prepares a disk for use by the system. Track and sector information is placed on the disk while bad areas are marked so that no data will be recorded on them.

formatting   The act of preparing a hard or floppy disk for use with an operating system. This operation places operating system-specific data tracking tables on the media and tests its storage locations (sectors or blocks) to make certain that they are reliable for holding data.

fragmentation   A condition that exists on hard disk drives after files are deleted, or moved, where areas of free disk space are scattered around the disk. These areas of disk space cause slower performance because the drive's read/write heads have to be moved more often to find the pieces of a single file.

frame   (1) A memory window that applications and the operating system exchange data through, such as the EMS frame in upper memory that expanded memory managers use to move data between conventional memory and additional memory beyond the 1MB mark. (2) The construction of a complete package of data with all overhead (headers) for transferring it to another location (that is, an Ethernet frame). (3) One screen of computer graphics data, or the amount of memory required to store it.

full-duplex   A method of data transmission that allows data flow in both directions simultaneously.

fully qualified domain name (FQDN)   A name that consists of the hostname and the domain name, including the top-level domain name (for instance, www.mic-inc.com; where www is the hostname, mic-inc is the second-level domain name, and com is the top-level domain name).

function keys   A special set of keyboard keys used to give the computer special commands. They are frequently used in combination with other keys, and can have different uses depending on the software application being run.

G

GDI.EXE   A Windows core component responsible for managing the operating system's/environment's graphical user interface.

General Protection Fault (GPF)   A Windows memory usage error that typically occurs when a program attempts to access memory currently in use by another program.

GHz (gigahertz)   One billion hertz or cycles per second.

graphical user interface (GUI)   A form of operating environment that uses a graphical display to represent procedures and programs that can be executed by the computer.

graphics   The creation and management of pictures using a computer.

ground   (1) Any point from which electrical measurements are referenced. (2) Earth ground is considered to be an electrical reference point of absolute zero, and is used as the electrical return path for modern power transmission systems. This ground, often incorporated by electronic devices to guard against fatal shock, is called chassis or protective ground. (3) An actual conductor in an electronic circuit being used as a return path, alternately called a signal ground.

Group Policies   Administrators use these tools to institute large numbers of detailed settings for users throughout an enterprise, without establishing each setting manually.

Group Policy Editor   Utility employed to establish policies in Windows 2000. Administrators use this editor to establish which applications different users have access to, as well as to control applications on the user's desktop.

groups   The administrative gathering of users that can be administered uniformly. In establishing groups, the administrator can assign permissions or restrictions to the entire body. The value of using groups lies in the time saved by being able to apply common rights to several users instead of applying them one by one.

H

HAL.DLL   HAL.DLL is the Hardware Abstraction Layer driver that holds the information specific to the CPU that the system is being used with.

half-duplex communication   Communications that occur in both directions, but can only occur in one direction at a time. Most older networking strategies were based on half-duplex operations.

handshaking   A system of signal exchanges conducted between the computer system and a peripheral device during the data-transfer process. The purpose of these signals is to produce as orderly a flow of data as possible.

hard disk   A metal disk for external storage purposes, coated with ferromagnetic coating and available in both fixed and removable format.

hardware   Any aspect of the computer operation that can be physically touched. This includes IC chips, circuit boards, cables, connectors, and peripherals.

Hardware Abstraction Layer (HAL)   The Windows NT HAL is a library of hardware drivers that operate between the actual hardware and the rest of the system. These software routines act to make every architecture look the same to the operating system. The HAL occupies the logical space directly between the system's hardware and the rest of the operating system's Executive Services. In Windows NT 4.0, the HAL enables the operating system to work with different types of microprocessors.

Hardware Compatibility List (HCL) The list of Microsoft-certified compatible hardware devices associated with Windows 2000 Professional and Windows 2000 Server products.

HIMEM.SYS The DOS memory manager that enables expanded and extended memory strategies for memory operations above the 1MB conventional memory range.

hives The five files that hold the contents of the Windows NT Registry. Hives represent the major divisions of all the Registry's keys, subkeys, subtrees, and values. The hives of the Windows NT Registry are the SAM hive, the Security hive, the Software hive, the System hive, and the Default hive. These files are stored in the \WINNT\System32\Config directory along with a backup copy and log file for each hive.

host Any device that communicates over the network using TCP/IP. The term refers to a device that has an assigned (dedicated) IP address.

I

icons Graphical symbols used to represent commands. These symbols are used to start and manipulate programs without knowing where that program is or how it is configured.

impact printer Any printer that produces a character image by hammering onto a combination of embossed character, ribbon, and paper.

Industry Standard Architecture (ISA) A term that refers to the bus structures used in the IBM PC series of personal computers. The PC and XT uses an 8-bit bus, whereas the AT uses a 16-bit bus.

Infrared Data Association (IrDA) A data-transmission standard for using infrared light. IrDA ports provide wireless data transfers between devices. These ports

support data-transfer rates roughly equivalent to traditional parallel ports. The only downside to using IrDA ports for data communications is that the two devices must be within one or two meters of each other and have a clear line of sight between them.

INI files Windows initialization text files that hold configuration settings that are used to initialize the system for Windows operation. Originally, these files form the basis of the Windows 3.x operating environments. They were mostly replaced in Windows 9x and NT/2000 by the Registry structure. However, some parts of the INI files still exist in these products.

initialization The process of supplying startup information to an intelligent device or peripheral (for instance, the system board's DMA controller or a modem), or to a software application, or applet.

ink-jet printer A high-resolution–type printer that produces its image by spraying a specially treated ink onto the paper.

input device Any computer input-generating peripheral device such as keyboard, mouse, light pen, scanner, or digitizer.

instruction word A class of binary coded data words that tells the computer what operation to perform and where to find any data needed to perform the operation.

integrated circuit (IC) The technical name for a chip. See chip.

Integrated Drive Electronics (IDE) A method of disk drive manufacturing that locates all the required controller circuitry on the drive itself, rather than on a separate adapter card. Also known as AT Attachment interface.

Integrated Services Digital Network (ISDN) A digital communications standard that can carry digital data over special telephone lines, at speeds much higher than those possible with regular analog phone lines.

intelligent controller   Usually an IC, or series of ICs, with built-in microprocessor capabilities dedicated to the controlling of some peripheral unit or process. Single-chip controllers are sometimes referred to as smart chips.

interface   The joining of dissimilar devices so that they function in a compatible and complementary manner.

interlaced   The method of rewriting the monitor screen repeatedly by alternately scanning every other line and then scanning the previously unscanned lines.

Internet   The most famous wide area network is actually a network of networks working together. The main communication path is a series of networks established by the U.S. government that has expanded around the world and offers access to computers in every part of the globe.

Internet Printing Protocol (IPP)   A protocol included with Windows 2000 that enables users to sort between different printers based on their attributes. This standards-based Internet protocol provides Windows users with the capability of printing across the Internet. With IPP, the user can print to a URL, view the print queue status using an Internet browser, and install print drivers across the Internet.

Internet Protocol (IP)   The network layer protocol where logical addresses are assigned. IP is one of the protocols that make up the TCP/IP stack.

Internet Protocol (IP) address   A 32-bit network address consisting of four dotted-decimal numbers, separated by periods, that uniquely identifies a device on the network. Each IP address consists of two parts: the network address and the host address. The network address identifies the entire network, whereas the host address identifies an intelligent member within the network (router, a server, or a workstation).

Internet service provider (ISP)   Companies that provide the technical gateway to the Internet. It connects all the users and individual networks together.

interrupt   A signal sent to the microprocessor from the interrupt controller or generated by a software instruction, which is capable of interrupting the microprocessor during program execution. An interrupt is usually generated when an input or output operation is required.

interrupt controller   A special programmable IC responsible for coordinating and prioritizing interrupt requests from I/O devices and sending the microprocessor the starting addresses of the interrupt service routines so that the microprocessor can service the interrupting device and then continue executing the active program.

interrupt request (IRQ)   Hardware interrupt request lines in a PC-compatible system. System hardware devices use these lines to request service from the microprocessor as required. The microprocessor responds to the IRQ by stopping what it is doing, storing its environment, jumping to a service routine, servicing the device, and then returning to its original task.

intranet   An intranet is a network built on the TCP/IP protocol that belongs to a single organization. It is, in essence, a private Internet. Like the Internet, intranets are designed to share information and are accessible only to the organization's members, with authorization.

I/O (input/output)   A type of data transfer occurring between a microprocessor and a peripheral device. Whenever any data transfer occurs, output from one device becomes an input to another.

I/O port   The external window or connector on a computer, used to effect an interface with a peripheral device. The I/O port might appear as either parallel data connections or serial data connections.

IO.SYS   A special hidden, read-only boot-up file that the Bootstrap Loader finds and moves into RAM to manage the boot-up process. After the bootup is complete, this file manages the basic input/output routines of the system. This includes communication between the system and I/O devices such as hard disks, printers, floppy disk drives, and so on.

IPCONFIG   A TCP/IP networking utility that can be used to determine the IP address of a local machine.

IPX/SPX   Internetwork Packet Exchange/Sequential Packet Exchange protocol. A proprietary transport protocol developed by Novell for the NetWare operating system. The IPX portion of the protocol is a connectionless, network layer protocol, which is responsible for routing. The SPX portion of the protocol is a connection oriented, transport layer protocol that manages error checking. These protocols are primarily found on local area networks that include NetWare servers.

J

joystick   A computer input device that offers quick, multidirectional movement of the cursor for CAD systems and video games.

jumper   Normally, a 2- or 4-pin BERG connector, located on the system board or an adapter card, which permits the attachment of a wired, hardware switch or the placement of a shorting bar to effect a particular hardware function or setting.

K

kernel   The Windows 3.x and 95 core files that are responsible for managing Windows resources and running applications.

kernel mode   The kernel mode is the operating mode in which the program has unlimited access to all memory, including those of system hardware, the user-mode applications and other processes (such as I/O operations). The kernel mode consists of three major blocks: the Win32k Executive Service module, the Hardware Abstraction Layer, and the microkernel.

keyboard   The most familiar computer input device, incorporating a standard typewriter layout with the addition of other specialized control and function keys.

L

laser printer   Any printer that utilizes the electrophotographic method of image transfer. Light dots are transferred to a photosensitive rotating drum, which picks up electrostatically charged toner before transferring it to the paper.

legacy devices   Adapter cards and devices that do not include PnP capabilities. These are typically older ISA expansion cards that are still being used for some reason.

letter quality   Refers to a print quality as good or better than that provided by an electric typewriter.

light-emitting diode (LED)   A particular type of diode that emits light when conducting, and used in computers and disk drives as active circuit indicators.

liquid-crystal display (LCD)   The type of output display created by placing liquid-crystal material between two sheets of glass. A set of electrodes is attached to each sheet of glass. Horizontal (row) electrodes are attached to one glass plate, whereas vertical (column) electrodes are fitted to the other plate. These electrodes are transparent and let light pass through. A pixel is created in the liquid-crystal material at each spot where a row and a column electrode intersect. When the pixel is energized, the liquid-crystal material bends and prevents light from passing through the display.

local area network (LAN)   A collection of local computers and devices that can share information. A LAN is normally thought of as encompassing a campus setting, room, or collection of buildings.

logical block addressing (LBA)   A hard disk drive organizational strategy that permits the operating system to access larger drive sizes than older BIOS/DOS FAT-management schemes could support.

logon   The process of identifying one's self to the network. Normally accomplished by entering a valid username and password that the system recognizes.

loopback   A modem test procedure that allows a transmitted signal to be returned to its source for comparison with the original data.

lost allocation units   Also referred to as lost clusters. File segments that do not currently belong to any file in the file allocation table. The DOS command CHKDSK/F can be used to locate and free these segments for future use.

LPT1   The label used in Microsoft DOS versions assigned to parallel port #1, usually reserved for printer operation.

M

magnetic disk   The most popular form of secondary data storage for computers. Shaped like a platter and coated with an electromagnetic material, magnetic disks provide direct access to large amounts of stored data and can be erased and rerecorded many times.

magnetic tape   Traditionally, one of the most popular forms of secondary data storage backup for computers. However, Windows 2000 offers a number of other backup capabilities that might render tape an undesirable backup media in the future. Because access to data is sequential in nature, magnetic tape is primarily used to restore a system that has suffered a catastrophic loss of data from its hard disk drive.

mapped drives   A technique employed to enable a local system to assign a logical drive letter to the remote disk drive or folder. This is referred to as mapping the drive letter to the resource. This will enable applications running on the local computer to use the resources across the network.

Master Boot Record (MBR)   Also referred to as the Master Partition Boot Sector. This file is located at the first sector of the disk. It contains a Master Partition Table that describes how the hard disk is organized. This table includes information about the disk's size, as well as the number and locations of all partitions on the disk. The MBR also contains the Master Boot Code that loads the operating system from the disk's active partition.

Master File Table (MFT)   The core component of the NTFS system, this table replaces the FAT in an MS-DOS–compatible system and contains information about each file being stored on the disk.

MEM.EXE   The DOS command that can be used to examine the total and used memory of the system.

memory   Computer components that store information for future use. In a PC, memory can be divided into two categories: primary and secondary (that is, semiconductor RAM and ROM and other devices). Primary memory can be divided into ROM, RAM, and cache groups. Likewise, secondary memory contains many types of storage devices such as floppy drives, hard disk drives, CD-ROM drives, DVD drives, tape drives, and so on.

memory management   Methodology used in handling a computer's memory resources, including bank switching, memory protection, and virtual memory.

memory map   A layout of the memory and/or I/O device addressing scheme used by a particular computer system.

memory-mapped I/O   An I/O addressing method in which I/O devices are granted a portion of the available address allocations, thus requiring no additional control lines to implement.

menu   A screen display of available program options or commands that can be selected through keyboard or mouse action.

metal-oxide semiconductor (MOS)   A category of logic and memory chip design that derives its name from the use of metal, oxide, and semiconductor layers. Among the various families of MOS devices are PMOS (P-Type semiconductor material), NMOS (N-Type semiconductor material), and CMOS (Complimentary/Symmetry MOS material). The first letter of each family denotes the type of construction used to fabricate the chip's circuits. MOS families do not require a highly regulated +5V DC power supply, like TTL devices.

MHz (megahertz)   One million hertz, or cycles per second.

microcomputer   The same thing as a personal computer, or a computer using a microprocessor as its CPU.

Microsoft Management Console (MMC)   A collection of manageability features that accompanies Windows 2000. These features exist as "snap-in" applets that can be added to the operating system through the MMC.

mirroring   A RAID fault-tolerance method in which an exact copy of all data is written to two separate disks at the same time.

modem (modulator-demodulator)   Also called a DCE device, it is used to interface a computer or terminal to the telephone system for the purpose of conducting data communications between computers often located at great distances from each other.

monitor   (1) A name for a CRT computer display. (2) Any hardware device, or software program, such as the Windows 95 System Resource Monitor, that checks, reports about, or automatically oversees a running program or system.

mouse   A popular computer I/O device used to point or draw on the video monitor by rolling it along a desktop as the cursor moves on the screen in a corresponding manner.

MSD (Microsoft Diagnostics)   Microsoft Diagnostic program that can be used from the command prompt to examine different aspects of a system's hardware and software configuration. The MSD utility has been included with MS-DOS 6.x, Windows 3.x, and Windows 9x.

MSDOS.SYS   One of the hidden, read-only system files required to boot the system. It is loaded by the IO.SYS file during the boot-up process. It handles program and file-management functions for MS-DOS systems. In Windows 95, its function is changed to that of providing pathways to other Windows files and supporting selected startup options.

multimedia   A term applied to a range of applications that bring together text, graphics, video, audio, and animation to provide interactivity between the computer and its human operator.

Multimedia Extensions (MMX) technology   An advanced Pentium microprocessor that includes specialized circuitry designed to manage multimedia operations. Its additional multimedia instructions speed up high-volume input/output needed for graphics, motion video, animation, and sound.

multitasking   The capability of a computer system to run two or more programs simultaneously.

N

National Television Standards Committee (NTSC)   This organization created the television standards in the United States, and is administered by the FCC.

near letter quality (NLQ)   A quality of printing nearly as good as an electric typewriter. The very best dot-matrix printers can produce NLQ.

Negative ACKnowledge (NAK)   A data communications code used by a receiver to tell the transmitter that the last message was not properly received.

NetBEUI (NetBIOS Extended User Interface)   The Microsoft networking protocol used with Windows-based systems.

NetBIOS   An emulation of IBM's NETwork Basic Input/Output System. NetBIOS represents the basic interface between the operating system and the LAN hardware. This function is implemented through ROM ICs, located on the network card.

NetWare   The Novell client/server network operating system.

Network Connection Wizard   Automated setup routine in Windows 2000 that can be invoked to guide the user through the process of creating a network connection.

Network Neighborhood   The Windows 95 utility used to browse and connect multiple networks to access shared resources on a server without having to map a network drive.

nibble   A 4-bit binary pattern, which can easily be converted into a single hexadecimal digit.

nonimpact printer   Any printer that does not form its characters by using a hammer device to impact the paper, ribbon, or embossed character.

nonmaskable interrupt (NMI)   A type of interrupt that cannot be ignored by the microprocessor during program execution. Three things can cause a nonmaskable interrupt to occur: (1) a numeric coprocessor installation error; (2) A RAM parity check error; (3) an I/O channel check error.

nonvolatile memory   Memory that is not lost after the power is turned off, such as ROM.

NT File System (NTFS)   The proprietary Windows NT file system. The NTFS structure is designed to provide better data security and to operate more efficiently with larger hard drives than FAT systems do. Its structure employs 64-bit entries to keep track of storage on the disk (as opposed to the 16- and 32-bit entries used in FAT and FAT32 systems).

NTDETECT   NTDETECT.COM is the Windows NT hardware-detection file. This file is responsible for collecting information about the system's installed hardware devices and passing it to the NTLDR program. This information is later used to upgrade the Windows NT Registry files.

NTLDR   NT Loader is the Windows NT Bootstrap Loader for Intel-based computers running Windows NT. It is the Windows NT equivalent of the DOS IO.SYS file and is responsible for loading the NT operating system into memory. Afterward, NTLDR passes control of the system over to the Windows NT operating system.

NTOSKRNL   NTOSKRNL.EXE is the Windows NT kernel file that contains the Windows NT core and loads its device drivers.

NTUSER.DAT   The Windows NT/2000 file that contains the User portion of the Windows NT Registry. This file contains the user-specific settings that have been established for this user. When a user logs on to the system, the User file and System hive portions of the Registry are used to construct the user-specific environment in the system.

null modem cable   A cable meeting the RS-232C specification, used to cross-connect two computers through their serial ports by transposing the transmit and receive lines. They must be physically located close to one another, eliminating the need for a modem.

O

odd parity   The form of parity checking in which the parity bit is used in order to make the total number of 1s contained in the character an odd number.

off-hook   A condition existing on a telephone line that is now capable of initiating an outgoing call, but unable to receive an incoming call.

offline   Any computer system or peripheral device that is not ready to operate, not connected, not turned on, or not properly configured.

on-hook   A condition that exists on any telephone line that is capable of receiving an incoming call.

online   Any computer system or peripheral device that is not only powered up, but also is ready to operate.

operating system   A special software program first loaded into a computer at power up and responsible for running it. The operating system also serves as the interface between the machine and other software applications.

optical mouse   A mouse that emits an infrared light stream to detect motion as it is moved around a special x-y matrix pad.

output device   Any peripheral device (such as a monitor, modem, or printer) that accepts computer output.

P

paging file   Also known as the swap file. The hidden file located on the hard disk that makes up half of the Windows 2000 virtual memory system. This file holds the programs and data that the operating system's virtual memory manager moves out of RAM memory and stores on to the disk as virtual memory.

parallel interface   The multiline channel through which the simultaneous transfer of one or more bytes occurs.

parallel mode   The mode of data transfer in which an entire word is transferred at once, from one location to another, by a set of parallel conductors.

parallel port   The external connector on a computer that is used to effect an interface between the computer and a parallel peripheral, such as a printer.

parity bit   Used for error checking during the sending and receiving of data within a system and from one system to another. The parity bit's value depends on how many 1 bits are contained in the byte it accompanies.

parity checking   A method to check for data-transmission errors by using a ninth bit to ensure that each character sent has an even (even parity) or odd (odd parity) number of logic 1s before transfer. The parity bit is checked for each byte sent.

parity error   This error occurs when a data transfer cannot be verified for integrity. At least one data bit or the parity bit has corrupted during the transfer process.

partition   A logical section of a hard disk. Partitioning allows a single, physical disk to be divided into multiple logical drives that can each hold a different operating system. Most disks contain a single partition that holds a single operating system.

Partition Boot Sector   The boot sector of that partition located in the first sector of the active partition. Here, the MBR finds the code to begin loading the Secondary Bootstrap Loader from the root directory of the boot drive.

partitioning   Partitioning establishes the logical structure of the hard disk in a format that conforms to the operating system being used with the computer. It is a function of the operating system being used. In the case of Microsoft operating systems, the FDISK utility is used to establish and manipulate partitions.

partition table   The table present at the start of every hard disk that describes the layout of the disk, including the number and location of all partitions on the disk.

passwords   Unique code patterns associated with a user's logon account that is used to access the resources of a network.

path   The location of the file on the disk in reference to the drive's root directory. The file's full path is specified by a logical drive letter and a listing of all directories between the root directory and the file.

PC bus   Refers to the bus architectures used in the first IBM PCs, the original 8-bit bus, and the 16-bit bus extension used with the AT.

peer-to-peer network   A network that does not have a centralized point of management and where each computer is equal to all the others. In this scenario, all the members can function as both clients and servers.

Peripheral Component Interconnect (PCI) bus   A low-cost, high-performance 32-/64-bit local bus developed jointly by IBM, Intel, DEC, NCR, and Compaq.

peripherals   Also called I/O devices, these units include secondary memory devices, such as hard disk drives, floppy disk drives, magnetic tape drives, modems, monitors, mice, joysticks, light pens, scanners, and even speakers.

permissions   A feature that enables security levels to be assigned to files and folders on the disk. These settings provide parameters for activities that users can conduct with the designated file or folder.

Personal Computer Memory Card International Association (PCMCIA) card   A credit-card–sized adapter card designed for use with portable computers. These cards slide into a PCMCIA slot and are used to implement modems, networks, and CD-ROM drives.

personal digital assistants (PDAs)   Handheld computing devices that typically include telephone, fax, and networking functions. A typical PDA can function as a cell phone, a fax, and a personal organizer. Most are pen-based devices that use a wand for input rather than a keyboard or mouse. PDAs are a member of the palmtop class of computers.

pin feed   A method of moving continuous forms through the print area of a printer by mounting pins on each side of a motorized platen to engage the holes on the right and left side of the paper.

PING Network troubleshooting utility command that is used to verify connections to remote hosts. The PING command sends Internet Control Message Packets to a remote location and then waits for echoed response packets to be returned. The command waits for up to one second for each packet sent and then displays the number of transmitted and received packets. The command can be used to test both the name and IP address of the remote unit. A number of switches can be used to set parameters for the ping operation.

pixel Also called a PEL, or picture element, it is the smallest unit (one dot for monochrome) into which a display image can be divided.

Plug and Play (PnP) A specification that requires the BIOS, operating system, and adapter cards to be designed so that the system automatically configures new hardware devices to eliminate system resource conflicts.

pointing device Any input device used for the specific purpose of moving the screen cursor or drawing an image.

Point-to-Point Protocol (PPP) A connection protocol that controls the transmission of data over the wide area network. PPP is the default protocol for the Microsoft Dial-Up adapter. In a dial-up situation, Internet software communicates with the service provider by embedding the TCP/IP information in a PPP shell for transmission through the modem in analog format. The communications equipment, at the ISP site, converts the signal back to the digital TCP/IP format. PPP has become the standard for remote access.

Point-to-Point Tunneling Protocol (PPTP) The de facto industry standard tunneling protocol first supported in Windows NT 4.0. PPTP is an extension of the Point-to-Point Protocol (PPP) and takes advantage of the authentication, compression, and encryption mechanisms of PPP. PPTP is installed with the Routing and Remote Access service. By default, PPTP is configured for five PPTP ports that can be enabled for inbound remote access and demand-dial routing connections through the Windows 2000 Routing and Remote Access Wizard. PPTP and Microsoft Point-to-Point Encryption (MPPE) provide the primary security technology to implement Virtual Private Network services of encapsulation and encryption of private data.

polarizer An optical device that either blocks or allows the passage of light through it, depending on the polarity of an electrical charge applied to it.

policies Network administrative settings that govern the rights and privileges of different users in multiuser operations.

PolEdit The system Policy Editor, used to establish or modify system policies, that governs user rights and privileges. The Policy Editor is another tool that can be used to access the information in the Registry. Unlike the RegEdit utility, however, PolEdit can access only subsets of keys. The Registry Editor can access the entire Registry.

polling A system of initiating data transfer between a computer system and a peripheral, in which the status of all the peripherals is examined periodically under software program control by having the microprocessor check the ready line. When it is activated by one of the peripherals, the processor begins the data transfer using the corresponding I/O port.

Power On Self Tests (POST) A group of ROM BIOS-based diagnostic tests performed on the system each time it is powered up. These tests check the PC's standard hardware devices, including the microprocessor, memory, interrupts, DMA, and video.

power supply The component in the system that converts the AC voltage from the wall outlet to the DC voltages required by the computer circuitry.

preventive maintenance   Any regularly scheduled checking and testing of hardware and software with the goal of avoiding future failure or breakdown.

primary domain controller (PDC)   Primary domain controllers contain the directory databases for the network. These databases contain information about user accounts, group accounts, and computer accounts. PDCs also are referred to as Security Accounts Managers.

primary partitions   Bootable partitions created from unallocated disk space. Under Windows 2000, up to four primary partitions can be created on a basic disk. The disk also can contain three primary partitions and an extended partition. The primary partition becomes the system's boot volume by being marked as Active. The free space in the extended partition can be subdivided into up to 23 logical drives.

printer   A peripheral device for the printing of computer text or graphics output.

printer font   A prescribed character set properly formatted for use by the printer.

profiles   Information about each user and group defined in the system that describes the resources and desktop configurations created for them. Settings in the profiles can be used to limit the actions users can perform, such as installing, removing, configuring, adjusting, or copying resources. When users log on to the system, it checks their profile and adjusts the system according to their information. This information is stored in the \WINNT\login_name\NTUSER.DAT file.

program   Any group of instructions designed to command a computer system through the performance of a specific task. Also called software.

Program Information Files (PIF)   Windows 3.x information files used to identify resources required for DOS-based applications.

programmed I/O   A system of initiating data transfer between a computer system and a peripheral, in which the microprocessor alerts the specific device by using an address call. The I/O device can signal its readiness to accept the data transfer by using its busy line. If busy is active, the microprocessor can perform other tasks until the busy line is deactivated; at which time, the transfer can begin.

prompt   A software-supplied message to the user, requiring some specific action or providing some important information. It also can be a simple symbol, indicating that the program is successfully loaded and waiting for a command from the user.

protected mode   An operational state that allows an 80286 or higher computer to address all of its memory, including that memory beyond the 1MB MS-DOS limit.

protocol   A set of rules that govern the transmitting and receiving of data communications.

Q

queue   A special and temporary storage (RAM or registers) area for data in printing or internal program execution operations.

quotas   Windows 2000 security settings that enable administrators to limit the amount of hard drive space users can have access to.

QWERTY keyboard   A keyboard layout that was originally designed to prevent typists from jamming old-style mechanical typewriters, it is still the standard English language keyboard. The name spells out the first six leftmost letters in the first alphabetic row of keys.

R

RAM disk An area of memory that has been set aside and assigned a drive letter to simulate the organization of a hard disk drive in RAM memory. Also referred to as a virtual disk.

random access memory (RAM) A type of semiconductor memory device that holds data on a temporary or volatile basis. Any address location in the RAM memory section can be accessed as fast as any other location.

raster graphics A graphics representation method that uses a dot matrix to compose the image.

raster scan The display of a video image, line by line, by an electron beam deflection system.

read-only (1) A file parameter setting that prevents a file from being altered. (2) Refers to data permanently stored on the media or to such media itself.

read-only memory (ROM) A type of semiconductor memory device that holds data on a permanent or non-volatile basis.

read/write head Usually abbreviated R/W head, the device by which a disk or tape drive senses and records digital data on the magnetic medium.

real mode A mode of operation in 80286 and higher machines in which the computer functions under the same command and addressing restrictions as an 8086 or 8088.

reboot To restart the computer or to reload the operating system.

Redundant Array of Inexpensive Disks (RAID) A set of specifications for configuring multiple hard drives to store data to increase storage capacity and improve performance. Some variations configure the drives in a manner to improve performance, whereas other levels concentrate on data security.

refresh A required way to re-energize a memory cell or display pixel so that its data is continually held.

Registry A multipart, hierarchical database established to hold system and user configuration information in Windows 9x, NT, and 2000.

Registry keys The Registries in Windows 9x, NT, and 2000 are organized into headkeys, subkeys, and values.

RegEdit The editing utility used to directly edit the contents of the Registry (`REGEDIT.EXE` and `REGEDIT32.EXE`). This file is located in the `WINNT\System32` folder.

RESET A control bus signal, activated either by a soft or hard switch, which sets the system microprocessor and all programmable system devices to their start-up, or initialization, values. This allows the computer to begin operation following the application of the RESET input signal.

resolution A measurement of the sharpness of an image or character—either of a printer or a display monitor. For a monitor, resolution consists of the number of dots per scan line, times the number of scans per picture. For a printer, resolution consists of the number of dots present per linear inch of print space.

ROM BIOS A collection of special programs (native intelligence) permanently stored in one or two ROM ICs installed on the system board. These programs are available to the system as soon as it is powered up, providing for initialization of smart chips, POST tests, and data-transfer control.

root directory The main directory of every logical disk. It follows the FAT tables and serves as the starting point for organizing information on the disk. The location of every directory, subdirectory, and file on the disk is recorded in this directory.

RS-232C The most widely used serial interface standard, it calls for a 25-pin D-type connector. Specific pins are designated for data transmission and receiving, as well as a number of handshaking and control lines. Logic voltage levels also are established for the data and the control signals on the pins of the connector.

RS-422 An enhancement to the original RS-232C interface standard and adopted by the EIA, it uses twisted-pair transmission lines and differential line voltage signals resulting in higher immunity for the transmitted data.

RS-423 Another enhancement to the original RS-232C interface standard and adopted by the EIA, it uses coaxial cable to provide extended transmission distances and higher data-transfer rates.

S

Safe mode A special Windows 95/98/2000 startup mode that starts the system by loading minimum configuration drivers. This mode is used to allow the correction of system errors when the system will not boot up normally. Safe mode is entered by pressing F5 or F8 when the Starting Windows message is displayed during bootup.

scan rate The total number of times per second that a video raster is horizontally scanned by the CRT's electron beam.

sector One of many individual data-holding areas into which each track of a disk is divided during the format process.

serial interface A channel through which serial digital data transfer occurs. Although multiple lines can be used, only one of these will actually carry the data. The most popular serial interface standard is the EIA RS-232C.

Serial Line Internet Protocol (SLIP) Older units running UNIX employ this Internet connection protocol for dial-up services. The protocol wraps the TCP/IP packet in a shell for transmission through the modem in analog format. The communications equipment, at the service provider's site, converts the signal back to the digital TCP/IP format.

serial mode The mode of data transfer in which the word bits are transferred one bit at a time, along a single conductor.

serial mouse A type of mouse that plugs in to a serial port rather than an adapter card.

serial port The external connector on a computer that is used to effect an interface between the computer and a serial device such as a modem. A typical serial port uses a DB-25 or a DB-9 connector.

servers Powerful network computers (or devices) that contain the network operating system and manage network resources for other computers (clients). Some servers take on special management functions for the network. Some of these functions include print servers, Web servers, file servers, database servers, and so on.

setup disks Disks created to get a failed Windows NT/2000 system restarted. These disks are created by the Windows 2000 Backup utility and contain information about the system's current Windows configuration settings.

shadow RAM An area of RAM used for copying the system's BIOS routines from ROM. Making BIOS calls from the RAM area improves the operating speed of the system. Video ROM routines are often stored in shadow RAM also.

shared resources A system resource (device or directory) that has been identified as being available for use by multiple individuals throughout the network environment.

shares   Resources, such as printers and folders, that are made available for use by other network users.

simplex communications   Communications that occur only in one direction. A public address system is an example of simplex communications.

single in-line memory module (SIMM)   A memory chip, circuit board module, containing eight (without parity) or nine (with parity) memory chips, and designed to plug in to special sockets.

Small Computer System Interface (SCSI) bus   A system-level interface standard used to connect different types of peripheral equipment to the system. The standard actually exists as a group of specifications (SCSI, SCSI-2, and SCSI-3) featuring several cabling connector schemes. Even within these three specifications, major variations can exist: Wide SCSI, Fast SCSI, and Fast/Wide SCSI. Apple was the first personal computer maker to select the SCSI interface as the bus standard for peripheral equipment that can provide high-speed, data-transfer control for up to seven devices while occupying only one expansion slot. The standard is gaining widespread support in the PC market, particularly in the area of portable PCs. See system-level interface.

SMARTDRV.EXE (SmartDrive)   A DOS driver program that establishes a disk cache in an area of extended memory as a storage space for information read from the hard disk drive. When a program requests more data, the SMARTDRV program redirects the request to check in the cache memory area to see whether the requested data is there.

software   Any aspect of the computer operation that cannot be physically touched. This includes bits, bytes, words, and programs.

speaker   The computer system's audio output device. Measuring 2 1/4 inches in diameter, and rated at 8 ohms, 1/2 watts, the speaker is usually used as a system prompt, and as an error indicator. It also can produce arcade sounds, speech, and music.

start bit   In asynchronous serial data transmission, this bit denotes the beginning of a character and is always a logic low pulse, or space.

static electricity   A stationary charge of electricity normally caused by friction and potentially very damaging to sensitive electronic components. It can be a serious problem in environments of low humidity.

static random-access memory (SRAM)   A type of RAM that can store its data indefinitely, as long as power to it is not interrupted.

stop bit   The bit, sent after each character in an asynchronous data-communications transmission, that signals the end of a character.

Stop errors   Errors that occur when Windows 2000 detects a condition from which it cannot recover. The system stops responding, and a screen of information with a blue, or black, background displays. Stop errors are also known as Blue Screen errors, or the Blue Screen of Death (BSOD).

subnet mask   The decimal number 255 is used to hide, or mask, the network portion of the IP address while still showing the host portions of the address. The default subnet mask for Class A IP addresses is 255.0.0.0. Class B is 255.255.0.0, and Class C is 255.255.255.0.

swap file   A special file established on the hard drive to provide virtual memory capabilities for the operating system. Windows 3.*x* can work with temporary or permanent swap files. Windows 95 uses a dynamically assigned, variable-length swap file.

synchronous transmission A method of serial data transmission in which both the transmitter and the receiver are synchronized by a common clock signal.

SYSEDIT.EXE A special Windows text editor utility that can be used to alter ASCII text files, such as CONFIG.SYS, AUTOEXEC.BAT, WIN.INI, and SYSTEM.INI files.

system board The large printed circuit board (motherboard) into which peripheral adapter boards (daughter boards) can plug in to, depending on the number of devices working with the system. The system board is populated with 100 or more IC chips, depending on how much onboard memory is installed. Besides RAM chips, the system board contains the microprocessor, BIOS ROM, several programmable controllers, system clock circuitry, switches, and various jumpers. Also, most system boards come with an empty socket into which the user can plug a compatible co-processor chip to give the computer some high-level number-crunching capabilities.

system files Files that possess the System attribute. These are normally hidden files used to boot the operating system.

system-level interface An interface that allows the system to directly access the I/O device through an expansion slot without an intermediate interface circuit. The system is isolated from the peripheral device and sees only its logical configuration.

system partitions Normally the same as the boot partition. More precisely, the disk partition that contains the hardware-specific files (NTLDR, OSLOADER, BOOT.INI, and NTDETECT) required to load and start Windows 2000.

system software A class of software dedicated to the control and operation of a computer system and its various peripherals.

system unit The main computer cabinet housing containing the primary components of the system. This includes the main logic board (system- or motherboard), disk drive(s), switching power supply, and the interconnecting wires and cables.

T

tape drive The unit that actually reads, writes, and holds the tape being used for backup purposes.

task switching The changing of one program or application to another either manually by the user or under the direction of a multitasking operating system environment.

telephony In the computer world, this term is used to refer to hardware and software devices that perform functions typically performed by telephone equipment. Microsoft offers the TAPI interface for both clients and servers. See Telephony API.

Telephony API (TAPI, Telephony Application Programming Interface) This software interface provides a universal set of drivers that enable modems and COM ports to control and arbitrate telephony operations for data, faxes, and voice. Through this interface, applications can cooperatively share the dial-up connections functions of the system.

TCP/IP (Transfer Control Protocol/Internet Protocol) A collection of protocols developed by the U. S. Department of Defense in the early days of the network that would become the Internet. It is the standard transport protocol used by many operating systems and the Internet.

toner A form of powdered ink that accepts an electrical charge in laser printers and photocopying machines. It adheres to a rotating drum containing an image that is given an opposite charge. The image is transferred to paper during the printing process.

TRACERT   A network troubleshooting utility that displays the route and a hop count taken to a given destination. The route taken to a particular address can be set manually using the ROUTE command. The TRACERT utility traces the route taken by ICMP packets sent across the network. Routers along the path return information to the inquiring system and the utility displays the host name, IP address, and round-trip time for each hop in the path.

track   A single disk or tape data-storage channel, upon which the R/W head places the digital data in a series of flux reversals. On disks, the track is a concentric data circle; whereas on tapes, it is a parallel data line.

trackball   (1) A pointing device that enables the user to control the position of the cursor on the video display screen by rotating a sphere (trackball). (2) The sphere inside certain types of mice that the mouse rides on. As the mouse moves across a surface, the trackball rolls, creating x-y movement data.

tractor feed   A paper-feeding mechanism for printers that use continuous forms. The left and right edges of the forms contain holes through which the tractor pins pull the paper through the print area.

transmit   Although this term usually means to send data between a transmitter and receiver over a specific communications line, it can also describe the transfer of data within the internal buses of a computer or between the computer and its peripheral devices.

Transport Control Protocol (TCP)   TCP is a transport layer protocol used to establish reliable connections between clients and servers.

trees   In Active Directory, a collection of objects that share the same DNS name. All the domains in a tree share a common security context and global catalog.

troubleshooters   A special type of Help utilities available in Windows 9x and 2000. These utilities enable the user to pinpoint problems and identify solutions to those problems by asking a series of questions and then providing detailed troubleshooting information based on the user responses.

U

Ultra DMA   A burst-mode DMA data transfer protocol used with Ultra ATA IDE devices to support data transfer rates of 33.3Mbps. Although the official name of the protocol is Ultra DMA/33, it is also referred to as UDMA, UDMA/33, and DMA mode 33.

Ultra SCSI   A series of advanced SCSI specifications that include (1) Ultra SCSI, which employs an 8-bit bus and supports data rates of 20Mbps; (2) SCSI-3 (also referred to as Ultra Wide SCSI), which widens the bus to 16 bits and supports data rates of 40Mbps; (3) Ultra2 SCSI, which uses an 8-bit bus and supports data rates of 40Mbps; and (4) Wide Ultra2 SCSI, which supports data rates of 80Mbps across a 16-bit bus.

uniform resource locator (URL)   A unique address on the World Wide Web used to access a Web site.

uninterruptible power supply (UPS)   A special power-supply unit that includes a battery to maintain power to key equipment in the event of a power failure. A typical UPS is designed to keep a computer operational after a power failure long enough for the user to save his or her current work and properly shut down the system. Many UPSs include software that provides automatic backup and shutdown procedures when the UPS senses a power problem.

Universal Asynchronous Receiver/Transmitter (UART)   A serial interface IC used to provide for the parallel-to-serial and serial-to-parallel conversions required for asynchronous serial data transmission. It also handles the parallel interface to the computer's bus, as well as the control functions associated with the transmission.

Universal Naming Convention (UNC)   A standardized way to specify a path to a network computer or a device (for instance, \\Computername\Sharename).

Universal Serial Bus (USB)   A specification for a high-speed, serial communication bus that can be used to link various peripheral devices to the system. The standard permits up to 127 USB-compliant devices to be connected to the system in a daisy chained or tiered-star configuration.

Universal Synchronous Asynchronous Receiver/Transmitter (USART)   A serial interface IC used to provide for the parallel-to-serial and serial-to-parallel conversions required for both asynchronous and synchronous serial data transmission. It also handles the parallel interface to the computer's bus, as well as the control functions associated with the transmission.

upgrading   The process of replacing an older piece of hardware or software with a newer version of that hardware or software. Upgrading also serves as an interim solution for bugs discovered in software.

upper memory area (UMA)   The area in the DOS memory map between 640KB and 1MB. This memory area was referred to as the reserved memory area in older PC and PC-XT systems. It typically contains the EMS page frame, as well as any ROM extensions and video display circuitry.

upper memory blocks (UMBs)   Special 16KB blocks of memory established in the upper memory area between the 640KB and 1MB marks.

user profiles   User profiles are records that permit each user who logs on to a computer to have a unique set of properties associated with him, such as particular desktop or Start menu configurations. In Windows 2000, user profiles are stored in C:\Documents and Settings by default. User profiles are local, meaning that they reside only on that computer. Therefore, users can have different profiles created and stored for them on each computer they log on to.

username   The public portion of the user logon name that identifies permissions and rights to network resources.

utility program   A term used to describe a program designed to help the user in the operation of the computer.

V

very large scale integration (VLSI)   IC devices containing a very large number of electronic components (from 100,000 to 1,000,000 approximately).

video adapter   Sometimes referred to as a display adapter, graphics adapter, or graphics card, it is a plug-in peripheral unit for computers, fitting in one of the system board option slots and providing the interface between the computer and the display. The adapter usually must match the type of display (digital or analog) with which it is used.

Video Electronics Standards Association (VESA) bus   A 64-bit local bus standard developed to provide a local bus connection to a video adapter. Its operation has been defined for use by other adapter types, such as drive controllers, network interfaces, and other hardware.

Video Graphics Array (VGA)   Another video standard, developed by IBM, providing medium and high text and graphics resolution. It was originally designed for IBM's high-end PS/2 line, but other vendors have created matching boards for PC and AT machines also, making it the preferred standard at this time. Requiring an analog monitor, it originally provided 16 colors at 640x480 resolution. Third-party vendors have boosted that capability to 256 colors, while adding an even greater 800x600 resolution, calling it Super VGA.

View menu   A Windows 2000 dialog box drop-down menu option enables the user to toggle screen displays between Large and Small Icons, Details, and Thumbnail views. The dialog boxes can be resized to accommodate as many thumbnail images as desired.

virtual disk   A method of using RAM as if it were a disk.

virtual memory   A memory technique that allows several programs to run simultaneously, even though the system does not have enough actual memory installed to do this. The extra memory is simulated using disk space.

Virtual Memory Manager (VMM)   The section of the Windows 9*x*, NT, and 2000 structure that assigns unique memory spaces to every active 32-bit and 16-bit DOS/Windows 3.*x* application. The VMM works with the environmental subsystems of the user mode to establish special environments for the 16-bit applications to run in.

virtual private network (VPN)   Virtual private networks use message encryption and other security techniques to ensure that only authorized users can intercept and access the message as it passes through public transmission media. In particular, VPNs provide secure Internet communications by establishing encrypted data tunnels across the WAN that cannot be penetrated by others.

virus   A destructive program designed to replicate itself on any machine that it comes into contact with. Viruses are spread from machine to machine by attaching themselves to (infect) other files.

volatile memory   Memory (RAM) that loses its contents as soon as power is discontinued.

volumes   Portions of disks signified by single drive designators. In the Microsoft environment, a volume corresponds to a partition.

volt ohm millimeter (VOM)   A basic piece of electronic troubleshooting equipment that provides for circuit measurements of voltage, current, and resistance in logarithmic analog readout form.

W

warm boot   Booting a computer that has already been powered up. This can be accomplished by pressing the Reset switch on the front of most computers or by selecting one of the Restart options from the Windows Exit Options dialog box.

Web sites   A location on the World Wide Web. Web sites typically contain a home page that displays when the site is accessed. It likely contains other pages and programs that can be accessed through the home page.

wildcards   Characters, such as * or ?, used to represent letters or words. Such characters are typically used to perform operations with multiple files.

Windows   A graphical user interface from Microsoft Corporation. It uses a graphical display to represent procedures and programs that can be executed by the computer. Multiple programs can run at the same time.

Windows Explorer   The Windows 95, Windows 98, and Windows NT/2000 utility that graphically displays the system as drives, folders, and files in a hierarchical tree structure. This enables the user to manipulate all the system's software using a mouse.

WINNT32   WINNT.EXE or WINNT32.EXE are the programs that can be run to initiate the installation of Windows 2000. The WINNT32.EXE program is designed to run under a 32-bit operating system and will not run from the command line. The WINNT.EXE program is designed to run under a 16-bit operating system and will not run from within a 32-bit operating system such as Windows NT.

WINS   A Microsoft-specific naming service that can be used to assign IP addresses to computer domain names within a LAN environment. The LAN must include a Windows NT name server running the WINS server software that maintains the IP address/domain name database for the LAN. Each client in the LAN must contain the WINS client software and be WINS enabled.

wizards   Special Windows routines designed to lead users through installation or setup operation using a menu style of selecting options. The wizards carry out these tasks in the proper sequence, requesting information from the user at key points in the process.

word   Refers to the amount of data that can be held in a computer's registers during a process, and is considered to be the computer's basic storage unit.

workgroups   A network control scenario in which all the nodes might act as servers for some processes and clients for others. In a workgroup environment, each machine maintains its own security and administration databases.

x-axis   (1) In a two-dimensional matrix, the horizontal row/rows such as on an oscilloscope screen. (2) The dimension of width in a graphics representation.

Xmodem   A very early and simple asynchronous data communications protocol developed for personal computers, and capable of detecting some transfer errors, but not all.

XON-XOFF   An asynchronous data communications protocol that provides for synchronization between the receiver and transmitter, requiring the receiver to indicate its capability to accept data by sending either an XON (transmit on-buffer ready) or XOFF (transmit off-buffer full) signal to the transmitter.

x-y matrix   Any two-dimensional form or image, where x represents width and y represents height.

y-axis   (1) In a two-dimensional matrix, the vertical column/columns such as on an oscilloscope screen. (2) The dimension of height in a graphics representation.

Ymodem   An improvement of the Xmodem protocol that increases the data block size from 128 bytes to 1,024 bytes. An off-shoot known as Ymodem Batch includes filenames in the transmission so that multiple files can be sent in a single transmission. Another variation, labeled Ymodem G, modified the normal Ymodem flow-control method to speed up transmissions.

Z

Zmodem   This dial-up protocol can be used to transmit both text and binary files (such as EXE files across telephone lines, not the Internet). It employs advanced error-checking/correcting schemes and provides Autofile Restart crash-recovery techniques.

Overview of the Certification Process

You must pass two certification exams to become an A+ certified technician. The Core Hardware Service Technician component is covered by exam number 220-201 and the Operating System Technologies component is covered by exam number 220-202. These closed-book exams provide a valid and reliable measure of your technical proficiency and expertise. Developed in consultation with computer-industry professionals who have on-the-job experience with multivendor hardware and software products in the workplace, the exams are conducted by two independent organizations, VUE and Prometric. VUE has more than 3,000 authorized testing centers serving more than 100 countries. Prometric has more than 4,800 testing centers.

The exam prices vary depending on your CompTIA member status:

> CompTIA members: $89 each
>
> Non-CompTIA members: $139 each

To schedule an exam, call VUE at 877-551-7587. You can also contact VUE or locate a convenient testing center through its Web site at www.vue.com. Schedule and exam with Prometric at 800-77-MICRO or www.prometric.com/default.asp.

ABOUT THE A+ CERTIFICATION PROGRAM

The A+ Certification is an internationally recognized industry-standard certification designed to measure the competency of an entry-level technician. Entry level in this case is defined as the equivalent knowledge of a technician with six months experience in a support role. This certification is attained by passing the two tests within 90 days of each other. Each of these tests covers a separate series of objectives, as described in this book's introduction.

The Computing and Technology Industry Association (CompTIA) developed the A+ Certification in response to several factors—not the least of which was the growing need for computer hardware and software manufacturers to create a standard curriculum. Prior to this standard, each manufacturer created individual lower-level courses to provide a logical path to their own product offerings. This caused entry-level courses to be duplicated by various manufacturers, albeit in many different ways and with many different results.

CompTIA itself provides the following reasons for the creation of the A+ Certification:

◆ To set an industry-wide, nationally recognized standard of basic competency levels in the field of computer service

◆ To maximize efficiency in recruiting, hiring, training, and promoting employees

◆ To help meet the needs of today's information technology workforce by providing individuals with in-demand skills

◆ To give job seekers identifiable career paths, transferable skills, and industry-recognized credentials

◆ To give educators and trainers the standards necessary to better prepare individuals to meet today's job-skill requirements

The A+ Certification has undergone a few changes since its inception. The most recent changes (the January 31, 2001 version) include dropping the Windows 3.*x* operating information from the test and upgrading the Operating System Technologies exam to include Windows 98 and Windows 2000 Professional questions. The Core Hardware Service Technician exam now includes a larger base of questions relating to newer bus systems and new hardware additions (such as the Intel Pentium III processor and its clones, as well as the IEEE-1394 FireWire bus specifications). Also, the customer satisfaction objectives have been removed from the Core Hardware Service Technician exam.

You might be asking why this exam is for you, and why now. Aside from joining the swelling ranks of A+ certified technicians (more than 260,000 members and ris-

ing), the A+ program gives you access to the CompTIA organization and to the benefits this access affords. CompTIA's Web site, for instance, identifies the following benefits for prospective A+ technicians:

◆ Recognized proof of professional achievement—A level of competence commonly accepted and valued by the industry.

◆ Enhanced job opportunities—Many employers give preference in hiring to applicants with certification. They view this as proof that a new hire knows the procedures and technologies required.

◆ Opportunity for advancement—The certification can be a plus when an employer awards job advancements and promotions.

◆ Training requirement—Certification might be required as a prerequisite to attending a vendor's training course, so employers will offer advance training to those employees who are already certified.

◆ Customer confidence—As the general public learns about certification, customers will require that only certified technicians be assigned to their accounts.

For any additional information or clarification of the CompTIA A+ Certification path and its history and benefits, consult the CompTIA home page at www.comptia.org.

What's on the CD-ROM

This appendix is a brief rundown of what you'll find on the CD-ROM that comes with this book. For a more detailed description of the *PrepLogic Practice Tests, Preview Edition* exam simulation software, see Appendix D, "Using the *PrepLogic Practice Tests, Preview Edition* Software." In addition to the *PrepLogic Practice Tests, Preview Edition*, the CD-ROM includes the electronic version of the book in Portable Document Format (PDF), several utility and application programs, and a complete listing of test objectives and where they are covered in the book. Finally, a pointer list to online pointers and references are added to this CD. You will need a computer with Internet access and relatively recent browser installed to use this feature.

PREPLOGIC PRACTICE TESTS, PREVIEW EDITION

PrepLogic is a leading provider of certification training tools. Trusted by certification students worldwide, PrepLogic is, we believe, the best practice exam software available. In addition to providing a means of evaluating your knowledge of the Training Guide material, *PrepLogic Practice Tests, Preview Edition* features several innovations that help you to improve your mastery of the subject matter.

For example, the practice tests allow you to check your score by exam area or domain to determine which topics you need to study more. Another feature allows you to obtain immediate feedback on your responses in the form of explanations for the correct and incorrect answers.

PrepLogic Practice Tests, Preview Edition exhibits most of the full functionality of the *Premium Edition* but offers only a fraction of the total questions. To get the complete set of practice questions and exam functionality, visit PrepLogic.com and order the *Premium Edition* for this and other challenging exam titles.

Again, for a more detailed description of the *PrepLogic Practice Tests, Preview Edition* features, see Appendix D.

EXCLUSIVE ELECTRONIC VERSION OF TEXT

The CD-ROM also contains the electronic version of this book in PDF. This electronic version comes complete with all figures as they appear in the book. You will find that the search capabilities of the reader come in handy for study and review purposes.

Easy Access to Online Pointers and References

The Suggested Reading section at the end of each chapter in this Training Guide, as well as Appendix B, "Overview of the Certification Process," contain numerous pointers to Web sites, newsgroups, mailing lists, and other online resources. To make this material as easy to use as possible, we include all this information in an HTML document entitled "Online Pointers" on the CD. Open this document in your favorite Web browser to find links you can follow through any Internet connection to access these resources directly.

Using the *PrepLogic Practice Tests, Preview Edition* Software

This Training Guide includes a special version of PrepLogic Practice Tests—a revolutionary test engine designed to give you the best in certification exam preparation. PrepLogic offers sample and practice exams for many of today's most in-demand and challenging technical certifications. This special Preview Edition is included with this book as a tool to use in assessing your knowledge of the Training Guide material while also providing you with the experience of taking an electronic exam.

This appendix describes in detail what *PrepLogic Practice Tests, Preview Edition* is, how it works, and what it can do to help you prepare for the exam. Note that although the Preview Edition includes all the test simulation functions of the complete, retail version, it contains only a single practice test. The Premium Edition, available at PrepLogic.com, contains the complete set of challenging practice exams designed to optimize your learning experience.

EXAM SIMULATION

One of the main functions of *PrepLogic Practice Tests, Preview Edition* is exam simulation. To prepare you to take the actual vendor certification exam, PrepLogic is designed to offer the most effective exam simulation available.

Question Quality

The questions provided in the *PrepLogic Practice Tests, Preview Edition* are written to highest standards of technical accuracy. The questions tap the content of the Training Guide chapters and help you review and assess your knowledge before you take the actual exam.

Interface Design

The *PrepLogic Practice Tests, Preview Edition* exam simulation interface provides you with the experience of taking an electronic exam. This enables you to effectively prepare for taking the actual exam by making the test experience a familiar one. Using this test simulation can help eliminate the sense of surprise or anxiety you might experience in the testing center because you will already be acquainted with computerized testing.

Effective Learning Environment

The *PrepLogic Practice Tests, Preview Edition* interface provides a learning environment that not only tests you through the computer, but also teaches the material you need to know to pass the certification exam.

Each question comes with a detailed explanation of the correct answer and often provides reasons the other options are incorrect. This information helps to reinforce the knowledge you already have and also provides practical information you can use on the job.

SOFTWARE REQUIREMENTS

PrepLogic Practice Tests requires a computer with the following:

◆ Microsoft Windows 98, Windows Me, Windows NT 4.0, Windows 2000, or Windows XP

◆ A 166MHz or faster processor is recommended.

◆ A minimum of 32MB of RAM

◆ As with any Windows application, the more memory, the better your performance.

◆ 10MB of Hard Drive space

Installing *PrepLogic Practice Tests, Preview Edition*

Install *PrepLogic Practice Tests, Preview Edition* by running the setup program on the *PrepLogic Practice Tests, Preview Edition* CD. Follow these instructions to install the software on your computer.

◆ Insert the CD into your CD-ROM drive. The Autorun feature of Windows should launch the software. If you have Autorun disabled, click Start and select Run. Go to the root directory of the CD and select setup.exe. Click Open, and then click OK.

◆ The Installation Wizard copies the *PrepLogic Practice Tests, Preview Edition* files to your hard drive; adds *PrepLogic Practice Tests, Preview Edition* to your Desktop and Program menu; and installs test engine components to the appropriate system folders.

Removing *PrepLogic Practice Tests, Preview Edition* from Your Computer

If you elect to remove the *PrepLogic Practice Tests, Preview Edition* product from your computer, an uninstall process has been included to ensure that it is removed from your system safely and completely. Follow these instructions to remove *PrepLogic Practice Tests, Preview Edition* from your computer:

◆ Select Start, Settings, Control Panel.

◆ Double-click the Add/Remove Programs icon.

◆ You are presented with a list of software installed on your computer. Select the appropriate *PrepLogic Practice Tests, Preview Edition* title you want to remove. Click the Add/Remove button. The software is then removed from your computer.

USING *PREPLOGIC PRACTICE TESTS, PREVIEW EDITION*

PrepLogic is designed to be user friendly and intuitive. Because the software has a smooth learning curve, your time is maximized because you start practicing almost immediately. *PrepLogic Practice Tests, Preview Edition* has two major modes of study: Practice Test and Flash Review.

Using Practice Test mode, you can develop your test-taking abilities as well as your knowledge through the use of the Show Answer option. While you are taking the test, you can expose the answers along with a detailed explanation of why the given answers are right or wrong. This gives you the ability to better understand the material presented.

Flash Review is designed to reinforce exam topics rather than quiz you. In this mode, you will be shown a series of questions but no answer choices. Instead, you will be given a button that reveals the correct answer to the question and a full explanation for that answer.

Starting a Practice Test Mode Session

Practice Test mode enables you to control the exam experience in ways that actual certification exams do not allow:

◆ **Enable Show Answer Button**—Activates the Show Answer button allowing you to view the correct answer(s) and full explanation for each question during the exam. When not enabled, you must wait until after your exam has been graded to view the correct answer(s) and explanation.

◆ **Enable Item Review Button**—Activates the Item Review button allowing you to view your answer choices, marked questions, and facilitating navigation between questions.

To begin studying in Practice Test mode, click the Practice Test radio button from the main exam customization screen. This will enable the options detailed above.

To your left, you are presented with the option of selecting the preconfigured Practice Test or creating your own Custom Test. The preconfigured test has a fixed time limit and number of questions. Custom Tests allow you to configure the time limit and the number of questions in your exam.

The Preview Edition included with this book includes a single preconfigured Practice Test. Get the compete set of challenging PrepLogic Practice Tests at PrepLogic.com and make certain you're ready for the big exam.

Click the Begin Exam button to begin your exam.

Starting a Flash Review Mode Session

Flash Review mode provides you with an easy way to reinforce topics covered in the practice questions. To begin studying in Flash Review mode, click the Flash Review radio button from the main exam customization screen. Select either the preconfigured Practice Test or create your own Custom Test.

Click the Best Exam button to begin your Flash Review of the exam questions.

Standard *PrepLogic Practice Tests, Preview Edition* Options

The following list describes the function of each of the buttons you see. Depending on the options, some of the buttons will be grayed out and inaccessible or missing completely. Buttons that are appropriate are active. The buttons are as follows:

◆ **Exhibit**—This button is visible if an exhibit is provided to support the question. An exhibit is an image that provides supplemental information necessary to answer the question.

◆ **Item Review**—This button leaves the question window and opens the Item Review screen. From this screen you will see all questions, your answers, and your marked items. You will also see correct answers listed here when appropriate.

◆ **Show Answer**—This option displays the correct answer with an explanation of why it is correct. If you select this option, the current question is not scored.

◆ **Mark Item**—Check this box to tag a question you need to review further. You can view and navigate your Marked Items by clicking the Item Review button (if enabled). When grading your exam, you will be notified if you have marked items remaining.

◆ **Previous Item**—View the previous question.

◆ **Next Item**—View the next question.

◆ **Grade Exam**—When you have completed your exam, click to end your exam and view your detailed score report. If you have unanswered or marked items remaining, you will be asked if you would like to continue taking your exam or view your exam report.

Time Remaining

If the test is timed, the time remaining is displayed on the upper-right corner of the application screen. It counts down minutes and seconds remaining to complete the test. If you run out of time, you will be asked if you want to continue taking the test or if you want to end your exam.

Your Examination Score Report

The Examination Score Report screen appears when the Practice Test mode ends—as the result of time expiration, completion of all questions, or your decision to terminate early.

This screen provides you with a graphical display of your test score with a breakdown of scores by topic domain. The graphical display at the top of the screen compares your overall score with the PrepLogic Exam Competency Score.

The PrepLogic Exam Competency Score reflects the level of subject competency required to pass this vendor's exam. While this score does not directly translate to a passing score, consistently matching or exceeding this score does suggest you possess the knowledge to pass the actual vendor exam.

Review Your Exam

From Your Score Report screen, you can review the exam that you just completed by clicking on the View Items button. Navigate through the items viewing the questions, your answers, the correct answers, and the explanations for those questions. You can return to your score report by clicking the View Items button.

Get More Exams

Each *PrepLogic Practice Tests, Preview Edition* that accompanies your training guide contains a single PrepLogic Practice Test. Certification students worldwide trust PrepLogic Practice Tests to help them pass their IT certification exams the first time. Purchase the Premium Edition of PrepLogic Practice Tests and get the entire set of all new challenging Practice Tests for this exam. PrepLogic Practice Tests—Because You Want to Pass the First Time.

CONTACTING PREPLOGIC

If you would like to contact PrepLogic for any reason including information about our extensive line of certification practice tests, we invite you to do so. Please contact us online at www.preplogic.com.

Customer Service

If you have a damaged product and need a replacement or refund, please call the following phone number:

800-858-7674

Product Suggestions and Comments

We value your input! Please email your suggestions and comments to the following address:

feedback@preplogic.com

LICENSE AGREEMENT

YOU MUST AGREE TO THE TERMS AND CONDITIONS OUTLINED IN THE END USER LICENSE AGREEMENT ("EULA") PRESENTED TO YOU DURING THE INSTALLATION PROCESS. IF YOU DO NOT AGREE TO THESE TERMS, DO NOT INSTALL THE SOFTWARE.

Index

SYMBOLS

A

applications
  AutoPlay function (Windows 9x), 797
  DOS-based, 798-800
  installing
    Windows 2000 applications, 800-801
    Windows NT applications, 800
APPS.INF file, 798
ARP (Address Resolution Protocol) utility, 944
ASCII (American Standard Code for Information Interchange), 1036
ASD (Automatic Skip Driver) utility, 708, 837
ASICs (Application-Specific Integrated Circuits), 32, 1036
ASKIR, 136
ASPICD.SYS file, 776, 987
asynchronous SRAM, 412
asynchronous transfer method, 154, 1036
AT Attachment (ATA) interface. See IDE devices
AT Attachment Packet Interface. See ATAPI
AT buses. See ISA (Industry Standard Architecture) buses
AT command set, 294-300
  Command mode, 294-295
  Communications mode, 294-295
  entering at command line, 295
  result codes, 297-299
  summary of, 295-297
  using, 299-300
AT form factor, 24-25, 28, 432-434
  ports, 147-151
  system board connectors, 36, 443-444
ATA (AT Attachment). See IDE devices
ATA-2 devices. See EIDE devices
ATA-3 devices, 177
ATA-4 devices, 178, 449-450
ATAPI, 177
ATDT*70 command, 300
Athlon CPUs, 389-390
ATTRIB command, 666, 838, 981, 990, 1036
attributes (file), 1036
  changing, 666, 982

ATX form factor, 28, 431-432, 1036
  mini-ATX specification, 431
  ports, 150-151
  power supply, 431-432
  system board connectors, 35, 445
  USB connectors, 134-135
ATZ command, 299
audio output devices. See speakers
Auto Detect option (BIOS), 466
AUTOCHK, 770
AUTOEXEC.BAT file, 584-585, 763, 1036
  error messages, 830
  MOUSE.COM driver file, 264
Automatic Skip Driver (ASD) utility, 708, 837
AutoPlay function (Windows applications), 797

B

B-cables, 179
Baby AT form factor, 430-432
back lighting, 55
backside buses, 436
Backup Domain Controllers (BDCs), 604-605, 1036
Backup utility, 346, 702-703, 983, 1037
backups, 702-704, 983-984, 1036
  Windows NT Registry, 611
"Bad File Allocation" error message, 328
"Bad or Missing Command Interpreter" error message, 328, 825, 828-829, 989
bandwidth, 418
Base-2 numbering system, 136-137
Base-16 numbering system, 136-137
basic disks, 695-696
Basic Input/Output System. See BIOS
basic volumes, 695, 697-699
.BAT file extension, 1037
batteries
  CMOS backup batteries, troubleshooting, 260, 465-466
  disposal procedures, 365

J-K

M

power-supply units, 28, 35-36, 1056
  ATX form factor, 431-432
  high-voltage hazards, 362-364
  installing, 93-94
  portable PCs, 107-108
  removing, 92-93
  SCSI devices, 180
  soft switch, 36
  surge suppressors, 359
  system board compatibility, 434
  troubleshooting, 251-252
    AC voltage readings, 321
    DC voltage readings, 319-320
    dot-matrix printers, 512
    laser printers, 520-521
  UPS (uninterruptible power supply), 359-361
  wattage ratings, 93
PPGA (Plastic Pin Grid Array), 370
  specification, 387
PPP (Point-to-Point Protocol), 924, 1056
PPTP (Point-to-Point Tunneling Protocol), 1056
Practice Test mode (PrepLogic Practice Tests), 1073
  customized tests, 1073
  Enable Item Review button, 1073
  Enable Show Answer button, 1073
  preconfigured tests, 1073
  starting, 1073
PrepLogic, contacting, 1075
PrepLogic Exam Competency Score, 1074
PrepLogic Practice Tests
  Examination Score Report, 1074
  Installation Wizard, 1072
  installing, 1072
  interface design, 1071
  obtaining additional exams, 1074
  options, 1073-1074
  PrepLogic Exam Competency Score, 1074
  reviewing test scores, 1074
  reviewing your exam, 1074
  Score Report, 1074
  software requirements, 1072
  study modes, 1072
  timed tests, 1074
  uninstalling, 1072
"Press F1 to Continue" error message, 327
preventive maintenance, 1057
  cleaning procedures, 339-340
  dust buildup, 341
  fast facts for, 966-968
  floppy disk drives, 346-347
  hard disk drives, 344-346
  heat buildup, 342-343
  input devices, 347-348
  monitors, 343
  printers, 525-526
Primary Bootstrap Loader, 1038
primary cache. *See* L1 cache
primary corona wires (laser printers), 494
Primary Domain Controllers (PDCs), 604-605, 1057
primary hard disk drive partitions, 103
Primary IDE interface, 177
Primary Network Logon window, 893
primary partitions, 686-687, 1057
Print Manager (Windows), 802-803, 988
print queue, 803
Print Server ports, 499
print servers, 989, 992
print sharing, 499
print spooler
  Windows 9x, 802-803
  Windows 2000, 804-805
Print Troubleshooter (Windows 9x), 284
"Printer Not Ready" error message, 497
PRINTER.SYS file, 584
printers, 26, 1057. *See also* printing
  cabling, 152-153, 496-498
  dot-matrix printers, 488-490, 972-974, 1042
    configuration settings, 511-512
    preventive maintenance, 526
    printhead mechanisms, 490
    troubleshooting, 511-515

Q

R

U

V

X-Y-Z

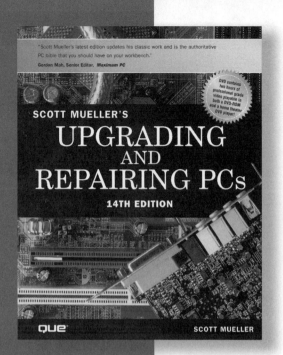

Upgrading & Repairing PCs has sold more than 2 Million Copies Worldwide.

Join the Loyal Following of St. Scott!

See what the buzz is all about... Get your copy of

UPGRADING AND REPAIRING PCs 14TH EDITION

Written by Scott Mueller, the most trusted, authoritative hardware voice in the industry.

Upgrading & Repairing PCs 14th Edition
$59.99 US
$89.99 CAN
£39.99 Net UK
ISBN: 0-7897-2745-5

The 14th Edition includes:

- All new content, including deep coverage of new Intel Northwood and AMD Athlon XP processors.
- Coverage of cutting edge technologies, including new motherboard chipsets from nVidia, VIA and Intel, Creative Labs Audigy sound card, hot broadband technologies, choosing the right PC case, advanced PC cooling techniques, and new hard disk drive technologies.
- A DVD containing two hours of professional video featuring Scott walking through complicated technologies inside your PC.

Get your copy today at the Que Web site or your favorite bookstore!

About Scott

Scott Mueller is president of Mueller Technical Research, an international research and corporate training firm. Since 1982, MTR has specialized in the industry's most in-depth, accurate, and effective corporate PC hardware and technical training seminars, maintaining a client list that includes Fortune 500 companies, the U.S. and foreign governments, major software and hardware corporations, as well as PC enthusiasts and entrepreneurs. His seminars have been presented to several thousands of PC support professionals throughout the world. Scott has developed and presented training courses in all areas of PC hardware and software.

  www.quepublishing.com   www.upgradingandrepairingpcs.com

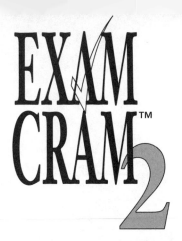

EXAM CRAM 2™

A+ Exam Cram2
(Exams 220-221 & 220-222)
James Jones and Craig Landes
0-7897-2867-2
$29.99 US/$46.99 CAN/£21.99 Net UK

The test is in 2 weeks – are you ready?

You need a quick and efficient way to make sure you have what it takes to pass.

Where do you go?

Exam Cram2!

Why?

Que Certification Exam Cram2 titles have exactly what you need to pass your exam:

- Key terms and concepts highlighted at the start of each chapter
- Notes, Exam Tips, and Alerts advise what to watch out for
- End-of-chapter sample Exam Questions with detailed discussions of all answers
- Complete text-based practice test with answer key at the end of each book
- The tear-out Cram Sheet condenses the most important items and information into a two-page reminder
- A CD that includes PrepLogic Practice Tests for complete evaluation of your knowledge
- Our authors are recognized experts in the field. In most cases, they are current or former instructors, trainers, or consultants— they know exactly what you need to know!

Que Certification: Your Complete Certification Resource!   www.examcram.com

What if Que

joined forces to deliver the best technology books in a common digital reference platform?

We have. Introducing
InformIT Online Books
powered by Safari.

■ **Specific answers to specific questions.**
InformIT Online Books' powerful search engine gives you relevance-ranked results in a matter of seconds.

■ **Immediate results.**
With InformIt Online Books, you can select the book you want and view the chapter or section you need immediately.

■ **Cut, paste, and annotate.**
Paste code to save time and eliminate typographical errors. Make notes on the material you find useful and choose whether or not to share them with your workgroup.

■ **Customized for your enterprise.**
Customize a library for you, your department, or your entire organization. You pay only for what you need.

POWERED BY Safari

InformIT Online Books

informit.com/onlinebooks

As an InformIT partner, Que has shared the knowledge and hands-on advice of our authors with you online. Visit InformIT.com to see what you are missing.

Get your first 14 days **FREE!**

InformIT Online Books is offering its members a 10-book subscription risk free for 14 days. Visit **http://www.informit.com/onlinebooks** for details.

informIT

www.informit.com

Your Guide to Information Technology Training and Reference

Que has partnered with **InformIT.com** to bring technical information to your desktop. Drawing on Que authors and reviewers to provide additional information on topics you're interested in, **InformIT.com** has free, in-depth information you won't find anywhere else.

Articles

Keep your edge with thousands of free articles, in-depth features, interviews, and information technology reference recommendations – all written by experts you know and trust.

Online Books

Answers in an instant from **InformIT Online Books'** 600+ fully searchable online books. Sign up now and get your first 14 days **free**.

POWERED BY
Safari

Catalog

Review online sample chapters and author biographies to choose exactly the right book from a selection of more than 5,000 titles.

As an **InformIT** partner, **Que** has shared the knowledge and hands-on advice of our authors with you online. Visit **InformIT.com** to see what you are missing.

Get Certified!

You have the experience and the training — now demonstrate your expertise and get the recognition your skills deserve. An IT certification increases your credibility in the marketplace and is tangible evidence that you have the know-how to provide top-notch support to your employer.

Visit www.vue.com

for a complete listing of

IT certification exams

offered by VUE

Why Test with VUE?

Using the speed and reliability of the Internet, the most advanced technology and our commitment to unparalleled service, VUE provides a quick, flexible way to meet your testing needs.

Three easy ways to register for your next exam, all in real time:

- Register online at www.vue.com

- Contact your local VUE testing center. There are over 3000 quality VUE testing centers in more than 130 countries. Visit www.vue.com for the location of a center near you.

- Call a VUE call center. In North America, call toll-free 800-TEST-NOW (800-837-8734). For a complete listing of worldwide call center telephone numbers, visit www.vue.com.

Call your local VUE testing center and ask about TESTNOW!™ same-day exam registration!

The VUE testing system is built with the best technology and backed by even better service. Your exam will be ready when you expect it and your results will be quickly and accurately transmitted to the testing sponsor. Test with confidence!

When IT really matters... Test with VUE!

■ TEST YOUR "IT" SKILLS

Play the Game!

WIN PRIZES & GET ON THE LIST ■

So you've read a book or two, worn out a couple of practice test disks, and memorized lots of stuff...now you think you're ready for the IT Certification test. Wait a minute!

Go to our games website.
www.eitgames.com is for IT certification* candidates.

Play a free demo game.
Gauge your skill level and challenge yourself.

Win great merchandise.
Test vouchers, reference books, software etc.

Get on our Top Performers list.
Our Top Performers list is one handy place for job recruiters to find the most knowledgeable IT people.

www.eitgames.com

THE OFFICIAL IT CERTIFICATION TEST GAMES SITE

*MCSE A+ NETWORK+ i-NET+ CCNA

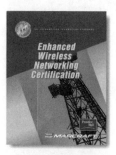

Wireless Networking Certification technology is one of the hottest technologies available today, used in electronic devices, such as cell phones and Personal Digital Assistants (PDA), to enable access to e-mail and the Internet. Wireless technology is also utilized in wireless Local Area Networks (LANs). With Marcraft's Wireless Networking Certification, you learn the entire process of designing, building, configuring, and managing a wireless network. This text combines into one place everything needed to successfully design, install, and troubleshoot a simple wireless solution. Keep on the cutting edge of wireless with Marcraft.

Security Installers Certification is an expert introduction to the security alarm industry, for those who have limited or no previous knowledge of the industry. After successfully completing the Security Installers Certification program, you'll be prepared for employment in the security industry as a technician or a field installer. This manual is also beneficial to sales reps for enhancing their technical knowledge. No matter what your background may be or what your educational intentions are, this manual offers you a wealth of information and will answer all of your security installation questions.

The Complete Introductory Computer Course is an entry-level course. It prepares students for the more challenging A+ Certification course. It also provides a careerlink™ into the fast-growing IT industry. The MC-2300 is a 45 hour, easy-to-understand exploration of basic computer hardware, software, and troubleshooting. This course helps build students confidence and basic computer literacy. The fully illustrated 198-page Theory Text/Lab Guide provides an easy-to understand exploration of the basics of computers: basic computer architecture and operation, step-by-step computer hardware assembly, computer hardware and functions, common software packages, consumer maintenance practices, and troubleshooting a "sick" computer. The reusable MC-2300 Intro Computer Trainer comes with all the necessary hardware, software, and tools to perform over 30 hands-on Lab Explorations.

The Complete Introductory Networking Course is a superbly-illustrated theory text and lab guide all in one. It not only provides a great way for students to explore over 45 hours of easy-to-understand basic Networking topics, but also develops job skills for starting them on the path towards a new high-tech career! This manual guides you through such activities as: installation and configuration of local, area network hardware, peer-to peer networking functions, sharing computer resources, mapping to remote resources, and consumer level network troubleshooting. The Complete Introductory Networking Course provides an excellent starting point for IT Certification including Microsoft's MCSE, Novell's CNA, and Cisco's CCNA.

The Complete Introductory Internet Course takes advantage of the growing demand for qualified Internet technicians. This 45 hour course explores easy-to-understand basic Internet topics and helps develop Internet skills. This manual guides you through such activities as: configure e-mail accounts, design a basic HTML page, setup basic firewall for security, and establish Internet connection slaving. The Complete Introductory Internet Course provides an excellent starting point for IT Certification including CompTIA's i-NET+ and Prosoft's Certified Internet Webmaster (CIW)

Network+ Certification is a CompTIA vendor-neutral certification that measures the technical knowledge of networking professionals with 18-24 months of experience in the IT industry. The test is administered by NCS/VUE and PrometricTM. Discount exam vouchers can be purchased from Marcraft. Earning the Network+ certification indicates that the candidate possesses the knowledge needed to configure and install the TCP/IP client. This exam covers a wide range of vendor and product neutral networking technologies that can also serve as a prerequisite for vendor-specific IT certifications. Network+ has been accepted by the leading networking vendors and included in many of their training curricula. The skills and knowledge measured by the certification examination are derived from industry-wide job task analyses and validated through an industry wide survey. The objectives for the certification examination are divided in two distinct groups, Knowledge of Networking Technology and Knowledge of Networking Practices.

CompTIA
seal of approval

i-Net+ Certification program is designed specifically for any individual interested in demonstrating baseline technical knowledge that would allow him or her to pursue a variety of Internet-related careers. i-Net+ is a vendor-neutral, entry-level Internet certification program that tests baseline technical knowledge of Internet, Intranet and Extranet technologies, independent of specific Internet-related career roles. Learning objectives and domains examined include: Internet basics, Internet clients, development, networking, security, and business concepts. Certification not only helps individuals enter the Internet industry, but also helps managers determine a prospective employee's knowledge and skill level.

CompTIA
seal of approval

Data Cabling Installer Certification provides the IT industry with an introductory, vendor-neutral certification for skilled personnel that install Category 5 copper data cabling.The Marcraft Enhanced Data Cabling Installer Certification Training Guide provides students with the knowledge and skills required to pass the Data Cabling Installer Certification exam and become a certified cable installer. The DCIC is recognized nationwide and is the hiring criterion used by major communication companies. Therefore, becoming a certified data cable installer will enhance your job opportunities and career advancement potential.

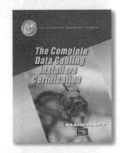

Server+ Certification deals with advanced hardware issues such as RAID, SCSI, multiple CPUs, SANs, and more. This certification is vendor-neutral with a broad range of support, including core support by 3Com, Adaptec, Compaq, Hewlett-Packard, IBM, Intel, EDS Innovations Canada, Innovative Productivity, and Marcraft. This book focuses on complex activities and solving complex problems to ensure servers are functional and applications are available. It provides an in-depth understanding of installing, configuring, and maintaining servers, including knowledge of server-level hardware implementations, data storage subsystems, data recovery, and I/O subsystems.

Fiber Cabling Installers Certification prepares technicians for the growing demand for qualified cable installers who understand and can implement fiber optic technologies. These technologies cover terminology, techniques, tools and other products in the fiber optic industry. This text/lab book covers the basics of fiber optic design, installations, pulling and prepping cables, terminations, testing, and safety considerations. Labs will cover ST-compatible and SC connector types, both multi- and single-mode cables and connectors. Learn about insertion loss, optical time domain reflectometry, and reflectance. This text covers mechanical and fusion splices and troubleshooting cable systems. This text/lab covers the theory and hands-on skills needed to prepare you for fiber optic entry-level certification.

MARCRAFT
Your IT Training Provider
(800) 441-6006 www.mic-inc.com

Complete and Affordable Classroom Management

Classroom management just got a heck of a lot easier. Thanks to TEAMS 32 you're relieved from many of the mundane and time-consuming tasks involved in managing a classroom. It can even eliminate a lot of the paperwork...maybe all of it! And you get back the time to do what you actually want to do: teach. TEAMS 32 is flexible enough to fit any classroom size or style. Whether traditional or a more complex rotational system. Manage your classroom the way you want! Classroom records are kept and updated automatically, including individual student test performance, attendance, class rosters, and other student information.

For more details and a sample CD, simply call

(800) 441-6006

A+ Computer Trainer

The Pentium III motherboard is custom designed with hundreds of built-in faults that can be controlled by the instructor. This makes a great trouble-shooting platform for teaching diagnostic techniques. It's fast, easy and realistic.

THIS TRAINER INCLUDES:
- System Board
- Pentium III Processor
- DIMM, 128 MB
- Case, ATX Full Tower w/Power Supply
- FDD, 3.5"
- HDD, 10 GB
- Video Card, 4 MB
- Keyboard, 101-key

- PS2 Mouse, 3-Button Serial
- Fax Modem, 56k
- Network Card, 10/100 Mbps
- Speakers
- Monitor, 15"

to order call Toll Free
1-800-441-6006
or go to: www.mic-inc.com
MARCRAFT

Marcraft International Corporation
100 N. Morain - 302, Kennewick, WA 99336

CramSession

– the difference between Pass
... or Fail

"On top of everything else, I find the best deals on training products and services for our CramSession members".

Jami Costin,
Product Specialist

CramSession.com is #1
for IT Certification on the 'Net.

There's no better way to prepare for success in the IT Industry. Find the best IT certification study materials and technical information at CramSession. Find a community of hundreds of thousands of IT Pros just like you who help each other pass exams, solve real-world problems, and discover friends and peers across the globe.

CramSession – #1 Rated Certification Site!

- *#1 by TechRepublic.com*
- *#1 by TechTarget.com*
- *#1 by CertMag's Guide to Web Resources.*

Visit Cramsession.com today!
...and take advantage of the best
IT learning resources.

CramSession has IT all!

- **The #1 study guides on the 'Net.** With over 250 study guides for IT certification exams, we are the web site every techie visits before passing an IT certification exam.

- **Practice questions.** Get the answers and explanations with our CramChallenge practice questions delivered to you daily.

- **The most popular IT Forums.** Cramsession has over 400 discussion boards loaded with certification infomation where our subscribers study hard, work hard, and play harder.

- **e-Newsletters.** Our IT e-Newsletters are written by techs for techs: IT certification, technology, humor, career and more.

- **Technical Papers and Product Reviews.** Find thousands of technical articles and whitepapers written by industry leaders, trainers, and IT veterans.

- **Exam reviews.** Get the inside scoop before you take that expensive certification exam.

- **And so much more!**

CramSession
Prepare for Success!

www.cramsession.com

coram deo
quixnet.net

Want to Pass Your Exam?

PrepLogic Practice Tests are trusted by certification candidates worldwide to prepare them for their upcoming exams. Developed by Certified IT Professionals, we've spent endless hours creating thousands of practice questions designed to give you the experience and challenge of the real exam. Best of all, we realize that using practice tests shouldn't cost you more than taking the actual exam. If you haven't experienced PrepLogic Practice Tests, visit PrepLogic.com and join the growing list of certification students who trust PrepLogic for their certification needs.

MCSE, Server+, MCSA, i-Net+, Linux+, CCNA, Network+, A+, and more...

Try the enclosed Preview Edition CD and then purchase the complete set of Practice Tests from PrepLogic. Brand new questions, brand new exams at preplogic.com.

Here are just a few of the reasons to buy PrepLogic Practice Tests:

- Prepares You for the Actual Exam
- Developed by Certified IT Professionals
- More Challenging Questions than the Competition
- Powerful, Full-Featured Test Engine
- Trusted by Students Worldwide
- PrepLogic Pass Guarantee

PrepLogic Guarantee

We are so confident in our ability to prepare you to pass your exam that we guarantee it.

Visit preplogic.com/guarantee for more information and let PrepLogic lead you towards success.

Prep Logic
Practice Tests

www.preplogic.com

···Because you Want to Pass the First Time.